012 345 678

Reward yourself

WITH $40 CASH OR A $50 ROOM VOUCHER

Easy Rewards is a simple new loyalty program from AmericInn. 10 nights earns you **$40 cash or a $50 room voucher**. No hassles, no black-out dates. Plus, each of AmericInn's 220 locations offer the amenities you want most:

FREE HOT BREAKFAST

FREE HIGH-SPEED INTERNET ACCESS

FRIENDLY SERVICE

A CLEAN, FUN POOL

Download a free QR code reader
app on your smart phone

AmericInn

Welcome to the end of the day.

Find our location listings in this book, or book now at AmericInn.com or by calling 800-634-3444

destination: unforgettable.

With Hampton as your home base, you'll get more out of every getaway. Save with valuable amenities like free hot breakfast, free high-speed internet access and great AAA rates. Plus, the linens and duvet are washed fresh for every guest. For reservations, call your AAA agent, visit **hampton.com** or call 1-800-hampton.

we love having you here.®

clean and fresh
Hampton bed™

FREE
hot breakfast

preferred
hotel

Find yourself.
Anywhere you like.

Offering great AAA rates and Hilton HHonors® points at over 3,600 hotels in 81 countries. Finding yourself will be as easy as finding a hotel in the Hilton Worldwide portfolio.

HHONORS
HILTON WORLDWIDE

WALDORF
ASTORIA

CONRAD

Hilton

DOUBLETREE

EMBASSY
SUITES

Hilton
Garden Inn

Hampton

HOMEWOOD
SUITES

HOME2

Hilton
Grand Vacations

Michigan & Wisconsin

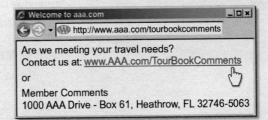

Welcome to aaa.com   _ □ x

http://www.aaa.com/tourbookcomments

Are we meeting your travel needs?
Contact us at: www.AAA.com/TourBookComments
or
Member Comments
1000 AAA Drive - Box 61, Heathrow, FL 32746-5063

Published by AAA Publishing

1000 AAA Drive, Heathrow, FL 32746-5063
Copyright AAA 2011, All rights reserved

The publisher has made every effort to provide accurate,
up-to-date information but accepts no responsibility for loss or
injury sustained by any person using this book. TourBook® guides
are published for the exclusive use of AAA members. Not for sale.

Advertising Rate and Circulation Information: (407) 444-8280

Printed in the USA by Quad/Graphics

Photo Credit: (Cover & Title Page)
Cana Island Lighthouse, Baileys Harbor, Door County, WI
© Tom Algire / Larry Ulrich Stock

Printed on recyclable paper.
Please recycle whenever possible.   Stock #4616

**This book is printed on paper certified by third-party standards
for sustainably-managed forestry and production.**

Michigan
& Wisconsin

■ *Wisconsin*

Featured Information

"TREES?
100 FEET UNDERWATER?"

MÉXICO

THE PLACE YOU THOUGHT YOU KNEW
DISCOVER MORE AT www.visitmexico.com

CENOTE ANGELITA, QUINTANA ROO

Welcome to Get Closer Country.

I love this Country.™

A splash in the pool. A free breakfast. Even free high-speed Internet access. Everything you need to make your family travels easier. Visit countryinns.com for AAA rates and a stay that will have everyone saying, "I love this Country."

Complimentary breakfast • Free high-speed Internet
Indoor pool & whirlpool • Free weekday newspaper

MICHIGAN	Iron Mountain	Chippewa Falls	Mauston	Schofield
Big Rapids	Jackson	East Troy	Menomonie	Sparta
Birch Run	Lansing	Eau Claire	Middleton	Stevens Point
Cascade	Marquette	Fond du Lac	Milwaukee	West Bend
Dundee	Novi	Germantown	Monona	
Grand Rapids	WISCONSIN	Green Bay*	Platteville	
Holland	Appleton	Kenosha	Port Washington	
Houghton	Brookfield	Little Chute	Prairie du Chien	

Amenities may vary by hotel location.
*Multiple locations

Scan code to receive member discount. Get the free mobile app at http://gettag.mobi

800-456-4000 • countryinns.com

Attractions, lodgings and restaurants are listed on the basis of merit alone after careful evaluation and approval by one of AAA/CAA's full-time, professionally trained inspectors. Evaluations are unannounced to ensure that we see an establishment just as you would see it.

An establishment's decision to advertise in the TourBook guide has no bearing on its evaluation or rating. Advertising for services or products does not imply AAA endorsement.

Information in this guide was believed accurate at the time of publication. However, since changes inevitably occur between annual editions, we suggest you work with your AAA travel professional or check on AAA.com to confirm prices and schedules.

How the TourBook Guide is Organized

The TourBook guide is organized into three distinct sections.

The **Points of Interest** section helps you plan daily activities and sightseeing excursions and provides details about the city or attraction you are visiting.

The **Lodgings and Restaurants** section helps you select AAA Approved accommodations and dining facilities meeting your specific needs and expectations.

The **Reference** section provides indexes for locating information within this guide and items to aid the trip planning process.

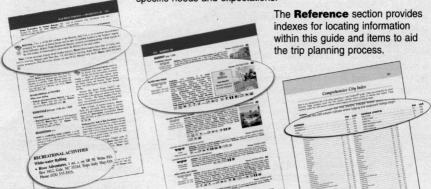

Locating the Attractions, Lodgings and Restaurants

Attractions, lodgings and restaurants are listed under the city in which they physically are located - or in some cases under the nearest recognized city. Most listings are alphabetically organized by state, province, region or island, then by city and establishment name.

A color is assigned to each state or province so that you can match the color bars at the top of the page to switch from the **Points of Interest** section to the **Lodgings and Restaurants** section.

Spotting maps help you physically locate points of interest, lodgings and restaurants in the major destinations.

The Comprehensive City Index located in the **Reference** section contains an A-to-Z list of cities.

Destination Cities and Destination Areas

Destination cities, established based on government models and local expertise, include metropolitan areas plus nearby vicinity cities. **Destination areas** are regions with broad tourist appeal; several cities will comprise the area.

If a city falls within a destination's vicinity, the city name will appear at its alphabetical location in the book, and a cross reference will give you the exact page on which listings for that city begin.

An Orientation map appears at the beginning of each destination section to familiarize you with that destination.

Understanding the Points of Interest Listing

GEM Designation

A ⬙ indicates the attraction has been rated a AAA GEM, a "must see" point of interest that offers a *Great Experience for Members®*. These attractions have been judged to be of exceptional interest and quality by AAA inspectors.

Discount Savings

The ⬛SAVE icon denotes those attractions offering AAA/CAA members or international Show Your Card & Save discount cardholders a discount off the attraction's standard admission. Present your membership card at the attraction's admission desk.

A list of participating points of interest appears in the Reference section of this guide.

Shopping establishments preceded by a ⬛SAVE icon also provide to AAA/CAA members a discount and/or gift with purchase; present your card at the mall's customer service center to receive your benefit.

Exceptions

- Members should inquire in advance concerning the validity of the discount for special rates.
- The ⬛SAVE discount may not be used in conjunction with other discounts.
- Attractions that already provide a reduced senior or child rate may not honor the ⬛SAVE discount for those age groups.
- All offers are subject to change and may not apply during special events, particular days or seasons or for the entire validity period of the TourBook guide.

Adventure Travel

There are inherent risks with adventure travel activities like air tours, hiking, skiing and white-water rafting. For your own safety, please read and adhere to all safety instructions. Mentions of these activities are for information only and do **not** imply endorsement by AAA.

BLUE RIDGE PA

Boone Convention & Visitors Bureau: 208 such as Howard St., Boone, NC 28607 **Phones:** (828) Laughing 555-5555 or (800) 555-5555

Sh

⬙GEM **RED OAK,** .7 mi. n. of US 421 via Horn in the West I portraying the struggle of Daniel Boone and his men chian Highlands. Hickory Ridge Homestead Museum ⬛SAVE the 18th century. Costumed guides demonstrate the lif **Time:** 2 hours minimum. Inquire about weather policies. H June to mid-Aug. Museum open Tues.-Sun. 1-8, mid-June to mission to museum) $18; $9 (senior citizens and ages 0-12),

onstra

Time: 2 hours minimum.
policies. **Hours:** Performances Tues.-Sun. at 8 p.m., mid-June to mid-Aug. Museum open Tues.-Sun. 1-8, mid-June to mid-Aug. **Cost:** Musical drama (includes admission to museum) $18; $9 (senior citizens and ages 0-12). Museum only $4.50. **Phone:** (800) 555-5555.

Sea
coa
me
Tr
la

RECREATIONAL ACTIVITIES

White-water Rafting

- **Wahoo's Adventures-Boone Outpost,** 1 mi. s. on US 321. **Hours:** Trips daily Apr.-Oct. **Phones:** (828) 555-5555 or (800) 555-5555.

a
p

BOONVILLE (B-4) pop. 1,138, elev. 1,066

WINERIES

- **RagApple Lassie Vineyards** is at 3724 RagApple Lassie Ln. **Hours:** Daily noon-6. Closed Easter, Thanksgiving and Dec. 25. **Phones:** (336) 555-5555 or (866) 555-5555.

BRASSTOWN (F-1)

JOHN C. CAMPBELL FOLK SCHOOL is in the center of town at 1 Folk School Rd. Visitors observe students at work in a variety of folk classes includ- ing cooking
potter

RECREATIONAL ACTIVIT

White-water Rafting

- **River Adventures,** 1 mi. s. o Box 1012, Gale, NC 35244. Phone (828) 555-5555.

Y — BRYSON CITY, NC   129

...stee Falls, Courthouse Falls and

...of Commerce

...n 2 mi. e., is an outdoor musical drama
...ablish freedom in the Southern Appala-
...ns a reconstructed log village typical of
of the early settlers.

Performances Tues.-Sun. at 8 p.m., mid-
Aug. Cost: Musical drama (includes ad-
...eum only $4.50. Phone: (800) 555-5555.

...28/13
...5555.

...reat Smoky Mountains Railroad, departing
...e Bryson City depot, operates various
...alf-day and full-day round-trip excursions.
...s offered in open cars, coaches, crown
...d club cars. On weekends there are Gour-
...ner Trains and Mystery Theatre Dinner
...he Polar Express runs early Nov. through

...uts—The Easter Beagle Express" and
...as the Tank," rides with kid-oriented themes,
...lable in the spring and summer with limited
..."Peanuts— The Great Pumpkin Patch Ex-
...runs weekends in October. An animal petting
...d musical entertainment also are offered.
...ne: 4 hours, 30 minutes minimum. Hours:
...s run year-round. Phone ahead to confirm
...ule. Cost: Sightseeing fares begin at $34; $19
...2-12). Reservations: recommended. Phone:
...555-5555, or (800) 555-5555 for reservations.

...dwater Ltd. Raft & Rail Excursion, departing
...railroad depot in Bryson City, combines rail and
...te-water excursions in one outing. The adventure
...ins with a scenic 2-hour train trip across Fontana
...ke to the top of Nantahala Gorge. Rafts are then
...ded for a guided 3-hour trip down the Nan-
... unch is included.

...minimum. Children under 60
...Hours: Trips daily mid-
...times vary. Cost: Fares
...-12). Phone: (828)

S

...R 50. Write P.O.
...ps daily May-Oct.   13 mi. s.w. on US
...daily 8-8, Apr.-Oct.
...ec. 25. Phones: (828)
...55.

Directions

Unless otherwise specified, directions are given from the center of town, using the following highway designations:

I=interstate highway	**US**=federal highway
SR=state route	**CR**=county road
FM=farm to market	**FR**=forest road
Mex.=Mexican highway	**Hwy.**=Canadian or Caribbean highway

Prices and Dates of Operation

Admission prices are quoted without sales tax. Children under the lowest age specified are admitted free when accompanied by an adult. Days, months and age groups written with a hyphen are inclusive.

Prices pertaining to points of interest in the United States are quoted in U.S. dollars; points of interest in Canada are quoted in Canadian dollars; prices for points of interest in Mexico and the Caribbean are quoted as an approximate U.S. dollar equivalent.

Schedules and admission rates may change throughout the validity period of this guide. Check AAA.com for the most current information.

Credit Card Information

Most establishments accept credit cards, but a small number require cash. If you want to use a specific credit card, call ahead to ensure it's accepted.

Icons

Attraction icons represent some of the services and facilities offered:

🏕 Camping facilities available

🍴 Food available on premises

🎿 Recreational activities available

🐾 Pets on leash allowed

⛱ Picnicking permitted

Bulleted Listings

Gambling establishments within hotels are presented for member information regardless of whether the lodging is AAA Approved.

Recreational activities of a participatory nature (requiring physical exertion or special skills) are not inspected.

Wineries are evaluated by AAA inspectors to ensure they meet listing requirements and offer tours.

All are presented in an abbreviated bulleted format for informational purposes.

Understanding the Lodging Listing

Local Member Value

Red Diamonds indicate lodgings that are AAA/CAA Official Appointment (OA) logo licensing partners. OA lodgings may list up to two free special amenities such as breakfast, room upgrade, preferred room or high-speed Internet.

OA lodgings with a SAVE icon offer members a rate guarantee: discounted standard room rate (usually based on last standard room availability) or the lowest public rate available at time of booking for dates of stay.

Diamond Rating

The number of Diamonds informs you of the overall complexity of a lodging's amenities and services. For detailed descriptions of each rating level, see page 18 or visit AAA.com/Diamonds.

An fyi in place of Diamonds indicates the property has not been rated but is included as an "information only" service.

Classification

All Diamond Rated lodgings are classified using three key elements: style of operation, overall concept and service level. See pages 20-21 for details.

Rates

The effective dates for a property's standard two-person rates are shown unless applicable all year.

Rates provided to AAA for each lodging represent the publicly available rate or ranges for a standard room. Rates are rounded to the nearest dollar and do not include taxes. U.S., Mexican and Caribbean rates are in U.S. dollars; rates for Canadian lodgings are in Canadian dollars.

Information about cancellation and minimum stay policies is provided in the **Terms** section of the property's listing.

Unit/Service Availability

Unit types, amenities and room features preceded by the word "some" are available on a limited basis, potentially as small as one.

Parking

Parking is free, on-site self parking unless otherwise noted.

474 MURPHY, NC

MURPHY pop. 1,568

FLORENCE RESORT

Vacation Rental Condominium

Address: 12550 Florence Resort Tr 2 on SR 528 (Beachline Expwy), exit 1 condominiums offer all the comforts of

HILTON PINE RIDGE

Hotel

$599-$3870 12/1-4/30
$399-$3600 5/1-11/30

Address: 5111 Tamiami Tr N 28 **Location:** Just s of jct CR 896 (Pine Ridge F **Facility:** Large pillars, ironwork Mediterranean-style archways enhance lobby. Designated smoking area. 199 units, stories, interior corridors. **Parking:** on-site s valet. **Amenities:** high-speed Intern **Dining:** Shula's America's Steak House, se separate listing. **Pool(s):** heated outdo basketball. **Fee:** massage. **Guest Services** valet laundry, beach shuttle, wireless interne **Free Special Amenities:** newspaper and high

SAVE ECO

HOLIDAY INN SUNSPREE RESORT

Resort Motel

$159-$199 12/1-4/11
$119-$149 4/12-11/30

Address: 6800 Sunshine Skyway Ln S 289 just e on Pinellas Point Dr S, then just s. ctivities are available at this 18-acre resort. 2 stories, interior/exterior corridors. **Terms: Amenities:** high-speed Internet, sales fishing, 5 lighted tennis courts, playground, e charter fishing, beach cruisers, personal w **Services:** valet and coin laundry, wireless Inte (see ad p. 477)

ECO / SOME UNITS

HOLIDAY INN EXPRESS HOTEL & SUITES

Hotel
Rates not provided

Address: 130 Holiday Dr 28906 **Location:** U **Amenities:** high-speed Internet. **Pool(s):** heati **Services:** coin laundry, wireless Internet.

HOWARD HOUSE VICTORIAN BED & BREAKFAST

Historic Bed & Breakfast
$119-$149

Address: 207 Pollock St 28906 **Location:** 0.3 **Facility:** The 1890 Queen Anne-influenced hom gourmet breakfast is served each morning in the (no elevator), interior/exterior corridors. **Terms: Services:** wireless Internet. / SOME UNITS

ROCK HOTEL AND CASINO

Hotel

$599-$3870 12/1-4/30
$359-$3600 5/1-11/30

Address: 5223 N Orient Rd 28906 **Location:** spacious, art deco-style rooms, a lush pool and cafe, market and shops. 250 units. 12 stories, Floyd's Restaurant & Night Club, see separate **Activities:** whirlpools, steamrooms, exercise roo Internet. **Free Special Amenities:** local telephon

SLEEP INN

Hotel
Rates not provided

Address: 710 Henderson St 28365 **Location:** Jct units. 2 stories (no elevator), interior corridors. **Pool** / SOME UNITS.

SOUTHERN COUNTRY INN

Motel
$65

Address: 8514 Hwy 49 28124 **Location:** Jct SR 7 stories (no elevator), exterior corridors.

Nationwide Member Value

The blue box in the listing identifies hotel brands that offer an everyday member benefit at all AAA Approved locations. (See page 17 for additional program benefits.)

Spotting Symbol

Black ovals with white numbers are used to locate, or "spot," lodgings on maps we provide for larger cities.

Credit Card Information

Most establishments accept credit cards, but a small number require cash. If you want to use a specific credit card, call ahead to ask if it's accepted.

Icons

Icons are used to indicate the availability of standard lodging services; where more information is needed, the icons may be preceded by CALL, FEE and/or SOME UNITS.

The **ECO** icon indicates lodgings that have been certified by well-established government and/or private eco-certification organizations. For more information, visit AAA.com/eco.

Member Services

⬆️ Airport transportation

🐾 Pets allowed (call property for restrictions and fees)

🍽️ Restaurant on premises

🍽️+ Restaurant off premises (walking distance)

24️⃣ 24-hour room service

🍸 Full bar

👶 Child care

BIZ Business services

♿M Accessible features (call property for available services and amenities)

Activities

🎲 Full-service casino

🏊 Pool

💪 Health club on premises

💪➡️ Health club off premises

In-Room Amenities

🚫 Designated non-smoking rooms

🎬 Movies

🧊 Refrigerator

🍽️ Microwave

☕ Coffee maker

🚫❄️ No air conditioning

📺 No TV

📺 No cable TV

📞 No telephones

Safety Features

(see page 22)

Mexico and Caribbean only:

S Sprinklers

D Smoke detectors

Phone: (555)555-5555 75

...cation: I-4, exit 72, just e ...mi s. **Facility:** Spacious ...cluding a modern decor, ...some three

Phone: 555/555-5555 11

🏨
Hilton

AAA Benefit:
Members save 5% or more everyday!

...d Internet. (see ad p. 479)

🚫 🐾 🧊 ☕ / SOME UNITS 👶 🍽️

Phone: (555)555-5555 9

...ation: I-275, exit 16, ...: Many recreational ...ts, some efficiencies. ...lation fee imposed. ...g: 2 restaurants. ...ool, beach access. ...room. Fee: marina, ...l, massage. Guest

🐾 ☕

Phone: 555/555-5555

...**Facility:** 51 units. 3 stories, interior corridors. ...or. **Activities:** whirlpool, exercise room. Guest

🚫

Phone: 555/555-5555

...of Tryon Palace; downtown; in historic district. ...ecorated with antiques and family heirlooms; a ...room. Smoke free premises. 6 units. 2 stories ...ancellation notice. **Activities:** bicycles. Guest

☕

Phone: 555/555-5555 18

...6, just w. **Facility:** The large facility boasts ...area and a 90,000-square-foot casino with a ...corridors. **Parking:** on-site (fee) and valet. ...safes, honor bars. **Dining:** 4 restaurants, also, ...g, entertainment. **Pool(s):** heated outdoor. ...**Guest Services:** valet laundry, wireless ...and high-speed Internet.
SOME UNITS FEE 🐾 🚫 👶 🍽️

Phone: 555/555-5555

...7, just e on SR 55, then just s. **Facility:** 68 ...tdoor. **Guest Services:** wireless Internet.

Phone: 555/555-5555

...n. **Facility:** 26 units, some kitchens. 1-2
🐾 / SOME UNITS 🚫 🧊

Understanding the Restaurant Listing

Official Appointment

Red Diamonds or text indicate restaurants that are AAA/CAA Official Appointment (OA) logo licensing partners. OA restaurants may display the AAA/CAA Approved Restaurant emblem and signage.

Diamond Rating

The number of Diamonds informs you of the overall complexity of food, presentation, service and ambience. For detailed descriptions of each rating level, see page 19 or visit AAA.com/Diamonds.

Cuisine Type

The cuisine type helps you select a dining facility that caters to your individual taste. AAA currently recognizes more than 100 different cuisine types.

Prices

Prices shown represent the minimum and maximum entree cost per person. Exceptions may include one-of-a-kind or special market priced items. Prices are rounded to the nearest dollar and do not include taxes. U.S., Mexican and Caribbean prices are in U.S. dollars; prices for Canadian restaurants are in Canadian dollars.

Dress Code

Dress is casual or dressy casual unless otherwise noted.

Parking

Parking is free, on-site self parking unless otherwise noted.

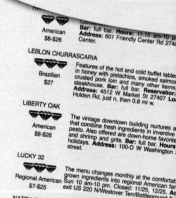

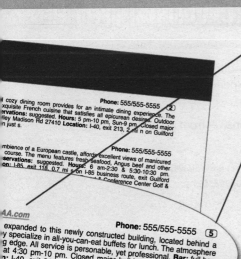

cozy dining room provides for an intimate dining experience. The xquisite French cuisine that satisfies all epicurean desires. The ervations: suggested. **Hours:** 5 pm-10 pm, Sun-9 pm. Closed major ley Madison Rd 27410 **Location:** I-40, exit 213, 2 mi n on Guilford n just s. **Phone:** 555/555-5555 ②

mbience of a European castle, afford excellent views of manicured course. The menu features fresh seafood, Angus beef and other ervations: suggested. **Hours:** 6 am-2:30 & 5:30-10:30 pm. on: I-85, exit 118, 0.7 mi s on I-85 business route, exit Guilford Conference Center Golf & **Phone:** 555/555-5555

AA.com

expanded to this newly constructed building, located behind a y specialize in all-you-can-eat buffets for lunch. The atmosphere g edge. All service is personable, yet professional. **Bar:** full bar. at 4:30 pm-10 pm. Closed major holidays; also 12/24 & Sun. n: I-40, exit 214 or 214B, 1.8 mi e on Wendover Ave, then 0.3 **Phone:** 555/555-5555 ⑤

& Sat-11 pm, Sun 10:30 am-10 pm. Closed: 11/25, 12/25. ation: Jct Wendover Ave, just w; in Friendly Center Shopping 555/555-5555 steak, seafood, chicken and salads.

de whipped sweet potatoes, fried bananas, salad fixings, Brie f lamb, flank steak, bacon-wrapped filet mignon, Parmesan-s are carved and served tableside at this upscale Brazilian gested. **Hours:** 5 pm-9:30 pm. Closed: 12/25; also Sun. I-40, exit 214 or 214B, 1.8 mi e on Wendover Ave, exit **Phone:** 555/555-5555 ④

ally upscale dining atmosphere. The menu features dishes such as in stuffed rainbow trout and lamb with honey-mint ared with flair, including roasted pulled pork, fried chicken am-9:30 pm, Fri & Sat-10 pm Sun-9 pm. Closed major 01 **Location:** Jct S Elm St, just w; downtown. **Parking:** **Phone:** 555/555-5555 ⑭

cale eatery, which focuses on incorporating fresh, locally : full bar. **Hours:** 11:15 am-10:30 pm, Fri & Sat-11 pm, s: 1421 Westover Terr 27408 **Location:** Wendover Ave, st n. **Phone:** 555/555-5555 ⑩

menu of burgers, wraps, sandwiches and hearty pub tdoor seating is offered during warm weather. **Bar:** full 1/25, 12/24, 12/25. **Address:** 345 S Elm St 27401 **Phone:** 555/555-5555 ⑯

stiest and is served with a smile in the comfortable, 11 am-3:30 & 5-9:30 pm, Fri-Sun 11 am-9:30 pm, I-40, exit 214 or 214B, 1.8 mi ne on Wendover Ave, **Phone:** 555/555-5555 ③

comfortable ste ives, the resta s are so tende and yummy de : 1051 W Inter 555-5555 ⑨ says no to a s lodge, with one. Also on **Hours:** 11 am-cation: I-20, exit

Menus
This notation indicates AAA/CAA members can conveniently view the restaurant's menu in a secure online environment at AAA.com.

Spotting Symbol
White ovals with black numbers serve as restaurant locators and are used to locate, or "spot," restaurants on maps for larger cities.

Classifications
If applicable, a restaurant may be defined as:

Classic - renowned and landmark restaurant operations in business longer than 25 years, known for unique style and ambience.

Historic - establishments must meet one of the following criteria:
- Listed on the National Register of Historic Places
- Designated a National Historic Landmark
- Located in a National Register Historic District

Separate criteria designate historic properties in Canada, Mexico and the Caribbean.

Credit Card Information
Most establishments accept credit cards, but a small number require cash. If you want to use a specific credit card, call ahead to ensure it's accepted.

Icons
Icons provide additional information about services and facilities.

SAVE Show Your Card & Save member discount

AC No air-conditioning

&M Accessible features offered (call property for available services and amenities)

Designated smoking section available

AAA BLOGGERS ARE Out There.

Find new trip ideas from AAA travel editors, counselors, inspectors and others with a passion for new experiences at AAATravelViews.com.

Q&A WITH AAA

Ask your travel question and get an answer from a AAA travel professional.

NEWS AND DEALS

The latest from AAA Travel and the AAA Newsroom, including Hot Deals, Diamond Award winners and travel forecasts.

SOME OF OUR CONTRIBUTORS

■ **Greg Seiter** – This self-proclaimed Disney fanatic has blogged about the Mouse from land and sea and about his native Indiana.

■ **Elizabeth Harryman** – Southern California's travel editor has met Prince Philip (no curtsy required) and written on a range of travel topics.

■ **Terence Baker** – New York's travel editor has been to 109 countries and written about his experiences near and far.

■ **Heidemarie Chernushin** – This Ohio contributor may be from the Midwest, but she has blogged from Boston to San Francisco and can make the most of a few days anywhere.

■ **Don Gleason** – This Arizona blogger has been known as a savvy traveler for many years and is always searching the globe for old, new and interesting destinations.

Visit AAATravelViews.com today!

AAA/CAA members can generally expect to pay no more than the maximum regular rate printed in the TourBook guide in each rate range for a standard room. On rare occasions AAA receives or inadvertently publishes incorrect rates.

Obtain current AAA/CAA member rates and make reservations at AAA.com. Rates may vary within the range, depending on season and room type. Listed rates are usually based on last standard room availability.

Discounts

Member discounts, when offered, will apply to rates quoted within the rate range and are applicable at the time of booking. Special rates used in advertising, as well as special short-term promotional rates lower than the lowest listed rate in the range, are not subject to additional member discounts.

Exceptions

Rates for properties operating as concessionaires for the U.S. National Park Service are not guaranteed due to governing regulations. Rates in the Mexico TourBook are not guaranteed and may fluctuate based on the exchange rate of the peso.

Lodgings may temporarily increase room rates, not recognize discounts or modify pricing policies during special events. Examples of special events range from Mardi Gras and the Kentucky Derby (including pre-Derby events) to college football games, holidays, holiday periods and state fairs. Although some special events are listed in AAA/CAA TourBook guides and on AAA.com, it is always wise to check in advance with AAA travel professionals for specific dates.

Get the Room You Reserved

When making your reservation, identify yourself as a AAA or CAA member and request written confirmation to guarantee: type of room, rate, dates of stay, and cancellation and refund policies. At registration, show your membership card.

When you find your room is not as specified, and you have written confirmation of reservations for a certain type of accommodation, you should be given the option of choosing a different room or finding one elsewhere. Should you choose to go elsewhere and a refund is refused or resisted, submit the matter to AAA/CAA within 30 days, along with complete documentation, including your reasons for refusing the room and copies of your written confirmation and any receipts or canceled checks associated with this problem.

If you are charged more than the maximum rate listed in the TourBook guide for a standard room, question the additional charge. If management refuses to adhere to the published rate, pay for the room and submit your receipt and membership number to AAA/CAA within 30 days. Include all pertinent information: dates of stay, rate paid, itemized paid receipts, number of persons in

your party and the room number you occupied, and list any extra room equipment used. A refund of the amount paid in excess of the stated maximum will be made if our investigation indicates that unjustified charging occurred.

Deposit, Refund and Cancellation Policies

Most establishments give full deposit refunds if they have been notified at least 48 hours before the normal check-in time. Listing prose will note if more than 48 hours' notice is required for cancellation. Some properties may charge a cancellation or handling fee. When this applies, "cancellation fee imposed" will appear in the **Terms** section of the listing. If you cancel too late, you have little recourse if a refund is denied.

When an establishment requires full or partial payment in advance and your trip is cut short, a refund may not be given.

When canceling a reservation, phone the lodging immediately. Make a note of the date and time you called, the cancellation number if there is one, and the name of the person who handled the cancellation. If your AAA/CAA club made your reservation, allow them to make the cancellation for you as well, so you will have proof of cancellation.

Check-in and Check-out Times

Check-in and check-out times are shown in the lodging listings, under **Terms**, only if they are after 3 p.m. or before 10 a.m., respectively.

Meeting Your Travel Needs

AAA is proud to stand behind the Approved hotels, restaurants, attractions and campgrounds listed in the TourBook and CampBook guides. If, however, your visit doesn't meet your expectations, now you can tell us about it immediately. Visit AAA.com/TourBookComments to complete an easy online form, or send written comments to: AAA Member Comments, 1000 AAA Dr., Heathrow, FL 32746.

Members Save With Our Partners

These Show Your Card & Save® partners provide the listed member benefits. Visit AAA.com/Discounts to discover all the great Show Your Card & Save® discounts in your area. Even greater discounts on theme park tickets may be available at your local AAA/CAA club. Discounts apply to a maximum of six tickets for Amtrak, Gray Line and the theme parks. Restaurant savings apply to AAA/CAA members and up to five guests. Other restrictions may apply.

SeaWorld, Busch Gardens, Sesame Place

SEAWORLD PARKS & ENTERTAINMENT

- Save on admission at the gate, at participating offices or online AAA.com/SeaWorld
- Save 10% on up-close dining; visit Guest Relations for details

Six Flags

- Save on admission at the gate, at participating offices or online AAA.com/SixFlags

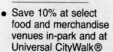

- Save 10% on merchandise purchases of $15 or more at in-park stores

Universal Orlando Resort and Universal Studios Hollywood

- Save on admission at the gate, at participating offices or online AAA.com/Universal

- Save 10% at select food and merchandise venues in-park and at Universal CityWalk®

Hard Rock Cafe

- Save 10% on food, non-alcoholic beverages and merchandise

at all U.S., Canadian and select international locations

Landry's Seafood House, The Crab House, Chart House, Saltgrass Steak House, Muer Seafood Restaurants and Aquarium Restaurants

- Save 10% on food and non-alcoholic beverages at all of the above restaurants
- Save 10% on merchandise at Aquarium and Downtown Aquarium restaurants

Amtrak

- 10% discount on rail fare when booked at least 3 days in advance of travel date

Grand Canyon Railway

- Save up to 20% on rail fare, hotel accommodations, restaurant and gift shop purchases sold outside of Grand Canyon National Park

Gray Line

AAA.com/GrayLine

- Save 10% on sightseeing tours of 1 day or less worldwide

Hertz

- Exclusive AAA member savings on daily, weekend, weekly and monthly rentals
AAA.com/hertz
or 1-800-654-3080

Tanger Outlet Centers

www.tangeroutlet.com

- Save up to 20% on total purchase at select merchants with FREE coupon booklet
- Member BONUS: FREE $5 gift card for each additional Tanger Outlet Center visited after first within same calendar year
- Show membership card and register at the AAA customer service desk when you visit

Show Your Card & Save!
Preferred Hotels

ASSURED STAY
Total Satisfaction Guarantee

AAA Preferred Lodging Partners

EXPECT SAVINGS, SELECTION, AND SATISFACTION

- **Best AAA/CAA member rates for your dates of stay.** Provide a valid membership number when placing your reservation and show your card at hotel check-in.
- **Total satisfaction guarantee.** If you book your stay with AAA Travel and your stay fails to meet your expectations, you can apply for a full refund for your night's stay. You must bring the complaint to the hotel's attention during the stay to provide the hotel an opportunity to correct the problem. If the complaint is not resolved by the participating hotel property, you can rest assured that the complaint will be resolved by AAA's Assured Stay program.
- **Seasonal promotions and special member offers.** Visit AAA.com to view current offers.
- **Everyday member benefit.** Look for the blue boxes in the TourBook listings for everyday values offered at all AAA Approved locations. *Offer good at time of publication: Chains and offers may change without notice. Preferred Hotel Partner discounts may vary in Mexico and the Caribbean.*

Up to 20% Off the Best Rates
Best Western, Best Western Plus, and Best Western Premier

5% or More Off Best Available Rates
Conrad Hotels & Resorts, Doubletree, Embassy Suites, Hampton Inns & Suites, Hilton Hotels & Resorts, Hilton Garden Inns, Hilton Grand Vacations, Home2 Suites, Homewood Suites, and Waldorf Astoria Collection

10% Off Best Available Rates
ANdAZ, Grand Hyatt, Hyatt Hotels & Resorts, Hyatt Place, Hyatt Regency, Hyatt Summerfield Suites, and Park Hyatt

5% or More Off Best Available Rates
Autograph Collection by Marriott, Courtyard, EDITION Hotels by Marriott, Fairfield Inn, JW Marriott, Marriott Hotels & Resorts, Renaissance Hotels, Residence Inn, Ritz Carlton Hotels, SpringHill Suites, and TownePlace Suites

5-15% Off Best Available Rates
Aloft, Element, Four Points, Le Meridien, Sheraton, St. Regis Hotels & Resorts, The Luxury Collection, Westin, and W Hotels

Visit Over 1,100 AAA Offices | **Click** AAA.com | **Call** 1-866-AAA-SAVE (222-7283)

Understanding the Diamond Ratings

AAA/CAA inspectors have evaluated and rated each of the 58,000 lodging and restaurant establishments in the TourBook series to ensure quality travel information for our members. All properties must meet AAA's minimum requirements (for lodgings) concerning cleanliness, comfort and security - or - AAA's minimum requirements (for restaurants) pertaining to cleanliness, food preparation and service.

Eligible applicants receive an unannounced evaluation by a AAA/CAA inspector that includes two distinct components:

- **AAA Approval:** The inspector first must determine whether the property meets the criteria required to be AAA Approved. Every establishment that meets these strict guidelines offers AAA members the assurance that, regardless of the Diamond Rating, it provides acceptable quality, cleanliness, service and value.
- **AAA Diamond Rating:** Once an establishment becomes AAA Approved, it is then assigned a rating of one to five Diamonds, indicating the extensiveness of its facilities, amenities and services, from basic to moderate to luxury. These Diamond Ratings guide members in selecting establishments appropriately matched to their needs and expectations.

LODGINGS

1 Diamond

One Diamond lodgings typically appeal to the budget-minded traveler. They provide essential, no-frills accommodations and basic comfort and hospitality.

2 Diamond

Two Diamond lodgings appeal to travelers seeking affordable yet more than the basic accommodations. Facilities, decor and amenities are modestly enhanced.

3 Diamond

Three Diamond lodgings offer a distinguished style. Properties are multi-faceted, with marked upgrades in physical attributes, amenities and guest comforts.

4 Diamond

Four Diamond lodgings are refined and stylish. Physical attributes are upscale. The fundamental hallmarks at this level include an extensive array of amenities combined with a high degree of hospitality, service and attention to detail.

5 Diamond

Five Diamond lodgings provide the ultimate in luxury and sophistication. Physical attributes are extraordinary in every manner. Service is meticulous, exceeding guest expectations and maintaining impeccable standards of excellence. Extensive personalized services and amenities provide first-class comfort.

The lodging listings with [fyi] in place of Diamonds are included as an *information only* service for members. The icon indicates that a property has not been rated for one or more of the following reasons: too new to rate, under construction, under major renovation, not evaluated, may not meet all AAA requirements.

A property not meeting all AAA requirements is included for either its member value or because it may be the only accommodation available in the area. Listing prose will give insight as to why the [fyi] designation was assigned.

4 Diamond

Four Diamond restaurants provide a distinctive fine-dining experience that is typically expensive. Surroundings are highly refined with upscale enhancements throughout. Highly creative chefs use imaginative presentations to augment fresh, top-quality ingredients. A proficient service staff meets or exceeds guest expectations. A wine steward may offer menu-specific knowledge to guide selection.

5 Diamond

Five Diamond restaurants are luxurious and renowned for consistently providing a world-class experience. Highly acclaimed chefs offer artistic menu selections that are imaginative and unique, using only the finest ingredients available. A maitre d' leads an expert service staff in exceeding guest expectations, attending to every detail in an effortless and unobtrusive manner.

The restaurants with 〔fyi〕 in place of Diamonds are included as an *information only* service for members. These listings provide additional dining choices but have not yet been evaluated.

RESTAURANTS

1 Diamond

One Diamond restaurants provide simple, familiar specialty food (such as burgers, chicken, pizza or tacos) at an economical price. Often self-service, basic surroundings complement a no-nonsense approach.

2 Diamond

Two Diamond restaurants offer a familiar, family-oriented experience. Menu selection includes home-style foods and family favorites, often cooked to order, modestly enhanced and reasonably priced. Service is accommodating yet relaxed, a perfect complement to casual surroundings.

3 Diamond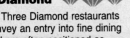

Three Diamond restaurants convey an entry into fine dining and are often positioned as adult-oriented experiences. The atypical menu may feature the latest cooking trends and/or traditional cuisine. Expanded beverage offerings complement the menu. The ambience is well coordinated, comfortable and enhanced by a professional service staff.

Understanding the Lodging Classifications

To ensure that your lodging needs and preferences are met, we recommend that you consider an establishment's classification when making your travel choices. While the quality and comfort at properties with the same Diamond Rating should be consistent (regardless of the classification), there are differences in typical decor/theme elements, range of facilities and service levels.

Lodging Classifications

Bed & Breakfast

Typically smaller scale properties emphasizing a high degree of personal touches that provide guests an "at home" feeling. Guest units tend to be individually decorated. Rooms may not include some modern amenities such as

1884 Paxton House Inn
Thomasville, GA

televisions and telephones, and may have a shared bathroom. Usually owner-operated with a common room or parlor separate from the innkeeper's living quarters, where guests and operators can interact during evening and breakfast hours. Evening office closures are normal. A continental or full, hot breakfast is served and is included in the room rate.

Cabin

Vacation-oriented, typically smaller scale, freestanding units of simple construction—roughly finished logs or stone—and basic design or décor. Often located in wooded, rural, or waterfront locations. As a rule, basic cleaning supplies, kitchen utensils, and complete bed and bath linens are

Greenbrier Valley Resorts
at Cobbly Nob / Gatlinburg, TN

supplied. The guest registration area may be located off site.

Condominium

Vacation-oriented—commonly for extended-stay purposes—apartment-style accommodations of varying design or décor. Routinely available for rent through a management company, units often contain one or more bedrooms, a living room, full kitchen, and an eating area. Studio-type models combine the

The Sands of Kahana
Kahana, Maui, HI

sleeping and living areas into one room. As a rule, basic cleaning supplies, kitchen utensils, and complete bed and bath linens are supplied. The guest registration area may be located off site.

Cottage

Vacation-oriented, typically smaller scale, freestanding units with home style enhancements in architectural design and interior décor. Often located in wooded, rural, or waterfront locations. Units may vary in design and décor. As a rule, basic cleaning supplies, kitchen

Paradise Villas, Little Cayman Island

utensils, and complete bed and bath linens are supplied. The guest registration area may be located off site.

Country Inn

Although similar in definition to a bed and breakfast, country inns are usually larger in scale with spacious public areas and offer a dining facility that serves—at a minimum—breakfast and dinner.

The Lodge at Moosehead Lake
Greenville, ME

Hotel

Commonly, a multistory establishment with interior room entrances offering a variety of guest unit styles. The magnitude of the public areas is determined by the overall theme, location and service level, but may include a variety of facilities such as a

The Grand America Hotel
Salt Lake City, UT

restaurant, shops, fitness center, spa, business center, and/or meeting rooms.

Motel

Commonly, a one- or two-story establishment with exterior room entrances and drive up parking. Typically, guest units have one bedroom with a bathroom of similar décor and design. Public areas and facilities are often limited in size and/or availability.

Best Western Sea Island Inn
Beaufort, SC

Ranch

Typically a working ranch with an obvious rustic, Western theme featuring equestrian-related activities and a variety of guest unit styles.

Lost Valley Ranch, Deckers, CO

Vacation Rental House

Vacation-oriented—commonly for extended-stay purposes—typically larger scale, freestanding, and of varying design or décor. Routinely available for rent through a management company, houses often contain two or more bedrooms, a living room, full kitchen, dining room, and multiple bathrooms. As a rule, basic cleaning supplies, kitchen utensils, and complete bed and bath linens are supplied. The guest registration area may be located off site.

ResortQuest, Hilton Head Island, SC

Lodging Sub-classifications

The following are sub-classifications that may appear along with the classifications listed previously to provide a more specific description of the lodging.

Boutique

Often thematic and typically an informal, yet highly personalized experience; may have a luxurious or quirky style which is fashionable or unique.

Casino

Extensive gambling facilities are available, such as: blackjack, craps, keno, and slot machines. **Note:** This sub-classification will not appear beneath its Diamond Rating in the listing. It will be indicated by a 🎰 icon and will be included in the row of icons following the lodging listing.

Classic

Renowned and landmark properties, older than 50 years, well-known for their unique style and ambience.

Contemporary

Overall design and theme reflects characteristics of the present era's mainstream tastes and style.

Extended Stay

Offers a predominance of long-term accommodations with a designated full-service kitchen area within each unit.

Historic

These properties are typically over 75 years of age and exhibit many features of a historic nature with respect to architecture, design, furnishings, public record, or acclaim. Properties must meet one of the following criteria:

- Maintain the integrity of the historical nature
- Be listed on the National Register of Historic Places
- Have a National Historic Landmark designation or be located in a National Register Historic District

Separate criteria designate historic properties in Canada, Mexico and the Caribbean.

Resort

Recreation-oriented, geared to vacation travelers seeking a specific destination experience. Travel packages, meal plans, themed entertainment, and social and recreational programs are typically available. Recreational facilities are extensive and may include spa treatments, golf, tennis, skiing, fishing, or water sports. Larger resorts may offer a variety of guest accommodations.

Retro

Overall design and theme reflect a contemporary design reinterpreting styles from a bygone era.

Vacation Rental

Typically houses, condos, cottages or cabins; these properties are a "home away from home" offering more room and greater value for the money. In general, they provide the conveniences of home, such as full kitchens and washers/dryers. Located in resort or popular destination areas within close proximity to major points of interest, attractions, or recreation areas, these properties may require a pre-arranged reservation and check-in at an off-site location. Housekeeping services may be limited or not included.

Vintage

Offers a window to the past and provides an experience reflecting a predominance of traits associated with the era of their origin.

Guest Safety

Room Security

In order to be approved for listing in AAA/CAA TourBook guides for the United States and Canada, accommodations must have deadbolt locks on all guest room entry doors and connecting room doors.

If the area outside the guest room door is not visible from inside the room through a window or door panel, viewports must be installed on all guest room entry doors. Bed and breakfast properties and country inns are not required to have viewports. Ground floor and easily accessible sliding doors must be equipped with some type of secondary security locks.

Even with those approval requirements, AAA cannot guarantee guest safety. AAA inspectors view a percentage of rooms at each property since it is not feasible to evaluate every room in every lodging establishment. Therefore, AAA cannot guarantee that there are working locks on all doors and windows in all guest rooms.

Fire Safety

Because of the highly specialized skills needed to conduct professional fire safety inspections, AAA/CAA inspectors cannot assess fire safety.

Properties must meet all federal, state/province and local fire codes. Each guest unit in all U.S. and Canadian lodging properties must be equipped with an operational, single-station smoke detector. A AAA/CAA inspector has evaluated a sampling of the rooms to verify this equipment is in place.

Mexico and the Caribbean

Requirements for some features differ in Mexico and the Caribbean. Examples include door locks and smoke detectors/sprinkler systems, denoted by icons. If a property met AAA's security requirements at the time of the evaluation, the phrase "Meets AAA guest room security requirements" appears in the listing.

Service Animals

Under the Americans with Disabilities Act (ADA), U.S. businesses that serve the public must allow people with disabilities to bring their service animals into all areas of the facility where customers are normally allowed to go.

Businesses may ask if an animal is a service animal and what tasks the animal has been trained to perform. Businesses may not ask about the person's disability, require special identification for the animal or request removal of the animal from the premises except in limited cases that require alternate assistance. Businesses may not charge extra fees for service animals, including standard pet fees, but may charge for damage caused by service animals if guests are normally charged for damage they cause.

Call the U.S. Department of Justice ADA Information Line: (800) 514-0301 or TTY (800) 514-0383, or visit ada.gov. Regulations may differ in Canada, Mexico or the Caribbean.

Frank Frand with his seeing eye dog, Cardinal.

Michigan

Touring at a Snail's Pace

Savor historic Mackinac Island on foot, on a bicycle or by carriage—it's the only way!

Museums, All in a Row

Buildings dedicated to science, surveying and transportation line Lansing's Museum Drive

Motors and Music

Explore Detroit's homes of the automobile barons and the birthplace of the Motown sound

The Unspoiled Upper

The Upper Peninsula preserves a national lakeshore, virgin forests, mountains and wildlife

Seeing the Soo

The Soo Locks can be observed from several vantage points in Sault Ste. Marie

Windmill Island, Holland
© David R. Frazier
Danita Delimont Stock
Photography

Oval Beach, Saugatuck / © Mark Cassino / SuperStock

Mitten-shaped Michigan greets visitors with a hearty wave hello.

When exploring the Wolverine State, start at the base of the thumb, where Henry Ford's jumpy Model T turned Detroit into the world's best known assembly line.

Head to the pinkie, where Sleeping Bear Dunes National Lakeshore is lapped by Lake Michigan, only one of the truly "great" lakes bordering the state. Lining the lakes are more than 100 lighthouses that illuminate the way for American and Canadian ships.

Near the heel of the hand is Holland, a town proud of its Dutch heritage. On any given day you can see shopkeepers scrubbing the cobblestone sidewalks and crafting wooden shoes.

Between the thumb and forefinger is Frankenmuth, which has a decidedly German flavor. Melodies ring through the streets from the 35 bells of the Bavarian Inn Glockenspiel Tower.

And at the fingertip, Mackinac Bridge, one of the longest suspension bridges in the world, connects Colonial-style Mackinaw City to the Upper Peninsula, where more than 150 cascading waterfalls, including spectacular Tahquamenon Falls, delight spectators. Here boats chug through Soo Locks and steep cliffs are dubbed Pictured Rocks.

Spend some time in Michigan; you'll find it carries a bit of everything in its hand.

Ever since Charles King drove the first "horseless carriage" down the streets of Detroit in 1896, Michigan has been synonymous with motoring. Henry Ford and Ransom E. Olds hopped on the wagon, so to speak, and before long, "merry Oldsmobiles" and "Tin Lizzies" came to represent a freedom not previously known to travelers—putting Michigan on the map and making millionaires of many.

Ford's assembly line concept made mass production of automobiles possible, bringing great wealth to auto barons. Visit Henry Ford's Fair Lane mansion in Dearborn to get a glimpse of how the Fords spent their earnings. If the house itself isn't enough to make your jaw drop, Clara Ford's formal rose garden should do it. It once was attended by 20 full-time gardeners.

Take a tour of Edsel and Eleanor Ford's sprawling estate in Grosse Pointe Shores. On its 87 acres is the Play House given to daughter Josephine on her seventh birthday. Constructed in mock-Tudor style and in three-fourths scale, the cottage is every little girl's dream—and is probably more expensive than most *real* houses.

Hit the Road, Jack

The automobile remains the most convenient form of travel, and there's no better means of visiting some of Michigan's smaller towns.

Take to the highway and explore Holland. Be sure to arrive in May, when millions of colorful tulips bloom during the spring festival. Slip into a pair of wooden shoes, clomp around the town's adorable restored downtown and check out the wee Dutch village surrounding De Zwaan windmill.

If you prefer sausage and sauerkraut, cruise to Frankenmuth, which sports a Bavarian architectural flair. You'll think you're smack in the middle of Munich when you hear the Glockenspiel Tower's twinkling bells. Sneak a smooch under the Holz-Brücke covered bridge before heading to giant Bronner's Christmas Wonderland, rumored to be the world's largest Christmas store. With a showroom bigger than a football field, the talk may be true.

Heading north, you'll reach Mackinaw City. Costumed guides at Fort Michilimackinac, built by the French in 1715, reenact life during Colonial days by launching cannons on

Father Jacques Marquette establishes the first settlement at Sault Ste. Marie.
1668

Travel Michigan

Lansing becomes the new state capital, succeeding Detroit.
1847

The Soo Locks are completed, marking the first continuous shipping route between lakes Superior and Huron.
1855

Jeffrey Foltice
Travel Michigan

1783
The Treaty of Paris awards land that includes future Michigan territory to the United States.

1837
Michigan is admitted as the nation's 26th state.

1894
The Kellogg brothers create a breakfast food industry when they develop a flake cereal for use at their Battle Creek Sanitarium.

Michigan Historical Timeline

Lake Huron's shore, cutting logs with cross-cut saws, peddling furs and singing French songs.

Bridge, Tunnel or Ferry

With most of Michigan surrounded by those "great" lakes, bridges provide another handy way to get around. For starters, take the Mackinac Bridge from Michigan's Lower Peninsula to the rugged Upper Peninsula (U.P.). The bridge, affectionately termed "Big Mac," stretches across the Straits of Mackinac, where lakes Michigan and Huron meet.

How about lunch in Canada? Drive over the Detroit River on the Ambassador Bridge or through the Detroit-Windsor Tunnel, both of which link Detroit and Windsor, Ontario. Impress friends back home with your fancy international itinerary.

To get to peaceful Mackinac Island, you'll have to take a ferry, catamaran or plane. Once you're there, ride in a horse-drawn carriage, bike or stroll—but leave your car behind, since no automobiles are allowed on this little island. Browse the boutiques in downtown's gingerbread-laced buildings, sampling home-made fudge at one of many candy shops.

Even if locals call you a "fudgie" (tourist), the chocolaty goodness will make up for it! Next, take a tour of the 1887 Grand Hotel, a beautiful white Victorian building with a sweeping 600-foot-long veranda topped by a sky-blue ceiling.

Outdoorsy folks will love Isle Royale National Park, off the western tip of the U.P. in Lake Superior; a ferry or floatplane can escort you. This roadless island is home to historic lighthouses, shipwrecks, ancient copper mining sites and lots of spots to see moose and wolves.

A unique mode of transit exists on the U.P.—the Soo Locks, which allow ships to navigate the rapids between lakes Huron and Superior. You can take a boat tour through the locks to experience a 21-foot lift to the level of Lake Superior. Adjacent St. Mary's Rapids are a frothy, delightful sight.

And there's more—from a stop on the Underground Railroad in Kalamazoo to Greenfield Village in Dearborn, where the Wright brothers tinkered with the airplane. Michigan will encourage you to gas up the ol' Chevy and put the "pedal to the metal."

Ransom E. Olds establishes the country's first automobile production factory in Lansing.
1900

The Mackinac Bridge opens, linking the Upper and Lower peninsulas.
1957

Randall McCune
Travel Michigan

Jennifer Granholm, who had been elected Michigan's first female attorney general in 1998, is elected as the state's first female governor.
2002

Library of Congress

1908
The General Motors Co. is organized in Flint by William Durant.

1997
Billed as the largest museum of its kind in the world, the 120,000-square-foot Museum of African American History opens in Detroit.

Recreation

You've gotta hand it to Michigan. Complete with three national forests, one national park and two national lakeshores—not to mention four Great Lakes and dozens of state parks from Bald Mountain to Sleepy Hollow—it's no wonder the state packs a punch when it comes to recreation options.

Water Watch

Perhaps the coolest outdoor activity here—literally—is donning wet suit and tanks to go **scuba diving** at one of more than 3,000 shipwrecks littering 38,000 square miles of Michigan's Great Lakes bottomlands. Largely dating to the last quarter of the 19th century, the wrecks are remarkably well-preserved due to the fresh and—here's the key—*extremely* cold waters of lakes Huron, Michigan and Superior. Depths range from 20 to 150 feet, and visibility varies from excellent to muddy.

Some ships worth looking for are the *Bermuda*, an 1880s schooner resting only 25 feet below the surface in Murray Bay, off Munising; and the skeletal *Michael Groh,* which met its fate on a Lake Superior sandbar in November 1895. Of more recent vintage is the *Cedarville*, a 700-foot ore carrier that sank intact after succumbing to Lake Huron's fury in 1966.

Non-diving adventurers aren't left out of the fun, though: **Glass-bottomed boat tours** can be chartered in Munising.

Downed ships aren't all you'll find in Michigan's many waterways; **fishing** is good, too. Along Lake Michigan's shoreline at South Haven and Saugatuck there are plenty of charters targeting coho salmon, which can top 25 pounds. For walleye, float your boat in the Tittabawassee River or Saginaw Bay.

Landlubbers can opt to try their luck on one of several fishing platforms. The 1,000-foot North Pier in St. Joseph and Grand Haven's South Pier are both renowned as perch hangouts. Near Rockford, a deck built specifically to accommodate wheelchairs borders the Rogue River's west bank. And at Lansing's Riverfront Park and Trail there's a water-level dock favored by local anglers.

Those who would rather swing a paddle than cast a line will find ideal conditions for **sea kayaking** off Pictured Rocks National Lakeshore on Lake Superior, whose waters lap sandy beaches and richly layered sandstone cliffs. But even in top-skirted kayaks a wet suit is standard equipment on frigid Superior, and all small-craft boaters are advised to avoid open water and stay well-informed of weather conditions. Popular put-in points include Sand Point, Miners Beach, the Munising Municipal Boat Ramp and Grand Island Landing. Twelvemile Beach Campground and Grand Marais Marina are at the park's east end.

Should you prefer rubbing shoulders with the big ships, board an authentic ferry steamer in Ludington for a Lake Michigan **cruise** with an "ocean liner" feel. Or head to Sault Ste. Marie, where 2-hour tours through the Soo Locks put you right alongside enormous freighters.

In addition to its border lakes, Michigan has many inviting interior waterways offering myriad **boating** options, from low-key **canoeing** on the Au Sable River, near Roscommon, to high-speed **water skiing** at Haughton Lake, the state's largest inland body of water.

Shore Leave

You can enjoy Michigan's wealth of water from a distance, too. **Climb** the dunes to a sweeping view of Lake Michigan at Sleeping Bear Dunes National Lakeshore. Or **hike** in sight of five waterfalls in the Ottawa National Forest's Black River Harbor area. Within Huron-Manistee National Forest, the Jewell Lake Trail is generally flat enough to allow for easy lakeside ambling. And **walkers** will enjoy Sault Ste. Marie's waterfront Locks Park Historic Walkway and Silver City's .5-mile elevated boardwalk, which follows the Presque Isle River and passes still more waterfalls.

Scenic drives do the job as well. Especially pretty are the lakeside highway north of Muskegon State Park and Bessemer's Black River National Forest Scenic Byway.

But to really get an overview of the landscape, visit Tower Hill, outside Bridgman, where perfectly placed winds lure **hang gliders** into the sky year-round.

Recreational Activities

Throughout the TourBook, you may notice a Recreational Activities heading with bulleted listings of recreation-oriented establishments listed underneath. Similar operations also may be mentioned in Destination City recreation sections. Since normal AAA inspection criteria cannot be applied, these establishments are presented only for information. Age, height and weight restrictions may apply. Reservations often are recommended and sometimes are required. Addresses and/or phone numbers are provided so visitors can contact the attraction for additional information.

Fast Facts

POPULATION: 9,938,444.

AREA: 56,804 square miles; ranks 23rd.

CAPITAL: Lansing.

HIGHEST POINT: 1,979 ft., Mount Arvon.

LOWEST POINT: 571 ft., Lake Erie.

TIME ZONE(S): Eastern/Central. DST.

TEEN DRIVING LAWS: Driving is not permitted midnight-5 a.m. Minimum age for an unrestricted driver's license is 17. For more information about Michigan driver's license regulations phone (888) 767-6424.

MINIMUM AGE FOR GAMBLING: 21.

SEAT BELT/CHILD RESTRAINT LAWS: Seat belts required for driver and front-seat passengers 16 and older. Children ages 8 until 16 are required to be in a seat belt; child restraints required for under 8 years old and less than 57 inches. Children under age 4 must be in rear seat of vehicle, if possible.

CELL PHONE RESTRICTIONS: Text messaging while driving is prohibited. In Detroit, drivers are banned from using handheld cell phones. In Troy, drivers are prohibited from using handheld cell phones or engaging in any activity that diverts driver attention.

HELMETS FOR MOTORCYCLISTS: Required for all riders.

RADAR DETECTORS: Permitted.

MOVE OVER LAW: Driver is required to slow down and vacate the lane nearest stopped police, fire and rescue vehicles using audible or flashing signals. The law includes tow trucks.

FIREARMS LAWS: Vary by state or county. Contact local law enforcement agencies or the Michigan Department of State Police, Statistical Records, Firearms Unit, P.O. Box 30634, Lansing, MI 48909; phone (517) 241-1917.

HOLIDAYS: Jan. 1; Martin Luther King Jr. Day, Jan. (3rd Mon.); Presidents' Day, Feb. (3rd Mon.); Memorial Day, May (last Mon.); July 4; Labor Day, Sept. (1st Mon.); Veterans Day, Nov. 11; Thanksgiving; Dec. 24; Christmas, Dec. 25.

TAXES: Michigan's statewide sales tax is 6 percent. Local options allow taxes ranging from 1.5 to 6 percent on lodgings in convention hotels and lodging taxes of up to 5 percent at other facilities. An additional 2 percent tax is charged in metropolitan areas.

INFORMATION CENTERS: State welcome centers are maintained all year on I-94 at New Buffalo; on I-69 at Coldwater; on US 23 at Dundee; on US 2 at Ironwood; on US 2 in Iron Mountain; on US 41S at Marquette; on US 41 in Menominee; on I-75N in St. Ignace; on I-75 at the south end of the International Bridge at Sault Ste. Marie; on I-94 at Water Street in Port Huron; on US 127 at a rest area 1 mile north of Clare; on I-75 in Mackinaw City; on I-75 at Monroe; and on I-75N in Detroit.

FURTHER INFORMATION FOR VISITORS:

Travel Michigan
Michigan Economic Development
  Corporation
300 N. Washington Sq.
Lansing, MI 48913
(888) 784-7328

RECREATION INFORMATION:

Parks and Recreation Division
Department of Natural Resources
Third Floor
P.O. Box 30257
Lansing, MI 48909-7757
(517) 373-9900
(800) 447-2757 (reservations)

FISHING AND HUNTING REGULATIONS:

Wildlife Division
Department of Natural Resources
Fourth Floor
P.O. Box 30444
Lansing, MI 48909-7544
(517) 373-1263

NATIONAL FOREST INFORMATION:

U.S. Forest Service
626 E. Wisconsin Ave.
Milwaukee, WI 53202
(414) 297-3600
(877) 444-6777 (reservations)

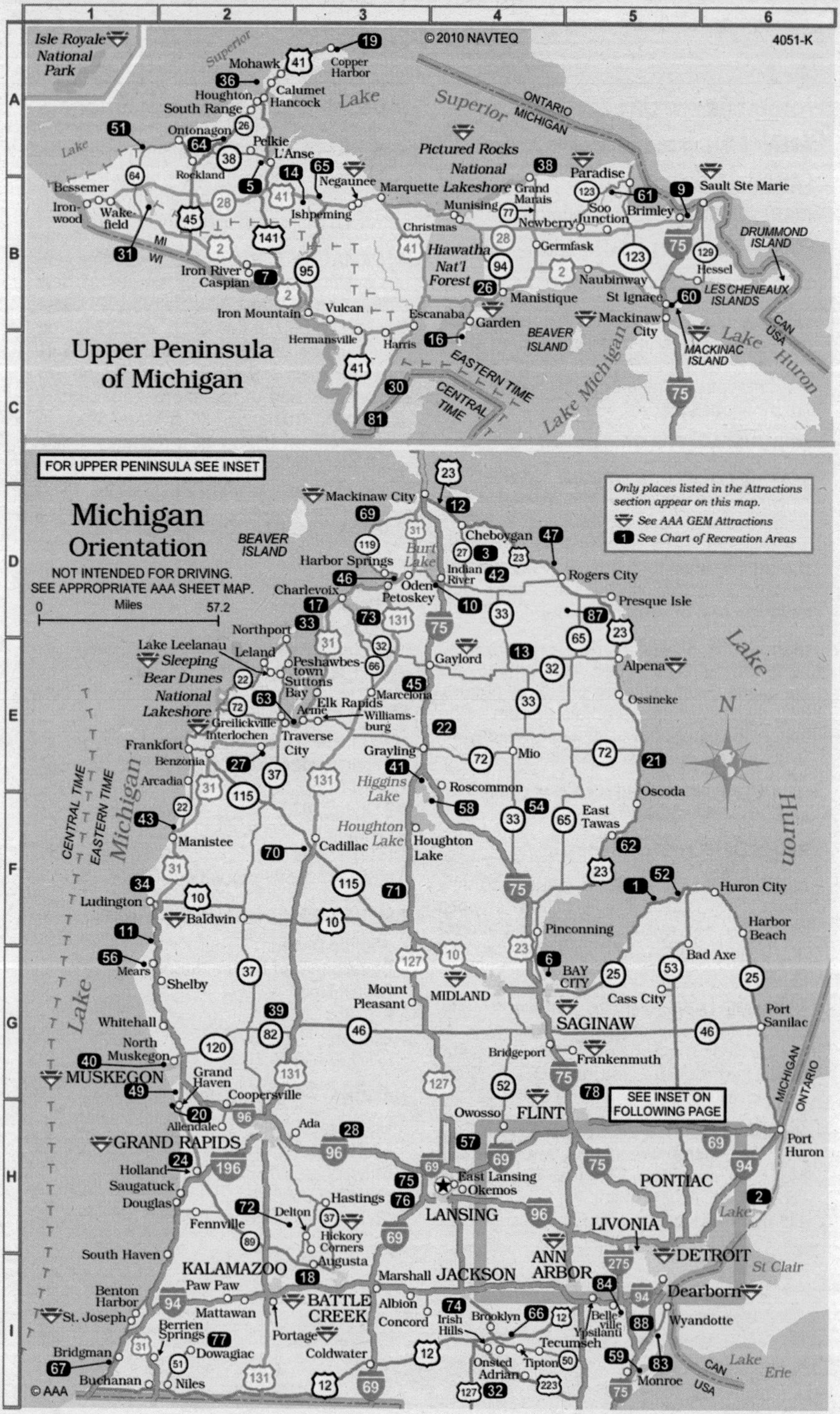

© 2010 NAVTEQ

4051-K

Isle Royale National Park

Mohawk 41 Copper Harbor 19
36
Houghton Calumet Hancock
South Range
51 Ontonagon 26
64 Pelkie
38 L'Anse 65 Negaunee
Rockland 5 14
Bessemer 141 Ishpeming
Iron-wood Wakefield 45 2
31 MI WI
Iron River 7 95
Caspian
Iron Mountain Vulcan
Hermansville Harris 16

Superior

Lake Superior

ONTARIO
MICHIGAN

Pictured Rocks National Lakeshore
Marquette Grand Marais 38 Paradise 61
Munising 77 Newberry Soo Junction 123 Brimley 9
Christmas Sault Ste Marie
Hiawatha Nat'l Forest 94 Germfask 123 75 129 Hessel
26 DRUMMOND ISLAND
Manistique 2 Naubinway LES CHENEAUX ISLANDS
Escanaba Garden St Ignace 60 CAN USA
BEAVER ISLAND Mackinaw City MACKINAC ISLAND
75 Lake Huron

Upper Peninsula of Michigan

EASTERN TIME
30 CENTRAL TIME
81

Lake Michigan

FOR UPPER PENINSULA SEE INSET

Michigan Orientation

NOT INTENDED FOR DRIVING.
SEE APPROPRIATE AAA SHEET MAP.

0 Miles 57.2

Only places listed in the Attractions section appear on this map.
See AAA GEM Attractions
1 See Chart of Recreation Areas

Mackinaw City 23
69 12
BEAVER ISLAND Cheboygan 47
Harbor Springs 119 27 3 23
Charlevoix 46 Oden Indian River 42 Rogers City
17 Petoskey 10 33 Presque Isle
Northport 33 73 131 75 13 87 23
Lake Leelanau 31 32 65 Alpena
Sleeping Bear Dunes Leland Peshawbestown 66 45 32
National Lakeshore 22 Suttons Bay Marcetona 33 Ossineke
63 Elk Rapids Williamsburg
Greilickville 72 Acme 22
Interlochen Traverse City Grayling 72 Mio 72 21
Frankfort 27 37 41 Oscoda
Benzonia 115 Higgins Lake Roscommon
Arcadia 31 131 58 54 East 65
22 Houghton Lake 33 Tawas
43 Manistee Cadillac 62
34 70 115 71 23 1 52 Huron City
Ludington 10 Harbor Beach
11 Baldwin 10 Pinconning
56 Mears 127 6 BAY CITY Bad Axe
Shelby 37 10 25 53 25
Whitehall 39 Mount Pleasant MIDLAND SAGINAW Cass City Port Sanilac
40 North Muskegon 82 46 75 46
MUSKEGON 120 Bridgeport Frankenmuth
49 Grand Haven 131 127 52 78 SEE INSET ON FOLLOWING PAGE
20 Coopersville Owosso FLINT Port Huron
GRAND RAPIDS Ada 28 57 PONTIAC 69 94
24 96 69 75 2
Holland 196 East Lansing Okemos LIVONIA DETROIT
Saugatuck Hastings 75 76 96 St Clair
Douglas 72 Delton 37 LANSING ANN ARBOR 275 Dearborn
Fennville 89 Hickory Corners 69 JACKSON 84 94
South Haven Augusta Marshall 74 66 Belleville 88 Wyandotte
KALAMAZOO 18 Albion Brooklyn 12 Ypsilanti
Benton Harbor Paw Paw BATTLE CREEK Concord Irish Hills Tecumseh 59 83
St. Joseph 94 Mattawan Portage 12 Onsted 50 Monroe
Bridgman 77 Dowagiac Coldwater Adrian Tipton
67 Berrien Springs 51 127 32 223 75 CAN USA
Buchanan Niles 131 69 Lake Erie

CENTRAL TIME EASTERN TIME

Lake Michigan

MICHIGAN ONTARIO

© AAA

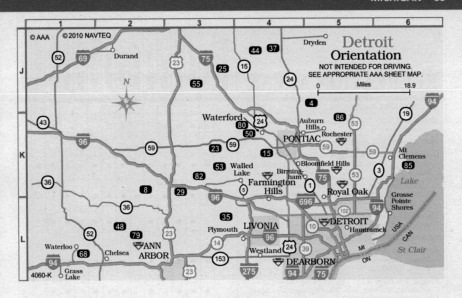

Michigan Temperature Averages
Maximum/Minimum
From the records of The Weather Channel Interactive, Inc.

	JAN	FEB	MAR	APR	MAY	JUNE	JULY	AUG	SEPT	OCT	NOV	DEC
Detroit	33 / 20	36 / 22	46 / 29	59 / 39	72 / 51	80 / 60	85 / 65	82 / 64	75 / 56	62 / 45	49 / 36	38 / 25
Grand Rapids	29 / 16	33 / 18	43 / 26	57 / 36	70 / 47	78 / 56	82 / 61	80 / 59	72 / 51	60 / 40	46 / 31	34 / 21
Houghton Lake	26 / 10	29 / 11	39 / 19	53 / 31	67 / 41	76 / 49	80 / 53	77 / 52	68 / 45	56 / 36	42 / 28	30 / 17
Marquette	25 / 11	29 / 14	37 / 22	48 / 33	61 / 42	70 / 51	76 / 57	74 / 57	66 / 49	55 / 40	40 / 28	30 / 17
Sault Ste. Marie	21 / 5	25 / 7	34 / 16	48 / 29	63 / 39	71 / 47	76 / 52	74 / 52	65 / 45	53 / 36	39 / 26	27 / 13

Stay. Play. Dine. Save. Visit AAA.com/Travel
or CAA.ca/Travel for Information To Go!

RECREATION AREAS

	MAP LOCATION	CAMPING	PICNICKING	HIKING TRAILS	BOATING	BOAT RAMP	BOAT RENTAL	FISHING	SWIMMING	PETS ON LEASH	BICYCLE TRAILS	WINTER SPORTS	VISITOR CENTER	LODGE/CABINS	FOOD SERVICE
NATIONAL PARKS *(See place listings)*															
Isle Royale (A-1) 571,790 acres in Lake Superior. Nature programs. Scuba diving.		•	•	•				•						•	•
NATIONAL FORESTS *(See place listings)*															
Hiawatha 893,348 acres in the Upper Peninsula. Canoeing, cross-country skiing, hunting, kayaking; horse trails, motorized vehicle trails.		•	•	•	•	•	•	•	•	•	•	•	•		•
Huron-Manistee 976,043 acres in the northern part of the Lower Peninsula. Canoeing, cross-country skiing, hunting, snowmobiling; horse trails, motorized vehicle trails.		•	•	•	•	•	•	•	•	•	•	•	•		•
Ottawa 986,518 acres in the Upper Peninsula. Cross-country skiing, hunting, snowmobiling, snowshoeing; horse trails.		•	•	•	•	•	•	•	•	•		•	•		
NATIONAL LAKESHORES *(See place listings)*															
Pictured Rocks (A-4) 70,822 acres along Lake Superior n.e. of Munising. Cross-country skiing, hunting, snowmobiling, snowshoeing, waterskiing.		•	•	•	•	•		•	•	•		•	•		•
Sleeping Bear Dunes (E-2) 71,105 acres along Lake Michigan n. of Frankfort. Nature programs. Cross-country skiing, ice fishing, snowshoeing; horse trails.		•	•	•	•	•		•	•	•		•	•	•	
STATE															
Albert E. Sleeper (F-5) 723 acres 5 mi. n.e. of Caseville on SR 25. Cross-country skiing.	❶	•	•	•				•	•	•		•	•		
Algonac (H-6) 1,450 acres 2 mi. n. of Algonac on SR 29. Cross-country skiing, hunting.	❷	•	•	•				•		•		•			
Aloha (D-4) 107 acres 9 mi. s. of Cheboygan on SR 33.	❸	•	•	•	•	•		•	•	•					
Bald Mountain (J-5) 4,637 acres 7 mi. n. of Pontiac off SR 24. Cross-country skiing, hunting, snowmobiling; shooting range.	❹		•	•	•	•		•	•	•		•	•		
Baraga (B-2) 56 acres 1 mi. s. of Baraga on US 41. Nature programs. Cross-country skiing.	❺	•	•	•	•	•		•		•		•	•		
Bay City (G-4) 2,100 acres 5 mi. n. of Bay City on SR 247. Cross-country skiing, hunting; nature center.	❻	•	•	•				•	•	•		•	•		
Bewabic (B-2) 315 acres 4 mi. w. of Crystal Falls on US 2. Cross-country skiing, tennis.	❼	•	•	•	•	•		•	•	•		•			
Brighton (K-2) 4,913 acres 3 mi. w. of Brighton on Main St. (Brighton Rd.), then s. on Chilson Rd. Cross-country skiing; horse rental.	❽	•	•	•	•	•	•	•	•	•	•	•	•		
Brimley (B-5) 160 acres 1 mi. e. of Brimley on SR 221. Hunting.	❾	•	•	•				•	•	•					
Burt Lake (D-4) 406 acres .5 mi. s.w. of Indian River on SR 68. Cross-country skiing.	❿	•	•	•	•	•		•	•	•		•			•
Charles Mears (F-1) 50 acres 1 mi. n. of Pentwater off US 31 Bus. Rte. Snowmobiling; playground.	⓫	•	•	•				•	•	•		•		•	•
Cheboygan (D-4) 1,250 acres 4 mi. e. of Cheboygan on US 23. Cross-country skiing, hunting.	⓬	•	•	•	•	•		•	•	•		•	•	•	
Clear Lake (E-4) 290 acres 9 mi. n. of Atlanta off SR 33. Cross-country skiing.	⓭	•	•	•	•	•		•	•	•		•	•		
Craig Lake (B-3) just n. of US 41 in Imperial Heights. Cross-country skiing, hunting, snowmobiling.	⓮		•	•	•			•				•		•	
Dodge No. 4 (K-4) 136 acres 6 mi. w. of Pontiac off SR 59. Cross-country skiing; playground.	⓯		•	•	•			•	•	•		•			•
Fayette (C-4) 711 acres in Garden off SR 183. Historic. Cross-country skiing, kayaking, scuba diving. *(See Garden p. 72)*	⓰	•	•	•	•	•		•	•	•		•	•		
Fisherman's Island (D-3) 2,678 acres 3 mi. s.w. of Charlevoix off US 31. Cross-country skiing, hunting.	⓱	•	•	•				•	•	•					
Fort Custer (I-3) 3,033 acres 8 mi. w. of Battle Creek on SR 96. Nature programs. Cross-country skiing, dogsledding, hunting, snowmobiling.	⓲	•	•	•	•	•	•	•	•	•	•	•	•		
Fort Wilkins (A-3) 700 acres 1 mi. e. of Copper Harbor on US 41. Historic. Cross-country skiing. *(See Copper Harbor p. 49)*	⓳	•	•	•	•	•		•	•	•	•	•	•	•	•

RECREATION AREAS

	MAP LOCATION	CAMPING	PICNICKING	HIKING TRAILS	BOATING	BOAT RAMP	BOAT RENTAL	FISHING	SWIMMING	PETS ON LEASH	BICYCLE TRAILS	WINTER SPORTS	VISITOR CENTER	LODGE/CABINS	FOOD SERVICE
Grand Haven (H-2) 48 acres 1 mi. w. of Grand Haven off US 31. Cross-country skiing.	20	•	•	•				•	•	•		•			•
Harrisville (E-5) 107 acres 1 mi. s. of Harrisville on US 23.	21	•	•	•					•	•					
Hartwick Pines (E-4) 9,672 acres 7 mi. n.e. of Grayling on SR 93. Historic. Cross-country skiing, hunting. *(See Grayling p. 76)*	22	•	•	•		•		•		•		•	•		
Highland (K-3) 5,524 acres 2 mi. e. of Highland off SR 59. Historic. Cross-country skiing; horse rental.	23	•	•	•	•			•	•	•		•		•	
Holland (H-2) 142 acres 7 mi. w. of Holland on US 31. Playground.	24	•	•						•	•					•
Holly (J-3) 7,670 acres about 7 mi. e. of I-75 in Holly. Cross-country skiing, disc golf, hunting, snowmobiling.	25	•	•	•	•	•	•	•	•	•		•		•	
Indian Lake (B-4) 567 acres 5 mi. w. of Manistique on SR 442. Nature programs.	26	•	•	•	•	•	•	•	•	•		•			
Interlochen (E-2) 187 acres 1 mi. s. of Interlochen on SR 137. Nature programs.	27	•	•	•	•	•		•	•	•				•	•
Ionia (H-3) 4,085 acres 2 mi. w. of Ionia on SR 66. Cross-country skiing, hunting, snowmobiling; horse trails, playground.	28	•	•	•	•			•	•	•	•	•		•	
Island Lake (K-3) 4,000 acres 4 mi. s.e. of Brighton off US 23. Canoeing, cross-country skiing, hunting, snowmobiling; shooting range.	29		•	•	•		•	•	•	•		•		•	
J.W. Wells (C-3) 678 acres 2 mi. s. of Cedar River on SR 35. Cross-country skiing.	30	•	•	•				•	•	•		•		•	
Lake Gogebic (B-1) 360 acres 12 mi. n.e. of Marenisco on SR 64. Cross-country skiing. *(See Ottawa National Forest p. 100)*	31	•	•	•	•	•		•	•	•		•		•	
Lake Hudson (I-4) 2,796 acres 6 mi. s.e. of Hudson on SR 156. Hunting.	32	•	•		•	•		•	•	•					
Leelanau (D-3) 1,350 acres 7 mi. n. of Northport on SR 201. Cross-country skiing, hunting; playground. *(See Northport p. 98)*	33	•	•					•	•	•		•		•	
Ludington (F-1) 5,300 acres 8 mi. n. of Ludington on SR 116. Cross-country skiing; nature center. *(See Ludington p. 87)*	34	•	•	•		•		•	•	•		•	•		•
Maybury (L-3) 944 acres w. of Detroit on I-96 to I-275N, then 5 mi. w. on Beck Rd. Cross-country skiing; horse rental, playground.	35		•	•				•		•	•	•	•		
McLain (A-2) 443 acres 8 mi. w. of Calumet on SR 203. Nature programs. Cross-country skiing, hunting, snowshoeing. *(See Hancock p. 77)*	36	•	•	•		•		•	•	•		•		•	
Metamora-Hadley (J-4) 723 acres 10 mi. s. of Lapeer off SR 24. Cross-country skiing, snowmobiling.	37	•	•	•	•			•	•	•		•			•
Muskallonge Lake (A-4) 217 acres just n. of Muskallonge Lake at 30042 CR 407 (Deer Park Truck Tr.). Nature programs. Snowmobiling.	38	•	•	•	•	•		•	•	•		•			
Muskegon (G-1) 1,165 acres 4 mi. w. of North Muskegon on Memorial Dr. Cross-country skiing. *(See Muskegon p. 96)*	39	•	•	•		•		•	•	•		•		•	
Newaygo (G-2) 257 acres 8 mi. w. of Morley off US 131 following signs. Playground.	40	•	•		•	•		•	•	•					
North Higgins Lake (E-3) 429 acres 7 mi. w. of Roscommon via US 127 and Military Rd. Cross-country skiing; playground. *(See Roscommon p. 105)*	41	•	•	•	•	•	•	•	•	•		•	•	•	•
Onaway (D-4) 158 acres on Black Lake 7 mi. n.w. of Onaway on SR 211. Cross-country skiing; playground.	42	•	•	•	•	•		•	•	•		•			
Orchard Beach (F-1) 201 acres 2 mi. n. of Manistee on SR 110. Cross-country skiing.	43	•	•	•					•	•		•		•	
Ortonville (J-4) 5,400 acres 4 mi. n.e. of Ortonville on SR 15. Cross-country skiing, equestrian camping, hunting; shooting range.	44	•	•	•	•			•	•	•		•		•	
Otsego Lake (E-3) 62 acres 3.8 mi. n. of Waters on S. Old 27.	45	•	•	•	•	•		•	•	•				•	•
Petoskey (D-3) 303 acres at Petoskey off SR 119. Cross-country skiing. *(See Petoskey p. 101)*	46	•	•	•					•	•	•	•		•	

RECREATION AREAS

	MAP LOCATION	CAMPING	PICNICKING	HIKING TRAILS	BOATING	BOAT RAMP	BOAT RENTAL	FISHING	SWIMMING	PETS ON LEASH	BICYCLE TRAILS	WINTER SPORTS	VISITOR CENTER	LODGE/CABINS	FOOD SERVICE
P.H. Hoeft (D-4) 301 acres 6 mi. n.w. of Rogers City on US 23. Nature programs. Cross-country skiing, hunting; Huron dunes. *(See Rogers City p. 105)*	47	•	•	•				•	•	•	•	•		•	
Pinckney (L-2) 10,201 acres 4 mi. s.w. of Pinckney via SR 36. Cross-country skiing; horse rental.	48	•	•	•	•	•	•	•	•	•		•		•	
P.J. Hoffmaster (G-1) 1,043 acres 10 mi. n.w. of Grand Haven off US 31. Cross-country skiing; nature center. *(See Muskegon p. 97)*	49	•	•	•					•	•		•	•	•	
Pontiac Lake (K-4) 3,745 acres 8 mi. w. of Pontiac on SR 59. Cross-country skiing, snowmobiling; archery and rifle ranges, horse rental, playground.	50	•	•	•	•	•	•	•	•	•	•	•		•	
Porcupine Mountains Wilderness (A-1) 60,000 acres 15.5 mi. w. of Ontonagon on Headquarters Rd. Scenic. Nature programs. Canoeing, cross-country skiing, hunting. *(See Ontonagon p. 99)*	51	•	•	•	•	•	•	•	•	•	•	•	•	•	•
Port Crescent (F-5) 600 acres 5 mi. s.w. of Port Austin on SR 25. Canoeing, cross-country skiing, hunting; playground.	52	•	•	•				•	•	•		•		•	
Proud Lake (K-3) 4,700 acres 4 mi. s.e. of Milford off I-96. Canoeing, cross-country skiing, hunting, snowmobiling; horse trails.	53	•	•	•	•	•	•	•	•	•		•		•	
Rifle River (F-4) 4,449 acres 6 mi. s.e. of Rose City on Rose City Rd. Cross-country skiing.	54	•	•	•	•			•	•	•		•		•	
Seven Lakes (J-3) 1,434 acres 1 mi. w. of Holly off US 23. Cross-country skiing, hunting; playground.	55	•	•	•	•	•	•	•	•	•		•		•	
Silver Lake (G-1) 2,936 acres on Silver Lake 7 mi. w. of Mears via US 31. Nature programs. Hunting; off-road vehicle area. *(See Mears p. 93)*	56	•	•	•	•	•	•	•	•	•				•	
Sleepy Hollow (H-4) 2,860 acres 15 mi. n.e. of Lansing off US 127. Cross-country skiing, hunting; playgrounds.	57	•	•	•	•	•	•	•	•	•		•			•
South Higgins Lake (F-4) 962 acres 8 mi. s.w. of Roscommon off US 127. Cross-country skiing, hunting; playground. *(See Roscommon p. 105)*	58	•	•	•	•	•	•	•	•	•		•			
Sterling (I-5) 1,300 acres e. of I-75 on the n. edge of Monroe on State Park Rd. Nature programs. Playground.	59	•	•	•	•			•	•	•				•	
Straits (B-5) 181 acres 1 mi. s.w. of St. Ignace on US 2. Playground.	60	•	•					•	•	•				•	
Tahquamenon Falls (B-5) 46,179 acres 12 mi. w. of Paradise on SR 123. Scenic. Nature programs. Canoeing, cross-country skiing, hunting, snowmobiling. *(See Paradise p. 101)*	61	•	•	•	•	•	•	•	•	•		•	•		•
Tawas Point (F-5) 183 acres 3 mi. e. of East Tawas off US 23. Nature programs. *(See East Tawas p. 68)*	62	•	•	•				•	•	•				•	
Traverse City (E-2) 47 acres 2 mi. e. of Traverse City on US 31. *(See Traverse City p. 112)*	63	•	•	•		•	•	•	•	•				•	•
Twin Lakes (A-2) 175 acres 25 mi. s. of Houghton on SR 26. Cross-country skiing, snowmobiling; playground.	64	•	•	•	•	•	•	•	•	•		•		•	
Van Riper (A-3) 1,044 acres 3 mi. w. of Champion on US 41. Nature programs. Cross-country skiing, hunting, snowmobiling.	65	•	•	•	•	•	•	•	•	•		•		•	•
Walter J. Hayes (I-4) 654 acres 9 mi. w. of Clinton off US 12. Playground.	66	•	•	•	•			•	•	•				•	
Warren Dunes (I-1) 1,952 acres on Lake Michigan 3 mi. s.w. of Bridgman via Red Arrow Hwy. Cross-country skiing, hunting. *(See Bridgman p. 45)*	67	•	•	•					•	•		•		•	•
Waterloo (L-1) 20,500 acres 7 mi. w. of Chelsea off I-94. Cross-country skiing, hunting, snowmobiling; geology center, horse rental, playground.	68	•	•	•	•	•	•	•	•	•		•	•	•	•
Wilderness (D-3) 10,512 acres 11 mi. w. of Mackinaw City on Wilderness Park Dr. Nature programs. Cross-country skiing, hunting.	69	•	•	•	•	•	•	•	•	•		•		•	
William Mitchell (F-2) 334 acres 4 mi. w. of Cadillac on SR 115. Cross-country skiing; museum. *(See Cadillac p. 46)*	70	•	•	•	•	•	•	•	•	•		•	•	•	•
Wilson (F-3) 36 acres 1 mi. n. of Harrison on US 127 Bus. Rte.	71	•	•		•			•	•	•				•	

RECREATION AREAS

	MAP LOCATION	CAMPING	PICNICKING	HIKING TRAILS	BOATING	BOAT RAMP	BOAT RENTAL	FISHING	SWIMMING	PETS ON LEASH	BICYCLE TRAILS	WINTER SPORTS	VISITOR CENTER	LODGE/CABINS	FOOD SERVICE
Yankee Springs (H-2) 5,200 acres 8 mi. e. of Bradley off A-42 following signs. Cross-country skiing, hunting; playground.	72	•	•	•	•	•		•	•	•	•	•		•	
Young (D-3) 563 acres 2 mi. n.w. of Boyne City on SR 75. Nature programs. Cross-country skiing.	73	•	•	•	•	•		•	•	•		•	•	•	•
OTHER															
Ella Sharp (I-4) 562 acres 2 mi. s. of Jackson on 4th St. Golf (18 holes), tennis; driving range, playground. *(See Jackson p. 84)*	74		•	•				•	•	•		•	•		•
Fitzgerald (H-3) 78 acres 2 mi. w. of Grand Ledge on SR 43. Nature programs. Cross-country skiing, sledding; playground.	75		•	•	•	•	•	•		•		•	•	•	
Fox Memorial (H-3) 35 acres 1 mi. n. of Potterville off SR 100. Cross-country skiing; playground.	76		•	•						•		•			
Fred Russ Forest (I-2) 13 acres on Marcellus Hwy., 8 mi. e. of Dowagiac. Canoeing, cross-country skiing; horse trails, playground	77		•	•	•			•				•			
Genesee (G-5) 4,540 acres 6 mi. n.e. of Flint off I-475 exit 13. Cross-country skiing, disc golf, snowmobiling, tennis; playground. *(See Flint p. 70)*	78		•	•	•	•		•	•	•	•	•	•		
Hudson Mills (L-2) 1,549 acres 12 mi. n.w. of Ann Arbor via US 23 and N. Territorial Rd. Nature programs. Canoeing, cross-country skiing, disc golf, golf (18 holes), kayaking; nature trails, playground.	79		•	•	•	•	•	•		•	•	•	•	•	•
Indian Springs (K-4) 2,215 acres 5 mi. s.w. of Clarkston on White Lake Rd. Nature programs. Cross-country skiing, golf (18 holes); nature trails.	80		•	•						•	•	•	•	•	
John Henes (C-3) 45 acres 2.5 mi. n.e. of Menominee off SR 35.	81		•	•				•	•	•		•	•		
Kensington (K-3) 4,481 acres 35 mi. n.w. of Detroit via I-96. Canoeing, cross-country skiing, disc golf, golf (18 holes), ice fishing, ice-skating, sledding; farm, horse trails, nature center.	82		•	•	•	•	•	•	•	•	•	•	•		•
Lake Erie (I-5) 1,607 acres near Gibraltar on W. Jefferson. Bird-watching, canoeing, cross-country skiing, golf (18 holes), kayaking, sledding; marina, nature center, playground, wave pool.	83		•	•	•	•	•	•	•	•	•	•	•		•
Lower Huron (I-5) 1,258 acres 5 mi. s. of Belleville via Huron River Dr. to Waltz Rd. Canoeing, cross-country skiing, golf (18 holes), ice-skating; nature trails, pool.	84		•	•				•	•	•	•	•			•
Metro Beach (K-6) 770 acres 3 mi. e. of Mount Clemens via Metropolitan Pkwy. (Sixteen Mile Rd.). Nature programs. Bird-watching, cross-country skiing, ice-skating; nature center, nature trails.	85		•	•	•	•		•	•	•	•	•	•		
Stony Creek (K-5) 4,461 acres near Utica on 26 Mile Rd. Bird-watching, canoeing, cross-country skiing, disc golf, golf (18 holes), ice-skating, kayaking, sledding; nature center, nature trails.	86		•	•	•	•	•	•	•	•	•	•	•		
Sunken Lake Campground (D-5) 160 acres 5 mi. s. of Posen on SR 65, 1 mi. w. on Maple Ln., then 2 mi. n. on Leer Rd. Playground.	87	•	•	•	•	•		•	•	•		•			
Willow Metropark (I-5) 1,525 acres 4 mi. n.w. of Flat Rock on Willow Rd. Cross-country skiing, disc golf, golf (18 holes), ice fishing, ice-skating, sledding, tobogganing; driving range, paddle boats, pool.	88		•	•	•			•	•	•	•	•	•		•

Points of Interest

ACME (E-3) pop. 4,332, elev. 604'

MUSIC HOUSE MUSEUM is 1.5 mi. n. of SR 72 at 7377 US 31N. The late 19th-century farm complex includes re-creations of a general store, saloon and lyric theater. Museum galleries showcase antique radios, phonographs, music boxes, nickelodeons and organs; a 1924 Wurlitzer Theater Organ and a 97-key Mortier Dance Organ, built in Antwerp in 1922, are highlights.

Entrance is by guided tour only. **Time:** Allow 1 hour, 30 minutes minimum. **Hours:** Tours are offered Mon.-Sat. 10-4, Sun. noon-4, May-Oct.; Sat. 10-4, Sun. noon-4, Nov.-Dec. Phone for holiday hours. Closed Thanksgiving and Dec. 25. **Cost:** $10; $3 (ages 6-15); $25 (family). **Phone:** (231) 938-9300.

ADA (H-3) pop. 9,882, elev. 664'

AMWAY CORP. WELCOME CENTER is 5 mi. e. of I-96 via SR 21 at 7575 Fulton St. E. The center offers interactive touch-screen displays and audiovisual presentations about product manufacturing and the history of the company. **Time:** Allow 1 hour minimum. **Hours:** Mon.-Fri. 8:30-noon and 1-5. **Cost:** Free. Ages 0-12 must be with an adult. **Phone:** (616) 787-6701.

ADRIAN (I-4) pop. 21,574, elev. 812'

Established in 1825, Adrian once was a bustling community of industry with three automobile manufacturing companies. Today the seat of Lenawee County is home to Adrian College and Siena Heights University. Located on the Raisin River, Adrian has an impressive historic district centered on Dennis and State streets. The 79 houses in the district exemplify the evolution of architectural styles in the area, from the Greek and Gothic revivals of the 1830s to Italianate to the Queen Anne-style houses that became popular after the Civil War. The houses are all privately owned.

The Croswell Opera House, 129 E. Maumee St., is an example of the utilitarian architecture prevalent after the Civil War. It has been offering musicals, plays, lectures and operas since 1866; phone (517) 264-7469.

Lenawee County Conference and Visitors Bureau: 209 N. Main St., Adrian, MI 49221. **Phone:** (517) 263-7747 or (800) 536-2933.

Shopping areas: Adrian Mall, at the junction of US 223 and SR 52, has Elder-Beerman, JCPenney and Sears.

LENAWEE COUNTY HISTORICAL SOCIETY MUSEUM, 110 E. Church St. at jct. SR 52 (S. Main St.), occupies the former library, an historic Richardson Romanesque building resembling a castle. The massive collection relates to local history from the mid-1800s to the mid-1900s and covers economic development, items used in everyday life, government and politics, transportation history and the Underground Railroad. Clothing, dentistry tools, dolls, furniture and toys are displayed.

The historical records and archives contain documents, photographs and postcards. **Time:** Allow 30 minutes minimum. **Hours:** Tues.-Sat. 10-2 (also Sat. 2-4). Closed Jan. 1, Memorial Day, July 4, Thanksgiving and Dec. 25. **Cost:** Free. **Phone:** (517) 265-6071.

ALBION (I-3) pop. 9,144, elev. 950'

Established at the forks of the Kalamazoo River, Albion retains its history in restored buildings along brick-lined Main Street. The Historic Walkway winds around and across the river to notable landmarks, including Albion College.

The Greater Albion Chamber of Commerce: 203 S. Superior St., P.O. Box 238, Albion, MI 49224. **Phone:** (517) 629-5533.

WHITEHOUSE NATURE CENTER is .25 mi. s.e. of the Albion College campus, just off Hannah St. The 135-acre outdoor education facility offers five self-guiding nature trails through a variety of natural and man-made habitats. The interpretive building houses a small observation room and exhibits; trail brochures are available.

Guided tours are available by appointment. **Time:** Allow 1 hour minimum. **Hours:** Building open daily 10:30-4:30; closed major and college holidays. Trails open daily dawn-dusk. Phone ahead to confirm schedule. **Cost:** Free. **Phone:** (517) 629-0582.

ALLENDALE (H-2) pop. 11,555, elev. 657'

In downtown Allendale, visitors will find the Engine House No. 5 Museum, 6610 Lake Michigan Dr., which displays firefighting equipment and memorabilia; phone (616) 895-4347.

VETERANS GARDEN OF HONOR is just off SR 45 (Lake Michigan Dr.) on 68th Ave., in Allendale Community Park. The memorial, dedicated to U.S. veterans, features nine life-size statues of soldiers placed in a circle surrounding an 18-foot-tall obelisk topped with an American eagle. The nine statues, including one of a woman to honor female veterans, represent those who served in our country's wars. **Hours:** Daily dawn-dusk. **Cost:** Free. **Phone:** (616) 895-6295.

ALPENA (E-5) pop. 11,304, elev. 594'

Settled in 1840 at the head of Thunder Bay, Alpena served the booming lumber enterprises in the late 19th century. It is a center for industry and recreational boating, diving, fishing, snowmobiling, cross-country skiing and hunting; diving and fishing charters are popular on Lake Huron. The area also is home to a number of lighthouses. Thunder Bay National Marine Sanctuary lies in northwest Lake Huron; it was the first NOAA (National Oceanic and Atmospheric Administration) sanctuary to be designated in the Great Lakes. These 448 square miles contain more than 100 shipwrecks, and there are opportunities for boating, diving, kayaking and snorkeling. The Great Lakes Maritime Heritage Center (see attraction listing) interprets the underwater sanctuary.

The 16.5-mile bicycling/hiking/in-line skating Alpena Bi-Path winds through some of the city's parks and beaches along Thunder Bay River and Lake Huron. A portion of the route includes the Maritime Heritage Trail, which runs along the Thunder Bay River downtown and showcases local maritime culture and history. It begins and ends in South Riverfront Park and includes a boardwalk, a pedestrian bridge and interpretive signage.

Duck Park and Island Park, US 23 and Long Rapids Road at the Thunder Bay River, occupy part of a 600-acre wildlife sanctuary and offer opportunities for fishing. Duck Park also has a picnic area and is a good locale for bird-watching. Island Park, which is across the bridge from Duck Park, features nature trails.

Limestone quarries remain important in the region. North and west of the city is an area of natural sinkholes created by the settling of the limestone crust into caverns formed by subterranean streams. Some of the sinkholes are more than 150 feet deep.

Alpena Area Convention & Visitors Bureau: 235 W. Chisholm St., Alpena, MI 49707. **Phone:** (989) 354-4181 or (800) 425-7362.

BESSER MUSEUM FOR NORTHEAST MICHIGAN is at 491 Johnson St. The museum is a regional center for the art, history and science of northeastern Michigan. Displays include Michigan wildlife paintings, sculpture and Native American artifacts as well as lumbering, agricultural and industrial equipment. On the grounds is a re-created 1890s street with period shops. Changing exhibits and a planetarium also are featured.

Time: Allow 1 hour minimum. **Hours:** Mon.-Sat. 10-5. Planetarium shows Sat. at 2. Closed major holidays. **Cost:** Museum $5; $3 (ages 5-17 and 60+); free (persons with disability and Wed. 3-5). Planetarium $3; $2 (ages 5-17 and 60+). **Phone:** (989) 356-2202.

GREAT LAKES MARITIME HERITAGE CENTER, 500 W. Fletcher St., showcases maritime history related to the Great Lakes, including Lake Huron's Thunder Bay National Marine Sanctuary, which protects 448 square miles with more than 100 shipwrecks. Exhibits detail the glacial period, early inhabitants in the area, fur traders and the shipping industry. "Tragedies in the Mist,"

a 27-minute documentary detailing various shipwrecks over the years, is shown in a 93-seat auditorium.

A highlight of the center is a full-scale re-creation of an 1880s Great Lakes schooner, where you can walk the deck and through the cabins to see what it was like to be aboard a ship during a storm. Other exhibits feature scale models of ships and images taken from shipwreck dives. Additional films and documentaries are shown, and educational programs are held throughout the year. **Time:** Allow 1 hour minimum. **Hours:** Mon.-Sat. 10-5, Sun. noon-5, Memorial Day weekend-Oct. 31; Mon.-Sat. 10-5, rest of year. **Cost:** Donations. **Phone:** (989) 356-8805.

ANN ARBOR (L-2) pop. 114,024, elev. 766′

Take one look at Michigan Stadium and you'll know Ann Arbor is one serious college town. The facility has a seating capacity for some 109,000 fans, many of whom wear or paint themselves the school colors of blue and maize during home football games. The University of Michigan's (see attraction listing) central and medical campuses occupy a large portion of downtown and play a big role in the city's cultural and sports scenes. The north campus lies northeast of downtown. Since its move from Detroit in 1837, the university has been the primary influence in the growth and life of the city.

City and county parks offer an array of recreational opportunities, including biking, hiking, horseback riding, fishing, swimming, ice-skating, cross-country skiing and sledding. Canoeing and kayaking on the Huron River, which flows through the city, are other options.

Near the junction of S. State Street, at 603 E. Liberty St., is the 1927 Michigan Theater, home to the Ann Arbor Symphony Orchestra and host of other music concerts throughout the year. The theater shows movies as well, including many documentary, independent, foreign and classic films. Near the same intersection is the 1942 Art Deco State Theater, which also shows movies. If you're looking for theater performances, you'll have a lot of venue choices between the city and university performing arts organizations.

Thanks to the creativity of a local resident, you may encounter some tiny decorated doors located on the interiors and exteriors of several downtown businesses. They are much too small to house people or animals, but they are just the right size to serve as dwellings for fairies. Nearly a dozen of these urban fairy doors have popped up in various Ann Arbor locations over the past several years, sparking delight and intrigue for the visitors who peer inside the small facades and see the intricate furnishings and details, which cleverly reflect the nature of the establishment they have selected. Four of these doors can be found downtown within one block of each other: at The Peaceable Kingdom shop; The Ark, a folk and roots music nightclub; Selo/Shevel Gallery;

and Sweetwaters Coffee & Tea. Another residence can be spotted about three blocks away at the main branch of the Ann Arbor Public Library. Keep your eyes peeled for the others. To aid your search, stop by the chamber of commerce or the convention and visitors bureau, both on W. Huron Street, for a map of the locations.

Another interesting aspect of the city is its fire hydrants. Many of them in the downtown, campus and outlying residential areas have been painted and decorated in a variety of colors and designs—a departure from the traditional solid reds and yellows. These brightly adorned hydrants are the result of a cleanup activity in spring several years back; some sport university colors, faces, flowers and geometric patterns.

A highlight among the city's special events is the Ann Arbor Art Fairs, held the third week in July, which is comprised of The Ann Arbor Street Art Fair, the Original; The State Street Area Art Fair; The Ann Arbor Summer Art Fair, and the Ann Arbor's South University Art Fair; phone (734) 994-5260.

Ann Arbor Area Convention & Visitors Bureau: 120 W. Huron St., Ann Arbor, MI 48104. **Phone:** (734) 995-7281 or (800) 888-9487. *(see ad)*

Shopping areas: Head downtown to Main, Liberty, and State streets as well as S. University Avenue for specialty stores, art galleries, bookstores and University of Michigan souvenirs. The historic Kerrytown district features a complex of more than 20 locally owned shops and restaurants housed in three renovated brick buildings on N. Fifth Avenue. A farmers market is held adjacent to the shops at 315 Detroit St. Wed. and Sat. 7-3, May through December, and Sat. 8-3 the rest of the year. The site also includes an artisan market Sun. 11-4 between late April and late December. More locally owned specialty shops are just across the street on Fourth Avenue.

While shopping at the Kerrytown complex, you may hear the ringing of nearby bells. The tower at the complex houses the Kerrytown Chime, a 7-ton musical instrument consisting of 17 bells, which the public is invited to play. You can select from a list of simple, well-known songs, which are written out as a series of numbers, and then play the corresponding levers to create the tune. For your efforts, you'll receive an "I played the bells at Kerrytown" sticker. The public has access to the chime and chime master Wed. and Fri. noon-12:30 and Sat. 10:30-11; phone (734) 662-5008 or (734) 369-3107.

JCPenney, Macy's, Sears and Von Maur can be found at Briarwood Mall, I-94 and State Street.

THE ANN ARBOR HANDS-ON MUSEUM is at 220 E. Ann St. The museum offers hundreds of opportunities to explore the worlds of science and technology. More than 250 interactive exhibits are featured, including an operating TV station where children assume roles of director, weatherperson or news anchor.

Energy exhibits include displays about hydrogen fuel cells, solar energy and energy from landfills. Visitors can explore the natural world in the Michigan Nature room. **Time:** Allow 2 hours minimum. **Hours:** Mon.-Sat. 10-5, Sun. noon-5. Closed major holidays. **Cost:** $9; free (ages 0-1). **Phone:** (734) 995-5439.

DOMINO'S PETTING FARM is off US 23 exit 41, .5 mi. e. on Plymouth Rd., then .9 mi. n. on Earhart Rd., following sign. Cows, ducks, goats, ponies and sheep are among the animals that can be seen here in barns and in open pastures. Such rare breeds as Watusi cattle and wild European hogs also are part of the farm. Hayrides are offered. Children's pony rides are available during weekends (weather permitting) for an additional fee.

Time: Allow 30 minutes minimum. **Hours:** Mon.-Fri. 9:30-4, Sat.-Sun. 10:30-5. Closed Jan. 1, Thanksgiving and Dec. 25. **Cost:** $5; $4.50 (ages 2-12 and 65+). **Phone:** (734) 998-0182. 🚻

GERALD R. FORD PRESIDENTIAL LIBRARY is at 1000 Beal Ave. at jct. Fuller Rd., on the University of Michigan's North Campus. The library opened in 1981 and is the only site in the presidential library system where the museum and library are not located together; the museum is in Ford's hometown of Grand Rapids, and the library is at his alma mater in Ann Arbor. The collection contains presidential archives, documents, transcripts, photos and video footage about domestic and foreign policies during the Cold War era as well as Ford administration papers.

Visitor displays include a timeline with photos and document images representing substantial events in Ford's life. Several cases include rotating exhibits, and video footage is shown as well. **Time:** Allow 30 minutes minimum. **Hours:** Mon.-Fri. 8:45-4:45. Closed federal holidays. **Cost:** Free. **Phone:** (734) 205-0555.

UNIVERSITY OF MICHIGAN is e. on Huron St. to State St. The campus was formed with 40 donated acres and now covers more than 2,800 acres. Highlights on the central campus include the Gothic buildings of the Law Quadrangle, Hill Auditorium, Power Center for the Performing Arts, Exhibit Museum of Natural History, Kelsey Museum of Archaeology, University of Michigan Museum of Art, William L. Clements Library and the 55-bell Baird Carillon at Burton Memorial Tower. Just east of the central campus is Matthaei Botanical Gardens.

The star of the south campus is Michigan Stadium, one of the largest college stadiums in the country with some 109,000 seats. Among the features on the North Campus are the 60-bell carillon at Lurie Tower, engineering research laboratories and the School of Music building, designed by Eero Saarinen. The School of Music offers free recitals and concerts. Nichols Arboretum is on the medical campus; the medical center's six hospitals serve more than a million patients annually.

Note: The Burton Tower carillon bells are undergoing renovations and will be silent until summer 2011. **Hours:** Burton Tower carillon bells play Mon.-Fri. noon-12:30. Lurie Tower carillon bells play Mon.-Fri. 1-1:30 (also Thurs. 5-5:30), Sun. 1:15-2. Carillons are closed during exams and university vacations. Michigan Stadium tours are available Mon. at 10 and Wed. at 1. **Cost:** Admission is charged at some sites. Reservations are required for stadium tours. **Phone:** (734) 764-4636 for general campus information, (734) 647-1172 for Burton Memorial and Lurie towers, or (734) 764-4599 for stadium tour information.

Exhibit Museum of Natural History is at 1109 Geddes Ave. at jct. Washtenaw Ave. on the University of Michigan central campus. The museum has a planetarium and exhibits about dinosaurs, prehistoric life, fossils, minerals, anthropology, astronomy, biology and Michigan wildlife. **Hours:** Museum Mon.-Sat. 9-5, Sun. noon-5. Phone for planetarium show schedule. **Cost:** Museum by donations. Planetarium $5. **Phone:** (734) 764-0478.

Kelsey Museum of Archaeology is at 434 S. State St. in Newberry Hall on the University of Michigan central campus. Displays feature pottery, glass, statues and other artifacts excavated at the university's Mediterranean and Near Eastern digs. Greek, Roman and Egyptian artifacts are showcased. Changing exhibits also are offered. The museum recently underwent an expansion and restoration project and reopened November 2009. **Hours:** Tues.-Fri. 9-4, Sat.-Sun. 1-4. Closed university and major holidays. **Cost:** Donations. **Phone:** (734) 764-9304.

Matthaei Botanical Gardens is e. of US 23 at 1800 N. Dixboro Rd., east of the University of Michigan central campus. Exotic plants from around the world bloom in the conservatory all year, and there are formal outdoor gardens. Along the nature trails are changing seasonal displays. **Hours:** Grounds daily dawn-dusk. Conservatory Tues.-Sun. 10-4:30 (also Wed. 4:30-8). **Cost:** Grounds free. Conservatory $5; $2 (ages 5-18); free (Wed. noon-8). **Phone:** (734) 647-7600.

Nichols Arboretum is at 1610 Washington Heights Rd. next to the University of Michigan hospital on the University of Michigan medical campus. Visitors can follow nature trails through the 123-acre grounds containing more than 400 labeled tree species. A peony garden blooms in early June. Education programs are scheduled throughout the year. **Hours:** Grounds open daily dawn-dusk. **Cost:** Donations. **Phone:** (734) 647-7600.

◆ **University of Michigan Museum of Art** is at 525 S. State St. at S. University Ave. on the University of Michigan central campus. In 2009 a renovation of the Beaux Arts-style Alumni Memorial Hall and the addition of the Maxine and Stuart Frankel and the Frankel Family Wing (a 53,000-square-foot expansion) were completed. The new space allows a greater number of works from the 18,000-piece permanent collection to be displayed. Visitors also have the opportunity to view storage items—like Chinese decorative arts and Arts and Crafts ceramics—through glass cabinets.

The objects represent key art schools and movements from African, Asian and Western traditions. Works by many of the great masters can be seen. Highlights include paintings by James Abbott McNeill Whistler and Pablo Picasso as well as works by Louis Comfort Tiffany, Congolese sculpture and East Asian paintings and ceramics. The museum also receives temporary exhibits throughout the year.

Guided tours, which last 45-60 minutes, are available. **Hours:** Tues.-Sat. 10-5, Sun. noon-5. Phone for guided tour schedule. Closed Jan. 1, July 4, Thanksgiving and Dec. 25. **Cost:** Donations. **Phone:** (734) 764-0395 Mon.-Fri. or (734) 763-8662.

William L. Clements Library is at 909 S. University Ave. on the University of Michigan central campus. The library houses notable collections of early Americana, including original manuscripts, maps, prints, photographs and rare books about the Revolution and the Civil War. **Hours:** Exhibits open Mon.-Fri. 1-4:45. Reading room open Mon.-Fri. 9-11:45 and 1-4:45. Closed holidays and Dec. 26-31. **Cost:** Free. **Phone:** (734) 764-2347.

ARCADIA (E-1) elev. 594′

Arcadia Township Hall 3422 Lake St., P.O. Box 318, Arcadia, MI 49613. **Phone:** (231) 889-4463.

Self-guiding tours: Walking tour maps covering a nearly 1.5-mile route of the town can be picked up at Arcadia Area Historical Museum. The tour features 35 stops, most of which are structures dating to the late 1800s and early 1900s.

ARCADIA AREA HISTORICAL MUSEUM, 3340 Lake St., is in a restored 1884 Victorian house that was moved from just northeast of Arcadia to its present location in 1994 to save it from demolition. The two floors contain antiques and historical exhibits, and the lookout tower houses a photo gallery. Collections feature such items as antique furniture, hats, shoes, toys and quilts; Native American artifacts; and Petoskey stones. Exhibits depict other stories about Arcadia, including shipwrecks, railroads and native Arcadian and aviation pioneer Harriet Quimby.

A recently constructed carriage house also contains exhibits, including information about hunting and lumbering. **Time:** Allow 45 minutes minimum. **Hours:** Thurs.-Sat. 1-4, Sun. 1-3, mid-June through Labor Day and by appointment mid-June through Dec. 1. **Cost:** Donations. **Phone:** (231) 889-4360.

AUBURN HILLS—*see Detroit p. 61.*

AUGUSTA (I-3) pop. 899, elev. 790′

The Barn Theatre, 13351 SR 96, is the home of the oldest professional resident summer theater in Michigan, which presents Broadway plays and musicals. Numerous alumni of the theater company are now stars in theater, film and television. Housed in a renovated dairy barn, the theater presents shows mid-May through August; phone (269) 731-4121.

W. K. KELLOGG BIRD SANCTUARY, part of Michigan State University's W.K. Kellogg Biological Station (*see attraction listing p. 79*), is on SR 89, following signs to 12685 E. C Ave., between 40th St. and E. Gull Lake Dr. This experimental facility is a 180-acre area inhabited by birds of prey, wild ducks, geese, swans, peacocks, pheasants and other upland species.

The sanctuary has displays and an observation deck. **Time:** Allow 1 hour, 30 minutes minimum. **Hours:** Daily 9-7, May-Oct.; 9-5, rest of year. **Cost:** $4; $2 (ages 65+); $1 (ages 2-12). **Phone:** (269) 671-2510.

W. K. KELLOGG EXPERIMENTAL FOREST, 7060 N. 42nd St., is part of the W.K. Kellogg Biological Station (*see attraction listing p. 79*). Since 1931 this area has been transformed from 283 acres of poor farmland into a 720-acre research and forest management demonstration site. The forest is made up of 150 tree species; the nearly 1.5-mile dirt/gravel Tree ID Trail introduces 31 of them.

More than 15 miles of hiking, jogging, mountain biking, horseback riding and cross-country ski trails are on the grounds. Bow hunting, trout fishing and picnicking also are permitted. **Time:** Allow 1 hour minimum. **Hours:** Daily 8 a.m.-dusk. **Cost:** Free. **Phone:** (269) 731-4597. 🅰

BALDWIN (F-2) pop. 1,107, elev. 841′

A railroad junction in earlier days, Baldwin offers access to the numerous lakes and streams of the surrounding Huron-Manistee National Forests (*see place listing p. 81*).

Lake County Chamber of Commerce and Tourist Center: 911 Michigan Ave., P.O. Box 130, Baldwin, MI 49304. **Phone:** (231) 745-4331 or (800) 245-3240.

SHRINE OF THE PINES is about 2.2 mi. s. at 8962 S. SR 37. Guided tours reveal this shrine created by R. W. Overholzer as a memorial to the white pine, the Michigan state tree. Furniture from tree stumps and roots gleaned from virgin stands of white pines cut in the early 1920s is displayed. All pieces were entirely worked by hand, and no metal fasteners or varnish were used.

Overholzer scraped the roots with broken glass, then rubbed each piece with handmade sandpaper and raw deer hide. From these pieces he fashioned beds, chairs, chandeliers and candlesticks. Particularly impressive is a dining room table with drawers carved from a 700-pound stump. A complete living room with a stone fireplace, dining room and game room are included. The museum is housed in a hunting lodge in a wooded park on the north bank of the Pere Marquette River. A wheelchair-accessible trail winds through the pines, and an observation deck overlooks the river. There also are opportunities for bird-watching.

Time: Allow 45 minutes minimum. **Hours:** Mon.-Sat. 10-6, Sun. 1:30-6, May 15-Oct. 15. Last tour begins 30 minutes before closing. **Cost:** $5; $4 (ages 55+); $2.50 (ages 6-17); $12.50 (family, two adults and children ages 6-17). **Phone:** (231) 745-7892. 🅰

BATTLE CREEK (I-3) pop. 53,364, elev. 819′

In 1894 two brothers named Kellogg, experimenting in the kitchens of the Battle Creek Sanitarium, developed a flake cereal. From this modest beginning grew the Kellogg Co., the Post Division of Kraft-General Foods Corp. and the Ralston Purina Co., which have made Battle Creek the breakfast food center of the nation.

Battle Creek residents' progressive attitudes are manifested in other issues. In the decades before the Civil War the city was an abolitionist stronghold and an overt station on the Underground Railroad. Thus the names Kellogg and Post are no more important than that of Sojourner Truth. An ex-slave, this tall, persuasive woman carried her crusade for truth and freedom from tiny rooms to President Lincoln's office. She came to Battle Creek in 1858 and died in 1883; her grave is in Oak Hill Cemetery at South Avenue and Oak Hill Drive. Statues in Monument Park and Linear Park honor her work.

Residents find respite from industrial and commercial activities in city parks. Bailey Park's C.O. Brown Stadium, between Capital Avenue and the Battle Creek River, is the setting for national amateur baseball tournaments. South of town on Goguac Lake, landscaped Willard Park offers water sports and picnicking. Linear Park extends across much of the city, offering 17 miles of landscaped walkways highlighted by gazebos, boardwalks and bridges, which provide opportunities for jogging, bicycling, walking and picnicking.

Guided tours are offered of the Historic Adventist Village, 480 W. Van Buren St. The religious community features restored and re-created 19th-century buildings; phone (269) 965-3000.

Battle Creek/Calhoun County Convention & Visitors Bureau: 77 E. Michigan Ave., Suite 100, Battle Creek, MI 49017. **Phone:** (269) 962-2240 or (800) 397-2240.

Shopping areas: Lakeview Square, east on Beckley Road from I-94 and Capital Avenue, has more than 90 stores, including JCPenney, Macy's and Sears.

ART CENTER OF BATTLE CREEK is at 265 E. Emmett St. Changing exhibits of works by regional and national artists as well as art of other cultures are featured. Works by 20th-century Michigan artists and craftspeople can be seen; classes and workshops also are offered. Guided tours are available upon request. **Hours:** Tues.-Fri. 10-5, Sat. 11-3. Closed major holidays. **Cost:** Donations. **Phone:** (269) 962-9511.

BINDER PARK ZOO is 3 mi. s. of I-94 exit 100 at 7400 Division Dr. Exotic animals live in a natural park setting. Visitors can board a train to tour the safari-style habitat of Wild Africa, where they can purchase biscuits to feed to the giraffes. Among the species represented in the zoo are the African wild dog, bald eagle, green iguana, Mexican wolf, Mongolian wild horse, red kangaroo and red panda.

The zoo has elevated wooden boardwalks and the wooden Binda Conservation Carousel. There are hands-on activities and regularly changing exhibits at the Conservation Discovery Center, a children's learning center. Zookeepers give talks twice daily at various animal exhibits. In the Wildlife Discovery Theater, with seating for 300, several animals are brought out to allow visitors to have a closer interaction and more in-depth understanding.

Time: Allow 2 hours minimum. **Hours:** Mon.-Fri. 9-5, Sat. and holidays 9-6, Sun. 11-6, late Apr.-early Oct. Last admission 30 minutes before closing. **Cost:** $12.50 (includes tram ride to Africa section and Miller Children's Zoo); $11.50 (ages 65+); $10.50 (ages 2-10). Railroad and carousel each additional $2. **Phone:** (269) 979-1351. ⫼

Miller Children's Zoo, 3 mi. s. of I-94 exit 100 at 7400 Division Dr., at the Binder Park Zoo, features a life-size dinosaur replica, a petting area, a miniature train and domestic animal exhibits. **Hours:** Mon.-Fri. 9-5, Sat. and holidays 9-6, Sun. 11-6, late Apr.-early Oct. Last admission 30 minutes before closing. **Cost:** $12.50 (includes Binder Park Zoo and its tram ride); $11.50 (ages 65+); $10.50 (ages 2-10). Miniature train additional $2. **Phone:** (269) 979-1351.

LEILA ARBORETUM is on W. Michigan Ave. at 20th St. A 72-acre tract of ornamental trees and shrubs, the arboretum is known for its collection of mature specimen trees and 10 perennial gardens, including a native flower garden and a living peace labyrinth, as well as sculptures and structures. A children's garden also is featured. Kingman Museum *(see attraction listing)* is on the grounds. **Hours:** Arboretum daily dawn-dusk. Children's garden Sat. 10-3, June-Aug; closed July 4 weekend. **Cost:** Free. **Phone:** (269) 969-0270.

Kingman Museum, at 175 Limit St. on the grounds of Leila Arboretum, features a Digistar III SP2 HD full dome planetarium and a variety of natural history exhibits. Science topics covered include biology, geology and paleontology, and exhibits range from a mounted polar bear and skeleton of a saber-toothed cat to a live feed from NASA.

Time: Allow 1 hour minimum. **Hours:** Tues.-Thurs. 11-4:30 (also first Tues. of the month 4:30-8), Fri. 11-6, Sat. 1-5. Closed major holidays. Phone ahead to confirm schedule. **Cost:** $6; $5 (ages 65+ and military with ID); $4 (ages 3-18); $18 (family, up to six members). **Phone:** (269) 965-5117.

BAY CITY (G-5) pop. 36,817, elev. 594'

Bay City is a major distribution point for the industrial and agricultural wealth of east-central Michigan. Many domestic and foreign freighters pass through the city's busy port, and boat races are often held on the river. Shipping and commerce have been the foundation of Bay City's prosperity since the demise of its lumber industry around 1900. Mansions built by the lumber barons can be seen along the tree-shaded residential streets in the city's three historic districts.

The Saginaw River and Saginaw Bay provide ample recreational opportunities. Bay City State Recreation Area *(see Recreation Chart)* is 5 miles north on SR 247 on the Lake Huron shore.

Bay City Convention & Visitors Bureau: 919 Boutell Pl., Suite 100, Bay City, MI 48708. **Phone:** (989) 893-1222 or (888) 229-8696.

HISTORICAL MUSEUM OF BAY COUNTY is at 321 Washington Ave. Displays, which trace the development of Bay County, include period rooms and exhibits pertaining to agriculture, maritime history, Native American culture and the fur trade as well as the lumber, shipbuilding and shipping industries. A research library also is included. **Time:** Allow 1 hour minimum. **Hours:** Museum Mon.-Fri. 10-5, Sat. noon-4. Library Tues.-Thurs. 1-5. **Cost:** Free. **Phone:** (989) 893-5733.

SAGINAW BAY VISITOR CENTER is 3 mi. n. in Bay City State Recreation Area. Permanent and changing exhibits depict life in the wetlands. A 15-minute multimedia presentation about wetlands development is offered. The paved Frank N. Anderson Nature Trail leads to Tobico Marsh, a 1,700-acre refuge for more than 100 species of birds and migratory waterfowl. Nature trails, observation towers and a boardwalk are included. The wetlands also contain a fishing pier. Visitors can walk to the marsh from the center, which offers a bird observation room and a wet lab.

Time: Allow 30 minutes minimum. **Hours:** Mon.-Sat. 10-6, Sun. noon-6, Memorial Day weekend-Labor Day; Tues.-Sun. noon-5, day after Labor Day-Nov. 30 and Jan. 1-day before Memorial Day weekend. **Cost:** Center free. Park entry fee $10 (per private in-state vehicle; Recreation Passport, valid for 1 year, allows entry into Michigan state parks); $8 (per private out-of-state vehicle). **Phone:** (989) 667-0717.

BEAVER ISLAND (C-4)

About 30 miles offshore in Lake Michigan, Beaver Island is the largest island of the Beaver Archipelago. The island is popular for fishing and hunting.

The French established the island's first settlement but abandoned it in 1603. The arrival of the Mormons in 1847, led by tyrannical king and politician James Jesse Strang, aroused resentment on the mainland, leading to dissolution of the colony by force in 1856. The island was eventually settled by Irish fishermen.

The 1850 print shop built by the Mormons now houses the museum for the Beaver Island Historical Society. Exhibits showcase Strang's place in local history as well as exhibits featuring other local history topics such as Native American stories, early Irish life and island musicians; some exhibits are rotated. Phone (231) 448-2254. St. James, the former Mormon capital and a pleasant vacation spot, is accessible from Charlevoix *(see place listing p. 46)* by boat or plane.

Beaver Island Chamber of Commerce: P.O. Box 5, Beaver Island, MI 49782. **Phone:** (231) 448-2505.

BELLEVILLE—*see Detroit p. 61.*

BENTON HARBOR (I-1)
pop. 11,182, elev. 594'

HOUSE OF DAVID MUSEUM is at 2251 Riverside Rd. The museum chronicles the lifestyle and legacy of the House of David, a Christian religious colony founded in 1903. The group, which reached its peak during the 1920s, lived a communal lifestyle, preached celibacy and was entrepreneurial in nature.

They built their own elaborate mansions and furniture and an amusement park. Their orchestra toured the country, as did their baseball team, whose players all sported long hair and beards. The museum displays memorabilia from the colony, including baseball artifacts, photographs and artwork. Shiloh House is where the group's leaders resided.

Time: Allow 45 minutes minimum. **Hours:** Mon.-Sat. 10-4 and by appointment. Closed major holidays. **Cost:** $5; $1 (ages 0-1). **Phone:** (269) 849-0739.

BENZONIA (E-2) pop. 519

BENZIE AREA HISTORICAL MUSEUM is 1 blk. w. of US 31 at 6941 Traverse Ave. (River Rd.). Housed in a century-old church, the museum contains a large display about the farmers, fishermen, lumberjacks and sailors who tamed the northern Michigan wilderness. Exhibits about local author Bruce Catton and artist Gwen Frostic also are included. **Time:** Allow 1 hour minimum. **Hours:** Tues.-Sat. 11-5, May-Dec. Closed major holidays. **Cost:** Donations. **Phone:** (231) 882-5539.

GWEN FROSTIC PRINTS is 2 mi. w. of US 31 on Traverse Ave. to 5140 River Rd. A small wooden building lies within a 285-acre wildlife sanctuary on the Betsie River. Carvings of wild birds and animals are among the collection and works of Gwen Frostic, an artist and poet who specialized in nature themes. Visitors can watch presses make prints from original blocks seasonally. Nature trails traverse the grounds and a nature library is available.

Time: Allow 30 minutes minimum. **Hours:** Daily 9-5:30, May-Oct.; schedule varies rest of year. Prints are made Mon.-Fri. 9-4:30, May-Oct. **Cost:** Free. **Phone:** (231) 882-5505.

BERRIEN SPRINGS (I-2)
pop. 1,862, elev. 671'

HISTORY CENTER AT COURTHOUSE SQUARE is at 313 N. Cass St. An 1870 sheriff's residence, an 1830s log house, a re-created county jail and the 1860 county office building are included. The 1839 courthouse contains local history exhibits and a courtroom restored to its original appearance. **Time:** Allow 1 hour minimum. **Hours:** Mon.-Sat. 10-5, June-Aug.; Mon.-Fri. 10-5, rest of year. **Cost:** Free. **Phone:** (269) 471-1202.

WINERIES
• **Lemon Creek Fruit Farm and Winery** is off I-94 exit 16, n. 2.5 mi. to Lemon Creek Rd., then 6 mi. e. to 533 Lemon Creek Rd. **Hours:** Mon.-Sat. 10-6, Sun. noon-6, May-Oct.; daily noon-5, rest of year. Phone ahead to confirm schedule. **Phone:** (269) 471-1321.

BESSEMER (B-1) pop. 2,148, elev. 1,437'

BLACK RIVER NATIONAL FOREST SCENIC BY-WAY (CR 513) follows the winding course of the Black River to Lake Superior. The scenic 11-mile drive within the Ottawa National Forest passes five waterfalls, which range from 25 to 40 feet high and are accessible by well-marked trails. Black River Harbor, at the end of Black River Drive, has picnicking and camping areas and a playground. **Cost:** Free. **Phone:** (906) 932-1330 (Bessemer Rangers District) or TTY (906) 663-4035. ⬠ 🚻

RECREATIONAL ACTIVITIES
Skiing
- **Big Powderhorn Mountain** is off US 2 at 11375 Powderhorn Rd. N. **Hours:** Daily 9-4, early Dec.-late Mar. (weather permitting). **Phone:** (906) 932-4838, or (800) 501-7669 from the Midwest.
- **Blackjack Ski Resort** is e. on US 2 to N. 11251 Blackjack Rd. **Hours:** Daily 9-4, mid-Dec. to late Mar. **Phone:** (906) 229-5115.

BIRMINGHAM —see Detroit p. 61.

BLOOMFIELD HILLS—see Detroit p. 61.

BRIDGEPORT (G-4) pop. 7,849, elev. 610'

JUNCTION VALLEY RAILROAD is 2 mi. s. on Dixie Hwy. Two-mile train rides are offered on a railroad built to one-quarter size. Trains wind past buildings and across bridges built to scale. Visitors may depart the train at a park equipped with picnic tables and a playground and return on a later train. Special excursions are scheduled during the Halloween season. **Time:** Allow 1 hour minimum. **Hours:** Mon.-Fri. 10-4, Sat. 10-5, Sun. 1-5, mid-May through Labor Day. **Cost:** $6.25; $6 (ages 65+); $5.25 (ages 18 months-2 years). Additional fares are charged for special excursions. **Phone:** (989) 777-3480. 🍴

BRIDGMAN (I-1) pop. 2,428

Hang gliders are a familiar sight in the sky south of Bridgman. Prevailing winds from Lake Michigan and a 240-foot vertical drop afforded by Tower Hill have made nearby Warren Dunes State Park (see Recreation Chart) a popular all-year locale for the sport. Flights more than an hour long have been recorded.

BRIMLEY (B-5) elev. 655'

GAMBLING ESTABLISHMENTS
- **Bay Mills Casino** is at 11386 W. Lakeshore Dr. **Hours:** Daily 24 hours. **Phone:** (906) 248-3715 or (888) 422-9645.

BROOKLYN (I-4) pop. 1,176, elev. 988'

MICHIGAN INTERNATIONAL SPEEDWAY is 1 mi. w. of SR 50 on US 12. The speedway has been hosting racing action since 1968. Among the events featured here are NASCAR Sprint Cup Series, Nationwide Series, Craftsman Truck Series and ARCA RE/MAX Series. After several expansions, the speedway's seating capacity is now more than 132,000. **Hours:** The race season runs Apr.-Oct.; gate opening times vary. Track viewing area Mon.-Fri. 9-4:30 (weather permitting). Phone ahead to confirm schedule. **Phone:** (517) 592-6666.

ST. JOSEPH'S SHRINE is at 8743 US 12. The shrine sits at the site of an early religious settlement visited by Father Gabriel Richard, minister to the Potawatomi Indians. The church is a combination of an original fieldstone chapel, erected by Irish settlers in the 1850s, and a 1928 addition.

On the grounds are a life-size crucifixion group, a monument to early Irish settlers, a memorial to the Irish "Great Hunger" of the 1840s and an outdoor Stations of the Cross overlooking Iron Lake. **Hours:** Church daily 7-dusk. **Cost:** Free. **Phone:** (517) 467-2183.

WALKER TAVERN HISTORIC SITE is at jct. US 12 and SR 50 in Cambridge Junction Historic State Park. The history of Michigan's stagecoach era is presented through exhibits, presentations and walking tours. The tavern is an 1840s clapboard house that was used as a stagecoach stop on the Detroit to Chicago path. A farmers market is held on Sundays. In late October a Victorian Halloween celebration for families features costumes, food, craft activities, parlor games and historic tours.

Hours: Tues.-Sun. 10-5, June-Aug. Farmers market Sun. 10-2, late May-late Sept. Closed holidays and some Michigan International Speedway race weekends. **Cost:** Free. **Phone:** (517) 467-4401. 🚻

BUCHANAN (I-1) pop. 4,681, elev. 732'

BEAR CAVE is 4 mi. n. on Red Bud Tr. to 4085 Bear Cave Rd. The 150-foot-long tufa rock cave is accessible by a 40-foot winding stairway. A taped narration plays continuously, guiding visitors past unique geological formations, including the 250,000-year-old Kansan Boulder. The cave was part of the Underground Railroad and a movie location for the 1903 film "The Great Train Robbery." The cave maintains a constant temperature of 58 F; suitable clothing is advised.

Portions of walkways are narrow, puddles can form when there has been heavy rain, and visitors should be aware that the cave contains bats. **Time:** Allow 30 minutes minimum. **Hours:** Mon.-Sat. 9-5, Sun. 1-4, Memorial Day-Labor Day. **Cost:** $2; $1 (ages 6-11). **Phone:** (269) 695-3050.

WINERIES
- **Tabor Hill Winery** is at 185 Mt. Tabor Rd. **Hours:** Tasting Mon.-Sat. 10-5 (also Wed.-Sat. 5-9), Sun. noon-9, May-Nov.; Mon.-Sat. 10-5 (also Wed.-Sat. 5-9), Sun. noon-6, rest of year. Tours daily noon-4:30, May-Nov.; Sat.-Sun. noon-4:30, rest of year. Closed Jan. 1, Easter, Thanksgiving, and Dec. 24-25 and 31. **Phone:** (800) 283-3363.

CADILLAC (F-3) pop. 10,000, elev. 1,292'

Begun as a lumber camp in 1871, Cadillac was named for the founder of Detroit, Antoine de la Mothe Cadillac. The rolling terrain of the Huron-Manistee National Forests *(see place listing p. 81)* and the proximity of Cadillac and Mitchell lakes *(see William Mitchell State Park listing on Recreation Chart)* have made the town a popular recreational center.

Cadillac Area Visitors Bureau: 222 N. Lake St., Cadillac, MI 49601. **Phone:** (231) 775-0657 or (800) 225-2537.

CARL T. JOHNSON HUNTING AND FISHING CENTER is at 6087 E. SR 115 in William Mitchell State Park. Featuring an exhibit hall, nature trail and auditorium, the modern facility gives visitors a variety of opportunities to experience the great outdoors. The history of hunting in the state and the conservation of Michigan's natural resources are presented through interactive wildlife exhibits and multimedia presentations. The Heritage Nature Trail offers 2.5 miles of plants and wildlife.

Guided hikes and interpretive programs are available; phone for information. **Time:** Allow 1 hour minimum. **Hours:** Daily 10-6, May-Nov.; Fri. and Sun. noon-5, Sat. 10-5, rest of year. **Cost:** Park entry fee $10 (per private in-state vehicle; Recreation Passport, valid for 1 year, allows entry into Michigan state parks); $8 (per private out-of-state vehicle). **Phone:** (231) 779-1321, or (231) 775-7911 for state park information.

JOHNNY'S WILD GAME AND FISH PARK is at 5465 E. 46 1/2 Rd. The park houses a variety of wild and domestic game animals in a natural setting. Visitors can feed and pet deer, goats, birds and other animals. Trout fishing and fish cleaning also are available. **Time:** Allow 30 minutes minimum. **Hours:** Daily 10-6, Memorial Day weekend-Labor Day. **Cost:** $5.75; $5.50 (ages 56+); $5.25 (ages 3-14). Phone ahead to verify rates. **Phone:** (231) 775-3700.

CALUMET (A-2) pop. 879, elev. 1,202'

Keweenaw Convention & Visitors Bureau: 56638 Calumet Ave., Calumet, MI 49913. **Phone:** (906) 337-4579 or (800) 338-7982.

CALUMET THEATRE is at 340 Sixth St. A variety of scheduled theater events is offered. The building opened in 1900 for stage performances and for a time was used as a motion picture theater. The theater is now used for concerts and stage performances.

Time: Allow 30 minutes minimum. **Hours:** Guided tours Mon.-Fri. 11-2, mid-June to mid-Sept. Self-guiding tours Mon.-Fri. 2-5, Sat. 11-5, mid-June to mid-Sept.; by appointment rest of year. Tours are limited on days when performances are scheduled; phone ahead for tour availability. Closed major holidays. **Cost:** Guided tour $6; $3 (ages 3-15). Self-guiding tour $4; $2 (ages 3-15). **Phone:** (906) 337-2610.

COPPERTOWN USA MINING MUSEUM is on Red Jacket Rd., 2 blks. w. of US 41. A heritage site of Keweenaw National Historical Park, Coppertown traces the evolution of mines and mining through displays of mining equipment. A simulated mine at the entrance provides a glimpse of the miner's world. **Time:** Allow 30 minutes minimum. **Hours:** Mon.-Sat. 10-5, June 1 to mid-Oct. (also Sun. 12:30-4, July-Aug.). **Cost:** $3. National Parks pass holders $2; $1 (ages 12-18). **Phone:** (906) 337-4354, or (800) 338-7982 during off-season.

CASPIAN (B-2) pop. 997

IRON COUNTY MUSEUM is 1.5 mi. s. of US 2 on SR 189, then e. on CR 424 to Museum Rd. at jct. Brady Ave. (also referred to as Museum St.) Outdoor complexes depict life in the late 1800s. Exhibits examine the lumber industry, farming, mining, transportation, domestic life and homesteading. Among the 23 structures are an 1890 train depot, the Caspian Mine Headframe Mining Memorial, a logging camp and the home of Carrie Jacobs-Bond, composer of such tunes as "I Love You Truly" and "End of a Perfect Day."

The Renaissance-style home of Brandon Giovanelli, the Bernhardt Collection with works by presidential portrait artist Simmi Knox, and the Lee Leblanc Memorial Art Gallery with one of the largest collections of wildlife art by a single artist in the country also can be seen. **Hours:** Mon.-Sat. 10-4, Sun. 1-4, June-Aug.; Tues.-Sat. noon-4, in Sept.; by appointment rest of year. **Cost:** $10; $5 (ages 5-18); $25 (family). **Phone:** (906) 265-2617, or (906) 265-3942 during the off-season.

CASS CITY (G-5) pop. 2,643, elev. 745'

SANILAC PETROGLYPHS HISTORIC STATE PARK is 3.9 mi. e. on SR 81, 4 mi. n. on SR 53 (Van Dyke Rd.), 4 mi. e. on W. Bay City Forestville Rd., then .5 mi. s. to 8251 Germania Rd. The park contains the Sanilac Petroglyphs, a series of Native American rock carvings on sandstone. The 300- to 1,000-year-old carvings consist of figures that resemble animals, birds and humans. A mile-long nature trail winds around the park. **Hours:** Park open daily 8 a.m.-10 p.m. Access to the petroglyph site is by reservation only. **Cost:** Free. **Phone:** (989) 856-4411.

CHARLEVOIX (D-2) pop. 2,994, elev. 592'

Its early history linked to the stormy affairs of the Mormon monarchy on Beaver Island *(see place listing p. 44),* Charlevoix is an enterprising resort center. Lakes Michigan and Charlevoix offer excellent beaches and opportunities for boating. Round Lake, lying between the two, provides the city with its fine yacht harbor. The city offers band shell musical entertainment during July and August.

Charlevoix is on US 31, a scenic route that follows the shore between Traverse City and Petoskey.

Beaver Island Boat Co., 103 Bridge Park Dr., offers ferry service to Beaver Island; phone (231) 547-2311 or (888) 446-4095.

Charlevoix Area Chamber of Commerce: 109 Mason St., Charlevoix, MI 49720. **Phone:** (231) 547-2101 or (800) 367-8557.

CASTLE FARMS is 2 mi. e. of US 31 at 5052 SR 66. The castle, modeled after châteaus in Normandy, France, was built in 1918 by Albert Loeb, the president of Sears, Roebuck and Co. The grounds served as a showcase for the company's innovative farm equipment. A brief film presents the farm's history and restoration, and then visitors can set off on their own to explore the castle, gardens, and a pond where fish can be fed. A hedge maze and garden railroad also are on the grounds. Festivals and shows are held throughout the year.

Tours: Guided tours are available. **Time:** Allow 1 hour minimum. **Hours:** Daily 10-4, May-Oct.; Mon.-Sat. 10-4, Sun. by appointment, rest of year. Hours may vary due to special events; phone ahead to confirm. **Cost:** $7; $5 (ages 2-12). **Phone:** (231) 237-0884. 🎟

CHEBOYGAN (D-4) pop. 5,295, elev. 600'

The crew members of the Coast Guard icebreaker *Mackinaw* make Cheboygan their home port. Specialized construction fits the ship for rescue towing as well as icebreaking; it is credited with extending the shipping season on the Great Lakes by 6 weeks. When in port, the *Mackinaw* is docked on the Cheboygan River; visitors are welcome.

This industrial and resort city is surrounded by some of Michigan's largest lakes. Mullett Lake and Burt Lake, both noted for bass and muskellunge, are part of the historic inland waterway. The waterway became a major transportation link in the late 19th century after a lock was built at Cheboygan. Traffic consists of pleasure boaters, who can still cruise as far as Conway.

One of the Great Lakes' largest cattail marshes, a nesting site for 54 bird species, can be viewed from a boardwalk in Gordon Turner Park at the north end of Huron Street. The Mackinac Bridge and Round and Bois Blanc islands also can be seen from the boardwalk and from the nearby fishermen's walkway.

Cheboygan Area Chamber of Commerce: 124 N. Main St., Cheboygan, MI 49721. **Phone:** (231) 627-7183 or (800) 968-3302.

CHEBOYGAN COUNTY HISTORICAL MUSEUM is at jct. Huron and Court sts. The 1882 two-story brick structure, which includes a county jail, served as the sheriff's home until 1969. The parlor, kitchen, schoolroom and bedrooms are re-created in period style. Logging, railroad, veterans' and marine displays are included.

A flower garden, country store and a 19th-century furnished log cabin are on the grounds. **Time:** Allow 30 minutes minimum. **Hours:** Tues.-Sat. 1-4, May-Sept.; by appointment rest of year. **Cost:** $5; free (children). **Phone:** (231) 627-9597, or (231) 625-2511 for appointments.

THE OPERA HOUSE is at 403 N. Huron St. The Victorian theater was constructed in 1877, rebuilt following a fire in 1888 and restored in 1984. Mary Pickford, Annie Oakley and Marie Dressler were among the theater's actors and entertainers; it now plays host to local and professional entertainment and arts events. **Hours:** Guided tours are given Tues.-Fri. 1-4, June-Sept. **Cost:** $1. **Phone:** (231) 627-5432, or (231) 627-5841 for the box office.

CHELSEA (L-2) pop. 4,398, elev. 935'

Chelsea Milling Co., 201 W. North St., is the producer of "Jiffy" baking mixes. Tours include a slide presentation, product sampling and a tour of the packaging facility. Children under age 6 are not permitted. Free 90-minute tours are offered Mon.-Fri. 9-1:30; reservations are required. Phone (734) 475-1361.

Chelsea is in the midst of Waterloo State Recreation Area *(see Recreation Chart).*

CHELSEA TEDDY BEAR CO. is at 400 N. Main St. The company features a museum that traces the evolution of toys from wood and tin creations from around the world to toys manufactured in the 1950s, including early Steiff teddy bears. Richard Steiff, who invented the teddy bear in 1906, emigrated from Germany to nearby Jackson.

The company, which calls teddy bears "the greatest toy in the world," also offers 1-hour guided tours of its factory during which visitors can see how these much-loved, furry creatures are made. **Time:** Allow 15 minutes minimum for the museum, 1 hour for the tour. **Hours:** Museum Mon.-Sat. 10-6, Sun. noon-5. Factory tours are given Sat. at 11, 1 and 3. Closed major holidays. Phone ahead to confirm schedule. **Cost:** Free. **Phone:** (734) 433-5499 or (800) 303-7255.

GERALD E. EDDY DISCOVERY CENTER is off I-94 exit 157, following signs to 17030 Bush Rd. in the Waterloo State Recreation Area. Hands-on exhibits and 17 miles of walking trails are featured. A slide presentation discusses the geology of Earth and of Michigan.

Time: Allow 1 hour minimum. **Hours:** Tues.-Sat. 10-5, Sun. noon-5, week after Easter-Sun. before Thanksgiving. **Cost:** Discovery Center free. Park entry fee $10 (per private in-state vehicle; Recreation Passport, valid for 1 year, allows entry into Michigan state parks); $8 (per private out-of-state vehicle). **Phone:** (734) 475-3170.

CHRISTMAS (B-3) elev. 619'

GAMBLING ESTABLISHMENTS

- **Christmas Kewadin Casino** is on SR 28. **Hours:** Daily 8 a.m.-3 a.m. Winter hours vary. Phone ahead to confirm schedule. **Phone:** (906) 387-5475 or (800) 539-2346.

COLDWATER (I-3) pop. 12,697

From cabin to inn to village was the early progression of Coldwater, on the Chicago Turnpike, a

48

AAA TRIPTIK® MOBILE
Navigation · Gas Prices · Hotels

Free app for your iPhone featuring:

· Maps and directions · Updated fuel prices
· Hotel reservations function · Voice guidance for next maneuver
· AAA inspector notes for lodgings and restaurants
· Location identification for member AAA roadside assistance

Download it FREE Today
From the iTunes Store

AAA.com/mobile

Scan this tag with your
iPhone to access app at
the iTunes Store.

Get the free mobile app at
http://gettag.mobi

primary east-west transportation route. By the 1880s the city had assumed its present character as a trading and supply center.

Branch County Area Chamber of Commerce: 20 Division St., Coldwater, MI 49036. **Phone:** (517) 278-5985.

TIBBITS OPERA HOUSE is at 14 S. Hanchett St. The theater opened in 1882 to house the many performers and theater companies that played Coldwater en route between Chicago and Detroit. Its excellent acoustics and sophisticated backstage equipment were widely acclaimed.

The renovated French-Victorian building presents a variety of concerts and art exhibitions. Theater tours are available by request. A professional summer stock series and a children's series are offered June through August. Community and youth productions are presented the rest of the year. **Hours:** Mon.-Fri. 9-5. **Cost:** Tours by donation. Performance admission prices vary. **Phone:** (517) 278-6029.

CONCORD (I-3) pop. 1,101, elev. 940'

MANN HOUSE MUSEUM is .2 mi. s. of SR 60 at 205 Hanover St. The 1883 house contains Mann family heirlooms dating from 1840 and depicts family life in the Midwest during the Victorian period. A carriage house and Victorian and herb gardens are on the grounds. **Tours:** Guided tours are available. **Time:** Allow 30 minutes minimum. **Hours:** Tues.-Sat. 10-4, Memorial Day-Labor Day. Phone ahead to confirm schedule. **Cost:** Free. **Phone:** (517) 524-8943 or TTY (517) 373-1592.

COOPERSVILLE (G-2) pop. 3,910

COOPERSVILLE AREA HISTORICAL SOCIETY MUSEUM is at 363 Main St. This former depot contains many area artifacts, including a railroad collection and re-creations of a local drugstore and the interior of a one-room schoolhouse. An exhibit is dedicated to Del Shannon, a member of the Rock and Roll Hall of Fame and a Coopersville native. An additional building contains a sawmill exhibit.

Tours: Guided tours are available. **Time:** Allow 30 minutes minimum. **Hours:** Tues. 3-8, Wed. 10-1, Sat. 10-4 (also Sun. 1-4, Aug. 1 to mid-Dec.). **Cost:** Donations. **Phone:** (616) 997-7240 or (616) 997-6978.

COPPER HARBOR (A-3) elev. 621'

Tales of copper lying on the lakeshore first drew explorers, then miners, to the remote Keweenaw Peninsula. The deposits proved scant, and Copper Harbor lost its vitality as its mines, timber and port activity successively dwindled.

Michigan's northernmost community is a popular summer vacation spot. Boat trips to Isle Royale National Park (see place listing p. 83) are available mid-May to late September. Lake Superior and the surrounding woodlands can be viewed along the 9.5-mile Brockway Mountain Drive, which runs

west from Copper Harbor and rejoins SR 26 about 10 miles east of Eagle Harbor.

The Astor House Museum at US 41 and SR 26 contains antique dolls, Native American relics and local historic artifacts; phone (906) 289-4449. The Estivant Pines, a grove of 100-foot-tall white pines, some 500 years old, grow along the Montreal River. See Upper Peninsula p. 114.

FORT WILKINS HISTORIC STATE PARK is 1 mi. e. at 15223 US 41. The 700-acre park contains the restored buildings of Fort Wilkins, the Army post established in 1844 to protect copper miners. The fort had no hostilities and was finally abandoned in 1870. Refurbished officers' quarters and other buildings can be visited; wildflower and historical exhibits also are included. From late June to late August costumed staff members portray life at the fort in the 1800s. Copper Harbor Lighthouse (see attraction listing) also is on the grounds. See Recreation Chart and the AAA Great Lakes CampBook.

Time: Allow 1 hour minimum. **Hours:** Daily 8 a.m.-dusk, mid-May to mid-Oct. **Cost:** Park entry fee $10 (per private in-state vehicle; Recreation Passport, valid for 1 year, allows entry into Michigan state parks); $8 (per private out-of-state vehicle). **Phone:** (906) 289-4215.

Copper Harbor Lighthouse is reached by boat departing from the Copper Harbor Marina within Fort Wilkins Historic State Park, .5 mi. w. on SR 26. Visitors can see the 1866 Copper Harbor Lighthouse, the 1848 lighthouse keeper's house and a 1933 steel light tower. Transportation to the lighthouse is by narrated cruise. A sunset tour also is offered.

Hours: Boats depart the harbor daily on the hour 10-5, July 1-Labor Day; at 10, noon, 2 and 4, Memorial Day-June 30 and day after Labor Day to mid-Oct. A sunset tour departs daily 90 minutes before dusk, July 1-Labor Day. **Cost:** Tour fee $15; $10 (ages 0-11). Sunset tour $18. Park entry fee $10 (per private in-state vehicle; Recreation Passport, valid for 1 year, allows entry into Michigan state parks); $8 (per private out-of-state vehicle). **Phone:** (906) 289-4966 for the marina, (906) 289-4215 for Fort Wilkins or TTY (517) 373-1592.

DEARBORN—see Detroit p. 62.

DELTON (H-2) elev. 935'

BERNARD HISTORICAL MUSEUM is at 7135 W. Delton Rd. Displays housed in a 1930s hospital include artifacts and items used in the facility. An 1873 schoolhouse, a 1900 country store and a blacksmith shop are nearby. A re-created seamstress cottage with sewing machines is featured.

Also on the grounds are a working windmill, a marked nature trail, a barn with farm equipment and handmade tools, and a house where visiting medical professionals resided. **Time:** Allow 1 hour minimum. **Hours:** Sat.-Sun. 1-5, June-Sept. **Cost:** Donations. **Phone:** (269) 623-2077.

Detroit

City Population: 951,270
Elevation: 600 ft.

Editor's Picks:

One of the world's greatest automobile manufacturing cities, Detroit is an international symbol of America's productive might. The spirit of Detroit—the automobile and the assembly line—has spread around the globe, profoundly changing the lives of millions of people.

The French settled the city in 1701 and called it *d'etroit* or city "of straits," referring to the 27-mile Detroit River that connects lakes Erie and St. Clair. The Detroit River, a segment of the international border between the United States and Canada, marks the only point where Canada lies directly south of the United States. A remnant of the early settlement is Ste. Anne de Detroit Catholic Church. Its original log chapel was built in 1701. Another historic place of worship is the Old Mariners' Church at 170 E. Jefferson Ave. Built in 1849, it was moved to its present location in 1955 to make way for the construction of the civic center. Tours are available; phone (313) 259-2206.

Strategically located, Detroit was the objective of several major campaigns during the struggle for supremacy between the French and British. During the Revolutionary War the community served as northwest headquarters for the British. The settlement took on new life following the War of 1812; the launching in 1818 of the first steam vessel on the Great Lakes and the subsequent expansion of shipbuilding and commerce helped to assure the future prosperity of the city.

However, at the turn of the 20th century Detroit was still a tree-shaded small town busily engaged in making stoves, beer and carriages. This serenity was broken by Henry Ford's creation, a practical vehicle propelled by power generated from within itself—the wheezing, sputtering Model T. Detroit was never the same.

With the growth of the automobile industry the town burst its river-hugging confines and absorbed

Detroit River / © David R. Frazier
Danita Delimont Stock Photography

surrounding communities. To augment local manpower for the assembly lines, Detroit turned to Europe for help and soon became one of the largest cities in the United States.

In recent years the auto industry has been struggling, and although such tags as the Motor City are foremost in outsiders' minds, Detroit residents are eager to point out that the port of Detroit is one of the world's busiest inland ports and ranks high in customs collection. New industries are springing up and expanding across metro Detroit in such areas as defense, entertainment, green technology, medical research and urban farming.

A polyglot community pulled together by high aspirations and hard work, Detroit has many sports and cultural activities. The city boasts a civic center complex as well as varied sports facilities, an excellent park system and numerous theaters, museums and galleries. The Detroit Civic Center covers 75 acres along the downtown riverfront. The center includes Cobo Center, phone (313) 877-8777; Cobo Arena, phone (313) 983-6616; Joe Louis Arena, phone (313) 983-6606; and GM Renaissance Center, phone (313) 567-3126. The GM Renaissance Center is home to a showroom featuring a display of current and vintage GM vehicles and GM engines; phone (313) 667-7151 for schedule information.

Getting There — starting on p. 51

Getting Around — starting on p. 51

What To See — starting on p. 55

What To Do — starting on p. 58

Where To Stay — starting on p. 255

Where To Dine — starting on p. 262

The simple and modest gravesites of Henry and Clara Ford and other members of the Ford family are in the Ford Family Cemetery at St. Martha's Episcopal Church at 15801 Joy Rd. The grounds are open daily dawn to dusk; phone (313) 273-9632.

Getting There

By Car

Interstate highway systems provide speedy access to Detroit from the north, south and west. I-75 enters Detroit from the south and the north; SR 10 also enters from the north. Approaching from the west and the northeast is I-94; also entering from the west is I-96. From the east, Canadian Hwy. 401 becomes SR 3 when entering Detroit from Windsor, Ontario, via the toll bridge, and SR 3B when entering via the toll tunnel.

Getting Around

Street System

City planners originally patterned Detroit after Washington, D.C., but abandoned this plan during its rapid growth. Instead, planners superimposed the basic grid system on Detroit's downtown streets. The result is confusing to drivers; since most of the downtown streets are one-way, a detailed map is necessary. Detroit's freeway system provides access to points within the city. Rush hours, 7-9 and 4-6:30, should be avoided.

Parking

Metered parking is minimal in downtown Detroit; most of the more than 8,000 meters are in the fringe

Detroit Zoo, Royal Oak / © Dennis MacDonald / Alamy

areas. To compensate for this, Detroit has many municipal and privately operated parking lots and garages. Rates range from approximately $2.50 to $5 for the first hour and average 50c to $1 for each additional hour. Daily rates run $10-$20 depending on the venue. Parking is free at all casinos.

Public Transportation

Considering the confusing maze of downtown streets and the hectic pace of traffic, Detroit's Department of Transportation (DDOT) might be the answer to getting from one place to another with minimal frustration. Bus fare is generally $1.50; 75c (Medicare cardholders and students with DDOT student ID); 50c (ages 65+ and disabled passengers); free (up to 3 children under 44 inches tall with adult). Transfers cost 25c; 10c (ages 65+, Medicare cardholders and students). Multiday passes also are available. For schedules, routes and fare information phone (313) 933-1300.

Destination Detroit

*I*t's the Motor City. Motown's hometown. And an inland port.

*B*ut Detroit is more than an industrial hub. Also assembled here are cultural diversions and sites embracing wonders of progress and reminders of the past.

Detroit Zoo, Royal Oak. (See listing page 65)

© Richard Cummins
Lonely Planet Images

© Detroit Institute of Arts

Detroit Institute of Arts. (See listing page 57)

Waterford •

Farmington Hills

See Vicinity map page 56

Livonia

Plymouth •

Westland

*P*laces included in this AAA Destination City:

Detroit Science Center. (See listing page 57)

The Henry Ford, Dearborn. (See listing page 62)

See Downtown Inset page 56

© Richard Cummins / Lonely Planet Images

Automotive Hall of Fame, Dearborn. (See listing page 62)

The Informed Traveler

Sales Tax: Detroit has a 6 percent lodging tax; a 5.9 percent tax is levied on automobile rentals.

WHOM TO CALL

Emergency: 911

Police (non-emergency): (313) 267-4600

Time: (313) 472-1111

Hospitals: Detroit Receiving Hospital/University Health Center, (313) 745-3000; Harper University Hospital, (313) 745-8040; Henry Ford Hospital, (313) 916-2600; St. John Hospital and Medical Center, (313) 343-4000 and Sinai-Grace Hospital, (313) 966-3300.

WHERE TO LOOK

Newspapers

The two daily newspapers—*The Detroit News* and *Detroit Free Press*—are supplemented with a variety of weekly papers.

Radio

Detroit radio station WWJ (950 AM) is an all-news/weather station; WDET (101.9 FM) is a member of National Public Radio.

Visitor Information

Detroit Metro Convention & Visitors Bureau: 211 W. Fort St., Suite 1000, Detroit, MI 48226. **Phone:** (313) 202-1800 or (800) 338-7648.

Maps, brochures, calendars of events, lists of sightseeing companies and hotel location maps are available from the visitors bureau.

TRANSPORTATION

Air Travel

Major commercial airlines have regularly scheduled flights to the Detroit Metropolitan Wayne County Airport, 21 miles west of downtown. Allow approximately 45 minutes travel time to the airport. Most taxi fares are on a meter system. The average fare between the airport and downtown is approximately $50; fuel surcharges may apply. Two companies include Metro Airport Taxi, (800) 745-5191, and Metro Detroit Taxi and Car Services, (866) 389-8294.

Car services also are available. Average fare between the airport and downtown is approximately $50-$64; fuel surcharges may apply. Companies include Metro Cars, (734) 946-5700 or (800) 456-1701, and Metro Cab, (734) 997-6500.

Rental Cars

Car rental companies may be found at the airport. Hertz, (800) 654-3131, offers discounts to AAA members.

Rail Service

Amtrak stations are at 11 W. Baltimore Ave. in the New Center area and in Dearborn at 16121 Michigan Ave. Train service to various parts of the country is provided; phone (800) 872-7245.

Buses

Greyhound Lines Inc. serves Detroit. The terminal is at 1001 Howard St.; for information about fares and schedules phone (800) 231-2222.

Taxis

Taxis operate on a meter system; the basic charge is $2.50, plus $1.60 per mile (no extra charge for additional riders). The largest companies are Checker Cab, (313) 963-7000, City Cab, (313) 833-7060, and Metro Cab, (734) 997-6500.

Boats

Detroit, one of the world's busiest inland freight ports, is linked by 25 steamship companies to more than 40 countries worldwide. Vessels ranging from ocean-going freighters to private craft dock in Detroit's well-protected harbor.

The automated People Mover, a 2.9-mile elevated light-rail system, operates through the central business district, including the Civic Center, Mon.-Thurs. 6:30 a.m.-midnight., Fri. 6:30 a.m.-2 a.m., Sat. 9 a.m.-2 a.m., Sun. noon-midnight. Hours are extended during events. The fare is 50c; free (ages 0-4), and must be in exact change or tokens. For more information phone (313) 962-7245.

The three-story Rosa Parks Transit Center at Michigan and Cass avenues, which opened July 2009, serves as a 24-hour connection hub for bus and People Mover traffic.

What To See

BELLE ISLE PARK is just s. over the MacArthur Bridge at jct. E. Jefferson Ave. This island in the Detroit River features 5 miles of scenic shoreline. A highlight is the Scott Memorial Fountain, which is made of white marble. The Anna Scripps Whitcomb Conservatory displays cacti, ferns, orchids and palms. The Belle Isle Nature Zoo features flora and fauna that can be found throughout Michigan. Various amphibians and reptiles are included, and deer reside on the grounds; visitors can watch deer feedings daily. There are children's playgrounds, and during the summer a children's dry slide and waterslides for children and adults are available for a fee.

The Dossin Great Lakes Museum, 100 Strand Dr., profiles local maritime history and includes an impressive collection of model ships as well as the reconstructed pilot house from the S.S. *William Clay Ford.*

Note: Visiting the island after dark is not recommended. **Time:** Allow 15 minutes minimum for the park and 30 minutes minimum for the museum. **Hours:** Park daily 6 a.m.-10 p.m. Conservatory and nature zoo daily 10-5; closed Jan. 1, Thanksgiving and Dec. 25. Deer feedings are given at 11, 1 and 3. Museum Sat.-Sun. 11-4; closed major holidays. **Cost:** Park and zoo free. Museum by donations. **Phone:** (313) 628-2081 for park information, (313) 821-2661 for the museum, or (313) 852-4056 for the nature zoo.

CHARLES H. WRIGHT MUSEUM OF AFRICAN AMERICAN HISTORY is at 315 E. Warren Ave. The featured exhibit, And Still We Rise: Our Journey Through African American History and Culture, includes nearly 100 mannequins in re-creations of such scenes as a slave ship, a slave auction and living quarters from a rice plantation. Four other galleries feature changing exhibits. A research library and archives contain materials relating to African and American history.

Time: Allow 1 hour minimum. **Hours:** Tues.-Sat. 9-5, Sun. 1-5. Closed major holidays. **Cost:** $8; $5 (ages 3-12 and 62+). **Phone:** (313) 494-5800.

DETROIT CHILDREN'S MUSEUM is off I-94 exit 215C (Woodward Ave./SR 1/John R. St.), just w. on Antoinette St., then just n. to 6134 Second Ave. Interactive exhibits showcase such topics as ancient civilizations, dinosaurs, Native American history and African-American leaders as well as the natural world, health and nutrition. A planetarium is on-site.

Cranbrook House and Gardens, Bloomfield Hills / © Dennis McDonald / Alamy

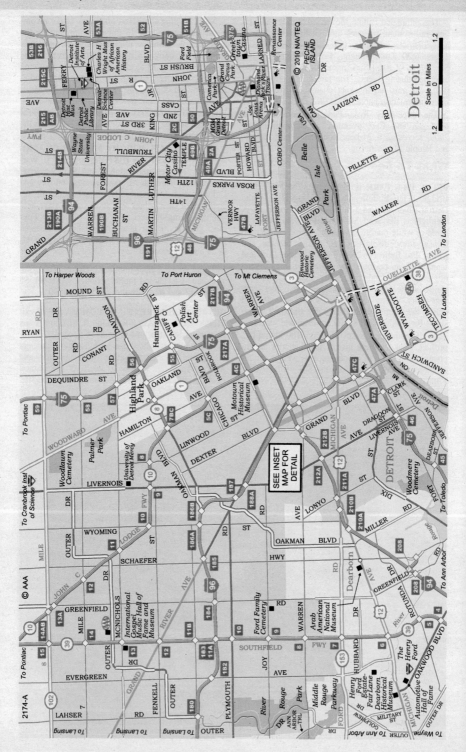

Time: Allow 30 minutes minimum. **Hours:** Mon.-Fri. 9-4, Sat. 10-4, June-Sept.; Tues.-Fri. 9-4, Sat. 10-4, rest of year. **Cost:** $5. **Phone:** (313) 873-8100.

DETROIT HISTORICAL MUSEUM is at 5401 Woodward Ave. at Kirby Ave. Museum exhibits depict more than 300 years of Detroit and southeastern Michigan history, showcasing its days as a fur trading outpost to the present. Automotive history also is profiled. Reconstructions of 19th- and early 20th-century streets as well as historic model railroads can be seen.

Films and educational programs are offered. **Time:** Allow 1 hour minimum. **Hours:** Wed.-Fri. 9:30-3, Sat. 10-5, Sun. noon-5. Closed major holidays. **Cost:** $6; $4 (ages 5-17 and 60+). **Parking:** $4. **Phone:** (313) 833-1805.

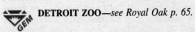 **DETROIT INSTITUTE OF ARTS** is at 5200 Woodward Ave. at Farnsworth Ave.

The more than 60,000 pieces in the museum's collection trace the development of art from ancient to modern times. The African, African-American, American, Asian, Dutch, Italian Renaissance and modern art collections are notable. The Diego Rivera murals representing Detroit industry are highlights. Some of the other renowned artists featured include Mary Cassatt, Edgar Degas, Claude Monet, Henri Matisse, Michelangelo, Henry Moore, Pablo Picasso, Rembrandt, Peter Paul Rubens, John Singer Sargent, Georges Seurat, Vincent van Gogh and Andy Warhol.

Interactive elements such as digital books and videos of artists demonstrating their techniques are scattered throughout the galleries. Live music and other activities are offered Friday evenings, and family activities are held on Sundays. Programs and concerts are also presented throughout the year.

Audio tours are available in English, Spanish and Japanese. **Time:** Allow 1 hour, 30 minutes minimum. **Hours:** Galleries open Wed.-Fri. 10-4 (also Fri. 4-10), Sat.-Sun. 10-5. Guided tours are given Wed.-Sun. at 1 (also Fri. at 6 and 7:30 p.m. and Sun. at 3). Closed major holidays. **Cost:** $8; $6 (ages 65+); $4 (ages 6-17). Guided tour $5. Audio tour $2. **Phone:** (313) 833-7900, (313) 833-7530 for weekend event information or TTY (313) 833-1454. 🍴

DETROIT PUBLIC LIBRARY is at 5201 Woodward Ave. at Kirby Ave. The Italian Renaissance building features white Vermont marble. Murals by Edwin H. Blashfield and Gari Melchers, painted-glass windows designed by Frederick J. Wiley, mosaic panels depicting Shakespeare's "Seven Ages of Man" and Pewabic tiles adorn the interior.

The Burton Historical Collection in the rare book room is of interest. The Hackley Collection focuses on African-Americans' contribution to the performing arts and includes rare books, manuscripts, photographs and recorded sounds. The Skillman Branch Library (121 Gratiot Ave.) houses the National Automotive History Collection. **Hours:** Main library open Tues.-Wed. noon-8, Thurs.-Sat. 10-6. Skillman Branch Library open Mon.-Fri. 10-6. Closed major holidays. **Cost:** Free. **Phone:** (313) 833-1000, or (313) 628-2750 for Skillman Branch Library.

DETROIT SCIENCE CENTER is at 5020 John R. St. at Warren Ave. in the midtown cultural center. The center features more than 200 hands-on exhibits, an IMAX dome theater and a planetarium. An exhibit collection entitled United States Steel Fun Factory is included. Live science programs are presented on the Science Stage, and electrical demonstrations are the focus in the Sparks Theater. A children's gallery also offers science exhibits designed for young minds. The Motorsports Hall of Fame of America is part of the center, too.

Time: Allow 2 hours minimum. **Hours:** Wed.-Fri. 9-3, Sat.10-6, Sun. noon-6. Closed July 4, Labor Day, Thanksgiving and Dec. 24-25. **Cost:** (includes one IMAX show and the planetarium) $13.95; $11.95 (ages 2-12 and 60+). Additional IMAX shows $5 each. **Parking:** $5. **Phone:** (313) 577-8400.

DETROIT ZOO—*see Royal Oak p. 65.*

ELMWOOD HISTORIC CEMETERY, 1200 Elmwood Ave., was established in 1846 and is the city's oldest continuously operating non-denominational cemetery. A creek on the grounds is now a serene feature but was the site of a battle between Chief Pontiac and the British during the French and Indian War.

The 86-acre parklike setting includes many tombs, grave markers and mausoleums that date to the mid- to late 1800s and are Victorian in style. Lewis Cass, the powerful 19th-century Michigan politician, and Martha Jean "The Queen" Steinberg, believed to be the first African-American woman to own a radio station, are two of the prominent individuals buried here. **Time:** Allow 15 minutes minimum. **Hours:** Daily 8-7, May-Sept.; 8-4, rest of year. **Cost:** Free. **Phone:** (313) 567-3453.

GM RENAISSANCE CENTER TOUR departs from the Pure Detroit/GM Collection store on Level 1 in Tower 400 at 100 Renaissance Center. Stops and points of interest on the 1-hour tour include GM Wintergarden, a tropical atrium; the Detroit River-Walk; the GM showroom; "Borealis," said to be the world's tallest vertical glass sculpture; and a view of Detroit and Windsor, Ontario from the building's 72nd floor.

Hours: Tours depart Mon.-Fri. at noon and 2. Closed major holidays. **Cost:** Free. Reservations are recommended. **Phone:** (313) 568-5624 or (313) 568-5740. 🍴

MODEL T AUTOMOTIVE HERITAGE COMPLEX, is off I-94 exit 215C (Woodward Ave./SR 1/John R St.), just n. on Brush St., then just e. to 461 Piquette Ave. The site is home to Henry Ford's 1904 plant, which was in operation for the Ford Motor Co. until 1910. It was the company's first plant built to assemble automobiles, and it represented a substantial space increase from the rented location on Mack Avenue. The new location was adjacent to the Michigan Central Railroad, which was extremely beneficial for shipping and receiving.

Historic Ford vehicles and interpretive panels recalling the early era of automotive production are displayed. The third floor is home to Henry Ford's "Experimental Room," where he worked on plans for the future.

One-hour guided tours as well as brochures for self-guiding tours are offered. The plant does not have a heating or cooling system. **Hours:** Wed.-Fri. 10-4, Sat. 9-4, Sun. noon-4, Apr. 1-Nov. 21; by appointment rest of year. Tour availability varies; phone for schedule. **Cost:** $10; $9 (senior citizens); $5 (students with ID); free (ages 0-16). Cash only. **Phone:** (313) 872-8759.

MOTOWN HISTORICAL MUSEUM is at 2648 W. Grand Blvd. The Motown sound of the early 1960s originated in this old brick house that is now home to the museum. Such entertainers as Marvin Gaye, Smokey Robinson, Diana Ross and the Supremes, and Stevie Wonder got their starts here under the direction of Motown Records founder Berry Gordy Jr.

The galleries contain a variety of musical instruments, photographs, artifacts and the original Studio A and control room. **Hours:** Mon.-Sat. 10-6, July-Aug.; Tues.-Sat. 10-6, rest of year. Closed major holidays. **Cost:** $10; $8 (ages 0-12 and 62+). **Phone:** (313) 875-2264.

PEWABIC POTTERY is at 10125 E. Jefferson Ave. The ceramics museum, gallery, workshop and studio offer changing contemporary exhibits. A collection of historic work by Mary Chase Perry Stratton, Pewabic's founder, also is displayed. **Hours:** Mon.-Sat. 10-4. Closed major holidays. **Cost:** Free. **Phone:** (313) 822-0954.

WOODLAWN CEMETERY, 19975 Woodward Ave., has ornate Victorian tombs, grave markers and mausoleums. Many famous individuals are buried here, including Civil Rights icon Rosa Parks; Edsel Ford and his wife and son Benson; and Obie Benson, a founding member of The Four Tops. **Time:** Allow 15 minutes minimum. **Hours:** Grounds daily dawn-dusk. Office Mon.-Fri. 9-4:30, Sat. 9-3. **Cost:** Free. **Phone:** (313) 368-0010.

WOODMERE CEMETERY is off I-75 exit 45 (Fort St.), just s. on Springwell, then 1 mi. w. to 9400 W. Fort St. This cemetery, dating to 1869, contains ornate Victorian grave markers, mausoleums and tombs. Some notable individuals interred here include David Dunbar Buick, founder of Buick Motors; James Vernor Sr., Detroit florist, pharmacist and inventor of Vernor's ginger ale; and Eugene Hamlet Krapp, an early 20th-century professional baseball player.

Time: Allow 15 minutes minimum. **Hours:** Grounds Mon.-Fri. 8:30-4:30, Sat.-Sun. 8:30 a.m.-dusk. Office Mon.-Fri. 8:30-4:30, Sat. 9-3. Phone ahead to confirm schedule. **Cost:** Free. **Phone:** (313) 841-0188.

GAMBLING ESTABLISHMENTS

- **Greektown Casino** is at 555 E. Lafayette Ave. **Hours:** Daily 24 hours. **Phone:** (888) 771-4386.
- **MGM Grand Detroit** is at 1777 Third St. **Hours:** Daily 24 hours. **Phone:** (313) 465-1777 or (877) 888-2121. *(see ad p. 257)*
- **Motor City Casino** is at 2901 Grand River Ave. **Hours:** Daily 24 hours. **Phone:** (313) 237-7711 or (866) 752-9622. *(see ad & starting p. 258)*

What To Do

Sightseeing

Boat Tours

SAVE **DIAMOND JACK'S RIVER TOURS** departs from Rivard Plaza dock at jct. Bates and Atwater sts., and from Bishop Park dock in Wyandotte at jct. Superior Blvd. and Van Alstyne. Passengers ride on a former Mackinac Island ferry for a 2-hour narrated cruise. The Detroit trip passes historic and modern buildings, shipyards and downtown Windsor, Ontario, as well as under the Ambassador Bridge and around

Belle Isle. The Wyandotte trip focuses on nature and wildlife.

Time: Allow 2 hours minimum. **Hours:** Cruises depart from Rivard Plaza and Bishop Park Thurs.-Sun. at 1 and 3:30, mid-June through Sun. before Labor Day. Passengers should phone ahead to verify departure location and arrive 30 minutes before departure. **Cost:** Fare for either trip $17; $15 (ages 61+); $13 (ages 6-16). **Phone:** (313) 843-9376, ext. 100.

Sports and Recreation

Sports enthusiasts can watch the Detroit Tigers **baseball** team at Comerica Park, (313) 962-4000. The Lions **football** team plays at Ford Field; phone (313) 262-2000, or (313) 262-2002 for ticket information. The eleven-time Stanley Cup champion Red Wings **hockey** team challenges rivals in the Joe Louis Arena; phone (313) 983-6606. The Palace of Auburn Hills is the home of the Detroit NBA Pistons **basketball** team; phone (248) 377-0100. Since Detroit sports are popular, tickets should be ordered at least a month before the scheduled date of the event.

Harness racing can be enjoyed at Northville Downs, (248) 349-1000; Hazel Park Harness Raceway, (248) 398-1000; Pinnacle Race Course in New Boston, (734) 543-3200; and Windsor Raceway in Windsor, Ontario, (313) 961-9545 or (519) 969-8311.

Note: Policies concerning admittance of children to pari-mutuel betting facilities vary. Phone ahead for information.

Biking and **walking** opportunities are continuing to grow in Detroit. Two popular options include the Detroit RiverWalk and Dequindre Cut Greenway. The more than 3-mile RiverWalk affords walkers and joggers views of the river as well as GM Renaissance Center, Joe Louis Arena and Cobo Center. The 1.35-mile, 20-foot-wide paved Dequindre Cut Greenway, which features designated lanes for pedestrians and bikers/in-line skaters, has several entrance ramps. It currently runs between the RiverWalk and Gratiot Avenue, with plans to extend it to Mack Avenue in the future. Both trails are open daily 6 a.m.-10 p.m., with extended hours during special events. For information about this area, contact the Detroit RiverFront Conservancy at (313)

566-8200. Wheelhouse Detroit, 1340 E. Atwater St. at Rivard Plaza on the RiverWalk, offers bicycle rentals. A valid ID and credit card deposit are required, and rentals include a helmet and lock; phone (313) 656-2453.

Several public courses offer **golf** in Detroit: Chandler Park, 12801 Chandler Park Dr., (313) 331-7755; Palmer Park, Woodward at Seven Mile Road, (313) 883-2525; Rackham, 10100 W. Ten Mile Rd. in Huntington Woods, (248) 543-4040; Rogell, 18601 Berg Rd., (313) 255-4653; and Rouge Park, 11701 Burt Rd., (313) 837-5900.

Swimming is permitted at Belle Isle and at the mile-long Metropolitan Beach Metropark; phone (586) 463-4581. Twelve other metro parks have playgrounds and facilities for swimming, golfing, **boating**, **ice-skating**, **picnicking** and nature study. Many parks have courts for **tennis** and **shuffleboard** in addition to winter recreation facilities.

Shopping

When Saturday rolls around, vendors open up their Eastern Market stalls to sell produce, meat, fish, nuts, bakery items and imported products between 5 a.m. and 5 p.m. Local artists sell their creations, too, and entertainment from buskers livens up the environment. Special events are held throughout the year. The market runs along Market Street between Wilkins and Winder streets. The market's welcome center is between Sheds 2 and 3 at 1445 Adelaide; phone (313) 833-9300.

The Stores of Renaissance Center are popular with shoppers. If you're after rock and roll merchandise, try the shop inside the SAVE Hard Rock Cafe at 45 Monroe St.

Suburban shopping centers contain many major department store chains and smaller specialty shops and theaters. Among the largest malls are Eastland, at SR 102 (Eight Mile Road) and Kelly Road; Fairlane Town Center, at SR 39 (Southfield) and US 12 (Michigan Avenue) in Dearborn; Lakeside, at SR 59 (Hall Road) and Schoenherr in Sterling Heights; The Mall at Partridge Creek, at SR 59 (Hall Road) and Partridge Creek Boulevard in Clinton Township; Northland, north of SR 102 at SR 10 (Northwestern Highway); The Somerset Collection and Somerset North, at Big Beaver (Sixteen Mile Road) and Coolidge in Troy; Southland, at Eureka and Pardee roads in Taylor; Twelve Oaks Mall, off I-96 Novi Road exit in Novi; and Westland, at Wayne Road and Warren Avenue.

Great Lakes Crossing Mall on Baldwin Road in Auburn Hills features more than 200 stores, restaurants and entertainment facilities. A combination of retail and outlet shopping opportunities is available.

Performing Arts

The industrial side of Detroit is tempered by the city's notable cultural offerings. The Detroit Symphony plays a full season of concerts, including children's concerts at Orchestra Hall; phone (313) 576-5111. Throughout the year the following theaters offer a variety of stage presentations, including concert artists, drama, opera and dance: The Fillmore Detroit, (313) 961-5451; Fox Theatre, (313) 471-3200; the Masonic Temple, (313) 832-7100; and the Music Hall Center for the Performing Arts, (313) 887-8500.

Detroit ranks high in sales of theater tickets. Professional repertory, including first-run and off-Broadway productions, can be enjoyed at the Fisher Theater at 3001 W. Grand Blvd.; phone (313) 872-1000. Evening and matinee performances are offered at the Detroit Repertory Theatre, (313) 868-1347, and at the Gem and Century theatres, (313) 963-9800.

Other area theaters offer concerts and plays sponsored by the drama departments of the University of Detroit-Mercy, (313) 993-3270, and Wayne State University, (313) 577-2972. Among the area's popular suburban venues are the Meadow Brook Music Festival, (248) 377-0100; the DTE Energy Music Theatre, (248) 377-0100; the Palace of Auburn Hills, (248) 377-0100; and the Freedom Hill Amphitheatre, (586) 268-5100, in Sterling Heights.

Several first-run multiple cinemas dot the suburbs. Local newspapers carry complete information about concerts, theater, movies and other events.

Special Events

Start the new year off right in the city built by cars with the North American International Auto Show held in mid-January at the Cobo Center.

Summers in Detroit, though at times hot and humid, are celebrated with a variety of events. Festivities include Flower Day at Eastern Market (see Shopping section) in May. Also in May is Detroit's Electronic Music Festival.

In late June (weather permitting) the riverfront is the place to be for ⬆ Detroit River Days. The celebration features family-friendly entertainment, music, and the River Days Boat Parade of Lights; it concludes with the Target Fireworks, a spectacular display above the river.

Watch the street rods cruise by on Woodward Avenue at the Woodward Dream Cruise in mid-August. For music lovers the Detroit International Jazz Festival is presented over Labor Day weekend. Also over Labor Day weekend is the ⬆ Arts, Beats & Eats Festival held in Royal Oak.

Initiating the holiday season is the America's Thanksgiving Parade on Thanksgiving Day. In late December the ⬆ Little Caesars Pizza Bowl (formerly called the Motor City Bowl) is held at Ford Field.

The Detroit Vicinity

AUBURN HILLS (K-5) pop. 19,837, elev. 975'

WALTER P. CHRYSLER MUSEUM is off I-75 exit 78, then 1.3 mi. e. to One Chrysler Dr. Interactive displays and vignettes relate the history of Walter P. Chrysler and the Chrysler Group LLP. The collection of more than 70 vehicles includes restored classics, muscle cars, trucks and race cars. Visitors may watch three 7-minute films in the theater. **Time:** Allow 30 minutes minimum. **Hours:** Tues.-Sat. 10-5, Sun. noon-5. Closed major holidays. **Cost:** $8; $7 (ages 62+); $4 (ages 6-12). **Phone:** (248) 944-0001 or (888) 456-1924.

BELLEVILLE (I-5) pop. 3,997, elev. 670'

YANKEE AIR MUSEUM is at 47884 D St. at Willow Run Airport. The museum features aircraft as well. as items related to aviation history. There are thousands of World War II artifacts and a variety of hands-on exhibits for children. **Hours:** Wed.-Sat. 10-4:30, Sun. noon-4. Hours may be expanded in summer. Closed major holidays. Phone ahead to confirm schedule. **Cost:** $3; $2 (students with ID); free (ages 0-17 with adult); $5 (family, two adults and children ages 0-17). **Phone:** (734) 483-4030.

BIRMINGHAM (K-5) pop. 19,291, elev. 778'

Shopping areas: More than a dozen art galleries and antique shops can be found downtown.

BIRMINGHAM HISTORICAL MUSEUM & PARK, 556 W. Maple Rd. at jct. Southfield Rd., features two furnished historical houses in a beautifully landscaped park. Guided tours of the 1822 John West Hunter House, the oldest house in Birmingham, reveal furnishings representative of the 1820s-80s. Visitors can tour the 1928 Allen House next door on their own. This house belonged to the city's first mayor and showcases a 1920s kitchen and changing exhibits regarding local history. **Time:** Allow 30 minutes minimum. **Hours:** Wed.-Sat. 1-4. Closed major holidays. **Cost:** $2; $1 (ages 6-18 and 65+). Cash only. **Phone:** (248) 530-1928.

BLOOMFIELD HILLS (K-5) pop. 3,940

In 1819 Judge Amasa Bagley cleared land for a tavern and a farm on what was to become known as Bagley's Corner. It remained an agricultural center until about 1900 when city dwellers from Detroit began to buy acreage for estates. In 1932 the name was changed to Bloomfield Hills.

Among the wealthy who were attracted to this quiet community during the first decade of the 20th century were the publisher of *The Detroit News*, George G. Booth, and his wife, Ellen Scripps Booth. Their estate, Cranbrook, has become a notable cultural and educational center.

CRANBROOK EDUCATIONAL COMMUNITY is at 39221 Woodward Ave. (SR 1). The 319-acre campus includes a college preparatory school and a graduate fine arts school. There is a modern and contemporary art museum, a natural science museum, two historic homes and more than 40 acres of sculpture-filled gardens *(see attraction listings)*. The buildings represent designs by prominent architects. **Hours:** Schedule varies per site. **Cost:** Admission is charged at the museums and historic houses. **Phone:** (248) 645-3000 or (877) 462-7262.

Cranbrook Art Museum, part of Cranbrook Educational Community, is at 39221 Woodward Ave. (SR 1). Changing displays of modern and contemporary art as well as faculty and student artwork are the focus of the museum's collection. Traveling exhibitions are featured throughout the year. Ninety-minute tours are available of the restored 1930 Art Deco Saarinen House, the home and studio of Eliel Saarinen, Cranbrook's resident architect 1925-50, and his wife Loja, who was head of the Department of Weaving.

CLOSURE INFORMATION: The museum is closed through spring 2011 for renovations. Phone for schedule and admission closer to reopening date. Tours of the Saarinen House continue to be offered during the art museum renovation. **Hours:** Saarinen House tours depart Thurs.-Sun. at 2, May-Oct. Closed major holidays. **Cost:** Saarinen House tour $10; $9 (ages 65+); $6 (students with ID); free (ages 0-12). **Phone:** (248) 645-3323, (248) 645-3210 for Saarinen House or (877) 462-7262.

Cranbrook House and Gardens, part of Cranbrook Educational Community, is at 380 Lone Pine Rd. Designed by Albert Kahn, the Arts and Crafts-style house is situated on 40 acres that include formal plantings, woods, sculpture, fountains, pine walks and two lakes.

Time: Allow 1 hour minimum. **Hours:** House tours depart Thurs. at 11 and 1:15, Fri. at 11 and 1, Sun. at 1 and 3, mid-June through Sept. 30; Thurs. at 11 and 1:15, Fri. at 11 and Sun. at 1, in Oct. **Cost:** (includes house and gardens) $10; $8 (ages 66+ and students with ID). **Phone:** (248) 645-3147 or (877) 462-7262.

Cranbrook Institute of Science, part of Cranbrook Educational Community, is at 39221 Woodward Ave. (SR 1). This museum of science and natural history boasts one of the country's largest mineral collections. Interactive and hands-on exhibits demonstrate such physical principles as the laws of gravity, motion, and plate tectonics and the creation of minerals and the Earth's crust. Entertainment light shows and a planetarium also are offered.

Earth's dynamic aspect is featured in several exhibits, one of which includes a skeleton cast of a full-size Tyrannosaurus rex. Another exhibit focuses on extinction and showcases animals that were extinct by the end of the last ice age. Climate changes and ice ages also are explored. The Bat Zone is home to bats, owls and a sloth. This exhibit highlights the characteristics of nocturnal animals.

Time: Allow 2 hours minimum. **Hours:** Tues.-Sat. 10-5 (also Fri. 5-10). Light and astronomy shows Fri. on the hour 7-9 p.m., Sat.-Sun. on the hour 11:30-3:30. Observatory Fri. 8:30 p.m.-10 p.m., first Sun. of the month 1-4. Bat Zone tour Sat.-Sun. at 12:30 and 2:30. Closed Jan. 1, Easter, July 4, Labor Day-Sept. 13, Thanksgiving, and Dec. 24-25 and 31.

Cost: $9.50; $7.50 (ages 2-12 and 65+). Admission Fri. 5-10 p.m. $5.50; $4.50 (ages 2-12 and 65+). Planetarium shows and Bat Zone tours each additional $4; $1 (ages 0-2). Some planetarium shows do not permit children under age 5; phone for details. **Phone:** (248) 645-3200 or (877) 462-7262. ⑪

KIRK IN THE HILLS is at 1340 W. Long Lake Rd. The cornerstone of this Presbyterian church was laid in 1951; the grounds occupy 40 acres on a lakefront. The church is Gothic in its design and was patterned after the 13th-century Melrose Abbey in Scotland. Stained-glass windows, a 77-bell carillon, a 5,000-pipe Moller organ, statues and multiple carvings are some of the highlights.

Walking tour brochures with information about the church's exterior as well as the narthex, nave and chancel are provided. **Time:** Allow 20 minutes minimum. **Hours:** Mon.-Fri. 10-noon and 2-4. **Cost:** Donations. **Phone:** (248) 626-2515. ⚏

DEARBORN (L-4) pop. 97,775, elev. 604'

While its giant neighbor Detroit absorbed adjoining townships, Dearborn—itself created from the merger of Fordson and Dearborn—did not lose its identity. It had a giant of its own, Henry Ford, who put Dearborn on the map by putting the nation on wheels.

During the holiday season (on select nights in December) you can relive the past as you stroll along the candle-lit paths, ride in a Model-T and listen to live musical performances at the ⚑ Holiday Nights in Greenfield Village, part of The Henry Ford *(see attraction listing).*

Dearborn Chamber of Commerce: 22100 Michigan Ave., Dearborn, MI 48124. **Phone:** (313) 584-6100.

ARAB AMERICAN NATIONAL MUSEUM is at 13624 Michigan Ave. across from City Hall. Various aspects of Arab-American history and culture, including the Arab immigrant experience and the culture's impact on American society, are portrayed through exhibits and interactive displays. Cultural artifacts and a gallery of works by contemporary Arab-American artists also are displayed.

Time: Allow 30 minutes minimum. **Hours:** Wed.-Sat. 10-6, Sun. noon-5. Closed Jan. 1, Thanksgiving and Dec. 25. **Cost:** $6; $3 (ages 6-12, senior citizens and students with ID). **Phone:** (313) 582-2266.

💾 **AUTOMOTIVE HALL OF FAME** is at 21400 Oakwood Blvd., adjacent to The Henry Ford. Plaques and memorabilia are dedicated to the men and women of the automotive industry. Honorees include designers, educators, inventors, journalists, manufacturers, race car drivers and automotive association members. **Time:** Allow 1 hour, 30 minutes minimum. **Hours:** Wed.-Sun. 9-5. Closed Jan. 1, Thanksgiving and Dec. 25. **Cost:** $8; $6 (ages 13-18 and 62+); $4 (ages 5-12). **Phone:** (313) 240-4000.

DEARBORN HISTORICAL MUSEUM has collections at 21950 Michigan Ave. and 915 Brady St. The museum includes two buildings of the original 1833 United States Government Arsenal. An exhibit annex has farm equipment, wagons and buggies. The Richard Gardner House, built in 1831 and furnished in period, belonged to the family of one of Henry Ford's childhood friends. The commandant's quarters contains period furnishings and military displays. The McFadden-Ross House depicts a 1900 farmhouse and holds the City of Dearborn Archive.

Guided tours are available by appointment. **Time:** Allow 30 minutes minimum. **Hours:** Commandant's quarters Tues.-Fri. 11-4, Sat. 9-1. McFadden-Ross House/Archives Mon.-Fri. 9-5, Sat.-Sun. by appointment. Closed major holidays. **Cost:** Free. **Phone:** (313) 565-3000, or (313) 565-0844 for commandant's quarters.

⚑💎 **THE HENRY FORD** is at 20900 Oakwood Blvd. This five-venue complex commemorates 300 years of the American experience through exhibits, tours, programs and special events.

Henry Ford Museum celebrates American innovative genius. National treasures include the Rosa Parks bus, presidential limousines, the chair in which Abraham Lincoln was assassinated and a folding camp bed used by George Washington. The museum includes permanent and temporary touring exhibits.

In Greenfield Village more than 90 acres include seven historic districts with buildings of historic significance. Vintage transportation, skilled artisans and costumed presenters can be seen daily. Important sites include the Ford Birthplace, Wright Cycle Shop and Noah Webster House. An IMAX theater is inside the museum. The Benson Ford Research Center's reading room is open to the public.

Comfortable shoes are recommended. **Time:** Allow a full day. **Hours:** Museum daily 9:30-5. Village daily 9:30-5, mid-Apr. through Oct. 31; Fri.-Sun. 9:30-5, in Nov. IMAX show times vary; phone ahead. Research center Tues.-Fri. 9-5; closed major holidays. All closed Thanksgiving and Dec. 25.

Cost: Museum: $15; $14 (ages 62+); $11 (ages 5-12). Village $22; $21 (ages 62+); $16 (ages 5-12). IMAX $10-$13.75; $9-$12.75 (ages 62+); $8.50-$9.75 (ages 5-12). Research center free. Individual and combination attraction admissions are available. **Phone:** (313) 982-6001, (313) 271-1570, (313)

271-1620 for recorded information, (800) 835-5237, (800) 747-4629 for IMAX or TTY (313) 271-2455. 🎭

Ford Rouge Factory Tour begins at The Henry Ford at 20900 Oakwood Blvd. At the factory visitors can see rare footage of the facility's history. A second theater features special virtual reality-type effects, allowing visitors to experience automobile production. An observation deck and walking tour of the assembly plant where F-150 trucks are assembled complete the tour.

Tours may not always coincide with vehicle production schedule. **Time:** Allow 2 hours minimum. **Hours:** Buses depart from the museum Mon.-Sat. every 30 minutes 9:20-3. Closed Thanksgiving and Dec. 25. Phone ahead to confirm schedule. **Cost:** $15; $14 (ages 62+); $11 (ages 3-12). Reservations are recommended. **Phone:** (313) 982-6001, (313) 271-1620 for recorded information, (800) 835-5237 or TTY (313) 271-2455.

HENRY FORD ESTATE—FAIR LANE is on the campus of the University of Michigan-Dearborn at 4901 Evergreen Rd. Clara and Henry Ford lived on this 32,000-square-foot estate, where they entertained such luminaries as Charles Lindbergh, the Duke of Windsor and President Herbert Hoover in their spacious mansion. Tours of the mansion and powerhouse are given, and visitors can walk the 300-foot underground tunnel connecting the two. Gardens and trails are on the grounds.

Time: Allow 1 hour, 30 minutes minimum. **Hours:** Self-guiding tours of the grounds are available Tues.-Sun. 9:30-5, Apr.-Dec. Estate tours depart Tues.-Sun. at 10:30, 11:30, 12:30, 1:30 and 2:30, Apr.-Dec.; Tues.-Sun. at 1:30, rest of year. Closed Jan. 1, Easter, Thanksgiving and Dec. 24-25. **Cost:** Estate tour $12; $11 (ages 62+ and students with ID); $8 (ages 6-12). Grounds only admission $2. **Phone:** (313) 593-5590. 🎭

FARMINGTON HILLS (K-4) pop. 82,111

HOLOCAUST MEMORIAL CENTER is at 28123 Orchard Lake Rd. The center's exterior is designed to resemble a Nazi concentration camp. Inside, powerful exhibits document the history of the Holocaust with videotape presentations, oral accounts, photographs, dioramas and a memorial flame. Dark, small areas are dedicated to life under the Nazi regime and describe the horrors incurred. Visitors then emerge into brighter exhibit areas, which include post-World War II displays; the Museum of European Jewish History; and the International Institute of the Righteous, which honors non-Jews who endangered their lives while attempting, some successfully, to save at least one Jew.

Also included is a library and archives dedicated to the study of the Holocaust and Jewish history, culture and genealogy. **Time:** Allow 2 hours minimum. **Hours:** Sun.-Thurs. 9:30-5, Fri. 9:30-3. Guided tours are offered Sun.-Thurs. at 1. Last admission 1 hour, 30 minutes before closing. Closed

religious and most federal holidays. **Cost:** Donations. **Phone:** (248) 553-2400, or (248) 553-2834 for the library.

MARVIN'S MARVELOUS MECHANICAL MUSEUM is at 31005 Orchard Lake Rd. Displays include antique slot and pinball machines and other mechanical memorabilia and video games, including nickelodeons, vintage neon signs and magic show posters. **Hours:** Mon.-Sat. 10-9 (also Fri.-Sat. 9-11 p.m.), Sun. 11-9. **Cost:** Free. **Phone:** (248) 626-5020. 🎭

GROSSE POINTE SHORES (L-6)
pop. 2,823, elev. 586'

EDSEL & ELEANOR FORD HOUSE is 1.5 mi. e. from I-94 Vernier/Eight Mile exit, then 1 mi. n. on Lake Shore Rd. The 60-room house, styled after houses in the Cotswold area of England, was built 1926-29 by the Ford Motor Co. executive and his wife. The estate and landscaped grounds were created to accommodate their family and an extensive collection of fine and decorative arts. Twenty of the rooms are shown on guided tours that begin with a 15-minute videotape presentation in the Activities Center.

Time: Allow 2 hours minimum. **Hours:** Tours are given Tues.-Sat. 10-4, Sun. noon-4, Apr.-Dec.; Tues.-Fri. at noon and 1:30, Sat.-Sun. noon-4, rest of year. Grounds open Tues.-Sat. 9:30-6, Sun. 11:30-6, Apr.-Dec.; Tues.-Sun. 11:30-4, rest of year. Closed Jan. 1, Thanksgiving and Dec. 25. **Cost:** (includes guided house tour and self-guiding grounds tour) $12; $11 (ages 60+); $8 (ages 6-12). Grounds only $5. **Phone:** (313) 884-4222.

HAMTRAMCK (L-5) pop. 22,976, elev. 630'

POLISH ART CENTER is off I-75 exit 55, .6 mi. e. on Caniff St., then .3 mi. s. to 9539 Joseph Campau St. Folk art and cultural artifacts celebrate the cultural heritage, traditions, history and art of the Polish community. Folk art classes, including Polish Easter egg making, are available; phone for schedule. **Time:** Allow 30 minutes minimum. **Hours:** Mon.-Sat. 9:30-5 (also Thurs.-Sat. 5-6), Sun. 11-3. **Cost:** Free. **Phone:** (313) 874-2242 or (888) 619-9771.

LIVONIA (L-4) pop. 100,545, elev. 638'

GREENMEAD HISTORICAL PARK is at 20501 Newburgh Rd. at jct. Eight Mile Rd. The 95-acre site was the 1820s homestead of Michigan pioneer Joshua Simmons. It includes the original farm complex, the Livonia Historical Village and a nature trail. The farm complex features an 1841 Greek Revival farmhouse with nine of the original 11 outbuildings still intact. Events are held throughout the year.

Time: Allow 2 hours minimum. **Hours:** Grounds open daily dawn-dusk. Tours of historic buildings Mon.-Fri. by appointment, Sun. 1-4, June-Oct. and in Dec. Closed holiday weekends. **Cost:** $3; $2 (ages 0-17). **Phone:** (248) 477-7375. 🅰

MOUNT CLEMENS (K-6)
pop. 17,312, elev. 604'

THE CROCKER HOUSE MUSEUM & MACOMB COUNTY HISTORICAL SOCIETY is at 15 Union St. Joshua Dickinson, the first mayor of Mount Clemens, built this Italianate house in 1869; his daughter Katherine and her husband moved into it after their marriage the following year. The house showcases artifacts, including rotating exhibits, that depict local history, especially the period of prosperity between the late 1800s and the Great Depression that resulted after the discovery of mineral water wells. The historical society's collections also are housed here.

Time: Allow 1 hour minimum. **Hours:** Tues.-Thurs. and first Sun. of the month 10-4. Closed major holidays. Phone ahead to confirm schedule. **Cost:** Donations. **Phone:** (586) 465-2488.

PLYMOUTH (L-3) pop. 9,022, elev. 741'

Plymouth was founded in 1867 by a group of settlers from Plymouth, Mass. Their Colonial influence can still be seen in the town's architecture.

After the holidays are over, there is still something to look forward to with the 🐸 Plymouth Ice Festival, which is held in Kellogg Park in late January.

Plymouth Community Chamber of Commerce: 850 W. Ann Arbor Tr., Plymouth, MI 48170. **Phone:** (734) 453-1540.

[SAVE] **PLYMOUTH HISTORICAL MUSEUM** is 1 blk. n. of Kellogg Park at 155 S. Main St. This 26,000-square-foot museum chronicles the history of early Plymouth. A gallery houses Main Street shops and offices reflecting many trades and professions of 19th-century Plymouth. Highlights include the Abraham Lincoln and Victorian Rooms exhibits. Among the Lincoln artifacts and archives are a lock of the president's hair and one of his childhood books. The museum is home to what is said to be the only Alter car, which was built in Plymouth 1916-17. A collection of Daisy air rifles also is displayed.

A library and archives are available. **Time:** Allow 1 hour minimum. **Hours:** Wed. and Fri.-Sun. 1-4. **Cost:** $5; $2 (ages 6-17); $10 (family). **Phone:** (734) 455-8940.

PONTIAC (K-4) pop. 66,337, elev. 933'

Pontiac was established in 1818 where the Pontiac Trail crossed the Clinton River. Settlers began pouring in, and by the 1880s the city entertained a major wagon and carriage-making industry. In a sense, it still does: What began as the Pontiac

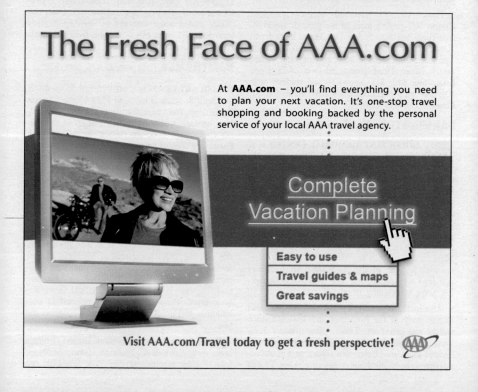

Spring Wagon Works is known as General Motors. The Pontiac Division of General Motors perpetuates the name of the great Ottawa Indian chief who reputedly spent his summers at nearby Orchard Lake.

A number of municipal parks and more than 400 nearby lakes that arc around the western side of the city offer outdoor recreation.

Pontiac Regional Chamber of Commerce: 402 N. Telegraph Rd., Pontiac, MI 48341. **Phone:** (248) 335-9600.

ROCHESTER (K-5) pop. 10,467, elev. 745'

Although on the fringe of metropolitan Detroit, Rochester lies among wooded hills—an apt home for Oakland University.

During the holiday season, downtown Rochester's buildings are festively dressed for the season with The Big, Bright Light Show. More than 1 million LED lights thoroughly cover the building exteriors. Also part of the extravaganza are the Dazzling Tree of Lights and the Snowflake Spectacular—light displays that are set to music. The lights can be seen daily 6 p.m.-midnight from late November to early January. The Annual Rochester Hometown Christmas Parade is another holiday favorite; it's held the first Sunday afternoon in December and runs through downtown along Main Street.

Rochester Regional Chamber of Commerce: 71 Walnut Blvd., Suite 110, Rochester, MI 48307. **Phone:** (248) 651-6700.

OAKLAND UNIVERSITY'S MEADOW BROOK HALL is 3 mi. e. via Walton Blvd., then .3 mi. s. on Adams Rd., on the eastern campus of Oakland University. This 1920s Tudor Revival-style mansion was once the residence of Matilda Dodge Wilson and lumber broker Alfred G. Wilson. The 80,000-square-foot, 100-room home boasts a two-story ballroom, 24 fireplaces, hand-carved paneling and sculptured ceilings as well as many original furnishings and works of art.

Knole Cottage, also on the premises, is a brick six-room playhouse built for the Wilsons' daughter. It is furnished in the same style as Meadow Brook Hall. Visitors can walk through the various gardens; spring, summer and autumn provide the best viewing opportunities.

Time: Allow 1 hour, 30 minutes minimum. **Hours:** Guided house tours are given daily at 11:30, 12:30, 1:30 and 2:30, Memorial Day-Aug. 31; Mon.-Fri. at 1:30, Sat.-Sun. at 11:30, 12:30 1:30 and 2:30, rest of year. Closed major holidays. **Cost:** House tour $15; $10 (ages 62+); free (ages 0-12). Gardens free. **Phone:** (248) 364-6200.

ROYAL OAK (K-5) pop. 60,062, elev. 661'

In early September, the Arts, Beats and Eats event features food, art and music in downtown Royal Oak.

DETROIT ZOO is at 8450 W. Ten Mile Rd. at Woodward Ave. One of the most modern zoos in the country, it features spacious, open exhibits. Designed to simulate natural environments, habitats are laid out over 125 acres of landscaped grounds. Highlights are a 4-acre great ape complex, a snow monkey area with a hot spring, a reptile house, a free-flight aviary, and penguin and polar bear exhibits.

A miniature railroad carries passengers across the grounds. A hands-on learning center also is available. The Wildlife Interpretive Gallery features art and an indoor butterfly garden. The Wild Adventure Ride is a virtual motion-simulated theater offering a variety of shows. The Wild Adventure 3-D/4-D Theater presents 3-D films enhanced with 4-D special effects.

Time: Allow 4 hours minimum. **Hours:** Daily 9-5 (also Wed. 5-8, July-Aug.), Apr. 1-Labor Day; daily 10-5, day after Labor Day-Oct. 31; daily 10-4, rest of year. Closed Jan. 1, Thanksgiving and Dec. 25. **Cost:** $11; $9 (ages 62+); $7 (ages 2-14). One-way railroad ride $3. Wild Adventure Ride $3. Wild Adventure 3-D/4-D Theater $3. **Parking:** $5. **Phone:** (248) 541-5717. 🍴 🎡

NATIONAL SHRINE OF THE LITTLE FLOWER is at 2100 W. 12 Mile Rd. at jct. SR 1 (Woodward Ave.). The shrine became known through the radio broadcasts of its pastor, Father Charles E. Coughlin, now deceased. A striking feature is the 104-foot crucifixion tower, girded by four crosses; below the figure is a carving of the last words of Christ.

The church is built of granite and limestone interspersed with stone blocks from America's states and territories; on each is carved the state name and flower. Guided tours are available by appointment. **Time:** Allow 30 minutes minimum. **Hours:** Mon.-Sat. 10-4. Phone ahead to confirm schedule. **Cost:** Free. **Phone:** (248) 541-4122.

WATERFORD (K-3) pop. 73,150

DRAYTON PLAINS NATURE CENTER is . 2 mi. s.w. on Hatchery Rd. off US 24 (Dixie Hwy.), just s.e. on Edmore Rd. and Oakdale Dr., .1 mi. w. on Denby Dr., .2 mi. s. on Fortress Dr., then just s.w. to 2125 Denby Dr. The grounds encompass 137 acres along the Clinton River and feature nearly 4 miles of marked trails with interpretive signs through woodlands and meadows. Ponds also are on the grounds. The interpretive center includes displays of specimens in their natural habitats.

Time: Allow 30 minutes minimum. **Hours:** Grounds daily dawn-dusk. Interpretive center open daily; hours vary. Phone ahead to confirm schedule. **Cost:** Free. **Phone:** (248) 618-3070.

WESTLAND (L-4) pop. 86,602, elev. 666'

NANKIN MILLS INTERPRETIVE CENTER is at 33175 Ann Arbor Tr. This historic structure was built in the mid-1800s as a mill, and in 1918 Henry

Ford purchased the building for use as a small automobile factory. It now houses three floors of exhibits and interactive displays profiling the Rouge River's history and the relationships that local Native American tribes and industry had with the water source.

An exhibit with fish, turtles, frogs and insects of the Rouge River is included. **Hours:** Mon.-Sat. 9-4. Closed major holidays. **Cost:** Donations. **Phone:** (734) 261-1990.

WYANDOTTE (I-5) pop. 28,006, elev. 590'

DIAMOND JACK'S RIVER TOURS—
see Detroit p. 58.

THE FORD-MacNICHOL HOME/WYANDOTTE MUSEUM is at 2610 Biddle Ave. The 1896 Victorian house includes original fixtures, furnishings, wallpaper and woodwork. The lower level houses a museum that chronicles the development of the town from a Native American village through the 19th century. **Time:** Allow 1 hour minimum. **Hours:** Thurs.-Sun. noon-4, Apr. 1-early Jan. Last tour begins 30 minutes before closing. Closed major holidays. **Cost:** Free. $2; 50c (ages 0-12). **Phone:** (734) 324-7284 for news and events, or (734) 324-7297 for general information.

National Shrine of the Little Flower, Royal Oak / © Jim West / age fotostock

This ends listings for the Detroit Vicinity.
The following page resumes the alphabetical listings of cities in Michigan.

DOUGLAS (H-1) pop. 1,214

Along with its neighbor, Saugatuck *(see place listing p. 108)*, Douglas is a popular destination for fans of art and beautiful natural scenery. The town is the site of Douglas Beach, and there are more than two dozen galleries between the two communities.

Saugatuck/Douglas Convention & Visitors Bureau: 2902 Blue Star Hwy., Douglas, MI 49406. **Phone:** (269) 857-1701.

Self-guiding tours: You can pick up a brochure for a self-guiding walking tour of historic Douglas at the convention and visitors bureau. The route includes more than three dozen sites.

Shopping areas: A variety of specialty stores lines Center Street.

SS *KEEWATIN* is moored off CR A2 (Blue Star Hwy.) at the Kalamazoo River s. of the Saugatuck-Douglas Bridge. One of the last of the classic steamships, it was built in 1907 for the Canadian Pacific Railway's upper Great Lakes passenger route. Now a marine museum, the 350-foot coal-burning vessel is maintained and preserved as it was during its 57 years of service on the lakes.

The upper deck can be seen by guided 45-minute tours. Other tours also are available. **Hours:** Tours daily 10:30-4:30, Memorial Day weekend-Labor Day. **Cost:** $12; $6 (ages 6-12). **Phone:** (269) 857-2464.

DOWAGIAC (I-2) pop. 6,147, elev. 772'

MUSEUM AT SOUTHWESTERN MICHIGAN COLLEGE is e. on SR 62 from SR 51, then .2 mi. s. to 58900 Cherry Grove Rd., following signs. The museum explores regional history through hands-on exhibits, artifacts and pictures. Permanent exhibits include displays about Native Americans, pioneers, the Underground Railroad, the Round Oak Stove Co., agriculture and industry. **Time:** Allow 1 hour minimum. **Hours:** Tues.-Fri. 10-5, Sat. 11-3. Closed major holidays and holiday weekends. **Cost:** Free. **Phone:** (269) 782-1374.

DRUMMOND ISLAND (B-6) pop. 500

Part of the rocky Manitoulin archipelago that separates Georgian Bay and the North Channel from the rest of Lake Huron, Drummond Island lies off the eastern tip of the Upper Peninsula at the mouth of the St. Marys River.

When the treaty ending the War of 1812 ousted the British from Mackinac Island, they re-established their garrison on the southwest promontory of Drummond Island, despite the fact that the boundary through the archipelago was still indefinite. British attempts to obtain the island failed, and in 1828 the Union Jack was lowered.

Anglers, boaters, hunters and vacationers are drawn to this cliff-bound, deeply indented wilderness isle. Its woodlands harbor deer, grouse and rabbits; duck hunting is particularly good. From the bays and inlets come bass, northern pike, yellow perch and walleye. Hiking in the summer and snowmobiling in the winter are favorite pastimes along the forest trails. Dolomite quarries augment the economy. The island is accessible by automobile ferry from De Tour Village on SR 134.

DRUMMOND ISLAND HISTORICAL MUSEUM is about 8 mi. e. of the ferry dock on SR 134, 1.2 mi. n. on S. Townline Rd., .2 mi. w. on E. Court St., .3 mi. n. on S. Lane Rd. then just w. on S. Water St.; the museum is on the n.w. end of Drummond Island. Exhibits showcase local history with artifacts from Native Americans and Finnish settlers, a display about Fort Drummond, marine and sportsman's exhibits, and a display about the lumbering era.

The building is made of hand-hewn Drummond Island logs and the fireplace was built with stones from a former chimney at Fort Drummond. **Time:** Allow 30 minutes minimum. **Hours:** Daily 1-5, Memorial Day weekend to mid-Oct. **Cost:** Donations. **Phone:** (906) 493-5746.

DRYDEN (J-5) pop. 815

SEVEN PONDS NATURE CENTER is at 3854 Crawford Rd. Various natural communities—Earl's Prairie, glacial lakes, an herb garden, wetlands, a wildflower garden and a butterfly garden—are accessible by 6 miles of trails contained within 468 acres. The nature center offers changing exhibits, and maps are available.

Time: Allow 1 hour minimum. **Hours:** Tues.-Sun. 9-5. Closed Jan. 1, Thanksgiving, day after Thanksgiving, and Dec. 24-25 and 31. **Cost:** $3; $1 (ages 0-12). **Phone:** (810) 796-3200.

DURAND (J-2) pop. 3,933, elev. 796'

MICHIGAN RAILROAD HISTORY MUSEUM AND DURAND UNION STATION is at 200 Railroad St. Railroad artifacts, a model railroad display, a library housing abundant literature and archives about railroads in Michigan, and a tribute to rail workers are included. **Time:** Allow 30 minutes minimum. **Hours:** Museum Fri.-Sat. 10-5, Tues.-Thurs. and Sun. 1-5. Library and archives Sat. 1-5 and by appointment. Model railroad exhibit Sat. 1-4. Closed major holidays. **Cost:** Donations. **Phone:** (989) 288-3561.

EAST LANSING (H-4) pop. 46,525

Primarily residential, East Lansing complements the governmental and industrial emphasis of Lansing *(see place listing p. 85)*, which it abuts. The creation of Michigan Agricultural College in 1855 spurred the town's growth; since then East Lansing's development has paralleled that of the school, which became Michigan State University.

MICHIGAN STATE UNIVERSITY is e. on Grand River Ave. (SR 43), following signs. The school is on a 5,320-acre educational campus; its housing complex lodges more than 15,000 students and student families. Points of interest include Abrams Planetarium, Beaumont Tower, Kresge Art Museum, MSU Museum and Television Studio (WKAR-TV) *(see attraction listings)*.

Additional facilities on the campus are the Kellogg Center for Continuing Education, the Munn Ice Arena, seasonal displays of the 1873 Beal Botanical Garden, and the Wharton Center for Performing Arts. Both men's and women's basketball is played at Breslin Student Events Center. Tours of the campus and Wharton Center are available by appointment. **Hours:** Schedule varies per attraction. **Cost:** All attractions are free, but admission is charged to view planetarium shows. **Phone:** (517) 355-1855 for general campus information, or (517) 353-1982 for the Wharton Center.

Abrams Planetarium is on the Michigan State University campus on Science Rd. between N. Shaw and S. Shaw lns., 1 blk. e. of Farm Ln. The planetarium offers a variety of exhibits about astronomy and features a Digistar II projector. A highlight is the black light gallery featuring astronomical paintings made with fluorescent paint, hung against black walls and lit with ultraviolet lights.

Hours: Exhibit hall and black light gallery open Mon.-Fri. 8:30-noon and 1-4:30, Sept.-July. Planetarium shows Fri.-Sat. at 8 p.m., Sun. at 4 (a family show designed for preschool and early elementary students is offered Sun. at 2:30), Sept.-July. Ticket sales begin 30 minutes prior to show times. **Cost:** Exhibit hall free. Planetarium shows $3; $2.50 (ages 65+ and students with ID); $2 (ages 0-12). **Phone:** (517) 355-4676 or (517) 355-4672.

Beaumont Tower is on the Michigan State University campus in Building 12 on W. Circle Dr. On the site of one of the Michigan Agricultural College's original buildings, the tower contains a 49-bell carillon. **Hours:** Performances are given weekly during the school year. Tours depart Tues. at noon during the school year; by appointment with one month's notice rest of year. Summer concerts and tours are offered Wed., in July; phone for hours. Phone ahead to confirm schedule. **Cost:** Free. **Phone:** (517) 353-9300, or (517) 432-4066 for tour information.

Kresge Art Museum is on the Michigan State University campus at jct. Auditorium and Physics rds. Noted for its comprehensive collections of art from many cultures, the museum contains exhibits spanning more than 5,000 years of art history. Changing exhibits are presented.

Guided tours are available by reservation. **Hours:** Mon.-Fri. 10-5 (also Thurs. 5-8), Sat.-Sun. noon-5, day after Labor Day-May 31; Tues.-Fri. 11-5, Sat.-Sun. noon-5, June-July. Closed Jan. 1-9, Easter, Memorial Day, July 4, Thanksgiving and Dec. 18-31. **Cost:** Free. **Parking:** Free Thurs. after 6 p.m. and Sat.-Sun. except during sporting events. **Phone:** (517) 355-7631 or (517) 353-9834.

MSU Museum is on the Michigan State University campus opposite the library on W. Circle Dr. Three floors display permanent and changing natural and cultural history exhibits. The museum features full dinosaur skeletons and audiovisual presentations. **Time:** Allow 30 minutes minimum. **Hours:** Mon.-Fri. 9-5, Sat. 10-5, Sun. 1-5. Closed major holidays. **Cost:** Donations. **Parking:** Two-hour parking permit $2 (sold in the museum store and at the visitor counter.) Limited metered parking is available. **Phone:** (517) 355-2370.

Television Studio (WKAR-TV) is on the Michigan State University campus in the MSU Communication Arts and Sciences Building at Wilson and Red Cedar rds. The station contains three studios and complete facilities for live programming and student training. Guided tours are available by appointment. **Hours:** Mon.-Fri. 8-5. **Cost:** Free. **Phone:** (517) 432-9527.

EAST TAWAS (F-5) pop. 2,951, elev. 588'

East Tawas, a resort community on Tawas Bay, offers opportunities for exploring the woodlands of nearby Huron-Manistee National Forests *(see place listing p. 81)*. Fishing is good, particularly for perch, salmon, trout and walleye. Recreational opportunities also are available at Tawas Point State Park *(see Recreation Chart and the AAA Great Lakes Camp-Book)*. The grounds offer scenic views, bird-watching opportunities (particularly during spring and fall) and a lighthouse that began operating in 1876.

ELK RAPIDS (E-3) pop. 1,700, elev. 587'

GUNTZVILLER'S SPIRIT OF THE WOODS MUSEUM is 2 mi. s. on US 31. The museum houses collections of Native American artifacts and dioramas displaying North American animals and fish. Arrowheads, pipes, ceremonial pieces, bows and moccasins are exhibited, while preserved beavers, otters, deer, bison, bears and minks are among the animals mounted in natural settings. Collections of early hunting and fishing gear also are displayed.

Time: Allow 1 hour minimum. **Hours:** Mon.-Sat. 9-5 (also Sun. 11-4, Memorial Day-Labor Day). Closed major holidays. **Cost:** $3; $2 (ages 65+); $1 (students with ID); $5 (two adults). **Phone:** (231) 264-5597.

ESCANABA (C-3) pop. 13,140, elev. 598'

The logging industry's hunger for the seemingly inexhaustible stands of Upper Peninsula pine spurred the establishment of Escanaba in the early 1800s. Its excellent deepwater harbor at the mouth of the Escanaba River on Little Bay de Noc also attracted the attention of the various iron enterprises; therefore, the town continued to flourish once the virgin forests were depleted.

Second growth forests are the basis for paper and lumber industries. The only ore port on Lake Michigan, Escanaba still ships several million tons of iron ore every year. North of town lies Hiawatha National Forest *(see place listing p. 78)*.

An especially scenic highway is the section of US 2 that extends 143 miles—about 50 of them along the Lake Michigan shore—between Escanaba and St. Ignace *(see place listing p. 106)*. *Also see Upper Peninsula p. 114.*

Bays de Noc Convention and Visitors Bureau: 230 Ludington St., Escanaba, MI 49829. **Phone:** (906) 789-7862 or (800) 533-4386.

DELTA COUNTY HISTORICAL MUSEUM is in Ludington Park at the e. end of Ludington St. Displays chronicle the development of Delta County and the Upper Peninsula. Items include agricultural, logging, railroad, shipping, military and household artifacts. A 1905 motor launch powered by a one-cylinder engine also is featured. **Time:** Allow 30 minutes minimum. **Hours:** Daily 10-5, Memorial Day-Labor Day; 1-4, in Sept. **Cost:** (includes Sand Point Lighthouse) $3; $1 (ages 0-13); $5 (family). **Phone:** (906) 786-6790.

Sand Point Lighthouse is next to the Delta County Historical Museum in Ludington Park at the e. end of Ludington St. Restored to its original 1867 appearance, the tower adjoins the keeper's house, furnished in period. Winding stairs lead to the tower's observation deck. A Coast Guard exhibit, an archives building with information about Delta County and a restored boathouse with original surfboat also are on the premises.

Time: Allow 30 minutes minimum. **Hours:** Lighthouse, boathouse and Coast Guard exhibit daily 10-5, Memorial Day-Labor Day; 1-4, in Sept. Archives Mon.-Fri. 1-5, June-Aug.; Mon.-Fri. 1-4, in Sept.; Mon. and Thurs. 1-5, in Oct. **Cost:** (includes Delta County Historical Museum) $3; $1 (ages 0-13); $5 (family). **Phone:** (906) 786-6790.

FARMINGTON HILLS—*see Detroit p. 63.*

FENNVILLE (H-2) pop. 1,459, elev. 664'

THE CHILDREN'S MUSEUM OF FENNVILLE is at 202 E. Main St. The museum's exhibits, planned by retired teachers, provide hands-on learning opportunities in a fun way. In the Local Environment area children can see artifacts from Native American and Hispanic cultures as well as climb into a real wigwam and imagine what it would be like to live in such a setting.

The Human Machine has an interactive display of a human skeleton, an area explaining how X-rays work and an exhibit about sign language and braille. Kids can also learn about space, gravity and U.S. presidents and play in a castle. **Time:** Allow 45 minutes minimum. **Hours:** Tues.-Sat. 10-3. Closed major holidays. **Cost:** $3.50; free (ages 0-1). **Phone:** (269) 561-8494.

WINERIES

• **Fenn Valley Vineyards** is at 6130 122nd Ave. **Hours:** Mon.-Sat. 11-5, Sun. 1-5. Closed Jan. 1, Easter, Thanksgiving and Dec. 25. Phone ahead to confirm schedule. **Phone:** (269) 561-2396 or (800) 432-6265.

FLINT (H-4) pop. 124,943, elev. 800'

From its inception Flint has been associated with transportation. In its early days the site was an important river crossing on the Pontiac Trail, one of the network of Native American routes that crisscrossed the wilderness. The logging boom created the need for katydids—two-wheeled log-hauling contrivances—in addition to road carts and wagons; Flint soon became a major center for their manufacture.

The city's subsequent carriage-making industry quickly gained international repute. Flint remains one of the world's largest manufacturers of carriages of the horseless variety and is where General Motors originated.

Flint Area Convention & Visitors Bureau: 502 Church St., Flint, MI 48503. **Phone:** (810) 232-8900 or (800) 253-5468.

Shopping areas: Genesee Valley Center, off I-75 at 3341 S. Linden Rd. at the junction of Miller Road, offers JCPenney, Macy's and Sears as well as nearly 130 specialty stores.

CROSSROADS VILLAGE AND HUCKLEBERRY RAILROAD is off I-475 exit 13, just n. on N. Saginaw Rd., 1.9 mi. e. on E. Stanley Rd., then 1.1 mi. s. to 6140 Bray Rd., following signs. The restored 1800s Genesee County community features 35 historic structures, including an operating blacksmith shop, cider mill, sawmill, gristmill, general store, school, church and residences.

Huckleberry Railroad, a steam train with antique passenger cars pulled by a steam-powered Baldwin locomotive, departs from the Crossroads Depot for 40-minute trips through the recreation area. A carousel, Ferris wheel, children's amusement rides and paddlewheel riverboat rides are available for an additional fee.

Time: Allow 4 hours minimum. **Hours:** Wed.-Sun. and holidays 10-5, Memorial Day weekend-Labor Day; Wed.-Fri. 5-9, Sat.-Sun. noon-9, early Oct.-Oct. 31; Wed.-Sun. 4-9, Mon. and Dec. 24 (drive-through only) 5-9, day after Thanksgiving-Dec. 30. Closed Dec. 25. Phone ahead to confirm schedule.

Cost: (includes village, train and boat ride) $16; $15 (ages 60+); $12.50 (ages 2-12). Village and train or boat ride $13; $12 (ages 60+); $10 (ages 2-12). Village only $10; $9 (ages 60+); $8 (ages 2-12). Other combination tickets also are available. Holiday rates vary; phone ahead. **Phone:** (810) 736-7100 or (800) 648-7275. 🎫

Genesee Belle is off I-475 exit 13, just n. on N. Saginaw Rd., 1.9 mi. e. on E. Stanley Rd., then 1.1 mi. s. to 6140 Bray Rd., following signs, docked within Crossroads Village and Huckleberry Railroad. Visitors can take 45-minute sightseeing cruises on Mott Lake. Lunch and evening cruises also are offered from Stepping Stone Falls within Genesee

Recreation Area. **Hours:** Sightseeing cruise departs Wed.-Sun. (also Memorial Day and Labor Day) on the hour 1-4, May-June and Aug.-Sept.; Thurs.-Sun. on the hour 1-4, Wed. on the hour 2-4, in July. Departure times may vary; phone ahead. Phone for lunch and evening cruise schedule.

Cost: Sightseeing fare (includes village and train ride) $16; $15 (ages 60+); $12.50 (ages 2-12). Sightseeing fare (includes village) $13; $12 (ages 60+); $10 (ages 2-12). Phone for lunch and evening cruise fares. Reservations are required for lunch cruise. **Phone:** (810) 736-7100 or (800) 648-7275.

THE FLINT CHILDREN'S MUSEUM is at 1602 W. Third Ave. on the Kettering University campus. The hands-on learning center has exhibits related to science, technology and the arts. Children should be accompanied by an adult. **Time:** Allow 2 hours minimum. **Hours:** Tues.-Fri. 9-5, Sat. 10-5. Closed major holidays. Phone ahead to confirm schedule. **Cost:** $4; free (under 1). **Phone:** (810) 767-5437.

FLINT CULTURAL CENTER is off I-475 exit 8A to 817 E. Kearsley St. The campus includes the Flint Institute of Arts, Longway Planetarium and Sloan Museum *(see attractions listings)* as well as an auditorium, youth theater and music center. **Hours:** Schedule varies per site. **Cost:** Admission varies per site. **Phone:** (810) 237-7333.

Flint Institute of Arts, part of the Flint Cultural Center, is at 1120 E. Kearsley St. African, American, Asian, European, Impressionist and contemporary art as well as a sculpture courtyard are featured. Special temporary exhibitions also are presented. An audio tour guide provides insights into the permanent collection. **Time:** Allow 30 minutes minimum. **Hours:** Mon.-Fri. noon-5 (also Thurs. 5-9), Sat. 10-5, Sun. 1-5. Closed major holidays. **Cost:** Free. Admission charged for special exhibits. **Phone:** (810) 234-1695. ⓘ

Longway Planetarium is part of the Flint Cultural Center at 1310 E. Kearsley St., across from Whiting Auditorium. Star and laser shows are given. The projector reproduces the night sky on a 60-foot dome. Family programs are offered throughout the year; phone for information. Traveling exhibits also are featured.

Hours: Planetarium Mon.-Fri. 9-5; planetarium closes during group tours, so phone for availability. Star and laser shows Sat.-Sun. at 12:30, 2 and 3:30; phone for programming schedule. **Cost:** $5; $4 (ages 3-11 and 56+). Combination ticket with Sloan Museum and one planetarium show $9; $6 (ages 3-11). **Phone:** (810) 237-3400.

Sloan Museum, part of the Flint Cultural Center, is at 1221 E. Kearsley St.; the Buick Gallery is a short walk away at 303 Walnut St. The museum has a variety of permanent and changing exhibits, highlighting fur trading and pioneer life to lumbering, carriage manufacturing and the General Motors automobile boom. A profile of Flint's 20th-century history is shared through more than 600 artifacts and photographs. Items relating to the automobile industry, particularly the local General Motors Corp., and everyday household items and clothing also capture the era.

The Discovery Center features hands-on science displays. The Hometown Gallery showcases temporary exhibits. Prehistoric stone implements also can be seen. The Buick Gallery displays vintage and experimental prototype vehicles, including a World War II tank destroyer and a restored 1905 Buick.

Visitors may be able to watch as museum staff and volunteers work on the automotive collection in the conservation and restoration shop. **Hours:** Museum Mon.-Fri. 10-5, Sat.-Sun. noon-5. Buick Gallery Mon.-Fri. 10-5, Sat. noon-5. Closed major holidays. **Cost:** (includes Buick Gallery) $6; $5 (ages 56+); $4 (ages 3-11). Combination ticket with one show at Longway Planetarium $9; $6 (ages 3-11). **Phone:** (810) 237-3450.

GENESEE RECREATION AREA is 6 mi. n.e. off I-475 exit 13. Covering 4,540 acres along the Flint River, the area contains beaches, bicycle paths, a boat launch, fishing sites, hiking and horse trails, disc golf course and picnic areas. *See Recreation Chart.* After sunset from Memorial Day through Labor Day colored lights play upon Stepping Stone Falls, a spillway impounding 600-acre Mott Lake. **Hours:** Daily dawn-dusk. **Cost:** Free. **Phone:** (810) 736-7100 or (800) 648-7275. ⊠ ⊞

FRANKENMUTH (G-5) pop. 4,838

Pastors in Bavaria, concerned over the religious life of Lutheran immigrants and their Native American neighbors, sent a colony to the United States to demonstrate their faith on a day-to-day basis. Fifteen Franconians from Bavaria arrived in the Saginaw Valley in 1845 and named their settlement Frankenmuth, meaning "courage of the Franconians."

The tribe soon moved elsewhere, but the Bavarian heritage remained and was reinforced by other arrivals from Germany. For many years after 1900 German remained the principal language of the community. The Old World atmosphere is still evident in the architecture.

The 35-bell automatic carillon in the Bavarian Inn Glockenspiel Tower plays selected melodies followed by a presentation of carved wooden figures depicting the legend of the Pied Piper of Hameln. Nearby is the 19th-century Holz-Brücke—Frankenmuth's wooden covered bridge that spans the Cass River.

Two annual events worth checking out if you are in the area at the right time are Frankenmuth Oktoberfest, held in mid-September at Heritage Park, and Zehnder's Snowfest, at Zehnder's Restaurant in late January. The former features traditions like dancing, polka music and German food, and the latter has ice carving and snow sculpting as well as entertainment and fireworks.

Frankenmuth Chamber of Commerce and Convention and Visitors Bureau: 635 S. Main St., Frankenmuth, MI 48734. **Phone:** (989) 652-6106 or (800) 386-8696.

Shopping areas: Between the downtown business district and Frankenmuth River Place—which is at 925 S. Main St. at the river—more than 100 shops can be found in Frankenmuth.

BRONNER'S CHRISTMAS WONDERLAND, 1 mi. s. at 25 Christmas Ln., was founded in 1945 by Wally Bronner. At the size of 1.5 football fields, this is billed as the world's largest Christmas store. More than 50,000 Christmas ornaments, gifts, lights, decorations and trees are featured.

An outdoor display with nearly 100,000 lights illuminates Christmas Lane every evening. The Bronner's Silent Night Memorial Chapel, a replica of the original in Oberndorf, Austria, also can be seen. Films about Wally Bronner, the store and the memorial chapel are shown daily.

Time: Allow 1 hour, 30 minutes minimum. **Hours:** Mon.-Sat. 9-9, Sun. noon-7, June-Dec.; Mon.-Sat. 9-5:30 (also Fri. 5:30-9), Sun. noon-5:30, rest of year. Closed Jan. 1, Easter, Thanksgiving and Dec. 25; open shorter hours on Good Friday and Dec. 24 and 31. **Cost:** Free. **Phone:** (989) 652-9931. *(see ad)*

FRANKENMUTH HISTORICAL MUSEUM is at 613 S. Main St. Permanent and changing exhibits depict the area's German ancestry and history from Native American mission days. Guided tours are available by appointment. **Hours:** Mon.-Sat. 10:30-5 (also Fri.-Sat. 5-8), Sun. 10-7. Closed Jan. 1, Easter, Thanksgiving and Dec. 25. **Cost:** $2; $1 (ages 5-12 and students with ID); $5 (family, two adults and up to four children). **Phone:** (989) 652-9701.

MICHIGAN'S OWN INC.—MILITARY AND SPACE MUSEUM is at 1250 Weiss St. The museum honors Michigan veterans of foreign wars and the space program. Visitors can see more than 100 exhibits featuring uniforms of Michigan heroes and heroines as well as what is said to be the largest collection of original Medals of Honor. The uniforms and flight suits of all thirteen Michigan astronauts are displayed. **Hours:** Mon.-Sat. 10-5, Sun. 11-5, Mar.-Dec. **Cost:** $5; $4 (ages 65+); $2 (ages 6-18). **Phone:** (989) 652-8005.

FRANKFORT (E-1) pop. 1,513, elev. 585'

High bluffs surround the natural harbor of Frankfort, one of northwest Michigan's busiest ports. Beach lovers are drawn to the area's sandy shores, and the city's natural harbor, yacht facilities and launching ramp accommodate boating and fishing. North of the city off SR 22 is the Point Betsie Lighthouse, near the entrance to Sleeping Bear Dunes National Lakeshore *(see place listing p. 111)*.

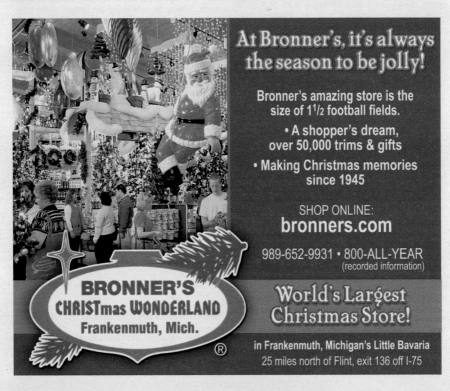

Some think that Jesuit explorer and missionary Pere Jacques Marquette died at the mouth of Betsie Bay in 1675; a marker and wooden cross signify the supposed site. It is generally believed that he died near Ludington *(see place listing p. 87)*, about 50 miles south.

GARDEN (C-4) pop. 240, elev. 591'

HISTORIC FAYETTE TOWNSITE is off SR 183 in Fayette Historic State Park *(see Recreation Chart)*. The preserved industrial community was founded in 1867 by Jackson Iron Co. manager Fayette Brown. The largely immigrant community thrived after the furnaces began smelting charcoal iron, but when the operation ceased in 1891 due to a decline in the charcoal iron market, the site was abandoned.

Historic buildings are showcased throughout the site, including a company office, furnace complex, hotel, town hall and workers' homes. A self-guiding walking tour begins at the interpretive museum. Along the walk are views of the cliffs and of Lake Michigan.

Guided tours are available mid-June through Labor Day; phone for details. **Hours:** Museum buildings open daily 9-dusk, mid-June through Labor Day; 9-5, mid-May to mid-June and day after Labor Day to mid-Oct. Park open daily 9 a.m.-10 p.m. **Cost:** Townsite free. Park entry fee $10 (per private in-state vehicle; Recreation Passport, valid for 1 year, allows entry into Michigan state parks); $8 (per private out-of-state vehicle). **Phone:** (906) 644-2603 or TTY (517) 373-1592.

GAYLORD (E-4) pop. 3,681, elev. 1,348'

In the center of the northern end of the Lower Peninsula, Gaylord is one of the highest incorporated communities in Michigan. The Black, Manistee, Pigeon and Sturgeon rivers and the North Branch of the Au Sable River all rise nearby and flow in different directions.

A sister city to Pontresina, Switzerland, Gaylord maintains the atmosphere of an Alpine village. Buildings of Swiss-style architecture line Main and surrounding streets. An average of nearly 180 inches of snow falls in Otsego County, so skiing, snowmobiling and snowshoeing in town and nearby areas are popular during the winter. The Gaylord Area Convention and Tourism Bureau has guides about local cross-country ski and snowmobile trails. A Swiss essence also pervades community activities throughout the year. Gaylord is the southern starting point for the North Central State Trail System which extends to Mackinaw City and offers great hiking and bicycling opportunities.

Gaylord Area Convention & Tourism Bureau: 101 W. Main St., Gaylord, MI 49735. **Phone:** (989) 732-4000 or (800) 345-8621.

CALL OF THE WILD MUSEUM is off I-75 exit 282, 3 blocks e., then 6 blocks s. to 850 S. Wisconsin Ave. More than 150 lifelike North American wild animals and game birds are featured in more than 60 displays, each with a hand-painted backdrop. Beavers, bobcats, coyotes, elk, moose and polar bears appear in re-created natural settings, many complete with sound effects. The Wildlife Theater shows short nature films. Also featured are two projected image presentations about Joseph Bailly, one of the first fur trappers who worked in Michigan in the early 19th century.

An interactive center encourages kids to learn through activity sheets and scavenger hunts. **Time:** Allow 1 hour minimum. **Hours:** Daily 9-9, mid-June through Labor Day; Mon.-Sat. 9:30-6, Sun. 11-5, rest of year. Closed Thanksgiving and Dec. 25. **Cost:** $7; $6.50 (ages 62+); $4.50 (ages 5-13). **Phone:** (989) 732-4336 or (800) 835-4347.

RECREATIONAL ACTIVITIES

Winter Activities

- **Treetops Resort** is at 3962 Wilkinson Rd. Downhill and cross-country skiing as well as snow tubing and snowboarding are offered. **Hours:** Winter activities late Dec. to mid-Mar. Schedule varies; phone ahead to confirm. **Phone:** (989) 732-6711 or (888) 873-3867.

GERMFASK (B-4) pop. 491

During the lumberjack era Germfask was on the old tote road from Manistique to Seney, 8 miles north. Named by combining the initials of the town founders, the settlement was referred to as the dump because logs were dropped into the Manistique River to be floated to the mill. *See Upper Peninsula p. 114.*

SENEY NATIONAL WILDLIFE REFUGE visitor center entrance is about 2 mi. n. on SR 77. More than 200 species of birds and other wildlife inhabit the 95,455-acre refuge. The site has one of the state's highest concentrations of nesting loons and is home to bald eagles, Canadian geese, ospreys and sandhill cranes. More than 200 adult trumpeter swans can be found. There are opportunities for biking, canoeing, fishing, hiking and hunting as well as skiing and snowshoeing in winter. A one-way 7-mile unpaved driving tour route also is available. An orientation program is shown at the visitor center.

Check with the visitor center for information about designated fishing and hunting areas as well as regulations. **Hours:** Visitor center open daily 9-5, mid-May to mid-Oct. Refuge office open Mon.-Fri. 8-4. Walking trail open daily dawn-dusk, year-round. Driving tour route open daily dawn-dusk, mid-May to mid-Oct. **Cost:** Free. **Phone:** (906) 586-9851 ⊠

GRAND HAVEN (G-2) pop. 11,168, elev. 603'

At the mouth of the Grand River, Grand Haven benefits equally from its busy port and from the tourists attracted to the beaches, bayous, rolling dunes and wooded hills along Lake Michigan,

Spring Lake and Ferrysburg. According to geologists, this is one of the few areas where singing sand is found. When walked upon the tiny sand particles emit a peculiar musical whistle.

Popular beach areas include Grand Haven State Park (see Recreation Chart and the AAA Great Lakes CampBook), 1 mile west, and P.J. Hoffmaster State Park, 10 miles northwest off US 31 (see Recreation Chart). Grand Haven State Park hosts the ≋Great Lakes Kite Festival in late May; the beach event benefits the Children's Leukemia Foundation.

A large musical fountain on Dewey Hill at the waterfront combines light, water and music in nightly concerts held at dusk, Memorial Day through Labor Day and weekends only the rest of May and September. During the holiday season it appears as a 40-foot nativity scene and offers evening performances during December.

Trolley car routes through Grand Haven, Spring Lake and Ferrysburg offer convenient access to area attractions and a pleasant way to tour the town. The Harbor Trolley operates from Memorial Day through Labor Day. For views from the water there are sailing charters on Lake Michigan. Peak fall color occurs early to mid-October.

Grand Haven Area Convention & Visitors Bureau: One S. Harbor Dr., Grand Haven, MI 49417. **Phone:** (616) 842-4499 or (800) 303-4092.

Shopping areas: Grand Haven's waterfront features shopping and dining areas and a 2.5-mile boardwalk along the Grand River. The city also has an open-air farmers market and Harbourfront Place, a renovated historic piano factory building containing shops and restaurants.

TRI-CITIES HISTORICAL MUSEUM—AKELEY BUILDING is at 200 Washington Ave. This 1871 building houses displays about local history. Exhibits profile Native American and early pioneers, and Victorian period rooms can be seen. Genealogical research material also is available. The museum also includes the nearby Train Depot Museum (see attraction listing). **Time:** Allow 30 minutes minimum. **Hours:** Tues.-Fri. 9:30-7:30, Sat.-Sun. 12:30-7:30, Memorial Day-Labor Day; Tues.-Fri. 9:30-5, Sat.-Sun. 12:30-5, rest of year. Closed major holidays. **Cost:** Donations. **Phone:** (616) 842-0700.

Tri-Cities Historical Museum—Train Depot Museum is at Harbor Dr. and Washington St. Displays about the railroad and shipping industries as well as exhibits about local history are in the 1870 Grand Trunk Railroad Depot. Exhibits about the local Coast Guard also are included. **Time:** Allow 30 minutes minimum. **Hours:** Tues.-Fri. 9:30-7:30, Sat.-Sun. 12:30-7:30, Memorial Day-Labor Day; Tues.-Fri. 11:30-4:30, Sat.-Sun. 12:30-5, rest of year. **Cost:** Donations. **Phone:** (616) 842-0700.

GRAND MARAIS (B-4) elev. 627'

LIGHTKEEPER'S HOUSE is .7 mi. n.e. at the end of Coast Guard Point Rd. The Lifesaving Service built this house in 1908 for the lighthouse keeper. Guided tours showcase what life was like in the early 1900s. Period pieces, including a crank telephone, an Edison Victrola and vacuums, can be seen and operated. The kitchen has an antique stove, sink and utensils. **Time:** Allow 30 minutes minimum. **Hours:** Daily 1-4, July-Aug.; Sat.-Sun. 1-4 in June and Sept. **Cost:** Donations. **Phone:** (906) 494-2404.

PICKLE BARREL HOUSE MUSEUM is at jct. Lake and Randolph sts. The house was built in 1926 for "The Teenie Weenies" comic strip creator, William Donahey. His characters also were used in Reid-Murdoch & Co. ads, one of which pictured a house that had been made from a sweet pickle keg.

Inside are Donahey's drawing chair, paints and chalks as well as a small original stove and period antiques. His wife, Mary Dickerson Donahey, was an author and several of her books can be seen. **Time:** Allow 30 minutes minimum. **Hours:** Guided tours daily 1-4, July-Aug.; Sat.-Sun. 1-4 in June and Sept. **Cost:** Donations. **Phone:** (906) 494-2404.

GRAND RAPIDS (H-1)
pop. 197,800, elev. 610'

Grand Rapids is a vigorous manufacturing, cultural and convention center. It owes its development and its name to the rapids of the Grand River, a place of gathering and exchange since Louis Campau established a trading post in 1826. The water power and transportation afforded by the river and the abundance of wood from the forests made the growth of the furniture industry almost inevitable. By 1900 the city was renowned as a producer of quality office furniture, a reputation it still maintains.

Downtown stands the Alexander Calder sculpture "La Grande Vitesse"; it pays homage to the rapids (vitesse). In contrast are the stolid lines of a reconstructed covered bridge that spans the Thornapple River at Ada, east of Grand Rapids via SR 21. Also downtown is DeVos Place, on Monroe Avenue, offering large convention and exhibit halls.

In the Heritage Hill historic district at 115 College Ave. S.E. is the three-story Voigt House Victorian Museum. Built in the late 19th century, the opulent house retains the original furnishings of the Voigt family. The home is only open during special events; phone (616) 456-3977 for more details. In nearby Lowell the James C. Veen Observatory is open to the public the second and last Saturdays of the month April through October (weather permitting); phone (616) 897-7065 after 7:30 p.m. for status.

Rosa Parks Circle, at Monroe Avenue and Pearl Street, includes an amphitheater and hosts special events and concerts throughout most of the year. In cold weather—typically late November through

March—the site is transformed into an outdoor ice rink. Much to skaters' delight, the floor features fiber-optic lighting that creates an image of how the sky appeared in Michigan on the first night in the year 2000. This artistic representation of stars, planets and constellations can be seen year-round.

Broadway shows and performances by the Grand Rapids Ballet, Opera Grand Rapids and the Grand Rapids Symphony are presented at DeVos Performance Hall, on Monroe Avenue N.W. The Grand Rapids Civic Theatre, 30 N. Division Ave., presents community theatrical performances. Concerts and sporting events are held at the Van Andel Arena, 130 W. Fulton St.

Grand Rapids/Kent County Convention and Visitors Bureau: 171 Monroe Ave. N.W., Suite 700, Grand Rapids, MI 49503. **Phone:** (616) 459-8287 or (800) 678-9859. *(see ad)*

Shopping areas: The Fulton Street Farmers Market, which has been operating since 1922, opens each May and runs until late December with vendors selling produce, eggs, meat and flowers as well as local arts and crafts. It's held at 1147 E. Fulton St. and opens Tues.-Wed. and Fri.-Sat. at 8.

BLANDFORD NATURE CENTER is at 1715 Hillburn Ave. N.W. The center is surrounded by 143 acres of fields, forests, ponds and streams. On the grounds are several self-guiding trails, a small farm and a visitor center with a wildlife care program where animals can be seen. Several heritage buildings include a log cabin, one-room schoolhouse, blacksmith shop and a general store.

Time: Allow 1 hour minimum. **Hours:** Grounds open daily dawn-dusk. Visitor center open Mon.-Fri. 9-5, Sat. noon-5. Historical Village open fourth Sat.

of the month and during festivals; phone for schedule. Closed major holidays. **Cost:** Free. **Phone:** (616) 735-6240.

FISH LADDER SCULPTURE is n. on the Grand River at jct. Fourth and Front sts. The concrete five-step environmental ladder was designed by local artist Joseph Kinnebrew to assist salmon in jumping over a 6-foot dam to reach their spawning grounds. Although the leaping fish can be viewed at any time, the best time to see them scale the aquatic steps is spring and late September through late October. **Hours:** Daily 24 hours. **Cost:** Free. **Phone:** (616) 456-3696.

FREDERIK MEIJER GARDENS & SCULPTURE PARK is n.e. of jct. I-96 exit 38 and E. Beltline at 1000 E. Beltline N.E. The 132-acre barrier-free gardens and sculpture park contain perennial, American, Victorian, shade and arid gardens; nature trails; a carnivorous plant house; and tropical plants in the five-story, 15,000-square-foot Lena Meijer Conservatory, said to be the state's largest. A 30-acre outdoor sculpture park boasts more than 30 bronze sculptures by such artists as Henry Moore, Claes Oldenburg and Auguste Rodin. Most notable is "The American Horse," a 24-foot-tall sculpture by Nina Akamu, which is reminiscent of a 1493 Leonardo da Vinci clay model.

A children's garden also is featured, and a tropical butterfly exhibit takes place March through April. Narrated tram tours are available. **Time:** Allow 2 hours minimum. **Hours:** Mon.-Sat. 9-5 (also Tues. 5-9), Sun. noon-5. Closed Jan. 1, Thanksgiving and Dec. 25. **Cost:** $12; $9 (ages 65+ and students with ID); $6 (ages 5-13); $4 (ages 3-4). Tram fee $3; $2 (ages 5-13). **Phone:** (616) 957-1580 or (888) 957-1580.

GERALD R. FORD PRESIDENTIAL MUSEUM is off US 131 exit 85B at 303 Pearl St. N.W. The triangular building has a glass wall that mirrors downtown from the west bank of the Grand River. Displays portray both the private life and public career of President Ford. Exhibits include a re-creation of the Ford Paint & Varnish Co. where the future president worked as a boy as well as information about the October 1973 vice-presidential confirmation hearings when Ford served as House Minority Leader.

Visitors can take a holographic tour of the White House, observe foreign policy procedures in the White House Situation Room and view the nomination of Ford at the Republican National Convention in 1976. In the presidential library system, Ford's is the only site where the museum and library are not located together; his library is in Ann Arbor at the University of Michigan, his alma mater.

Time: Allow 1 hour minimum. **Hours:** Daily 9-5. Closed Jan. 1, Thanksgiving and Dec. 25. **Cost:** $7; $6 (ages 63+ and military with ID); $5 (college students with ID); $3 (ages 6-18). **Phone:** (616) 254-0400. *(see ad)*

GRAND RAPIDS ART MUSEUM, at 101 Monroe Center, is a 125,000-square-foot concrete and glass building and is the first art museum to have its entire facility attain LEED (Leadership in Energy and Environmental Design) Gold certification. The collection contains more than 5,000 works of art, with a focus on works of art on paper. Art periods represented include European art since 1500, American and American regional art since 1840 and International Modernism. Art by Richard Diebenkorn and Pablo Picasso is included along with a 25-foot wall sculpture by Ellsworth Kelly. Changing exhibits also are presented.

Tours: Guided tours are available. **Time:** Allow 1 hour minimum. **Hours:** Museum Tues.-Sat. 10-5 (also Fri. 5-9), Sun. noon-5. **Cost:** $8; $7 (ages 62+ and college students with ID); $5 (ages 6-17). **Phone:** (616) 831-1000. 🍴

GRAND RAPIDS CHILDREN'S MUSEUM is at 11 Sheldon Ave. N.E. In colorful play areas children can make giant bubbles, perform in costumes on stage and paint in a hands-on environment. Seasonal exhibits also are presented. **Time:** Allow 1 hour, 30 minutes minimum. **Hours:** Mon.-Sat. 9:30-5 (also Thurs. 5-8), Sun. noon-5, early June-late Aug.; Tues.-Sat. 9:30-5 (also Thurs. 5-8), Sun. noon-5, rest of year. Phone ahead to confirm schedule. **Cost:** $6.50; free (ages 0-1); $1.50 (Thurs. 5-8). Phone ahead to verify rates. **Phone:** (616) 235-4726.

GRAND RAPIDS PUBLIC MUSEUM is at 272 Pearl St. N.W. Exhibits depict various aspects of Grand Rapids history. The local furniture industry is showcased with more than 120 pieces of wooden furniture and a partially operational reconstruction of an early 20th-century furniture factory. Visitors can walk through a recreation of an 1890s downtown Grand Rapids street, which includes a theater, funeral parlor, department store, drug store and other shops.

Local Native American history is shared through artifacts and features insights from their descendants still living in the area. The museum also has an exhibit dedicated to the area's immigrant history, which includes more than 600 artifacts and photographs; video clips provide a visual history of ethnic traditions. Another exhibit details the state's natural habitats. A 76-foot finback whale skeleton can be seen and visitors can take a ride on an operational 1928 Spillman carousel.

Time: Allow 2 hours minimum. **Hours:** Mon.-Sat. 9-5 (also Tues. 5-8), Sun. noon-5. Closed Jan. 1, Easter, Thanksgiving and Dec. 25. Phone ahead to confirm schedule. **Cost:** $8; $7 (ages 62+); $3 (ages 3-17 and students with ID). Carousel ride $1. **Phone:** (616) 929-1700. ⓣ

The Roger B. Chaffee Planetarium is within the Grand Rapids Public Museum at 272 Pearl St. N.W. Equipped with technical sound, laser and videotape projection equipment, the dome sky theater features performances related to space technology. **Hours:** Museum open Mon.-Sat. 9-5 (also Tues. 5-8), Sun. noon-5. Show times vary. Closed Jan. 1, Easter, Thanksgiving and Dec. 25. Phone ahead to confirm schedule. **Cost:** Sky show $3. Laser light show $7; $5 (Tues.). **Phone:** (616) 929-1700.

JOHN BALL ZOO is at jct. I-196 and SR 45. One of the largest zoos in the state, it houses more than 2,000 animals from many parts of the world. Of particular interest are a troop of seven chimpanzees, a lion exhibit, a tropics building and aquarium as well as a 300-foot zipline and climbing ropes course. Two petting corrals are open mid-May through early September.

Time: Allow 1 hour minimum. **Hours:** Daily 9-6, mid-May through Labor Day; 10-4, day after Labor Day-early Dec. and Mar. 1 to mid-May. Phone ahead to confirm schedule. **Cost:** Mid-May to early Sept. $7.50; $6.50 (ages 62+); $5.50 (ages 3-13). Admission day after Labor Day through early Dec. and Mar. 1 to mid-May $3.50; $3 (ages 3-13). **Phone:** (616) 336-4300 or (616) 336-4301.

MEYER MAY HOUSE is at 450 Madison Ave. at jct. Logan St.; tours begin from the visitor center. This prairie-style house designed by Frank Lloyd Wright was built in 1909. The architecture features natural materials, horizontal lines, and design and material uniformity. A 30-minute film entitled "The Renewing of a Vision" is shown to highlight the restoration process.

Time: Allow 2 hours minimum. **Hours:** Tues. and Thurs. 10-2, Sun. 1-5. Last tour begins 1 hour before closing. Closed major holidays. Phone ahead to confirm schedule. **Cost:** Free. **Phone:** (616) 246-4821.

GRASS LAKE (L-1) pop. 1,082, elev. 994′

WATERLOO FARM MUSEUM is at 13493 Waterloo Munith Rd. Several buildings comprise this complex dedicated to Michigan's pioneer farm families: an 1850s farmhouse, a restored Perkins wooden windmill, a log house with a stone fireplace, a bake house with a working brick oven and a blacksmith's workshop as well as an icehouse, corncrib, milk cellar and barn. The one-room Dewey School Museum is 3 miles north of the farm.

Time: Allow 1 hour minimum. **Hours:** Farm Museum guided tours Sat.-Sun. 1-5, Memorial Day-Aug. and other times by appointment. Last tour departs 30 minutes before closing. Dewey School open

during special events and by appointment. Phone ahead to confirm schedule. **Cost:** $4; $3 (ages 62+); $2 (ages 5-17). **Phone:** (517) 596-2254.

GRAYLING (E-3) pop. 1,952, elev. 1,132′

Grayling is on the Au Sable River in one of the Lower Peninsula's leading recreation regions. Although the game fish for which it was named no longer inhabit nearby rivers, the town remains a starting point for trout fishing, canoeing, kayaking, hunting, cross-country skiing and snowmobiling expeditions. Canoeing is especially popular; canoes, supplies and guides are available in the community.

In spring the rare Kirtland's warbler nests in a restricted area east of Grayling. This tiny, elusive songbird winters in the Bahamas. Guided tours of the area are offered by the United States Fish & Wildlife Service along with the Michigan Audubon Society from mid-May through July 4.

Grayling Visitors Bureau: 2405 S. Grayling Rd., P.O. Box 217, Grayling, MI 49738. **Phone:** (989) 348-4945 or (800) 937-8837.

HARTWICK PINES STATE PARK is 7 mi. n.e. on SR 93. The 9,672-acre park contains stands of virgin pine and hemlock. The Michigan Forest Visitor Center, a chapel and reproductions of a kitchen, mess hall and workshop from an early logging camp and sawmill are on the grounds. The Hartwick Pines Logging Museum contains displays depicting the state's 19th-century logging industry. Recreational activities include 20 miles of hiking trails, fishing, mountain biking, cross-country skiing and camping. *See Recreation Chart and the AAA Great Lakes CampBook.*

Hours: Park open daily 8 a.m.-10 p.m. Museum open daily 10-6, Memorial Day-Labor Day; daily 9-4, May 1-day before Memorial Day and day after Labor Day-Oct. 31. **Cost:** Museum free. Park entry fee $10 (per private in-state vehicle; Recreation Passport, valid for 1 year, allows entry into Michigan state parks); $8 (per private out-of-state vehicle). **Phone:** (989) 348-7068. ⊠

GREILICKVILLE (E-2) elev. 584′

GREAT LAKES CHILDREN'S MUSEUM is 2.6 mi. n. on SR 22 at 13240 S. West Bay Shore Dr. Hands-on activities are the focus of the more than 30 exhibits and activities here, all of which have a connection to water and the Great Lakes. A favorite is Listening to the River, where five different games and mazes help youngsters learn about their environment and the concept of a watershed. Kids can also see what a drop of water looks like through a microscope and visit a child-size lighthouse and keeper's quarters.

Time: Allow 2 hours minimum. **Hours:** Tues.-Sat. 10-5, Sun. 1-5. Closed Jan. 1 and Dec. 25. **Cost:** $6; free (ages 0-2). **Phone:** (231) 932-4526.

TALL SHIP *MANITOU* is docked at 13390 S. West Bay Shore Dr. (SR 22); the office is across the street in Dockside Plaza. The vessel, which can hold 62 passengers, is a replica of the types of cargo schooners that sailed the Great Lakes and the Atlantic Ocean in the 19th-century. Two-hour trips explore the lower West Grand Traverse Bay. The crew invites passengers to help with rigging the sails. Dinner is served on the evening cruise. Several specialty cruises also are offered.

Hours: Departures require a minimum of 8 passengers. Sails daily at noon, 3 and 6:30, Memorial Day weekend-Labor Day weekend. Spring and fall schedules vary; phone ahead. Passengers should arrive 30 minutes prior to departure time to check in at the office to receive boarding passes. Phone for schedules for specialty cruises. **Cost:** Afternoon sail $35; $18 (ages 0-12). Evening sail $45; $26 (ages 0-12). Phone for specialty cruise fares. **Phone:** (231) 941-2000 or (800) 678-0383.

GROSSE POINTE SHORES—
see Detroit p. 63.

HAMTRAMCK—*see Detroit p. 63.*

HANCOCK (A-2) pop. 4,323, elev. 607'

Among the many groups of Europeans who settled the Upper Peninsula during the mid-1800s copper boom were Finnish farmers and Cornish miners. Traces of their influence remain. A pasty, the meat pie that often was the lunch of the tough Cornish miners, can still be found. Finlandia University (originally called Suomi College) was founded in 1896 and is the only college in the country founded by Americans of Finnish descent.

Like its sister city Houghton *(see place listing p. 80)*, Hancock depends on tourism and commerce along the Keweenaw Waterway. Created by dredging Portage Lake and cutting a canal to Lake Superior, the waterway bypasses the dangerous waters off Keweenaw Point. Rock hounds can find agates along the beach at McLain State Park, north on SR 203 *(see Recreation Chart and the AAA Great Lakes CampBook)*. Also north, on US 41, is the Lookout-Historic Monument, which provides fine views of the waterway. *See Upper Peninsula p. 114.*

QUINCY MINE HOIST is 1 mi. n. on US 41. A guided tour takes visitors to the seventh level of the mine, about 360 feet below the surface. The mine houses what is believed to be the largest steam-powered hoist ever manufactured. Historical structures, which date from 1846 to 1920, house exhibits. Tours also feature a scenic ride on the Midwest's only operating cogwheel tram. Other tours are available.

Time: Allow 2 hours minimum. **Hours:** Daily 9:30-5, mid-June to late Oct.; Fri.-Sun. 9:30-5, late Apr. to mid-June. **Cost:** $15; $14 (ages 55+); $8 (ages 6-12). **Phone:** (906) 482-3101.

HARBOR BEACH (F-6) pop. 1,837, elev. 610'

FRANK MURPHY MEMORIAL MUSEUM is at 142 S. Huron Ave. A collection of historical items relating to Murphy (1890-1949)—a Democratic politician who served as an associate justice of the Supreme Court, mayor of Detroit, governor-general of the Philippines, governor of Michigan and U.S. attorney general—are housed in the family home. **Hours:** Guided tours are given Tues.-Fri. noon-4, Sat.-Sun. 10-4, Memorial Day-Labor Day. **Cost:** $2; $1 (ages 5-12). **Phone:** (989) 479-3363.

HARBOR SPRINGS (D-3) pop. 1,567

On the north shore of Little Traverse Bay, Harbor Springs is both a center for winter recreation and a summer resort. SR 119, a scenic lakeshore drive through the tunnel of trees, passes through Harbor Springs as it travels north to Cross Village.

Harbor Springs Area Chamber of Commerce: 368 E. Main St., Harbor Springs, MI 49740. **Phone:** (231) 526-7999.

RECREATIONAL ACTIVITIES

Skiing

• **Nub's Nob Ski Area** is at 500 Nub's Nob Rd. Cross-country and downhill skiing are available. **Hours:** Daily 9-4:30, late Nov. to mid-Apr. (also daily 6-10 p.m., in late Dec.; Mon. and Wed.-Thurs. 4-9, Fri.-Sat. 6-10 p.m., early Jan. to mid-Mar.), weather permitting. Phone ahead to confirm schedule. **Phone:** (231) 526-2131 or (800) 754-6827.

HARRIS (C-3) pop. 1,895, elev. 790'

GAMBLING ESTABLISHMENTS

• **Island Resort and Casino** is at W399 US 2/41. **Hours:** Daily 24 hours. **Phone:** (906) 466-2941 or (800) 682-6040.

HASTINGS (H-3) pop. 7,095, elev. 790'

HISTORIC CHARLTON PARK VILLAGE MUSEUM AND RECREATION AREA is 2 mi. s. on SR 37, then 4 mi. e. on SR 79, following signs. The 300-acre complex includes a re-created turn-of-the-20th-century rural Midwestern village and a recreation area with nature trails, picnic areas, playgrounds, a beach and boat launch. The village contains 16 buildings—a general store, hardware store, stagecoach inn, one-room school, church, town hall and residences. The museum is furnished in period and contains Civil War artifacts. Farm implements are housed in a separate building.

Hours: Village and museums daily 9-4, Memorial Day-Labor Day. Recreation area daily 8 a.m.-9 p.m., Memorial Day-Labor Day. **Cost:** Village, museums, beach and recreation area free. Admission charged for special events. **Phone:** (269) 945-3775. ⊞

HERMANSVILLE (C-2) elev. 887'

IXL HISTORICAL MUSEUM is s. from US 2 to First St., then 2.5 blks. w. to IXL Dr. and W. River St. The museum is housed in the 1881 office buildings of the Wisconsin Land & Lumber Co., once the largest hardwood flooring plant in the country. Begun in the 1880s, the brand name was derived from the phrase "I excel."

Exhibits include a company house, warehouse, train caboose and depot, late 19th-century furnishings and office equipment, tools and equipment used in the early lumber era and the second-story living quarters of the owners and company executives. All the buildings are original but have been relocated to this site except for the IXL office (now the museum) and the carriage house, which were originally built on the grounds. **Time:** Allow 1 hour minimum. **Hours:** Daily 12:30-4, Memorial Day-Labor Day. **Cost:** $3. **Phone:** (906) 498-2181.

HESSEL (B-6) elev. 603'

GAMBLING ESTABLISHMENTS

• **Hessel Kewadin Casino** is 3 mi. n. on Three Mile Rd. **Hours:** Daily 24 hours. **Phone:** (800) 539-2346.

HIAWATHA NATIONAL FOREST

Elevations in the forest range from 580 ft. at Lake Michigan to 960 ft. next to Lake Superior in Munising. Refer to AAA maps for additional elevation information.

With shorelines on lakes Huron, Michigan and Superior, the two portions of the Hiawatha National Forest embrace 893,348 acres of the Upper Peninsula and feature the only Great Lakes lighthouses in the national forest system. The broad western unit extends southward from Munising to Rapid Rivers and includes Big Bay de Noc and Little Bay de Noc. The eastern unit reaches from St. Ignace (see place listing p. 106) north to Whitefish Bay.

The forest also manages Government Island, one of Les Cheneaux Islands (see place listing p. 87), which offers an unspoiled environment for boating and other outdoor activities. Grand Island National Recreation Area near Munising is adjacent to Pictured Rocks National Lakeshore.

Recreational opportunities in the forest include hunting for black bears, deer, grouse, turkeys and rabbits; fishing for bass, pike, trout and walleye; cross-country skiing and snowmobiling; camping; canoeing along canoe routes and boating on more than 400 lakes; and hiking or bicycling along miles of trails. Visitors may enjoy a drive along the Lake Superior shoreline on the Whitefish Bay Scenic Byway.

West of Munising near the town of Christmas is Bay Furnace Historic Site where the remains of an 1870s iron furnace can be seen. Forest daily 24 hours. Furnace daily dawn-dusk. Free. For further information contact the Forest Supervisor, 2727 N. Lincoln Rd., Escanaba, MI 49829; phone (906) 786-4062. See Upper Peninsula, Recreation Chart and the AAA Great Lakes CampBook.

HICKORY CORNERS (H-3) elev. 967'

GILMORE CAR MUSEUM is at 6865 Hickory Rd. Housed in restored historic buildings on a 90-acre parklike setting, the collection of more than 200 automobiles ranges from the Ford Model T to the muscle cars of the 1960s and '70s and includes an 1899 Locomobile,

Duesenbergs and a 1948 Tucker. Other highlights include a 1918 Franklin car dealership and a re-created early 1930s Shell gas station, complete with vintage gas pumps, full-service garage tools and Shell memorabilia.

The museum also is home to several national collections, including the Classic Car Club of America Museum, the Pierce-Arrow Museum and the Franklin Collection. The Tucker Historical Collection and Library displays a re-creation of Preston Tucker's office, automotive mascots and hood ornaments, an 1890s train depot, an operating 1940s diner and a vintage Disney movie set. The Miniatures Museum features an array of furnished miniature buildings, including a Victorian toy store and an Irish farm cottage.

Time: Allow 2 hours minimum. **Hours:** Daily 9-5 (also Sat.-Sun. 5-6), May-Oct. Miniatures Museum open Wed.-Sun. only. **Cost:** $10; $9 (ages 62+); $7 (ages 7-15). **Phone:** (269) 671-5089. [T]

W. K. KELLOGG BIOLOGICAL STATION is 2 mi. n. off SR 89 to 3700 E. Gull Lake Dr. This site is Michigan State University's largest off-campus field station and includes the Kellogg Farm Dairy Center and W.K. Kellogg Manor House in Hickory Corners as well as W.K. Kellogg Bird Sanctuary and W.K. Kellogg Experimental Forest in Augusta *(see place listing p. 42)*. Cereal magnate W.K. Kellogg was an environmentalist who donated many of the station's facilities. **Hours:** Daily 9 a.m.-dusk. **Cost:** Admission is charged at W.K. Kellogg Bird Sanctuary and W. K. Kellogg Manor House. **Phone:** (269) 671-5117.

Kellogg Farm Dairy Center, part of W. K. Kellogg Biological Station, is 1 mi. n. from jct. SR 89 at 10461 N. 40th St. From April through October cows can be viewed in the pasture-based grazing facility. Several barns as well as a nursery for calves are on-site. An observation room allows visitors to watch the robotic milking of cows. A visitor center also is available. **Time:** Allow 1 hour minimum. **Hours:** Farm open daily 8 a.m.-dusk. Visitor center open daily 8-5. Phone ahead to confirm schedule. **Cost:** Free. **Phone:** (269) 671-2507.

W. K. Kellogg Manor House, part of W. K. Kellogg Biological Station, is 1 mi. n. off SR 89 on 40th St., then 1 mi. w. on B Ave. to 3700 E. Gull Lake Dr. This 1925-26 Tudor Revival house was Kellogg's summer estate; he shared it with employees and Battle Creek residents, who often visited and enjoyed the amenities. A boathouse, caretaker's cottage, carriage house with chauffeur's residence, Dutch windmill, greenhouse, lakeside pagoda and gardens also adorn the 32-acre grounds. Guided walks also are available; hot spice tea and cookies are provided after holiday tours.

Time: Allow 1 hour minimum. **Hours:** Guided tours are offered by appointment as well as select days throughout the year. Phone ahead to confirm schedule. **Cost:** Guided tour $5; $4 (ages 6-18 and 65+). Guided holiday walk $7; $5 (ages 6-18 and 65+). **Phone:** (269) 671-2416.

HOLLAND (H-1) pop. 35,048, elev. 612'

Settled by Dutch immigrants in 1847, Holland retains the essence of a Dutch town. Even if you do nothing more than drive or walk around looking at scenery, you'll be greatly rewarded. The Victorian architecture is one of the appeals of downtown—along, of course, with all those springtime tulips. Millions of blooming tulips in the parks and neighborhoods provide a spectacular floral display from late April to mid-May. Markers and plaques document local heritage and some of the historic buildings. When you're downtown you won't have far to go before encountering a piece of public art; there are more than a dozen sculptures and statues. Hope College, Lake Michigan, Lake Macatawa, sand dunes and a lighthouse (affectionately called "Big Red") add to the area's picturesque attributes.

Holland has three public beaches: Holland State Park *(see Recreation Chart)* at 2215 Ottawa Beach Rd., Tunnel Park at 66 N. Lakeshore Dr., and Laketown Beach, west off 64th Street on 142nd Avenue. The 157-foot Mount Pisgah sand dune, just east of Holland State Park in neighboring Park Township, affords a panoramic view of Holland via a boardwalk and stair system; Lake Michigan, Big Red and Lake Macatawa can be seen. Park in the lot near Black Lake Avenue and Ottawa Beach Road.

There is no shortage of recreational opportunities. You can go biking, hiking, fishing, golfing, cross-country skiing, snowshoeing and snowboarding; the Holland Area Convention and Visitors Bureau has brochures about bike paths, fishing and winter activities. Boat launches for Lake Macatawa are at Dunton Park; Kollen Park; and on Ottawa Beach Road near Anchorage Marina, on the northwest section of the lake.

On Thursday evenings in summer (6:30-8:30, early June through late August), buskers perform downtown.

Tulip Time Festival, held in early May (May 7-14, 2011), features a flower show, carnival, klompen dancing, art exhibits, parades, trolley tours, concerts, fireworks and more.

Holland Area Convention & Visitors Bureau: 76 E. 8th St., Holland, MI 49423. **Phone:** (616) 394-0000 or (800) 506-1299.

Self-guiding tours: The visitor guides available at the convention and visitors bureau contain self-guiding routes mapping out several of the historic downtown buildings as well as the public art locations.

Shopping areas: There are several art galleries downtown, and the many boutiques sell a wide assortment of merchandise, including apparel, books, cards, gift items, home furnishings and jewelry. From mid-May to mid-December a farmers market offers fresh finds. Winter shopping is simple thanks to the town's snowmelt system, which keeps downtown streets and sidewalks snow-free during the winter.

Westshore Mall, across the street from Nelis' Dutch Village *(see attraction listing)*, has specialty stores as well as JCPenney and Younkers department stores.

CAPPON & SETTLERS HOUSE MUSEUMS are at 228 and 190 W. 9th St. The Cappon House, built in 1874 in the Italianate Victorian style, was the family residence of Isaac Cappon, a Dutch immigrant and the city's first mayor. A nursery, kitchen, parlor and sitting room contain nearly all original woodwork and furnishings. Displays in the tiny Settlers House reflect the hardships early settlers faced.
Time: Allow 30 minutes minimum. **Hours:** Fri.-Sat. noon-4, May-Nov. Phone ahead for extended schedule during the Tulip Time Festival. Closed major holidays. **Cost:** (includes both houses) $5; free (ages 0-5). **Phone:** (616) 392-9084.

DE KLOMP WOODEN SHOE AND DELFTWARE FACTORY is at 12755 Quincy St. at US 31. Visitors can walk through the premises to see craftspeople demonstrate wooden shoe carving and the making of blue and white Delftware. **Time:** Allow 30 minutes minimum. **Hours:** Daily 8-8, May 7-14 during Tulip Time Festival; Mon.-Sat. 9-5, Sun. 10-3, Apr. 1-May 6 and May 15-Dec. 31; Mon.-Fri. 9-5, rest of year. Phone ahead to verify schedule and demonstration times. Closed Jan. 1, Easter, Thanksgiving and Dec. 25. **Cost:** Free. **Phone:** (616) 399-1900.

THE HOLLAND MUSEUM is at 31 W. 10th St. and occupies the former 1914 post office building. Exhibits depict the progression from the days of early Dutch settlement to the current city of Holland. Dutch paintings, decorative arts and historical collectibles are featured. The archives and research library includes an extensive collection of items dating back to the mid-17th century. Temporary exhibits also are offered throughout the year.
Time: Allow 1 hour minimum. **Hours:** Museum open Mon. and Wed.-Sat. 10-5, Sun. 2-5. Archives and library open Mon. and Wed.-Fri. 10-5 and other days and times by appointment. Closed major holidays. **Cost:** Museum $7; $6 (ages 65+); $4 (students with ID); free (ages 0-5). Archives and library free. **Phone:** (616) 392-9084 or (888) 200-9123.

NELIS' DUTCH VILLAGE is at 12350 James St. The village features canals, gardens, windmills, museums, a movie theater, klompen dancers, carving exhibits, a Gouda cheese factory tour, a Frisian farmhouse, a 1924 Herschell-Spillman carousel, a petting zoo and children's rides. **Time:** Allow 2 hours minimum. **Hours:** Daily 10-5, mid-Apr. through Labor Day. **Cost:** $10; $9 (ages 59+); $7 (ages 3-15). **Phone:** (616) 396-1475. ⏹️

VELDHEER TULIP GARDENS is 3 mi. n. on US 31 at Quincy St. On display are more than 275 varieties of tulips and daffodils in a setting of windmills, drawbridges and canals. The main flowering season, with 15 acres of blooms, is late April through early May. A wide selection of bulbs and flowering plants replaces the tulips for the remainder of the year. A herd of 19 bison can be seen on the grounds.
Hours: Daily 8-8, May 7-14 during Tulip Time Festival; Mon.-Sat. 9-5, Sun. 10-3, Apr. 1-May 6 and May 15-Dec. 31; Mon.-Fri. 9-5, rest of year. Closed Jan. 1, Easter, Thanksgiving and Dec. 25. Phone ahead to confirm schedule. **Cost:** $8; $4 (ages 3-13). Phone to confirm prices. **Phone:** (616) 399-1900.

WINDMILL ISLAND is at 7th St. and Lincoln Ave. The island is an unusual 36-acre park. Canals, a drawbridge, a miniature Dutch village and spring tulip gardens surround the park's main feature, a 1780s operating windmill brought from the Netherlands. Called De Zwaan, the mill produces a fine graham flour. The post house is a replica of a 14th-century Netherlands wayside inn. A slide presentation is presented all year.

Klompen dancing and organ concerts are presented seasonally. **Tours:** Guided tours are available. **Time:** Allow 2 hours minimum. **Hours:** Daily 9:30-5, late Apr.-early Oct. **Cost:** $7.50; $4.50 (ages 5-15). **Phone:** (616) 355-1030.

HOUGHTON (A-2) pop. 7,010, elev. 637'

Houghton shares its multinational origins, copper mining heritage and guardianship of the Keweenaw Waterway with nearby Hancock *(see place listing p. 77).* The Portage Lake Vertical Lift Bridge links the two cities. Mineralogical interests are served at Michigan Technological University.

The city is the mainland headquarters of Isle Royale National Park *(see place listing p. 83).* Boat service is available between Houghton and the park June to mid-September. Float plane service is available mid-May through September. *Also see Upper Peninsula p. 114.*

Keweenaw Peninsula Chamber of Commerce: 902 College Ave., P.O. Box 336, Houghton, MI 49931. **Phone:** (906) 482-5240.

A.E. SEAMAN MINERAL MUSEUM is on the fifth floor of the Electrical Energy Resources Center at Michigan Technological University; metered parking is available on Townsend Dr. (US 41). Displays include copper and silver specimens native to the Upper Peninsula, celestite, fluorescent minerals and natural copper crystals. **Hours:** Mon.-Fri. 9-4:30, Apr.-Oct. (also Sat.-Sun. noon-4:30, July-Sept.). Closed university holidays. Phone ahead to confirm schedule. **Cost:** Donations. **Phone:** (906) 487-2572.

HOUGHTON LAKE (F-3) pop. 3,749

Sportsmen and vacationers have replaced the loggers and commercial anglers who once were the vital elements of Houghton Lake. The village is the core of a year-round resort area that borders the lake of the same name. Michigan's largest inland lake,

Houghton Lake is 10 miles long and 6 miles wide with a 32-mile shoreline.

Summer brings boaters and water skiers, and winter attracts snowmobilers, snowshoers, skiers and ice-skaters, but fishing knows no season. Ice fishing for bluegill, crappie and walleye is popular.

Houghton Lake Chamber of Commerce: 1625 W. Houghton Lake Dr., Houghton Lake, MI 48629. **Phone:** (989) 366-5644 or (800) 248-5253.

HURON CITY (F-6) elev. 604'

In 1871 and 1881 catastrophic forest fires twice destroyed Huron City, dashing its hopes of becoming a prosperous lumber center. It was reconstructed after these disasters only to be abandoned a short time later when the wells dried up. Not quite a ghost town, Huron City is owned by the William Lyon Phelps Foundation, which operates the remaining buildings as a museum.

HURON CITY MUSEUMS are about 9 mi. e. at jct. SR 25 and Huron City Rd. at 7995 Pioneer Dr. The area consists of several restored buildings—a general store, log cabin, church, carriage shed, inn, U.S. Lifesaving Station, barns and an information center—containing a variety of artifacts. The House of Seven Gables is a restored 1881 Victorian mansion with original furnishings.

Tours: Guided tours are available. **Hours:** Fri.-Sat. 10-4, July-Aug. **Cost:** Combination buildings and mansion admission $10; $8 (ages 62+); $5 (ages 10-15). Buildings or mansion admission $6; $5 (ages 62+); $3 (ages 10-15). Phone to confirm prices. **Phone:** (989) 428-4123.

HURON-MANISTEE NATIONAL FORESTS

Elevations in the forest range from 580 ft. around Lake Michigan to 1,407 ft. at Briar Hills north of Harrietta. Refer to AAA maps for additional elevation information.

In the northern part of the Lower Peninsula, Huron-Manistee National Forests extend over 976,043 acres. Through the Huron National Forest flows the Au Sable River, once heavily used to float logs to the sawmills at East Tawas and Oscoda. The river provides electricity generated by the dams along its course.

The forests offer a variety of outdoor recreational opportunities, including hunting for the morel mushroom in the spring, swimming in lakes Huron and Michigan in the summer and cross-country skiing in the winter. Trout fishing is excellent in many lakes and streams as well as in the Au Sable River. The Au Sable, Manistee, Pine and Pere Marquette rivers in the Manistee National Forest are favorites of canoeists; from mid-May to early September a permit is required to canoe on the Pine and Pere Marquette rivers.

The Nordhouse Dunes are spread across a mile of undeveloped shoreline along Lake Michigan in the Manistee National Forest. The dunes provide opportunities for solitude and seasonal deer hunting. The Loda Lake Wildflower Sanctuary offers a 1-mile trail through marsh, forest and orchard. An 11.5-mile trail offers hiking along the Manistee River and connects to the North Country Trail via a wooden suspension bridge across the river. Together the trails make a 22-mile loop.

The River Road Scenic Byway, in the Huron National Forest, runs 22 miles along the south bank of the Au Sable River. The byway provides vistas of tree-banked reservoirs and offers views of bald eagles, spawning salmon, the Canoeists Memorial and the Lumberman's Monument. Part of the Shore-to-Shore Hiking-Riding Trail also traverses the forest. The North Country Trail offers snowshoeing, camping, backpacking and hiking in the Manistee National Forest.

The Lumberman's Monument, a bronze statue depicting early loggers, overlooks the river valley 10 miles northwest of East Tawas. A visitor center at the monument houses interpretive displays that explore the rich logging legacy of the Au Sable River.

The forests are open daily 24 hours. Information and maps of the Huron National Forest can be obtained at district offices in Oscoda and Mio. Offices in Baldwin, Cadillac and Manistee provide information on the Manistee National Forest.

Some areas require a vehicle pass. A day pass costs $5 and offers access to trailheads, boat and canoe launches, and other day-use recreation sites; passes for other lengths of time also are available. A fee is charged for camping and for watercraft permits. Contact the Huron-Manistee National Forests Headquarters, 1755 S. Mitchell St., Cadillac, MI 49601; phone (231) 775-2421, (800) 821-6263 or TTY (231) 775-3183. *See Recreation Chart and the AAA Great Lakes CampBook.*

INDIAN RIVER (D-4) pop. 2,008

Today's and yesterday's highways intersect at the heart of the inland waterway in Indian River: I-75 crosses the inland waterway that was once used by Native Americans to avoid the Straits of Mackinac. Nearby Burt Lake State Park offers recreational opportunities *(see Recreation Chart and the AAA Great Lakes CampBook).*

Indian River Chamber of Commerce and Tourist Bureau: 3435 S. Straits Hwy., P.O. Box 57, Indian River, MI 49749. **Phone:** (231) 238-9325 or (800) 394-8310.

THE CROSS IN THE WOODS is 1 mi. w. of I-75. Said to be the world's largest crucifix, the 55-foot-high cross is made from one California redwood tree and features a 7-ton bronze figure of Christ attached; the entire structure weighs 14 tons. The cross is set atop a 15-foot-high mound. The 13-acre site has an outdoor church, flower gardens and several shrines. A museum features more than 525 nun and priest dolls dressed in the traditional habits of 217 different religious orders.

Time: Allow 30 minutes minimum. **Hours:** Church open daily dawn-dusk. Museum open daily 9-6, Apr.-Oct.; 9-4, rest of year. **Cost:** Donations. **Phone:** (231) 238-8973 or (231) 238-8722.

INTERLOCHEN (E-2) elev. 849'

The northern Michigan village of Interlochen is headquarters for the Interlochen Center for the Arts, which includes Interlochen Arts Camp, Interlochen Arts Academy and Interlochen Public Radio. Founded in 1928, the camp enrolls students in music, art, dance and drama for 8 weeks each summer. During the winter students participate in academics, fine arts and motion picture classes at the academy.

The 1,200-acre campus includes two large outdoor concert halls, a theater, an art gallery, an indoor auditorium, a chapel/recital hall and a complex of buildings that contains classrooms and studios. For further information contact the Interlochen Center for the Arts, P.O. Box 199, Interlochen, MI 49643; phone (231) 276-7200.

Interlochen Area Chamber of Commerce: 2120 S. SR 137, P.O. Box 13, Interlochen, MI 49643. **Phone:** (231) 276-7141.

IRISH HILLS (I-4)

In the verdant, rolling region of the same name, Irish Hills has many lakes and is a popular vacation center. Recreational facilities are available at nearby Walter J. Hayes State Park *(see Recreation Chart)*.

IRON MOUNTAIN (B-2) pop. 8,154

Iron Mountain was established in 1879 following the discovery of rich iron deposits. The mines continued to operate into the 1940s. *See Upper Peninsula p. 114.*

Dickinson Area Partnership: 600 S. Stevenson Ave., Iron Mountain, MI 49801. **Phone:** (906) 774-2002.

SAVE **CORNISH PUMPING ENGINE AND MINING MUSEUM** is 2 blks. w. of US 2 on Kent St. The museum features one of the largest steam engines built in North America. Displays of mining equipment and artifacts relate the history of mining in the eastern Menominee Range. A World War II glider exhibit also is on display.

Hours: Mon.-Sat. 9-5, Sun. noon-4, Memorial Day-Labor Day; otherwise varies. Phone ahead to confirm schedule. **Cost:** $5; $4.50 (ages 65+); $3 (ages 10-18). Combination ticket with the Menominee Range Historical Foundation Museum $8; $7 (ages 65+); $4 (ages 10-18). Phone to confirm prices. **Phone:** (906) 774-1086.

SAVE **MENOMINEE RANGE HISTORICAL FOUNDATION MUSEUM** is at 300 E. Ludington St. The museum depicts local history from Native American habitation to the present with chronological displays and re-created period rooms. **Hours:**

Tues.-Sat. noon-4, mid-May through Labor Day. Phone ahead to confirm schedule. **Cost:** $5; $4.50 (ages 65+); $3 (children). Combination ticket with the Cornish Pumping Engine and Mining Museum $8; $7 (ages 65+); $4 (ages 10-18). Phone to confirm prices. **Phone:** (906) 774-4276.

IRON RIVER (B-2) pop. 1,929, elev. 1,512'

RECREATIONAL ACTIVITIES

Skiing

• **Ski Brule** is at 397 Brule Mountain Rd. Other activities also are available. **Hours:** Daily 9-4, mid-Nov. to late Apr. (weather permitting). Schedule may vary depending on activity; phone ahead. **Phone:** (800) 362-7853.

IRONWOOD (B-1) pop. 6,293, elev. 1,500'

The largest city in the Gogebic Range, Ironwood grew with the iron mining boom of the 1880s. It is the main trading, lumber and winter recreation center of the region. An imposing local landmark is the 52-foot colored fiberglass statue of Hiawatha on Houk Street. *See Upper Peninsula p. 114.*

Western Upper Peninsula Convention & Visitors Bureau: 648 W. Cloverland Dr., P.O. Box 706, Ironwood, MI 49938. **Phone:** (906) 932-4850 or (800) 522-5657.

BLACK RIVER NATIONAL FOREST SCENIC BYWAY—*see Bessemer p. 45.*

RECREATIONAL ACTIVITIES

Skiing

• **Mount Zion Ski Resort** is at 4946 Jackson Rd. Downhill and cross-country skiing as well as snow tubing are offered. **Hours:** Daily 9-4 (also Fri.-Sat. 4-9), mid-Dec. through Dec. 31; Tues.-Fri. 2-6, Sat. 9-9, Sun noon-4, Jan.-Mar. Closed Dec. 25. Phone ahead to confirm schedule. **Phone:** (906) 932-4231, ext. 269, or (906) 932-3718 for the ski chalet.

ISHPEMING (B-3) pop. 6,686, elev. 1,434'

In accordance with its name, which is thought to mean heaven, the Marquette iron range city of Ishpeming has become a well-known ski center. Organized skiing began in Ishpeming in 1887, when three Norwegians formed a ski club that eventually grew into a national ski association. Cross-country ski and snowmobile trails abound; brochures are available at the chamber of commerce. Cross-country skis, snowshoes and snowmobiles can be rented in town. Al Quaal Recreation Area at 525 Poplar St. is open weekends and has cross-country ski trails, a small downhill ski area and a tube slide; phone (906) 486-6181. *See Upper Peninsula p. 114.*

Marquette County Chamber of Commerce: 215 W. Hematite Dr., Ishpeming, MI 49849. **Phone:** (906) 486-4841 or (888) 578-6489.

U.S. SKI AND SNOWBOARD HALL OF FAME AND MUSEUM is on US 41 between Second and Third sts. at 610 Palms Ave. The greats of American skiing and snowboarding are honored here. The development of the sport is shown through photographs, antique grooming equipment, a cable car, trophies and other memorabilia. An 18-minute orientation videotape also is available. **Time:** Allow 1 hour minimum. **Hours:** Mon.-Sat. 10-5. Closed Jan. 1, July 4, Thanksgiving and Dec. 25. **Cost:** Donations. **Phone:** (906) 485-6323.

ISLE ROYALE NATIONAL PARK (A-1)

Elevations in the park range from 600 ft. at Lake Superior to 1,394 ft. at Mt. Desor. Refer to AAA maps for additional elevation information.

Northwest of the Upper Peninsula, Isle Royale is the largest island in Lake Superior. Dedicated as a national park in 1940, the main island is about 45 miles long and 8.5 miles across at the widest point. The park boundary extends 4.5 miles offshore. A rugged coastline and numerous crags and ridges add to the park's beauty; 99 percent of the island is wilderness.

Beginning some 4,000 years ago, the park was mined for copper—evidence that the island might have been the source of much of the copper used by early Native Americans. The metal has been found throughout the Ohio and Mississippi valleys. Mining activity also took place in the late 1800s on Isle Royale.

Although the soil is only a few inches to a few feet deep, Isle Royale is covered with dense growths of spruce and balsam fir softened by carpets of wildflowers. Beavers, loons, wolves, moose, red foxes and snowshoe hares are abundant in the park. The island is an important research site and is designated as a U.S. Biosphere Reserve.

General Information and Activities

The park is open mid-April through October, with full services July through August. The park's 165 miles of trails are rocky and often wet and slippery; proper footwear should be worn when hiking. Visitors planning hiking trips should write for information. Camping is based on a first-come, first-served basis and is free. Permits are required and are available at ranger stations. Campfires are prohibited at most campgrounds, so visitors should bring self-contained fuel stoves; check with park headquarters or ranger stations.

All surface drinking water must be boiled for 2 minutes or filtered with a .4-micron filter before consumption. Chemical purification will not kill the tapeworm eggs that may exist in the water. No medical facilities are available on Isle Royale.

Swimming in the park is undesirable due to low water temperatures in Lake Superior (35-60 F).

Swimming is allowed in the inland lakes; however, there are no lifeguards or beaches. Scuba diving should be attempted only by experienced divers; charters are available. Though a license is not necessary for fishing in the park's inland lakes and streams, Michigan state fishing regulations apply. Only artificial lures and bait are permitted on inland waters. A Michigan state license is required for fishing in Lake Superior's waters. Guides are available for fishing trips.

Travel in the park is on foot or by boat. Canoes, kayaks, boats and motors can be rented and gasoline purchased at Rock Harbor Lodge from late May to mid-September and at Windigo from early June to mid-September. The marina at Rock Harbor Lodge is open from mid-May to mid-September.

Transportation to the park is by boat or seaplane; reservations are recommended. Boat service to the island is available from Copper Harbor aboard the *Isle Royale Queen IV* mid-May through September. Crossings take 3 hours each way. Boat service is available from Houghton aboard the park-owned *Ranger III* early June to mid-September. Crossings take 5 hours each way. From Grand Portage, Minn., service is available from the *Wenonah* mid-June to mid-September, or *Voyageur II* mid-June to mid-October. Crossings to Windigo take 2-3 hours while the voyage to Rock Harbor takes 7 hours.

Float plane service also is available from Houghton mid-May to mid-September. Schedules and information for all vessels can be obtained from park headquarters, or contact Royale Air Service at P.O. Box 15184, Duluth, MN 55815; phone (218) 721-0405 or (877) 359-4753. *See Upper Peninsula, the Recreation Chart and the AAA Great Lakes CampBook.*

WARNING Crossing Lake Superior to the park in a craft less than 20 feet long is not advised. Private outboards, canoes, kayaks and boats up to 20 feet long may be transported on the *Ranger III* out of Houghton. Gasoline is available on the island but may not be carried on private boats.

ADMISSION is $4 per day; free (ages 0-11). There are costs for transportation to the park.

PETS are not permitted in the park, including 4.5 miles offshore and on private or commercial vessels going to the park.

ADDRESS inquiries to park headquarters at Isle Royale National Park, 800 E. Lakeshore Dr., Houghton, MI 49931-1869; phone (906) 482-0984. Reservations for Rock Harbor Lodge or housekeeping cabins should be made with Forever Resorts, P.O. Box 27, Mammoth Cave, KY 42259-0027, (866) 644-2003, or from mid-May to mid-September with Rock Harbor Lodge, P.O. Box 605, Houghton, MI 49931-0605, (906) 337-4993.

GREENSTONE RIDGE AND MINONG TRAILS, within Isle Royale National Park, generally follow the prominent ridges after which they are named.

The Greenstone Ridge Trail permits access to points at either end of the island. **Note:** The park's trails are rocky and often wet and slippery; proper footwear should be worn when hiking. Visitors should contact the park for hiking information. **Hours:** National park open mid-Apr. through Oct. 31, with full services available July-Aug. **Cost:** Park admission $4 (per day); free (ages 0-11). There are costs for transportation to the park. **Phone:** (906) 482-0984.

MOUNT FRANKLIN, along the Greenstone Ridge within Isle Royale National Park, is reached by a scenic hike from the head of Tobin Harbor or by trail from Rock Harbor. **Note:** The park's trails are rocky and often wet and slippery; proper footwear should be worn when hiking. Visitors should contact the park for hiking information. **Hours:** National park open mid-Apr. through Oct. 31, with full services available July-Aug. **Cost:** Park admission $4 (per day); free (ages 0-11). There are costs for transportation to the park. **Phone:** (906) 482-0984.

MOUNT OJIBWAY within Isle Royale National Park, is reached by a 1.7-mile hike from Daisy Farm Campground. The peak affords a view of the surrounding countryside. **Note:** The park's trails are rocky and often wet and slippery; proper footwear should be worn when hiking. Visitors should contact the park for hiking information. **Hours:** National park open mid-Apr. through Oct. 31, with full services available July-Aug. **Cost:** Park admission $4 (per day); free (ages 0-11). There are costs for transportation to the park. **Phone:** (906) 482-0984.

ROCK HARBOR LIGHTHOUSE within Isle Royale National Park, is 6 mi. by launch from Rock Harbor Lodge. The restored 1855 lighthouse is reached by a .3-mile trail from the Edisen Fishery. **Note:** The park's trails are rocky and often wet and slippery; proper footwear should be worn when hiking. Visitors should contact the park for hiking information. **Hours:** National park open mid-Apr. through Oct. 31, with full services available July-Aug. **Cost:** Park admission $4 (per day); free (ages 0-11). There are costs for transportation to the park. **Phone:** (906) 482-0984.

JACKSON (I-4) pop. 36,316, elev. 942′

Although the Republican Party itself was founded in Ripon, Wis., in 1854, Jackson played host to the party's first formal meeting. The city also was one of the key stops on the Underground Railroad. Some of the houses that served as way stations and sanctuaries still can be seen. Today diversified industry and transportation services anchor Jackson's economy. With 188 lakes, the area offers plenty of recreational opportunities.

Jackson County Convention and Visitors Bureau: 141 S. Jackson St., Jackson, MI 49201. **Phone:** (517) 764-4440 or (800) 245-5282.

Shopping areas: Jackson Crossing Mall, at the junction of US 127 and I-94, features Kohl's and Sears; Westwood Mall, at Michigan Avenue and Brown Street, features Elder-Beerman and JCPenney.

SAVE **CASCADE FALLS AT CASCADES PARK** is s.w. at jct. Brown and Denton sts. The park occupies 457 acres and contains the man-made illuminated cascades—a giant waterfall and six fountains over which water tumbles in continually changing patterns, accompanied by music. There also is a small museum depicting the history of Cascades Falls, a golf course, a basketball court, lagoons, paddleboats, a fishing pier and a miniature golf course. Concerts and entertainment are offered during the summer.

Hours: Park open daily 8 a.m.-dusk. Illuminated Cascade Falls can be seen 8:30-11 p.m., Memorial Day-Labor Day. Phone ahead to verify schedule after Labor Day. **Cost:** Park free. Admission to Cascades Falls $3; free (ages 0-10); $5 (on nights with fireworks). **Phone:** (517) 788-4320, or (517) 788-4323 for golf course. ⊠ ⛽

ELLA SHARP PARK is 2 mi. s. on 4th St. The largest park in the city, it covers 562 partially wooded acres. On the grounds are athletic fields, bicycle and jogging paths, cross-country ski trails, an 18-hole golf course, a driving range, a golf learning center, a miniature golf course, picnic areas, nature trails and a swimming pool. *See Recreation Chart.* **Hours:** Daily 5 a.m.-10 p.m. **Cost:** Free. **Phone:** (517) 788-4343. ⛽ ⊠ ⛽

SAVE **Ella Sharp Museum of Art and History** is at 3225 4th St., within Ella Sharp Park. The museum provides a look at 19th-century farmstead life and also features art and history in several exhibition galleries. A tour of a Victorian house; a pioneer log house; a barn with 1800s carriages, sleighs and farm implements; a wood shop; an 1885 one-room schoolhouse; and a country store complex featuring a print shop and doctor's office is offered.

Hours: Tues.-Fri. 10-4, Sat. 11-4, Sun. noon-4. House tour departs at 11, 12:30, 2 and 3. Closed major holidays. **Cost:** (includes museum and house tour) $7; $5 (ages 5-12). Museum only $5; $3 (ages 5-12). House tour only $3; free (ages 0-4). **Phone:** (517) 787-2320. ⛽

KALAMAZOO (I-2) pop. 77,145, elev. 792′

Springs bubbling up in the riverbed are said to have been the inspiration for Kalamazoo's catchy name, a Native American word meaning "place where the water boils." Whatever its origin, Kalamazoo has enlivened many a poem and song.

Produce from the nearby vegetable-growing region and the diverse yields of many industries provide the basis of Kalamazoo's economy. Western Michigan University and other schools contribute to the city's cultural life. River Oaks Park and Bronson Park are sites for numerous festivals.

Discover Kalamazoo 141 E. Michigan Ave., Suite 100, Kalamazoo, MI 49007. **Phone:** (269) 488-9000 or (800) 888-0509.

KALAMAZOO INSTITUTE OF ARTS is at 314 S. Park St. The complex combines galleries, a school, a library and an auditorium in a contemporary structure. Displayed in the galleries are permanent and temporary exhibits of 20th-century American art, European prints and works from Michigan artists. The galleries and library are open to the public. **Hours:** Tues.-Sat. 10-5, Sun. noon-5. Closed major holidays. **Cost:** Donations. **Phone:** (269) 349-7775.

KALAMAZOO NATURE CENTER is at 7000 N. Westnedge Ave. The area's natural history is illustrated through an interactive exhibit at the center, which is situated on a preserve encompassing more than 1,000 acres. Fourteen nature trails and an 11-acre arboretum with a hummingbird and butterfly garden are offered. A sun/rain room features turtles and native fish. The popular Big Gray Barn houses live animals and is operated May through September. A restored pioneer homestead is open during special events.

Guided tours are available by appointment. **Hours:** Nature center and grounds open Mon.-Sat. 9-5, Sun. 1-5, with extended hours in summer. Closed Jan. 1, Thanksgiving and Dec. 24-25. **Cost:** $6; $5 (ages 55+); $4 (ages 4-13). **Phone:** (269) 381-1574.

KALAMAZOO VALLEY MUSEUM is at 230 N. Rose St. on the Arcadia Commons Campus of the Kalamazoo Valley Community College. Permanent exhibits include a 2,500-year-old mummy and science and history galleries that house interactive exhibits, photographs and artifacts. Mini-missions simulate a trip to Mars in the Challenger Learning Center. The Digistar 4 Planetarium and Theater also are available.

Hours: Mon.-Sat. 9-5 (also Fri. 5-9), Sun. 1-5. Phone for program schedules. Closed Easter, Thanksgiving and Dec. 24-25. **Cost:** Museum free. Planetarium admission $3; free (ages 0-2). **Phone:** (269) 373-7990, (800) 772-3370 or TTY (269) 373-7982.

LAKE LEELANAU (E-2) elev. 614'

WINERIES

• **Good Harbor Vineyards** is .9 mi. s. on SR 22. **Hours:** Mon.-Sat. 11-5, Sun. noon-5, late May-Nov. 30; Sat. 11-5, rest of year. **Phone:** (231) 256-7165.

L'ANSE (A-2) elev. 620'

THE SHRINE OF THE SNOWSHOE PRIEST is at jct. US 41 and Lambert Rd. The six-story structure includes a 35-foot-tall brass statue featuring Bishop Frederic Baraga, a Catholic priest who moved to the Great Lakes region in 1830 and devoted his life to American Indians. He earned his nickname because he traveled by snowshoe up to 700 miles to visit the tribes. The statue overlooks Keweenaw Bay. **Time:** Allow 30 minutes minimum. **Hours:** Daily 24 hours. **Cost:** Free. **Phone:** (906) 524-7021.

LANSING (H-4) pop. 119,128, elev. 843'

Lansing Township became the permanent state capital in 1847 when it was moved from Detroit to a more centralized and protected location. Once the decision was made to make the small settlement of less than 20 residents the new capital, the town began to grow. By the time the city of Lansing was incorporated in 1859, there were some 3,000 enterprising residents, an increasing number of small

industries, a new capitol building and two newspapers that provided more political entertainment than news.

The real industrial flowering of the city is credited to R.E. Olds, whose buggy was one of the first practical motor vehicles. By the early 1900s Lansing was a leading maker of automobiles and gasoline engines. Although its economy is more diversified, Lansing is still a stronghold of the automotive industry. The atmosphere of manufacturing and government is leavened with that of education by Michigan State University and its many points of interest *(see East Lansing p. 67).*

Greater Lansing Convention and Visitors Bureau: 500 E. Michigan Ave., Suite 180, Lansing, MI 48906. **Phone:** (517) 487-6800 or (888) 252-6746.

CARL G. FENNER NATURE CENTER is at 2020 E. Mount Hope Rd. The center has 4 miles of nature trails, an herb garden, a butterfly garden and a visitor center building with some native reptiles, amphibians and birds as well as environmental displays. **Hours:** Grounds open daily 8-dusk. Visitor center open Tues.-Fri. 10-4, Sat.-Sun. noon-4. Closed Jan. 1, Easter, Thanksgiving, day after Thanksgiving and Dec. 22-25 and 29-31. **Cost:** Free. **Phone:** (517) 483-4224.

IMPRESSION 5 SCIENCE CENTER, 200 Museum Dr., is housed in a century-old lumber mill with original wood floors and brick walls. Interactive hands-on exhibits include the Giant Eye, Water Room, Bubble Room, Simple Machines and Throwing Things. Other engaging activities and workshops are related to health, electricity, magnetism, physics and chemistry.

Time: Allow 2 hours minimum. **Hours:** Mon.-Sat. 10-5 (also Sat. 5-7), Sun. noon-5. Closed major holidays. **Cost:** $5; $4.50 (ages 65+); pay your age (ages 1-4). **Phone:** (517) 485-8116.

MICHIGAN LIBRARY AND HISTORICAL CENTER is at 702 W. Kalamazoo St. The museum has displays about state history from prehistoric times to the late 20th century. Twenty-six permanent galleries and a temporary exhibit area feature a three-story relief map; a re-created, walk-through copper mine; a one-room schoolhouse; a 1920s street scene; and a large diorama. The center also houses the state library and archives.

Hours: Museum open Mon.-Fri. 9-4:30, Sat. 10-4, Sun. 1-5. Library open Mon.-Sat. 10-5. Closed major holidays. **Cost:** Free. **Phone:** (517) 373-3559 for the museum, (517) 373-1300 for the library, or (517) 373-1408 for the archives.

THE MICHIGAN MUSEUM OF SURVEYING is .2 mi. w. on Michigan Ave., then .2 mi. s. to 220 S. Museum Dr. The museum, at the MSPS Institute, houses a collection of historical land surveying artifacts. Educational programs, archives and a videotape library also are available. Guided tours are available upon request. **Time:** Allow 30 minutes

minimum. **Hours:** Mon.-Fri. 9-4, Sat.-Sun. by appointment. Closed major holidays. **Cost:** Free. **Phone:** (517) 484-6605.

MICHIGAN SUPREME COURT LEARNING CENTER is at 925 W. Ottawa St. Interactive exhibits teach young visitors about the judicial branch of state government, including the roles of judge, jury and defendant. A short film is shown. **Time:** Allow 30 minutes minimum. **Hours:** Mon.-Fri. 9-4. Closed state holidays. **Cost:** Free. **Phone:** (517) 373-7171.

MICHIGAN WOMEN'S HISTORICAL CENTER & HALL OF FAME is at 213 W. Main St. Special exhibits highlight the lives, history and achievements of Michigan women. An art gallery features the work of the state's outstanding female artists. The Michigan Women's Hall of Fame honors those who have made significant contributions to the state and to the world in nearly 40 fields.

Time: Allow 30 minutes minimum. **Hours:** Wed.-Sat. noon-4, Sun. 2-4. Closed major holidays and holiday weekends. **Cost:** $2.50; $2 (ages 65+); $1 (ages 5-18). **Phone:** (517) 484-1880.

POTTER PARK ZOO is at 1301 S. Pennsylvania Ave. Primates, lions, penguins, snow leopards, camels, tigers, wolves, reptiles, farm animals, exotic fish and birds live at the zoo. Pony and camel rides are offered in summer, and light shows are presented late November to late December.

Time: Allow 1 hour minimum. **Hours:** Park open daily 9-6, Apr.-Oct.; 10-4, rest of year. Schedules for pony and camel rides vary; phone ahead. Light shows presented Thurs.-Sun., late Nov.-late Dec.; phone for times. **Cost:** Apr.-Oct. $10; $8 (ages 60+); $2 (ages 3-16). Admission free rest of year. Pony ride $3. Camel ride $4. **Parking:** $4. **Phone:** (517) 483-4222.

R.E. OLDS TRANSPORTATION MUSEUM is .2 mi. w. on Michigan Ave., then .2 mi. s. to 240 Museum Dr. Artifacts and documents trace the history of area transportation since 1883. Antique vehicles and automotive memorabilia as well as aircraft, bicycles and carriages are displayed. Automobiles exhibited range from the first Oldsmobile, built in 1897, to contemporary vehicles.

Guided tours are available by request. **Time:** Allow 30 minutes minimum. **Hours:** Tues.-Sat. 10-5, Sun. noon-5, Apr.-Oct.; Tues.-Sat. 10-5, rest of year. Closed major holidays. **Cost:** $5; $3 (ages 6-17, ages 66+ and students with ID); $10 (family). **Phone:** (517) 372-0422.

STATE CAPITOL is at Capitol and Michigan aves. One of the first state capitols designed to resemble the U.S. Capitol, it was dedicated in 1879 and since has been restored to reflect that period. **Hours:** Mon.-Fri. 8-5. Guided tours lasting 45-60 minutes are offered every 30 minutes 9-4. **Cost:** Free. **Phone:** (517) 373-2353.

LELAND (E-2) pop. 2,033, elev. 656'

The village of Leland, bordered by Lake Michigan to the west and Lake Leelanau to the east, is a popular departure point for lake cruises and fishing charters. Settled in 1853, Leland was named by the many sailors who used the harbor. On the harbor is Fishtown, a collection of shops, galleries and art studios in a rustic fishing village setting.

Passenger ferry service is available to the North and South Manitou islands *(see Sleeping Bear Dunes National Lakeshore p. 111)* by Manitou Island Transit. Daily service is provided to South Manitou Island June-Aug.; limited service is available in May and Sept.-Oct. Transportation to North Manitou Island is available daily July-Aug., with limited service also available May-June and Sept.-Oct. Fare $32; $18 (ages 0-12). National park $10 per vehicle admission fee (valid for 7 days) is additional. Parking $2 per day. Reservations are recommended. Tours of South Manitou Island also are available. Phone (231) 256-9061.

LEELANAU HISTORICAL MUSEUM is at 203 E. Cedar St. The museum, on the Leland River, offers changing displays in addition to the permanent Anishnabek Basket exhibit. Traditional and folk arts exhibits also are included. **Time:** Allow 30 minutes minimum. **Hours:** Wed.-Fri. 10-4, Sat. 10-2. Closed major holidays. **Cost:** Donations. **Phone:** (231) 256-7475.

LES CHENEAUX ISLANDS (B-6)

The many bays and channels *(cheneaux)* created by the 36 wooded islands that dot Lake Huron off the south shore of the eastern Upper Peninsula account for the islands' name as well as their popularity. This is one of the most scenic snowmobiling, boating, paddling and fishing areas in the state. Government Island is maintained as an uninhabited isle by the Hiawatha National Forest *(see place listing p. 78).*

Marinas in both Hessel and Cedarville offer boater access to the channels and islands. An information center on SR 134 at Cedarville is open Mon.-Fri. 9-5.

Les Cheneaux Area Welcome Center: 680 W. SR 134, P.O. Box 10, Cedarville, MI 49719. **Phone:** (906) 484-3935 or (888) 364-7526.

LIVONIA—*see Detroit p. 63.*

LUDINGTON (F-1) pop. 8,357, elev. 593'

Ludington is a popular fishing center and port on the western shore of Lake Michigan at the mouth of the Pere Marquette River. Freighters and pleasure craft find safe deepwater harborage in Pere Marquette Lake. Chinook, coho and king salmon can be caught in Lake Michigan and in the Pere Marquette River. Waterfront Park features an amphitheater for summer concerts, a playground, picnic tables, scenic walkways, eight bronze statues designed to celebrate the city's heritage and future, and views of the harbor and automobile ferry.

The SS *Badger*, operated by the Lake Michigan Carferry Service, offers 4-hour cruises and automobile ferry service from Ludington to Manitowoc, Wis. For information and fares phone (800) 841-4243.

The huge illuminated cross that overlooks the harbor marks the spot where Pere Jacques Marquette is thought to have died in 1675.

Ludington Area Convention & Visitors Bureau: 5300 W. US 10, Ludington, MI 49431. **Phone:** (800) 542-4600.

SAVE **HISTORIC WHITE PINE VILLAGE** is 2 mi. s. via Pere Marquette Hwy. to Iris Rd., then 1.5 mi. w. to 1687 S. Lakeshore Dr. This reconstructed community of 29 buildings dating 1850-1950 overlooks Lake Michigan. Included are a blacksmith shop, farmstead complex, courthouse, hardware store, fire hall, chapel and schoolhouse as well as music, logging, car, lumber and maritime museums. Interpretive signs enhance the self-guiding tour.

Time: Allow 1 hour, 30 minutes minimum. **Hours:** Tues.-Sat. 10-5, early May to mid-Oct. (also Sun. 1-5, Memorial Day-Labor Day). **Cost:** $9; $6 (ages 6-17); $25 (family, parents or grandparents and children ages 0-17). Admission is slightly higher during events. **Phone:** (231) 843-4808. 🅰️

LUDINGTON NORTH BREAKWATER LIGHTHOUSE is near Stearns Dr. and W. Ludington Ave. (US 10) at Stearns Park. To reach this squat, pyramid-shaped lighthouse, visitors must walk almost a mile along a breakwater wall which affords sweeping views of Lake Michigan, a sandy beach and the town. Visitors enjoy an even better vista from the top of the 25-foot-tall tower.

The steep climb to the top is relieved by landings with viewing portholes. Historic information is posted on the walls, and knowledgeable volunteers supplement this with their own descriptions of the lighthouse, its function and its background. **Time:** Allow 30 minutes minimum. **Hours:** Wed.-Sun. 10-5, late May-Labor Day (weather permitting). Phone ahead to confirm schedule. **Cost:** $2; $1 (ages 0-11). Children under 36 inches tall are not permitted. Cash only. **Phone:** (231) 845-7343.

LUDINGTON STATE PARK is 8 mi. n. at 8800 W. SR 116. This 5,300-acre park borders Lake Michigan and Hamlin Lake and features fine beaches, sand dunes, year-round camping and miles of hiking, biking, cross-country skiing and canoe trails. The park's Great Lakes Visitor Center offers slide and video presentations as well as an array of educational displays about the park's wildlife, geology and history. *See Recreation Chart and the AAA Great Lakes CampBook.*

Picnic shelters, both open and enclosed, are available. **Time:** Allow 1 hour, 30 minutes minimum. **Hours:** Day-use daily 8 a.m.-10 p.m. Open daily 24 hours for overnight camping. Visitor center daily 10-5, Memorial Day-Labor Day; hours vary Mar. 1-day before Memorial Day and day after Labor Day-Dec. 30. **Cost:** Park entry fee $10 (per private in-state vehicle; Recreation Passport, valid for 1 year, allows entry into Michigan state parks); $8 (per private out-of-state vehicle). **Phone:** (231) 843-2423. ⬙ 🍴 ⌧ ⛱

Big Sable Point Lighthouse is within Ludington State Park, 8 mi. n. at 8800 W. SR 116. Visitors reach the black-and-white banded lighthouse, completed in 1867, by way of a 1.5-mile beach hike that begins near the state park headquarters. The 112-foot brick structure was clad in steel plates in the early 1900s, giving it a distinctive ribbed look. Visitors can climb up to the lantern room for sweeping views of Lake Michigan, Hamlin Lake and the surrounding state park.

Hours: Daily 10-5, May-Oct. **Cost:** Park entry fee $10 (per private in-state vehicle; Recreation Passport, valid for 1 year, allows entry into Michigan state parks); $8 (per private out-of-state vehicle). Lighthouse $2; $1 (children at least 36 inches tall and under age 12). Children under 36 inches tall are not permitted. **Phone:** (231) 843-2423.

MACKINAC ISLAND (C-5) pop. 523

Native Americans called it Michilimackinac, or "Great Turtle," but time and usage have shortened the island's name to Mackinac (MACK-i-naw). This limestone outcrop became a frontier outpost in 1780, when the English moved the old French garrison on the mainland to the more strategic island. It remained the stronghold of the Straits of Mackinac for 115 years.

The island, 3 miles long and 2 miles wide with high cliffs fronting the shore, can be reached by boat from St. Ignace or Mackinaw City *(see place listings p. 106 and p. 90)*. Once on the island, transportation is by horse-drawn carriage, bicycle or saddle horse; no motorized vehicles are permitted, except for a public utilities truck, a fire truck and an ambulance. For this reason, SR 185, which rims the island, is possibly the only state highway in the nation on which a motor vehicle accident has never occurred. Bicycles may be brought over on the ferry or rented on the island.

Usually during the coldest winter months, visitors can travel across the ice bridge, a three-mile section of Lake Huron where the water freezes solid. Christmas trees, saved from the holidays, line the "highway" where snowmobiles venture between Mackinac Island and St. Ignace. Depending on the weather, the bridge can last from a few days to two months.

Ravines, natural bridges, caves and strange rock formations—particularly Arch Rock and Sugar Loaf—add to this destination's scenic appeal. Mackinac Island State Park is especially attractive in mid-June when the lilacs bloom. The island's ⚑Lilac Festival, held early to mid-June each year (June 10-19, 2011), features concerts, comedy shows, lilac symposiums, hiking and biking tours, architectural tours, a parade and more. Summer sports facilities include a yacht harbor and golf courses. Pets must be physically restrained at all times. Most accommodations are only available from mid-May to late October and mid-December to March, but a few are open year-round.

The 1980 romance "Somewhere in Time," starring Jane Seymour and Christopher Reeve, was filmed on Mackinac Island, an ideal location for a story set in the early 1900s. Fans of the film will definitely want to visit the monument placed underneath the cedar tree where the main characters, Elise

McKenna and Richard Collier, first met. The marker is at the west end of the boardwalk along the Straits of Mackinac and features a photo and quote from the memorable scene. The nearby Grand Hotel served as another filming spot; this beautiful Victorian hotel hosts the movie's fan club for a weekend each October. Stop by Mackinac Island State Park to see another connection to the film—a gazebo used in several scenes now resides here on a wooded bluff.

Ferry service from St. Ignace to Mackinac Island operates from early May through October. For schedules and prices, contact Arnold Transit Co., (906) 847-3351 or (800) 542-8528; Shepler's Mackinac Island Ferry, (231) 436-5023 or (800) 828-6157; or Star Line Mackinac Island Hydro-Jet Ferry, (906) 643-7635 or (800) 638-9892. (see ad p. 88)

Mackinac Island Tourism Bureau: 7274 Main St., P.O. Box 451, Mackinac Island, MI 49757. **Phone:** (877) 847-0086.

EARLY MISSIONARY BARK CHAPEL is in Marquette Park. The church is a reconstruction patterned after chapels built on the island in the late 1600s. The original was erected by early Jesuit missionaries. **Hours:** Daily 9:30-4:30, mid-May to mid-Oct. **Cost:** Free. **Phone:** (906) 847-3328.

FORT MACKINAC is on a bluff overlooking the harbor. The restored 18th- and 19th-century British and American military outpost is preserved as a museum. All the buildings are original; their history is interpreted through period settings, audiovisual presentations and the Kids' Quarters exhibit. Costumed guides offer reenactments, military music, and cannon and rifle firings.

Hours: Daily 9:30-6, mid-June to late Aug.; 9-4:30, early May to mid-June; 9:30-4:30, late Aug.-early Oct. **Cost:** (includes all Fort Mackinac sites) $10.50; $6.50 (ages 5-17). Combination ticket, valid for 7 days, $23; $14 (ages 5-17); ticket allows admission to three of the following four attractions: Fort Mackinac, Colonial Michilimackinac, Old Mackinac Point Lighthouse and Historic Mill Creek Discovery Park. **Phone:** (906) 847-3328 or (231) 436-4100.

Benjamin Blacksmith Shop, at Fort Mackinac, is on Market St. Demonstrations using original 19th- and 20th-century blacksmith equipment are offered. **Hours:** Daily 11-6, early June-late Aug. **Cost:** (includes all Fort Mackinac sites) $10.50; $6.50 (ages 5-17). Combination ticket, valid for 7 days, $23; $14 (ages 5-17); ticket allows admission to three of the following four attractions: Fort Mackinac, Colonial Michilimackinac, Old Mackinac Point Lighthouse and Historic Mill Creek Discovery Park. **Phone:** (906) 847-3328 or (231) 436-4100.

Biddle House, at Fort Mackinac, is on Market St. The house contains early 19th-century furnishings. Domestic craft demonstrations are offered. **Hours:** Daily 11-6, early June-late Aug. **Cost:** (includes all Fort Mackinac sites) $10.50; $6.50 (ages 5-17). Combination ticket, valid for 7 days, $23; $14 (ages 5-17); ticket allows admission to three of the following four attractions: Fort Mackinac, Colonial Michilimackinac, Old Mackinac Point Lighthouse and Historic Mill Creek Discovery Park. **Phone:** (906) 847-3328 or (231) 436-4100.

Dr. Beaumont Museum/1820s American Fur Co. Store, at Fort Mackinac, is on Market St. Housed in the restored 1820 American Fur Co. Store, the museum is dedicated to Dr. William Beaumont, who pioneered studies of the human digestive system. His medical instruments are displayed and are explained by costumed interpreters.

Hours: Daily 11-6, early June-late Aug. **Cost:** (includes all Fort Mackinac sites) $10.50; $6.50 (ages 5-17). Combination ticket, valid for 7 days, $23; $14 (ages 5-17); ticket allows admission to three of the following four attractions: Fort Mackinac, Colonial Michilimackinac, Old Mackinac Point Lighthouse and Historic Mill Creek Discovery Park. **Phone:** (906) 847-3328 or (231) 436-4100.

McGulpin House, at Fort Mackinac, is on Fort St. An example of French-Canadian architecture, the house may have been one of the buildings brought to Mackinac Island from Fort Michilimackinac, established in 1780. The architecture of the house is showcased with a model of the structure as well as an exhibit detailing the restorations that have been performed. Some original rafters, plaster and wallpaper can be seen.

Hours: Daily 11-6, early June-late Aug. **Cost:** (includes all Fort Mackinac sites) $10.50; $6.50 (ages 5-17). Combination ticket, valid for 7 days, $23; $14 (ages 5-17); ticket allows admission to three of the following four attractions: Fort Mackinac, Colonial Michilimackinac, Old Mackinac Point Lighthouse and Historic Mill Creek Discovery Park. **Phone:** (906) 847-3328 or (231) 436-4100.

Mission Church, at Fort Mackinac, is 1 mi. e. on Huron St. The church is the first Protestant work of the Native Americans at Fort Mackinac and is said to be the oldest surviving church in the state. It was built in 1829 by local residents in the New England Colonial style and contains an antique organ.

Time: Allow 30 minutes minimum. **Hours:** Daily noon-4, early June-late Aug. **Cost:** (includes all Fort Mackinac sites) $10.50; $6.50 (ages 5-17). Combination ticket, valid for 7 days, $23; $14 (ages 5-17); ticket allows admission to three of the following four attractions: Fort Mackinac, Colonial Michilimackinac, Old Mackinac Point Lighthouse and Historic Mill Creek Discovery Park. **Phone:** (906) 847-3328 or (231) 436-4100.

MACKINAC ISLAND CARRIAGE TOURS departs from the center of the shopping district on Main St. Narrated 2-hour tours visit Mackinac Island's scenic and historic points of interest. Stops include Surrey Hill Square Carriage Museum, Wings of Mackinac

Butterfly Conservatory, Arch Rock and Fort Mackinac. The museum features more than a dozen historic carriages, and the butterfly conservatory houses several hundred butterflies.

Hours: Guided carriage tours daily 9-5, mid-June through Labor Day; 9-3, early May to mid-June and day after Labor Day-Sept. 30; 9-2, in Oct. (weather permitting). Horse-drawn taxi service available by appointment year-round. **Cost:** Guided carriage tour $23.50; $9 (ages 5-12). Prices may vary; phone ahead. Additional fee for butterfly conservatory and Fort Mackinac. **Phone:** (906) 847-3307. ⫟

ORIGINAL MACKINAC ISLAND BUTTERFLY HOUSE & INSECT WORLD is on McGulpin St., behind St. Anne's Church. More than 800 butterflies from Africa, Asia and the Americas inhabit this tropical garden. Several small displays detail the lives of butterflies. An exhibit featuring giant insects from around the world also is included. **Time:** Allow 30 minutes minimum. **Hours:** Daily 10-6, May 5-Oct. 30 (also 6-7 p.m., Memorial Day-Labor Day). **Cost:** $8.50; $4 (ages 4-11). **Phone:** (906) 847-3972.

THE RICHARD AND JANE MANOOGIAN MACKINAC ART MUSEUM is at the Indian Dormitory just e. of the ferry docks in Marquette Park, near the Mackinac Island State Park visitor center. Exhibits exemplify the history, culture and scenery of the island. Native American works, photographs and 18th-century maps are part of the collection, which is accompanied by interactive computer displays offering additional insights into the pieces. The museum also contains the interactive Kids' Art Studio with an art educator, which is available during the summer season.

Time: Allow 30 minutes minimum. **Hours:** Daily 10-4, mid-May to mid-Oct. Phone ahead to confirm schedule. **Cost:** $5; $3.50 (ages 5-17). A combination ticket with other local attractions is available. **Phone:** (906) 847-3328 May-Sept., or (231) 436-4100 rest of year.

MACKINAW CITY (D-3) pop. 859, elev. 591'

First a guardian of the Straits of Mackinac, now a destination for thousands of northbound vacationers, Mackinaw City was once a trading post established by early French settlers; the post became Fort Michilimackinac in 1715. During the ensuing decades the strategically situated garrison was held successively by the French, the British, the Native Americans, then the British again. The British moved the fort to Mackinac Island 1780-81.

The city is connected to the Upper Peninsula by way of the Mackinac Bridge. One of the longest suspension spans in the world, it stretches for 5 miles. Opened in 1957, it provided a convenient means of transportation between the two peninsulas. The passenger vehicle toll is $1.75 per axle or $4.50 per car. All other vehicles are $3.50 per axle. Bicycles and snowmobiles are not permitted on the

bridge, but transport services are provided. Pedestrians and drivers who prefer not to drive across the bridge may take advantage of this driver assistance program as well. Drivers are available daily 24 hours, and snowmobile transportation is available daily 8-8. A fee is charged for bicyclists ($2), pedestrians ($2) and snowmobilers ($10). To request a driver, phone (906) 643-7600 or use the phone located at the south entrance to the bridge; if you're entering from the north, a toll collector can assist. Each Labor Day morning thousands participate in the Mackinac Bridge Walk, from St. Ignace to Mackinaw City.

In late May the ⫸ Fort Michilimackinac Pageant, a living history event, is held on the grounds of Colonial Michilimackinac *(see attraction listing)*.

Mackinaw Area Visitors Bureau: 10800 W. US 23, Mackinaw City, MI 49701. **Phone:** (231) 436-5664 or (800) 750-0160.

Shopping areas: Mackinaw Crossings, at 248 S. Huron Ave., is a shopping, dining and entertainment complex containing a five-screen movie theater, restaurants, stores, a free nightly laser show and live theater. More than 100 shops line Central Avenue (Main Street).

COLONIAL MICHILIMACKINAC is on the site of Fort Michilimackinac. The fort comprises 27 acres. Built by the French in 1715, it was occupied by British forces 1761-81. Among the 13 reconstructed buildings are a priest's house, a guardhouse, blockhouses, barracks, a storehouse, a blacksmith shop, a French church and a British trader's house.

Costumed reenactments, an audiovisual program and exhibits illustrate the history of the fort. Other programs include blacksmithing and cooking demonstrations, musket and cannon firings, a Colonial wedding and dance, a Native American encampment, an archeological tunnel exhibit and the arrival of French voyageurs. Archeological excavations are conducted daily mid-June through Labor Day. Kids' Rendezvous appeals to the younger crowd.

Time: Allow 2 hours minimum. **Hours:** Daily 9-6, mid-June to late Aug.; 9-4, early May to mid-June and late Aug.-early Oct. **Cost:** $10.50; $6.50 (ages 5-17). Combination ticket, valid for 7 days, $23; $14 (ages 5-17); ticket allows admission to three of the following four attractions: Fort Mackinac, Colonial Michilimackinac, Old Mackinac Point Lighthouse and Historic Mill Creek Discovery Park. **Phone:** (231) 436-4100 or (906) 847-3328. ⫟

HISTORIC MILL CREEK DISCOVERY PARK is 3 mi. s.e. on US 23. This is the site of an 18th-century industrial complex believed to be the oldest in the Great Lakes region. A water-powered sawmill built about 1790 provided lumber for construction on Mackinac Island. Archeological evidence of the sawmill, a dam and several houses was discovered in 1972 by a Cheboygan high school history teacher.

There is a 12-minute audiovisual orientation. Demonstrations of sawmill operations are given daily. The reconstructed millwright's house is near the sawmill. Interpretive nature trails lead to scenic overlooks, including a view of the Mackinac Bridge and a beaver colony. The guided 40-minute Adventure Tour combines hiking and zipline exploration of local wildlife and plants as well as a visit to the Forest Canopy Bridge and the Natural Trail climbing wall.

Note: Adventure Tour participants must weigh between 50 and 250 pounds and be at least 4 feet tall. Clothing items that are not permitted on Adventure Tours include skirts, dresses, flip-flops and loose-fitting sandals; shoes must be securely attached. A liability waiver must be signed. **Hours:** Daily 9-5, mid-June to late Aug.; 9-4, early May to mid-June and late Aug. to mid-Oct. Adventure Tours are available daily (weather permitting). **Cost:** $8; $4.75 (ages 5-17). Combination ticket, valid for 7 days, $23; $14 (ages 5-17); ticket allows admission to three of the following four attractions: Fort Mackinac, Colonial Michilimackinac, Old Mackinac Point Lighthouse and Historic Mill Creek Discovery Park. Adventure Tour additional $7. **Phone:** (231) 436-4100 or (906) 847-3328. 🛈

ICEBREAKER *MACKINAW* **MARITIME MUSEUM** is moored at the historic Chief Wawatam railroad dock at 131 S. Huron St. A brief video showcasing the World War II ship is shown at the beginning of the tour and then a guide takes visitors to the engine room, crew quarters, galley, mess deck and office areas. After the tour visitors may climb to view the pilot house and other topside areas.

Note: Closed-toe shoes are recommended. The ship includes confined spaces, open steel decking, steep ladders and strong magnets. **Time:** Allow 45 minutes minimum. **Hours:** Daily 9-7, late June-early Sept.; 9-5, late May-late June and early Sept. to mid-Oct. Phone ahead to confirm schedule. **Cost:** $10; $6 (ages 0-17); $35 (family, two adults and children). Under 42 inches are not permitted. **Phone:** (231) 436-9825.

OLD MACKINAC POINT LIGHTHOUSE is just e. of the s. end of Mackinac Bridge on Huron St. This lighthouse resembling a castle was in operation 1890-1957. It is filled with various relics as well as such interactive exhibits as the Night Time Navigator, which allows guests to try guiding a ship using navigational aids. Costumed interpreters guide visitors up to the tower's lantern room for views of the Mackinac Straits.

Note: The top of the tower is accessed via 51 steps and a vertical ladder through a narrow opening; climbers should not be barefoot or wearing flip-flops. **Hours:** Daily 9-5, early June-late Aug.; 9-4, mid-May to early June and late Aug. to mid-Oct.

Cost: $6; $3.50 (ages 5-17). Combination ticket, valid for 7 days, $23; $14 (ages 5-17); ticket allows admission to three of the following four attractions: Fort Mackinac, Colonial Michilimackinac, Old

Mackinac Point Lighthouse and Historic Mill Creek Discovery Park. Under 4 feet tall are not permitted to climb to the top of the tower. **Phone:** (231) 436-4100 or (906) 847-3328.

MANCELONA (E-3) pop. 1,408, elev. 1,125'

RECREATIONAL ACTIVITIES

Skiing

- **Shanty Creek Resorts** is at 1826 Schuss Mountain Ln. Alpine and cross-country skiing and snow tubing are offered. **Hours:** Skiing Tues.-Thurs. and Sat. 9-9, Fri. 9 a.m.-10 p.m., Sun.-Mon. 9-4:30, Thanksgiving to mid-Mar., with extended hours during holiday periods. Tubing Wed. and Fri. 4-9, Sat. 10-9, Sun. 9-4, Thanksgiving to mid-Mar. Phone ahead to confirm schedule. **Phone:** (800) 678-4111.

MANISTEE (F-2) pop. 6,586, elev. 598'

As early as 1790 French and English fur traders inhabited the area that the Chippewa called Manistee, "spirit of the woods." Thousands of scenic acres of Huron-Manistee National Forests *(see place listing p. 81)* still stand in preservation today. The 19th-century logging frenzy ensured that the name would outlive the woods, yet the people–mainly Swedes and Norwegians–who came to shear the timber stayed to develop the city.

With the end of the logging era, the "Victorian Port City" turned to other industries, including the production of salt and a paper mill. Manistee, on the eastern shore of Lake Michigan, is a popular fishing location with access to numerous waterways. Vast brine deposits still make Manistee a primary producer of salt.

The North Pierhead Lighthouse, first lit in 1927, welcomes freighters, fishermen, and pleasure craft to the Manistee River channel and the safe harbor found in Manistee Lake.

Manistee County Convention and Visitors Bureau: 310 1st St., Manistee, MI 49660. **Phone:** (231) 398-9355 or (877) 626-4783.

Self-guiding tours: Relics of the logging era, many ornate Victorian mansions lining the residential streets, and refurbished buildings can be found in the commercial section. Walking tour brochures are available at the convention and visitors bureau, chamber of commerce (11 Cypress St.) and the Manistee County Historical Museum.

MANISTEE COUNTY HISTORICAL MUSEUM is at 425 River St. Historical exhibits are housed in the old A.H. Lyman Co. store. Displays include the fittings of an 1885 drugstore and general store, photographs and exhibits of Civil War and pioneer memorabilia. The museum also includes the nearby Water Works Building *(see attraction listing)*.

Time: Allow 1 hour minimum. **Hours:** Mon.-Sat. 10-5, June-Sept.; Tues.-Sat. 10-5, Apr.-May and Oct.-Dec.; Thurs.-Sat. 10-5, rest of year. Closed Jan.

1, Labor Day, Thanksgiving, and Dec. 24-25 and 31. **Cost:** $3; $1 (students with ID); $5 (adult couple); $7 (family). **Phone:** (231) 723-5531.

Water Works Building is .6 mi. w. of the Manistee County Historical Museum at 540 W. First St. It was built in 1882 and houses logging, maritime and railroad exhibits as well as other memorabilia. **Time:** Allow 30 minutes minimum. **Hours:** Tues.-Sat. 10:30-4:30, late June-late Aug. Phone ahead to confirm schedule. **Cost:** $1. **Phone:** (231) 723-5531.

GAMBLING ESTABLISHMENTS
• **Little River Casino** is at 2700 Orchard Hwy. **Hours:** Daily 24 hours. **Phone:** (888) 568-2244.

MANISTIQUE (B-4) pop. 3,583, elev. 613′

Manistique provides access to the 300 lakes and numerous streams of the Lake Superior State Forest and 135 miles of maintained snowmobile trails. The bridge carrying SR 94 across the Manistique River is unusual in that its floor is below river level.

Palms Book State Park, 11 miles northwest, is best known for Kitch-iti-kipi, a clear, cold spring 200 feet wide and 42 feet deep. Seven miles southwest via US 2 and SR 149 is the state fish hatchery that introduced the coho salmon into Michigan waters to counteract the invasion of alewives that followed the opening of the St. Lawrence Seaway.

A scenic portion of US 2 passes through Manistique on its way from Escanaba *(see place listing p. 68)* to St. Ignace *(see place listing p. 106)*. About one-third of the distance follows the shore of Lake Michigan. *See Upper Peninsula p. 114.*

Schoolcraft County Chamber of Commerce: 1000 W. Lakeshore Dr., Manistique, MI 49854. **Phone:** (906) 341-5010 or (888) 819-7420.

GAMBLING ESTABLISHMENTS
• **Kewadin Casino** is at 5630 W. US 2. **Hours:** Daily 8 a.m.-3 a.m. **Phone:** (906) 341-5510 or (800) 539-2346.

MARQUETTE (B-3) pop. 19,661, elev. 636′

First settled in 1849 as a shipping center, Marquette was named for the French missionary and explorer Father Jacques Marquette. Surrounded by the rugged Laurentian Uplands on the southern shore of Lake Superior, the city is regarded as the medical, shopping and political center of the Upper Peninsula. The wooden dome at Northern Michigan University's Great Lakes Sports Training Center offers football, soccer and an Olympic training facility.

Marquette is the western terminus of a scenic 42-mile drive that is US 41 for a few miles south, then SR 28 along the lakeshore to Munising *(see place listing p. 96)*. Also see Upper Peninsula p. 114.

Marquette Country Convention and Visitors Bureau: 337 W. Washington St., Marquette, MI 49855. **Phone:** (906) 228-7749 or (800) 544-4321.

Self-guiding tours: Walking tour maps of historic Marquette can be purchased at the Marquette County Historical Society and Museum.

MARQUETTE COUNTY HISTORICAL SOCIETY AND MUSEUM is at 145 W. Spring St. Visitors can see an Ojibwa village, a fur-trading post, equipment of the first survey party to the Upper Peninsula, pioneer artifacts and mining and lumber displays.

Hours: Mon.-Fri. 10-5 (also third Thurs. of the month 5-9), Sat. 11-4, June-Aug.; Mon.-Fri. 10-5 (also third Thurs. of the month 5-9), rest of year. Closed Jan. 1, Presidents' Day, Good Friday, Memorial Day, July 4, Labor Day, Thanksgiving weekend, Dec. 24-25 and 31 and on Marquette area public school snow days. **Cost:** $3; $1 (students with ID); free (ages 0-12). **Phone:** (906) 226-3571.

MARQUETTE MARITIME MUSEUM is at 300 Lakeshore Blvd. Displays in an 1890s water works building describe the maritime heritage of Marquette and Lake Superior. A film is shown. Dockside offices of Marquette's first commercial fishing and passenger freight companies are re-created; a fishing shanty contains sport fishing gear. A Coast Guard lighthouse is adjacent to the museum; guided tours of the lighthouse and grounds are available.

Time: Allow 30 minutes minimum. **Hours:** Daily 10-5, late May to mid-Oct. **Cost:** (includes museum and lighthouse) $7; $5 (ages 0-12). Museum or lighthouse $4; $3 (ages 0-12). **Phone:** (906) 226-2006.

PRESQUE ISLE PARK is n. of the city at the end of Lakeshore Blvd. This 328-acre wooded peninsula juts into Lake Superior. The park offers picnic facilities and rock hunting; facilities include an outdoor pool with a waterslide. Nature trails wind throughout the park and are used for bog walks in the summer and snowshoeing and cross-country skiing in winter. **Time:** Allow 30 minutes minimum. **Hours:** Daily 7 a.m.-11 p.m. **Cost:** Free. **Phone:** (906) 228-0460. ☒ ⌂

[SAVE] **THE UPPER PENINSULA CHILDREN'S MUSEUM** is at 123 W. Baraga Ave. Interactive displays were designed with input from local children and families. Subjects range from reptiles and forests to trains and planes to the human body. Kids can slide down a giant intestine in the Incredible Journey exhibit or check out a real ambulance and a re-created airplane cockpit.

Time: Allow 1 hour minimum. **Hours:** Mon.-Wed. and Sat. 10-6, Thurs. 10-7:30, Fri. 10-8, Sun. noon-5. Closed Jan. 1, Memorial Day, July 4, Labor Day, Thanksgiving and Dec. 24-25. **Cost:** $5; $25 (family); free (ages 0-1). **Phone:** (906) 226-3911.

RECREATIONAL ACTIVITIES
Skiing
- **Marquette Mountain** is at 4501 SR 553. **Hours:** Mon. 10-5, Tues.-Fri. 10-9:30, Sat. 9:30-9:30, Sun. 9:30-8, mid-Dec. to late Mar.; Thurs.-Fri. 10-5, Sat.-Sun. 9:30-5, late Mar. to mid-Apr. and late Nov. to mid-Dec. **Phone:** (906) 225-1155 or (800) 944-7669.

MARSHALL (I-3) pop. 7,459, elev. 898'

In 1846 near the site of Triangle Park, an event occurred that bore nationwide import. Adam Crosswhite, a Marshall resident, was seized by agents of the Kentucky slaveholder from whom he had escaped 2 years earlier. The townsfolk sprang to his defense, sending the slave hunters home without him and providing the Crosswhite family with passage to freedom in Canada.

Sued by the former slave owner, the Marshall abolitionists lost. The Crosswhite case was instrumental in the creation of the 1850 Fugitive Slave Act, which in turn contributed to tensions that led to the Civil War.

A historic houses tour held the first weekend after Labor Day focuses on one of Marshall's hallmarks: an unusual number of excellent, well-preserved examples of Greek and Gothic revival, Italianate and Queen Anne architecture. Their survival resulted in part from the dashing of two 19th-century dreams: Marshall failed to become the capital, and the railroad boom collapsed. Foresight has since supplanted chance, and the structures are carefully protected.

Marshall Area Chamber of Commerce: 424 E. Michigan Ave., Marshall, MI 49068. **Phone:** (269) 781-5163 or (800) 877-5163.

Self-guiding tours: A map detailing a tour of Marshall is available at local shops and inns, the chamber of commerce and the Honolulu House Museum.

HONOLULU HOUSE MUSEUM is off Fountain Cir. at 107 N. Kalamazoo Ave. The home was built in 1860 for Judge Abner Pratt, a chief justice of the Michigan Supreme Court who later became U.S. Consul to Hawai'i. A blend of Victorian, Italianate and island living styles, the house was influenced by his Hawaiian house.

A raised veranda, pagoda-capped tower and rooms with elaborate 15-foot ceilings hand-painted in high Victorian style are highlights. **Hours:** Daily noon-5, June-Aug.; Thurs.-Sun. noon-5 in May and Sept.-Oct. **Cost:** $5; $4 (ages 12-18 and 65+). **Phone:** (269) 781-8544.

MATTAWAN (I-2) pop. 2,536, elev. 869'

WOLF LAKE STATE FISH HATCHERY & VISITOR CENTER is 6 mi. w. off US 131 on SR 43, then just s. on Fish Hatchery Rd. to 34270 CR 652. The hatchery helps replenish depleted stocks in the wild, and visitors will learn about all the phases that occur before the fish are released into the Great Lakes as well as inland lakes. The visitor center includes an interactive museum and display showcasing fish life cycles and habitats, human impacts on fish environments and the history of fish hatcheries on the Great Lakes. Hiking and nature trails also are on the grounds.

Time: Allow 30 minutes minimum. **Hours:** Visitor center Mon.-Sat. 10-6, Sun. noon-6, June-Aug.; Tues.-Sat. 10-4, Sun. noon-4, Mar.-May and Sept.-Oct.; Sat.-Sun., first three weekends in Nov. (phone for hours). Special weekend programs are offered Sat.-Sun., Dec.-Feb. Guided tours depart on the hour Tues.-Sat. 10-11 and 1-3, Sun. 1-3. Tour times may vary. Phone ahead to confirm schedule. **Cost:** Free. **Phone:** (269) 668-2876. ⌂

MEARS (G-1)

MAC WOOD'S DUNE RIDES is 9 mi. w. of US 31 on Silver Lake. Guides take passengers on 40-minute scenic rides over 8 miles of shifting sand dunes. **Hours:** Daily 9:30-dusk, Memorial Day-Labor Day; daily 10-4, early May-day before Memorial Day and day after Labor Day-early Oct. Phone ahead to confirm schedule. **Cost:** $16; $11 (ages 3-11). **Phone:** (231) 873-2817.

SILVER LAKE STATE PARK is off US 31 Hart or Shelby exit, then 7 mi. w., following signs. Of the park's 3,400 acres, approximately 1,800 are covered in sweeping sand dunes. The dunes can be explored in off-road vehicles in the northern portion of the park or on foot in the center section. Silver Lake is a good place for swimming, fishing and boating. *See Recreation Chart.* The 107-foot red brick Little Sable Point Light Station, built in 1873, overlooks a scenic portion of Lake Michigan. Lighthouse tours allow visitors to go up to the top of the structure.

Phone ahead for off-road vehicle area hours and specific rules. **Hours:** Daily 8 a.m.-10 p.m., Apr.-Oct. Lighthouse tours are given daily 10-6, mid-May through Sept. 30. **Cost:** Park entry fee $10 (per private in-state vehicle; Recreation Passport, valid for 1 year, allows entry into Michigan state parks; $8 (per private out-of-state vehicle). **Phone:** (231) 873-3083, or (800) 447-2757 for reservations. ⊠

MIDLAND (G-4) pop. 41,685, elev. 610'

The development of Midland from a lumber town into a handsome, well-planned and culturally active city is entwined with the growth of the Dow Chemical Co. Large brine deposits precipitated the establishment of the company in Midland.

The Tridge, a three-legged pedestrian bridge, is at the confluence of the Tittabawassee and Chippewa rivers. The Pere Marquette Rail-Trail provides 30 miles of paved hiking trails between the Tridge and Clare. The riverfront area also features picnic facilities, a spray park, walking trails, an outdoor concert park and a farmers market.

Midland County Convention & Visitors Bureau: 300 Rodd St., Suite 101, Midland, MI 48640. **Phone:** (989) 839-9522 or (888) 464-3526.

ALDEN B. DOW HOME AND STUDIO, 315 Post St., integrates organic textures, geometric angles and rich colors with the natural surroundings. The building was designed by Dow, who apprenticed with Frank Lloyd Wright. **Time:** Allow 1 hour, 30 minutes minimum. **Hours:** Tours are given Mon.-Sat. at 2 (also Fri.-Sat. at 10), Feb.-Dec. Closed Memorial Day, July 4, Labor Day, Thanksgiving and Dec. 25. **Cost:** $12; $7 (children and students with ID). Ages 0-7 are not permitted. Reservations are required. **Phone:** (989) 839-2744 or (866) 315-7678.

CHIPPEWA NATURE CENTER is 3.5 mi. s.w. at 400 S. Badour Rd. More than 1,300 acres of woods, fields, ponds, rivers and wetlands as well as hiking and cross-country skiing trails are featured. A museum has interactive exhibits, a library, a restored 1870s farm, an 1880s log school house, a sugarhouse and a wigwam. The Howard L. Garrett Arboretum features Michigan tree and shrub specimens.

Time: Allow 2 hours minimum. **Hours:** Visitor center open Mon.-Fri. 8-5, Sat. 9-5, Sun. and holidays 1-5. Grounds open daily dawn-dusk. Closed Thanksgiving and Dec. 25. **Cost:** Donations. **Phone:** (989) 631-0830.

DOW GARDENS is next to Midland Center for the Arts at 1809 Eastman Ave.; Whiting Forest is .25 mi. n. on Eastman Ave. On display are 600 species of flowers and shrubs on 110 landscaped acres. Whiting Forest offers seven different types of forest, hiking trails, ponds, covered bridges, a visitor center, children's play forts and an observation tower.

Guided tours of Dow Gardens, Whiting Forest or both locations are available by appointment and require a minimum of five people. **Time:** Allow 1 hour minimum. **Hours:** Gardens daily 9-8:30, Apr. 15-Labor Day; 9-6:30, day after Labor Day-Oct. 31; 9-4:15, rest of year. Whiting Forest daily 10-6, Apr. 15-Labor Day; 10-5, day after Labor Day-Oct. 31;

10-4, rest of year. Closed Jan. 1, Thanksgiving and Dec. 25. **Cost:** $5; $1 (ages 6-17 and students with ID). Guided tour additional $2 (per person). **Phone:** (989) 631-2677 or (800) 362-4874.

HERITAGE PARK is at 3417 W. Main St. Three separate attractions located in a campus setting give visitors a chance to discover Midland County's history. Hands-on exhibits and Victorian relics can be found within the park's history center and carriage house. Also on the property are two museums and mid-Michigan's largest working blacksmith shop.

Time: Allow 3 hours, 30 minutes minimum. **Hours:** Thurs.-Sat. 11-4, Mar. 16-Nov. 14. Closed major holidays. Phone ahead to confirm schedule. **Cost:** (includes 1874 Bradley Home Museum & Carriage House, Herbert D. Doan Midland County History Center, and Herbert H. Dow Historical Museum) $5; $3 (ages 4-14). **Phone:** (989) 631-5930, ext. 1310.

1874 Bradley Home Museum & Carriage House is at 3417 W. Main St. in Heritage Park. The 1874 Victorian house contains Victorian furnishings, fixtures, costumes and hands-on displays. The Carriage House exhibits 15 horse-drawn vehicles, blacksmithing equipment and related items. Mid-Michigan's largest working blacksmith shop also can be seen.

Time: Allow 1 hour minimum. **Hours:** One-hour guided tours depart Thurs.-Sat. at 11, 1 and 3, Mar. 16-Nov. 14. Closed major holidays. Phone ahead to confirm schedule. **Cost:** (includes Herbert D. Doan Midland County History Center and Herbert H. Dow Historical Museum) $5; $3 (ages 4-14). **Phone:** (989) 631-5930, ext. 1310.

Herbert D. Doan Midland County History Center is at 3417 W. Main St. in Heritage Park. At the entrance to the park, the center houses a gallery offering interactive exhibits. The history of Midland is depicted through vignettes and re-created 20th-century city streets that visitors can roam. Guests to the center also learn about Midland's founders.

Hours: Thurs.-Sat. 11-4, Mar. 16-Nov. 14. Closed major holidays. Phone ahead to confirm schedule. **Cost:** (includes 1874 Bradley Home Museum & Carriage House and Herbert H. Dow Historical Museum) $5; $3 (ages 4-14). **Phone:** (989) 631-5930, ext. 1310.

Herbert H. Dow Historical Museum is at 3417 W. Main St. in Heritage Park. Displays chronicle the life of the founder of Dow Chemical Co., Herbert H. Dow, who conducted his pioneering chemical experiments in a nearby shed. The museum is housed in a replica of a gristmill. Exhibits include Dow's first office and his father's workshop. A 12-minute videotape presentation features a miniature image of Dow explaining his contributions to chemistry.

Next to the mill is a replica of the 1890 Midland Chemical Co., Dow's first manufacturing plant. A laboratory, steam engine and chemical tank help convey the humble beginnings of the Dow Chemical

Co. **Time:** Allow 1 hour, 30 minutes minimum. **Hours:** Thurs.-Sat. 11-4, Mar. 16-Nov. 14. Closed major holidays. Phone ahead to confirm schedule. **Cost:** (includes 1874 Bradley Home Museum & Carriage House and Herbert D. Doan Midland County History Center) $5; $3 (ages 4-14). **Phone:** (989) 631-5930, ext. 1310.

MIDLAND CENTER FOR THE ARTS is 2 mi. s. of US 10 at 1801 W. St. Andrews Rd. at jct. Eastman Ave. Concerts, plays and musicals are presented here. The center also houses the Alden B. Dow Museum of Science & Art, which features changing exhibits about science, technology, health, art and history. Many include interactive displays. A highlight is ViewSpace, which is a wall-mounted screen continually showing images of the universe from NASA's Hubble Space Telescope.

Tours: Guided tours are available. **Time:** Allow 2 hours minimum. **Hours:** Alden B. Dow Museum of Science & Art open Wed.-Sat. 10-4 (also Thurs. 4-6), Sun. 1-4, Labor Day-Memorial Day; Wed.-Sat. 10-4 (also Thurs. 4-6), rest of year. Ticket office open Mon.-Fri. noon-6, Sat. noon-4, and 1 hour before performances. Closed major holidays. Phone ahead to confirm schedule. **Cost:** Museum $8; $5 (ages 4-14). Audio tour $3. Performance ticket prices vary. **Phone:** (989) 631-8250, or (800) 523-7649 for ticket information.

MIO (E-4) pop. 2,016

Surrounded by the Huron-Manistee National Forests *(see place listing p. 81)* and with the Au Sable River nearby, Mio is a popular departure point and equipment rental center for fishing and canoeing expeditions. In spring the rare Kirtland's warbler nests in protected areas south of Mio near Mack Lake. Guided tours of the nesting area leave from the U.S. Forest Service station; phone (989) 826-3252.

Chamber of Commerce for Oscoda County: 201 S. Morenci, P.O. Box 670, Mio, MI 48647. **Phone:** (989) 826-3331 or (800) 800-6133.

OUR LADY OF THE WOODS SHRINE is 1.5 blks. w. of SR 33 on SR 72. Visitors can see replicas of Roman Catholic Marian shrines from around the world. Our Lady of Czestochowa, Our Lady of Fatima, Our Lady of Guadalupe, Our Lady of LaSalette, Our Lady of Lourdes and Our Lady of Mt. Carmel are represented. There also is a statue of the Assumption, two interior grottoes, and a tubular cross with representations of the Ten Commandments. Guided tours are available by appointment. **Hours:** Daily dawn-dusk. **Cost:** Free. **Phone:** (517) 826-5509.

MOHAWK (A-2) elev. 1,033'

DELAWARE COPPER MINE TOURS is at 7804 Delaware Mine Rd. Visitors can take a self-guiding underground walking tour into a mid-1800s copper mine where veins of copper can be seen. Above

ground there are walking trails past mine ruins and mining equipment. The mine temperature averages 45 F. **Note:** Warm clothing is recommended. **Time:** Allow 1 hour minimum. **Hours:** Daily 10-6, June-Aug.; 10-5, Sept.-Oct. Last admission 45 minutes before closing. **Cost:** $10; $6 (ages 6-12). **Phone:** (906) 289-4688.

MONROE (I-5) pop. 22,076, elev. 590'

One of the oldest communities in the state, Monroe was founded in 1780 by the French at the site of a Native American village where the River Raisin enters Lake Erie. The settlement, originally called Frenchtown, was the scene of the River Raisin Massacre in 1813 during the War of 1812. Gen. George Custer lived in Monroe for many years before his Army service. A 1920 bronze statue of Custer titled "Sighting the Enemy" is on the southwest corner of N. Monroe Street and W. Elm Avenue.

A Vietnam War Memorial is off I-75 exit 15, then one-fourth mile west on SR 50 in Heck Park.

Monroe County Convention and Tourism Bureau: 103 W. Front St., Monroe, MI 48161. **Phone:** (734) 457-1030 or (800) 252-3011.

Shopping areas: Monroe Factory Shops, I-75 exit 11 at 14500 LaPlaisance Rd., offers more than a dozen factory outlet stores such as Carter's Children, Gap Outlet and Reebok.

MONROE COUNTY HISTORICAL MUSEUM is at 126 S. Monroe St. Exhibits in the old Georgian-style post office building focus on the family of Gen. George A. Custer as well as on area history. The museum also contains local maps, Victorian furnishings and displays about Native American and French pioneer history. **Time:** Allow 1 hour minimum. **Hours:** Wed.-Sun. 10-5, May-Dec.; Wed.-Sat. 10-5, rest of year. Closed major holidays. Phone ahead to confirm schedule. **Cost:** $2; $1 (ages 7-17). **Phone:** (734) 240-7780.

RIVER RAISIN BATTLEFIELD VISITOR CENTER is off I-75 exit 14 at 1403 E. Elm Ave. Displays depict the Battle of the River Raisin, one of the largest engagements of the War of 1812. Exhibits include dioramas, fiber-optic maps, firearms and mannequins. A 15-minute auditorium presentation explains the major turning points of that war. The center also provides information about Monroe County. River Raisin National Battlefield Park has recently become part of the National Park Service.

Time: Allow 30 minutes minimum. **Hours:** Visitor center open Fri.-Tues. 10-5, June-Aug. Sat.-Sun. 10-5, Sept.-Oct. Grounds open year-round. Closed major holidays. **Cost:** Donations. **Phone:** (734) 243-7136 or (734) 240-7780.

MOUNT CLEMENS—*see Detroit p. 64.*

MOUNT PLEASANT (G-3)
pop. 25,946, elev. 761'

Originally known as Ojibway Besse, Mount Pleasant was a hunting ground for the Chippewa Indians. Magnificent pine and hardwoods destined the town to become a major lumber center. Mount Pleasant is home to Central Michigan University, founded in 1892, and the Saginaw Chippewa Indian Tribe on the Isabella Indian Reservation.

Horse racing takes place at Mount Pleasant Meadows weekends May through September; phone (989) 773-0012.

Note: Policies concerning admittance of children to pari-mutuel betting facilities vary. Phone ahead for information.

Mount Pleasant Area Convention and Visitors Bureau: 200 E. Broadway, Mount Pleasant, MI 48858. **Phone:** (989) 772-4433 or (888) 772-2022.

GAMBLING ESTABLISHMENTS

- **Soaring Eagle Casino & Resort** is at 6800 Soaring Eagle Blvd. **Hours:** Daily 24 hours. **Phone:** (888) 732-4537. *(see ad & p. 397)*

RECREATIONAL ACTIVITIES

Canoeing

- **Chippewa River Outfitters** is 2 mi. w. on Broomfield Rd., then .3 mi. n. to 3763 S. Lincoln Rd. Other activities are offered. **Hours:** Daily 10-5, May-Sept. Last departure is at 5; boaters must be off the river by 8. Open by appointment rest of year. Reservations are recommended. **Phone:** (989) 772-5474 or (888) 775-6077.

MUNISING (B-4) pop. 2,539, elev. 626'

Munising's harbor is protected from the brunt of Lake Superior's gales by Grand Island; the town is guarded on the landward side by a ring of sharply rising hills. A number of waterfalls cascade down the slopes within the city limits. Grand Island is a national recreation area; Munising also provides access to Hiawatha National Forest *(see place listing p. 78)* and is the eastern gateway to Pictured Rocks National Lakeshore *(see place listing p. 102)*.

The city is the eastern terminus of a scenic section of SR 28 that skirts the shore of Lake Superior to US 41 and Marquette *(see place listing p. 92)*. *Also see Upper Peninsula p. 114.*

Greater Munising Bay Partnership for Commerce Development: 129 E. Munising Ave., P.O. Box 405, Munising, MI 49862. **Phone:** (906) 387-2138.

PICTURED ROCKS CRUISES depart from Municipal Pier. Cruises, which cover 37 miles and last approximately 2 hours and 40 minutes, follow the colorful rock formations that rise sharply from Lake Superior to heights of 200 feet. Sunset cruises also are available.

Hours: Cruises depart daily at 10, noon, 1, 2, 3, 5 and at sunset, July 1 to mid-Aug.; at 11, 1, 3, 5 and at sunset, mid-Aug. through Labor Day; at 10, 1 and 4, mid-June through June 30 and day after Labor Day to early Oct.; at 10 and 2, Fri. before Memorial Day to mid-June; at 2, May 15-20; at 1, Oct. 11-17. Phone for sunset cruise times and to confirm schedule. **Cost:** $33; $10 (ages 6-12). **Phone:** (906) 387-2379 or (800) 650-2379.

SHIPWRECK TOURS is at 1204 Commercial St. Passengers ride in a glass-bottom boat for narrated tours of three Lake Superior shipwrecks. Additional highlights include views of the South Lighthouse and an original settlement on Grand Island. Narrated 2.5-hour evening cruises travel around Grand Island and the East Channel and North Light lighthouses.

Hours: Two-hour cruises depart daily at 10, 12:30, 1 and 4, July 1-Labor Day; at 10 and 1, second week in June-June 30 and day after Labor Day-Sept. 30; at 1, Memorial Day weekend-first week in June and Oct. 1-10. Phone for evening cruise schedule. **Cost:** $30; $27 (senior citizens); $12 (ages 6-12). Phone for evening cruise fare. **Phone:** (906) 387-4477.

MUSKEGON (G-1) pop. 40,105, elev. 599'

Formerly known as the Lumber Queen of the World, Muskegon produced 665 million board feet of lumber in 1888 alone. Although the languishing of the logging boom severely affected the town, the excellence of its harbor and success in attracting new enterprises prospered it. Muskegon is the largest city on the eastern shore of Lake Michigan, with

a diversified mix of industry, tourism, culture and recreational activities comprising its economy.

More than 3,000 acres of recreational land balance Muskegon's industrial image. Pere Marquette Park occupies the southern flank of the channel; Muskegon State Park (see Recreation Chart) is to the north. The lakeside highway leading north from Muskegon State Park is an especially scenic drive.

The Muskegon River offers fishing for walleyed pike, boating and canoeing; numerous lakes and streams are restocked yearly. Hundreds of anglers line the channel and breakwater walls on Lake Michigan during the perch and salmon runs.

The Lake Express, a high-speed car ferry, connects Muskegon with Milwaukee, saving travelers a 286-mile drive around the southern end of the lake through Chicago. The ferry, which travels 76 nautical miles in 2.5 hours, makes several round-trips daily May through October; phone (866) 914-1010 for schedule and fares.

Muskegon Summer Celebration—held at Heritage Landing and featuring family activities, food and music—lasts from late June to early July.

Muskegon County Convention and Visitors Bureau: 610 W. Western Ave., Muskegon, MI 49440. **Phone:** (231) 724-3100 or (800) 250-9283.

GILLETTE SAND DUNE VISITOR CENTER is in P.J. Hoffmaster State Park, about 2 mi. w. off US 31 Pontaluna exit. Hands-on exhibits, displays and a multimedia presentation illustrate the history and ecology of sand dunes and plant and animal life. Nature trails lead from the center to observation decks. See Recreation Chart.

Time: Allow 2 hours minimum. **Hours:** Center open daily 10-5, Memorial Day-Labor Day; Tues.-Fri. noon-4, Sat. 10-4, mid-Jan. through day before Memorial Day and day after Labor Day to mid-Nov. Park open daily 8 a.m.-dusk. **Cost:** Park entry fee $10 (per private in-state vehicle; Recreation Passport, valid for 1 year, allows entry into Michigan state parks); $8 (per private out-of-state vehicle). **Phone:** (231) 798-3573.

GREAT LAKES NAVAL MEMORIAL AND MUSEUM is on the south side of the channel at 1346 Bluff St. The memorial includes the USS Silversides, a restored, much-decorated World War II submarine and the McClain, a Coast Guard cutter. Guided tours through the sub's compartments explain how sailors lived and worked despite cramped quarters. The Robert G. Morin Sr. building houses military artifacts, and a presentation demonstrating life in the 1940s during the war is shown.

Time: Allow 1 hour minimum. **Hours:** Daily 10-5:30, June-Aug.; daily 10-4, Apr.-May and Sept.-Oct.; Mon.-Fri. 10-4, Sat.-Sun. 10-noon, rest of year. **Cost:** $15; $12.50 (ages 12-18 and 62+); $10.50 (ages 5-11). **Phone:** (231) 755-1230.

LAKESHORE MUSEUM CENTER is at 430 W. Clay Ave. Exhibits highlight the natural and cultural

history of the region. The display Coming to the Lakes reveals why people have been coming to the region for more than 10,000 years. Other topics showcased include birds, dinosaurs, mammals, minerals and rocks. Interactive science and health exhibits also can be explored. **Hours:** Mon.-Fri. 9:30-4:30, Sat.-Sun. noon-4. Closed major holidays. **Cost:** Free. **Phone:** (231) 722-0278 or (888) 843-5661.

MICHIGAN'S ADVENTURE AMUSEMENT PARK is 8 mi. n. via US 31 exit 121 (Russell Rd.). The park has more than 60 rides and attractions. Its seven roller coasters include the Thunderhawk, Wolverine Wildcat and Shivering Timbers. Several rides are appropriate for small children. The WildWater Adventure Water Park features 20 slides, three wave pools, a lazy river and two play areas.

Lockers are available. Sunscreen is recommended. Life jackets are provided. **Time:** Allow a full day. **Hours:** Amusement park open daily at 11, mid-May through Labor Day. Water park open daily at noon. Closing times for both parks vary. Phone ahead to confirm schedule. **Cost:** $26; free (ages 0-2). Locker rental $10. **Parking:** $8. **Phone:** (231) 766-3377. [T]

MUSKEGON MUSEUM OF ART is at 296 W. Webster Ave. Works of such American artists as Ralph Albert Blakelock, Winslow Homer, Edward Hopper and James Abbot McNeill Whistler are displayed. John Steuart Curry's "Tornado Over Kansas" also can be seen. A European collection has objects ranging from ancient glass to contemporary art.

Guided tours are available by appointment. **Hours:** Tues.-Sat. 10-4:30 (also Thurs. 4:30-8), Sun. noon-4:30. Closed major holidays. **Cost:** $5; free (ages 0-17, students with ID and to all Thurs.). **Phone:** (231) 720-2570.

NAUBINWAY (B-5) elev. 595'

GARLYN ZOOLOGICAL PARK is 6 mi. e. on US 2. Among the animals living in this wooded park setting are alligators, camels, cougars, ring-tailed lemurs, river otters, tortoises, wallabies and wolves. Visitors can feed deer, goats, llamas and even a bear. **Hours:** Daily 10-6, Apr.-Sept.; daily 10-5, in Oct.; Fri.-Sun., 10-5, in Mar. and Nov. **Cost:** $9; $8 (ages 3-13); $30 (family, up to six people). **Phone:** (906) 477-1085.

NEGAUNEE (B-3) pop. 4,576, elev. 1,400'

Negaunee, the first mining city on the Marquette Range, was brought into being in 1844 by a group of explorers who were led to the ore beds by a Native American chief from the Keweenaw country. See Upper Peninsula p. 114.

MICHIGAN IRON INDUSTRY MUSEUM is 3 mi. e. off US 41E to Maas St., then n. to 73 Forge Rd. Forested ravines of the Marquette Iron Range provide the setting for this museum overlooking the Carp River and the site of the first iron forge in the Lake Superior region. Through exhibits, audiovisual programs and interpretive outdoor trails, the museum presents the history of Michigan's three iron ranges from their geologic origins through the 20th century and showcases the people who worked them. "The Yankee"—an 1860s vertical boiler locomotive from the Jackson Mine—as well as underground mine cars, mining equipment and artifacts also are displayed.

Time: Allow 1 hour, 30 minutes minimum. **Hours:** Daily 9:30-4:30, June-Sept.; daily 9:30-4 in May and Oct.; Mon.-Fri. and first Sat. of the month 9:30-4, rest of year. Closed major holidays except Memorial Day, July 4 and Labor Day. **Cost:** Donations. **Phone:** (906) 475-7857.

NEWBERRY (B-4) pop. 2,686, elev. 788′

OSWALD'S BEAR RANCH is 4 mi. n. on SR 123 to Four Mile Corner, then 4.5 mi. w. to 13814 CR 407. Thirty American black bears, ranging in age from cubs to adults, are raised and kept on the 80-acre ranch. Visitors may view them in re-created natural habitats. **Time:** Allow 30 minutes minimum. **Hours:** Daily 9:30-5, Memorial Day weekend-Sept. 30. **Cost:** $15 (per private vehicle) or $10 (per person). **Phone:** (906) 293-3147.

TAHQUAMENON LOGGING MUSEUM is 1 mi. n. on SR 123. The complex, situated on 29 acres, includes a museum with logging memorabilia, a horse-drawn steam engine, a one-room schoolhouse, a memorial to the Depression-era Civilian Conservation Corps program, a bunkhouse, a cook shack and a log cabin from the late 19th century. A slide presentation also is offered. **Time:** Allow 1 hour minimum. **Hours:** Thurs.-Sat. 10-4, Memorial Day-Labor Day. **Cost:** $3; $1.50 (ages 6-12). **Phone:** (906) 293-3700.

NILES (I-2) pop. 12,204, elev. 659′

Because the banners of France, England, Spain and the United States have flown successively over this region, Niles is called the City of Four Flags. Its position as a stop on the 1830s Detroit-to-Chicago stagecoach route encouraged industrial and commercial development. Author Ring Lardner and the Dodge brothers of automobile fame were born in Niles. The town was also the childhood home of Aaron Montgomery Ward, who founded his mail-order business in 1872.

Four Flags Area Council on Tourism: 404 E. Main St., P.O. Box 1300, Niles, MI 49120. **Phone:** (269) 684-7444.

FERNWOOD BOTANICAL GARDENS AND NATURE PRESERVE is off US 31 (St. Joseph Valley Pkwy.) exit 7 to 13988 Range Line Rd. The 105-acre nature preserve offers gardens, woodland trails and prairie. A visitor center includes gallery shows, exhibits and a fern conservatory.

Time: Allow 2 hours minimum. **Hours:** Daily noon-5, in Dec.; Tues.-Sat. 10-6, Sun. noon-6, May-Oct.; Tues.-Sat. 10-5, Sun. noon-5, rest of year. Closed major holidays. **Cost:** $7; $5 (ages 65+); $4 (ages 13-18); $3 (ages 6-12). Rates increase during special events. **Phone:** (269) 695-6491. 🍴

FORT ST. JOSEPH MUSEUM is at 508 E. Main St. The museum, located in the carriage house of the 1882 Chapin home, contains more than 10,000 historic items, including Lakota and Potawatomi Indian relics, artifacts from the site of Fort St. Joseph, and Sitting Bull pictographs. **Time:** Allow 30 minutes minimum. **Hours:** Wed.-Fri. 10-4, Sat. 10-3. Closed major holidays. **Cost:** Free. **Phone:** (269) 683-4702.

NORTH MUSKEGON (G-1)
pop. 4,031, elev. 621′

RECREATIONAL ACTIVITIES
Winter Activities

- **Muskegon Winter Sports Complex** is in Muskegon State Park at 442 N. Scenic Dr. Cross-country skiing, ice-skating, a luge track and snow-shoeing are offered. **Hours:** Ski trails open daily 10-10, Dec.-Mar. Phone for hours of other facilities. **Phone:** (231) 744-9629 or (877) 879-5843.

NORTHPORT (D-2) pop. 648

The coastal community of Northport lies in the northern end of the Leelanau Peninsula. The town is noted for its sandy beaches and spectacular sunsets. Leelanau State Park (see Recreation Chart) is 7 miles north on SR 201. The Grand Traverse Lighthouse and Museum, within the park, offers tours.

Leelanau Peninsula Chamber of Commerce: 5046 S. West Bayshore Dr., Suite G, Suttons Bay, MI 49682. **Phone:** (231) 271-9895.

ODEN (D-3) elev. 617′

ODEN STATE FISH HATCHERY AND MICHIGAN FISHERIES VISITOR CENTER is at 3377 US 31. The Michigan Fisheries Visitor Center houses interactive exhibits. Just outside is a reproduction of a train car used 1914-35 to transport fish for stocking throughout the state. A .5-mile nature trail running by a stream leads visitors to the hatchery, which can be seen on guided tours only. Visitors also can drive to the hatchery. The facility raises brown and rainbow trout. The Stream Viewing Chamber allows visitors to watch fish swimming in the Oden River.

Time: Allow 2 hours minimum. **Hours:** Daily 10-6, Memorial Day weekend-Labor Day; Tues.-Sat. 10-5, Sun. noon-5, day after Labor Day-Nov. 1. Hatchery tours by appointment in May and Sept.-Oct. **Cost:** Free. **Phone:** (231) 348-0998 for the visitor center.

OKEMOS (H-4) elev. 840′

Shopping areas: Meridian Mall, 1982 W. Grand River Ave., features several dozen stores along with mall anchors JCPenney, Macy's and Younkers.

NOKOMIS LEARNING CENTER is at 5153 Marsh Rd., just n. of jct. SR 43 (Grand River Ave.). Various rotating exhibits present the history, art and culture of the Ottawa, Potawatomi and Ojibway, separate Native American groups who spoke similar dialects and held many common beliefs.

Artifacts and contemporary Native American artwork are displayed. Regular events enhance the appeal of the center, which is in a parklike setting. **Time:** Allow 30 minutes minimum. **Hours:** Mon., Wed. and Fri. 10-5. Closed major holidays. **Cost:** Donations. **Phone:** (517) 349-5777. 🅰

ONSTED (I-4) pop. 813, elev. 1,010'

SAVE **MYSTERY HILL** is at 7611 US 12 opposite Walter J. Hayes State Park. Twenty-minute guided tours are offered through exhibits that seem to defy the laws of gravity, such as water running uphill. A 19-hole miniature golf course is offered for an extra fee. **Hours:** Tues.-Sun. 11-4 (also Fri.-Sun. 4-7), Mother's Day-Labor Day. Phone ahead to confirm schedule. **Cost:** Tour $8; $7 (children). **Phone:** (517) 467-2517.

ONTONAGON (A-2) pop. 1,769, elev. 605'

Named "Place of the Bowl" by Native Americans due to the shape of the river's mouth, Ontonagon was visited frequently from the 1600s to the mid-1800s by voyageurs and Jesuits. All who came took note of a huge copper boulder that measured 50 inches by 41 inches. Native Americans believed the boulder to be the mediator between them and the Great Spirit. Publication of the discovery of copper led to an influx of prospectors and settlers on Lake Superior. Within the county that shares Ontonagon's name are 45 waterfalls. *See Upper Peninsula p. 114.*

Ontonagon County Chamber of Commerce: 424 River St., P.O. Box 266, Ontonagon, MI 49953. **Phone:** (906) 884-4735.

ONTONAGON COUNTY HISTORICAL MUSEUM is at 422 River St. Artifacts reflect the history of the county. Exhibits include photographs, Finnish items, logging and mining equipment and a replica of the Ontonagon copper boulder, which was recorded in 1843 as weighing 3,708 pounds. A lighthouse also is on the grounds.

Guided tours of the museum are available. **Hours:** Museum Mon.-Fri. 10-5, Sat. 10-4. Tours of the lighthouse are given Mon.-Sat. at 11, 1:30 and 3:30, Memorial Day weekend-Labor Day. **Cost:** Museum $3; free (ages 0-17). Lighthouse $5; free (ages 0-17). **Phone:** (906) 884-6165.

PORCUPINE MOUNTAINS WILDERNESS STATE PARK is at 33303 Headquarters Rd. The 60,000-acre park is popular for camping, skiing and backpacking; natural history programs are offered. Lake of the Clouds Scenic Overlook, on an escarpment above the lake at the western end of SR 107, offers an excellent view. Panoramas also can be enjoyed from Summit Peak. A .75-mile boardwalk along Presque Isle River passes several waterfalls. Interpretive programs are available in summer; phone ahead for schedule. More than 28 miles of hiking and cross-country skiing trails run throughout the park. *See Recreation Chart and the AAA Great Lakes CampBook.*

Hours: Park open daily 24 hours. Visitor center open daily 10-8, late May to mid-Oct. **Cost:** Park entry fee $10 (per private in-state vehicle; Recreation Passport, valid for 1 year, allows entry into Michigan state parks); $8 (per private out-of-state vehicle). **Phone:** (906) 885-5275. 🅰 🅧

OSCODA (E-5) pop. 992

Oscoda is a resort community, offering access to the Huron-Manistee National Forests *(see place listing p. 81).*

Fishing and canoeing on the Au Sable River are especially popular. Winter brings cross-country skiing and snowmobiling opportunities. The town also is a major sport fishing center for Lake Huron, with chinook salmon and lake and brown trout the main catches.

Oscoda-Au Sable Chamber of Commerce: 4440 N. US 23, Oscoda, MI 48750. **Phone:** (989) 739-7322 or (800) 235-4625.

AU SABLE RIVER QUEEN departs Foote Dam, 7 mi. w. to 1775 W. River Rd. on the Au Sable River. The 19-mile, round-trip cruise, which provides a narrative about historic and scenic points of interest, lasts approximately 2 hours. The *Au Sable River Queen of Oscoda* features a cocktail bar and glass-enclosed decks.

Hours: Trips depart daily at noon and 3, Memorial Day weekend and late June-Aug.; at 1, day after Memorial Day-late June and in Sept. Fall color tours Mon.-Fri. at noon and 3, Sat.-Sun. at 10:30, 1 and 4, late Sept. to mid-Oct. (weather permitting). **Cost:** Tour fare $14; $10 (ages 61+); $6 (ages 5-12). Fall color tour fare $14; $10 (ages 61+ Mon.-Thurs.); $6 (ages 5-12). Reservations are required for fall color tours and recommended for regular tours. **Phone:** (989) 739-7351, (989) 728-3131 or (989) 728-6558.

OSSINEKE (E-5) pop. 1,059, elev. 604'

At the mouth of the Devil River and the site of a Native American village in 1839, Ossineke was named for a native word, *wawsineke,* meaning "image stones," which referred to a prominent landmark. The pair of boulders were thought to encase the spirit of Chief Shinggabaw, who had promised to return there after death.

When a rival tribe removed the sacred stones during a raid, the waters of Thunder Bay are said to have destroyed the raiders and returned the stones to their original site at the village. An angler later used the boulders to anchor fishing nets; the stones now repose at the bottom of Lake Huron.

DINOSAUR GARDENS PREHISTORICAL ZOO Allow 1 hour minimum. **Hours:** Daily 9-6, Memorial Day weekend-Labor Day; daily 9-4, mid-May through day before Memorial Day weekend; Sat.-Sun. 9-4, day after Labor Day-Sept. 30. **Cost:** $5; $4 (ages 6-11); $3 (ages 0-5). Miniature golf additional $4; $3 (ages 6-11); $2 (ages 0-5). **Phone:** (989) 471-5477 or (877) 823-2408.

OTTAWA NATIONAL FOREST

Elevations in the forest range from 602 ft. at Lake Superior, Black River Harbor to 1,826 ft. at Wolfe Mountain. Refer to AAA maps for additional elevation information.

In the Upper Peninsula, the 986,518 acres of the Ottawa National Forest are intermingled with approximately 606,300 acres of state, county and privately owned land. Included are Lake Gogebic State Park *(see Recreation Chart and the AAA Great Lakes CampBook)* near Marenisco and Sylvania Wilderness and Sturgeon Gorge Wilderness.

In excess of 50,000 acres in the forest remain as a federally designated wilderness, with pristine lakes and old growth trees. More than 35 waterfalls within the forest are accessible by woodland trails. Those falls that can be reached by road include Potawatomi Conglomerate, Gorge, Sandstone and Rainbow on the Black River north of US 2 on CR 513

north of Ironwood and Bessemer; the Agate Falls observation deck west on SR 28 near Trout Creek; and Bond Falls via Bond Falls Road.

More than 500 named lakes and more than 2,000 miles of rivers and streams yield varieties of panfish and trout. Fishing for coho salmon and rainbow trout is good on Lake Superior. Hunting for deer, bears and small game is permitted. Snowmobiling, snowshoeing, cross-country skiing and ice fishing are popular winter sports.

The J.W. Toumey Forest Nursery in Watersmeet supplies seed and tree stock to Great Lakes state forests; guided and self-guiding tours are offered on request; phone (906) 358-4523. The Ottawa National Forest Visitor Center, junction US 2 and US 45 in Watersmeet, has exhibits, an interpretive trail, audiovisual programs and scheduled naturalist-conducted activities. The visitor center is open daily 9-5 (also Thurs. 5-8), late May-Labor Day; Mon.-Sat. 9-5, rest of year. Admission free. Phone (906) 358-4724.

For further information contact the Forest Supervisor, Ottawa National Forest, E6248 US 2, Ironwood, MI 49938; phone (906) 932-1330 or TTY (906) 932-0301. *See Recreation Chart and the AAA Great Lakes CampBook.*

OWOSSO (H-4) pop. 15,713, elev. 728'

Shiawassee County Convention & Visitors Bureau: 215 N. Water St., Owosso, MI 48867. **Phone:** (989) 723-1199.

Self-guiding tours: A self guiding walking/driving tour brochure of many historic sites, including homes of architectural and historical interest, is available at the convention and visitors bureau and at Curwood Castle.

CURWOOD CASTLE is at 224 Curwood Castle Dr. at jct. Main St. Built in 1922, this castle was the writing studio of author James Oliver Curwood. His stories are mainly adventure tales set in the Canadian North, reflecting his interest in nature, and many of the novels were made into films. Historical documents and photographs are among the artifacts representing his writing, film and conservation pursuits. **Time:** Allow 30 minutes minimum. **Hours:** Tues.-Sun. 1-5, Feb.-Dec. Closed major holidays. **Cost:** $2; $1 (ages 0-11). **Phone:** (989) 725-0597.

STEAM RAILROADING INSTITUTE'S VISITOR CENTER & MUSEUM is at 405 S. Washington St., just n. of Corunna Ave. Tours, videos, model railroad exhibits and steam railroad memorabilia contribute to the visitor's experience. The visitor center is home to the Pere Marquette 1225 steam locomotive, prototype for the animated film "The Polar Express," and a collection of rolling stock and cabooses.

Time: Allow 30 minutes minimum. **Hours:** Wed.-Sun. 10-5, Memorial Day-Labor Day; Fri.-Sun. 10-4, rest of year. Phone ahead to confirm schedule. **Cost:** Museum $5. **Phone:** (989) 725-9464.

PARADISE (B-5) pop. 4,191, elev. 623'

The town's name is derived from a conversation between two of Paradise's pioneer developers who were commenting about the area's natural beauty. "This is a regular paradise," one said, and the name stuck. Snowmobilers and cross-country skiers enjoy the recreational facilities provided by the state and national forests that surround the village. *See Upper Peninsula p. 114.*

GREAT LAKES SHIPWRECK MUSEUM is at 18335 N. Whitefish Point Rd. Artifacts and pictures chronicle Great Lakes shipping disasters. A memorial to the *Edmund Fitzgerald* features the ship's bell, and the Shipwreck Theater offers a short videotape presentation about the *Edmund Fitzgerald.* Visitors also can tour the Lifesaving Surfboat House, which profiles the late 19th- and early 20th-century U.S. Lifesaving Service, the organization that became the Coast Guard. Equipment and a replica of a boat can be seen. A boardwalk extends to Lake Superior.

Hours: Daily 10-6, May-Oct. **Cost:** (includes Whitefish Point Light Station) $12; $8 (ages 6-17); $32 (family, two adults and two or more children ages 0-16). **Phone:** (888) 492-3747.

Whitefish Point Light Station is at the Great Lakes Shipwreck Museum at jct. SR 123 and Whitefish Point Rd. The restored light station began operation in 1849 and is the oldest working lighthouse on Lake Superior. Overlooking the graveyard of the Great Lakes, it marks the critical turning point for all ships leaving and entering Lake Superior. Visitors can tour the restored 1861 lighthouse keeper's quarters; it houses artifacts and period furnishings. Exhibits detail the stories of the former keepers and their families.

Tours: Guided tours are available. **Hours:** Daily 10-6, May-Oct. **Cost:** (includes Great Lakes Shipwreck Museum) $13; $9 (ages 6-17); $35 (family, two adults and two or more children ages 0-16). **Phone:** (888) 492-3747.

TAHQUAMENON FALLS STATE PARK is 12 mi. w. on SR 123. The 46,000-acre park includes two waterfalls on the Tahquamenon River. The Upper Falls are nearly 50 feet high and 200 feet wide at the crest. The Lower Falls, divided by an island, are a series of rapids and cascades. The park offers a variety of recreational opportunities. *See Recreation Chart.* **Hours:** Daily 8 a.m.-10 p.m. **Cost:** Park entry fee $10 (per private in-state vehicle; Recreation Passport, valid for 1 year, allows entry into Michigan state parks); $8 (per private out-of-state vehicle). **Phone:** (906) 492-3415.

PAW PAW (I-2) pop. 3,363, elev. 739'

WINERIES

- **St. Julian Winery** is off I-94 exit 60 at 716 S. Kalamazoo St. **Hours:** Tours are given Mon.-Sat. on the half-hour 10-noon and 1-4, Sun. 12:30-4. Tastings Mon.-Sat. 9-6 (also Fri.-Sat. 6-7 p.m.), Sun. noon-6. Closed Jan. 1, Easter, Thanksgiving and Dec. 25. **Phone:** (269) 657-5568.

- **Warner Vineyards** is off I-94 exit 60 at 706 S. Kalamazoo St. **Hours:** Mon.-Sat. 10-5, Sun. noon-5. Closed major holidays. **Phone:** (800) 756-5357.

PELKIE (A-2)

HANKA FINNISH HOMESTEAD MUSEUM is 7 mi. w. of US 41 on Arnheim Rd., following signs. The century-old Finnish farming homestead is restored to its 1920s appearance and includes a number of outbuildings. **Tours:** Guided tours are available. **Time:** Allow 1 hour minimum. **Hours:** Tues., Thurs., Sat.-Sun. and holidays noon-4 and by appointment, Memorial Day-Labor Day. **Cost:** $3; $1.50 (ages 5-12). **Phone:** (906) 353-6239.

PESHAWBESTOWN (E-2) elev. 610'

GAMBLING ESTABLISHMENTS

- **Leelanau Sands Casino & Lodge** is at 2521 N.W. Bayshore Dr. **Hours:** Fri.-Sat. 8 a.m.-4 a.m., Sun.-Thurs. 8 a.m.-2 a.m. **Phone:** (231) 534-8100 or (800) 922-2946.

PETOSKEY (D-3) pop. 6,080, elev. 636'

Petoskey is a resort center on Little Traverse Bay. On the bottom of the bay at a depth of 34 feet, an 11-foot figure of Christ serves as the Skin Divers' Shrine. Rock hounds crowd the Petoskey State Park *(see Recreation Chart)* and Magnus Park in spring, sorting through winter's debris for Petoskey stones. The remains of an extinct coral that inhabited the shallow waters of 350 million years ago, the stones were designated Michigan's state stone in 1965.

Fishing in Little Traverse Bay and area rivers and lakes yields bass, blue gill, lake and rainbow trout, perch, salmon and walleye. A number of scenic drives can be enjoyed in the other seasons: The lakeshore routes along US 31 west through Charlevoix then south to Traverse City *(see place listing p. 112)* and SR 119 north through Harbor Springs *(see place listing p. 78)* to Cross Village are particularly enjoyable. Closer to town, US 131 and Walloon Lake Drive provide a pleasant loop.

Petoskey Area Visitors Center: 401 E. Mitchell St., Petoskey, MI 49770. **Phone:** (231) 348-2755 or (800) 845-2828. *(see ad p. 102)*

Shopping areas: The Gaslight Shopping District along Lake, Howard and Bay streets offers more than 60 shops. Shopping also is available in the Village at Bay Harbor.

LITTLE TRAVERSE HISTORY MUSEUM is on the waterfront at Bayfront Park. Housed in an 1892 railroad depot, the museum features exhibits from the area's Odawa Indian, pioneer and Victorian past as well as exhibits about Ernest Hemingway, Civil War author Bruce Catton and the area's lumber and resort industries. **Time:** Allow 30 minutes minimum. **Hours:** Mon.-Fri. 10-4, Sat. 1-4, Memorial Day to mid-Oct.; by appointment rest of year. **Cost:** $2.50; $1 (ages 5-17). **Phone:** (231) 347-2620.

PICTURED ROCKS NATIONAL LAKESHORE (A-4)

Pictured Rocks National Lakeshore extends 40 miles along Lake Superior from Grand Marais to Munising *(see place listing p. 96)*. The Pictured Rocks cliffs rise to 200 feet above the lake, a spectacular example of the erosive action of waves, wind and ice. The Grand Sable Dunes expose part of a glacial deposit up to 200 feet high. Five square miles of dunes that once edged an ancient predecessor of Lake Superior top the banks by another 100 feet. The area includes Beaver Basin Wilderness, an 11,740-acre area recently granted protection from development when President Obama signed the Omnibus Public Land Management Act of 2009.

Lake Superior and the many inland lakes and streams harbor a variety of fish. Fishing is excellent in spring and fall; a Michigan license is required. Summer months offer swimming, hiking, picnicking, backpacking and a scenic boat ride along the Pictured Rocks.

Twenty-one miles of cross-country ski trails, abundant off-trail skiing and a yearly snowfall approaching 200 inches accommodate winter sports enthusiasts. Snowshoeing and ice fishing are popular activities.

Park rangers conduct campfire programs and guided walks in summer. Drive-in camping areas are at Hurricane River, Little Beaver Lake and Twelvemile Beach; roads to these areas are closed by snow from November through April. Backcountry, hike-in permits are required. Advance reservations are accepted; the fee is $15. Upon arrival, the additional user fee is $5 per person, per night. The fee for drive-in camping is $14-$16 per night and is on a first-come, first-served basis. Phone (906) 387-3700.

The Hiawatha National Forest/Pictured Rocks National Lakeshore Visitor Information Center, SR 28 and CR-H58 in Munising, is open daily 8-6, mid-June to mid-Sept.; Mon.-Sat. 9-4:30, rest of year; phone (906) 387-3700. The Munising Falls Interpretive Center at the beginning of Sand Point Road is not staffed but is open daily, Fri. before Memorial Day-Labor Day; phone (906) 387-4310. The Grand Sable Visitor Center, on CR-H58 1 mile west of Grand Marais, is open daily 9-5, Memorial Day-Labor Day; Sat.-Sun. 9-5, May 1-day before Memorial Day and day after Labor Day-Oct. 31. Phone (906) 494-2660. The Au Sable Maritime Museum in Grand Marais offers maps of the area and staff

members can provide information about the area, including about hiking trails. The center is open Wed.-Sun. 11-5, Memorial Day-Labor Day.

Park headquarters on Sand Point Road near Munising is open Mon.-Fri. 8-4:30. The park is open daily 24 hours. For more information contact Pictured Rocks National Lakeshore, P.O. Box 40, Munising, MI 49862; phone (906) 387-3700. *See Upper Peninsula p. 114 and the Recreation Chart.*

AU SABLE LIGHT STATION is about 12 mi. w. of Grand Marais; tours begin from the east porch of the lighthouse, which is on Au Sable Point in Pictured Rocks National Lakeshore. Tours of the 87-foot structure, which was built 1873-74, last 30-40 minutes. The keeper's quarters have been restored, and restoration work is under way on the assistant keeper's quarters. The light has been automatic since 1958.

Visitors must walk 1.5 miles on a wooded footpath to reach the light station. Au Sable Maritime Museum, an information center, is on the grounds. **Time:** Allow 1 hour minimum. **Hours:** Tours are offered Wed.-Sun. and holidays 11-5, Memorial Day-Labor Day. Tour schedule may vary based on volunteer availability and road conditions; phone ahead to confirm. **Cost:** $3; free (ages 0-5). Cash only. Reservations are recommended. **Phone:** (906) 387-3700.

PICTURED ROCKS begins 5 mi. n.e. of Munising within Pictured Rocks National Lakeshore. These cliffs, from Longfellow's "The Song of Hiawatha," are notable for their rich color and interesting formations. Except for Miners Castle, they are accessible only by boat or on foot. Pictured Rocks Cruises offers 2.5-hour tours of the formations leaving from Munising *(See Upper Peninsula p. 114 and Recreation Chart).* **Hours:** Park daily 24 hours. Boat tour schedule varies throughout the season. **Cost:** A fee is charged for boat tours. **Phone:** (906) 387-3700.

PINCONNING (F-4) pop. 1,386, elev. 596'

Once an important railhead during the lumber era, Pinconning serves the surrounding agricultural and dairy region and is known as the cheese capital of Michigan. It also is known for perch and walleye fishing on Saginaw Bay.

Pinconning Area Chamber of Commerce: P.O. Box 856, Pinconning, MI 48650. **Phone:** (989) 879-2816.

WOODLAND ADVENTURE AMUSEMENT PARK is 3 mi. s on SR 13 at 2346 N. Huron Rd. Storybook characters are the focus of the park, which includes a playground. There are some 40 animals representing 16 different species on-site. Other amusements are train, antique car and safari rides; a moon walk; miniature golf; a Ferris wheel and a carousel. Additional activities are offered during the Halloween and Christmas seasons.

Time: Allow 1 hour minimum. **Hours:** Daily 10-7, May-Sept.; phone ahead for schedule in Oct. and Dec. **Cost:** $8; free (ages 0-1). **Phone:** (989) 879-2849. 🍴 🎡

PLYMOUTH—*see Detroit p. 64.*

PONTIAC—*see Detroit p. 64.*

PORTAGE (I-2) pop. 44,897, elev. 879'

AIR ZOO is off I-94 exit 78, then 1 mi. s. to 6151 Portage Rd. This attraction showcases the history of aviation, immersing visitors in the world of flight with indoor amusement park-style rides, a 4-D theater, full-motion flight simulators and a 3-D ride depicting a space shuttle mission to the International Space Station.

The Air Zoo features rare and historic aircraft, many of which flew during World War II. Other aircraft on display include an F-14 Tomcat, the kind portrayed in the film "Top Gun," and an SR-71 Blackbird spy plane, which is still unmatched in speed and altitude. Exhibits and thousands of artifacts can be seen. "Century of Flight" holds the Guinness World Record for the largest hand-painted indoor mural.

Hours: Mon.-Sat. 9-5, Sun. noon-5. Closed Thanksgiving and Dec. 24-25. **Cost:** Museum free. Ride ticket (unlimited rides on amusement park-style attractions) $12.95. Other ticket options are available. **Phone:** (269) 382-6555 or (866) 524-7966. *(see ad p. 85)* 🍴

PORT HURON (H-6) pop. 32,338, elev. 596'

Linked by the Blue Water International Bridge with Sarnia, Ontario, at the point where Lake Huron empties into the St. Clair River, Port Huron is the center of the St. Clair River manufacturing district. It is one of the oldest settlements in the state, dating from 1686 when the French built Fort St. Joseph to guard against possible British incursions into their fur trade. The first permanent colony, however, was not established until 1790.

The fact that Thomas Edison spent his youth in Port Huron seems to reflect the city's proclivity for electrical pioneering. One of the earliest electrical utilities was formed in 1844. The 1891 railway tunnel, built beneath the St. Clair River, is considered to have been the first electrified underwater tunnel.

Some of Port Huron's popular parks are Lakeside Park, with opportunities for swimming and picnicking, and Lighthouse Park, which surrounds Fort Gratiot Lighthouse, one of the oldest working lighthouses on the Great Lakes. Contact the Port Huron Museum *(see attraction listing)*, (810) 982-0891, for tour availability. Another popular spot is Pine Grove Park, where the *Huron (see attraction listing),* the last commissioned lightship, is docked.

Blue Water Area Convention and Visitors Bureau: 520 Thomas Edison Pkwy., Port Huron, MI 48060. **Phone:** (810) 987-8687 or (800) 852-4242.

Shopping areas: The historic downtown district offers specialty shops, restaurants and art galleries. Port Huron Factory Outlet Center, west on Range Road at I-94 exit 269 in nearby Kimball, offers factory outlet shops. Birchwood Mall, north on SR 25 at Keewahdin Road in nearby Fort Gratiot, features 70 specialty stores as well as JCPenney, Macy's, Sears and Younkers. Discounts are offered to international travelers on merchandise at Duty Free Americas at 2425 Pine Grove Ave.

PORT HURON MUSEUM occupies four sites within a 3-mile area along the St. Clair River. CGC *Bramble* Museum, *Huron* Lightship Museum, Main Museum and Thomas Edison Depot Museum are included (*see attraction listings*). Allow 45-60 minutes minimum at each site. **Time:** Allow 30 minutes minimum. **Hours:** Schedules vary per location. Closed major holidays. **Cost:** Per site $7; $5 (ages 60+ and students with ID); free (ages 0-4). Combination ticket to all 4 sites $15; $12 (ages 60+); $10 (students with ID); free (ages 0-4). **Phone:** (810) 982-0891.

CGC *Bramble* Museum is moored at the Seaway Terminal dock on the St. Clair River at 2336 Military St. Now part of the Port Huron Museum, the *Bramble* was commissioned in 1944 and participated in atomic testing at Bikini Island. It was one of the first vessels to circumnavigate the North American continent. The cutter served on the Great Lakes for nearly 30 years before its retirement in 2003.

Time: Allow 30 minutes minimum. **Hours:** Daily 11-5, Memorial Day-Labor Day; Thurs.-Mon. 11-5, Apr. 1-day before Memorial Day and day after Labor Day-Dec. 1. Closed major holidays. **Cost:** $7; $5 (ages 60+ and students with ID); free (ages 0-4). Combination ticket with *Huron* Lightship Museum, Main Museum, and Thomas Edison Depot Museum $15; $12 (ages 60+); $10 (students with ID); free (ages 0-4). **Phone:** (810) 982-0891.

***Huron* Lightship Museum** is in Pine Grove Park at jct. Prospect Pl. and Thomas Edison Pkwy. The vessel was built in 1920 and decommissioned in 1970; at that time the lightship was the last one on the Great Lakes. It is now part of the Port Huron Museum. **Time:** Allow 30 minutes minimum. **Hours:** Daily 11-5, Memorial Day-Labor Day; Thurs.-Mon. 11-5, Apr. 1-day before Memorial Day and day after Labor Day-Dec. 1. Closed major holidays.

Cost: $7; $5 (ages 60+ and students with ID); free (ages 0-4). Combination ticket with CGC *Bramble* Museum, Main Museum, and Thomas Edison Depot Museum $15; $12 (ages 60+); $10 (students with ID); free (ages 0-4). **Phone:** (810) 982-0891.

Main Museum is at 1115 Sixth St. between Wall and Court sts. This museum is housed in the former Port Huron Public Library, which was donated to the city by philanthropist Andrew Carnegie in 1904. The building features a columned rotunda and a glass floor on the mezzanine. Displays include local artifacts, art, prehistoric woolly mammoth bones,

marine items, musical instruments and a Victorian parlor. The Frank Crevier Pilot House offers visitors a turn-of-the-century look at a ship's pilot house and cabin as well as the views seen by crew maneuvering into Lake Huron. A restored 1850s log house also is on the grounds. The site is part of the Port Huron Museum.

Time: Allow 30 minutes minimum. **Hours:** Daily 11-5. Closed major holidays. **Cost:** $7; $5 (ages 60+ and students with ID); free (ages 0-4). Combination ticket with CGC *Bramble* Museum, *Huron* Lightship Museum, and Thomas Edison Depot Museum $15; $12 (ages 60+); $10 (students with ID); free (ages 0-4). **Phone:** (810) 982-0891.

Thomas Edison Depot Museum is at 510 Edison Pkwy. under the Blue Water Bridge. Housed in the Fort Gratiot Railroad Station where Thomas Edison worked, the museum features re-created period displays, hands-on activities that focus on his inventions and a vintage baggage car that contains a mock-up of Edison's first laboratory. A videotape presentation also is offered. The museum is now part of the Port Huron Museum.

Time: Allow 30 minutes minimum. **Hours:** Daily 11-5, Memorial Day-Labor Day; Thurs.-Mon. 11-5, Mar. 1-day before Memorial Day and day after Labor Day-Dec. 1; Sat.-Sun. 11-5, rest of year. Closed major holidays. **Cost:** $7; $5 (ages 60+ and students with ID); free (ages 0-4). Combination ticket with CGC *Bramble* Museum, *Huron* Lightship Museum, and Main Museum $15; $12 (ages 60+); $10 (students with ID); free (ages 0-4). **Phone:** (810) 982-0891.

PORT SANILAC (G-6) pop. 658

Until 1857 when Port Sanilac was allegedly renamed for a well-known Wyandotte Indian chief, this locale was called Bark Shanty Point, a name stoutly defended in one issue of the village's newspaper, the *Bark Shanty Times.*

No editors, reporters, printers or editorial policies complicated the production of the paper, which was known throughout the region. Everyone who came through the general store/post office simply wrote news or commentary on a sheet of newsprint paper kept on the counter. Once thoroughly perused, the edition was bound and filed, and a new one was begun.

SANILAC COUNTY HISTORIC VILLAGE AND MUSEUM is at 228 S. Ridge St. (SR 25). The Victorian 1875 Loop-Harrison House contains original furnishings. Displays include medical instruments, antique glassware and marine, military and Native American artifacts.

On the village grounds are a dairy museum, two 19th-century log cabins, a 1920s-era lakefront cabin, a one-room schoolhouse, historic train depot, carriage barn and a general store. The carriage barn contains exhibits. A monthly concert series takes place in the village's church. Guided tours of the mansion and village are available. **Time:** Allow 1 hour minimum. **Hours:** Wed.-Fri. 11-4, Sat.-Sun. noon-4, mid-June through Labor Day. **Cost:** Fee for either mansion or village tour $5; $4 (ages 62+); $2 (ages 6-12). **Phone:** (810) 622-9946.

PRESQUE ISLE (D-5) pop. 1,691

Presque Isle, on the eastern shore of Grand Lake, is a supply center for the surrounding resort area. Three miles north is Presque Isle Harbor, an active lumber port in the mid-1800s, with a full marina facility.

OLD PRESQUE ISLE LIGHTHOUSE PARK AND MUSEUM stands on the northern arm of land enclosing the harbor. Built in 1840, the lighthouse was replaced in 1870 by the current lighthouse a mile north on the tip of the peninsula. The tower and 1905 keeper's house are restored in the new lighthouse. A 3,425-pound bronze bell, larger than the Liberty Bell, is displayed in the old lighthouse. Both lighthouses offer exhibits.

Time: Allow 30 minutes minimum. **Hours:** Old and new lighthouses open daily 9-6, mid-May to mid-Oct. Keeper's house open Tues.-Sat. 11-5, Sun. 1-5, Memorial Day-Labor Day. Phone ahead to confirm schedule. **Cost:** Old lighthouse $2.50; $1 (ages 6-12). Fee to climb new lighthouse tower $2.50; $2 (children). Keeper's house by donations. Phone ahead to verify prices. **Phone:** (989) 595-9917 for new lighthouse, (989) 595-5419 for general information, or (989) 595-6979 for old lighthouse.

ROCHESTER—*see Detroit p. 65.*

ROCKLAND (B-2) pop. 324, elev. 1,093'

OLD VICTORIA, 4 mi. s.w. on a paved road near the Victoria dam, is a partially restored late 19th-century company town. Mines opened 1847-49 and operated until 1921. Guided tours include a house tour, where three houses, a sauna and barn can be seen; a ruins walk which explores the ruins of the mining town of Victoria; and a tour of a cabin, now the visitor center, which includes displays, pictures and books showcasing mining days.

Hiking trails are on the grounds. Comfortable walking shoes are recommended. **Hours:** Daily 11-5, Memorial Day weekend-early Oct. **Cost:** House tour $5; $2 (ages 6-12). **Phone:** (906) 886-2617. 🅰

ROGERS CITY (D-5) pop. 3,322, elev. 655'

Rogers City's principal industry is readily apparent: Possibly the world's largest open limestone quarry—more than 3 miles long and nearly 2 miles across at its widest point—extends southeastward from the city limits. The quarry has been worked continuously since 1912. Operations can be seen from the rim of the pit at Quarry View, on Petersville Road (US 23 Business Route). The viewing area is always open, but most activity begins in the afternoon and continues into the evening. The docking and loading of the huge freighters are visible

from Harbor View, a fenced area a half-mile past the plant gate, which is accessed via Calcite Road. The site is closed in winter but otherwise is open in the morning and throughout the day until around 10 p.m.

Established during the 1870s lumber boom, Rogers City remains the largest community in Presque Isle County. Recreational opportunities abound year-round for those interested in ATV trails, biking, boating, camping, canoeing, fishing, hiking, hunting, kayaking, skiing, snowboarding and swimming. P.H. Hoeft State Park *(see Recreation Chart and the AAA Great Lakes CampBook)* is 6 miles northwest on US 23 and includes a section of Huron dunes. Ocqueoc Falls, the largest falls in the Lower Peninsula, is 12 miles west of Rogers City off SR 68. A 7-mile self-guiding trail originates there.

Rogers City Area Chamber of Commerce: 292 S. Bradley Hwy., P.O. Box 55, Rogers City, MI 49779. **Phone:** (989) 734-2535 or (800) 622-4148.

GREAT LAKES LORE MARITIME MUSEUM, 367 N. 3rd St., honors those who served the Great Lakes and remembers those who lost their lives. Four centuries of history are chronicled through exhibits, models and artifacts. A memorial hall pays tribute to the crews of the last four ships lost in the Great Lakes: *Carl D. Bradley,* SS *Cedarville, Daniel J. Morrell* and *Edmund Fitzgerald.* The museum also houses a maritime library.

Tours: Guided tours are available. **Time:** Allow 45 minutes minimum. **Hours:** Daily 11-4, May 1-early Dec.; Mon. 11-4, rest of year. **Cost:** $3; free (ages 0-17). **Phone:** (989) 734-0706.

PRESQUE ISLE COUNTY HISTORICAL MUSEUM is at 176 W. Michigan Ave. Exhibits about maritime and local history are in the restored Bradley House. Three floors are furnished in the style of the 1920s, while others re-create a general store and a Victorian sitting room. Displays include Native American artifacts as well as carpentry, farming, household and lumber-related items. **Hours:** Tues.-Sat. noon-4, May-Sept. Also open select dates late Nov. to mid-Dec. for Christmas at the Bradley House; phone for schedule. **Cost:** Donations. **Phone:** (989) 734-4121.

ROSCOMMON (E-4) pop. 1,133, elev. 1,123'

A resort area and starting point for canoe trips down the Au Sable River, Roscommon is near both North Higgins Lake and South Higgins Lake state parks *(see Recreation Chart and the AAA Great Lakes CampBook).*

CIVILIAN CONSERVATION CORPS MUSEUM is across the street from the main entrance to North Higgins Lake State Park. Housed in replica barracks, the museum showcases the accomplishments of the men who helped "put Americans back to work." Many photographs were donated by CCC alumni. Two original buildings used during the 1930s are on the grounds. Hiking trail maps are available for self-guiding tours.

Time: Allow 30 minutes minimum. **Hours:** Daily 10-4, Memorial Day-Labor Day. **Cost:** Park entry fee $10 (per private in-state vehicle; Recreation Passport, valid for 1 year, allows entry into Michigan state parks); $8 (per private out-of-state vehicle). Museum admission is free. **Phone:** (989) 821-6125. 🏕

MICHIGAN FIREMEN'S MEMORIAL is 2.5 mi. s. on CR 18, then .5 mi. e. on Robinson Lake Rd. The 12-foot bronze statue was created by Detroit's Edward Chesney. **Hours:** Daily 8-6, May-Nov. **Cost:** Free. **Phone:** (810) 635-9513 or (989) 275-5880.

ROYAL OAK—see Detroit p. 65.

SAGINAW (G-5) pop. 61,799, elev. 592'

When the Saginaw Valley was shorn of its pine forests, the once busy lumber center of Saginaw turned to the processing and shipping of shorter crops such as beans and sugar beets. Tourism contributes heavily to the economy.

The city's Celebration Square is home to attractions and parks, including the Lucille E. Andersen Memorial Garden, 120 Ezra Rust Drive, which adorns the top of the city's 20-million-gallon underground reservoir; phone (989) 759-1362.

Saginaw Valley Convention and Visitors Bureau: 515 N. Washington Ave., 3rd Floor, Saginaw, MI 48607. **Phone:** (989) 752-7164 or (800) 444-9979.

THE CASTLE MUSEUM is at 500 Federal Ave. The renovated 1897 post office building was designed in French château style and sports a spiral staircase and corner towers. Permanent and changing exhibits trace the social and industrial development of the Saginaw Valley. Guided tours are available by appointment. **Time:** Allow 1 hour minimum. **Hours:** Tues.-Sat. 10-4:30, Sun. 1-4:30. Closed major holidays. **Cost:** $1; 50c (ages 5-18). **Phone:** (989) 752-2861.

CHILDREN'S ZOO AT CELEBRATION SQUARE, 1730 S. Washington Ave., features 24 exhibits, including more than 80 Adopt-a-Gardens, a walkthrough butterfly encounter, timber wolf and monkey exhibits and six warm-water penguins. Other residents include alligators, bald eagles, bobcats and kangaroos. Carousel and miniature train rides are offered.

Time: Allow 1 hour, 30 minutes minimum. **Hours:** Mon.-Fri. 10-5, Sat. 10-6, Sun. noon-5, Memorial Day-Labor Day; Mon.-Sat. 10-5, Sun. noon-5, May 1-day before Memorial Day and day after Labor Day-Sept. 30; Mon.-Sat. 10-4, Sun. noon-4, Oct.-Dec. Closed Thanksgiving and Dec. 25. **Cost:** $7; free (under 1). Carousel or train ride $2; free (under 1); $5 (all-day ride pass). **Phone:** (989) 759-1408. 🍴

JAPANESE CULTURAL CENTER AND TEA HOUSE is at the corner of Ezra Rust Dr. and S. Washington Ave. The center offers insights into Japanese culture and the ritual ceremony of tea (*chanoyu*). Saginaw's ties with Tokushima, its sister city in Japan, were the impetus for the establishment of the Friendship Garden; many of the trees, bridges and stones used in the garden came from Japan.

Time: Allow 1 hour minimum. **Hours:** Gardens and Tea House open Tues.-Sat. noon-4, Apr.-Oct. Traditional tea ceremony is given the second Sat. of the month; phone for schedule. **Cost:** Gardens free. Tea house tour $3. Full tea ceremony $8. Reservations are required for tea ceremony. **Phone:** (989) 759-1648.

◤GEM◥ **JOHNNY PANTHER QUESTS ADVENTURE TRIPS** departs from 101 Lee St. and, on occasion, other points in the Saginaw River valley. Personalized boat tours through the Shiawassee National Wildlife Refuge include narration and put visitors up close to bald eagles, beavers, deer and their natural surroundings. Hiking, dune climbing and recreational water activities can be incorporated on scenic tours. Fall color tours also are available.

Tours ranging from 3 hours to several days can be customized depending on size of party and preferred destination. A jacket is recommended for afternoon cruises. **Hours:** Daily dawn-dusk. **Cost:** $45-$100 (per person). Reservations are required. **Phone:** (810) 653-3859.

MARSHALL M. FREDERICKS SCULPTURE MUSEUM is in the Arbury Fine Arts Center at 7400 Bay Rd. (SR 84) on the Saginaw Valley State University campus. The Main Exhibit Gallery has more than 200 works, most of which are plaster original models. The Sculptor's Studio features tools, equipment and sculptures from Fredericks' Royal Oak studio. An outdoor sculpture garden includes more than 20 monumental bronze sculptures.

Two galleries are devoted to three traveling exhibitions annually. **Time:** Allow 1 hour minimum. **Hours:** Mon.-Sat. noon-5. Closed major holidays. **Cost:** Free. **Phone:** (989) 964-7125.

SAGINAW ART MUSEUM is at 1126 N. Michigan Ave. Housed in a 1904 Georgian-revival mansion and two modern wings, the museum's permanent collection numbers more than 2,500 objects covering 4,500 years. There is a children's hands-on interactive gallery. The garden is landscaped to its original Italianate design.

Regularly changing traveling exhibits also are featured. **Tours:** Guided tours are available. **Hours:** Wed.-Thurs. noon-8, Fri.-Sat. 10-5, Sun. 1-5. Last admission 30 minutes before closing. Closed major holidays. **Cost:** $5; $3 (ages 65+ and students with ID); free (ages 0-15). An additional fee may be charged for some special exhibitions. **Phone:** (989) 754-2491.

ST. IGNACE (B-5) pop. 2,678, elev. 592'

St. Ignace's strategic location on the north shore of the Straits of Mackinac was quickly recognized by explorers. The town was founded in 1671 when Father Jacques Marquette established a mission; a fortress was built shortly thereafter. In 1701 the garrison moved to Detroit and St. Ignace's military importance became a thing of the past; by 1706 the mission had been abandoned.

St. Ignace, on the Upper Peninsula, is joined to the Lower Peninsula by the 5-mile-long Mackinac Bridge, which links the town with Mackinaw City. It opened in 1957 and is one of the longest suspension spans in the world. The passenger vehicle toll is $1.75 per axle or $3.50 per car. All other vehicles are $4.50 per axle. Bicycles and snowmobiles are not permitted on the bridge, but transport services are provided. Pedestrians and drivers who prefer not to drive across the bridge may take advantage of this driver assistance program as well. Drivers are available daily 24 hours, and snowmobile transportation is available daily 8-8. A fee is charged for bicyclists ($2), pedestrians ($2) and snowmobilers ($10). To request a driver, phone (906) 643-7600 or use the phone located at the south entrance to the bridge; if you're entering from the north, a toll collector can assist. Each Labor Day morning thousands participate in the Mackinac Bridge Walk, from St. Ignace to Mackinaw City.

Ferry service to Mackinac Island is available from the downtown harbor until ice forms on Moran Bay and the Straits of Mackinac, usually in late December or early January.

Scenic US 2, heading west from St. Ignace, winds down to the sand dunes and up into the wooded hills along Lake Michigan to Escanaba *(see place listing p. 68)*. Castle Rock, 4 miles north, was an ancient lookout of the Algonquin Indians and offers a scenic view.

St. Ignace is home to what is reportedly the world's largest all-category auto show on the last Saturday in June. *See Upper Peninsula p. 114.*

St. Ignace Area Chamber of Commerce: 560 N. State St., St. Ignace, MI 49781. **Phone:** (906) 643-8717.

FATHER MARQUETTE NATIONAL MEMORIAL is .2 mi. n.w. of the bridge via US 2; exit in the Marquette unit of Straits State Park. The memorial honors Jacques Marquette, the French explorer who established the state's first European settlements at Sault Ste. Marie and St. Ignace. Interpretive trails through the 52-acre park provide panoramic views of the straits and Mackinac Bridge.

Time: Allow 1 hour minimum. **Hours:** Park open daily 9:30-5, Memorial Day-Labor Day. Hours are extended into the evening mid-June to mid-Aug.; phone for schedule. **Cost:** Memorial free. Park entry fee $10 (per private in-state vehicle; Recreation Passport, valid for 1 year, allows entry into Michigan state parks); $8 (per private out-of-state vehicle). **Phone:** (906) 643-8620 for Straits State Park, or (800) 827-7007 for general information. 🅿️

FORT DE BUADE INDIAN MUSEUM, 334 N. State St., houses displays and dioramas depicting the lives of the area's early inhabitants. Local beadwork, stonework and weapons are displayed. **Hours:** Daily 9-9, Memorial Day weekend-Oct. 1. **Cost:** Free. **Phone:** (906) 643-6622.

SAVE **MARQUETTE MISSION PARK AND MUSEUM OF OJIBWA CULTURE** is at 500 N. State St. The park is the presumed site of Father Jacques Marquette's grave. A statue, interpretive kiosk about his life and a garden are on the grounds. The museum, in a restored 19th-century Jesuit church, is dedicated to the Ojibwa—the original inhabitants of the upper Great Lakes region. Displays include artifacts, some dating from 6000 B.C., and reproductions. The site has yielded important archeological finds—most dating back to the Huron, Ottawa and French settlements of the late 1600s. A typical Ojibwa family is portrayed in an 8-minute film.

Time: Allow 30 minutes minimum. **Hours:** Daily 9-6, late June-Labor Day; 9-5, Memorial Day weekend-late June; 10-3, day after Labor Day to mid-Oct. **Cost:** $2; $1 (ages 0-11); $5 (family). **Phone:** (906) 643-9161.

MYSTERY SPOT is .5 mi. n. of US 2 at 150 Martin Lake Rd. Guided tours are given in an area where gravity seems to play tricks on people by creating optical contradictions. A maze through the woods and miniature golf also are offered.

Time: Allow 15 minutes minimum. **Hours:** Daily 8 a.m.-9 p.m., mid-June through Labor Day; 9-8, mid-May to mid-June; 9-7, day after Labor Day to mid-Oct. Phone ahead to confirm schedule. **Cost:** Mystery Spot only $7; $5 (ages 5-11). Maze additional $2. Combination ticket (includes Mystery Spot, maze and miniature golf) $9.50; $7.50 (ages 5-11). Phone ahead to verify rates. **Phone:** (906) 643-8322.

GAMBLING ESTABLISHMENTS

- **Kewadin Shores Casino & Hotel** is at 3015 Mackinac Tr. **Hours:** Daily 24 hours. **Phone:** (906) 643-7071 or (800) 539-2346.

ST. JOSEPH (I-1) pop. 8,789, elev. 591'

In 1833 Newberryport was renamed St. Joseph after the St. Joseph River bordering the peninsular city along with Lake Michigan. Originally St. Joseph grew as a stopping place for travelers between Chicago and Detroit. Today there are a variety of beaches and parks.

Silver Beach Amusement Park was in operation 1891-1971, and nearly 40 years after it was torn down, nostalgia set a project in motion to bring back three of the park's features: a boardwalk, a carousel and a dance/meeting/reception pavilion. The nearly 250-foot re-creation of the original boardwalk parallels the Lake Michigan bluff and Silver Beach County Park. Six of the carousel's hand-carved and hand-painted horses are replicas of originals. The new carousel rounding boards showcase historic area images. The Whirlpool Compass Rose Fountain, across from the carousel, is a multi-arm fountain; each arm shoots water 35 feet in the air, creating a mist that rains down from where they meet. The fountain and carousel are open daily; phone (269) 982-8500.

St. Joseph Today Welcome Center: 120 State St., St. Joseph, MI 49085. **Phone:** (269) 985-1111.

Self-guiding tours: Brochures about walking tours past several historic houses can be obtained from the welcome center.

Shopping areas: Downtown St. Joseph features nearly 60 specialty shops, including antique, fashion, home furnishing and jewelry stores.

CURIOUS KIDS' MUSEUM is at 415 Lake Blvd. Curiosity and learning is encouraged through hands-on exhibits that change often. Some exhibits come with their own costumes for young visitors to wear. Children can serve customers in their own diner, use simple machines, type their names in Braille, experiment with sound production, learn about earthquakes and volcanoes, see what space is like in an interactive shuttle, and play with bubbles and shadows.

Children can pick apples from simulated trees, follow the crop through processing and then sell apple-related products at a market stand. An international culture is profiled for one year at a time, showcasing that culture's history as well as what the everyday lives of its children are like. Curious Kids' Discovery Zone *(see attraction listing)*, a companion site, is nearby.

Time: Allow 2 hours minimum. **Hours:** Mon.-Sat. 10-5, Sun. noon-5, June 1-Labor Day; Wed.-Sat. 10-5, Sun. noon-5, rest of year. **Cost:** June 1-Labor Day $6; free (under 1). Combination ticket with Curious Kids' Discovery Zone $10; free (under 1). Admission rest of year $4; free (under 1). Combination ticket with Curious Kids' Discovery Zone $7; free (under 1). **Phone:** (269) 983-2543.

Curious Kids' Discovery Zone, 333 Broad St. at Silver Beach, just w. of the Curious Kids' Museum. This companion site to the children's museum is intended to appeal to older children and adolescents. It features water and virtual reality exhibits as well as a climbing wall. There also are exhibits about the Great Lakes, the local watershed and the science behind wave formation. Temporary exhibits are presented regularly.

Time: Allow 1 hour minimum. **Hours:** Mon.-Sat. 10-5, Sun. noon-5, June 1-Labor Day; Wed.-Sat. 10-5, Sun. noon-5, rest of year. Closed major holidays. **Cost:** June 1-Labor Day $6; free (under 1). Combination ticket with Curious Kids' Museum $10; free (under 1). Admission rest of year $4; free (under 1). Combination ticket $7; free (under 1). **Parking:** $2 per hour (June 1-Labor Day). **Phone:** (269) 983-2543.

KRASL ART CENTER is at 707 Lake Blvd. Three galleries and an outdoor sculpture collection contain folk art, traditional art and works by regional artists. Traveling exhibitions from such major museums as the Smithsonian Institution and the Detroit Institute of Arts also are included. **Time:** Allow 30 minutes minimum. **Hours:** Mon.-Sat. 10-4 (also Thurs. 4-9), Sun. 1-4. Closed major holidays. **Cost:** Donations. **Phone:** (269) 983-0271.

SILVER BEACH MUSEUM, 333 Broad St., recalls the glory days of St. Joseph's Silver Beach Amusement Park, which was a resort destination frequented in great numbers by Chicagoans in the late 19th- and early 20th centuries. Photographs showcase the appeal of this spot on Lake Michigan. The restored 1910 carousel, featuring 48 hand-carved animals and two chariots, is a highlight.

Time: Allow 1 hour minimum. **Hours:** Mon.-Sat. and holidays 10-10, Sun. noon-10. Closed Dec. 25. **Cost:** Museum by donation. One carousel token $2; three tokens $5; seven tokens $10; 15 tokens $20. **Parking:** $2 per hour. **Phone:** (269) 982-8500.

SAUGATUCK (H-1) pop. 1,065

Saugatuck is a picturesque small town overflowing with nostalgic charm thanks to sand dunes, Lake Michigan, an array of boutiques and beautiful 19th-century architecture as well as orchards in the outlying areas. A particularly scenic view awaits those who are willing to climb the 282 steps to the top of Mt. Baldhead sand dune, which hovers above Oval Beach. This 2-mile stretch of beach with sand dunes has received high rankings for its beautiful undeveloped shoreline.

Along with neighboring Douglas *(see place listing p. 67)*, Saugatuck is a popular resort area. The Kalamazoo River connects Lake Michigan to the harbor, which is the focal point of downtown. Here you can stroll along the boardwalk and find nearly 1,000 docked boats. Since the early 1900s artists have been drawn to Saugatuck and Douglas for the abundance of natural scenery, and this lakeside environment where art continues to thrive has become known as The Art Coast of Michigan. Together the two towns boast more than 35 craft, fine art, specialty and studio art galleries. Ox-bow, an art school founded in the early 20th century by artists from the Art Institute of Chicago, is still offering summer classes at its campus off Park Street; phone (269) 857-5811.

The definition of art for which the area is known is expanding beyond visual arts to also include cinematic and performing arts. If you're a film festival buff, you might want to visit in mid-June to experience the Waterfront Film Festival. Opening night begins in Cook Park with an outdoor screening at dusk. The laid-back festival continues for three days of screenings, post-screening parties, seminars, and question and answer sessions with film directors. For live summer theater, see a performance at Mason Street Warehouse, which is in the Saugatuck Center for the Arts across from Coughlin Park at 400 Culver St. at the junction of Griffith Street. The center offers concerts, theater productions and rotating exhibits in a small gallery; phone (269) 857-4898. The Red Barn, 3657 63rd St., is another destination for theater productions; phone (269) 857-5300.

Outdoor enthusiasts can take advantage of opportunities for boating, fishing, hiking, biking, horseback riding and golf. Bicycles, canoes, kayaks and mopeds can be rented downtown. In winter, nearby Saugatuck Dunes State Park offers cross-country skiing.

Just west of Water Street is the departure point for the Victorian hand-cranked chain ferry that transports pedestrians and their bicycles to the other side of the Kalamazoo River. The ferry operates daily dawn to dusk Memorial Day through Labor Day; the season may be extended in May or September, weather permitting.

Self-guiding tours: A walking tour brochure can be picked up from the information booth at Culver and Butler streets, the Saugatuck-Douglas Historical Museum, and in downtown Douglas at the convention and visitors bureau at 2902 Blue Star Hwy. The route highlights 50 sites depicting local history since the pioneer era. During July and August (except July 4), guided tours following the same route depart from the information booth Wed. and Fri.-Sun. at 2; a $5 fee is charged. Phone (269) 857-5751 for more information.

Shopping areas: Butler, Water, Culver, Hoffman, Main and Mason streets in downtown Saugatuck feature an array of specialty shops.

A farmers market is held at the Saugatuck Center for the Arts parking lot Fri. 8-2 from early June to early Oct. as well as Mon. 3-7 between early July and Aug. 30.

THE HARBOR DUCK ADVENTURES TOUR departs from Coughlin Park at jct. Culver and Griffith sts.; tours also depart from Center St. at Berry Field in Douglas. Trips are given aboard a DUKW, an amphibious vehicle from World War II, which seats 28. The route encompasses downtown Saugatuck and makes a brief stop in Douglas, where visitors may explore the area on their own. The tour guide offers information about the area, and the highlight of the trip for many is when the vehicle splashes into the water.

Tickets can be purchased at the ticket booth at 121 Griffith St. **Time:** Allow 45 minutes minimum. **Hours:** Tours depart from Saugatuck daily on the hour 10-dusk, May-Oct.; tours depart from Douglas at 15 minutes past the hour (weather permitting). Departure times may vary 15-20 minutes; phone ahead to confirm schedule. **Cost:** $16; $8 (ages 6-12); $5 (ages 3-5). **Phone:** (269) 857-3825.

SAUGATUCK-DOUGLAS HISTORICAL MUSEUM, 735 Park St. at Mt. Baldhead Park, is housed in the historic pump house next to the Kalamazoo River. Each year this small museum features a different exhibit related to local history. There also are artifacts, a brief film about the area, and large illustrated wall map depicting Saugatuck and Douglas. A computer next to the map lets visitors access further historical information. The grounds feature a nice garden with benches and interpretive signs relaying the history of the pump house and the river as well as information about local history, birds and wildlife.

Time: Allow 30 minutes minimum. **Hours:** Daily noon-4, Memorial Day-Aug. 31; Sat.-Sun. noon-4, Sept.-Oct. Closed major holidays. **Cost:** Donations. **Phone:** (269) 857-7900.

SAUGATUCK DUNE RIDES, off I-196 exit 41, then about .5 mi. s.w. on Blue Star Hwy., offers rides on open-air vehicles that seat up to 18. The guide stops periodically throughout the trip to talk about the history of the dunes and the local plants and wildlife, and at one stop visitors can get out at the top of a dune to take pictures and climb the dunes. The route also includes forested areas.

Note: The ride includes some high speeds and quick turns. **Time:** Allow 45 minutes minimum. **Hours:** Mon.-Sat. 10-7:30, Sun. noon-7:30, July-Aug.; Mon.-Sat. 10-5:30, Sun. noon-5:30, Apr.-June and in Sept. (also Fri.-Sat. of Labor Day weekend 10-7:30, Sun. 11:30-7:30); Sat.-Sun. 10-5:30, Oct. 1 to mid-Oct. Trips depart every 30 minutes. Phone ahead to confirm schedule. **Cost:** $17; $10 (ages 3-10). **Phone:** (269) 857-2253.

STAR OF SAUGATUCK **BOAT CRUISES** departs from 716 Water St. The approximately 1.5-hour tour aboard the 150-passenger stern-wheeler travels the Kalamazoo River and enters Lake Michigan (conditions permitting).

Hours: Cruises depart (weather permitting) daily at 11, 1, 3, 5 and 8, in July; daily at 11, 1, 3, 5 and 7:30, Aug. 1-day before Labor Day (11, 1, 3 and 5 on Labor Day); Sat.-Sun. at 11, 1, 3, 5 and 8:15, Mon.-Fri. at 1, 3 and 8, day after Memorial Day-June 30; Sun.-Fri. at 1 and 3, Sat. at 1, 3, 5 and 8, first Sat. in May-Fri. before Memorial Day weekend (11, 1, 3, 5 and 8, on Memorial Day weekend); Sun.-Fri. at 1 and 3, Sat. at 11, 1, 3, 5 and dusk, day after Labor Day-Sept. 30; Fri.-Mon. at 1 and 3, Oct. 1 to mid-Oct. Hours may vary. Phone ahead to confirm schedule. **Cost:** $17; $9 (ages 6-12); $5 (ages 3-5). Phone ahead to verify rates. **Phone:** (269) 857-4261.

SAULT STE. MARIE (B-6)
pop. 16,542, elev. 617'

The oldest town in the state, Sault Ste. Marie was first visited by a European about 1620 when the French *voyageur* Étienne Brulé passed through the area on his way to the Lake Superior region. The first Jesuit missionaries, Isaac Jogues and Charles Raymbault, arrived about 1641; the first mission was established in 1668 by fathers Jacques Marquette and Claude Dablon, who named the town in honor of the Virgin Mary.

The French and British competed for the profitable fur trade in the upper Great Lakes. The Treaty of Paris established the Michigan Territory as part of America, and in 1820 a treaty with the Chippewa Indians brought the area and its inhabitants under government regulation. Fort Brady was built shortly thereafter and trade increased. The first American lock was built in 1855, and later sailors and travelers began referring to the town as the Soo. Railroad and highway bridges link the city with its Canadian twin, Sault Ste. Marie, Ontario.

The rapids of the St. Marys River, which drop some 21 feet from Lake Superior to Lake Huron, are the reason for the town's greatest attraction, the Soo Locks. Four locks on the U.S. side bypass this beautiful barrier. The MacArthur and Poe locks are used for shipping, while the Sabin and Davis locks are in the process of being replaced; the Canadian lock is for pleasure craft. More than 95 million tons of freight pass through the Soo every year.

Parkland parallels the locks; in the upper park are three observation platforms and a Corps of Engineers information center. Originating at the information center, the Locks Park Historic Walkway follows the waterfront for about a mile. It links many historic attractions and four main points of interest: the Locks Overlook; Plank Alley, site of the original business district which includes the restored historic John Johnson Home and the office of the Schoolcraft County Indian Agency; Fort Brady, site of both French and American forts; and the Johnston Homestead, a preserved neighborhood. *See Upper Peninsula p. 114.*

Sault Ste. Marie Convention & Visitors Bureau: 536 Ashmun St., Sault Ste. Marie, MI 49783. **Phone:** (906) 632-3366 or (800) 647-2858.

KEMP MINERAL RESOURCES MUSEUM is on the first floor of Crawford Hall at Lake Superior State University. Named after Prof. Ernest Kemp, a geologist and founder of the earth sciences program at LSSU, the museum contains examples of minerals and ore indigenous to Sault Ste. Marie and upper Michigan and features a history of the area from its formation to the present.

Exhibits in the museum's three sections—geology, resources and society—demonstrate how mineral and energy resources are non-renewable and should be maintained and protected. Visitors are introduced to the immensity of geologic time, familiar products and their mineral origins and the positive social impacts of the extraction and use of selected regional resources.

Time: Allow 45 minutes minimum. **Hours:** Mon.-Fri. 9-4, Sat.-Sun. by appointment, May 1-Labor Day; by appointment only, rest of year. Closed major holidays. **Cost:** Donations. **Phone:** (906) 635-2267.

MUSEUM SHIP *VALLEY CAMP* is e. of the Soo Locks at 501 E. Water St. Walk-in tours of the retired Great Lakes freighter include the pilot house, captain's quarters, the Marine Museum and an aquarium. Also on board are two lifeboats recovered

from the *Edmund Fitzgerald,* a freighter that sank with all hands during a storm on Lake Superior in 1975.

Hours: Mon.-Sat. 10-5, Sun. 11-5, July-Aug.; Mon.-Sat. 10-4, Sun. 11-4, mid-May through June 30 and Sept. 1 to mid-Oct. Last admission 1 hour before closing. **Cost:** $11; $5.50 (ages 6-17). Combination ticket with Tower of History $16; $7.75 (ages 6-17). Combination ticket with River of History Museum and Tower of History $22; $10.50 (ages 6-17). **Phone:** (906) 632-3658 or (888) 744-7867.

RIVER OF HISTORY MUSEUM is at 531 Ashmun St. Galleries chronicle more than 8,000 years of St. Marys River history. The valley's development is traced from the Anishnabeg (Chippewa) Indians—the area's first settlers—through the 18th-century French fur trade to modern industrial and environmental issues. An audio system re-creates sounds of history.

Time: Allow 30 minutes minimum. **Hours:** Mon.-Sat. noon-5. Phone ahead to confirm schedule. **Cost:** $6.50; $3.25 (ages 6-17). Combination ticket with Museum Ship *Valley Camp* and Tower of History $22; $10.50 (ages 6-17). **Phone:** (906) 632-1999 or (906) 632-3658.

SOO LOCKS BOAT TOURS departs from the docks at 515 and 1157 E. Portage Ave. Two-hour narrated tours take visitors through the Soo Locks and alongside giant ships. A narrator explains the operation and the history of the locks, St. Marys Rapids, the waterfronts of the Michigan and Ontario cities of Sault Ste. Marie that face each other across the St. Marys River, Algoma Steel Plant and other sights. A sunset dinner cruise along the St. Marys River (including a locks tour) is available. A lighthouse cruise passes U.S. and Canadian lighthouses in Whitefish Bay.

Hours: Locks tours depart daily 10-4:30, June 21-Sept. 30; 10:30-3:30, mid-May through June 20 and in Oct. (Sun. schedule may vary; phone to confirm). **Cost:** Locks tour $21; $10.50 (ages 5-12). Reservations are recommended for dinner and lighthouse cruises. **Phone:** (906) 632-6301 or (800) 432-6301.

TOWER OF HISTORY is e. of Soo Locks at 326 E. Portage Ave. The 21-story structure offers a panoramic view of the locks, the St. Marys River and rapids, and the city's historical sites. The tower has artifacts and a videotaped show depicting the history of the Great Lakes and Sault Ste. Marie. The ride to the top is by elevator.

Time: Allow 30 minutes minimum. **Hours:** Mon.-Sat. 10-5, Sun. 11-5, July-Aug.; Mon.-Sat. 10-4, Sun. 11-4, mid-May through June 30 and Sept. 1 to mid-Oct. Last admission 30 minutes before closing. **Cost:** $6.50; $3.25 (ages 6-17). Combination ticket with Museum Ship *Valley Camp* $16; $7.75 (ages 6-17). Combination ticket with Museum Ship *Valley Camp* and River of History Museum

$22; $10.50 (ages 6-17). **Phone:** (906) 632-3658 or (888) 744-7867.

GAMBLING ESTABLISHMENTS

- **Kewadin Casino Hotel & Convention Center** is 7 mi. e. on Marquette St. at 2186 Shunk Rd. **Hours:** Daily 24 hours. **Phone:** (906) 632-0530.

SHELBY (G-2) pop. 1,914

Orchards and asparagus farms form a backdrop for this small western Michigan town.

SHELBY GEM FACTORY is n. of Shelby Rd. at 1330 Industrial Park Dr. Visitors can see gem-producing equipment and gems that are made on the premises. An audiovisual presentation about artificial gem making is offered. **Time:** Allow 30 minutes minimum. **Hours:** Mon.-Fri. 9-5:30, Sat. noon-4. Closed holidays and Dec. 26-Dec. 31. **Cost:** Free. **Phone:** (231) 861-2165.

SLEEPING BEAR DUNES NATIONAL LAKESHORE (E-2)

Sleeping Bear Dunes National Lakeshore lies along 35 miles of the Lower Peninsula's northwestern shore and includes the Manitou Islands. The name is derived from an Ojibway Indian legend that tells of a bear and her two cubs forced to swim across Lake Michigan to escape a forest fire. The mother reached the shore safely and climbed to the top of a dune to await the cubs, who lagged behind and never arrived. She still maintains her vigil in the form of a dark hill of sand atop a plateau, while the errant cubs have become the North and South Manitou islands.

The dunes are the product of several glacial assaults that ended 11,000 years ago. The glaciers left a legacy of rock, sand and silt as they melted. Rugged bluffs rise as high as 480 feet above the lake. Among the dunes are ghost forests, the bleached remains of trees that were once covered by advancing dunes, then exposed as the sand moved on. The 7.4-mile Pierce Stocking Scenic Drive, open late April to early November (9 a.m.-30 minutes after dusk), provides access to the high dunes of Sleeping Bear Plateau and affords views from the bluffs overlooking the lake. The Dune Climb on SR 109 is open daily 24 hours.

Fishing and canoeing are popular on the Platte and Crystal rivers and adjoining lakes, as are hiking and cross-country skiing on the park's 55 miles of marked trails. On South Manitou Island is a lighthouse, the wreck of the Liberian freighter *Francisco Morazan* and the Valley of Giants—a virgin white-cedar forest. North Manitou Island, 15,000 acres of wilderness, attracts backpackers. The islands are accessible by passenger ferry from Leland *(see place listing p. 87).*

Several attractions are in Glen Haven. The Cannery Boathouse Museum has boats as well as equipment and motors; the site is open daily 11-5, late May-Labor Day. A restored 1920s blacksmith shop

offers demonstrations, which are usually given daily 11-5 early June-early October if staff is available. Glen Haven General Store on SR 209 is also reminiscent of the 1920s. The Maritime Museum at the Sleeping Bear Point Coast Guard Station, 1 mile west of Glen Haven, has displays depicting the maritime history of the area, including Great Lakes shipping, the U.S. Coast Guard and the U.S. Life-Saving Service. It is open daily 11-5, mid-May through Labor Day and then on weekends noon-5 until mid-October.

The Philip A. Hart Visitor Center, on SR 72 in Empire, has exhibits about the region's natural history and a slide program about the park. It is open daily except for Jan. 1, Thanksgiving and Dec. 25 (8-6, Memorial Day-Labor Day and 8:15-4 the rest of the year).

Other recreational opportunities include camping, horseback riding, ice fishing, snowshoeing and swimming. Picnic facilities are available at various places throughout the park, and there are several beaches.

A pass, valid for 7 days, is $10 per private vehicle. For further information contact the Superintendent, Sleeping Bear Dunes National Lakeshore, 9922 Front St., Empire, MI 49630; phone (231) 326-5134. *See Recreation Chart and the AAA Great Lakes CampBook.*

SOO JUNCTION (B-5)

TAHQUAMENON FALLS RIVERBOAT TOUR AND THE FAMOUS TOONERVILLE TROLLEY is 2 mi. n. of SR 28 to the end of CR 381. Tour 1 is a 6.5-hour narrow-gauge train trip and riverboat ride to private access at the Upper Tahquamenon Falls. Tour 2, offered in the summer, is a wilderness train ride to the riverside park and back, lasting approximately 1 hour, 45 minutes.

Hours: Tour 1 departs Mon., Wed. and Sat. at 10:30, early Sept.-early Oct. Tour 2 departs Mon.-Wed. and Sat. at 12:30, July 1-late Aug. and Sat.-Sun. before Labor Day. Phone ahead to confirm schedule. **Cost:** Tour 1 fare $45; $42.50 (ages 62+); $29 (ages 9-15); $20 (ages 4-8). Tour 2 fare $15; $14 (ages 62+); $9 (ages 9-15); $7 (ages 4-8). **Phone:** (906) 876-2311 or (888) 778-7246.

SOUTH HAVEN (H-1) pop. 5,021, elev. 589'

MICHIGAN MARITIME MUSEUM is off I-196 exit 20, then w. to 260 Dyckman Ave. Exhibits inform about the people who built and used boats on the Great Lakes and about changes in fishing history. U.S. Coast Guard exhibits also are displayed. *Friends Good Will*, a replica of a 60-foot sloop from the early 1800s, is on the premises; sailing trips are available.

Hours: Daily 10-5, May 1-Columbus Day. Closed major holidays. **Cost:** $5; $4 (ages 65+); $3.50 (ages 6-17). **Phone:** (269) 637-8078 or (800) 747-3810.

SOUTH RANGE (A-2) pop. 727, elev. 1,138'

COPPER RANGE HISTORICAL SOCIETY MUSEUM, 44 Trimountain Ave., showcases past South Range inhabitants and copper mining history in southern Houghton County. Mining, farming, ice harvesting, logging and banking are profiled as is barrel making, which was necessary for shipping the ore and supplies to and from the area. **Time:** Allow 30 minutes minimum. **Hours:** Mon.-Sat. noon-3, July-Aug.; Tues.-Sat. noon-3, in June and Sept.-early Oct. **Cost:** $1; free (ages 0-12). **Phone:** (906) 482-6125.

SUTTONS BAY (E-2) pop. 589

Suttons Bay Chamber of Commerce: 201 W. Broadway, P.O. Box 46, Suttons Bay, MI 49682. **Phone:** (231) 271-5077.

Shopping areas: Farm markets and antique shops can be found along SR 22 between Suttons Bay and Northport.

TECUMSEH (I-4) pop. 8,574, elev. 795'

TECUMSEH AREA HISTORICAL MUSEUM is at 302 E. Chicago Blvd. The museum is housed in Tecumseh's first Catholic church, which was built in 1913 by local farmers with stones from their fields. Displays include 19th-century dresses, Civil War items, arrowheads, old quilts and the surveying equipment used to lay out the town in 1824. Changing exhibits also are featured. **Time:** Allow 30 minutes minimum. **Hours:** Wed.-Sat. 11-3. Closed major holidays. Phone ahead to confirm schedule. **Cost:** Free. **Phone:** (517) 423-2374.

TIPTON (I-4)

HIDDEN LAKE GARDENS is 8 mi. w. of SR 52 on SR 50. The 755-acre garden is part of Michigan State University and has a greenhouse complex displaying plants from arid, tropical and temperate climates. There also are gardens, natural and developed landscapes, an all-America display, a lake, several hiking trails and a 6-mile scenic drive.

There are thousands of labeled trees, shrubs and flowers and a display of dwarf and unusual evergreens, including a bonsai courtyard. **Hours:** Daily 8-dusk, Apr.-Oct.; 8-4, rest of year. **Cost:** $3; free (ages 0-2 and first Mon. of the month except holidays). **Phone:** (517) 431-2060. 🎟

TRAVERSE CITY (E-2)
pop. 14,532, elev. 589'

Named for the local bay, Traverse City began as a lumber mill in the mid-1800s. As the need for lumber diminished, the town became the center of a flourishing cherry-growing region.

The city's setting at the base of Grand Traverse Bay makes it a busy resort in all seasons. Winter sports are widely available. In summer the bay provides good sailing and fishing. Traverse City State Park (*see Recreation Chart and the AAA Great Lakes CampBook*) is 2 miles east. The area has more than 30 golf courses, including courses designed by Jack Nicklaus, Arnold Palmer and Gary Player.

Particularly picturesque among the area's many scenic drives is the 36-mile trip on SR 37 through Old Mission Peninsula, which splits the bay into two long, narrow arms. It is especially lovely when the cherry trees bloom in mid-May and when leaves take on their fall colors, beginning in September. The tip of the peninsula, marked by a lighthouse, is equidistant from the equator and the North Pole. At

Online & On the Go!

Travel smarter with **AAA Mobile Web** for your Internet-capable cell or smartphone. Find a AAA Approved restaurant or hotel, get local event and attraction information from our trusted TourBook® guides and locate it all on AAA maps.

AAA Mobile Web also displays Show Your Card & Save® discount locations, AAA Approved repair shops and has one-touch access to AAA Emergency Road Service.

Go to AAA.com on your Internet-connected device or visit AAA.com/mobile for more on-the-go solutions.

AAA Mobile Web

Wherever you go, AAA is right there with you.

Access to AAA Mobile Web requires a Web-enabled device with a data plan. Usage is free, but charges from your carrier may apply.

Scan this tag using your Web-enabled smartphone to access AAA Mobile Web now.

Get the free mobile app at
http://gettag.mobi

Old Mission is a reconstructed Native American mission originally built in 1836. Another scenic route along the lakeshore is US 31 between Traverse City and Petoskey, then SR 119 to Cross Village.

The  National Cherry Festival, a weeklong event held downtown in early July, celebrates the long heritage of Traverse City's cherry growing industry that began when the first cherry trees were planted in 1852. The festival features more than 150 activities, including cherry recipe contests, an arts and crafts show, concerts, air shows, parades and sporting events.

Traverse City Convention & Visitors Bureau: 101 W. Grandview Pkwy., Traverse City, MI 49684-2252. **Phone:** (231) 947-1120 or (800) 872-8377.

CLINCH PARK is at jct. Cass St. and Grandview Pkwy. at 400 Boardman Ave. A steam train, the "Spirit of Traverse City," circles the park, offering views of the harbor and Clinch Park Beach. **Hours:** Train runs daily 10-4:30, Memorial Day weekend-Labor Day. **Cost:** Train ride $3; $2 (ages 2-12). **Phone:** (231) 922-4905.

DENNOS MUSEUM CENTER is at 1701 E. Front St. on the campus of Northwestern Michigan College. Permanent and changing art exhibits in the galleries include the Discovery Gallery, offering hands-on art and science exhibits; and the Inuit Art Gallery, featuring an extensive collection of Canadian Aboriginal art. **Time:** Allow 1 hour minimum. **Hours:** Mon.-Sat. 10-5 (also Thurs. 5-8), Sun. 1-5. Closed major holidays. **Cost:** $6; $4 (ages 0-12); $20 (family). **Phone:** (231) 995-1055.

GREAT LAKES CHILDREN'S MUSEUM — *see Greilickville p. 76.*

TALL SHIP MANITOU— *see Greilickville p. 77.*

WINERIES

• **Chateau Chantal Winery** is 12 mi. n. on SR 37 to 15900 Rue de Vin. **Hours:** Mon.-Sat. 11-8, Sun. noon-5, mid-June through Aug. 31; Mon.-Sat. 11-7, Sun. noon-5, Sept.-Oct.; Mon.-Sat. 11-5, Sun. noon-5, rest of year. Tours daily at 1, 2 and 3, mid-June through Aug. 31. Closed Jan. 1, Easter, Thanksgiving and Dec. 25. **Phone:** (231) 223-4110 or (800) 969-4009.

• **Chateau Grand Traverse Winery and Vineyards** is 8.5 mi. n. on SR 37 at 12239 Center Rd. **Hours:** Winery open Mon.-Sat. 10-7, Sun. noon-6, June-Aug.; Mon.-Sat. 10-6, Sun. noon-5 in May and Sept.-Oct.; Mon.-Sat. 10-5, Sun. noon-5, rest of year. Tours offered daily on the hour noon-4, June-Aug.; Mon.-Fri. at 1 and 3, Sat.-Sun. on the hour noon-4 in May and Sept.-Oct.; Sat. at 1 and 3, rest of year. **Phone:** (231) 223-7355 or (800) 283-0247.

UPPER PENINSULA

That the Upper Peninsula is part of Michigan at all was the result of the unpopular compromise that won Michigan its statehood. The crucial issue at stake was the sole proprietorship of a strip of territory along the Michigan-Ohio border that included the city of Toledo. The bitterly fought Toledo War (contested in Congress with blazing words, not in Toledo with bullets) resulted in Michigan's ceding that land to Ohio in exchange for statehood.

Michigan somewhat grudgingly accepted the Upper Peninsula—then considered a barren wasteland—as a consolation prize. Hardly a Michigander today would have it any other way. In terms of natural resources alone the raw deal turned out to be a steal. When Michigan became a state in 1837, the Upper Peninsula's fabulous deposits of pure copper were already being uncovered; the deposits were, however, not news to Native Americans, who had mined the metal thousands of years before.

In 1957 the slender strand of the Mackinac Bridge anchored the Upper Peninsula to the Lower, making the U.P.—as locals call it—easily accessible from the south. Recreation and tourism have since helped alleviate some of the region's economic slack.

Known now for its unspoiled beauty rather than its industrial scars, the Upper Peninsula is a popular haven for outdoors enthusiasts. State and national forests cover much of the land; Isle Royale National Park *(see place listing p. 83)* and Pictured Rocks National Lakeshore *(see place listing p. 102)* preserve some of the rugged peninsula's most impressive terrain. Aspen, birch, fir, maple and spruce trees shelter such animals as black bears, Eastern timber wolves, white-tailed deer and moose.

The Porcupine Mountains in the west have a large stand of virgin hemlock and one of the largest relatively undisturbed northern hemlock hardwood forests west of New York's Adirondack Mountains. Recreational opportunities range from swimming to skiing, with almost legendary popularity in fishing.

The following places in the Upper Peninsula are listed separately under their individual names:

DID YOU KNOW

Henry Ford's estate in Dearborn is called Fair Lane, a name he also gave to one of his automobile models.

Bessemer, Calumet, Caspian, Copper Harbor, Escanaba, Germfask, Hancock, Hiawatha National Forest, Houghton, Iron Mountain, Iron River, Ironwood, Ishpeming, Isle Royale National Park, Manistique, Marquette, Munising, Negaunee, Ontonagon, Paradise, Pictured Rocks National Lakeshore, Rockland, St. Ignace, Sault Ste. Marie, Soo Junction and South Range.

VULCAN (B-3) elev. 968′

IRON MOUNTAIN IRON MINE is on US 2. The mine, which operated 1877-1945, produced some 21,625,000 tons of ore. Guided tours along the same railway system that transported miners takes visitors 400 feet underground along 2,600 feet of drifts. Demonstrations show how the mining machinery extracted the ore. Visitors should wear warm clothing; raincoats and hard hats are provided. **Hours:** Daily 9-5, June 1 to mid-Oct. **Cost:** $10; $7.50 (ages 6-12). **Phone:** (906) 563-8077 in season, or (906) 774-7914 off-season.

WAKEFIELD (B-1) pop. 2,085

RECREATIONAL ACTIVITIES
Skiing
• **Indianhead Mountain Resort** is off US 2 at 500 Indianhead Rd. **Hours:** Daily 9-4, late Nov.-early Apr. **Phone:** (800) 346-3426.

WATERFORD—*see Detroit p. 65.*

WATERLOO (L-1) pop. 3,069

Plentiful game attracted many of the Great Lakes Indian tribes to Waterloo, an area of low hills and marshes that divides the headwaters of the westward-flowing Grand River from the eastbound Huron River. Waterloo is in the midst of Waterloo State Recreation Area *(see Recreation Chart).*

WESTLAND—*see Detroit p. 65.*

WHITEHALL (G-1) pop. 2,884, elev. 599′

WHITE RIVER LIGHT STATION MUSEUM is at 6199 Murray Rd. This 1875 lighthouse displays photographs, paintings and marine artifacts from and about steamships and Great Lakes vessels. Local shipping activity history also is profiled. The collection includes the original Fresnel lens and artifacts from the United States Lighthouse Service and the Coast Guard as well as a life ring from the *Edmund Fitzgerald*. Visitors can climb the spiral stairway to view the dunes along Lake Michigan's coastline.

Phone ahead for parking information for large campers and RVs. **Time:** Allow 30 minutes minimum. **Hours:** Tues.-Fri. 11-5, Sat.-Sun. noon-6, Memorial Day weekend-Aug. 31; Tues.-Fri. 11-4, Sat.-Sun. noon-5, Sept.-Oct. **Cost:** $4; $2 (ages 8-18); $10 (family, two adults and two children ages 8-18). **Phone:** (231) 894-8265.

WILLIAMSBURG (E-3) elev. 732′

GAMBLING ESTABLISHMENTS
• **Turtle Creek Casino & Hotel** is at 7741 SR 72E. **Hours:** Daily 24 hours. **Phone:** (800) 922-2946.

WYANDOTTE—*see Detroit p. 66.*

YPSILANTI (I-5) pop. 22,362, elev. 720′

When the youthful Greek revolutionary general Demetrios Ypsilanti held the entire Turkish Army at bay and escaped without losing even one of his 300 soldiers, he had no idea that his bravery would

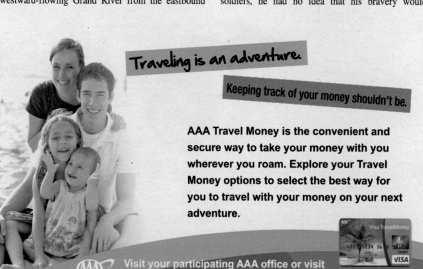

cause a muddy but energetic village in the wilds of southeastern Michigan to become his namesake in 1832. This city on the Huron River is an industrial center and the home of 880-acre Eastern Michigan University. Ford Gallery, on campus at 114 Ford Hall, features works by students and faculty as well as artists of local interest. The gallery is usually open Monday through Saturday, but exhibits rotate regularly, so you should call ahead to make sure the facility is open before visiting; (734) 487-0465. Ypsilanti is also home to Riverside Park and the 1890s Water Tower.

The city's 40-block historic district, centered around Huron Street, contains some 700 restored buildings in the Greek Revival, Gothic Revival, Italianate, Second Empire, Queen Anne and Tudor Revival architectural styles.

Ypsilanti Area Convention and Visitors Bureau: 106 W. Michigan Ave., Ypsilanti, MI 48197. **Phone:** (734) 483-4444.

MICHIGAN FIREHOUSE MUSEUM is at 110 W. Cross St. Housed in an original 1898 fire station with a 10,000-square-foot addition, the museum contains exhibits about firefighting, which include equipment and a number of antique vehicles. A large collection of vintage toys and model trucks related to firefighting are displayed. **Time:** Allow 30 minutes minimum. **Hours:** Tues.-Sat. 10-4, Sun. noon-4. Closed major holidays. **Cost:** $3; $2 (ages 55+ and students with ID). **Phone:** (734) 547-0663.

WIARD'S ORCHARDS & COUNTRY FAIR is s. of I-94 exit 183 (Huron St.) following signs to 5565 Merritt Rd. The property has been owned and operated by the Wiard family since 1853. Nearly 100 acres contain apple orchards, a pumpkin patch and a cider mill. Additional features include a corn maze, pony rides, petting zoo, wagon rides, giant inflatable creations, a labyrinth and a karaoke cabin.

Hours: Country Store Tues.-Sun. 10-6. Country Fair Fri.-Sun. 10-6, mid-Sept. through Oct. 31. Closed major holidays. **Cost:** Orchards free. Country fair admission Sat.-Sun. (includes rides) $11.99; free (ages 0-2). Country fair Wed.-Fri. (includes rides) $8.50; free (ages 0-2). **Phone:** (734) 390-9211. 🍴

YPSILANTI AUTOMOTIVE HERITAGE MUSEUM AND MILLER MOTORS HUDSON is at 100 E. Cross St. Housed in the last Hudson dealership, the museum contains more than 35 original and restored cars, from a copy of the Tucker Torpedo to an original Kaiser. Corvairs, Chevy IIs and Hudsons also are on display, along with Hudson memorabilia. **Hours:** Mon.-Fri. 1:30-5, Sat. 10-5, Sun. noon-5. Closed major holidays. **Cost:** $4; free (ages 0-12). **Phone:** (734) 482-5200.

YPSILANTI HISTORICAL MUSEUM AND ARCHIVES is just n. of Michigan Ave. at 220 N. Huron St. The 1860 house is filled with collections representing 19th-century life in Ypsilanti. Each room focuses on a different aspect of history; the parlor features antique furniture and art; a bedroom showcases antique quilts and the nursery displays antique toys. There also is a room dedicated to historic tools. The archives are housed in the basement, and the collection includes genealogical information.

Guides provide information about architectural details as well as the antique collection. **Time:** Allow 30 minutes minimum. **Hours:** Tues.-Sun. 2-5. Closed major holidays. **Cost:** Donations. **Phone:** (734) 482-4990.

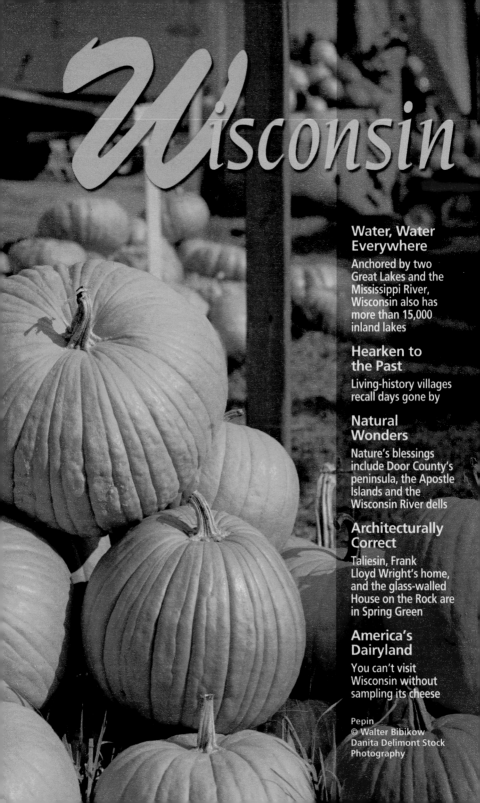

Wisconsin

Water, Water Everywhere

Anchored by two Great Lakes and the Mississippi River, Wisconsin also has more than 15,000 inland lakes

Hearken to the Past

Living-history villages recall days gone by

Natural Wonders

Nature's blessings include Door County's peninsula, the Apostle Islands and the Wisconsin River dells

Architecturally Correct

Taliesin, Frank Lloyd Wright's home, and the glass-walled House on the Rock are in Spring Green

America's Dairyland

You can't visit Wisconsin without sampling its cheese

Pepin
© Walter Bibikow
Danita Delimont Stock
Photography

Whitefish Dunes State Park / © Todd Phillips / Photolibrary

I n America's Dairyland, there are lots of reasons to say "cheese."

Smiles, rest and relaxation are a way of life in the communities along the Door County peninsula. Although square in the Midwest, you'll experience the flavor of New England in a rugged landscape peppered with fishing villages, farms, lighthouses and sand beaches.

The state's biggest city, Milwaukee, reflects a decidedly German heritage. Key players in its development—such sudsy names as Miller, Pabst and Schlitz—are sure to elicit a grin or two.

Noted architect Frank Lloyd Wright left his mark in the middle of the state.

The Richland Center native brought his visions to life in such cities as Madison and Spring Green.

Affectionately called "cheeseheads," fans of the Green Bay Packers (the oldest team in the NFL) cheer wildly and beam like Cheshire cats.

Stretching along the western border is the St. Croix River, a recreational hot spot with scenic gorges, rock formations and waterfalls.

And like sprinkled Parmesan, the intriguing Apostle Islands top the state. The national lakeshore features more lighthouses than any other national park.

Wisconsin. It's whey more than dairy.

Milk Wisconsin for all it's worth, and you end up with more than just cheese.

Sure, the state earned its nickname as America's Dairyland by being a leader in dairy production. However, it's also a big processor of snap beans, sweet corn, hay, oats, cranberries, ginseng and potatoes. It manufactures much of the nation's mining machinery, x-ray equipment and power cranes. And its economy thrives on a booming tourism business—which is no small wonder, given the seemingly endless number of things you can do.

Take steps into the past. A replica of the log cabin in which "Little House" books author Laura Ingalls Wilder was born is in Pepin. Historic lighthouses line the Door Peninsula. Costumed interpreters perform daily chores around the 360-acre grounds of the 1851 Wade House in Greenbush.

Explore another culture. A strong Norwegian influence embraces Blue Mounds. Scandinavian customs prevail on Washington Island, the country's oldest Icelandic settlement. New Glarus, often called "Little Switzerland," reflects a decidedly Swiss heritage. German, Danish, Polish and Finnish homesteads are among the more than 65 preserved buildings at the 1870s rural village in Eagle.

Awakening the Senses

Admire great architecture. Massive fireplaces, waterfalls and a windowed room that juts out over Wyoming Valley are among the wonders of Alex Jordan's The House on the Rock, south of Spring Green. Richland Center native Frank Lloyd Wright designed buildings in Madison, Milwaukee, Racine and Spring Green. The State Capitol in Madison shows a Roman Renaissance flair. A 40-foot circular stairway winds among five floors of the 1854 Octagon House in Watertown.

Give your palate a treat. Sip apple, cherry and grape wines in Algoma, Barneveld, Cedarburg, Prairie du Sac and St. Croix. Taste brewery samples in the city made famous for beer: Milwaukee. Nibble on cheese in Monroe and Rudolph. Savor cranberry refreshments made from berries cultivated in marshes around Manitowish Waters and Warrens.

Play the slots and scream out "Bingo!" Casinos in Baraboo, Carter, Green Bay, Keshena and Milwaukee invite you to test your luck.

Learn about locomotives. You can ride the rails through the St. Croix River Valley in Osceola and the lake country of Spooner, where

French explorer Jean Nicolet leads an expedition ashore near Green Bay.
1634

Jacques Marquette and Louis Joliet leave De Pere on their historic journey to the Mississippi River.
1673

Wisconsin becomes the nation's 30th state.
1848

Library of Congress

1867
Architect Frank Lloyd Wright is born in Richland Center.

1783
Following the Treaty of Paris, the U.S. takes ownership of the Wisconsin territory.

Wisconsin Historical Timeline

a former train depot holds railroad memories. Iron horses from the steam and diesel eras also are preserved at museums in Green Bay and North Freedom.

Focus on other transportation. Aircraft are showcased at an Oshkosh museum. Classic automobiles beg to be admired in Hartford. Maritime vessels are centerpieces at museums in Gills Rock, Manitowoc, Sturgeon Bay and Superior. Circus wagons have a big-top home in Baraboo.

Remember veterans. Museums and parks in King, Madison and Neillsville pay tribute to those who served in conflicts.

Trees, Caves and Wildlife

Trace the papermaking trade. The Lumberjack Steam Train carries visitors from the historic depot in Laona to the Logging Museum Complex, where logging artifacts and an audiovisual presentation detail the history of an industry that feeds off 15 million acres of forestland.

Get back to nature. Rose-colored cliffs punctuate the weathered caves and hollows at Apostle Islands National Lakeshore. Part of Wisconsin's Ice Age National Scientific Reserve, the glacial phenomena of Devil's Lake State Park and Kettle Moraine State Forest are a sight to behold. River tours wander among unusual rock formations and caverns in Wisconsin Dells.

Confront a local legend. The folksy myth of the Hodag, a creature once said to have inhabited the forests around Rhinelander, is kept very much alive in the area.

Study native wildlife. Cruises departing from Horicon bring you face-to-face with all kinds of creatures. Bird-watchers gather on the shores of St. Croix National Scenic Riverway and in a Waupun refuge.

Catch a great view. On a clear day, you can see practically forever from the lofty vantage point atop Granddad Bluff, which towers 600 feet above La Crosse.

When it comes to family fun, America's Dairyland may just be the cream of the crop.

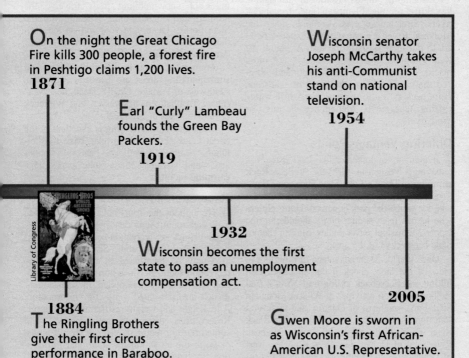

On the night the Great Chicago Fire kills 300 people, a forest fire in Peshtigo claims 1,200 lives.
1871

Earl "Curly" Lambeau founds the Green Bay Packers.
1919

Wisconsin senator Joseph McCarthy takes his anti-Communist stand on national television.
1954

Library of Congress

1932
Wisconsin becomes the first state to pass an unemployment compensation act.

1884
The Ringling Brothers give their first circus performance in Baraboo.

2005
Gwen Moore is sworn in as Wisconsin's first African-American U.S. Representative.

Recreation

With 15,000 inland lakes and 25,000 miles of waterways—plus borders touching lakes Michigan and Superior, the Brule, St. Croix and Menominee rivers and the mighty Mississippi—Wisconsin is an H_2O utopia.

Sailing enthusiasts float through the steely waters of Chequamegon and Sturgeon bays, while **windsurfers** unfurl sails of their own around the southern tip of Lake Winnebago and at Kohler-Andrae State Park, on the shores of Lake Michigan. Surprisingly, **surfing** is a popular sport along the Lake Michigan beaches around Sheboygan.

Break the surface during a **scuba diving** trip along Apostle Islands National Lakeshore, or explore the shipwrecks lining "death's door," the nautical passage between Door County and Washington Island.

Such lazy rivers as the Apple and Crystal are prime territory for **tubing.** Moderate currents enhance the **canoeing** experience on the Baraboo, Black, Chippewa, Grant, La Crosse, Oconto, St. Croix, Upper Bois Brule and Wisconsin rivers. The winding Kickapoo—dubbed the "crookedest river in the world"—is navigable its entire length.

Challenging rapids result in irresistible **kayaking** on the Flambeau and Tomahawk rivers. Stretches of class V rapids make the Montreal River a great spot for expert kayakers to put their skills to the test. Although the waters around the Apostle Islands are more placid, paddlers won't be disappointed. Rugged sea caves riddling the bases of sandstone cliffs beckon you to explore. For **white-water rafting,** take on the Menominee, Peshtigo or Wolf rivers.

Differing Vantage Points

If thoughts of lofty heights don't leave you quivering, Wisconsin delivers thrills. **Rock climbing** in Devil's Lake State Park, near Baraboo, leads you atop 500-foot bluffs around the lake for which the park is named. **Hang gliders** who launch from similar bluffs shouldering the Upper Mississippi River Valley enjoy a memorable perspective of the area.

Once you've taken advantage of a bird's-eye view of the land, check it out up close from **hiking** and **horseback riding** trails. You'll find facilities for both activities at Wildcat Mountain State Park, southeast of Ontario, and at several state forests, including Black River, near Black River Falls; Brule River, in Brule; Flambeau River, east of Draper; Governor Knowles, west of Grantsburg; and Kettle Moraine near Greenbush and Eagle.

On-road **bicycling** trails paint a fitting picture of the varied landscape. The 22-mile High Falls Tour, which weaves through Marinette County, passes the cascade of Veterans Falls and the glimmering waters of High Falls Reservoir. Take your bike over an original covered bridge on the 30-mile trail that begins at Cedar Creek Park in Cedarburg, or pedal through the stone railroad tunnels of the 32-mile Elroy-Sparta Trail.

For off-road excitement, **mountain biking** trails cater to cyclists of all abilities. The Boulder Junction Area Trail System, or B.A.T.S., covers 10 mostly easy miles around Boulder Junction. Skilled riders favor the tough Washburn Lake trails, near Rhinelander, or the wild and jarring experience afforded by the Swiss-cheeselike terrain of Kettle Moraine State Forest, much of which only extreme adventurers would like.

"Snow" Much Fun

During winter, the groomed trails at many state parks entice **cross-country skiers** and **snowshoers.** Some of the more extensive systems trek through Governor Dodge State Park, north of Dodgeville; Mirror Lake State Park, southwest of Lake Delton; and Newport State Park, northeast of Ellison Bay. Nearly 120 miles of snowmobiling trails traverse the northern and southern units of Kettle Moraine State Forest. Quadruple your fun on the 480-plus miles of trails in Northern Highland-American Legion State Forest.

Among the popular **downhill skiing** and **snowboarding** areas are Cascade Mountain, southwest of Portage; Devil's Head, near Merrimac; Trollhaugen, in Dresser; and Whitecap Mountain, west of Montreal.

Trout and salmon **fishing** is excellent in the Great Lakes. For northern pike, bass, muskellunge, perch and walleye, head to smaller lakes and streams. Many state parks have **camping** facilities.

Recreational Activities

Throughout the TourBook, you may notice a Recreational Activities heading with bulleted listings of recreation-oriented establishments listed underneath. Similar operations also may be mentioned in Destination City recreation sections. Since normal AAA inspection criteria cannot be applied, these establishments are presented only for information. Age, height and weight restrictions may apply. Reservations often are recommended and sometimes are required. Visitors should phone or write the attraction for additional information; the address and phone number are provided for this purpose.

Fast Facts

POPULATION: 5,363,675.

AREA: 56,154 square miles; ranks 26th.

CAPITAL: Madison.

HIGHEST POINT: 1,953 ft., Timm's Hill.

LOWEST POINT: 581 ft., Lake Michigan.

TIME ZONE(S): Central. DST.

TEEN DRIVING LAWS: The minimum age for an unrestricted driver's license is 16 years, 9 months. No more than one unrelated passenger is permitted (family members are exempt). Driving is not permitted midnight-5 a.m. For more information about Wisconsin driver's license regulations contact (800) 924-3570.

MINIMUM AGE FOR GAMBLING: 18; 21 if alcohol is served on the premises.

SEAT BELT/CHILD RESTRAINT LAWS: Seat belts required for driver and front-seat passengers 8 and older. Child restraints required for under age 8, less than 57 inches tall and under 80 pounds.

CELL PHONE RESTRICTIONS: Text messaging while driving is not permitted. In Marshfield, drivers are not permitted to use handheld cell phones.

HELMETS FOR MOTORCYCLISTS: Required for all riders under 18 and all drivers during the learner permit stage.

RADAR DETECTORS: Permitted.

MOVE OVER LAW: Driver is required to slow down and vacate a lane nearest police, fire and rescue vehicles stopped on the side of the road using audible or flashing signals. The law includes recovery vehicles, such as tow trucks.

FIREARMS LAWS: Vary by state and/or county. Contact Wisconsin State Patrol Headquarters, 4802 Sheboygan Ave., Room 551, Madison, WI 53707; phone (608) 266-3212.

HOLIDAYS: Jan. 1; Martin Luther King Jr. Day, Jan. (3rd Mon.); Presidents' Day, Feb. (3rd Mon.); Memorial Day, May (last Mon.); July 4; Labor Day, Sept. (1st Mon.); Columbus Day, Oct. (2nd Mon.); Veterans Day, Nov. 11; Thanksgiving; Christmas, Dec. 25.

TAXES: Wisconsin's statewide sales tax is 5 percent, with local options for an additional increment of 0.5 percent, plus a lodgings tax. Car rentals are subject to a 5 percent state tax as well as an airport tax ranging from 6.5 to 9 percent. The city of Milwaukee levies an additional 3 percent car rental tax.

INFORMATION CENTERS: The state of Wisconsin has closed all border welcome centers. Please refer to the AAA TourBook listings for visitor information bureaus in the cities of Hudson, Hurley, Kenosha, La Crosse, Marinette, Platteville and Prairie du Chien, or phone the Wisconsin Department of Tourism for further assistance with your travel plans.

FURTHER INFORMATION FOR VISITORS:
Wisconsin Department of Tourism
P.O. Box 8690
Madison, WI 53708-8690
(608) 266-2161
(800) 432-8747

FISHING AND HUNTING REGULATIONS:
Wisconsin Department of Natural Resources
P.O. Box 7921
Madison, WI 53707-7921
(608) 266-2621

NATIONAL FOREST INFORMATION:
U.S. Forest Service, Eastern Region
626 E. Wisconsin Ave., Room 9
Milwaukee, WI 53202
(414) 297-3600
(877) 444-6777 (for reservations)
(866) 377-8642

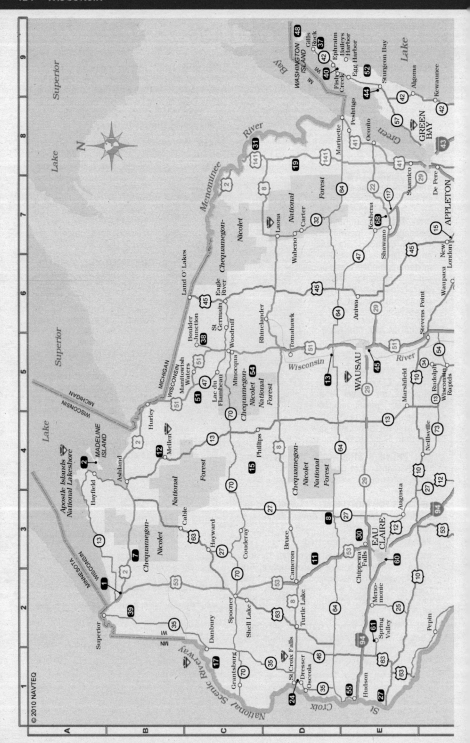

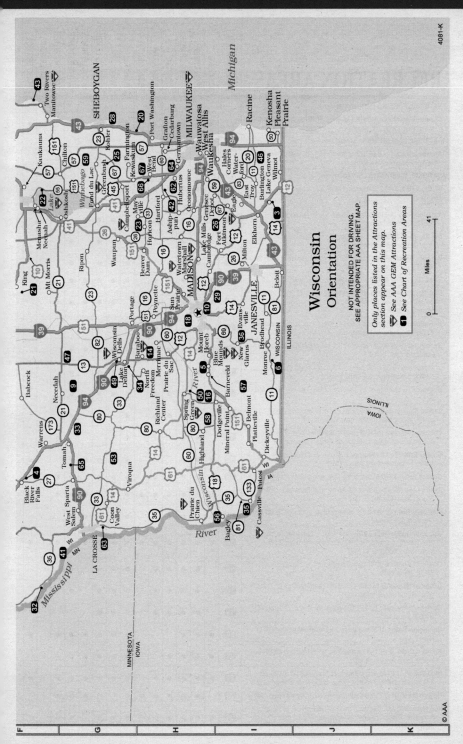

Wisconsin Orientation

NOT INTENDED FOR DRIVING.
SEE APPROPRIATE AAA SHEET MAP.

Only places listed in the Attractions section appear on this map.

See AAA GEM Attractions

See Chart of Recreation Areas

0 — Miles — 41

4081-K

© AAA

RECREATION AREAS

RECREATION AREAS	MAP LOCATION	CAMPING	PICNICKING	HIKING TRAILS	BOATING	BOAT RAMP	BOAT RENTAL	FISHING	SWIMMING	PETS ON LEASH	BICYCLE TRAILS	WINTER SPORTS	VISITOR CENTER	LODGE/CABINS	FOOD SERVICE
NATIONAL FORESTS *(See place listings)*															
Chequamegon-Nicolet 1,518,138 acres. North-central and northeastern Wisconsin. Horse rental.		•	•	•	•	•		•	•	•	•	•			•
NATIONAL LAKESHORES *(See place listings)*															
Apostle Islands (A-3) 69,372 acres off northern Wisconsin's Bayfield peninsula in Lake Superior.		•	•	•	•	•	•	•	•	•			•	•	
NATIONAL RIVERWAYS *(See place listings)*															
St. Croix (E-1, C-1) 252 mi. from Cable to Prescott.		•	•	•	•	•	•	•	•	•					
STATE															
Amnicon Falls (A-2) 825 acres 10 mi. s.e. of Superior on US 2. Scenic. Covered bridge.	❶	•	•	•				•	•	•					
Big Bay (A-4) 2,358 acres e. of Bayfield on Madeline Island via ferry. Cross-country skiing.	❷	•	•	•				•	•	•					
Big Foot Beach (I-7) 271 acres 2.5 mi. s. of Lake Geneva on SR 120.	❸	•	•	•				•	•	•			•		
Black River (F-4) 68,000 acres. *(See Black River Falls p. 135)*	❹	•	•	•	•			•	•	•		•			
Blue Mound (H-5) 1,153 acres off US 18/151 in Blue Mounds. Scenic. Cross-country skiing, mountain biking. *(See Blue Mounds p. 135)*	❺	•	•	•					•	•	•	•	•		
Browntown-Cadiz Springs (I-5) 644 acres 1 mi. e. of Browntown off SR 11. Canoeing. Playground.	❻		•	•	•	•		•	•	•					
Brule River (B-3) 40,367 acres at Brule. Canoeing, cross-country skiing, mountain biking.	❼	•	•	•	•			•	•	•		•			
Brunet Island (D-3) 1,200 acres 1 mi. n. of Cornell off SR 27. Historic. Canoeing, cross-country skiing.	❽	•	•	•	•	•		•	•	•		•			
Buckhorn (G-5) 2,507 acres 13 mi. n. of Mauston on CRs Q and G.	❾	•	•	•	•	•		•	•	•					
Capital Springs (H-6) 3,000 acres just s. of Madison. Cross-country skiing; bike rentals, observation tower.	❿		•	•	•	•		•		•		•	•		
Chippewa Moraine Ice Age (D-3) 3,063 acres 7 mi. e. of New Auburn and 1.9 mi. e. of SR 40 on CR M. Canoeing.	⓫		•	•				•					•		
Copper Falls (B-4) 3,100 acres 2 mi. n.e. of Mellen on SR 169. Nature programs. *(See Mellen p. 162)*	⓬	•	•	•				•	•	•		•	•		•
Council Grounds (D-5) 508 acres 2 mi. n.w. of Merrill on SR 107.	⓭	•	•	•	•	•		•	•	•		•	•		•
Devil's Lake (H-5) 10,000 acres 3.5 mi. s. of Baraboo on SR 123. Scenic. *(See Baraboo p. 133)*	⓮	•	•	•	•		•	•	•	•		•	•		•
Flambeau River (C-4) 89,914 acres 5 mi. e. of Draper on SR 70. Cross-country skiing.	⓯	•	•	•	•	•		•	•	•		•			
Governor Dodge (H-5) 5,270 acres 4 mi. n. of Dodgeville on SR 23N. Nature programs. Scenic. Cross-country skiing. Bridle trails. *(See Dodgeville p. 140)*	⓰	•	•	•	•	•	•	•	•	•	•	•	•		
Governor Knowles (C-1) 19,343 acres 5 mi. w. of Grantsburg on SR 70. Bridle trails.	⓱	•	•	•	•			•		•					
Governor Nelson (H-6) 5140 CR M, on Lake Mendota in Waunakee. Pet swimming area.	⓲		•	•	•	•		•	•	•		•			
Governor Thompson (D-8) 2,800 acres 15 mi. n.w. of Crivitz at N10008 Paust Ln.	⓳	•	•	•	•	•		•	•	•					
Harrington Beach (H-8) 636 acres 2 mi. e. of Belgium on CR O. Nature trails.	⓴	•	•	•				•	•	•			•		
Hartman Creek (F-6) 1,417 acres 6 mi. w. of Waupaca on SR 54. Nature programs. Horse trails.	㉑	•	•	•	•	•		•	•	•					
High Cliff (F-7) 1,145 acres 3 mi. s. of Sherwood off SR 55. Nature programs. Cross-country skiing. Bridle trails. Effigy mounds.	㉒	•	•	•	•	•		•	•	•		•	•		•
Horicon Marsh (H-7) 11,000 acres n. of Horicon. *(See Horicon p. 149)*	㉓		•	•	•			•		•			•		
Interstate (D-1) 1,377 acres .5 mi. s. of US 8 on SR 35. Nature programs. Scenic. Ice Age geological formations. *(See St. Croix Falls p. 191)*	㉔	•	•	•	•	•		•	•	•		•	•		•

RECREATION AREAS

Recreation Area	MAP LOCATION	CAMPING	PICNICKING	HIKING TRAILS	BOATING	BOAT RAMP	BOAT RENTAL	FISHING	SWIMMING	PETS ON LEASH	BICYCLE TRAILS	WINTER SPORTS	VISITOR CENTER	LODGE/CABINS	FOOD SERVICE
Kettle Moraine North (G-8) 29,268 acres. Nature programs. Bridle trails, horse rental. Ice Age geological formations. *(See Campbellsport p. 137)*	25	•	•	•	•	•		•	•	•	•	•	•		•
Kettle Moraine South (I-7) 18,391 acres at Eagle. Nature programs. Bridle trails.	26	•	•	•	•	•		•	•	•	•	•	•		
Kinnickinnic (E-1) W11983 820th Ave. in River Falls. Boat-in camping, cross-country skiing, sledding, snowshoeing, wind-surfing.	27	•	•	•	•			•	•						
Kohler-Andrae (G-8) 879 acres 6 mi. s.e. of Sheboygan off US 141. Nature programs.	28	•	•					•	•	•	•		•		•
Lake Kegonsa (I-6) 343 acres 10 mi. s. of Madison off CR N.	29	•	•	•	•	•		•	•	•			•		
Lake Wissota (E-3) 1,062 acres 5 mi. e. of Chippewa Falls on SR 29. Nature programs. Horse rental.	30	•	•	•	•	•		•	•	•			•	•	
Menominee River Natural Resources Area (C-8) 1,922 acres e. of Pembine. Waterfalls. Primitive camping, canoeing, hunting.	31	•		•	•			•							
Merrick (F-2) 322 acres 2 mi. n.w. of Fountain City off SR 35. Canoe rental.	32	•	•	•	•	•		•	•	•			•		
Mill Bluff (G-4) 1,258 acres 4 mi. n.w. of Camp Douglas off I-90. Ice Age geological formations, scenic bluffs.	33	•	•	•					•	•					
Mirror Lake (H-5) 2,200 acres 4 mi. s.w. of Lake Delton on SR 23. Nature programs. Cross-country skiing.	34	•	•	•	•	•		•	•	•	•	•	•		
Nelson Dewey (I-3) 756 acres 1.2 mi. n.w. of Cassville on CR VV. *(See Cassville p. 137)*	35	•	•	•				•		•			•		
New Glarus Woods (I-5) 431 acres 1.5 mi. s. of New Glarus via SR 69 on CR NN.	36	•	•	•						•	•				
Newport (D-9) 2,368 acres n.e. of Ellison Bay via SR 42. Cross-country skiing.	37	•	•	•				•	•	•	•	•	•		
Northern Highland-American Legion (C-5) 225,000 acres 3 mi. w. of Eagle River on SR 70. Nature programs.	38	•	•	•	•	•		•	•	•	•	•	•		
Pattison (B-2) 1,436 acres 10 mi. s. of Superior on SR 35. Nature programs. Waterfalls.	39	•	•	•				•	•	•			•	•	
Peninsula (D-9) 3,763 acres 2 mi. n.e. of Fish Creek on SR 42. Nature programs. Golf, cross-country skiing, snowmobiling, tennis. Bike, canoe, kayak and paddleboat rentals. Nature trails. *(See Fish Creek p. 142)*	40	•	•	•	•	•	•	•	•	•	•	•	•		•
Perrot (G-3) 1,270 acres 1 mi. n. of Trempealeau off SR 35. Nature programs. Historic.	41	•	•	•	•	•		•		•			•		
Pike Lake (H-7) 678 acres 2 mi. e. of Hartford on SR 60.	42	•	•	•				•	•	•			•		
Point Beach (F-9) 2,903 acres 6 mi. n.e. of Two Rivers. Nature programs. Lighthouse.	43	•	•	•				•	•	•	•		•		•
Potawatomi (E-9) 1,226 acres 2 mi. n.w. of Sturgeon Bay on CR M. Downhill and cross-country skiing, snowmobiling.	44	•	•	•	•	•		•		•		•	•		
Rib Mountain (E-5) 1,600 acres 4 mi. s.w. of Wausau on CR N. Amphitheater. *(See Wausau p. 200)*	45	•	•	•						•		•	•		•
Richard Bong (I-8) 4,515 acres 4 mi. s. of Kansasville on SR 142. Horse rental.	46	•	•	•	•			•	•	•	•	•	•		
Roche-A-Cri (G-5) 605 acres 2 mi. n. of Friendship on SR 13.	47	•	•	•				•		•			•		
Rock Island (D-9) 912 acres on Rock Island via ferry. Historic.	48	•	•	•				•	•	•			•		
Rocky Arbor (G-5) 244 acres 2 mi. n.w. of Wisconsin Dells off I-90.	49	•	•										•		
Tower Hill (H-5) 77 acres 3 mi. s.e. of Spring Green on SR 23.	50	•	•	•	•	•		•		•			•		
Turtle Flambeau Scenic Waters Area (C-5) S.W. of Mercer. Boat-in camping only; bird and wildlife spotting.	51	•		•	•			•				•			
Whitefish Dunes (E-9) 863 acres 10 mi. n.e. of Sturgeon Bay via SR 57. Cross-country skiing.	52		•	•				•	•	•	•		•		
Wildcat Mountain (G-4) 3,603 acres 3 mi. s.e. of Ontario off SR 33. Canoeing, cross-country skiing; bridle trails.	53	•	•	•	•	•		•		•		•	•		

RECREATION AREAS

	MAP LOCATION	CAMPING	PICNICKING	HIKING TRAILS	BOATING	BOAT RAMP	BOAT RENTAL	FISHING	SWIMMING	PETS ON LEASH	BICYCLE TRAILS	WINTER SPORTS	VISITOR CENTER	LODGE/CABINS	FOOD SERVICE
Willow Flowage Scenic Waters Area (C-5) 17,000 acres s.w. of Hazelhurst. Cross-country skiing, hunting, mountain biking, snowshoeing.	54	•		•	•			•				•	•		
Willow River (E-1) 2,891 acres 7 mi. n.e. of Hudson. Nature programs.	55	•	•	•	•	•		•	•	•	•	•	•		•
Wyalusing (I-3) 2,628 acres 7 mi. s.e. of Prairie du Chien on US 18 and SR 35, then 5 mi. w. on CR C. Nature programs. Scenic. Canoe and kayak rental, canoe trail, Indian mounds. *(See Bagley p. 132)*	56	•	•	•	•	•		•		•	•	•	•		•
Yellowstone Lake (I-5) 1000 acres 7 mi. n.w. of Argyle on CR N.	57	•	•	•	•	•	•	•	•	•		•			
OTHER															
Blackhawk Lake Recreation Area (H-4) 2,200 acres 3.5 mi. n. of Cobb via SR 80, then e. on CR BH. Cross-country skiing.	58	•	•	•	•	•	•	•	•	•		•			
Broughton Sheboygan Marsh (G-8) 30 acres 1 mi. w. of Elkhart Lake. Cross-country skiing, hunting, snowmobiling.	59	•	•	•	•	•		•		•		•			•
Carson (E-3) 135 acres. Cross-country skiing. No motor vehicles. *(See Eau Claire p. 144)*	60		•	•	•	•		•		•	•	•	•		
Eau Galle Lake (E-2) n.w. of Spring Valley via CR CC (Van Buren Rd.). Ice fishing, snowmobiling; bridle trails.	61	•	•	•	•	•		•	•	•		•			
Glacier Hills (H-7) 140 acres 10 mi. w. of Richfield on Freiss Lake Rd. Nature programs. Cross-country skiing.	62		•	•	•			•	•	•	•	•	•		
Goose Island (G-3) 3 mi. s. of La Crosse on SR 35, then 2.5 mi. w. on CR GI. Cross-country skiing.	63	•	•	•	•	•		•	•	•		•			
Homestead Hollow (H-8) 105 acres 20 mi. n. of Milwaukee on US 41.	64		•	•						•					
Pine View (G-4) 200 acres on the Fort McCoy Base, 6 mi. e. of Sparta. Miniature golf; canoe rental.	65	•	•	•	•	•	•	•	•	•		•		•	
Ridge Run (H-7) 140 acres on University Dr. in West Bend. Nature trails.	66		•	•				•		•		•			
Sandy Knoll (H-8) 267 acres 1 mi. n.w. on SR 28, then 1 mi. e. on Wallace Lake Rd. Cross-country skiing, snowmobiling.	67		•	•				•	•	•		•			
Shawano Lake (E-7) 6,062 acres 3 mi. n.e. of Shawano via SR 29 on CR H. Cross-country skiing, golf, snowmobiling, tennis; bridle trails.	68	•	•							•	•	•	•		

Wisconsin Temperature Averages Maximum/Minimum

From the records of The Weather Channel Interactive, Inc.

	JAN	FEB	MAR	APR	MAY	JUNE	JULY	AUG	SEPT	OCT	NOV	DEC
Green Bay	24/7	29/12	40/23	55/34	68/45	77/54	81/59	79/57	70/48	58/37	42/26	29/13
La Crosse	26/6	33/13	45/24	60/37	72/49	81/58	85/63	83/61	74/52	61/40	44/27	30/14
Madison	27/5	33/10	45/22	58/33	70/44	80/53	84/58	82/56	74/47	62/36	46/25	32/12
Milwaukee	27/13	32/18	42/27	54/38	67/50	77/59	82/66	80/64	73/55	61/44	46/31	33/19

Points of Interest

ALGOMA (E-9) pop. 3,357, elev. 600'.

On the shore of Lake Michigan, Algoma began with a sawmill and a store in the 1850s. To get a sense of the town's past, take a walking tour downtown and check out its well-preserved historic churches, hotels and shops, built 1860-1880 and in the early 1900s. Notice the colorful murals replicating old-time signs on some of the brick walls, part of an ongoing beautification project. Spend some time in the charming boutiques and restaurants that have replaced the dry goods stores of yesteryear.

Recreation in Algoma centers on Lake Michigan, drawing anglers, beachgoers and boaters alike. Take your pick from a bounty of fishing charters and marinas; reel in brown trout, rainbow trout, chinook salmon and trophy steelhead. The winding 15-mile Ahnapee Trail, which follows the Ahnapee River, attracts hikers, bikers and snowmobilers with its vistas of farms, marshes and woodlands. If you prefer more leisurely pursuits, experience a sunset over Lake Michigan while strolling on the Crescent Beach boardwalk.

Algoma Area Chamber of Commerce: 1226 Lake St., Algoma, WI 54201. **Phone:** (920) 487-2041 or (800) 498-4888.

WINERIES

- **Von Stiehl Winery** is at 115 Navarino St. **Hours:** Tours are given daily at 9:30, 10:30, 11:30, 1, 2, 3 and 4, May-Oct. Tastings are given daily 9-5:30, July-Aug.; 9-5, May-June and Sept.-Oct.; 11-5, Nov.-Dec.; 11-4, rest of year. **Phone:** (920) 487-5208 or (800) 955-5208.

ANIWA (E-6) pop. 272, elev. 1,414'

DELLS OF THE EAU CLAIRE PARK is 6 mi. w. on Sportsman Dr., then .5 mi. n. on CR Y following signs. Trails crisscross the 192-acre park, noted for its unusual rock formations, turbulent and tumbling waters at the "falls," nature trails and rare plants. A segment of the Ice Age National Scenic Trail winds through the park. *See the AAA Great Lakes CampBook.* **Hours:** Daily 6 a.m.-11 p.m., May-Oct. **Cost:** Free. **Phone:** (715) 261-1550.

◥ APOSTLE ISLANDS NATIONAL LAKESHORE (A-3)

The Apostle Islands lie offshore from Bayfield Peninsula in Lake Superior in northwestern Wisconsin. There are 22 Apostle Islands ranging in size from 3 acres to 14,000 acres. All but Madeline Island (*see place listing p. 155*) are within the national lakeshore, which also includes a 12-mile strip of shoreline on the peninsula.

The Apostles are the result of an ice age, when huge ice sheets gouged channels into the bedrock and then left piles of debris in their wakes. As the glaciers retreated, the islands were exposed, revealing rose-colored cliffs that the lake's waters since have shaped into twisted formations, caves and hollows.

Fur trading began here as early as the 17th century, and commercial fishing continues around the islands today. For the early traders the islands offered plentiful game and refuge from the lake's storms. Later developers harvested such resources as timber and sandstone. The latter became the brownstone used extensively in buildings in Chicago and other Midwestern cities in the late 19th century.

By the beginning of the 20th century, wealthy city dwellers had transformed the remote islands into a fashionable retreat, building summer cottages on Madeline Island. This idyllic period ended with the Great Depression.

Once again sugar maple, birch, balsam fir, red pine and an array of wildflowers blanket the islands, and with the second-growth forest are renewed populations of deer, bear and a variety of birds.

Stockton Island, the largest island in the lakeshore, has the most extensive trail system and such facilities as docks, campgrounds and a regular camper shuttle service from the mainland. Recreational activities on the other islands vary and can include hiking, camping, sailing, kayaking and fishing. Lake Superior rarely is warm enough for swimming, and the area's treacherous weather can make canoeing and boating hazardous.

Note: Taking pets to the lakeshore is not advised. The boat service will not accept pets on scheduled trips. Pets must always be on a 6-foot or shorter leash and must never be unattended.

There are scheduled ranger programs on some of the islands, including Raspberry and Stockton. For additional information write the Superintendent, Apostle Islands National Lakeshore, 415 Washington Ave, Bayfield, WI 54814; phone (715) 779-3397. *See Recreation Chart and the AAA Great Lakes CampBook.*

◥ **APOSTLE ISLANDS CRUISE SERVICE** departs the Bayfield Dock. The company offers a variety of narrated, scenic cruises of Apostle Islands National Lakeshore. The Grand Tour cruises past the 22 Apostle Islands with views of historic Raspberry Island Lighthouse, Devils Island Lighthouse and sea caves. Island shuttles for hiking and camping, lighthouse tours, sunset cruises and the annual Lighthouse Celebration in September are provided.

Time: Allow 1 hour, 30 minutes minimum. **Hours:** Grand Tour departs daily (weather permitting) at 10, mid-May to mid-Oct. **Cost:** Grand Tour

$40; $24 (ages 6-12). Reservations are recommended. **Phone:** (715) 779-3925 or (800) 323-7619.

APOSTLE ISLANDS NATIONAL LAKESHORE VISITOR CENTER AND HEADQUARTERS is at 4th St. and Washington Ave. in Bayfield. The Apostle Islands are detailed in exhibits, a movie and publications. Maps, weather information and a schedule of naturalist programs also are available.

Hours: Visitor center open daily 8-4:30, mid-June through Labor Day; Mon.-Fri. 8-4:30 (if staff is available), rest of year. Little Sand Bay Information Center, off SR 13, offers similar services to visitors early June-late Sept. Phone ahead to confirm schedule. **Cost:** Free. **Phone:** (715) 779-3397.

HOKENSON FISHERY HISTORIC SITE is in the Apostle Islands at Little Sand Bay. This complex of buildings was used for more than 30 years by the Hokenson Brothers Fishery. During the summer, guided tours describe the tools and techniques of the rigorous family occupation. A visitor center displays historic artifacts and lakeshore exhibits. **Time:** Allow 1 hour minimum. **Hours:** Grounds open year-round. Visitor center daily 9-5, mid-June through Labor Day; Fri.-Sun. 9-5, day after Labor Day-Sept. 30. Phone ahead to confirm schedule. **Cost:** Free. **Phone:** (715) 779-3397.

APPLETON (F-7) pop. 70,087, elev. 714'

The largest of the five cities along the Fox River, Appleton and its neighboring communities make up the third largest metropolitan area in Wisconsin. Early settlers and French explorers quickly learned the economic value of the "water highway" that tumbles from Lake Winnebago toward Green Bay.

As the lumber industry became established in the mid-19th century, many mills were built along the river's shores. Now known as "Paper Valley," the area supports numerous paper mills and related industries. With the construction of a hydroelectric station in 1882, Appleton became the first city in North America to generate its electricity with water power.

The city is home to Wisconsin's first co-educational institution of higher learning, Lawrence University, which is noteworthy for the Henry M. and Ruth B. Wriston Art Center at Alton and Law streets. Edna Ferber's family moved to Appleton in 1897 when she was 12; it was here that she wrote her first published short story and novel in 1910. Sen. Joe McCarthy, a fervent anti-communist during the 1950s, also hailed from Appleton.

The diverse cultural population lends a distinct ethnic flavor to the area. Descendants of the original New England settlers mingle with Dutch, German, Polish and Vietnamese immigrants.

Fox Cities Convention & Visitors Bureau: 3433 W. College Ave., Appleton, WI 54914. **Phone:** (920) 734-3358 or (800) 236-6673.

Shopping areas: Fox River Mall, 1 block off US 41 on Wisconsin Avenue, has more than 180 stores, including JCPenney, Macy's, Sears and Younkers. Vande Walle's Candies, 400 Mall Dr., offers self-guiding tours through its candy-manufacturing areas.

THE BUILDING FOR KIDS is at 100 W. College Ave. This two-story children's museum features a giant tree with tree houses for climbing and exploration. Exhibits include a golf simulator, airplane and control tower, crane and big dig play area, kids town, art and science studio, fire truck, balls and water play activities, and a play area for toddlers. **Time:** Allow 1 hour minimum. **Hours:** Tues.-Fri. 9-5, Sat. 10-5, Sun. noon-5. **Cost:** $7.25; $6 (ages 65+); free (under 1). **Phone:** (920) 734-3226.

THE GORDON BUBOLZ NATURE PRESERVE is 1.5 mi. n. of US 41 on CR A. This privately maintained non-profit reserve covers 775 acres and provides 8.5 miles of trails for year-round outdoor activities. Trails range from a half-mile to 4.5 miles in length and accommodate cross-country skiers and snowshoers in winter. Wildlife viewing includes a wide variety of native birds and animals. Exhibits at the nature center describe the seasonal changes of indigenous plants and animals.

Time: Allow 1 hour minimum. **Hours:** Preserve open daily dawn-dusk. Nature center open Tues.-Fri. 8-4:30, Sat. 11-4, Sun. 12:30-4. Closed major holidays. **Cost:** Donations. Fee for cross-country skiing. **Phone:** (920) 731-6041. 🖝

SAVE **HEARTHSTONE HISTORIC HOUSE MUSEUM** is at 625 W. Prospect Ave. Hearthstone was the first house in the world to be lit by a water-powered electric central station using the Thomas Edison System. Visitors can explore electricity in the hands-on hydroadventure center. The restored 1882 structure contains period furniture, intricate woodwork, Minton tiles and original light switches and fixtures designed by the Edison Co. Special events, including Victorian Christmas, as well as changing exhibits are offered.

Time: Allow 1 hour minimum. **Hours:** Guided tours begin every half-hour Tues.-Fri. 10-3:30, Sat. 11-3:30, Sun. 1-3:30. Closed last two weeks in Jan. **Cost:** Fee $6; $3 (ages 5-17). Christmas tours $7; $4 (ages 5-17). **Phone:** (920) 730-8204.

SAVE **THE HISTORY MUSEUM AT THE CASTLE** is at 330 E. College Ave. The museum's A.K.A. Houdini exhibit recounts the life of magician Harry Houdini, who claimed Appleton as his hometown, and reveals how he performed his most spectacular illusions. The Sports and Spirit exhibit features individual and team sports from the late 19th century to the present and explores how organized, competitive sports create ties that build a community. The Tools of Change exhibit includes a reproduction of a 19th-century paper shop, an 1896 wire-weaving loom, a 1926 Model-T Ford, a 1920s newspaper composing room and a 1930s bulletproof bank.

Time: Allow 1 hour, 30 minutes minimum. **Hours:** Mon.-Sat. 10-4 (also Thurs. 4-8), Sun. noon-4, June-Aug.; Tues.-Sat. 10-4, Sun. noon-4, rest of year. Closed major holidays. **Cost:** $7.50; $5.50 (ages 65+ and students with ID); $3.50 (ages 5-17); $20 (family). **Phone:** (920) 735-9370.

PAPER DISCOVERY CENTER is at 425 W. Water St. Housed in a renovated paper mill on the banks of the Fox River, this science and technology museum celebrates all things paper. Enjoy interactive exhibits while learning about the science, history and art of paper. Design and create a sheet of paper in the Purdy-Weissenborn paper lab.

Time: Allow 1 hour minimum. **Hours:** Mon.-Sat. 10-4; closed Jan. 1, Easter, Memorial Day, July 4, Labor Day, Thanksgiving and Dec. 24-25 and 31. **Cost:** $5; $4 (ages 62+); $3 (students with ID); $12 (family). **Phone:** (920) 380-7491.

ASHIPPUN (H-7) pop. 2,308, elev. 858'

HONEY ACRES MUSEUM is 2 mi. n. on SR 67. The history and techniques of beekeeping are preserved at Honey Acres, which has been owned by the same family of beekeepers and honey packers since 1852. A 20-minute multimedia presentation and various displays highlight pollination and the enemies of the bee. Visitors can taste five varieties of honey and four varieties of mustard and view an active beehive. A nature trail is on the grounds.

Time: Allow 30 minutes minimum. **Hours:** Mon.-Fri. 9-3:30, Sat.-Sun. noon-4, mid-May through Oct. 31; Mon.-Fri. 9-3:30, rest of year. Closed major holidays. **Cost:** Free. **Phone:** (920) 474-4411 or (800) 558-7745.

ASHLAND (B-4) pop. 8,620, elev. 660'

Whether Fourth of July festivities on Madeline Island inspired Asaph Whittlesey to establish a new town is uncertain, but on July 5, 1854, he arrived on the southeast shore of Chequamegon Bay of Lake Superior, built a cabin and founded Ashland. Once his cabin was complete, Whittlesey opened negotiations with the railroad in Chicago to provide an outlet for the area's timber, brownstone and iron ore.

The railroad, completed in 1877, combined with Ashland's natural harbor, soon made the community a thriving port; millions of tons of iron ore and timber were shipped annually. Legacies of this prosperous period are the distinctive facades of preserved, early 20th-century commercial buildings in the Main Street Historic District. Ten murals painted on historic buildings in the eight-block business district portray scenes from local history as part of the Ashland Mural Walk.

Although the area's commercial resources are important, its other resources—local parks, national forests, Lake Superior and Chequamegon Bay—have made Ashland an active recreation center. Trout, walleye, perch, salmon, northern pike and muskellunge thrive in Lake Superior and inland lakes and streams. Lake Superior charter excursions can be arranged in Ashland.

Prentice Park, 100 acres at the west edge of town, is a refuge for ducks and swans; camping, hiking and picnicking are available. Band concerts take place at the historic band shell in Memorial Park Thursday evenings in the summer.

Ashland is part of a statewide network of well-groomed snowmobile trails, which include the Tri-County Trail and the Mount Valhalla Recreational Area in Chequamegon-Nicolet National Forest *(see place listing p. 138)*. A map outlining area snowmobile touring loops and cross-country ski trails is available from the chamber of commerce.

Ashland Area Chamber of Commerce: 1716 W. Lakeshore Dr., P.O. Box 746, Ashland, WI 54806. **Phone:** (715) 682-2500 or (800) 284-9484.

NORTHERN GREAT LAKES VISITOR CENTER is 2.5 mi. w. on US 2 to CR G. Exhibits, special programs and a theater show featuring lighting and sound effects illustrate the region's cultural and natural history. The center also offers visitor information services, nature trails, a research area, a five-story observation tower and Nature's Discovery Area, an outside exploration area for children. **Time:** Allow 1 hour minimum. **Hours:** Visitor center open daily 9-5. Archives Tues.-Fri. 1-4:30. **Cost:** Free. **Phone:** (715) 685-9983.

AUGUSTA (E-3) pop. 1,186, elev. 972′

DELL'S MILL HISTORICAL LANDMARK & MUSEUM is 3 mi. n. on SR 27, then w. on CR V. This flour and feed mill served the community for 145 years. No major commercial milling has been done since the building was converted to a museum in 1968. The machinery still is in working order and a small amount of milling continues. Visitors can tour the five-story 1864 structure to observe how the water-powered parts—including 3,000 feet of belting and 175 pulleys—interact. **Time:** Allow 1 hour

DID YOU KNOW

Wisconsin, "America's Dairyland," produces more cheese than any other state.

minimum. **Hours:** Daily 10-5, May-Oct. **Cost:** $7; $3.50 (ages 6-18); $1.50 (ages 3-5). **Phone:** (715) 286-2714.

BABCOCK (F-5) elev. 975′

SANDHILL WILDLIFE AREA is on CR X. Automobile and hiking trails with observation towers permit visitors to view the woods and wide marshes of this 9,150-acre wildlife refuge, home to geese, ducks, sand hill cranes, bison, deer and other native flora and fauna. **Time:** Allow 2 hours minimum. **Hours:** Park open daily dawn-dusk. Automobile trails open daily, mid-Apr. through Oct. 31; also mid-Dec. to mid-Mar. for cross-country skiing. **Cost:** Donations. **Phone:** (715) 884-2437.

BAGLEY (I-3) pop. 339, elev. 630′

WYALUSING STATE PARK is 6 mi. n. on CR X (N. Bagley Ave.) to 13081 State Park Ln. The 2,628-acre park encompasses the spot where Father Jacques Marquette and Louis Joliet discovered the Mississippi River. Prehistoric mounds lie on Sentinel Ridge, 520 feet above the Mississippi. Interesting rock formations, bluffs and lookouts are found throughout the park. Camping, picnicking, canoeing and hiking are popular. *See Recreation Chart and the AAA Great Lakes CampBook.*

Hours: Daily 6 a.m.-11 p.m. **Cost:** Day-use fee (per private vehicle) $10; $7 (state residents); $3 (resident seniors ages 65+). Annual permit $35; $25 (state residents); $10 (resident seniors ages 65+). Hourly fee $5. **Phone:** (608) 996-2261.

BAILEYS HARBOR—

see Door County p. 141.

BARABOO (H-5) pop. 10,711, elev. 879′

The river, the nearby mountains of purplish quartzite and the trim little city of Baraboo all took their name from the French trader Baribault, whose post stood here in the early 19th century.

Baraboo also is the hometown of the Ringling Brothers. Fond memories of a circus boat they had seen in Iowa spurred five sons of a German harnessmaker to present their first "Classic and Comic Concert Company" show in 1882. From 1884 to 1918 Baraboo was home to their enterprise, which ultimately became Ringling Bros. and Barnum & Bailey Circus. The tradition continues today with live circus shows in the summer.

Baraboo Area Chamber of Commerce: 600 W. Chestnut St., P.O. Box 442, Baraboo, WI 53913. **Phone:** (608) 356-8333 or (800) 227-2266.

CIRCUS WORLD MUSEUM is at 550 Water St., following signs. Preserving the original winter quarters of the Ringling Brothers, the museum celebrates the history of the American circus. Throughout the summer season the museum offers big-top circus performances, hands-on programs and exhibits, including what is described as the world's largest collection of circus wagons.

Time: Allow 4 hours minimum. **Hours:** Daily 9-6, third weekend in May-Aug. 29; Mon.-Fri. 10-4, Aug. 30-Sept. 30 **Cost:** $14.95 (third weekend in May-Aug. 29); $12.95 (ages 65+); $7.95 (ages 5-11). Admission rest of year $7; $6 (ages 65+); $3.50 (ages 5-11). **Phone:** (608) 356-8341 or (866) 693-1500.

DEVIL'S LAKE STATE PARK is 2.5 mi. s. on SR 123. Devil's Lake, spring fed and having no visible outlet, is bounded on three sides by the quartzite cliffs of the Baraboo Range. Bear, Lynx and Eagle Indian mounds were created by ancient tribes. The 10,000-acre park is one of several units of the Ice Age National Scientific Reserve, which is under development. In summer naturalist programs and exhibits explain the area's glacial phenomena.

This popular park features 29 miles of hiking trails including paths leading to such whimsically named rock formations as Elephant Rock and Devil's Doorway. Visitors also have access to large lakeshore picnic areas and more than 400 family campsites. *See Recreation Chart and the AAA Great Lakes CampBook.*

Hours: Park open daily 6 a.m.-11 p.m. **Cost:** $10 (per private vehicle); $7 (state residents); $3 (resident seniors ages 65+). Annual permit $35; $25 (state residents); $10 (resident seniors ages 65+). **Phone:** (608) 356-8301.

THE INTERNATIONAL CRANE FOUNDATION is 5.2 mi. n. on US 12, then 1.2 mi. e. on Shady Lane Rd.; from I-90/94 exit 92, 1.5 mi. s. on US 12, then 1.2 mi. e. on Shady Lane Rd. This nonprofit center works worldwide to conserve cranes and the wetlands, grassland and other ecosystems on which they depend.

According to the foundation, it maintains the world's only collection of all 15 crane species. Visitors can see rare whooping cranes in a natural wetland and learn about the Wisconsin-based whooping crane reintroduction program. The Spirit of Africa contains four outdoor exhibits featuring magnificent African cranes as well as a family education center. Interpretive nature trails wind through a restored tallgrass prairie and oak savanna.

Guided tours are available. **Hours:** Open daily 9-5, Apr. 15-Oct. 31. Guided 90-minute tours are given daily at 10, 1 and 3, Memorial Day-Labor Day; Sat.-Sun. at 10, 1 and 3, April-May and Sept.-Oct. **Cost:** $9.50; $8 (ages 62+); $5 (ages 5-11). **Phone:** (608) 356-9462.

MID-CONTINENT RAILWAY MUSEUM—
see North Freedom p. 184.

SAUK COUNTY HISTORICAL MUSEUM is at 531 4th Ave. Housed in a 1903 mansion, the museum displays American Indian and pioneer artifacts, Civil War equipment, household furnishings, toys, textiles

and genealogical records. **Hours:** Wed.-Sat. noon-4. **Cost:** Donations. A fee is charged to use genealogical records. **Phone:** (608) 356-1001.

WISCONSIN OPRY Allow 2 hours minimum. **Hours:** Mon.-Sat. at 8 p.m. (dinner at 6 p.m.), some Sun. at 3 and 8 p.m., Memorial Day weekend-late Sept. Performance days and hours may vary. Phone ahead to confirm schedule. **Cost:** Mon.-Sat. $31.50 (including meal); $19 (without meal). Rates vary on Sun. depending on show. **Phone:** (608) 254-7951 for schedule information.

GAMBLING ESTABLISHMENTS

• **Ho-Chunk Casino and Bingo,** S3214A Hwy. 12. **Hours:** Daily 24 hours. **Phone:** (800) 746-2486.

BARNEVELD (I-5) pop. 1,088

WINERIES

• **Botham Vineyards & Winery** is off US 18/151; take CR K 1.7 mi. s. to Langberry Rd., then .2 mi. w. to 8180 Langberry Rd. **Hours:** Wed.-Sun. 10-5, Apr. 1-Dec 24; Sat.-Sun. 10-5, in Mar. **Phone:** (608) 924-1412 or (888) 478-9463.

BAYFIELD (A-3) pop. 611, elev. 607'

Mansions grace the side streets of Bayfield, once the main shipping point for regionally produced lumber and sandstone. The town now relies on fishing, fruit crops and the annual throng of summer vacationers.

Bayfield has been dubbed Wisconsin's Berry Capital; throughout the summer, visitors may choose from picking cherries, blueberries, raspberries, strawberries or blackberries at local farms. In the autumn, apples, pumpkins and squash are ripe for harvesting.

Sightseeing cruises among the Apostle Islands *(see Apostle Islands National Lakeshore p. 129)* and ferry service to Madeline Island *(see place listing p. 155)*, both offshore in Lake Superior, depart from Bayfield. In the winter a motorized windsled offers transportation to the island until the lake freezes and cars can travel on an ice highway.

From mid-May through mid-October, Bayfield Heritage Tours offers guided tours of the town: Ghost and Legends of Old Bayfield, Dying to Get in Cemetery Tour, A Lighthearted Walk through Bayfield and Sven's Architect Tour. Phone (715) 779-0299 for further information.

The area affords good hunting, fishing, skiing, snowmobiling, kayaking, boating and sailing. Deepwater fishing trips leave the pier daily; a fishing license is required.

Bayfield Chamber of Commerce & Visitors Bureau: 42 S. Broad St., P.O. Box 138, Bayfield, WI 54814. **Phone:** (715) 779-3335 or (800) 447-4094.

APOSTLE ISLANDS CRUISE SERVICE—
see Apostle Islands National Lakeshore p.
129.

APOSTLE ISLANDS NATIONAL LAKESHORE
VISITOR CENTER AND HEADQUARTERS—
see Apostle Islands National Lakeshore p. 130.

LAKE SUPERIOR BIG TOP CHAUTAUQUA is 3.5
mi. s. on SR 13, then 2 mi. w. on Ski Hill Rd., at
the foot of Mount Ashwabay. The performing arts
organization presents a summer season of original
musicals, variety shows and national touring acts at
least 4 nights a week in a state-of-the-art, all-canvas
tent.

A free shuttle from Ashland, Washburn and Bayfield is available. **Time:** Allow 2 hours, 30 minutes
minimum. **Hours:** Shows at 7:30 p.m., mid-June to
early Sept. Matinee schedule varies; phone ahead to
confirm. **Cost:** Shows $18; $9 (ages 3-17); free
(ages 0-2 on parent's lap). Prices are higher for visiting artists. **Phone:** (715) 373-5552 or (888)
244-8368. [T]

BEAVER DAM (H-6) pop. 15,169, elev. 872′

A retail and manufacturing center, Beaver Dam
serves the surrounding dairy region. The Dodge
County Historical Society, in an 1890 Romanesque
library at 105 Park Ave., houses more than 4,000
items relating to city and county history; phone
(920) 887-1266. Nearby Beaver Dam Lake is noted
for good fishing and recreational boating; public
boat launches are available in the city.

Beaver Dam Area Chamber of Commerce: 127
S. Spring St., Beaver Dam, WI 53916. **Phone:** (920)
887-8879.

BELMONT (I-4) pop. 871, elev. 1,063′

Belmont had high hopes for growth and promi-
nence when the first session of the Wisconsin Territorial legislature met there in 1836. But after long
debate by the legislators, Madison was selected as
the permanent capital, although at the time it existed
only on paper. Contemporary Belmont is an agricultural village.

Visitors to Belmont Mound State Park, at E.
Mountain Road and CR G, can climb a 64-foot observation tower atop a 400-foot mound for unob-
structed views of the town and surrounding countryside. One corner of the park has been designated a
state natural area because of the diversity of plant
species there. Phone (608) 523-4427.

FIRST CAPITOL HISTORIC SITE is 3 mi. n.w. of
US 151 on CR G. Two restored buildings stand on
the site where the first territorial legislature met in
1836. In the Council House the legislature drafted
many laws and fixed the permanent government seat
in Madison. The lodging house contains displays
about Wisconsin's early territorial government and
history. **Hours:** Wed.-Sun. 10-4, mid-June through

Labor Day. Phone ahead to confirm schedule. **Cost:**
Donations. **Phone:** (608) 987-2122.

BELOIT (I-6) pop. 35,775, elev. 745′

The agent for New England Emigrating Co. must
be credited with having a silver tongue, for nearly
the entire town of Colebrook, N.H., moved to this
site on the Rock River in 1837. Determined to sus-
tain "science and religion and all the adjuncts that
contribute to the elevation of society," the cultured
arrivals promptly established a church and chartered
Beloit College in 1846.

The college is the site of more than two dozen
American Indian effigy mounds built between A.D.
700 and A.D. 1200. The Wright Museum of Art on
the Beloit College campus exhibits Asian art, graph-
ics and sculpture.

Other points of interest in town include the Near
East Side and Bluff Street historic districts, which
feature rare 19th-century cobblestone houses. The
Rock River offers boating and fishing opportunities.
The riverfront is the site of festivals as well as biking and walking paths and a lagoon with
paddleboats.

Just west of Beloit is Beckman Mill, a restored,
operating 1868 gristmill within a 50-acre county
park. The site also features a rebuilt dam with a
creamery, mill pond, picnic area and a one-of-a-kind
fish ladder; phone (608) 751-1551.

Home games for the minor-league baseball team
the Beloit Snappers, a Class A affiliate of the Minnesota Twins, are played at Pohlman Field.

Visit Beloit: 500 Public Ave., Beloit, WI 53511.
Phone: (608) 365-4838 or (800) 423-5648.

Self-guiding tours: Walking tour brochures about
local historic districts are available from the convention and visitors bureau.

THE ANGEL MUSEUM is at 656 Pleasant St.
(US 51). Housed in a renovated historic
church built by Italian immigrants in 1914, the museum features more than 12,000 angels including the
Berg Angel Collection as well as nearly 500 black
angels donated by Oprah Winfrey. **Time:** Allow 1
hour minimum. **Hours:** Thurs.-Sat. 10-4, Mar.-Dec.
Hours vary on Sun. in summer; phone ahead for
schedule. Closed major holidays. **Cost:** $7; $6 (ages
62+); $5 (students with ID); free (ages 0-5). **Phone:**
(608) 362-9099 or (877) 412-6435.

LOGAN MUSEUM OF ANTHROPOLOGY is in
Memorial Hall at Bushnell and College sts. on the
Beloit College campus. The 1869 building houses a
highly regarded collection of more than 225,000 artifacts, including Paleolithic art, jewelry from ancient civilizations, pre-Columbian ceramics and
American Indian beadwork, baskets and clothing.
Visitors can see the pieces and watch ongoing research through a two-story glass cube.

Time: Allow 30 minutes minimum. **Hours:**
Tues.-Sun. 11-4. Closed Thanksgiving and college
holidays. **Cost:** Donations. **Phone:** (608) 363-2677.

BLACK RIVER FALLS (F-3)
pop. 3,618, elev. 809'

Vast Black River State Forest *(see attraction listing)* and adjoining Jackson County Forest provide 188,000 acres of public lands full of wilderness trails, trout creeks and beautiful rock outcroppings. The winding Black River is a favorite with canoeists and kayakers, and clear Wazee Lake is not only the deepest lake in Wisconsin, it is said to be one of the best scuba diving destinations in the Midwest.

One of the first sawmills in Wisconsin was built here in 1819; the city was a busy logging center throughout the 19th century. Field of Honor Veterans Memorial, behind the chamber of commerce on Water Street, honors veterans and their families.

Black River Area Chamber of Commerce: 120 N. Water St., Black River Falls, WI 54615. **Phone:** (715) 284-4658 or (800) 404-4008.

BLACK RIVER STATE FOREST is e. on US 12. The forest encompasses 68,000 acres of diverse habitats. It lies in a transitional zone between Wisconsin's Driftless area and its glaciated central plain, which contributes to its unique geology. The forest offers camping, hiking, mountain bike trails, horseback riding trails, ATV riding, cross-country skiing, hunting, fishing and several other activities *(see Recreation Chart and the AAA Great Lakes CampBook).*

Vehicle permits are required in designated areas. **Hours:** Daily 6 a.m.-11 p.m. **Cost:** $10 (per private vehicle); $7 (state residents); $3 (resident seniors ages 65+). Annual permit $35; $25 (state residents); $10 (resident seniors ages 65+). Fees are charged for camping, bicycling and cross-country skiing. **Phone:** (715) 284-4103.

BLUE MOUNDS (I-5) pop. 708, elev. 1,296'

Serving as landmarks for Winnebago Indians and lead miners following the ore veins from Galena, Ill., two blue hills, the highest in southern Wisconsin, attracted Ebenezer Brigham in 1828. Using nothing more than a windlass, rope and tub, Brigham extracted more than 4 million pounds of lead from the ground. With his establishment of a smelting furnace, the town of Blue Mounds took shape.

When the Black Hawk War threatened, settlers built Fort Blue Mounds, which successfully defended the town during an ambush by Sac Indians. The fort later helped supply the troops who drove Black Hawk out of the state. A bronze plaque now commemorates the site.

BLUE MOUND STATE PARK is off US 18/151. The 1,153-acre park's centerpiece is 1,716-foot Blue Mound, the highest point in southern Wisconsin. According to legend, Winnebago treasure is buried in the mound. The summit offers views of the Baraboo Range and Wisconsin River Valley. *See Recreation Chart and the AAA Great Lakes CampBook.* **Hours:**

Park open daily 6 a.m.-11 p.m. **Cost:** $10 (per private vehicle); $7 (state residents); $3 (resident seniors ages 65+). Annual permit $35; $25 (state residents); $10 (resident seniors ages 65+). **Phone:** (608) 437-5711.

CAVE OF THE MOUNDS NATIONAL NATURAL LANDMARK is off US 18/151 on Cave of the Mounds Rd. This National Natural Landmark has theatrical lighting enhancing a variety of brilliantly colored stalactites, stalagmites and underground pools. A short film explains the history of the cave and its formation. Guided 1-hour tours follow concrete walkways through the cave, which maintains a uniform temperature of 50 F. The grounds also offer rock gardens, a gemstone mine, a fossil dig, hiking trails and picnic areas.

Food is available in summer. **Hours:** Tours depart every 20 min. daily 9-6, Memorial Day weekend-Labor Day; on the hour Mon.-Fri. 10-4, every 30 min. Sat.-Sun. 9-5, day after Labor Day-Nov. 15 and Mar. 15-day before Memorial Day weekend; Mon.-Fri. at 2, Sat.-Sun. on the hour 10-4, rest of year. Closed Jan. 1, Thanksgiving and Dec. 25. **Cost:** $15; $7.50 (ages 4-12). **Phone:** (608) 437-3038.

LITTLE NORWAY is off US 18/151 between Mount Horeb and Blue Mounds; exit Cave of the Mounds Rd. and follow signs to CR JG. This farmstead, known as Nissedahle ("Valley of the Elves"), was built by Norwegian settlers in the mid-1800s and houses pioneer furnishings, arts and crafts. On the grounds is a replica of a stave church built in Norway for the 1893 World's Columbian Exposition. Costumed guides conduct 45-minute tours.

Hours: Daily 9-7, July-Aug.; 9-5, May-June and Sept.-Oct. Last tour leaves 1 hour before closing. **Cost:** $12; $11 (ages 63+); $5 (ages 5-12). **Phone:** (608) 437-8211.

BOULDER JUNCTION (C-5)
pop. 958, elev. 1,648'

Boulder Junction is surrounded by the woodlands and lakes of the Northern Highland-American Legion State Forest *(see Recreation Chart and the AAA Great Lakes CampBook).* Recreational activities include hiking, bicycling, boating, cross-country skiing and snowmobiling. Fishing for muskellunge is particularly rewarding in the area, which bills itself as the "Musky Capital of the World." There are nearly 200 lakes within a 9-mile radius of Boulder Junction. The forest is a major producer of seedling pines for state reforestation programs.

Boulder Junction Chamber of Commerce: 5352 Park St., P.O. Box 286, Boulder Junction, WI 54512. **Phone:** (715) 385-2400 or (800) 466-8759.

BRODHEAD (I-5) pop. 3,180, elev. 792'

Edward Brodhead, chief engineer of the Milwaukee and Minnesota Railroad, is credited with having brought the railroad into the treeless sand prairie where the town began in 1856. Ancient trails already crossed the area, known to American Indians as the halfway point between the Mississippi and Lake Michigan. Both American Indians and European settlers once collected sap from the hard maples lining the Sugar River to make maple syrup and sugar.

The First Brigade Band, organized in 1857, achieved considerable popularity. Enlisted in the Civil War, the six-horse bandwagon followed Union general William T. Sherman on his Atlanta campaign and marched in the grand review in Washington, D.C., at the war's end.

The 23-mile Sugar River Trail, built on an abandoned railroad bed, follows the meandering river from Brodhead to New Glarus *(see place listing p. 183).*

Take a tour of the factory at Decatur Dairy, W1668 CR F, and see how fine Wisconsin cheese is made; phone (608) 897-8661 for reservations.

Brodhead Chamber of Commerce: P.O. Box 16, Brodhead, WI 53520. **Phone:** (608) 897-8411.

Self-guiding tours: Brodhead's Exchange Square and North Residential historic districts can be explored on a self-guiding walking tour. Maps are available from Brodhead Historical Depot Museum in the old railroad depot on SR 11; phone (608) 897-2549 or (608) 897-8411.

BRUCE (D-3) pop. 787, elev. 1,106'

RECREATIONAL ACTIVITIES
Skiing and Snowboarding
- **Christie Mountain** 8 mi. n.w. of jct. US 8 and SR 40 at W13755 CR O, Bruce, WI 54819. **Hours:** Skiing and snowboarding Wed.-Thurs. 5 p.m.-9 p.m., Fri. 5 p.m.-10 p.m., Sat. 10-10, Sun. 10-5 (tubing Fri. 5 p.m.-10 p.m., Sat. noon-10, Sun. noon-5), Fri. after Thanksgiving-third or fourth Sun. in Mar. (weather permitting). **Phone:** (715) 868-7800.

BURLINGTON (I-7) pop. 9,936, elev. 790'

Burlington, home to the Nestle Co., has been celebrating chocolate for more than 30 years and was designated by the Governor of Wisconsin as "Chocolate City USA." The town celebrates Chocolate Fest on Memorial Day weekend; phone (262) 763-6044.

Burlington has long been noted as the home of the Burlington Liars' Club, an organization that encourages contributors from around the world to write tall tales in the classic country manner, a tradition it has sustained since 1929 when the first competition gained national attention. Each year scores of tall-tale tellers vie for first place, and the winner is announced each New Year's Eve. Visitors can explore the "Tall Tale Trail," a trail through town featuring tall tales on bronze plaques at various businesses.

Another popular Burlington attraction is the dramatic offerings of the Haylofters—one of the oldest community theater groups in Wisconsin—presented from May through October at Malt House Theatre. Free water-skiing performances by the Aquaducks are offered at Fischer Park on Browns Lake Thursday at 6, Memorial Day through Labor Day.

Burlington Area Chamber of Commerce: 113 E. Chestnut St. Suite B, P.O. Box 156, Burlington, WI 53105. **Phone:** (262) 763-6044.

Self-guiding tours: Maps describing a walking and driving tour linking sites important to Underground Railroad history in Racine County are available from the chamber of commerce.

LOGIC PUZZLE MUSEUM is at 533 Milwaukee Ave. Visitors can exercise their gray matter trying to solve 60 hands-on puzzles and may make a puzzle to take home. Exhibits feature vintage mechanical puzzles, sliding block puzzles, Chinese checkers and Victorian parlor toys and puzzles. **Hours:** Open Tues.-Wed. 1-6, Sat. 10-1, June-Aug.; Sat. 10-1, rest of year. Closed major holidays. Phone ahead to confirm schedule. **Cost:** $6. Children must be with an adult. Reservations are required. **Phone:** (262) 763-3946.

CABLE (B-3) pop. 836, elev. 1,370'

The Cable vicinity is a popular year-round vacation area in northwest Wisconsin set in the heart of Chequamegon-Nicolet National Forest. Fine hunting and fishing are available along more than 150 lakes. More than 300 miles of mapped and marked trails are available for mountain bicyclists, hikers and cross-country skiers. The Cable area also has over 600 miles of groomed snowmobile trails. Hiking trails in the area include the demanding North Country National Scenic Trail.

Cable Area Chamber of Commerce: 13380 CR M, P.O. Box 217, Cable, WI 54821. **Phone:** (715) 798-3833 or (800) 533-7454.

CABLE NATURAL HISTORY MUSEUM is at 13470 CR M. Exhibits about northern Wisconsin wildlife include displays of native birds of prey, songbirds and mammals mounted in natural settings. Special workshops and outdoor programs offer natural history and science education. **Hours:** Tues.-Sat. 10-4. Closed Jan. 1, Thanksgiving weekend, Dec. 24-25 and 31. **Cost:** Donations. **Phone:** (715) 798-3890.

CAMBRIDGE (H-6) pop. 1,101, elev. 855'

Founded in the mid-1800s, Cambridge has long been a popular vacation spot for Chicagoans and other city dwellers lured to the spring-fed waters of nearby Lake Ripley. Ripley Park, on the lake's western shore, encompasses sandy beaches and a swimming area. The Cambridge area also is popular with cross-country skiers and hikers. The Glacial Drumlin Bike Trail, which follows the path of the 19th-century Chicago & Northwestern Railway, provides a winding, 47-mile-long scenic trail for bicyclists. Hiking and mountain biking trails, canoeing and picnicking are available.

Cambridge is noted for its pottery, antiques and artwork displayed in historic buildings along its Victorian-style Main Street.

Cambridge Chamber of Commerce: 102 W. Main St., P.O. Box 572, Cambridge, WI 53523. **Phone:** (608) 423-3780.

CAMERON (D-2) pop. 1,546, elev. 998'

PIONEER VILLAGE MUSEUM is 1.5 mi. w. on CR W (Museum Rd.). The pioneer street setting features 35 old buildings, including a train depot, church, general store, town hall, smithy, farmstead and late 19th-century house. Most buildings are furnished in period. Five display buildings house additional items relating to the county's settlement. An exhibit hall contains 40 display cases with historic artifacts. **Hours:** Thurs.-Sun. 1-5, early June-day before Labor Day. **Cost:** $5; $3 (ages 5-12). **Phone:** (715) 642-1327 or (715) 458-2080.

CAMPBELLSPORT (G-7)
pop. 1,913, elev. 1,062'

KETTLE MORAINE STATE FOREST—NORTHERN UNIT is 7 mi. e. on SR 67. Visitors can take a self-guiding automobile tour to view such geological formations as eskers, kames and kettles, created by glaciers more than 20,000 years ago. Henry Reuss Ice Age Visitor Center provides information about the forest's geological history. Recreational activities include boating, camping, fishing, hiking, horseback riding, mountain biking, swimming, cross-country skiing and snowmobiling (*see Recreation Chart*).

Time: Allow 3 hours minimum. **Hours:** Visitor center open Mon.-Fri. 8:30-4, Sat.-Sun. 9:30-5, Apr.-Nov. Hours vary rest of year. Mauthe Lake and Long Lake recreation areas open daily 6 a.m.-11 p.m. **Cost:** $10 (per private vehicle); $7 (state residents). Annual permit $35; $25 (state residents). $4 (additional trail fee for horseback riding or mountain biking). **Phone:** (262) 626-2116 Mon.-Fri. or (920) 533-8322. ⚐

CARTER (D-7) elev. 1,516'

GAMBLING ESTABLISHMENTS
• **Potawatomi Bingo Northern Lights Casino** is at 618 SR 32. **Hours:** Casino open daily 24 hours. Closed Dec. 25. **Phone:** (715) 473-2021 or (800) 487-9522.

CASSVILLE (I-3) pop. 1,085, elev. 622'

In the 1830s the Mississippi River community of Cassville was among several towns that vied for the status of territorial capital. It lost, but continued its existence as grain port and trading center for the surrounding farms.

Cassville Car Ferry, which departs from the Prime Street landing, makes trips across the Mississippi River to Turkey River Landing, near Millville, Iowa. The ferry operates daily Memorial Day weekend through Labor Day; Friday through Sunday in spring and fall. Phone (608) 725-5180.

STONEFIELD HISTORIC SITE is 1.2 mi. n.w. on CR VV, next to Nelson Dewey State Park (*see Recreation Chart and the AAA Great Lakes CampBook*). The first of the site's three parts is Stonefield, the reconstructed home of Nelson Dewey, Wisconsin's first governor. The second part, the State Agricultural Museum, exhibits

farm tools and machinery, manufacturers' models and domestic items tracing the evolution of agriculture and rural life from the 19th-century frontier days.

A covered bridge leads to the third section, a turn-of-the-20th-century rural village. More than 30 reconstructed buildings are furnished in period and include a bank, saloon, newspaper office, smithy and general store.

Time: Allow 2 hours minimum. **Hours:** Daily 10-4, Memorial Day weekend to mid-Oct. Last admission 2 hours before closing. **Cost:** $8; $6.75 (students with ID and ages 65+); $4 (ages 5-17); $22 (family). **Phone:** (608) 725-5210.

Governor Nelson Dewey Homesite is at 12195 CR VV. The Gothic Revival home of Wisconsin's first governor has been reconstructed on the site. The original red brick house burned in 1873, but the doors, walls and millwork that remained intact were used in the reconstruction. Books and personal belongings of the Dewey family are displayed. The 2,000-acre estate was one of the few Midwestern farms planned in the manner of a Virginia plantation. **Hours:** Tours are given daily at 11 and 2, Memorial Day weekend to mid-Oct. Last tour begins 1 hour before closing.

CEDARBURG—*see Milwaukee p. 177.*

CHEQUAMEGON-NICOLET NATIONAL FOREST

Elevations in the forest range from 600 ft. at Lake Superior to 1,860 ft. near Twin Lake. Refer to AAA maps for additional elevation information.

In north-central and northeastern Wisconsin, the Chequamegon-Nicolet National Forest comprises 1.5 million acres in four separate regions. The Chequamegon (she-Wa-ma-gon) area covers 856,938 acres east, south and northwest of Park Falls on SRs 182 and 13; the Nicolet (nik-oh-LAY) area totals 661,200 acres east of Rhinelander and is accessible via several major highways.

More than 800 lakes dot the Chequamegon forest, where tree species include maple, aspen, pine, spruce, balsam, oak and birch. Licensed hunting and fishing are available in season. The Chippewa, Flambeau, Jump, St. Croix and Yellow rivers provide good canoeing in the spring and early summer. Muskellunge fishing is excellent.

An extensive 200-mile trail system threads through the Chequamegon, where a 49-mile segment of the Ice Age National Scenic Trail follows the terminal moraines of the last glaciers. Providing a system of loops used for cross-country skiing as well as hiking, the Rock Lake National Recreation Trail passes near Cable. Maps of snowmobile and cross-country ski trails are available at the forest supervisor headquarters.

The North Country National Scenic Trail traverses 34 miles of the northern part of the forest, roughly between Mellen and Iron River. Part of this route crosses the Rainbow Lake and Porcupine Lake wildernesses. Together covering about 11,000 acres of glaciated, lake-dotted woodlands, the wilderness areas offer an opportunity to experience a Northern hardwood forest free of development.

Primitive trails thread through the Nicolet region's three wilderness areas: Whisker Lake Wilderness Area, 8 miles west of Florence on SR 70, containing Riley and Whisker lakes; Blackjack Springs Wilderness Area, 8 miles east of Eagle River on SR 70, containing spring ponds; and the 22,000-acre Headwaters Wilderness Area, 8 miles east of Three Lakes on SR 32 and FR 2183.

With 1,200 lakes, 1,100 miles of trout streams and more than 400 spring ponds, the Nicolet forest also offers good fishing; there is hunting for deer, bears and upland game in season. Canoeing on the Wolf and Peshtigo rivers provides white-water excitement, while the Oconto, Pine, Popple and Wisconsin rivers are gentler.

The Great Divide Scenic Byway (SR 77) provides visitors with some of the most picturesque scenery in Wisconsin. The portion of this route between Hayward and Glidden is punctuated by several highlands known as the Penokee Range. The byway takes its name from the ridges that form the Great Divide, which separates waters flowing north to Lake Superior from waters flowing south to the Mississippi River.

There are more than 50 developed campgrounds in the combined forests; campsites are available on a first-come, first-served basis, but a limited number may be reserved in advance. For reservations phone, (877) 444-6777 daily 10-8.

For information about Chequamegon-Nicolet campgrounds and facilities, contact the forest headquarters at 500 N. Hanson Lake Rd., Rhinelander, WI 54501; phone (715) 362-1300, Mon.-Fri. 8-4:30.

Information also is available from district ranger offices in Eagle River, Florence, Glidden, Hayward, Lakewood, Laona, Medford, Park Falls, Washburn and the Northern Great Lakes Visitor Center in Ashland. *See Recreation Chart and the AAA Great Lakes CampBook.*

CHILTON (G-7) pop. 3,708, elev. 902'

Chilton began in 1845 when Moses Stanton built a cabin and grist mill on the banks of the Manitowoc River. Today the town is home to many year-round and seasonal activities including cave exploration at Ledge View Nature Center *(see attraction listing p. 139)*, canoeing and ice skating on the river and extreme motocross racing at Gravity Park USA.

Calumet County Tourism: 206 Court St., P.O. Box 24, Chilton, WI 53014. **Phone:** (920) 849-1493, ext. 790.

LEDGE VIEW NATURE CENTER is 1 mi. s. of jct. SRs 32 and 57, then 1.2 mi. s. on Irish Rd. to W2348 Short Rd., following signs. Just inside the nature center, a stream runs though a large rock formation surrounded by mounted wildlife. Displays feature live animals including snakes, a large aquarium stocked with sturgeon, and bees swarming in a glass-enclosed hive. Visitors can learn about echolocation and hibernation while observing flying bats. A 60-foot-tall observation tower provides views of the surrounding grounds, caves and rock ledges. There also are 2.5 miles of trails and an arboretum. In winter months, there are opportunities for snowshoeing and cross-country skiing.

Note: Insect repellant is recommended in summer months. **Tours:** Guided tours are available. **Time:** Allow 1 hour, 30 minutes minimum. **Hours:** Park open daily dawn-dusk. Nature center open Mon.-Fri. 8-4:30, Sat.-Sun. 10-4:30. Cave tours Sat.-Sun., May-Oct. Guided 1- to 2-hour snowshoe hikes Sun., mid-Jan. through mid-Feb. Closed major holidays. **Cost:** Cave tours $7. Snowshoe hike (includes instruction and rental) $5. Nature center free. **Phone:** (920) 849-7094. 🅰

CHIPPEWA FALLS (E-2)
pop. 12,925, elev. 848'

That several locally made beverages have attained critical acclaim is credited to the purity of Chippewa Falls' ground water. It was not the clear water, however, that first attracted settlement to the banks of the Chippewa in 1837, but the vast white-pine forests and the river's potential for producing power.

With the passing of the logging era, attention turned to serving the local farmers, generating electricity for use throughout the region and developing diversified industry—including brewing and spring water bottling. Premium Waters, Inc./Chippewa Spring Water, which still operates today, was founded in 1880 by Thaddeus Pound—former Wisconsin lieutenant governor and grandfather of poet Ezra Pound.

Impounded by the Chippewa Falls dam, Lake Wissota provides fishing and other recreational activities. Lake Wissota State Park *(see Recreation Chart and the AAA Great Lakes CampBook)* is on the east shore. At the Chippewa Rose Society Garden, Jefferson Avenue and Bridgewater, see a beautiful collection of more than 500 roses, including teas, floribunda, grandifloras, miniatures and climbers. If you're interested in hiking or bicycling, try out the paved 19.5-mile Old Abe State Trail or the 5-mile Duncan Creek Trail.

Chippewa Falls Area Chamber of Commerce: 10 S. Bridge St., Chippewa Falls, WI 54729. **Phone:** (715) 723-0331 or (888) 723-0024.

IRVINE PARK AND ZOO is .5 mi. n. on SR 124. The 318-acre park offers picnic facilities and multiple cross-country ski and walking trails. The zoo offers a look at Wisconsin wildlife with bears, deer, geese, ducks, elk and native birds present. The park also features a selection of exotic animals including tigers, cougars and buffaloes. Thousands of Christmas lights and decorations transform the park into a Christmas Village from Thanksgiving through New Year's Day.

Hours: Park open daily 7 a.m.-dusk. Petting zoo open 10-6, June-Aug. **Cost:** Free. **Phone:** (715) 723-0051.

LEINENKUGEL BREWERY TOURS is on SR 124 at 124 E. Elm St. Guided 1-hour tours detail the brewing process. Displays depict the history of brewing in the area. Tastings are available. **Hours:** Guided tours are given every half-hour Mon.-Thurs. 9:30-4, Fri. 9:30-6:30, Sat. 9:30-4, Sun. 11:30-3. Closed Jan. 1, Easter, Thanksgiving and Dec. 25. **Cost:** Free. Reservations are recommended. **Phone:** (715) 723-5557 or (888) 534-6437.

COON VALLEY (G-3) pop. 714, elev. 735'

In a valley laced with numerous springs and surrounded by high bluffs, Coon Valley lies in a landscape forever captured in the books of Hamlin Garland, who grew up on a farm in nearby West Salem *(see place listing p. 200).* Reminiscent of the valleys of Norway, the ravines in the Coon Valley area attracted Norwegian and Bohemian immigrants beginning in 1849.

The hills around the village are among the highest along US 14/61. Between the bluffs are tobacco and dairy farms run by descendants of the village's original settlers.

SAVE **NORSKEDALEN NATURE & HERITAGE CENTER** is 3 mi. n.e. via CRs P and PI, nestled in Poplar Coulee. The 400-acre educational, nature and heritage center offers trails, museums, an arboretum, a visitor center and a restored 1890s pioneer log homestead. Norskedalen's Skumsrud Heritage Farm, west of Coon Valley and south of Norskedalen off US 14/61, offers seasonal self-guiding tours through 12 historic buildings. Programs are offered Sundays at 2, April through November. Special events are featured throughout the year.

A trail is available for the physically impaired. Leashed pets are permitted on the grounds but not in the buildings. **Time:** Allow 1 hour minimum. **Hours:** Mon.-Fri. 9-5, Sat. 10-5, Sun. noon-5, May-Oct.; Mon.-Fri. 8-4, Sun. noon-4, rest of year. Homestead open daily 10-5, May-Oct. Skumsrud Heritage Farm open Fri. noon-6, Sat. 10-5, Sun. noon-5, June-Aug. Phone ahead to confirm schedule. **Cost:** $6 (including Skumsrud); $3 (ages 5-17); $15 (family). **Phone:** (608) 452-3424. ⊞

DANBURY (C-2) elev. 947′

FORTS FOLLE AVOINE HISTORICAL PARK is 2.5 mi. w. on CR U from jct. SR 35. This 80-acre living history site includes reconstructions of an Ojibwe Indian village and fur trading posts that flourished along the Yellow River 1802-04. Costumed interpreters provide guided tours of the park, which includes museum displays, archeological exhibits and a research library.

Time: Allow 1 hour minimum. **Hours:** Park open Wed.-Sun. 10-4, Memorial Day weekend-Labor Day weekend; Sat.-Sun. 10-4, day after Labor Day-Sept. 30. Tours depart on the hour 10-3. **Cost:** $7; $5 (ages 6-12); $20 (family, two adults and two children). **Phone:** (715) 866-8890.

DE PERE (F-7) pop. 20,559, elev. 595′

De Pere originally was called "Rapides des Pères" for the Jesuits who established the first mission in the state in 1669. From here explorers Jacques Marquette and Louis Joliet departed on their voyage of discovery.

Tours of the St. Joseph National Shrine are free and can be arranged at St. Norbert Abbey, 1016 N. Broadway; phone (920) 337-4300. Small stores and restaurants line the streets of downtown De Pere, offering boutique shopping in a scenic small-town atmosphere.

ONEIDA NATION MUSEUM is 5 mi. w. on SR 54 from US 41 exit 168, then 5 mi. s. on CR E and just w. on CR EE. This museum has displays and hands-on exhibits tracing the history and culture of the Oneida Indian Nation as it moved from New York to Wisconsin. Two nature trails are on the grounds.

Guided tours are available by appointment. **Time:** Allow 1 hour minimum. **Hours:** Tues.-Sat. 9-5, June-Aug.; Tues.-Fri. 9-5, rest of year. **Cost:** $2; $1 (ages 0-17 and 55+). Guided tour $3. **Phone:** (920) 869-2768. ⊞

WHITE PILLARS is at 403 N. Broadway. Built in 1836 and remodeled in 1912, this building once housed the first bank offices in Wisconsin. It is now home to the De Pere Historical Society and its Historical Museum. An extensive collection includes rare documents, photographs and archives. **Time:** Allow 30 minutes minimum. **Hours:** Mon.-Thurs. 2-6; Fri. 11-3. Closed major holidays. **Cost:** Donations. **Phone:** (920) 336-3877.

DICKEYVILLE (I-4) pop. 1,043, elev. 955′

DICKEYVILLE GROTTO is on US 61/151 and SR 35. Made of costume jewelry, knickknacks, colorful bits of stone, glass and shell from around the world, the grotto was built 1925-30 by Father Mathias Wernerus as an expression of unity between religion and patriotism. **Time:** Allow 30 minutes minimum. **Hours:** Grotto open daily 24 hours. Guided tours daily 11-4, June-Aug.; Sat.-Sun. 11-4, Sept.-Oct. Last tour leaves one hour before closing. **Cost:** Donations. **Phone:** (608) 568-3119.

DODGEVILLE (I-4) pop. 4,220, elev. 1,249′

Along with Mineral Point *(see place listing p. 182)*, Dodgeville was a metropolis of the lead-mining region in the 1820s and 1830s during which its population was larger than Milwaukee and Chicago. The town bears the name of Henry Dodge, a colorful frontiersman who pioneered the mining industry, figured prominently in the defeat of Black Hawk and served as the first territorial governor of Wisconsin and later as a U.S. senator.

The 40-mile Military Ridge State Trail connects Dodgeville with Madison passing along the boundaries of Governor Dodge State Park *(see attraction listing)* and Blue Mound State Park *(see attraction listing p. 135)*. Hikers and bicyclists use the gravel-paved trail until winter, when it is opened to cross-country skiers and snowmobilers.

The town is home to the corporate headquarters for the Lands' End clothing company.

Dodgeville Area Chamber of Commerce & Information Center: 338 N. Iowa St., Dodgeville, WI 53533. **Phone:** (608) 935-9200 or (877) 863-6343.

GOVERNOR DODGE STATE PARK is 4 mi. n. at 4175 SR 23N. This unglaciated area of hills, bluffs and valleys contains two lakes, picturesque Stephens Falls and scenic rock formations, which can be seen from the network of hiking and riding trails. *See Recreation Chart and the AAA Great Lakes CampBook.* **Hours:** Daily 6 a.m.-11 p.m. **Cost:** $10 (per private vehicle); $7 (state residents); $3 (resident seniors ages 65+). Annual permit $35; $25 (state residents); $10 (resident seniors ages 65+). **Phone:** (608) 935-2315.

MUSEUM OF MINERALS AND CRYSTALS is 4 mi. n. on SR 23. Displayed are more than 3,000 rock, mineral and crystal specimens mostly from Africa, Australia, Brazil, China, England, Mexico and the United States. A 90-pound quartz crystal, a 315-pound agate, a 215-pound a geode amethyst and gemstone picture of Man o' War are highlights. Fluorescent material is displayed in a black-lit room. Horseback riding is available.

Time: Allow 1 hour minimum. **Hours:** Mon.-Sat. 9-5, June-Aug.; Mon.-Sat. 9-4, Apr.-May and Sept.-Oct. **Cost:** $5; $4.50 (ages 65+); $4 (ages 6-18). Horseback rides $25 (1 hour); $20 (45 minutes). Trail pass $4. **Phone:** (608) 935-5205.

DOOR COUNTY

Door County stretches from about 15 miles south of Sturgeon Bay to the islands that lie off the northern tip of the Door Peninsula. Wisconsin's most conspicuous feature extends like the spout of a teapot into Green Bay and Lake Michigan. The waters on either side of the 70-mile-long peninsula have carved much of its rocky shoreline into caves, arches and cliffs. The overall effect is that this rugged landscape—dotted with fishing villages, beaches, farms and orchards—resembles New England more than the Midwest.

Despite its scenic allure, the treacherously narrow channel between the peninsula's end and its outlying rocky islands was feared by American Indians and trappers. They named the channel *porte des morts,* or death's door, from which the peninsula and county take their names.

According to legend 17th-century French fur traders first ran afoul of the strait when Robert La Salle's ship *Griffin* sank. To circumvent the straits and the tedious trip around the peninsula, traders followed the American Indians' portage at Sturgeon Bay, which allowed easier passage to the important trade route at the head of Green Bay.

Fur trading dominated the area for 200 years, and it was not until the 19th century that Moravians, Scandinavians and other immigrants settled the peninsula and its surrounding islands. Around the turn of the 20th century wealthy city dwellers discovered the region's charms, transforming rustic villages into resorts.

Much of the peninsula and its islands cater to vacationers. Sailing on the surrounding waters, hiking and golf in one of the nearby state parks, as well as such cultural activities as summer theater, concerts and fish boils are area draws. Historic lighthouses, cherry blossoms and more than 50 sand beaches along Lake Michigan and Green Bay further accentuate the allure.

Door County Visitor Bureau: 1015 Green Bay Rd., P.O. Box 406, Sturgeon Bay, WI 54235. **Phone:** (920) 743-4456, or (800) 527-3529 for a vacation planning guide.

Baileys Harbor (D-9) pop. 1,003, elev. 595'

During a fierce storm in 1848, Captain Justice Bailey found a safe port for his schooner on the Lake Michigan coast. Baileys Harbor, as the place came to be known, is the oldest village in the Door County. The scenic harbor, notched into the Door Peninsula, is a popular vacation center.

A half-mile north, the Ridges Sanctuary offers hiking trails in a natural wildlife area where wildflowers and species of native orchids can be seen from May to September. Tours are conducted during the summer and early fall and guided snowshoe hikes take place in January and February.

Nearby recreational activities include salmon and trout fishing, bicycling, sea kayaking, windsurfing,

kite boarding, snowmobiling and cross-country skiing. The Cana Island Lighthouse, about 4 miles northeast of Baileys Harbor via CR Q, was built in 1869. Stroll through the keepers' house, climb the lighthouse tower and explore the rocky shore which surrounds this glorious island. There is a minimal entry fee. Daily 10-5, early May-late Oct. Phone (920) 743-5958.

Egg Harbor (E-9) pop. 250, elev. 635'

Although some sources credit Increase Claflin, the first settler of Door County, with naming the town for a nest of duck eggs, one legend claims the "Battle of the Eggs" gave Egg Harbor its name. A group of Green Bay men supposedly sailed into the harbor in 1825 and engaged in an egg-throwing fight when they reached the townsite.

From mid-June to mid-August, Birch Creek Music Performance Center, a performing arts school and concert venue 3 miles east via CR E, presents symphony, percussion/steel band and big band performances in an early 1900s barn adapted as a concert hall; phone (920) 868-3763.

Ephraim (D-9) pop. 353, elev. 710'

Founded in 1853 by Moravians from Norway, Ephraim is a resort village. A monument to the Moravian founders overlooks the harbor. South of town is Peninsula State Park. *See Recreation Chart and Door County as well as Fish Creek in the AAA Great Lakes CampBook.*

Guided walking tours of Ephraim's historic district are offered Tuesday through Friday at 10:30, mid-June through the Saturday before Labor Day; tram tours are offered Tuesday through Friday at 10 and Saturday at 11. Both tours depart from the Ephraim Historical Foundation's Anderson Barn History Center. For further information, phone (920) 854-9688.

ANDERSON BARN HISTORY CENTER is at 3060 Anderson Ln. The history center is the starting point for guided 1.3-mile walking and tram tours of historic Ephraim, featuring the Anderson Store, Pioneer Schoolhouse and Goodletson Cabin. The center features a timeline of Ephraim history, a special exhibit each year, hands-on activities for children and an interactive touch screen exhibit. **Hours:** Tues.-Sat. 11-4, mid-June through Labor Day; Fri.-Sat. 11-4, weekend after Labor Day through Columbus Day weekend. **Cost:** $5 (includes Anderson Barn History Center, Anderson Store, Pioneer Schoolhouse and Goodletson Cabin); $3 (ages 6-18). **Phone:** (920) 854-9688.

The Anderson Store is .5 mi. n. on SR 42. The restored 1858 general store displays retail items typical of the 1940s, antiques, clothes, tools and possessions of Ephraim's settlers.

Tours: Guided tours are available. **Time:** Allow 30 minutes minimum. **Hours:** Tues.-Sat. 11-4, mid-June through Labor Day; Fri.-Sat. 11-4, weekend after Labor Day-Columbus Day weekend. **Cost:** $5 (includes Anderson Barn History Center, Anderson Store, Pioneer Schoolhouse and Goodletson Cabin); $3 (ages 6-18). **Phone:** (920) 854-9688.

Pioneer Schoolhouse and Goodletson Cabin is 1.5 mi. e. of SR 42 at 9998 E. Moravia St. Built in 1880, the one-room schoolhouse operated until 1949. Exhibits include memorabilia, photographs and costumes of local origin. The Goodletson Cabin, located behind the school, offers a glimpse into how families lived during the era.

Hours: Tues.-Sat. 11-4, mid-June through Labor Day; Fri.-Sat. 11-4, weekend after Labor Day-Columbus Day weekend. **Cost:** $5 (includes Anderson Barn History Center, Anderson Store, Pioneer Schoolhouse and Goodletson Cabin); $3 (ages 6-18). **Phone:** (920) 854-9688.

Fish Creek (D-9) elev. 583'

A huge castellated cliff rising above Green Bay dominates Fish Creek's western waterfront. Sheltered coves provide the finest natural harbors on this side of the peninsula, augmented by the town's marina.

The Peninsula Players, (920) 868-3287, the oldest resident professional summer stock company in the country, performs a variety of comedies, musicals and drama at Theatre in a Garden Tuesday through Sunday evenings, mid-June to mid-October.

PENINSULA STATE PARK is 2 mi. n.e. on SR 42. Established in 1909, Peninsula has 150-foot-high rocky bluffs and 8 miles of shoreline on Green Bay. A favorite with campers, the state park also draws those in search of hiking and biking (the park has 20 miles of trails), boating, fishing, picnicking, bird-watching and golfing (18 holes) in summer and cross-country skiing, sledding, tubing, snowmobiling and snowshoeing in winter.

Nature lovers will want to visit the park's two state natural areas, White Cedar Forest and Beech Maple Forest, as well as the White Cedar Nature Center, which has historic photos, mounted animals and birds and summer nature programs. If you're lucky, you might spot a deer wandering nearby.

Touring the historic Eagle Bluff Lighthouse, boating to Horseshoe Island and climbing up 75-foot Eagle Tower for panoramic views and to watch the sunsets over the waters of Green Bay are also popular activities. In summer catch one of the original 90-minute musical productions presented by the American Folklore Theatre at the park's outdoor amphitheater. *See Recreation Chart and the AAA Great Lakes CampBook.*

Hours: Park open daily 6 a.m.-11 p.m. Nature center daily 10-2, Memorial Day-Labor Day. Nature center schedule varies, rest of year; phone ahead. Theater productions are presented mid-June to late Aug. **Cost:** $10 (day use fee per private vehicle); $7 (state residents). Annual permit $35; $25 (state residents). **Phone:** (920) 868-3258 for the park headquarters, (920) 854-5976 for the nature center, (920)

854-6117 for the theater, or (888) 947-2757 for camping reservations. ▲ ⌦ ⌧ ⌸ ⌹

Eagle Bluff Lighthouse is off SR 42 to Peninsula State Park entrance, then 3.5 mi. n. on Shore Rd. Built in 1868, the restored lighthouse is furnished with early 1900s antiques and memorabilia. Tour guides regale visitors with stories about the exploits of lighthouse keeper William Duclon's family, including his seven sons, who lived here 1883-1918. **Hours:** Tours are given daily on the half-hour 10-3:30, early June to mid-Oct.; Sat.-Sun. on the hour 10-4, mid-May to early June. **Cost:** Park access fee $5. Lighthouse tour $5; $2 (ages 13-18); $1 (ages 6-12). **Phone:** (920) 421-3636.

Gills Rock (D-9) elev. 594'

DOOR COUNTY MARITIME MUSEUM AT GILLS ROCK is just e. off SR 42 at 12724 Wisconsin Bay Rd. This museum on the tip of the Door Peninsula chronicles the area's fishing heritage with displays featuring shipwreck artifacts, navigational instruments, antique motors and models and an exhibit entitled Piracy on the Great Lakes. The *Hope,* a restored commercial fishing tug, is featured.

Time: Allow 30 minutes minimum. **Hours:** Daily 10-5, Memorial Day weekend-late Oct. **Cost:** $4.50; $2 (ages 5-17); $10.50 (family, two adults and children ages 0-17). **Phone:** (920) 854-1844.

Sturgeon Bay (E-9) pop. 9,437, elev. 922'

Where once a tedious portage was necessary to avoid the 100-mile voyage around the tip of the Door Peninsula, today boats and giant freighters easily ply the ship canal between Green Bay and Lake Michigan. Sturgeon Bay, named for its fine natural harbor, is one of the largest shipbuilding ports on the Great Lakes.

Sturgeon Bay also processes the ruby yield of Door county's cherry orchards. Some 2,200 acres of cherry trees produce from 8 to 14 million pounds of fruit annually. The trees bloom in mid-May, carpeting the peninsula in blossoms; harvest occurs from mid-July to early August.

During the annual chinook salmon spawning run each fall, as many as 500 anglers attack the waters daily in Sturgeon Bay Harbor in search of the 20- to 40-pound fish. Abundant winter recreation opportunities are available, including cross-country skiing and snowmobiling.

On the shore of Sturgeon Bay, Potawatomi State Park *(see Recreation Chart and the AAA Great Lakes CampBook)* offers 9 miles of hiking trails, 8 miles of mountain biking trails and more than 8 miles of groomed ski trails and snowmobile trails. Visitors can take in scenic views of Sawyer Harbor from the park's 75-foot-tall observation tower.

DOOR COUNTY FIREBOAT CRUISES leave the city dock adjacent to the Door County Maritime Museum at 120 N. Madison Ave. A fire-engine red 1937 fireboat takes passengers on narrated tours through the Sturgeon Bay Ship Canal or to the Sherwood Point Lighthouse.

Time: Allow 1 hour, 30 minutes minimum. **Hours:** One-and-a-half-hour tours depart daily at 10:30 and 12:30, Memorial Day weekend-Labor Day; at 10:30, day after Labor Day-early Oct. (weather permitting). Phone ahead to confirm Sept.-Oct. schedule. **Cost:** $20 (for one cruise); $18 (ages 60+); $15 (ages 10-17); $5 (ages 5-9). $30 (for both cruises); $28 (ages 60+); $20 (ages 10-17); $10 (ages 5-9). **Phone:** (920) 495-6454.

DOOR COUNTY HISTORICAL MUSEUM is at 18 N. Fourth Ave. A wildlife diorama, pioneer items, an early firehouse and videos pertinent to Door County are among the exhibits. **Time:** Allow 1 hour minimum. **Hours:** Daily 10-4:30, May-Oct. **Cost:** Donations. **Phone:** (920) 743-5809.

DOOR COUNTY MARITIME MUSEUM is on the waterfront at 120 N. Madison Ave. Exhibits span the nautical history of Door County from early American Indian canoes to post-World War II bulk carriers and yachts. The museum features a model ship gallery, a small craft workshop, a lighthouse exhibit, an art gallery and vintage outboard motors and marine engines. The pilot house from a Great Lakes ore carrier is on display, part of the exhibit entitled Ghosts! Haunted Lighthouses of the Great Lakes. The nuclear ballistic submarine periscope offers a bay area view. Tours of the 150-foot tug *John Purves* are offered seasonally.

Time: Allow 1 hour, 30 minutes minimum. **Hours:** Daily 9-6, Memorial Day weekend-Labor Day; 10-5, rest of year. **Cost:** $7.50; $4 (ages 5-17). Tug tour $5. **Phone:** (920) 743-5958.

THE FARM is 4 mi. n. at 4285 SR 57N. The 40-acre rural environment includes various farm buildings, a pioneer homestead and farm animals, including young animals that can be held and fed. Particularly noteworthy are the nature cabin, with displays about the natural attractions of Door County, and the woodshed, with farm tools and utensils. There also are milking demonstrations, nature trails and vegetable, flower and herb gardens.

Time: Allow 1 hour minimum. **Hours:** Daily 9-5, Memorial Day weekend to mid-Oct. **Cost:** $8; $6.40 (ages 63+); $4 (ages 4-13). **Phone:** (920) 743-6666.

MILLER ART MUSEUM is in the Door County Public Library at 107 S. Fourth Ave. Permanent and changing exhibits include works in various media by Door County and other Midwestern artists. The main gallery also serves as a community center for museum-sponsored arts and education programs. **Time:** Allow 30 minutes minimum. **Hours:** Mon. 10-8, Tues.-Sat. 10-5. Closed major holidays. **Cost:** Donations. **Phone:** (920) 746-0707.

WINERIES

• **Door Peninsula Winery** is 6 mi. n. at 5806 SR 42. **Hours:** Daily 9-5. Tours are given daily on the hour 10-4. Last tour departs at 4. **Phone:** (920) 743-7431 or (800) 551-5049.

Washington Island (D-9)

Six miles off the tip of the Door Peninsula, Washington Island is surrounded by the waters of Lake Michigan and Green Bay. More than 200 years ago Potawatomi Indians inhabited the island. The tribe almost was destroyed by a sudden, severe squall that swamped the canoes of a war party as it crossed what is now known as Death's Door Strait, en route to the mainland.

The island's population is predominantly Scandinavian and constitutes the oldest Icelandic settlement in the United States. It is reached by daily ferry service from the Northport Pier, 2 miles east of Gills Rock on SR 42; phone (800) 223-2094. For narrated sightseeing tram tours of the island, board at the Washington Island dock. Providers include the Cherry Train, (920) 847-2546 or (800) 223-2094; and the Viking Tour Train, (920) 854-2972. Passenger excursion service to Rock Island State Park *(see Recreation Chart)* also is offered late May to mid-October.

Washington Island Chamber of Commerce: 2206 W. Harbor Rd., Box 222, Washington Island, WI 54246. **Phone:** (920) 847-2179.

JACOBSEN'S MUSEUM is 6 mi. n. of the ferry dock on Little Lake Rd. A cedar log building houses American Indian artifacts, antiques, rocks and fossils gathered on the island. **Time:** Allow 30 minutes minimum. **Hours:** Daily 10-4, Memorial Day weekend to mid-Oct. **Cost:** Donations. **Phone:** (920) 847-2213.

WASHINGTON ISLAND FARM MUSEUM is 5.4 mi. n. of the ferry dock at jct. Jackson Harbor and Airport rds. The museum provides a detailed look at Washington Island's farming history. Items displayed include horse-drawn farm equipment, log buildings, tools, a weaving loom and historic photographs. Farm animals and a blacksmith shop also are on the property. **Hours:** Daily 9:30-dusk, Memorial Day weekend-Columbus Day. **Cost:** Donations. **Phone:** (920) 847-2179.

DRESSER (D-1) pop. 732, elev. 973'

RECREATIONAL ACTIVITIES
Skiing and Snowboarding

• **Trollhaugen Winter Recreation Area**, CR F e. to 2232 100th Ave., Dresser, WI 54009. **Hours:** Sun.-Thurs. 9:30-9, Fri.-Sat. 9:30 a.m.-10 p.m., late Nov. through mid-Mar. (weather permitting). **Phone:** (715) 755-2955 or (800) 826-7166.

EAGLE—*see Milwaukee p. 177.*

EAGLE RIVER (C-6) pop. 1,443, elev. 1,628'

Eagle River is in an all-year resort area. The Eagle chain of lakes, consisting of 28 navigable lakes, is one of the best known boating and fishing areas in northern Wisconsin, and in winter the Eagle River vicinity boasts 500 miles of groomed snowmobile trails. At 519 Sheridan St. E. is the Trees for Tomorrow Natural Resource Specialty School, which has a self-guiding demonstration forest trail; phone (715) 479-6456.

The U.S. Forest Service maintains about 40 miles of cross-country ski trails in nearby Chequamegon-Nicolet National Forest *(see place listing p. 138);* there also are 600 miles of groomed trails in the area.

Eagle River Area Chamber and Visitors Center: 201 N. Railroad St., P.O. Box 1917, Eagle River, WI 54521. **Phone:** (800) 359-6315.

Shopping areas: Antiques and arts and crafts can be found on Wall Street and in the surrounding area.

NORTHWOODS CHILDREN'S MUSEUM is just n. on US 45 to Willow St., following signs to 346 W. Division St. The museum features 22 interactive exhibits for children including a camping exhibit, a pioneer cabin, a medical center, an art center and a grocery store. **Time:** Allow 1 hour minimum. **Hours:** Mon.-Sat. 10-5 (also Fri. 5-8), Sun. noon-5, Memorial Day-Labor Day; Tues.-Fri. 10-3 (also Fri. 3-8), Sat. 10-5, Sun. noon-5, rest of year. Closed Jan. 1, Easter, Mother's Day, Memorial Day, Labor Day, Thanksgiving and Dec. 24-26 and 31. **Cost:** $6. **Phone:** (715) 479-4623.

EAST TROY (I-7) pop. 3,564, elev. 860′

EAST TROY ELECTRIC RAILROAD departs 2002 Church St. The railroad preserves 19th- and 20th-century history through its museum, restoration efforts and 15 active interurban trolleys and coaches offering 10-mile round-trip rides between the depots in East Troy and Mukwonago. Special events include dinner trains, wine trains, Halloween and Santa trains. The depot has exhibits that can be toured while waiting for the train.

Time: Allow 1 hour, 30 minutes minimum. **Hours:** Trains depart Wed.-Fri. at 10, Sat.-Sun. at 11:30, June-Aug.; Fri. at 10, Sat.-Sun. at 11, Sept.-Oct. **Cost:** Round-trip trolley rides $12.50; $10.50 (ages 65+); $8 (ages 3-11). All-inclusive dinner trip $72. **Phone:** (262) 642-3263.

EAU CLAIRE (E-3) pop. 61,704, elev. 796′

Relations with Eau Claire's upstream neighbor, Chippewa Falls *(see place listing p. 139),* were not always amicable in the days when rival logging companies from both towns drove their cuts down the *eau claire* ("clear water") of the Chippewa River. A number of midnight log drives and battles took place before cooperation supplanted warfare. When the timber was exhausted, Eau Claire, like Chippewa Falls, turned to diversified manufacturing.

Eau Claire's position at the confluence of the Chippewa and Eau Claire rivers enhances its status as a gateway to the resort areas of northwestern Wisconsin. Outdoor activities, such as bicycling, hiking, fishing and skiing, abound throughout the year. If you prefer to do your stargazing inside, the L.E. Phillips Planetarium on the University of Wisconsin-Eau Claire campus offers programs to the public Tuesdays at 7 p.m. during the fall and spring semesters; phone (715) 836-3727 for directions to the box office and to the planetarium.

Visit Eau Claire: 4319 Jeffers Rd., Suite 201, Eau Claire, WI 54703. **Phone:** (715) 831-2345 or (888) 523-3866.

Shopping areas: Oakwood Mall, at US 53 and Golf Road, has more than 100 stores, including JCPenney, Macy's, Sears and Younkers.

CARSON PARK is a 135-acre peninsula on Half Moon Lake. Hank Aaron started his professional baseball career at the park with the Eau Claire Bears; a sculpture of Aaron is in front of Carson Park Stadium. Sports events, recreational activities and train rides are available at the park *(see Recreation Chart).* **Hours:** Daily 4 a.m.-11 p.m. **Cost:** Park free. **Phone:** (888) 523-3866.

SAVE **Chippewa Valley Museum** is in Carson Park at 1204 Carson Park Dr. This regional history museum includes exhibits about the Ojibwe Indians, European settlement and farm life. The museum also offers a working 1950s ice cream parlor, and an 8-foot long, 22-room dollhouse furnished with hundreds of miniatures. An 1880s one-room school and 1860s Norwegian log home on the grounds are open for tours April through October.

Hours: Mon.-Sat. 10-5 (also Tues. 5-8), Sun. 1-5, Memorial Day weekend-Labor Day; Tues.-Fri. 1-5 (also Tues. 5-8), Sat. 10-5, Sun. 1-5, rest of year. Closed Jan. 1, Easter, Thanksgiving and Dec. 24-25. **Cost:** $4; $2 (ages 4-17); free (Tues. 5-8). **Phone:** (715) 834-7871.

Paul Bunyan Logging Camp and Interpretive Center is in Carson Park at 1110 Carson Park Dr. The center features a re-created 1890s logging camp. Historic items are displayed in the cook shanty, bunkhouse, barn, blacksmith shop, filer's shanty, wanigan (store), foreman's office and heavy equipment shed. The Interpretive Center introduces visitors to the logging industry by means of a movie, an exhibit room, a tall tales playroom and a forest history exhibit. **Hours:** Daily 10-4:30, May-Sept. **Cost:** $5; $2 (ages 5-17). **Phone:** (715) 835-6200.

FOSTER GALLERY AT THE UNIVERSITY OF WISCONSIN-EAU CLAIRE is in the Haas Fine Arts Center, 121 Water St. The permanent collection displays more than 700 pieces in campus buildings. Eight rotating exhibits are displayed in the gallery during the academic year. **Hours:** Open Mon.-Fri. 10-4:30 (also Thurs. 6-8 p.m.), Sat.-Sun. 1-4:30, early Sept.-early Aug. Closed holidays, examination weeks and during school breaks. **Cost:** Free. **Phone:** (715) 836-2328.

EGG HARBOR—*see Door County p. 141.*

ELKHORN (I-7) pop. 7,305, elev. 996'

A busy industrial community, Elkhorn traditionally has been associated with the manufacture of band instruments. Joseph Philbrick Webster, a popular Civil War era composer, wrote "Lorena" and "The Sweet Bye and Bye" while living in Elkhorn.

Elkhorn Area Chamber of Commerce: 203 E. Walworth St., P.O. Box 41, Elkhorn, WI 53121. **Phone:** (262) 723-5788.

WEBSTER HOUSE MUSEUM is at 9 E. Rockwell St. Built in 1836 as the local land office during Wisconsin's territorial years, the house was moved from the public square to its present site in 1840. It was the home of parlor music composer Joseph Webster until his death in 1875 and contains some of his memorabilia. Visitors can also see American Indian, Civil War and Victorian items along with a carriage display and a 400-piece mounted bird collection. Costumed interpreters depict the Civil War era.

Guided tours are available by appointment. **Time:** Allow 1 hour minimum. **Hours:** Wed.-Sat. 1-5, mid-May to mid-Oct. **Cost:** $5; $4 (senior citizens); $2 (ages 6-12); $15 (family). **Phone:** (262) 723-4248.

RECREATIONAL ACTIVITIES
Skiing and Snowboarding
- **Alpine Valley Resort** W2501 CR D Elkhorn, WI 53121. **Hours:** Mon.-Fri. 10-10, Sat.-Sun. and holidays 9 a.m.-11 p.m., Thanksgiving weekend through mid-Mar. (weather permitting). **Phone:** (262) 642-7374 or (800) 227-9395.

EPHRAIM—*see Door County p. 141.*

EVANSVILLE (I-6) pop. 4,039, elev. 893'

Reports of prime agricultural land drew New Englanders from New York and Vermont during the 1840s to "The Grove," so named for the abundant forest edging part of the prairie belt settlement. The early economy of Evansville rested on wheat but was replaced by tobacco during the Civil War era.

With the arrival of the railroad in 1864, tobacco warehouses and other commercial enterprises clustered around the tracks. On the main line of the North Western Railroad, the city became Wisconsin's largest shipping point for wool and a major distribution center for livestock during the mid-19th century.

Evansville's development is reflected in its wide range of architecture, spanning more than 125 years. The 22-block historic district has many unaltered structures in such diverse styles as Greek Revival, Italianate, late Picturesque, Neoclassic and Prairie. Along the shores of Lake Leota are park and recreational facilities. An 18-hole golf course is 2 miles from Lake Leota Park.

Evansville Area Chamber of Commerce & Tourism: 8 W. Main St., Evansville, WI 53536. **Phone:** (608) 882-5131.

Self-guiding tours: A brochure describing residential and commercial structures in Evansville's historic district can be obtained at city hall, 31 S. Madison St., and the chamber of commerce.

FARMINGTON—*see Milwaukee p. 178.*

FISH CREEK—*see Door County p. 142.*

FOND DU LAC (G-7) pop. 42,203, elev. 765'

The French traders who first visited this region referred to it as the *fond,* or "far end," of Lake Winnebago, Wisconsin's largest freshwater lake; hence the name Fond du Lac. In 1835 Wisconsin's first judge and later territorial governor, James D. Doty, laid out the town in hopes of it becoming the state capital; it lost to Madison in 1848.

Today mansions of industrial barons line Division Street. Fond du Lac offers a diversity of industry and business, including Mercury Marine and MAG Giddings & Lewis, a supplier of industrial automation products and machine tools.

Fond du Lac Area Convention & Visitors Bureau: 171 S. Pioneer Rd., Fond du Lac, WI 54935-3871. **Phone:** (920) 923-3010 or (800) 937-9123.

Self-guiding tours: Fond du Lac County's Talking Country Roads CD-guided tour includes the history of the area from the ice age to the present and features a front-porch view of Horicon National Wildlife Refuge. The Lake Winnebago Road Trip guides visitors on a scenic driving tour around the lake. Contact the convention and visitors bureau for information.

Shopping areas: Downtown Main Street offers specialty boutiques including antiques, gourmet coffee, stained glass and quilting shops. Kristmas Kringle Shoppe, at 1330 S. Main Street at the entrance to the city, features a large assortment of glass ornaments, trees, animated figures and collectibles displayed in a Bavarian village setting. Forest Mall, off US 41 at Johnson Street, has more than 60 stores including JCPenney, Kohl's, Sears and Younkers.

GALLOWAY HOUSE AND VILLAGE AND BLAKELY MUSEUM is on the s. city limits at 336 Old Pioneer Rd.; from US 41 take the Hickory St. exit to Pioneer Rd., then 1.5 mi. e. following signs. The Galloway House is an elaborate 1847, 30-room mansion surrounded by 29 buildings from the late 19th century. The museum traces area history. A replica of barracks used by the Civilian Conservation Corps of the 1930s-40s is on the grounds, along with a bronze statue of a typical CCC worker.

Under 12 must be with an adult. **Time:** Allow 1 hour, 30 minutes minimum. **Hours:** Daily 10-4, Memorial Day weekend-Labor Day; Sat.-Sun. 10-4, day after Labor Day-Sept. 30. **Cost:** $7; $6 (ages 62+);

$5 (ages 5-17); $25 (family, two adults and all children). **Phone:** (920) 922-1166 or (920) 922-0991.

LAKESIDE PARK is 650 N. Main St. The 400-acre park on Lake Winnebago contains a white-tailed deer enclosure, a playground, miniature train rides, a carousel, gardens, covered wooden bridges, a lighthouse and a scenic drive. Aqua bikes and canoes can be rented. Boats can launch from a number of launch ramps. **Hours:** Park open daily 7 a.m.-11 p.m. Lighthouse open daily 8-dusk (weather permitting), Apr. 15-Oct. 15. **Cost:** Free. **Phone:** (800) 937-9123.

ST. PAUL'S EPISCOPAL CATHEDRAL is at 51 W. Division St. This interior features American and German woodcarvings and stained-glass windows from European and American studios. A 1-hour guided tour is available by reservation. Check in at the office for self-guiding tour information. **Hours:** Office open Tues.-Fri. 9-4 during the school year; Mon.-Thurs. 9-1, rest of year. **Cost:** Donations. Guided tour $2. **Phone:** (920) 921-3363.

FORT ATKINSON (I-7)
pop. 11,621, elev. 790'

American Indian effigy mounds are numerous in the Fort Atkinson area. Panther Intaglio, west on SR 106 at 1236 Riverside Dr., is of interest: Rather than forming a mound on the site, Indians dug an effigy into the earth. Poet Lorine Faith Niedecker was born on Blackhawk Island southwest of town in 1903 and lived most of her life along the banks of Rock River.

The Glacial River Trail is an 8.6-mile bike trail on a former rail bed running south from downtown Fort Atkinson to the Jefferson County line. The northernmost 4.5 miles are asphalt, the balance is crushed limestone. The trail features an archway, bronze sculptures, rest areas and fountains.

DID YOU KNOW

Ringling Bros. and Barnum & Bailey Circus was born in Baraboo.

Fort Atkinson Area Chamber of Commerce: 244 N. Main St., Fort Atkinson, WI 53538. **Phone:** (920) 563-3210 or (888) 733-3678.

HOARD HISTORICAL MUSEUM AND NATIONAL DAIRY SHRINE'S VISITORS CENTER is at 401 Whitewater Ave. (US 12). The museum's galleries feature exhibits about Abraham Lincoln and the 1832 Black Hawk War. The Mysteries of the Mounds gallery interprets life in the area between 10,000 B.C. and 1600 A.D. and includes a video and woodland diorama. Two historic homes interpret local and area history.

Time: Allow 1 hour minimum. **Hours:** Tues.-Sat. 9:30-4:30. Closed holidays and first 2 weeks of Jan. **Cost:** Donations. **Phone:** (920) 563-7769.

GENESEE DEPOT—*see Milwaukee p. 178.*

GERMANTOWN—*see Milwaukee p. 178.*

GILLS ROCK—*see Door County p. 142.*

GRAFTON—*see Milwaukee p. 178.*

GRANTSBURG (C-1) pop. 1,369, elev. 940'

Named after General Ulysses S. Grant's victory at Vicksburg, the village of Grantsburg was incorporated in 1886. One resident of notable stature was Gust Anderson, local marshal and lamplighter, who stood 7 1/2 feet tall. A wooden statue of "Big Gust" is in front of the community center on Pine Street.

CREX MEADOWS WILDLIFE AREA is .5 mi. n. at the corner of CR D and CR F (follow the geese silhouette signs). More than 30,000 acres of wetlands, brush prairie and forests are accessible via a 40-mile road system. Some 270 species of birds have been observed, including blue herons, trumpeter swans, sharp-tailed grouse, bald eagles, Canada geese, ospreys, sandhill cranes and migrating waterfowl. River otters, wolves and bears also call Crex Meadows home. The Wildlife Education Center features wildlife and landscape displays, a prairie garden and education films. An Auto Tour Guide, maps and education brochures are available.

Time: Allow 1 hour, 30 minutes minimum. **Hours:** Wildlife area open daily 24 hours. Wildlife Education Center open Mon.-Fri. 8-4:30, Sat.-Sun. 10-4. **Cost:** Donations. **Phone:** (715) 463-2739 or (715) 463-2896. ♿

GREEN BAY (F-8) pop. 102,313, elev. 604'

Green Bay, at the head of its namesake bay, has two claims to fame that no other town in the state can match: its longevity and the Green Bay Packers. Green Bay had for centuries been an important site for a number of American Indian tribes. The first permanent European settlement was founded in 1669 when Father Allouez established a mission. By the time the United States assumed dominance in 1816, the town—a major fur trading and military post—had changed nationalities three times.

In 1850 Norwegian Otto Tank came to Green Bay to serve as a Moravian missionary to about 50 families of farmers. Bringing with him a large amount of development capital, Tank bought 800 acres of land along the west bank of the Fox River and parceled them out to members of his religious colony. When the city of Green Bay was officially founded in 1854, the city boasted a lumber mill, steel foundry, and a population of more than 2,000.

Christ Church (Episcopal), at Cherry and Madison streets, was established in 1829. It is the oldest permanent church site in the state. Phone (920) 432-0042 for information.

In addition to its success as a paper- and cheese-producing and shipping center, the enthusiasm generated by the Green Bay Packers, one of the oldest professional football teams in the National Football League, helps keep the old town young. The team was founded in 1919 and plays at Lambeau Field. Guided tours of the stadium depart from the Lambeau Field Atrium; phone (920) 569-7513.

Greater Green Bay Convention & Visitors Bureau: 1901 S. Oneida St., P.O. Box 10596, Green Bay, WI 54307. **Phone:** (920) 494-9507 or (888) 867-3342.

Shopping areas: Bay Park Square, south of Lambeau Field on Oneida Street, houses more than 90 stores, including Kohl's, Old Navy, ShopKo and Younkers. In the area surrounding the mall are well-known shops including Barnes & Noble, JCPenney, Best Buy and Dick's Sporting Goods. Shoppers in downtown Green Bay can spend time in boutiques, galleries and gift shops.

BAY BEACH AMUSEMENT PARK, 1313 Beach Rd., features 16 rides for children and adults including a merry-go-round, a miniature train, a 100-foot slide, a ferris wheel, bumper cars and a Tilt-A-Whirl. **Hours:** Daily 10-9, early June to mid-Aug.; daily 10-6, Memorial Day-early June and mid-Aug. through Aug. 31; Sat.-Sun. 10-6, early May-day before Memorial Day and in Sept. Phone ahead to confirm schedule. **Cost:** Park free; individual ride tickets 25¢ (some rides require two tickets). **Phone:** (920) 448-3365. ⑪ ⌗

BAY BEACH WILDLIFE SANCTUARY, 1660 E. Shore Dr., features nature programs, wildlife exhibits and cross-country ski trails on its 700 acres. A nature center has interactive exhibits, including a two-story forest with otter slide, walk-in bee tree, a waterfall, crawl-through burrow and habitat house. Nocturnal animals, a wolf pack, deer herd, songbird aviary, fruit bat colony, large snakes, native fish aquarium and bird-of-prey trail exhibits also can be seen.
Hours: Daily 8-7:30, Apr. 15-Sept. 15; 8-4:30, rest of year. **Cost:** Free. **Phone:** (920) 391-3671. ⌗

GREEN BAY BOTANICAL GARDEN is at 2600 Larsen Rd. Forty-seven acres of landscaped grounds include a four seasons garden with magnolias, crab apples, lilacs and perennials; a contemporary rose garden with shrub and English varieties; an American perennial garden; a cottage garden; a children's garden; a woodland garden featuring plants and wildflowers native to Wisconsin; a color and foliage garden and the memorial grove.
Hours: Daily 9-8, June-Aug.; daily 9-5 in May and Sept.-Oct.; Mon.-Sat. 9-4, Jan.-Apr.; Mon.-Fri. 9-4, rest of year. Closed Jan. 1, Thanksgiving and Dec. 25. **Cost:** $7; $5 (ages 65+); $2 (ages 5-12). **Phone:** (920) 490-9457 or (877) 355-4224.

HAZELWOOD HISTORIC HOUSE is at 1008 S. Monroe Ave. Overlooking the Fox River, the 10-room Greek Revival home was the residence of Morgan L. Martin, a prominent politician, businessman, attorney and judge for 60 years, and his wife Elizabeth. The 1837 house, which contains many items belonging to the family, depicts the 1890s period. **Hours:** Guided tours are given Thurs.-Sun. noon-4, June-Aug.; Sat.-Sun. noon-4, in May. Tours are available some weekends in Dec.; phone ahead for schedule. **Cost:** $4; $3.50 (ages 55+); $2.50 (ages 6-12). **Phone:** (920) 437-1840.

HERITAGE HILL STATE PARK is e. of the Fox River at 2640 S. Webster Ave. at jct. SR 172. A 48-acre complex of furnished historical buildings is grouped into four themed areas including La Baye, Fort Howard, A Growing Community and Ethnic Agricultural Area.

La Baye includes a fur trader's cabin, a bark chapel, a log sugaring house and a reproduction of Wisconsin's first courthouse. Fort Howard consists of a hospital, officers' quarters, school and company kitchen in use during the 1830s. A Growing Community depicts a busy community that includes print shop, blacksmith shop, hose company and Tank Library.

The Ethnic Agricultural areas contain a Belgian farmhouse, log barns, a stone summer kitchen, and Cotton House, a home that served as the center of social life in Green Bay for many years. A visitor's/education center is on the grounds. A schedule of events is available at the park.

Pets are not permitted. **Time:** Allow 2 hours minimum. **Hours:** Tues.-Sat. 10-4:30, Sun. noon-4:30, first Sunday in May-Labor Day; Sat. 10-4:30, Sun. noon-4:30, day after Labor Day-Sept. 30. Grounds only are open for Stroll through the Park Mon.-Fri. 10-4, rest of year. **Cost:** $8; $7 (ages 62+); $6 (ages 5-17); $4 (Stroll through the Park). **Phone:** (920) 448-5150 or (800) 721-5150.

LAMBEAU FIELD is at 1265 Lombardi Ave. Built in 1957 with a major renovation in 2003, Lambeau Field is home to the National Football League's Green Bay Packers. The renovation included the addition of the Lambeau Field Atrium, home to the Packers Hall of Fame and stadium tours. Fourteen-foot-high bronze statues of Curly Lambeau, the team's founder, and coach Vince Lombardi, are found outside the atrium. **Phone:** (920) 569-7500 for information, or (920) 569-7501 🚻

Green Bay Packers Hall of Fame is located in the Lambeau Field Atrium at 1265 Lombardi Ave. The hall of fame features a wide variety of Packers memorabilia, including mementos chronicling the team's history through NFL championships and Super Bowl victories, as well as interactive and historical displays. Several videos, including game highlights, are available for viewing. **Time:** Allow 2 hours minimum. **Hours:** Mon.-Sat. 9-6, Sun. 10-5; hours vary on holidays. Phone ahead for game day hours. Closed Easter, Thanksgiving and Dec. 25. **Cost:** $10; $8 (ages 12-17, ages 62+, college students and military with ID); $5 (ages 6-11). Combination ticket with stadium tour $19. **Phone:** (920) 569-7512 or (888) 442-7225.

Lambeau Field Stadium Tours is at 1265 Lombardi Ave. This behind-the-scenes guided tour of the atrium, the players' tunnel, the exclusive Legends Club and private game-day suite teaches visitors about the Green Bay Packers' history. Fans may sit in the bleachers and get a great view of the gridiron. **Time:** Allow 1 hour minimum. **Hours:** Tours depart daily 10-4. Tickets are sold on a first-come, first-served basis and go on sale beginning Mon.-Sat. at 9, Sun. at 10 in the atrium. There are no tours on game days. **Cost:** $11; $10 (ages 12-17, ages 62+, college students and military with ID); $8 (ages 6-11). Combination ticket with Hall of Fame $19. **Phone:** (920) 569-7513.

NATIONAL RAILROAD MUSEUM is at 2285 S. Broadway, .2 mi. e. of Ashland Ave. via Cormier. The museum houses more than 60 locomotives and rail cars from the steam and diesel eras. Highlights include a Union Pacific "Big Boy," reputedly the world's largest steam locomotive, Dwight D. Eisenhower's British World War II command train and a 1920s Pullman sleeping car exhibit. A reception center has an exhibit hall and theater featuring an audiovisual presentation. A 3-mile ride on a standard-gauge train is available. On the grounds, a 65-foot tower overlooks the Fox River.

Time: Allow 2 hours minimum. **Hours:** Mon.-Sat. 9-5, Sun. 11-5, May-Dec. (house closes at 2 on Dec. 31); Tues.-Sat. 9-5, Sun. 11-5, rest of year. Train rides depart daily at noon, 2 and 4 (also Mon.-Sat. at 10), May-Sept.; Sat.-Sun. at noon, 2 and 4 (also Sat. at 10) in Oct. Closed Jan. 1, Easter, Thanksgiving and Dec. 24-25. **Cost:** $9; $8 (ages 62+); $6.50 (ages 4-12). Train ticket $1. **Phone:** (920) 437-7623. 🅿️

NEVILLE PUBLIC MUSEUM OF BROWN COUNTY is at 210 Museum Pl. Galleries on two floors are devoted to art, history and science. Major traveling exhibits complement art, natural science, history and changing displays of local art and artifacts. Particularly noteworthy is the exhibit "On the Edge of the Inland Sea," which traces 12,000 years of northeast Wisconsin's development.

Time: Allow 2 hours minimum. **Hours:** Mon.-Sat. 9-5 (also Wed. 5-8), Sun. noon-5. Closed Jan. 1, Memorial Day, Labor Day, Thanksgiving and Dec. 25. **Cost:** $4; $2 (ages 6-15). **Phone:** (920) 448-7842.

NEW ZOO—*see Suamico p. 196.*

GAMBLING ESTABLISHMENTS

• **Oneida Bingo & Casino** is at 2020/2100 Airport Dr. **Hours:** Daily 24 hours. **Phone:** (920) 494-4500 or (800) 238-4263.

GREENBUSH (G-7)

WADE HOUSE & WESLEY JUNG CARRIAGE MUSEUM is off SR 23 at Plank Rd. Built in 1850 along the plank road that linked Sheboygan and Fond du Lac, the 27-room Wade House stagecoach inn is the centerpiece of this 240-acre state historic site. Authentically costumed guides bring to life the everyday world of a small 1860's Wisconsin community, leading tours at the Stagecoach Inn, forging iron at the Dockstader Blacksmith Shop, and demonstrating the sawyer's craft at the Herrling Sawmill—a working reproduction of a muley-type up-and-down sawmill.

Visitors enjoy a relaxing horse-drawn carriage ride (included with admission) to the Wesley Jung Carriage Museum, featuring more than 100 carriages, wagons and sleighs dating from 1870-1915. **Hours:** Site open daily 10-5, mid-May through mid-Oct. **Cost:** $11; $9.25 (ages 65+); $5.50 (ages 5-17); $30 (family, two adults and children ages 5-17). **Phone:** (920) 526-3271. 🚻

HALES CORNERS—*see Milwaukee p. 178.*

HARTFORD—*see Milwaukee p. 178.*

HAYWARD (C-3) pop. 2,129, elev. 1,192'

East of Hayward, the vast Chippewa Flowage spreads out over 15,300 acres. Created in 1924 as part of a hydropower project, the reservoir—affectionately called "The Big Chip"—is Wisconsin's third largest lake. It boasts an irregular, 233-mile wooded shoreline and 200 undeveloped islands. Visitors come mainly to enjoy the natural scenery and the fishing; the lake is particularly known for its record-breaking muskellunge.

FRED SCHEER'S LUMBERJACK SHOWS are 1 mi. e. on CR B at Lumberjack Village. Plaid-clad lumberjacks demonstrate their skills for viewers in a competitive yet humorous atmosphere. Children may help lumberjacks saw trees and receive souvenirs as a prize. **Time:** Allow 2 hours minimum. **Hours:** Tues., Thurs. and Sat. at 2 and Fri. at 7:30 p.m., mid-June through late Aug. Phone ahead for early June to mid-June and late Aug.-late Sept. schedules. **Cost:** $9.95; $8.95 (ages 62+); $7.95 (ages 4-11). **Phone:** (715) 634-6923. 🚻

FRESH WATER FISHING HALL OF FAME is at jct. SR 27/CR B. Housed in a building designed to resemble a muskellunge, the museum includes an observation deck in the mouth of the giant fish. Five other buildings on 6 acres of landscaped grounds display more than 400 specimens of fish from around the world, as well as angling equipment, trophies and other items.

Time: Allow 1 hour minimum. **Hours:** Daily 9:30-4:30, June-Aug.; 9:30-4, Apr. 15-May 30 and Sept.-Oct. **Cost:** $6.50; $6 (ages 65+); $3.75 (ages 10-17); $2.75 (ages 2-9). **Phone:** (715) 634-4440.

WILDERNESS WALK is 3 mi. s. on SR 27. This 35-acre park features live animals in natural habitats, an animal nursery and the Old West Town. Ages 0-11 must be accompanied by an adult. **Time:** Allow 1 hour minimum. **Hours:** Daily 10-5:30, mid-May through Labor Day. Last admission 1 hour before closing. **Cost:** $11; $10 (ages 65+); $8 (ages 2-11). Rates may vary; phone ahead. **Phone:** (715) 634-2893. [⋔] [⊼]

HIGHLAND (H-4) pop. 855, elev. 1,194'

WINERIES

• **Spurgeon Vineyards & Winery** is 4 mi. w. on CR Q, then 2.1 mi. n. to 16008 Pine Tree Rd. **Hours:** Daily 10-5. Closed Jan. 1, Easter, Thanksgiving and Dec. 25. **Phone:** (608) 929-7692, or (800) 236-5555 from the Midwest.

HORICON (H-7) pop. 3,775, elev. 886'

The Horicon area's location on the southern fringe of the Horicon Marsh and on both sides of the Rock River presents visitors with many sightseeing opportunities.

Horicon Chamber of Commerce: 620 Washington St., P.O. Box 23, Horicon, WI 53032. **Phone:** (920) 485-3200.

HORICON MARSH BOAT TOURS departs from the bridge at SR 33. Narrated 1-hour pontoon boat tours explore Horicon Marsh, a wetland inhabited by more than 280 species of birds. A 2-hour birding tour and 1.5-hour sunset cruise also are available weekends May through September. Canoe and kayak rentals are available April through September.

Reservations are required for birding and sunset tours. **Hours:** Marsh tours depart daily at 1, May-Sept.; Mon.-Fri. at 1, Sat.-Sun. at 10, 1 and 3, Oct. 1-fourth Sun. in Oct. Phone ahead to confirm schedule. **Cost:** Marsh tour $10; $6.25 (ages 12-15); $5.25 (ages 4-11). Birding tour $18; $10 (ages 12-15); $8 (ages 4-11). Sunset cruise $18. **Phone:** (920) 485-4663 or (800) 814-4474.

HORICON MARSH WILDLIFE AREA AND INTERNATIONAL EDUCATION CENTER is at N7725 SR 28. The southernmost third of the Horicon Marsh, an 11,000-acre state-owned area, is primarily used for recreation. Activities include nature study, fishing, hunting, canoeing, hiking, birdwatching and photography (see Recreation Chart). Naturalist programs on the weekends in the spring

and fall also are offered. **Time:** Allow 1 hour minimum. **Hours:** Marsh open daily dawn-dusk. Office open Tues.-Fri. 8:15-1 and 2-4, Sat.-Mon. 9-3. **Cost:** Free. **Phone:** (920) 387-7860.

HUBERTUS—see Milwaukee p. 179.

HUDSON (E-1) pop. 8,775, elev. 669'

Founded by fur traders on the St. Croix River in the 1840s, Hudson developed into a prosperous steamboat and lumbering center within 20 years. Evoking the Victorian era are renovated historic buildings in the downtown and residential areas. The stately houses along Third and Vine streets were the showplaces of wealthy merchants and lumber barons.

Phipps Center for the Arts, First and Locust streets, presents theatrical productions, concerts, art exhibitions and other cultural programs. Lakefront Park along the St. Croix River offers fishing, boating and swimming. Just outside of town is Willow River State Park (see Recreation Chart and the AAA Great Lakes CampBook).

Hudson Area Chamber of Commerce & Tourism Bureau: 502 Second St., Hudson, WI 54016. **Phone:** (715) 386-8411 or (800) 657-6775.

Self-guiding tours: Maps outlining walking, bicycling and driving tours of historic Hudson are available at the chamber of commerce and tourism bureau.

[SAVE] **THE OCTAGON HOUSE MUSEUM,** 1004 Third St., represents architectural styles of the 1850s. It contains dolls and Victorian-era furnishings. The Garden House displays a general store, a blacksmith shop and a woodworking area. The house is decorated for Christmas from late November through December.

Tours: Guided tours are available. **Time:** Allow 30 minutes minimum. **Hours:** Wed.-Sat. noon-4:30, Sun. 2-4:30, May-Aug.; Sat. noon-4:30, Sun. 2-4:30, Sept.-Oct. and in Dec. Last tour departs 30 minutes before closing. Closed major holidays. **Cost:** $7; $3 (ages 13-18); $2 (ages 5-12). **Phone:** (715) 386-2654.

HURLEY (B-4) pop. 1,818, elev. 1,502'

Begun as an iron-mining and logging town around 1884, Hurley enjoyed more than 30 years of prosperity and high living—its main street once was studded with 76 saloons and taverns along a five-block stretch.

The town's colorful past is celebrated in several books, including Pulitzer Prize-winner Edna Ferber's "Come and Get It." The movie version of Ernest Hemingway's novel "Adventures of a Young Man" was filmed in Hurley. The Iron County Historical Museum, in the old county courthouse at Iron Street and 3rd Avenue, contains artifacts recalling Hurley's mining and logging heritage; phone (715) 561-2244.

Summer adventurers can try out miles of hiking, mountain bicycling and all-terrain vehicle trails, or explore more than 50 waterfalls in the area. During winter, skiers can visit Whitecap Mountain in nearby Ironbelt. Hurley also is a convenient base for exploring Iron County's 450 miles of snowmobile trails.

Hurley Area Chamber of Commerce: 316 Silver St., Hurley, WI 54534. **Phone:** (715) 561-4334 or (866) 340-4334.

JANESVILLE (I-6) pop. 59,498, elev. 804'

Soldiers returning home from the Black Hawk War were the first to promote Janesville's fertile valley on the Rock River. One who heard their praise was pioneer and visionary Henry F. Janes, who arrived in 1836, became the town's first postmaster and started a ferry and tavern. In 1892 George Parker opened Parker Pen Co., and 1919 brought the arrival of General Motors Corp., which became the town's largest employer.

Several accomplished women hail from Janesville. Born here in 1862 was Carrie Jacobs Bond, one of the first female songwriters to become published and writer of "A Perfect Day," which sold more than 5 million copies in 10 years. In 1846 the family of 7-year-old Frances Willard moved to Janesville where she remained until 1864; she later became the national president of the Women's Christian Temperance Union and a relentless suffragist. Born in 1850 in nearby Johnstown Center, poet Ella Wheeler Wilcox sent the public stampeding to the bookstores after her "Poems of Passion" was printed by a progressive publisher.

Free water-skiing shows are performed at Traxler Park on Wednesday and Sunday evenings in summer. Janesville also offers 25 miles of hiking, biking, and cross-country skiing trails, the eight-mile Wisconsin Ice Age Trail, and 14 area golf courses.

Janesville Area Convention & Visitors Bureau: 20 S. Main St., Suite 17, Janesville, WI 53545. **Phone:** (608) 757-3171 or (800) 487-2757.

Self-guiding tours: The Janesville Historic Commission has identified nine residential and four downtown commercial historic districts. Brochures describing each district and the downtown self-guiding tour map are available from the Janesville Historic Commission, 18 N. Jackson St., P.O. Box 5005; phone (608) 755-3107.

Shopping areas: Janesville Mall, 2500 Milton Ave., is anchored by Boston Store, JCPenney and Sears, and has more than 60 stores.

HELEN JEFFRIS WOOD MUSEUM CENTER is at 426 N. Jackson St. Housed in the 1912 Prairie-style home of Stanley Dexter Tallman, the Rock County Historical Society museum offers temporary and permanent exhibits and educational programs. Facilities include the Lincoln-Tallman Restorations visitor and ticketing center *(see attraction listing),*

the Pauline Pottery Exhibit and the Parker Pen Exhibit Room.

Hours: Mon.-Fri. 10-4, Sat.-Sun. 10-3, June-Sept.; Mon.-Fri. 10-4, rest of year. Closed major holidays. **Cost:** Donations. **Phone:** (608) 756-4509 or (800) 577-1859.

THE LINCOLN-TALLMAN RESTORATIONS is at 440 N. Jackson St., on US 14 Bus. Rte., 2 blks. n.e. of jct. US 51. The 26-room Italian Villa-style house was built by William Morrison Tallman, a wealthy attorney and abolitionist from New York. When the house was built 1855-57, it had such conveniences as running water, a communication system, central heating, plumbing and gas lighting. Abraham Lincoln was a weekend guest in 1859.

Hours: Tours are given daily on the hour 10-3, June-Sept. Holiday tours are offered daily mid-Nov. through Dec. 30. Closed major holidays. **Cost:** $8 (includes Helen Jeffris Wood Museum Center admission); $7.50 (ages 62+); $4 (grades K-12). **Phone:** (608) 756-4509.

ROTARY GARDENS is .7 mi. w. of I-90 via SR 11, then .7 mi. sw. at 1455 Palmer Dr. The 20-acre ornamental botanic garden with an international theme features Japanese, Scottish, French, Italian and English Cottage gardens. Other areas are dedicated to ferns and mosses, shade plants, prairie grasses and woodlands. The garden also features extensive collections of perennials, trees and shrubs and changing seasonal displays. Events and activities are held throughout the year.

Time: Allow 1 hour minimum. **Hours:** Gardens open daily dawn-dusk. Visitor center open daily 8:30-8, Jun.-Aug.; 8:30-6, mid-Apr. through Apr. 30 and in Oct.; 8:30-7 in May and Sept.; 8:30-4:30, rest of year. **Cost:** $5; $3 (ages 6-12); $15 (family). Rates may vary; phone ahead. **Phone:** (608) 752-3885.

KAUKAUNA (F-8) pop. 12,983, elev. 712'

Five gallons of rum was the price paid for the parcel of land that became Kaukauna in 1793, in the first deeded transaction executed in Wisconsin. On the portage that bypassed the long rapids of the Fox River, the community developed into a busy trading and milling center. The cascade that once hampered travel long since has been tamed for industrial use.

1000 ISLANDS ENVIRONMENTAL CENTER is at 1000 Beaulieu Ct. This 350-acre center features an indoor exhibition of mounted animals from Africa, Asia and North America. The collection includes antelopes, lions, polar bears, rhinoceroses, tigers and zebras. Bald eagles, deer, ducks, herons and owls can be seen on the grounds. Nature trails follow the Fox River and go through the woods. Snowshoes can be rented. **Time:** Allow 2 hours minimum. **Hours:** Mon.-Fri. 8-4, Sat.-Sun. 10-3:30. Closed Jan. 1, Easter, Memorial Day, Labor Day, Thanksgiving, day after Thanksgiving and Dec. 24-25. **Cost:** Free. **Phone:** (920) 766-4733.

KENOSHA (I-8) pop. 90,352, elev. 611'

Wisconsin's southernmost Lake Michigan port, Kenosha was settled in 1835. The area maintains its historic charms with shaded residential streets, a nostalgic downtown with cobblestone walks and an authentic electric streetcar system. Nearly 90 percent of Kenosha's lakefront is dedicated to such public spaces as parks and beaches as well as museums, and the city offers an array of festivals, fairs and markets throughout the year.

Children will enjoy the life-size dinosaur replicas as well as the working paleontology lab at the Dinosaur Discovery Museum, 5608 Tenth Ave.; phone (262) 653-4450.

Kenosha Area Convention & Visitors Bureau: 10519 120th Ave., Kenosha, WI 53158. **Phone:** (262) 857-7164 or (800) 654-7309.

Shopping areas: Nike, Polo/Ralph Lauren, Banana Republic, Gap and Guess are just some of the nearly 100 stores that can be found at Prime Outlets at Pleasant Prairie, I-94 and SR 165 exit 347.

SAVE **BRISTOL RENAISSANCE FAIRE** is at 12550 120th Ave.; take I-94 s. to exit 347 (SR 165), then take SR 165 w. to Frontage Rd., then 2 mi. s., following signs. This site depicts a 16th-century English village; costumed performers provide entertainment on 16 stages and in the streets. Visitors experience the food, games and crafts of Elizabethan England. Highlights include Queen Elizabeth I and her court, jousting, sword fighting, juggling and the Kids Kingdom.

Allow a full day. **Hours:** Sat.-Sun. and Labor Day 10-7, July 10-Labor Day. **Cost:** $18.95; $16.95 (ages 55+ and students with ID); $9.50 (ages 5-12). **Phone:** (847) 395-7773.

CIVIL WAR MUSEUM, 5400 First Ave in Harbor-Park, demonstrates how culture, politics and the economy contributed to the Civil War through interactive exhibits, dioramas with life-size figures, and high-tech displays. The museum concentrates on the role of the upper Middle West in the Civil War. **Time:** Allow 1 hour, 30 minutes minimum. **Hours:** Tues.-Sat. 9-5, Sun.-Mon. noon-5. Closed major holidays. **Cost:** $7; free (ages 0-15). **Phone:** (262) 653-4141.

KENOSHA PUBLIC MUSEUM is at 5500 First Ave. in HarborPark. A two-story atrium cuts through the center of this museum, an architectural representation of the glacier that sculpted Wisconsin during the Ice Age. Natural history exhibits include the Schaefer mammoth, excavated in Kenosha County. A walk-through model of an American Indian village recreates life in the early 1800s. An art gallery features temporary exhibits. **Time:** Allow 1 hour minimum. **Hours:** Tues.-Sat. 9-5, Sun.-Mon. noon-5. Closed major holidays. **Cost:** Free. **Phone:** (262) 653-4140.

KESHENA (E-7) pop. 1,394, elev. 825'

GAMBLING ESTABLISHMENTS

- **Menominee Casino Bingo Hotel**, 1.5 mi. s. on SR 47/55. **Hours:** Daily 24 hours; closed noon Dec. 24-noon Dec. 25. **Phone:** (715) 799-3600 or (800) 343-7778.

KEWASKUM—see Milwaukee p. 179.

KEWAUNEE (F-9) pop. 2,806, elev. 672'

Kewaunee's history dates back to 1634, when French explorer Jean Nicolet arrived for a visit, but Europeans began to settle here permanently beginning in 1836. From the late 1800s through the early 1900s Kewaunee became a prosperous community, and well-to-do businessmen built grand homes to reflect their wealth. Walk or drive through the Marquette Historic District to see these beautifully maintained residences, where you will find such styles as Queen Anne, American Foursquare, Period Revival and Craftsman.

Water sports reign supreme in Kewaunee — launch a boat from the marina, catch the big one from a chartered fishing boat in Lake Michigan, or cast a lure from the lakeshore or on the Kewaunee River. Father Marquette Memorial Park and Pioneer Park feature wide sandy beaches on the western shore of Lake Michigan, where you can go for a dip in the cool lake water and dig your toes in the soft sand.

Kewaunee Chamber of Commerce: 308 N. Main St., P.O. Box 243, Kewaunee, WI 54216. **Phone:** (920) 388-4822 or (800) 666-8214.

Self-guiding tours: A booklet detailing a walking tour of 43 homes and a school in Kewaunee's Marquette Historic District is available from the Kewaunee County Historical Museum and Old Jail in Court House Square.

KEWAUNEE COUNTY HISTORICAL MUSEUM AND OLD JAIL is in Court House Sq. at 613 Dodge St. Housed in the 1876 former sheriff's house and jail wing, the museum displays area artifacts and antiques. Notable are a large basswood carving, "Custer's Last Stand," and four life-size carvings of Father Marquette and American Indians, depicting his landing in 1674. **Time:** Allow 30 minutes minimum. **Hours:** Daily noon-4, Memorial Day weekend-Labor Day. Phone ahead to confirm schedule. **Cost:** $2. **Phone:** (920) 388-3858.

KING (F-6)

WISCONSIN VETERANS MUSEUM is at N2665 CR QQ in Marden Memorial Center of the Wisconsin Veterans Home. Dedicated to veterans of all wars, this museum displays memorabilia and weapons from nations involved in those wars. **Time:** Allow 30 minutes minimum. **Hours:** Daily 8-4. **Cost:** Free. **Phone:** (715) 258-5586, ext. 2369.

KOHLER (G-8) pop. 1,926, elev. 680'

Kohler is a planned, landscaped, incorporated village surrounding the factories of Kohler Co., manufacturers of plumbing and leisure products, engines and generators. The model village has won national recognition for its architecture.

KOHLER DESIGN CENTER is at 101 Upper Rd. A multi-level showroom features designer bathrooms and kitchens, plumbing products, artifacts from Kohler's early factory and village, a theater and an Arts/Industry ceramics display. Departing from the Design Center, the 3-hour Industry in Action factory tour takes visitors through the Pottery, Brass and Foundry Buildings, where items such as china lavatories, faucets and cast-iron tubs are created.

Note: Enclosed footwear is required for walking tour. **Hours:** Design center open Mon.-Fri. 8-5, Sat.-Sun. and holidays 10-4 (10-3 on Dec. 24). Factory tour offered Mon.-Fri. at 8:30 a.m. Closed Thanksgiving and Dec. 25. **Cost:** Free. Under 14 are not permitted on factory tour. Reservations are required. **Phone:** (920) 457-3699.

WAELDERHAUS is reached from I-43 exit 126 (Kohler Memorial Dr.), w. on SR 23 to Highland Dr., then 1.2 mi. s. This house employs a style of architecture found in Bregenzerwald, Austria. Waelderhaus is a replica of the John M. Kohler house. **Time:** Allow 1 hour minimum. **Hours:** Guided tours are given daily at 2, 3 and 4. Closed major holidays. **Cost:** Free. **Phone:** (920) 453-2851.

LAC DU FLAMBEAU (C-5)
pop. 1,646, elev. 1,609'

Lac du Flambeau literally means "lake of the torch." The name was given to this area by French fur traders who saw the Ojibwe fishing at night with torches. The town is home to the Lac du Flambeau Band of Lake Superior Chippewa Indians. Within the surrounding reservation's borders are more than 250 lakes and 71 miles of rivers and streams, giving visitors many options to enjoy the area's natural beauty. Powwow's are held throughout the summer.

Downtown's Woodland Indian Art Center, 562 Peace Pipe Rd. in native-owned Adaawe Place, carries traditional American Indian artwork and offers classes, workshops and demonstrations of native artistry; phone (715) 588-3700.

Lac du Flambeau Chamber of Commerce: 602 Peace Pipe Rd., P.O. Box 456, Lac du Flambeau, WI 54538. **Phone:** (715) 588-3346 or (877) 588-3346.

GEORGE W. BROWN JR. OJIBWE MUSEUM & CULTURAL CENTER is 2 blks. s. of SR 47 at 603 Peace Pipe Rd., just s. of the Indian Bowl. A collection of American Indian artifacts dates to the mid-18th century. A four-seasons display demonstrates Indian activities, clothing and living arrangements. Of interest is a 24-foot dugout canoe discovered off the shores of Strawberry Island and thought to be 200 years old.

Tours: Guided tours are available. **Time:** Allow 1 hour minimum. **Hours:** Mon.-Fri. 10-4, Sat. 10-2 and by appointment, May-Oct.; Tues.-Thurs. 10-2, rest of year. **Cost:** $4; $3 (ages 5-15 and 56+). **Phone:** (715) 588-3333.

RECREATIONAL ACTIVITIES
Fishing

- **William J. Poupart Fish Hatchery** is at 2500 SR 47 N, at the lower end of Pokegama Lake. **Hours:** Mon.-Fri. 7-3, Sat.-Sun. 7-5, Memorial Day-Labor Day. **Phone:** (715) 588-4223.

LA CROSSE (G-2) pop. 51,818, elev. 640'

On the Mississippi River where the Black and La Crosse rivers meet, La Crosse was founded in 1842 as an American Indian trading post. Serious development began a decade later, when settlers from New York, Ohio and Vermont established sawmills and gristmills and spurred the arrival of the railroad. The Easterners were joined by German and Norwegian immigrants attracted by the extensive pine groves.

La Crosse was faced with a crippling depression when the La Crosse and Milwaukee Railroad Co. went bankrupt in 1857. However, when the Civil War closed river traffic on the Mississippi below the Ohio River, La Crosse provided a major link with the East, thus ensuring the town's economic recovery. A railroad bridge erected over the Mississippi in 1876 precipitated a dramatic increase in trade and manufacturing, as the network of railroads radiating from La Crosse found new markets.

Overseeing all river traffic is a 25-foot carved wooden American Indian in Riverside Park at the base of State Street near the downtown area. Lock and Dam No. 7, a U.S. Army Corps of Engineers project 5 miles north of La Crosse, has an observation deck.

Goose Island County Park (see Recreation Chart and the AAA Great Lakes CampBook) offers developed recreational facilities and a wildlife refuge. During the winter downhill and cross-country skiing are available in the area.

Tours of the University of Wisconsin-La Crosse campus are available; phone (608) 785-8067. The university's art gallery exhibits works by prominent artists September through May. Cultural events also take place at Viterbo University.

The city lies on a scenic route that follows the Mississippi. The route consists of SR 35, which heads southeast to Prairie du Chien, and US 53, which runs northwest to its junction with SR 54/35.

La Crosse Area Convention & Visitors Bureau: Riverside Park, 410 Veterans Memorial Dr., La Crosse, WI 54601. **Phone:** (608) 782-2366 or (800) 658-9424.

Shopping areas: Valley View Mall, I-90 exit 5 on US 16, has more than 90 stores, including JCPenney, Macy's and Sears. Downtown La Crosse, off I-90, exit 3, is one of the largest commercial historic districts in the state with unique shops, galleries and award-winning restaurants.

GRANDAD BLUFF is 2 mi. e. off Main St., which turns into Bliss Rd. Follow Grandad Bluff Rd. e. to the entrance. Towering about 600 feet above the city, the summit offers a panoramic view of three states—Wisconsin, Minnesota and Iowa. **Note:** The direct route may be under construction, but short detours are available. **Hours:** The bluff can be visited daily 24 hours. **Cost:** Free. 🏕

THE HIXON HOUSE AND MUSEUM is at jct. Badger and 7th sts. at 429 N. 7th St. This mid-19th-century Italianate house reflects the lifestyle of lumberman and banker Gideon Hixon and his wife Ellen. Approximately 90 percent of the furnishings are original, including a "Turkish Nook," Oriental rugs, ceramics from Europe and Asia and furniture of the Victorian period. Guided tours lasting 45 minutes are available.

Hours: Tues.-Sun. 10-5, Memorial Day-Labor Day. Last tour begins 1 hour before closing. Phone ahead to confirm schedule. **Cost:** $8; $7 (ages 56+); $6 (students 13+ with ID); $4 (ages 5-12). **Phone:** (608) 782-1980.

LA CROSSE QUEEN departs at the n. end of Riverside Park, 3 blks. w. of US 53 off State St. An authentic paddlewheeler offers 90-minute narrated sightseeing cruises on the Mississippi River. Weekend brunch, dinner and lunch cruises, cocktail cruises and 3-hour cruises also are available. Reservations are required for meal cruises. **Hours:** Sightseeing cruises depart daily May-Oct. Phone ahead to confirm schedule. **Cost:** Sightseeing cruise fare $14.50; $13.95 (ages 60+); $7.25 (ages 1-11). Other cruise fares vary; phone ahead. **Phone:** (608) 784-2893 or (608) 784-8523.

MYRICK HIXON ECOPARK is at 789 Myrick Park Dr. The EcoPark is an entry point for La Crosse's hiking, bicycling and skiing trails. An interpretive center contains educational displays, maps and information about the Hixon Forest and the La Crosse River Marsh. Also available are a variety of educational programs, lectures and guided talks for children and adults. **Note:** The park is currently undergoing renovations and expansion. **Hours:** Mon.-Fri. 9-4, Sat.-Sun. 9-noon. **Cost:** Free (building entry and trail access). Prices vary for educational programs. **Phone:** (608) 784-0303.

PUMP HOUSE REGIONAL ARTS CENTER is 1 blk. w. of US 53 at 119 King St. Built in the Romanesque Revival style, the 1880 waterworks building now houses a performing arts theater and three visual arts galleries. **Time:** Allow 30 minutes minimum. **Hours:** Tues.-Sat. 11-7. **Cost:** Donations. **Phone:** (608) 785-1434.

RIVERSIDE MUSEUM is at the base of State St. in Riverside Park at 410 E. Veterans Memorial Dr. The museum features articles brought up from the wreck of the steamboat *War Eagle*, along with exhibits about local river history and American Indian artifacts. Visitors also can watch a video presentation about the *War Eagle*.

Time: Allow 30 minutes minimum. **Hours:** Tues.-Sat. 10:30-4:30, Sun. 10:30-4, Memorial Day-Labor Day; Sat. 10:30-4:30, Sun. 10:30-4, day after Labor Day-Oct. 31. Closed July 4. **Cost:** $2; $1 (ages 3-12); $5 (family). **Phone:** (608) 782-1980.

SWARTHOUT MUSEUM is next to the La Crosse Public Library at 9th and Main sts. Featured are changing exhibits that relate to local history, including such topics as early social customs, American Indians, transportation, river life, agriculture, industry and commerce. **Time:** Allow 30 minutes minimum. **Hours:** Tues.-Fri. 10-5, Sat.-Sun. 1-5. Closed Jan. 1, Easter, Memorial Day weekend, Labor Day weekend, Thanksgiving and Dec. 25. **Cost:** Donations. **Phone:** (608) 782-1980.

RECREATIONAL ACTIVITIES
Skiing and Snowboarding

• **Mount La Crosse Ski Area** is 6 mi. s. at N5549 Old Town Hall Rd. Write P.O. Box 9, La Crosse, WI 54602. **Hours:** Mon.-Fri. 10-9, Sat.-Sun. 9-9, weekend after Thanksgiving through mid-Mar. **Phone:** (608) 788-0044 or (800) 426-3665.

LAKE DELTON (G-5) pop. 1,982, elev. 894'

LOST CANYON is .5 mi. e. on Canyon Rd. Horse-drawn wagons leaving every 15 minutes tour the sandstone formations in the canyon. The walls of the canyon reach 80 feet in height. **Time:** Allow 30 minutes minimum. **Hours:** Daily 8:30-7:30, mid-May through Labor Day; 10-6, mid-Apr. to mid-May and day after Labor Day-Oct. 31. **Cost:** Fare $9.50; $5 (ages 4-11). Phone to verify prices. **Phone:** (608) 254-8757. 🏕

RECREATIONAL ACTIVITIES
Horseback Riding

• **Canyon Creek Riding Stables** are at 60 Hillman Rd. **Hours:** Daily 9-7, Memorial Day-Labor Day; daily hours vary, rest of year. **Phone:** (608) 253-6942.

LAKE GENEVA (I-7) pop. 7,148, elev. 864'

Nicknamed the "Newport of the West," Lake Geneva has been a resort community since just after the Civil War when wealthy Chicago families discovered the site and began building summer homes here. Today the elegant, often historic estates still ring the lake and can best be viewed by tour boat or via the 21-mile Geneva Lake Shore Path.

The area boasts golf courses designed by such icons as Lee Trevino, Gary Player, Arnold Palmer, Jack Nicklaus and Pete Dye. In winter Lake Geneva is host to legions of downhill skiers, cross-country skiers, ice skaters and snowmobilers. Big Foot Beach State Park is 2.5 miles south of Lake Geneva *(see Recreation Chart and the AAA Great Lakes CampBook).*

Lake Geneva Area Convention & Visitors Bureau: 201 Wrigley Dr., Lake Geneva, WI 53147-2004. **Phone:** (262) 248-4416 or (800) 345-1020.

SAVE **LAKE GENEVA CRUISE LINE** departs from the Riviera Docks at 812 Wrigley Dr. One- and 2-hour sightseeing trips on Geneva Lake are offered aboard yachts. U.S. Mailboat, Black Point Estate, Luncheon, Dixieland Jazz dinner, and Ice Cream Social tours as well as Sunday brunch cruises also are available.

Reservations are recommended for all cruises, and are required for food cruises. **Hours:** Tours daily mid-Apr.-early Nov., with times and frequency depending upon the season. Phone for departure times. **Cost:** Fares $20-$60. **Phone:** (262) 248-6206 or (800) 558-5911.

Black Point Estate Boat and House Tour departs from the Riviera Docks at 812 Wrigley Dr. Located on a bluff overlooking Lake Geneva, the 4-story, 13-bedroom 1888 Black Point Mansion was home to wealthy brewer Conrad Seipp and his family. A 1.5-hour tour is offered of the mansion's first two floors and its grounds. Visitors arrive by boat; the 45-minute ride is narrated each way. A series of about 100 stairs connect the pier to the house; comfortable walking shoes are recommended.

Tours: Guided tours are available. **Time:** Allow 3 hours, 30 minutes minimum. **Hours:** Tours depart daily at 11:10 and 1:10, late May-late Aug.; at 11:10, late Aug.-late Oct. **Cost:** Fare $36; $34 (ages 65+); $31 (ages 13-17); $24 (ages 4-12). Reservations are recommended. **Phone:** (262) 248-6206 or (800) 558-5911.

RECREATIONAL ACTIVITIES
Skiing and Snowboarding

• **The Mountain Top at Grand Geneva Resort** is at jct. SR 50 and US 12 at 7036 Grand Geneva Way, Lake Geneva, WI 53147. **Hours:** Fri.-Mon. and holidays 10-10, Tues.-Thurs. noon-10, mid-Dec. to mid-Mar. **Phone:** (262) 249-4726 or (888) 392-8000.

LAKE MILLS (H-7) pop. 4,843, elev. 857′

Archeologists theorize that Aztalan, 3 miles east of Lake Mills on CR B, then right on CR Q, was the northernmost city of the Middle Mississippian Phase Indians, a culture influenced by the Aztecs in Mexico. Established 1075-1175, a 21-acre stockaded village once was occupied by about 500 Aztalan Indians. The Aztalans had a settled farming culture characterized by pyramidal mounds, complex pottery and crafts, and cannibalism.

After the Black Hawk War ended in 1836, settlers flooding into the area founded the second village of Aztalan at the junction of two stagecoach roads just northwest of the stockade. By 1842, the pioneer town had evolved into an industrial center, with Jefferson County's first post office, two hotels, a brickyard and five small factories. Aztalan's downfall came in 1859, after the railroad bypassed the town.

Truncated mounds and stockade sections of the ancient Indian village are identified with markers in Aztalan State Park, a quarter-mile south of the Aztalan Museum *(see attraction listing).* Phone (920) 648-8774.

Lake Mills Area Chamber of Commerce: 200 C Water St., Lake Mills, WI 53551-0125. **Phone:** (920) 648-3585.

AZTALAN MUSEUM is 3 mi. e. on CR B at jct. CR Q, next to Aztalan State Park. The only remaining building from the 1830s pioneer village of Aztalan, this former Baptist church houses a collection of Aztalan and Woodland Indian artifacts, as well as exhibits, maps and documents relating to Aztalan and early Lake Mills. Four log cabins on the 4-acre site date from the mid- to late 1800s. The Pettey cabin has furnishings of the 1840s, the Zickert house is outfitted with items from the late 19th century and the Bornell cabin is furnished as an early 20th-century store.

Time: Allow 1 hour minimum. **Hours:** Thurs.-Sun. noon-4, mid-May to late Sept. **Cost:** $3; $1 (ages 6-17). **Phone:** (920) 648-4632 mid-May to late Sept., or (920) 648-8575 rest of year.

LAND O'LAKES (B-6) pop. 882, elev. 1,709′

Heart of the region of the same name, the attractive village of Land O'Lakes is surrounded by some 135 lakes. To the west, the Cisco Chain of 17 lakes forms the second longest chain in Wisconsin. Lac Vieux Desert, east of town, is the source of the Wisconsin River. A popular resort center, the region offers summer and winter sports.

Land O'Lakes Chamber of Commerce: CR B at US 45, P.O. Box 599, Land O'Lakes, WI 54540. **Phone:** (715) 547-3432 or (800) 236-3432.

LAONA (D-7) pop. 1,367, elev. 1,580′

Laona is a lumbering and vacation center providing access to the varied recreational opportunities available in Chequamegon-Nicolet National Forest *(see place listing p. 138).*

GEM **LUMBERJACK STEAM TRAIN AND LOGGING MUSEUM COMPLEX TOUR** is on US 8 just w. of jct. SR 32 and US 8. Riders aboard the Laona and Northern Railroad's "Lumberjack Steam Train" travel from the historic depot in Laona to the museum complex. A logging museum at the complex contains logging artifacts from the river and railroad eras through the gasoline era as well as an active blacksmith and harness shop, transportation and agricultural displays, a lumber company money collection and an audiovisual presentation about logging history.

The complex also includes an early 20th-century country store, animal corral and a nature center. A 30-minute forest tour by surrey and a haywagon/ pontoon boat ride along banks of wild rice and through a bird refuge are available.

Time: Allow 2 hours minimum. **Hours:** Mon.- Sat. 11-4, June 22-Aug. 27. Trains depart at 11, noon, 1 and 2. Fall color tours are offered on Sat., Sept. 17 and 24 and Oct. 1. **Cost:** Museum, surrey ride and round-trip train ride $19; $17 (senior citizens); $8 (ages 4-12); $56 (family, two adults and 3+ children ages 4-12); free (active military with ID). Hayrack/pontoon ride $5; $3 (ages 4-12). Phone to verify prices and schedules. **Phone:** (715) 674-3414.

MADELINE ISLAND (A-4)

Madeline Island is east of the Bayfield Peninsula in Lake Superior. The largest of the Apostle Islands group *(see Apostle Islands National Lakeshore p. 129)*, Madeline has a permanent population of about 250 residents. The island was the focus of some of the earliest trading, missionary activity and commercial fishing in the interior of North America. It is possible that Etienne Brule visited the region as early as 1622 in his attempt to find the mythical Northwest Passage to China and the East Indies.

The French explorers Radisson and Groseilliers explored Madeline in 1659. Trading posts were established by the French in 1693 and by the British in 1793. La Pointe became headquarters for a post of the American Fur Co. in 1816. It currently serves the thousands of summer visitors to the island. Big Bay State Park *(see Recreation Chart)* is on the east shore of the island. Just across the lagoon is Big Bay Town Park.

Ferries operate between Bayfield *(see place listing p. 133)* and the island town of La Pointe daily from April to early January (weather permitting). They run about every 30 minutes during the peak season, mid-June to early October; phone (715) 747-2051. In the winter a motorized windsled offers transportation to the island until the lake freezes and cars can travel on an ice highway.

Free guided walking tours of downtown La Pointe depart twice daily, late June through August, from the Madeline Island Ferry Lines office near the ferry landing; phone (715) 747-2051 or (715) 747-6801.

Madeline Island Chamber of Commerce: 794 Main St., P.O. Box 274, La Pointe, WI 54850. **Phone:** (715) 747-2801 or (888) 475-3386.

Shopping areas: During the summer Woods Hall Craft Shop, 3 blocks south of the ferry landing, features craftspersons displaying their wares.

MADELINE ISLAND MUSEUM is 1 blk. from the ferry landing in La Pointe. Surrounded by a log stockade, this state historic site consists of an American Fur Co. warehouse, the island jail, a barn and the old Sailors' Home. Exhibits and programs explore more than 350 years of human interaction with the land and waters of the Lake Superior region from early American Indian habitation to the present. A 20-minute film also is available.

Hours: Daily 10-5, late June-last Sat. in Aug.; 10-4, late May-late June and day after last Sat. in Aug.-first Sat. in Oct. Last admission 30 minutes before closing. **Cost:** $7; $6 (students with ID and ages 65+); $3.50 (ages 5-17); $19 (family). **Phone:** (715) 747-2415.

MADISON (H-6) pop. 208,054, elev. 845'

See map page 156.

Madison existed only as a plan when it was selected as the territorial capital in 1836. By 1838 there was one inn and a general store, and construction had just begun on the Capitol. The going was slow, and the legislature, weary of cold, crowded and bedless accommodations, repeatedly threatened to move the capital elsewhere.

With the completion of the statehouse, Wisconsin's attainment of statehood and the establishment of the University of Wisconsin in 1848, the city began to assume some of its present character. Landscape architect John Nolen unveiled a city plan in 1910 presenting Madison as a model city that would be a place for politics, education and living. Today Madison is a center for business, cultural arts, government and education.

The city center is on an eight-block-wide isthmus between two glacial lakes: Mendota and Monona. By ordinance, the city's skyline is dominated by the 2,500-ton dome of the state Capitol. Capitol Square is connected to the University of Wisconsin-Madison campus by State Street, a tree-lined shopping district with import shops, ethnic restaurants, coffeehouses and galleries.

The Unitarian Meeting House at 900 University Bay Dr. is an especially noteworthy example of Frank Lloyd Wright's architectural style. Wright intended its ascending triangular forms to symbolize unity and prayer.

Much of the city's recreation is available on more than 26,748 acres of lake surface within surrounding Dane County. The "Five Lakes of Madison" are Kegonsa, Mendota, Monona, Waubesa and Wingra. Mendota, with 21 miles of shoreline, is the largest. More than 260 city parks and 120 miles of shared-use biking and walking trails are open year-round. Visitors can enjoy a spectacular view of the city from Picnic Point, a narrow spit jutting into Lake Mendota.

Fans of spectator sports cheer on the Madison Mallards minor-league baseball team at Warner Park. Professional women's football team the Wisconsin Wolves take the field at Lussier Stadium.

Greater Madison Convention & Visitors Bureau: 615 E. Washington Ave., Madison, WI 53703. **Phone:** (608) 255-2537 or (800) 373-6376.

Shopping areas: Madison has four major shopping centers. East Towne, at I-90/94 and US 151, has 100 stores, and West Towne, at Gammon and Mineral Point roads, features more than 100 stores. Anchor stores at these are Boston Store, JCPenney and Sears.

Hilldale Mall, at Midvale Boulevard and University Avenue, features more than 50 stores including Macy's. Greenway Station, at US 12/14 West and Greenway Boulevard, includes Ann Taylor Loft, Jos. A Bank, Marshalls and Orvis as well as several restaurants.

 CAVE OF THE MOUNDS NATIONAL NATURAL LANDMARK— *see Blue Mounds p. 135.*

HENRY VILAS ZOO is on Lake Wingra at 702 South Randall Ave. Founded in 1911, the 30-acre park contains more than 700 animals. Major attractions include a great ape primate center, tropical rain

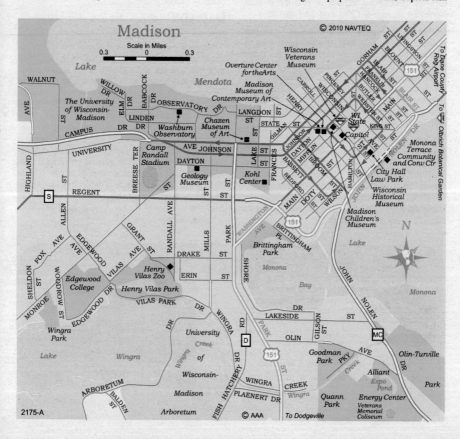

forest aviary, Herpetarium, Discovery Center and a wildlife-themed carousel.

Hours: Grounds open daily 9:30-5. Buildings open daily 10-4. Closed Jan. 1, Martin Luther King Jr. Day, Thanksgiving, day after Thanksgiving, Dec. 24-25 and 31. **Cost:** Free. **Phone:** (608) 266-4732. ⊞

MADISON CHILDREN'S MUSEUM is at 100 N. Hamilton St. on the Capitol Square. This educational, hands-on museum is designed for adults and children to learn and play together. Exhibits include Possible-opolis, a whimsical environment for ages 6 and older that celebrates the wonders of invention and creativity; the Wildernest, a global village with huts, music and a water play area for children under age 6; the Community Concourse, a free area full of surprises for those visiting briefly; a drop-in Art Studio; Rooftop Ramble, a four-season park in the sky with animals, gardens and energy-saving demonstrations; and the Log Cabin, which takes visitors back to Madison life in the 1840s.

Time: Allow 1 hour minimum. **Hours:** Daily 9:30-5 (also 5-8 on Thurs.). Closed major holidays. Phone ahead to confirm schedule. **Cost:** $6.95; $5.95 (ages 55+); free (ages 0-1 and from 5-8 on first Thurs. of the month). **Phone:** (608) 256-6445.

MADISON MUSEUM OF CONTEMPORARY ART is at 227 State St. Designed by architect Cesar Pelli, the museum presents modern and contemporary art in. various media including paintings, photography and sculpture. The collection features works by Deborah Butterfield, Frida Kahlo, Diego Rivera and Cindy Sherman. An illuminated sculpture garden covers 7,100 square feet on the museum roof. **Time:** Allow 1 hour minimum. **Hours:** Tues.-Fri. noon-5 (also Fri. 5-8), Sat. 10-8, Sun. noon-5. **Cost:** Free. **Phone:** (608) 257-0158.

MONONA TERRACE COMMUNITY AND CONVENTION CENTER is 2 blks. e. of Capitol Sq. at 1 John Nolen Dr. Frank Lloyd Wright proposed this 250,000-square-foot civic center on the shore of Lake Monona in 1938 but it was not completed until 1997. The complex bears Wright's signature style of dramatic open spaces, circular forms and expansive views of the outdoors. The rooftop garden has a memorial to Otis Redding, who died in a Lake Monona plane crash in 1967.

Hours: Center open daily 8-5. Guided tours are offered daily at 1. **Cost:** Tours $3; $2 (ages 6-17). **Phone:** (608) 261-4000. ⊞

OLBRICH BOTANICAL GARDENS is at 3330 Atwood Ave. This oasis on the shores of Lake Monona includes 16 acres of specialty gardens, a 50-foot-high glass conservatory and what is said to be the only Thai pavilion and garden in the continental United States. A two-acre rose garden features hardy shrub roses in mixed borders with fountains and a two-story stone tower overlook. Other gardens display herbs, hostas, perennials, wildflowers and annuals.

The conservatory simulates a rain-forest atmosphere and contains tropical plants, bamboo arbors, a waterfall, palm trees and free-flying birds. Flower shows, concerts and special events are offered throughout the year.

Guided tours are available by appointment. **Time:** Allow 2 hours minimum. **Hours:** Outdoor gardens open daily 8-8, Apr.-Sept.; 9-6 in Oct.; 9-4, rest of year. Conservatory open Mon.-Sat. 10-4, Sun. 10-5. Closed Jan. 1, Thanksgiving and Dec. 25. **Cost:** Outdoor gardens and Thai pavilion admission free. Conservatory $1; free (Wed. and Sat. 10-noon except during special exhibits). **Phone:** (608) 246-4550.

OVERTURE CENTER FOR THE ARTS is at 201 State St. Ten arts organizations, including the symphony, opera, ballet and a children's theater, reside at the center. The complex includes the historic 1928 Capitol Theater, the 2,251-seat Overture Hall, the 345-seat Playhouse and the Madison Museum of Contemporary Art. The Watrous Gallery exhibits the work of Wisconsin artists. Visitors can also see works by local and regional artists in the four Overture Galleries.

Tours: Guided tours are available. **Time:** Allow 1 hour minimum. **Hours:** Mon.-Sat. 9-5, Sun. 11-5. Overture galleries Mon.-Sat. 9-5 (also Fri.-Sat. 5-9), Sun. noon-5. **Cost:** Free. Guided tour $3; free (ages 0-5). **Phone:** (608) 258-4177. ⊞

THE UNIVERSITY OF WISCONSIN-MADISON is on the shores of Lake Mendota at the end of State St. Opened in 1848 with 17 students, the university now occupies a 935-acre campus with an enrollment of more than 42,000. The Kohl Center Arena, on campus, is home to the university's basketball and hockey teams, while Camp Randall Stadium hosts Big Ten football games. The University Welcome Center is at 21 N. Park St. and the Campus Information Center is at 716 Langdon St.

Hours: Welcome Center is open Mon.-Fri. 9-4:30. Campus Information Center is open Mon.-Fri. 8-5, Sat.-Sun. 11-2:30. Hours vary during university breaks and holidays. Phone ahead to confirm schedule. **Phone:** (608) 263-2400.

Chazen Museum of Art is on the University of Wisconsin-Madison campus at 800 University Ave. Artworks in the permanent collection date from 2300 B.C. to the present. American and western European paintings, sculpture, prints and drawings are featured as well as ancient, Asian and African art. Temporary exhibits change frequently and the Kohler Art Library houses more than 155,000 volumes. **Hours:** Tues.-Fri. 9-5, Sat.-Sun. 11-5. Closed Jan. 1, Thanksgiving and Dec. 24-25. **Cost:** Free. **Phone:** (608) 263-2246.

Geology Museum is on the University of Wisconsin-Madison campus in Weeks Hall at Charter and W. Dayton sts. Mineral, rock and fossil exhibits include the skeletons of a 33-foot-long duckbilled dinosaur and a Wisconsin mastodon.

Additional highlights include a 6-foot rotating globe and a walk-through model of a limestone cave. **Hours:** Mon.-Fri. 8:30-4:30, Sat. 9-1. Closed major holidays. **Cost:** Free. **Phone:** (608) 262-1412 or (608) 262-2399.

University of Wisconsin-Madison Arboretum Visitor Center is near the University of Wisconsin-Madison campus at 1207 Seminole Hwy. Covering 1,260 acres along Lake Wingra and south of the West Beltline Highway, the arboretum acts as a research and study area and features natural plant and animal communities native to Wisconsin. The Longenecker Horticultural Gardens includes flowering trees, shrubs and a renowned lilac collection. Surrounding the visitor center, the 4-acre Wisconsin Native Plant Gardens feature a collection of nearly 500 native Wisconsin plant species and serve as an introduction to ecological restoration.

Bimonthly exhibits in the visitor center feature nature-themed art and photography. Free naturalist-led tours are offered on Sundays. Pets and picnicking are not permitted. **Hours:** Grounds daily dawn-dusk. Visitor center Mon.-Fri. 9:30-4, Sat.-Sun. 12:30-4. Closed major holidays. **Cost:** Free. **Phone:** (608) 263-7888.

Washburn Observatory is on the University of Wisconsin-Madison campus at 1401 Observatory Dr. Objects can be viewed through a 15-inch telescope. Astronomers are available to answer questions.

Hours: Open in clear weather every Wed. at 9 p.m., June-Aug.; first and third Wed. at 9 p.m., Sept.-Oct. and April-May; first and third Wed. at 7:30 p.m., Nov.-Mar. Closed Jan. 1, July 4, Dec. 24-25 and 31. **Cost:** Free.

WISCONSIN HISTORICAL MUSEUM is at 30 N. Carroll St. on Capitol Sq. Permanent and changing exhibits illustrate Wisconsin's history from prehistoric times and territorial days to the present. **Time:** Allow 1 hour minimum. **Hours:** Tues.-Sat. 9-4; closed Jan. 1, July 4, Thanksgiving, Dec. 24-25 and 31. **Cost:** $4; $3 (ages 3-17); $10 (family). **Phone:** (608) 264-6555.

WISCONSIN STATE CAPITOL is on Capitol Sq. at 2 East Mifflin St. This example of Beaux Arts architecture was completed in 1917. The white granite dome is topped by Daniel Chester French's "Wisconsin," a gilded bronze allegorical statue. Guided tours of the rotunda, the governor's conference room, the Supreme Court of Wisconsin and the Senate and Assembly chambers include commentary about the building's history and the artworks in the various rooms. Summer tours include the sixth floor museum and observation deck.

Time: Allow 1 hour minimum. **Hours:** Building open Mon.-Fri. 8-6, Sat.-Sun. and holidays 8-4. Tours are given on the hour Mon.-Sat. 9-11 and 1-3,

Sun. 1-3 (also Mon.-Fri. at 4, Memorial Day-Labor Day). **Cost:** Free. **Phone:** (608) 266-0382.

WISCONSIN VETERANS MUSEUM is downtown at 30 W. Mifflin St. The museum is dedicated to the men and women of Wisconsin who served in America's conflicts from the Civil War to the present. The 19th Century Gallery houses exhibits recounting events of the Civil War and Spanish American War; it features a diorama dramatizing the Battle of Antietam. Visitors can use the Civil War database to look up service records of family members.

The 20th Century Gallery displays illustrate the Mexican Border Campaign, World War I, World War II, the Korean War, the Vietnam War and the Persian Gulf War. Dioramas depict the Battle of the Bulge in Europe and jungle warfare in Papua New Guinea. A Sopwith "Camel" biplane from World War I, a P-51 "Mustang" from World War II, a "Huey" helicopter from the Vietnam War and a Cold War-era periscope are suspended from the gallery ceiling.

Time: Allow 1 hour minimum. **Hours:** Mon.-Sat. 9-4:30, Sun. noon-4, Apr.-Sept.; Mon.-Sat. 9-4:30, rest of year. Closed major holidays. **Cost:** Free. **Phone:** (608) 267-1799.

MANITOWISH WATERS (B-5)
pop. 646, elev. 1,640′

A year-round vacation center, Manitowish Waters is in the Northern Highland-American Legion State Forest *(see Recreation Chart and the AAA Great Lakes CampBook)*. One of the area's highlights is its interconnected chain of 10 lakes that together cover 4,265 acres. The area offers water sports, tennis, hiking, biking and fishing in summer and cross-country skiing, ice fishing and snowmobiling in winter.

Mountain bikers, hikers, snowshoers and cross-country skiers pass by a lake, a bog and the Manitowish River on 12 miles of winding forest trails at the North Lakeland Discovery Center on CR W, 1.2 miles north of FR 51. Programs, events and activities offer learning adventures for adults and children year-round; donations are accepted.

Part of the Great Wisconsin Birding & Nature Trail, Powell Marsh Wildlife Area lies north of Lac du Flambeau and provides a home for waterfowl, deer, ruffed grouse, fur-bearing animals, raptors, shorebirds, songbirds and other wildlife; phone (715) 358-9207.

A free cranberry marsh tour is offered Fridays at 10, early July to early October. A video, cranberry refreshments and a question-and-answer session are offered at the community center before vehicles motorcade to a marsh for an up-close look. Contact the chamber of commerce for further information.

Manitowish Waters Chamber of Commerce: 4 S. US 51, P.O. Box 251, Manitowish Waters, WI 54545. **Phone:** (715) 543-8488 or (888) 626-9877.

MANITOWOC (F-8) pop. 34,053, elev. 595′

Manitowoc, an American Indian name meaning "the home of the Great Spirit Manitou," is a leading industrial and shipping center. Its harbor at the mouth of the Manitowoc River has made it an important port since the early 1830s. Hundreds of ships, including 28 submarines, have been built at local shipyards since the schooner *Citizen* was launched in 1848; Burger Boat shipyard still is in operation.

Formerly distinguished as one of the world's largest producers of aluminum ware, the city balances its commercial enterprises with refuges for both animals and nature lovers. Collins Marsh Wildlife Refuge, 16 miles west of Manitowoc on CR JJ, is a natural haven for wildfowl; it is open May through October on a limited basis.

The SS Badger, operated by the Lake Michigan Carferry Service, offers a 4-hour cross-lake car-ferry service from Manitowoc to Ludington, Mich. from late May to early October. For information and fares phone (800) 841-4243. Several charter fishing associations also operate out of the town.

Manitowoc Area Visitor & Convention Bureau & Visitor Information Center: 4221 Calumet Ave., P.O. Box 966, Manitowoc, WI 54221-0966. **Phone:** (920) 686-3070 or (800) 627-4896.

Shopping areas: Browse boutiques and galleries in downtown's quaint 8th Street Historic District; a farmer's market is open Tuesday and Saturday mornings from May through November.

PINECREST HISTORICAL VILLAGE is 3 mi. w. of I-43 via CR JJ to Pine Crest Ln. The village, which depicts rural life in Manitowoc County from the 1850s to the early 1900s, contains a collection of restored buildings relocated to this 60-acre site. Structures include three log houses, a smokehouse, cheese factory, church, school, blacksmith shop, harness shop, saloon, general store, firehouse, town hall, an octagonal dancehall and a train depot with a caboose and an 1887 engine.

Time: Allow 1 hour minimum. **Hours:** Daily 9-4, May 1-Oct. 24. **Cost:** $7; $5 (ages 6-17); $18 (family, two adults and dependent children ages 6-17). **Phone:** (920) 684-5110 or (920) 684-4445.

RAHR-WEST ART MUSEUM is at 610 N. 8th St. Housed in an 1893 Victorian mansion, the museum contains period furnishings, Chinese ivory, dolls and porcelain objects. **Hours:** Mon.-Fri. 10-4 (also Wed. 4-8), Sat.-Sun. 11-4. Closed Jan. 1, Easter, Memorial Day, July 4, Labor Day, Thanksgiving and Dec. 24-25. **Cost:** Donations. **Phone:** (920) 686-3090.

WISCONSIN MARITIME MUSEUM is off I-43 exit 152, 4 mi. e. on US 10, then 1 mi. s. to 75 Maritime Dr. The museum's 12 galleries are dedicated to the maritime heritage of the Great Lakes region and the submarine culture of the area. Operate a steam engine, learn how ships navigate through locks, view life in a re-created 19th-century shipbuilding town and tour a restored World War II submarine, the USS *Cobia*, which is docked at the museum.

In the Children's Waterways Room, youngsters can build model boats to navigate through miniature rivers and locks. Adults and children can experience the thrill of landing a "big one" at the realistic, multimedia sport fishing simulator. Allow 2 hours minimum for the museum, 1 hour additional for the submarine. **Hours:** Museum daily 9-6, Memorial Day weekend-Labor Day; 9-5, rest of year. Tours of the submarine are included in museum tour (weather permitting). Closed Jan. 1, Easter, Thanksgiving and Dec. 25. Phone ahead to confirm schedule. **Cost:** $12 (includes submarine); $10 (ages 6-15). **Phone:** (920) 684-0218 or (866) 724-2356.

The USS *Cobia* is docked in the Manitowoc River at the Wisconsin Maritime Museum, 75 Maritime Dr. The 45-minute tour of the USS *Cobia*, believed to be the nation's most completely restored WW II submarine, begins in the interpretive center where exhibits and a multimedia theater tell the story of submarine war patrols in the Pacific Ocean, the role U.S. Navy subs played in World War II and how the Manitowoc Shipbuilding Company came to build 28 submarines during the war years. The tour provides an up-close look at life in the "silent service."

Time: Allow 1 hour minimum. **Hours:** Tours daily 9:30-4:30, Memorial Day-Labor Day; 10-3 (also Sat. 10-4), March 1-day before Memorial Day and day after Labor Day-Oct. 31; Mon.-Thurs. 11:30-1, Fri.-Sat. 11-2, Sun. at 1, rest of year (weather permitting). Closed Jan. 1, Easter, Thanksgiving and Dec. 25. Phone ahead to confirm schedule. **Cost:** Included in the Wisconsin Maritime Museum admission. **Phone:** (866) 724-2356.

MARINETTE (D-8) pop. 11,749, elev. 597'

Marinette was named for Queen Marinette, a woman of French and Chippewa Indian extraction who operated a trading post in the area with her husband, William Farnsworth, during the 1820s.

From the mid-19th to the early 20th century, Marinette and neighboring Menominee, Mich. experienced a lumber boom, relying on the area's abundance of white pine. Dozens of lumber mills lined both sides of the Menominee River, which separates Wisconsin and Michigan; sawmills, lumber mills and door factories employed thousands of woodsmen, sawyers and scalers.

Marinette is the gateway to Marinette County, which encompasses 250 lakes, 50 trout streams and 14 waterfalls.

Marinette-Menominee Area Chamber of Commerce: 601 Marinette Ave., Marinette, WI 54143. **Phone:** (715) 735-6681 or (800) 236-6681.

MARINETTE COUNTY HISTORICAL MUSEUM is downtown on US 41 in Stephenson Island Park. The museum houses early farming and logging tools, hand-carved miniatures of logging operations, American Indian items and furniture and other household items. On the premises is the fully-furnished restored Evancheck log cabin of the 1800s. Stephenson Island Park offers picnic facilities, a playground and a boat ramp.

Time: Allow 1 hour minimum. **Hours:** Mon.-Fri. 10-4, Memorial Day weekend-Labor Day; otherwise by appointment. **Cost:** $3; $1 (ages 12-17). **Phone:** (715) 732-0831.

MARSHALL (H-6) pop. 3,432, elev. 879'

LITTLE AMERRICKA AMUSEMENT PARK, 700 E. Main St. (SR 19), features more than 20 rides including a Ferris wheel, wooden rollercoaster, a parachute tower, a carousel, bumper boats and cars, a haunted house, miniature golf and go-carts. An elevated monorail circles the park, and the Mad Mouse is a single-car roller coaster. Passengers may ride on a miniature railroad through Wisconsin farmland and see llamas, peacocks, ducks, geese, cattle, emus, donkeys and a zebra along the way.

Hours: Daily noon-6, June-Sept. Phone ahead to confirm schedule. **Cost:** (includes all rides except go-carts and miniature golf) $13.95; $11.95 (ages 60+ and children 36-42 inches tall); $9.95 (children under 36 inches tall). Gold Pass (includes all rides) $19.95. **Phone:** (608) 655-3181.

MARSHFIELD (E-5) pop. 18,800, elev. 1,276'

Marshfield once was a railroad hub with 50 trains stopping daily as hotels were crowded with passengers awaiting connections to go "out West" or "back East." In the early days of the Marshfield Clinic, one of the country's largest medical clinics, physicians rode the trains to serve patients in smaller outlying communities.

At the junction of Vine Avenue and East 17th Street is the Central Wisconsin State Fair Round Barn, reputed to be the largest round barn in existence.

Hiking, bicycling, camping and swimming are popular during summer. In winter Marshfield provides ample opportunity for cross-country skiing, snowmobiling and hunting. Marshfield Super Speedway is host to stock car races; phone (715) 384-8325.

Marshfield Convention & Visitors Bureau: 700 S. Central Ave., P.O. Box 868, Marshfield, WI 54449. **Phone:** (715) 384-4314 or (800) 422-4541.

NEW VISIONS GALLERY is 8 blks. n. of SR 13 in the Marshfield Clinic at 1000 N. Oak Ave. Permanent displays include posters by Marc Chagall, West African sculpture, Japanese prints, Haitian paintings, Australian aboriginal art and original prints by modern artists. Temporary exhibits change every 6 to 8-

weeks. **Time:** Allow 1 hour minimum. **Hours:** Permanent and temporary exhibits Mon.-Fri. 9-5:30. Closed major holidays. **Cost:** Free. **Phone:** (715) 387-5562.

WILDWOOD PARK & ZOO is at 608 W. 17th St. Home to numerous species of free-range and exhibited animals, this 60-acre park also offers picnic facilities, tennis courts, fishing, playgrounds, nature trails and disc golf. **Time:** Allow 1 hour minimum. **Hours:** Park open daily 6 a.m.-10:30 p.m. Zoo open daily 7:30-7:30, late Apr. through mid-Sept.; 7:30-6, late Sept. to mid-Oct.; 7:30-2:45, rest of year. Closed Jan. 1, Thanksgiving, Dec. 24-25 and 31. **Cost:** Free. **Phone:** (715) 384-4642.

MELLEN (B-4) pop. 835, elev. 1,240′

Home of Copper Falls State Park *(see attraction listing)* and surrounded by the wooded hills of the Penokee Mountain Range, Mellen is a lumbering town as well as an eastern gateway to Chequamegon-Nicolet National Forest *(see place listing p. 138)*, where all-terrain vehicle and snowmobile trails crisscross the area. The red and black granite quarried in the area is used widely for monuments and buildings.

Mellen Area Chamber of Commerce: Main St., P.O. Box 193, Mellen, WI 54546. **Phone:** (715) 274-2330.

COPPER FALLS STATE PARK is 2 mi. n.e. on SR 169. This 3,100-acre park is named for falls where the Bad and Tyler Forks rivers flow over the edge of a rock outcropping into a canyon. The Doughboy Nature Trail follows the top of the Bad River canyon to scenic views of waterfalls. Loon Lake has a sand beach for swimming, a canoe launch and access to the Red Granite Trail which leads to a series of cascades over red granite rock.

Loon Lake has largemouth bass, northern pike and panfish and is a good spot for ice fishing. Bad and Tyler Forks rivers both offer fishing for rainbow, brown and brook trout. Denizens of the woods include black bears, deer, grey wolves and raccoons. The park has 5 miles of cross-country ski trail loops, a 2.5-mile snowshoe trail, 5 miles of mountain bike trails, hiking trails and a backpack campsite. *See Recreation Chart and the AAA Great Lakes CampBook.*

Hours: Daily 6 a.m.-11 p.m. **Cost:** Day-use fee (per private vehicle) $10; $7 (state residents); $3 (residents ages 65+). Annual permit $35; $25 (state residents); $10 (residents ages 65+). **Phone:** (715) 274-5123.

MENASHA (F-7) pop. 16,331

Located on the north shore of Lake Winnebago, Wisconsin's largest lake, Menasha enjoys a beautiful waterfront setting. Water power afforded by the Fox River helped establish Menasha as an industrial center in the mid to late 19th century, and today the city retains elements of its historic character in its rejuvenated downtown. The navigable waterway running through the heart of Menasha provides recreational opportunities.

WEIS EARTH SCIENCE MUSEUM AND BARLOW PLANETARIUM are at 1478 Midway Rd., on the University of Wisconsin-Fox Valley campus. Wisconsin's official state mineralogical museum offers interactive and hands-on exhibits about geology and mining history. The planetarium offers a variety of astronomy, family laser and rock laser shows.

Hours: Museum open Mon.-Thurs. noon-4, Fri. noon-7, Sat. 10-5, Sun. 1-5. Planetarium and museum closed all school holidays. Phone for planetarium show times and to confirm schedule. **Cost:** Museum $2; $1.50 (ages 13-17 and 65+); $1 (ages 3-12). Astronomy, family, and rock laser shows $7; $6 (ages 60+ and students with ID); $5 (ages 0-12). **Phone:** (920) 832-2925 for the museum, or (920) 832-2848 for the planetarium.

MENOMONIE (E-2) pop. 14,937, elev. 794′

Menomonie began as a lumber mill settlement on the Red Cedar River in 1830. Almost 50 years later the town's lumber corporation had become one of the largest in the world. Dairying later replaced lumbering as the city's economic mainstay.

Several 19th-century attractions downtown recall the days of the early lumber barons. Near Lake Menomin stand the 1868 John Holly Knapp House and the 1846 Wilson Place, stately Victorian mansions of the founders of Knapp Stout & Co. At 101 Wilson Ct., Wilson Place, now a museum depicting the early settlement era, was the estate of Sen. James H. Stout, founder of the University of Wisconsin-Stout in Menomonie; phone (715) 235-2283.

Of humbler origin is the home of Caddie Woodlawn, the subject of the 1935 Newbury Award-winning children's book "Caddie Woodlawn" by Carol Ryrie Brink. The Caddie Woodlawn Home and Park, 8 miles south on SR 25, contains the pioneer girl's home and provides picnic facilities.

Bordering the Red Cedar River along the western city limits is the 14-mile limestone-surfaced Red Cedar State Trail for bicyclists, hikers and cross-country skiers. Lake Menomin offers boating, and the Red Cedar River provides good fishing. Hoffman Hills State Recreation Area, 9 miles northeast, has 8 miles of trails. During the summer the Ludington Guard Band performs every Tuesday evening at 8 in the Wilson Park band shell.

Greater Menomonie Area Chamber of Commerce/ Visitor Center: 342 E. Main St., Menomonie, WI 54751. **Phone:** (715) 235-9087 or (888) 595-4223.

THE MABEL TAINTER CENTER FOR THE ARTS is at 205 Main St. Built in 1889, this Richardsonian Romanesque building contains a public reading room, an artist gallery with temporary exhibits and the Victorian Landmark Theater. Decorated with white pine, oak, Italian marble, Tiffany stained-glass windows and polished brass, the theater features an 1889 Steere & Turner pipe organ with 1,597 pipes and 25 stops. Performing arts programs are presented year-round.

Time: Allow 1 hour minimum. **Hours:** Mon.-Sat. 10-5, Sun. 1-5. Closed Dec. 25. **Cost:** Free. **Phone:** (715) 235-0001.

RUSSELL J. RASSBACH HERITAGE MUSEUM is at 1820 Wakanda St. in Wakanda Park. The museum features an exhibit detailing the life of Sen. James H. Stout, founder of the University of Wisconsin. The many other exhibits include the Oscar Brekke Bicycle Shop, a turn of the 20-century livery, an old gas station with antique cars and Rivers, Routes, Rails & Roads—Transportation in Dunn County.

Hours: Wed.-Sun. 10-5, Memorial Day-Sept. 30; Wed.-Sun. noon-4, rest of year. Closed Jan. 1, Easter, Thanksgiving and Dec. 25. **Cost:** $5; $3 (ages 13-18); $1 (ages 6-12); $12 (family). **Phone:** (715) 232-8685.

MERRIMAC (H-5) pop. 416, elev. 810′

RECREATIONAL ACTIVITIES

Skiing and Snowboarding

- **Devil's Head Resort** S6330 Bluff Rd., Merrimac, WI 53561. **Hours:** Mon.-Fri. 10-10, Sat.-Sun. and holidays 9 a.m.-10 p.m., day after Thanksgiving-Mar. 31 (weather permitting). **Phone:** (608) 493-2251 or (800) 472-6670.

MILTON (I-6) pop. 5,132, elev. 875′

Joseph Goodrich, an abolitionist from New York, fostered the growth of Milton when he established a stagecoach inn in 1844 on the site of three well-traveled trails. That same year marked the founding of Milton College, which closed in 1982. The former campus now accommodates a museum and visitor center as well as antiques and crafts shops. Milton is a leading manufacturer of electronic medical instruments. Agribusiness also supports the community.

The Milton area provides many opportunities for recreation, including hiking through the Storrs Lake nature preserve, traversing the Ice Age Trail, golfing or boating on one of five nearby lakes.

Milton Area Chamber of Commerce, Industry & Tourism: 508 Campus St., P.O. Box 222, Milton, WI 53563. **Phone:** (608) 868-6222.

MILTON HOUSE MUSEUM is at 18 S. Janesville St. Built by Joseph Goodrich in 1844, this six-sided, 20-room structure was the first poured-concrete home in the United States and operated as a stagecoach inn. A guided tour includes the house, an Underground Railroad tunnel, an 1837 log cabin and a country store. Also featured is a miniature replica of the original inn. **Time:** Allow 1 hour minimum. **Hours:** Guided tours every half-hour daily 10-5, Memorial Day-Labor Day. Last tour begins 1 hour before closing. **Cost:** $6; $5 (ages 62+); $3 (ages 5-17). **Phone:** (608) 868-7772.

Milwaukee

City Population: 596,974
Elevation: 740 ft.

Editor's Picks:

Miller Brewery Tour & Visitor
Center................................*(see p. 174)*
Milwaukee Art Museum ....*(see p. 170)*
Milwaukee County Zoo ....*(see p. 170)*

Historic Third Ward / © Walter Bibikow / age fotostock

During the 19th century immigrants from more than 30 European countries flocked to Milwaukee, bringing with them their skills, arts and cuisines. Germans were the largest group; as the decades passed their *gemütlichkeit* (hospitality) assumed Italian, Polish, Scandinavian, Irish and other national overtones.

Milwaukee's watery surroundings, while a boon to its eventual development as a river port, posed a few problems during its early years. A fierce rivalry developed over the question of payment for the Milwaukee River bridges that connected the two villages of Juneautown and Kilbourntown. The Great Bridge War was settled by the legislature in 1845, but not before both factions angrily had torn down every bridge and the residents of Juneautown had trained a loaded cannon on Kilbourntown.

The new city of Milwaukee witnessed the arrival of the Forty-eighters, refugees from unsuccessful revolutionary movements against German monarchies in 1848. This intellectual minority launched the city into new cultural and political directions, endowing the city with theaters, music societies, athletic clubs and Freethinker groups. They also established a reform tradition that later gave rise to Milwaukee's distinctive brand of socialism.

During the last half of the 19th century, the reference to Milwaukee as the German Athens was hardly an exaggeration. Only the Polish and Irish populations came close in number. English was almost never heard in some neighborhoods, especially on the northwest side. By the late 1870s Milwaukee had six daily newspapers published in German.

Public schools zealously enforced their requirement that German be taught from kindergarten on. Ever-popular were family picnics at such open-air beer gardens as the Schlitz Palm Garden. By the end of the century, however, German cultural allegiances

had begun to fade. The decision of the Stadt Theater, pride of Milwaukee's German culture, to alternate plays in German and English was an indisputable sign of changing times.

In reality Milwaukee's northern European heritage never disappeared. Its influence survived, despite such setbacks as World War I's repressive effect on the German community and Prohibition's nearly fatal blow to the city's brewing industry. The period following World War II brought massive development.

Today, Milwaukee is the largest city in Wisconsin, and while formerly known as the "machine shop of America," the service and technology sectors have experienced the most rapid growth in recent years. Some of the companies that call Milwaukee home include Briggs & Stratton, Harley-Davidson, Johnson Controls, Manpower, Northwestern Mutual and Rockwell Automation.

But what really has made Milwaukee famous is beer. Though other industries have dethroned the king since 1889, the brewing industry remains synonymous with the city. Milwaukee's beer heritage can be explored at the Captain Frederick Pabst Mansion, the Miller Brewery Tour & Visitor Center *(see attraction listings p. 168 and p. 174)* and smaller microbreweries found throughout the city. Lakefront

Getting There — *starting on p. 165*

Getting Around — *starting on p. 165*

What To See — *starting on p. 168*

What To Do — *starting on p. 172*

Where To Stay — *starting on p. 315*

Where To Dine — *starting on p. 319*

Brewery, 1872 N. Commerce St., and Sprecher Brewing Co., 701 W. Glendale Ave. are microbreweries that offer tours and tastings; phone (414) 372-8800 and (414) 964-2739, respectively. While City Hall *(see attraction listing p. 170)* and the ornate Pabst Theater, both built in the 1890s in the Flemish Renaissance style, reflect Milwaukee's European heritage, the city's newest icon is the Milwaukee Art Museum expansion *(see attraction listing p. 170)* with its unusual wings that open and close over a sunlit atrium on the Lake Michigan shore.

Bastille Days / © Susan Ruggles / Photolibrary

The 90-acre lakefront park area also boasts the science and technology museum Discovery World at Pier Wisconsin *(see attraction listing p. 169)*, along with the 75-acre Henry Maier Festival Park, home to the city's numerous ethnic festivals. In the heart of the city, visitors can stroll along an impressive two-mile-long Riverwalk to restaurants and microbrew pubs. Stop at Wells Street along the river for a look at the brass, life-sized statue of Fonzie – an homage to one of television's favorite characters from the show "Happy Days."

Getting There

By Car

From the north I-43 provides controlled access into downtown Milwaukee. I-94 affords direct access to the downtown area from Chicago and other southern points. From the west I-94 is the controlled-access highway into the city. Bypassing the metropolitan area to the south and west, I-894 provides the best connection for the I-94 through corridor. Lake Express offers 2.5-hour car-ferry trips from Muskegon, Mich., to Milwaukee; phone (866) 914-1010 for rates and schedule.

Getting Around

Street System

Lake Michigan flanks the city on the east, and Wisconsin Avenue is the main downtown east-west thoroughfare. The Milwaukee River divides the downtown area into approximately equal east and west sections; I-94 is the approximate dividing line between north and south street addresses. Streets are numbered in ascending order west of the Milwaukee River and continue well into the suburbs to the Milwaukee County line.

The official, unposted speed limit is 25 mph; other limits are posted. Rush hours are 7-9 a.m. and 3:30-6 p.m. Right turns are permitted on red unless otherwise posted.

Parking

Private commercial lots are scattered throughout the downtown area and near the airport. Lot rates

Destination Milwaukee

Milwaukee has a lot to offer visitors—from art museums to a variety of parks, gardens and nature centers.

Sightseeing is at its best here; horse-and-carriage tours, cruises and scenic drives are offered. The young and young-at-heart can enjoy an impressive zoo, an enormous ice-skating facility and a mansion built by a sea captain.

Milwaukee Public Museum.
(See listing page 171)

© Richard Cummins
Lonely Planet Images

Old World Wisconsin, Eagle.
(See listing page 177)

© Richard Cummins
Lonely Planet Images

Kewaskum • • Farmington
57
West Bend 33
41
Port Washington 43
45
Cedarburg • Grafton
Hartford • 60
Germantown
Hubertus • 41 **Milwaukee**
83

Oconomowoc
45
94 16 Wauwatosa •
Genesee Depot 59 Waukesha
83 894
Hales Corners 41
Eagle 43 94

See Downtown map page 169

Places included in this AAA Destination City:

Mitchell Park Horticultural Conservatory—"The Domes," Milwaukee.
(See listing page 171)

Visit Milwaukee

The Informed Traveler

Sales Tax: The sales tax in Milwaukee is 5.6 percent. In addition there is a 9.5 percent tax on hotel rooms, a 3 percent tax on car rentals and a .5 percent tax on food and beverage purchases.

WHOM TO CALL

Emergency: 911

Police (non-emergency): (414) 933-4444

Hospitals: Aurora St. Luke's Medical Center, (414) 649-6000; Aurora Sinai Medical Center, (414) 219-2000; Columbia St. Mary's Hospital, (414) 291-1000; Froedtert Hospital, (414) 805-3000; and St. Francis Hospital, (414) 647-5000.

WHERE TO LOOK

Newspapers

The morning daily *Milwaukee Journal/Sentinel* is Milwaukee's major newspaper.

Radio

Milwaukee radio station WTMJ (620 AM) is an all-news/weather/sports station; WUWM (89.7 FM) is a member of National Public Radio.

Visitor Information

VISIT Milwaukee Administrative Center: 648 N. Plankinton Ave., Suite 425, Milwaukee, WI 53203-2501. **Phone:** (800) 231-0903.

The VISIT Milwaukee Visitor Center is downtown at the Frontier Airlines Center, 400 W. Wisconsin Ave. The center is open daily 9-5; phone (800) 554-1448.

TRANSPORTATION

Air Travel

General Mitchell International Airport, 8 miles south via I-94 East, is served by several major domestic and international passenger carriers. Transportation to and from the airport by GO Airport Connection shuttle or by taxi takes about 20 minutes. One-way fares range from $12 to $35 by shuttle and $19 to $25 by taxi. Phone (800) 236-5450 for GO Airport Connection. The Milwaukee County Transit System operates buses to and from the airport from all points on its system via transfers from 5 a.m. to 12:30 a.m.; the fare is $2.25. Phone (414) 344-6711.

Rental Cars

Hertz, at the airport, (414) 747-5200 or (800) 654-3080, offers discounts to AAA members.

Rail Service

Amtrak, 433 W. St. Paul Ave. at the Milwaukee Intermodal Station, provides railroad passenger service to the city; phone (414) 271-9037, or (800) 872-7245 for reservations.

Buses

The Greyhound Lines Inc. terminal is at 433 W. St. Paul Ave. at the Milwaukee Intermodal Station; phone (414) 272-2156 or (800) 231-2222.

Taxis

All taxis in Milwaukee use the meter system. The fare is $6.75 for the first mile, $2.25 for each additional mile and $1 for each additional person. Taxis can be ordered by phone or hired at taxi stands at most major hotels. American United is the city's major taxi service; phone (414) 220-5000.

Public Transport

The Milwaukee County Transit System, 1942 N. 17th St., operates 22-hour service throughout Milwaukee County and eastern Waukesha County. The fare is $2.25; $1.10 (ages 6-11, ages 65+ and disabled persons with ID). Exact fare is required. For schedule and route information, phone (414) 344-6711 daily Mon.-Fri. 6 a.m.-7 p.m., Sat.-Sun. 8-4:30.

are $3-$4 per hour and $7-$14 for all-day parking. Private lots within four blocks of the Frontier Airlines Center and Bradley Center provide parking for functions at the centers.

What To See

BASILICA OF ST. JOSAPHAT is at 601 W. Lincoln Ave. Built in 1901 by Polish immigrants, this Romanesque basilica was designed after St. Peter's in Rome and features one of the largest domes in the world. The interior is noted for its hand-carved marble pulpit, ornate stained glass, murals and gilded plasterwork.

A guided tour is available after the Sunday 10 a.m. mass and daily by appointment. Tours begin at The Pope John Paul II Pavilion, the basilica's visitor center. **Time:** Allow 30 minutes minimum. **Hours:** Visitor center open Mon.-Fri. 9-4. Masses are open to the public Sat. at 4:30, Sun. at 8, 10 and noon. Closed major holidays. **Cost:** Free. **Phone:** (414) 902-3523.

BETTY BRINN CHILDREN'S MUSEUM is at 929 E. Wisconsin Ave. in the Miller Pavilion at O'Donnell Park. This museum offers hands-on exhibits and educational programs for children ages 10 and younger. Exhibit areas include Home Town; WBB-TV; It's Artastic!; Kohl's Healthy Kids; It's Your Move!; Let's Play Railway; and Betty's Busy Backyard, a play area for children ages 3 and younger.

Children not admitted without an adult. **Hours:** Mon.-Sat. 9-5, Sun. noon-5, June-Aug.; Tues.-Sat. 9-5, Sun. noon-5, rest of year. Closed major holidays. **Cost:** $6; $5 (ages 55+); free (ages 0-11 months). **Phone:** (414) 390-5437.

THE CAPTAIN FREDERICK PABST MANSION is at 2000 W. Wisconsin Ave. In 1892 Capt. Frederick Pabst of Pabst Brewing Co. fame built a 37-room Flemish Renaissance Revival mansion on aptly named Grand Avenue, a tree-line boulevard lined with extravagant, upper-class homes.

The street, now known as Wisconsin Avenue, would seem to have lost all evidence of its Gilded Age opulence if it weren't for Pabst's mansion tucked in among the low-rise commercial buildings and concrete parking garages. Preservationists saved the home from demolition in the 1970s, and since then they have returned several rooms to their former splendor complete with meticulously crafted wood details, lovely stained glass and fine wall coverings.

Time: Allow 1 hour, 30 minutes minimum. **Hours:** Mansion open Mon.-Sat. 10-4, Sun. noon-4, Mar. 1-early Jan.; Tues.-Sat. 10-4, Sun. noon-4, rest of year. Guided tours depart on the hour. Closed Jan. 1, Easter, Thanksgiving and Dec. 25. **Cost:** $9; $8 (ages 63+ and students with ID); $5 (ages 6-17). Christmas season tours are $1 additional. **Phone:** (414) 931-0808.

THE CHARLES ALLIS ART MUSEUM is at 1801 N. Prospect Ave. at the corner of E. Royall Pl. This Tudor-style mansion with original furnishings was

Harley-Davidson Museum / © Michael DeFreitas / Robert Harding

completed in 1911 for Charles Allis, the first president of Allis-Chalmers Manufacturing Co., and his wife Sarah. The art collection, spanning more than 2,000 years, emphasizes the fine arts—drawing, painting, photography, printmaking and sculpture. Changing exhibitions of Wisconsin artists are presented.

Docent-led, 45-minute tours are available upon request. **Time:** Allow 30 minutes minimum. **Hours:** Wed.-Sun. 1-5. Closed major holidays. **Cost:** $5; $3 (ages 63+, military and students with ID); free (ages 0-12). **Phone:** (414) 278-8295.

COOL WATERS FAMILY AQUATIC PARK is at 2028 S. 124th St. in Greenfield Park. The park features a heated zero-depth, beach-style entry pool with tube and body waterslides, tube rentals, a children's aquatic area with waterslides and a playground, and sand volleyball courts. **Time:** Allow 1 hour minimum. **Hours:** Mon.-Thurs. 10-8, Fri.-Sun. 10-6, Memorial Day weekend-Labor Day. **Cost:** $6.75; $5 (ages 3-11 and ages 60+). **Phone:** (414) 321-7530. 🍴 🎦

DISCOVERY WORLD is at 500 N. Harbor Dr. Exhibit areas focus on automation in the modern world; the Great Lakes watershed featuring a scale model with live animals; modern medicine including genetics and microscope technology; energy's uses and sources; and water and its environmental importance. The 120,000-square-foot facility also contains fresh and saltwater aquariums, an amphitheater and The HIVE, a multimedia virtual reality theater. Biking, fishing and walking are popular activities at a lakefront promenade, which also features a boat landing.

Hours: Tues.-Fri. 9-4, Sat.-Sun. 10-5. Closed July 4, Thanksgiving and Dec. 25. **Cost:** $16.95; $14.95 (ages 60+); $12.95 (ages 3-17); $9.95 (college students with ID). **Phone:** (414) 765-9966.

S/V *Denis Sullivan* is docked next to Discovery World at Pier Wisconsin. Visitors can tour the recreation of a 19th-century three-masted cargo schooner. Two-hour cruises aboard the schooner also are available. Passengers may help steer and set sails, or they may choose to sit back and enjoy the leisurely cruise on Lake Michigan.

Reservations are recommended for tours and cruises. **Time:** Allow 1 hour minimum. **Hours:** Cruises depart mid-May through Sept. 30. Phone ahead to confirm schedule. **Cost:** Fare for cruise $40; $20 (ages 0-11). Fee for deck tour $5. **Phone:** (414) 765-8625 for tour and cruise reservations or (414) 765-9966.

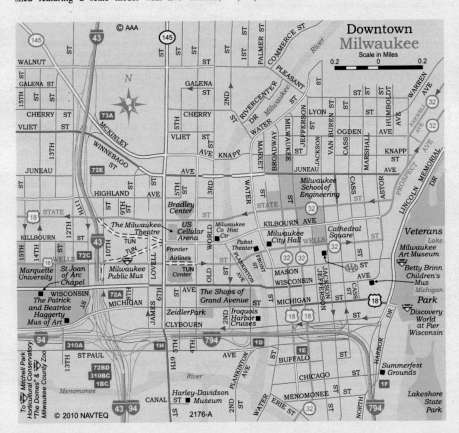

HARLEY-DAVIDSON MUSEUM is at 400 Canal St. The 130,000-square-foot museum features a collection of more than 450 motorcycles. Highlights include Elvis Presley's 1956 model KH motorcycle, the 13-foot-long customized King Kong with two engines, and the 1903 Serial Number One, the oldest known bike in existence. Exhibits including The Engine Room, Women at the Handlebars, and The Design Lab explore the company's history, culture and design.

Time: Allow 1 hour, 30 minutes minimum. **Hours:** Daily 9-6 (also Tues.-Thurs. 6-8 p.m.), May-Sept.; 10-6 (also Thurs. 6-8 p.m.), rest of year. **Cost:** $16; $12 (ages 65+ and military and students with ID); $10 (ages 5-17). **Phone:** (877) 436-8738.
🍴

HAVENWOODS STATE FOREST is at 6141 N. Hopkins St. Tread a path on foot or via bicycle on more than 6 miles of nature trails through grasslands, wetlands and a forest on the park's 237 acres. Cross-country skiers may traverse 2.5 miles of snow-covered trails in the winter. The habitats are home to a wide variety of birds, butterflies and wildflowers; trail maps and wildlife lists are available at the Environmental Awareness Center. An urban arboretum and garden areas are on the property.

Time: Allow 1 hour minimum. **Hours:** Daily 6 a.m.-8 p.m. Environmental Awareness Center Mon.-Fri. 7:45-4:30, Sat. 9-noon. **Cost:** Free. **Phone:** (414) 527-0232. 🐾 🏕

MARQUETTE UNIVERSITY is at 1250 W. Wisconsin Ave. Established in 1881 as a Catholic, Jesuit college, Marquette University was named after the 17th-century French Jesuit missionary and explorer, Father Jacques Marquette. The campus covers 90 acres in downtown Milwaukee; campus tours are available. **Phone:** (414) 288-7302, or (800) 222-6544 for the Office of Undergraduate Admissions.

The Patrick and Beatrice Haggerty Museum of Art is on the e. mall of the Marquette University campus at 530 N. 13th St. at Clybourn St. More than 4,500 works of art are included in four main galleries. The permanent collection includes European and American contemporary art, old master paintings, photography and works on paper. **Time:** Allow 1 hour minimum. **Hours:** Mon.-Sat. 10-4:30 (also Thurs. 4:30-8), Sun. noon-5. Closed major holidays. Phone ahead to confirm schedule. **Cost:** Free. **Phone:** (414) 288-1669.

St. Joan of Arc Chapel is on the campus of Marquette University. This Gothic, 15th-century French chapel stood in the Rhone River Valley until it was moved in 1927 to a Long Island estate and then in 1965 to Marquette University. Incorporated within the structure is the Joan of Arc Stone, before which the saint supposedly prayed. The small stone building contains items from the 11th to 15th centuries; four stained-glass windows were designed in the 20th-century by Charles J. Connick. Part of the floor is the tomb of the Companion of Bayard, a French knight.

Hours: Open Mon.-Sat. 10-4, Sun. noon-4, during the school year; Mon.-Fri. 10-4, rest of year. Closed Good Friday, Easter, Memorial Day weekend, July 4, Labor Day weekend, Thanksgiving weekend and Dec. 24-Jan. 1. **Cost:** Donations. **Phone:** (414) 288-6873.

◢◣GEM **MILWAUKEE ART MUSEUM** is at 700 N. Art Museum Dr. A suspended pedestrian bridge links the museum to downtown Milwaukee at Wisconsin Avenue. The graceful, postmodern Quadracci Pavilion was designed by Spanish architect Santiago Calatrava. Soaring above this white marble and glass pavilion is the Burke Brise Soleil, a winglike sunscreen with a 217-foot wingspan that unfolds twice daily. Windhover Hall is a magnificent cathedral-like space with a vaulted 90-foot-high glass ceiling.

More than forty galleries on four floors hold the museum's vast collection of nearly 20,000 works from antiquity to the present. Permanent collections include Old Masters and 19th- and 20th-century art, American decorative arts, German Expressionism, folk and Haitian art, and American art after 1960. Artists on exhibit include Wisconsin native Georgia O'Keeffe as well as Winslow Homer, Claude Monet, Pablo Picasso, Henri de Toulouse-Lautrec and Andy Warhol.

Time: Allow 2 hours minimum. **Hours:** Tues.-Sun. 10-5 (also Thurs. 5-8). The museum is open on Martin Luther King Jr. Day, Memorial Day and Labor Day. Closed Thanksgiving and Dec. 25. **Cost:** $12; $10 (ages 65+, active military and students with ID); free (ages 0-12 with adult). **Phone:** (414) 224-3200.

MILWAUKEE CITY HALL is at 200 E. Wells St. Built in 1895 in the Flemish Renaissance style, this building is noted for its stained-glass windows, ornately carved woodwork and stenciled ceilings in the Common Council Chamber and anteroom. A self-guiding tour pamphlet is available. **Hours:** Open Mon.-Fri. 8-4:45. Closed major holidays. **Cost:** Free. **Phone:** (414) 286-3285.

MILWAUKEE COUNTY HISTORICAL CENTER is at 910 N. Old World 3rd St. The county's past is preserved through permanent and rotating exhibits. Displays chronicle Milwaukee's culture, architecture and significant individuals and events. There is an extensive research library on the second floor. Guided tours are available by appointment. **Note:** The center is open while undergoing renovations, which are scheduled for completion spring 2011. **Hours:** Mon.-Fri. 9:30-5, Sat. 10-5. Closed major holidays. **Cost:** $5; $4 (ages 65+ and students with ID.) Phone: (414) 273-8288.

◢◣GEM **MILWAUKEE COUNTY ZOO** is 6 mi. w. on US 18 between US 45 and SR 100 at 10001 W. Bluemound Rd. More than 2,200 animals are displayed in five continental groupings. Among the animals are Humboldt penguins, African elephants and Alaska brown bears.

Apes of Africa features lowland gorillas and pygmy chimpanzees. The Wolf Woods exhibit is home to a pack of three timber wolves. North American river otters, meerkats and ring-tailed lemurs are in the Small Mammals Building. The Aquatic and Reptile Center features endangered Chinese alligators and a 23,000-gallon Pacific Coast aquarium. Other highlights include the "Big Cat Country" feline building and the Giraffe Experience.

The Oceans of Fun Show is a 20-minute show featuring California sea lions and harbor seals. Also included is an educational dairy complex, a petting zoo and a miniature train that circles the zoo. The Sky Safari chair lift carries passengers above several animal habitats including the rhinoceros, wolf and sea lion enclosures.

Stroller and wheelchair rentals are available. **Time:** Allow 3 hours minimum. **Hours:** Zoo open daily 9-5, May 29-Sept. 6; daily 9-4:30, Mar. 1-May 28 and Sept. 7-Oct. 31; Mon.-Fri. 9:30-2:30, Sat.-Sun. 9:30-4:30, rest of year. Sky Safari, petting zoo and miniature train daily Memorial Day weekend-Labor Day; Sat.-Sun. in spring and fall. Animals in Action shows daily 10:30-3 (weather permitting). Oceans of Fun Show Mon.-Sat. at 10:30, noon, 1:30 and 3, Sun. at 10, 11:30, 1, 2:30 and 4, Memorial Day-Labor Day (weather permitting).

Cost: Apr.-Oct. $13.25; $12.25 (ages 60+); $10.25 (ages 3-12). Admission rest of year $11.75; $10.25 (ages 60+); $8.75 (ages 3-12). Zoomobile $3; $2 (ages 3-12). Miniature train $2.50; $1.50 (ages 3-12). **Parking:** $11. **Phone:** (414) 771-3040. [T]

 MILWAUKEE PUBLIC MUSEUM is at 800 W. Wells St. Natural and cultural history are featured on three floors of walk-through exhibits and galleries. Visitors can stroll through a large diorama with life-size dinosaur models, explore North American Indian history and visit Egyptian mummies up close. Other walk-through exhibits include a Costa Rican rainforest, streets recreating turn-of-the-20th-century Milwaukee and a tropical garden filled with hundreds of live butterflies. The museum houses the Humphrey IMAX Dome Theater and the Daniel M. Soref Planetarium and features traveling exhibitions.

Tours: Guided tours are available. **Hours:** Open Mon.-Sat. 9-5, Sun. noon-5. Closed July 4, Thanksgiving and Dec. 25. **Cost:** $12.50; $11 (ages 13-17, ages 60+ and college students with ID); $9 (ages 3-12). IMAX movies and planetarium shows are additional. Hours and admission prices may vary during special exhibitions. **Phone:** (414) 278-2702 or (888) 700-9069. [T]

Daniel M. Soref Planetarium is at 800 W. Wells St. The state-of-the-art dome theater uses an advanced, full-color projection system to create stunning views of the night sky and show audiences remote regions of the universe. **Hours:** Shows take place daily at various times. Closed July 4, Thanksgiving and Dec. 25. **Cost:** $8; $7 (ages 13-17, ages 60+ and college students with ID); $6 (ages 3-12). **Phone:** (414) 319-4629.

Humphrey IMAX Dome Theater is at 800 W. Wells St. The theater shows high-resolution, large-format films on a 74-foot-diameter, hemispheric screen. **Hours:** Films are shown daily at various times. Closed July 4, Thanksgiving and Dec. 25. **Cost:** $8; $7 (ages 13-17, ages 60+ and college students with ID); $6 (ages 3-12). **Phone:** (414) 319-4629.

MITCHELL PARK HORTICULTURAL CONSERVATORY—"THE DOMES" is off I-94 exit 309B, just w. on St. Paul Ave., then .7 mi. s. on 27th St. to 524 S. Layton Blvd.

Three glass domes, each seven stories high and 140 feet in diameter, house a variety of exotic gardens; the tops of the domes are highlighted by halo lights.

The Arid Dome features plants from the world's deserts, such as cactuses, succulents, palms and grasses. More than 750 species of plants, including orchids, thrive in the Tropical Dome; birds, lizards and frogs also inhabit this rain forest-like environment. Five themed floral displays each year are presented in the Show Dome; the displays of lilies and poinsettias are spectacular at Easter and Christmas.

Picnicking is allowed by permit. **Time:** Allow 1 hour, 30 minutes minimum. **Hours:** Mon.-Fri. 9-5, Sat.-Sun. 9-4. **Cost:** $6.50; $5 (ages 6-17 and 60+). **Phone:** (414) 649-9830, (414) 257-8005 for a picnic permit, or (414) 649-9800 for the conservatory's 24-hour hotline.

PETTIT NATIONAL ICE CENTER is s. of I-94 exit 306 at 500 S. 84th St. The 200,000-square-foot U.S. Olympic training site houses one of three 400-meter speed skating ovals in North America, and two full-internationally-sized rinks for hockey, figure skating and short-track speed skating. The center hosts local, regional, national and international competitions in skating sports. The center also is open to the public for skating nearly every day as well as for use of an indoor track for walking and running; phone for times.

Guided tours are available by appointment only. **Time:** Allow 30 minutes minimum. **Hours:** Daily 8 a.m.-9 p.m. Phone for public skating times. **Cost:** Spectators free except during special events. Guided tours $3. Skating $7; $5 (ages 0-12 and 61+). Skate rentals $3. **Phone:** (414) 266-0100.

SAVE **SCHLITZ AUDUBON NATURE CENTER** is 1 mi. e. of I-43 exit 82A at 1111 E. Brown Deer Rd. This 185-acre nature center and sanctuary on the shores of Lake Michigan has about 6 miles of trails. Hiking, snowshoeing and cross-country skiing are popular. The sanctuary provides habitats for native animals and features a 60-foot observation tower offering views of the lake, the city and its surrounding suburbs. The sustainable Dorothy K. Vallier Environmental Learning Center houses natural sciences exhibits. **Hours:** Center and trails open daily 9-5. Closed Jan. 1, Thanksgiving and Dec. 25. **Cost:** $6; $4 (ages 2-12 and 62+). **Phone:** (414) 352-2880.

UNIVERSITY OF WISCONSIN-MILWAUKEE encompasses 90 acres bounded by N. Cramer St., E. Hartford Ave., N. Maryland Ave., N. Edgewood Ave., N. Downer Ave. and E. Kenwood Blvd. Founded in 1885 as the Milwaukee Normal School, UWM now has an enrollment of more than 29,000 students. The university's programs in architecture and urban planning are considered among the best in the country. The Institute of Visual Arts offers contemporary exhibitions at several sites on campus. **Phone:** (414) 229-5070 for information about Institute of Visual Arts exhibitions.

American Geographical Society Library is at 2311 E. Hartford Ave. in the Golda Meir Library on the University of Wisconsin-Milwaukee campus. An exceptional collection of material relates to geography, exploration, map making, earth science and history. Highlights include maps, globes and geography-related books, including many rare items. Exhibitions change several times throughout the year. **Hours:** Mon.-Fri. 8-4:30. Closed major holidays. **Cost:** Free. **Phone:** (414) 229-6282.

VILLA TERRACE DECORATIVE ARTS MUSEUM is at 2220 N. Terrace Ave. This 16th-century Italian Renaissance-style villa was designed and built by architect David Adler in 1923 for metals mogul Lloyd Smith of the A.O. Smith Corp. The museum features fine and decorative arts from the 15th through the 20th centuries, wrought-iron masterpieces by Cyril Colnik and a formal garden. Changing exhibits emphasize decorative arts plus drawing, painting, photography, printmaking and sculpture with architectural, European and garden-themed subject matter.

Docent-led, 45-minute tours are available upon request. **Time:** Allow 30 minutes minimum. **Hours:** Wed.-Sun. 1-5. Closed major holidays. **Cost:** $5; $3 (ages 63+, military and students with ID); free (ages 0-12). **Phone:** (414) 271-3656.

WISCONSIN BLACK HISTORICAL SOCIETY/MUSEUM is at 2620 West Center St. The museum houses changing exhibits about the history of African-Americans in Wisconsin with an emphasis on civil rights, the Underground Railroad and the contribution of African-Americans to America's labor force. **Time:** Allow 1 hour minimum. **Hours:** Mon.-Fri. 11-4, Sat. 11-1. Closed Jan. 1, Thanksgiving and Dec. 25. **Cost:** $5; $4 (senior citizens); free (ages 0-12). **Phone:** (414) 372-7677.

GAMBLING ESTABLISHMENTS

- **Potawatomi Bingo Casino** is .5 mi. s of I-94 exit 309 at 1721 W. Canal St. **Hours:** Daily 24 hours. **Phone:** (800) 729-7244.

What To Do

Sightseeing

Boat Tours

IROQUOIS HARBOR CRUISES departs from the RiverWalk between the Michigan and Clybourn St. bridges on the w. bank of the Milwaukee River at 505 N. Riverwalk Way. Narrated 90-minute sightseeing cruises feature the Milwaukee Art Museum, Pier Wisconsin, the breakwater, lighthouse and harbor. Summer sunset cruises are available. **Hours:** Trips depart daily at noon, 2 and 4, May-Sept. Summer sunset cruises depart at 6. **Cost:** Fare $14; $13 (ages 62+); free (ages 0-12 with adult, otherwise $7). **Phone:** (414) 294-9450. ⓣ

Bus and Limousine Tours

Several public and private charter transportation companies offer sightseeing tours that explore the

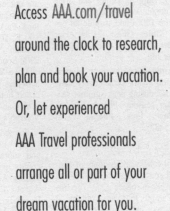

city. Customized tours devoted to Milwaukee's industrial, cultural, civic and residential sights are available, often complemented by lunch or dinner.

Carriage Tours

Horse-drawn carriages offer a memorable mode of transportation through downtown and along the shores of Lake Michigan. Milwaukee Coach & Carriage, (414) 272-6873, provides nightly service (weather permitting).

Driving Tours

A scenic drive extends from the downtown area at Lincoln Memorial Drive, north to SR 32 through beautiful parks and past the lakeside mansions of the early brewers to Brown Deer Road. North Lake Drive along the bluffs is particularly attractive.

Industrial Tours

MILLER BREWERY TOUR & VISITOR CENTER is at 4251 W. State St. A 1-hour indoor/outdoor guided walking tour of the facility includes a 3-screen theater presentation, as well as visits to the south packaging facility, shipping center and brew house facilities. Tours conclude with a stop in the historic caves built in the 1800s and include an appearance by Frederick Miller. Guests 21 or older with ID may sample beer at the end of each tour in the Bavarian-style Miller Inn.

Strollers are not permitted on the tour. **Hours:** Tours generally depart the visitor center every half-hour Mon.-Sat. 10:30-3:30 during peak summer season; times vary all other seasons. Phone ahead to confirm schedule. **Cost:** Free. **Phone:** (414) 931-2337 or (800) 944-5483.

Walking Tours

Brochures outlining historic walking tours of Milwaukee's east, west and south sides are available at the Visit Milwaukee walk-in office (*see The Informed Traveler box*). Campus tours are available at the University of Wisconsin-Milwaukee, (414) 229-2222, and at Marquette University, (414) 288-7302.

Historic Milwaukee Inc. offers guided walking tours concentrating on the city's historical and architectural heritage. Tours last 1.5 hours and include Milwaukee's downtown, skywalk system, the city's historic German neighborhood and East Town, mansions along Lake Drive and North Point, historic districts such as Walker's Point, the Third Ward, Brady Street, Yankee Hill and local cemeteries. Brochures are available at businesses throughout the city. Phone (414) 277-7795.

Sports and Recreation

Milwaukee sports fans enthusiastically support their professional teams. **Baseball** fans make their pilgrimage to Miller Park, where the beloved Milwaukee Brewers play from April through September; phone (414) 902-4000. Almost before the last baseball game's bratwurst can be digested, the NBA's Milwaukee Bucks begin **basketball** exhibition games. Regular season games are played until April at the Bradley Center, 1001 N. 4th St.; phone (414) 227-0400 or (414) 227-0500. The Marquette University Golden Eagles also play at the Bradley Center; phone (414) 227-0400 or (414) 288-7127.

The Milwaukee Wave play indoor **soccer** October through April in the U.S. Cellular Arena; phone (414) 224-9283. At the Bradley Center the Milwaukee Admirals compete with other teams of the American **Hockey** League October through April; phone (414) 227-0550 or (414) 227-0400.

Spectators are outdoors again in the spring and the fall to watch fierce **rugby** matches at the lakefront. National championship **automobile races** are held at the Milwaukee Mile, (414) 266-7107, from May through September; the Izod IndyCar Series is scheduled for mid-June. **Sailboat races** skirt Lake Michigan's shoreline, off N. Lincoln Memorial Drive, weekends during the summer.

The lakefront also is the playground of anglers, sailors and swimmers during the warm months. **Swimming** is possible at five beaches (lifeguards are not on duty except for Bradford Beach): Bradford Beach, 2400 N. Lincoln Memorial Dr.; Doctor's Park Beach, 1870 E. Fox Ln.; Grant Beach, 100 E. Hawthorne Ave.; McKinley Beach, 1750 N. Lincoln Memorial Dr.; and South Shore Beach, 2900 South Shore Dr. Bradford Beach, on the shores of Lake Michigan, offers festivals, concerts and free activities as well as 17 sand volleyball courts and a beach house. At McKinley Beach, rent jet skis, bicycles and paddleboats; hydrobikes are available at Veteran's Park.

For those who cannot adjust to Lake Michigan's chilly waters, there are 8 outdoor and 2 indoor pools and more than 20 wading pools throughout the county park system. The county also runs three Family Aquatic Water Parks: Cool Waters Family Aquatic Park in Greenfield Park at 2028 S. 124th; David F. Schulz Family Aquatic Center in Lincoln Park at 1301 W. Hampton Ave.; and Pelican Cove Family Water Park in Kosciuszko Park at 2201 S. 7th St.

Sailors with their own **boating** craft may use the launch ramps at Bender, Riverfront, McKinley Marina and South Shore Yacht Club for a fee. Paddle boat rentals are available at the Juneau Lagoon in Veterans Park. **Fishing** in Lake Michigan can reward anglers with prize catches of salmon and trout as big as 30 pounds. Full- and half-day charters are offered by numerous companies; check the telephone directory.

Tennis is available at 28 county parks; many courts are lighted. Court use is free, though a fee is charged for reserving a court and for lighted courts; phone (414) 257-8030. North Shore Elite Fitness and Racquet Club, (414) 351-2900, at 5750 N. Glen Park Rd., is one of several clubs that offers indoor tennis courts. Lawn bowling is popular during the summer. **Sand volleyball** courts are found at 17 county parks.

About two-thirds of the **golf** courses in the Milwaukee vicinity are 18-hole courses. Brown Deer Golf Course, (414) 352-8080, 7625 N. Range Line Rd., is a premier-level municipal course open to the public. The county also maintains par-three and regulation 18-hole courses and an 18-hole pitch-and-putt course. November through April, the Currie Park Golf Dome, 3535 N. Mayfair Rd., offers an indoor driving range; phone (414) 453-1742.

The Milwaukee County Park System offers a variety of public facilities among its more than 140 parks, including beaches, swimming pools, golf courses, tennis courts, soccer fields, **hiking** trails and the 106-mile Oak Leaf Trail, a paved path for **bicycling**, inline skating and jogging that encircles the city. The 3-mile Alpha Trail provides mountain bikers with tricky terrain to negotiate; it begins near Whitnall Park *(see attraction listing p. 178)*. Bicycles, in-line skates and Segways can be rented in Juneau Park at the lakefront. For information about county park facilities phone (414) 257-6100.

The Hank Aaron State Trail follows portions of the Menomonee River through a former industrial area and the Historic Third Ward warehouse district to the Lake Michigan shore, providing a 7-mile paved route closed to motorized traffic for most its length. Popular with walkers, runners, skaters and bicyclists, the trail passes Miller Park Stadium, the Marquette University athletic fields and Potawatomi Bingo Casino *(see attraction listing p. 172)* and connects to the Oak Leaf Trail. For information about the trail, phone (414) 263-8559.

Although Milwaukee's winters are somewhat formidable, the lure of various winter sports entices even the frostbite-prone outdoors. Milwaukee County Parks has seven lagoons that freeze for **ice skating.** The premier site, however, is Pettit National Ice Center *(see attraction listing p. 172)*. Wilson Park Center and Slice of Ice at Red Arrow Park also offer skating.

Most of the county parks allow **cross-country skiing,** with Whitnall Park providing lightly groomed trails. Old World Wisconsin *(see Eagle p. 177)* and Schlitz Audubon Nature Center *(see attraction listing p. 172)* also provide cross-country ski trails. Favorite weekend destinations for Milwaukee residents include Kettle Moraine State Forest *(see Recreation Chart and Campbellsport p. 137)* and any of the 60 inland lakes in the metropolitan area.

Shopping

In the heart of Milwaukee, legacy cobblestone streets and ethnic specialty shops blend gracefully with the skywalks and covered malls that characterize the modern emporiums. The city's centerpiece is The Shops of Grand Avenue, a three-block multilevel marketplace on Wisconsin Avenue between N. 4th Street and the Milwaukee River that incorporates the historic Plankinton Arcade. It is anchored by Boston Store and encloses more than 70 shops and eateries.

Such modern shopping malls as The Shops of Grand Avenue have not displaced Milwaukee's traditional shopping areas. Old World 3rd Street, just north of Wisconsin Avenue between Wells and Juneau, is known for its cobblestone street and late 19th-century buildings housing specialty stores and eateries. Shops include Usinger's Famous Sausage, the Wisconsin Cheese Mart and the Spice House.

Across the Milwaukee River in East Town, the elegant shops along Jefferson Street include George Watts' china and crystal and shops offering antiques,

furnishings and other items. Two other colorful east-side neighborhoods are Brady Street, between Farwell Avenue and Marshall Street, where Old World tradition meets a trendy Bohemian lifestyle, and Downer Avenue, between E. Webster and E. Park, home to students and faculty of the University of Wisconsin-Milwaukee.

An archway welcomes shoppers to the Historic Third Ward, the city's original commercial district and now Milwaukee's "SoHo." Renovated warehouses and factories now house art galleries, antiques stores, restaurants, specialty shops and performing arts centers along streets lined with old-fashioned street lights. Anchoring the Ward is the Milwaukee Public Market at 400 N. Water Street, a year-round enclosed market selling fresh produce, meats, cheeses, spices and ethnic foods. Downtown, the Milwaukee River and Lake Michigan form the boundaries for the Third Ward's 17-block shopping area.

Cedar Creek Settlement *(see Cedarburg p. 177)* offers a delightful step back in time. Stonewood Village, 17700 W. Capitol Dr. in Brookfield, markets Colonial wares.

Shopping centers in the metropolitan area are Bayshore Town Center, 5900 N. Port Washington Rd.; Brookfield Square, 95 N. Moorland Rd.; and Southridge, 5300 S. 76th St. Mayfair Mall, 2500 N. Mayfair Rd. in Wauwatosa, is anchored by Macy's and Boston Store along with eateries and an 18-screen theater.

Performing Arts

Milwaukee boasts several nationally acclaimed performing arts companies. The Marcus Center for the Performing Arts, 929 N. Water St., is home to many of these, including the Florentine Opera Company, Milwaukee Ballet Company, First Stage Children's Theater and the Milwaukee Symphony Orchestra. The orchestra's regular season is early September through June; phone (800) 291-7605 or (888) 612-3500.

Among Milwaukee's free outdoor summer concerts are River Rhythms on Wednesday evenings at the riverside Pere Marquette Park and Jazz in the Park on Thursdays at Cathedral Square. The county parks department also sponsors free concerts at various parks during the summer.

The Milwaukee Repertory Theater performs a variety of dramatic productions at The Milwaukee Center at 108 E. Wells St. from early September to mid-May; phone (414) 224-9490. The splendidly restored late 19th-century Pabst Theater at 144 E. Wells St., presents theatrical, jazz and modern music productions. Tours of the theater are offered Saturday at noon; phone (414) 286-3663. The Ko-Thi Dance Co. is among the groups performing at the Pabst Theater.

The Helfaer Theater, (414) 288-7504, at 13th and Clybourn on the Marquette University campus, presents quality theater and concert offerings. The Milwaukee Theatre, (414) 908-6001, at 500 W. Kilbourn Ave., presents touring Broadway shows and

musical artists. Marcus Amphitheater, (414) 273-2600, in Henry Maier Festival Park at 200 N. Harbor Dr., and the Milwaukee Riverside Theater, (414) 224-3000, at 116 W. Wisconsin Ave., feature nationally known touring bands.

Musicals and operettas are staged by the Skylight Opera Theater, which performs at the Broadway Theatre Center, 158 N. Broadway in the Historic Third World; phone (414) 291-7800. The Broadway Theatre Center also is home to the Chamber Theatre, which stages both classical and contemporary works, phone (414) 291-7800. The Off Broadway Theater at 342 N. Water St. is home to the cutting edge Next Act Theater, (414) 278-0765, and Renaissance Theaterworks, (414) 291-7800.

The events section of the city's newspaper carries current information about local cultural activities. Visitors also can contact VISIT Milwaukee for an update; phone (800) 554-1448.

Special Events

The regular sports calendar includes the Milwaukee Journal/Sentinel Sports Show, which draws crowds to the Wisconsin State Fair Park in mid-March. The Greater Milwaukee Auto Show at the Midwest Airlines Center is held every February.

Two of Milwaukee's top cultural events are the Lakefront Festival of the Arts in June and 🎵 Summerfest, held from late June to early July. Ethnic festivals include 🎵 Polish Fest in June and 🎵 Festa Italiana, Bastille Days and 🎵 German Fest in July.

Big-name entertainment is a given during August's 🎵 Wisconsin State Fair in West Allis. Also in August are the African World Festival, Arab World Festival, the Irish Fest and Mexican Fiesta. Indian Summer and Oktoberfest take place in September.

More than 50 ethnic groups gather in mid-November for the Holiday Folk Fair, which salutes Old World culture. Colorful floats and other displays launch yuletide festivities at the Christmas Parade, traditionally held in late November.

Each season of the year is celebrated with a spectacular flower show at Mitchell Park Horticultural Conservatory—"The Domes." Waves of color and fragrance delight the senses during the Spring Flower Show, late March to mid-May, and the Summer Flower Show, held from June to mid-September. The Fall Flower Show takes place from late September to mid-November. The Christmas Flower Show is held from Thanksgiving to early January, and the Winter Flower Show, held mid-January to mid-March, closes the season.

The Milwaukee Vicinity

CEDARBURG (H-8) pop. 10,908, elev. 778'

Thanks to the water power provided by Cedar Creek and an abundant supply of limestone, Cedarburg had become a busy milling, textile, quarrying and industrial center by the 1850s. The original center of activity was New Dublin, later renamed Hamilton, southeast of the present downtown section. Now designated a historic district, Hamilton includes the 1853 Concordia Mill and several other historic stone buildings.

The 1855 Cedarburg Mill, used as a refuge for families during the Great Indian Scare of 1862, still stands near the Columbia Road bridge over Cedar Creek.

One of the last two surviving covered bridges in the state crosses Cedar Creek about 3 miles north via CR NN and Covered Bridge Road. The other spans the Crystal River in Waupaca (*see place listing p. 198*). The Cedarburg Cultural Center at W62 N546 Washington Ave. features four galleries with changing art and history exhibits and serves as a venue for special events and musical performances; phone (262) 375-3676.

Lime Kiln Park, on Green Bay Road in nearby Grafton, features restored lime kiln chimneys and a picturesque dam. The park, on the Milwaukee River, offers a picnic area and a canoe launch. Landmark Tours provides guided tours of Cedarburg and Ozaukee County; phone (262) 375-1426.

Cedarburg Chamber of Commerce: Washington Ave. and Spring St., P.O. Box 104, Cedarburg, WI 53012. **Phone:** (262) 377-9620 or (800) 237-2874.

Self-guiding tours: Several brochures outlining a walking tour and describing Cedarburg's historic district and architecture are available from the visitor center on the corner of Washington Avenue and Spring Street.

Shopping areas: Hidden treasures can be found in the numerous shops and galleries lining Washington Avenue in the historic district.

CEDAR CREEK SETTLEMENT is downtown at jct. Bridge Rd. and Washington Ave. at N70 W6340 Bridge Rd. Built in 1864 and in operation until 1969, the old Wittenberg Woolen Mill was restored in the early 1970s to house nearly 30 retail establishments, including Cedar Creek Winery. **Hours:** Mon.-Thurs. 10-5, Fri.-Sat. 10-6, Sun. 11-5. **Cost:** Free. **Phone:** (262) 377-4763 or (866) 626-7005.

THE OZAUKEE ART CENTER/BREWERY WORKS ARTS COMPLEX is at W62 N718 Riveredge Dr. An 1843 brewery has been converted into the art studios of sculptor Paul J. Yank and the Ozaukee County Art Center. Working artisans sometimes can be seen. **Time:** Allow 1 hour minimum. **Hours:** Wed.-Sun. 1-4. Closed Jan. 1, Thanksgiving and Dec. 25. **Cost:** Donations. **Phone:** (262) 377-8230 or (262) 377-7220.

WINERIES

- **Cedar Creek Winery** is at jct. Bridge Rd. and Washington Ave. at N70 W6340 Bridge Rd. **Hours:** Mon.-Sat. 10-5, Sun. 11-5 (also Fri.-Sat. 5-6, Apr.-Dec.). Closed Jan. 1, Easter, Thanksgiving and Dec. 25. **Phone:** (262) 377-8020 or (800) 827-8020.

EAGLE (I-7) pop. 1,707, elev. 947'

KETTLE MORAINE STATE FOREST—SOUTHERN UNIT is 3 mi. w. of the village of Eagle; forest headquarters are at S91 W39091 SR 59. The 20,000-acre, 30-mile-long southern unit runs from Dousman, Wisconsin, to a point near Whitewater. With an array of habitats ranging from glacial hills, lakes, and prairie to pine and hardwood forests, the area is popular with outdoor sports lovers who enjoy mountain biking, horseback riding, cross-country skiing, snowmobiling and winter hiking/snowshoeing trails as well as the Ice Age National Scenic Trail.

The forest is also home to Old World Wisconsin (*see attraction listing*), a state historic site with restored 19th-century buildings. The headquarters for both the southern and northern units (*see Campbellsport p. 137*) of the state forest are located here; a museum offers interpretive programs. **Hours:** Daily 6 a.m.-11 p.m. **Cost:** $10 (per private vehicle); $7 (state residents). Annual permit $35; $25 (state residents). **Phone:** (262) 594-6200. 🅰 ⊠ 🄿

OLD WORLD WISCONSIN is 1.5 mi. s. at S103 W37890 SR 67. This 576-acre state historic site consists of more than 65 preserved and furnished buildings erected by 19th- and early 20th-century Wisconsin immigrants. Nearly a dozen ethnic groups are represented at the 1870s Crossroads Village and 10 working farmsteads, stocked with rare breeds of horses, oxen, chickens and hogs. The gardens and fields are planted with many heirloom varieties of grains, flowers, fruits, herbs and vegetables. Period-clad interpreters demonstrate the work and crafts of the immigrants.

A 15-minute orientation film about 19th-century Wisconsin is offered on the lower level of Ramsey Barn Visitor Center. If walking, allow 4 to 6 hours and wear comfortable shoes. Tram service is available. Seasonal events take place throughout the year. The nearly 6-mile Aldo Leopold Environmental History Trail includes interpretive signs about the area's heritage and habitats.

Hours: Mon.-Sat. 10-5, Sun. noon-5, June 14-Sept. 6; Mon.-Fri. 10-3, Sat. 10-5, Sun. noon-5, May 1-June 13 and Sept. 7-Oct. 31. Special events Sun. 10-5. **Cost:** $16 (includes all-day tram pass); $14 (ages 65+ and students with ID); $9 (ages

5-17); $43 (family, two adults and all dependent children ages 5-17). **Phone:** (262) 594-6300. ⊤

FARMINGTON (G-8) pop. 3,239

LIZARD MOUND COUNTY PARK is on CR A, 1 mi. e. of SR 144. The archeological site is named after its most prominent effigy mound. Between A.D. 400 and 1200, American Indians built the mounds to cover their burial and ceremonial sites. Designed in animal, bird and geometric shapes, the 31-acre park's 28 mounds and earthworks are among the best preserved in Wisconsin. A nature trail is on the grounds. **Time:** Allow 1 hour minimum. **Hours:** Daily 6 a.m.-9 p.m., Apr. 1 to mid-Nov. **Cost:** Free. **Phone:** (262) 335-4445. ⍑

GENESEE DEPOT (H-7) elev. 909′

TEN CHIMNEYS is just w. of SR 83 at S43 W31575 Depot Rd., following signs. The romance of the 1930s and '40s permeates the estate of Broadway legends Alfred Lunt and Lynn Fontanne. The narrated Full Estate Tour includes the three-story Main House, the rustic Studio, the enchanting Cottage, gardens, and the exteriors of the Poolhouse, Greenhouse and Creamery. The couple's personal effects and original furnishings are displayed in the Main House. There are no ropes and nothing is under glass on the estate, so guests enjoy a barrier-free view of the décor.

Ages 0-11 are not permitted. Walk-ins are welcome, but reservations are strongly recommended. Tours run regardless of weather conditions. **Time:** Allow 1 hour, 30 minutes minimum. **Hours:** Guided tours are offered Tues.-Sat. 10-2:30, May 1 to mid-Nov. Last tour begins no later than 2:45. **Cost:** Full Estate Tour (2 hours) $35. Main House Tour (90 minutes) $28. **Phone:** (262) 968-4110.

GERMANTOWN (H-8) pop. 13,700

SILA LYDIA BAST BELL MUSEUM, on Holy Hill Rd., 2 miles e. of US 41/45 exit 57, is in a restored 1870 building. More than 5,000 bells in the collection range in size from 1,063 pounds to just several ounces. Bells made of metals, wood, stone, ceramic and volcanic rock as well as bells from South America, Indonesia, China, Holland, Sweden, Africa and the United States are featured. The building also houses exhibits from the Germantown Volunteer Fire Co., including an 1871 fire engine. An 1854 German *fachwerk* building is on the property; its style is reminiscent of English Tudor.

Time: Allow 1 hour minimum. **Hours:** Wed.-Sun. 1-4 and by appointment, Apr.-Nov.; by appointment rest of year. Closed major holidays. **Cost:** $6; $5 (ages 65+); $2 (ages 5-12). **Phone:** (262) 628-3170. ⍑

GRAFTON (H-8) pop. 10,312, elev. 757′

THE FAMILY FARM is at 328 W. Port Washington Rd. This 40-acre restored turn-of-the-20th-century farmstead has a farm zoo with livestock including goats, chickens, sheep, draft horses, pigs and calves. Antique tools and murals are displayed. Wagon rides are offered. A .75-mile nature walk winds through prairie, wetland and woodland habitat.

Time: Allow 1 hour minimum. **Hours:** Wed.-Sat. 9-4, Sun. 11-4, mid-May through Sept. 30; Tues.-Fri. 9-4, Sat. 9-5, Sun. 11-5 in Oct. Closed Memorial Day, July 4 and Labor Day. Phone ahead to confirm schedule. **Cost:** $6.25; $5.25 (ages 62+); $3.75 (ages 2-12). Wagon rides $1. **Phone:** (262) 377-6161. ⊤

HALES CORNERS (I-8)
pop. 7,765, elev. 800′

WHITNALL PARK is at 5879 S. 92nd St. One of the largest municipal parks in the nation, the 625-acre grounds encompass an 18-hole golf course, an archery range, a 3-mile bike trail, a variety of all-year recreational facilities, picnic areas, nature trails, an environmental education center and botanical gardens. In winter the park is popular for cross-country skiing and sledding. A toboggan slide features a groomed ice track with rentable sleds that can reach speeds close to 40 miles per hour. **Hours:** Park open daily dawn-dusk. **Cost:** Free. **Phone:** (414) 425-7303.

Boerner Botanical Gardens, 9400 Boerner Dr. in Whitnall Park, feature more than 1,000 perennials and a rose garden with more than 3,000 rose plants; each year more than 11,000 annuals are planted for seasonal floral exhibitions. Also included are herb gardens, a trial garden and a butterfly garden as well as a tulip display and a crab apple collection. Free outdoor concerts take place Thursday evenings in summer. The Garden House contains art exhibits.

Time: Allow 1 hour minimum. **Hours:** Formal gardens and Garden House open daily 8 a.m.-dusk, mid-Apr. through Oct. 31; otherwise varies. **Cost:** $5; $4 (Milwaukee County residents ages 60+); $3 (ages 6-17). **Phone:** (414) 525-5601.

Wehr Nature Center is in the center of Whitnall Park at 9701 W. College Ave. Natural history displays are featured at the center, which includes a 30-acre prairie restoration site and more than 5 miles of nature trails in its surrounding woodlands and wetlands. Seasonal hikes and lectures are conducted by naturalists. **Hours:** Daily 8-4:30. Closed Thanksgiving and Dec. 24-26. **Cost:** Donations. Fee for special events. **Parking:** $3. **Phone:** (414) 425-8550.

HARTFORD (H-7) pop. 10,905, elev. 988′

Pike Lake State Park, 2 miles east on SR 60, offers a variety of recreational activities year-round, including camping, picnicking, hiking, fishing, swimming and cross-country skiing. *See Recreation Chart and the AAA Great Lakes CampBook.*

WISCONSIN AUTOMOTIVE MUSEUM is at 147 N. Rural St. More than 100 antique and classic automobiles are exhibited, including Austin-Americans,

Fords, Hudsons, Wisconsin-built Nashes and reputedly the largest collection of the locally manufactured Kissel. Also displayed are single-cylinder farm engines, automotive artifacts, outboard motors, gas pumps; modified stock cars, a 250-ton steam locomotive and a train layout exhibit.

Time: Allow 1 hour minimum. **Hours:** Mon.-Sat. and holidays 10-5, Sun. noon-5, May-Sept.; Wed.-Sat. 10-5, Sun. noon-5, rest of year. Closed Jan. 1, Easter, Thanksgiving and Dec. 24-25 and 31. **Cost:** $8; $7 (ages 63+); $6 (ages 8-16). **Phone:** (262) 673-7999.

HUBERTUS (H-7) elev. 1,014'

BASILICA AT HOLY HILL is w. on SR 167 to 1525 Carmel Rd. The Basilica of the National Shrine to Mary, Help of Christians, is staffed by Discalced Carmelites. Settlers erected a 15-foot oak cross and chapel on the 1,350-foot summit in the early 19th century. The log chapel evolved into a Romanesque church, a national shrine to the Virgin Mary and a monastery for the friars who staff the shrine. A tower affords picturesque views.

Food is available daily, May-Oct; Fri.-Sun., rest of year. **Time:** Allow 1 hour minimum. **Hours:** Shrine and Church open daily 6 a.m.-5 p.m. Scenic tower open Mon.-Sat. 9-4:45, Sun. 1:30-4:45, May-Oct. (weather permitting). **Cost:** Donations. **Phone:** (262) 628-1838.

KEWASKUM (G-8) pop. 3,274, elev. 960'

RECREATIONAL ACTIVITIES
Skiing and Snowboarding
- **Sunburst Ski and Recreation Area** 1 mi. s. on US 45, then w. on Badger Rd., then s. to 8355 Prospect Dr., Kewaskum, WI 53040. **Hours:** Mon.-Thurs. 4-10, Fri.-Sun. and holidays 10-10; late Nov. through mid-Mar. **Phone:** (262) 626-8404.

OCONOMOWOC (H-7) pop. 12,382, elev. 869'

Surrounded by lakes and easily accessible from Milwaukee, Chicago and other cities, Oconomowoc was a wealthy resort community in the late 19th century. The most fashionable people of the period built their elaborate summer cottages on the nearby lakes. Many of these houses remain and lend their charm to this popular vacation community.

Oconomowoc Convention & Visitors Bureau: 174 E. Wisconsin Ave., Oconomowoc, WI 53066. **Phone:** (800) 524-3744.

Self-guiding tours: The historic houses around Fowler Lake can be viewed on a self-guiding 2-mile-long walking tour. Maps are available from the convention and visitors bureau.

OCONOMOWOC AREA HISTORICAL SOCIETY MUSEUM is at 103 W. Jefferson St. The history of Oconomowoc and Lake Country are depicted in permanent and temporary exhibits. Displays include an

HO-scale model railroad layout. Murals from the Oconomowoc Canning Co. painted by artist Schomer Lichtner are featured in the theater area. A representation of historic Oconomowoc includes a Victorian house and five historic businesses including a general store. **Hours:** Fri.-Sun. 1-5, early May to mid-Dec.; other times by appointment. **Cost:** Donations. **Phone:** (262) 569-0740.

PORT WASHINGTON (H-8)
pop. 10,467, elev. 668'

Patriotic fervor was hardly the reaction of Ozaukee County farmers when the governor ordered all able-bodied citizens to enroll for service during the Civil War. On Nov. 10, 1862, an angry mob stampeded Port Washington's courthouse and destroyed the draft rolls.

Lest their point of view go unacknowledged, they later seized the small cannon ordinarily used for Fourth of July celebrations and positioned it on the south bluff overlooking the harbor. The rebels were no match for government troops, however, who sailed into the harbor by night and easily subdued the small group.

Port Washington is a fishing and yachting center on Lake Michigan distinguished by many pre-Civil War buildings, including the 19th-century Eghart House, 316 Grand Ave. On a hill overlooking the downtown area is St. Mary's Church, a much-photographed Gothic church built in 1882.

The city is home to a working 1935 Art Deco-style automated beacon in the middle of the harbor. The 1860 Port Washington Historical Society Light Station Museum, 311 Johnson St., has been restored in the style of a lighthouse keeper's quarters from the 1880s; phone (262) 284-7240 for tour information.

Numerous charter boats operate from the marina during the summer and fall; fishing for trout as well as coho and chinook salmon is popular all year. Festivals and free concerts occur throughout the summer in parks along the lake including late August's Maritime Heritage Festival featuring tall ships and schooner replicas from days of yore.

Port Washington Tourism & Chamber of Commerce: 126 E. Grand Ave., P.O. Box 153, Port Washington, WI 53074. **Phone:** (262) 284-0900 or (800) 719-4881.

Self-guiding tours: Maps of the historic district for self-guiding walking tours are available at the chamber of commerce and visitor center.

WAUKESHA (H-8) pop. 64,825, elev. 867'

Waukesha takes its name from an American Indian word meaning "by the Little Fox." Although the Fox River has been important in the city's steady industrial growth, it was the many mineral springs and their purported curative powers that brought Waukesha its fame as the elegant "Saratoga of the West" during the late 19th century. Plants bottling carbonated beverages are the only vestiges of those halcyon days.

Another small reminder of the past is a marker in Cutler Park honoring a local citizen who safely transported the first slave through Wisconsin into Canada. Waukesha was an important station on the Underground Railroad and an abolitionist stronghold; the *American Freeman* was published in the town 1844-48.

Waukesha is an industrial and college town serving the surrounding dairying and farming area. Colleges include Carroll University, University of Wisconsin-Waukesha and Waukesha County Technical College. Frame Park, the largest of 45 municipal parks, is noted for its formal garden.

Waukesha and Pewaukee Convention & Visitors Bureau: N14 W23755 Stone Ridge Dr., Suite 225, Waukesha, WI 53188. **Phone:** (262) 542-0330 or (800) 366-8474.

WAUKESHA COUNTY MUSEUM is at 101 W. Main St. at East Ave. Housed in an 1893 castle-like building downtown, the former courthouse features three floors of changing displays and interactive exhibits about the American Civil War, early technology, dollhouses, antique toys, architecture, fur trading and the area's historic mineral springs. Nationally touring exhibits also are hosted at the museum. Vintage photos and records are available in the museum's research center.

Time: Allow 30 minutes minimum. **Hours:** Museum open Tues.-Sat. 10-4:30. Research center Fri.-Sat. and Tues. 10-4:30, Thurs. 12:30-4:30. Closed major holidays. **Cost:** Museum $5; $4 (ages 62+); $3 (ages 6-17). Research center $5 per day. **Phone:** (262) 521-2859.

WEST BEND (H-8) pop. 28,152, elev. 906'

Challenging terrain makes the area popular with cyclists and hikers. The town boasts a rails-to-trails bike/walking trail and the "Labyrinth Garden Earth Sculpture," a series of concentric pathways lined with flowering plants and herbs. In Regner Park, sledding and skiing keep adventure seekers busy in winter.

Riverfront Parkway, a trail that winds along the Milwaukee River through West Bend, can be enjoyed by joggers, walkers or those on bicycles. In addition to the scenic beauty of the trail is a series of sculptures at the river's edge. The 25-mile Eisenbahn Trail extends from West Bend into the scenic countryside of eastern Wisconsin and can be used for walking, bicycling, in-line skating and snowmobiling.

Washington County Convention and Visitors Bureau: 3000 Hwy. PV, West Bend, WI 53095. **Phone:** (262) 677-5069 or (888) 974-8687.

LIZARD MOUND COUNTY PARK— *see Farmington p. 178.*

MUSEUM OF WISCONSIN ART is at 300 S. 6th Ave. The museum features a survey collection of historic Wisconsin art (1800-present) particularly the works of Milwaukee-Munich artist Carl von Marr. Numerous group exhibitions and the monthly "One from Wisconsin" solo exhibition series feature contemporary Wisconsin artists. The museum also houses the state's primary research archive on Wisconsin art.

Time: Allow 1 hour minimum. **Hours:** Wed.-Sat. 10-4:30, Sun. 1-4:30. Closed major holidays. **Cost:** $5; $3 (students with ID and ages 62+); $15 (family, two adults and ages 0-17). **Phone:** (262) 334-9638.

OLD COURTHOUSE SQUARE MUSEUM is at 320 S. Fifth Ave. This restoration of the 1889 Romanesque-revival courthouse contains a variety of permanent and temporary exhibits centering on local history. A research library is available. Adjacent to the museum is the restored 1886 Sheriff's Residence and Jail. **Hours:** Wed.-Fri. 11-5, Sat. 9-1, Sun. 1-4:30. **Cost:** Museum free. Jail $4; $3 (ages 55+); $2 (ages 13-19); $10 (family, one adult and all children). $3 (research fee). **Phone:** (262) 335-4678.

Miller Brewery Tour and Visitor Center / © Scott White / Photolibrary

This ends listings for the Milwaukee Vicinity.
The following page resumes the alphabetical listings of cities in Wisconsin.

MINERAL POINT (I-4)
pop. 2,617, elev. 1,041'

Some of the early surface miners who came to Mineral Point in search of "mineral," or lead, lived in crude shelters that were dug in hillsides—and provided the source for Wisconsin's nickname, "The Badger State." Beginning in the early 1830s they were joined by Cornish miners skilled in hard-rock mining.

Their Cornish heritage survives in the town's stone houses, colorful stories and traditional pasties (PAST-ees), saffron cakes and tea biscuits. Folklore claims the name of Shake Rag Street stems from the Cornish wives' custom of waving rags to summon their men working on the opposite hillside.

Mineral Point has become a center for the arts, with some of the many restored buildings now home to working art studios and galleries and a Center for the Arts that offers classes year-round.

Mineral Point Chamber of Commerce: 225 High St., Mineral Point, WI 53565. **Phone:** (608) 987-3201 or (888) 764-6894.

PENDARVIS HISTORIC SITE is at 114 Shake Rag St. In the 1830s and 1840s, settlers from other areas of the country and Europe arrived in the Wisconsin Territory, lured by the plentiful amounts of lead easily found in shallow diggings. As the lead became scarce, and more technical knowledge was needed to work the earth for its deeper deposits, immigrants from Cornwall, England filled the need. At Pendarvis, you can see five of their restored stone and log cottages furnished in period and also view abandoned mine shafts and "badger holes," crude shelters dug by miners.

Tours: Guided tours are available. **Hours:** Open daily 10-5, mid-May through Oct. 31. Hours may vary. Last tour begins 1 hour before closing. Phone ahead to confirm schedule. **Cost:** Fee $9; $7.75 (ages 65+); $4.50 (ages 5-17); $24 (family, two adults and dependent children ages 5-17). **Phone:** (608) 987-2122.

MINOCQUA (C-5) pop. 4,859, elev. 1,603'

Calling itself the "Island City," Minocqua is in the Lakeland area, which has more than 3,200 lakes. The region is known for fishing and boating in summer and cross-country skiing and snowmobiling in winter. Minocqua Winter Park *(see attraction listing)* offers 75 miles of groomed cross-country trails.

Northern Lights Playhouse, 10 miles south at 5611 US 51 in nearby Hazelhurst, presents Broadway musicals and comedies nightly from Memorial Day weekend to mid-September; phone (715) 356-7173.

Minocqua-Arbor Vitae-Woodruff Area Chamber of Commerce: 8216 US 51S, P.O. Box 1006, Minocqua, WI 54548. **Phone:** (715) 356-5266 or (800) 446-6784.

WILDWOOD WILDLIFE PARK AND NATURE CENTER is 2 mi. w. of US 51 at 10094 SR 70 W. More than 700 mammals, birds and reptiles live in the 25-acre park. Visitors to the animal encounter area can pet a porcupine, tortoise, skunk, woodchuck and other animals. Visitors also can walk among deer, feed the bear "bear juice," feed the camel, and visit the primate and reptile educational centers. Nature programs are offered daily. Boat rides, a safari train ride and trout fishing are available.

Hours: Daily 9-5:30, June-Aug.; 9-4:30 in May and Sept.-Oct. **Cost:** $12; $8 (ages 2-11). **Phone:** (715) 356-5588. ⛺

RECREATIONAL ACTIVITIES
Skiing (Cross-country)
* **Minocqua Winter Park,** 6 mi. w. on SR 70, then 6 mi. s. on Squirrel Lake Rd. to 12375 Scotchman Lake Rd., Minocqua, WI 54548. **Hours:** Daily 9-5 (also Thurs. 5-7 and Sat. 5-8), Dec.-Mar. **Phone:** (715) 356-3309.

MONROE (I-5) pop. 10,843, elev. 1,050'

Monroe and its environs are known as the Swiss cheese capital of the United States. Many inhabitants are of Swiss descent, and old customs prevail at certain festivals. Some of the shops on the business square that surrounds the red brick courthouse have ornate Swiss-style facades. Of note is the Old Methodist Church, designed by Milwaukee architect E. Townsend Mix in 1869. The architecturally interesting 1891 Romanesque Green County courthouse is at 1610 16th Ave.

The Roth Kase Cheese Factory/Alp and Dell Cheese Factory Store, north on SR 69, offers two viewing halls where visitors can watch the cheesemaking process; phone (608) 328-3355. The Minhas Brewery, 1208 14th Ave., offers guided tours and beer and soda tastings Friday and Saturday; phone (608) 325-3191.

Monroe Chamber of Commerce and Industry: 1505 9th St., Monroe, WI 53566. **Phone:** (608) 325-7648.

NATIONAL HISTORIC CHEESEMAKING CENTER is at 2108 6th Ave. Located in a restored railroad depot, the museum explores the history of cheesemaking. See a replica of a late 1900's cheese factory and cheesemaking equipment, including huge copper kettles used in the process, as well as a restored caboose and a cow named Honey Belle. Exhibits provide information about dairy farming, local history and the railroad. The restored early 20th-century Farmstead Cheese Factory and its original contents is now part of the center's campus.

Hours: Daily 9-4, Apr.-Oct. **Cost:** $5; free (ages 0-16). **Phone:** (608) 325-4636. 🅰

MOUNT HOREB (H-5)
pop. 5,860, elev. 1,240'

The town's name was chosen in 1861 from a Biblical passage in reference to its relatively high elevation. Although settled by people of English, German, Irish, Scottish and Swiss descent, the largest percentage of residents originally came from Norway. Evidence of the town's Scandinavian heritage can be seen along its main thoroughfare, which is known as "The Trollway" thanks to all the carved wooden troll statues that line it. According to Norwegian folklore, the trolls bring good luck.

Mount Horeb Area Chamber of Commerce: 300 E. Main St., Mount Horeb, WI 53572. **Phone:** (608) 437-5914 or (888) 765-5929.

RECREATIONAL ACTIVITIES

Skiing and Snowboarding

- **Tyrol Basin Ski and Snowboard Area** 3487 Bohn Rd., Mount Horeb, Wisconsin 53572. **Hours:** Open Mon.-Fri. 10-9; Sat.-Sun. 9-9; late Nov.-Mar. 31 (weather permitting). Phone ahead to confirm schedule. **Phone:** (608) 437-4135.

MOUNT MORRIS (F-6)
pop. 1,092, elev. 1,137′

RECREATIONAL ACTIVITIES

Skiing and Snowboarding

- **Nordic Mountain Ski, Snowboarding and Tubing Area** e. off CR W at 5806 CR W, Wild Rose, WI 54984. **Hours:** Mon.-Thurs. 4:30-9:30, Fri.-Sat. 10-10, Sun. 10-8, Dec. 1 through mid-Mar. **Phone:** (800) 253-7266.

NECEDAH (F-5) pop. 888, elev. 919′

NECEDAH NATIONAL WILDLIFE REFUGE, W7996 20th St. W., offers plenty of wildlife viewing opportunities. The refuge is home to a diverse mixture of plants and animals, including the endangered Karner blue butterfly, trumpeter swans, flying squirrels, whooping cranes, wolves, white-tailed deer, bobcats, foxes and otters. A tower off Grand Dike Road faces a marsh. Three trails are available and may be used for hiking as well as for winter activities such as snowshoeing and ungroomed cross-country skiing.

Visitors may take a self-guiding automobile tour of the refuge and visit outdoor facilities year-round. Hunting and fishing are permitted. **Hours:** Visitor center open daily 7:30-4. Closed Jan. 1 and Dec. 25. **Cost:** Free. **Phone:** (608) 565, 2551.

NEENAH (F-7) pop. 24,507, elev. 753′

The cities of Neenah and Menasha (population 16,331) meet at the junction of Nicolet Boulevard and Abbey Avenue, on the island separating the two channels through which Lake Winnebago empties into the Fox River. Although they have separate governments, the cities share many civic and industrial enterprises, including their reputation as Wisconsin's papermaking center.

It was the possibility of water power that spurred the birth of the two villages in the 1840s. Neenah was incorporated in 1873. A year later Menasha was established and awarded the charter to develop the water power for the area. Historic mansions once belonging to area paper barons surround Riverside Park and Kimberly Point Park.

BERGSTROM-MAHLER MUSEUM is at 165 N. Park Ave. on Lake Winnebago. Collections within this Tudor-style mansion include antique and modern glass paperweights, Germanic glass and contemporary glass. Changing exhibitions also are featured. **Time:** Allow 1 hour minimum. **Hours:** Tues.-Sat. 10-4:30, Sun. 1-4:30. Closed major holidays. **Cost:** Free. **Phone:** (920) 751-4658.

DOTY CABIN is at 701 Lincoln St. at Fifth St. in Doty Park. This replica of the home of James Doty, second territorial governor, contains American Indian artifacts, belongings of the Doty family and other historical items. **Time:** Allow 30 minutes minimum. **Hours:** Daily noon-4, June to mid-Aug.; Sat.-Sun. in May. **Cost:** Donations. **Phone:** (920) 886-6060.

NEILLSVILLE (F-4) pop. 2,731, elev. 977′

The Wisconsin Pavilion from the 1964-65 New York World's Fair is at 1200 E. Division St. The angular, futuristic building houses the central studios for three radio stations and a collection of New York World's Fair memorabilia. Outside stands Chatty Belle, a 20-foot-long mechanical talking cow. The restored 1915 Reed School on US 10 and Cardinal Avenue is a one-room schoolhouse containing original and period 1930s furnishings; phone (608) 253-3523 for tour information.

Neillsville Area Chamber of Commerce: 106 W. Division St., P.O. Box 52, Neillsville, WI 54456. **Phone:** (715) 743-6444.

THE HIGHGROUND is 4 mi. w. on US 10. This veterans memorial park features national tributes to Wisconsin's Vietnam veterans, Native American Vietnam Veterans and veterans of World War I and II and Korea as well as Women Airforce Service Pilots (WASPs). Visitors can see a replica Liberty Bell and enjoy a meditation garden and effigy mounds.

The 146-acre park offers 4 miles of hiking trails, a handicapped-accessible tree house and picnic shelters. Changing exhibits are shown at the Learning Center. **Tours:** Guided tours are available. **Time:** Allow 1 hour minimum. **Hours:** Grounds open daily 24 hours; Learning Center daily 10-5. **Cost:** Donations. Guided tours $4. **Phone:** (715) 743-4224.

NEW GLARUS (I-5) pop. 2,111, elev. 859′

Impelled by economic adversity in Switzerland, 118 emigrants from the canton of Glarus settled New Glarus in 1845. "Little Switzerland," as the community often is called, remains essentially Swiss in character. Emblems of the Swiss cantons adorn buildings and street signs. Dairying and cheesemaking brought New Glarus its prosperity.

In late June the community celebrates its heritage with 3 days of food, music and other entertainment during the Heidi Festival. The Friday, Saturday and Sunday of Labor Day weekend, the highlight of the Wilhelm Tell Festival is the outdoor performance of the Wilhelm Tell drama; other events include a yodel contest and an art fair.

New Glarus is a popular departure point for the Sugar River State Trail, a 23-mile hiking, bicycling and snowmobiling route leading to Brodhead.

New Glarus Chamber of Commerce: 418 Railroad St., P.O. Box 713, New Glarus, WI 53574-0713. **Phone:** (608) 527-2095 or (800) 527-6838.

SWISS HISTORICAL VILLAGE is at 612 7th Ave. Fourteen buildings on the landscaped grounds include a firehouse, smithy, log church, butcher shop, machine shed, general store, print shop, Swiss bee house and cheese factory. A log cabin and schoolhouse are original. The Hall of History contains displays tracing Swiss immigration to America and the settlement of the New Glarus area. Self-guiding tours are available. **Time:** Allow 1 hour, 30 minutes minimum. **Hours:** Daily 10-4, May 1-Oct. 15. **Cost:** $9; $3 (ages 6-13). **Phone:** (608) 527-2317.

NEW LONDON (F-7) pop. 7,085, elev. 758′

New London, on the Wolf River near its junction with the Embarrass River, witnessed the booming days when great log drives traveled down both streams. Agribusiness and timber-related industries employ much of the area's population. The area offers numerous recreational opportunities, including cross-country skiing, snowmobiling, white-water rafting and fishing.

The New London Heritage Historical Village, just east of Mill Street at 900 Montgomery St., consists of five historical buildings—a log cabin, an octagon-shaped house, a chapel, a school and a railroad depot—all moved to the site. The village is open several Sundays a month June through August and by appointment; phone (920) 982-5186 or (920) 982-8557.

New London Area Chamber of Commerce: 301 E. Beacon Ave., New London, WI 54961. **Phone:** (920) 982-5822.

MOSQUITO HILL NATURE CENTER is 2 mi. e. off CR S at N3880 Rogers Rd. Several miles of paved and unpaved nature trails wind through the center's 430 acres along the Wolf River. This year-round environmental education facility features prairie plantings, bottomland hardwood forest and scenic views from the top of Mosquito Hill. An 11,000-square-foot interpretive building has hands-on educational exhibits, a nature library and an art gallery. A butterfly house also is available. Snowshoeing along marked trails can be enjoyed during the winter months.

Hours: Tues.-Fri. 8-4:30, Sat.-Sun. 10-3. Butterfly house open Sat.-Sun. and Wed. 11-3, July-Aug. Closed major holidays. **Cost:** Donations. A fee may

be charged during special events. **Phone:** (920) 779-6433.

NEW LONDON PUBLIC MUSEUM is on US 45 Bus. Rte. at 406 S. Pearl St. The museum contains American Indian artifacts, minerals, fossils, shells, examples of taxidermy and regional historical items. Regular changing exhibits are featured. **Time:** Allow 1 hour minimum. **Hours:** Tues.-Fri. 10-5 (also Tues. 5-7), Sat. 10-2. Closed major holidays. **Cost:** Free. **Phone:** (920) 982-8520.

NICOLET NATIONAL FOREST—
see Chequamegon-Nicolet National Forest p. 138.

NORTH FREEDOM (H-5)
pop. 649, elev. 867′

MID-CONTINENT RAILWAY MUSEUM is w. on W. Walnut St. to E8948 Diamond Hill Rd. Vintage trains take passengers on a 50-minute ride. The museum includes an 1894 depot and restored rolling stock. A winter ride runs the second weekend in February; an autumn color train ride takes place the second and third weekends in October, and a Pumpkin Special runs on the fourth weekend. The Santa Claus Express is Thanksgiving weekend. Dinner train rides also are available.

Hours: Museum open daily 10-5, Memorial Day-Labor Day; Sat.-Sun. 10-5, mid-May to day before Memorial Day and day after Labor Day to mid-Oct. Trains depart at 11, 1 and 3, mid-May to Labor Day. Passengers should arrive at least 20 minutes prior to departure. Phone ahead to confirm schedule. **Cost:** Museum free. Train fare $16; $15 (ages 63+); $14 (ages 13-18); $10 (ages 3-12). Caboose rides $18; $17 (ages 63+); $16 (ages 13-18); $13 (ages 3-12). Phone ahead to verify fares. **Phone:** (608) 522-4261 or (800) 930-1385.

OCONOMOWOC—see Milwaukee p. 179.

OCONTO (E-8) pop. 4,708, elev. 590′

Nearly 6,000 years ago, ancient American Indians known for the copper artifacts they left behind used a site in what is now Oconto to bury their dead. Copper Culture Park, on N. River Road near SR 22 (Charles Street), preserves this prehistoric cemetery within its 48 acres. A small museum displays items recovered from the site; phone (920) 834-6206.

Modern by comparison is the West Main Street Historic District, a three-block area lined with elegant houses marking the period when lumber was supreme in Oconto. Among the houses dating 1860-1928 is one that belonged to Edward Scofield, the last of Wisconsin's lumberman governors. The first church built by the Christian Science denomination is at Chicago and Main streets.

Oconto Visitors Center: 110 Brazeau Ave., Oconto, WI 54153. **Phone:** (920) 834-6254 or (888) 626-6862.

BEYER HOME MUSEUM is at 917 Park Ave. The 1868 brick home is furnished to reflect the Victorian period. A museum annex on the grounds contains Old Main Street and its shops, Copper Culture artifacts, and displays about Oconto County history. A barn/carriage house houses tools and historic vehicles, including two antique electric cars. A restored log cabin reflects life on the frontier.

Time: Allow 1 hour minimum. **Hours:** Tours are given daily noon-4, June 1-Labor Day; Sat.-Sun. noon-4, day after Labor Day to mid-Oct. **Cost:** $4; $2 (students with ID); $10 (family, two adults and all children). **Phone:** (920) 834-6206.

OSCEOLA (D-1) pop. 2,421, elev. 809'

On the bluffs of the St. Croix River, Osceola was a popular stop for late 19th-century excursion steamboats. Passengers disembarked to follow a boardwalk to scenic Cascade Falls. Visitors today can duplicate that hike along a path leading to the waterfall. Interstate State Park, known for its cliffs, potholes and hiking trails, is a short drive north *(see St. Croix Falls p. 191)*.

Osceola Chamber of Commerce: 550 Chieftain St., Osceola, WI 54020. **Phone:** (715) 755-3300 or (800) 947-0581.

OSCEOLA & ST. CROIX VALLEY RAILWAY departs from 114 Depot Rd. Scenic 50- and 90-minute excursions aboard restored diesel-powered trains take passengers through the St. Croix River Valley between Wisconsin and Minnesota. Special event rides and brunch, dinner and pizza trips also are offered. **Hours:** Trips depart Sat.-Sun. and holidays at 11, 1:15 and 2:30, May-Oct. **Cost:** Fare $12-$17; $11-$15 (ages 62+); $6-$8 (ages 5-15); $30-$45 (family). **Phone:** (715) 755-3570.

OSHKOSH (G-7) pop. 62,916, elev. 755'

Oshkosh is an important manufacturing center on the west shore of Lake Winnebago at the mouth of the upper Fox River. Because the Fox and its tributaries and the Wolf River could transport logs, and because nearby lakes Poygan and Butte des Morts provided natural storage facilities, the lumbering boom lasted longer in Oshkosh than in other central Wisconsin sawmill towns.

Streets inches deep in sawdust prompted the nickname "Sawdust City" and probably contributed to the fact that the downtown area was destroyed by fire five times 1859-75. After the last conflagration, rebuilding was done with brick.

A noted Oshkosh resident, Helen Farnsworth Mears, won national acclaim for her sculpture "Genius of Wisconsin," now at the Capitol in Madison. More than 240 acres of municipal parks and the University of Wisconsin-Oshkosh enhance the community. Campus tours are offered; phone (920) 424-0202.

Menominee Park, 109 acres along the shores of Lake Winnebago, includes such recreational facilities as a marina, paddleboats, amusement ride and children's zoo. Also featured is Little Oshkosh, a playground complete with castles, mazes, tunnels and a lighthouse.

A collection of nativity scenes, including one made by German POWs in World War II, is displayed at the 1892 limestone Algoma Boulevard United Methodist Church at 1174 Algoma Blvd. Viewing is available during church office hours; phone (920) 231-2800.

Oshkosh Convention & Visitors Bureau: 2401 W. Waukau Ave., Oshkosh, WI 54904. **Phone:** (920) 303-9200 or (877) 303-9200.

Shopping areas: The Outlet Shoppes at Oshkosh, US 41 and SR 44, offers more than 55 outlet stores.

EAA AIRVENTURE MUSEUM is at 3000 Poberezny Rd., .2 mi. s.e. of jct. US 41/SR 44. A collection of more than 150 aircraft includes home-built sport planes, gliders, barnstormers, helicopters, tracers and aerobatic planes as well as antique, military, solar-powered and ultralight aircraft. KidVenture and Willan Space Gallery offer hands-on exhibits for children. The museum also has a multimedia exhibit as well as models, engines, propellers, components and cutaways to show structural design.

Time: Allow 1 hour, 30 minutes minimum. **Hours:** Mon.-Sat. 8:30-5, Sun. 10-5. Airplane rides are available May-Oct. (weather permitting). Closed Jan. 1, Easter, Thanksgiving and Dec. 25. **Cost:** $12.50; $10.50 (ages 62+); $9.50 (ages 6-17); $31 (family). Aircraft rides $30-$70. **Phone:** (920) 426-4818.

GRAND OPERA HOUSE is at 100 High Ave. The restored 1883 660-seat Victorian theater offers concerts, plays and community events. Public performances by national and international touring artists are held here. **Time:** Allow 30 minutes minimum. **Hours:** Box office hours Mon.-Fri. 11:30-5, Sat. 11-2; guided tours available by appointment. **Cost:** Tour $2. **Phone:** (920) 424-2355 for tours and information, or (866) 964-7263 for tickets.

MENOMINEE PARK ZOO is in Menominee Park at the corner of Hazel St. and Merritt Ave. This small zoo houses a variety of animals native to Wisconsin. Recreational activities are available in the park. **Time:** Allow 1 hour minimum. **Hours:** Daily 9-7:30, first Sat. in May-last Sun. in Sept. **Cost:** Free. **Phone:** (920) 236-5082.

OSHKOSH PUBLIC MUSEUM is at 1331 Algoma Blvd. The exploration and settlement of the Lake Winnebago Region is described through numerous objects, paintings and photographs as well as family-friendly interactive exhibits. The museum includes the 1908 Edwardian Sawyer mansion with interiors by Tiffany Studios. The 8-foot-tall Apostles Clock, created by German immigrant Mathias Kitz in 1895, is a prized example of Wisconsin folk art.

Time: Allow 1 hour minimum. **Hours:** Tues.-Sat. 10-4:30, Sun. 1-4:30. Closed major holidays. **Cost:**

$7; $5 (ages 62+); $3.50 (ages 6-17). Prices may vary during special events. **Phone:** (920) 236-5799.

PAINE ART CENTER AND GARDENS is at 1410 Algoma Blvd. Referred to as one of "America's Castles," this is a combination of a historic 1920's mansion, art galleries and seasonal display gardens. The Paine also presents changing art exhibits, and the Family Discovery Gallery offers creative, hands-on activities for children dealing with the subjects of architecture, art and gardens. Throughout the holiday season, the Nutcracker story unfolds in the elaborately decorated mansion.

Time: Allow 1 hour, 30 minutes minimum. **Hours:** Tues.-Sun. 11-4. Phone for Nutcracker in the Castle schedule and rates. Closed major holidays. **Cost:** $9; $5 (ages 5-17). **Phone:** (920) 235-6903.

PEPIN (F-2) pop. 878, elev. 688'

Charles Ingalls acquired a small tract of land near Pepin in 1863, where he built his "Little House in the Big Woods." His daughter, author Laura Ingalls Wilder, was born there in 1867. A replica of the log cabin is on the site at Little House Wayside—north of town off CR CC. The "beautiful lake" about which she wrote is scenic Lake Pepin, a wide spot on the Mississippi River that still attracts nature lovers. In mid-September Laura Ingalls Wilder Days celebrates the author with activities including arts and crafts, a fiddle contest, a quilt show, a parade and demonstrations of traditional crafts such as blacksmithing and hand-spinning yarn.

Pepin Visitor Information Center: P.O. Box 277, Pepin, WI 54759. **Phone:** (715) 442-3011 or (800) 442-3011.

LAURA INGALLS WILDER HISTORICAL MUSEUM is at 306 Third St./SR 35. Items pertain to the history of Pepin County as well as memorabilia

of Laura Ingalls Wilder, author of the "Little House" books. A kitchen and bedroom are furnished in period. **Time:** Allow 1 hour minimum. **Hours:** Daily 10-5, May 15-Oct. 15. **Cost:** Donations. **Phone:** (715) 442-2142 or (800) 442-3011.

PESHTIGO (E-8) pop. 3,357, elev. 600'

On Oct. 8, 1871, Chicago was not the only community in flames. About 270 miles to the north was a forest area that had been plagued for days with small fires in the dry woodlands. On that October day winds whipped the small blazes into great ones; towns were leveled and more than 1,200 people perished. In Peshtigo alone 800 residents died.

A monument to the dead is in the Peshtigo Fire Cemetery. The Peshtigo Fire Museum, containing local items relating to the tragedy, is on Oconto Avenue; phone (715) 582-3244. The Peshtigo Wildlife Area, about 6 miles southeast on CR BB, is primarily a waterfowl habitat and refuge.

Peshtigo Chamber of Commerce: P.O. Box 36, Peshtigo, WI 54157. **Phone:** (715) 582-0327.

PHILLIPS (C-4) pop. 1,675, elev. 1,444'

Phillips offers year-round outdoor recreational opportunities. In the winter, the area's ice-fishing, 500 miles of snowmobile trails and 70 miles of cross-country ski trails beckon those not afraid of Jack Frost, while other seasons lure visitors with hunting and fishing.

Phillips Chamber of Commerce: 305 South Lake Ave., Phillips, WI 54555. **Phone:** (715) 339-4100 or (888) 408-4800.

WISCONSIN CONCRETE PARK is .5 mi. s. on SR 13. In 1949, retired lumberjack Fred Smith began creating embellished concrete sculptures that he decorated with such found objects as glass bottles, metals, shards of glass and rocks. Smith chose to depict such diverse subjects as Ben-Hur, a team of eight life-size Clydesdale horses pulling a beer wagon and the Iwo Jima Monument. Today visitors can see more than 200 life-size examples of his work surrounding the Smith family's former home. **Time:** Allow 1 hour minimum. **Hours:** Daily dawn-dusk. **Cost:** Donations. **Phone:** (715) 339-6371 or (800) 269-4505.

PLATTEVILLE (I-4) pop. 9,989, elev. 968'

On hillsides where dairy cattle now graze, miners once burrowed for lead. Platteville was settled in 1827, following John Rountree's discovery of "mineral" nearby. Rountree had the small mining town designed in the 1820s by an English architect who incorporated features of his native village of Yorkshire into the town plan.

Although some lead and zinc are still mined, cheese production is a more common industry. The town is a trading center for the surrounding agricultural and dairying region. Platteville also has the University of Wisconsin-Platteville.

DID YOU KNOW

Wisconsin's nickname,
the Badger State,
is derived from
early lead miners
who lived in caves
they burrowed out
of the hillsides.

Platteville Area Chamber of Commerce: 275 W. US 151, P.O. Box 724, Platteville, WI 53818. Phone: (608) 348-8888.

THE MINING MUSEUM is at 385 E. Main St. The development of lead and zinc mining in the area is traced through dioramas, models, artifacts and photographs. A guided tour includes a walk into the Bevans Lead, an 1845 lead mine 50 feet underground; a visit to the hoist house; and a train ride around the museum grounds in ore cars pulled by a 1931 mine locomotive. Changing art exhibits are offered on the second floor in the Rountree Gallery.

Time: Allow 1 hour, 30 minutes minimum. Hours: Museum self-guiding exhibits open daily 9-5, May-Oct.; Mon.-Fri. 9-4, rest of year. Guided mine tours daily 9-5, May-Oct. Closed Jan. 1, Good Friday, Veteran's Day, Thanksgiving, day after Thanksgiving and Dec. 24-25. Cost: Museum $9 (including the Rollo Jamison Museum); $7.75 (ages 65+); $4.50 (ages 5-15); $24 (family). Rountree Gallery free. Phone: (608) 348-3301.

Rollo Jamison Museum is next to the Mining Museum at 405 E. Main St. Exhibits include military items, carriages, farm implements, tools, a kitchen and parlor, a schoolroom and mechanical music boxes. Hours: Daily 9-5, May-Oct.; Mon.-Fri. 9-4, rest of year. Closed Jan. 1, Veterans Day, Thanksgiving, day after Thanksgiving and Dec. 24-25. Cost: $9 (including The Mining Museum); $7.75 (ages 65+); $4.50 (ages 5-15). Phone: (608) 348-3301.

PLEASANT PRAIRIE (I-8)
pop. 16,136, elev. 700'

JELLY BELLY VISITOR CENTER is 3 mi. e. off I-94 exit 347 (SR 165) at 10100 Jelly Belly Ln. Visitors ride on an indoor train that travels through the company's distribution center where the secrets of making Jelly Belly jelly beans are told in video presentations. Time: Allow 30 minutes minimum. Hours: Tours daily 9-4. Closed Jan. 1, Easter, Thanksgiving and Dec. 25. Cost: Free. Phone: (866) 868-7522.

PORTAGE (G-6) pop. 9,728, elev. 798'

In 1673 Jacques Marquette and Louis Joliet were probably the first Europeans to make the portage between the Fox and Wisconsin rivers, thus linking the Great Lakes with the Mississippi River. This junction rapidly developed into an important trade route. By 1835 the portage had become a plank road, which was replaced by a canal in the 1870s.

The town of Portage grew up around Fort Winnebago, which was built to protect the stream of commerce. Jefferson Davis, a young West Point lieutenant, was assigned in 1829 to cut logs for the barracks. He later became president of the Confederacy.

Modern and attractive, Portage acknowledges its origins with several restorations and the Marquette Trail, a portion of the Ice Age National Scenic Trail

that follows the Fox River from the Governor's Bend Locks to the Historic Indian Agency House (see attraction listing). The city attends to the present by serving the surrounding farming and dairying area.

Portage Area Chamber of Commerce: 104 W. Cook St., Suite A, Portage, WI 53901. Phone: (608) 742-6242 or (800) 474-2525.

FORT WINNEBAGO SURGEONS' QUARTERS is 2 mi. e. on SR 33. One of the oldest homes in Wisconsin still standing on its original foundation, the early 1800s French Colonial log building was erected by Francis LeRoi, a fur trader and portaging businessman. Acquired by the U.S. Army in 1828, it housed the fort surgeons 1834-1848. A fire in 1856 destroyed much of the fort, but the surgeons' quarters remains. Exhibits include period furnishings, original fort artifacts, and medical and dental equipment. The site also includes the Garrison School, a one-room schoolhouse used continually 1848-1960.

Time: Allow 1 hour minimum. Hours: Mon.-Sat. 10-4, Sun. 11-4, May 15-Oct. 15; by appointment Oct. 16-Nov. 1. Cost: $6; $5 (ages 60+); $3 (ages 6-18); $15 (family, two adults and three children); $10 (combination ticket with Historic Indian Agency House). Phone: (608) 742-2949.

HISTORIC INDIAN AGENCY HOUSE is .2 mi. e. on SR 33, then .5 mi. n. along the canal. The house was built in 1832 by the U.S. government for John Kinzie, agent to the Ho-Chunk (Winnebago) Indians, and his wife, Juliette. The structure has been restored and furnished in period and has a visitor center. Their granddaughter, Juliette Gordon Low, founded the Girl Scouts of the United States.

Tours: Guided tours are available. Time: Allow 1 hour minimum. Hours: Mon.-Sat. 10-4, Sun. 11-4, May 15-Oct. 15; by appointment rest of year. Cost: $6; $5 (ages 60+); $3 (ages 6-18); $15 (family, two adults and three children); $10 (combination ticket with Fort Winnebago Surgeons' Quarters). Phone: (608) 742-6362.

RECREATIONAL ACTIVITIES
Skiing and Snowboarding

• Cascade Mountain W10441 Cascade Mountain Rd., Portage, WI 53901-9633. Hours: Mon.-Thurs. 10-9, Fri.-Sat. and holidays 9 a.m.-10 p.m., Sun. 9-9, mid-Nov. to mid-Mar. (weather permitting). Phone: (608) 742-5588 or (800) 992-2754.

PORT WASHINGTON—
see Milwaukee p. 180.

POTOSI (I-3) pop. 711, elev. 794'

Potosi is home to the St. John Mine, 129 S. Main St. Between 1828-1848, this natural cave was a rich source of lead ore; hundreds of miners flocked to the area and began settling in Potosi.

NATIONAL BREWERY MUSEUM, 209 S. Main St., is part of the Potosi Brewing Company complex, which opened in 2008 following a $7.5 million restoration. The collection of breweriana includes beer bottles and cans, signs, glassware, trays and advertisements from the 1850s to the present. Flat-screen televisions show videos about the history of the area's beer industry from the days of prohibition to modern advertising. The museum also is home to the Great River Road Interpretive Center; displays delve into the history of the brewery and the Great River Road.

Hours: Daily 10-9. Phone ahead to confirm schedule. **Cost:** $7; $4 (ages 7-17); $22 (family, two adults and all children). **Phone:** (608) 763-4002.
🍴

Potosi Brewing Company Transportation Museum, 209 S. Main St., explores the role and various modes of transportation in the history of brewing from the early years of delivery by horse-drawn wagons and steamboats to today's methods via trucks and the railroad. **Hours:** Daily 10-9. **Cost:** Free. **Phone:** (608) 763-4002. 🍴

POYNETTE (H-6) pop. 2,266, elev. 852′

Poynette is the southeastern terminus of a scenic stretch of I-94, which follows the Wisconsin River and ends at the junction with I-90.

Poynette Area Chamber of Commerce: P.O. Box 625, Poynette, WI 53955. **Phone:** (608) 635-2425.

MACKENZIE ENVIRONMENTAL EDUCATION CENTER, 2 mi. e. on CRs CS and Q, includes a wildlife exhibit with live animals native to Wisconsin, a model forest nursery, a fire tower and an arboretum. The center also has logging and conservation museums, hiking trails and picnic facilities.

Time: Allow 2 hours minimum. **Hours:** Grounds open daily dawn-dusk, except deer gun season. Exhibits open daily 8-4, May-Oct.; Mon.-Fri. 8-4, rest of year. Exhibits closed off-season holidays. **Cost:** Donations. **Phone:** (608) 635-8110 or (608) 635-8105.

PRAIRIE DU CHIEN (H-3)
pop. 6,018, elev. 635′

Dating from 1673, when Jacques Marquette and Louis Joliet reached this site at the confluence of the Mississippi and Wisconsin rivers, Prairie du Chien is the oldest community on the Upper Mississippi River. Traditionally, the name of Prairie du Chien came from the French for "prairie of the dog," a Fox chief who lived on the prairie. The oldest part of the town is on St. Feriole Island along the Mississippi.

Prairie du Chien became a flourishing fur market soon after the French explorers' visit, attracting American Indians from the remote upper reaches of the Mississippi and Wisconsin rivers, as well as traders and settlers. From 1685 to 1831 four forts were built and occupied at various times by French, British and American forces. It was at Fort Crawford that Jefferson Davis and Zachary Taylor were stationed.

Prairie du Chien is the southern terminus of an especially scenic route that follows the Mississippi River. The route consists of SR 35 running north to La Crosse, then northwest along the Mississippi River to Prescott.

Prairie du Chien Chamber of Commerce: 211 S. Main St., Prairie du Chien, WI 53821. **Phone:** (608) 326-8555 or (800) 732-1673.

FORT CRAWFORD MUSEUM is at 717 S. Beaumont Rd. Located in the hospital of the second Fort Crawford built 1829-33, the museum chronicles area history, including the American Indian treaties, the first and second Fort Crawford, the Blackhawk War and the Civil War. Local collections and exhibits related to Prairie du Chien history also are displayed. Other highlights include a reconstructed pharmacy of the 1890s, dioramas illustrating the progress of surgery, and models of the human body depicting functions of the various systems and organs.

Time: Allow 1 hour minimum. **Hours:** Daily 9-4, May-Oct. **Cost:** $5; $4 (ages 55+); $3 (ages 5-12); $15 (family, two adults and dependent children ages 0-17). **Phone:** (608) 326-6960.

VILLA LOUIS is 1 mi. n.w. at 521 N. Villa Louis Rd. on St. Feriole Island. Villa Louis was the 19th-century home of the Dousman family, who made a fortune in the fur trade and through timely investments in land, steamboats and railroads. Four buildings in the mansion complex are open, exhibiting a collection of Victorian decorative arts original to the property. Restoration has replicated many original wallpapers, textiles and decorative treatments reflecting the design of William Morris and the British Arts and Craft Movement.

In addition to guided tours of the mansion complex, visitors may also tour the restored grounds and gardens and the Fur Trade Museum. Tours begin in the elevated visitor center and are conducted by costumed guides.

Time: Allow 1 hour, 30 minutes minimum. **Hours:** Daily 9:30-5, first Sat. in May-Oct. 31. Tours are given on the hour 10-4. **Cost:** Tour $9; $7.75 (students with ID and ages 65+); $4.50 (ages 5-17); $24 (family, two adults and children ages 5-17). **Phone:** (608) 326-2721.

WYALUSING STATE PARK—
see Bagley p. 132.

PRAIRIE DU SAC (H-5)
pop. 3,231, elev. 767′

Prairie du Sac and its neighbor Sauk City, on the high-bluffed west bank of the Wisconsin River, share a colorful historical character, Agoston Haraszthy. Arriving in 1841 with flamboyant attire, an international perspective and high ideals, the Hungarian nobleman fostered free thought in the Wisconsin wilderness. He also established some of the first vineyards in this fertile area before moving on to California, where his vineyards became the foundation of the wine industry.

The towns are the eastern terminus of scenic route the Lower Wisconsin River Road that follows SR 60 west along the Wisconsin River and ends in Prairie du Chien; it is the first Wisconsin state highway designated as a scenic byway. The 92 miles of free-flowing water between the dam at Prairie du Sac and the river's mouth near Prairie du Chien—along with a large swath of land along both sides—have been designated as the Lower Wisconsin State Riverway. Nearly 80,000 acres are within the Riverway's boundaries, which encompass fisheries, undeveloped land filled with wildlife and historical and archeological sites.

A portion of the Lower Wisconsin State Riverway includes the Battle of Wisconsin Heights site. Led by Chief Black Hawk, a small band of American Indian warriors fought federal and state forces in what would be the last such battle in the region. Black Hawk's defeat led to the continued westward expansion of the United States. The chief directed his forces from atop his white stallion near a spot where five effigy mounds can be seen today.

Canoeing, fishing, hiking and horseback riding are popular activities along the river, and campers can pitch their tents on most state-owned lands. For information, contact the Wisconsin Department of Natural Resources, Lower Wisconsin State Riverway, 1500 N. Johns St., Dodgeville, WI 53533; phone (608) 935-3368.

Sauk-Prairie Area Chamber of Commerce: 421 Water St., Suite 105, Prairie du Sac, WI 53578. **Phone:** (608) 643-4168 or (800) 683-2453.

Self-guiding tours: Brochures describing bald eagle watching in winter and a walking tour of Prairie du Sac's historic homes and businesses are available from the chamber of commerce.

WINERIES

- **Wollersheim Winery** is .2 mi e. on SR 60, then .7 mi. s. on SR 188. **Hours:** Tastings are available daily 10-5. Guided tours are given daily at 10:15, 11:15, 12:15, 1:15, 2:15, 3:15 and 4:15. Closed Jan. 1, Easter, Thanksgiving and Dec. 25. **Phone:** (608) 643-6515 or (800) 847-9463.

RACINE (I-8) pop. 81,855, elev. 626'

This once industrial port has transformed its lakefront into a recreation area that includes North Beach, which boasts 50 acres of fine, white sand. Racine's lakefront also is a great place for salmon and trout fishing.

Bisected by the winding Root River, the city has many residential areas and about 900 acres of parkland. Like many Wisconsin cities, it has a multiethnic population, but the emphasis is Danish. West Racine is often dubbed "Kringleville" for its bakeries specializing in Danish kringle. Filled with fruit and sweet nut fillings, the pastry can be enjoyed at any number of area bakeries.

Racine boasts a rich industrial history that includes Case Tractors, In-Sink-Erator food waste disposers and S.C. Johnson (formerly Johnson Wax) household products of, all which had their humble beginnings in Racine County.

Racine's architectural legacy includes five buildings designed by Frank Lloyd Wright, among them the landmark S.C. Johnson Administration Building at 1525 Howe St. The outstanding architectural features are highlighted along with a look at the company's history and philosophies. Guided tours are offered most Fridays and Saturdays. Reservations are required; phone (262) 260-2154.

The 1880 Wind Point Lighthouse is said to be the oldest and tallest in operation on Lake Michigan. The grounds are open to the public, but reservations are required to tour the building; phone (262) 639-2026. Downtown Racine is the site of Reefpoint Marina, with some 1,000 boat slips, and Racine Civic Centre Festival Park.

Racine County Convention & Visitors Bureau: 14015 Washington Ave., Sturtevant, WI 53177. **Phone:** (262) 884-6400 or (800) 272-2463.

Shopping areas: The Regency Mall, I-94 exit 335 on US 11, includes JCPenney and Sears among its 115 stores. The shops in 7-Mile Fair, I-94 at 7 Mile Road, feature antiques and collectibles. Downtown Racine offers a variety of boutiques.

RACINE ART MUSEUM (RAM) is at 441 Main St. Rotating exhibits highlight contemporary crafts constructed of ceramic, fiber, glass, metal and wood. Pieces by Dale Chihuly, Carol Eckert, Arline Fisch, John McQueen and Toshiko Takazu are represented. In November 1933, when the building was the American Trades Bank, it was the scene of an armed robbery by the Dillinger gang.

Time: Allow 30 minutes minimum. **Hours:** Tues.-Sat. 10-5, Sun. noon-5. Closed major holidays. **Cost:** $5; $3 (ages 63+ and students with ID); free (ages 0-11). **Phone:** (262) 638-8300.

RACINE HERITAGE MUSEUM is at 701 S. Main St. at 7th St. The museum exhibits include Frank Lloyd Wright in Racine, Racine County's Underground Railroad History and An Amazing Journey: the Life and Legacy of Astronaut Laurel Clark. Other exhibits describe Racine's manufacturing innovations, inventions and cultural heritage.

Time: Allow 30 minutes minimum. **Hours:** Museum open Tues.-Fri. 9-5, Sat. 10-3, Sun. noon-4. Archives open Tues. 1-4:30, Sat. 10-1 and by appointment. Closed major holidays. **Cost:** Donations. **Phone:** (262) 636-3926.

RACINE ZOOLOGICAL GARDENS is at 2131 N. Main St. This 25-acre park on the shore of Lake Michigan is home to 250 animals representing 76 species, including orangutans, African penguins, Andean bears, black rhinos and Masai giraffes.

Time: Allow 1 hour minimum. **Hours:** Daily 9-8, Apr. 1-Labor Day; 9-6, day after Labor Day-Oct. 31; 9-4, rest of year. Last admission one hour before closing. **Cost:** $6; $5 (ages 62+); $4 (ages 3-15). **Phone:** (262) 636-9189. 🍴

RAM'S CHARLES A. WUSTUM MUSEUM OF FINE ARTS is at 2519 Northwestern Ave. (SR 38). The museum offers several annual exhibitions of national, regional and local artists. The 13-acre grounds also accommodate the Racine Theater Guild. **Hours:** Museum open Tues.-Sat. 10-5; closed federal holidays and during exhibition changes. **Cost:** Donations. **Phone:** (262) 636-9177, or (262) 633-4218 for the Racine Theater Guild.

RHINELANDER (C-5) pop. 7,735, elev. 1,553'

Rhinelander had its beginning in the 1880s during the days of the pioneer lumber industry. Besides lumber, the area's forests yielded the Hodag, a creature that became the town's beloved mascot. Finally exposed as a hoax composed of wood and ox hides, the Hodag myth is kept alive in local symbols and also can be seen in statue form at the Rhinelander Logging Museum *(see attraction listing)* and the Rhinelander Area Chamber of Commerce.

Within a radius of 12 miles are 232 lakes, 11 trout streams and two rivers offering nearly every type of water sport. More than 1,000 miles of snowmobile trails traverse all of northern Wisconsin, some of which run through Rhinelander. The region also is noted for its scenic hiking, mountain bicycling and cross-country ski trails.

Nicolet College, on CR G and Oneida Avenue, is noted for its architecture, which blends into the surrounding woods. The college's art gallery features exhibits throughout the year, while the Nicolet Live Arts & Speakers series offers a mix of entertaining events. Free campus tours are given by appointment; phone (715) 365-4410.

Rhinelander Area Chamber of Commerce: 450 Kemp St., P.O. Box 795, Rhinelander, WI 54501. **Phone:** (715) 365-7464 or (800) 236-4386.

PIONEER PARK HISTORICAL COMPLEX is in Pioneer Park at jct. US 8 Bus. Rte./CR G. This reproduction of an 1870s logging camp features the Sioux Line Depot, built in 1892, loggers' living quarters, a cook's shack, schoolhouse, smithy and all the tools of their respective trades. Displays include a narrow-gauge engine built in 1879 and a replica of the Hodag.

Time: Allow 1 hour minimum. **Hours:** Daily 10-5, Memorial Day-Labor Day. **Cost:** Donations. **Phone:** (715) 369-5004.

THE RHINELANDER HISTORICAL SOCIETY MUSEUM is at 9 S. Pelham St. Housed in a restored 1894 boarding house, the museum portrays area history from the late 19th century to the present.

Hours: Tues. and Thurs. 10-4 and by appointment, June-Aug.; Tues. 10-4, rest of year. **Cost:** Donations. **Phone:** (715) 369-3833.

RICHLAND CENTER (H-4)
pop. 5,114, elev. 736'

Richland Center was settled in 1849. It is the birthplace of Frank Lloyd Wright, whose fine early work is represented by the 1915 design of the A.D. German Warehouse adjacent to downtown. Another noted resident was Ada James, an avid suffragette. Upon learning of Wisconsin's ratification of the 19th Amendment, James quickly put her 76-year-old father on the first train to Washington to present the ratification papers before any other state could secure the honor.

In an unglaciated corner of Wisconsin, Richland Center is surrounded by countryside characterized by fruit orchards, hardwood trees, steep hills, deep valleys, trout streams and unusual rock formations. A natural bridge can be seen in Pier County Park, 9 miles north on SR 80 near Rockbridge. Scenic SR 60 follows the Wisconsin River south from Richland Center.

Running between Richland Center and the town of Lone Rock, the Pine River Recreation Trail follows its namesake river for 15 miles, affording hikers, bicyclists and snowmobilers scenic views of wildlife in their natural habitat. Along the way, the well-groomed trail crosses 15 bridges.

Richland County Visitor Center: 397 W. Seminary St., P.O. Box 128, Richland Center, WI 53581-0128. **Phone:** (608) 647-6205.

Self-guiding tours: A map outlining a historical and architectural tour of Richland Center is available at the county visitor center.

RIPON (G-7) pop. 6,828, elev. 932'

Ripon began as an experiment in communal living called Ceresco, established in 1844 by 200 followers of the 19th-century socialist philosopher Charles Fourier. On the west edge of town stands one of the longhouses of the commune, which disbanded in 1851.

The Republican Party was founded in Ripon in 1854 at a local political meeting, which was called to organize against the extension of slavery. Alvan E. Bovay, a local lawyer and prominent Whig, proposed the party name. Four months later the name "Republican" was formally adopted at a state party convention in Jackson, Mich.

Ripon College, established in 1851, occupies a 250-acre campus on the highest hill in the city. A highlight of the college is C.J. Rodman Center for the Arts, with two Anthony Van Dyck portraits and changing exhibits. Free guided tours of the campus can be arranged; phone (920) 748-8364.

Ripon Area Chamber of Commerce: 127 Jefferson St., P.O. Box 305, Ripon, WI 54971. **Phone:** (920) 748-6764.

Self-guiding tours: Brochures outlining walking tours of the city are available from the chamber of commerce.

SAVE **LARSON'S FAMOUS CLYDESDALES** is 4 mi. s. on SR 44/49, then 1.6 mi. e. to W12654 Reeds Corner Rd. A 90-minute behind-the-scenes guided tour and show about Clydesdales includes performances by a horse, explanations of the Clydesdales' history and how they are prepared for show and judged. The barn, where Clydesdale colts can be seen and petted, is open after the program. A small museum is available.

Video cameras are prohibited. Reservations are preferred. **Hours:** Shows Mon.-Sat. at 1, May 15-Oct. 15. **Cost:** $15; $5 (ages 0-11). **Phone:** (920) 748-5466.

LITTLE WHITE SCHOOL HOUSE is at 303 Blackburn St. This mid-19th-century schoolhouse was the birthplace of the Republican Party. **Time:** Allow 30 minutes minimum. **Hours:** Daily 10-4, June 1-Labor Day; Sat.-Sun. 10-4, in May and day after Labor Day-Oct. 31 or by appointment. **Cost:** $1; free (ages 0-11). **Phone:** (920) 748-6764.

RUDOLPH (F-5) pop. 423, elev. 1,139'

DAIRY STATE CHEESE CO. is at SR 34 and CR C. An observation area and a multimedia presentation about cheesemaking are offered. **Hours:** Mon.-Fri. 8-5:15, Sat. 8-5, Sun. 9-noon. **Cost:** Free. **Phone:** (715) 435-3144.

GROTTO GARDENS AND WONDER CAVE is on SR 34 to 6957 Grotto Ave. The 12-acre site includes the Shrine of Peace and Our Lady of Lourdes Shrine and Museum, which contains pictures, plans and tools depicting the history of the grounds. The lush gardens of St. Phillips Church contain several other shrines and St. Jude's Chapel, constructed entirely of hand-cut logs. The quarter-mile-long Wonder Cave contains 26 shrines depicting the life and teachings of Jesus.

Hours: Wonder Cave open daily 10-5, Memorial Day weekend-mid Sept; by appointment rest of year. Grounds open 24 hours. **Cost:** Wonder Cave $2.50; $1.25 (ages 12-17); 25¢ (ages 6-11). Grotto Gardens by donation. **Phone:** (715) 435-3120.

ST. CROIX FALLS (D-1)
pop. 2,033, elev. 884'

St. Croix Falls is a center for outdoor recreation in the scenic valley of the St. Croix River. Long noted for excellent lake and stream fishing, the area is gaining popularity as a winter playground, with more than 350 miles of groomed snowmobile trails. The area also boasts several picturesque hiking and biking trails, including the nearly 50-mile Gandy Dancer State Bicycle Trail and the southern terminus of the Ice Age National Scenic Hiking Trail. Canoeing and kayaking are also popular activities.

Two state fish hatcheries are easily accessible from St. Croix Falls. On River Street downtown, the St. Croix Falls Fish Hatchery stocks brook and brown trout. Osceola Fish Hatchery, 7 miles south on CR S, breeds all of the state's rainbow trout.

Polk County Information Center: 710 US 35S, St. Croix Falls, WI 54024. **Phone:** (715) 483-1410 or (800) 222-7655.

 INTERSTATE STATE PARK is .5 mi. s. of US 8 on SR 35. This 1,377-acre park lies along the east side of the Dalles of the St. Croix River, a scenic gorge carved out of bedrock by glacial meltwater. The canyon walls rise 200 feet above the river. On the other side of the river is Minnesota's Interstate Park. The Old Man of the Dalles, a unique rock formation, and potholes formed by the swirling current of glacial meltwaters are in the park.

The area is one of nine units that make up the Ice Age National Scientific Reserve. A 20-minute film about the reserve is shown in the Ice Age Interpretive Center, near the park entrance off SR 35. Naturalist programs are offered year-round. The park has several hiking trails, and the lake offers a beach and bathhouse. *See Recreation Chart and the AAA Great Lakes CampBook.*

Hours: Park open daily 6 a.m.-11 p.m. Interpretive center open Mon.-Fri. 8:30-4:30, Sat.-Sun. 9-5, Memorial Day-Labor Day; hours vary, rest of year. Boat trips through the Dalles of the St. Croix River leave Taylors Falls, Minn., daily May 1 to mid-Oct. **Cost:** Day-use fee per private vehicle $10; $7 (state residents); $3 (residents ages 65+). Annual permit $35; $25 (state residents); $10 (residents ages 65+). **Phone:** (715) 483-3747.

ST. CROIX RIVER VISITOR CENTER— *see St. Croix National Scenic Riverway p. 192.*

WINERIES

- **Chateau St. Croix Winery & Vineyard** is 7 mi. n. on SR 87 to 1998A SR 87. **Hours:** Mon.-Sat. 11-6 (also Fri.-Sat. 6-7 p.m.), Sun. noon-4, June 1-Oct. 15; Mon.-Fri. noon-5, Sat. 11-6, Sun. noon-4, Oct. 16-Dec. 31 and Feb. 1-May 31. Tours are given Mon.-Sat. on the half-hour 11:30-3:30 (also Sat. at 4:30), Sun. at 12:30, 1:30 and 2:30. Closed Jan. 1, Easter, Thanksgiving and Dec. 25. **Phone:** (715) 483-2556.

ST. CROIX NATIONAL SCENIC RIVERWAY (E-1, B-2)

Flowing from the highlands of northern Wisconsin and central Minnesota to the St. Croix's juncture with the Mississippi River just s.e. of Minneapolis-St. Paul, the St. Croix National Scenic Riverway is a 255-mile river reserve. The Upper St. Croix River and its tributary, the Namekagon River, were among the original eight rivers designated as National Wild and Scenic Rivers in 1968. Four years later the Lower St. Croix River from St. Croix Falls to Prescott was added to the system by the National Park Service.

For hundreds of years the St. Croix and Namekagon were an important link between the Mississippi and Lake Superior. Besides being a major waterway, the St. Croix had marshes, pools and rapids that provided a wealth of food and fur for the Ojibwe and other American Indian tribes who once lived in this area. Beaver, otter and other pelts became the currency of a profitable trade with the French.

During the 17th and 18th centuries the river rang with the raucous songs of *voyageurs* as they paddled their loaded canoes up the St. Croix and down the Brule River to Lake Superior and eventually to Fort William. By the mid-19th century a new sound was heard, as logs thundered down the St. Croix from the logging camps of the North Woods.

Other than the development along its lower portion and the legacy of dams, the river retains much of its pristine nature. Both the Namekagon and St. Croix begin as narrow streams winding through forests, marshes and wide valleys. When the two rivers join, the St. Croix becomes wider, deeper and slower, making the area popular for small power-boats and canoes. The last segment below St. Croix Falls becomes even wider and more populated, marked by towns and pleasure craft.

General Information and Activities

The upper reaches of the St. Croix Riverway are canoe waters, with only a few rapids and none classified as white water. The canoeing season generally begins in May and ends in September; outfitters can be found in Hayward, Trego, Grantsburg and other towns on the riverway.

Canoe-access primitive camping predominates; permits are required for camping between St. Croix Falls/Taylors Falls and the Soo Line High Bridge north of Stillwater. Along the Wisconsin-Minnesota border several state forests and parks offer developed campgrounds, hiking and cross-country skiing.

Bass and muskellunge can be found along the entire riverway; trout are found in the headwaters. Anglers favor the upper reaches. Otters and such birds as bald eagles and osprey compete with the anglers for fish. The presence of these and other animals and waterfowl draws both bird-watchers and hunters. Fishing and hunting licenses are required within the riverway.

The proximity to urban areas and the river's width and placidity make the lower reaches below St. Croix Falls a popular area for boaters, water skiers and sailors. Highlights in this area include the scenic gorge in Interstate State Park *(see St. Croix Falls p. 191)* and the Apple River, which joins the St. Croix and is one of the most popular rivers in the state for tubing.

ADDRESS inquiries to the Superintendent, St. Croix National Scenic Riverway, 401 Hamilton St., St. Croix Falls, WI 54024; phone (715) 483-2274.

NAMEKAGON RIVER VISITOR CENTER is in Trego on US 63. Exhibits installed in 2010 help visitors explore river habitats and 10,000 years of human history, and also highlight how the Namekagon River is a part of a larger watershed and what people can do to protect the river. In addition to the exhibits, the visitor center features the 18-minute film "The St. Croix: A Northwoods Journey." **Hours:** Daily 9-5, Memorial Day weekend-Labor Day; Sat.-Sun. 9-5, May 1-day before Memorial Day and day after Labor Day-Sept. 30. Hours may vary. Phone ahead to confirm schedule. **Phone:** (715) 635-8346.

ST. CROIX RIVER VISITOR CENTER is in St. Croix Falls at 401 Hamilton St. The center features an aquarium with river fish, an aerial map of the riverway and displays about mussels. A movie about the riverway also is available. **Hours:** Daily 9-5, early May to mid-Oct.; Mon.-Fri. 9-4, rest of year. Closed federal holidays. Phone ahead to confirm schedule. **Phone:** (715) 483-2274.

ST. GERMAIN (C-5) pop. 1,932, elev. 1,631'

SNOWMOBILE HALL OF FAME is at 8481 W. SR 70 at Sled World Blvd. The hall of fame contains a theater where visitors can enjoy racing videos. Many types and brands of snowmobiles are on display as well as historic championship race sleds, trophies, snowmobile apparel, a photo collection and other memorabilia. **Time:** Allow 30 minutes minimum. **Hours:** Mon.-Fri. 10-5, Sat. 10-3, Memorial Day-Labor Day and Dec. 15-Mar. 15; Thurs.-Fri. 10-5, Sat. 10-3, rest of year. Closed major holidays. **Cost:** Free. **Phone:** (715) 542-4488.

SHAWANO (E-7) pop. 8,298, elev. 822'

Shawano has grown from a lumber boomtown into a retail trade center for the region's small farms. Shawano is among Wisconsin's leading dairy counties.

With its rolling hills beckoning cross-country skiers and its 300 miles of groomed snowmobile trails, Shawano is popular for winter recreation. Summer water sports include whitewater rafting on the Wolf River, trout fishing on the Embarrass and Red rivers and boating on 6,100-acre Shawano Lake *(see Recreation Chart)*. The Navarino Nature Center, 10 miles south on CR K, offers bicycling and nature trails as well as cross-country skiing in winter.

Two former railroad corridors, now serving as recreational trails, pass through Shawano. The Mountain Bay Trail and the Wiouwash Trail are open to hikers all year and to other recreational users seasonally; a fee is charged.

Shawano Country Chamber of Commerce and Visitor Center: 1263 S. Main St., P.O. Box 38, Shawano, WI 54166. **Phone:** (715) 524-2139 or (800) 235-8528.

Shopping areas: Downtown Shawano's Historic Main Street area features a collection of antique and specialty shops.

SHEBOYGAN (G-8) pop. 50,792, elev. 625'

Although the sound of nearby falls on the Sheboygan River may have inspired an American Indian term (Shawb-wa-way-going—"rumbling underground") for this location, the town means sausage and cheese to many people because of its industries. In addition to its savories, it produces and distributes steel, furniture, plastic products and in nearby Kohler, plumbing products.

The area's top-rated courses attract golfers as well as professional golf tournaments, and for fans of motorcycle and auto racing, Road America in nearby Elkhart Lake offers thrills mid-April through mid-September; phone (800) 365-7223. Kids can play in an indoor tree house, activate characters in a miniature circus and create metal sculptures using a giant horseshoe magnet at downtown's Above & Beyond Children's Museum, 902 N. 8th St.; phone (920) 458-4263.

Scenic drives along the lakeshore include Broughton Drive, Lakeshore Drive, and North 3rd Street. The Kettle Moraine State Forest also provides scenic views for drivers. Located on the shore of Lake Michigan, the city offers outstanding waterfront activities, including boating and fishing; other recreational pastimes are available at nearby Kohler-Andrae State Park *(see Recreation Chart and the AAA Great Lakes CampBook)*.

Sheboygan Chamber of Commerce: 621 S. 8th St. Sheboygan, WI 53081. **Phone:** (920) 457-9491 or (800) 457-9497.

JOHN MICHAEL KOHLER ARTS CENTER is at 608 New York Ave. This art museum and performing arts center presents exhibitions of contemporary art, as well as art by self-taught, folk and vernacular artists. With a 99,000-square-foot facility and 12 galleries, the arts center boasts six artist-commissioned public washrooms, a year-round performing arts series and an annual summer arts festival the third weekend in July. **Hours:** Center open Mon.-Fri. 10-5 (also Tues. and Thurs. 5-8), Sat.-Sun. 10-4. Closed major holidays. **Cost:** Donations. **Phone:** (920) 458-6144.

MAYWOOD—ELLWOOD H. MAY ENVIRONMENTAL PARK, 3615 Mueller Rd., is a 135-acre park where visitors can participate in environmental activities, take a self-guiding nature walk and utilize trails for cross-country skiing and hiking. Various habitats, including a prairie, ponds, wetlands, woodlands and the Pigeon River corridor provide ample opportunities to see wildlife such as amphibians, birds, coyotes, foxes, whitetail deer, raccoons, squirrels and wild turkeys. Educational exhibits are found at the Ecology Center.

Tours: Guided tours are available. **Time:** Allow 2 hours minimum. **Hours:** Park and trails daily 6 a.m.-10 p.m. Ecology Center Mon.-Fri. 9-4, Sat.-Sun. 1-4. **Cost:** Free. **Phone:** (920) 459-3906.

SHEBOYGAN COUNTY HISTORICAL SOCIETY MUSEUM is at 3110 Erie Ave. The museum includes an 1850s Victorian mansion, an 1860s log house furnished with pioneer items, an 1867 cheese factory and an 1890s barn that houses farm tools and machinery used by early settlers. Other exhibits highlight American Indian history, ice harvesting, immigration, the circus, sports, maritime history and early agriculture.

Time: Allow 1 hour minimum. **Hours:** Open Mon.-Fri. 10-5 (guided tours at 11, 1 and 3), Apr.-Oct.; daily noon-5, day after Thanksgiving-Dec. 30. Phone to confirm schedule during the school year and holiday season. **Cost:** $4; $2 (ages 7-12). Holiday season $4. **Phone:** (920) 458-1103.

SHEBOYGAN INDIAN MOUND PARK (Kletzien Mound Group) is just s. of Panther Ave. at 5000 S. 9th St. American Indian burial mounds in the park are shaped like panthers and deer. Dating from A.D. 500 to 1000, this is one of the few mound groups still intact. A nature trail leads to the lush valley of Hartman Creek, where both upland and lowland plant communities are identified. **Hours:** Self-guiding tours daily 10-10. **Cost:** Free. **Phone:** (920) 459-3444.

SHELL LAKE (C-2) pop. 1,309, elev. 1,241'

MUSEUM OF WOODCARVING is .5 mi. n. at 539 SR 63 at jct. CR B. The collection of Joseph Barta's hand-carved wood figurines depicts such Biblical events as The Last Supper. Barta created the 400 miniature figures over a span of 30 years, using oak, poplar, walnut and basswood. One hundred life-size figurines were created from ponderosa and sugar pine. **Time:** Allow 30 minutes minimum. **Hours:** Daily 9-6, May-Oct. **Cost:** $6.50; $4.50 (ages 0-11). **Phone:** (715) 468-7100.

SPARTA (G-3) pop. 8,648, elev. 793'

Sparta calls itself "the bicycling capital of the world" and is at the junction of the Elroy-Sparta State Trail and the La Crosse River State Trail. Running through Kendall, the 32-mile Elroy-Sparta Bicycling Trail was the nation's first to be converted from an abandoned railroad bed. For maps and information, phone (800) 354-2453 May through October.

The Deke Slayton Memorial Space & Bicycle Museum displays artifacts, documents and photographs related to the Sparta native's career as an aviator and astronaut, as well as exhibits related to the history of the bicycle. The exhibits are on the second floor of the Monroe County Museum at 200 W. Main St.; phone (608) 269-0033.

Six miles east of Sparta is Fort McCoy, the state's only U.S. Army installation. Two recreation areas on the base are open to the public: Pine View, (608) 388-3517, offers camping, hiking, boating, swimming, fishing and hunting; Whitetail Ridge, (608) 388-3517, is a winter facility for downhill and cross-country skiing, snow-tubing and snowmobiling.

Sparta Area Chamber of Commerce: 111 Milwaukee St., Sparta, WI 54656. **Phone:** (608) 269-4123 or (800) 354-2453.

SPOONER (C-2) pop. 2,653, elev. 1,065'

A railroad junction during the lumbering era, Spooner was named after John Coit Spooner, a railroad attorney elected to the U.S. Senate in 1885 and 1897. Spooner now is a popular resort community in the wooded lake district of northwestern Wisconsin. More than 900 lakes attract tourists to Washburn County. A float trip down the Namekagon River is a popular pastime; access landings are in Trego at the junction of US 53 and US 63, and on CR K, 10 miles north of Spooner.

Washburn County Tourist Information Center: 122 N. River St., Spooner, WI 54801. **Phone:** (715) 635-9696 or (800) 367-3306.

Self-guiding tours: The Spooner Heritage Walking Tour showcases some of the city's oldest homes and businesses. Also on the tour are the sites of Spooner's first school and church services. The tour guidebook can be obtained from the tourist information center.

GOVERNOR TOMMY G. THOMPSON STATE FISH HATCHERY is .5 mi. w. of US 63 on SR 70 to 951 W. Maple St. Said to be the world's largest muskellunge-raising facility, the hatchery also produces Northern pike and walleye. The best viewing opportunities are available from late April through early May. **Hours:** Visitor center open Mon.-Fri. 8-4; closed holidays. Visitor center observation deck open Sat.-Sun., late Apr.-early May. **Cost:** Free., **Phone:** (715) 635-4147.

RAILROAD MEMORIES MUSEUM is at 424 Front St. behind the post office parking lot. This museum in the former Chicago and Northwestern Depot displays 13 rooms of railroad memorabilia including tools used by track workers, firemen and brakemen; headlights; lanterns; uniforms; railroad logos; and office equipment. A library, an art room featuring railroad prints and originals, and a video room are offered. **Time:** Allow 30 minutes minimum. **Hours:** Daily 10-5, Memorial Day-Labor Day. **Cost:** $4; 50¢ (ages 6-12). **Phone:** (715) 635-3325 or (715) 635-2752.

WISCONSIN GREAT NORTHERN RAILROAD is at 426 N. Front St. Round-trip sightseeing excursions travel from Spooner to Trego and Springbrook and last from 1.5 to 2.5 hours. The historic train features a 1940 locomotive with restored cars from 1912 and 1918. Elegant Dinner trains, Sunday Brunch trains, pizza trains and family-oriented special events also are offered. Reservations are required for all meal trips and are recommended for sightseeing trips.

Time: Allow 3 hours minimum. **Hours:** Sightseeing trips depart Tues. and Thurs. at noon and 3, Sat. at 10, late June-late Aug.; Sat. at 10, early May-late June and late Aug.-late Sept. Two-hour Family Pizza Train trips depart Tues. and Thurs. at 5, Sat. at noon, late June-late Aug.; Sat. at noon, early May-late June and late Aug.-early Oct. Three-hour Sunday Brunch train departs at noon, early May-late Dec. Three-hour Elegant Dinner train departs Fri.-Sat. at 6, early May-late Dec. **Cost:** Fares $15-$50; $12-$25 (ages 3-12). **Phone:** (715) 635-3200.

SPRING GREEN (H-4) pop. 1,444, elev. 729'

Frank Lloyd Wright chose this farming community on the Wisconsin River as the site for his home, Taliesin, and for his architectural school. As a result,

Spring Green has a great concentration of Wright-influenced structures.

Across the river is Tower Hill State Park *(see Recreation Chart and the AAA Great Lakes Camp-Book)*. The restored Civil War shot tower is the last vestige of the town of Helena, a busy river port and railhead that once contended for the status of territorial capital.

In contrast to Wright's break with tradition, Spring Green's American Players Theatre bases its reputation on its adherence to the classics, with up to eight plays performed in rotating repertory. Staged in an amphitheater, the season generally is from the first Saturday in June through the first Saturday in October. The box office opens in late February; phone (608) 588-2361.

Spring Green Area Chamber of Commerce/Visitors Council: 259 E. Jefferson St., P.O. Box 3, Spring Green, WI 53588. **Phone:** (608) 588-2054 or (800) 588-2042.

FRANK LLOYD WRIGHT'S TALIESIN is 3 mi. s. on SR 23. The architect's primary home and studio was designed in 1902 out of sandstone and native oak. Wright enhanced the site throughout his life. Included on the grounds are a school, small theater, living and dining rooms, drafting studios, a gallery containing furniture Wright designed, artwork from his Asian collection and photograph murals and models of buildings he designed.

The visitor center, designed by Wright in 1953, overlooks the Wisconsin River and is the origin of Taliesin's various guided tours, including the House Tour, which explores the house Wright designed and updated over a 48-year period. The Hillside Tour gives an introduction to Wright and his work. Phone for information about Taliesin's other tours.

Time: Allow 1 hour minimum. **Hours:** Visitor center open daily 9-5:30, May-Oct. The 2-hour House Tour departs daily at noon and 3, May-Oct. The 1-hour Hillside Tour departs daily at 11:30, 1:30 and 3:30, May-Oct. Hours may vary. Phone ahead to confirm schedule. **Cost:** Tour fees $16-$80. Ages 0-11 are not permitted on House Tour. Reservations are recommended. **Phone:** (608) 588-7900 or (877) 588-7900. 🏠

THE HOUSE ON THE ROCK is 9 mi. s. on SR 23. Designed and built by Alex Jordan, this unusual house perched atop a rock pinnacle is at the center of a complex of interconnected buildings featuring themed rooms filled with eclectic collections.

The Gate House serves as an entryway to the original 14-room Main House, which incorporates natural rock walls and a waterfall. A highlight is the cantilevered Infinity Room, which extends 218 feet out over the valley and 156 feet above the forest floor, offering scenic views through floor-to-ceiling windows.

Note: From early May-early Nov., House on the Rock offers three tour options that include different portions of the complex. From early Nov.-early May, two tour options are offered. Each self-guiding tour takes at least 1 hour to complete.

Hours: Daily 9-6, May 1-Labor Day; daily 9-5, mid-Mar. through Apr. 30 and day after Labor Day-early Nov.; Thurs.-Mon. 9-5, early Nov.-early Jan.; Fri.-Mon. 9-5, rest of year. Last admission 1 hour before closing. Closed Thanksgiving and Dec. 24-25. Phone ahead to confirm schedule.

Cost: Tour of entire complex $28.50; $15.50 (ages 4-17). Partial tours of the complex also are available; phone ahead for rates. Rates may vary in winter. **Phone:** (608) 935-3639.

SPRING VALLEY (E-2)
pop. 1,189, elev. 1,100′

CRYSTAL CAVE is 1 mi. w. at 965 SR 29. Passageways meander through several "rooms" carved by an underground river, where thousands of formations can be seen on a narrated tour that descends 70 feet underground. **Time:** Allow 1 hour minimum. **Hours:** Guided 1-hour tours depart daily 9:30-5:30, Memorial Day-Labor Day; daily 10-4:30, day after Labor Day-Oct. 31; Sat.-Sun. 10-4:30, Apr. 1-day before Memorial Day. **Cost:** $11; $9 (ages 13-17); $7 (ages 4-12). Rates may vary; phone ahead. **Phone:** (715) 778-4414 or (800) 236-2283. 🏠

STEVENS POINT (F-6)
pop. 24,551, elev. 1,084′

Stevens Point was founded by George Stevens as a trading post on the Wisconsin River in 1838. Since its incorporation as a city in 1858, Stevens Point has fostered many industries including Worzalla Publishing; Herrschners, a needlecraft distribution center; Sentry Insurance; and the Stevens Point Brewery.

For recreation there are 11 swimming areas and 19 public parks in or around Stevens Point; lakes DuBay, Emily and Sunset are particularly popular. In winter cross-country skiers glide along more than 36 miles of trails that lace the surrounding countryside, and downhill skiers enjoy the two nearby slopes. In summer hiking and biking take over the trails, especially the Green Circle Trail, a 30.5-mile path linking scenic natural areas along the Wisconsin and Plover rivers.

The University of Wisconsin-Stevens Point campus offers a wealth of activities at minimal or no cost. "E Pluribus Unum," a mosaic mural on the wall of the College of Natural Resources, depicts the university and its environs using 25 tons of tiled panels. In nearby Custer, The ReNew the Earth Institute allows visitors to explore energy efficiency and other environmental issues; phone (715) 592-6595.

Stevens Point Area Convention & Visitors Bureau: 340 Division St. N., Stevens Point, WI 54481. **Phone:** (715) 344-2556 or (800) 236-4636.

MUSEUM OF NATURAL HISTORY is in the Albertson Learning Resources Center at 900 Reserve St. on the University of Wisconsin-Stevens Point campus. Exhibits include a regional collection of mounted raptors, waterfowl and songbirds as well as an extensive exhibit of bird eggs. Displays include geologic and mineral specimens; invertebrate, dinosaur and megafaunal fossils; and ecosystem dioramas of the upper Great Lakes, Arctic tundra, the desert, temperate and tropical rainforests and an African savannah. **Time:** Allow 1 hour minimum. **Hours:** Mon.-Fri. 7:45 a.m.-9 p.m., Sat. 9-9, Sun. 11 a.m.-1 a.m., early Sept. to mid-May. Closed holidays, examination weeks and during school breaks. Summer schedule varies; phone ahead. **Cost:** Free. **Phone:** (715) 346-2858.

SCHMEECKLE RESERVE is at 2419 North Point Dr. on the University of Wisconsin-Stevens Point campus. This 275-acre wildlife preservation area offers 5 miles of trails and boardwalks and a 24-acre lake for fishing and canoeing. A visitor center with interactive exhibits and the Wisconsin Conservation Hall of Fame are on the grounds. **Hours:** Visitor center open daily 8-5. Grounds open daily dawn-dusk. Phone for visitor center holiday schedule. **Cost:** Free. **Phone:** (715) 346-4992. 🚫

STEVENS POINT BREWERY is at 2617 Water St. Guided 45-minute tours detail the history of this brewery, in operation since 1857, and explain the process of making and distributing beer. **Time:** Allow 1 hour minimum. **Hours:** Brewery tours Mon.-Sat. at 11, noon, 1 and 2, June-Aug.; Mon.-Fri. at 1, Sat. at 11, noon, 1 and 2, rest of year. Hours may vary. Phone ahead to confirm schedule. **Cost:** Tour $3; $1 (ages 5-11). Reservations are required. **Phone:** (715) 344-9310 or (800) 369-4911.

STURGEON BAY —*see Door County p. 142.*

SUAMICO (E-7) pop. 8,686

NEW ZOO is off US 41 exit 176, 2.5 mi. w. on CR B, then 1 mi. n. on CR IR to 4418 Reforestation Rd. The zoo, located within the Brown County Reforestation Camp, features 1,600 acres of trails, trout ponds and animal exhibits. The Wisconsin Trails exhibit features bears, endangered red pandas, lynxes, foxes and game birds. The Prairie Grasslands Area is home to prairie dogs, buffaloes, elk, pronghorns and swans. The International Trail section features giraffes in a hand-feeding interactive exhibit as well as lions, snow monkeys, albino alligators and penguins. A children's area offers the opportunity to feed goats, llamas and zebu. **Time:** Allow 1 hour, 30 minutes minimum. **Hours:** Daily 9-6 (also Wed. 6 p.m.-8 p.m.), June-Aug.; daily 9-6, Apr.-May and Sept.-Oct.; daily 9-4, rest of year. **Cost:** $5; $3 (ages 3-15 and 62+); $15 (family). **Phone:** (920) 434-7841. 🍴

SUN PRAIRIE (H-6) pop. 20,369, elev. 958′

In a farmhouse on a dairy farm on the outskirts of Sun Prairie, artist Georgia Totto O'Keeffe was born Nov. 15, 1887; her family lived here until 1902 when they moved to Virginia. A historical marker is located at the site of the O'Keeffe's home at Town Hall Road and CR T.

The roar of midget auto racing at Angell Park Speedway announces the arrival of summer. The Midget Auto Racing Hall of Fame also is located at the speedway; phone (608) 837-5252.

Sun Prairie Chamber of Commerce: 109 E. Main St., Sun Prairie, WI 53590. **Phone:** (608) 837-4547 or (800) 400-6162.

SUPERIOR (A-2) pop. 27,368, elev. 638′

By the millions of tons, ore, grain and coal pour through the great port at Superior-Duluth. This excellent deepwater harbor at the head of Lake Superior ranks among the nation's leading ports in tonnage. Along the 28 miles of shoreline in Superior are shipyards, grain elevators, many heavy industries and some of the world's largest docks.

Accessible from the mainland via US 2/53, Barker's Island combines a 420-slip marina, a hotel, an 18-hole miniature golf course, playground, 5-mile paved recreation trail, picnic area, beach, fishing pier, outdoor performance pavilion and the SS *Meteor* Maritime Museum *(see attraction listing).* Also available are a public boat launch, sailing lessons and charters for fishing and sailing. Phone (715) 392-2773 or (800) 942-5313.

The campus of the University of Wisconsin-Superior and a number of parks are part of the municipal geography. Billings Park, at the west end of 21st Street, includes many lagoons and gardens.

Scenic Amnicon Falls highlights nearby Amnicon Falls State Park. Pattison State Park, south of the city, offers varied summer and winter recreation and is home to Big Manitou Falls, the highest waterfall in the state at 165 feet. Both parks feature year-round camping. *See Recreation Chart and the AAA Great Lakes CampBook.*

Superior also boasts one of the largest municipal forests in the country. The 4,400-acre Superior Municipal Forest offers 17 miles of trails for cross-country skiing and hiking. The Wild Rivers State Trail and the Tri-County Corridor are both multi-use recreation trails available year-round and are part of the more than 300 miles of seasonal all-terrain vehicle and snowmobile trails in Douglas County.

Superior/Douglas County Visitors Center: 205 Belknap St., Superior, WI 54880. **Phone:** (715) 392-2773 or (800) 942-5313.

FAIRLAWN MANSION is off US 2/53 to 906 E. 2nd St. The 42-room mansion overlooking Lake Superior was built in 1890 as the family home for lumber and mining baron Martin Pattison and his wife Grace. Fairlawn recalls the elegance and prosperity of Superior's early boomtown days as well as the mansion's unique history as the Superior Children's Home and Refuge 1920-62.

The first-floor rooms have been restored, revealing the lavish use of carved wood, marble, silver trim, brass, English tile and Victorian paintings. A permanent children's home exhibit is housed on the museum's third floor.

Time: Allow 1 hour minimum. **Hours:** Guided tours begin on the hour Mon.-Sat. 9-5, Sun. 11-5, mid-May through Dec. 31; Sun.-Thurs. noon-4, Fri.-Sat. 10-4, rest of year. The mansion closes at times for private events. Last tour begins 1 hour before closing. Closed Jan. 1, Easter, Thanksgiving and Dec. 25. Phone ahead to confirm schedule. **Cost:** Fee $8; $6.50 (ages 6-18 and 63+). **Phone:** (715) 394-5712.

THE OLD FIREHOUSE AND POLICE MUSEUM is at 402 23rd Ave. Housed in an 1898 firehouse known as Station No. 4, the museum contains exhibits pertaining to firefighting and the police. Photographs and artifacts provide details about the daily life of firefighters and police officers, local fire department history and changes in technology. A 1906 horse-drawn steam pumper, a 1944 Mack fire engine and a 1919 ladder truck are on display. **Hours:** Thurs.-Sat. 10-5, Sun. noon-5, mid-May through Aug. 31; Sat. 10-5, Sun. 11-5, Sept. 1 to mid-Oct. **Cost:** Free. **Phone:** (715) 394-5712.

SAVE **RICHARD I. BONG VETERANS HISTORICAL CENTER** is at 305 Harbor View Pkwy. The center honors those who participated in World War II and later conflicts both at home and on the front lines. Named for America's Ace of Aces and Medal of Honor recipient, Maj. Richard Bong, the center is located in Bong's birth city. Items on display include a rare 1945 P-38 *Lightning* fighter aircraft as well as uniforms, weapons and accoutrements from the center's collection of more than 6,000 artifacts. **Hours:** Mon.-Sat. 9-5, Sun. noon-5, mid-May to mid-Oct.; Tues.-Sat. 9-5, rest of year. Closed Jan. 1, Easter, Thanksgiving and Dec. 25. **Cost:** $9; $8 (age 65+ and students with ID); $6 (ages 6-12). **Phone:** (715) 392-7151 or (888) 816-9944.

SS *METEOR* **MARITIME MUSEUM** is on US 2/53 on Barker's Island. The last remaining whaleback ship, a type of vessel that was innovative in the late 19th century, the *Meteor* was launched from Superior in 1896, and for the next 73 years it sailed the Great Lakes with cargoes of iron ore, oil, grain and automobiles. **Tours:** Guided tours are available. **Hours:** Mon.-Sat. 9-5, Sun. 11-5, mid-May to mid-Oct. **Cost:** Tour $6; $5 (ages 6-18 and 63+). Exhibit area only $4. **Phone:** (715) 394-5712.

TOMAH (G-4) pop. 8,419, elev. 980'

Tomah is the crossroads for west-central Wisconsin, midway between Minnesota's Twin Cities and Milwaukee, and is where I-90/I-94 separates into two distinct highways. In the spring of 1856, Robert E. Gillett and his son, Robert A. Gillett, began planning the city they were to lay out on this site. Legend had it that years before the great Indian Chief Tomah had built a council house near the creek, and the Menomonee and the Winnebago had met there in peace. The Gilletts decided to name the town after this man of strong character and high ideals.

Frank King, the creator of the innovative "Gasoline Alley" cartoon strip grew up in Tomah but later moved to the Chicago area to work for the Chicago Tribune. First published in 1919, "Gasoline Alley" characters and locales were drawn from King's youth in Tomah and reflected life in a small American town. The most notable innovation was that the characters aged over the life of the strip.

Tomah Convention & Visitor Bureau: 901 Kilbourn Ave., P.O. Box 625, Tomah, WI 54660. **Phone:** (608) 372-2166 or (800) 948-6624.

TOMAHAWK (D-5) pop. 3,770, elev. 1,450'

On Lake Mohawksin near the confluence of three rivers—the Tomahawk, Somo and Wisconsin—the city of Tomahawk developed as a lumber town after the first mill was built in 1888. Today its location makes it a popular all-year North Woods retreat. Game fish, deer and small game are abundant, and eleven local parks provide opportunities for picnicking and other outdoor activities. The Hiawatha Trail, a 6.6-mile bicycle, hiking and snowmobile trail, begins in Tomahawk and extends northward to Lake Nokomis.

Water ski shows are held 3 nights a week Memorial Day through Labor Day at Kwahamot Bay. Winter sports activities include snowmobiling, cross-country skiing, ice skating and ice fishing.

Tomahawk Regional Chamber of Commerce: 208 N. 4th St., P.O. Box 412, Tomahawk, WI 54487. **Phone:** (715) 453-5334 or (800) 569-2160.

TURTLE LAKE (D-2) pop. 1,065, elev. 1,260'

GAMBLING ESTABLISHMENTS
• **St. Croix Casino** is at 777 US 8, near jct. US 63. **Hours:** Daily 24 hours. **Phone:** (800) 846-8946.

TWO RIVERS (F-8) pop. 12,639, elev. 587'

As it has been since the 1830s, the harbor at Two Rivers is the home of an important commercial fishing fleet. Light, diversified industry augments the economy. Point Beach State Forest (*see Recreation Chart and the AAA Great Lakes CampBook*) lies along Lake Michigan north of town.

Woodland Dunes Nature Center, west off SR 310 at 3000 Hawthorne Ave., is a 1,200-acre wildlife preserve featuring woodland and meadow habitats with walking trails, nature displays and a butterfly garden; phone (920) 793-4007.

HAMILTON WOOD TYPE AND PRINTING MUSEUM is at 1619 Jefferson St. Housed in a 1926 Hamilton factory, this museum includes what is reputed to be the world's largest collection of wood

type and wood type patterns. It also contains 19th-
and 20th-century printing equipment, much of which
works and is used in demonstrations. Exhibits include hand-operated printing presses, artisan tools;
cutting patterns and rare type specimen catalogs.

Time: Allow 30 minutes minimum. **Hours:**
Tues.-Sat. 9-5, Sun. 1-5, Apr.-Oct.; Tues.-Sat. 10-4,
rest of year. Closed Dec. 25. **Cost:** Free. **Phone:**
(920) 794-6272.

POINT BEACH ENERGY CENTER is 10 mi. n. of
Two Rivers, just e. of SR 42, at 6400 Nuclear Rd.
Hands-on displays reveal facts about electrical
power generation, the history of electricity, nuclear
fission and energy, fossil fuels and renewable
sources. An interactive display allows guests to generate electricity. View the inside of a simulated
nuclear reactor while learning how it works. An
eight-foot-tall Jacob's Ladder is on display. **Time:**
Allow 1 hour minimum. **Hours:** Tues.-Sat. 9:30-4.
Closed major holidays. Phone ahead to confirm
schedule. **Cost:** Free. **Phone:** (920) 755-6400 or
(800) 880-8463.

VIROQUA (G-4) pop. 4,335, elev. 1,280′

Following the initial wave of Eastern settlers,
Norwegian immigrants successfully introduced to-
bacco farming and dairying into the region around
Viroqua. Arriving by covered wagon in 1853 was
Jeremiah McLain Rusk, who served in Congress for
6 years and as governor for three successive terms.

VERNON COUNTY HISTORICAL MUSEUM is at
410 S. Center Ave. Housed in a former teachers college built in 1919, the museum depicts county history through displays about pioneer farming, Civil
War history and American Indians. A genealogy library is available. Guided tours are available by appointment. **Hours:** Mon.-Sat. noon-4, May 15-Sept.
15; Tues.-Thurs. noon-4, rest of year. Closed major
holidays. **Cost:** Donations. **Phone:** (608) 637-7396.

WARRENS (F-4) pop. 286, elev. 1,024′

WISCONSIN CRANBERRY DISCOVERY CENTER
is in the historic Union Cranberry Warehouse at 204
Main St. Hands-on exhibits, a 6-minute videotape
and other displays describe how cranberries are cultivated and harvested, as well as the industry's history. Guests can sample various products. **Hours:**
Daily 9-5, Aug.-Oct.; Mon.-Sat. 10-4, May-July and
Nov.-Dec. Hours may vary. Phone ahead to confirm
schedule. **Cost:** $4; $3.50 (ages 65+); $3 (ages
6-12). **Phone:** (608) 378-4878. 🎟

WASHINGTON ISLAND—
see Door County p. 143.

WATERFORD (I-8) pop. 4,048, elev. 949′

GREEN MEADOWS PETTING FARM is 3 mi. w.
on SR 20. This working farm has more than 300
farm animals. Self-guiding tours include tractor-
drawn hay rides, pony rides, a petting farm, milking

demonstrations followed by hands-on experience,
and, in October, pumpkin picking. **Hours:** Daily
10-3, late Sept.-Oct. 31; Tues.-Fri. 10-1, Sat. 10-2,
May-Aug. Phone ahead to confirm schedule. **Cost:**
$12; $10 (ages 65+); free (ages 0-1). **Phone:** (262)
534-2891.

WATERTOWN (H-6) pop. 21,598, elev. 825′

Watertown was founded in the 1830s when settlers from New England harnessed the rapids of the
Rock River to produce power for sawmills, wagon
works and other factories. By the early 1900s, the
mainly agricultural area had changed to an industrial
one. Many of the town's most influential citizens
were German intellectuals fleeing the political situation in their fatherland after an 1848 revolution. A
wave of Irish immigrants in the latter 1800s also
helped shape the community.

Carl Schurz, an early German settler, entered local politics on the new Republican ticket and ultimately became minister to Spain under President
Abraham Lincoln. It is his wife, however, who is re-
membered: While living in Watertown in 1856, Mar-
garethe Meyer established what is considered to be
the nation's first kindergarten. She was a student of
Fredrich Froebel, the renowned German pioneer of
infant education.

Watertown Area Chamber of Commerce: 519
E. Main St., Watertown, WI 53094. **Phone:** (920)
261-6320.

OCTAGON HOUSE is at 919 Charles St.
This 1854 dwelling includes five floors furnished with antiques. The house was constructed with central heating and running
water, and contains a central 40-foot circular stairway. What is considered to have been the nation's
first kindergarten as certified by the Library of Congress also is on the grounds and is furnished in
period. A late 1800s barn, moved from the old
Watertown-Milwaukee Plank Road, houses farm
implements and exhibits.

Time: Allow 1 hour, 30 minutes minimum.
Hours: Daily 10-4, Memorial Day-Labor Day; 11-3,
May 1-day before Memorial Day and day after Labor Day-Oct. 31. Tours are given on the hour. **Cost:**
$7; $6 (ages 66+); $4 (ages 6-17). **Phone:** (920)
261-2796.

WAUKESHA—*see Milwaukee p. 180.*

WAUPACA (F-6) pop. 5,676, elev. 868′

The resort community of Waupaca, near a chain
of 22 lakes to the southwest, supposedly was named
after Sam Waupaca, a Potawatomi chief credited
with persuading his braves not to massacre the
white settlers in the area. The chief collapsed and
died at the conclusion of the speech.

Waupaca is a popular departure point for canoe
and launch trips through the spring-fed lakes and
along Crystal River; canoe rentals are available locally. The area's well-stocked trout streams, also

filled with pickerel, bass and small pan fish, are extremely popular with anglers.

Nearby Hartman Creek State Park *(see Recreation Chart and the AAA Great Lakes CampBook)* has developed recreational facilities, including snowmobile trails that connect with 288 miles of groomed trails and 150 miles of club trails throughout Waupaca County. This 1,417-acre park also offers seven lakes, four of which are spring-fed and off-limits to gas boat motors and are therefore ideal for kayakers and canoeists; 10 miles of hiking trails, 7 miles of bridle trails, 5 miles of off-road bicycle trails provide diversions for landlubbers. Largemouth bass, perch, bluegill, and other panfish are the catch of the day. For more information phone (715) 258-2372.

Near the property of The Red Mill, 3 miles south on CR K, are the quaint Chapel in the Woods and, spanning the Crystal River, one of the two surviving covered bridges in Wisconsin *(see also Cedarburg p. 177)*. The old mill, built in 1855, has a 24-foot waterwheel, one of the largest in America. Friday night band concerts are performed in the summer in the Gay '90s bandstand in City Square.

Waupaca Area Chamber of Commerce: 221 S. Main St., Waupaca, WI 54981. **Phone:** (715) 258-7343 or (888) 417-4040.

CHIEF WAUPACA **STERNWHEELER CRUISE** is at Clear Water Harbor, 3.7 mi. s.w. of US 10 at N2757 CR QQ. Narrated 90-minute cruises travel the Waupaca Chain o' Lakes. Brunch cruises also are available. **Hours:** Cruises depart daily at 11:30, 1, 2:30 and 4, Memorial Day weekend-Labor Day; Sat.-Sun. at 1, weekend after Labor Day through mid-Oct. Phone ahead to confirm schedule. **Cost:** Sightseeing fare $9.95; $6.50 (ages 3-12). Rates may vary; phone ahead. **Phone:** (715) 258-2866.

WAUPUN (G-7) pop. 10,718, elev. 894'

Known as the "City of Sculpture," Waupun is home to an outdoor sculpture gallery with pieces located throughout the city in parks or parklike settings. Statues that have been presented to the city by local industrialist Clarence Shaler include the first bronze casting of James Earl Fraser's "End of the Trail," given to the city in 1929. "The Recording Angel," by Lorado Taft, stands in the Forest Mound Cemetery.

Shaler himself was a sculptor; some of his works include "Dawn of Day" on the City Hall terrace, "The Pioneers" in Wilcox Park and "Doe and Fawn" at Rock River Country Club. Others include "Who Sows Believes in God" and "The Citadel" as well as two of his other sculptures found on the campus of Ripon College in Ripon *(see place listing p. 190)*.

Waupun Chamber of Commerce: 324 E. Main St., Waupun, WI 53963. **Phone:** (920) 324-3491.

HORICON MARSH, entered e. on SR 49, occupies 32,000 acres of wetlands and uplands. During the annual spring and fall migrations more than one million Canada geese travel through the marsh. As many as 200,000 geese can be seen at a time along with many other bird species who use the marsh as a stopover. Mallards, redheads, ruddy ducks and blue-wing teals nest during the summer; egrets, herons, muskrats and deer also are common.

A self-guiding auto tour winds through 3.2 miles of the national refuge; three hiking trails and a floating boardwalk are accessible from the route. Maps are available at the refuge visitor center on County Route Z. **Hours:** Hiking trails open dawn-dusk. **Cost:** Free. **Phone:** (920) 387-2658 or (920) 387-7860.

MARSH HAVEN NATURE CENTER is adjacent to the Horicon Marsh on SR 49. A 30-foot-tall observation tower, theater, wildlife dioramas, art exhibits and a display of mounted birds are housed at the center, which offers information about American Indian history, glaciers and area wildlife. The Wild Goose Recreation Trail runs adjacent to the center. **Hours:** Mon.-Fri. noon-4, Sat.-Sun. and holidays 9-5, mid-Apr. to mid-Nov. **Cost:** $2; $1 (ages 0-12). **Phone:** (920) 324-5818. 🅰️

WAUSAU (E-5) pop. 38,426, elev. 1,204'

No longer considered far away (Wausau means "far away place"), Wausau ranks among the state's major industrial centers. This busy Wisconsin Valley city began as a sawmill settlement called Big Bull Falls. After the timber supply was depleted, farming and diversified manufacturing sustained the economy. Marathon County continues to be one of the nation's leading producers of cheddar cheese and ginseng.

Glimpses of the town's past can be seen in the Andrew Warren Historic District, a 10-block area of Wausau that preserves more than 60 historic buildings.

Wausau/Central Wisconsin Convention & Visitors Bureau: 219 Jefferson St., Wausau, WI 54403. **Phone:** (715) 355-8788 or (888) 948-4748.

Shopping areas: Cedar Creek Mall, US 51 exit 185, offers outlet shopping. Wausau Center, 3rd and Washington streets, features more than 50 stores, including JCPenney, Sears and Younkers.

DELLS OF THE EAU CLAIRE PARK— *see Aniwa p. 129.*

MARATHON COUNTY HISTORICAL MUSEUM is at 403 and 410 McIndoe St. The Yawkey House Museum preserves the 1900 neoclassical house of Cyrus Yawkey, a wealthy lumberman. Ionic columns and elaborate door and window frames mark the entrance. The house is furnished and painted in authentic 1910 colors, and the basement contains a model railroad display. The Woodson History Center across the street features a library and exhibit area.

Hours: Open Tues.-Thurs. 9-4:30, Sat.-Sun. 1-4:30. Tours are given on the hour Tues.-Thurs.

Last tour begins at 3. Closed major holidays. **Cost:** $7 for Yawkey house; $6 (ages 65+); $5 (ages 6-17). **Phone:** (715) 842-5750.

RIB MOUNTAIN STATE PARK is near the jct. US 51 and CR N. Rising to 1,940 feet, Rib Mountain is one of the highest points in Wisconsin. This 1,600-acre park has hiking trails, an observation tower and two observation decks offering a view of the scenic Wisconsin River valley, camping sites, a 170-seat amphitheater and one of the Midwest's finest ski areas. *See Recreation Chart and the AAA Great Lakes CampBook.*

Note: The campground may be closed in 2011; phone ahead to verify reopening date. **Hours:** Open daily 6 a.m.-11 p.m. **Cost:** Day-use fee (per private vehicle) $10; $7 (state residents); $3 (resident seniors ages 65+). Annual permit $35; $25 (state residents); $10 (resident seniors ages 65+). **Phone:** (715) 842-2522.

WOODSON ART MUSEUM is at jct. Franklin and 12th sts. at 700 N. 12th St. Housed in a Tudor-style building, the museum presents changing exhibitions by national and international artists. Birds in Art, presented each fall, is recognized as one of the finest exhibitions of bird paintings and sculpture in the world. Permanent collection highlights include bird-themed paintings and sculptures and decorative arts.

The 1.5-acre Sculpture Garden and lawns are the settings for bronze and stone sculpture. **Time:** Allow 1 hour minimum. **Hours:** Tues.-Fri. 9-4, Sat.-Sun. noon-5. Closed major holidays. **Cost:** Free. **Phone:** (715) 845-7010.

RECREATIONAL ACTIVITIES
Skiing and Snowboarding
- **Granite Peak Ski Area** 3605 North Mountain Rd., P.O. Box 5010 Wausau, WI 54402-5010. **Hours:** Mon.-Thurs. 10-4 (also Tues.-Thurs. 4-9), Fri.-Sat. 9-9, Sun. 9-4, Thanksgiving-early April. **Phone:** (715) 845-2846.

WEST BEND—*see Milwaukee p. 180.*

WEST SALEM (G-3) pop. 4,540, elev. 746'

When the railroad was laid a mile south of Neshonoc in 1858, the village's population of Easterners and Norwegians packed up and moved to West Salem near the tracks. Thomas Leonard, West Salem's founder, had offered the railroad free land if it would build a station in West Salem rather than in one of the neighboring towns. The railroad accepted Leonard's offer, ensuring the town's growth. Historic Salem, 99 Jefferson St., is Leonard's 1859 home.

This farm trade center became best known for its creamery, capable of producing a million pounds of butter annually. Emerging from this rural environment was one of Wisconsin's foremost authors, Hamlin Garland, born here in 1860. Deeply influenced by his childhood on the frontier, Garland set his autobiographical "Middle Border" books and some dozen short stories in the coulee area around La Crosse.

HAMLIN GARLAND HOMESTEAD is at 357 W. Garland St. The house, purchased by Garland in 1893 as a residence for his mother, has been restored as a memorial to this winner of a 1922 Pulitzer Prize. Of particular note is the upstairs study where Garland did much of his writing. **Time:** Allow 30 minutes minimum. **Hours:** Guided tours Mon.-Sat. 10-4:30, Sun. 1-4:30, Memorial Day weekend-Labor Day; by appointment rest of year. **Cost:** Admission $1; 50c (ages 6-18); $2.50 (family). **Phone:** (608) 786-1399 or (608) 786-1675.

PALMER-GULLICKSON OCTAGON HOUSE is at 360 N. Leonard St. Built in 1856, this eight-sided house displays original Victorian furnishings. **Time:** Allow 30 minutes minimum. **Hours:** Guided tours Mon.-Sat. 10-4:30, Sun. 1-4:30, Memorial Day weekend-Labor Day; by appointment rest of year. **Cost:** $1; 50c (ages 6-18); $2.50 (family). **Phone:** (608) 786-1675 or (608) 786-1399.

WILMOT (I-8) elev. 750'

RECREATIONAL ACTIVITIES
Skiing and Snowboarding
- **Wilmot Mountain Ski & Snowboard Area** .5 mi. s. on CR W to entrance on the e. side. Write P.O. Box 177, Wilmot WI 53192. **Hours:** Daily 8 a.m.-11 p.m., late Nov. through mid-Mar. **Phone:** (262) 862-2301.

WISCONSIN DELLS (G-5)
pop. 2,418, elev. 899'

"One more time! *Please?*" You can bet that somewhere in Wisconsin Dells a boy or girl is making just such a plea for another turn on a waterslide, rollercoaster or go-cart track. There are more kid-pleasing attractions in this south central Wisconsin community than you can shake a candy apple on a stick at, and even when temperatures plummet, the summery fun continues inside the area's indoor water parks. And as if that weren't more than enough for a family vacation already, ski and acrobatic shows, dinner theaters and animal parks round out the various diversions here.

At first glance you might wonder why this small town without a skyline to speak of—unless you count the towering steel skeletons supporting the tracks and tubes of thrill rides—has lured travelers for more than a century, way before the first amusement parks were built. The answer lies along the Wisconsin River, which flows through the center of town. A catastrophic flood many thousands of years ago cut a channel (French-Canadian fur trappers called such features *dalles* or dells) through soft sandstone 150 feet deep in places, leaving behind fantastic rock formations along 15 miles of the river's length.

Complementing the imitation Greek temples, medieval castles and garish amusement park signs competing for highway-side real estate here are the dells' natural landmarks, many with names every bit as fanciful as those of the man-made attractions: Witches Gulch, Steamboat Rock and Giants Shield, to name just a few. Boat tours highlighting these picturesque sights have been a chief draw since the 1870s, and today high-speed jet boats and vintage World War II amphibious vehicles known as Ducks offer exciting alternatives to the traditional leisurely scenic cruise.

The same ice age forces that shaped the dells also created nearby Devil's Lake *(see attraction listing p. 133)*, set amid 500-foot-high bluffs in Baraboo, and tree-lined Mirror Lake in the town of Lake Delton. Both are centerpieces of state parks *(see Recreation Chart and Baraboo and Lake Delton in the AAA Great Lakes CampBook)* and both offer fun in the outdoors ranging from fishing, off-road biking, hiking, canoeing and camping in summer to cross-country skiing and snowshoeing in winter. Speaking of skiing, three downhill ski areas are within a 20-mile radius of Wisconsin Dells: Christmas Mountain Village, 6 miles west of downtown; Cascade Mountain in Portage; and Devil's Head Resort in Merrimac *(see listings p. 204, p. 187 and p. 163)*.

Offering both an abundance of scenic natural beauty and human-engineered thrills, Wisconsin Dells makes it nearly impossible for anyone to respond to "One more time?" with anything but an enthusiastic "Yes!"

Wisconsin Dells Visitor & Convention Bureau: 701 Superior St., Wisconsin Dells, WI 53965. **Phone:** (608) 254-4636 or (800) 223-3557.

Shopping

Nike, Polo/Ralph Lauren, Banana Republic, Gap and Tommy Hilfiger are just a few of the more than 60 stores that can be found at [SAVE] Tanger Outlet Center, I-90/94 exit 92 and US 12 on Gasser Rd. Sweet shops, gift boutiques and swim apparel stores line the boardwalk in the downtown shopping district.

DELLS ARMY DUCKS is off I-90 exit 92, then n. on US 12 to 1550 Wisconsin Dells Pkwy. The tour company offers scenic trips aboard open-air amphibious vehicles built during World War II. Tours begin with a short, bumpy drive through woods before splashing into the Wisconsin River's Lower Dells. Each vehicle's driver provides an often humorous narration during the 1-hour journey.

Hours: Duck rides daily 9-6, Memorial Day-Labor Day; 10-3, Apr. 1-day before Memorial Day and day after Labor Day-Oct. 31. **Cost:** Fare $25; $15 (ages 4-11). **Phone:** (608) 254-6080.

Mark Twain **Upper Dells Tour** departs from the Dells Army Ducks ticket office at 1550 Wisconsin Dells Pkwy. After a brief shuttle ride to the boat dock, passengers board the *Mark Twain* for a leisurely 1-hour, 15-minute tour through the Upper Dells of the Wisconsin River. Knowledgeable guides describe how the towering sandstone bluffs along the river were formed and point out landmarks with such whimsical names as Steamboat Rock and the Giant's Shield. **Time:** Allow 1 hour, 30 minutes minimum. **Hours:** Cruises depart daily at noon, 2 and 4, Memorial Day-Labor Day; at noon, day after Labor Day-Oct. 31. **Cost:** Fare $25; $15 (ages 4-11). **Phone:** (608) 254-6080.

DELLS BOAT TOURS depart from the center of town at the Upper Dells Dock on SR 13 (Broadway), and from the Lower Dells Dock at jct. US 12 and SR 13/16/23. The sightseeing trips offer guided tours through the Upper and Lower Dells of the Wisconsin River. The 2-hour Upper Dells tour includes sandstone cliffs, rock formations and stops at Witches Gulch and Stand Rock. The 1-hour, non-stop Lower Dells tour cruises past unusual rock formations, Hawks Bill and the Rocky Islands. Tickets are available at booths throughout the Dells area. Dells Boat Tours also offers a 50-minute Jet Boat Adventures trip that hurtles along at 40 mph.

Hours: Boats depart daily every 30-45 minutes 10-7, June-Aug.; less frequently Apr.-May and Sept.-Oct. **Cost:** Fare for 2-hour Upper Dells tour $23; $11.50 (ages 6-11). Fare for 1-hour Lower Dells tour $18.31; $9.20 (ages 6-11). Combination Upper and Lower Dells tour $30.99; $15.53 (ages 6-11). Jet boat tour $23; $11.50 (ages 6-11). **Phone:** (608) 254-8555.

H.H. BENNETT STUDIO is at 215 Broadway. Henry Hamilton Bennett is known as "the man who made Wisconsin Dells famous" thanks to his spectacular landscape photos of the Dells area in the 19th century. Photography, equipment and his restored 1875 studio explain the life and contributions of Bennett to the photography world. **Time:** Allow 1 hour minimum. **Hours:** Daily 10-8, mid-June to mid-Aug.; 10-5, May 1 to mid-June and mid-Aug. to Oct. 31. **Cost:** $7; $6 (ages 65+); $3.50 (ages 5-17); $19 (family). **Phone:** (608) 253-3523.

LOST CANYON—*see Lake Delton p. 153.*

MT. OLYMPUS WATER & THEME PARK, 1 mi. s. on US 12, is said to offer the Wisconsin Dells' largest collection of indoor and outdoor waterpark rides, roller coasters, go-karts and other amusements. Highlights include 37 slippery water slides at Zeus' Playground, Poseidon's Rage Surf Pool, six hair-raising rollercoasters, eight go-kart tracks and kid's rides. **Hours:** Outdoor parks open daily at 10, Memorial Day weekend-Labor Day. Indoor parks open year-round. Closing times and schedules may vary; phone ahead. **Cost:** $15-$40. **Phone:** (608) 254-2490.

NOAH'S ARK WATERPARK is 1.5 mi. s. on US 12 and SR 23 at 1410 Wisconsin Dells Pkwy. The 70-acre park features 49 waterslides, two endless rivers, four children's water play areas, three group amusement rides, three arcades, an 18-hole miniature golf course, bumper boats and many other attractions. **Time:** Allow 5 hours minimum. **Hours:** Daily 9-8, Memorial Day weekend-Labor Day. Phone ahead to confirm schedule. **Cost:** All-day pass $35.99; $28.79 (ages 55+ and under 47 inches tall); free (ages 0-2). Rates may vary; phone ahead. **Phone:** (608) 254-6351. 🍴 ⛱

ORIGINAL WISCONSIN DUCKS INC. is 1 mi. s. on US 12 and SR 23 to 1890 Wisconsin Dells Pkwy.

The tour includes 8.5 miles of breathtaking views of towering sandstone cliffs and wilderness trails as well as splashdowns into the Wisconsin River and Lake Delton. **Hours:** Daily 8-7, June-Aug.; 9-5 in May; 9-4 in Apr. and Sept. 1-first Sun in Nov. **Cost:** Fare $23; $11.50 (ages 6-11). **Phone:** (608) 254-8751.

RIPLEY'S BELIEVE IT OR NOT! is downtown at 115 Broadway. The museum displays strange and unusual items and relates events of the type featured in the well-known comic strip and TV show. Videos and exhibits throughout the two-story building describe items discovered by Robert L. Ripley. Visitors to the 2,500-square-foot Temple of Discovery take part in an interactive mission to retrieve rare artifacts, uncovering clues and solving puzzles along the way.

Time: Allow 1 hour minimum. **Hours:** Daily 9 a.m.-11 p.m., Memorial Day weekend-Labor Day; daily 10-5, Mar. 1-day before Memorial Day weekend and day after Labor Day-Oct. 31; Fri.-Mon. 10-5, rest of year. Phone ahead to confirm schedule. **Cost:** $12.95; $10.95 (ages 5-11). **Phone:** (608) 253-7556.

RIVERSIDE & GREAT NORTHERN RAILWAY departs from Hyde Park Station at N115 CR N. Passengers ride a 15-gauge railroad on a scenic 3-mile round trip through canyons, forests and rock cuts near the Wisconsin River dells. The steam-operated locomotive is turned by hand on a turntable twice during the trip. **Time:** Allow 1 hour minimum. **Hours:** Railroad and museum open at 9:30. Trains depart daily on the hour 10-5, Memorial Day weekend-Labor Day; Sat.-Sun. on the hour 10-4, Apr. 1-day before Memorial Day weekend and day after Labor Day-early Dec. (weather permitting). **Cost:** $12; $9 (ages 61+); $8 (ages 4-12). **Phone:** (608) 254-6367. ⛱

RIVERVIEW PARK AND WATERWORLD is .2 mi. s. on US 12. This 35-acre park offers racing vehicles such as Grand Prix cars and high-speed go-carts. Waterworld has the Hurricane water coaster, two speed slides, three curved waterslides, a rapids tube ride, a children's pool and a wave pool.

Time: Allow 4 hours minimum. **Hours:** Go-cart tracks open daily at 10 a.m., Memorial Day weekend-Labor Day; Sat.-Sun. at 10 a.m. May 1-late May and Sat. after Labor Day-early Sept. Closing times vary. Water park open daily noon-4, Memorial Day weekend-Labor Day. **Cost:** $12; $5 (ages 0-5) for unlimited all-day pass for go-carts and water park. $4 (go-cart ticket). Phone to verify schedule and prices. **Phone:** (608) 254-2608.

TIMBAVATI WILDLIFE PARK AT STORYBOOK GARDENS is at 1500 Wisconsin Dells Pkwy. The wildlife park is home to a variety of exotic animals including anteaters, kangaroos, lemurs, colobus monkeys, giraffes, zebras, tigers, white lions and a menagerie of birds. Park visitors can watch live wildlife shows and ride camels. The gardens contain

a petting zoo and life-size statues that depict nursery rhyme characters. Miniature train rides also are featured. **Hours:** Daily 9-7, May 1 to mid-Sept. **Cost:** $12.95; $9.95 (ages 2-12). **Phone:** (608) 253-2391.

TIMBER FALLS ADVENTURE PARK is at Stand Rock Rd. and Broadway at the Wisconsin River Bridge. The park features a roller coaster with 70-degree banks and 10-story drops, the Skyscraper thrill ride, a log-flume ride, bumper boats and four 18-hole miniature golf courses. **Time:** Allow 1 hour minimum. **Hours:** Daily 11 a.m.-10 p.m., May-Oct. (weather permitting). Phone ahead to confirm schedule. **Cost:** All-day pass $19.99; $18.99 (senior citizens); $14.99 (under 46 inches tall). Skyscraper thrill ride $22; $11 (with all-day pass). Miniature golf $7.75-$19.37; $5.75-$14.37 (ages 6-12). **Phone:** (608) 254-8414.

TOMMY BARTLETT EXPLORATORY is 3 mi. s. on US 12 at 560 Wisconsin Dells Pkwy N. Visitors can experience more than 150 interactive activities at this playground for the imagination, including those exploring music, puzzles, holograms, static electricity and virtual reality. Visitors also can tour an original Russian space station MIR core module as well as an exact replica of the United States' first manned spacecraft, the Mercury space capsule; operate a pint-size backhoe in the Big Dig; and, in season, ride the High-Wire SkyCycle positioned on a 1-inch cable 12 feet in the air.

Hours: Daily 9-9, Memorial Day weekend-Labor Day weekend; 10-4, rest of year. **Cost:** $12; $9.60 (ages 65+); $9 (ages 6-11). **Phone:** (608) 254-2525.

TOMMY BARTLETT SHOW is 3 mi. s. on US 12 at 560 Wisconsin Dells Pkwy N. This 90-minute live performance takes place on water, on stage and high in the sky. Visitors witness professional water skiers and daredevil entertainers from around the world as they perform wakeboard and barefooting stunts, jumps, twists, flips and spins and build a three-tier human pyramid. Performances also feature daredevil entertainers, comedy and stage acts.

Hours: In 2011 shows are daily at 4:30 and 8:30, Memorial Day weekend-Labor Day weekend. **Cost:**

$16-$23; $12.80-$19.80 (ages 65+); $9-$16 (ages 6-11); free (ages 0-5 on adult lap). Upgraded seating is available. **Phone:** (608) 254-2525.

WISCONSIN DEER PARK is 1 mi. s. on US 12 at 583 Wisconsin Dells Pkwy. This 28-acre wildlife area is home to more than 100 deer of many varieties. Visitors may feed and pet the deer. **Time:** Allow 1 hour minimum. **Hours:** Daily 9-7, Memorial Day-Labor Day; 10-4, day after Labor Day to mid-Oct. **Cost:** $12; $8 (ages 3-11). **Phone:** (608) 253-2041.

WISCONSIN OPRY—*see Baraboo p. 133.*

RECREATIONAL ACTIVITIES
Fishing

- **B & H Trout Fishing & Bait Shop** is 7 mi. n. to 3640 SR 13. **Hours:** Daily 8-dusk. **Phone:** (608) 254-7280.

- **Beaver Springs Fishing Park** is at 600 Trout Rd. **Hours:** Daily 9-7, June-Aug.; 10-5, Apr.-May and Sept.-Oct.; 10-4, rest of year. **Phone:** (608) 254-2735.

Horseback Riding

- **Beaver Springs Riding Stable** is at 615 Trout Rd. **Hours:** Daily 10-7, June-Aug.; 10-5, Apr.-May and Sept.-Oct.; 10-4, rest of year. **Phone:** (608) 254-2735.

Skiing and Snowboarding

- **Christmas Mountain Village** is at S944 Christmas Mountain Rd., Wisconsin Dells, WI 53965. **Hours:** Sat.-Sun. and holidays 10-9, Mon.-Fri. noon-9, late Nov. to early Mar. (weather permitting). **Phone:** (608) 254-3971 or (608) 253-1000.

WISCONSIN RAPIDS (F-5)
pop. 18,435, elev. 1,028′

Wisconsin Rapids, on the Wisconsin River, is in the center of the world's largest inland cranberry-producing area. Cranberry harvests take place from late September through October. Glacial Lake Cranberries offers guided tours of a cranberry marsh during harvest season; phone (715) 887-2095.

Wisconsin Rapids Municipal Zoo, 1911 Gaynor Ave., is open from Memorial Day-Labor Day; a petting zoo, playground and picnic facilities are available. Visitors can learn about area history Tuesday, Thursday and Sunday afternoons Memorial Day through Labor Day at South Wood County Historical Society Museum, 540 3rd St. S.; phone (715) 423-1580.

Wisconsin Rapids Area Convention & Visitors Bureau: 841 Goodnow Ave., Suite 103, Wisconsin Rapids, WI 54494. **Phone:** (715) 422-4650, (888) 393-9792 for tourism information or (800) 554-4484.

Self-guiding tours: Three historic walking tours in Wisconsin Rapids all have the Wisconsin River as their focal point. Brochures can be obtained from the convention and visitors bureau.

WOODRUFF (C-5) pop. 1,982, elev. 1,618′

Once a roistering settlement whose establishments provided for the pleasures of loggers in from the woods, Woodruff now caters to outdoors enthusiasts and vacationers enjoying the nearby forest and lake country. The area boasts one of the largest concentrations of freshwater lakes in the world. Old logging trails are groomed in the winter for cross-country skiing and snowmobiling, while bicyclists and hikers use them in the summer.

A unit of the Chequamegon-Nicolet National Forest *(see place listing p. 138)* and the Northern Highland-American Legion State Forest *(see Recreation Chart and the AAA Great Lakes CampBook)* flank the community.

ART OEHMCKE STATE FISH HATCHERY is .7 mi. s.e. on SR 47, then 1.5 mi. e. at 8770 CR J. Muskellunge, walleye and suckers are produced at the facility; more than 100 million fish can be hatched annually. **Time:** Allow 1 hour minimum. **Hours:** Mon.-Fri. 8-4:30, Memorial Day-Labor Day. Tours are given at 11 and 2. Closed major holidays. **Cost:** Free. **Phone:** (715) 356-5211.

Ships' Registry: The Bahamas

No matter the Disney destination,
the smiles are always the same.

Let a AAA/CAA Travel professional help you get there.

A Disney vacation can take you to the world's greatest Theme
Parks, *Walt Disney World* Resort in Florida and *Disneyland*
Resort in California, and much, much more. Chart a course for
magic on *Disney Cruise Line*, featuring fun for every member
of the family. Or immerse your family in the stories of some of
the world's greatest destinations with *Adventures by Disney*.
A brand-new way for you to travel the globe.

Whatever you choose, make sure you book
through your AAA/CAA Travel professional to
receive exclusive benefits.

Where dreams come true

DISNEYLAND® • WALT DISNEY WORLD® • DISNEY CRUISE LINE® • ADVENTURES BY DISNEY

Michigan

Windmill Island, Holland
© David R. Frazier
Danita Delimont Stock
Photography

ACME pop. 4,332

GRAND TRAVERSE RESORT & SPA

Resort
Hotel
$135-$339

Phone: (231)534-6000

Address: 100 Grand Traverse Village Blvd 49610 **Location:** On US 31, 0.5 mi n of jct SR 72. **Facility:** Extensive recreational facilities are featured at this resort, which is on spacious, manicured grounds. Smoke free premises. 590 units, some two bedrooms, three bedrooms, efficiencies, kitchens and houses. 3-17 stories, interior/exterior corridors. **Terms:** check-in 4 pm, 3 day cancellation notice-fee imposed. **Amenities:** video games (fee). **Dining:** 4 restaurants, also, Aerie, see separate listing. **Pool(s):** 2 heated outdoor, 2 heated indoor. **Activities:** saunas, whirlpools, waterslide, beach access, fishing, cross country skiing, snowmobiling, ice skating, recreation programs, hiking trails, jogging, spa, volleyball. *Fee:* charter fishing, kayaks, personal watercraft, golf-54 holes, golf equipment & instruction, 9 tennis courts (5 indoor), ski equipment, skate equipment rental, game room. **Guest Services:** valet laundry, area transportation-within 3 mi, wireless Internet. Affiliated with A Preferred Hotel. *(see ad p. 435)*

FREE high-speed Internet and airport transportation

HOLIDAY INN EXPRESS HOTEL & SUITES

Hotel
$99-$239

Phone: (231)938-2600

Address: 3536 Mount Hope Rd 49610 **Location:** Jct US 31 and SR 72, 0.5 mi sw. **Facility:** Smoke free premises. 81 units. 3 stories, interior corridors. **Amenities:** *Some:* high-speed Internet. **Pool(s):** heated indoor. **Activities:** whirlpool, exercise room. **Guest Services:** coin laundry, wireless Internet. *(see ad p. 433)*

SLEEP INN & SUITES

Hotel
$45-$200

Phone: (231)938-7000

Address: 5520 US 31 N 49610 **Location:** Jct US 31 and SR 72, 0.5 mi sw. Opposite the bay. **Facility:** Smoke free premises. 74 units. 3 stories, interior corridors. **Terms:** check-in 4 pm, cancellation fee imposed. **Amenities:** safes (fee). **Pool(s):** heated indoor. **Activities:** whirlpool, exercise room. **Guest Services:** coin laundry, wireless Internet. **Free Special Amenities:** expanded continental breakfast and high-speed Internet.

—— WHERE TO DINE ——

AERIE

American
$19-$34

Phone: 231/534-6000

The busy restaurant is popular for its fantastic, 16th-floor view of the bay and its surroundings. Such dishes as rack of lamb are well-presented and tasty. Utilizing fresh ingredients, the menu represents regional specialties. **Bar:** full bar. **Reservations:** suggested. **Hours:** 6 pm-10 pm. **Address:** 100 Grand Traverse Village Blvd 49610 **Location:** On US 31, 0.5 mi n of jct SR 72; in Grand Traverse Resort & Spa.

TRAVINO TRAVERSE WINE & GRILLE

American
$8-$23

Phone: 231/938-9496

The wine list includes a number of local wines in addition to other domestic and international selections. The menu features salads, tapas, grilled steaks and fish prepared in the Old World style. **Bar:** full bar. **Hours:** 11 am-10 pm, Fri & Sat-11 pm. Closed: 11/24, 12/25. **Address:** 4341 M-72 E 49690 **Location:** On SR 72, 0.5 mi e of US 31.

ADRIAN pop. 21,574

CARLTON LODGE

Hotel
Rates not provided

Phone: 517/263-7000

Address: 1629 W Maumee St 49221 **Location:** Jct US 223 and SR 52, 3 mi w on US 223. **Facility:** Smoke free premises. 98 units. 2 stories (no elevator), interior corridors. **Amenities:** safes (fee). **Pool(s):** heated indoor/outdoor. **Activities:** exercise room. **Guest Services:** valet laundry, wireless Internet.

HOLIDAY INN EXPRESS

Hotel
$114-$119

Phone: (517)265-5700

Address: 1077 W US 223 49221 **Location:** Jct US 223 and SR 52, just w. **Facility:** Smoke free premises. 60 units. 3 stories, interior corridors. **Terms:** cancellation fee imposed. **Pool(s):** heated indoor. **Activities:** exercise room. **Guest Services:** valet laundry, wireless Internet.

SUPER 8

Hotel
$76-$248

Phone: (517)265-8888

Address: 1091 W US 223 49221 **Location:** Jct US 223 and SR 52, just w. **Facility:** Smoke free premises. 51 units. 2 stories (no elevator), interior corridors. **Guest Services:** valet laundry, wireless Internet.

ALANSON pop. 700

CROOKED RIVER LODGE

Hotel
$80-$295

Phone: (231)548-5000

Address: 6845 US 31 49706 **Location:** On US 31, just n. **Facility:** Smoke free premises. 40 units, some two bedrooms and efficiencies. 3 stories, interior corridors. **Parking:** winter plug-ins. **Terms:** 2 night minimum stay - seasonal and/or weekends. **Pool(s):** heated indoor. **Activities:** whirlpool, snowmobiling. **Guest Services:** wireless Internet.

ALGONAC pop. 4,613

LINDA'S LIGHTHOUSE INN

Bed & Breakfast
$95-$135

Phone: (810)794-2992

Address: 5965 Pointe Tremble Rd (SR 29) 48001 **Location:** I-94, exit 243 (23 Mile Rd), 14.3 mi e. **Facility:** Smoke free premises. 4 units. 2 stories (no elevator), interior corridors. **Terms:** open 5/1-10/31, check-in 4 pm, 1-2 night minimum stay - seasonal and/or weekends, 14 day cancellation notice-fee imposed. **Activities:** whirlpool, boat dock, fishing, croquet, bicycles. **Guest Services:** wireless Internet.

ALLEGAN pop. 4,050

CASTLE IN THE COUNTRY B & B INN

Historic Bed
& Breakfast
$139-$269

Phone: 269/673-8054

Address: 340 M-40 S 49010 **Location:** On SR 40 S, 6 mi s. Located in a quiet rural area. **Facility:** Most rooms at this 1906 Queen Anne-style home on 5 farmland acres have Italian-tile fireplaces and whirlpool tubs. Pets are only accepted in one room. Designated smoking area. 10 units. 3 stories (no elevator), interior corridors. **Terms:** check-in 4 pm, 2-3 night minimum stay - weekends, age restrictions may apply, 7 day cancellation notice-fee imposed. **Activities:** paddleboats, kayaks, snowshoes, hiking trails, spa. **Guest Services:** wireless Internet.

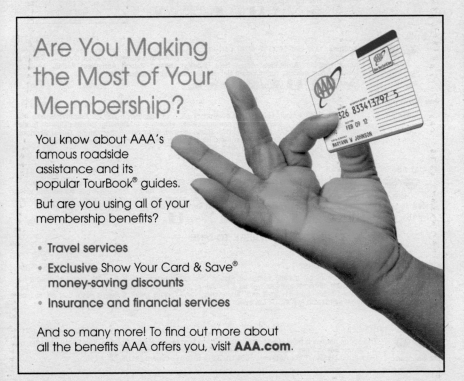

ALLENDALE pop. 11,555

SLEEP INN & SUITES

◆◆ ◆◆
Hotel
$74-$129

Phone: (616)892-8000

Address: 4869 Becker Dr 49401 **Location:** I-96, exit 16, 6 mi s, then 2.5 mi e on SR 45. Opposite Grand Valley State University. **Facility:** Smoke free premises. 60 units. 3 stories, interior corridors. **Parking:** winter plug-ins. **Terms:** cancellation fee imposed. **Amenities:** high-speed Internet, safes (fee). **Pool(s):** heated indoor. **Activities:** bicycle trails, exercise room. **Guest Services:** valet and coin laundry, wireless Internet.

ALLEN PARK —See Detroit p. 268.

ALMA pop. 9,275

TRIANGLE MOTEL

◆◆
Motel
$45-$50

Phone: 989/463-2296

Address: 131 W Lincoln Rd 48801 **Location:** US 127, exit 123 (Lincoln Rd) northbound; exit 124 (State Rd) southbound, just w on US business route 127. **Facility:** Smoke free premises. 10 units. 1 story, exterior corridors. *Bath:* shower only. **Guest Services:** wireless Internet. **Free Special Amenities: local telephone calls and high-speed Internet.**

ALPENA pop. 11,304

40 WINKS MOTEL

◆
Motel
$49-$69 4/1-10/15
$39-$49 10/16-4/30

Phone: 989/354-5622

Address: 1021 State St 49707 **Location:** 1 mi s on US 23. Opposite Lake Huron public beach. **Facility:** Smoke free premises. 15 units. 1 story, exterior corridors. **Terms:** 3 day cancellation notice. **Guest Services:** wireless Internet.

BEST WESTERN OF ALPENA

◆◆ ◆◆
Motel
$79-$92

Phone: (989)356-9087

Address: 1286 Hwy M-32 W 49707 **Location:** 2.3 mi w of jct US 23. **Facility:** Smoke free premises. 40 units. 1-2 stories (no elevator), interior/exterior corridors. **Parking:** winter plug-ins. **Amenities:** *Some:* high-speed Internet. **Pool(s):** heated indoor. **Activities:** whirlpool, picnic area with gas grill, playground, limited exercise equipment. **Guest Services:** coin laundry, wireless Internet. **Free Special Amenities: expanded continental breakfast and high-speed Internet.**

AAA Benefit:
Members save up to 20%, plus 10% bonus points with free rewards program.

DAYS INN

◆◆
Hotel
$67-$108

Phone: (989)356-6118

Address: 1496 Hwy M-32 W 49707 **Location:** 2.5 mi w of jct US 23. **Facility:** Smoke free premises. 77 units, some two bedrooms and efficiencies. 1-2 stories (no elevator), interior corridors. **Parking:** winter plug-ins. **Amenities:** safes (fee). **Pool(s):** heated indoor. **Activities:** sauna, whirlpool, snowmobiling, exercise room. **Guest Services:** coin laundry, wireless Internet.

DEW DROP INN

◆
Motel
$45-$65

Phone: 989/356-4414

Address: 2469 French Rd 49707 **Location:** 1 mi n of hospital on US 23. **Facility:** Smoke free premises. 14 units. 1 story, exterior corridors. *Bath:* shower only. **Parking:** winter plug-ins. **Terms:** office hours 8 am-11 pm. **Amenities:** high-speed Internet. **Activities:** snowmobiling. **Guest Services:** wireless Internet. **Free Special Amenities: local telephone calls and high-speed Internet.**

HOLIDAY INN

◆◆ ◆◆
Hotel
$109-$119 5/25-4/30
$99-$109 4/1-5/24

Phone: (989)356-2151

Address: 1000 Hwy 23 N 49707 **Location:** On US 23, 1 mi n. Located close to hospital. **Facility:** 148 units. 2 stories, interior corridors. **Parking:** winter plug-ins. **Terms:** video games (fee). **Pool(s):** heated indoor. **Activities:** sauna, whirlpool, putting green, indoor recreation area, exercise room. *Fee:* game room. **Guest Services:** valet and coin laundry, wireless Internet.

—— WHERE TO DINE ——

JOHN A LAU SALOON & STEAKHOUSE

◆◆ ◆◆
American
$7-$27

Phone: 989/354-6898

Housed in the oldest historic saloon in Alpena, this microbrewery offers a varied menu of classic bar favorites such as hamburgers as well as a number of daily specials. **Bar:** full bar. **Hours:** 11:30 am-9 pm, Fri & Sat-10 pm, Sun 11 am-8 pm; hours may vary. Closed major holidays; also Sun off season. **Address:** 414 N 2nd Ave 49707 **Location:** In Old Town section.

TWIN ACRES - 19TH HOLE

◆◆ ◆◆
American
$6-$25

Phone: 989/356-3712

This sports bar has a family tradition of serving good food for more than 48 years. The Friday night fish fry is popular. **Bar:** full bar. **Hours:** 11 am-11 pm, Fri & Sat-midnight, Sun 2:30 pm-9:30 pm; hours may vary. Closed: 1/1, 11/24, 12/25. **Address:** 1081 US 31 N 49707 **Location:** On US 23, 1.4 mi n.

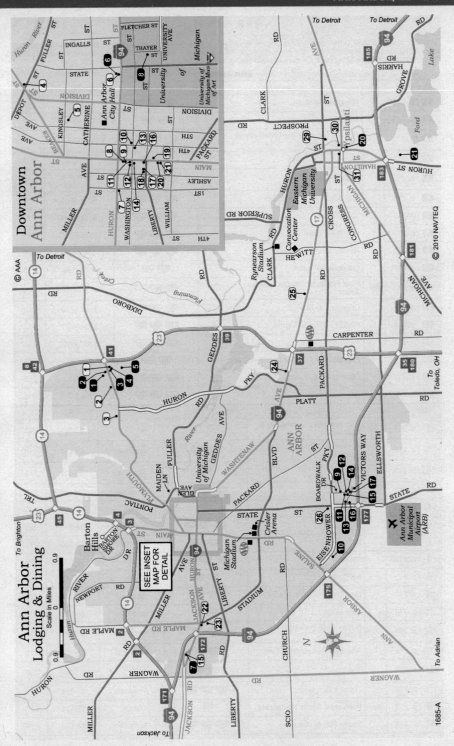

Ann Arbor
Lodging & Dining

Downtown
Ann Arbor

Ann Arbor

This index helps you "spot" where approved lodgings and restaurants are located on the corresponding detailed maps. Lodging daily rate range is for comparison only and show the property's high season. Restaurant rate range is a combination of lunch and/or dinner. Turn to the listing page for more detailed rate information and consult display ads for special promotions.

ANN ARBOR

Map Page	OA	Lodgings	Diamond Rated	High Season	Page
1 / p. 213		Hampton Inn-North	◆◆◆	$89-$269	216
2 / p. 213	AAA	**Red Roof Inn #7045**	◆◆	$60-$190 SAVE	217
3 / p. 213	AAA	**Holiday Inn Near the University of Michigan** - see ad p. 217	◆◆·◆	$139-$199 SAVE	217
4 / p. 213		Microtel Inn & Suites	◆◆	$56-$65	217
5 / p. 213		Hawthorn Suites	◆◆◆	Rates not provided	216
6 / p. 213		The Dahlmann Campus Inn	◆◆◆	$222-$245	215
7 / p. 213		Weber's Inn	◆◆◆	$195-$350	217
8 / p. 213		Bell Tower Hotel	◆◆◆	$185-$307	215
9 / p. 213		Holiday Inn Hotel & Suites	◆◆◆	$99-$149	216
10 / p. 213		Candlewood Suites	◆◆	$69-$180	215
11 / p. 213	AAA	**Four Points by Sheraton-Ann Arbor**	◆◆◆	$89-$250 SAVE	216
12 / p. 213		Courtyard by Marriott	◆◆◆	$149-$159	215
13 / p. 213		Residence Inn by Marriott	◆◆◆	$134-$171	217
14 / p. 213		Fairfield Inn by Marriott	◆◆◆	$107-$137	216
15 / p. 213		Extended Stay Deluxe Detroit-Ann Arbor	◆◆	$77-$87	216
16 / p. 213		Comfort Inn & Suites	◆◆◆	$90-$150	215
17 / p. 213		Hampton Inn-South	◆◆◆	$119-$169	216

Map Page	OA	Restaurants	Diamond Rated	Cuisine	Meal Range	Page
1 / p. 213	AAA	**Guy Hollerin's Sports Bar & Restaurant**	◆◆	American	$7-$21	219
2 / p. 213		Carson's American Bistro	◆◆	American	$8-$27	218
3 / p. 213		Flim Flam Family Restaurant & Deli	◆	American	$6-$11	218
4 / p. 213		Gandy Dancer	◆◆◆	American	$10-$32	218
5 / p. 213		Zingerman's Deli	◆	Deli	$6-$14	220
6 / p. 213		Victors	◆◆◆	American	$8-$35	220
7 / p. 213		Miki	◆◆	Japanese	$8-$26	219
8 / p. 213		Vinology	◆◆	American	$8-$28	220
9 / p. 213		Kai Garden	◆◆	Chinese	$8-$10	219
10 / p. 213		Blue Tractor BBQ & Brewery	◆◆	Barbecue	$7-$24	218
11 / p. 213		Café Zola	◆◆	American	$8-$32	218
12 / p. 213		Grizzly Peak Brewing Company	◆◆	American	$8-$20	219
13 / p. 213		Amadeus Restaurant & Cafe	◆◆	Hungarian	$6-$23	218
14 / p. 213		The Earle	◆◆	Provincial French	$15-$29	218
15 / p. 213		Weber's Restaurant	◆◆◆	American	$7-$29	220
16 / p. 213	AAA	**Parthenon Gyros Restaurant**	◆	Greek	$7-$20	219
17 / p. 213		Pacific Rim by Kana	◆◆◆	Pacific Rim	$8-$29	219

Map Page	OA	Restaurants (cont'd)	Diamond Rated	Cuisine	Meal Range	Page
⑱ / p. 213		Grange Kitchen & Bar	▽▽▽	American	$21-$33	218
⑲ / p. 213		La Dolce Vita	▽▽▽	Breads/Pastries	$6-$15	219
⑳ / p. 213		The Chop House	▽▽▽	Steak	$25-$40	218
㉑ / p. 213		Gratzi	▽▽▽	Italian	$8-$33	218
㉒ / p. 213		Zingerman's Roadhouse	▽▽	American	$12-$40	220
㉓ / p. 213		The Quarter Bistro & Tavern	▽▽▽	American	$10-$30	220
㉔ / p. 213		Paesano's Restaurant & Wine Bar	▽▽▽	Italian	$8-$35	219
㉕ / p. 213		Smokehouse Blues	▽▽	American	$7-$20	220
㉖ / p. 213		Mediterrano	▽▽▽	Mediterranean	$8-$25	219

YPSILANTI

Map Page	OA	Lodgings	Diamond Rated	High Season	Page
⑳ / p. 213		Parish House Inn	▽▽	$99-$150	445
㉑ / p. 213	ⒶⒶⒶ	**Ann Arbor Marriott Ypsilanti at Eagle Crest**	▽▽▽	$159-$169 SAVE	445

Map Page	OA	Restaurants	Diamond Rated	Cuisine	Meal Range	Page
㉙ / p. 213		Cafe Luwak	▽	Deli	$4-$6	446
㉚ / p. 213	ⒶⒶⒶ	**Haab's**	▽▽	American	$6-$27	446
㉛ / p. 213		Pub 13 Restaurant & Dueling Pianos	▽▽	American	$5-$20	446

ANN ARBOR pop. 114,024   (See map and index starting on p. 213)

BELL TOWER HOTEL
▽▽▽▽
Hotel
$185-$307 1/2-4/30
$180-$302 4/1-12/19

Phone: (734)769-3010   **8**

Address: 300 S Thayer St 48104 **Location:** Just e of downtown. Located on University of Michigan campus. **Facility:** Smoke free premises. 66 units, some two bedrooms. 3-4 stories, interior corridors. **Parking:** on-site (fee) and valet. **Terms:** open 4/1-12/19 & 1/2-4/30, check-in 4 pm. **Amenities:** high-speed Internet. *Some:* safes, honor bars. **Activities:** exercise room. **Guest Services:** valet laundry, wireless Internet.

CANDLEWOOD SUITES
▽▽▽ ▽▽▽
Extended Stay Hotel
$69-$180

Phone: (734)663-2818   **10**

Address: 701 Waymarket Way 48103 **Location:** I-94, exit 175 (Ann Arbor/Saline Rd), just e on Eisenhower Rd. **Facility:** Smoke free premises. 122 efficiencies. 3 stories, interior corridors. **Terms:** office hours 7 am-11 pm. **Amenities:** high-speed Internet. **Activities:** exercise room. **Guest Services:** complimentary and valet laundry, wireless Internet.

COMFORT INN & SUITES
▽▽▽▽
Hotel
$90-$150

Phone: (734)761-8838   **16**

Address: 3501 S State St 48108 **Location:** I-94, exit 177 (State St), just ne. **Facility:** Smoke free premises. 83 units. 3 stories, interior corridors. **Amenities:** high-speed Internet. **Pool(s):** heated indoor. **Activities:** whirlpool, exercise room. **Guest Services:** valet laundry, wireless Internet.

COURTYARD BY MARRIOTT
▽▽▽▽
Hotel
$149-$159

Phone: (734)995-5900   **12**

Address: 3205 Boardwalk St 48108 **Location:** I-94, exit 177 (State St), just n, then just e on Victors Way. **Facility:** Smoke free premises. 160 units. 4 stories, interior corridors. **Terms:** cancellation fee imposed. **Amenities:** video games (fee). **Pool(s):** heated indoor. **Activities:** whirlpool, exercise room. **Guest Services:** valet and coin laundry, wireless Internet.

> **AAA Benefit:**
> Members save a minimum 5% off the best available rate.

THE DAHLMANN CAMPUS INN
▽▽▽▽
Hotel
$222-$245

Phone: (734)769-2200   **6**

Address: 615 E Huron St 48104 **Location:** Jct E Huron and State sts. Adjacent to University of Michigan campus. **Facility:** Smoke free premises. 208 units. 15 stories, interior corridors. **Terms:** check-in 4 pm, cancellation fee imposed. **Amenities:** high-speed Internet. *Some:* safes, honor bars. **Dining:** Victors, see separate listing. **Pool(s):** outdoor. **Activities:** saunas, exercise room. **Guest Services:** valet laundry, wireless Internet.

(See map and index starting on p. 213)

EXTENDED STAY DELUXE DETROIT-ANN ARBOR

Extended Stay
Hotel
$77-$87

Phone: (734)997-7623 — **15**

Address: 3265 Boardwalk St 48108 **Location:** I-94, exit 177 (State St), just n, then just e on Victors Way. Adjacent to train tracks. **Facility:** Smoke free premises. 71 kitchen units. 3 stories, interior corridors. **Terms:** cancellation fee imposed. **Activities:** limited exercise equipment. **Guest Services:** coin laundry, wireless Internet.

FAIRFIELD INN BY MARRIOTT

Hotel
$107-$137

Phone: (734)995-5200 — **14**

Address: 3285 Boardwalk St 48108 **Location:** I-94, exit 177 (State St), just n, then just e on Victors Way. **Facility:** Smoke free premises. 110 units. 4 stories, interior corridors. **Terms:** cancellation fee imposed. **Pool(s):** heated indoor. **Activities:** whirlpool. **Guest Services:** valet laundry, wireless Internet.

AAA Benefit:
Members save a minimum 5% off the best available rate.

FOUR POINTS BY SHERATON-ANN ARBOR

Hotel
$89-$250

Phone: (734)996-0600 — **11**

Address: 3200 Boardwalk St 48108 **Location:** I-94, exit 177 (State St), just ne. **Facility:** Smoke free premises. 197 units. 6 stories, interior corridors. **Terms:** cancellation fee imposed. **Amenities:** video games (fee), high-speed Internet, safes. **Pool(s):** heated indoor/outdoor. **Activities:** sauna, whirlpool, exercise room. **Guest Services:** valet laundry, area transportation-within 10 mi, wireless Internet.

FOUR POINTS
BY SHERATON

AAA Benefit:
Members get up to 15% off, plus Starwood Preferred Guest® bonuses.

HAMPTON INN-NORTH

Hotel
$89-$269

Phone: (734)996-4444 — **1**

Address: 2300 Green Rd 48105 **Location:** US 23, exit 41 (Plymouth Rd), just nw. **Facility:** Smoke free premises. 129 units. 4 stories, interior corridors. **Terms:** 1-7 night minimum stay, cancellation fee imposed. **Pool(s):** heated indoor. **Activities:** whirlpool, in-room fitness kits, exercise room. **Guest Services:** valet and coin laundry, area transportation-within 5 mi, wireless Internet.

AAA Benefit:
Members save up to 10% everyday!

HAMPTON INN-SOUTH

Hotel
$119-$169

Phone: (734)665-5000 — **17**

Address: 925 Victors Way 48108 **Location:** I-94, exit 177 (State St), just ne. **Facility:** Smoke free premises. 149 units. 4 stories, interior corridors. **Terms:** 1-7 night minimum stay, cancellation fee imposed. **Amenities:** video games (fee). **Pool(s):** heated indoor. **Activities:** whirlpool, exercise room. **Guest Services:** valet and coin laundry, wireless Internet.

AAA Benefit:
Members save up to 10% everyday!

HAWTHORN SUITES

Hotel
Rates not provided

Phone: 734/327-0011 — **5**

Address: 3535 Green Ct 48105 **Location:** US 23, exit 41 (Plymouth Rd), just sw. **Facility:** Smoke free premises. 82 units, some two bedrooms, efficiencies and kitchens. 3 stories, interior corridors. **Pool(s):** heated indoor. **Activities:** whirlpool, barbecue grills, exercise room, sports court. **Guest Services:** valet and coin laundry, area transportation-city area, wireless Internet.

HOLIDAY INN HOTEL & SUITES

Hotel
$99-$149

Phone: (734)213-1900 — **9**

Address: 3155 Boardwalk St 48108 **Location:** I-94, exit 177 (State St), just n, then just e on Victors Way. **Facility:** Smoke free premises. 107 units. 5 stories, interior corridors. **Amenities:** high-speed Internet. **Pool(s):** heated indoor. **Activities:** whirlpool, exercise room. **Guest Services:** valet laundry, wireless Internet.

(See map and index starting on p. 213)

HOLIDAY INN NEAR THE UNIVERSITY OF MICHIGAN
Phone: (734)769-9800

Hotel
$139-$199

Address: 3600 Plymouth Rd 48105 **Location:** US 23, exit 41 (Plymouth Rd), just sw. **Facility:** Smoke free premises. 225 units. 2-5 stories, interior corridors. **Dining:** Guy Hollerin's Sports Bar & Restaurant, see separate listing. **Pool(s):** heated indoor/outdoor. **Activities:** whirlpool, 2 tennis courts, exercise room, basketball, volleyball. *Fee:* game room. **Guest Services:** valet and coin laundry, area transportation-within 10 mi, wireless Internet, beauty salon. *(see ad below)*

FREE high-speed Internet and local transportation

MICROTEL INN & SUITES
Phone: (734)997-9100

Hotel
$56-$65

Address: 3610 Plymouth Rd 48105 **Location:** US 23, exit 41 (Plymouth Rd), just sw. **Facility:** Smoke free premises. 83 units. 3 stories, interior corridors. **Terms:** cancellation fee imposed. **Guest Services:** valet laundry, area transportation-city area, wireless Internet.

RED ROOF INN #7045
Phone: (734)996-5800

Motel
$60-$190

Address: 3621 Plymouth Rd 48105 **Location:** US 23, exit 41 (Plymouth Rd), just nw. **Facility:** Smoke free premises. 108 units. 2 stories (no elevator), exterior corridors. **Amenities:** *Fee:* video games, safes. **Guest Services:** wireless Internet. **Free Special Amenities:** local telephone calls.

RESIDENCE INN BY MARRIOTT
Phone: (734)996-5666

Extended Stay
Hotel
$134-$171

Address: 800 Victors Way 48108 **Location:** I-94, exit 177 (State St), just ne. **Facility:** Smoke free premises. 114 kitchen units, some two bedrooms. 2-3 stories, interior/exterior corridors. **Terms:** cancellation fee imposed. **Amenities:** video games (fee). **Pool(s):** heated outdoor. **Activities:** whirlpool, barbecue grill, exercise room, sports court. **Guest Services:** valet and coin laundry, wireless Internet.

AAA Benefit:
Members save a minimum 5% off the best available rate.

WEBER'S INN
Phone: (734)769-2500

Hotel
$195-$350

Address: 3050 Jackson Ave 48103 **Location:** I-94, exit 172 (Jackson Ave), just n. **Facility:** Smoke free premises. 158 units. 4 stories, interior corridors. **Terms:** check-in 4 pm. **Amenities:** high-speed Internet, safes. **Dining:** restaurant, see separate listing. **Pool(s):** heated indoor. **Activities:** sauna, whirlpool, sun deck, indoor recreation area, exercise room. *Fee:* game room. **Guest Services:** valet laundry, wireless Internet.

▼ See AAA listing above ▼

(See map and index starting on p. 213)

—— WHERE TO DINE ——

AMADEUS RESTAURANT & CAFE

Hungarian
$6-$23

Phone: 734/665-8767 ⑬

This cozy, European-style restaurant features Polish and Central European cuisine, including fabulous pastry creations. The Hungarian combination plate is a fine example of a distinctive recipe prepared with care and fresh ingredients. Entertainment. **Bar:** full bar. **Hours:** 11:30 am-2:30 & 5-10 pm, Sat-11 pm, Sun 11 am-3 pm; Sunday brunch. Closed major holidays; also Mon. **Address:** 122 E Washington St 48104 **Location:** Between Main St and Fourth Ave; downtown. **Parking:** street only.

BLUE TRACTOR BBQ & BREWERY

Barbecue
$7-$24

Phone: 734/222-4095 ⑩

Country comforts meet urban chic in the surprisingly large and cool dining room of this hot local spot. The walls are lined with reclaimed barnyard timbers, adorned with grills from old tractors and huge black and white photos. The menu focuses on comfort foods, with ribs, mac and cheese and a variety of decked out burgers. In addition to a number of beers brewed on site, there also are some nice sipping whiskeys available. **Bar:** full bar. **Reservations:** required. **Hours:** 11 am-11 pm, Fri & Sat-midnight, Sun noon-10 pm. Closed major holidays. **Address:** 207 Washington St E 48104 **Location:** Between Main St and Fourth Ave; downtown. **Parking:** street only.

CAFÉ ZOLA

American
$8-$32

CALL

Phone: 734/769-2020 ⑪

Locals unwind in the trendy cafe's dining room or on the seasonal sidewalk patio over specialty teas and coffees and dishes made from organic foods and free-range meats. Omelets made from organic, free-range eggs are served daily until 4 pm. **Bar:** full bar. **Hours:** 7 am-10 pm, Fri & Sat-11 pm. Closed major holidays. **Address:** 112 W Washington St 48104 **Location:** Just w of Main St; downtown. **Parking:** street only.

CARSON'S AMERICAN BISTRO

American
$8-$27

Phone: 734/622-0537 ②

A casual dining setting with an upscale feel, the dining room has the atmosphere of a refined hunter's cabin complete with a chandelier made from antlers. Specialties here are steaks and fish, with alternatives such as pasta, chicken and burgers. **Bar:** full bar. **Hours:** 11 am-11 pm, Fri-midnight, Sat 4 pm-midnight, Sun 11:30 am-10 pm. Closed major holidays. **Address:** 2000 Commonwealth Blvd 48105 **Location:** US 23, exit 41 (Plymouth Rd), 0.5 mi e. CALL

THE CHOP HOUSE

Steak
$25-$40

Phone: 734/669-8826 ⑳

The perfect spot for that special dinner, this trendy, yet refined, restaurant offers an excellent selection of steak, seafood and poultry as well as extensive wine pairings. Patrons come here to be seen. **Bar:** full bar. **Hours:** 5 pm-10 pm, Fri & Sat-11 pm, Sun 4 pm-9 pm. Closed: 1/1, 11/24, 12/25. **Address:** 322 S Main St 48104 **Location:** Downtown. **Parking:** street only.

THE EARLE

Provincial French
$15-$29

Phone: 734/994-0211 ⑭

Provincial French and Italian cuisine are the specialties of this cellar-level restaurant. Candlelight and live jazz music fill this space with warmth and energy, serving as a popular escape from the hustle and bustle of the outside world. Entertainment. **Bar:** full bar. **Hours:** 5:30 pm-10 pm, Fri & Sat-11 pm, Sun 5 pm-9 pm. Closed major holidays. **Address:** 121 W Washington St 48104 **Location:** Just w of Main St; downtown. **Parking:** street only.

FLIM FLAM FAMILY RESTAURANT & DELI

American
$6-$11

Phone: 734/994-3036 ③

In a strip mall, the comfortable family restaurant has developed a loyal following of regulars who appreciate its extensive menu of well-prepared dishes. Enormous eclairs are a popular choice for dessert. **Hours:** 6 am-8 pm, Sun 7:30 am-3 pm. Closed major holidays. **Address:** 2707 Plymouth Rd 48105 **Location:** US 23, exit 41 (Plymouth Rd), 1 mi w; at Plymouth Mall.

GANDY DANCER

American
$10-$32

Phone: 734/769-0592 ④

Located near the University of Michigan, this restored 1886 railroad depot with its beautifully appointed dining room features stained-glass windows and red oak ceilings. The menu offers a tempting selection of fresh seafood specialties including shrimp fettuccine verde, potato-encrusted whitefish and crab-stuffed rainbow trout. **Bar:** full bar. **Reservations:** suggested. **Hours:** 11 am-10 pm, Fri-11 pm, Sat 4:30 pm-11 pm, Sun 10 am-2 & 3:30-9 pm. Closed: 12/25. **Address:** 401 Depot St 48104 **Location:** Jct State and Fuller sts. **Parking:** valet and street only. CALL

GRANGE KITCHEN & BAR

American
$21-$33

Phone: 734/995-2107 ⑱

The emphasis is on creative preparations of farm fresh foods at this small but trendy restaurant in the heart of the downtown district. Menu selections change seasonally and vary depending on local market ingredients. The chef-owner has a particular interest in making use of the whole animal, so in addition to steak, chicken and fish, dishes incorporating more unusual items such as bone marrow or pork belly are often available. House-made charcuterie is a popular specialty. **Bar:** full bar. **Hours:** 5 pm-10 pm, Fri & Sat-11 pm. Closed major holidays; also Sun. **Address:** 118 W Liberty 48104 **Location:** Between S Ashley and S Main sts; downtown. **Parking:** street only.

GRATZI

Italian
$8-$33

Phone: 734/663-6387 ㉑

Housed in a former theater space, this dramatic restaurant comes complete with bold trompe l'oeil effects and larger-than-life framed mirrors. Regional Italian cuisine, such as veal, seafood and pasta, is presented with flair. **Bar:** full bar. **Hours:** 11:30 am-9 pm, Fri & Sat-10 pm, Sun 4 pm-9 pm. Closed: 1/1, 12/25 & Easter. **Address:** 326 S Main St 48104 **Location:** Downtown. **Parking:** street only.

(See map and index starting on p. 213)

GRIZZLY PEAK BREWING COMPANY　　　　　　　　**Phone:** 734/741-7325　

American
$8-$20

Copper kettles dominate the front windows of this local microbrewery that specializes in handcrafted beers, and as much attention has been placed into the Continental menu that serves both daily specials and bar favorites. **Bar:** full bar. **Hours:** 11 am-11 pm, Fri & Sat-midnight, Sun noon-11 pm. Closed: 11/24, 12/24, 12/25. **Address:** 120 W Washington St 48104 **Location:** Downtown. **Parking:** street only.

GUY HOLLERIN'S SPORTS BAR & RESTAURANT　　　　　　**Phone:** 734/769-4323　

American
$7-$21

The vibrant and noisy dining room is a popular spot to catch the game, or simply share a plate of nachos and brews with friends. The menu focuses on pub favorites such as burgers and panini sandwiches at lunch, fish and chips, steaks and fajitas at dinner, and "anytime" bar favorites including wings, chicken fingers and cheese sticks. Friday and Saturday nights typically feature live music and drink specials. **Bar:** full bar. **Hours:** 6:30 am-10 pm, Fri-11 pm, Sat 7:30 am-11 pm, Sun 7:30 am-9 pm. **Address:** 3600 Plymouth Rd 48105 **Location:** US 23, exit 41 (Plymouth Rd), just sw; in Holiday Inn Near the University of Michigan. CALL (&M)

KAI GARDEN　　　　　　　　　　　　　　　**Phone:** 734/995-1786　

Chinese
$8-$10

Underneath the surface of this quiet and unassuming restaurant, which serves a menu of contemporary Chinese-American favorites, is the second menu. Focusing on authentic Cantonese and Taiwanese food, the "little menu," as regulars call it, offers adventurous diners such choices as fried taro with duck, shangtun chicken and pig's ear. **Bar:** full bar. **Hours:** 11 am-10 pm, Fri & Sat-11 pm, Sun noon-10 pm. Closed major holidays. **Address:** 116 S Main St 48104 **Location:** Just s of jct W Huron and S Main sts; downtown. **Parking:** street only.

LA DOLCE VITA　　　　　　　　　　　　　**Phone:** 734/669-8826　

Breads/Pastries
$6-$15

Squeezed between Gratzi and The Chop House, this after-dinner restaurant is reminiscent of a beautifully appointed living room. Overstuffed chairs, coffee tables, intimate lighting and a fireplace make for a perfect place to relax and enjoy house-made desserts and an extensive designer drink menu. A well-ventilated downstairs cigar bar is a popular hangout for aficionados. **Bar:** full bar. **Hours:** 5 pm-midnight, Fri & Sat-1 am, Sun 4 pm-10 pm. Closed major holidays. **Address:** 322 S Main St 48104 **Location:** Downtown. **Parking:** street only.

MEDITERRANO　　　　　　　　　　　　　　**Phone:** 734/332-9700　

Mediterranean
$8-$25

The theme is decidedly Greek in this cozy dining room, decorated with colorful landscapes and statues of mythological figures, while the summer patio resembles a gazebo. Such dishes as Moroccan sea bass are colorful and tasty. **Bar:** full bar. **Hours:** 11 am-10 pm, Fri-11 pm, Sat noon-11 pm, Sun noon-9 pm. Closed major holidays. **Address:** 2900 S State St 48104 **Location:** I-94, exit 177 (State St), just n; corner of State St and Eisenhower Pkwy. CALL (&M)

METZGER'S GERMAN RESTAURANT　　*Menu on AAA.com*　　　**Phone:** 734/668-8987

German
$6-$20

After enjoying a brief retirement, the owners have returned to this new location at the request of their many friends and fans. The comfy dining room features brief glimpses of local and personal history culled over the many years this restaurant has been serving fine German cuisine. **Bar:** full bar. **Hours:** 11 am-9:30 pm, Thurs-Sat to 10 pm, Sun-8 pm. Closed: 7/4, 11/24, 12/24, 12/25. **Address:** 305 N Zeeb Rd 48103 **Location:** I-94, exit 169 (Zeeb Rd); in Baxter's Plaza. CALL (&M)

MIKI　　　　　　　　　　　　　　　　　　**Phone:** 734/665-8226　

Japanese
$8-$26

The restaurant presents a menu of Japanese classics and more adventurous dishes, including sushi, sashimi and teriyaki beef and chicken. The showpiece of the subtle dining room, the sushi bar enables diners to watch their sushi being prepped and rolled. **Bar:** full bar. **Hours:** 11:30 am-2 & 5-10 pm, Fri-10:30 pm, Sat noon-2:30 & 5-10:30 pm, Sun 5 pm-9:30 pm. Closed major holidays. **Address:** 106 S First St 48104 **Location:** Jct First and Huron sts; downtown. **Parking:** street only.

PACIFIC RIM BY KANA　　　　　　　　　　　**Phone:** 734/662-9303　

Pacific Rim
$8-$29

Rather than traveling to California to experience the fusion of Asian and American ingredients with French culinary techniques, the chef/owner brings the latest trends to this warm, inviting restaurant. Among selections are firecracker prawns, Pacific Rim salmon and Malaysian barbecue ribs. **Bar:** full bar. **Hours:** 5:30 pm-11 pm, Fri & Sat-midnight, Sun 5 pm-9 pm. Closed major holidays. **Address:** 114 W Liberty St 48104 **Location:** Between S Ashley and S Main sts; downtown. **Parking:** street only.

PAESANO'S RESTAURANT & WINE BAR　　　　　　**Phone:** 734/971-0484　

Italian
$8-$35

This contemporary restaurant bustles with festive action. The menu runs the gamut of Italian specialties, sampling preparations of veal, seafood and chicken. Pasta is made in many varieties, such as lasagna and fettuccine. Salads are innovative and tasty. **Bar:** full bar. **Hours:** 11 am-10 pm, Fri-midnight, Sat noon-midnight, Sun noon-10 pm. Closed major holidays. **Address:** 3411 Washtenaw Ave 48104 **Location:** US 23, exit 37B (Washtenaw Ave), 0.3 mi w. CALL (&M)

PARTHENON GYROS RESTAURANT　　　　　　　**Phone:** 734/994-1012　

Greek
$7-$20

What college town doesn't have at least one Greek restaurant? Not to be left out, this place, decorated in the whites and blues of the Mediterranean, is downtown and just a short walk from campus. Diners will not be disappointed to find all the Greek favorites on the extensive menu, as well as a range of American standards. **Bar:** full bar. **Reservations:** required. **Hours:** 11 am-10 pm, Fri & Sat-11 pm, Sun noon-10 pm. Closed: 12/25 & Easter. **Address:** 226 S Main St 48104 **Location:** Jct Washington St; downtown. **Parking:** street only.

(See map and index starting on p. 213)

THE QUARTER BISTRO & TAVERN

Phone: 734/929-9200 (23)

American
$10-$30

A New Orleans-inspired menu features Cajun and Creole favorites including steak, chicken, pasta, crawfish, alligator and seafood entrees. Hand-painted murals, papier-mache roses and dried garlic hanging from rustic wooden beams over a semi-open kitchen provide a homey touch to the otherwise upscale, trendy bistro. **Bar:** full bar. **Hours:** 11 am-10 pm, Fri & Sat-midnight, Sun 10 am-9 pm; Sunday brunch. Closed major holidays. **Address:** 300 S Maple Rd 48103 **Location:** I-94, exit 172 (Jackson Ave), just n, then just e; in Westgate Shopping Plaza. CALL

SMOKEHOUSE BLUES

Phone: 734/434-5554 (25)

American
$7-$20

With a blues bar theme, the casual dining setting allows guests to relax while browsing a menu of Southern specialties, including slow-roasted ribs, hand-pulled pork and deep-fried okra. Sandwiches, burgers, salads and desserts are other options. **Bar:** full bar. **Hours:** 11 am-10 pm, Fri & Sat-11 pm, Sun noon-10 pm. Closed: 11/24, 12/25. **Address:** 4855 Washtenaw Ave 48108 **Location:** US 23, exit 37A (Washtenaw Ave), 1 mi e. CALL

VICTORS

Phone: 734/769-2282 (6)

American
$8-$35

The refined dining atmosphere—with its ornately framed paintings of jazz scenes and comfortable arm chairs—may seem at odds with its sports-themed name, but discussions of MSU's sporting heroes often thrive in this off-campus dining room. The menu offers modern variations of classics such as salmon with orange-ginger relish, duck with red mole, chicken with grapefruit and pink peppercorns, lobster ravioli, beef tenderloin and strip steak. Vegetarian options are also offered. **Bar:** full bar. **Hours:** 6:30 am-2 & 5-10 pm, Sat from 7 am, Sun 7 am-2 pm. Closed major holidays. **Address:** 615 E Huron St 48104 **Location:** Jct E Huron and State sts; in The Dahlmann Campus Inn.

VINOLOGY

Phone: 734/222-9841 (8)

American
$8-$28

This ultra-trendy restaurant ties earthy design elements into the celebration of wine. The wine list educates guests with icons describing the prominent features of the extensive offerings. On the menu are dishes made primarily from ingredients procured from local organic farmers. Entree options include dishes centered on organic bison or beef, and varied small plates range from quail to sweetbreads to a trio of mini-burgers with homemade ketchups. The in-house pastry chef makes desserts daily. **Bar:** full bar. **Hours:** 11 am-11 pm, Fri-midnight, Sat 4 pm-midnight, Sun 4 pm-10 pm. Closed major holidays. **Address:** 110 S Main St 48104 **Location:** Just s of jct W Huron and S Main sts; downtown. **Parking:** street only.

WEBER'S RESTAURANT

Phone: 734/665-3636 (15)

American
$7-$29

Prime rib, fresh fish, pasta and lobster are among dishes on the menu of this well-known restaurant, a local fixture since the early 1930s. Pleasing food is served in a comfortable, well-illuminated dining room. The outdoor terrace opens seasonally. Entertainment. **Bar:** full bar. **Hours:** 6:30 am-midnight, Sun 8 am-9:30 pm. Closed: 12/25. **Address:** 3050 Jackson Ave 48103 **Location:** I-94, exit 172 (Jackson Rd), just n; in Weber's Inn.

ZINGERMAN'S DELI

Phone: 734/663-3354 (5)

Deli
$6-$14

It's not unusual to see a long queue outside this hugely popular deli/gourmet grocery. A wide selection of made-to-order sandwiches are prepared using house-made bread and imported meats and cheeses. A good selection of gourmet groceries also is available. **Hours:** 7 am-10 pm. Closed: 11/24, 12/25. **Address:** 422 Detroit St 48104 **Location:** Jct Detroit and Kingsley sts; downtown. **Parking:** street only.

ZINGERMAN'S ROADHOUSE

Phone: 734/663-3663 (22)

American
$12-$40

The neon sign perched over the roof of this roadhouse-inspired restaurant says it all, but first-timers have to visit to see what it says. Hardwood floors, a sexy bar and an open kitchen area characterize the comfortable dining room, a great place to relax and enjoy everyday American cuisine prepared with a twist. The beef for burgers, which comes from a certified organic farm, is ground twice a day, while goat cheese and four-year-aged cheddar makes its way into the classic macaroni and cheese. **Bar:** full bar. **Hours:** 7 am-10 pm, Fri-11 pm, Sat 10 am-11 pm, Sun 10 am-9 pm. Closed: 5/30, 11/24, 12/25. **Address:** 2501 Jackson Ave 48103 **Location:** I-94, exit 172 (Jackson Rd), just n, then just e; in Westgate Shopping Plaza. CALL

AUBURN HILLS —See Detroit p. 268.

AU GRES pop. 1,028

ECONO LODGE INN

Phone: 989/876-4060

Hotel
Rates not provided

Address: 510 W US 23 48703 **Location:** On US 23, just w. **Facility:** Smoke free premises. 30 units. 1 story, interior corridors. **Parking:** winter plug-ins. **Pool(s):** heated indoor. **Activities:** whirlpool. **Guest Services:** coin laundry, wireless Internet.

BAD AXE pop. 3,462

ECONO LODGE INN & SUITES

Phone: 989/269-3200

Hotel
Rates not provided

Address: 898 N Van Dyke Rd 48413 **Location:** 1.3 mi n of jct SR 142 and 53 (Van Dyke Rd). **Facility:** Smoke free premises. 38 units. 2 stories (no elevator), interior corridors. **Pool(s):** heated indoor. **Activities:** whirlpool. **Fee:** game room. **Guest Services:** wireless Internet.

HOLIDAY INN EXPRESS HOTEL & SUITES

Phone: (989)269-5293

Hotel
$89-$94

Address: 55 Rapson Ln W 48413 **Location:** 1 mi n of jct SR 142 and 53 (Van Dyke Rd). **Facility:** Smoke free premises. 65 units. 2 stories, interior corridors. **Pool(s):** heated indoor. **Activities:** whirlpool, exercise room. **Fee:** game room. **Guest Services:** wireless Internet.

BARAGA pop. 1,285

BEST WESTERN BARAGA LAKESIDE INN

Phone: (906)353-7123

Hotel
$84-$94

Address: 900 US 41 S 49908 **Location:** On US 41, 0.8 mi s of SR 38. Located on shores of Keweenaw Bay. **Facility:** Smoke free premises. 68 units. 3 stories, interior corridors. **Parking:** winter plug-ins. **Amenities:** Some: high-speed Internet. **Dining:** restaurant, see separate listing. **Pool(s):** heated indoor. **Activities:** sauna, whirlpool, marina, fishing, snowmobiling, exercise room. **Guest Services:** wireless Internet. **Free Special Amenities:** local telephone calls and high-speed Internet.

AAA Benefit:
Members save up to 20%, plus 10% bonus points with free rewards program.

------ **WHERE TO DINE** ------

BEST WESTERN BARAGA LAKESIDE INN

Phone: 906/353-7123

American
$6-$21

During breakfast, lunch or dinner, patrons can enjoy the beautiful Keweenaw Bay while they eat. **Bar:** full bar. **Hours:** 7 am-9 pm; hours may vary. **Address:** 900 US 41 S 49908 **Location:** On US 41, 0.8 mi s of SR 38; in Best Western Baraga Lakeside Inn.

BATTLE CREEK pop. 53,364

BAYMONT INN & SUITES-BATTLE CREEK

Phone: (269)979-5400

Hotel
$79-$143

Address: 4725 Beckley Rd 49015 **Location:** I-94, exit 97 (Capital Ave), just sw. **Facility:** Smoke free premises. 88 units, some kitchens. 3 stories, interior corridors. **Pool(s):** heated indoor. **Activities:** whirlpool. **Guest Services:** valet and coin laundry, wireless Internet.

BAYMONT INN & SUITES DOWNTOWN

Phone: (269)565-0500

Hotel
$62-$80

Address: 182 W Van Buren 49017 **Location:** I-94, exit 98B, 4 mi n, then 0.5 mi w. **Facility:** Smoke free premises. 61 units. 2 stories (no elevator), interior corridors. **Terms:** cancellation fee imposed. **Pool(s):** heated indoor. **Activities:** whirlpool, exercise room. **Guest Services:** valet laundry, wireless Internet.

BEST WESTERN EXECUTIVE INN

Phone: (269)979-8506

Hotel
$80-$90

Address: 5090 Beckley Rd 49015 **Location:** I-94, exit 97 (Capital Ave), just s. **Facility:** Smoke free premises. 60 units. 2 stories (no elevator), interior corridors. **Pool(s):** heated indoor. **Activities:** whirlpool. **Fee:** game room. **Guest Services:** wireless Internet.

AAA Benefit:
Members save up to 20%, plus 10% bonus points with free rewards program.

FREE full breakfast and high-speed Internet

FAIRFIELD INN BY MARRIOTT

Phone: (269)979-8000

Hotel
$109-$119

Address: 4665 Beckley Rd 49015 **Location:** I-94, exit 97 (Capital Ave), 0.3 mi sw. Located in a quiet area. **Facility:** Smoke free premises. 74 units. 3 stories, interior corridors. **Terms:** check-in 4 pm, cancellation fee imposed. **Pool(s):** heated indoor. **Activities:** whirlpool, exercise room. **Guest Services:** valet and coin laundry, wireless Internet.

AAA Benefit:
Members save a minimum 5% off the best available rate.

HAMPTON INN BY HILTON

Hotel
$98-$103

Phone: (269)979-5577

Address: 1150 Riverside Dr 49015 **Location:** I-94, exit 97 (Capital Ave), 0.3 mi e on Beckley Rd. **Facility:** Smoke free premises. 64 units. 3 stories, interior corridors. **Terms:** 1-7 night minimum stay, cancellation fee imposed. **Pool(s):** heated indoor. **Activities:** whirlpool. **Guest Services:** valet laundry, wireless Internet.

HOLIDAY INN BATTLE CREEK

Hotel
$109-$169

Phone: (269)979-0500

Address: 12812 Harper Village Dr 49014 **Location:** I-94, exit 98A (SR 66 S), just s, then 0.3 mi e on Beckley Rd. Adjacent to Meijer's Shopping Center. **Facility:** Smoke free premises. 120 units, some two bedrooms. 5 stories, interior corridors. **Parking:** winter plug-ins. **Amenities:** video games (fee), high-speed Internet. *Some:* safes. **Pool(s):** heated indoor. **Activities:** exercise room. *Fee:* game room. **Guest Services:** valet and coin laundry, wireless Internet.

—— WHERE TO DINE ——

BARISTA BLUES CAFE

Deli
$6-$10

Phone: 269-968-8430

Close to the Kellogg Foundation, this popular downtown deli serves soups, salads, sandwiches and a few breakfast items. Curbside dining is a seasonal possibility. **Hours:** 7:30 am-4 pm. Closed major holidays; also Sat & Sun. **Address:** 21 W Michigan Ave 49017 **Location:** Downtown. **Parking:** street only.

CLARA'S RESTAURANT

American
$5-$20

Phone: 269/963-0966

This refurbished train depot is appointed with stained glass, old wood and antiques. Its lengthy menu includes a little bit of everything, from burgers and steak to seafood and enchiladas. The focus is on fun, rather than fine, family dining. **Bar:** full bar. **Reservations:** suggested. **Hours:** 11 am-10 pm, Fri & Sat-midnight, Sun 10 am-10 pm; Sunday brunch. Closed: 11/24, 12/25. **Address:** 44 McCamly St N 49017 **Location:** Downtown; across from McCamly Plaza Hotel.

FINLEY'S AMERICAN GRILL

American
$7-$20

Phone: 269/968-3938

This is a busy restaurant that is packed most evenings, so diners should expect a short wait. It's famous for award-winning, fork-tender baby back ribs. So tender, in fact, that the meat falls right off the bone. **Bar:** full bar. **Hours:** 11 am-10 pm, Fri & Sat-11 pm. Closed: 11/24, 12/25. **Address:** 140 E Columbia Ave 49015 **Location:** I-94, exit 97 (Capital Ave), 2 mi n, then 0.3 mi e.

THE WATERFRONT & SEASIDE SPORTS

American
$8-$23

Phone: 269/962-7622

This casual dining retreat has floor-to-ceiling windows affording panoramic views of the adjacent lake. Come for the popular lunch buffet or dinner menu featuring steaks and seafood. Either way, you'll see lots of locals packing in for the good food. **Bar:** full bar. **Reservations:** suggested, weekends. **Hours:** 11 am-10 pm, Sat & Sun from 4 pm. Closed: 12/25. **Address:** 315 W Columbia Ave 49015 **Location:** I-94, exit 97 (Capital Ave), 2 mi n, then 0.3 mi w.

BAY CITY pop. 36,817

BAY MOTEL

Motel
$39-$65

Phone: (989)684-4100

Address: 910 S Euclid Ave 48706 **Location:** Jct I-75 and US 10, 1.8 mi e on SR 25, then 0.5 mi s on SR 13. **Facility:** Smoke free premises. 18 units. 1 story, exterior corridors. **Parking:** winter plug-ins. **Terms:** 5 day cancellation notice. **Amenities:** high-speed Internet. **Guest Services:** wireless Internet. **Free Special Amenities:** preferred room (subject to availability with advance reservations) and high-speed Internet.

BAY VALLEY RESORT & CONFERENCE CENTER

Resort Hotel
$69-$139

Phone: (989)686-3500

Address: 2470 Old Bridge Rd 48706 **Location:** 0.3 mi nw of jct I-75 and SR 84, exit 160. **Facility:** Opened in 1973, the resort is convenient to Bay City, Midland and Saginaw; its 18-hole golf course was designed by Desmond Muirhead. Smoke free premises. 145 units. 3 stories, interior corridors. **Parking:** winter plug-ins. **Terms:** 7 day cancellation notice-fee imposed. **Pool(s):** heated indoor/outdoor. **Activities:** saunas, whirlpool. *Fee:* golf-18 holes, game room. **Guest Services:** valet laundry, wireless Internet. **Free Special Amenities:** expanded continental breakfast and airport transportation.

DOUBLETREE BAY CITY RIVERFRONT HOTEL

Hotel
$119-$159

Address: One Wenonah Park Pl 48708 **Location:** Center line on I-75 business loop, SR 15 and 25; downtown. Located on Saginaw River. **Facility:** Smoke free premises. 150 units. 6 stories, interior corridors. **Terms:** 1-7 night minimum stay, cancellation fee imposed. **Amenities:** video games, high-speed Internet. **Dining:** The Riverfront Grille, see separate listing. **Pool(s):** heated indoor. **Activities:** whirlpool, exercise room. **Guest Services:** valet and coin laundry, wireless Internet.

Phone: (989)891-6000

EUCLID MOTEL

Motel
$40-$60

Address: 809 N Euclid Ave 48706 **Location:** Jct I-75 and US 10, 1.8 mi e on SR 25, then 0.8 mi n on SR 13. **Facility:** Smoke free premises. 36 units. 1 story, exterior corridors. **Parking:** winter plug-ins. **Terms:** 7 day cancellation notice-fee imposed. **Amenities:** high-speed Internet. **Pool(s):** heated outdoor. **Activities:** playground, basketball. **Guest Services:** wireless Internet. *(see ad below)*

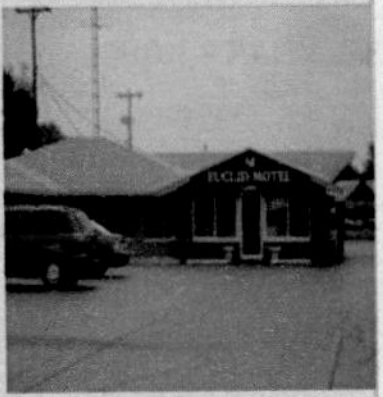

Phone: (989)684-9455

FAIRFIELD INN BY MARRIOTT

Hotel
$95-$121

Address: 4015 E Wilder Rd 48706 **Location:** 1 mi e of SR 13. Located at the Bay City Mall. **Facility:** Smoke free premises. 64 units. 3 stories, interior corridors. **Terms:** cancellation fee imposed. **Pool(s):** heated indoor. **Activities:** whirlpool. **Guest Services:** valet laundry, wireless Internet.

Phone: (989)667-7050

HOLIDAY INN EXPRESS & SUITES

Hotel
$99-$159

Address: 3959 Traxler Ct 48706 **Location:** I-75, exit 164 (SR 13/Wilder Rd), 0.3 mi e. **Facility:** Smoke free premises. 77 units. 3 stories, interior corridors. **Amenities:** high-speed Internet. **Pool(s):** heated indoor. **Activities:** exercise room. **Guest Services:** valet and coin laundry, wireless Internet.

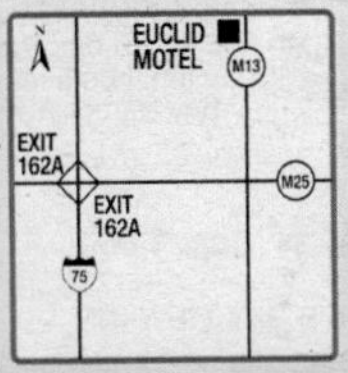

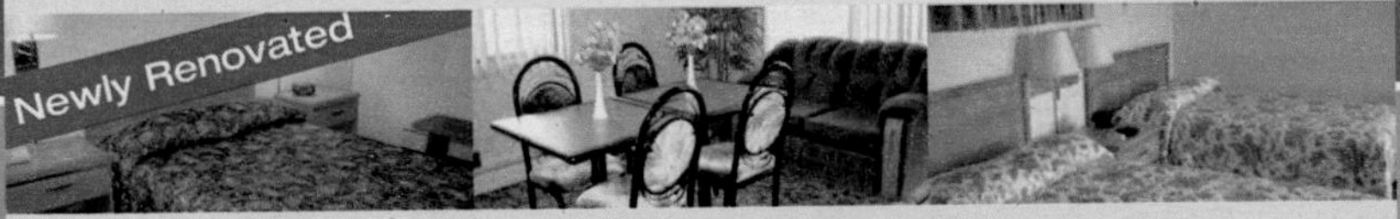

Phone: (989)667-3800

—— WHERE TO DINE ——

BERGER'S FAMILY RESTAURANT

Phone: 989/686-0224

American
$6-$14

On the south bank of Squaconning Creek, this restaurant has been owned and operated through four generations of the same family and is a local favorite for fish, steak, sandwiches and delicious homemade pie. **Bar:** full bar. **Hours:** 10 am-11 pm, Sun noon-8 pm; to 7:30 pm in winter. **Address:** 6387 W Side Saginaw St 48706 **Location:** Jct I-75 and SR 84, 0.3 mi s.

CHAR HOUSE

Phone: 989/893-5881

American
$6-$23

Tried-and-true American staples-steak, seafood, chops and chicken-are at the heart of the family-oriented restaurant's menu. A nautical theme is prevalent in the comfortable dining room, which is decorated with some shipwreck memorabilia. Breakfast is available all day. **Bar:** full bar. **Reservations:** suggested. **Hours:** 8 am-9 pm, Fri & Sat-10 pm. Closed: 11/24, 12/25. **Address:** 432 N Tuscola Rd 48708 **Location:** On SR 15, 1.5 mi s of SR 25.

KRZYSIAK'S HOUSE RESTAURANT

Phone: 989/894-5531

Polish
$6-$15

Lively and upbeat, the friendly restaurant is a favorite for family dining. The menu meshes the cuisines of Poland and America. The seafood buffet on Friday and Saturday evenings draws a good crowd. Colorful hand-painted murals decorate the walls. **Bar:** full bar. **Reservations:** suggested, weekends. **Hours:** 6:30 am-9 pm, Fri & Sat-10 pm, Sun-8 pm; hours may vary. Closed: 5/30, 12/25. **Address:** 1605 S Michigan Ave 48708 **Location:** On SR 13, 2.3 mi s, then 0.5 mi e on Cass Ave.

LOS CUATRO AMIGOS

Phone: 989/686-8630

Mexican
$6-$16

As the name might suggest, this is a place for friends. The popular eatery serves all of the traditional Mexican dishes. **Bar:** full bar. **Hours:** 11 am-10 pm, Fri & Sat-11 pm. Closed: 11/24, 12/25. **Address:** 305 N Euclid Ave 48706 **Location:** Jct I-75 and US 10, 1.8 mi e on SR 25, 0.5 mi n on SR 13.

THE RIVERFRONT GRILLE

Phone: 989/891-6000

American
$7-$30

This dining room offers diners a choice of a riverfront view or a seat away from the windows. Entrees include dishes such as chicken breast seasoned with citrus herb butter or a chargrilled venison chop accented with a Michigan cherry sauce. **Bar:** full bar. **Hours:** 6 am-1:30 & 5-10 pm; hours may vary. **Address:** One Wenonah Park Pl 48708 **Location:** Center line on I-75 business loop, SR 15 and 25; downtown; in Doubletree Bay City Riverfront Hotel. CALL 🉑Ⓜ

BAY HARBOR

THE INN AT BAY HARBOR-A RENAISSANCE GOLF RESORT

Phone: (231)439-4000

Resort
Hotel
$151-$193

Address: 3600 Village Harbor Dr 49770 **Location:** On US 31; center. Located on Little Traverse Bay. **Facility:** Nestled among village shops, a marina and a yacht club. Smoke free premises. 136 units, some two bedrooms and efficiencies. 6 stories, interior corridors. **Parking:** on-site and valet. **Terms:** check-in 4 pm, cancellation fee imposed. **Amenities:** video games (fee), high-speed Internet. **Dining:** 2 restaurants, also, Sagamore's, see separate listing. **Pool(s):** heated outdoor. **Activities:** whirlpool, beach access, snowmobiling, recreation programs in season, jogging, exercise room, spa. *Fee:* charter fishing, golf-45 holes, bicycles. **Guest Services:** valet and coin laundry, area transportation-downtown Petoskey & casino, wireless Internet. **Free Special Amenities:** high-speed Internet. SAVE ECO 🍽 🍷 📶 CALL 🉑Ⓜ 🏊 🖥 BIZ ✖ 📷 🔌 🖳 / SOME UNITS 📼

R
RENAISSANCE
HOTELS & RESORTS

AAA Benefit:
Members save a minimum 5% off the best available rate.

—— WHERE TO DINE ——

SAGAMORE'S

Phone: 231/439-4059

American
$18-$39

Handsome French doors in the dining room open out to a view of the bay. The restaurant specializes in delightful regional cuisine. The chef pairs classics such as whitefish with an international palette of flavors. **Bar:** full bar. **Reservations:** suggested. **Hours:** 7 am-11 & 5:30-9 pm, Fri & Sat-10 pm, Sun 7 am-1 & 5:30-9 pm; hours may vary. **Address:** 3600 Village Harbor Dr 49770 **Location:** On US 31; center; in The Inn at Bay Harbor-A Renaissance Golf Resort. **Parking:** on-site and valet.

BAY VIEW pop. 1,000

STAFFORD'S BAY VIEW INN

Phone: (231)347-2771

Historic
Country Inn
$99-$255

Address: 2011 Woodland Ave 49770 **Location:** 0.5 mi n on US 31. **Facility:** Rooms and furnishings at this historic 1886 inn have an ambience of nostalgia. Smoke free premises. 31 units. 3 stories, interior corridors. **Terms:** 2 night minimum stay - seasonal, 7 day cancellation notice-fee imposed. **Activities:** Bay View Association privileges, bicycles. **Guest Services:** wireless Internet. 🍽 ✖ 🅆 🎫

—— WHERE TO DINE ——

LA SEÑORITA

Phone: 231/347-7750

Mexican
$6-$15

Mexican knickknacks adorn the walls of the dining room, creating a friendly and warm atmosphere. There's a good variety of reasonably priced Mexican dishes, snacks and salad. Mesquite cooked dishes are a specialty. Smoking permitted in the lounge only. **Bar:** full bar. **Hours:** 11 am-10 pm, Fri & Sat-11 pm, Sun noon-10 pm; Fri & Sat-midnight 5/29-9/4. Closed: 11/24, 12/25 & Easter. **Address:** 1285 US 31 N 49770 **Location:** Jct US 31 and SR 119.

BEAR LAKE pop. 318

BELLA VISTA INN

Phone: 231/864-3000

Motel
$60-$106 4/1-10/31
$55-$65 11/1-4/30

Address: 12273 US 31 49614 **Location:** On US 31; center. **Facility:** Smoke free premises. 20 units. 1 story, exterior corridors. **Terms:** office hours 8 am-11 pm, 7 day cancellation notice, 6/16-9/14-fee imposed. **Pool(s):** outdoor. **Activities:** snowmobiling. **Guest Services:** wireless Internet. **Free Special Amenities: continental breakfast and high-speed Internet.**

BELLEVILLE —See Detroit p. 270.

BENTON HARBOR pop. 11,182

COMFORT SUITES ST. JOSEPH/BENTON HARBOR

Phone: 269/925-8800

Hotel
Rates not provided

Address: 1825 Meadowbrook Rd 49022 **Location:** I-94, exit 29 (Pipestone Rd), just s. **Facility:** Smoke free premises. 62 units. 3 stories, interior corridors. **Amenities:** video games (fee). **Pool(s):** heated indoor. **Activities:** sauna, whirlpool, exercise room. **Guest Services:** valet and coin laundry, wireless Internet.

COURTYARD BY MARRIOTT BENTON HARBOR/ST JOSEPH

Phone: (269)925-3000

Hotel
$120-$140

Address: 1592 Mall Dr 49022 **Location:** I-94, exit 29 (Pipestone Rd), just n to Mall Dr, then just w. **Facility:** Smoke free premises. 98 units. 2 stories (no elevator), interior corridors. **Terms:** cancellation fee imposed. **Amenities:** video games (fee). **Pool(s):** heated indoor/outdoor. **Activities:** whirlpool, exercise room. **Guest Services:** valet and coin laundry, wireless Internet.

AAA Benefit:
Members save a minimum 5% off the best available rate.

HOLIDAY INN EXPRESS

Phone: (269)927-4599

Hotel
$119-$159

Address: 2276 Pipestone Rd 49022 **Location:** I-94, exit 29 (Pipestone Rd), just s. **Facility:** Smoke free premises. 79 units. 3 stories, interior corridors. **Terms:** 7 day cancellation notice. **Amenities:** high-speed Internet. **Pool(s):** heated indoor. **Activities:** whirlpool, exercise room. **Guest Services:** valet and coin laundry, wireless Internet.

BERKLEY —See Detroit p. 270.

BEULAH pop. 363

BEST WESTERN SCENIC HILL RESORT

Phone: (231)882-7754

Hotel
$75-$250

Address: 1400 US Hwy 31 49617 **Location:** On US 31, 0.8 mi e. **Facility:** Smoke free premises. 43 units. 3 stories, interior corridors. **Parking:** winter plug-ins. **Terms:** cancellation fee imposed. **Amenities:** high-speed Internet. **Pool(s):** heated indoor. **Activities:** whirlpool, snowmobiling, exercise room, spa. **Guest Services:** wireless Internet. **Free Special Amenities: continental breakfast and high-speed Internet.**

AAA Benefit:
Members save up to 20%, plus 10% bonus points with free rewards program.

BEVERLY HILLS —See Detroit p. 271.

BIG RAPIDS pop. 10,849

COUNTRY INN & SUITES BY CARLSON

Phone: (231)527-9000

Hotel
$89-$109

Address: 15344 Waldron Way 49307 **Location:** US 131, exit 139, just e. Located next to Meijer's Shopping Center. **Facility:** Smoke free premises. 63 units. 3 stories, interior corridors. **Parking:** winter plug-ins. **Terms:** check-in 4 pm. **Amenities:** safes. **Pool(s):** heated indoor. **Activities:** whirlpool, exercise room. **Guest Services:** valet and coin laundry, wireless Internet. *(see ad p. 6)*

HOLIDAY INN HOTEL & CONFERENCE CENTER

Phone: (231)796-4400

Hotel
$105-$160

Address: 1005 Perry St 49307 **Location:** US 131, exit 139, 1.3 mi e on SR 20. Located at Ferris State University. **Facility:** Smoke free premises. 118 units. 4 stories, interior corridors. **Terms:** check-in 4 pm. **Pool(s):** heated indoor. **Activities:** whirlpool, exercise room. *Fee:* golf-18 holes, game room. **Guest Services:** valet and coin laundry, wireless Internet.

QUALITY INN & SUITES

Phone: (231)592-5150

Motel
$59-$79

Address: 1705 S State St 49307 **Location:** US 131, exit 139, 1.5 mi e on SR 20, then 0.8 mi s. Located close to Ferris State University. **Facility:** Smoke free premises. 93 units. 2-3 stories, interior/exterior corridors. **Parking:** winter plug-ins. **Pool(s):** heated outdoor. **Activities:** exercise room. **Guest Services:** valet and coin laundry, wireless Internet.

BIRCH RUN pop. 1,653

AMERICAS BEST VALUE INN & SUITES

Hotel
$61-$129

Phone: (989)624-4440

Address: 9235 E Birch Run Rd 48415 **Location:** I-75, exit 136 (Birch Run Rd), just e. **Facility:** Smoke free premises. 109 units. 2 stories (no elevator), interior corridors. **Parking:** winter plug-ins. **Terms:** cancellation fee imposed. **Activities:** sauna, whirlpool. **Fee:** game room. **Guest Services:** wireless Internet.

BEST WESTERN BIRCH RUN-FRANKENMUTH

Hotel
$70-$140

Phone: (989)624-9395

Address: 9087 Birch Run Rd 48415 **Location:** I-75, exit 136 (Birch Run Rd), just e. **Facility:** Smoke free premises. 107 units. 2 stories (no elevator), interior/exterior corridors. **Terms:** check-in 4 pm, 2 night minimum stay - seasonal. **Amenities:** Some: high-speed Internet. **Pool(s):** heated indoor. **Activities:** whirlpool, exercise room. **Fee:** game room. **Guest Services:** coin laundry, wireless Internet. **Free Special Amenities: local telephone calls and high-speed Internet.**

AAA Benefit:
Members save up to 20%, plus 10% bonus points with free rewards program.

COMFORT INN

Hotel
$70-$130

Phone: (989)624-7777

Address: 11911 Dixie Hwy 48415 **Location:** I-75, exit 136 (Birch Run Rd), just e. **Facility:** Smoke free premises. 99 units. 3 stories, interior corridors. **Amenities:** safes (fee). **Pool(s):** heated indoor. **Activities:** whirlpool, exercise room. **Fee:** game room. **Guest Services:** coin laundry, wireless Internet.

COUNTRY INN & SUITES BY CARLSON

Hotel
$69-$159

Phone: (989)624-8000

Address: 12112 S Beyer Rd 48415 **Location:** I-75, exit 136 (Birch Run Rd), just w; at entrance to Birch Run Outlet Mall. **Facility:** Smoke free premises. 71 units. 3 stories, interior corridors. **Pool(s):** heated indoor. **Activities:** whirlpool. **Guest Services:** wireless Internet. *(see ad p. 6)*

HAMPTON INN

Hotel
Rates not provided

Phone: 989/624-2500

Address: 12130 Tiffany Blvd 48415 **Location:** I-75, exit 136 (Birch Run Rd), just e. **Facility:** Smoke free premises. 89 units. 3 stories, interior corridors. **Terms:** check-in 4 pm. **Pool(s):** heated indoor. **Activities:** whirlpool, exercise room. **Fee:** game room. **Guest Services:** valet and coin laundry, wireless Internet.

Phone: 989/624-2500

AAA Benefit:
Members save up to 10% everyday!

HOLIDAY INN EXPRESS

Hotel
Rates not provided

Phone: 989/624-9300

Address: 12150 Dixie Hwy 48415 **Location:** I-75, exit 136 (Birch Run Rd), just e. **Facility:** Smoke free premises. 95 units. 3 stories, interior corridors. **Terms:** check-in 4 pm. **Pool(s):** heated indoor. **Activities:** whirlpool, exercise room. **Fee:** game room. **Guest Services:** coin laundry, wireless Internet.

——— WHERE TO DINE ———

THE EXIT RESTAURANT

American
$5-$10

Phone: 989/624-9652

This quaint, country-style diner features large portions of comfort foods as well as its own bake shop. Fresh pies and other treats are baked every day. **Hours:** 6 am-11 pm, Thurs-Sat 24 hours. Closed major holidays. **Address:** 9143 Birch Run Rd 48415 **Location:** I-75, exit 136 (Birch Run Rd), just e.

TONY'S

American
$5-$10

Phone: 989/624-5860

Known for large portions, this popular burger joint is a community staple that has been in business for more than 50 years. Representative of massive plates include the omelet, served with a one-pound side of bacon, and the banana split made with a half-gallon of ice cream. In addition to burgers and omelets, the menu also features pastas, steaks, fried fish and a variety of sandwiches. **Hours:** 7 am-9 pm, Fri & Sat-10 pm; 6 am-10 pm, Fri & Sat-11 pm in summer. Closed major holidays. **Address:** 8781 Main St 48415 **Location:** I-75, exit 136 (Birch Run Rd), just w.

BIRMINGHAM —See Detroit p. 271.

BLANCHARD

——— WHERE TO DINE ———

MAXFIELD'S RESTAURANT

American
$7-$25

Phone: 989/427-5630

An area institution since 1959, the family-oriented restaurant is adorned with paintings and tapestries created by the owner's mother. More than 100 homemade items line the tempting salad bar—the cornerstone of guests' dining experience. **Bar:** full bar. **Hours:** 11 am-8 pm, Fri & Sat-9 pm, Sun noon-5 pm. Closed: 12/24, 12/25; also Mon & Tues. **Address:** 11228 Wyman Rd 49310 **Location:** 3 mi n of SR 46 and blinking light.

BLISSFIELD pop. 3,223

—— WHERE TO DINE ——

HATHAWAY HOUSE
Phone: 517/486-2141

American
$19-$32

You'll find several inviting period dining rooms in this 1851 Greek revival mansion. The menu lists imaginatively prepared soups, salads, seafood, beef and poultry. Try the broiled whitefish; its delicate flavors will please you. Semi-formal attire. **Bar:** full bar. **Hours:** 5 pm-9 pm, Sun noon-8 pm. Closed: 1/1, 12/25; also Mon. **Address:** 424 W Adrian St (US 223) 49228 **Location:** 0.3 mi w of town on US 223. **Historic**

MAIN STREET STABLE & TAVERN
Phone: 517/486-2144

American
$8-$23

This rustic, restored carriage house is a fitting spot for meal and a drink. The menu offers light fare like snacks, soups, sandwiches and salads as well as entrees from salmon to steak. The banana cream pie is to die for. **Bar:** full bar. **Hours:** 11 am-9 pm, Fri & Sat-10 pm; Sunday brunch. Closed: 1/1, 12/25. **Address:** 116 N Main St 49228 **Location:** 0.3 mi w of town on US 223; adjacent to Hathaway House. **Historic**

BLOOMFIELD HILLS —See Detroit p. 272.

BOYNE CITY pop. 3,500

—— WHERE TO DINE ——

RED MESA GRILL
Phone: 231/582-0049

International
$6-$15

The menu displays a mix of Cajun, Creole and Mexican dishes. **Bar:** full bar. **Hours:** 11 am-11 pm; hours may vary. Closed: 11/24, 12/25. **Address:** 117 Water St 49712 **Location:** Downtown.

BRIDGEPORT pop. 7,849

BAYMONT INN & SUITES-FRANKENMUTH/BRIDGEPORT
Phone: (989)777-3000

Hotel
$62-$159

Address: 6460 Dixie Hwy 48722 **Location:** I-75, exit 144A. **Facility:** Smoke free premises. 100 units. 3 stories, interior corridors. **Pool(s):** heated indoor. **Activities:** whirlpool, exercise room. **Guest Services:** coin laundry, wireless Internet.

BRIGHTON pop. 6,701

COURTYARD BY MARRIOTT
Phone: (810)225-9200

Hotel
$98-$125

Address: 7799 Conference Center Dr 48114 **Location:** I-96, exit 145 (Grand River Ave S), just ne. **Facility:** Smoke free premises. 90 units. 3 stories, interior corridors. **Terms:** cancellation fee imposed. **Amenities:** video games (fee), high-speed Internet. **Pool(s):** heated indoor. **Activities:** whirlpool, exercise room. **Guest Services:** valet and coin laundry, wireless Internet.

AAA Benefit:
Members save a minimum 5% off the best available rate.

FREE full breakfast and high-speed Internet

HOLIDAY INN EXPRESS HOTEL & SUITES
Phone: (810)225-4300

Hotel
$99-$169

Address: 8285 Movie Dr 48114 **Location:** I-96, exit 145 (Grand River Ave S), just s. Located in Towne Square Shopping Plaza. **Facility:** Smoke free premises. 106 units, some efficiencies. 2 stories, interior corridors. **Terms:** cancellation fee imposed. **Amenities:** video games (fee). **Pool(s):** heated indoor. **Activities:** whirlpool, exercise room. **Guest Services:** valet and coin laundry, wireless Internet. **Free Special Amenities:** expanded continental breakfast and high-speed Internet.

HOMEWOOD SUITES BY HILTON
Phone: (810)225-0200

Extended Stay Hotel
$99-$139

Address: 8060 Challis Rd 48116 **Location:** I-96, exit 145 (Grand River Ave S), just s. **Facility:** Smoke free premises. 94 units, some two bedrooms and efficiencies. 3 stories, interior corridors. **Terms:** 1-7 night minimum stay, cancellation fee imposed. **Amenities:** high-speed Internet, safes. **Pool(s):** heated indoor. **Activities:** whirlpool, barbecue area, exercise room. **Guest Services:** complimentary and valet laundry, wireless Internet. **Free Special Amenities:** expanded continental breakfast and manager's reception.

AAA Benefit:
Members save 5% or more everyday!

—— WHERE TO DINE ——

THE BREAKFAST CLUB

American
$7-$10

Phone: 810/229-8877

Beige walls and floral sheer curtains give the comfortable little restaurant plenty of charm. In addition to classic, well-prepared breakfast and lunch choices, guests can experience a delightful change from the ordinary with such daily specials as baked French toast with seasonal fruit, a crab omelet or linguine tossed with fresh pesto. **Hours:** 7 am-2 pm. Closed: 11/24, 12/25. **Address:** 676 W Grand River Ave 48116 **Location:** I-96, exit 145 (Grand River Ave S), 1 mi s.

THE BRIGHTON HOUSE

American
$8-$23

Phone: 810/229-9390

Don't let the vintage decor lead you astray. While the decorations may be somewhat dated, the food reflects contemporary trends in American roadhouse dining with everything from burgers and wraps to steaks and salmon. Prices are reasonable, and the friendly staff are well-versed in making patrons feel like longtime locals. **Bar:** full bar. **Hours:** 11 am-11 pm; Sunday brunch 10:30 am-1 pm. Closed major holidays. **Address:** 10180 Grand River Ave 48116 **Location:** Jct Old US 23, just e.

CIAO AMICI'S

Italian
$8-$25

Phone: 810/227-9000

With the soft strains of Frank Sinatra playing in the background and gold-framed pictures of the Rat Pack decorating the elegant walls, it would be hard not to guess this is an Italian restaurant. Traditional recipes employ fresh pasta, homemade sauces and seasonal produce. **Bar:** full bar. **Hours:** 11:30 am-10 pm, Fri-11 pm, Sat noon-11 pm, Sun noon-9 pm. Closed major holidays. **Address:** 217 W Main St 48116 **Location:** I-96, exit 145 (Grand River Ave S); downtown. **Parking:** on-site and street. CALL 〔M〕

THE GRAND TRAVERSE PIE COMPANY

Deli
$6-$8

Phone: 810/225-7437

A large open working bakery greets guests as they enter into this cute, cozy cafe. The aromas of freshly baked fruit pies, spinach quiche and made-to-order sandwiches stimulate the appetite. **Hours:** 7:30 am-8 pm, Sat from 8 am, Sun 11 am-6 pm. Closed major holidays. **Address:** 9912 E Grand River Ave 48116 **Location:** Old US 23 and E Grand River Ave, 0.5 mi w.

STILLWATER GRILL

American
$12-$24

Phone: 810/225-1800

The huge restaurant became popular almost immediately, which translates to a short wait for seating, even on weeknights. Northwood accents with green and tan walls and a fieldstone fireplace give the room a stylish air, and the open kitchen prepares a menu that focuses on both steaks and several nightly fresh fish or pasta specials. **Bar:** full bar. **Hours:** 11 am-10 pm, Fri-11 pm, Sat 3 pm-11 pm, Sun 2 pm-9 pm. Closed: 11/24, 12/25. **Address:** 503 W Grand River Ave 48116 **Location:** I-96, exit 145 (Grand River Ave S), 1 mi s. CALL 〔M〕

BRIMLEY

WILLABEE'S MOTEL

Motel
Rates not provided

Phone: 906/248-3090

Address: 9903 W 6 Mile Rd 49715 **Location:** At the end of SR 221. Located on the river. **Facility:** Smoke free premises. 36 units, some two bedrooms. 2 stories (no elevator), exterior corridors. **Terms:** office hours 7 am-11 pm. **Activities:** boat dock, fishing, snowmobiling. **Guest Services:** wireless Internet. 〔↑⊷〕 ⊠ / SOME UNITS 〔〕

BROOKLYN pop. 1,176

SUPER 8 - BROOKLYN

Hotel
$54-$135

Phone: (517)592-0888

Address: 155 Wamplers Rd 49230 **Location:** Jct SR 50 (Main St) and 124; downtown. **Facility:** Smoke free premises. 52 units, some kitchens. 2 stories (no elevator), interior corridors. **Guest Services:** coin laundry, wireless Internet. CALL 〔M〕 ⊠ 〔〕 / SOME UNITS FEE 〔〕 〔〕 〔〕

BYRON CENTER pop. 3,777 (See map and index starting on p. 324)

BAYMONT INN & SUITES GRAND RAPIDS SOUTHWEST/BYRON CENTER

Hotel
$71-$107

Phone: (616)583-9535

Address: 8282 Pfeiffer Farms Dr SW 49315 **Location:** US 131, exit 74, just w. **Facility:** Smoke free premises. 84 units. 4 stories, interior corridors. **Parking:** winter plug-ins. **Terms:** 3 day cancellation notice. **Amenities:** high-speed Internet. **Pool(s):** heated indoor. **Activities:** whirlpool, sun deck, exercise room. **Guest Services:** valet and coin laundry. 〔↑〕 CALL 〔M〕 ⊷ ⊠ 〔꙰〕 〔〕 / SOME UNITS 〔〕 〔〕

COMFORT SUITES-GRAND RAPIDS SOUTH

Hotel
$80-$100

Phone: (616)301-2255

Address: 7644 Caterpillar Ct SW 49548 **Location:** US 131, exit 75. Located in a business park. **Facility:** Smoke free premises. 76 units. 3 stories, interior corridors. **Amenities:** high-speed Internet. **Pool(s):** heated indoor. **Activities:** sauna, whirlpool, exercise room. **Guest Services:** valet and coin laundry, wireless Internet. CALL 〔M〕 ⊷ ⊠ 〔꙰〕 〔〕 〔〕 〔〕 / SOME UNITS FEE 〔〕

HOLIDAY INN EXPRESS INN & SUITES

Hotel
$99-$159

Phone: (616)871-9700 〔54〕

Address: 6565 Clay Ave SW 49548 **Location:** US 131, exit 76, just e, then 0.3 mi n. **Facility:** 79 units. 4 stories, interior corridors. **Terms:** check-in 4 pm, cancellation fee imposed. **Amenities:** high-speed Internet. **Pool(s):** heated indoor. **Activities:** whirlpool, waterslide, lifeguard on duty, exercise room. **Fee:** game room. **Guest Services:** valet and coin laundry, wireless Internet. CALL 〔M〕 ⊷ ⊠ 〔꙰〕 〔〕 〔〕 〔〕 〔〕

CADILLAC pop. 10,000

HOLIDAY INN EXPRESS

Phone: (231)779-4656

Hotel
$119-$289 6/17-4/30
$114-$239 4/1-6/16

Address: 7642 S Business Rt US 131 49601 **Location:** US 131, exit 177, 0.7 mi n. **Facility:** Smoke free premises. 70 units. 3 stories, interior corridors. **Amenities:** high-speed Internet. **Pool(s):** heated indoor. **Activities:** whirlpool, snowmobiling, exercise room. **Guest Services:** valet and coin laundry.

MCGUIRES RESORT

Phone: (231)775-9947

Resort
Hotel
$79-$109

Address: 7880 Mackinaw Tr 49601 **Location:** US 131, exit 177, 0.7 mi n, then 0.5 mi w. **Facility:** A variety of rooms, some with patios, is offered at this resort set on spacious grounds. Smoke free premises. 120 units. 2-3 stories (no elevator), interior corridors. **Parking:** winter plug-ins. **Terms:** check-in 4 pm, 7 day cancellation notice-fee imposed. **Pool(s):** heated indoor. **Activities:** sauna, whirlpool, driving range, snowmobiling, tobogganing, exercise trail, exercise room, basketball, horseshoes, shuffleboard, volleyball. **Fee:** golf-27 holes, 2 lighted tennis courts, cross country skiing, cross country skis & snowshoes, game room. **Guest Services:** valet laundry, wireless Internet.

—— WHERE TO DINE ——

HERMANN'S EUROPEAN CAFE & INN

Phone: 231/775-9563

International
$8-$29

The Austrian chef-owner prepares an interesting array of European dishes, such as schnitzel, wild boar, pork loin and apple strudel. Couples favor the quiet restaurant for moderately upscale fine dining. Attentive servers provide good follow-up. **Bar:** full bar. **Hours:** 11 am-9:30 pm, Fri & Sat-10 pm. Closed: 1/1, 11/24, 12/25; also Sun & for dinner 12/24. **Address:** 214 N Mitchell St 49601 **Location:** Center. **Parking:** street only.

LAKESIDE CHARLIES

Phone: 231/775-5332

American
$6-$18

Overlooking Lake Mitchell, the restaurant has three dining rooms decorated with hunting and fishing memorabilia and various antiques. The focus of the menu is on beef and seafood. The basic ice cream fudge sundae is hard to beat. **Bar:** full bar. **Reservations:** required. **Hours:** 11:30 am-9 pm, Fri & Sat-10 pm, Sun-8 pm; hours may vary. Closed: 11/24, 12/25. **Address:** 301 S Lake Mitchell 49601 **Location:** Jct SR 55 and 115.

MAGGIE'S TAVERN

Phone: 231/775-1810

American
$6-$14

The downtown tavern is decorated with mounted animal heads and beer-ad pictures. New York steak with a brown-sugar-topped baked sweet potato makes a delicious meal. **Bar:** full bar. **Hours:** 11 am-10:30 pm, Fri & Sat-11:30 pm; hours may vary. Closed major holidays; also Sun. **Address:** 523 N Mitchell St 49601 **Location:** Downtown.

THE TIMBERS

Phone: 231/775-6751

American
$5-$23

The restaurant's specialties include seasoned, slow-roasted prime rib, tasty steaks, and chicken and pasta dishes. **Bar:** full bar. **Hours:** 11:30 am-9 pm, Fri & Sat-10 pm, Sun-8 pm. Closed: 11/24, 12/25; also Mon. **Address:** 5535 E M-115 49601 **Location:** Between Division and 13th sts.

CALUMET pop. 879

AMERICINN LODGE & SUITES OF CALUMET

Phone: (906)337-6463

Hotel
$95-$146

Address: 56925 S 6th St 49913 **Location:** On US 41; just w of Visitors Center. Located next to Mine St Station Complex. **Facility:** Smoke free premises. 67 units. 2 stories (no elevator), interior corridors. **Parking:** winter plug-ins. **Terms:** cancellation fee imposed. **Pool(s):** heated indoor. **Activities:** sauna, whirlpool, snowmobiling. **Fee:** game room. **Guest Services:** coin laundry, wireless Internet.

CANNONSBURG

—— WHERE TO DINE ——

HONEY CREEK INN

Phone: 616/874-7849

American
$8-$23

This quaint, inviting tavern is well known for its Kobe beef burgers and many brews on tap. For dinner, menu items include pan-fried walleye, parsley linguine chicken and a Polish favorite: kielbasa. **Bar:** full bar. **Hours:** 11 am-11 pm, Fri & Sat-midnight. Closed: 11/24, 12/25; also Sun. **Address:** 8000 Cannonsburg NE 49317 **Location:** Center.

CANTON —See Detroit p. 273.

CASCADE (See map and index starting on p. 324)

BAYMONT INN-GRAND RAPIDS AIRPORT

Phone: (616)956-3300

Hotel
$58-$146

Address: 2873 Kraft Ave SE 49512 **Location:** I-96, exit 43B, just e. **Facility:** Smoke free premises. 93 units, some kitchens. 3 stories, interior corridors. **Amenities:** video games. **Activities:** exercise room. **Guest Services:** valet and coin laundry, wireless Internet.

(See map and index starting on p. 324)

BEST WESTERN HOSPITALITY HOTEL & SUITES

Hotel
$59-$99

Phone: (616)949-8400 [22]

Address: 5500 28th St SE 49512 **Location:** I-96, exit 43B, just e on SR 11. **Facility:** Smoke free premises. 120 units. 2 stories, interior corridors. **Pool(s):** heated indoor. **Activities:** sauna, whirlpool, exercise room. **Guest Services:** valet and coin laundry, wireless Internet.

AAA Benefit:
Members save up to 20%, plus 10% bonus points with free rewards program.

FREE full breakfast and airport transportation

CLARION INN & SUITES GRAND RAPIDS AIRPORT

Hotel
$90-$150

Phone: (616)956-9304 [24]

Address: 4981 28th St SE 49512 **Location:** I-96, exit 43A, 0.5 mi w on SR 11. **Facility:** Smoke free premises. 106 units. 2 stories, interior corridors. **Amenities:** Some: safes. **Pool(s):** heated outdoor. **Activities:** exercise room. **Guest Services:** valet and coin laundry, wireless Internet.

COUNTRY INN & SUITES BY CARLSON

Hotel
$79-$114

Phone: (616)977-0909 [19]

Address: 5399 28th St SE 49512 **Location:** I-96, exit 43B, just e on SR 11. Located next to a Meijer's Shopping Center. **Facility:** Smoke free premises. 61 units. 3 stories, interior corridors. **Amenities:** safes (fee). **Pool(s):** heated indoor. **Activities:** whirlpool, exercise room. **Guest Services:** valet and coin laundry, wireless Internet. **Free Special Amenities:** full breakfast and airport transportation. *(see ad p. 6)*

CROWNE PLAZA GRAND RAPIDS

Hotel
$95-$189

Phone: (616)957-1770 [20]

Address: 5700 28th St SE 49546 **Location:** I-96, exit 43B, 0.3 mi e on SR 11. **Facility:** Smoke free premises. 320 units. 5 stories, interior corridors. **Parking:** on-site and valet. **Terms:** check-in 4 pm. **Pool(s):** heated indoor/outdoor. **Activities:** sauna, whirlpool, exercise room. *Fee:* game room. **Guest Services:** valet laundry, area transportation-within 3 mi, wireless Internet.

HAMPTON INN & SUITES GRAND RAPIDS AIRPORT

Hotel
$89-$139

Phone: (616)575-9144 [26]

Address: 5200 28th St SE 49512 **Location:** I-96, exit 43A, 0.3 mi w on SR 11, then just s. Located next to Target Shopping Center. **Facility:** Smoke free premises. 98 units. 3 stories, interior corridors. **Terms:** 1-7 night minimum stay, cancellation fee imposed. **Amenities:** high-speed Internet. **Pool(s):** heated indoor. **Activities:** whirlpool, exercise room. **Guest Services:** valet laundry, wireless Internet.

AAA Benefit:
Members save up to 10% everyday!

HOLIDAY INN EXPRESS SUITES AIRPORT

Hotel
$89-$159

Phone: (616)940-8100 [18]

Address: 5401 28th Ct SE 49546 **Location:** I-96, exit 43B, just e on SR 11. Located next to Meijer's Shopping Center. **Facility:** Smoke free premises. 121 units. 3 stories, interior corridors. **Amenities:** safes. **Pool(s):** heated indoor. **Activities:** whirlpool, exercise room, basketball, volleyball. **Guest Services:** valet and coin laundry, area transportation-within 3 mi, wireless Internet.

RED ROOF INN #7011

Motel
$53-$70 8/31-4/30
$52-$66 4/1-8/30

Phone: (616)942-0800 [23]

Address: 5131 28th St SE 49512 **Location:** I-96, exit 43A, 0.3 mi w on SR 11. **Facility:** Smoke free premises. 107 units. 2 stories (no elevator), exterior corridors. **Amenities:** video games. **Guest Services:** wireless Internet. **Free Special Amenities:** local telephone calls.

SPRINGHILL SUITES GRAND RAPIDS AIRPORT

Hotel
$125-$160

Phone: (616)464-1130 [27]

Address: 5250 28th St SE 49512 **Location:** I-96, exit 43, 0.3 mi w on SR 11, then just s. Located next to Target Shopping Center. **Facility:** Smoke free premises. 109 units. 3 stories, interior corridors. **Terms:** cancellation fee imposed. **Pool(s):** heated indoor. **Activities:** whirlpool, exercise room. **Guest Services:** valet and coin laundry, wireless Internet.

AAA Benefit:
Members save a minimum 5% off the best available rate.

SUPER 8

Hotel
$44-$53

Phone: (616)957-3000 [21]

Address: 4855 28th St SE 49512 **Location:** I-96, exit 43A, 0.5 mi w on SR 11. **Facility:** Smoke free premises. 107 units. 2 stories (no elevator), interior corridors. **Activities:** limited exercise equipment. **Guest Services:** coin laundry, wireless Internet.

(See map and index starting on p. 324)

—— WHERE TO DINE ——

NOTO'S OLD WORLD ITALIAN DINING   **Phone:** 616/493-6686

Italian
$15-$33

The high-end restaurant serves steak, chops and seafood with fine Italian wines and homemade-style desserts. **Bar:** full bar. **Hours:** 4 pm-10 pm. Closed major holidays; also Sun. **Address:** 6600 28th St SE 49546 **Location:** I-96, exit 43B, 1.5 mi e on SR 11. CALL 🚭M

CASEVILLE pop. 888

—— WHERE TO DINE ——

BAY CAFE   **Phone:** 989/856-3705

American
$5-$15

Burgers, steak, seafood and pasta make up the bulk of the family restaurant's traditional menu. An outdoorsy decor, with fish and wildlife, punctuates the relaxed dining room. The summer patio is popular in season. For dessert, have a slice of homemade pie. **Hours:** 6 am-8 pm; hours may vary. Closed: 11/24, 12/25; also Sun in winter. **Address:** 6750 Main St 48725 **Location:** Center. **Parking:** street only.

CHARLEVOIX pop. 2,994

AMERICINN LODGE & SUITES OF CHARLEVOIX   **Phone:** 231/237-0988

Hotel
Rates not provided

Address: 11800 US 31 N 49720 **Location:** On US 31, 2.4 mi n. **Facility:** Smoke free premises. 52 units. 2 stories (no elevator), interior corridors. **Amenities:** high-speed Internet, safes (fee). **Pool(s):** heated indoor. **Activities:** sauna, whirlpool. **Guest Services:** valet and coin laundry.

CALL 🚭M 🏊 ✕ 🎇 💻 / SOME UNITS FEE 🐾 🛗 📺 💻

WEATHERVANE TERRACE INN & SUITES   **Phone:** (231)547-9955

Motel
$55-$270

Address: 111 Pine River Ln 49720 **Location:** Just off US 31; at Harbor Bridge. Opposite Pine River Channel. **Facility:** Smoke free premises. 68 units, some efficiencies and kitchens. 2-3 stories, exterior corridors. **Parking:** winter plug-ins. **Terms:** office hours 7 am-11 pm, check-in 4 pm, 2 night minimum stay - seasonal and/or weekends, 7 day cancellation notice. **Pool(s):** heated outdoor. **Activities:** whirlpool. **Guest Services:** wireless Internet. *(see ad below)*

SAVE 🍴 🏊 ✕ 🎇 🛗 📺 💻

FREE expanded continental breakfast and high-speed Internet

▼ See AAA listing above ▼

Unique Atmosphere · Unparalleled Amenities

Weathervane
Terrace Inn & Suites

**Plush "Weathervane Wonder" Beds
with Triple Sheeting
32" Flat Screen TV in All Rooms**

- Fireplaces in all 1 Bedroom Suites and Jacuzzi Rooms
- Free Deluxe Continental Breakfast
- Free Wireless Internet Property-wide
- Great Hospitality/Meeting Room
- Indoor 8 Person Hot Tub Area
- Outdoor Pool with Harbor View
- Adjacent to Miles of Sandy Lake Michigan Beach and Downtown

**The Only AAA Rated Property Located
In Downtown Charlevoix**

231-547-9955 Email: info@weathervane-chx.com 111 Pine River Lane, Charlevoix, MI

Call Direct for Rates: 800-552-0025   www.weathervane-chx.com

—— **WHERE TO DINE** ——

STAFFORD'S WEATHERVANE RESTAURANT

Phone: 231/547-4311

American
$9-$40

Weathervane scallops and planked whitefish stand out on a menu of mostly steak and seafood selections. The nautical theme is evident in the dining room decor, as well as in the seagull-shaped roof of the building itself. Families are welcomed. **Bar:** full bar. **Hours:** 11 am-3 & 4:30-10 pm; hours vary off season. Closed: 12/25. **Address:** 106 Pine River Ln 49720 **Location:** US 31 at Pine River Bridge; downtown.

CHARLOTTE pop. 8,389

COMFORT INN

Phone: (517)543-7307

Hotel
$79-$149

Address: 1302 E Packard Hwy 48813 **Location:** I-69, exit 61 (Lansing Rd), 0.5 mi e. Located in a commercial/residential area. **Facility:** Smoke free premises. 61 units. 3 stories, interior corridors. **Amenities:** high-speed Internet. **Pool(s):** heated indoor. **Activities:** exercise room. **Guest Services:** coin laundry, wireless Internet. **Free Special Amenities:** expanded continental breakfast and high-speed Internet.

HOLIDAY INN EXPRESS HOTEL & SUITES

Phone: (517)541-5000

Hotel
$109-$119

Address: 500 Meijer St 48813 **Location:** I-69, exit 60 (SR 50), just e. Adjacent to Meijer Shopping Mall. **Facility:** Smoke free premises. 67 units. 3 stories, interior corridors. **Terms:** cancellation fee imposed. **Amenities:** high-speed Internet. **Pool(s):** heated indoor. **Activities:** whirlpool, exercise room. **Guest Services:** coin laundry, wireless Internet.

SUPER 8

Phone: (517)543-8288

Hotel
$62-$122

Address: 828 E Shepherd St 48813 **Location:** I-69, exit 60 (SR 50), just w. Located in a quiet area. **Facility:** Smoke free premises. 49 units. 2 stories (no elevator), interior corridors. **Terms:** cancellation fee imposed. **Guest Services:** wireless Internet.

—— **WHERE TO DINE** ——

THE GAVEL

Phone: 517/543-1620

American
$5-$10

Wide storefront windows are a good spot for people watching at this neighborhood eatery. **Bar:** full bar. **Hours:** 7 am-9:30 pm, Fri-10:30 pm. Closed major holidays; also Sun. **Address:** 112 S Cochran St 48813 **Location:** I-69, exit 61, jct Lansing Rd; downtown. **Parking:** street only.

CHEBOYGAN pop. 5,295

BEST WESTERN RIVER TERRACE

Phone: (231)627-5688

Motel
$89-$179

Address: 847 S Main St 49721 **Location:** 1 mi s on SR 27. Located on the Cheboygan River. **Facility:** Smoke free premises. 53 units. 2 stories (no elevator), interior/exterior corridors. **Terms:** office hours 6 am-1 am. **Amenities:** *Some:* high-speed Internet. **Pool(s):** heated indoor. **Activities:** whirlpool, boat dock, snowmobiling, exercise room. **Guest Services:** wireless Internet. *(see ad below)*

AAA Benefit:
Members save up to 20%, plus 10% bonus points with free rewards program.

/ SOME UNITS FEE

FREE expanded continental breakfast and high-speed Internet

BIRCH HAUS MOTEL

Phone: (231)627-5862

Motel
$40-$80

Address: 1301 Mackinaw Ave 49721 **Location:** On US 23, 0.8 mi nw. **Facility:** Smoke free premises. 13 units, some two bedrooms. 1 story, exterior corridors. **Parking:** winter plug-ins. **Terms:** cancellation fee imposed. **Activities:** snowmobiling. **Guest Services:** wireless Internet.

/ SOME UNITS FEE

CONTINENTAL INN

Phone: 231/627-7164

Motel
$39-$99

Address: 613 N Main St 49721 **Location:** Jct US 23 and SR 27. **Facility:** Smoke free premises. 41 units, some two bedrooms. 2 stories (no elevator), exterior corridors. **Terms:** office hours 7 am-11 pm. **Amenities:** high-speed Internet. **Pool(s):** heated outdoor. **Activities:** snowmobiling. **Guest Services:** coin laundry, wireless Internet.

/ SOME UNITS FEE

WHERE TO DINE

HACK-MA-TACK INN

 *Menu on AAA.com*

Phone: 231/625-2919

American
$18-$29

This historic 1894 log lodge overlooks the Cheboygan River, sitting amid a mature cedar, pine and birch setting. Rustic appointments, a moose head mounted on a stone fireplace, a canoe and racing boat hanging from the log rafters all add to the ambience. Prime rib and whitefish are house specialties. **Bar:** full bar. **Hours:** Open 5/1-10/15; 5 pm-10 pm; hours may vary. **Address:** 8131 Beebe Rd 49721 **Location:** On SR 27, 3.3 mi s, 0.3 mi e on US 33, then 2 mi sw, follow signs. **Historic**

CHELSEA pop. 4,398

CHELSEA COMFORT INN & VILLAGE CONFERENCE CENTER

Phone: (734)433-8000

Hotel
$99-$299

Address: 1645 Commerce Park Dr 48118 **Location:** I-94, exit 159 (SR 52/Main St), just n. **Facility:** Smoke free premises. 82 units, some two bedrooms. 3 stories, interior corridors. **Amenities:** high-speed Internet. **Pool(s):** heated indoor. **Activities:** whirlpool, exercise room. **Guest Services:** valet laundry, wireless Internet.

HOLIDAY INN EXPRESS

Phone: (734)433-1600

Hotel
$94-$266

Address: 1540 Commerce Park Dr 48118 **Location:** I-94, exit 159 (SR 52/Main St), 0.3 mi n. **Facility:** Smoke free premises. 65 units. 3 stories, interior corridors. **Terms:** cancellation fee imposed. **Pool(s):** heated indoor. **Activities:** exercise room. **Guest Services:** valet laundry, wireless Internet.

—— WHERE TO DINE ——

THE COMMON GRILL

Phone: 734/475-0470

American
$10-$32

This busy eatery has a trendy look and an imaginative menu. Exotic spices give American classics a new twist. The owner constantly searches the markets of such cities as Los Angeles and San Francisco, to bring back fresh new recipes. **Bar:** full bar. **Hours:** 11 am-10 pm, Fri & Sat-11 pm, Sun-9 pm. Closed major holidays; also Mon. **Address:** 112 S Main St 48118 **Location:** I-94, exit 159 (SR 52/Main St), 2 mi n.

CHESANING pop. 2,548

COLONIAL MOTEL

Phone: 989/845-3292

Motel
$60-$130

Address: 9475 E M-57 48616 **Location:** On SR 57, 0.5 mi e. **Facility:** Smoke free premises. 14 units. 1 story, exterior corridors. **Terms:** 3 day cancellation notice-fee imposed. **Guest Services:** wireless Internet. **Free Special Amenities:** expanded continental breakfast and high-speed Internet.

CHESTERFIELD —See Detroit p. 274.

CHRISTMAS

—— WHERE TO DINE ——

FOGGY'S STEAK HOUSE

Phone: 906/387-3357

American
$5-$20

Along the main highway and the snowmobile trails, the steak house offers cuts of beef and other traditional dishes. Guests can sip a drink in the active sports bar before dinner, then grill their own steak. **Bar:** full bar. **Hours:** 11 am-11 pm; hours may vary. Closed: 11/24, 12/25. **Address:** E7876 WM-M28 49862 **Location:** On SR 28; center.

CLARE pop. 3,000

DAYS INN

Phone: 989/802-0144

Hotel
$58-$67

Address: 10100 S Clare Ave 48617 **Location:** On Business Rt US 10 and 127, just w of jct US 127 and Old US 27. **Facility:** Smoke free premises. 60 units. 2 stories (no elevator), interior corridors. **Parking:** winter plug-ins. **Activities:** whirlpool, snowmobiling. **Guest Services:** coin laundry, wireless Internet.

DAYS INN OF CLARE

Phone: (989)386-1111

Hotel
$70-$120

Address: 10318 S Clare Ave 48617 **Location:** On Business Rt US 10 and 127; just w of jct US 127 and Old US 27. **Facility:** Smoke free premises. 85 units. 2 stories (no elevator), interior corridors. **Parking:** winter plug-ins. **Amenities:** safes (fee). **Pool(s):** heated indoor. **Activities:** whirlpool, snowmobiling. **Guest Services:** coin laundry, wireless Internet.

CLARKSTON —See Detroit p. 275.

CLAWSON —See Detroit p. 275.

CLINTON TOWNSHIP

—— WHERE TO DINE ——

TIN FISH

Phone: 586/286-2600

Seafood
$9-$28

Those looking for a chic place to relax and unwind after a long day of shopping should head to this hip spot featuring seasonal fish that can be cooked in any preparation style. The house specialties, such as tuna au poivre, bacon-wrapped scallops or surf and turf, provide plenty of temptation as well. Patrons not in the mood for fish can look toward the long list of pasta dishes or the menu's "Land Lovers" section that includes steaks, ribs and cashew chicken. **Bar:** full bar. **Reservations:** required. **Hours:** 11 am-10 pm, Fri & Sat-11 pm, Sun-9 pm. Closed major holidays. **Address:** 17470 Hall Rd 48038 **Location:** Between Garfield and Romeo Plank rds; in The Mall at Partridge Creek.

Don't Take a Vacation From Your Car Seat

Vacations should be fun and hassle-free.
Hertz provides free use of a child seat for AAA/CAA members!
Contact your AAA/CAA travel counselor or visit us at
AAA.com/hertz or CAA.ca/hertz for reservations.

CLIO pop. 2,483

—— WHERE TO DINE ——

LUCKY'S STEAKHOUSE

American
$8-$20

Phone: 810/686-8600

Big portions are the norm at this family-oriented local favorite where service is quick and attentive. Local, black-and-white historical photos are on display in the dining room. **Bar:** full bar. **Reservations:** required. **Hours:** 11 am-10 pm, Fri-11 pm, Sat noon-11 pm, Sun noon-9 pm. Closed major holidays. **Address:** 11451 Linden Rd 48420 **Location:** I-75, exit 131, just w. CALL

COLDWATER pop. 12,697

HAMPTON INN

Hotel
$89-$129

Phone: (517)279-9800

AAA Benefit:
Members save up to 10% everyday!

Address: 391 N Willowbrook Rd 49036 **Location:** I-69, exit 13 (US 12), just e. **Facility:** Smoke free premises. 66 units. 3 stories, interior corridors. **Terms:** 1-7 night minimum stay, cancellation fee imposed. **Amenities:** high-speed Internet. **Pool(s):** heated indoor. **Activities:** exercise room. **Guest Services:** valet laundry, wireless Internet.

HOLIDAY INN EXPRESS

Hotel
$99-$159

Phone: (517)279-0900

Address: 630 E Chicago St 49036 **Location:** I-69, exit 13 (US 12), just sw. **Facility:** Smoke free premises. 80 units. 3 stories, interior corridors. **Terms:** 9 day cancellation notice. **Pool(s):** heated indoor. **Activities:** whirlpool, exercise room. **Guest Services:** valet and coin laundry, wireless Internet.

SUPER 8

Hotel
$45-$126

Phone: (517)278-8833

Address: 600 Orleans Blvd 49036 **Location:** I-69, exit 13 (US 12), 0.3 mi w on E Chicago St, just n on N Michigan Ave, then just e. **Facility:** Smoke free premises. 52 units. 2 stories (no elevator), interior corridors. **Guest Services:** wireless Internet.

—— WHERE TO DINE ——

NORTHWOODS COFFEE COMPANY

Deli
$4-$8

Phone: 517/278-1998

Part gift shop and part coffee shop, the downtown establishment serves made-to-order sandwiches, homemade soups and salads and desserts in a relaxing and inviting environment. **Hours:** 7 am-6 pm, Sat 8 am-5 pm. Closed major holidays; also Sun. **Address:** 34 W Chicago St 49036 **Location:** I-69, exit 13 (US 12), 2 mi w on E Chicago St; downtown. **Parking:** street only.

COMMERCE —See Detroit p. 275.

COMSTOCK PARK pop. 10,674 (See map and index starting on p. 324)

COMFORT SUITES GRAND RAPIDS NORTH

Hotel
$65-$179

Phone: (616)785-7899

Address: 350 Dodge St 49321 **Location:** US 131, exit 91. **Facility:** Smoke free premises. 86 units, some two bedrooms and kitchens. 4 stories, interior corridors. **Parking:** winter plug-ins. **Amenities:** high-speed Internet. **Pool(s):** heated indoor. **Activities:** whirlpool, movie theater, exercise room. **Guest Services:** valet and coin laundry, wireless Internet.

—— WHERE TO DINE ——

EMPIRE CHINESE BUFFET II

Chinese
$6-$11

Phone: 616/785-8880   (33)

The family restaurant offers a daily lunch and dinner buffet at a reasonable price. A take-out buffet also is available. **Hours:** 11 am-10 pm, Fri & Sat-11 pm; hours may vary. Closed: 11/24. **Address:** 4255 Alpine Ave NW 49321 **Location:** Jct I-96 and Alpine Ave, 2 mi n on SR 37.

COPPER HARBOR

LAKE FANNY HOOE RESORT

Motel
$90-$125

Phone: 906/289-4451

Address: 505 2nd St 49918 **Location:** Just s on Manganese Rd. **Facility:** Smoke free premises. 17 units, some efficiencies and cabins. 1-2 stories (no elevator), exterior corridors. **Terms:** office hours 8 am-10 pm, 7 day cancellation notice-fee imposed. **Activities:** beach access, rental boats, rental canoes, rental paddleboats, boat dock, fishing, cross country skiing, snowmobiling, hiking trails. **Fee:** game room. **Guest Services:** coin laundry, wireless Internet.

—— **WHERE TO DINE** ——

TAMARACK INN

American
$5-$19

Phone: 906/289-4522

In the heart of the small, remote town, the relaxed restaurant is a nice spot for an informal meal. Menu offerings include broasted chicken, prime rib and fresh whitefish and trout from Lake Superior. Wait times are typically short, even during summer. **Hours:** 6:30 am-8 pm; seasonal hours may vary. **Address:** 571 Gratiot Ave 49918 **Location:** Jct US 41 and SR 26.

CROSS VILLAGE pop. 100

—— **WHERE TO DINE** ——

LEGS INN

Polish
$7-$19

Phone: 231/526-2281

More than 100 varieties of beer and wine complement authentic entrees of Polish and American cuisine. The historic stone and timber landmark is decorated with distinctive driftwood furniture. The outdoor patio and gardens overlook the lake. **Bar:** full bar. **Hours:** Open 5/21-10/31; noon-9 pm; hours may vary. **Address:** 6425 Lake Shore Dr 49723 **Location:** At end of SR 119; center.

DAVISON pop. 5,536

COMFORT INN DAVISON

Hotel
$89-$155

Phone: (810)658-2700

Address: 10082 Lapeer Rd 48423 **Location:** I-69, exit 145 (S State Rd), just n on SR 15, then e. Located in a quiet area. **Facility:** Smoke free premises. 66 units. 2 stories (no elevator), interior corridors. **Pool(s):** heated outdoor. **Guest Services:** valet laundry, wireless Internet. **Free Special Amenities:** continental breakfast and high-speed Internet.

—— **WHERE TO DINE** ——

ITALIA GARDENS

Italian
$7-$17

Phone: 810/653-6899

The small restaurant serves up many favorite entrees such as spaghetti, ribs, manicotti and pizza. The casually upscale dining room features a modern Italian theme, which is evident in the stone columns and candle-topped pedestal tables. **Bar:** beer & wine. **Hours:** 11 am-9 pm, Fri & Sat-10 pm, Sun noon-8 pm. Closed major holidays. **Address:** 1141 S State Rd 48423 **Location:** I-69, exit 145 (SR 15), 0.4 mi n.

LUCKY'S STEAKHOUSE

Steak
$7-$21

Phone: 810/653-4300

Big portions are the trademark for this local family-oriented favorite, where service is quick and attentive. Local black-and-white historical photos are on display in the dining room. **Bar:** full bar. **Hours:** 11 am-10 pm, Fri-11 pm, Sat noon-11 pm, Sun noon-9 pm. Closed major holidays. **Address:** 10098 E Lapeer Rd 48423 **Location:** I-69, exit 145 (S State Rd), just n on SR 15, then e. CALL

DEARBORN —See Detroit p. 276.

Destination Detroit
pop. 951,270

*I*n addition to the attractions on your list of places to visit, consider the city's musical, theatrical and recreational offerings.

*C*atch a symphony or theater performance. If you're into pro sports, take your pick between baseball, basketball, football and hockey.

Detroit skyline.

Detroit Historical Museum.
(See listing page 57)

© Richard Cummins / Lonely Planet Images

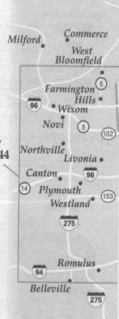

*P*laces included in this AAA Destination City:

See Vicinity map page 244

Holly

Clarkston

Waterford

Milford   Commerce
           West Bloomfield

Farmington Hills   Wixom

Novi

Northville   Livonia

Canton   Plymouth
          Westland

Romulus

Belleville

Greektown Casino, Detroit.
(See listing page 58)

Comerica Park, Detroit.
(See mention page 59)

See Downtown
map page 240

Eastern Market, Detroit.
(See mention page 59)

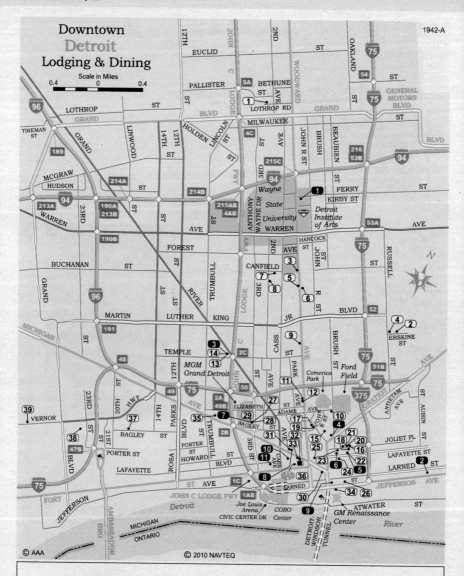

Downtown
Detroit
Lodging & Dining

Scale in Miles
0.4 0 0.4

1942-A

Downtown Detroit

This index helps you "spot" where approved lodgings and restaurants are located on the corresponding detailed maps. Lodging daily rate range is for comparison only and show the property's high season. Restaurant rate range is a combination of lunch and/or dinner. Turn to the listing page for more detailed rate information and consult display ads for special promotions.

DOWNTOWN DETROIT

Map Page	OA	Lodgings	Diamond Rated	High Season	Page
1 / p. 240	(AAA)	**The Inn on Ferry Street**	◆◆◆	$119-$169 SAVE	255
2 / p. 240		Detroit Regency Hotel	◆◆	$70-$130	255
3 / p. 240	(AAA)	**MotorCity Casino Hotel - see ad starting on p. 258, p. 58**	◆◆◆◆	$179-$599 SAVE	256
4 / p. 240		Hilton Garden Inn Detroit/Downtown	◆◆◆	$119-$239	255
5 / p. 240		Greektown Casino-Hotel	◆◆◆	$139-$229	255
6 / p. 240		The Atheneum Suite Hotel & Conference Center	◆◆◆	$159-$340	255
7 / p. 240	(AAA)	**MGM Grand Detroit - see ad p. 257**	◆◆◆◆	$249-$299 SAVE	256
8 / p. 240	(AAA)	**The Westin Book Cadillac Detroit - see ad p. 261**	◆◆◆◆	$179-$409 SAVE	261
9 / p. 240		Detroit Downtown Courtyard by Marriott	◆◆◆	$159-$169	255
10 / p. 240		Holiday Inn Express	◆◆◆	$99-$199	255
11 / p. 240		Doubletree Guest Suites Detroit Downtown/ Fort Shelby	◆◆◆	$129-$229	255

Map Page	OA	Restaurants	Diamond Rated	Cuisine	Meal Range	Page
1 / p. 240		Cuisine	◆◆◆	French	$22-$33	263
2 / p. 240		Roma Cafe	◆◆	Italian	$8-$25	265
3 / p. 240		The Whitney	◆◆◆	American	$9-$37	266
4 / p. 240		Sala Thai	◆◆	Thai	$7-$13	265
5 / p. 240		Union Street	◆◆	American	$9-$21	266
6 / p. 240		Majestic Cafe	◆◆	American	$8-$25	264
7 / p. 240		Traffic Jam & Snug	◆◆	American	$8-$18	266
8 / p. 240		Mario's	◆◆	Italian	$7-$35	264
9 / p. 240		Atlas Global Bistro	◆◆	American	$7-$35	262
10 / p. 240		The Elwood Bar & Grill	◆	American	$5-$12	263
11 / p. 240		Hockeytown Cafe	◆◆	American	$7-$24	264
12 / p. 240		DaEdoardo's Foxtown Grille	◆◆◆	Italian	$7-$36	263
13 / p. 240	(AAA)	**Iridescence Restaurant**	◆◆◆◆	American	$28-$42	264
14 / p. 240		Assembly Line Buffet	◆◆	American	$19-$27	262
15 / p. 240		Coaches Corner	◆◆	American	$6-$10	263
16 / p. 240		Pizza Papalis	◆◆	Pizza	$8-$22	265
17 / p. 240		Detroit Beer Co.	◆◆	American	$8-$18	263
18 / p. 240		Pegasus Taverna Restaurant	◆◆	Greek	$6-$27	265
19 / p. 240		Small Plates	◆◆	American	$10-$15	265
20 / p. 240		Astoria Pastry Shop	◆	Breads/Pastries	$2-$5	262
21 / p. 240	(AAA)	**Mosaic**	◆◆◆	International	$8-$65	265

Map Page	OA	Restaurants (cont'd)	Diamond Rated	Cuisine	Meal Range	Page
㉒ / p. 240		Bistro 555	▼▼	American	$8-$36	262
㉓ / p. 240		Fishbone's Rhythm Kitchen Cafe	▼▼	Cajun	$6-$25	263
㉔ / p. 240		Loco Bar & Grill	▼▼	Tex-Mex	$6-$18	264
㉕ / p. 240		Hard Rock Cafe	▼▼	American	$12-$24 [SAVE]	263
㉖ / p. 240		Tom's Oyster Bar	▼▼	Seafood	$11-$24	265
㉗ / p. 240		Wolfgang Puck Grille - see ad p. 257	▼▼▼	American	$15-$50	266
㉘ / p. 240		Bourbon Steak - see ad p. 257	▼▼▼	Steak	$30-$52	262
㉙ / p. 240		Saltwater - see ad p. 257	▼▼▼▼	Seafood	$30-$52	265
㉚ / p. 240		Checker Bar & Grill	▼▼	American	$6-$10	263
㉛ / p. 240		Michael Symon's Roast	▼▼▼	American	$14-$38	265
㉜ / p. 240		American Coney Island	▼	American	$3-$10	262
㉝ / p. 240		Lafayette Coney Island	▼	American	$3-$8	264
㉞ / p. 240		Coach Insignia	▼▼▼	Steak	$23-$50	263
㉟ / p. 240		Nemo's Bar & Grill	▼	American	$4-$8	265
㊱ / p. 240		Caucus Club	▼▼	American	$9-$28	262
㊲ / p. 240	⏛	**Mexican Village Restaurant**	▼▼	Mexican	$6-$20	264
㊳ / p. 240		Evie's Tamales	▼	Mexican	$6-$8	263
㊴ / p. 240		Armando's	▼▼	Mexican	$5-$28	262

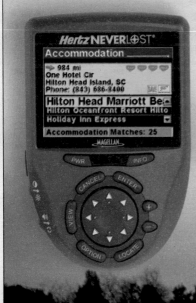

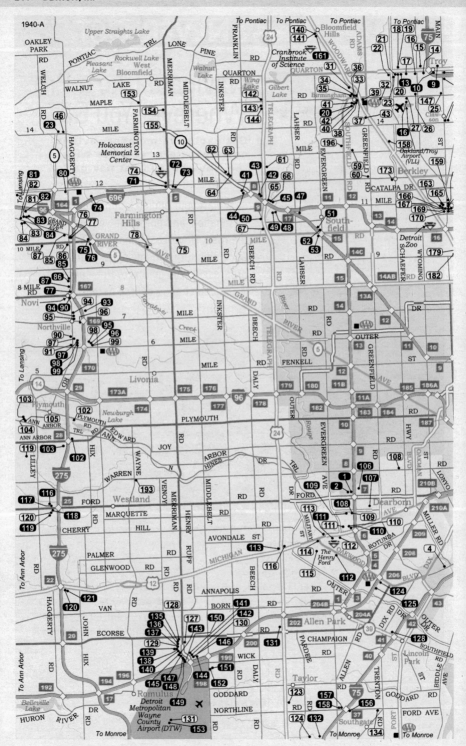

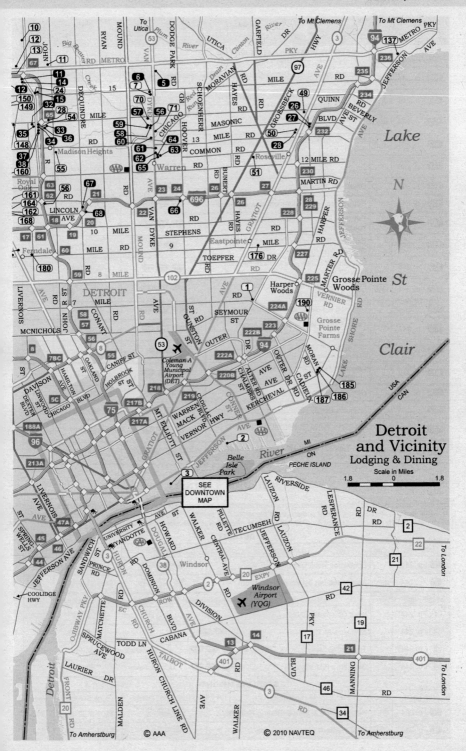

Detroit
and Vicinity
Lodging & Dining

Scale in Miles

© AAA

© 2010 NAVTEQ

✈ Airport Accommodations

Map Page	OA	DETROIT METROPOLITAN WAYNE COUNTY	Diamond Rated	High Season	Page
148 / p. 244		Baymont Inn & Suites Detroit-Airport, opposite airport	▼▼	$44-$71	293
150 / p. 244	◉	**Best Western Gateway International Hotel, opposite airport**	▼▼	$75-$149 SAVE	293
143 / p. 244	◉	**Clarion Hotel Detroit Metro Airport, opposite airport**	▼▼▼	$55-$100 SAVE	293
142 / p. 244		Courtyard by Marriott-Metro Airport, opposite airport	▼▼▼	$107-$137	293
137 / p. 244		Crowne Plaza Hotel Detroit Metro Airport, opposite airport	▼▼▼	$89-$169	293
151 / p. 244		Days Inn, opposite airport	▼▼	$54-$63	293
146 / p. 244		Detroit Metro Airport Marriott, opposite airport	▼▼▼	$152-$194	293
145 / p. 244		Embassy Suites-Detroit Metro Airport, opposite airport	▼▼▼	$99-$159	294
144 / p. 244		Extended StayAmerica Detroit-Metro Airport, opposite airport	▼▼	$60-$70	294
136 / p. 244		Fairfield Inn & Suites by Marriott, opposite airport	▼▼▼	$98-$125	294
147 / p. 244	◉	**Four Points by Sheraton Detroit Metro Airport, opposite airport**	▼▼▼	$85-$180 SAVE	294
138 / p. 244		Hampton Inn & Suites, Opposite airport	▼▼▼	$79-$129	294
139 / p. 244		Hilton Garden Inn-Detroit Metro Airport, opposite airport	▼▼▼	$79-$139	294
135 / p. 244		La Quinta Inn Detroit Airport Romulus, opposite airport	▼▼	$84-$126	294
141 / p. 244		Lexington Hotel-Detroit Metro Airport, opposite airport	▼▼▼	$45-$99	294
149 / p. 244		Red Roof Inn, opposite airport	▼▼	$39-$60	294
152 / p. 244		Romulus Quality Inn & Suites, opposite airport	▼▼	$60-$80	295
140 / p. 244		SpringHill Suites by Marriott Detroit Metro Airport Romulus, opposite airport	▼▼▼	$107-$137	295
153 / p. 244	◉	**The Westin Detroit Metropolitan Airport, in terminal**	▼▼▼▼	$99-$329 SAVE	295

Detroit and Vicinity

This index helps you "spot" where approved lodgings and restaurants are located on the corresponding detailed maps. Lodging daily rate range is for comparison only and show the property's high season. Restaurant rate range is a combination of lunch and/or dinner. Turn to the listing page for more detailed rate information and consult display ads for special promotions.

DETROIT

Map Page	OA	Lodgings	Diamond Rated	High Season	Page
1 / p. 244		Doubletree Hotel Dearborn	▼▼▼	$99-$199	266
2 / p. 244	◉	**Residence Inn by Marriott-Dearborn**	▼▼▼	$139-$149 SAVE	267

Map Page	OA	Restaurants	Diamond Rated	Cuisine	Meal Range	Page
1 / p. 244		Milt's Gourmet Barbecue	▼	Barbecue	$6-$23	267
2 / p. 244		Sindbad's At The River	▼▼	American	$6-$28	267
3 / p. 244		The Rattlesnake Club	▼▼▼	American	$12-$46	267
4 / p. 244		Giovanni's Ristorante	▼▼▼	Italian	$11-$33	267

STERLING HEIGHTS

Map Page	OA	Lodgings	Diamond Rated	High Season	Page
5 / p. 244	◉	**Hampton Inn & Suites-Sterling Heights**	▼▼▼	$109-$139 SAVE	302
6 / p. 244	◉	**Best Western Plus Sterling Inn**	▼▼▼	$130-$190 SAVE	302

Map Page	OA	Restaurant	Diamond Rated	Cuisine	Meal Range	Page
⑦ / p. 244		Loon River Cafe	▽▽	American	$7-$20	303

TROY

Map Page	OA	Lodgings	Diamond Rated	High Season	Page
❾ / p. 244		Troy Marriott	▽▽▽	$189-$199	305
❿ / p. 244		Drury Inn & Suites-Troy	▽▽▽	$80-$229	304
⓫ / p. 244		Quality Inn	▽▽	$79-$135	304
⓬ / p. 244		The Gatehouse Suites Troy Hotel	▽▽▽	$152-$186	304
⓭ / p. 244		Somerset Inn	▽▽▽	$99-$194	305
⓮ / p. 244	🚺	**Red Roof Inn-Troy #7021**	▽▽	$56-$66 🆂🅰🆅🅴	305
⓯ / p. 244		Courtyard by Marriott	▽▽▽	$129-$139	304
⓰ / p. 244		Homewood Suites by Hilton Detroit/Troy	▽▽▽	$99-$169	304

Map Page	OA	Restaurants	Diamond Rated	Cuisine	Meal Range	Page
⑩ / p. 244		Ridley's Bakery Cafe	▽	Deli	$5-$10	307
⑪ / p. 244		Joe Kool's	▽▽	American	$8-$17	306
⑫ / p. 244		Big Beaver Tavern	▽▽	American	$8-$25	305
⑬ / p. 244		Kona Grill	▽▽▽	New American	$9-$30	306
⑭ / p. 244		Ruth's Chris Steak House	▽▽▽	Steak	$20-$45	307
⑮ / p. 244		Morton's The Steakhouse	▽▽▽	Steak	$33-$48	306
⑯ / p. 244		Recipes	▽▽	American	$6-$13	307
⑰ / p. 244		Maggiano's Little Italy	▽▽▽	Italian	$11-$38	306
⑱ / p. 244		J. Alexander's Restaurant	▽▽▽	American	$12-$27	305
⑲ / p. 244		The Capital Grille	▽▽▽	American	$11-$45	305
⑳ / p. 244		Zodiac at Neiman Marcus	▽▽▽	American	$12-$40	307
㉑ / p. 244		P.F. Chang's China Bistro	▽▽▽	Chinese	$10-$21	306
㉒ / p. 244		Ocean Prime	▽▽▽	Seafood	$12-$48	306
㉓ / p. 244		McCormick & Schmick's	▽▽▽	Seafood	$7-$32	306
㉔ / p. 244		Mon Jin Lau	▽▽▽	Chinese	$7-$26	306
㉕ / p. 244		Priya	▽▽	Indian	$8-$17	306
㉖ / p. 244	🚺	**Shield's of Troy**	▽▽	Pizza	$7-$13	307
㉗ / p. 244		Café Sushi	▽▽	Japanese	$6-$25	305
㉘ / p. 244		Lakeshore Grill	▽▽	American	$9-$14	306

BIRMINGHAM

Map Page	OA	Lodging	Diamond Rated	High Season	Page
⑳ / p. 244	🚺	**The Townsend Hotel**	▽▽▽▽	$299-$375 🆂🅰🆅🅴	271

Map Page	OA	Restaurants	Diamond Rated	Cuisine	Meal Range	Page
㉛ / p. 244		Old Woodward Deli	▽	Deli	$6-$8	272
㉜ / p. 244	🚺	**Big Rock Chop House**	▽▽▽	Steak	$8-$35	271
㉝ / p. 244		Hunter House	▽	American	$5-$10	272
㉞ / p. 244		Mitchell's Fish Market	▽▽▽	Seafood	$17-$30	272
㉟ / p. 244		Cameron's Steakhouse	▽▽▽	Steak	$20-$44	271
㊱ / p. 244		New Bangkok Thai Bistro	▽▽	Thai	$8-$12	272

Map Page	OA	Restaurants (cont'd)	Diamond Rated	Cuisine	Meal Range	Page
㊲ / p. 244		Peabody's	◆◆	American	$6-$27	272
㊳ / p. 244		Forte'	◆◆	American	$8-$32	271
㊴ / p. 244		Forest Grill	◆◆◆	Continental	$14-$48	271
㊵ / p. 244		220	◆◆	Italian	$9-$35	271
㊶ / p. 244		Streetside Seafood	◆◆◆	Seafood	$8-$28	272
㊷ / p. 244	AAA	**Rugby Grille**	◆◆◆◆	American	$10-$40	272
㊸ / p. 244		?How About Lunch	◆	Deli	$5-$7	272

COMMERCE

Map Page	OA	Lodging	Diamond Rated	High Season	Page
㉓ / p. 244		Hampton Inn - Detroit / Novi - see ad p. 288	◆◆◆	$89-$179	275

Map Page	OA	Restaurant	Diamond Rated	Cuisine	Meal Range	Page
㊻ / p. 244		Gest Omelettes	◆	Breakfast	$5-$10	276

ROSEVILLE

Map Page	OA	Lodgings	Diamond Rated	High Season	Page
㉖ / p. 244		Holiday Inn Express & Suites	◆◆◆	$99-$199	296
㉗ / p. 244	AAA	**Red Roof Inn #7012**	◆◆	$57-$74 [SAVE]	296
㉘ / p. 244	AAA	**Best Western Plus Georgian Inn**	◆◆◆	$69-$99 [SAVE]	296

Map Page	OA	Restaurants	Diamond Rated	Cuisine	Meal Range	Page
㊾ / p. 244		Sea Breeze Diner	◆	American	$5-$14	296
㊿ / p. 244		Olives Mediterranean	◆◆	Mediterranean	$6-$22	296
51 / p. 244		Mr. Paul's Chophouse	◆◆◆	American	$9-$50	296

MADISON HEIGHTS

Map Page	OA	Lodgings	Diamond Rated	High Season	Page
㉜ / p. 244	AAA	**Best Western Troy-Madison Inn**	◆◆	$60-$100 [SAVE]	284
㉝ / p. 244		Motel 6 Madison Heights #1109	◆	$42-$52	285
㉞ / p. 244		Fairfield Inn by Marriott	◆◆	$80-$102	284
㉟ / p. 244	AAA	**Econo Lodge**	◆◆	$36-$140 [SAVE]	284
㊱ / p. 244	AAA	**Red Roof Inn #7084**	◆◆	$49-$85 [SAVE]	285
㊲ / p. 244		Residence Inn by Marriott-Detroit Troy/ Madison Heights	◆◆◆	$170-$217	285
㊳ / p. 244	AAA	**Hampton Inn Detroit/Madison Heights - see ad p. 285**	◆◆◆	$58-$121 [SAVE]	285

Map Page	OA	Restaurants	Diamond Rated	Cuisine	Meal Range	Page
54 / p. 244		Big Fish Seafood Bistro	◆◆	Seafood	$6-$24 [SAVE]	286
55 / p. 244		The Breakfast Club	◆◆	American	$6-$10	286
56 / p. 244		Boodle's Restaurant	◆◆	American	$8-$28	286

SOUTHFIELD

Map Page	OA	Lodgings	Diamond Rated	High Season	Page
㊶ / p. 244	AAA	**SpringHill Suites by Marriott Detroit/ Southfield**	◆◆◆	$108-$138 [SAVE]	300
㊷ / p. 244		Marvin's Garden Inn	◆◆	Rates not provided	299
㊸ / p. 244	AAA	**Red Roof Inn-Southfield #7133**	◆◆	$41-$111 [SAVE]	299
㊹ / p. 244	AAA	**Embassy Suites Detroit-Southfield**	◆◆◆	$68-$95 [SAVE]	299
㊺ / p. 244		Hampton Inn-Southfield	◆◆◆	$79-$109	299

SOUTHFIELD (cont'd)

Map Page	OA	Lodgings (cont'd)	Diamond Rated	High Season	Page
47 / p. 244		Candlewood Suites	◈◈	$69-$129	298
48 / p. 244		Courtyard by Marriott-Southfield	◈◈◈	$89-$114	298
49 / p. 244		Detroit Marriott Southfield	◈◈◈	$161-$206	298
50 / p. 244		Quality Inn Southfield	◈◈◈	$79-$99	299
51 / p. 244	⟨AAA⟩	**The Westin Hotel Southfield-Detroit -** see ad p. 300	◈◈◈◈	Rates not provided [SAVE]	300
52 / p. 244	⟨AAA⟩	**Holiday Inn Express Hotel & Suites**	◈◈◈	$119-$169 [SAVE]	299
53 / p. 244		Comfort Suites	◈◈◈	$89-$230	298

Map Page	OA	Restaurants	Diamond Rated	Cuisine	Meal Range	Page
59 / p. 244		Tavern on 13	◈◈	American	$6-$20	301
60 / p. 244		Sweet Lorraine's Cafe & Bar	◈◈	Continental	$9-$17	301
61 / p. 244		Shiraz	◈◈◈	American	$8-$36	301
62 / p. 244		Beans & Cornbread: A Soulful Bistro	◈◈	Soul Food	$6-$18	301
63 / p. 244		Bacco Ristorante	◈◈◈	Italian	$10-$35	301
64 / p. 244		Fishbone's Rhythm Kitchen Cafe	◈◈	Cajun	$8-$23	301
65 / p. 244		New Seoul Garden	◈◈	Asian	$9-$25	301
66 / p. 244		Copper Canyon Brewery & Restaurant	◈◈	American	$11-$24	301
67 / p. 244		C.A. Muer's Merriwether	◈◈◈	American	$7-$30	301

WARREN

Map Page	OA	Lodgings	Diamond Rated	High Season	Page
56 / p. 244	⟨AAA⟩	**Baymont Inn & Suites Warren**	◈◈◈	Rates not provided [SAVE]	308
57 / p. 244		Comfort Inn	◈◈	Rates not provided	309
58 / p. 244		Fairfield Inn by Marriott	◈◈	$80-$102	309
59 / p. 244		Candlewood Suites-Detroit Warren	◈◈	$69-$109	308
60 / p. 244	⟨AAA⟩	**TownePlace Suites by Marriott-Warren**	◈◈◈	$107-$137 [SAVE]	310
61 / p. 244		La Quinta Inn Detroit Warren Tech Center	◈◈	$49-$89	309
62 / p. 244		Courtyard by Marriott-Warren	◈◈◈	$114-$124	309
63 / p. 244		Hawthorn Suites	◈◈◈	Rates not provided	309
64 / p. 244		Extended Stay Deluxe Detroit-Warren	◈◈	$68-$78	309
65 / p. 244		Holiday Inn Hotel & Suites	◈◈◈	$89-$114	309
66 / p. 244		Holiday Inn Express	◈◈◈	$104-$114	309
67 / p. 244	⟨AAA⟩	**Red Roof Inn-Warren #070**	◈◈	$54-$74 [SAVE]	309
68 / p. 244	⟨AAA⟩	**Comfort Suites**	◈◈◈	$80-$200 [SAVE]	309

Map Page	OA	Restaurants	Diamond Rated	Cuisine	Meal Range	Page
70 / p. 244		Andiamo	◈◈◈	Italian	$9-$30	310
71 / p. 244		Michelle's Restaurant & Sweetheart Bakery	◈◈	American	$6-$13	310

FARMINGTON HILLS

Map Page	OA	Lodgings	Diamond Rated	High Season	Page
71 / p. 244		Courtyard by Marriott Detroit Farmington Hills	◈◈◈	$121-$154	279
72 / p. 244	⟨AAA⟩	**Fairfield Inn & Suites by Marriott**	◈◈◈	$98-$125 [SAVE]	279

FARMINGTON HILLS (cont'd)

Map Page	OA	Lodgings (cont'd)	Diamond Rated	High Season	Page
73 / p. 244		Extended StayAmerica Detroit-Farmington Hills	◆◆	$55-$65	279
74 / p. 244		Candlewood Suites	◆◆	$77-$124	279
75 / p. 244	AAA	**Red Roof Inn-Farmington Hills #7038**	◆◆	$48-$73 SAVE	279
76 / p. 244		Holiday Inn & Suites	◆◆◆	$79-$140	279
77 / p. 244		Holiday Inn Express Hotel & Suites	◆◆◆	$81-$144	279

Map Page	OA	Restaurants	Diamond Rated	Cuisine	Meal Range	Page
74 / p. 244		Hong Hua	◆◆◆	Cantonese	$7-$35	280
75 / p. 244		Café Cortina	◆◆◆◆	Traditional Italian	$12-$40	280
76 / p. 244		Recipes	◆◆	American	$5-$10	280
77 / p. 244		Alfoccino	◆◆	Italian	$8-$20	280
78 / p. 244		John Cowley & Sons Irish Pub	◆◆	Irish	$8-$25	280

NOVI

Map Page	OA	Lodgings	Diamond Rated	High Season	Page
80 / p. 244		Holiday Inn Express & Suites	◆◆	$89-$129	289
81 / p. 244	AAA	**The Baronette Renaissance**	◆◆◆	$119-$199 SAVE	287
82 / p. 244	AAA	**Doubletree Hotel Detroit/Novi - see ad p. 288**	◆◆◆	$89-$129 SAVE	288
83 / p. 244		TownePlace Suites	◆◆	$89-$114	289
84 / p. 244		Courtyard by Marriott	◆◆◆	$112-$143	287
85 / p. 244		Country Inn & Suites By Carlson - see ad p. 6	◆◆◆	Rates not provided	287
86 / p. 244		Extended StayAmerica-Detroit-Novi	◆◆	$70-$80	288
87 / p. 244	AAA	**Sheraton-Detroit-Novi**	◆◆◆	$85-$189 SAVE	289

Map Page	OA	Restaurants	Diamond Rated	Cuisine	Meal Range	Page
81 / p. 244		Diamond Jim Brady's Bistro	◆◆	American	$8-$27	290
82 / p. 244		Steve & Rocky's	◆◆◆	American	$8-$29	290
83 / p. 244		Gus O'Connor's Irish Pub	◆◆	Irish	$8-$19	290
84 / p. 244		W.F. Bi Bim Bab	◆◆	Korean	$6-$25	290
85 / p. 244		Picasso Café	◆	Deli	$4-$8	290
86 / p. 244		Moe's On Ten	◆◆	Seafood	$7-$20	290
87 / p. 244		Ah Wok	◆◆	Chinese	$6-$35	289

NORTHVILLE

Map Page	OA	Lodging	Diamond Rated	High Season	Page
90 / p. 244		Hampton Inn	◆◆◆	$99-$139	286

Map Page	OA	Restaurants	Diamond Rated	Cuisine	Meal Range	Page
90 / p. 244		P.F. Chang's China Bistro	◆◆◆	Chinese	$10-$21	287
91 / p. 244		Papa Vino's Italian Kitchen	◆◆	Italian	$7-$18	286

LIVONIA

Map Page	OA	Lodgings	Diamond Rated	High Season	Page
93 / p. 244		Embassy Suites Hotel	◆◆◆	$80-$134	282
94 / p. 244	AAA	**Hyatt Place Detroit/Livonia**	◆◆◆	$69-$169 SAVE	282
95 / p. 244		Courtyard by Marriott	◆◆◆	$116-$148	282

LIVONIA (cont'd)

Map Page	OA	Lodgings (cont'd)	Diamond Rated	High Season	Page
96 / p. 244		Livonia Marriott	▽▽▽	$152-$194	282
97 / p. 244		TownePlace Suites by Marriott	▽▽	$110-$120	283
98 / p. 244		Fairfield Inn Detroit/Livonia	▽▽	$89-$114	282
99 / p. 244		Residence Inn Detroit-Livonia	▽▽▽	$152-$194	283

Map Page	OA	Restaurants	Diamond Rated	Cuisine	Meal Range	Page
94 / p. 244		Bahama Breeze	▽▽▽	Caribbean	$11-$22	283
95 / p. 244		J. Alexander's Restaurant	▽▽▽	American	$8-$26	283
96 / p. 244		Andiamo	▽▽▽	Italian	$12-$30	283
97 / p. 244		Mitchell's Fish Market	▽▽▽	Seafood	$17-$30	283
98 / p. 244		The Traveling Fork	▽▽	American	$10-$26	283
99 / p. 244		Sweet Lorraine's Cafe & Bar	▽▽	American	$8-$20	283

PLYMOUTH

Map Page	OA	Lodgings	Diamond Rated	High Season	Page
102 / p. 244	◉	**Red Roof Inn-Plymouth #7016**	▽▽	$45-$110 [SAVE]	291
103 / p. 244		Comfort Inn Plymouth Clocktower	▽▽	$45-$110	290

Map Page	OA	Restaurants	Diamond Rated	Cuisine	Meal Range	Page
102 / p. 244		La Bistecca Italian Grille	▽▽▽	Steak	$12-$53	291
103 / p. 244		Sean O'Callaghan's	▽▽	Irish	$7-$23	291
104 / p. 244		Compari's on the Park	▽▽	Italian	$7-$27	291
105 / p. 244		Fiamma Grille	▽▽▽	Continental	$12-$35	291

DEARBORN

Map Page	OA	Lodgings	Diamond Rated	High Season	Page
106 / p. 244		TownePlace Suites	▽▽	$130-$140	278
107 / p. 244	◉	**Courtyard by Marriott-Dearborn**	▽▽▽	$134-$144 [SAVE]	276
108 / p. 244	◉	**The Henry - see ad p. 277**	▽▽▽▽	$179-$199 [SAVE]	277
109 / p. 244		Extended StayAmerica Detroit Dearborn	▽▽	$85-$95	276
110 / p. 244	◉	**Hyatt Regency Dearborn**	▽▽▽▽	$99-$399 [SAVE]	277
111 / p. 244		Dearborn West Village Hotel	▽▽▽	$85-$140	276
112 / p. 244	◉	**The Dearborn Inn, A Marriott Hotel**	▽▽▽▽	$169-$179 [SAVE]	276
113 / p. 244	◉	**Red Roof Inn-Dearborn #7182**	▽▽	$65-$86 [SAVE]	277

Map Page	OA	Restaurants	Diamond Rated	Cuisine	Meal Range	Page
108 / p. 244		New Yasmeen Flying Carpet Café	▽	Lebanese	$6-$10	279
109 / p. 244	◉	**The Grill at The Henry**	▽▽▽▽	Continental	$18-$40	278
110 / p. 244	◉	**Giulio & Sons**	▽▽▽	American	$10-$35	278
111 / p. 244		Big Fish Seafood Bistro	▽▽	Seafood	$6-$24 [SAVE]	278
112 / p. 244		Michigan Café	▽	American	$6-$9	278
113 / p. 244		Andiamo	▽▽▽	Italian	$12-$30	278
114 / p. 244		Kiernan's Steak House	▽▽	American	$7-$25	278
115 / p. 244	◉	**Mati's Deli**	▽	Deli	$6-$8	278
116 / p. 244		Richter's Chalet	▽▽	German	$6-$19	279

CANTON

Map Page	OA	Lodgings	Diamond Rated	High Season	Page
116 / p. 244		Comfort Suites of Canton	▼▼▼	$85-$130	273
117 / p. 244		Fairfield Inn by Marriott	▼▼	$98-$125	273
118 / p. 244		La Quinta Inn Detroit Canton	▼▼	$49-$105	274
119 / p. 244		Hampton Inn & Suites	▼▼▼	$79-$154	273
120 / p. 244	△△△	**Holiday Inn Express Hotel & Suites**	▼▼▼	$99-$109 SAVE	274
121 / p. 244		Super 8-Canton	▼▼	Rates not provided	274

Map Page	OA	Restaurants	Diamond Rated	Cuisine	Meal Range	Page
119 / p. 244		Izakaya Sanpei	▼▼	Japanese	$11-$24	274
120 / p. 244		Ashoka Indian Cuisine	▼▼	Indian	$9-$17	274

ALLEN PARK

Map Page	OA	Lodgings	Diamond Rated	High Season	Page
124 / p. 244	△△△	**Best Western Greenfield Inn**	▼▼▼	$79-$109 SAVE	268
125 / p. 244	△△△	**Holiday Inn Express & Suites**	▼▼▼	$99-$149 SAVE	268

LINCOLN PARK

Map Page	OA	Lodging	Diamond Rated	High Season	Page
128 / p. 244	△△△	**Magnuson Hotel**	▼▼▼	Rates not provided SAVE	282

TAYLOR

Map Page	OA	Lodgings	Diamond Rated	High Season	Page
131 / p. 244	△△△	**Comfort Inn & Suites of Taylor**	▼▼▼	$90-$100 SAVE	303
132 / p. 244	△△△	**Red Roof Inn-Taylor #7189**	▼▼	$38-$75 SAVE	303

Map Page	OA	Restaurants	Diamond Rated	Cuisine	Meal Range	Page
123 / p. 244		Pete's Place	▼▼	American	$5-$12	303
124 / p. 244		Little Daddy's Family Dining	▼	American	$5-$12	303

ROMULUS

Map Page	OA	Lodgings	Diamond Rated	High Season	Page
135 / p. 244		La Quinta Inn Detroit Airport Romulus	▼▼	$84-$126	294
136 / p. 244		Fairfield Inn & Suites by Marriott	▼▼▼	$98-$125	294
137 / p. 244		Crowne Plaza Hotel Detroit Metro Airport	▼▼▼	$89-$169	293
138 / p. 244		Hampton Inn & Suites	▼▼▼	$79-$129	294
139 / p. 244		Hilton Garden Inn-Detroit Metro Airport	▼▼▼	$79-$139	294
140 / p. 244		SpringHill Suites by Marriott Detroit Metro Airport Romulus	▼▼▼	$107-$137	295
141 / p. 244		Lexington Hotel-Detroit Metro Airport	▼▼▼	$45-$99	294
142 / p. 244		Courtyard by Marriott-Metro Airport	▼▼▼	$107-$137	293
143 / p. 244	△△△	**Clarion Hotel Detroit Metro Airport**	▼▼▼	$55-$100 SAVE	293
144 / p. 244		Extended StayAmerica Detroit-Metro Airport	▼▼	$60-$70	294
145 / p. 244		Embassy Suites-Detroit Metro Airport	▼▼▼	$99-$159	294
146 / p. 244		Detroit Metro Airport Marriott	▼▼▼	$152-$194	293
147 / p. 244	△△△	**Four Points by Sheraton Detroit Metro Airport**	▼▼▼	$85-$180 SAVE	294
148 / p. 244		Baymont Inn & Suites Detroit-Airport	▼▼	$44-$71	293
149 / p. 244		Red Roof Inn	▼▼	$39-$60	294

ROMULUS (cont'd)

Map Page	OA	Lodgings (cont'd)	Diamond Rated	High Season	Page
150 / p. 244	🔷	**Best Western Gateway International Hotel**	🔷🔷	$75-$149 SAVE	293
151 / p. 244		Days Inn	🔷🔷	$54-$63	293
152 / p. 244		Romulus Quality Inn & Suites	🔷🔷	$60-$80	295
153 / p. 244	🔷	**The Westin Detroit Metropolitan Airport -** see ad p. 266	🔷🔷🔷🔷	$99-$329 SAVE	295

Map Page	OA	Restaurants	Diamond Rated	Cuisine	Meal Range	Page
127 / p. 244		Leonardo's Pizzeria & Ristorante	🔷🔷	American	$8-$15	295
128 / p. 244	🔷	**Merriman Street Grill**	🔷🔷	American	$6-$12	295
129 / p. 244		Bistro 94	🔷🔷	American	$6-$18	295
130 / p. 244		Ha' Penny Pub	🔷🔷	American	$10-$15	295
131 / p. 244		Dema at the Westin	🔷🔷	American	$13-$42	295

SOUTHGATE

Map Page	OA	Lodgings	Diamond Rated	High Season	Page
156 / p. 244		Holiday Inn Southgate Banquet & Conference Center	🔷🔷🔷	$99-$199	302
157 / p. 244		Comfort Suites	🔷🔷🔷	Rates not provided	302
158 / p. 244		La Quinta Inn Detroit Southgate	🔷🔷🔷	$55-$109	302

Map Page	OA	Restaurant	Diamond Rated	Cuisine	Meal Range	Page
134 / p. 244	🔷	**Hungarian Rhapsody**	🔷🔷	Hungarian	$5-$19	302

BLOOMFIELD HILLS

Map Page	OA	Lodging	Diamond Rated	High Season	Page
161 / p. 244		Radisson Hotel Detroit-Bloomfield Hills	🔷🔷🔷	$139	272

Map Page	OA	Restaurants	Diamond Rated	Cuisine	Meal Range	Page
140 / p. 244		Northern Lakes Seafood Company	🔷🔷🔷	Seafood	$8-$38	273
141 / p. 244		Deli Unique	🔷🔷	Deli	$5-$10	273
142 / p. 244		Beau Jack's Food & Spirits	🔷🔷	American	$7-$17	273
143 / p. 244		Steve's Deli	🔷	Deli	$10-$24	273
144 / p. 244		Andiamo	🔷🔷🔷	Italian	$10-$35	273

MOUNT CLEMENS

Map Page	OA	Restaurant	Diamond Rated	Cuisine	Meal Range	Page
137 / p. 244		Luigi's "The Original"	🔷🔷	Italian	$12-$37	286

CLAWSON

Map Page	OA	Restaurants	Diamond Rated	Cuisine	Meal Range	Page
147 / p. 244		Shilla Korean and Japanese Cuisine	🔷🔷🔷	Korean	$6-$19	275
148 / p. 244		Clawson Steak House	🔷🔷	Steak	$6-$33	275
149 / p. 244		Noble Fish	🔷	Japanese	$5-$16	275
150 / p. 244		Black Lotus Brewing Company	🔷	American	$4-$8	275

WEST BLOOMFIELD

Map Page	OA	Restaurants	Diamond Rated	Cuisine	Meal Range	Page
153 / p. 244	🔷	**The Lark**	🔷🔷🔷🔷	Continental	$65-$80	311
154 / p. 244		Deli Unique	🔷	Deli	$7-$9	311
155 / p. 244		J. Alexander's Restaurant	🔷🔷🔷	American	$8-$25	311

ROYAL OAK

Map Page	OA	Restaurants	Diamond Rated	Cuisine	Meal Range	Page
158 / p. 244		RedCoat Tavern	◆◆	American	$6-$16	297
159 / p. 244		Zumba Mexican Grille	◆	Mexican	$3-$8	297
160 / p. 244		Andiamo	◆◆◆	Italian	$8-$35	296
161 / p. 244		Little Tree Sushi Bar	◆◆	Sushi	$8-$14	297
162 / p. 244		Comet Burger	◆	American	$4-$8	297
163 / p. 244		D'Amato's Neighborhood Restaurant	◆◆◆	Italian	$14-$23	297
164 / p. 244		Royal Oak Brewery	◆◆	American	$8-$14	297
165 / p. 244		Tom's Oyster Bar	◆◆	Seafood	$9-$27	297
166 / p. 244		Astoria Bakery & Cafe	◆	Breads/Pastries	$2-$6	296
167 / p. 244		Lily's Seafood	◆◆	Seafood	$9-$25	297
168 / p. 244		Café Habana	◆◆	Cuban	$7-$13	297
169 / p. 244		Bastone	◆◆	Belgian	$7-$22	296
170 / p. 244		Pronto!	◆◆	Deli	$7-$15	297

BERKLEY

Map Page	OA	Restaurant	Diamond Rated	Cuisine	Meal Range	Page
173 / p. 244		O'Mara's	◆◆	Irish	$6-$25	270

EASTPOINTE

Map Page	OA	Restaurant	Diamond Rated	Cuisine	Meal Range	Page
176 / p. 244		Weekday Cafe	◆◆	Deli	$5-$12	315

FERNDALE

Map Page	OA	Restaurants	Diamond Rated	Cuisine	Meal Range	Page
179 / p. 244		Toast	◆◆	American	$6-$10	281
180 / p. 244		Christine's Cuisine	◆◆	Continental	$5-$17	280
182 / p. 244		Assaggi Mediterranean Bistro	◆◆◆	Mediterranean	$12-$35	280

GROSSE POINTE FARMS

Map Page	OA	Restaurants	Diamond Rated	Cuisine	Meal Range	Page
185 / p. 244	AAA	The Hill Seafood and Chop House	◆◆◆	Seafood	$10-$39	281
186 / p. 244		Lucy's Tavern On The Hill	◆◆	American	$8-$23	281
187 / p. 244		Jumps	◆◆	American	$4-$25	281

GROSSE POINTE WOODS

Map Page	OA	Restaurant	Diamond Rated	Cuisine	Meal Range	Page
190 / p. 244		Mack Avenue Diner	◆	American	$5-$10	281

WESTLAND

Map Page	OA	Restaurant	Diamond Rated	Cuisine	Meal Range	Page
193 / p. 244		Alexander the Great	◆◆	American	$6-$15	311

BEVERLY HILLS

Map Page	OA	Restaurant	Diamond Rated	Cuisine	Meal Range	Page
196 / p. 244		Beverly Hills Grill	◆◆◆	American	$8-$36	271

Visit AAA.com or CAA.ca for one-stop travel planning and reservations.

DOWNTOWN DETROIT (See map and index starting on p. 240)

THE ATHENEUM SUITE HOTEL & CONFERENCE CENTER

Phone: (313)962-2323 **6**

Hotel
$159-$340

Address: 1000 Brush Ave 48226 **Location:** Jct Brush Ave and Lafayette Blvd. Located in the heart of Greektown and opposite Greektown Casino. **Facility:** Smoke free premises. 174 units. 10 stories, interior corridors. **Parking:** on-site (fee) and valet. **Terms:** cancellation fee imposed. **Amenities:** safes, honor bars. **Dining:** Fishbone's Rhythm Kitchen Cafe, see separate listing. **Activities:** exercise room. **Guest Services:** valet laundry, area transportation-downtown, wireless Internet. Affiliated with A Preferred Hotel.

DETROIT DOWNTOWN COURTYARD BY MARRIOTT

Phone: (313)222-7700 **9**

Hotel
$159-$169

Address: 333 E Jefferson Ave 48226 **Location:** In Millender Center. Opposite Renaissance Center. **Facility:** Smoke free premises. 260 units. 21 stories, interior corridors. **Parking:** on-site (fee) and valet. **Terms:** cancellation fee imposed. **Amenities:** video games (fee), high-speed Internet, safes. **Pool(s):** heated indoor. **Activities:** saunas, whirlpool, steamroom, 2 tennis courts, jogging. *Fee:* aerobic instruction. **Guest Services:** valet laundry, wireless Internet.

> **AAA Benefit:**
> Members save a minimum 5% off the best available rate.

DETROIT REGENCY HOTEL

Phone: (313)567-8888 **2**

Hotel
$70-$130

Address: 1999 E Jefferson Ave 48207 **Location:** I-375, exit E Jefferson Ave, 0.5 mi e. **Facility:** Smoke free premises. 78 units. 3 stories, interior corridors. **Terms:** cancellation fee imposed. **Amenities:** safes (fee). *Some:* high-speed Internet. **Activities:** limited exercise equipment. **Guest Services:** valet and coin laundry, wireless Internet.

DOUBLETREE GUEST SUITES DETROIT DOWNTOWN/FORT SHELBY

Phone: (313)963-5600 **11**

Historic
Hotel
$129-$229

Address: 525 W Lafayette Blvd 48226 **Location:** Jct First Ave. **Facility:** Not a typical Doubletree, this hotel has spacious, upscale rooms with a separate living room area with a sleeper sofa and oversize chair. Smoke free premises. 206 units. 22 stories (no elevator), exterior corridors. **Parking:** valet only. **Terms:** 1-7 night minimum stay, cancellation fee imposed. **Amenities:** video games (fee), high-speed Internet, safes. **Activities:** exercise room. **Guest Services:** valet laundry, area transportation-downtown area, wireless Internet.

> **AAA Benefit:**
> Members save 5% or more everyday!

GREEKTOWN CASINO-HOTEL

Phone: (313)223-2999 **5**

Contemporary
Hotel
$139-$229

Address: 1200 St Antoine 48226 **Location:** Jct Lafayette Blvd and Beaubien St. Located in the heart of Greektown. **Facility:** The swanky hotel's impressive three-story lobby makes the first impression, while well-appointed rooms feature sophisticated Europe-inspired decor. Designated smoking area. 400 units. 30 stories, interior corridors. **Parking:** on-site and valet. **Terms:** check-in 4 pm, cancellation fee imposed. **Amenities:** high-speed Internet (fee), safes, honor bars. **Dining:** Bistro 555, see separate listing. **Activities:** exercise room. **Guest Services:** valet laundry, wireless Internet.

HILTON GARDEN INN DETROIT/DOWNTOWN

Phone: (313)967-0900 **4**

Hotel
$119-$239

Address: 351 Gratiot Ave 48226 **Location:** Jct Randolph St and Gratiot Ave, just e; in Harmonie Park. **Facility:** Smoke free premises. 198 units. 10 stories, interior corridors. **Parking:** on-site (fee) and valet. **Terms:** 1-7 night minimum stay, cancellation fee imposed. **Amenities:** video games (fee), high-speed Internet. **Pool(s):** heated indoor. **Activities:** whirlpool, exercise room. **Guest Services:** valet and coin laundry, wireless Internet.

> **AAA Benefit:**
> Members save 5% or more everyday!

HOLIDAY INN EXPRESS

Phone: (313)887-7000 **10**

Hotel
$99-$199

Address: 1020 Washington Blvd 48226 **Location:** Corner of Washington Blvd and Michigan Ave. **Facility:** Smoke free premises. 240 units, some efficiencies. 17 stories, interior corridors. **Parking:** valet only. **Amenities:** high-speed Internet. **Pool(s):** heated indoor. **Activities:** exercise room. **Guest Services:** valet and coin laundry, wireless Internet.

THE INN ON FERRY STREET

Phone: (313)871-6000 **1**

Historic
Hotel
$119-$169

Address: 84 E Ferry St 48202 **Location:** Jct Woodward Ave and Ferry St, just e. **Facility:** Walking distance from The Detroit Institute of Arts, these four restored Victorian mansions and two carriage houses offer elegant rooms. Smoke free premises. 40 units, some two bedrooms. 2-3 stories (no elevator), interior corridors. **Terms:** cancellation fee imposed. **Guest Services:** valet laundry, area transportation-within 5 mi, wireless Internet. **Free Special Amenities:** full breakfast and high-speed Internet.

(See map and index starting on p. 240)

MGM GRAND DETROIT

Hotel
$249-$299

Address: 1777 3rd St 48226 **Location:** Jct Bagley St. **Phone:** (313)465-1777

Facility: Spacious guest rooms exude contemporary chic design with custom lighting, extra-large showers and TV screens built into the bathroom mirror. Designated smoking area. 400 units, some two bedrooms. 17 stories, interior corridors. **Parking:** on-site and valet. **Amenities:** high-speed Internet, safes, honor bars. **Dining:** 2 restaurants, also, Bourbon Steak, Saltwater, Wolfgang Puck Grille, see separate listings, nightclub, entertainment. **Pool(s):** heated indoor. **Activities:** whirlpools, steamrooms, exercise room, spa. **Guest Services:** valet laundry, area transportation-within 5 mi, wireless Internet. *(see ad p. 257)*

FREE newspaper and high-speed Internet

MOTORCITY CASINO HOTEL

Hotel
$179-$599

Address: 2901 Grand River Ave 48201 **Location:** Jct SR 10 (Lodge Frwy). **Phone:** (313)237-7711

Facility: Spacious guest rooms boast an ultra-chic decor with leather-padded headboards, flat-panel televisions and a cordless telephone. Designated smoking area. 400 units. 22 stories, interior corridors. **Parking:** on-site and valet. **Amenities:** high-speed Internet, safes, honor bars. **Dining:** 7 restaurants, also, Assembly Line Buffet, Iridescence Restaurant, see separate listings, nightclub, entertainment. **Activities:** saunas, whirlpools, steamrooms, exercise room, spa. **Guest Services:** valet laundry, wireless Internet. *(see ad starting on p. 258 & p. 58)*

FREE newspaper and high-speed Internet

TOUCH PERFECTION IN DETROIT

You'll see it in the hottest lounges and largest gaming floor in the Midwest. Taste it in the three signature restaurants from legends Michael Mina and Wolfgang Puck. And luxuriate in it in our multiple award-winning, 400-room hotel with its spectacular views, resort-style spa, and salon staffed by highly trained stylists. It's called perfection. And it's everywhere you turn at MGM Grand Detroit. Come feel what it's like to be the center of the universe. Come touch the Lion.

MGM GRAND
DETROIT

1.877.888.2121
mgmgranddetroit.com

We offer our hotel guests a whole lot more than cable TV and an ice machine.

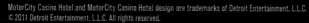

With fine dining, gaming, nightlife, headline entertainment and a decadent spa, MotorCity Casino Hotel brings together excitement, luxury and pleasure to create an experience you can't get anywhere else.
866-STAY-MCC **MotorCityCasino.com**

MotorCity
CASINO · HOTEL ™

A MILLION MILES AWAY,
RIGHT DOWN THE STREET.

If you're texting
or talking on the phone
while you drive,
who's focusing on driving?

Stay Focused
Keep your mind on the road.

(See map and index starting on p. 240)

THE WESTIN BOOK CADILLAC DETROIT

Hotel
$179-$409

Phone: (313)442-1600   8

Address: 1114 Washington Blvd 48226
Location: Corner of Washington Blvd and Michigan Ave. **Facility:** The historic, neoclassical facade of this landmark hotel remains, while the interior is contemporary and luxurious. Rooms are well appointed. Smoke free premises. 453 units. 29 stories, interior corridors. **Parking:** valet only. **Terms:** cancellation fee imposed. **Amenities:** high-speed Internet (fee), safes. *Some:* honor bars. **Dining:** 2 restaurants, also, Michael Symon's Roast, see separate listing. **Pool(s):** heated indoor. **Activities:** whirlpool, exercise room, spa. **Guest Services:** valet laundry, wireless Internet. *(see ad below)*

WESTIN
HOTELS & RESORTS

AAA Benefit:
Enjoy up to 15% off your next stay, plus Starwood Preferred Guest® bonuses.

FREE newspaper

(See map and index starting on p. 240)

─────── *The following lodging was either not evaluated or did not* ───────
meet AAA rating requirements but is listed for your information only.

DETROIT MARRIOTT RENAISSANCE CENTER　　　　　　　　　　**Phone:** 313/568-8000

[fyi]　　Not evaluated. **Address:** Renaissance Center 48243 **Location:** In
Renaissance Center. Facilities, services, and decor characterize a
mid-scale property. [ECO]

> **AAA Benefit:**
> Members save 5% or more off
> best available rate.

──────── **WHERE TO DINE** ────────

AMERICAN CONEY ISLAND　　　　　　　　　　　　　　　　　**Phone:** 313/961-7758　　(32)

◆
American
$3-$10

Stretch limousines still idle at 3 am in front of the famous hot dog and chili compound. The restaurant does a fine job with its steamed buns, spicy chili, onions, mustard and natural casings that snap when bitten. The décor is red, white and blue. **Bar:** beer only. **Hours:** 24 hours. **Address:** 114 W Lafayette Blvd 48226 **Location:** Corner of Griswold St. **Parking:** street only.

ARMANDO'S　　　　　　　　　　　　　　　　　　　　　　**Phone:** 313/554-0666　　(39)

◆◆
Mexican
$5-$28

This local favorite offers a menu largely of Mexican dishes, with specialty cuisine from Cuba, Guatemala and other Latin American countries. **Bar:** full bar. **Hours:** 10:30 am-2 am, Fri & Sat-4 am. Closed: 11/24, 12/25. **Address:** 4242 W Vernor Hwy 48209 **Location:** Between Clark and Scotten sts.

ASSEMBLY LINE BUFFET　　　　　　　　　　　　　　　　　**Phone:** 313/237-7711　　(14)

◆◆
American
$19-$27

With such a large and varied selection, it can be hard to know where to start. The massive buffet area offers a variety of international and American choices, ranging from sushi and seafood to pastas and roast meats to burgers and pizza. The dessert station is loaded with cakes, cookies and pies and even offers a make-your-own sundae station. The all-you-can-eat seafood buffet on Friday is quickly becoming legendary for its seemingly endless supply of crab legs. **Hours:** 8 am-11, noon-4 & 5-10 pm, Fri & Sat-midnight. **Address:** 2901 Grand River Ave 48201 **Location:** Jct SR 10 (Lodge Frwy); in MotorCity Casino. **Parking:** on-site and valet. CALL

ASTORIA PASTRY SHOP　　　　　　　　　　　　　　　　　**Phone:** 313/963-9603　　(20)

◆
Breads/Pastries
$2-$5

For those who need to satisfy a sweet tooth, this bakery cafe serves a large variety of elegant-looking cakes and pastries. Cappuccino and ice cream also are available. **Hours:** 8 am-midnight, Fri & Sat-1 am. Closed major holidays. **Address:** 541 Monroe St 48226 **Location:** Between Beaubien and St. Antoine sts; in Greektown. **Parking:** street only.

ATLAS GLOBAL BISTRO　　　　　　　　　　　　　　　　　**Phone:** 313/831-2241　　(9)

◆◆
American
$7-$35

In a rehabilitated beaux-arts building a few blocks north of Fox Theatre and Comerica Park, the restaurant employs floor-to-ceiling windows and flickering candlelight to set a dramatic stage for self-described "globetrotting fare." Such dishes as Yucatecan duck, paella Valencia and Mediterranean crab cakes draw inspiration from the world at large. **Bar:** full bar. **Hours:** 11 am-3 & 4:30-10 pm, Thurs-11 pm, Fri-midnight, Sat 4:30 pm-midnight, Sun 10 am-3 & 4:30-9 pm; Sunday brunch. Closed major holidays. **Address:** 3111 Woodward Ave 48201 **Location:** Jct Charlotte St, 0.5 mi n of Comerica Park. CALL

BISTRO 555　　　　　　　　　　　　　　　　　　　　　　**Phone:** 313/223-2999　　(22)

◆◆
American
$8-$36

Swanky surroundings distinguish the contemporary dining room on the fifth floor of the hotel. This is even more true in the bar area, which is separated from the dining room by a hanging curtain of glittering gold beads. The menu lists favorites including steaks, surf and turf, club sandwiches, pasta and pizza, as well as some more unusual combinations such as lobster pizza, beer chicken sandwich and fennel-scented salmon. **Bar:** full bar. **Reservations:** required. **Hours:** 6:30 am-10 pm, Fri & Sat-midnight. **Address:** 1200 St. Antoine St 48226 **Location:** Jct Lafayette Blvd and Beaubien St; in Greektown Casino-Hotel. **Parking:** on-site and valet. CALL

BOURBON STEAK　　　　　　　　　　　　　　　　　　　　**Phone:** 313/465-1777　　(28)

◆◆◆
Steak
$30-$52

With its upscale brick and glass decor, acclaimed chef Michael Mina's steakhouse concept offers diners a sophisticated escape from the casino floor. Whether indulging in prime rib, short ribs or one of the many Angus beef steak offerings, a perfect yet unusual pairing is to be found in the signature duck fat fries, truffle mac n' cheese or spinach soufflé. An extensive wine list is also offered. **Bar:** full bar. **Reservations:** suggested. **Hours:** 5 pm-10 pm, Fri & Sat-11 pm. **Address:** 1777 Third St 48226 **Location:** Jct Bagley St; in MGM Grand Detroit. **Parking:** on-site and valet. *(see ad p. 257)* CALL

CAUCUS CLUB　　　　　　　　　　　　　　　　　　　　　**Phone:** 313/965-4970　　(36)

◆◆
American
$9-$28

Low lighting and attractive antiques give the club-like dining room a sophisticated atmosphere. Standard favorites, such as barbecue pork ribs, Dover sole and fresh perch, are well-prepared, consistent and appropriately seasoned. **Bar:** full bar. **Hours:** 11:30 am-8 pm, Fri-9 pm, Sat 5 pm-9 pm, Mon 11:30 am-3 pm. Closed major holidays; also Sun. **Address:** 150 W Congress 48226 **Location:** In Penobscot Building. **Parking:** street only.

(See map and index starting on p. 240)

CHECKER BAR & GRILL

American
$6-$10

Phone: 313/961-9249   ③⓪

Hailed by locals as the home of the best burger in town, this cozy, family run restaurant with its menu featuring a variety of comfort foods serves the infamous Checker Burger, a half-pound behemoth smothered in the toppings of your choice. A favorite spot for locals to gather before the big game, a small TV over the bar keeps diners up-to-date on the sporting action. **Bar:** full bar. **Hours:** 11 am-8 pm. Closed major holidays; also Sat & Sun. **Address:** 124 Cadillac Square 48266 **Location:** Just w of Randolph St. **Parking:** street only.

COACHES CORNER
American
$6-$10

Phone: 313/963-4000   ①⑤

This sports bar's prime location in Harmonie Park puts the diner's seat in the middle of all the action. Flanked by Ford Field and Comerica Park, guests won't have to keep their eyes on the big screen TV or plethora of smaller screens to know if the Lions or Tigers have won—the shouts of fans from the field or as they stream past the restaurant are sure to give the game result away. The menu offers a variety of pub classics ranging from finger foods to deli sandwiches to burgers and Coneys. **Bar:** full bar. **Hours:** 11 am-midnight, Wed-Sat to 2 am. Closed: 12/25. **Address:** 1465 Centre St 48226 **Location:** Jct E Grand River Ave. **Parking:** street only. CALL &M

COACH INSIGNIA
Steak
$23-$50

Phone: 313/567-2622   ③④

On the 72nd floor of GM's global headquarters at the Renaissance Center, the restaurant makes a trip up the high-speed elevator worthwhile for the spectacular 360-degree views of Detroit, the Detroit River and Windsor, Canada. On the menu are sumptuous high-grade steaks and seafood and a wine list with more than 300 selections. The location is ideal for special occasions and romantic nights out. Artwork on the interior walls celebrates the history of the automobile from 1900 to the present day. **Bar:** full bar. **Reservations:** suggested. **Hours:** 5 pm-10 pm, Fri & Sat-11 pm. Closed major holidays; also Sun. **Address:** 100 Renaissance Center 48266 **Location:** Center. **Parking:** on-site (fee) and valet. CALL &M

CUISINE
French
$22-$33

Phone: 313/872-5110   ①

Hidden from view behind the Fisher Theatre, the chef/owner of this upscale converted house has turned French-American cuisine completely on its head. Using premium ingredients and boundless creativity, even classically prepared dishes such as beef Rossini find a new and exciting life when paired with seared foie gras, a potato-daikon cake and topped with black truffle demi glace. **Bar:** full bar. **Reservations:** suggested. **Hours:** 5 pm-10 pm; hours may vary. Closed major holidays; also Mon & Tues. **Address:** 670 Lothrop Rd 48202 **Location:** Jct 2nd St and Lothrop Rd. **Parking:** valet and street only.

DAEDOARDO'S FOXTOWN GRILLE
Italian
$7-$36

Phone: 313/471-3500   ①②

With large picture windows overlooking Comerica Park and right next door to the Fox Theatre, the tastefully decorated and intimate Italian restaurant is in the heart of the city's action. Well-prepared Italian favorites include gnocchi with bolognese sauce and chicken saltimbocca. **Bar:** full bar. **Hours:** 11:30 am-10 pm, Fri-11 pm, Sat 5 pm-11 pm, Mon 11:30 am-3 pm. Closed major holidays. **Address:** 2203 Woodward Ave 48201 **Location:** In Fox Theatre Building; across from Comerica Park. **Parking:** valet and street only.

DETROIT BEER CO.
American
$8-$18

Phone: 313/962-1529   ①⑦

Across from the Detroit Opera House, the historic building was restored to keep its original character of red exposed-brick walls and a roomy, slightly industrial feel. This place functions as a brewpub, with a menu of standards such as beer-battered fish and chips, beer cheese soup and beer grain pizza. **Bar:** full bar. **Hours:** 11 am-midnight, Fri & Sat-2 am. Closed: 12/25 & Easter. **Address:** 1529 Broadway 48226 **Location:** Between John R St and Park Ave; across from Detroit Opera House. **Parking:** street only. CALL &M

THE ELWOOD BAR & GRILL
American
$5-$12

Phone: 313/962-2337   ①⓪

Built in 1936, the art deco diner was moved from its original location at the corner of Elizabeth Street and Woodward Avenue in 1997 to make room for Comerica Park. Just behind left field, this is a popular meeting place before games. Patrons can enjoy an extensive menu of burgers, sandwiches and salads. **Bar:** full bar. **Hours:** 11 am-8 pm, Mon & Tues-2 pm. Closed major holidays; also Sun. **Address:** 300 E Adams Ave 48226 **Location:** Jct Brush Ave; between Comerica Park and Ford Field. **Parking:** street only.

EVIE'S TAMALES
Mexican
$6-$8

Phone: 313/843-5056   ③⑧

Patrons can eat inside this tiny, cozy restaurant, or pick up the perfectly seasoned and nearly grease-free, steamed corn-husk-wrapped pork and cornmeal delights by the bag for carryout. Another flavorful Mexican selection is the chicken enchilada suiza. **Hours:** 6 am-6 pm, Sun 8 am-3 pm. Closed major holidays. **Address:** 3454 Bagley St 48216 **Location:** Corner of Bagley and 24th sts; in Mexicantown. **Parking:** street only.

FISHBONE'S RHYTHM KITCHEN CAFE

Cajun
$6-$25

Phone: 313/965-4600   ②③

The restaurant lures a loud and lively crowd eager to dine on New Orleans Cajun specialties, such as whiskey barbecue ribs, chicken and seafood gumbo. **Bar:** full bar. **Hours:** 6:30 am-midnight, Fri & Sat-2 am, Sun 10:30 am-midnight. Closed: 11/24, 12/25. **Address:** 400 Monroe St 48226 **Location:** Jct Brush Ave and Lafayette Blvd; in The Atheneum Suite Hotel & Conference Center. **Parking:** on-site (fee). CALL &M

HARD ROCK CAFE

American
$12-$24

Phone: 313/964-7625   ②⑤

Rock 'n' roll memorabilia decorates the walls of the popular theme restaurant. Live music on the weekends contributes to the bustling atmosphere. On the menu is a wide variety of American cuisine—from burgers and sandwiches to seafood, steaks and pasta. **Bar:** full bar. **Hours:** 11 am-midnight. **Address:** 45 Monroe St 48226 **Location:** Jct Monroe St and Woodward Ave; in CompuWare World Headquarters. **Parking:** on-site (fee) and street. SAVE CALL &M

(See map and index starting on p. 240)

HOCKEYTOWN CAFE

 American $7-$24

Phone: 313/965-9500 ⑪

First-timers can't miss the 60-by-16-foot sign with the rotating puck and massive TV screens that herald the shrine of all things: Red Wings. Lending to the lively atmosphere are the blaring sounds of 30 TVs, the cheering fans watching live feeds of games from nearby Cobo Hall, and three floors of Red Wing memorabilia. The menu ranges from sports grub, such as wings and burgers, to New York strip steaks and pork chops. **Bar:** full bar. **Hours:** 11 am-9 pm. **Address:** 2301 Woodward Ave 48201 **Location:** Across from Fox Theater and Comerica Park. **Parking:** on-site (fee). CALL ⓁⓂ

IRIDESCENCE RESTAURANT *Menu on AAA.com*

 American $28-$42

Phone: 313/237-7711 ⑬

On the top floor of a casino hotel in a former Wonder Bread factory, this upscale, richly appointed restaurant will make guests feel as if they are on top of the world. While overlooking views of the Ambassador Bridge and the Detroit skyline, diners partake in cuisine that focuses on organic, sustainable foods from the global marketplace. Menu items change often, but some features include sashimi, Vietnamese lobster roll, sea bass, Alaskan halibut, beef filet, rack of lamb and Amish chicken. **Bar:** full bar. **Reservations:** required. **Hours:** 5 pm-10 pm, Fri & Sat-11 pm. Closed: Mon. **Address:** 2901 Grand River Ave 48201 **Location:** Jct SR 10 (Lodge Frwy); in MotorCity Casino. **Parking:** on-site and valet. CALL ⓁⓂ

LAFAYETTE CONEY ISLAND

 American $3-$8

Phone: 313/964-8198 ㉝

Stretch limousines still idle at 3 am in front of the famous hot dog and chili compound. The restaurant does a fine job with its steamed buns, spicy chili, onions, mustard and natural casings that snap when bitten. **Bar:** beer only. **Hours:** 24 hours. Closed: 12/25. **Address:** 118 W Lafayette Blvd 48226 **Location:** Corner of Griswold St. **Parking:** street only.

LOCO BAR & GRILL

 Tex-Mex $6-$18

Phone: 313/965-3737 ㉔

The rough-and-tumble cowboy bar serves up tasty renditions of Tex-Mex cuisine, with a large selection of hot sauces and beer. Patrons can sink their teeth into zippy enchiladas, quesadillas, tacos, chunky salsa and spicy Mexican sausage with rice and beans. **Bar:** full bar. **Hours:** 11 am-2 am, Fri & Sat-3 am. Closed major holidays. **Address:** 454 E Lafayette Blvd 48226 **Location:** At Lafayette Blvd and Beaubien St. **Parking:** street only.

MAJESTIC CAFE

 American $8-$25

Phone: 313/833-9700 ⑥

Big, bright windows and cool, faux-Miro murals lend to the casually upscale feel of the dining room. The spicy menu falls somewhere between Midwest and Middle Eastern. Symphony and cultural crowds frequent the reserved restaurant before shows. **Bar:** full bar. **Reservations:** suggested, weekends. **Hours:** 11 am-2 am, Sun from 10:30 am; Sunday brunch. Closed major holidays. **Address:** 4140 Woodward Ave 48202 **Location:** Between Alexandrine and Canfield sts.

MARIO'S

 Italian $7-$35

Phone: 313/832-1616 ⑧

Dark and romantic, Old Blue Eyes himself could have patronized this local institution, famous for its 1960s-style Italian dishes and ambiance. The lasagna and fettuccine alfredo have been untouched by time. Valet parking is a must at this restaurant located halfway between the theatre district and Wayne State University. **Bar:** full bar. **Reservations:** suggested. **Hours:** 11:30 am-10 pm, Fri-midnight, Sat noon-midnight, Sun noon-10 pm. Closed: 12/25. **Address:** 4222 2nd Ave 48201 **Location:** 1.5 mi n of civic center. **Parking:** valet and street only.

MEXICAN VILLAGE RESTAURANT

 Mexican $6-$20

Phone: 313/237-0333 ㊲

In business since 1943, the restaurant is an established favorite for fajitas, burritos, nachos and combination plates. White stucco arches, paintings depicting Mexican history and colorful decorations add to the lively ambience of the dining room. **Bar:** full bar. **Hours:** 11 am-11 pm, Fri & Sat-1 am. Closed: 1/1, 11/24, 12/24, 12/25. **Address:** 2600 Bagley St 48216 **Location:** Jct Bagley and 18th sts; near Ambassador Bridge; in Mexican Village.

(See map and index starting on p. 240)

MICHAEL SYMON'S ROAST
Phone: 313/961-2500 ㉛

American
$14-$38

Bold and sophisticated, the interior of chef-owner Michael Symon's new venture affords floor-to-ceiling street views and a huge rotisserie showcasing the "roasted beast of the day." The menu features high-quality artisanal meats including goat, wild boar and suckling pig complemented with an impressive wine list. **Bar:** full bar. **Reservations:** suggested. **Hours:** 5 pm-10 pm, Fri & Sat-11 pm, Sun-9 pm. **Address:** 1128 Washington Blvd 48226 **Location:** Corner of Washington Blvd and Michigan Ave; in The Westin Book Cadillac Detroit. **Parking:** on-site and valet. CALL ⑤M

MOSAIC
Phone: 313/962-9366 ㉑

International
$8-$65

Aptly named, the pastiche theme present in the upscale decor of this sophisticated restaurant- located in the heart of Greektown-is echoed in the eclectic menu offerings. With foods inspired by cultures from around the world, the robust menu offers a variety of cuisines ranging from Asian to Greek to French to Italian to classic American surf and turf, all skillfully prepared and artfully presented. Not to be missed is the decadent lobster grilled cheese sandwich. **Bar:** full bar. **Hours:** 11 am-11 pm, Fri-midnight, Sat 4 pm-midnight. Closed major holidays; also Sun. **Address:** 501 Monroe St 48226 **Location:** Jct Beaubien St; in Greektown. **Parking:** street only. CALL ⑤M

NEMO'S BAR & GRILL
Phone: 313/965-3180 ㉟

American
$4-$8

Touted as being one of the best sports bars in the country, this Detroit landmark across from the old Tiger Stadium remains the sports bar of choice for die-hard fans. The menu is simple, focusing on burgers and sandwiches, but on game days patrons line up down the street for their chance to score one of the city's best cheeseburgers. The retro Irish turn-of-the-century decor with its walls documenting legendary Detroit sports moments provides a perfect backdrop for a rowdy game-day experience. **Bar:** full bar. **Hours:** 11 am-11 pm; extended hours on game days. Closed major holidays; also Sun. **Address:** 1384 Michigan Ave 48226 **Location:** Jct 8th St.

PEGASUS TAVERNA RESTAURANT
Phone: 313/964-6800 ⑱

Greek
$6-$27

This Greektown restaurant offers intimate, couples-friendly booth seating and a wide selection of authentic Greek dishes and desserts. **Bar:** full bar. **Hours:** 11 am-1 am, Fri & Sat-3 am, Sun-midnight. **Address:** 558 Monroe St 48226 **Location:** In Greektown. **Parking:** no self-parking. CALL ⑤M

PIZZA PAPALIS
Phone: 313/961-8020 ⑯

Pizza
$8-$22

With reasonable prices, a family-friendly atmosphere and a close proximity to Ford Field and Comerica Park, this Greektown restaurant is a favorite spot for locals who warm up over steaming pizza before or after the big game. **Bar:** full bar. **Hours:** 11 am-1 am. Closed: 12/25. **Address:** 553 Monroe St 48226 **Location:** Between Beaubien and St. Antoine sts; in Greektown. **Parking:** street only.

ROMA CAFE
Phone: 313/831-5940 ②

Italian
$8-$25

Homemade pasta and a flavorful house meat sauce add to the great taste of such dishes as spaghetti and lasagna. Attractive prints and a hand-carved bar decorate the appealingly unpretentious dining room. Tuxedoed servers are friendly and efficient. **Bar:** full bar. **Reservations:** suggested. **Hours:** 11 am-10 pm, Sat-11 pm. Closed major holidays; also Sun. **Address:** 3401 Riopelle St 48207 **Location:** Jct Riopelle and Erskine sts; near Eastern Market area. **Parking:** on-site and valet.

SALA THAI
Phone: 313/831-1302 ④

Thai
$7-$13

The symbolism behind the former fire-station location may become immediately obvious after a few bites of several of the hot dishes at this local favorite. Steps away from the Eastern Market, this place includes market-fresh ingredients in its classic Thai dishes, which can be ordered in various degrees of heat. Semi-formal attire. **Bar:** full bar. **Reservations:** suggested. **Hours:** 10:30 am-9:30 pm, Sat from 11 am, Sun noon-9 pm. Closed major holidays. **Address:** 3400 Russell St 48207 **Location:** I-75, exit 52 (Mack Ave); just s of jct Russell St and Mack Ave. **Parking:** on-site and street. CALL ⑤M

SALTWATER
Phone: 313/465-1777 ㉙

Seafood
$30-$52

Famed chef Michael Mina has created a truly exceptional seafood experience in this restaurant tucked away off the casino floor behind a modern art sculpture of an oversized fish. The elegant dining room features an underwater motif, complete with textured walls resembling circular sandstone, and a cascading mosaic tile ceiling. The menu focuses on high quality, fresh seafood flown in from around the world on a near daily basis; a tasting menu is offered regularly. **Bar:** full bar. **Reservations:** suggested. **Hours:** 5 pm-10 pm, Fri & Sat-11 pm. Closed: Sun & Mon. **Address:** 1777 Third St 48226 **Location:** Jct Bagley St; in MGM Grand Detroit. **Parking:** on-site and valet. *(see ad p. 257)* CALL ⑤M

SMALL PLATES
Phone: 313/963-0497 ⑲

American
$10-$15

Within easy strolling distance of downtown's major entertainment venues, the casually upscale restaurant takes its cue from Spanish tapas and adds a creative American twist. Portion sizes are large enough to be comfortably shared. **Bar:** full bar. **Hours:** 11 am-10 pm, Fri-midnight, Sat noon-midnight. Closed major holidays; also Sun & Mon. **Address:** 1521 Broadway St 48226 **Location:** Jct Park St; across from Detroit Opera House. **Parking:** street only. CALL ⑤M

TOM'S OYSTER BAR
Phone: 313/964-4010 ㉖

Seafood
$11-$24

From tin ceilings to checkered tablecloths, the local chain of raw bars has more than a slight resemblance to New England fish houses. Fresh oysters are the signature item on a menu of diverse seafood selections, including panko-fried shrimp and grilled yellowfin tuna. Other choices on the menu include burgers and pasta. **Bar:** full bar. **Hours:** 11 am-11 pm, Fri-midnight, Sat noon-midnight. Closed major holidays; also Sun. **Address:** 519 E Jefferson Ave 48226 **Location:** Jct Beaubien St; across from GM World Headquarters at the Renaissance Center. **Parking:** on-site (fee) and valet. CALL ⑤M

(See map and index starting on p. 240)

TRAFFIC JAM & SNUG

Phone: 313/831-9470   (7)

♦♦♦ American
$8-$18

On the end of a cobblestone street of restored turn-of-the-20th-century Victorian mansions, the restaurant serves complex and creative preparations, such as the smoked turkey Reuben with sauerkraut and melted Swiss cheese on a potato roll. **Bar:** full bar. **Hours:** 11 am-10:30 pm, Fri & Sat-midnight, Sun-8 pm. Closed major holidays. **Address:** 511 W Canfield St 48201 **Location:** W Canfield St at 2nd Ave. CALL 🛒M

UNION STREET

Phone: 313/831-3965   (5)

♦♦ American
$9-$21

Loud, noisy and fun, the energetic restaurant is a hangout for students and professionals. Seafood bisque, pasta with flavorful sauces, and fiery foods, such as ribs slathered with hot sauce, are representative of the menu choices. Servers are upbeat. **Bar:** full bar. **Hours:** 11:30 am-midnight, Sat 4 pm-1 am, Sun 11:30 am-7 pm. Closed major holidays. **Address:** 4145 Woodward Ave 48201 **Location:** Between Alexandrine and Canfield sts. **Parking:** on-site (fee) and street. CALL 🛒M

THE WHITNEY

Phone: 313/832-5700   (3)

♦♦♦ American
$9-$37

The chef uses fresh ingredients in creative preparations of contemporary cuisine. In a restored 1894 Victorian mansion, the restaurant exudes elegant charm. Stained glass windows, lovely woodwork and a hand-laid mosaic tile floor enhance the decor. Semi-formal attire. **Bar:** full bar. **Reservations:** suggested. **Hours:** 11:30 am-3 & 5-10 pm, Sat 5 pm-11 pm, Sun 11 am-3 pm. Closed major holidays; also Mon. **Address:** 4421 Woodward Ave 48201 **Location:** Between Mack and Warren aves. **Parking:** valet and street only. **Historic**

WOLFGANG PUCK GRILLE

Phone: 313/465-1777   (27)

♦♦♦ American
$15-$50

Billed as an upscale "bar and grill," the restaurant is accessible from the hotel lobby and is the only casino restaurant that allows children. Famous for wood-oven baked pizzas, this place also entices diners with casual classics such as burgers, rib-eye steak sandwiches or flat-iron steak, in addition to the lobster club sandwich, angel hair pasta with truffle oil, pan-roasted organic chicken, seafood risotto, sauteed salmon or New York steak. Among house specialties is butternut squash soup. **Bar:** full bar. **Hours:** 5 pm-10 pm, Fri & Sat-11 pm. Closed: Tues. **Address:** 1777 Third St 48226 **Location:** Jct Bagley St; in MGM Grand Detroit. **Parking:** on-site and valet. *(see ad p. 257)* CALL 🛒M

DETROIT pop. 951,270   (See map and index starting on p. 244)

DOUBLETREE HOTEL DEARBORN

Phone: (313)336-3340   ①

♦♦♦ Hotel
$99-$199

Address: 5801 Southfield Expwy 48228 **Location:** SR 39 (Southfield Frwy), exit 7 (Ford Rd), just w. **Facility:** Smoke free premises. 347 units. 2-6 stories, interior corridors. **Terms:** 1-7 night minimum stay, cancellation fee imposed. **Pool(s):** heated outdoor, heated indoor. **Activities:** whirlpools, exercise room. **Guest Services:** valet laundry, wireless Internet.

> **AAA Benefit:**
> Members save 5% or more everyday!

🍴 🍸 CALL 🛒M 🐕 BIZ ✕ 🎿 ▭ / SOME UNITS 🅱

▼ *See AAA listing p. 295* ▼

(See map and index starting on p. 244)

RESIDENCE INN BY MARRIOTT-DEARBORN

Extended Stay
Hotel

$139-$149

Phone: (313)441-1700

Address: 5777 Southfield Service Dr 48228 **Location:** SR 39 (Southfield Frwy), exit Ford Rd, just w. **Facility:** Smoke free premises. 128 kitchen units. 2 stories, exterior corridors. **Terms:** cancellation fee imposed. **Amenities:** high-speed Internet. **Pool(s):** heated outdoor. **Activities:** whirlpool, gas barbecue grills, outdoor patio area, exercise room, sports court. **Guest Services:** valet and coin laundry, wireless Internet. **Free Special Amenities:** expanded continental breakfast and high-speed Internet.

AAA Benefit:
Members save a minimum 5% off the best available rate.

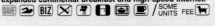

—— WHERE TO DINE ——

GIOVANNI'S RISTORANTE

Italian
$11-$33

Phone: 313/841-0122 (4)

A favorite haunt of Frank Sinatra when he came to town, the completely remodeled restaurant exudes refinement. It continues to delight diners with its food and polished service. **Bar:** full bar. **Reservations:** suggested. **Hours:** 11 am-9 pm, Fri-10 pm, Sat 4 pm-10 pm. Closed major holidays; also Sun & Mon. **Address:** 330 S Oakwood Blvd 48217 **Location:** Between Schaefer Rd and Fort St. **Parking:** valet and street only.

MILT'S GOURMET BARBECUE

Barbecue
$6-$23

Phone: 313/521-5959 (1)

First-timers shouldn't let the lack of décor-nor the fact that everything is served in foam containers-scare them away. Patrons often share a table in the small neighborhood barbecue joint. The food isn't fancy, but it's definitely good. Regulars line up for ample servings of barbecue ribs and chicken and in-house-made sides. Diners should save room for a slice of one of Delores' incredible pies. **Hours:** noon-8 pm, Fri & Sat-10 pm. Closed: 11/24, 12/25; also Sun, Mon & week of 7/4. **Address:** 19143 Kelly Rd 48224 **Location:** I-94, exit 223 (Moross Rd), 1 mi n. **Parking:** street only.

THE RATTLESNAKE CLUB

American
$12-$46

Phone: 313/567-4400 (3)

Trendy and cutting edge, this riverside restaurant located in Detroit's river place area, offers sophisticated American cuisine geared toward the hip and lively. Semi-formal attire. **Bar:** full bar. **Reservations:** suggested. **Hours:** 11:30 am-10 pm, Fri-11 pm, Sat 5:30 pm-11 pm. Closed: 12/24; also Sun & Mon. **Address:** 300 River Place Dr 48207 **Location:** 1.5 mi on E Jefferson Ave, then 4 blks s on Joseph Campau St. **Parking:** valet only. CALL

SINDBAD'S AT THE RIVER

American
$6-$28

Phone: 313/822-7817 (2)

On the banks of the Detroit River, the restaurant has been an area institution for casual dining and great waterfront views since 1949. The menu centers on a good selection of seafood and steaks. Outdoor dining is popular during pleasant weather. **Bar:** full bar. **Hours:** 11 am-11 pm, Fri & Sat-midnight. Closed major holidays. **Address:** 100 St. Clair St 48214 **Location:** Jct E Jefferson Ave and Marquette Dr, e on Marquette Dr to St. Clair St. **Parking:** valet only.

The Detroit Vicinity

ALLEN PARK pop. 29,376   (See map and index starting on p. 244)

BEST WESTERN GREENFIELD INN

Hotel
$79-$109

Phone: (313)271-1600   **124**

Address: 3000 Enterprise Dr 48101 **Location:** I-94, exit 206 (Oakwood Blvd), just s, then just w. **Facility:** Smoke free premises. 209 units. 3 stories, interior corridors. **Amenities:** safes. *Some:* high-speed Internet. **Pool(s):** heated indoor. **Activities:** sauna, whirlpool, exercise room. **Guest Services:** valet and coin laundry, area transportation-The Henry Ford Museum, wireless Internet. **Free Special Amenities: high-speed Internet and airport transportation.**

 / SOME UNITS

AAA Benefit:
Members save up to 20%, plus 10% bonus points with free rewards program.

HOLIDAY INN EXPRESS & SUITES

Hotel
$99-$149

Phone: (313)323-3500   **125**

Address: 3600 Enterprise Dr 48101 **Location:** I-94, exit 206 (Oakwood Blvd), just s, then just w. **Facility:** Smoke free premises. 121 units. 3 stories, interior corridors. **Amenities:** high-speed Internet, safes. **Pool(s):** heated indoor. **Activities:** whirlpool, exercise room. **Guest Services:** valet and coin laundry, area transportation-The Henry Ford Museum, wireless Internet. **Free Special Amenities: continental breakfast and high-speed Internet.**

 CALL / SOME UNITS

AUBURN HILLS pop. 19,837

CANDLEWOOD SUITES

Extended Stay
Hotel
$59-$94

Phone: (248)373-3342

Address: 1650 N Opdyke Rd 48326 **Location:** I-75, exit 79 (University Dr), just w, then 0.4 mi n. **Facility:** Smoke free premises. 110 efficiencies. 3 stories, interior corridors. **Amenities:** high-speed Internet. **Activities:** exercise room. **Guest Services:** complimentary and valet laundry.

 / SOME UNITS FEE

COURTYARD BY MARRIOTT DETROIT AUBURN HILLS

Hotel
$107-$137

Phone: (248)373-4100

Address: 1296 Opdyke Rd 48326 **Location:** I-75, exit 79 (University Dr), just w, then 0.3 mi s. **Facility:** Smoke free premises. 148 units. 2-3 stories, interior corridors. **Terms:** cancellation fee imposed. **Amenities:** video games (fee), high-speed Internet. **Pool(s):** heated indoor. **Activities:** whirlpool, exercise room. **Guest Services:** valet and coin laundry, wireless Internet. ECO CALL / SOME UNITS

AAA Benefit:
Members save a minimum 5% off the best available rate.

CROWNE PLAZA AUBURN HILLS

Hotel
$79-$134

Phone: (248)373-4550

Address: 1500 Opdyke Rd 48326 **Location:** I-75, exit 79 (University Dr). **Facility:** Smoke free premises. 190 units. 8 stories, interior corridors. **Terms:** check-in 4 pm. **Amenities:** high-speed Internet. **Pool(s):** heated indoor. **Activities:** sauna, whirlpool, exercise room. **Guest Services:** valet and coin laundry, wireless Internet.

 CALL / SOME UNITS

EXTENDED STAY DELUXE-DETROIT AUBURN HILLS-FEATHERSTONE

Extended Stay
Hotel
$70-$80

Phone: (248)335-5200

Address: 2100 Featherstone Rd 48326 **Location:** I-75, exit 79 (University Dr), just w to Opdyke Rd, s to Featherstone, then just e. **Facility:** Smoke free premises. 139 efficiencies. 3 stories, interior corridors. **Terms:** cancellation fee imposed. **Pool(s):** heated outdoor. **Activities:** exercise room. **Guest Services:** valet and coin laundry, wireless Internet.

CALL / SOME UNITS FEE

FAIRFIELD INN BY MARRIOTT-AUBURN HILLS

Hotel
$80-$102

Phone: (248)373-2228

Address: 1294 Opdyke Rd 48326 **Location:** I-75, exit 79 (University Dr), just w, then 0.3 mi s. **Facility:** Smoke free premises. 119 units. 3 stories, interior/exterior corridors. **Parking:** winter plug-ins. **Terms:** cancellation fee imposed. **Pool(s):** heated outdoor. **Activities:** exercise room. **Guest Services:** valet and coin laundry, wireless Internet.

AAA Benefit:
Members save a minimum 5% off the best available rate.

HAMPTON INN

Hotel
$99-$139 1/1-4/30
$89-$129 4/1-12/31

Address: 1461 N Opdyke Rd 48326 **Location:** I-75, exit 79 (University Dr), just w, then just n. **Facility:** Smoke free premises. 124 units. 3 stories, interior corridors. **Terms:** 1-7 night minimum stay, cancellation fee imposed. **Pool(s):** heated outdoor. **Activities:** exercise room. **Guest Services:** valet laundry, wireless Internet.

Phone: (248)370-0044

AAA Benefit:
Members save up to 10% everyday!

HILTON SUITES AUBURN HILLS

Hotel
$79-$149

Address: 2300 Featherstone Rd 48326 **Location:** I-75, exit 79 (University Dr), just w, 0.5 mi s on Opdyke Rd, then just e. **Facility:** Smoke free premises. 224 units. 5 stories, interior corridors. **Terms:** 1-7 night minimum stay, cancellation fee imposed. **Some:** high-speed Internet (fee). **Pool(s):** heated indoor. **Activities:** sauna, whirlpool, billiards, exercise room. **Guest Services:** complimentary and valet laundry, area transportation-within 5 mi, wireless Internet.

Phone: (248)334-2222

AAA Benefit:
Members save 5% or more everyday!

HOLIDAY INN EXPRESS HOTEL & SUITES

Hotel
$65-$169

Address: 3990 Baldwin Rd 48326 **Location:** I-75, exit 84B (Baldwin Rd S), just s. **Facility:** Smoke free premises. 93 units. 4 stories, interior corridors. **Amenities:** high-speed Internet. **Pool(s):** heated indoor. **Activities:** whirlpool, exercise room. **Guest Services:** valet and coin laundry, area transportation-within 5 mi, wireless Internet.

Phone: (248)322-7000

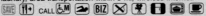

FREE full breakfast and high-speed Internet

HOMESTEAD STUDIO SUITES HOTEL-DETROIT/AUBURN HILLS

Extended Stay Hotel
$65-$75

Address: 3315 University Dr 48326 **Location:** I-75, exit 79 (University Dr), 0.9 mi e. **Facility:** Smoke free premises. 134 efficiencies. 3 stories, interior corridors. **Terms:** cancellation fee imposed. **Guest Services:** coin laundry, wireless Internet.

Phone: (248)340-8888

HYATT PLACE DETROIT/AUBURN HILLS

Hotel
$79-$169

Address: 1545 N Opdyke Rd 48326 **Location:** I-75, exit 79 (University Dr), just w, then just n. **Facility:** Smoke free premises. 127 units. 6 stories, interior corridors. **Terms:** cancellation fee imposed. **Amenities:** Some: high-speed Internet. **Pool(s):** heated indoor. **Activities:** exercise room. **Guest Services:** valet laundry, wireless Internet. **Free Special Amenities: continental breakfast and high-speed Internet.**

Phone: (248)475-9393

AAA Benefit:
Ask for the AAA rate and save 10%.

STAYBRIDGE SUITES

Extended Stay Hotel
$79-$139

Address: 2050 Featherstone Rd 48326 **Location:** I-75, exit 79 (University Dr), just w, 0.5 mi s on Opdyke Rd, then just e. **Facility:** Smoke free premises. 118 efficiencies, some two bedrooms. 3 stories, interior corridors. **Amenities:** high-speed Internet. **Pool(s):** heated outdoor. **Activities:** exercise room, sports court. **Guest Services:** complimentary and valet laundry, wireless Internet.

Phone: (248)322-4600

WINGATE BY WYNDHAM

Hotel
$72-$90

Address: 2200 Featherstone Rd 48326 **Location:** I-75, exit 79 (University Dr), just w, 0.5 mi s on Opdyke Rd, then just e. **Facility:** Smoke free premises. 102 units. 4 stories, interior corridors. **Amenities:** high-speed Internet, safes. **Pool(s):** heated indoor. **Activities:** whirlpool, exercise room. **Guest Services:** valet and coin laundry, wireless Internet.

Phone: (248)334-3324

—— WHERE TO DINE ——

LELLI'S INN OF AUBURN HILLS

Italian
$15-$40

A Detroit legend in a new location overlooking the Pontiac Silverdome, this place still serves the filet mignon and shrimp Lelli that made the original restaurant famous. Many come here for special occasions. **Bar:** full bar. **Reservations:** suggested. **Hours:** 11 am-10 pm, Sat 3 pm-11 pm, Sun noon-9 pm. Closed major holidays. **Address:** 885 N Opdyke Rd 48326 **Location:** I-75, exit 79 (University Dr), just w, then 0.5 mi s. **Parking:** on-site and valet.

Phone: 248/373-4440

O'BRIEN'S CRABHOUSE

American
$7-$25

Phone: 248/332-7744

In a shopping plaza not far from the Pontiac Silverdome, this modest, nautically themed restaurant is popular with the pre- and postgame crowd. Specialty crab dishes such as Alaskan crab legs and crab cakes dominate the menu. A large wood bar is the dining area's focal point, and a few fish trophies decorate the wall. **Bar:** full bar. **Hours:** 11 am-10 pm, Sat 3 pm-11 pm, Sun 4 pm-9 pm. Closed: 11/24, 12/25 & Easter. **Address:** 621 S Opdyke Rd 48342 **Location:** I-75, exit 79 (University Dr), just w, then 1 mi s.

RAINFOREST CAFE

American
$15-$25

Phone: 248/333-0280

The tropical rainforest setting, which incorporates animated jungle animals and birds, offers a distinctive experience for families and special parties. The eclectic menu lists a large variety of fun dishes. **Bar:** full bar. **Hours:** 11 am-9 pm, Sun-6 pm. Closed: 11/24, 12/25. **Address:** 4310 Baldwin Rd 48326 **Location:** I-75, exit 84 (Baldwin Rd), just w; in Great Lakes Crossing Mall in Area 6. CALL ⓒM

RANGOLI INDIAN CUISINE

Indian
$9-$20

Phone: 248/377-3800

Named for a type of traditional Indian folk painting, this attractive restaurant showcases India's widely varied regional cuisines. Expert waiters help guide patrons through the extensive menu. **Bar:** full bar. **Hours:** 11 am-3 & 5-9:30 pm, Fri-10:30 pm, Sat 11:30 am-3 & 5-10:30 pm, Sun 11:30 am-3 & 5-9:30 pm. Closed: 12/25. **Address:** 3055 E Walton Blvd 48326 **Location:** I-75, exit 79 (University Dr), 1 mi n on Opdyke Rd, then 0.5 mi e; in Walton Village Plaza. CALL ⓒM

BELLEVILLE pop. 3,997

HAMPTON INN

Hotel
$99-$109

Phone: (734)699-2424

Address: 46280 N I-94 Service Dr 48111 **Location:** I-94, exit 190 (Belleville Rd), just n, then just w. **Facility:** Smoke free premises. 90 units. 3 stories, interior corridors. **Terms:** 1-7 night minimum stay, cancellation fee imposed. **Pool(s):** heated indoor. **Activities:** whirlpool, exercise room. **Guest Services:** valet and coin laundry, area transportation-within 5 mi, wireless Internet. **Free Special Amenities: expanded continental breakfast and airport transportation.**

AAA Benefit:
Members save up to 10% everyday!

SAVE ✚ ⑪ CALL ⓒM ⌁ ✕ ▦ ▤ ▭ ▭

HOLIDAY INN EXPRESS HOTEL & SUITES

Hotel
Rates not provided

Phone: 734/857-6200

Address: 46194 N I-94 Service Dr 48111 **Location:** I-94, exit 190 (Belleville Rd), just n, then just w. **Facility:** Smoke free premises. 108 units. 3 stories, interior corridors. **Pool(s):** heated indoor. **Activities:** saunas, whirlpool, steamrooms, exercise room. **Guest Services:** valet and coin laundry, area transportation-within 5 mi, wireless Internet.

✚ ⑪ CALL ⓒM ⌁ BIZ ✕ ▦ ▤ ▭ ▭ / SOME UNITS FEE 🐾

RED ROOF INN METRO AIRPORT #7183

Motel
$53-$75

Phone: (734)697-2244

Address: 45501 N I-94 Service Dr 48111 **Location:** I-94, exit 190 (Belleville Rd), just n. **Facility:** Smoke free premises. 112 units. 2 stories, exterior corridors. **Amenities:** video games (fee). **Guest Services:** wireless Internet. **Free Special Amenities: local telephone calls.**

SAVE ⑪ ✕ ▦ / SOME UNITS 🐾 ▤ ▭

—— **WHERE TO DINE** ——

DIMITRI'S KITCHEN

American
$5-$12

Phone: 734/699-7555

The diner-style restaurant serves wholesome, reasonably priced food, including eggs, omelets, sandwiches and burgers, as well as steaks, ribs and chicken. **Hours:** 24 hours. Closed major holidays. **Address:** 11511 Belleville Rd 48111 **Location:** I-94, exit 190 (Belleville Rd), just s.

DOS PESOS RESTAURANT

Mexican
$5-$15

Phone: 734/697-5777

In a small shopping plaza, this casual Mexican eatery serves modestly prepared Mexican fare including unique renditions of flautas, quesadillas and enchiladas. **Bar:** full bar. **Hours:** 11 am-9:30 pm, Fri & Sat-10 pm, Sun noon-8 pm. Closed major holidays. **Address:** 11800 Belleville Rd 48111 **Location:** I-94, exit 190 (Belleville Rd), just s; in shopping plaza. CALL ⓒM

BERKLEY pop. 15,531 (See map and index starting on p. 244)

—— **WHERE TO DINE** ——

O'MARA'S

Irish
$6-$25

Phone: 248/399-6750 (173)

With bagpipes and photographs on the wall, the typical Irish pub's homelike and spacious dining room often moves to the beat of live music. The rather extensive menu lists everything from Irish stew in a bread bowl to noteworthy crab cakes with papaya, mango and chutney. **Bar:** full bar. **Hours:** 11 am-11 pm, Fri & Sat-midnight. Closed: 12/25. **Address:** 2555 W 12 Mile Rd 48072 **Location:** Jct 12 Mile Rd and Coolidge Hwy; 1 mi w of Woodward Ave. CALL ⓒM

BEVERLY HILLS pop. 10,437 (See map and index starting on p. 244)

—— WHERE TO DINE ——

BEVERLY HILLS GRILL

American
$8-$36

Phone: 248/642-2355 (196)

Well known for its breakfast specials, such as bananas Foster French toast and eggs Benedict, this somewhat trendy diner also offers a California-influenced lunch and dinner menu that has developed an ardent following, with specials such as spicy rock shrimp on angel hair pasta. **Bar:** full bar. **Hours:** 7 am-11 pm, Fri-midnight, Sat 8 am-midnight, Sun 8 am-9 pm. Closed major holidays. **Address:** 31471 Southfield Rd 48025 **Location:** Just n of jct 13 Mile Rd. CALL [&M]

BIRMINGHAM pop. 19,291 (See map and index starting on p. 244)

THE TOWNSEND HOTEL

Hotel
$299-$375

Phone: (248)642-7900 (20)

Address: 100 Townsend St 48009 **Location:** Center. **Facility:** Exuding style and class, this beautiful European-style hotel has traditional guest rooms with luxurious baths marked by marble floors and vanities. Smoke free premises. 150 units, some two bedrooms and kitchens. 6 stories, interior corridors. **Parking:** valet and street only. **Terms:** check-in 4 pm, cancellation fee imposed. **Amenities:** safes, honor bars. *Fee:* video games, high-speed Internet. **Dining:** Rugby Grille, see separate listing. **Activities:** *Fee:* massage. **Guest Services:** valet laundry, wireless Internet. *Fee:* area transportation. Affiliated with A Preferred Hotel.

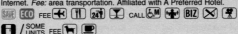

FREE newspaper and early check-in/late check-out

—— WHERE TO DINE ——

220

Italian
$9-$35

Phone: 248/645-2150 (40)

Paying homage to the inventor of the light bulb, this comfortable "see and be seen" restaurant offers a creative Italian-Continental menu featuring risotto, pasta, veal chops and a variety of fish dishes. A walk-down martini-cigar bar is popular with the often-boisterous cell phone set. **Bar:** full bar. **Hours:** 11 am-11 pm, Thurs-Sat to midnight. Closed: Sun. **Address:** 220 Merrill St 48009 **Location:** Jct Old Woodward Ave; downtown. **Parking:** street only. CALL [&M]

BIG ROCK CHOP HOUSE

Steak
$8-$35

Phone: 248/647-7774 (32)

A sophisticated interpretation of the microbrewery-steakhouse concept, the restaurant serves some very fine beef cooked the way meat lovers like it. Patrons will find award-winning beer to sample and an upstairs cigar and martini lounge for connoisseurs of those particular pleasures. All the above, combined with a whimsical flying buffalo, make for an above-average dining experience. **Bar:** full bar. **Reservations:** required. **Hours:** 11 am-11 pm, Fri & Sat-midnight. Closed major holidays; also Sun. **Address:** 245 S Eton St 48009 **Location:** 1 mi e of jct Woodward Ave and Maple Rd. **Parking:** on-site and valet. CALL [&M]

CAMERON'S STEAKHOUSE

Steak
$20-$44

Phone: 248/723-1700 (35)

In a posh downtown area, the steakhouse encourages guests to valet park rather than look for street parking. Inside the clubby restaurant, a waterfall cascades silently down one wall, and it's easy to imagine the Rat Pack nursing martinis at the bar. The menu covers all the bases that a top-notch steakhouse should, touching on enormous prime steaks, a few non-beef entrees and raw selections on the oyster bar. Such desserts as cheesecake and crème brûlée are large enough to share. **Bar:** full bar. **Reservations:** suggested. **Hours:** 5 pm-10 pm, Thurs-Sat to 11 pm, Sun-9 pm. Closed major holidays. **Address:** 115 Willits St 48009 **Location:** Just w of jct Old Woodward Ave; center. **Parking:** valet and street only. CALL [&M]

FOREST GRILL

Continental
$14-$48

Phone: 248/258-9400 (39)

"Cooking what nature provides" is the motto of this place, where diners look forward to an ultra-chic and first-rate dining experience. The menu focuses on simple, contemporary preparations of local and organic ingredients using traditional French and Italian cooking techniques. Portion sizes are small, making sampling a tempting possibility for those with a budget and a necessity for those with an appetite. Menu items change seasonally. **Bar:** full bar. **Reservations:** suggested. **Hours:** 11:30 am-2:30 & 5-11 pm, Fri-midnight, Sat 5 pm-midnight. Closed major holidays; also Sun. **Address:** 735 Forest Ave 48009 **Location:** Just s of jct Woodward Ave and Maple Rd. **Parking:** valet and street only. CALL [&M]

FORTE'

American
$8-$32

Phone: 248/594-7300 (38)

A loud, trendy "see and be seen" bar overlooks the elegant and somewhat eclectic dining room. A mix of styles ranging from French and Mediterranean to Californian combine into diverse menu offerings. Guests will find everything from tapas to brick-oven roasted, rosemary-rubbed chicken breast. **Bar:** full bar. **Hours:** 11 am-10 pm, Fri-midnight, Sat 9 am-midnight, Sun 9 am-9 pm. Closed major holidays. **Address:** 201 S Old Woodward Ave 48009 **Location:** Center. **Parking:** street only.

(See map and index starting on p. 244)

?HOW ABOUT LUNCH
Phone: 248/645-6644 **43**

Deli
$5-$7

The take-out-only spot is especially popular with diners looking to grab a quick picnic in one of the local parks. Ever-changing selections of sandwiches, soups and salads are made daily, and the restaurant has developed a reputation for its homemade baked goods, including brownies and cookies. Credit cards are not accepted. **Hours:** 10 am-3 pm. Closed major holidays; also Sat & Sun. **Address:** 33757 Woodward Ave 48009 **Location:** Just s of 14 1/2 Mile Rd (Lincoln Rd).

HUNTER HOUSE
Phone: 248/646-7121 **33**

American
$5-$10

A Birmingham landmark, the tiny white diner has been serving sliders, small hamburgers with onions, to loyal followers for decades. **Hours:** 8 am-10 pm, Fri & Sat-midnight, Sun noon-5 pm. Closed major holidays. **Address:** 35075 Woodward Ave 48009 **Location:** Jct W Maple Rd.

MITCHELL'S FISH MARKET
Phone: 248/646-3663 **34**

Seafood
$17-$30

A variety of fresh, never-frozen fish is flown in daily, and market availability determines the daily specials. Diners may order fish grilled, broiled, blackened or steamed in the Shanghai style with ginger, spinach and sticky rice. Among other choices are steak, pasta and chicken selections. **Bar:** full bar. **Reservations:** suggested. **Hours:** 11 am-10 pm, Fri & Sat-11 pm, Sun-9 pm. **Address:** 117 Willits St 48009 **Location:** Just e of jct Old Woodward Ave; downtown. **Parking:** valet only. CALL

NEW BANGKOK THAI BISTRO
Phone: 248/644-2181 **36**

Thai
$8-$12

Across from a theater, the attractively decorated restaurant displays Thai artwork. For those looking to experience Thai food for the first time, the restaurant offers both a lunchtime buffet and well-prepared standards, such as chicken satay and Thai pepper steak. **Hours:** 11 am-10 pm, Fri-11 pm, Sat 4 pm-11 pm, Sun 4 pm-9 pm. Closed major holidays. **Address:** 183 N Old Woodward Ave 48009 **Location:** Jct Old Woodward Ave and Maple Rd, just n; center. **Parking:** street only. CALL

OLD WOODWARD DELI
Phone: 248/642-0768 **31**

Deli
$6-$8

The cozy, upscale delicatessen is a popular stop for a quick sandwich prepared fresh on homemade bread. The glass counter displays meats available that day. Homemade soups and dessert items are other options that can be enjoyed on site or for carry-out. **Hours:** 9 am-3 pm. Closed major holidays; also Sat & Sun. **Address:** 768 N Old Woodward Ave 48009 **Location:** Jct Maple Rd, just n. **Parking:** street only.

PEABODY'S
Phone: 248/644-5222 **37**

American
$6-$27

At this well-known local eating and drinking establishment you will find a friendly, yet dressy tavern atmosphere. Great food is served in generous portions by a congenial staff that delivers what you order quickly. **Bar:** full bar. **Hours:** 11 am-10 pm, Fri & Sat-10:30 pm. Closed major holidays; also Sun. **Address:** 34965 Woodward Ave 48009 **Location:** Jct Maple Rd.

RUGBY GRILLE
Phone: 248/642-7900 **42**

American
$10-$40

Evocative of an English Country Club, the elegant dining room is marked by large hunting murals, a fireplace, dark woods and richly painted walls. The tuxedoed waiters, formal but not snooty, concentrate on preparing such traditional tableside favorites as steak tartare, Chateaubriand for two and cherries jubilee. **Bar:** full bar. **Reservations:** suggested. **Hours:** 6:30 am-midnight, Fri & Sat-1 am. **Address:** 100 Townsend St 48009 **Location:** Center; in The Townsend Hotel. **Parking:** valet and street only. CALL

SALVATORE SCALLOPINI
Phone: 248/644-8977

Italian
$7-$18

Popular and informal, the family-friendly restaurant delivers fresh entrees from a lengthy menu of traditional favorites. Seafood linguine is served piping hot with fresh mussels and squid. The waitstaff is professional and friendly. **Hours:** 11 am-9 pm, Thurs-10 pm, Fri & Sat-11 pm, Sun noon-9 pm. Closed: 11/24, 12/25 & Easter. **Address:** 505 N Old Woodward Ave 48009 **Location:** 0.5 mi n of jct Old Woodward Ave and Maple Rd; center. **Parking:** street only.

STREETSIDE SEAFOOD
Phone: 248/645-9123 **41**

Seafood
$8-$28

Rough brick walls, crackle-painted fish trophies and worn wood floors give this tiny restaurant plenty of charm. With only 60 seats, the dining room often fills to the gills with locals who appreciate the care and attention to detail that is taken to prepare the constantly changing 14 or so creative and tasty entrees of incredibly fresh fish and seafood. **Bar:** full bar. **Hours:** 11 am-11 pm, Fri-midnight, Sat 4 pm-midnight, Sun 4 pm-10 pm. Closed major holidays. **Address:** 273 Pierce St 48009 **Location:** Between Merrill St and Maple Rd; downtown. **Parking:** street only.

BLOOMFIELD HILLS pop. 3,940 (See map and index starting on p. 244)

RADISSON HOTEL DETROIT-BLOOMFIELD HILLS
Phone: (248)644-1400 **161**

Hotel
$139

Address: 39475 Woodward Ave 48304 **Location:** On SR 1 (Woodward Ave), just s of jct Long Lake Rd. **Facility:** Smoke free premises. 151 units. 2-4 stories, interior corridors. **Amenities:** video games (fee), high-speed Internet, safes. **Dining:** Deli Unique, Northern Lakes Seafood Company, see separate listings. **Pool(s):** heated indoor. **Activities:** whirlpool, exercise room. **Guest Services:** valet laundry, area transportation-within 10 mi, wireless Internet.

(See map and index starting on p. 244)

———— **WHERE TO DINE** ————

ANDIAMO

Italian
$10-$35

Phone: 248/865-9300 ⟨144⟩

With its upscale artwork and comfortable furnishings, the restaurant's dining room is an ideal setting for an intimate dinner. The menu features traditional Italian dishes, such as ravioli and lasagna, prepared using authentic recipes. **Bar:** full bar. **Reservations:** suggested. **Hours:** 11:30 am-10 pm, Fri-11 pm, Sat 4 pm-11 pm, Sun 4 pm-9 pm. Closed major holidays. **Address:** 6676 Telegraph Rd 48301 **Location:** Just s of jct US 24 (Telegraph Rd). **Parking:** on-site and valet. CALL ⟨&M⟩

BEAU JACK'S FOOD & SPIRITS

American
$7-$17

Phone: 248/626-2630 ⟨142⟩

The rustic restaurant, relaxed in its sports tavern decor, encourages laid-back dining. Menu choices range from burgers and steaks to seafood and stir-fry. A pianist further adds to the boisterous and noisy atmosphere Thursdays through Saturdays. Entertainment. **Bar:** full bar. **Hours:** 11:30 am-10 pm, Fri & Sat-11 pm, Sun 4 pm-9 pm. Closed major holidays. **Address:** 4108 W Maple Rd 48301 **Location:** Just w of jct US 24 (Telegraph Rd).

DELI UNIQUE

Deli
$5-$10

Phone: 248/646-7923 ⟨141⟩

The upscale diner has exposed-brick walls and framed artwork that set it apart from typical delicatessens. Fresh ingredients, including some made in house, go into the enormous portions of daily specials and sandwiches. **Hours:** 6:30 am-2:30 pm, Sat & Sun from 7:30 am. Closed major holidays. **Address:** 39495 N Woodward Ave 48304 **Location:** On SR 1 (Woodward Ave), just s of jct Long Lake Rd; in Radisson Hotel Detroit-Bloomfield Hills. CALL ⟨&M⟩

THE MOOSE PRESERVE BAR & GRILL

American
$8-$20

Phone: 248/858-7688

As the name might suggest, the boisterous, northwoods-inspired sports bar and lodge features plenty of duck prints and mounted trophy heads. Farmed game-such as elk, emu, venison, buffalo and duck-highlight a menu that also lists beef steaks, chicken and burgers. Outdoor dining is available in season. **Bar:** full bar. **Hours:** 11 am-midnight, Thurs-Sat to 2 am. Closed: 12/25. **Address:** 43034 Woodward Ave 48302 **Location:** Jct Square Lake Rd.

NORTHERN LAKES SEAFOOD COMPANY

Seafood
$8-$38

Phone: 248/646-7900 ⟨140⟩

This popular restaurant features a comfortable dining room decorated with marine accents, like light globes that include a glass octopus. They serve generous portions of deliciously prepared fish, shrimp and lobster. Their special "martini menu" includes a spectacular selection of variations on the basic drink that you can enjoy, like olives stuffed with blue cheese or anchovies. It is a great place for that special family dinner. **Bar:** full bar. **Reservations:** suggested, weekends. **Hours:** 11 am-2:30 & 5-10 pm, Fri-11 pm, Sat 5 pm-11 pm, Sun 5 pm-9 pm. Closed major holidays. **Address:** 39495 Woodward Ave 48304 **Location:** On SR 1 (Woodward Ave), just s of jct Long Lake Rd; in Radisson Hotel Detroit-Bloomfield Hills. **Parking:** on-site and valet. CALL ⟨&M⟩

STEVE'S DELI

Deli
$10-$24

Phone: 248/932-0800 ⟨143⟩

Featuring everything a diner could want a delicatessen to have-from corned beef to knishes to matzo ball soup-the strip-mall location doesn't stop patrons from waiting for one of the tightly packed tables. The lengthy menu lists daily specials and delicatessen favorites. **Hours:** 9 am-8 pm. Closed: 1/1, 11/24, 12/25. **Address:** 6646 Telegraph Rd 48301 **Location:** Just s of W Maple Rd; in Bloomfield Plaza.

CANTON pop. 76,366   (See map and index starting on p. 244)

COMFORT SUITES OF CANTON

Hotel
$85-$130

Phone: (734)981-1010 ⟨116⟩

Address: 5730 Haggerty Rd 48187 **Location:** I-275, exit 25 (Ford Rd), just w on SR 153. **Facility:** Smoke free premises. 66 units, some efficiencies. 3 stories (no elevator), interior corridors. **Terms:** cancellation fee imposed. **Amenities:** high-speed Internet. **Pool(s):** heated indoor. **Activities:** exercise room. **Guest Services:** valet and coin laundry, area transportation-within 3 mi, wireless Internet. ⟨🍴⟩ CALL ⟨&M⟩ ⟨➔⟩ ⟨✕⟩ ⟨📷⟩ ⟨🗄⟩ ⟨🖥⟩ ⟨💻⟩

FAIRFIELD INN BY MARRIOTT

Hotel
$98-$125

Phone: (734)981-2440 ⟨117⟩

Address: 5700 Haggerty Rd 48187 **Location:** I-275, exit 25 (Ford Rd), just w on SR 153. **Facility:** Smoke free premises. 117 units. 3 stories, interior/exterior corridors. **Terms:** cancellation fee imposed. **Pool(s):** heated outdoor. **Activities:** exercise room. **Guest Services:** valet and coin laundry, area transportation-within 3 mi, wireless Internet. ⟨🍴⟩ CALL ⟨&M⟩ ⟨➔⟩ ⟨✕⟩ ⟨📷⟩ ⟨🗄⟩ ⟨🖥⟩ ⟨💻⟩

AAA Benefit:
Members save a minimum 5% off the best available rate.

HAMPTON INN & SUITES

Hotel
$79-$154

Phone: (734)844-1111 ⟨119⟩

Address: 1950 Haggerty Rd N 48187 **Location:** I-275, exit 25 (Ford Rd), just w on SR 153. **Facility:** Smoke free premises. 90 units. 4 stories, interior corridors. **Terms:** 1-7 night minimum stay, cancellation fee imposed. **Amenities:** high-speed Internet. **Pool(s):** heated indoor. **Activities:** exercise room. **Guest Services:** valet and coin laundry, area transportation-within 5 mi, wireless Internet. ⟨✈⟩ ⟨🍴⟩ CALL ⟨&M⟩ ⟨➔⟩ ⟨BIZ⟩ ⟨✕⟩ ⟨📷⟩ ⟨💻⟩ / SOME UNITS ⟨🗄⟩ ⟨🖥⟩

AAA Benefit:
Members save up to 10% everyday!

(See map and index starting on p. 244)

HOLIDAY INN EXPRESS HOTEL & SUITES

Phone: (734)721-5500   **120**

Hotel
S99-$109

Address: 3950 Lotz Rd 48188 **Location:** I-275, exit 22 (Michigan Ave), just e. **Facility:** Smoke free premises. 81 units. 3 stories, interior corridors. **Terms:** cancellation fee imposed. **Amenities:** video games (fee), high-speed Internet. **Pool(s):** heated indoor. **Activities:** whirlpool, exercise room. **Guest Services:** valet laundry, wireless Internet.

FREE expanded continental breakfast and use of on-premises laundry facilities

LA QUINTA INN DETROIT CANTON

Phone: (734)981-1808   **118**

Hotel
$49-$105

Address: 41211 Ford Rd 48187 **Location:** I-275, exit 25 (Ford Rd), just w to jct Haggerty Rd. Located behind White Castle. **Facility:** Smoke free premises. 98 units. 3 stories, interior corridors. **Amenities:** video games (fee). *Some:* high-speed Internet. **Guest Services:** valet and coin laundry, wireless Internet.

SUPER 8-CANTON

Phone: 734/722-8880   **121**

Hotel
Rates not provided

Address: 3933 Lotz Rd 48188 **Location:** I-275, exit 22 (Michigan Ave), just e on US 12, then just s. **Facility:** Smoke free premises. 69 units. 3 stories, interior corridors. **Amenities:** safes (fee). **Guest Services:** complimentary and valet laundry, wireless Internet.

—— WHERE TO DINE ——

ASHOKA INDIAN CUISINE

Phone: 734/844-3100   **120**

Indian
$9-$17

Across from several hotels, the restaurant draws a strong crowd for its lunchtime buffet. The expansive evening menu lists both Northern and Southern Indian cuisine as well as a variety of tandoori and Indian-style Chinese dishes. **Bar:** full bar. **Hours:** 11 am-2:30 & 5:30-9:30 pm, Fri-10:30 pm, Sat 11:30 am-3 & 5:30-10:30 pm, Sun 11:30 am-3 & 5:30-9 pm. **Address:** 2100 Haggerty Rd 48187 **Location:** I-275, exit 25 (Ford Rd), just w, then just s.

IZAKAYA SANPEI

Phone: 734/416-9605   **119**

Japanese
$11-$24

Known for its karaoke bar, this small, traditionally decorated sushi bar is a regular hangout for visiting Japanese businessmen. In addition to an extensive menu of sushi and sashimi, the restaurant offers well-prepared tempura dishes and other Japanese specialties. **Bar:** full bar. **Hours:** 11:30 am-2 & 5:30-10:30 pm, Sat 5:30 pm-11 pm, Sun 5 pm-10 pm. Closed major holidays. **Address:** 43327 Joy Rd 48187 **Location:** I-275, exit 28 (Ann Arbor Rd), just w to Main St, then 0.5 mi s; in Country Commons Strip Mall.

ROSE'S RESTAURANT & LOUNGE

Phone: 734/981-9904

Italian
$8-$18

Since 1993, this family-run restaurant has specialized in Italian dishes from the region between Rome and Naples. In addition to homemade pastas, pizzas and a variety of traditional Italian chicken and fish dishes, the menu also boasts American favorites such as grilled steaks and burgers. Entrees are accompanied by a delicious loaf of homemade bread served in a long and skinny paper bag. A small patio is available seasonally for outdoor seating. **Bar:** full bar. **Reservations:** required. **Hours:** 11 am-9 pm, Thurs-Sat to 10 pm, Sun noon-9 pm. Closed major holidays. **Address:** 201 N Canton Center Rd 48187 **Location:** Jct Cherry Hill Rd.

THAI BISTRO

Phone: 734/416-2122

Thai
$6-$12

Tucked away in a strip mall, this unassuming but pleasant dining room serves a strong menu of Thai specialties. Using fresh ingredients and stellar sauces, the chef/owner faithfully re-creates the flavors of Thailand. **Bar:** beer only. **Hours:** 11:30 am-2:30 & 4:30-9 pm, Fri-10 pm, Sat 4:30 pm-10 pm. Closed major holidays; also Sun. **Address:** 45620 Ford Rd 48187 **Location:** I-275, exit 25 (Ford Rd), 2 mi w; jct Canton Center Rd.

CHESTERFIELD pop. 37,405

HOLIDAY INN EXPRESS & SUITES

Phone: (586)598-4000

Hotel
$129-$159

Address: 45805 Marketplace Blvd 48051 **Location:** I-94, exit 240B (SR 59), 0.3 mi w, then 0.3 mi n. **Facility:** Smoke free premises. 77 units. 3 stories, interior corridors. **Amenities:** high-speed Internet. **Pool(s):** heated indoor. **Activities:** exercise room, game room. **Guest Services:** valet and coin laundry, wireless Internet.

CLARKSTON pop. 1,000

—— **WHERE TO DINE** ——

THE CLARKSTON UNION   Phone: 248/620-6100

American
$8-$23

Savor hearty, homemade comfort foods in a resurrected 1840s church. An extensive selection of European and American microbrewed beer complements a limited offering of pub-type food. A nice variety of teas and gourmet coffees are also available. **Bar:** full bar. **Hours:** 11 am-10 pm, Fri & Sat-11 pm, Sun 9 am-9 pm. Closed major holidays. **Address:** 54 S Main St 48346 **Location:** Downtown. CALL 🅼

MESQUITE CREEK STEAKS & SEAFOOD   Phone: 248/620-9300

American
$8-$30

There's an upscale atmosphere at this popular dining spot but decidedly reasonable prices and generous portions. Prime steaks and seafood selections are the focus, but the menu also offers a variety of Southwest-inspired options such as quesadillas, crab macao and fajitas. For those counting their calories, a "lean" menu offers tasty, healthful options for three-course meals at less than 600 calories. **Bar:** full bar. **Hours:** 11 am-10 pm, Thurs-Sat to 11 pm, Sun noon-9 pm. Closed major holidays. **Address:** 7228 N Main St 48346 **Location:** I-75, exit 91 (Clarkston/Davison), just w. CALL 🅼

UNION WOODSHOP   Phone: 248/625-5660

Barbecue
$8-$25

It's all about the almighty pig at this trendy barbecue joint, where this "magical" animal is celebrated in all its glorious iterations. On the menu is everything from pulled pork sandwiches and proscuitto on pizza, to bacon sprinkled over caesar salad, to falling-off-the-bone ribs. Smoked meats, mouth-watering brisket and a selection of gourmet or build-your-own wood-fired pizzas round out the impressive array of selections. A children's menu also is available. **Bar:** full bar. **Hours:** 4 pm-10 pm, Fri-11 pm, Sat noon-11 pm, Sun noon-9 pm. Closed major holidays. **Address:** 18 S Main St 48346 **Location:** Downtown. **Parking:** on-site and street. CALL 🅼

CLAWSON pop. 12,732 (See map and index starting on p. 244)

—— **WHERE TO DINE** ——

BLACK LOTUS BREWING COMPANY   Phone: 248/577-1878   (150)

American
$4-$8

With its visible brew works and live entertainment, this is a popular spot for locals to gather. They chat over a pint of one of the brewpub's seasonally-inspired specialties, like Green Jasmine Tea, Sun Ra Summer Wheat, Top Shelf Smoked Scotch Ale or Ms. Michigan Pale. Menu offerings are simple and range from burgers, panini and chips and salsa to cheese and crackers. Talented local bands are featured regularly. **Bar:** beer & wine. **Hours:** noon-midnight, Fri & Sat-2 am. Closed major holidays. **Address:** 1 E 14 Mile Rd 48017 **Location:** Jct Main St.

CLAWSON STEAK HOUSE   Phone: 248/588-5788   (148)

Steak
$6-$33

Reminiscent of a 1950s supper club, the mauve dining room has been popular with locals of all ages for more than 40 years. Live music is featured Wednesday through Saturday after 8 pm to enhance meals of traditional steak house favorites. Entertainment. **Bar:** full bar. **Hours:** 11 am-11 pm, Fri & Sat-midnight. Closed: Sun. **Address:** 56 S Rochester Rd 48017 **Location:** I-75, exit 65 (14 Mile Rd), 1 mi w of jct Rochester Rd. **Parking:** on-site and valet.

NOBLE FISH   Phone: 248/585-2314   (149)

Japanese
$5-$16

Hidden in the back of a Japanese grocery store where many local sushi restaurants are reputed to obtain their ingredients, the revered spot lures discerning diners who grab a seat when one is available to enjoy fresh and creative sushi and sashimi. **Hours:** 11 am-2:30 & 4:30-7:30 pm. Closed major holidays; also Mon. **Address:** 45 E 14 Mile Rd 48017 **Location:** Jct N Main St. **Parking:** street only.

SHILLA KOREAN AND JAPANESE CUISINE   Phone: 248/655-0120   (147)

Korean
$6-$19

Named for what Korea once was called, the restaurant presents an extensive menu of Korean and Japanese fare. A ceiling resembling a ship's hull—in addition to dark woods, original artwork and a long sushi bar—helps create a relaxed but upscale environment. Diners can watch a talented chef create gem-like morsels of sushi and sashimi. Half of the menu features Korean dishes, and barbecues in most tabletops enable patrons to grill their own dishes. **Bar:** full bar. **Hours:** 11 am-10 pm, Fri-11 pm, Sat noon-11 pm, Sun noon-10 pm. Closed: 1/1, 11/24. **Address:** 1119 W Maple Rd 48017 **Location:** Just e of jct N Crooks Rd. CALL 🅼

COMMERCE pop. 34,764 (See map and index starting on p. 244)

HAMPTON INN - DETROIT / NOVI   Phone: (248)624-8100   23

Hotel
$89-$179

Address: 169 Loop Rd 48390 **Location:** Jct SR 5 and 14 Mile Rd. **Facility:** Smoke free premises. 106 units. 4 stories, interior corridors. **Terms:** 1-7 night minimum stay, cancellation fee imposed. **Amenities:** video games (fee), high-speed Internet. **Pool(s):** heated indoor. **Activities:** whirlpool, exercise room. **Guest Services:** valet and coin laundry, area transportation-within 7 mi, wireless Internet. *(see ad p. 288)*

(See map and index starting on p. 244)

―――― **WHERE TO DINE** ――――

GEST OMELETTES

Breakfast
$5-$10

Phone: 248/926-0717 [46]

This is the spot to nosh on an omelet. In addition to standards such as Spanish and Western omelets, patrons can select from a variety of specialties including a Greek omelet with seasoned ground beef and black olives; an Oriental omelet with shrimp, water chestnuts and pea pods; a Coney Island omelet with hot dogs and cheese; or the Popeye's favorite omelet with, of course, spinach. Also available are pancakes, waffles and cooked-to-order eggs as well as a few lunch offerings. **Hours:** 6:30 am-4 pm. Closed major holidays. **Address:** 39560 W 14 Mile Rd 48390 **Location:** Just e of jct SR 5; in Newberry Square Shopping Plaza. CALL [&M]

DEARBORN pop. 97,775 (See map and index starting on p. 244)

COURTYARD BY MARRIOTT-DEARBORN

Hotel
$134-$144

Phone: (313)271-1400 [107]

Address: 5200 Mercury Dr 48126 **Location:** SR 39 (Southfield Frwy), exit 7 (Ford Rd), just e, then s. **Facility:** Smoke free premises. 147 units. 1-3 stories, interior corridors. **Terms:** cancellation fee imposed. **Amenities:** high-speed Internet. **Pool(s):** heated indoor. **Activities:** whirlpool, exercise room. **Guest Services:** valet and coin laundry, wireless Internet. **Free Special Amenities: early check-in/late check-out and high-speed Internet.**

AAA Benefit:
Members save a minimum 5% off the best available rate.

[SAVE] [ECO] [Y] CALL [&M] [🏊] [✕] [📷] [📶] [💻] / SOME UNITS [📷]

THE DEARBORN INN, A MARRIOTT HOTEL

Historic
Hotel
$169-$179

Phone: (313)271-2700 [112]

Address: 20301 Oakwood Blvd 48124 **Location:** SR 39 (Southfield Frwy), exit Oakwood Blvd, 1 mi w. **Facility:** Built in 1931 by Henry Ford, the contemporary hotel's stunning historic lobby is a wonderful example of Georgian-style architecture and opulence. Smoke free premises. 229 units, some two bedrooms. 2-4 stories, interior/exterior corridors. **Parking:** on-site and valet. **Terms:** check-in 4 pm, cancellation fee imposed. **Amenities:** high-speed Internet (fee). **Pool(s):** heated outdoor. **Activities:** exercise room. **Guest Services:** valet laundry, area transportation-within 3 mi, wireless Internet.

Marriott.
HOTELS & RESORTS
AAA Benefit:
Members save 5% or more off best available rate.

[SAVE] [ECO] FEE[🔌] [🍴] [Y] CALL [&M] [🏊] [BIZ] [✕] [📷] [💻] / SOME UNITS [📷] [📷]

DEARBORN WEST VILLAGE HOTEL

Hotel
$85-$140

Phone: (313)436-9600 [111]

Address: 20061 Michigan Ave 48124 **Location:** SR 39 (Southfield Frwy), exit Michigan Ave, just w. **Facility:** Smoke free premises. 119 units. 4 stories, interior corridors. **Terms:** cancellation fee imposed. **Amenities:** video games (fee). **Pool(s):** heated indoor. **Activities:** exercise room. **Guest Services:** valet and coin laundry, wireless Internet.

[🍴➕] [🏊] [✕] [📷] [💻] / SOME UNITS [📷] [📷]

EXTENDED STAYAMERICA DETROIT DEARBORN

Extended Stay
Hotel
$85-$95

Phone: (313)336-0021 [109]

Address: 260 Towne Center Dr 48126 **Location:** SR 39 (Southfield Frwy); between Ford Rd and Michigan Ave exits; just w of jct Service and Hubbard drs. Adjacent to shopping mall. **Facility:** Smoke free premises. 93 efficiencies. 4 stories, interior corridors. **Terms:** cancellation fee imposed. **Guest Services:** coin laundry, wireless Internet.

[🍴➕] CALL [&M] [✕] [📷] [📷] [📷] [💻] / SOME UNITS FEE[🐕]

(See map and index starting on p. 244)

THE HENRY

Hotel
$179-$199

Phone: (313)441-2000   108

Address: 300 Town Center Dr 48126
Location: SR 39 (Southfield Frwy); between
Ford Rd and Michigan Ave exits, on Service Dr.
Facility: Refined atmosphere with a traditional
elegance adorn the property. Smoke free
premises. 308 units. 11 stories, interior corridors.
Parking: on-site and valet. **Terms:** cancellation
fee imposed. **Amenities:** video games (fee),
high-speed Internet, safes. **Dining:** The Grill at
The Henry, see separate listing. **Pool(s):** heated
indoor. **Activities:** saunas, whirlpool, tennis &
racquetball privileges, exercise room.
Fee: massage. **Guest Services:** valet laundry,
area transportation-within 5 mi, wireless Internet. *(see ad below)*

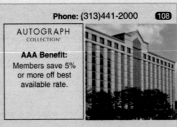

AUTOGRAPH
COLLECTION®

AAA Benefit:
Members save 5%
or more off best
available rate.

FREE local telephone calls and high-speed Internet

HYATT REGENCY DEARBORN

Hotel
$99-$399

Phone: (313)593-1234   110

Address: 600 Town Center Dr 48126 **Location:** Jct SR 39
(Southfield Frwy), 0.3 mi w on Michigan Ave, 0.3 mi n on
Evergreen Rd, then e on Fairlane Rd. Opposite Ford Motor
Company World Headquarters. **Facility:** A spectacular 16-story
atrium and a chic lobby with stainless steel, polished wood and
dramatic lighting give the hotel an up-to-date, sophisticated feel.
Smoke free premises. 772 units. 13 stories, interior corridors.
Parking: on-site and valet. **Terms:** cancellation fee imposed.
Amenities: video games (fee). *Some:* safes. *Fee:* high-speed
Internet. **Dining:** Giulio & Sons, see separate listing.
Pool(s): heated indoor. **Activities:** sauna, whirlpool, exercise room. **Guest Services:** valet laundry,
wireless Internet. *Fee:* area transportation-within 5 mi.

HYATT
HOTELS & RESORTS®

AAA Benefit:
Ask for the AAA rate and save
10%.

RED ROOF INN-DEARBORN #7182

Motel
$65-$86

Phone: (313)278-9732   113

Address: 24130 Michigan Ave 48124 **Location:** Jct US 24 (Telegraph Rd) and 12 (Michigan Ave).
Facility: Smoke free premises. 111 units. 2 stories, exterior corridors. **Amenities:** *Fee:* video games,
safes. **Guest Services:** wireless Internet. **Free Special Amenities:** local telephone calls.

▼ *See AAA listing above* ▼

(See map and index starting on p. 244)

TOWNEPLACE SUITES

Extended Stay
Hotel
$130-$140

Address: 6141 Mercury Dr 48126 **Location:** SR 39 (Southfield Frwy), exit 7 (Ford Rd), just e, then 0.8 mi n. **Facility:** Smoke free premises. 148 kitchen units, some two bedrooms. 3 stories, interior corridors. **Terms:** cancellation fee imposed. **Amenities:** high-speed Internet. **Pool(s):** outdoor. **Activities:** barbecue grills, exercise room. **Guest Services:** valet and coin laundry, wireless Internet.

Phone: (313)271-0200   106

> **AAA Benefit:**
> Members save a minimum 5% off the best available rate.

 / SOME UNITS FEE

—— WHERE TO DINE ——

ANDIAMO

Italian
$12-$30

Part of a local restaurant chain, the classy yet casual restaurant serves traditional Italian dishes, such as ravioli and lasagna, prepared using authentic recipes and high-quality ingredients. The spacious dining room, with its upscale artwork and comfortable furnishings, is an ideal setting for an intimate dinner. Entertainment. **Bar:** full bar. **Reservations:** suggested. **Hours:** 11 am-10 pm, Fri-11 pm, Sat 4 pm-11 pm, Sun 4 pm-9 pm. Closed major holidays. **Address:** 21400 Michigan Ave 48124 **Location:** SR 39 (Southfield Frwy), exit Michigan Ave, just w. **Parking:** on-site and valet.

Phone: 313/359-3300   113

BIG FISH SEAFOOD BISTRO

Seafood
$6-$24

Popular with local corporate types, the eclectic restaurant is dotted with stylized fish and nautical memorabilia. Specializing in fresh seafood, the daily catch menu changes constantly, but the varied steak, chicken and pasta dishes are reliable choices. Hot and cold soups, varied appetizers and creative desserts complement such innovatively prepared seafood entrees as whitefish Oscar. **Bar:** full bar. **Hours:** 11 am-10 pm, Fri & Sat-11 pm, Sun 1 pm-9 pm. Closed: 12/25. **Address:** 700 Town Center Dr 48126 **Location:** At Fairlane Town Center near Evergreen Rd. **Parking:** on-site and valet. SAVE

Phone: 313/336-6350   111

BUDDY'S RESTAURANT PIZZERIA

Pizza
$6-$17

In business since 1946, the pizzeria is known for its square, deep-dish pizza with crispy, buttery crust and a blend of four cheeses. Diners might want to save room for the huge brownie sundae, which could probably serve a family of four. The decor is styled after an old-time diner and soda fountain, making this a great place for a casual dinner with friends or family. Nine locations are in the greater Detroit area, so finding a convenient one shouldn't be difficult. **Bar:** full bar. **Hours:** 11 am-10 pm, Sat 11:30 am-11 pm, Sun noon-10 pm. Closed: 11/24, 12/25 & Easter. **Address:** 22148 Michigan Ave 48124 **Location:** Jct US 24 (Telegraph Rd), 0.3 mi e.

Phone: 313/562-5900

GIULIO & SONS

American
$10-$35

On the second floor just above the hotel lobby, the dining room's hand-painted murals of pastoral countryside scenes create a relaxing setting to enjoy one of the many American favorites or Northern Italian-inspired dishes on the menu. Selections range from steaks and chops to chicken, pasta and a variety of fresh fish and seafood. A sweet shop in the reception area is home to a dessert buffet as well as jar after jar of candy just waiting to be sampled. **Bar:** full bar. **Hours:** 6:30 am-3 & 5-10 pm, Fri & Sat-10:30 pm. **Address:** 600 Town Center Dr 48126 **Location:** Jct SR (Southfield Frwy), 0.3 mi w on Michigan Ave, 0.3 mi n on Evergreen Rd, then just e on Fairlane Rd; in Hyatt Regency Dearborn.

Phone: 313/593-1234   110

THE GRILL AT THE HENRY

Continental
$18-$40

This elegant restaurant, reminiscent of an English country club, offers impeccable service and creative takes on a Continental menu that emphasizes organic ingredients and sustainable agriculture. The menu changes frequently, but usually features classics such as filet mignon, Bay of Fundy salmon, rack of lamb, organic chicken and Dover sole. **Bar:** full bar. **Reservations:** suggested. **Hours:** 6:30 am-2:30 & 5-10 pm, Sun-2:30 pm. **Address:** 300 Town Center Dr 48126 **Location:** SR 39 (Southfield Frwy); between Ford Rd and Michigan Ave exits, on Service Dr; in The Henry, Autograph Collection. **Parking:** on-site and valet.

Phone: 313/441-2000   109

KIERNAN'S STEAK HOUSE

American
$7-$25

As its name suggests, the restaurant focuses on steakhouse fare: veal, pork, chicken, seafood and, of course, beef. Silk lampshades and subtle illumination add to the romantic ambience of the tavern-like dining room. Servers are friendly and attentive. **Bar:** full bar. **Reservations:** suggested. **Hours:** 11 am-10 pm, Fri-11 pm, Sat 5 pm-11 pm, Sun 5 pm-9 pm. Closed major holidays. **Address:** 21931 Michigan Ave 48124 **Location:** On US 12 (Michigan Ave), 1 mi w of jct SR 39 (Southfield Frwy). **Parking:** on-site and valet.

Phone: 313/565-4260   114

MATI'S DELI

Deli
$6-$8

Diners should all be so lucky as to have a New York delicatessen in their neighborhood. Featuring scratch-made soups and fresh breads, the tiny eatery in the middle of a residential area often has lines of customers out the front door eager for its custom-made sandwiches and desserts. **Hours:** 10 am-6 pm, Sat-3 pm. Closed major holidays; also Sun. **Address:** 1842 Monroe 48124 **Location:** Jct US 12 (Michigan Ave), 0.5 mi s. **Parking:** on-site and street.

Phone: 313/277-3253   115

MICHIGAN CAFÉ

American
$6-$9

In the foyer of The Henry Ford Museum, this family friendly, cafeteria-style restaurant plays whimsical tribute to Detroit and Michigan's motoring past through historic murals and photos that line the walls of the dining area. Menu items also pay tribute to local influences, offering regionally inspired cuisine such as the Dearborn sausage and kraut, Hammtramck cabbage roll, Great Lakes whitefish cake, Motown pulled pork and Sander's hot fudge cream puff. Museum admission is not required. **Bar:** beer only. **Hours:** 9:30 am-4:30 pm. Closed: 11/24, 12/25. **Address:** 20900 Oakwood Blvd 48124 **Location:** SR 39 (Southfield Frwy), exit 4 (Oakwood Blvd), 1.8 mi w; jct Village Rd; in The Henry Ford Museum.

Phone: 313/982-6001   112

(See map and index starting on p. 244)

NEW YASMEEN FLYING CARPET CAFÉ
Phone: 313/582-6035 (108)

Lebanese
$6-$10

Diners are greeted by dessert and delicatessen counters that showcase more than 30 varieties of Lebanese and French sweets, platters of hot and cold items and an oven that continually turns out fresh pitas. The restaurant prepares the standard chicken shawarma and shish tawook, in addition to a variety of new dishes. All meat dishes are cooked to order. A commitment to preparing food in the traditional handmade manner takes such items as baba ghanouj to unparalleled levels. **Hours:** 5:30 am-9:45 pm; open 24 hours during Ramadan. **Address:** 13900 W Warren Ave 48126 **Location:** 1.5 mi e of jct Greenfield Rd. **Parking:** on-site and street.

RICHTER'S CHALET
Phone: 313/565-0484 (116)

German
$6-$19

The cozy restaurant offers a menu of such authentic German dishes as potato pancakes, Wiener schnitzel and sauerbraten sprinkled with a handful of American dishes. Light background music and Bavarian appointments set the tone in the dining room, and the staff is friendly and efficient. **Bar:** beer & wine. **Hours:** 11 am-8:30 pm, Fri & Sat-9 pm, Sun noon-7 pm. Closed: 12/24, 12/25; also Mon. **Address:** 23920 Michigan Ave 48124 **Location:** Jct US 24 (Telegraph Rd), just e.

FARMINGTON HILLS pop. 82,111 (See map and index starting on p. 244)

CANDLEWOOD SUITES
Phone: (248)324-0540 (74)

Extended Stay Hotel
$77-$124

Address: 37555 Hills Tech Dr 48331 **Location:** I-696, exit I-96 E/I-275 S/SR 5, just s to SR 5 N, 2 mi n to 12 Mile Rd, 1.3 mi e, then 0.3 mi s on Halsted Rd. **Facility:** Smoke free premises. 125 efficiencies. 4 stories, interior corridors. **Terms:** office hours 7 am-11 am. **Amenities:** high-speed Internet. **Activities:** exercise room. **Guest Services:** valet and coin laundry.

CALL 🛗Ⓜ ✕ 🎥 🖥 🖥 🖥 / SOME UNITS FEE 🐾

COURTYARD BY MARRIOTT DETROIT FARMINGTON HILLS
Phone: (248)553-0000 (71)

Hotel
$121-$154

Address: 31525 12 Mile Rd 48334 **Location:** I-696, exit 5 (Orchard Lake Rd), just w. **Facility:** Smoke free premises. 203 units. 3 stories, interior corridors. **Terms:** cancellation fee imposed. **Amenities:** Some: high-speed Internet. **Pool(s):** heated indoor. **Activities:** whirlpool, exercise room. **Guest Services:** valet and coin laundry, area transportation-within 5 mi, wireless Internet.

🍸 🏊 BIZ ✕ 🎥 🖥 / SOME UNITS 🖥

AAA Benefit:
Members save a minimum 5% off the best available rate.

EXTENDED STAYAMERICA DETROIT-FARMINGTON HILLS
Phone: (248)473-4000 (73)

Extended Stay Hotel
$55-$65

Address: 27775 Stansbury Blvd 48334 **Location:** I-696, exit 5 (Orchard Lake Rd), just n, just e on 12 Mile Rd, then just s. **Facility:** Smoke free premises. 113 efficiencies. 3 stories, interior corridors. **Terms:** cancellation fee imposed. **Guest Services:** coin laundry, wireless Internet.

🍴 CALL 🛗Ⓜ ✕ 🎥 🖥 🖥 🖥 / SOME UNITS FEE 🐾

FAIRFIELD INN & SUITES BY MARRIOTT
Phone: (248)442-9800 (72)

Hotel
$98-$125

Address: 27777 Stansbury Blvd 48334 **Location:** I-696, exit 5 (Orchard Lake Rd), just n, just e on 12 Mile Rd, then just s. **Facility:** Smoke free premises. 90 units. 3 stories, interior corridors. **Terms:** cancellation fee imposed. **Amenities:** video games (fee), high-speed Internet. **Pool(s):** heated indoor. **Activities:** whirlpool, exercise room. **Guest Services:** valet and coin laundry, wireless Internet. **Free Special Amenities:** expanded continental breakfast and high-speed Internet.

SAVE 🍴 CALL 🛗Ⓜ 🏊 ✕ 🎥 🖥 🖥 🖥

AAA Benefit:
Members save a minimum 5% off the best available rate.

HOLIDAY INN & SUITES
Phone: (248)477-7800 (76)

Hotel
$79-$140

Address: 37529 Grand River Ave 48335 **Location:** I-275, exit 165 (SR 5/Grand River Ave), 1 mi e. **Facility:** Smoke free premises. 137 units. 4 stories, interior corridors. **Terms:** cancellation fee imposed. **Amenities:** Some: high-speed Internet. **Pool(s):** heated indoor. **Activities:** whirlpool, exercise room. **Guest Services:** valet and coin laundry, area transportation-within 5 mi, wireless Internet.

🍴 🍸 CALL 🛗Ⓜ 🏊 ✕ 🎥 🖥 / SOME UNITS FEE 🐾

HOLIDAY INN EXPRESS HOTEL & SUITES
Phone: (248)675-1020 (77)

Hotel
$81-$144

Address: 21100 Haggerty Rd 48167 **Location:** I-275, exit 167 (8 Mile Rd), just w. **Facility:** Smoke free premises. 105 units. 3 stories, interior corridors. **Amenities:** safes. **Pool(s):** heated indoor. **Activities:** exercise room. **Guest Services:** valet laundry, wireless Internet.

🍴 CALL 🛗Ⓜ 🏊 BIZ ✕ 🎥 🖥 🖥 / SOME UNITS 🖥

RED ROOF INN-FARMINGTON HILLS #7038
Phone: (248)478-8640 (75)

Motel
$48-$73

Address: 24300 Sinacola Ct 48335 **Location:** I-96/275 and SR 5, exit 165 (Grand River Ave), just w. **Facility:** Smoke free premises. 108 units. 2 stories, interior corridors. **Terms:** cancellation fee imposed. **Amenities:** Fee: video games, safes. **Guest Services:** wireless Internet. **Free Special Amenities:** local telephone calls. SAVE 🍴 CALL 🛗Ⓜ ✕ 🎥 / SOME UNITS 🐾 🖥 🖥

(See map and index starting on p. 244)

—— **WHERE TO DINE** ——

ALFOCCINO

Italian
$8-$20

Phone: 248/476-0044　⑦

The warm and cozy dining room's relaxed atmosphere hints at Old World charm. Dishes range from pizza and pasta to steaks, seafood, burgers and sandwiches. Among house specialties are veal, chicken and eggplant parmigiana and veal or chicken piccata or Marsala. **Bar:** full bar. **Hours:** 11 am-10 pm, Sat from 3 pm, Sun from noon. Closed major holidays. **Address:** 39205 Grand River Ave 48335 **Location:** I-96/275 and SR 5, exit 165 (Grand River Ave), 1 mi w. CALL ♿M

CAFÉ CORTINA

Traditional Italian
$12-$40

Phone: 248/474-3033　⑦⑤

While the area by the fireplace is the most requested, there isn't a bad seat in the dimly lit, demurely elegant dining room. Northern Italian cuisine reflects a few Southern accents and employs fresh herbs and vegetables grown in the kitchen's own garden. Both homemade and luxurious imported ingredients abound. While attentive and professional, service lends to a relaxed and unobtrusive experience. **Bar:** full bar. **Reservations:** required. **Hours:** 11 am-10:30 pm, Sat from 5 pm. Closed major holidays; also Sun. **Address:** 30715 W 10 Mile Rd 48336 **Location:** I-696, exit 5 (Orchard Lake Rd), 1 mi s to jct W 10 Mile Rd, then 0.3 mi e. **Parking:** on-site and valet. CALL ♿M

FAMILY BUGGY RESTAURANT

American
$7-$16

Phone: 248/553-9090

Antique furnishings and decorations give you the feeling that you've slipped into yesteryear. The homey, family-oriented restaurant is a comfortable place in which to enjoy such reliable favorites as smothered chicken breast and barbecue ribs. **Hours:** 11 am-9 pm, Fri & Sat-10 pm; Sun-Thurs to 9:30 pm in summer. Closed: 1/1, 11/24, 12/25. **Address:** 29335 Orchard Lake Rd 48334 **Location:** I-696, exit 5 (Orchard Lake Rd), 1 mi n, jct 13 Mile Rd. CALL ♿M

HONG HUA

Cantonese
$7-$35

Phone: 248/489-2280　⑦④

An exacting eye for detail is evident in this upscale, white-tableclothed Cantonese restaurant. Everything from the "floral" arrangements of carved vegetables to the fresh fish kept in aerated freshwater tanks in the kitchen speak volumes about the 120-item menu. Offering specialties such as shark's fin and bird's nest soups, and fresh abalone, the menu also gives a brief nod to hot and spicy Szechuan-style dishes and lists some more traditional Chinese-American fare. **Bar:** full bar. **Hours:** 11 am-10:30 pm, Fri & Sat-midnight, Sun noon-midnight. Closed major holidays. **Address:** 27925 Orchard Lake Rd 48334 **Location:** I-696, exit 5 (Orchard Lake Rd), just n. CALL ♿M

JOHN COWLEY & SONS IRISH PUB

Irish
$8-$25

Phone: 248/474-5941　⑦⑧

Split between a more formal dining area downstairs and a more casual space upstairs, the restaurant is decorated with Dublin street signs that point the way to an enjoyable Irish-American dining experience. House specialties include potato soup, a blarney crock and trifecta of beef tenderloin. Chicken, pork and fish are other options. **Bar:** full bar. **Hours:** 11 am-10 pm, Sat from noon. Closed major holidays; also Sun. **Address:** 33338 Grand River Ave 48336 **Location:** Jct Farmington Rd; downtown Farmington. **Parking:** on-site and street. CALL ♿M

RECIPES

American
$5-$10

Phone: 248/477-2600　⑦⑥

Open for breakfast and lunch, the cozy restaurant offers the standards of eggs and pancakes. However, by using fresh ingredients and influences ranging from Southern and Southwestern to vegetarian and Asian, patrons get to experience more exotic flavors than those typically offered in standard breakfast and lunch fare. **Reservations:** required. **Hours:** 7 am-2:30 pm, Sat & Sun-3 pm. Closed major holidays. **Address:** 39297 Grand River Ave 48335 **Location:** I-96/275 and SR 5, exit 165 (Grand River Ave), 1 mi w. CALL ♿M

FERNDALE pop. 22,105　(See map and index starting on p. 244)

—— **WHERE TO DINE** ——

ASSAGGI MEDITERRANEAN BISTRO

Mediterranean
$12-$35

Phone: 248/584-3499　⑱②

Using fresh herbs and vegetables grown in a kitchen garden, this chef at this storefront restaurant highlights an innovative menu that mixes and matches such Mediterranean styles as French, Spanish, Greek and Lebanese. **Bar:** full bar. **Hours:** 11 am-2 & 5-10 pm, Fri-11 pm, Sat 5 pm-11 pm, Sun 4 pm-9 pm. Closed major holidays; also Mon. **Address:** 330 W 9 Mile Rd 48220 **Location:** Jct Woodward Ave, just w. **Parking:** valet and street only. CALL ♿M

CHRISTINE'S CUISINE

Continental
$5-$17

Phone: 248/584-3354　⑱⓪

In a nondescript strip mall, the small but cheerful restaurant displays a revolving collection of local artwork on its walls. Maybe best described as international comfort food, the offerings pick and choose influences from a dozen or so countries, as well as the Eastern Europe region. The results are such dishes as linguine with tomato-basil-garlic sauce, meatloaf with wild mushroom stuffing and "Baba's" own cheddar and potato pierogies. **Hours:** 11 am-9 pm, Sat from 9 am, Sun 9 am-3 pm. Closed major holidays. **Address:** 729 E 9 Mile Rd 48220 **Location:** 1 mi e of jct Woodward Ave; in Ferndale Plaza.

(See map and index starting on p. 244)

TOAST   Phone: 248/398-0444   (179)

American
$6-$10

True to its namesake, the cheerful restaurant displays a collection of toasters on one wall as a gentle reminder that breakfast is indeed the most important meal of the day. In addition to classic breakfast items, the menu lists such creative takes as Grand Marnier or bananas Foster French toast and breakfast burritos. **Hours:** 7 am-3 pm, Sat & Sun from 8 am. Closed major holidays. **Address:** 23144 Woodward Ave 48220 **Location:** Just n of 9 Mile Rd. **Parking:** on-site and street.

GROSSE POINTE FARMS pop. 9,764   (See map and index starting on p. 244)

—— WHERE TO DINE ——

THE HILL SEAFOOD AND CHOP HOUSE   Phone: 313/886-8101   (185)

Seafood
$10-$39

A country club atmosphere exudes through this comfortable and subtly upscale space. Simple and classic dishes such as Dover sole meuniere are prepared from the freshest fish, while the 20-ounce rib chop is prepared with a light bourbon-butter sauce. **Bar:** full bar. **Reservations:** suggested. **Hours:** 11:30 am-3 & 5-10 pm, Fri-11 pm, Sat 5 pm-11 pm. Closed major holidays; also Sun, except Easter & Mothers Day. **Address:** 123 Kercheval Ave 48236 **Location:** Center. **Parking:** on-site and valet. CALL 🔊M

JUMPS   Phone: 313/882-9555   (187)

American
$4-$25

This popular restaurant prepares most items from scratch. Fresh local ingredients are paired with global accents. The skill and imagination of the kitchen really shines on the chalkboard menu of daily specials. **Bar:** full bar. **Hours:** 8 am-10 pm, Sun-2 pm. Closed major holidays; also Mon. **Address:** 63 Kercheval Ave 48236 **Location:** Jct McKinley Ave. **Parking:** street only.

LUCY'S TAVERN ON THE HILL   Phone: 313/640-2020   (186)

American
$8-$23

A popular local drinking and dining establishment, the tavern features a cozy, friendly pub-like atmosphere and sophisticated tavern-style meals. A scrumptious steak is complemented by tasty waffle fries and a favorite beer or wine. **Bar:** full bar. **Hours:** 11 am-10 pm, Fri & Sat-11 pm, Sun 2 pm-10 pm. Closed: 11/24, 12/25. **Address:** 115 Kercheval Ave 48236 **Location:** Center. **Parking:** street only.

GROSSE POINTE WOODS pop. 17,080   (See map and index starting on p. 244)

—— WHERE TO DINE ——

MACK AVENUE DINER   Phone: 313/886-0680   (190)

American
$5-$10

The occasional wait for one of the limited number of tables may be an indication of the popularity of this place. While the decor is straightforward, it's the homemade daily specials and desserts that bring regulars back. **Hours:** 7 am-8 pm. Closed: 12/25 & Easter. **Address:** 19841 Mack Ave 48236 **Location:** Just e of Moross Rd. **Parking:** street only. CALL 🔊M

HOLLY pop. 6,135

—— WHERE TO DINE ——

THE HOLLY HOTEL   Phone: 248/634-5208

American
$27-$36

Late Queen Anne Victorian architecture is the hallmark of this historic former inn, which has provided hospitality service for three centuries. Every aspect of the three formal dining rooms, from lace-covered windows to delicate tea cups and saucers, is a nod to the restaurant's historic past. The menu changes daily, but always available signature dishes include rack of lamb, Lake Superior whitefish and tournedos of beef tenderloin. Legend has it that ghosts often appear while guests are dining. **Bar:** full bar. **Reservations:** suggested. **Hours:** 4 pm-10 pm, also for tea 2 pm-5 pm, Sun 10:30 am-2:30 & 4-8 pm; Sunday brunch. Closed: 1/1, 5/30, 12/25. **Address:** 110 Battle Alley 48442 **Location:** I-75, exit 98 (E Holly Rd), 4.8 mi w, then just s on Broad St.

LAKE ORION pop. 2,715

BEST WESTERN PALACE INN   Phone: (248)391-2755

Hotel
$69-$79

Address: 2755 N Lapeer Rd 48360 **Location:** I-75, exit 81 (Lapeer Rd), 3.3 mi n. **Facility:** Smoke free premises. 76 units. 2 stories, interior/exterior corridors. **Amenities:** Some: high-speed Internet. **Pool(s):** heated indoor. **Activities:** exercise room. Fee: game room. **Guest Services:** valet and coin laundry, area transportation-within 3 mi, Great Lakes Crossings & The Palace of Auburn Hills, wireless Internet. **Free Special Amenities:** full breakfast and high-speed Internet.

/ SOME UNITS FEE

AAA Benefit:
Members save up to 20%, plus 10% bonus points with free rewards program.

SPRINGHILL SUITES BY MARRIOTT

▼▼▼▼
Contemporary
Hotel
$107-$137

Address: 4919 Interpark Dr 48359 **Location:** I-75, exit 81 (Lapeer Rd), 1.5 mi n. **Facility:** Smoke free premises. 102 units. 4 stories, interior corridors. **Terms:** cancellation fee imposed. **Amenities:** high-speed Internet. **Pool(s):** heated indoor. **Activities:** whirlpool, exercise room. **Guest Services:** valet and coin laundry, area transportation-within 10 mi, wireless Internet.

CALL 🛗M 🏊 ✕ 🎥 🖥 🍽 🖵

Phone: (248)475-4700

AAA Benefit:
Members save a minimum 5% off the best available rate.

LINCOLN PARK pop. 40,008 (See map and index starting on p. 244)

MAGNUSON HOTEL

▼▼▼▼
Hotel
Rates not provided

Address: 1805 John A Papalas Dr 48146 **Location:** I-75, exit 41 (Southfield Frwy). Located in front of the railway tracks. **Facility:** Smoke free premises. 82 units. 3 stories, interior corridors. **Amenities:** safes (fee). *Some:* high-speed Internet. **Pool(s):** heated indoor. **Activities:** sauna, exercise room. **Guest Services:** valet and coin laundry, wireless Internet. **Free Special Amenities: expanded continental breakfast and high-speed Internet.**

SAVE CALL 🛗M 🏊 ✕ 🎥 🖥 🍽 🖵

Phone: 313/381-5600 [128]

LIVONIA pop. 100,545 (See map and index starting on p. 244)

COURTYARD BY MARRIOTT

▼▼▼▼
Hotel
$116-$148

Address: 17200 N Laurel Park Dr 48152 **Location:** I-275, exit 170 (6 Mile Rd), just e. Located beside the Laurel Park Mall. **Facility:** Smoke free premises. 149 units. 2-3 stories, interior corridors. **Terms:** cancellation fee imposed. **Amenities:** high-speed Internet. **Pool(s):** heated indoor. **Activities:** whirlpool, exercise room. **Guest Services:** valet and coin laundry, wireless Internet. ECO 🍽 🏊 ✕ 🎥 🖥 🖵 / SOME UNITS 🍽

Phone: (734)462-2000 [95]

AAA Benefit:
Members save a minimum 5% off the best available rate.

EMBASSY SUITES HOTEL

▼▼▼▼
Hotel
$80-$134

Address: 19525 Victor Pkwy 48152 **Location:** I-275, exit 169 (7 Mile Rd), just e, then 0.5 mi n. Located in Victor Corporate Park. **Facility:** Smoke free premises. 239 units. 5 stories, interior corridors. **Terms:** 1-7 night minimum stay, cancellation fee imposed. **Amenities:** video games (fee). **Pool(s):** heated indoor. **Activities:** whirlpool, exercise room. **Guest Services:** valet and coin laundry, area transportation-within 5 mi, wireless Internet.

🍴 🍽 🏊 BIZ ✕ 🎥 🖥 🍽 🖵 / SOME UNITS FEE 🐾

Phone: (734)462-6000 [93]

AAA Benefit:
Members save 5% or more everyday!

FAIRFIELD INN DETROIT/LIVONIA

▼▼ ▼▼
Hotel
$89-$114

Address: 17350 Fox Dr 48152 **Location:** I-275, exit 170 (6 Mile Rd), just w. **Facility:** Smoke free premises. 103 units. 4 stories, interior corridors. **Terms:** cancellation fee imposed. **Pool(s):** heated indoor. **Activities:** whirlpool, exercise room. **Guest Services:** valet and coin laundry, wireless Internet.

🍴 CALL 🛗M 🏊 ✕ 🎥 🖵 / SOME UNITS 🖥 🍽

Phone: (734)953-8888 [98]

AAA Benefit:
Members save a minimum 5% off the best available rate.

HYATT PLACE DETROIT/LIVONIA

▼▼▼▼
Hotel
$69-$169

Address: 19300 Haggerty Rd 48152 **Location:** I-275, exit 169 (7 Mile Rd), just w. **Facility:** Smoke free premises. 127 units. 6 stories, interior corridors. **Terms:** cancellation fee imposed. **Amenities:** video games (fee). *Some:* high-speed Internet. **Pool(s):** heated indoor. **Activities:** exercise room. **Guest Services:** valet laundry, wireless Internet. **Free Special Amenities: continental breakfast and high-speed Internet.**

SAVE 🍴 🍽 CALL 🛗M 🏊 BIZ ✕ 🎥 🖥 🖵

Phone: (734)953-9224 [94]

HYATT
PLACE

AAA Benefit:
Ask for the AAA rate and save 10%.

LIVONIA MARRIOTT

▼▼▼▼
Hotel
$152-$194

Address: 17100 Laurel Park Dr N 48152 **Location:** I-275, exit 170 (6 Mile Rd), just w. Located in the Laurel Park Mall. **Facility:** Smoke free premises. 224 units. 6 stories, interior corridors. **Terms:** check-in 4 pm, cancellation fee imposed. **Amenities:** *Fee:* video games, high-speed Internet. **Dining:** Sweet Lorraine's Cafe & Bar, see separate listing. **Pool(s):** heated indoor. **Activities:** whirlpool, exercise room. **Guest Services:** valet laundry, wireless Internet. ECO 🍴 🍽 🏊 ✕ 🎥 🖵 / SOME UNITS FEE 🐾 🖥

Phone: (734)462-3100 [96]

AAA Benefit:
Members save 5% or more off best available rate.

(See map and index starting on p. 244)

RESIDENCE INN DETROIT-LIVONIA

Extended Stay
Hotel
$152-$194

Address: 17250 Fox Dr 48152 **Location:** I-275, exit 170 (6 Mile Rd), just w. **Facility:** Smoke free premises. 112 units, some two bedrooms, efficiencies and kitchens. 4 stories, interior corridors. **Terms:** cancellation fee imposed. **Amenities:** video games (fee). **Pool(s):** heated outdoor. **Activities:** whirlpool, exercise room, sports court. **Guest Services:** valet and coin laundry, wireless Internet.

Phone: (734)462-4201 99

| AAA Benefit: |
| Members save a minimum 5% off the best available rate. |

TOWNEPLACE SUITES BY MARRIOTT

Extended Stay
Hotel
$110-$120

Address: 17450 Fox Dr 48152 **Location:** I-275, exit 170 (6 Mile Rd), just nw. **Facility:** Smoke free premises. 94 kitchen units, some two bedrooms. 3 stories, interior corridors. **Terms:** cancellation fee imposed. **Amenities:** high-speed Internet. **Pool(s):** heated outdoor. **Activities:** exercise room. **Guest Services:** valet and coin laundry, wireless Internet.

Phone: (734)542-7400 97

| AAA Benefit: |
| Members save a minimum 5% off the best available rate. |

—— WHERE TO DINE ——

ANDIAMO

Italian
$12-$30

Part of a local chain, the classy yet casual restaurant serves traditional dishes, such as ravioli and lasagna, which are prepared using authentic recipes and high-quality ingredients and accented with Parmesan cheese. The spacious dining room, with its upscale artwork and comfortable furnishings, is an ideal setting for an intimate dinner. **Bar:** full bar. **Reservations:** suggested. **Hours:** 11:30 am-10 pm, Fri-11 pm, Sat 4 pm-11 pm, Sun 4 pm-9 pm. Closed major holidays. **Address:** 38703 7 Mile Rd 48152 **Location:** I-275, exit 169 (7 Mile Rd), just w.

Phone: 734/953-3200 96

BAHAMA BREEZE

Caribbean
$11-$22

Capturing the sights, sounds and sensations of the Caribbean, the restaurant caters to those seeking an exciting evening out. In addition to delicious food, such as fresh mahi mahi and Key lime pie, patrons will find a full bar and scheduled live entertainment. **Bar:** full bar. **Hours:** 11 am-11 pm, Fri & Sat-midnight. Closed: 11/24, 12/25. **Address:** 19600 Haggerty Rd 48152 **Location:** I-275, exit 169 (7 Mile Rd), just w, then 0.5 mi n.

Phone: 734/542-0891 94

THE CLADDAGH IRISH PUB

Irish
$8-$19

Nooks and crannies dotted throughout lend to the Irish pub's character. A large selection of imported beers complements typical pub food, including fish and chips, shepherd's pie, Celtic corned beef and cabbage, beef and Guinness stew, bangers and mash, and an array of sandwiches and burgers. **Bar:** full bar. **Hours:** 11 am-2 am, Sun & Mon-midnight. Closed: 12/25. **Address:** 17800 Haggerty Rd 48152 **Location:** I-275, exit 170 (6 Mile Rd), 0.5 mi w, then 0.4 mi n.

Phone: 734/542-8141

J. ALEXANDER'S RESTAURANT

American
$8-$26

The busy and casual restaurant prepares classic fare—including steak, grilled fish and prime rib—in the open kitchen. The dessert menu is excellent. **Bar:** full bar. **Hours:** 11 am-10:30 pm, Fri & Sat-11:30 pm, Sun-10 pm. Closed: 11/24, 12/25. **Address:** 19200 Haggerty Rd 48152 **Location:** I-275, exit 169 (7 Mile Rd), 0.5 mi w, then just n.

Phone: 734/464-9220 95

MITCHELL'S FISH MARKET

Seafood
$17-$30

A variety of fresh, never-frozen fish is flown in daily, and market availability determines the daily specials. Diners may order fish grilled, broiled, blackened or steamed in the Shanghai style with ginger, spinach and sticky rice. Among other choices are steak, pasta and chicken selections. **Bar:** full bar. **Hours:** 11:30 am-10 pm, Fri & Sat-11 pm, Sun-9 pm. Closed: 11/24, 12/25. **Address:** 17600 Haggerty Rd 48152 **Location:** I-275, exit 170 (6 Mile Rd), just w.

Phone: 734/464-3663 97

SWEET LORRAINE'S CAFE & BAR

American
$8-$20

A step above the typical hotel restaurant, this bright and cheery space serves an eclectic menu of Continental standards such as steak and seafood as well as globally influenced items like French pot pie or Spanish paella. **Bar:** full bar. **Reservations:** suggested. **Hours:** 6:30 am-11 pm, Fri-midnight, Sat 7 am-midnight, Sun 7 am-11 pm. **Address:** 17100 N Laurel Park Dr 48152 **Location:** I-275, exit 170 (6 Mile Rd), just w; in Livonia Marriott.

Phone: 734/953-7480 99

THE TRAVELING FORK

American
$10-$26

As its name suggests, the restaurant "travels" nationwide to find reasonably priced choices for its diverse menu. Items range from Alaskan king crab cakes, Louisiana gumbo and Wisconsin cheese fondue to Hawaiian ahi tuna, Lake Huron perch, Texas rib-eye and the all-American burger. Multiple TV screens in the friendly, casual setting give patrons a good place to keep an eye on the action. **Bar:** full bar. **Hours:** 7 am-midnight. **Address:** 17123 Laurel Park Dr N 48152 **Location:** I-275, exit 170 (6 Mile Rd), just e.

Phone: 734/462-2196 98

MACOMB

—— **WHERE TO DINE** ——

EASTSIDE GRILL

American
$5-$17

Phone: 586/566-1800

Specializing in freshly baked desserts, it's the tantalizing dessert case that's the first thing to greet diners as they walk through the door. House specialties include a 12-layer chocolate cake, homemade cheesecakes with hand-crumbled crusts, and a variety of cream and fruit pies. Dessert selections change regularly, and full cakes and pies can be ordered. Entree selections offer very good value, and include burgers, steaks, chicken and a variety of soups and sandwiches. **Hours:** 10:30 am-10 pm, Fri-Sun from 8 am. Closed major holidays. **Address:** 47250 Hayes Rd 48044 **Location:** Jct Van Dyke Ave (SR 53) and Hall Rd (SR 59), 1 mi e, then 0.5 mi n. CALL 🗃M

MADISON HEIGHTS pop. 31,101   (See map and index starting on p. 244)

BEST WESTERN TROY-MADISON INN

Hotel
$60-$100

Phone: (248)583-7000   **32**

Address: 1331 W 14 Mile Rd 48071 **Location:** I-75, exit 65B (14 Mile Rd), just w. **Facility:** Smoke free premises. 86 units. 2 stories, interior corridors. **Amenities:** safes. **Pool(s):** heated indoor. **Activities:** limited exercise equipment. *Fee:* game room. **Guest Services:** valet laundry, wireless Internet. **Free Special Amenities: expanded continental breakfast and high-speed Internet.** SAVE 🍴 🏊 BIZ ✕ 📹 🔌 🖥 📺

AAA Benefit:
Members save up to 20%, plus 10% bonus points with free rewards program.

ECONO LODGE

Motel
$36-$140

Phone: (248)583-7700   **35**

Address: 32703 Stephenson Hwy 48071 **Location:** I-75, exit 65B (14 Mile Rd), just w, then just s. **Facility:** Designated smoking area. 148 units, some kitchens. 1 story, exterior corridors. **Pool(s):** outdoor. **Guest Services:** wireless Internet. **Free Special Amenities: expanded continental breakfast and high-speed Internet.** SAVE 🍴 🏊 ✕ 📹 🖥 / SOME UNITS 🔌 🖥

FAIRFIELD INN BY MARRIOTT

Hotel
$80-$102

Phone: (248)588-3388   **34**

Address: 32800 Stephenson Hwy 48071 **Location:** I-75, exit 65B (14 Mile Rd), just w, then just s. **Facility:** Smoke free premises. 120 units. 3 stories, interior/exterior corridors. **Terms:** cancellation fee imposed. **Amenities:** video games (fee). **Pool(s):** heated outdoor. **Activities:** exercise room. **Guest Services:** valet and coin laundry, wireless Internet.

🍴 🏊 ✕ 📹 🔌 🖥 📺

AAA Benefit:
Members save a minimum 5% off the best available rate.

(See map and index starting on p. 244)

HAMPTON INN DETROIT/MADISON HEIGHTS

Hotel
$58-$121

Phone: (248)585-8881   **38**

Address: 32420 Stephenson Hwy 48071 **Location:** I-75, exit 65B (14 Mile Rd), just w, then just s. **Facility:** Smoke free premises. 123 units. 4 stories, interior corridors. **Terms:** 1-7 night minimum stay, cancellation fee imposed. **Amenities:** video games (fee). **Pool(s):** heated outdoor. **Activities:** sauna, exercise room. **Guest Services:** valet laundry, wireless Internet. *(see ad below)*

AAA Benefit:
Members save up to 10% everyday!

FREE expanded continental breakfast and high-speed Internet

MOTEL 6 MADISON HEIGHTS #1109

Motel
$42-$52

Phone: (248)583-0500   **33**

Address: 32700 Barrington Rd 48071 **Location:** I-75, exit 65A (14 Mile Rd), just e. Opposite shopping mall. **Facility:** Smoke free premises. 100 units. 2 stories (no elevator), exterior corridors. **Guest Services:** coin laundry, wireless Internet.

RED ROOF INN #7084

Motel
$49-$85

Phone: (248)583-4700   **36**

Address: 32511 Concord Dr 48071 **Location:** I-75, exit 65A (14 Mile Rd), just e, then just s. Opposite shopping mall. **Facility:** Smoke free premises. 108 units. 2 stories, exterior corridors. **Amenities:** *Fee:* video games, safes. **Guest Services:** wireless Internet. **Free Special Amenities: local telephone calls.**

RESIDENCE INN BY MARRIOTT-DETROIT TROY/MADISON HEIGHTS

Extended Stay
Hotel
$170-$217

Phone: (248)583-4322   **37**

Address: 32650 Stephenson Hwy 48071 **Location:** I-75, exit 65B (14 Mile Rd), just w, then just s. **Facility:** Smoke free premises. 96 kitchen units. 2 stories (no elevator), exterior corridors. **Terms:** cancellation fee imposed. **Pool(s):** heated outdoor. **Activities:** whirlpool, limited exercise equipment, sports court. **Guest Services:** valet and coin laundry, wireless Internet.

AAA Benefit:
Members save a minimum 5% off the best available rate.

─────────── ▼ *See AAA listing above* ▼ ───────────

(See map and index starting on p. 244)

────── WHERE TO DINE ──────

BIG FISH SEAFOOD BISTRO

Phone: 248/585-9533   54

Seafood
$6-$24

Popular with local corporate types, the eclectic restaurant is dotted with stylized fish and nautical memorabilia. Specializing in fresh seafood, the daily catch menu changes constantly, but the varied steak, chicken and pasta dishes are reliable choices. Hot and cold soups, varied appetizers and creative desserts complement such innovatively prepared seafood entrees as whitefish Oscar. **Bar:** full bar. **Reservations:** suggested. **Hours:** 11 am-10 pm, Fri & Sat-11 pm, Sun 3 pm-9 pm. Closed: 12/25. **Address:** 1111 W 14 Mile Rd 48071 **Location:** I-75, exit 65B (14 Mile Rd), just w. SAVE

BOODLE'S RESTAURANT

Phone: 248/399-5960   56

American
$8-$28

A wide selection of well-prepared entrees-from steak Diane to Alaskan crab legs to seafood pasta-line the restaurant's menu. The dark-stained walls give the dining room a warm, comfortable feel. Dessert choices are tempting and tasty. Entertainment. **Bar:** full bar. **Reservations:** suggested, weekends. **Hours:** 11 am-11 pm, Fri-midnight, Sat 4 pm-midnight, Sun 4 pm-10 pm. Closed: 1/1, 12/25. **Address:** 935 W 11 Mile Rd 48071 **Location:** I-75, exit 62 (11 Mile Rd), just e.

THE BREAKFAST CLUB

Phone: 248/307-9090   55

American
$6-$10

Pale yellow walls and lace curtains give the comfortable little restaurant plenty of charm. In addition to classic, well-prepared breakfast and lunch choices, guests can experience a delightful change from the ordinary with such daily specials as baked French toast with seasonal fruit, a crab omelet or linguine tossed with fresh pesto. **Hours:** 7 am-2 pm. Closed major holidays. **Address:** 30600 John R Rd 48071 **Location:** 0.5 mi s of jct 13 Mile Rd. CALL

MILFORD pop. 6,272

────── WHERE TO DINE ──────

CINCO LAGOS

Phone: 248/684-7455

Mexican
$8-$14

Cinco Lagos' upbeat storefront dining room is a bright and cheerful spot for enjoying Mexican favorites such as fajitas, quesadillas, burritos and tacos. If you're looking for delicious and authentic fare, you can't beat the stuffed fried peppers and fish tacos. **Bar:** full bar. **Hours:** 4 pm-10 pm, Fri & Sat-11 pm. Closed major holidays; also Sun. **Address:** 424 N Main St 48381 **Location:** At Main St and Commerce Rd. **Parking:** on-site and street. CALL

MOUNT CLEMENS pop. 17,312   (See map and index starting on p. 244)

CONCORDE INN OF CLINTON TOWNSHIP

Phone: (586)493-7300

Hotel
$90-$190

Address: 44315 Gratiot Ave 48036 **Location:** I-94, exit 240B (SR 59), 0.3 mi w, then 0.3 mi s. **Facility:** Smoke free premises. 160 units, some kitchens. 4 stories, interior corridors. **Pool(s):** heated indoor. **Activities:** sauna, spa. **Fee:** game room. **Guest Services:** valet and coin laundry, wireless Internet, tanning facilities.

────── WHERE TO DINE ──────

LUIGI'S "THE ORIGINAL"

Phone: 586/468-7711   137

Italian
$12-$37

The tiny restaurant often is crowded with boaters from nearby Lake St. Clair, so diners should be prepared to wait awhile to get in. The family-owned restaurant rises above its setting—low ceilings, basement-like panel-board walls, red vinyl booths, and red and green Christmas lights—with its extensive menu of well-prepared, mainly Northern Italian favorites. Choices also include at least 20 daily specials and varied pizzas. **Bar:** full bar. **Hours:** 4 pm-10:30 pm, Fri & Sat-11:30 pm, Sun 3 pm-10 pm. **Address:** 36691 Jefferson Ave 48045 **Location:** I-94, exit 236 (Metro Pkwy), just e to Crocker Blvd, 1 mi s to Jefferson Ave, then just n.

NORTHVILLE pop. 6,459   (See map and index starting on p. 244)

HAMPTON INN

Phone: (734)462-1119   90

Hotel
$99-$139 11/1-4/30
$89-$129 4/1-10/31

Address: 20600 Haggerty Rd 48167 **Location:** I-275, exit 167 (8 Mile Rd), just w. **Facility:** Smoke free premises. 124 units. 4 stories, interior corridors. **Terms:** 1-7 night minimum stay, cancellation fee imposed. **Amenities:** video games (fee). **Pool(s):** heated outdoor. **Activities:** sauna, exercise room. **Guest Services:** valet laundry, wireless Internet.

AAA Benefit:
Members save up to 10% everyday!

────── WHERE TO DINE ──────

PAPA VINO'S ITALIAN KITCHEN

Phone: 248/449-4664   91

Italian
$7-$18

The spacious dining room is a warm and relaxing gathering place for groups, families and couples alike. Menu specialties include such American favorites as personal pizzas, lasagna, cannelloni, ravioli and sandwiches on Italian bread. **Bar:** full bar. **Hours:** 11 am-10 pm, Fri & Sat-11 pm. Closed: 11/24, 12/25. **Address:** 17107 Haggerty Rd 48167 **Location:** I-275, exit 170 (6 Mile Rd), 0.5 mi w, then 0.3 mi n. CALL

(See map and index starting on p. 244)

P.F. CHANG'S CHINA BISTRO   Phone: 248/675-0066

Chinese
$10-$21

Trendy, upscale decor provides a pleasant backdrop for New Age Chinese dining. Appetizers, soups and salads are a meal by themselves. Vegetarian plates and sides, noodles, meins, chicken and meat dishes are created from exotic, fresh ingredients. **Bar:** full bar. **Hours:** 11 am-11 pm, Fri & Sat-11:30 pm, Sun 11:30 am-10 pm. Closed: 11/24, 12/25. **Address:** 17905 Haggerty Rd 48167 **Location:** I-275, exit 170 (6 Mile Rd), 0.5 mi w, then 0.3 mi n. CALL

NOVI pop. 47,386   (See map and index starting on p. 244)

THE BARONETTE RENAISSANCE   Phone: (248)349-7800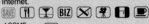

Hotel
$119-$199

Address: 27790 Novi Rd 48377 **Location:** I-96, exit 162 (Novi Rd), 0.4 mi n. Located beside 12 Oaks Mall. **Facility:** Smoke free premises. 155 units. 3 stories, interior corridors. **Terms:** cancellation fee imposed. **Amenities:** high-speed Internet, safes. **Activities:** exercise room. **Guest Services:** valet laundry, wireless Internet.

AAA Benefit:
Members save a minimum 5% off the best available rate.

/ SOME UNITS   FEE

FREE newspaper

COUNTRY INN & SUITES BY CARLSON   Phone: 248/596-9800

Hotel
Rates not provided

Address: 21625 Haggerty Rd 48375 **Location:** I-275, exit 167 (8 Mile Rd), just w, then 0.5 mi n. **Facility:** Smoke free premises. 100 units. 4 stories, interior corridors. **Amenities:** high-speed Internet. **Pool(s):** heated indoor. **Activities:** whirlpool, exercise room. **Guest Services:** valet and coin laundry, wireless Internet. *(see ad p. 6)*   CALL   / SOME UNITS

COURTYARD BY MARRIOTT   Phone: (248)380-1234   84

Hotel
$112-$143

Address: 42700 11 Mile Rd 48375 **Location:** I-96, exit 162 (Novi Rd), just s, 0.5 mi e on Crescent Dr, then just s on Town Center Dr. Across from Novi Town Center. **Facility:** Smoke free premises. 122 units. 4 stories, interior corridors. **Terms:** cancellation fee imposed. **Amenities:** high-speed Internet. **Pool(s):** heated indoor. **Activities:** whirlpool, exercise room. **Guest Services:** valet and coin laundry, wireless Internet.

AAA Benefit:
Members save a minimum 5% off the best available rate.

CALL   / SOME UNITS

(See map and index starting on p. 244)

DOUBLETREE HOTEL DETROIT/NOVI

Phone: (248)344-8800   82

Hotel
$89-$129

Address: 42100 Crescent Blvd 48375 **Location:** I-96, exit 162 (Novi Rd), just s, then 0.5 mi e. Located behind the Novi Town Center. **Facility:** Smoke free premises. 148 units. 2 stories (no elevator), interior corridors. **Terms:** 1-7 night minimum stay, cancellation fee imposed. **Amenities:** high-speed Internet (fee). **Pool(s):** heated indoor. **Activities:** sauna, whirlpool. **Guest Services:** valet laundry, area transportation-within 5 mi, wireless Internet. *(see ad below)*

AAA Benefit:
Members save 5% or more everyday!

FREE newspaper and high-speed Internet

EXTENDED STAYAMERICA-DETROIT-NOVI

Phone: (248)305-9955   86

Extended Stay
Hotel
$70-$80

Address: 21555 Haggerty Rd 48375 **Location:** I-275, exit 167 (8 Mile Rd), just w, then 0.5 mi n. **Facility:** Smoke free premises. 125 efficiencies. 3 stories, interior corridors. **Terms:** cancellation fee imposed. **Guest Services:** coin laundry, wireless Internet.

CALL ... / SOME UNITS FEE

▼ See AAA listing above ▼

Welcome to Doubletree.

- Heated pool, sauna and whirlpool
- Local area transportation
- Advance reservations with one call to the dedicated Doubletree AAA number, **1-877-655-5697** or your local AAA travel office. Or visit online at doubletree.com.

DOUBLETREE®
HOTELS·SUITES·RESORTS·CLUBS

42100 Crescent Blvd. Novi, MI 48375 • 248-344-8800

HHONORS
HILTON WORLDWIDE
©2010 Hilton Worldwide

▼ See AAA listing p. 275 ▼

want a better getaway?

Wake up at Hampton for friendly surprises like free hot breakfast! Plus a great night's sleep and free wired and wireless Internet. We're delighted to offer special rates for AAA members.*

Hampton Inn

Hampton Inn - Detroit / Novi
169 Loop Rd. Novi, MI 48390
1-800-Hampton • 248-624-8100
we love having you here™ www.detroitnovi.hamptoninn.com

©2010 Hilton Worldwide. *Rates from $89-$179 Standard/Suites, 1 to 4 people. Subject to availability. Valid for stays April 1, 2011 - April 30, 2012. Rates exclude taxes, gratuities and incidental charges. Offer valid for AAA members only and is not transferable. AAA card required at check-in.

(See map and index starting on p. 244)

HILTON GARDEN INN DETROIT/NOVI

Hotel
$99-$139

Address: 27355 Cabaret Dr 48377 **Location:** I-96, exit 162 (Novi Rd), just n to 12 Mile Rd, then just w. **Facility:** Smoke free premises. 148 units. 4 stories, interior corridors. **Terms:** 1-7 night minimum stay, cancellation fee imposed. **Amenities:** high-speed Internet. **Pool(s):** heated indoor. **Activities:** whirlpool, exercise room. **Guest Services:** valet and coin laundry, wireless Internet.

Phone: (248)348-3840

AAA Benefit:
Members save 5% or more everyday!

HOLIDAY INN EXPRESS & SUITES

Hotel
$89-$129

Address: 39675 12 Mile Rd 48377 **Location:** Just e of jct SR 5. **Facility:** Smoke free premises. 92 units. 3 stories (no elevator), interior corridors. **Amenities:** high-speed Internet. **Pool(s):** heated indoor. **Activities:** exercise room. **Guest Services:** valet laundry, wireless Internet.

Phone: (248)344-8204   80

RESIDENCE INN BY MARRIOTT-DETROIT/NOVI

Extended Stay Hotel
$144-$184

Address: 27477 Cabaret Dr 48377 **Location:** I-96, exit 162 (Novi Rd), just n to 12 Mile Rd, then just w. Across shopping mall. **Facility:** Smoke free premises. 107 units, some two bedrooms, efficiencies and kitchens. 4 stories, interior corridors. **Terms:** cancellation fee imposed. **Pool(s):** heated indoor. **Activities:** whirlpool, exercise room. **Guest Services:** valet and coin laundry, wireless Internet.

Phone: (248)735-7400

AAA Benefit:
Members save a minimum 5% off the best available rate.

SHERATON-DETROIT-NOVI

Hotel
$85-$189

Address: 21111 Haggerty Rd 48375 **Location:** I-275, exit 167 (8 Mile Rd), just w to Haggerty Rd, then just n. **Facility:** Smoke free premises. 238 units. 7 stories, interior corridors. **Terms:** cancellation fee imposed. **Pool(s):** heated indoor. **Activities:** whirlpool, exercise room. **Guest Services:** valet laundry, area transportation-within 5 mi, wireless Internet. **Free Special Amenities:** newspaper and manager's reception.

Phone: (248)349-4000   87

 Sheraton
HOTELS & RESORTS

AAA Benefit:
Members get up to 15% off, plus Starwood Preferred Guest® bonuses.

STAYBRIDGE SUITES

Extended Stay Hotel
$125-$199

Address: 27000 Providence 48374 **Location:** I-96, exit 160 (Beck Rd), just s to Grand River Ave, then 0.6 mi w. **Facility:** Smoke free premises. 108 efficiencies, some two bedrooms. 3 stories, interior corridors. **Terms:** cancellation fee imposed. **Amenities:** high-speed Internet. **Pool(s):** heated indoor. **Activities:** whirlpool, gas barbecue grills, exercise room, basketball. **Guest Services:** valet and coin laundry, area transportation-within 5 mi, wireless Internet.

Phone: (248)349-4600

TOWNEPLACE SUITES

Extended Stay Hotel
$89-$114

Address: 42600 11 Mile Rd 48375 **Location:** I-96, exit 162 (Novi Rd), just s, 0.5 mi e on Crescent Dr, then just s on Town Center Dr. Across Novi Town Center. **Facility:** Smoke free premises. 95 kitchen units, some two bedrooms. 3 stories, interior corridors. *Bath:* some shared. **Terms:** cancellation fee imposed. **Amenities:** high-speed Internet. **Pool(s):** heated outdoor. **Activities:** limited exercise equipment. **Guest Services:** valet and coin laundry, wireless Internet.

Phone: (248)305-5533   83

AAA Benefit:
Members save a minimum 5% off the best available rate.

—— **WHERE TO DINE** ——

AH WOK

Chinese
$6-$35

Phone: 248/349-9260   87

Located in a small shopping plaza, the dining room sports pink, white and black décor with a few artificial plants, but its menu is less standard, listing creative takes on Chinese fare. The adventurous diner will find such new and interesting choices as winter melon soup and eight treasures taro nest, but the menu lists plenty of traditional dishes as well. **Bar:** full bar. **Hours:** 11 am-9:30 pm, Fri-11:30 pm, Sat noon-11:30 pm, Sun 2 pm-9 pm. **Address:** 41563 W 10 Mile Rd 48375 **Location:** Jct Haggerty Rd, 1 mi w.

CHERRY BLOSSOM

Japanese
$6-$34

Phone: 248/380-9160

Squeezed between two big box stores in the West Oaks II Shopping Center, the restaurant draws many Japanese business travelers who bear witness to the authenticity of the food. While standard dishes of yakitori, tempura and teriyaki are prominently displayed on the menu, it's the incredibly fresh sushi, prepared by a chef reputed to have cooked for the emperor of Japan, that stands out. **Bar:** full bar. **Hours:** 11:30 am-2 & 5:30-10:30 pm, Fri & Sat-11 pm, Sun 4 pm-10 pm. Closed major holidays. **Address:** 43588 W Oaks Dr 48377 **Location:** I-96, exit 162 (Novi Rd), just n; at west end of West Oaks II Shopping Center.

(See map and index starting on p. 244)

DIAMOND JIM BRADY'S BISTRO

Phone: 248/380-8460 ⑧①

American
$8-$27

Somewhat difficult to find, the restaurant is behind the Novi Shopping Center and beside the movie theater. Those willing to search for this gem can expect to be rewarded for their efforts. Most items are homemade, and the wide ranging menu lists everything from standard bar food, such as Buffalo wings, to British Isles fish and chips and shepherd's pie. **Bar:** full bar. **Reservations:** required. **Hours:** 11 am-10 pm, Fri & Sat-11 pm, Sun 4 pm-8 pm. Closed major holidays. **Address:** 26053 Town Center Dr 48375 **Location:** I-96, exit 162 (Novi Rd), just s, 0.5 mi e on Crescent Dr, then just s. CALL ⬛M

GUS O'CONNOR'S IRISH PUB

Phone: 248/465-9670 ⑧③

Irish
$8-$19

Each element of the pub's design and decor was built in Ireland then reassembled in Novi by Irish craftsmen. House specialties include an assortment of boxties, Irish pancakes, shepherd's pie, Irish stew, corned beef and cabbage, beer-battered fish and a pub steak with whiskey sauce. **Bar:** full bar. **Hours:** 11 am-11 pm, Fri & Sat-midnight, Sun noon-11 pm. Closed major holidays. **Address:** 42875 Grand River Ave, Suite 103 48375 **Location:** I-96, exit 162 (Novi Rd), 1 mi s, then just e. CALL ⬛M

MOE'S ON TEN

Phone: 248/478-9742 ⑧⑥

Seafood
$7-$20

The elegant dining room—with burgundy, terra cotta and cream colors and balloon-like draperies—does not resemble a typical seafood restaurant. Creatively prepared fresh fish and other seafood dishes include Lake Superior whitefish, which is given a crunch with panko breadcrumbs, and Alaskan salmon with mango chutney. The restaurant also offers steak, chicken and pasta dishes. **Bar:** full bar. **Hours:** 7 am-10 pm, Fri & Sat-11 pm, Sun-9 pm. Closed major holidays. **Address:** 39455 W 10 Mile Rd 48375 **Location:** Jct Haggerty Rd. CALL ⬛M

NO. VI CHOP HOUSE & LOBSTER BAR

Phone: 248/305-5210

Steak
$21-$49

The dramatic and somewhat seductive interior mirrors the creativity found in the food. Using high-quality ingredients, such as USDA prime cuts of beef, and a global palette of influences, the kitchen not only prepares varied steaks, which range in size from 7-ounce filets to massive 20-ounce porterhouses, but also hoisin-glazed beef short ribs, steak au poivre, coriander- and lime-grilled ahi tuna and fresh lobster. **Bar:** full bar. **Reservations:** suggested. **Hours:** 5 pm-10 pm, Fri & Sat-11 pm, Sun 5 pm-9 pm. Closed major holidays. **Address:** 27000 Sheraton Dr 48377 **Location:** I-96, exit 162 (Novi Rd), 0.4 mi n; in Crowne Plaza Hotel. **Parking:** on-site and valet. CALL ⬛M

PICASSO CAFÉ

Phone: 248/427-0600 ⑧⑤

Deli
$4-$8

Works by local artists, all available for purchase, decorate the walls of this trendy, upscale cafe, where diners enjoy sandwiches, wraps and homemade soups and cookies. **Hours:** 6 am-7 pm, Sat 9 am-3 pm. Closed major holidays; also Sun. **Address:** 39915 Grand River Ave, Suite 800 48375 **Location:** I-275, exit 165 (SR 5/Grand River Ave), 0.5 mi e.

STEVE & ROCKY'S

Phone: 248/374-0688 ⑧②

American
$8-$29

Bright contrasting colors and an eclectic decor set the tone for this restaurant known for its fresh fish and seafood. Emphasizing fresh food, the kitchen shows its creative side in both food presentation and creation. Daily specials such as the "just today" or "just tonight" highlight an ever-changing menu. Entertainment. **Bar:** full bar. **Hours:** 11 am-10 pm, Fri-11 pm, Sat noon-11 pm, Sun 1 pm-9 pm. Closed: 1/1, 12/25. **Address:** 43150 Grand River Rd 48375 **Location:** I-96, exit 162 (Novi Rd), 1 mi s, then just e. CALL ⬛M

W.F. BI BIM BAB

Phone: 248/348-6800 ⑧④

Korean
$6-$25

It's easy to overlook this bright and lively space. Specializing in Korean barbecue, where diners grill their own meat and seafood from barbecue tops set into most tables, the restaurant also offers sushi, plus its namesake dish, which has been described as offering a different taste with every bite. **Bar:** full bar. **Hours:** 11:30 am-11 pm, Sat-11:30 pm, Sun-10 pm. Closed: 11/24, 12/25. **Address:** 43155 Main St, Suite 300 48375 **Location:** I-96, exit 162 (Novi Rd), 1 mi s, then just e on Grand River Rd; at rear and inside of Main St Development Mall. CALL ⬛M

PLYMOUTH pop. 9,022 (See map and index starting on p. 244)

COMFORT INN PLYMOUTH CLOCKTOWER

Phone: (734)455-8100 ⑩③

Hotel
$45-$110

Address: 40455 Ann Arbor Rd 48170 **Location:** I-275, exit 28 (Ann Arbor Rd), just w; entry on Massey Dr. **Facility:** Smoke free premises. 123 units. 2 stories, interior corridors. **Terms:** cancellation fee imposed. **Amenities:** high-speed Internet. **Pool(s):** outdoor. **Activities:** exercise room. **Guest Services:** valet laundry, wireless Internet. ⬛ ⬛ BIZ ⬛ ⬛ ⬛ / SOME UNITS ⬛ ⬛

HILTON GARDEN INN - PLYMOUTH

Phone: (734)354-0001

Hotel
$89-$149

Address: 14600 Sheldon Rd 48170 **Location:** SR 14, exit 20 (Sheldon Rd), just n. **Facility:** Smoke free premises. 157 units. 6 stories, interior corridors. **Terms:** 1-7 night minimum stay, cancellation fee imposed. **Amenities:** high-speed Internet. **Pool(s):** heated indoor. **Activities:** whirlpool, exercise room. **Guest Services:** valet and coin laundry, area transportation-within 5 mi, wireless Internet. ⬛ ⬛ CALL ⬛M ⬛ BIZ ⬛ ⬛ ⬛ ⬛ ⬛

AAA Benefit:
Members save 5% or more everyday!

(See map and index starting on p. 244)

THE INN AT ST. JOHN'S   Phone: (734)414-0600

Hotel
$129-$199 4/1-10/31
$99-$189 11/1-4/30

Address: 44045 Five Mile Rd 48170 **Location:** SR 14, exit 20 (Sheldon Rd), 0.3 mi n, then just e. **Facility:** Smoke free premises. 118 units. 7 stories, interior corridors. **Terms:** cancellation fee imposed. **Amenities:** high-speed Internet, safes. **Dining:** 5ive Restaurant, see separate listing. **Pool(s):** heated indoor. **Activities:** whirlpool, lazy river, resistance pool, bubble lounger, exercise room. *Fee:* golf-27 holes. **Guest Services:** valet laundry, wireless Internet.

RED ROOF INN-PLYMOUTH #7016   Phone: (734)459-3300   102

Motel
$45-$110

Address: 39700 Ann Arbor Rd 48170 **Location:** I-275, exit 28 (Ann Arbor Rd), just e. **Facility:** Smoke free premises. 109 units. 2 stories, exterior corridors. **Amenities:** *Fee:* video games, safes. **Guest Services:** wireless Internet. **Free Special Amenities:** local telephone calls.

———— WHERE TO DINE ————

5IVE RESTAURANT   Phone: 734/414-0600

American
$10-$33

The cozy and elegant atmosphere of the dining room provides a sophisticated backdrop to the adventurous menu, which offers items ranging from tempura calamari sticks to chicken quesadillas, from apple-wood-smoked chicken, smoked trout and St. Louis-style dry-rubbed ribs to filet mignon, duck, venison and lamb. Also among choices are varied seafood selections, in addition to create-your-own pasta dishes. **Bar:** full bar. **Reservations:** suggested. **Hours:** 6 am-11 pm, Sun-10 pm. **Address:** 44045 Five Mile Rd 48170 **Location:** SR 14, exit 20 (Sheldon Rd), 0.3 mi n, then just e; in The Inn at St. John's.

COMPARI'S ON THE PARK   Phone: 734/416-0100   104

Italian
$7-$27

Exposed brick walls, murals and large picture windows that overlook the city park give this upscale restaurant a comfortable feel. Focusing on well-prepared Italian specialties and pizza, this restaurant is popular with the local crowd. **Bar:** full bar. **Hours:** 11 am-10 pm, Thurs-Sat to 11 pm, Sun noon-10 pm. Closed: 12/25. **Address:** 350 S Main St 48170 **Location:** Jct Ann Arbor Tr; downtown.

FIAMMA GRILLE   Phone: 734/416-9340   105

Continental
$12-$35

The motto at this family-run restaurant is: "At Fiamma, eating and drinking is always a pleasure." Many folks choose this place for its selection of aged steaks, but as regulars will attest, the other choices are difficult to pass up. The menu changes seasonally, offering options such as Colorado lamb, braised short ribs, sauteed walleye, lobster tails and a handful of vegan-friendly fare. Delicious desserts are designed to tempt. **Bar:** full bar. **Hours:** 5 pm-10 pm. Closed major holidays. **Address:** 380 S Main St 48170 **Location:** Jct Ann Arbor Tr; downtown. **Parking:** street only.

LA BISTECCA ITALIAN GRILLE   Phone: 734/254-0400   102

Steak
$12-$53

An open ceiling, dark woods, fine art, attentive service and soft background music combine to give this Italian chophouse a warm, intimate feeling. Featuring certified Piedmontese beef exclusively, the menu also lists creative daily specials and a number of fresh fish, lamb and chicken selections. **Bar:** full bar. **Reservations:** suggested. **Hours:** 5 pm-11 pm. Closed major holidays; also Sun. **Address:** 39405 Plymouth Rd 48170 **Location:** Jct Eckles Rd; between Haggerty and Newburgh rds. **Parking:** on-site and valet.

SEAN O'CALLAGHAN'S   Phone: 734/459-6666   103

Irish
$7-$23

With its warm, cozy atmosphere, dark cherry and mahogany woods, stained glass and Irish memorabilia, this place would be hard to mistake for anything other than an Irish pub. Classic dishes range from bangers and mash to fish and chips. An impressive array of Irish whiskeys is offered. **Bar:** full bar. **Hours:** 11 am-11 pm. Closed major holidays. **Address:** 821 Penniman Ave 48170 **Location:** Between Main and Harvey sts; downtown. **Parking:** street only.

PONTIAC pop. 66,337

COURTYARD BY MARRIOTT DETROIT PONTIAC/BLOOMFIELD   Phone: (248)858-9595

Hotel
$99-$127

Address: 3555 Centerpoint Pkwy 48341 **Location:** I-75, exit 75 (Square Lake Rd), w via Opdyke Rd. **Facility:** Smoke free premises. 110 units. 4 stories, interior corridors. **Parking:** winter plug-ins. **Terms:** cancellation fee imposed. **Amenities:** video games (fee). **Pool(s):** heated indoor. **Activities:** whirlpool, exercise room. **Guest Services:** valet and coin laundry, wireless Internet.

AAA Benefit:
Members save a minimum 5% off the best available rate.

DETROIT MARRIOTT PONTIAC AT CENTERPOINT   Phone: (248)253-9800

Hotel
$153-$196

Address: 3600 Centerpoint Pkwy 48341 **Location:** I-75, exit 75 (Square Lake Rd), w via Opdyke Rd. **Facility:** Smoke free premises. 290 units. 11 stories, interior corridors. **Terms:** cancellation fee imposed. **Amenities:** safes. *Fee:* video games, high-speed Internet. **Dining:** Parkway Grille, see separate listing. **Pool(s):** heated outdoor, heated indoor. **Activities:** whirlpool, exercise room. *Fee:* massage. **Guest Services:** valet and coin laundry, wireless Internet.

AAA Benefit:
Members save 5% or more off best available rate.

RESIDENCE INN BY MARRIOTT DETROIT PONTIAC/AUBURN HILLS

Extended Stay Hotel
$126-$161

Phone: (248)858-8664

Address: 3333 Centerpoint Pkwy 48341 **Location:** I-75, exit 75 (Square Lake Rd), w via Opdyke Rd. **Facility:** Smoke free premises. 114 units, some two bedrooms, efficiencies and kitchens. 3 stories, interior corridors. **Terms:** check-in 4 pm, cancellation fee imposed. **Amenities:** video games (fee), high-speed Internet. **Pool(s):** heated indoor. **Activities:** whirlpool, barbecue grills, patio area, playground, exercise room, sports court. **Guest Services:** valet and coin laundry, wireless Internet.

> **AAA Benefit:**
> Members save a minimum 5% off the best available rate.

--- **WHERE TO DINE** ---

BO'S BREWERY BISTRO

Barbecue
$8-$23

Phone: 248/338-6200

The menu at this popular, youthful restaurant features a wide selection of barbecue and bar classics such as ribs, brisket and pulled pork, as well as chicken sandwiches, burgers, quesadillas and nachos. The large vats where fresh microbrews are prepared are a focal point in the dining room. **Bar:** full bar. **Hours:** 11 am-10 pm, Fri & Sat-11 pm. Closed major holidays; also Sun. **Address:** 51 N Saginaw 48342 **Location:** Jct SR 59 (Huron) and Saginaw; downtown. **Parking:** street only.

PAPA VINO'S ITALIAN KITCHEN

Italian
$8-$23

Phone: 248/333-3606

The spacious dining room is a warm and relaxing gathering place for groups, families and couples alike. Menu specialties include such American favorites as personal pizzas, lasagna, cannelloni, ravioli and sandwiches on Italian bread. **Bar:** full bar. **Hours:** 11 am-10 pm, Fri & Sat-11 pm. Closed major holidays. **Address:** 3900 Centerpoint Pkwy 48341 **Location:** I-75, exit 75 (Square Lake Rd), w via Opdyke Rd.

PARKWAY GRILLE

American
$9-$32

Phone: 248/648-6034

This upmarket and lively space is a definite step-above the typical hotel restaurant. The gently trendy and daring menu offers a signature "Napoleon" of tri-colored tomatoes, rack of lamb with mustard, mint and rosemary crust, and sinful and creative desserts such as white-chocolate cherry bread pudding. **Bar:** full bar. **Hours:** 6:30 am-11 pm, Sun-9 pm. **Address:** 3600 Centerpoint Pkwy 48341 **Location:** I-75, exit 75 (Square Lake Rd), w via Opdyke Rd; in Detroit Marriott Pontiac at Centerpoint.

ZOUP!

Deli
$5-$8

Phone: 248/874-1111

One of several Detroit locations, the restaurant encourages diners to sample any of a dozen hand-crafted soups served daily from a rotation of just about 200 varieties. **Hours:** 10:30 am-8 pm, Sun 11 am-5 pm. Closed major holidays. **Address:** 3999 Centerpoint Pkwy 48341 **Location:** I-75, exit 75 (Square Lake Rd), w via Opdyke Rd.

ROCHESTER pop. 10,467

ROYAL PARK HOTEL

Hotel
$199-$329

Phone: (248)652-2600

Address: 600 E University Dr 48307 **Location:** Just e of jct S Main St (SR 150); center. **Facility:** In a parklike setting, the luxurious full-service hotel is just a short walk from the quaint shops and restaurants of downtown Rochester. Smoke free premises. 143 units, some efficiencies. 4 stories, interior corridors. **Terms:** check-in 4 pm. **Amenities:** high-speed Internet, safes. **Dining:** Brookshire, see separate listing. **Activities:** fly fishing equipment rentals, putting green, bocci, croquet, bicycles, hiking trails, exercise room. **Guest Services:** valet laundry, area transportation-within 10 mi, wireless Internet. **Free Special Amenities:** high-speed Internet.

--- **WHERE TO DINE** ---

ANDIAMO

Italian
$8-$31

Phone: 248/601-9300

With its upscale artwork and comfortable furnishings, the restaurant's dining room is an ideal setting for an intimate dinner. The menu features traditional Italian dishes, such as ravioli and lasagna, prepared using authentic recipes. **Entertainment. Bar:** full bar. **Reservations:** suggested. **Hours:** 11:30 am-10 pm, Fri & Sat-11 pm, Sun 10 am-9 pm. Closed: 1/1, 12/25. **Address:** 401 N Main St 48307 **Location:** Just s of jct Walton Blvd; downtown. **Parking:** valet and street only.

BROOKSHIRE

French
$9-$50

Phone: 248/652-2600

The elegant dining room provides a sophisticated backdrop to a menu featuring such rich delectables as foie gras and roasted duck. Menu selections vary seasonally. **Bar:** full bar. **Reservations:** suggested. **Hours:** 6:30 am-10 pm. **Address:** 600 E University Dr 48307 **Location:** Just e of jct Main St (SR 150); center; in Royal Park Hotel. **Parking:** on-site and valet.

ROCHESTER MILLS BEER CO.

American
$7-$19

Phone: 248/650-5080

In downtown's historic Western Knitting Mill, the restaurant retains many of the building's historic features, including hardwood floors, columns, beams and exposed brick walls. Among the more modern amenities are an outdoor patio overlooking a park, pool tables, wall-mounted TVs and a complete microbrewery facility. The menu focuses on pub favorites, with hand-made pizzas and beer-and-cheese soup definitely worth a taste. **Bar:** full bar. **Hours:** 11:30 am-10 pm, Fri & Sat-11 pm, Sun noon-10 pm. Closed major holidays. **Address:** 400 Water St, Suite 101 48307 **Location:** Jct of E University Dr; downtown. **Parking:** street only.

ROCHESTER HILLS pop. 68,825

RED ROOF INN #7191
Phone: (248)853-6400

♦♦ ♦♦
Motel
$49-$89

Address: 2580 Crooks Rd 48309 **Location:** Jct Hall Rd (SR 59). **Facility:** Smoke free premises. 111 units. 2 stories, exterior corridors. **Amenities:** Fee: video games, safes. **Guest Services:** wireless Internet. **Free Special Amenities: local telephone calls.**

[SAVE] [X] [icons] / SOME UNITS [icons]

ROMULUS pop. 22,979   (See map and index starting on p. 244)

BAYMONT INN & SUITES DETROIT-AIRPORT
Phone: (734)722-6000   `148`

♦♦ ♦♦
Hotel
$44-$71

Address: 9000 Wickham Rd 48174 **Location:** I-94, exit 198 (Merriman Rd), just n, then just w. **Facility:** Smoke free premises. 100 units. 3 stories, interior corridors. **Amenities:** video games (fee). **Guest Services:** valet and coin laundry, wireless Internet.

[icons] / SOME UNITS [icons]

BEST WESTERN GATEWAY INTERNATIONAL HOTEL
Phone: (734)728-2800   `150`

♦♦ ♦♦
Hotel
$75-$149

Address: 9191 Wickham Rd 48174 **Location:** I-94, exit 198 (Merriman Rd), just n, then just w. **Facility:** 232 units. 2 stories, interior corridors. **Terms:** 3 day cancellation notice. **Amenities:** Some: safes. **Pool(s):** outdoor, heated indoor. **Activities:** sauna, whirlpool, atrium recreation room, pool table, exercise room. **Guest Services:** valet and coin laundry, wireless Internet, tanning facilities. **Free Special Amenities: continental breakfast and high-speed Internet.**

AAA Benefit:
Members save up to 20%, plus 10% bonus points with free rewards program.

[SAVE] [icons] [BIZ] [icons] / SOME UNITS FEE [icons]

CLARION HOTEL DETROIT METRO AIRPORT
Phone: (734)728-7900   `143`

♦♦ ♦♦
Hotel
$55-$100

Address: 8600 Merriman Rd 48174 **Location:** I-94, exit 198 (Merriman Rd), just n. **Facility:** Smoke free premises. 153 units. 3 stories (no elevator), interior corridors. **Amenities:** safes (fee). **Pool(s):** outdoor. **Activities:** exercise room. **Guest Services:** valet and coin laundry, wireless Internet. **Free Special Amenities: expanded continental breakfast and airport transportation.**

[SAVE] [icons] [BIZ] [X] [icons] / SOME UNITS [icons]

COURTYARD BY MARRIOTT-METRO AIRPORT
Phone: (734)721-3200   `142`

♦♦ ♦♦
Hotel
$107-$137

Address: 30653 Flynn Dr 48174 **Location:** I-94, exit 198 (Merriman Rd), just n, then just e. **Facility:** Smoke free premises. 146 units. 3 stories, interior corridors. **Terms:** cancellation fee imposed. **Amenities:** high-speed Internet. **Pool(s):** heated indoor. **Activities:** whirlpool, exercise room. **Guest Services:** valet and coin laundry, wireless Internet.

AAA Benefit:
Members save a minimum 5% off the best available rate.

[ECO] [icons] CALL [icons] [X] [icons] / SOME UNITS [icons]

CROWNE PLAZA HOTEL DETROIT METRO AIRPORT
Phone: (734)729-2600   `137`

♦♦ ♦♦
Hotel
$89-$169

Address: 8000 Merriman Rd 48174 **Location:** I-94, exit 198 (Merriman Rd), 0.4 mi n. **Facility:** Smoke free premises. 359 units. 11 stories, interior corridors. **Terms:** cancellation fee imposed. **Amenities:** high-speed Internet. **Dining:** Bistro 94, see separate listing. **Pool(s):** heated indoor. **Activities:** whirlpool, exercise room. **Guest Services:** valet laundry, wireless Internet.

[icons] [BIZ] [X] [icons] / SOME UNITS [icons]

DAYS INN
Phone: (734)946-4300   `151`

♦♦ ♦♦
Hotel
$54-$63

Address: 9501 Middlebelt Rd 48174 **Location:** I-94, exit 199 (Middlebelt Rd), 0.4 mi s. **Facility:** Smoke free premises. 126 units. 3 stories, interior corridors. **Amenities:** safes (fee). **Activities:** exercise room. **Guest Services:** valet and coin laundry, wireless Internet.

[icons] [X] [icons] / SOME UNITS FEE [icons]

DETROIT METRO AIRPORT MARRIOTT
Phone: (734)729-7555   `146`

♦♦ ♦♦
Hotel
$152-$194

Address: 30559 Flynn Dr 48174 **Location:** I-94, exit 198 (Merriman Rd), just n, then 0.3 mi e. **Facility:** Smoke free premises. 245 units. 4 stories, interior corridors. **Terms:** cancellation fee imposed. **Dining:** Ha' Penny Pub, see separate listing. **Pool(s):** heated indoor. **Activities:** whirlpool, exercise room. **Guest Services:** valet laundry, area transportation-within 2 mi, wireless Internet.

AAA Benefit:
Members save 5% or more off best available rate.

[icons] CALL [icons] [BIZ] [X] [icons] / SOME UNITS FEE [icons]

(See map and index starting on p. 244)

EMBASSY SUITES-DETROIT METRO AIRPORT

Hotel
$99-$159

Address: 8600 Wickham Rd 48174 **Location:** I-94, exit 198 (Merriman Rd), 0.4 mi n, then just e. **Facility:** Smoke free premises. 151 units. 3 stories, interior corridors. **Terms:** 1-7 night minimum stay, cancellation fee imposed. **Pool(s):** heated indoor/outdoor. **Activities:** whirlpool, exercise room. **Guest Services:** valet and coin laundry, area transportation-within 5 mi, wireless Internet.

Phone: (734)728-9200 **145**

EXTENDED STAYAMERICA DETROIT-METRO AIRPORT

Extended Stay Hotel
$60-$70

Address: 30325 Flynn Dr 48174 **Location:** I-94, exit 198 (Merriman Rd), just n, then 0.4 mi e. **Facility:** Smoke free premises. 109 efficiencies. 3 stories, interior corridors. **Terms:** cancellation fee imposed. **Guest Services:** coin laundry, wireless Internet.

Phone: (734)722-7780 **144**

FAIRFIELD INN & SUITES BY MARRIOTT

Hotel
$98-$125

Address: 7800 Merriman Rd 48174 **Location:** I-94, exit 198 (Merriman Rd), 0.4 mi n. **Facility:** Smoke free premises. 106 units. 3 stories, interior corridors. **Terms:** cancellation fee imposed. **Amenities:** high-speed Internet. **Pool(s):** heated indoor. **Activities:** whirlpool, exercise room. **Guest Services:** valet and coin laundry, wireless Internet.

Phone: (734)467-7601 **136**

FOUR POINTS BY SHERATON DETROIT METRO AIRPORT

Hotel
$85-$180

Address: 8800 Wickham Rd 48174 **Location:** I-94, exit 198 (Merriman Rd), just n, then just e. **Facility:** Smoke free premises. 173 units. 7 stories, interior corridors. **Terms:** cancellation fee imposed. **Amenities:** video games (fee). **Pool(s):** heated indoor. **Activities:** whirlpool, exercise room. **Guest Services:** valet and coin laundry, area transportation-within 2 mi, wireless Internet. **Free Special Amenities: high-speed Internet and airport transportation.**

Phone: (734)729-9000 **147**

HAMPTON INN & SUITES

Contemporary Hotel
$79-$129

Address: 31700 Smith Rd 48174 **Location:** I-94, exit 198 (Merriman Rd), 0.4 mi n, then just w. **Facility:** Smoke free premises. 126 units. 6 stories, interior corridors. **Terms:** 1-7 night minimum stay, cancellation fee imposed. **Amenities:** high-speed Internet. **Pool(s):** heated indoor. **Activities:** whirlpool, exercise room. **Guest Services:** valet laundry, wireless Internet.

Phone: (734)595-0033 **138**

HILTON GARDEN INN-DETROIT METRO AIRPORT

Hotel
$79-$139

Address: 31800 Smith Rd 48174 **Location:** I-94, exit 198 (Merriman Rd), 0.4 mi n, then just w. **Facility:** Smoke free premises. 165 units. 6 stories, interior corridors. **Terms:** 1-7 night minimum stay, cancellation fee imposed. **Amenities:** high-speed Internet. **Pool(s):** heated indoor. **Activities:** whirlpool, exercise room. **Guest Services:** valet and coin laundry, area transportation-within 3 mi, wireless Internet.

Phone: (734)727-6000 **139**

LA QUINTA INN DETROIT AIRPORT ROMULUS

Hotel
$84-$126

Address: 7680 Merriman Rd 48174 **Location:** I-94, exit 198 (Merriman Rd), 0.4 mi n. **Facility:** Smoke free premises. 111 units. 3 stories, interior corridors. **Amenities:** video games (fee). *Some:* high-speed Internet. **Activities:** exercise room. **Guest Services:** wireless Internet.

Phone: (734)641-9006 **135**

LEXINGTON HOTEL-DETROIT METRO AIRPORT

Hotel
$45-$99

Address: 30847 Flynn Dr 48174 **Location:** I-94, exit 198 (Merriman Rd), just n, then just e. **Facility:** Smoke free premises. 135 units. 3 stories, interior corridors. **Terms:** 1-30 night minimum stay, cancellation fee imposed. **Amenities:** video games (fee). **Pool(s):** outdoor. **Activities:** exercise room. **Guest Services:** valet laundry, wireless Internet.

Phone: (734)721-1100 **141**

RED ROOF INN

Hotel
$39-$60

Address: 9095 Wickham Rd 48174 **Location:** I-94, exit 198 (Merriman Rd), just n, then just w. **Facility:** Smoke free premises. 76 units. 3 stories, interior corridors. **Activities:** exercise room. **Guest Services:** valet and coin laundry, wireless Internet.

Phone: (734)595-7400 **149**

(See map and index starting on p. 244)

ROMULUS QUALITY INN & SUITES
Phone: (734)946-1400   **152**

WWW
Hotel
$60-$80

Address: 9555 Middlebelt Rd 48174 **Location:** I-94, exit 199 (Middlebelt Rd), 0.4 mi s. **Facility:** Smoke free premises. 116 units. 3 stories, interior corridors. **Amenities:** safes (fee). **Activities:** exercise room. **Guest Services:** valet and coin laundry, wireless Internet.

 / SOME UNITS FEE

SPRINGHILL SUITES BY MARRIOTT DETROIT METRO AIRPORT ROMULUS
Phone: (734)326-7500   **140**

WWW
Contemporary
Hotel
$107-$137

Address: 8280 Merriman Rd 48174 **Location:** I-94, exit 198 (Merriman Rd), 0.4 mi n. **Facility:** Smoke free premises. 118 units. 4 stories, interior corridors. **Terms:** cancellation fee imposed. **Amenities:** high-speed Internet. **Pool(s):** heated indoor. **Activities:** whirlpool, exercise room. **Guest Services:** valet and coin laundry, wireless Internet.

> **AAA Benefit:**
> Members save a minimum 5% off the best available rate.

THE WESTIN DETROIT METROPOLITAN AIRPORT
Phone: (734)942-6500   **153**

WWW WWW
Hotel
$99-$329

Address: 2501 Worldgateway Pl 48242 **Location:** I-94, exit 198 (Merriman Rd); at McNamara Terminal. **Facility:** The Asia-inspired hotel features a large serenity pool and a bamboo forest in the lobby. Smoke free premises. 404 units. 11 stories, interior corridors. **Parking:** on-site (fee) and valet. **Terms:** cancellation fee imposed. **Amenities:** high-speed Internet (fee), safes, honor bars. **Dining:** Dema at the Westin, see separate listing. **Pool(s):** heated indoor. **Activities:** whirlpool, exercise room. **Guest Services:** valet laundry, wireless Internet. *(see ad p. 266)*

> **AAA Benefit:**
> Enjoy up to 15% off your next stay, plus Starwood Preferred Guest® bonuses.

FREE airport transportation

—— WHERE TO DINE ——

BISTRO 94
Phone: 734/729-2600   **129**

WW
American
$6-$18

Nestled away from traffic at the back of a hotel lobby, this casual restaurant is open for breakfast, lunch and dinner and offers a range of favorites ranging from steaks and chicken to fish and pastas. The breakfast menu offers a breakfast buffet with an "omelet to go" station. **Bar:** full bar. **Hours:** 6 am-2 & 6-10 pm. **Address:** 8000 Merriman Rd 48174 **Location:** I-94, exit 198 (Merriman Rd), 0.4 mi n; in Crowne Plaza Hotel Detroit Metro Airport.

DEMA AT THE WESTIN
Phone: 734/942-6500   **131**

WW
American
$13-$42

The hip restaurant opens into the Asia-inspired minimalist hotel lobby. Examples of contemporary American cuisine prepared with Asian influences include stir-fries, noodle dishes and wasabi-mashed potatoes. Also on the menu are offerings of timeless American fare. **Bar:** full bar. **Hours:** 6 am-11 pm. **Address:** 2501 Worldgateway Pl 48242 **Location:** I-94, exit 198 (Merriman Rd); at McNamara Terminal; in The Westin Detroit Metropolitan Airport. **Parking:** on-site (fee) and valet.

HA' PENNY PUB
Phone: 734/729-7555   **130**

WW
American
$10-$15

As its Irish-inspired name implies, the casual, yet elegant, pub evokes a "cottage-on-the-Emerald Isle" atmosphere, with wood-paneled walls and classic pub foods at moderate prices. The menu features cabbage soup, shepherd's pie and a black and tan strip steak, as well as pub classics like fish and chips, burgers and rotisserie chicken. **Bar:** full bar. **Hours:** 6:30 am-2 & 5-10 pm, Sat & Sun from 7 am. **Address:** 30559 Flynn Rd 48174 **Location:** I-94, exit 198 (Merriman Rd), just n, then 0.3 mi e; in Detroit Metro Airport Marriott.

LEONARDO'S PIZZERIA & RISTORANTE
Phone: 734/326-2560   **127**

WW
American
$8-$15

Near a number of airport hotels, this family-oriented restaurant specializes in home-style Italian food such as fettuccine Alfredo, lasagna and pizza. Green and white decor characterizes the inviting environment. Smartly dressed servers are pleasant and professional. **Bar:** full bar. **Hours:** 11 am-10 pm, Fri-midnight, Sat 4 pm-midnight, Sun 4 pm-10 pm. Closed major holidays. **Address:** 7575 Merriman Rd 48174 **Location:** I-94, exit 198 (Merriman Rd), 0.4 mi n.

MERRIMAN STREET GRILL
Phone: 734/595-6166   **128**

WW
American
$6-$12

Located in a small strip mall near a number of airport hotels, this restaurant is a nice change from the deluge of fast-food places and airport food. Fairly standard bar food and a number of daily specials are served by a friendly and helpful staff. **Bar:** full bar. **Hours:** 11 am-midnight, Sun 4 pm-10 pm. Closed major holidays. **Address:** 7660 Merriman Rd 48174 **Location:** I-94, exit 198 (Merriman Rd), 0.4 mi n.

ROSEVILLE pop. 48,129 (See map and index starting on p. 244)

BEST WESTERN PLUS GEORGIAN INN

Motel
$69-$99

Phone: (586)294-0400 [28]

Address: 31327 Gratiot Ave 48066 **Location:** I-94, exit 232 (Little Mack Ave), just s, 0.5 mi n on 13 Mile Rd, then just n. **Facility:** Smoke free premises. 111 units, some efficiencies. 2 stories, exterior corridors. **Terms:** cancellation fee imposed. **Amenities:** *Some:* high-speed Internet. **Pool(s):** heated outdoor. **Activities:** exercise room. *Fee:* game room. **Guest Services:** valet and coin laundry, wireless Internet. **Free Special Amenities: early check-in/late check-out and room upgrade (subject to availability with advance reservations).**

AAA Benefit:
Members save up to 20%, plus 10% bonus points with free rewards program.

 / SOME UNITS FEE

HOLIDAY INN EXPRESS & SUITES

Hotel
$99-$199

Phone: (586)285-5800 [26]

Address: 31900 Little Mack Ave 48066 **Location:** I-94, exit 232 (Little Mack Ave), just n. **Facility:** Smoke free premises. 90 units. 3 stories, interior corridors. **Amenities:** video games (fee). *Some:* high-speed Internet. **Pool(s):** heated indoor. **Activities:** whirlpool, exercise room. **Guest Services:** valet and coin laundry, wireless Internet.

CALL BIZ / SOME UNITS

RED ROOF INN #7012

Motel
$57-$74

Phone: (586)296-0310 [27]

Address: 31800 Little Mack Ave 48066 **Location:** I-94, exit 232 (Little Mack Ave), just n. **Facility:** Smoke free premises. 109 units. 2 stories (no elevator), exterior corridors. **Amenities:** *Fee:* video games, safes. **Guest Services:** wireless Internet. **Free Special Amenities: local telephone calls.** / SOME UNITS

—— WHERE TO DINE ——

MR. PAUL'S CHOPHOUSE

American
$9-$50

Phone: 586/777-7770 [51]

Don't let the industrial corridor location be a determent. Inside, wonderful tableside preparations of Chateaubriand for two and cherries jubilee make this restaurant perfect for special occasions. **Bar:** full bar. **Reservations:** suggested. **Hours:** 11 am-10 pm, Sat 4 pm-11 pm. Closed major holidays; also Sun. **Address:** 29850 Groesbeck Hwy 48066 **Location:** I-94, exit 232 (Little Mack Ave), 0.3 mi n, 1.5 mi w on 13 Mile Rd, then 1 mi s. **Parking:** on-site and valet.

OLIVES MEDITERRANEAN

Mediterranean
$6-$22

Phone: 586/293-3444 [50]

American and Middle Eastern classics—such as steak, ribs, pecan chicken, kebabs, shish kafta and grape leaves stuffed with lamb—are served in an informal atmosphere marked by a Mediterranean flair. **Bar:** full bar. **Hours:** 11 am-11 pm, Fri & Sat-midnight, Sun noon-10 pm. Closed: 1/1, 5/30, 12/25. **Address:** 31531 Gratiot Ave 48066 **Location:** I-94, exit 232 (Little Mack Ave), just s, 0.5 mi w on 13 Mile Rd, then just n.

SEA BREEZE DINER

American
$5-$14

Phone: 586/294-6760 [49]

A classic diner experience with a nautical twist, the booths in this casual restaurant are often filled with locals. The menu features a variety of wholesome dishes ranging from eggs, omelets and pancakes for breakfast, to chicken, ribs, seafood, steaks, sandwiches and burgers for lunch or dinner. Patrons should save room for a slice of homemade pie. **Hours:** 7 am-10 pm. Closed major holidays. **Address:** 32773 Gratiot Ave 48066 **Location:** I-94, exit 232 (Little Mack Ave), just s, 0.5 mi w on 13 Mile Rd, then 1 mi n.

CALL

ROYAL OAK pop. 60,062 (See map and index starting on p. 244)

—— WHERE TO DINE ——

ANDIAMO

Italian
$8-$35

Phone: 248/582-9300 (160)

Decorated with sunflower inspired artwork, this stylish upscale restaurant, part of a local chain, is an ideal spot to enjoy an intimate meal with friends or family. Traditional dishes, such as gnocchi, ravioli and lasagna, are prepared using high-quality ingredients. **Bar:** full bar. **Hours:** 11:30 am-11 pm, Sat from 4 pm, Sun 4 pm-9 pm. Closed major holidays. **Address:** 129 S Main St 48067 **Location:** Just s of 11 Mile Rd; downtown. **Parking:** valet and street only. CALL

ASTORIA BAKERY & CAFE

Breads/Pastries
$2-$6

Phone: 248/582-9220 (166)

For those who need to satisfy a sweet tooth, the bakery cafe serves a large variety of elegant-looking cakes and pastries. **Hours:** 8 am-midnight, Fri & Sat-1 am; to 11 pm, Fri & Sat-midnight 9/15-4/15. Closed: 11/24, 12/25. **Address:** 320 S Main St 48067 **Location:** Downtown. **Parking:** street only. CALL

BASTONE

Belgian
$7-$22

Phone: 248/544-6250 (169)

The quirky atmosphere of the Belgian brewpub could have been lifted from the streets of New York. While beer is brewed on the premises, the Belgian food is the real crowd-pleaser. German and French influences show themselves in moules, tarte flambé and twice-fried Belgian frites with tarragon-seasoned mayonnaise. **Bar:** full bar. **Hours:** 11 am-11 pm, Fri & Sat-midnight, Sun noon-10 pm. Closed major holidays. **Address:** 419 S Main St 48067 **Location:** Jct 5th St; center. **Parking:** street only. CALL

(See map and index starting on p. 244)

CAFÉ HABANA

Cuban
$7-$13

Phone: 248/544-6255 [168]

Just behind its sister restaurant, Bastone, the cozy cafe is decorated with colorful murals and lots of chrome. An open kitchen and energetic salsa music create a lively environment. One of the state's few Cuban restaurants, this place features many fresh fruits and vegetables, including fried plantain chips with a citrus dipping sauce; an array of Cuban sandwiches and salads; and a few daily specials, such as pork in adobo. **Bar:** full bar. **Hours:** 11 am-11 pm, Fri & Sat-midnight, Sun-10 pm. Closed major holidays. **Address:** 419 S Main St 48067 **Location:** Jct 4th St; behind Bastone. **Parking:** street only. CALL &M

COMET BURGER

American
$4-$8

Phone: 248/414-4567 [162]

The claims to fame for the stereotypical hole-in-the-wall restaurant aren't the homages to Elvis, Buddy or Marilyn that adorn the walls but rather the quintessential sliders, a perfect match to satisfy late-night cravings. **Hours:** 11 am-midnight, Thurs-Sat to 3 am. Closed: 12/25, 12/26. **Address:** 207 S Main St 48307 **Location:** Just s of 11 Mile Rd; downtown. **Parking:** street only. CALL &M

D'AMATO'S NEIGHBORHOOD RESTAURANT

Italian
$14-$23

Phone: 248/584-7400 [163]

The friendly restaurant delivers large portions of simple favorites: light bites, salad, pizza, pasta, chicken, fish and sausage. The atmosphere is warm and inviting. Diners can watch the cooking through a partial wall and enjoy delectable desserts. **Bar:** full bar. **Hours:** 5 pm-10 pm, Thurs-Sat to 11 pm, Sun 11 am-3 pm. Closed major holidays. **Address:** 222 S Sherman Dr 48067 **Location:** Corner of S Washington Ave and Sherman Dr; downtown. **Parking:** street only.

LILY'S SEAFOOD

Seafood
$9-$25

Phone: 248/591-5459 [167]

Besides brewing its own beers and sodas on site, the casual yet chic restaurant with exposed brick walls and aquariums offers a diverse menu of fresh seafood. Also offered is a limited selection of pasta and steaks. Among the choices are Creole soup with homemade seafood sausage, Prince Edward Island mussels, seafood boil and mom's key lime cheesecake, all of which are reminiscent of the East Coast. **Bar:** full bar. **Hours:** 11 am-10:30 pm, Fri & Sat-2 am. Closed major holidays. **Address:** 410 S Washington St 48067 **Location:** Jct W 4th St; downtown. **Parking:** street only. CALL &M

LITTLE TREE SUSHI BAR

Sushi
$8-$14

Phone: 248/586-0994 [161]

Nestled amid the quaint downtown shops of Royal Oak, the trendy dining room provides a relaxed atmosphere for experimenting with different types of sushi. Knowledgeable staffers help acquaint the uninitiated with the basics of sushi. A few options from Thailand and the Philippines round out the menu, such as pad thai and deep-fried spring rolls. **Bar:** full bar. **Hours:** 11:30 am-11 pm, Fri & Sat-midnight, Sun 4:30 pm-10 pm. Closed major holidays. **Address:** 107 S Main St 48067 **Location:** Corner of E 11 Mile Rd and Main St; downtown. **Parking:** street only. CALL &M

PRONTO!

Deli
$7-$15

Phone: 248/544-7900 [170]

Much of the produce that goes into the sandwiches and limited selection of entrees is specially grown for this fun and informal restaurant. While known for the enormous choices of sandwiches, the restaurant also offers a good selection of homemade desserts. **Bar:** full bar. **Hours:** 9 am-10 pm, Fri & Sat-midnight. Closed major holidays. **Address:** 608 S Washington St 48067 **Location:** Jct 6th St; center. **Parking:** street only.

REDCOAT TAVERN

American
$6-$16

Phone: 248/549-0300 [158]

Patrons can watch for the red-coated soldier at the entrance to the British-style tavern. Deep red lights, dark woods and brick walls give the place a charming atmosphere. While there are plenty of other items on the menu, burgers with a slightly spicy secret sauce are the main draw. **Bar:** full bar. **Hours:** 11 am-2 am. Closed major holidays; also Sun. **Address:** 31542 Woodward Ave 48073 **Location:** 1 mi n of jct W 13 Mile Rd.

ROYAL OAK BREWERY

American
$8-$14

Phone: 248/544-1141 [164]

A dozen rotating microbrewed ales complement selections of lighter fare: soup, salad, sandwiches, appetizers, pasta dishes and gourmet pizza. The freshly baked pita bread is delicious. The cozy patio is a great place to unwind after a long day. **Bar:** full bar. **Hours:** 11:30 am-10 pm, Fri & Sat-11 pm. Closed major holidays. **Address:** 215 E 4th St 48067 **Location:** Just e of jct Main St; downtown. **Parking:** street only.

TOM'S OYSTER BAR

Seafood
$9-$27

Phone: 248/541-1186 [165]

From tin ceilings to checkered tablecloths, the local chain of raw bars bears more than a slight resemblance to New England fish houses. Fresh oysters are the signature item on a menu of diverse seafood selections, including crunchy panko-fried shrimp and grilled yellowfin tuna. Among other delightful choices are burgers and pasta. **Bar:** full bar. **Hours:** 11 am-midnight, Fri-2 am, Sat noon-2 am, Sun noon-midnight. Closed major holidays. **Address:** 318 S Main St 48607 **Location:** 0.3 mi s of jct 11 Mile Rd; downtown. **Parking:** street only.

ZUMBA MEXICAN GRILLE

Mexican
$3-$8

Phone: 248/542-1400 [159]

The artsy/industrial roadside shack, with its concrete and stainless-steel interior, presents a simple menu of incredibly fresh Mexican street food, such as quesadillas, burritos and Baja- or American-style tacos prepared to order. **Hours:** 11 am-10 pm, Fri & Sat-11 pm, Sun noon-9 pm. Closed major holidays. **Address:** 121 N Main St 48067 **Location:** Just n of jct 11 Mile Rd; downtown. **Parking:** on-site and street. CALL &M

SOUTHFIELD pop. 78,296   (See map and index starting on p. 244)

CANDLEWOOD SUITES

Extended Stay
Hotel
$69-$129

Phone: (248)945-0010   **47**

Address: 1 Corporate Dr 48076 **Location:** SR 10 (Northwestern Hwy), exit Lahser Rd, just e. **Facility:** Smoke free premises. 121 efficiencies. 3 stories, interior corridors. **Terms:** office hours 7 am-11 pm. **Amenities:** high-speed Internet. **Activities:** exercise room. **Guest Services:** complimentary and valet laundry.

COMFORT SUITES

Hotel
$89-$230

Phone: (248)357-9990   **53**

Address: 24977 Northwestern Hwy 48076 **Location:** SR 10 (Northwestern Hwy), exit 10 Mile Rd. **Facility:** Smoke free premises. 81 units. 3 stories, interior corridors. **Terms:** cancellation fee imposed. **Amenities:** high-speed Internet, safes (fee). **Pool(s):** heated indoor. **Activities:** whirlpool, exercise room. **Guest Services:** valet and coin laundry, wireless Internet.

COURTYARD BY MARRIOTT-SOUTHFIELD

Hotel
$89-$114

Phone: (248)358-1222   **48**

Address: 27027 Northwestern Hwy 48033 **Location:** SR 10 (Northwestern Hwy), exit Lahser Rd, just sw. **Facility:** Smoke free premises. 147 units. 2-3 stories, interior corridors. **Terms:** cancellation fee imposed. **Amenities:** high-speed Internet. **Pool(s):** heated indoor. **Activities:** whirlpool, exercise room. **Guest Services:** valet and coin laundry, wireless Internet.

> **AAA Benefit:**
> Members save a minimum 5% off the best available rate.

DETROIT MARRIOTT SOUTHFIELD

Hotel
$161-$206

Phone: (248)356-7400   **49**

Address: 27033 Northwestern Hwy 48033 **Location:** SR 10 (Northwestern Hwy), exit Lahser Rd, just nw. **Facility:** Smoke free premises. 226 units. 6 stories, interior corridors. **Terms:** cancellation fee imposed. **Amenities:** video games (fee). *Some:* high-speed Internet. **Pool(s):** heated indoor. **Activities:** whirlpool, exercise room. **Guest Services:** valet laundry, wireless Internet.

> **AAA Benefit:**
> Members save 5% or more off best available rate.

(See map and index starting on p. 244)

EMBASSY SUITES DETROIT-SOUTHFIELD

Hotel
$68-$95

Address: 28100 Franklin Rd 48034 **Location:** I-696, exit 8, 0.5 mi nw on SR 10. **Facility:** Smoke free premises. 239 units, some two bedrooms. 9 stories, interior corridors. **Terms:** 1-7 night minimum stay, cancellation fee imposed. **Amenities:** video games (fee), high-speed Internet. **Pool(s):** heated indoor. **Activities:** whirlpool, exercise room. **Guest Services:** valet and coin laundry, area transportation-within 5 mi, wireless Internet.

Phone: (248)350-2000   44

EMBASSY SUITES
HOTELS®
AAA Benefit:
Members save 5% or more
everyday!

HAMPTON INN-SOUTHFIELD

Hotel
$79-$109

Address: 27500 Northwestern Service Dr 48034 **Location:** I-696, exit 9 (Telegraph Rd N), just n to 11 Mile Rd, then 0.5 mi e. **Facility:** Smoke free premises. 154 units. 2 stories, interior corridors. **Terms:** 1-7 night minimum stay, cancellation fee imposed. **Pool(s):** heated indoor. **Activities:** whirlpool, exercise room. **Guest Services:** valet and coin laundry, wireless Internet.

Phone: (248)356-5500   45

AAA Benefit:
Members save up to 10%
everyday!

HOLIDAY INN EXPRESS HOTEL & SUITES

Hotel
$119-$169

Address: 25100 Northwestern Hwy 48075 **Location:** SR 10 (Northwestern Hwy), exit 10 Mile Rd. **Facility:** Smoke free premises. 91 units, some efficiencies. 3 stories, interior corridors. **Amenities:** high-speed Internet. **Pool(s):** heated indoor. **Activities:** whirlpool, exercise room. **Guest Services:** valet and coin laundry, wireless Internet. **Free Special Amenities:** full breakfast and high-speed Internet.

Phone: (248)350-2400   52

MARVIN'S GARDEN INN

Motel
Rates not provided

Address: 27650 Northwestern Hwy 48034 **Location:** I-696, exit 9 (Telegraph Rd), just nw. **Facility:** Smoke free premises. 110 units. 2 stories (no elevator), interior/exterior corridors. *Bath:* shower only. **Parking:** winter plug-ins. **Guest Services:** valet and coin laundry, wireless Internet.

Phone: 248/353-6777   42

QUALITY INN SOUTHFIELD

Hotel
$79-$99

Address: 26111 Telegraph Rd 48034 **Location:** I-696, exit 10, just s. **Facility:** Smoke free premises. 105 units. 3 stories, interior corridors. **Activities:** exercise room. **Guest Services:** valet laundry, wireless Internet.

Phone: 248/368-6130   50

RED ROOF INN-SOUTHFIELD #7133

Motel
$41-$111

Address: 27660 Northwestern Hwy 48034 **Location:** I-696, exit 9 (Telegraph Rd), just nw. **Facility:** Smoke free premises. 113 units. 3 stories, exterior corridors. **Amenities:** *Fee:* video games, safes. **Guest Services:** valet laundry, wireless Internet. **Free Special Amenities:** local telephone calls.

Phone: (248)353-7200   43

(See map and index starting on p. 244)

SPRINGHILL SUITES BY MARRIOTT DETROIT/SOUTHFIELD

Hotel
$108-$138

Address: 28555 Northwestern Hwy 48034 **Location:** I-696, exit 9 (Telegraph Rd), 0.5 mi nw on SR 10. **Facility:** Smoke free premises. 84 units. 3 stories, interior corridors. **Terms:** cancellation fee imposed. **Pool(s):** heated indoor. **Activities:** whirlpool, exercise room. **Guest Services:** valet and coin laundry, wireless Internet. **Free Special Amenities:** expanded continental breakfast and high-speed Internet.

Phone: (248)352-6100 **41**

AAA Benefit:
Members save a minimum 5% off the best available rate.

THE WESTIN HOTEL SOUTHFIELD-DETROIT

Hotel
Rates not provided

Address: 1500 Town Center 48075 **Location:** SR 10 (Northwestern Hwy), exit 10 (10 Mile Rd/Evergreen Rd), 0.3 mi n. **Facility:** This distinctive hotel in the Southfield Town Center Complex offers easy access to the Detroit-area business community. Smoke free premises. 389 units, some two bedrooms. 12 stories, interior corridors. **Parking:** on-site and valet. **Amenities:** high-speed Internet (fee), safes, honor bars. **Dining:** 2 restaurants. **Pool(s):** heated indoor. **Activities:** whirlpool. **Guest Services:** valet laundry, area transportation-within 3 mi, wireless Internet. *(see ad below)*

Phone: 248/827-4000 **51**

AAA Benefit:
Enjoy up to 15% off your next stay, plus Starwood Preferred Guest® bonuses.

FREE newspaper and high-speed Internet

▼ *See AAA listing above* ▼

---

soothe your soul

Wake restored in 10 layers of comfort on our Heavenly Bed‡ and feel refreshed with the soothing elements of our Heavenly Bath.

Book the AAA member rate at The Westin Southfield Detroit by calling 888-627-8558 or visiting westinsouthfielddetroit.com

spg₊
Starwood
Preferred
Guest

THE WESTIN
SOUTHFIELD
DETROIT

©2010 Starwood Hotels & Resorts Worldwide, Inc. All Rights Reserved.

Plan. Map. Go.
TripTik® Travel Planner on AAA.com or CAA.ca

(See map and index starting on p. 244)

—— **WHERE TO DINE** ——

BACCO RISTORANTE

Italian
$10-$35

Phone: 248/356-6600 63

"Modern" and "progressive" might be among words used to describe the restaurant, whose owners regularly travel to Italy to keep abreast of the ongoing evolution in Italian cuisine. An attractive yet comfortable dining room—brought to life with a large stylized mural and folds of fabric over the floor-to-ceiling windows—is the perfect venue in which diners can savor simple, lighter, modern fare with an expansive wine list. **Bar:** full bar. **Reservations:** required. **Hours:** 11:30 am-10 pm, Fri-11 pm, Sat 5 pm-11 pm. Closed major holidays; also Sun. **Address:** 29410 Northwestern Hwy 48034 **Location:** Jct SR 10 (Northwestern Hwy) and I-696, 1 mi n. **Parking:** on-site and valet. CALL ♿M

BEANS & CORNBREAD: A SOULFUL BISTRO

Soul Food
$6-$18

Phone: 248/208-1680 62

Cozy like a family room, the dining area has purple walls that display a collection of vintage magazine covers. Lines can be long, but lovers of Southern home cooking will find the wait well worth the effort. Items such as barbecue ribs, filet mignon and fried pork chops are served with traditional home-style accompaniments—from collard greens, black-eyed peas and grits to macaroni and cheese and candied sweet potatoes. **Hours:** 11 am-9 pm, Fri-10 pm, Sat noon-10 pm, Sun 10:30 am-9 pm. Closed major holidays. **Address:** 29508 Northwestern Hwy 48034 **Location:** Jct SR 10 (Northwestern Hwy) and I-696, 1 mi n; in Sunset Strip Plaza.

C.A. MUER'S MERRIWETHER

American
$7-$30

Phone: 248/358-1310 67

The surroundings are festive and upbeat in the English-style restaurant. Preparations of fowl, pork, beef and seafood are as eye-popping as they are palate-pleasing. Tantalizing desserts show the same artistic flair. Service is friendly and prompt. **Bar:** full bar. **Reservations:** suggested. **Hours:** 11 am-10 pm, Sat from noon, Sun 2 pm-8 pm. Closed: 12/25. **Address:** 25485 Telegraph Rd 48034 **Location:** I-696, exit US 9 (Telegraph Rd), 0.3 mi s. **Parking:** valet only.

COPPER CANYON BREWERY & RESTAURANT

American
$11-$24

Phone: 248/223-1700 66

In the spirit of a copper mine, the expansive restaurant, decorated with brick and copper accents, also serves as a brewpub. Among the menu favorites are buffalo wings, sandwiches, pasta, seafood and 16-ounce steaks. A separate children's menu is available. **Bar:** full bar. **Hours:** 11 am-11 pm, Sun 1 pm-9 pm. Closed major holidays. **Address:** 27522 Northwestern Hwy 48034 **Location:** I-696, exit 9 (Telegraph Rd N), just n to 11 Mile Rd, then 0.5 mi e on Northwestern Service Dr. CALL ♿M

FISHBONE'S RHYTHM KITCHEN CAFE

Cajun
$8-$23

Phone: 248/351-2925 64

The restaurant lures a loud and lively crowd eager to dine on New Orleans Cajun specialties, such as whiskey barbecue ribs, chicken and seafood gumbo. **Bar:** full bar. **Reservations:** required. **Hours:** 11 am-10:30 pm, Fri & Sat-midnight. Closed major holidays. **Address:** 29244 Northwestern Hwy 48034 **Location:** Jct SR 10 (Northwestern Hwy) and I-696, 1 mi n. CALL ♿M

NEW SEOUL GARDEN

Asian
$9-$25

Phone: 248/827-1600 65

A sushi bar and the tempura choices distinguish this restaurant, which delivers Korean and Japanese cuisine. Potted plants, natural lighting and attractive, solid-wood grill tables decorate the dining areas. Service is professional. **Bar:** full bar. **Hours:** 11:30 am-10:30 pm, Fri & Sat-11 pm, Sun noon-10 pm. Closed major holidays. **Address:** 27566 Northwestern Hwy 48034 **Location:** I-696, exit 9 (Telegraph Rd), just n to 11 Mile Rd, then 0.5 mi e on Northwestern Service Dr. CALL ♿M

SHIRAZ

American
$8-$36

Phone: 248/645-5289 61

Named after a grape variety, this corkscrew- and wine-themed restaurant, not surprisingly, offers an extensive selection of wines and employs a knowledgeable staff. Using high-quality ingredients, such as USDA Prime cuts of beef and a global palette of influences, the kitchen prepares not only varied steaks, which range in size from 7-ounce filets to massive 24-ounce porterhouses, but also fresh Asia-influenced seafood and lobster. **Bar:** full bar. **Hours:** 11 am-10 pm, Fri-11 pm, Sat 5 pm-11 pm. Closed major holidays; also Sun. **Address:** 30100 Telegraph Rd 48025 **Location:** I-696, exit 9 (Telegraph Rd), 1 mi n. **Parking:** on-site and valet. CALL ♿M

SWEET LORRAINE'S CAFE & BAR

Continental
$9-$17

Phone: 248/559-5985 60

One of the first locations for the small chain, the attractive, yet casual, restaurant serves an eclectic menu of continental standards, such as steak and seafood. Other choices include globally influenced items along the lines of French pot pie and Spanish paella. Desserts are dreamily good. **Bar:** full bar. **Hours:** 11 am-10 pm, Sat & Sun from 8 am. Closed major holidays. **Address:** 29101 Greenfield Rd 48076 **Location:** Jct Greenfield and 12 Mile rds. CALL ♿M

TAVERN ON 13

American
$6-$20

Phone: 248/647-7747 59

This casual tavern-on the backside of a strip mall-specializes in seafood. Although Asia-influenced seafood and standard fish and chips are crowd favorites, patrons also can try grilled chicken, ribs and pasta. **Bar:** full bar. **Hours:** 11 am-9 pm, Fri-11 pm, Sat 2 pm-11 pm, Sun 4 pm-9 pm. Closed major holidays. **Address:** 17600 W 13 Mile Rd 48025 **Location:** Jct Southfield Rd; northeast side of shopping plaza. CALL ♿M

ZOUP!

Deli
$5-$9

Phone: 248/799-2800

One of several Detroit locations, the restaurant encourages patrons to sample any of a dozen hand-crafted soups served daily from a rotation of nearly 200 varieties. **Hours:** 11 am-8 pm, Sun noon-5 pm. Closed: 7/4, 11/24, 12/25. **Address:** 29177 Northwestern Hwy 48034 **Location:** I-696 W, exit 10, 0.6 mi w to SR 10 (Northwestern Hwy), then 1.1 mi n; in Franklin Plaza Shopping Center. CALL ♿M

SOUTHGATE pop. 30,136   (See map and index starting on p. 244)

COMFORT SUITES
Phone: 734/287-9200   157

Hotel
Rates not provided

Address: 18950 Northline Rd 48195 **Location:** I-75, exit 37 (Northline Rd), just w. **Facility:** Smoke free premises. 78 units. 3 stories, interior corridors. **Amenities:** high-speed Internet, safes (fee). **Pool(s):** heated indoor. **Activities:** sauna, exercise room. **Guest Services:** valet and coin laundry, wireless Internet.

HOLIDAY INN SOUTHGATE BANQUET & CONFERENCE CENTER
Phone: (734)283-4400   156

Hotel
$99-$199

Address: 17201 Northline Rd 48195 **Location:** I-75, exit 37 (Northline Rd), just e. **Facility:** Smoke free premises. 160 units. 2 stories (no elevator), interior corridors. **Terms:** check-in 4 pm, cancellation fee imposed. **Amenities:** video games (fee). **Dining:** entertainment. **Pool(s):** heated indoor. **Activities:** whirlpool, sun deck, exercise room. *Fee:* game room. **Guest Services:** valet and coin laundry, area transportation-within 5 mi, wireless Internet.

LA QUINTA INN DETROIT SOUTHGATE
Phone: (734)374-3000   158

Hotel
$55-$109

Address: 12888 Reeck Rd 48195 **Location:** I-75, exit 37 (Northline Rd), just w. **Facility:** Smoke free premises. 100 units, some kitchens. 3 stories, interior corridors. **Amenities:** video games (fee). *Some:* high-speed Internet. **Guest Services:** coin laundry, wireless Internet.

——— WHERE TO DINE ———

HUNGARIAN RHAPSODY
Phone: 734/283-9622   134

Hungarian
$5-$19

Hand-embroidered tablecloths are framed and hung as artwork along walls also decorated with memorabilia from the old country. One of only a few Hungarian restaurants in the area, this place serves gulyas (beef goulash) in the traditional kettle over a campfire and is known for its paprikas and Old World pastries. **Bar:** full bar. **Hours:** 11 am-10 pm, Sun 11:30 am-7:30 pm. Closed: 12/25; also Mon. **Address:** 14315 Northline Rd 48195 **Location:** I-75, exit 37 (Northline Rd), 0.4 mi w of Toledo-Dix Hwy.

STERLING HEIGHTS pop. 124,471   (See map and index starting on p. 244)

BEST WESTERN PLUS STERLING INN
Phone: (586)979-1400   6

Hotel
$130-$190

Address: 34911 Van Dyke Ave 48312 **Location:** I-696, exit 23, 4 mi n on SR 53 (Van Dyke Ave), jct 15 Mile Rd. **Facility:** Smoke free premises. 246 units. 2-5 stories, interior/exterior corridors. **Terms:** cancellation fee imposed. **Amenities:** safes. *Some:* high-speed Internet. **Dining:** Loon River Cafe, see separate listing. **Pool(s):** heated indoor. **Activities:** whirlpools, steamrooms, waterslide, indoor water park, jogging, exercise room. *Fee:* game room. **Guest Services:** valet and coin laundry, wireless Internet.

AAA Benefit:
Members save up to 20%, plus 10% bonus points with free rewards program.

FREE newspaper and high-speed Internet

HAMPTON INN & SUITES-STERLING HEIGHTS
Phone: (586)276-0600   5

Hotel
$109-$139

Address: 36400 Van Dyke Ave 48312 **Location:** 0.5 mi s of 16 Mile Rd (Metro Pkwy). Across from Daimler-Chrysler Sterling Stamping Plant. **Facility:** Smoke free premises. 76 units. 3 stories, interior corridors. **Terms:** 1-7 night minimum stay, cancellation fee imposed. **Amenities:** video games (fee), high-speed Internet. **Pool(s):** heated indoor. **Activities:** exercise room. **Guest Services:** valet and coin laundry, wireless Internet. **Free Special Amenities:** expanded continental breakfast and high-speed Internet.

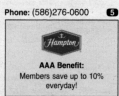

AAA Benefit:
Members save up to 10% everyday!

(See map and index starting on p. 244)

TOWNEPLACE SUITES

Extended Stay
Hotel
$120-$130

Phone: (586)566-0900

AAA Benefit:
Members save a minimum 5%
off the best available rate.

Address: 14800 Lakeside Cir 48313 **Location:** 1 mi e of jct SR 53 (Van Dyke Ave) and 59 (Hall Rd). Across from Lakeside Mall. **Facility:** Smoke free premises. 95 kitchen units, some two bedrooms. 3 stories, interior corridors. **Terms:** cancellation fee imposed. **Amenities:** video games (fee), high-speed Internet. **Pool(s):** heated outdoor. **Activities:** exercise room. **Guest Services:** valet and coin laundry, wireless Internet.

WHERE TO DINE

ANDIAMO

Italian
$12-$25

Phone: 586/532-8800

The upscale, trendy dining room with its sunflower-inspired artwork and comfortable furnishings is an ideal spot to unwind after a day of shopping or to enjoy an intimate dinner with friends or family. Part of a local chain, the restaurant's menu offers such traditional dishes as gnocci, ravioli and lasagna, all of which are prepared using authentic recipes and high-quality ingredients. **Bar:** full bar. **Hours:** 11:30 am-10 pm, Fri-midnight, Sat 3 pm-midnight, Sun 1 pm-9 pm. Closed major holidays. **Address:** 14425 Lakeside Cir 48313 **Location:** 1 mi e of jct SR 53 (Van Dyke Ave) and 59 (Hall Rd). CALL

LOON RIVER CAFE

American
$7-$20

Phone: 586/979-1420   ⑦

The rustic 1930s hunting lodge offers a quaint setting for enjoying specialties of local wild game and other creative dishes, such as lasagna soup and snake cakes. The master chef whips up all of the tantalizing desserts on the premises. **Bar:** full bar. **Hours:** 6 am-10 pm, Fri-11 pm, Sat 7 am-11 pm, Sun 7 am-9 pm. **Address:** 34911 Van Dyke Ave 48312 **Location:** I-696, exit 23, 4 mi n on SR 53 (Van Dyke Ave), jct 15 Mile Rd; in Best Western Plus Sterling Inn. CALL

TAYLOR pop. 65,868   (See map and index starting on p. 244)

COMFORT INN & SUITES OF TAYLOR

Hotel
$90-$100

Phone: (313)292-6730   131

Address: 6778 S Telegraph Rd 48180 **Location:** I-94, exit 202B (Telegraph Rd), just s. **Facility:** Smoke free premises. 78 units. 3 stories, interior corridors. **Amenities:** high-speed Internet, safes (fee). **Pool(s):** heated indoor. **Activities:** sauna, whirlpool, exercise room. **Guest Services:** valet and coin laundry, wireless Internet. **Free Special Amenities:** full breakfast and high-speed Internet.

RED ROOF INN-TAYLOR #7189

Motel
$38-$75

Phone: (734)374-1150   132

Address: 21230 Eureka Rd 48180 **Location:** I-75, exit 36 (Eureka Rd), just w. **Facility:** Smoke free premises. 111 units. 2 stories, exterior corridors. **Amenities:** Fee: video games, safes. **Guest Services:** wireless Internet. **Free Special Amenities:** local telephone calls.

WHERE TO DINE

LITTLE DADDY'S FAMILY DINING

American
$5-$12

Phone: 734/287-8600   124

Inviting to families, the restaurant prepares moderately priced sandwiches, burgers and hot dogs, as well as chicken, steaks and ribs. **Bar:** beer & wine. **Hours:** 7 am-9:30 pm, Sat from 8 am, Sun 8 am-9 pm. Closed major holidays. **Address:** 22250 Eureka Rd 48180 **Location:** I-75, exit 36 (Eureka Rd), 0.4 mi w.

PETE'S PLACE

American
$5-$12

Phone: 734/374-0088   123

The trendy coffee shop has an upscale appeal and plenty of homemade offerings, such as soups, salads, sandwiches, chili and burgers. **Hours:** 6 am-9 pm, Fri-10 pm, Sat 7 am-10 pm, Sun 7 am-9 pm. Closed major holidays. **Address:** 12245 Telegraph Rd 48180 **Location:** I-75, exit 37 (Northline Rd), 1.5 mi w, then just n.

TRENTON pop. 19,584

―――― WHERE TO DINE ――――

FRATELLO'S

Italian
$8-$23

Phone: 734/692-1730

Specializing in steak and fresh seafood, with popular Italian items to choose from. Comfortable dining room with contemporary decor and warm, cozy foyer fireplace. Cheerful and friendly wait staff. **Bar:** full bar. **Reservations:** suggested. **Hours:** 11 am-10 pm, Fri & Sat-11 pm, Sun-8 pm, Mon 3 pm-8 pm; Sunday brunch. Closed major holidays. **Address:** 4501 Fort St 48183 **Location:** Jct SR 85 (Fort St) and Van Horn Rd.

SIBLEY GARDENS
Italian
$8-$32

Phone: 734/285-1707

Just north of downtown, this local favorite serves up traditional Italian fare such as veal piccata and fettuccine Alfredo in a dark and romantic atmosphere. **Bar:** full bar. **Hours:** 11 am-11 pm, Sat from 3 pm. Closed major holidays; also Sun. **Address:** 916 W Jefferson Ave 48183 **Location:** 1 mi n of downtown.

TROY pop. 72,900   (See map and index starting on p. 244)

COURTYARD BY MARRIOTT
Hotel
$129-$139

Phone: (248)528-2800 **15**

Address: 1525 E Maple Rd 48083 **Location:** I-75, exit 67 (Rochester Rd), 1 mi s on Stephenson Hwy, then just e. **Facility:** Smoke free premises. 147 units. 3 stories, interior corridors. **Terms:** cancellation fee imposed. **Amenities:** high-speed Internet. **Pool(s):** heated indoor. **Activities:** whirlpool, exercise room. **Guest Services:** valet and coin laundry, wireless Internet.

AAA Benefit:
Members save a minimum 5% off the best available rate.

DRURY INN & SUITES-TROY
Hotel
$80-$229

Phone: (248)528-3330 **10**

Address: 575 W Big Beaver Rd 48084 **Location:** I-75, exit 69 (Big Beaver Rd), just e. **Facility:** Smoke free premises. 217 units. 4 stories, interior corridors. **Terms:** cancellation fee imposed. **Amenities:** high-speed Internet. **Pool(s):** heated indoor. **Activities:** whirlpool, exercise room. **Guest Services:** valet and coin laundry, wireless Internet.

EMBASSY SUITES
Hotel
$91-$151

Phone: (248)879-7500

Address: 850 Tower Dr 48098 **Location:** I-75, exit 72 (Crooks Rd), just s. **Facility:** Smoke free premises. 251 units, some two bedrooms. 8 stories, interior corridors. **Terms:** 1-7 night minimum stay, cancellation fee imposed. **Pool(s):** heated indoor. **Activities:** whirlpool, sun deck, exercise room. **Guest Services:** valet and coin laundry, area transportation-within 5 mi, wireless Internet.

AAA Benefit:
Members save 5% or more everyday!

THE GATEHOUSE SUITES TROY HOTEL
Extended Stay Hotel
$152-$186

Phone: (248)689-6856 **12**

Address: 2600 Livernois Rd 48083 **Location:** I-75, exit 69 (Big Beaver Rd), 0.5 mi e to Livernois Rd, then 0.5 mi s. **Facility:** Smoke free premises. 152 kitchen units, some two bedrooms. 2 stories, exterior corridors. **Terms:** cancellation fee imposed. **Pool(s):** heated outdoor. **Activities:** whirlpool, exercise room, sports court, horseshoes. **Guest Services:** valet and coin laundry, wireless Internet.

HOMEWOOD SUITES BY HILTON DETROIT/TROY
Extended Stay Hotel
$99-$169

Phone: (248)816-6500 **16**

Address: 1495 Equity Dr 48084 **Location:** Just s of Maple Rd; between Crooks Rd and Coolidge Hwy. Adjacent to Cambridge Commons Shopping Plaza. **Facility:** Smoke free premises. 150 efficiencies, some two bedrooms. 4 stories, interior corridors. **Terms:** 1-7 night minimum stay, cancellation fee imposed. **Amenities:** video games (fee), high-speed Internet. **Pool(s):** heated indoor. **Activities:** exercise room. **Guest Services:** valet and coin laundry, wireless Internet.

AAA Benefit:
Members save 5% or more everyday!

THE MET HOTEL TROY DETROIT
Hotel
Rates not provided

Phone: 248/879-2100

Address: 5500 Crooks Rd 48098 **Location:** I-75, exit 72 (Crooks Rd), just n. **Facility:** 185 units. 3 stories, interior corridors. **Dining:** Charley's Crab, see separate listing. **Pool(s):** heated indoor. **Activities:** sauna, exercise room. **Guest Services:** valet and coin laundry, area transportation-within 5 mi, wireless Internet.

QUALITY INN
Hotel
$79-$135

Phone: (248)689-7500 **11**

Address: 2537 Rochester Ct 48083 **Location:** I-75, exit 67 (Rochester Rd), 0.3 mi sw, then just w. Located in a secluded area. **Facility:** Smoke free premises. 150 units. 4 stories, interior corridors. **Amenities:** high-speed Internet. **Pool(s):** heated outdoor. **Activities:** exercise room. **Guest Services:** valet and coin laundry, wireless Internet.

(See map and index starting on p. 244)

RED ROOF INN-TROY #7021   Phone: (248)689-4391

▼▼ Motel
$56-$66

Address: 2350 Rochester Ct 48083 **Location:** I-75, exit 67 (Rochester Rd), 0.3 mi sw. **Facility:** Smoke free premises. 109 units. 2 stories, exterior corridors. **Amenities:** *Fee:* video games, safes. **Guest Services:** wireless Internet.

SOMERSET INN   Phone: (248)643-7800   ⑬

▼▼▼▼ Hotel
$99-$194

Address: 2601 W Big Beaver Rd 48084 **Location:** I-75, exit 69 (Big Beaver Rd), 1 mi w. Adjacent to Somerset Collection South. **Facility:** Smoke free premises. 250 units. 14 stories, interior corridors. **Terms:** cancellation fee imposed. **Amenities:** high-speed Internet. **Pool(s):** 5 heated outdoor. **Activities:** golf-9 holes, exercise room. **Guest Services:** valet laundry, wireless Internet.

TROY MARRIOTT   Phone: (248)680-9797   ⑨

▼▼▼▼ Hotel
$189-$199

Address: 200 W Big Beaver Rd 48084 **Location:** I-75, exit 69 (Big Beaver Rd), just e. **Facility:** Smoke free premises. 350 units. 17 stories, interior corridors. **Terms:** cancellation fee imposed. **Amenities:** high-speed Internet (fee). **Pool(s):** heated indoor. **Activities:** whirlpool, exercise room. **Guest Services:** valet and coin laundry, area transportation-within 5 mi, wireless Internet.

AAA Benefit:
Members save 5% or more off best available rate.

——— WHERE TO DINE ———

BIG BEAVER TAVERN   Phone: 248/680-0066   ⑫

▼▼▼ American
$8-$25

This casual eatery focuses on sports and fun, with multiple TVs hanging from the ceiling broadcasting the day's game, and ongoing competitions of darts keeping patrons occupied. The menu focuses on pub favorites such as cheese sticks, chicken tenders, burgers and sandwiches, plus steaks and chicken. The dessert selections are available as carry out. **Bar:** full bar. **Reservations:** required. **Hours:** 11 am-11 pm, Sun noon-9 pm. Closed major holidays. **Address:** 645 E Big Beaver Rd 48083 **Location:** I-75, exit 65 (Beaver Rd), 1.3 mi e.

CAFÉ SUSHI   Phone: 248/280-1831   ㉗

▼▼ Japanese
$6-$25

In a small mall across from several automobile dealerships, the restaurant draws patrons primarily for its super-fresh sushi. Also offered are tempura, noodles and teriyaki. Dark and pale-green striped wallpaper and Impressionist paintings, belie the fact that this is first and foremost a Japanese restaurant, complete with two tatami rooms and a sushi bar. **Bar:** full bar. **Reservations:** suggested. **Hours:** 11:30 am-2 & 5:30-10:30 pm, Fri & Sat-11 pm, Sun 4 pm-10 pm. Closed major holidays. **Address:** 1933 W Maple Rd 48084 **Location:** Between Crooks Rd and Coolidge Hwy; in Cambridge Crossings Shopping Plaza.

CAMP TICONDEROGA   Phone: 248/828-2825

▼▼▼ American
$8-$25

As the name might suggest, the boisterous, northwoods-inspired sports bar and lodge features plenty of duck prints and mounted trophy heads. Farmed game-such as elk, emu, venison, buffalo and duck-highlight a menu that also lists beef steaks, chicken and burgers. **Bar:** full bar. **Hours:** 11 am-10 pm, Fri & Sat-11 pm, Sun-9 pm. **Address:** 5725 Rochester Rd 48085 **Location:** Between Long Lake and Square Lake rds; at Sylvan Glen Golf Course.

THE CAPITAL GRILLE   Phone: 248/649-5300   ⑲

▼▼▼▼ American
$11-$45

Cherry wood and red leather assist in making this "clubby" dining room a beautiful spot to dine on excellent cuts of dry-aged beef. The staff is highly attentive and knowledgeable. **Bar:** full bar. **Hours:** 11 am-10 pm, Fri & Sat-11 pm, Sun 5 pm-9 pm; holiday hours may vary. Closed: 11/24, 12/25. **Address:** 2800 W Big Beaver Rd 48084 **Location:** I-75, exit 69 (Big Beaver Rd), 1 mi w; at Somerset Collection North; between Hudson's and Nordstrom. **Parking:** on-site and valet.

CHARLEY'S CRAB   Phone: 248/879-2060

▼▼▼▼ Seafood
$7-$43

The comfortable restaurant is known for creative preparations of fresh seafood, such as tuna schimini, crab-stuffed trout and the signature Charley's chowder. A good variety of wine is available. Service is attentive, friendly and fittingly inquisitive. **Bar:** full bar. **Reservations:** suggested, weekends. **Hours:** 11 am-10 pm, Fri-11 pm, Sat 5 pm-11 pm, Sun 10 am-2 & 3-9 pm. Closed: 12/25. **Address:** 5498 Crooks Rd 48098 **Location:** I-75, exit 72 (Crooks Rd); in Ramada Plaza Troy/Detroit. **Parking:** on-site and valet.

CHINESE KENO   Phone: 248/879-3232

▼▼▼ Chinese
$6-$12

This attractively decorated restaurant features a wide range of Cantonese, Hong Kong and Szechuan cuisine on its menu. **Hours:** 11 am-9 pm, Fri-10:30 pm, Sat noon-10:30 pm, Sun noon-9 pm. Closed: 7/4, 11/24. **Address:** 2081 South Blvd W 48098 **Location:** I-75, exit 72 (Crooks Rd), 1.4 mi n; jct Crooks Rd.

J. ALEXANDER'S RESTAURANT   Phone: 248/816-8379   ⑱

▼▼▼ American
$12-$27

The busy and casual restaurant prepares classic fare—including steak, grilled fish and prime rib—in the open kitchen. The dessert menu is excellent. **Bar:** full bar. **Hours:** 11 am-10 pm, Fri & Sat-11 pm, Sun 11:30 am-9 pm. Closed major holidays. **Address:** 2800 W Big Beaver Rd 48084 **Location:** I-75, exit 69 (Big Beaver Rd), 1 mi w; in Somerset Collection North. **Parking:** on-site and valet.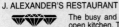

(See map and index starting on p. 244)

JOE KOOL'S
Phone: 248/526-5665   (11)

American
$8-$17

The emphasis is on fun at this popular pub, where a menu strewn with tongue-in-cheek sayings such as "better than hospital food" and "no pants, no service" draw smiles. Not surprisingly, the menu focuses on pub foods ranging from burgers and pizzas to wings and quesadillas. **Bar:** full bar. **Hours:** 11 am-2 am, Sun from noon. Closed: 11/24, 12/25 & Easter. **Address:** 1835 E Big Beaver Rd 48083 **Location:** I-75, exit 69 (Big Beaver Rd), 2 mi e.

KONA GRILL
Phone: 248/619-9060   (13)

New American
$9-$30

The eclectic menu reflects Pacific influences. In addition to noodle dishes and sushi, it lists specialties of macadamia nut chicken and lemon grass-encrusted swordfish. The dining room has a large aquarium, a private area and a sushi bar. The patio opens during warm weather. **Bar:** full bar. **Hours:** 11 am-11 pm, Fri & Sat-midnight, Sun-10 pm. Closed: 11/24, 12/25. **Address:** 30 E Big Beaver Rd 48083 **Location:** I-75, exit 69 (Big Beaver Rd), 0.5 mi e.

LAKESHORE GRILL
Phone: 248/597-2040   (28)

American
$9-$14

This bright, open dining room overlooks the courtyard of the mall. The menu is anything but department store, as several world famous chefs have collaborated to create a well-designed menu of comfort food ranging from backyard barbecue chicken quesadillas, the flagship steak salad, slow-roasted breast of turkey and lake perch fish and chips. Desserts include banana splits and pineapple upside down cake. **Bar:** full bar. **Hours:** 11 am-8 pm, Sun noon-4 pm. Closed: 11/24, 12/25 & Easter. **Address:** 500 W 14 Mile Rd (Oakland Mall) 48083 **Location:** I-75, exit 65 (W 14 Mile Rd), just e; in Oakland Mall, 2nd floor of Macy's.

MAGGIANO'S LITTLE ITALY
Phone: 248/205-1060   (17)

Italian
$11-$38

Diners savor scrumptious, traditional favorites served in a bustling atmosphere reminiscent of Little Italy. The dining area projects an early-20th-century feel; loud conversations bouncing off high ceilings evoke a sense of the Roaring '20s. **Bar:** full bar. **Hours:** 11 am-10 pm, Fri & Sat-11 pm, Sun noon-9 pm. Closed: 12/25. **Address:** 2089 W Big Beaver Rd 48084 **Location:** I-75, exit 69 (Big Beaver Rd), 1 mi w.

McCORMICK & SCHMICK'S
Phone: 248/637-6400   (23)

Seafood
$7-$32

This place is all about seafood, which is imported from all over the world. Among good choices are Washington state oysters, Maine clams, delicate Hawaiian escolar and tuna from Ecuador. The club-like decor is cozy, and expert staff provide able assistance. **Bar:** full bar. **Hours:** 11:30 am-10 pm, Sun noon-8 pm. Closed: 12/25. **Address:** 2850 Coolidge Hwy 48084 **Location:** I-75, exit 69 (Big Beaver Rd), 1 mi w to jct Big Beaver Rd; behind Saks at Somerset Collection South.

MON JIN LAU
Phone: 248/689-2332   (24)

Chinese
$7-$26

This restaurant offers food that is so original that the term "Nu-Asian" was coined just to describe the endless influences that exert themselves in these dishes. Prompt, friendly servers deliver Asian cuisine with a creative bent as well as sushi items. **Bar:** full bar. **Reservations:** suggested, weekends. **Hours:** 11 am-11 pm, Fri-midnight, Sat & Sun 4 pm-midnight. Closed: 11/24, 12/25. **Address:** 1515 E Maple Rd 48083 **Location:** I-75, exit 67 (Stephenson Hwy), 1 mi s.

MORTON'S THE STEAKHOUSE
Phone: 248/404-9845   (15)

Steak
$33-$48

Patrons should make sure to reserve ahead for the popular, well-known steakhouse. Large portions, including huge cuts of fine beef and plentiful seafood, are the norm. Even the vegetables are oversized, with baked potatoes big enough for sharing. **Bar:** full bar. **Hours:** 5:30 pm-11 pm, Sun 5 pm-10 pm. Closed major holidays. **Address:** 888 W Big Beaver Rd 48084 **Location:** I-75, exit 69 (Big Beaver Rd), just w.

OCEAN PRIME
Phone: 248/458-0500   (22)

Seafood
$12-$48

A self-proclaimed reinvention of the American supper club, the restaurant combines elegant surroundings and servers in white jackets with sumptuous seafood and steak selections, all with the soft notes of live jazz music hanging in the background. Menu selections include truffled deviled eggs, oysters Rockefeller, prime steaks and in-season line-caught fish ranging from Chilean sea bass to king salmon to Atlantic halibut to mountain trout. A raw bar is also offered. Entertainment. **Bar:** full bar. **Hours:** 11:30 am-10 pm, Fri-11 pm, Sat 4 pm-11 pm, Sun 4 pm-9 pm. Closed major holidays. **Address:** 2915 Coolidge Hwy 48084 **Location:** I-75, exit 69 (Big Beaver Rd), 1.5 mi w. **Parking:** on-site and valet.

P.F. CHANG'S CHINA BISTRO
Phone: 248/816-8000   (21)

Chinese
$10-$21

Trendy, upscale decor provides a pleasant backdrop for New Age Chinese dining. Appetizers, soups and salads are a meal by themselves. Vegetarian plates and sides, noodles, meins, chicken and meat dishes are created from exotic, fresh ingredients. **Bar:** full bar. **Hours:** 11 am-11 pm, Fri & Sat-midnight, Sun-10 pm. Closed: 11/24, 12/25. **Address:** 2801 W Big Beaver Rd 48084 **Location:** I-75, exit 69 (Big Beaver Rd), 1 mi w; at Somerset Collection South. **Parking:** on-site and valet.

PRIYA
Phone: 248/269-0100   (25)

Indian
$8-$17

Intriguing South Indian dishes are delightful in fragrance, appearance and taste. The menu lists seven kinds of dosas served with sambar and little bowls of tomato, coconut and mint sauces. The dining room is pretty, stylish and quietly serene. **Bar:** full bar. **Hours:** 11 am-2:30 & 5-10 pm, Sat 11 am-10 pm, Sun 11 am-9 pm. Closed: 11/24, 12/25. **Address:** 72 W Maple Rd 48084 **Location:** Just w of jct Livernois Rd.

(See map and index starting on p. 244)

RECIPES
American
$6-$13

Phone: 248/614-5390   (16)

Open for breakfast and lunch, the cozy restaurant offers the standards of eggs and pancakes. However, by using fresh ingredients and influences ranging from Southern and Southwestern to vegetarian and Asian, this place enables diners to experience their meal from a different culture. **Hours:** 7 am-2:30 & 5-10 pm, Sat 7 am-3 & 5-10 pm, Sun & Mon 7 am-2:30 pm. Closed major holidays. **Address:** 2919 Crooks Rd 48084 **Location:** I-75, exit 69 (Big Beaver Rd), 0.5 mi w to Crooks Rd, then just s. CALL ⑤M

RIDLEY'S BAKERY CAFE
Deli
$5-$10

Phone: 248/689-8638   (10)

First-timers shouldn't mistake this little spot, with only a few tables, for anything other than a tempting bakery. The beautiful displays of fancy-looking desserts will surely tug at the sweet tooth after a meal of a gourmet sandwich, soup or salad. **Hours:** 6 am-6 pm, Sat 7 am-4 pm. Closed major holidays; also Sun. **Address:** 4054 Rochester Rd 48085 **Location:** Jct Wattles Rd. CALL ⑤M

RUTH'S CHRIS STEAK HOUSE
Steak
$20-$45

Phone: 248/269-8424   (14)

The main fare is steak, which is prepared from several cuts of prime beef and cooked to perfection, but the menu also lists lamb, chicken and seafood dishes. Guests should come hungry because the side dishes, which are among the a la carte offerings, could make a meal in themselves. **Bar:** full bar. **Reservations:** suggested. **Hours:** 5 pm-10 pm, Sat 4:30 pm-11 pm, Sun 4:30 pm-9 pm. Closed major holidays. **Address:** 755 W Big Beaver Rd, Suite 151 48084 **Location:** I-75, exit 69 (Big Beaver Rd), just w. **Parking:** on-site and valet. CALL ⑤M

SHIELD'S OF TROY
Pizza
$7-$13

Phone: 248/637-3131   (26)

Part of metro Detroit since 1937, the family-oriented restaurant specializes in mouthwatering deep-dish square pizza and specialty salads. Other notable menu items include pasta and barbecue pork ribs. **Bar:** full bar. **Hours:** 11 am-11 pm, Fri & Sat-midnight, Sun noon-9:30 pm. Closed major holidays. **Address:** 1476 W Maple Rd 48084 **Location:** I-75, exit 69 (Big Beaver Rd), 0.7 mi w, 1 mi s on Crooks Rd, then w. CALL ⑤M

SUSHI DO
Japanese
$7-$12

Phone: 248/265-4400

Often packed with local office workers at lunch time, the small Japanese grocery store boasts a small, attractively decorated sushi bar, where guests can sample an extensive array of incredibly fresh sushi and noodle dishes. **Hours:** 11 am-8 pm. Closed major holidays. **Address:** 5365 Crooks Rd 48098 **Location:** I-75, exit 72 (Crooks Rd), just w. CALL ⑤M

ZODIAC AT NEIMAN MARCUS
American
$12-$40

Phone: 248/643-3300   (20)

Hidden away on the third floor of Neiman Marcus, the tiny but quietly elegant dining room serves lunch almost exclusively. Attentive service and a superbly executed menu—which lists offerings ranging from rib-eye steak sandwiches to soft-shell crabs to desserts made in house—make this a spot worth seeking out. **Bar:** wine only. **Hours:** 11 am-3 pm, Fri & Sat-4 pm. Closed major holidays; also Sun. **Address:** 2705 W Big Beaver Rd 48084 **Location:** I-75, exit 69 (Big Beaver Rd), 1 mi w; on 3rd Floor of Neiman Marcus Department Store. **Parking:** on-site and valet. CALL ⑤M

ZOUP!
Deli
$4-$8

Phone: 248/435-5300

One of several Detroit locations, the restaurant encourages diners to sample any of a dozen hand-crafted soups served daily from a rotation nearly 200 varieties. **Hours:** 11 am-8 pm. Closed major holidays; also Sun. **Address:** 2873 W Maple Rd 48084 **Location:** Jct Coolidge Hwy. CALL ⑤M

UTICA pop. 4,577

COMFORT INN
Hotel
$80-$110

Phone: (586)739-7111

Address: 11401 Hall Rd 48317 **Location:** Jct Van Dyke Ave (SR 53). **Facility:** Smoke free premises. 101 units, some kitchens. 3 stories, interior corridors. **Terms:** cancellation fee imposed. **Amenities:** video games (fee). *Some:* safes. **Activities:** exercise room. **Guest Services:** valet and coin laundry, wireless Internet. **Free Special Amenities:** expanded continental breakfast and high-speed Internet. SAVE BIZ ⊠ ⚒ ▤ /SOME UNITS FEE 🐾 🛗 🖥

COURTYARD BY MARRIOTT
Hotel
$121-$154

Phone: (586)997-6100

Address: 46000 Utica Park Blvd 48315 **Location:** Jct Van Dyke Ave (SR 53) and Hall Rd (SR 59), just n. **Facility:** Smoke free premises. 90 units. 3 stories, interior corridors. **Terms:** cancellation fee imposed. **Amenities:** high-speed Internet. **Pool(s):** heated indoor. **Activities:** whirlpool, exercise room. **Guest Services:** valet and coin laundry, wireless Internet.

AAA Benefit:	Members save a minimum 5% off the best available rate.

 🍴 CALL ⑤M 🛏 BIZ ⊠ ⚒ ▤ /SOME UNITS 🛗 🖥

HAMPTON INN DETROIT/SHELBY TOWNSHIP

Hotel
$79-$99

Phone: (586)731-4267

Address: 51620 Shelby Pkwy 48315 **Location:** Jct Van Dyke Ave (SR 53) and 23 Mile Rd, just e. **Facility:** Smoke free premises. 90 units. 4 stories, interior corridors. **Terms:** 1-7 night minimum stay, cancellation fee imposed. **Amenities:** high-speed Internet. **Pool(s):** heated indoor. **Activities:** whirlpool, exercise room. **Guest Services:** valet and coin laundry, wireless Internet.

> **AAA Benefit:**
> Members save up to 10% everyday!

HOLIDAY INN EXPRESS HOTEL & SUITES

Hotel
$89-$135

Phone: (586)803-0400

Address: 45555 Utica Park Blvd 48315 **Location:** Jct Van Dyke Ave (SR 53) and Hall Rd (SR 59), just n. **Facility:** Smoke free premises. 104 units. 4 stories, interior corridors. **Terms:** 3 day cancellation notice. **Amenities:** high-speed Internet. **Pool(s):** heated indoor. **Activities:** exercise room. **Guest Services:** valet and coin laundry, wireless Internet.

HYATT PLACE DETROIT/UTICA

Hotel
$69-$169

Phone: (586)803-0100

Address: 45400 Park Ave 48315 **Location:** Jct Van Dyke Ave (SR 53) and Hall Rd (SR 59). **Facility:** Smoke free premises. 123 units. 6 stories, interior corridors. **Terms:** cancellation fee imposed. **Amenities:** Some: high-speed Internet. **Pool(s):** heated indoor. **Activities:** exercise room. **Guest Services:** valet laundry, wireless Internet. **Free Special Amenities: continental breakfast and high-speed Internet.**

HYATT PLACE
AAA Benefit:
Ask for the AAA rate and save 10%.

LA QUINTA INN & SUITES DETROIT UTICA

Hotel
$65-$119

Phone: (586)731-4700

Address: 45311 Park Ave 48315 **Location:** Jct Van Dyke Ave (SR 53) and Hall Rd (SR 59), just n. **Facility:** Smoke free premises. 102 units. 4 stories, interior corridors. **Amenities:** video games (fee). Some: high-speed Internet. **Pool(s):** heated indoor. **Activities:** whirlpool. **Guest Services:** valet and coin laundry, wireless Internet.

STAYBRIDGE SUITES-UTICA

Extended Stay
Hotel
$119-$189

Phone: (586)323-0101

Address: 46155 Utica Park Blvd 48315 **Location:** Jct Van Dyke Ave (SR 53) and Hall Rd (SR 59), just n. **Facility:** Smoke free premises. 91 units, some two bedrooms and efficiencies. 3 stories, interior corridors. **Amenities:** high-speed Internet, safes. Fee: video games. **Pool(s):** heated outdoor. **Activities:** whirlpool, exercise room. **Guest Services:** complimentary and valet laundry, wireless Internet.

—— WHERE TO DINE ——

FILIPPA'S WINE BARREL

American
$9-$35

Phone: 586/254-1311

The warm, vintage surroundings invite diners to unwind while enjoying a wide array of choices from fowl to beef. The cool, delicious gazpacho is an excellent contrast to the well-seasoned encrusted, stuffed salmon. Service is attentive and adaptable. **Bar:** full bar. **Hours:** 11 am-11 pm, Fri & Sat-midnight, Sun noon-9 pm. Closed: 7/4, 12/25; also Super Bowl Sun. **Address:** 45125 Mound Rd 48317 **Location:** Jct Mound and Hall rds (SR 59).

RISTORANTE PICCIRILLI

Italian
$9-$28

Phone: 586/731-0610

The intimate dining room is a cozy setting in which to savor homemade Italian fare. Strolling musicians enhance the romantic ambience on Saturday evenings. In addition to a nice list of wines, the restaurant rolls out a tempting assortment of desserts. **Bar:** full bar. **Reservations:** suggested, weekends. **Hours:** 4:30 pm-10 pm, Sun 2 pm-8:30 pm. Closed major holidays; also Mon. **Address:** 52830 Van Dyke Ave 48316 **Location:** Jct Van Dyke Ave (SR 53) and 24 Mile Rd, just s.

WARREN pop. 138,247 (See map and index starting on p. 244)

BAYMONT INN & SUITES WARREN

Hotel
Rates not provided

Phone: 586/977-7270   **56**

Address: 7447 Convention Blvd 48092 **Location:** I-696, exit 23 (Van Dyke Ave), 2.8 mi n. **Facility:** Smoke free premises. 123 units. 3 stories, interior corridors. **Pool(s):** heated indoor. **Activities:** whirlpool, exercise room. **Guest Services:** valet laundry, wireless Internet. **Free Special Amenities: full breakfast and high-speed Internet.**

CANDLEWOOD SUITES-DETROIT WARREN

Extended Stay
Hotel
$69-$109

Phone: (586)978-1261   **59**

Address: 7010 Convention Blvd 48092 **Location:** I-696, exit 23 (Van Dyke Ave), 2.8 mi n. **Facility:** Smoke free premises. 122 efficiencies. 3 stories, interior corridors. **Terms:** office hours 7 am-11 pm. **Amenities:** high-speed Internet. **Activities:** gazebo with barbecue grill, exercise room. **Guest Services:** complimentary laundry, wireless Internet.

(See map and index starting on p. 244)

COMFORT INN

Hotel
Rates not provided

Phone: 586/268-9020 **57**

Address: 7001 Convention Blvd 48092 **Location:** I-696, exit 23 (Van Dyke Ave), 2.8 mi n. **Facility:** Smoke free premises. 97 units. 4 stories, interior corridors. **Amenities:** video games (fee), high-speed Internet. **Activities:** exercise room. **Guest Services:** valet and coin laundry, wireless Internet.

COMFORT SUITES

Hotel
$80-$200

Phone: (586)427-7000 **68**

Address: 2020 Walter Ruether Service Dr 48091 **Location:** I-696, exit 20 (Dequindre Rd). **Facility:** Smoke free premises. 65 units. 2 stories, interior corridors. **Terms:** cancellation fee imposed. **Pool(s):** heated indoor. **Guest Services:** valet laundry, wireless Internet. **Free Special Amenities: full breakfast and high-speed Internet.**

COURTYARD BY MARRIOTT-WARREN

Hotel
$114-$124

Phone: (586)751-5777 **62**

Address: 30190 Van Dyke Ave 48093 **Location:** I-696, exit 23 (Van Dyke Ave), 1.6 mi n. **Facility:** Smoke free premises. 147 units. 2-3 stories, interior corridors. **Terms:** cancellation fee imposed. **Amenities:** video games (fee), high-speed Internet. **Pool(s):** heated indoor. **Activities:** whirlpool, exercise room. **Guest Services:** valet and coin laundry, wireless Internet.

AAA Benefit:
Members save a minimum 5% off the best available rate.

EXTENDED STAY DELUXE DETROIT-WARREN

Extended Stay
Hotel
$68-$78

Phone: (586)558-5554 **64**

Address: 30125 N Civic Center Blvd 48093 **Location:** I-696, exit 23 (Van Dyke Ave), 1.5 mi n, then just e. **Facility:** Smoke free premises. 59 kitchen units. 3 stories, interior corridors. **Terms:** office hours 7 am-11 pm, cancellation fee imposed. **Activities:** barbecue grills, limited exercise equipment. **Guest Services:** coin laundry, wireless Internet.

FAIRFIELD INN BY MARRIOTT

Hotel
$80-$102

Phone: (586)939-1700 **58**

Address: 7454 Convention Blvd 48092 **Location:** I-696, exit 23 (Van Dyke Ave), 2.8 mi n. **Facility:** Smoke free premises. 115 units. 3 stories, interior/exterior corridors. **Terms:** cancellation fee imposed. **Pool(s):** heated outdoor. **Activities:** exercise room. **Guest Services:** valet laundry, wireless Internet.

AAA Benefit:
Members save a minimum 5% off the best available rate.

HAWTHORN SUITES

Extended Stay
Hotel
Rates not provided

Phone: 586/558-7870 **63**

Address: 30180 N Civic Center Blvd 48093 **Location:** I-696, exit 23 (Van Dyke Ave), 1.8 mi n. **Facility:** Smoke free premises. 76 units, some efficiencies. 2-3 stories, interior/exterior corridors. **Amenities:** safes (fee). *Some:* high-speed Internet. **Pool(s):** heated outdoor. **Activities:** exercise room, sports court. **Guest Services:** valet and coin laundry, wireless Internet.

HOLIDAY INN EXPRESS

Hotel
$104-$114

Phone: (586)754-9700 **66**

Address: 11500 11 Mile Rd 48089 **Location:** I-696, exit 24 (Hoover Rd), just s. **Facility:** Smoke free premises. 123 units. 2 stories, interior corridors. **Amenities:** video games (fee). **Pool(s):** outdoor. **Activities:** exercise room. **Guest Services:** valet and coin laundry, wireless Internet.

HOLIDAY INN HOTEL & SUITES

Hotel
$89-$114

Phone: (586)573-7600 **65**

Address: 30000 Van Dyke Ave 48093 **Location:** I-696, exit 23 (Van Dyke Ave), 1.5 mi n. **Facility:** Smoke free premises. 127 units. 6 stories, interior corridors. **Amenities:** video games (fee). **Pool(s):** heated indoor. **Activities:** whirlpool, exercise room. **Guest Services:** valet and coin laundry, wireless Internet.

LA QUINTA INN DETROIT WARREN TECH CENTER

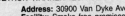

Hotel
$49-$89

Phone: (586)574-0550 **61**

Address: 30900 Van Dyke Ave 48093 **Location:** I-696, exit 23 (Van Dyke Ave), 1.8 mi n on SR 53. **Facility:** Smoke free premises. 97 units. 3 stories, interior corridors. **Amenities:** video games (fee). **Guest Services:** valet and coin laundry, wireless Internet.

RED ROOF INN-WARREN #070

Motel
$54-$74

Phone: (586)573-4300 **67**

Address: 26300 Dequindre Rd 48091 **Location:** I-696, exit 20 (Dequindre Rd), just ne. **Facility:** Smoke free premises. 136 units. 2 stories (no elevator), exterior corridors. **Amenities:** *Fee:* video games, safes. **Guest Services:** wireless Internet. **Free Special Amenities: local telephone calls.**

(See map and index starting on p. 244)

TOWNEPLACE SUITES BY MARRIOTT-WARREN

Extended Stay
Hotel
$107-$137

Phone: (586)264-8800   [60]

Address: 7601 Chicago Rd 48092 **Location:** I-696, exit 23 (Van Dyke Ave), 2 mi n. **Facility:** Smoke free premises. 79 efficiencies. 3 stories, interior corridors. **Terms:** cancellation fee imposed. **Amenities:** video games (fee), safes. **Pool(s):** heated indoor. **Activities:** exercise room. **Guest Services:** valet and coin laundry, wireless Internet.

SAVE ⓉⓁ CALL Ⓜ ☜ BIZ ✕ ⚓ ▤ ▣ ▱ / SOME UNITS FEE 🐕

AAA Benefit:
Members save a minimum 5% off the best available rate.

--- WHERE TO DINE ---

ANDIAMO

Italian
$9-$30

Phone: 586/268-3200   [70]

Andiamo is an Italian ristorante that combines a sophisticated atmosphere and skilled use of traditional Mediterranean ingredients to produce unique creations that will satisfy your craving for Italian-style fare. Entertainment. **Bar:** full bar. **Reservations:** suggested. **Hours:** 11:30 am-10 pm, Fri-11 pm, Sun 4 pm-9 pm. Closed major holidays. **Address:** 7096 E 14 Mile Rd 48092 **Location:** Jct Van Dyke Ave, just w. **Parking:** on-site and valet. CALL Ⓜ

BUDDY'S RESTAURANT PIZZERIA

Pizza
$8-$18

Phone: 586/574-9200

In business since 1946, the pizzeria is known for its square, deep-dish pizzas with crispy, buttery crust and a blend of four cheeses. Patrons should save room for the huge brownie sundae, which probably could serve a family of four. The decor is styled after an old-time diner and soda fountain, making this a great place for a casual dinner with friends or family. Nine locations are in the greater Detroit area, so finding a convenient one shouldn't be difficult. **Bar:** full bar. **Hours:** 11 am-10 pm, Fri-11 pm, Sat noon-11 pm, Sun noon-10 pm. Closed: 11/24, 12/25 & Easter. **Address:** 8100 Old 13 Mile Rd 48093 **Location:** I-696, exit 23 (Van Dyke Ave), 2 mi n. CALL Ⓜ

MICHELLE'S RESTAURANT & SWEETHEART BAKERY

American
$6-$13

Phone: 586/795-1665   [71]

Business executives sit side by side with moms and their toddlers at this popular local eatery. The menu may be basic and straightforward—with items such as meatloaf, burgers and sandwiches—but having an attached bakery might complicate the decision process. Open and somewhat noisy, the well-lit dining area has large slanted windows and is tended by a casual, efficient staff. **Bar:** full bar. **Hours:** 7 am-9 pm, Sun & Mon-8 pm. Closed: 9/5, 12/25. **Address:** 31920 Van Dyke Ave 48093 **Location:** I-696, exit 23 (Van Dyke Ave), 2.7 mi n.

WATERFORD pop. 73,150

COMFORT INN

Hotel
$90-$200

Phone: (248)666-8555

Address: 7076 Highland Rd 48327 **Location:** Jct SR 59 (Highland Rd) and Airport Rd, 1 mi w. Adjacent to shopping plaza. **Facility:** Smoke free premises. 111 units. 3 stories, interior corridors. **Terms:** cancellation fee imposed. **Amenities:** high-speed Internet. **Pool(s):** heated indoor. **Activities:** sauna, exercise room. **Fee:** game room. **Guest Services:** valet and coin laundry, area transportation-within 5 mi, wireless Internet.

HOLIDAY INN EXPRESS & SUITES

Hotel
$114-$154

Phone: (248)674-3434

Address: 4350 Pontiac Lake Rd 48328 **Location:** Jct SR 59 (Highland Rd). **Facility:** Smoke free premises. 83 units. 3 stories, interior corridors. **Terms:** cancellation fee imposed. **Amenities:** video games (fee), high-speed Internet. **Pool(s):** heated indoor. **Activities:** exercise room. **Guest Services:** valet laundry, wireless Internet.

—— WHERE TO DINE ——

LION'S DEN

American
$8-$25

Phone: 248/674-2251

Tables at the casual restaurant often are packed with locals, and lines are not uncommon. The menu lists fish, steaks, chicken and burgers. **Bar:** full bar. **Hours:** 11 am-10 pm, Fri 4 pm-11 pm, Sun 4 pm-9 pm. Closed major holidays. **Address:** 4444 Highland Rd 48328 **Location:** Jct Pontiac Lake Rd, just w.

WEST BLOOMFIELD pop. 64,862 (See map and index starting on p. 244)

—— WHERE TO DINE ——

DELI UNIQUE

Deli
$7-$9

Phone: 248/737-3890 (154)

Several twists set the upscale diner's fare apart from that of typical delicatessens. Fresh ingredients, including some made in house, go into the daily specials and sandwiches, which are served in enormous portions. **Hours:** 10 am-9 pm, Sat & Sun from 9 am. Closed major holidays. **Address:** 6724 Orchard Lake Rd 48322 **Location:** Just s of jct W Maple Rd.

J. ALEXANDER'S RESTAURANT

American
$8-$25

Phone: 248/538-8349 (155)

The busy and casual restaurant prepares classic fare—including steak, grilled fish and prime rib—in the open kitchen. The dessert menu is excellent. **Bar:** full bar. **Hours:** 11 am-10 pm, Fri & Sat-11 pm. Closed: 11/24, 12/25. **Address:** 7440 Orchard Lake Rd 48322 **Location:** Jct Northwestern Hwy (US 10), just n of W 14 Mile Rd.

THE LARK

Continental
$65-$80

Phone: 248/661-4466 (153)

The dining room has the ambience of an intimate Portuguese country inn. The menu of classic European selections, which changes bimonthly, might include such selections as rack of lamb. The pre-appetizer and dessert carts are loaded with temptations. Formal attire. **Bar:** full bar. **Reservations:** required. **Hours:** 6 pm-9 pm. Closed major holidays; also Sun & Mon. **Address:** 6430 Farmington Rd 48322 **Location:** Just n of jct Maple Rd.

WESTLAND pop. 86,602 (See map and index starting on p. 244)

—— WHERE TO DINE ——

ALEXANDER THE GREAT

American
$6-$15

Phone: 734/326-5410 (193)

Although the family-run restaurant offers a variety of Italian-American dishes, long lines of diners regularly visit on weekends for the house specialty of barbecue ribs and chicken. **Bar:** full bar. **Hours:** 11 am-10 pm, Sun from noon. Closed major holidays. **Address:** 34733 Warren Rd 48185 **Location:** Just e of jct Wayne Rd.

WIXOM pop. 13,263

COMFORT SUITES

Hotel
Rates not provided

Phone: 248/504-5080

Address: 28049 Wixom Rd 48393 **Location:** I-96, exit 159 (Wixom Rd), just s. **Facility:** Smoke free premises. 92 units. 4 stories, interior corridors. **Amenities:** high-speed Internet. **Pool(s):** heated indoor. **Activities:** exercise room. **Fee:** game room. **Guest Services:** valet and coin laundry, wireless Internet.

HOLIDAY INN EXPRESS

Hotel
$95-$159

Phone: (248)735-2781

Address: 48953 Alpha Dr 48393 **Location:** I-96, exit 159 (Wixom Rd), just n. Located in a business park. **Facility:** Smoke free premises. 110 units. 4 stories, interior corridors. **Terms:** 3 day cancellation notice. **Amenities:** high-speed Internet. **Pool(s):** heated indoor. **Activities:** whirlpool, exercise room. **Guest Services:** valet and coin laundry, wireless Internet. **Free Special Amenities:** expanded continental breakfast and high-speed Internet.

———— WHERE TO DINE ————

LEON'S FAMILY DINING

American
$7-$20

Phone: 248/926-5880

Across from the Ford plant, the comfortable family restaurant is a popular spot for locals to stop and grab lunch. The lunch menu offers a good value as the sandwich menu includes all-you-can-eat soup from a soup buffet. A variety of pasta dishes, steaks and grilled meats are staples on a menu that includes a wide selection of fish. Brunch is offered on weekends. **Bar:** full bar. **Hours:** 11 am-10 pm, Fri & Sat-11 pm, Sun-9 pm. Closed major holidays. **Address:** 29710 Wixom Rd 48393 **Location:** I-96, exit 159 (Wixom Rd), 0.5 mi n. CALL

WOODHAVEN pop. 12,530

BEST WESTERN WOODHAVEN INN

Hotel
$69-$76

Phone: (734)676-8000

Address: 21700 West Rd 48183 **Location:** I-75, exit 32 (West Rd), just w. **Facility:** Smoke free premises. 119 units. 2 stories (no elevator), interior corridors. **Parking:** winter plug-ins. **Terms:** 7 day cancellation notice. **Amenities:** video games (fee), safes. *Some:* high-speed Internet. **Pool(s):** heated indoor. **Activities:** sauna, exercise room. *Fee:* game room. **Guest Services:** valet laundry, wireless Internet. **Free Special Amenities:** local telephone calls and high-speed Internet.

AAA Benefit:
Members save up to 20%, plus 10% bonus points with free rewards program.

HOLIDAY INN EXPRESS HOTEL & SUITES

Hotel
$96-$110

Phone: (734)362-0933

Address: 21500 West Rd 48183 **Location:** I-75, exit 32 (West Rd), just w. **Facility:** Smoke free premises. 77 units. 3 stories, interior corridors. **Amenities:** video games (fee), high-speed Internet. **Pool(s):** heated indoor. **Activities:** whirlpool, exercise room. **Guest Services:** valet and coin laundry, wireless Internet.

National Shrine of the Little Flower, Royal Oak / © Jim West / age fotostock

This ends listings for the Detroit Vicinity.
The following page resumes the alphabetical listings of cities in Michigan.

DEWITT pop. 4,702

BAYMONT INN & SUITES DE WITT/LANSING NORTH

Hotel
$67-$116

Phone: (517)374-0000

Address: 1055 Aaron Dr 48820 **Location:** I-69, exit 87 (Old US 27), just s. Across from outlet mall. **Facility:** 75 units. 3 stories, interior corridors. **Parking:** winter plug-ins. **Amenities:** safes (fee). **Pool(s):** heated indoor. **Activities:** whirlpool, limited exercise equipment. **Guest Services:** valet laundry, wireless Internet. CALL ⬥M ⬥ ⬥ ⬥ / SOME UNITS FEE ⬥ ⬥ ⬥ ⬥

SLEEP INN

Hotel
$69-$129 4/1-10/31
$69-$99 11/1-4/30

Phone: (517)669-8823

Address: 1101 Commerce Park Dr 48820 **Location:** I-69, exit 87 (Old US 27), 0.8 mi n. **Facility:** Smoke free premises. 61 units. 2 stories (no elevator), interior corridors. **Parking:** winter plug-ins. **Terms:** cancellation fee imposed. **Amenities:** safes (fee). **Pool(s):** outdoor. **Guest Services:** coin laundry, wireless Internet. **Free Special Amenities:** expanded continental breakfast and high-speed Internet. SAVE ⬥ ⬥ ⬥ ⬥ ⬥ ⬥ / SOME UNITS FEE ⬥ ⬥ ⬥

DIMONDALE pop. 1,342

COMFORT INN & SUITES OF LANSING

Hotel
$79-$109

Phone: (517)345-6101

Address: 9742 Woodlane Dr 48821 **Location:** I-96, exit 98B (Lansing Rd N), just n. **Facility:** Smoke free premises. 82 units. 3 stories, interior corridors. **Terms:** cancellation fee imposed. **Amenities:** high-speed Internet, safes (fee). **Pool(s):** heated indoor. **Activities:** whirlpool, exercise room. **Guest Services:** valet and coin laundry, wireless Internet. **Free Special Amenities:** full breakfast and high-speed Internet.

SAVE ECO ⬥ CALL ⬥M ⬥ BIZ ⬥ ⬥ ⬥ ⬥ ⬥ / SOME UNITS FEE ⬥

DOLLAR BAY

—— WHERE TO DINE ——

QUINCY'S DINING COMPANY

American
$7-$22

Phone: 906/482-2118

On the snowmobile trail, the restaurant is filled with historic mining memorabilia. Charbroiled steaks, pasta, seafood and Chicago-style thin-crust pizza are among offerings. **Bar:** full bar. **Hours:** 11:30 am-11 pm; hours may vary. Closed: 12/25. **Address:** 48660 Hwy M-26 49922 **Location:** Center.

DOUGLAS pop. 1,214—See also Saugatuck p. 422

AMERICINN LODGE & SUITES OF DOUGLAS

Hotel
Rates not provided

Phone: 269/857-8581

Address: 2905 Blue Star Hwy 49406 **Location:** I-196, exit 36, 0.3 mi n. **Facility:** Smoke free premises. 45 units. 2 stories (no elevator), interior corridors. **Amenities:** safes (fee). **Pool(s):** heated indoor. **Activities:** sauna, whirlpool. **Guest Services:** coin laundry, wireless Internet. CALL ⬥M ⬥ ⬥ ⬥ / SOME UNITS FEE ⬥ ⬥ ⬥

THE KIRBY HOUSE

Bed & Breakfast
$100-$225 4/1-10/31
$100-$200 11/1-4/30

Phone: 269/857-2904

Address: 294 W Center St 49406 **Location:** Center. **Facility:** Three rooms of this Victorian manor have fireplaces. Smoke free premises. 6 units. 2 stories (no elevator), interior corridors. **Terms:** 2 night minimum stay - weekends, age restrictions may apply, 14 day cancellation notice-fee imposed. **Pool(s):** heated outdoor. **Activities:** whirlpool, bicycles, horseshoes. **Guest Services:** wireless Internet. ⬥ ⬥ ⬥ ⬥ ⬥ / SOME UNITS FEE ⬥

ROSEMONT INN RESORT

Bed & Breakfast
$165-$350 4/1-9/2
$160-$305 9/3-4/30

Phone: (269)857-2637

Address: 83 Lakeshore Dr 49406 **Location:** CR A2, 1 mi w on Center St, just n. Opposite Lake Michigan. **Facility:** Cozy accommodations are offered at this turn-of-the-century house opposite Lake Michigan. All rooms have fireplaces and many offer window seats. Smoke free premises. 14 units. 2 stories (no elevator), interior corridors. **Terms:** 1-3 night minimum stay - seasonal and/or weekends, age restrictions may apply, 14 day cancellation notice-fee imposed. **Pool(s):** heated outdoor. **Activities:** sauna, whirlpool, beach access, croquet, bocci, patio lounge, bicycles. **Guest Services:** wireless Internet. ⬥ ⬥

SHERWOOD FOREST BED & BREAKFAST

Bed & Breakfast
$110-$205 4/1-10/31
$110-$185 11/1-4/30

Phone: (269)857-1246

Address: 938 Center St 49406 **Location:** CR A2, 1 mi w. **Facility:** The Victorian-style property has rooms in unique decor themes, such as the log cabin, and some of them have fireplaces. Smoke free premises. 6 units, some cottages. 2 stories (no elevator), interior corridors. **Terms:** 2 night minimum stay - weekends, age restrictions may apply, 14 day cancellation notice-fee imposed. **Pool(s):** heated outdoor. **Activities:** bicycles. **Guest Services:** wireless Internet. ⬥ ⬥ ⬥ ⬥ / SOME UNITS ⬥ ⬥ ⬥

—— WHERE TO DINE ——

EVERYDAY PEOPLE CAFE

American
$16-$30

Phone: 269/857-4240

A cozy two-room restaurant located near the waterfront, this cafe offers filet saltimboca, gorgonzola pork chops, vegetarian pad thai and ahi tuna served rare. Tables on the patio are available for summer dining. **Bar:** full bar. **Hours:** 5:30 pm-10 pm, Fri & Sat-11 pm. Closed major holidays. **Address:** 11 Center St 49406 **Location:** Jct Main St; downtown. **Parking:** street only.

DOWAGIAC pop. 6,147

─── **WHERE TO DINE** ───

WOOD FIRE ITALIAN TRATTORIA

Italian
$11–$23

Phone: 269/782-0007

The restaurant's more formal Pompeii room offers décor meant to reflect the grandeur of its namesake, while its more casual room provides better seating for the live jazz or blues bands that perform on Wednesday, Friday and Sunday nights. Most menu offerings prepared in the open kitchen take advantage of the traditional, wood-fired oven. Light Italian cuisine includes antipasti, salads, pizzas and traditional pastas as well as some not-so-Italian entrées. **Bar:** full bar. **Hours:** 11 am-9 pm, Sat-11 pm, Sun 4 pm-10 pm. Closed major holidays. **Address:** 134 S Front St 49047 **Location:** Between Commercial and Beeson sts; center. **Parking:** street only. CALL 🔵M

DUNDEE pop. 3,522

COUNTRY INN & SUITES BY CARLSON

Hotel
$89–$104

Phone: (734)529-8822

Address: 665 Tecumseh St 48131 **Location:** US 23, exit 17 (SR 50), just w. **Facility:** Smoke free premises. 70 units. 3 stories, interior corridors. **Terms:** 3 day cancellation notice-fee imposed. **Amenities:** high-speed Internet. **Pool(s):** heated indoor. **Activities:** whirlpool, exercise room. **Guest Services:** valet and coin laundry, wireless Internet. *(see ad p. 6)*

HOLIDAY INN EXPRESS SPLASH UNIVERSE RESORT-DUNDEE

Hotel
$79–$159

Phone: (734)529-5100

Address: 100 White Tail Dr 48131 **Location:** US 23, exit 17 (SR 50), just w. **Facility:** Smoke free premises. 163 units. 3 stories, interior corridors. **Terms:** check-in 4 pm, cancellation fee imposed. **Amenities:** high-speed Internet. **Pool(s):** 3 heated indoor. **Activities:** whirlpools, waterslide, indoor water park, exercise room. *Fee:* game room. **Guest Services:** valet and coin laundry, wireless Internet.

─── **WHERE TO DINE** ───

MUY LOCO BURRITO BAR

Mexican
$4–$8

Phone: 734/529-7330

The fun, casual restaurant adjoins a sports bar. On the menu are such favorites as nachos, quesadillas, tamales, fajitas, burritos, tacos, tostadas and enchiladas. Take-out also is available. **Bar:** full bar. **Hours:** 11 am-9 pm, Fri & Sat-10 pm. Closed major holidays. **Address:** 103 Cabela Blvd E 48131 **Location:** US 23, exit 17 (SR 50), just w. CALL 🔵M

WILDERNESS SPORTS BAR & GRILLE

American
$4–$12

Phone: 734/529-7220

A hunting-and-fishing-themed restaurant, the menu offers a modest selection of regional seafood and traditional bar foods. **Bar:** full bar. **Hours:** 11 am-10 pm, Fri-11 pm. Closed major holidays. **Address:** 103 Cabela Blvd E 48131 **Location:** US 23, exit 17 (SR 50), just w.

EAST GRAND RAPIDS pop. 10,764 (See map and index starting on p. 324)

─── **WHERE TO DINE** ───

ROSE'S

American
$8–$27

Phone: 616/458-1122 (30)

The noisy, bustling bistro and its breezy outdoor deck, overlook Reed's Lake. Pizzas cooked in a brick oven and homemade pasta dishes are at the center of a menu that features daily fish specials. Tiramisu and creme brulee are delicious dessert choices. **Bar:** full bar. **Hours:** 11 am-11 pm, Sun 9 am-9 pm. Closed: 1/1, 12/25. **Address:** 550 Lakeside Dr 49506 **Location:** 1.4 mi w of E Belt Line, just nw.

EAST LANSING pop. 46,525—See also Lansing p. 349

CANDLEWOOD SUITES

Extended Stay
Hotel
$59–$189

Phone: (517)351-8181

Address: 3545 Forest Rd 48910 **Location:** I-496, exit 11 (Jolly Rd), just e to Collins Rd, 0.3 mi n, then just e. Located in a quiet area. **Facility:** Smoke free premises. 128 efficiencies. 3 stories, interior corridors. **Terms:** cancellation fee imposed. **Amenities:** high-speed Internet. **Guest Services:** complimentary and valet laundry, area transportation-within 5 mi. **Free Special Amenities:** local telephone calls and high-speed Internet.

EAST LANSING MARRIOTT AT UNIVERSITY PLACE

Hotel
$180–$230

Phone: (517)337-4440

Address: 300 Michigan Agricultural College Ave 48823 **Location:** Just n of Grand River Ave; downtown. **Facility:** Smoke free premises. 180 units. 7 stories, interior corridors. **Parking:** on-site (fee). **Terms:** cancellation fee imposed. **Amenities:** *Fee:* video games, high-speed Internet. **Pool(s):** heated indoor. **Activities:** sauna, whirlpool, exercise room. **Guest Services:** valet and coin laundry, area transportation-within 2 mi, wireless Internet.

AAA Benefit:
Members save 5% or more off best available rate.

GATEHOUSE SUITES EAST LANSING

Phone: 517/332-7711

Extended Stay
Hotel
Rates not provided

Address: 1600 E Grand River Ave 48823 **Location:** US 127, exit Grand River Ave, 2.6 mi se on SR 43. **Facility:** Smoke free premises. 60 kitchen units, some two bedrooms. 2 stories (no elevator), exterior corridors. **Pool(s):** heated outdoor. **Activities:** whirlpool, limited exercise equipment, sports court. **Guest Services:** valet and coin laundry, wireless Internet.

 / SOME UNITS FEE

HAMPTON INN

Phone: (517)324-2072

Hotel
$87-$151

Address: 2500 Coolidge Rd 48823 **Location:** US 127, exit Lake Lansing Rd, just e. **Facility:** Smoke free premises. 86 units. 4 stories, interior corridors. **Terms:** 1-7 night minimum stay, cancellation fee imposed. **Amenities:** video games (fee). **Pool(s):** heated indoor. **Activities:** whirlpool, exercise room. **Guest Services:** valet laundry, wireless Internet.

> **AAA Benefit:**
> Members save up to 10% everyday!

 CALL / SOME UNITS

HOWARD JOHNSON INN

Phone: (517)351-5500

Motel
$67-$143

Address: 1100 Trowbridge Rd 48823 **Location:** US 127, exit Trowbridge Rd, just e. **Facility:** Smoke free premises. 55 units. 2 stories (no elevator), interior/exterior corridors. **Terms:** cancellation fee imposed. **Amenities:** high-speed Internet, safes (fee). **Pool(s):** heated indoor. **Activities:** whirlpool, exercise room. **Guest Services:** wireless Internet.

 / SOME UNITS FEE

KELLOGG HOTEL AND CONFERENCE CENTER

Phone: (517)432-4000

Hotel
$124-$199 4/1-12/31
$124-$194 1/1-4/30

Address: 55 S Harrison Rd 48824 **Location:** I-496, exit 9 (Trowbridge Rd), just e, then 0.5 mi n. Located on Michigan State University campus. **Facility:** Smoke free premises. 160 units. 7 stories, interior corridors. **Terms:** check-in 4 pm, cancellation fee imposed. **Dining:** The State Room, see separate listing. **Activities:** recreational privileges, exercise room. **Guest Services:** valet laundry, area transportation-within 5 mi, wireless Internet. **Free Special Amenities: high-speed Internet and airport transportation.**

SAVE ECO CALL / SOME UNITS

—— WHERE TO DINE ——

BEGGAR'S BANQUET

Phone: 517/351-4573

American
$9-$20

In business since the mid-1970s, the casual restaurant has two dining rooms: one classy and one rustic. Such dishes as baked chili and chicken Kiev make up the traditional menu. Artwork created and donated by local students decorates the walls. **Bar:** full bar. **Reservations:** suggested, weekends. **Hours:** 11 am-11:30 pm, Fri-midnight, Sat 10 am-midnight, Sun 10 am-10:30 pm. Closed: 12/25. **Address:** 218 Abbott Rd 48823 **Location:** Just n of Grand River Ave; center. **Parking:** street only. CALL

DUBLIN SQUARE

Phone: 517/351-2222

American
$8-$27

The interior of this boisterous bar and restaurant is set up as a large, open square, with polished wood floors, wainscoting and a vaulted ceiling fitted with stained-glass skylights over the massive mahogany bar, which was hand-carved in Dublin. Guests tuck into small recessed areas around the central bar to enjoy steaks, shepherd's pie, bangers and mash, fish and chips, or the specialty blackberry barbecue ribs. A game room with a dartboard and pool table is at the back of the bar. **Bar:** full bar. **Hours:** 11 am-midnight, Sun-10 pm. Closed major holidays. **Address:** 327 Abbott Rd 48823 **Location:** Just n of Grand River Ave; center. CALL

THE STATE ROOM

Phone: 517/432-5049

American
$9-$25

This quietly upscale restaurant offers relaxed dining for all three meals. Focusing on seasonal Michigan products, the menu is further supplemented by a visiting chef series which has brought exciting and innovative chefs to the restaurant. **Bar:** full bar. **Hours:** 6:30 am-10 pm, Sun-2 pm. Closed major holidays. **Address:** 55 S Harrison Rd 48824 **Location:** I-496, exit 9 (Trowbridge Rd), just e, then 0.5 mi n; in Kellogg Hotel and Conference Center. **Parking:** on-site (fee).

EASTPOINTE   (See map and index starting on p. 244)

—— WHERE TO DINE ——

WEEKDAY CAFE

Phone: 586/778-6433   176

Deli
$5-$12

Making most of his items from scratch, the chef/owner even takes the time to grind his own sirloin steak for hamburgers. Featuring at least four daily soups, the menu applies a few unusual twists to regular items, such as fish and chips made with whitefish, grilled chicken paired with chili mole and a ham sandwich made with zucchini bread and pineapple cream cheese. True to its name, the bright, cheery restaurant is not open on weekends. **Hours:** 7 am-7 pm. Closed major holidays; also Sat & Sun. **Address:** 16749 E 9 Mile Rd 48021 **Location:** I-94, exit 227 (E 9 Mile Rd), 1 mi w.

EAST TAWAS pop. 2,951

BAMBI MOTEL

Phone: 989/362-4582

Motel
$49-$99

Address: 1100 E Bay St 48730 **Location:** 0.5 mi n on US 23. **Facility:** Smoke free premises. 15 units. 1 story, exterior corridors. **Terms:** office hours 8 am-11 pm, 2 night minimum stay - seasonal and/or weekends, cancellation fee imposed. **Guest Services:** wireless Internet.

 / SOME UNITS FEE   FEE

TAWAS BAY BEACH RESORT

Hotel
$70-$189

Phone: (989)362-8601

Address: 300 E Bay St 48730 **Location:** On US 23 W. Located on Lake Huron, next to state park marina. **Facility:** Smoke free premises. 103 units. 2 stories (no elevator), interior corridors. **Terms:** check-in 4 pm, 3 day cancellation notice-fee imposed. **Pool(s):** heated indoor. **Activities:** sauna, whirlpool, beach access, rental paddleboats, playground, exercise room, shuffleboard. *Fee:* boat dock, personal watercraft, game room. **Guest Services:** coin laundry, wireless Internet. **Free Special Amenities: local telephone calls and high-speed Internet.**

EDMORE pop. 1,244

MAXFIELD'S INN

Hotel
$70-$140 4/1-9/30
$60-$140 10/1-4/30

Phone: (989)427-8888

Address: 1106 E Main St 48829 **Location:** On SR 46; center. **Facility:** Smoke free premises. 50 units. 2 stories (no elevator), interior corridors. **Terms:** cancellation fee imposed. **Pool(s):** heated indoor. **Activities:** whirlpool, steamrooms, exercise room, massage. **Guest Services:** coin laundry, wireless Internet.

ELK RAPIDS pop. 1,700

—— **WHERE TO DINE** ——

PEARL'S

Cajun
$5-$20

Phone: 231/264-0530

Voodoo dolls, Mardi Gras beads, papier-mache doodads and the music all add up to a taste of the Big Easy. On the menu is a variety of Cajun and Creole selections, from spicy gumbo ya ya and pasta jambalaya, to beef brisket and muffuletta sandwiches. The scratch-made desserts are to die for. **Bar:** full bar. **Hours:** 11 am-10 pm, Fri & Sat-11 pm, Sun 10 am-10 pm. Closed: 11/24, 12/24, 12/25. **Address:** 617 Ames St 49629 **Location:** From US 31, 0.5 mi e of stoplight.

ESCANABA pop. 13,140

BAY VIEW MOTEL

Motel
$55-$65 4/1-9/15
$45-$65 9/16-4/30

Phone: 906/786-2843

Address: 7110 US Hwy 2 & 41 & M35 49837 **Location:** 4.5 mi n on US 2/41 and SR 35. **Facility:** Smoke free premises. 19 units. 1-2 stories (no elevator), interior/exterior corridors. **Parking:** winter plug-ins. **Terms:** 4 day cancellation notice. **Activities:** sauna, basketball. **Guest Services:** wireless Internet.

BEST WESTERN PIONEER INN & SUITES

Motel
$84-$114

Phone: (906)786-0602

Address: 2635 Ludington St 49829 **Location:** 1 mi w on US 2/41. **Facility:** Smoke free premises. 88 units. 2 stories (no elevator), interior corridors. **Parking:** winter plug-ins. **Terms:** cancellation fee imposed. **Amenities:** *Some:* high-speed Internet. **Pool(s):** heated indoor. **Guest Services:** valet laundry, wireless Internet. **Free Special Amenities: full breakfast and high-speed Internet.**

AAA Benefit:
Members save up to 20%, plus 10% bonus points with free rewards program.

COMFORT SUITES

Hotel
$90-$170

Phone: (906)786-9630

Address: 3600 Ludington St 49829 **Location:** 1.5 mi w on US 2/41. **Facility:** Smoke free premises. 60 units. 3 stories, interior corridors. **Terms:** check-in 4 pm. **Amenities:** high-speed Internet, safes (fee). **Pool(s):** heated indoor. **Activities:** whirlpool, waterslide, snowmobiling, exercise room. **Guest Services:** coin laundry, wireless Internet, tanning facilities.

ECONO LODGE

Hotel
$60-$109

Phone: (906)789-1066

Address: 921 N Lincoln Rd 49829 **Location:** 0.5 mi n on US 2/41 and SR 35. Located next to the U.P. State Fairgrounds. **Facility:** 50 units. 2 stories (no elevator), interior corridors. **Activities:** sauna, whirlpool. **Guest Services:** wireless Internet. **Free Special Amenities: continental breakfast and high-speed Internet.**

HIAWATHA MOTEL

Motel
$50-$125

Phone: (906)786-1341

Address: 2400 Ludington St 49829 **Location:** 0.5 mi w on US 2/41. **Facility:** Smoke free premises. 20 units. 1 story, exterior corridors. **Terms:** office hours 7 am-11 pm. **Guest Services:** wireless Internet.

—— **WHERE TO DINE** ——

FERDINAND'S

Mexican
$7-$15

Phone: 906/786-8484

Located in the downtown area, the restaurant serves Mexican and American dishes. **Bar:** full bar. **Hours:** 11 am-9 pm, Fri & Sat-10 pm. Closed major holidays. **Address:** 1318 Ludington St 49829 **Location:** Downtown.

GREAT NORTHERN BUFFET

Phone: 906/789-0630

American
$6-$12

The popular family restaurant offers travelers a chance to make a quick stop for reasonably priced eats. **Hours:** 11 am-9 pm, Sun from 8:30 am; hours may vary. Closed: 12/25. **Address:** 521 N Lincoln Rd 49829 **Location:** 0.4 mi n on US 2/41 and SR 35.

HEREFORD AND HOPS

Phone: 906/789-1945

American
$5-$22

Patrons of the brew pub and restaurant can barbecue their own steaks, kebabs or catch of the day on the charcoal grill. **Bar:** full bar. **Hours:** 11 am-10 pm, Sun 4 pm-9 pm. **Address:** 624 Ludington St 49829 **Location:** Downtown.

HONG KONG BUFFET

Phone: 906/233-9999

International
$6-$10

The buffet at this casual restaurant lays out a wide selection of Chinese, American, Japanese and Cantonese dishes. Take-out service is also available. **Bar:** full bar. **Hours:** 11 am-10 pm; hours may vary. **Address:** 2100 Ludington St 49829 **Location:** Just e of jct US 2/41 and SR 35.

THE STONEHOUSE

Phone: 906/786-5003

American
$6-$28

The cozy dining room is a casual, informal spot for enjoying thoughtful preparations of chicken, seafood and steak. The house specialty is succulent prime rib. Diners should take time to check out the artwork and appreciate the attentive, efficient service. **Bar:** full bar. **Hours:** 11 am-2 & 5-9:30 pm, Fri-10 pm, Sat 5 pm-10 pm. Closed major holidays; also Sun. **Address:** 2223 Ludington St 49829 **Location:** 0.3 mi n at jct US 2/41 and SR 35.

SWEDISH PANTRY   *Menu on AAA.com*

Phone: 906/786-9606

Swedish
$6-$14

Recently recognized as one of the top twenty restaurants in Michigan, the cozy dining room is filled with unusual gifts and clocks as well as apples for good luck. On the menu are some of the area's best homemade dishes and bakery items. **Hours:** 8 am-7:30 pm, Sat-3 pm; hours may vary. Closed major holidays. **Address:** 819 Ludington St 49829 **Location:** Between S 8th and 7th sts; downtown.

EVART pop. 1,738

THE OSCEOLA GRAND HOTEL

Phone: (231)734-0470

Hotel
$79-$129

Address: 940 W 7th St 49631 **Location:** 0.8 mi w on US 10. **Facility:** Smoke free premises. 50 units. 2 stories (no elevator), interior corridors. **Parking:** winter plug-ins. **Terms:** 6 day cancellation notice. **Pool(s):** heated indoor. **Activities:** whirlpool, exercise room. **Guest Services:** coin laundry, wireless Internet.

FAIR HAVEN pop. 1,500

—— WHERE TO DINE ——

TIN FISH RESORT

Phone: 586/725-7888

Seafood
$8-$24

Patrons should never get lost in the nautical restaurant, as the circular dining room has compass points around the border and nautical charts on the wall. Views of the lake are spectacular. True to the theme, fresh fish prepared in varied manners is the house specialty, but a number of steaks and pasta dishes also share space on the menu. **Bar:** full bar. **Reservations:** suggested. **Hours:** Open 4/27-9/30; 11:30 am-10 pm. Closed major holidays. **Address:** 10069 Dixie Hwy 48023 **Location:** Just e of jct Church Rd and SR 29 (Dixie Hwy).

FARMINGTON HILLS —See Detroit p. 279.

FENNVILLE pop. 1,459

—— WHERE TO DINE ——

CRANE'S PIE PANTRY RESTAURANT & BAKERY

Phone: 269/561-2297

American
$7-$10

Settled at the back of the big "red barn," this popular restaurant serves freshly baked breads, seasonal fruit pies, fresh cider and hearty soups along with a section of hot or cold sandwiches. **Hours:** 9 am-8 pm, Sun from 11 am; 10 am-6 pm, Sun from 11 am 11/1-12/31; seasonal hours may vary. Closed: 11/24, 12/25 & Easter; also Mon in winter. **Address:** 6054 124th Ave (SR 89) 49408 **Location:** I-196, exit 34 (SR 89), 4 mi e.

FENTON pop. 10,582

HOLIDAY INN EXPRESS HOTEL & SUITES

Phone: (810)714-7171

Hotel
$99-$129 4/1-9/30
$89-$129 10/1-4/30

Address: 17800 Silver Pkwy 48430 **Location:** US 23, exit 78 (Owen Rd), just w, then 0.4 mi n. Across from a shopping mall. **Facility:** Smoke free premises. 69 units. 2 stories, interior corridors. **Pool(s):** heated indoor. **Activities:** whirlpool, limited exercise equipment. **Guest Services:** valet and coin laundry, wireless Internet.

—— WHERE TO DINE ——

FENTON HOTEL TAVERN & GRILLE
Phone: 810/750-9463

American
$10-$25

Allegedly haunted by two ghosts, one of which occasionally orders a drink at the bar, the hotel is home to a charming Victorian-style restaurant with a hint of intrigue. **Bar:** full bar. **Hours:** 4 pm-10 pm, Fri & Sat-11 pm, Sun 3 pm-9 pm. Closed: major holidays, 12/24. **Address:** 302 N Leroy St 48430 **Location:** US 23, exit 78 (Owen Rd), 1.1 mi e on Silver Lake Rd, then just n.

THE FRENCH LAUNDRY
Phone: 810/629-8852

Deli
$7-$26

Not far from the center of town, the loud, crowded, fun and trendy delicatessen serves a good variety of made-to-order sandwiches, salads and daily specials. Also offered are several Zingerman's products. **Bar:** full bar. **Hours:** 7 am-10 pm, Fri & Sat-11 pm, Sun-9 pm. Closed major holidays. **Address:** 125 W Shiawassee Ave 48430 **Location:** US 23, exit 78 (Owen Rd), 1 mi e. **Parking:** street only.

LUCKY'S STEAKHOUSE
Phone: 810/750-1400

American
$8-$25

Big portions are the trademark at the family-oriented favorite, where service is quick and attentive. **Bar:** full bar. **Hours:** 11 am-10 pm, Fri-11 pm, Sat noon-11 pm, Sun noon-9 pm. Closed major holidays. **Address:** 17500 Silver Pkwy 48430 **Location:** US 23, exit 78 (Owen Rd), just w, then 0.4 mi n. CALL [M]

FERNDALE —See Detroit p. 280.

FERRYSBURG pop. 3,040

—— WHERE TO DINE ——

ARBOREAL INN
Phone: 616/842-3800

American
$11-$33

Established in 1981, the moderately upscale restaurant is a favorite of the local crowd. There are several dining areas, including one with a warm, cozy fireplace. An extensive selection of wine accompanies choices on the diverse menu. **Bar:** full bar. **Reservations:** suggested, weekends. **Hours:** 4:30-9 pm, Wed & Thurs also 11 am-2 pm, Fri 11 am-2 & 4:30-10 pm, Sat 5 pm-10 pm; hours may vary. Closed major holidays; also Sun. **Address:** 18191 Old Grand Haven Rd 49456 **Location:** 1 mi n from US 31, exit Van Wagoner Rd W, 0.3 mi n on 174th Ave.

FLINT pop. 124,943

AMERICINN MOTEL & SUITES OF FLINT
Phone: (810)233-9000

Hotel
$79-$109

Address: 6075 Hill 23 Dr 48507 **Location:** US 23, exit 90 (Hill Rd), just w. **Facility:** Smoke free premises. 71 units. 3 stories, interior corridors. **Terms:** cancellation fee imposed. **Pool(s):** heated indoor. **Activities:** sauna, whirlpool. **Guest Services:** valet and coin laundry, wireless Internet. **Free Special Amenities: expanded continental breakfast and high-speed Internet.**

[SAVE] CALL [M] [symbols] / SOME UNITS FEE [symbols] FEE [symbols] FEE [symbols]

BAYMONT INN & SUITES-FLINT
Phone: (810)732-2300

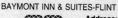
Hotel
$62-$107

Address: 4160 Pier North Blvd 48504 **Location:** I-75, exit 122 (Pierson Rd), just w. **Facility:** Smoke free premises. 88 units, some kitchens. 4 stories, interior corridors. **Pool(s):** heated indoor. **Activities:** whirlpool, exercise room. **Guest Services:** valet and coin laundry, wireless Internet.

[symbols] [symbols] [symbols] [symbols] [symbols] [symbols] / SOME UNITS FEE [symbols]

COURTYARD BY MARRIOTT
Phone: (810)232-3500

Hotel
$107-$137

Address: 5205 Gateway Center 48507 **Location:** US 23, exit 90 (Hill Rd), just e to Gateway Center, then just n. **Facility:** Smoke free premises. 102 units. 3 stories, interior corridors. **Terms:** cancellation fee imposed. **Pool(s):** heated indoor. **Activities:** whirlpool, exercise room. **Guest Services:** valet and coin laundry, wireless Internet.

> **AAA Benefit:**
> Members save a minimum 5% off the best available rate.

[symbols] CALL [M] [symbols] [symbols] [symbols] [symbols] / SOME UNITS FEE [symbols] [symbols] [symbols]

HAMPTON INN & SUITES
Phone: 810/234-8400

Hotel
Rates not provided

Address: 6060 Rashelle Dr 48507 **Location:** US 23, exit 90 (Hill Rd), just w. **Facility:** Smoke free premises. 100 units. 4 stories, interior corridors. **Terms:** check-in 4 pm. **Amenities:** high-speed Internet. **Pool(s):** heated indoor. **Activities:** whirlpool, exercise room. **Guest Services:** valet and coin laundry, wireless Internet.

> **AAA Benefit:**
> Members save up to 10% everyday!

CALL [M] [symbols] [BIZ] [symbols] [symbols] [symbols] / SOME UNITS [symbols] [symbols]

HOLIDAY INN EXPRESS FLINT CAMPUS AREA
Phone: (810)238-7744

Hotel
$79-$189 6/2-4/30
$79-$129 4/1-6/1

Address: 1150 Robert T Longway Blvd 48503 **Location:** I-475, exit 8A (Robert T Longway Blvd), just w. Located in a commercial area. **Facility:** Smoke free premises. 119 units. 5 stories, interior corridors. **Amenities:** safes. **Activities:** exercise room. **Guest Services:** valet and coin laundry, area transportation-within 5 mi, wireless Internet.

 [symbols] [symbols] CALL [M] [symbols] [symbols] [symbols] [symbols] [symbols] / SOME UNITS FEE [symbols]

RESIDENCE INN BY MARRIOTT

▼▼▼▼
Extended Stay
Hotel
$116-$148

Phone: (810)424-7000

Address: 2202 W Hill Rd 48507 **Location:** US 23, exit 90 (Hill Rd), just e. Located in a commercial area. **Facility:** Smoke free premises. 87 units, some two bedrooms, efficiencies and kitchens. 3 stories, interior corridors. **Terms:** cancellation fee imposed. **Pool(s):** heated indoor. **Activities:** whirlpool, exercise room, sports court. **Guest Services:** valet and coin laundry, wireless Internet. CALL 🆒Ⓜ 🛁 ✖ 📶 🅱 🖥 🖳 / SOME UNITS FEE 🐾

SLEEP INN FLINT AIRPORT

▼▼▼▼
Hotel
$60-$80

Phone: (810)232-7777

Address: 2325 Austin Pkwy 48507 **Location:** I-75, exit 117B (Miller Rd) northbound; exit 117 (Miller Rd) southbound, just e. Located in a commercial area. **Facility:** Smoke free premises. 60 units. 3 stories, interior corridors. **Amenities:** safes (fee). **Pool(s):** heated indoor. **Activities:** whirlpool, recreational privileges, exercise room. **Guest Services:** valet and coin laundry, wireless Internet.

✈ 🛁 ✖ 📶 🖥

—— WHERE TO DINE ——

ITALIA GARDENS

▼▼ ▼▼
Italian
$8-$16

Phone: 810/720-4112

The small restaurant serves up many favorite entrees, such as spaghetti, ribs, manicotti and pizza. A modern Italian theme is evident in the casually upscale dining room, which is decorated with stone columns and candle-topped pedestal tables. **Bar:** beer & wine. **Hours:** 11 am-9 pm, Fri & Sat-10 pm, Sun noon-8 pm. Closed major holidays. **Address:** G-3273 Miller Rd 48507 **Location:** I-75, exit 117 (Miller Rd) southbound; exit 117B (Miller Rd) northbound, just w.

MAKUCH RED ROOSTER

▼▼ ▼▼
American
$7-$40

Phone: 810/742-9310

The building may be small and unassuming, but the flavors are big and bold in innovative specialties prepared by the creative chef. Such dishes as the fruit, vegetable and salmon platter are colorful, fresh and tasty. Service is friendly and efficient. **Bar:** full bar. **Hours:** 11 am-9 pm, Sat from 5 pm. Closed major holidays; also Sun. **Address:** 3302 Davison Rd 48506 **Location:** I-69, exit 138 (Dort Hwy), 1 mi n, then 1 mi e.

REDWOOD LODGE MESQUITE GRILL & BREW PUB

▼▼ ▼▼
American
$9-$38

Phone: 810/233-8000

The warm hunting lodge theme of this microbrewery sets the stage for a menu dedicated to mesquite-grilled specialties, including wild game, steak, seafood and wood-fired pizza. Hand-crafted beers and a laid-back cigar lounge add to the dining experience. **Bar:** full bar. **Hours:** 11 am-midnight, Fri & Sat-1 am, Sun noon-10 pm. Closed: 11/24, 12/25. **Address:** 5304 Gateway Center Dr 48507 **Location:** US 23, exit 90 (Hill Rd), just e; jct I-75 N and 475, 1 mi n on I-475, then 2 mi w on Hill Rd. CALL 🆒Ⓜ

SALVATORE SCALLOPINI

▼▼ ▼▼
Italian
$8-$17

Phone: 810/732-1070

Popular and informal, the family-oriented restaurant delivers fresh and authentic entrees from a lengthy menu of traditional specialties. Seafood linguine is served piping hot with fresh mussels and squid. The wait staff is friendly and efficient. **Bar:** full bar. **Hours:** 11 am-10 pm, Fri & Sat-11 pm, Sun noon-10 pm. Closed: 11/24, 12/25 & Easter. **Address:** G-3227 Miller Rd 48507 **Location:** I-75, exit 117 (Miller Rd).

FOWLERVILLE pop. 2,972

MAGNUSON HOTEL FOWLERVILLE

▼▼ ▼▼
Motel
Rates not provided

Phone: 517/223-9165

Address: 950 S Grand Ave 48836 **Location:** I-96, exit 129 (Fowlerville), just n. **Facility:** Smoke free premises. 60 units. 2 stories (no elevator), exterior corridors. **Amenities:** Some: high-speed Internet. **Pool(s):** heated indoor. **Guest Services:** coin laundry, wireless Internet. 🖥 🛁 ✖ 🅱 🖥 🖳 / SOME UNITS FEE 🐾

FRANKENMUTH pop. 4,838

BAVARIAN INN LODGE

▼▼ ▼▼
Resort
Hotel
$110-$195 4/1-12/31
$89-$185 1/1-4/30

Phone: (989)652-7200

Address: 1 Covered Bridge Ln 48734 **Location:** Just e across covered bridge. Located along the river within walking distance of downtown area. **Facility:** This riverfront resort offers extensive recreational facilities. Smoke free premises. 360 units. 5 stories, interior corridors. **Parking:** winter plug-ins. **Terms:** 3 day cancellation notice-fee imposed. **Dining:** 2 restaurants, entertainment. **Pool(s):** 5 heated indoor. **Activities:** whirlpools, miniature golf, 4 tennis courts (2 lighted), exercise room, basketball. **Fee:** family fun center, game room. **Guest Services:** area transportation-within 0.3 mi, wireless Internet. *(see ad p. 320)*

SAVE FEE ✈ 🖥 🍸 CALL 🆒Ⓜ 🛁 ✖ 🅱 🖥

FREE high-speed Internet and children's activities

DRURY INN & SUITES

Hotel
$110-$199

Phone: (989)652-2800

Address: 260 S Main St 48734 **Location:** On SR 83; downtown. **Facility:** Smoke free premises. 78 units. 5 stories, interior corridors. **Parking:** winter plug-ins. **Terms:** check-in 4 pm, cancellation fee imposed. **Amenities:** high-speed Internet. **Pool(s):** heated indoor. **Activities:** whirlpool. **Guest Services:** wireless Internet.

FAIRFIELD INN BY MARRIOTT

Hotel
$74-$109

Phone: (989)652-5000

Address: 430 S Main St 48734 **Location:** On SR 83; downtown. **Facility:** Smoke free premises. 62 units. 3 stories, interior corridors. **Terms:** cancellation fee imposed. **Amenities:** high-speed Internet. **Pool(s):** heated indoor. **Activities:** whirlpool, exercise room. **Guest Services:** valet laundry, wireless Internet.

AAA Benefit:
Members save a minimum 5% off the best available rate.

▼ See AAA listing p. 319 ▼

FRANKENMUTH MOTEL

Motel
$50-$99

Phone: (989)652-6171

Address: 1218 Weiss St 48734 **Location:** Just e of SR 83. Located close to the downtown area. **Facility:** 53 units. 1 story, exterior corridors. **Parking:** winter plug-ins. **Activities:** horseshoes. **Guest Services:** wireless Internet.

MARV HERZOG HOTEL

Hotel
$89-$219 1/1-4/30
$89-$209 4/1-12/31

Phone: (989)652-4700

Address: 501 S Main St 48734 **Location:** On SR 83; downtown. **Facility:** Smoke free premises. 38 units. 3 stories, interior corridors. **Terms:** check-in 4 pm, 1-2 night minimum stay - seasonal and/or weekends, cancellation fee imposed. **Guest Services:** wireless Internet. Affiliated with Drury Inns, Inc.

SPRINGHILL SUITES BY MARRIOTT

Hotel
$89-$129

Phone: (989)652-7500

Address: 530 S Main St 48734 **Location:** On SR 83; center. **Facility:** Smoke free premises. 64 units. 3 stories, interior corridors. **Terms:** cancellation fee imposed. **Amenities:** high-speed Internet. **Pool(s):** heated indoor. **Activities:** whirlpool, exercise room. **Fee:** game room. **Guest Services:** valet and coin laundry, wireless Internet.

> **AAA Benefit:**
> Members save a minimum 5% off the best available rate.

ZEHNDER'S SPLASH VILLAGE HOTEL & WATERPARK

Hotel
Rates not provided

Phone: 989/652-0470

Address: 1365 S Main St 48734 **Location:** 0.5 mi s on SR 83. Located beside Bronner's Christmas Wonderland. **Facility:** Smoke free premises. 146 units, some two bedrooms. 2-4 stories, interior corridors. **Terms:** check-in 4 pm. **Amenities:** video games. *Some:* high-speed Internet. **Pool(s):** heated indoor. **Activities:** sauna, whirlpools, waterslide, indoor water park, exercise room. **Fee:** golf-18 holes, game room. **Guest Services:** area transportation-within 3 mi, wireless Internet.

—— WHERE TO DINE ——

BAVARIAN INN RESTAURANT   *Menu on AAA.com*

German
$7-$23

Phone: 989/652-9941

A dozen German-themed dining rooms are decorated with hand-painted murals, steins and other Bavarian decor. The menu lists a good selection of American comfort foods—such as chicken, mashed potatoes and applesauce—as well as German entrees. **Bar:** full bar. **Reservations:** suggested. **Hours:** 11 am-9 pm, Fri & Sat-9:30 pm. **Address:** 713 S Main St 48734 **Location:** On SR 83.

FRANKENMUTH BREWERY

American
$8-$23

Phone: 989/262-8300

The restaurant offers a riverfront setting and serves mainly American dishes with a few German classics thrown in, such as bratwurst and sauerkraut. Staff are happy to assist patrons in selecting one of the many beers brewed on site to accompany any of the pub classics on the menu, such as burgers, sandwiches, pizzas and ribs. Patio seating overlooking the Cass River is available in season. **Bar:** full bar. **Hours:** 11 am-10 pm, Fri & Sat-11 pm, Sun-9 pm; hours may vary. Closed: 11/24, 12/25. **Address:** 425 S Main St 48734 **Location:** On SR 83; downtown. CALL

SULLIVAN'S BLACK FOREST BREW HAUS & GRILL   *Menu on AAA.com*

American
$7-$21

Phone: 989/652-6060

The city's oldest brewpub serves a number of finger foods, seafood, pasta, pizza and barbecue combinations. **Bar:** full bar. **Hours:** 11:30 am-9 pm, Fri & Sat-10 pm, Sun-8 pm; hours may vary. Closed: 1/1, 12/25. **Address:** 281 Heinlein Strasse 48734 **Location:** 0.9 mi se; corner of Weiss and Heinlein Strasse. CALL

ZEHNDER'S

American
$8-$22

Phone: 989/652-9925

One of America's largest family restaurants. This popular, well-established restaurant has a very good selection of main dishes. Specializing in all-you-can-eat family-style chicken dinners. Zehnder's Marketplace and Z Chef's Cafe is open 8 am-9 pm daily. **Bar:** full bar. **Hours:** 11 am-9:30 pm. Closed: for dinner 12/24. **Address:** 730 S Main St 48734 **Location:** On SR 83.

FREELAND pop. 5,147

—— WHERE TO DINE ——

RIVERSIDE FAMILY RESTAURANT

American
$5-$12

Phone: 989/695-5563

Beside the Tittabawassee River, this casual restaurant offers up-close views of the water, woods and wildlife. Country-style decorations complement country-style cooking in such daily specials as meatloaf and pot roast. Save room for homemade pie. **Hours:** 6 am-9 pm. **Address:** 8295 Midland Rd 48623 **Location:** 0.5 mi nw on SR 47.

GAYLORD pop. 3,681

ALPINE LODGE

Hotel
$69-$119

Phone: (989)732-2431

Address: 833 W Main St 49735 **Location:** I-75, exit 282, 0.3 mi e on SR 32. **Facility:** Smoke free premises. 130 units. 2 stories (no elevator), interior/exterior corridors. **Terms:** check-in 4 pm, 14 day cancellation notice. **Amenities:** safes (fee). **Pool(s):** heated indoor. **Activities:** sauna, whirlpool, snowmobiling, indoor recreational area, pool table, exercise room. **Fee:** game room. **Guest Services:** coin laundry, wireless Internet. **Free Special Amenities:** expanded continental breakfast and high-speed Internet.

DOWNTOWN MOTEL

Motel
$40-$66

Phone: (989)732-5010

Address: 208 S Otsego Ave 49735 **Location:** I-75, exit 282, 0.5 mi e, then 0.3 mi s on I-75 business loop. **Facility:** Smoke free premises. 13 units. 2 stories (no elevator), exterior corridors. **Terms:** cancellation fee imposed. **Activities:** snowmobiling. **Guest Services:** wireless Internet. **Free Special Amenities: continental breakfast and high-speed Internet.**

SAVE ⏰ ✕ 🐾 🛏 🖥 / SOME UNITS FEE 🐕

HAMPTON INN

Hotel
Rates not provided

Phone: 989/731-4000

AAA Benefit:
Members save up to 10% everyday!

Address: 230 Dickerson Rd 49735 **Location:** I-75, exit 282, just w. **Facility:** Smoke free premises. 83 units. 3 stories, interior corridors. **Pool(s):** heated indoor. **Activities:** whirlpool, snowmobiling, exercise room. **Guest Services:** valet and coin laundry, wireless Internet.

⏰ 🏊 ✕ 🐾 🖥 / SOME UNITS FEE 🛏 FEE 🖥

ROYAL CREST MOTEL

Hotel
Rates not provided

Phone: 989/732-6451

Address: 803 S Otsego Ave 49735 **Location:** I-75, exit 279, 2.3 mi ne on I-75 business loop. **Facility:** Smoke free premises. 44 units. 2 stories (no elevator), interior corridors. **Parking:** winter plug-ins. **Terms:** office hours 6:30 am-midnight. **Pool(s):** heated indoor. **Activities:** sauna, whirlpool, snowmobiling. **Fee:** game room. **Guest Services:** wireless Internet.

⏰ 🏊 ✕ 🖥 / SOME UNITS FEE 🐕 🛏 🖥

──── **WHERE TO DINE** ────

BIG BUCK BREWERY & STEAKHOUSE

American
$7-$22

Phone: 989/732-5781

The brewery produces fine brews, bound to please the beer connoisseur, and features the finest Sterling Silver certified USDA choice beef for its steaks. **Bar:** full bar. **Hours:** 11 am-11 pm, Fri & Sat-midnight, Sun-10 pm; hours may vary. **Closed:** 12/25. **Address:** 550 S Wisconsin Ave 49735 **Location:** I-75, exit 282, just e on SR 32, then 0.5 mi s. CALL ♿ M

LA SEÑORITA

Mexican
$6-$15

Phone: 989/732-1771

This family-friendly restaurant offers such traditional favorites as burritos, enchiladas and fajitas, as well as mesquite-grilled entrees served in a festive, lively atmosphere. **Bar:** full bar. **Hours:** 11 am-10 pm, Fri & Sat-11 pm, Sun noon-10 pm; to 11 pm, Fri & Sat-midnight 5/29-9/4. **Closed:** 11/24, 12/25 & Easter. **Address:** 737 W Main St 49735 **Location:** I-75, exit 282, just e on SR 32.

SUGAR BOWL

American
$6-$26

Phone: 989/732-5524

Established in 1919, the casual spot is one of Michigan's oldest family-owned restaurants. The menu includes Greek and American selections, with such popular choices as ribs, whitefish, perch and prime rib. Sink your teeth into homemade raspberry pie. **Bar:** full bar. **Hours:** 7 am-11 pm, Sun-10 pm; hours may vary. **Closed:** 11/24, 12/25. **Address:** 216 W Main St 49735 **Location:** I-75, exit 282, 0.5 mi e on SR 32.

GRAND BLANC

GRAND BLANC COMFORT INN & SUITES

Hotel
Rates not provided

Phone: 810/694-0000

Address: 9040 Holly Rd 48439 **Location:** I-75, exit 108 (Holly Rd), just e. Located in a quiet area. **Facility:** Smoke free premises. 58 units. 2 stories (no elevator), interior corridors. **Amenities:** safes (fee). **Pool(s):** heated indoor. **Activities:** whirlpool. **Guest Services:** valet laundry, wireless Internet.

🏊 ✕ 🐾 🛏 🖥 🖥

HOLIDAY INN EXPRESS HOTEL & SUITES

Hotel
$99-$139

Phone: (810)695-3000

Address: 3405 Regency Park Dr 48439 **Location:** I-75, exit 108 (Holly Rd), just e. **Facility:** Smoke free premises. 77 units. 3 stories, interior corridors. **Amenities:** high-speed Internet. **Pool(s):** heated indoor. **Activities:** exercise room. **Guest Services:** valet and coin laundry, wireless Internet.

CALL ♿ M 🏊 ✕ 🐾 🖥 / SOME UNITS 🛏 🖥

WINGATE BY WYNDHAM

Hotel
$76-$93

Phone: (810)694-9900

Address: 1359 Grand Pointe Ct 48439 **Location:** I-475, exit 2 (Hill Rd), just e. Located in a quiet area. **Facility:** Smoke free premises. 82 units. 3 stories, interior corridors. **Amenities:** video games (fee), high-speed Internet, safes. **Pool(s):** heated indoor. **Activities:** whirlpool, exercise room. **Guest Services:** valet and coin laundry, area transportation-within 3 mi, wireless Internet.

✈ ⏰ CALL ♿ M 🏊 BIZ ✕ 🐾 🛏 🖥 🖥

──── **WHERE TO DINE** ────

DA EDOARDO NORTH

Italian
$8-$35

Phone: 810/694-1300

With large picture windows overlooking a large reeded pond, it might be hard to remember that you are inside a tastefully upscale Italian restaurant rather than outside. Gnocchi with Bolognese sauce or chicken saltimbocca highlight a menu that features a wide selection of Italian favorites. **Bar:** full bar. **Hours:** 11:30 am-10 pm, Fri-11 pm, Sat 4 pm-11 pm, Sun 4 pm-9 pm. **Closed:** 1/1, 11/24, 12/25. **Address:** 8185 Holly Rd, Suite 7 48439 **Location:** I-75, exit 108 (Holly Rd), 2 mi e. CALL ♿ M

GRAND HAVEN pop. 11,168

BEST WESTERN BEACON INN

Hotel
$65-$170

Phone: (616)842-4720

Address: 1525 S Beacon Blvd 49417 **Location:** 1.5 mi s on US 31. **Facility:** Smoke free premises. 105 units. 1-3 stories, interior/exterior corridors. **Terms:** check-in 4 pm, 2-3 night minimum stay - seasonal and/or weekends. **Pool(s):** heated indoor. **Activities:** whirlpool, exercise room. *Fee:* game room. **Guest Services:** valet laundry, wireless Internet. **Free Special Amenities: continental breakfast and high-speed Internet.**

AAA Benefit:
Members save up to 20%, plus 10% bonus points with free rewards program.

DAYS INN

Hotel
$73-$145

Phone: (616)842-1999

Address: 1500 S Beacon Blvd 49417 **Location:** 1.5 mi s on US 31. **Facility:** Smoke free premises. 100 units. 2 stories (no elevator), interior corridors. **Terms:** check-in 4 pm. **Amenities:** safes (fee). **Pool(s):** heated indoor. **Activities:** whirlpool. *Fee:* game room. **Guest Services:** valet and coin laundry, wireless Internet.

HARBOR HOUSE INN

Bed & Breakfast
$99-$275

Phone: 616/846-0610

Address: 114 S Harbor Dr 49417 **Location:** Corner of Harbor Dr and Clinton. Opposite Lake Michigan. **Facility:** This attractive, modern Victorian-style house is located across from the water, just steps from the downtown shops; some rooms have fireplaces. Smoke free premises. 20 units, some cottages. 3 stories (no elevator), interior/exterior corridors. **Terms:** office hours 7:30 am-10 pm, 2 night minimum stay - seasonal and/or weekends, age restrictions may apply, 7 day cancellation notice-fee imposed. **Guest Services:** wireless Internet. **Free Special Amenities: expanded continental breakfast and preferred room (subject to availability with advance reservations).**

───── WHERE TO DINE ─────

KIRBY HOUSE

American
$8-$22

Phone: 616/846-3299

Old pictures and advertisements hang on the walls of the 1873 building in the heart of downtown. Such specialties as white chili and fresh fish and lobster are favorites. Homemade cheesecakes, such as raspberry chocolate black bottom, are delicious. **Bar:** full bar. **Hours:** 11:30 am-10 pm, Fri & Sat-11 pm, Sun-9 pm. **Address:** 2 Washington St 49417 **Location:** 0.7 mi w of US 31. **Parking:** street only.

THE STABLE INN

American
$5-$16

Phone: 616/846-8581

Chicken Monterey, beer-battered shrimp and the 10-ounce rib-eye are representative of menu selections. The decor is Western, with plenty of American Indian accents. The large, open dining room is inviting to families. Service is friendly and prompt. **Bar:** full bar. **Hours:** 11 am-10 pm; hours may vary. Closed major holidays; also Sun. **Address:** 11880 US 31 49417 **Location:** On US 31, 5 mi s.

GRAND MARAIS

VOYAGEUR'S MOTEL

Motel
$85-$95

Phone: 906/494-2389

Address: 21914 E Wilson St 49839 **Location:** 0.5 mi e of SR 77. Located high on a ridge overlooking the harbor. **Facility:** Smoke free premises. 10 units. 2 stories (no elevator), exterior corridors. **Terms:** office hours 8 am-10 pm, cancellation fee imposed. **Activities:** sauna, whirlpool, snowmobiling. **Guest Services:** wireless Internet.

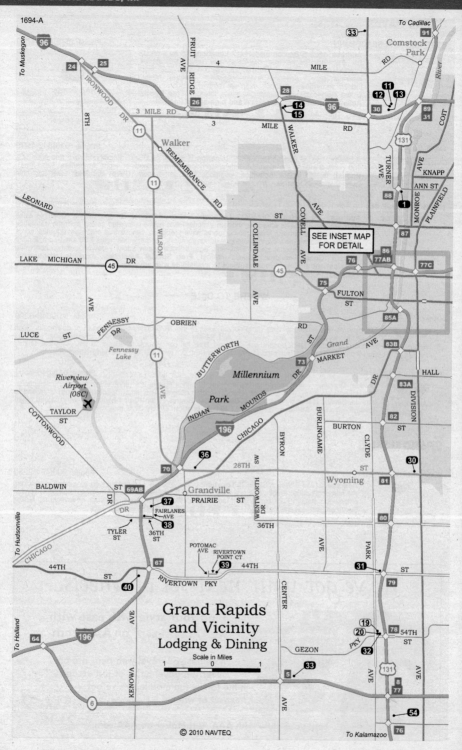

Grand Rapids and Vicinity
Lodging & Dining

Scale in Miles

© 2010 NAVTEQ

1694-A

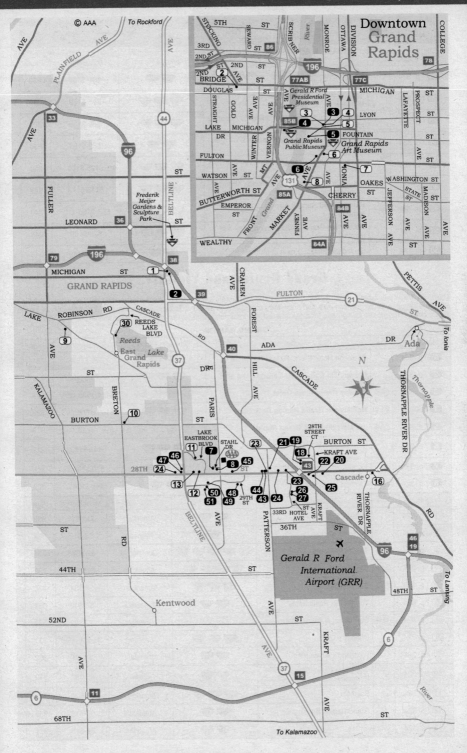

© AAA

To Rockford

Downtown Grand Rapids

GRAND RAPIDS

MICHIGAN ST

Frederik Meijer Gardens & Sculpture Park

To Ionia

To Lansing

Gerald R Ford International Airport (GRR)

Kentwood

To Kalamazoo

✈ Airport Accommodations

Map Page	OA	GERALD R FORD INTERNATIONAL AIRPORT	Diamond Rated	High Season	Page
24 / p. 324		Clarion Inn & Suites Grand Rapids Airport, 2 mi n of terminal	◆◆	$90-$150	230
20 / p. 324		Crowne Plaza Grand Rapids, 2 mi n of terminal	◆◆◆	$95-$189	230
26 / p. 324		Hampton Inn & Suites Grand Rapids Airport, 2 mi n of terminal	◆◆◆	$89-$139	230
18 / p. 324		Holiday Inn Express Suites Airport, 2 mi n of terminal	◆◆	$89-$159	230
27 / p. 324		SpringHill Suites Grand Rapids Airport, 2 mi n of terminal	◆◆◆	$125-$160	230
44 / p. 324		Courtyard by Marriott Grand Rapids Airport, 2 mi n of terminal	◆◆◆	$135-$173	347
43 / p. 324	AAA	**Hilton Grand Rapids Airport, 2 mi n of terminal**	◆◆◆	$88-$166 (SAVE)	348
51 / p. 324		Holiday Inn Grand Rapids Airport, 2 mi n of terminal	◆◆◆	$79-$169	348
50 / p. 324		Staybridge Suites, 2 mi n of terminal	◆◆	$119-$149	348

Grand Rapids and Vicinity

This index helps you "spot" where approved lodgings and restaurants are located on the corresponding detailed maps. Lodging daily rate range is for comparison only and show the property's high season. Restaurant rate range is a combination of lunch and/or dinner. Turn to the listing page for more detailed rate information and consult display ads for special promotions.

GRAND RAPIDS

Map Page	OA	Lodgings	Diamond Rated	High Season	Page
1 / p. 324		Radisson Hotel Grand Rapids Riverfront	◆◆	$89-$139	331
2 / p. 324		Country Inn & Suites By Carlson - see ad p. 6	◆◆◆	$99-$149	329
3 / p. 324	AAA	**Amway Grand Plaza Hotel**	◆◆◆◆	$144-$525 (SAVE)	329
4 / p. 324	AAA	**Holiday Inn Grand Rapids Downtown**	◆◆◆	$129-$179 (SAVE)	329
5 / p. 324	AAA	**JW Marriott Hotel Grand Rapids**	◆◆◆◆	$197-$252 (SAVE)	329
6 / p. 324		Courtyard by Marriott Grand Rapids Downtown	◆◆◆	$143-$183	329
7 / p. 324		Homewood Suites by Hilton	◆◆◆	$70-$140	329
8 / p. 324		Fairfield Inn by Marriott	◆◆	$81-$104	329

Map Page	OA	Restaurants	Diamond Rated	Cuisine	Meal Range	Page
1 / p. 324		Malarky's	◆◆	American	$10-$17	332
2 / p. 324		Maggie's Kitchen	◆	Mexican	$3-$12	332
3 / p. 324	AAA	**The 1913 Room**	◆◆◆◆◆	Continental	$20-$75	331
4 / p. 324	AAA	**Cygnus 27**	◆◆◆	American	$15-$39	332
5 / p. 324	AAA	**Six One Six**	◆◆◆	American	$8-$34	332
6 / p. 324		The B.O.B. Restaurants	◆◆	American	$6-$42	331
7 / p. 324	AAA	**San Chez, A Tapas Bistro**	◆◆	Spanish	$7-$22	332
8 / p. 324		Charley's Crab	◆◆◆	Seafood	$9-$39 (SAVE)	331
9 / p. 324		Wolfgang's Restaurant	◆◆	Breakfast	$4-$8	332
10 / p. 324		The Great Lakes Shipping Company	◆◆	Steak	$8-$37	332
11 / p. 324		Sayfee's	◆◆◆	American	$6-$29	332
12 / p. 324		Grand Rapids Brewing Co.	◆◆	American	$6-$19	332
13 / p. 324		Arnie's	◆◆	American	$6-$15	331

WALKER

Map Page	OA	Lodgings	Diamond Rated	High Season	Page
11 / p. 324		Holiday Inn Express Hotel & Suites	◆◆◆	$89-$189	443
12 / p. 324		SpringHill Suites by Marriott	◆◆◆	$116-$148	443
13 / p. 324		Hampton Inn- Grand Rapids North	◆◆◆	$99-$124	443
14 / p. 324		Baymont Inn & Suites-Grand Rapids North	◆◆	$76-$134	443
15 / p. 324		Quality Inn Grand Rapids North	◆◆	$70-$84	443

CASCADE

Map Page	OA	Lodgings	Diamond Rated	High Season	Page
18 / p. 324		Holiday Inn Express Suites Airport	◆◆	$89-$159	230
19 / p. 324	AAA	**Country Inn & Suites By Carlson** - see ad p. 6	◆◆	$79-$114 SAVE	230
20 / p. 324		Crowne Plaza Grand Rapids	◆◆◆	$95-$189	230
21 / p. 324		Super 8	◆	$44-$53	230
22 / p. 324	AAA	**Best Western Hospitality Hotel & Suites**	◆◆	$59-$99 SAVE	230
23 / p. 324	AAA	**Red Roof Inn #7011**	◆	$53-$70 SAVE	230
24 / p. 324		Clarion Inn & Suites Grand Rapids Airport	◆◆	$90-$150	230
25 / p. 324		Baymont Inn-Grand Rapids Airport	◆◆	$58-$146	229
26 / p. 324		Hampton Inn & Suites Grand Rapids Airport	◆◆◆	$89-$139	230
27 / p. 324		SpringHill Suites Grand Rapids Airport	◆◆◆	$125-$160	230

Map Page	OA	Restaurant	Diamond Rated	Cuisine	Meal Range	Page
16 / p. 324	AAA	**Noto's Old World Italian Dining**	◆◆◆	Italian	$15-$33	231

WYOMING

Map Page	OA	Lodgings	Diamond Rated	High Season	Page
30 / p. 324	AAA	**Travelodge**	◆	$45-$67 SAVE	445
31 / p. 324		Super 8	◆	$42-$53	445
32 / p. 324		Hampton Inn Grand Rapids South	◆◆	$99-$139	445
33 / p. 324	AAA	**Hyatt Place Grand Rapids - South**	◆◆◆	$89-$179 SAVE	445

Map Page	OA	Restaurants	Diamond Rated	Cuisine	Meal Range	Page
19 / p. 324		Oriental Forest	◆	Chinese	$6-$12	445
20 / p. 324		Arnie's	◆◆	American	$6-$15	445

GRANDVILLE

Map Page	OA	Lodgings	Diamond Rated	High Season	Page
36 / p. 324	AAA	**Days Inn & Suites**	◆	$60-$63 SAVE	333
37 / p. 324	AAA	**Grandvillage Inn**	◆◆	$79-$89 SAVE	333
38 / p. 324		Holiday Inn Express	◆◆	$109-$189	333
39 / p. 324	AAA	**Residence Inn by Marriott Grand Rapids West**	◆◆◆	$134-$171 SAVE	333
40 / p. 324	AAA	**Comfort Suites-Grandville**	◆◆	$85-$250 SAVE	333

KENTWOOD

Map Page	OA	Lodgings	Diamond Rated	High Season	Page
43 / p. 324	AAA	**Hilton Grand Rapids Airport**	◆◆◆	$88-$166 SAVE	348
44 / p. 324		Courtyard by Marriott Grand Rapids Airport	◆◆◆	$135-$173	347
45 / p. 324		Comfort Inn	◆◆	$67-$126	347
46 / p. 324		The Gatehouse Suites	◆◆	Rates not provided	348

KENTWOOD (cont'd)

Map Page	OA	Lodgings (cont'd)	Diamond Rated	High Season	Page
47 / p. 324	AAA	**Ramada Plaza Hotel**	◆◆	$64-$144 SAVE	348
48 / p. 324		Sleep Inn	◆◆	$56-$63	348
49 / p. 324		Extended StayAmerica Grand Rapids-Kentwood	◆	$43-$70	347
50 / p. 324		Staybridge Suites	◆◆	$119-$149	348
51 / p. 324		Holiday Inn Grand Rapids Airport	◆◆◆	$79-$169	348

Map Page	OA	Restaurants	Diamond Rated	Cuisine	Meal Range	Page
23 / p. 324	AAA	**Spinnaker**	◆◆	American	$8-$40	348
24 / p. 324		Seoul Garden	◆◆	Asian	$6-$18	348

BYRON CENTER

Map Page	OA	Lodging	Diamond Rated	High Season	Page
54 / p. 324		Holiday Inn Express Inn & Suites	◆◆◆	$99-$159	228

EAST GRAND RAPIDS

Map Page	OA	Restaurant	Diamond Rated	Cuisine	Meal Range	Page
30 / p. 324		Rose's	◆◆	American	$8-$27	314

COMSTOCK PARK

Map Page	OA	Restaurant	Diamond Rated	Cuisine	Meal Range	Page
33 / p. 324		Empire Chinese Buffet II	◆	Chinese	$6-$11	236

GRAND RAPIDS pop. 197,800 (See map and index starting on p. 324)

AMWAY GRAND PLAZA HOTEL

Hotel
$144-$525

Phone: (616)774-2000 **3**

Address: 187 Monroe Ave NW 49503 **Location:** Pearl St at Monroe Ave; US 131, exit Pearl St; downtown. **Facility:** On the Grand River, the tower section of this elegant, service-oriented hotel houses a number of guest rooms with water views. Smoke free premises. 682 units, some two bedrooms. 12-29 stories, interior corridors. **Parking:** on-site (fee) and valet. **Terms:** check-in 4 pm, cancellation fee imposed. **Amenities:** high-speed Internet (fee). **Dining:** 7 restaurants, also, The 1913 Room, Cygnus 27, see separate listings. **Pool(s):** heated indoor. **Activities:** sauna, whirlpools, steamroom, 2 lighted tennis courts, racquetball court, spa. **Guest Services:** valet laundry, wireless Internet, tanning facilities. *Fee:* area transportation-within 1 mi. Affiliated with A Preferred Hotel.

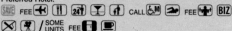

COUNTRY INN & SUITES BY CARLSON

Hotel
$99-$149

Phone: (616)942-7000 **2**

Address: 3251 Deposit Dr NE 49546 **Location:** I-96, exit 38, just s on SR 37 (E Beltline). **Facility:** Smoke free premises. 154 units. 5 stories, interior corridors. **Terms:** cancellation fee imposed. **Amenities:** high-speed Internet. **Pool(s):** heated indoor. **Activities:** whirlpool, exercise room. *Fee:* game room. **Guest Services:** valet and coin laundry, wireless Internet. *(see ad p. 6)*

COURTYARD BY MARRIOTT GRAND RAPIDS DOWNTOWN

Hotel
$143-$183

Phone: (616)242-6000 **6**

Address: 11 Monroe Ave NW 49503 **Location:** Corner of Fulton St and Monroe Ave; downtown. **Facility:** Smoke free premises. 214 units. 7 stories, interior corridors. **Parking:** on-site (fee). **Terms:** cancellation fee imposed. **Pool(s):** heated indoor. **Activities:** sauna, whirlpool, steamroom, 2 lighted tennis courts, sports deck, exercise room, basketball. **Guest Services:** valet and coin laundry, wireless Internet.

> **AAA Benefit:**
> Members save a minimum 5% off the best available rate.

FAIRFIELD INN BY MARRIOTT

Hotel
$81-$104

Phone: (616)940-2700 **8**

Address: 3930 Stahl Dr SE 49546 **Location:** I-96, exit 43A (28th St SW), 1.5 mi w on SR 11, just n on E Paris, then just w. Located in an upscale office park. **Facility:** Smoke free premises. 82 units. 3 stories, interior corridors. **Terms:** cancellation fee imposed. **Pool(s):** heated indoor. **Activities:** whirlpool. **Guest Services:** valet laundry, wireless Internet.

> **AAA Benefit:**
> Members save a minimum 5% off the best available rate.

HOLIDAY INN GRAND RAPIDS DOWNTOWN

Hotel
$129-$179

Phone: (616)235-7611 **4**

Address: 310 Pearl St NW 49504 **Location:** US 131, exit 85B (Pearl St), just e. **Facility:** Smoke free premises. 175 units. 8 stories, interior corridors. **Pool(s):** heated indoor. **Activities:** whirlpool, exercise room. **Guest Services:** valet and coin laundry, wireless Internet. **Free Special Amenities:** newspaper and high-speed Internet.

HOMEWOOD SUITES BY HILTON

Extended Stay
Hotel
$70-$140

Phone: (616)285-7100 **7**

Address: 3920 Stahl Dr SE 49546 **Location:** I-96, exit 43A (28th St SW), 1.5 mi w to E Paris Ave, then just n. Located in an upscale office park. **Facility:** Smoke free premises. 78 units, some two bedrooms, efficiencies and kitchens. 3 stories, interior corridors. **Terms:** 1-7 night minimum stay, cancellation fee imposed. **Pool(s):** heated indoor. **Activities:** whirlpool, exercise room. **Guest Services:** valet and coin laundry, wireless Internet.

> **AAA Benefit:**
> Members save 5% or more everyday!

JW MARRIOTT HOTEL GRAND RAPIDS

Hotel
$197-$252

Phone: (616)242-1500 **5**

Address: 235 Louis NW 49503 **Location:** US 131, exit Pearl St; downtown. Located along the Grand River. **Facility:** Guest rooms at the newer property feature modern, up-to-date amenities like no other hotel; an amazing Art Deco theme adorns the public areas. Smoke free premises. 337 units. 23 stories, interior corridors. **Parking:** on-site (fee) and valet. **Terms:** check-in 4 pm, cancellation fee imposed. **Amenities:** high-speed Internet, safes, honor bars. **Dining:** Six One Six, see separate listing. **Pool(s):** heated indoor. **Activities:** whirlpool, steamrooms, exercise room, spa. **Guest Services:** valet laundry, wireless Internet.

> **JW MARRIOTT**
> **AAA Benefit:**
> A deluxe level of comfort and a Member rate.

KEEP YOUR CHILDREN SAFE IN THE CAR

AAA and the timeless characters of Richard Scarry, one of the best-selling children's authors of all time, have partnered to promote child passenger safety. To keep your child safe, use the right car seat and follow the guidelines at AAA.com/SafeSeats4Kids. To install your car safety seat correctly, call an expert at **866-SEAT-CHECK(732-8243)** or visit seatcheck.org. Remember, car seats save lives!

Visit BusytownMysteries.com
for more on best-selling children's author Richard Scarry.

RADISSON HOTEL GRAND RAPIDS RIVERFRONT

Hotel
$89-$139 1/2-4/30
$84-$129 4/1-1/1

Phone: (616)363-9001 **1**

Address: 270 Ann St NW 49504 **Location:** US 131, exit 88, 1.8 mi n. **Facility:** Smoke free premises. 162 units. 7 stories, interior corridors. **Terms:** cancellation fee imposed. **Amenities:** *Some:* safes. **Pool(s):** heated indoor. **Activities:** whirlpool, exercise room. **Guest Services:** valet and coin laundry, wireless Internet. / SOME UNITS FEE

—— WHERE TO DINE ——

THE 1913 ROOM   *Menu on AAA.com*

Continental
$20-$75

Phone: 616/774-2000 **3**

Business professionals and couples frequent this elegant dining room with Louis XVI decor. The continental menu offers a number of exquisite dishes, many with a French influence, as well as intriguing selections from the chef's tasting menu. For dessert, savor the forbidden apple or rich Viennese chocolate cake. **Bar:** full bar. **Reservations:** suggested. **Hours:** 5:30 pm-10 pm, Fri & Sat from 5 pm. Closed: 12/25; also Sun. **Address:** 187 Monroe Ave NW 49503 **Location:** Pearl St at Monroe Ave; US 131, exit Pearl St; downtown; in Amway Grand Plaza Hotel. **Parking:** on-site and valet. CALL

ARNIE'S

American
$6-$15

Phone: 616/956-7901 **13**

Freshly baked artisan breads and Scandinavian danish complement the sandwiches, salads and soups, as well as other traditional dishes. **Hours:** 7 am-10 pm, Fri-10:30 pm, Sat 8 am-10:30 pm, Sun 9 am-3 pm. Closed: 11/24, 12/25. **Address:** 3561 28th St SE 49512 **Location:** I-96, exit 43A, 2 mi w on SR 11; at Centerpointe Mall.

THE B.O.B. RESTAURANTS

American
$6-$42

Phone: 616/356-2000 **6**

B.O.B. stands for "big old building," and that's just what it is: a big old building with several restaurants inside. There's a cornucopia of food selections offered, and the place also is a hotbed of multifaceted entertainment. **Bar:** full bar. **Hours:** 11:30 am-11 pm, Sat & Sun from 4 pm. Closed: 1/1, 11/24, 12/25. **Address:** 20 Monroe Ave NW 49503 **Location:** Downtown; across from Van Andel Arena. **Parking:** street only.

CHARLEY'S CRAB

Seafood
$9-$39

Phone: 616/459-2500 **8**

Overlooking the Grand River, the restaurant is known for creative preparations of fresh seafood, such as crab and avocado timbale and lobster ravioli. The eclectic decor includes items from a mansion that was torn down. **Bar:** full bar. **Reservations:** suggested. **Hours:** 11:30 am-10 pm, Fri-11 pm, Sat 4:30 pm-11 pm, Sun 10 am-9 pm. Closed: 12/25. **Address:** 63 Market Ave SW 49503 **Location:** Jct US 131 and SR 45, exit 85. **Parking:** on-site and valet. SAVE

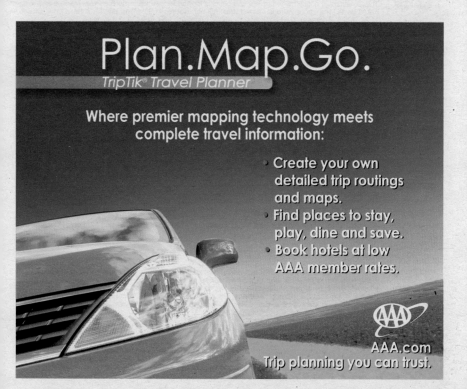

CYGNUS 27 *Menu on AAA.com*   **Phone:** 616/776-6425   (4)

American
$15–$39

High atop the Amway Grand Plaza Hotel, this 27th-floor restaurant offers outstanding views and a menu featuring well-prepared beef, poultry and seafood entrees. Service is friendly and efficient. A recent renovation has resulted in a restaurant that remains upscale, but is no longer being presented as high-end fine dining. **Bar:** full bar. **Reservations:** suggested. **Hours:** 5:30 pm-10 pm, Sun 10:30 am-2 pm. Closed: 1/1, 11/24, 12/25; also Mon & Sun 5/7-9/9. **Address:** 187 Monroe Ave NW 49503 **Location:** Pearl St at Monroe Ave; US 131, exit Pearl St; downtown; in Amway Grand Plaza Hotel. **Parking:** on-site and valet.

CALL M

GRAND RAPIDS BREWING CO.   **Phone:** 616/285-5970   (12)

American
$6–$19

The brew pub is decorated with photographs and pictures of the original Grand Rapids Brewing Co., which prospered in the early 1900s. Menu choices range from typical starters to sandwiches, steaks, perch and the popular rotisserie chicken dishes. **Bar:** full bar. **Hours:** 11 am-10 pm, Fri & Sat-11 pm. Closed: 11/24, 12/24, 12/25. **Address:** 3689 28th St SE 49512 **Location:** I-96, exit 43A, 2 mi w on SR 11; at Centerpointe Mall.

THE GREAT LAKES SHIPPING COMPANY   **Phone:** 616/949-9440   (10)

Steak
$8–$37

Five fireplaces and nautical decorations give the restaurant a cozy, rustic flavor. Menu specialties include prime rib, pan-fried walleye and filet tenderloin. **Bar:** full bar. **Reservations:** suggested, weekends. **Hours:** 11:30 am-10 pm, Sat 5 pm-11 pm. Closed major holidays; also Sun. **Address:** 2455 Burton St SE 49546 **Location:** US 131, exit 82A, 3.8 mi e; jct Breton Ave and Burton St.

MAGGIE'S KITCHEN   **Phone:** 616/458-8583   (2)

Mexican
$3–$12

This fast-food restaurant offers a good selection of Mexican dishes, which can be enjoyed in a simple, unpretentious dining room. **Hours:** 9 am-7 pm, Sun 8 am-4 pm; hours may vary. Closed major holidays; also Mon. **Address:** 636 Bridge St NW 49504 **Location:** 0.6 mi w on Michigan and Bridge sts; center. **Parking:** street only.

MALARKY'S   **Phone:** 616/808-2956   (1)

American
$10–$17

This restaurant is just off the highway and has plenty of parking. It offers pizzas, salads, some pasta entrees, sandwiches and paninis. **Bar:** full bar. **Hours:** 11 am-10 pm, Sun-8 pm. Closed: 11/24, 12/25 & Easter. **Address:** 3210 Deposit Dr NE 49546 **Location:** I-96, exit 38, just s on SR 37 (E Beltline).

PIETRO'S ITALIAN RESTAURANT   **Phone:** 616/452-3228

Italian
$8–$17

The restaurant is popular with families and couples looking for specialties such as veal Marsala and oven-baked pasta. The atmosphere is relaxed. **Bar:** full bar. **Hours:** 11:30 am-10 pm, Fri & Sat-11 pm. Closed: 11/24, 12/25. **Address:** 2780 Birchcrest Dr 49506 **Location:** I-96, exit 43A, 3.8 mi w on SR 11.

RIO GRAND STEAKHOUSE   **Phone:** 616/364-6266

American
$8–$24

The West River location prepares large cuts of charbroiled mesquite steak, barbecue ribs, rotisserie chicken and a variety of seafood entrees. **Bar:** full bar. **Hours:** 11 am-10 pm, Fri & Sat-11 pm. Closed: 11/24, 12/25. **Address:** 5501 Northland Dr 49525 **Location:** I-96, exit 38, 6.5 mi n on SR 37.

SAN CHEZ, A TAPAS BISTRO *Menu on AAA.com*   **Phone:** 616/774-8272   (7)

Spanish
$7–$22

So many tapas, so little time. Guests can prepare their taste buds for an explosion of flavorful options in the lively, energetic bistro. The specialty is tapas, available either hot or cold. **Bar:** full bar. **Hours:** 8 am-10 pm, Fri-11 pm, Sat 10 am-11 pm, Sun 9 am-10 pm. Closed major holidays. **Address:** 38 W Fulton St 49503 **Location:** Just e of Van Andel Arena; downtown. **Parking:** street only.

SAYFEE'S   **Phone:** 616/949-5750   (11)

American
$6–$29

The casually elegant restaurant has been around for years. The refined menu of steaks, chops, prime rib and seafood include standouts such as escargots, oysters boursin, sautéed frog legs, duck a l'orange, veal Oscar and walleye. The wine selection incorporates some less-than-$20 bottles. Diners may dance on Friday and Saturday evenings. A large deck overlooks the sparkling water. Entertainment. **Bar:** full bar. **Reservations:** suggested. **Hours:** 11 am-10 pm, Fri & Sat-11 pm; hours may vary. Closed: 12/25; also Sun. **Address:** 3555 Lake Eastbrook Blvd 49546 **Location:** 0.7 mi ne of jct SR 11 and 37; behind Centerpointe Mall.

SIX ONE SIX   **Phone:** 616/242-1500   (5)

American
$8–$34

This modern, signature hotel restaurant offers inspired, fresh, locally grown cuisine. The most popular dish is the New York strip steak, one of the best steaks in the city, served with heirloom tomatoes, fingerling potatoes, balsamic onions and arugula and topped with onion rings and blue cheese butter. **Bar:** full bar. **Hours:** 7 am-4 & 5:30-10 pm. **Address:** 235 Louis St NW 49503 **Location:** US 131, exit Pearl St; downtown; in JW Marriott Hotel Grand Rapids. **Parking:** on-site (fee) and valet. CALL M

WOLFGANG'S RESTAURANT   **Phone:** 616/454-5776   (9)

Breakfast
$4–$8

Breakfast is the specialty at this restaurant, which opens early. The menu features lots of interesting choices, all for less than ten dollars. Patrons seeking lunch will find a limited menu with service beginning at 11 am. **Hours:** 6:30 am-2:30 pm, Sat & Sun 7 am-4 pm. Closed: 11/24, 12/25. **Address:** 1530 Wealthy St SE 49506 **Location:** Corner of Wealthy St and Lake Dr SE. **Parking:** street only.

GRANDVILLE pop. 16,263 (See map and index starting on p. 324)

COMFORT SUITES-GRANDVILLE

Hotel
$85-$250

Phone: (616)667-0733 **40**

Address: 4520 Kenowa Ave SW 49418 **Location:** I-196, exit 67, just sw. Located next to Wal-Mart Shopping Center. **Facility:** Smoke free premises. 66 units. 3 stories, interior corridors. **Amenities:** video games (fee), high-speed Internet. **Pool(s):** heated indoor. **Activities:** whirlpool, exercise room. **Guest Services:** valet and coin laundry, wireless Internet. **Free Special Amenities: expanded continental breakfast and high-speed Internet.**

DAYS INN & SUITES

Hotel
$60-$63

Phone: (616)531-5263 **36**

Address: 3825 28th St SW 49418 **Location:** I-196, exit 70/70A, 0.5 mi e. **Facility:** 88 units, some two bedrooms. 3 stories, interior corridors. **Terms:** cancellation fee imposed. **Activities:** exercise room. **Guest Services:** coin laundry, wireless Internet. **Free Special Amenities: continental breakfast and high-speed Internet.**

GRANDVILLAGE INN

Hotel
$79-$89

Phone: (616)532-3222 **37**

Address: 3425 Fairlanes Ave 49418 **Location:** I-196, exit 69A, just e to Fairlanes Ave, then just s. **Facility:** Smoke free premises. 80 units. 2 stories (no elevator), interior corridors. **Amenities:** safes (fee). *Some:* high-speed Internet. **Pool(s):** heated indoor. **Activities:** whirlpool, limited exercise equipment. *Fee:* game room. **Guest Services:** coin laundry, wireless Internet. **Free Special Amenities: full breakfast and high-speed Internet.**

HOLIDAY INN EXPRESS

Hotel
$109-$189

Phone: (616)532-0202 **38**

Address: 4651 36th St 49418 **Location:** I-196, exit 69A, just e to Fairlanes Ave, then 0.4 mi s. **Facility:** Smoke free premises. 78 units. 3 stories, interior corridors. **Pool(s):** heated indoor. **Activities:** whirlpool, sun deck, exercise room. **Guest Services:** valet and coin laundry, wireless Internet.

RESIDENCE INN BY MARRIOTT GRAND RAPIDS WEST

Extended Stay
Hotel
$134-$171

Phone: (616)538-1100 **39**

Address: 3451 Rivertown Point Ct SW 49418 **Location:** I-196, exit 67, 1.7 mi e. Opposite River Town Crossings Mall. **Facility:** Smoke free premises. 90 units, some two bedrooms, efficiencies and kitchens. 3 stories, interior corridors. **Terms:** cancellation fee imposed. **Amenities:** high-speed Internet. **Pool(s):** heated outdoor. **Activities:** whirlpool, exercise room, sports court, basketball, volleyball. **Guest Services:** valet and coin laundry, wireless Internet. **Free Special Amenities: full breakfast and high-speed Internet.**

AAA Benefit:
Members save a minimum 5%
off the best available rate.

GRAYLING pop. 1,952

AUSABLE VALLEY RAMADA INN & CONFERENCE CENTER

Hotel
Rates not provided

Phone: 989/348-7611

Address: 2650 S Business Loop 49738 **Location:** I-75 business loop, 0.8 mi s. **Facility:** Smoke free premises. 151 units. 2 stories (no elevator), interior/exterior corridors. **Parking:** winter plug-ins. **Dining:** entertainment. **Pool(s):** heated indoor. **Activities:** sauna, whirlpool, snowmobiling, lighted cross country ski trails, recreation area, playground, exercise room, basketball, shuffleboard, volleyball. *Fee:* ski equipment, game room. **Guest Services:** valet laundry, wireless Internet.

SUPER 8

Hotel
$48-$101

Phone: (989)348-8888

Address: 5828 Nelson A Miles Pkwy 49738 **Location:** I-75, exit 251, just w. **Facility:** Smoke free premises. 60 units. 2 stories (no elevator), interior corridors. **Parking:** winter plug-ins. **Pool(s):** heated indoor. **Activities:** whirlpool, snowmobiling, hiking trails. *Fee:* game room. **Guest Services:** coin laundry, wireless Internet.

GREENBUSH

—— WHERE TO DINE ——

RED ROOSTER

Italian
$4-$15

Phone: 989/739-7659

The dining room is homey and offers a view of Lake Huron. Selections of wholesome Italian cuisine are prepared with homemade pasta and sauces. Delicious cream pies melt in your mouth. **Bar:** full bar. **Hours:** 8 am-9 pm; hours may vary. Closed: Mon. **Address:** 3228 S US 23 48738 **Location:** On US 23, 1.8 mi s.

GREENVILLE pop. 7,935

AMERICINN LODGE & SUITES OF GREENVILLE

Hotel
$90–$105
Phone: (616)754-4500

Address: 2525 W Washington 48838 **Location:** US 131, exit 101 (SR 57), 13 mi e. **Facility:** Smoke free premises. 69 units. 3 stories, interior corridors. **Terms:** cancellation fee imposed. **Amenities:** high-speed Internet. **Pool(s):** heated indoor. **Activities:** sauna, whirlpool. **Guest Services:** valet and coin laundry, wireless Internet.

— WHERE TO DINE —

RUMNEY'S FIESTA CAFE

American
$3–$8
Phone: 616/754-3302

A local favorite, this quaint little eatery has dishing up down-home foods at great prices since 1986. The menu focuses on freshly prepared soups, sandwiches on bakery fresh bread, a variety of comfort foods like meatloaf and fried chicken, plus several Mexican items like burritos and quesadillas. The house specialty is a vegetarian olive burger, a must-try. **Hours:** 11:30 am-8 pm, Fri-9 pm. Closed major holidays; also Sat & Sun. **Address:** 129 S Lafayette St 48838 **Location:** Downtown. **Parking:** street only.

GROSSE POINTE FARMS —See Detroit p. 281.

GROSSE POINTE WOODS —See Detroit p. 281.

HANCOCK pop. 4,323

BEST WESTERN COPPER CROWN MOTEL

Hotel
$71
Phone: (906)482-6111

Address: 235 Hancock St 49930 **Location:** On US 41 S; downtown. **Facility:** Smoke free premises. 46 units. 2 stories (no elevator), interior/exterior corridors. **Parking:** winter plug-ins. **Terms:** cancellation fee imposed. **Pool(s):** heated indoor. **Activities:** saunas, whirlpool, snowmobiling. **Guest Services:** wireless Internet.

AAA Benefit:
Members save up to 20%, plus 10% bonus points with free rewards program.

FREE continental breakfast and high-speed Internet

RAMADA WATERFRONT

Hotel
$77–$162
Phone: (906)482-8400

Address: 99 Navy St 49930 **Location:** Off US 41, just nw of bridge. Located along the canal. **Facility:** Smoke free premises. 51 units. 2 stories (no elevator), interior corridors. **Dining:** The Waterfront, see separate listing. **Pool(s):** heated indoor. **Activities:** sauna, whirlpool, boat dock, fishing, snowmobiling. **Guest Services:** coin laundry, wireless Internet.

— WHERE TO DINE —

THE WATERFRONT
American
$7–$25
Phone: 906/482-8494

The restaurant and lounge offers a view of the water, particularly from the seasonal patio. Dishes include steaks, seafood, sandwiches and daily specials. **Bar:** full bar. **Hours:** 11 am-10 pm, Sat & Sun from 8 am. **Address:** 99 Navy St 49930 **Location:** Off US 41, just nw of bridge; in Ramada Waterfront.

HARBOR SPRINGS pop. 1,567

BEST WESTERN OF HARBOR SPRINGS

Motel
$74–$240
Phone: (231)347-9050

Address: 8514 M-119 49740 **Location:** On SR 119, 3 mi se. **Facility:** Smoke free premises. 50 units, some kitchens. 1 story, exterior corridors. **Parking:** winter plug-ins. **Terms:** office hours 7 am-11 pm, 2 night minimum stay - seasonal, 3 day cancellation notice. **Amenities:** high-speed Internet. **Pool(s):** heated indoor. **Activities:** whirlpool, snowmobiling, playground, exercise room. **Guest Services:** coin laundry, wireless Internet. **Free Special Amenities:** continental breakfast and high-speed Internet.

AAA Benefit:
Members save up to 20%, plus 10% bonus points with free rewards program.

—— WHERE TO DINE ——

THE NEW YORK RESTAURANT   Phone: 231/526-1904

American
$19-$33

Menu selections, such as Colorado lamb shank, Great Lakes whitefish, wolverine pork loin and petite filet of beef, are full in flavor and attractively presented. An antique bar and tin ceiling are charming characteristics of the vintage 1904 building. **Bar:** full bar. **Reservations:** suggested. **Hours:** 5 pm-10 pm; hours may vary. Closed: 11/24, 12/25. **Address:** 101 State St 49740 **Location:** Just s of jct SR 119 and State St; center. **Parking:** street only.

STAFFORD'S PIER RESTAURANT   Phone: 231/526-6201

American
$9-$42

The restaurant offers casual upscale dining in a building that overlooks the marina. Two menu favorites are the whitefish and rack of lamb. The homemade pies are the best when served with a scoop of ice cream. **Bar:** full bar. **Reservations:** suggested. **Hours:** 11:30 am-9:30 pm. Closed: 12/25. **Address:** 102 Bay St 49740 **Location:** Just s of jct SR 119 and State St; center.

HARRISON (CLARE COUNTY)

LAKESIDE MOTEL & COTTAGES   Phone: 989/539-3796

Motel
$62-$99

Address: 515 E Park St, Business US 127, M-61 48625 **Location:** US 127, exit US 127 business route/SR 61, 2.2 mi w. Located on Budd Lake. **Facility:** Smoke free premises. 15 units, some cottages. 1 story, exterior corridors. *Bath:* shower only. **Parking:** winter plug-ins. **Terms:** office hours 9 am-10 pm. **Activities:** beach access, rental boats, rental canoes, rental paddleboats, snowmobiling. **Guest Services:** wireless Internet. **Free Special Amenities: local telephone calls and high-speed Internet.**

HARRISVILLE pop. 514

—— WHERE TO DINE ——

THE OLD PLACE INN   *Menu on AAA.com*   Phone: 989/724-6700

American
$5-$17

The building that houses the restaurant has stood on Main Street since the 1870s, surviving all of the town's fires. On the menu are traditional beef, pork and chicken dishes, as well as a vegetarian stir-fry and sweet treats. **Bar:** full bar. **Hours:** 11:30 am-9 pm; hours may vary. Closed: Mon. **Address:** 309 E Main St 48740 **Location:** Just e of US 23; downtown.

HART pop. 1,950

AMERICAN HOST INN OF HART   Phone: 231/873-1855

Hotel
$59-$124 4/1-9/10
$49-$89 9/11-4/30

Address: 4143 W Polk Rd 49420 **Location:** US 31, exit Mears/Hart, just e on US 31 business route. **Facility:** Smoke free premises. 22 units. 2 stories (no elevator), interior corridors. **Terms:** 2 night minimum stay - seasonal and/or weekends, 14 day cancellation notice-fee imposed. **Activities:** rental bicycles. **Guest Services:** wireless Internet.

HARTLAND

BEST WESTERN HARTLAND   Phone: (810)632-7177

Motel
$85-$112

Address: 10087 M-59 48353 **Location:** On SR 59, at US 23, exit 67. **Facility:** Smoke free premises. 60 units. 2 stories (no elevator), exterior corridors. **Terms:** check-in 4 pm, 10 day cancellation notice-fee imposed. **Amenities:** safes. *Some:* high-speed Internet. **Pool(s):** heated indoor. **Guest Services:** coin laundry, wireless Internet. **Free Special Amenities: expanded continental breakfast and high-speed Internet.**

AAA Benefit:
Members save up to 20%, plus 10% bonus points with free rewards program.

HILLMAN pop. 685

THUNDER BAY GOLF RESORT   Phone: (989)742-4502

Resort Motel
$69-$89

Address: 27800 Hwy M-32 E 49746 **Location:** On SR 32, just e. **Facility:** Condominium-type units. Smoke free premises. 34 units, some two bedrooms and kitchens. 2 stories (no elevator), exterior corridors. **Terms:** 2 night minimum stay - weekends, 14 day cancellation notice-fee imposed. **Activities:** whirlpool, 2 tennis courts, cross country skiing, snowmobiling, hiking trails. *Fee:* golf-18 holes, carriage & sleigh rides. **Guest Services:** wireless Internet.

HILLSDALE pop. 8,233

DAYS INN HILLSDALE   Phone: (517)439-3297

Hotel
$33-$122

Address: 3241 Carleton Rd 49242 **Location:** 2 mi n of town. Located in a commercial area. **Facility:** Smoke free premises. 49 units. 1-2 stories (no elevator), interior corridors. **Terms:** 3 day cancellation notice. **Pool(s):** heated indoor. **Activities:** whirlpool, exercise room. **Guest Services:** wireless Internet.

HOLLAND pop. 35,048

BEST WESTERN HOLLAND INN & SUITES

Hotel
$65-$139

Address: 2888 W Shore Dr 49424 **Location:** US 31, exit Felch St E, just n. **Facility:** Smoke free premises. 80 units. 3 stories, interior/exterior corridors. **Terms:** 10 day cancellation notice. **Amenities:** video games. **Pool(s):** heated indoor. **Activities:** whirlpool, exercise room. **Guest Services:** valet and coin laundry, wireless Internet. **Free Special Amenities: local telephone calls and high-speed Internet.**

Phone: (616)994-0400

AAA Benefit:
Members save up to 20%, plus 10% bonus points with free rewards program.

BONNIE'S (THE) PARSONAGE 1908 B&B

Historic Bed
& Breakfast

$110-$140 4/1-10/31
$100-$120 11/1-4/30

Address: 6 E 24th St & Central Ave 49423 **Location:** US 31, 1 mi w. Located in a quiet residential area. **Facility:** This property is a former parsonage built in 1908. Smoke free premises. 3 units. 2 stories (no elevator), interior corridors. *Bath:* some shared. **Terms:** office hours 9 am-10 pm, check-in 4 pm, 2 night minimum stay - seasonal, age restrictions may apply.

Phone: (616)396-1316

COUNTRY INN & SUITES BY CARLSON

Hotel
$63-$135

Address: 12260 James St 49424 **Location:** Jct US 31 N and James St, just e. Located at the Horizon Outlet Mall. **Facility:** Smoke free premises. 116 units. 2 stories (no elevator), interior corridors. **Terms:** cancellation fee imposed. **Pool(s):** heated indoor. **Guest Services:** valet laundry, wireless Internet.

(see ad p. 6) / SOME UNITS FEE

Phone: (616)396-6677

FAIRFIELD INN BY MARRIOTT

Hotel
$90-$115

Address: 2854 W Shore Dr 49424 **Location:** Jct US 31 and Felch St. **Facility:** Smoke free premises. 64 units. 3 stories, interior corridors. **Parking:** winter plug-ins. **Terms:** cancellation fee imposed. **Pool(s):** heated indoor. **Activities:** whirlpool. **Guest Services:** valet laundry, wireless Internet.

/ SOME UNITS

Phone: (616)786-9700

AAA Benefit:
Members save a minimum 5% off the best available rate.

HAMPTON INN OF HOLLAND

Hotel
Rates not provided

Address: 12427 Felch St 49424 **Location:** Jct US 31 and Felch St. **Facility:** Smoke free premises. 178 units. 4 stories, interior corridors. **Amenities:** video games (fee). *Some:* high-speed Internet. **Pool(s):** heated indoor. **Activities:** whirlpools, exercise room. *Fee:* pool table, game room. **Guest Services:** valet and coin laundry, wireless Internet.

/ SOME UNITS FEE FEE

Phone: 616/399-8500

AAA Benefit:
Members save up to 10% everyday!

HOLIDAY INN EXPRESS

Hotel
$139-$259 4/1-9/30
$109-$189 10/1-4/30

Address: 12381 Felch St 49424 **Location:** Jct US 31. **Facility:** Smoke free premises. 118 units. 4 stories, interior corridors. **Amenities:** high-speed Internet. **Pool(s):** heated indoor. **Activities:** sauna, whirlpool, exercise room, sports court. *Fee:* game room. **Guest Services:** valet and coin laundry, wireless Internet.

Phone: (616)738-2800

RESIDENCE INN BY MARRIOTT

Extended Stay
Hotel
$119-$159

Address: 631 Southpoint Ridge Rd 49423 **Location:** I-196, exit 49, 0.7 mi n on SR 40. **Facility:** Smoke free premises. 78 efficiencies, some two bedrooms. 3 stories, interior corridors. **Terms:** cancellation fee imposed. **Amenities:** high-speed Internet. **Pool(s):** heated indoor. **Activities:** whirlpool, exercise room, sports court. **Guest Services:** valet and coin laundry.

/ SOME UNITS FEE

Phone: (616)393-6900

AAA Benefit:
Members save a minimum 5% off the best available rate.

—— WHERE TO DINE ——

BOATWERKS WATERFRONT RESTAURANT

American
$6-$24

On the banks of Lake Macatawa, this modern restaurant offers a number of tasty, well-executed dishes, such as seafood linguine or sauteed petit filet mignon. **Bar:** full bar. **Hours:** Open 4/12-1/31; 11 am-9 pm, Fri-10 pm, Sat 9 am-10 pm, Sun 9 am-9 pm; hours may vary in winter. Closed: 12/25. **Address:** 216 Van Raalte Ave 49423 **Location:** Next to Kollen Park; end of 10th St; downtown.

Phone: 616/396-0600

CHINA INN

Chinese
$6-$20

The casual restaurant's menu incorporates Mandarin, Szechuan, Hunan and Cantonese dishes. **Bar:** full bar. **Hours:** 11 am-9:30 pm, Fri & Sat-10:30 pm, Sun-8:30 pm. Closed: 11/24. **Address:** 2863 W Shore Dr 49424 **Location:** Jct US 31 and Felch St; in West Shore Shopping Center.

Phone: 616/786-9230

CRAZY HORSE STEAKHOUSE & SALOON
Phone: 616/395-8393

American
$6-$16

The tavern has a Country-and-Western theme and serves a delicious sirloin (cattle baron) steak with mashed red-skin potatoes and a mix of colorful vegetables. **Bar:** full bar. **Hours:** 11 am-9:30 pm, Fri & Sat-10 pm; hours may vary. Closed major holidays; also Sun. **Address:** 2027 N Park Dr 49424 **Location:** US 31, exit Lakewood Blvd, just w. CALL

HOLLY —See Detroit p. 281.

HOUGHTON pop. 7,010

COUNTRY INN & SUITES BY CARLSON
Phone: (906)487-6700

Hotel
$99-$179 4/1-10/23
$89-$179 10/24-4/30

Address: 919 Razorback Dr 49931 **Location:** 1.3 mi w on SR 26. **Facility:** Smoke free premises. 75 units. 3 stories, interior corridors. **Parking:** winter plug-ins. **Terms:** cancellation fee imposed. **Amenities:** high-speed Internet. **Pool(s):** heated indoor. **Activities:** whirlpool, snowmobiling, exercise room. **Guest Services:** valet and coin laundry, wireless Internet. *(see ad p. 6)* CALL

THE DOWNTOWNER MOTEL
Phone: 906/482-4421

Motel
$58-$148

Address: 110 Shelden Ave 49931 **Location:** On US 41; downtown. **Facility:** Smoke free premises. 27 units, some two bedrooms. 2 stories (no elevator), exterior corridors. **Parking:** winter plug-ins. **Activities:** sun deck, snowmobiling. **Guest Services:** wireless Internet. **Free Special Amenities:** local telephone calls and high-speed Internet.

FRANKLIN SQUARE INN
Phone: 906/487-1700

Hotel
$90-$110

Address: 820 Shelden Ave 49931 **Location:** On US 41; downtown. **Facility:** Smoke free premises. 105 units. 7 stories, interior corridors. **Parking:** winter plug-ins. **Pool(s):** heated indoor. **Activities:** sauna, whirlpool, snowmobiling, exercise room. **Guest Services:** valet laundry, wireless Internet, tanning facilities.

—— WHERE TO DINE ——

THE LIBRARY
Phone: 906/487-5882

American
$6-$18

Pizza, steak, seafood and Mexican dishes—as well as on-site microbrews—are served at this restaurant. **Bar:** full bar. **Hours:** 11:30 am-10 pm, Fri & Sat-11 pm. Closed: 11/24, 12/25. **Address:** 62 N Isle Royale 49931 **Location:** Just n of US 41; downtown. **Parking:** street only.

PILGRIM RIVER STEAKHOUSE
Phone: 906/482-8595

American
$8-$27

The rustic restaurant specializes in fine steaks and fresh Lake Superior fish, but also prepares sandwiches and salads for guests with lesser appetites. In the wintertime, guests like to get cozy by the fireplace in the lounge section. **Bar:** full bar. **Hours:** 11 am-10 pm, Fri & Sat-11 pm, Sun noon-9:30 pm. Closed: 11/24, 12/25. **Address:** 47409 Hwy US 41 S 49931 **Location:** On US 41, 2.5 mi s.

——— *The following restaurant has not been evaluated by AAA* ———
but is listed for your information only.

AMBASSADOR
Phone: 906/482-5054

fyi

Not evaluated. The popular downtown restaurant, with its antique bar and view of the canal, serves a number of snacks, salads and pizzas, as well as daily pasta specials. **Address:** 126 Shelden Ave 49931 **Location:** Downtown.

HOUGHTON LAKE pop. 3,749

SUPER 8
Phone: (989)422-3119

Hotel
$54-$99

Address: 9580 W Lake City Rd 48629 **Location:** Jct US 127 and SR 55. **Facility:** Smoke free premises. 69 units. 2 stories (no elevator), interior corridors. **Parking:** winter plug-ins. **Pool(s):** heated indoor. **Activities:** sauna, whirlpool, snowmobiling, playground. **Fee:** game room. **Guest Services:** coin laundry, wireless Internet.

Plan. Map. Go.
TripTik® Travel Planner on AAA.com or CAA.ca

—— WHERE TO DINE ——

COYLES RESTAURANT   Phone: 989/422-3812

American
$5-$20

Pick and choose from the wide assortment of tempting options on the lunch and dinner buffets, or order from a menu that includes Alaskan king crab, frog legs and steak dinners. Meals are reasonably priced and please every member of the family. **Bar:** full bar. **Hours:** 8 am-9 pm, Fri & Sat-10 pm; hours may vary. Closed: 12/25. **Address:** 9074 Old US 27 48629 **Location:** Just n of jct SR 55.

HOWELL pop. 9,232

BAYMONT INN & SUITES-HOWELL   Phone: (517)546-0712

Hotel
$67-$95

Address: 4120 Lambert Dr 48843 **Location:** I-96, exit 133 (US 59/Grand River Ave), just n, then 0.5 mi e. Adjacent to Outlet Mall. **Facility:** Smoke free premises. 75 units. 3 stories, interior corridors. **Amenities:** safes (fee). **Pool(s):** heated indoor. **Activities:** whirlpool, limited exercise equipment. **Guest Services:** wireless Internet.

BEST WESTERN HOWELL   Phone: (517)548-2900

Motel
$89-$165

Address: 1500 Pinckney Rd 48843 **Location:** I-96, exit 137 (Pinckney Rd), just s on CR D19. Located in a semi-rural area. **Facility:** Smoke free premises. 59 units. 2 stories (no elevator), exterior corridors. **Terms:** cancellation fee imposed. **Amenities:** high-speed Internet. **Pool(s):** heated outdoor. **Guest Services:** coin laundry, wireless Internet. **Free Special Amenities:** early check-in/late check-out and high-speed Internet.

AAA Benefit:
Members save up to 20%, plus 10% bonus points with free rewards program.

HOLIDAY INN EXPRESS & SUITES   Phone: (517)548-0100

Hotel
$86-$129

Address: 1397 N Burkhart Rd 48855 **Location:** I-96, exit 133 (US 59/Grand River Ave), just n, then 0.5 mi e. **Facility:** Smoke free premises. 77 units. 3 stories, interior corridors. **Amenities:** high-speed Internet. **Pool(s):** heated indoor. **Activities:** exercise room. **Guest Services:** valet and coin laundry, wireless Internet.

—— WHERE TO DINE ——

CHINESE DELIGHT   Phone: 517/545-9988

Chinese
$6-$14

Rustic brick walls and hardwood floors give this space a cheerful ambience. Locally popular, the Cantonese/American-based menu offers a wide selection of traditional dishes. **Bar:** full bar. **Hours:** 11 am-9 pm, Fri & Sat-10 pm, Sun noon-9 pm. Closed: 11/24. **Address:** 111 W Grand River Ave 48843 **Location:** Downtown. **Parking:** street only.

HUDSONVILLE pop. 7,160

QUALITY INN-HUDSONVILLE   Phone: 616/662-4000

Hotel
Rates not provided

Address: 3301 Highland Dr 49426 **Location:** I-196, exit 62 (32nd Ave), just nw. **Facility:** Smoke free premises. 58 units. 2 stories (no elevator), interior corridors. **Pool(s):** heated indoor. **Activities:** whirlpool. **Guest Services:** valet and coin laundry, wireless Internet.

—— WHERE TO DINE ——

HUDSONVILLE GRILLE   Phone: 616/662-9670

American
$6-$17

This restaurant offers a variety of moderately priced dishes in a casual setting. Service is friendly and attentive. **Hours:** 6 am-9 pm, Fri & Sat-10 pm. Closed major holidays; also Sun. **Address:** 4676 32nd Ave 49426 **Location:** I-196, exit 62 (32nd Ave), 0.6 mi n.

IMLAY CITY pop. 3,869

SUPER 8-IMLAY CITY   Phone: (810)724-8700

Hotel
$48-$68

Address: 6951 Newark Rd 48444 **Location:** I-69, exit 168 (SR 53/Van Dyke Rd), then just e. Located in a quiet area. **Facility:** Smoke free premises. 60 units. 2 stories (no elevator), interior corridors. **Activities:** whirlpool, playground. **Guest Services:** coin laundry, wireless Internet.

—— WHERE TO DINE ——

LUCKY'S STEAKHOUSE   Phone: 810/724-4100

American
$8-$21

Big portions are the trademark at this local family-oriented favorite where service is quick and attentive. Mainstays such as prime rib, steaks and burgers populate the menu, while historical pictures of Imlay City dot the walls. The restaurant is located just off the state road and close to several motels. **Bar:** full bar. **Hours:** 11 am-10 pm, Fri-11 pm, Sat noon-11 pm, Sun noon-9 pm. Closed major holidays. **Address:** 2000 S Cedar St 48444 **Location:** I-69, exit 168 (SR 53/Van Dyke Rd), just n.

INDIAN RIVER pop. 2,008

——— WHERE TO DINE ———

THE BROWN TROUT   Phone: 231/238-9441

American
$7-$26

Just south of town, the restaurant serves steaks, fresh seafood and prime rib in an up-north atmosphere. **Bar:** full bar. **Reservations:** required. **Hours:** 11 am-10 pm. Closed major holidays. **Address:** 4653 S Straits Hwy 49749 **Location:** I-75, exit 310, 0.3 mi w, then 1.8 mi s on Old US 27. CALL

VIVIO'S NORTHWOOD INN   Phone: 231/238-9471

American
$10-$30

The rustic log cabin is decorated with wall-mounted wildlife, including deer heads and a black bear cub. Shaded lamps throw adequate, yet modest, light. American and Italian cuisine, such as the specialty pizza, make up the restaurant's menu. **Bar:** full bar. **Hours:** 5 pm-11 pm; hours may vary. **Address:** 4531 S Straits Hwy 49749 **Location:** I-75, exit 310, 0.3 mi w, then 1 mi s.

WILSON'S RIVER'S EDGE   Phone: 231/238-8111

American
$4-$16

The popular restaurant serves reasonably priced dishes and delicious homemade-style desserts and pies. **Bar:** full bar. **Hours:** 7 am-10 pm; hours may vary. Closed: 11/24, 12/25. **Address:** 4208 S Straits Hwy 49749 **Location:** I-75, exit 310, just w, then just s.

IRON MOUNTAIN pop. 8,154

BUDGET HOST INN   Phone: (906)774-6797

Motel
$52-$60

Address: 1585 N Stephenson Ave 49801 **Location:** On US 2 and 141, 1.5 mi nw. **Facility:** Smoke free premises. 19 units, some kitchens. 1 story, exterior corridors. **Parking:** winter plug-ins. **Terms:** cancellation fee imposed. **Activities:** snowmobiling. **Guest Services:** wireless Internet. **Free Special Amenities: continental breakfast and high-speed Internet.**

COMFORT INN   Phone: 906/774-5505

Hotel
Rates not provided

Address: 1565 N Stephenson Ave 49801 **Location:** On US 2, 1.3 mi nw. Located next to a bowling alley/lounge. **Facility:** Smoke free premises. 60 units. 2 stories (no elevator), interior corridors. **Parking:** winter plug-ins. **Amenities:** safes (fee). **Activities:** snowmobiling, exercise room. **Guest Services:** coin laundry, wireless Internet. **Free Special Amenities: expanded continental breakfast and high-speed Internet.**

COUNTRY INN & SUITES BY CARLSON   Phone: (906)774-1900

Hotel
$86-$160

Address: 2005 S Stephenson Ave 49801 **Location:** Jct SR 141, 0.8 mi w on US 2. **Facility:** Smoke free premises. 84 units. 3 stories, interior corridors. **Parking:** winter plug-ins. **Terms:** cancellation fee imposed. **Amenities:** high-speed Internet. **Pool(s):** heated indoor. **Activities:** whirlpool, exercise room. **Guest Services:** valet and coin laundry, wireless Internet. *(see ad p. 6)*

HOLIDAY INN EXPRESS HOTEL & SUITES   Phone: (906)774-1668

Hotel
$85-$105

Address: 1535 N Stephenson Ave 49801 **Location:** On US 2, 1.2 mi nw. Located next to a bowling alley/lounge. **Facility:** Smoke free premises. 61 units. 3 stories, interior corridors. **Pool(s):** heated indoor. **Activities:** snowmobiling, exercise room. **Guest Services:** wireless Internet. **Free Special Amenities: expanded continental breakfast and high-speed Internet.**

——— WHERE TO DINE ———

FONTANA'S SUPPER CLUB   Phone: 906/774-0044

Italian
$9-$55

Noted for charbroiled steaks and house-made Italian dishes, the restaurant is a favorite spot for casual, intimate dining. Attractive paintings and soft background music set a romantic tone in the casually upscale dining room. **Bar:** full bar. **Hours:** 5 pm-10 pm; hours may vary. Closed: 11/24, 12/24, 12/25; also Sun. **Address:** 115 S Stephenson Ave 49801 **Location:** On US 2; center.

IRON RIVER pop. 1,929

AMERICINN LODGE & SUITES OF IRON RIVER   Phone: (906)265-9100

Hotel
$95-$136 7/1-4/30
$89-$126 4/1-6/30

Address: 40 E Adams St 49935 **Location:** On US 2; downtown. Located on the banks of Iron River. **Facility:** Smoke free premises. 66 units. 3 stories, interior corridors. **Parking:** winter plug-ins. **Terms:** cancellation fee imposed. **Activities:** sauna, whirlpool, snowmobiling, exercise room. **Guest Services:** coin laundry, wireless Internet.

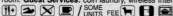

IRONWOOD pop. 6,293

AMERICAS BEST VALUE INN

Hotel
$60-$120

Phone: (906)932-3395

Address: 160 E Cloverland Dr 49938 **Location:** Jct US 2 and 2 business route. **Facility:** Smoke free premises. 42 units. 2 stories (no elevator), interior corridors. **Parking:** winter plug-ins. **Activities:** sauna, whirlpool, snowmobiling. **Guest Services:** wireless Internet.

AMERICINN OF IRONWOOD

Hotel
$69-$185

Phone: (906)932-7200

Address: 1117 E Cloverland Dr 49938 **Location:** 0.8 mi e on US 2. **Facility:** Smoke free premises. 49 units. 2 stories (no elevator), interior corridors. **Parking:** winter plug-ins. **Terms:** cancellation fee imposed. **Amenities:** high-speed Internet. **Pool(s):** heated indoor. **Activities:** sauna, whirlpool, snowmobiling, limited exercise equipment. **Guest Services:** wireless Internet.

COMFORT INN
Hotel
Rates not provided

Phone: 906/932-2224

Address: 210 E Cloverland Dr 49938 **Location:** Jct US 2 and 2 business route. **Facility:** Smoke free premises. 61 units. 2 stories (no elevator), interior corridors. **Parking:** winter plug-ins. **Pool(s):** heated indoor. **Activities:** whirlpool, snowmobiling. **Guest Services:** valet laundry, wireless Internet.

—— WHERE TO DINE ——

THE BREAKWATER
American
$4-$14

Phone: 906/932-8400

There is nothing fancy about this family restaurant, but the food is good, the service friendly and the prices very reasonable. **Hours:** 6 am-10 pm. Closed: 11/24, 12/25. **Address:** 1111 E Cloverland Dr 49938 **Location:** 0.8 mi e on US 2.

DON & GG'S FOOD & SPIRITS
American
$8-$18

Phone: 906/932-2312

This friendly neighborhood restaurant and bar is right off the main highway. It's a great place to stop for house-made salads and nightly specials, not to mention the local favorite called "cheese curds.". **Bar:** full bar. **Hours:** 10 am-11 pm, Fri & Sat-midnight, Sun 11 am-10 pm. Closed major holidays. **Address:** 1300 Cloverland Dr 49938 **Location:** 0.9 mi e on US 2.

THE PINES CAFE
American
$5-$9

Phone: 906/932-4207

The family restaurant offers ample portions of reasonably priced home-style food. **Hours:** 6 am-3 pm. Closed: 12/25. **Address:** 120 S Suffolk St 49938 **Location:** On US 2 business route; downtown. **Parking:** street only.

ISHPEMING pop. 6,686

BEST WESTERN COUNTRY INN
Hotel
$94-$113

Phone: (906)485-6345

Address: 850 US 41 W 49849 **Location:** US 41, just n of town. Located next to outdoor mall. **Facility:** Smoke free premises. 60 units. 2 stories (no elevator), interior corridors. **Parking:** winter plug-ins. **Pool(s):** heated indoor. **Activities:** whirlpool. **Guest Services:** wireless Internet. **Free Special Amenities:** local telephone calls and high-speed Internet.

AAA Benefit:
Members save up to 20%, plus 10% bonus points with free rewards program.

—— WHERE TO DINE ——

JASPER RIDGE BREWERY
American
$8-$17

Phone: 906/485-6017

Within walking distance of several area lodgings, the new brew pub pairs a number of traditional dishes with freshly brewed beer. **Bar:** full bar. **Hours:** 11 am-11 pm; hours may vary. Closed: 12/25. **Address:** 1035 Country Ln 49849 **Location:** Off US 41, just n of town.

ISLE ROYALE NATIONAL PARK

ROCK HARBOR LODGE
Resort Motel
$245-$252 7/5-9/9
$220-$227 5/27-7/4

Phone: (906)337-4993

Address: Isle Royale 49931 **Location:** Northeast end of island; accessible by boat or sea plane only. Located on Lake Superior. **Facility:** An exceptionally scenic wilderness island is the setting for this lodge. Smoke free premises. 80 units, some efficiencies. 1-2 stories (no elevator), exterior corridors. **Terms:** open 5/27-9/9, office hours 7 am-8 pm, cancellation fee imposed. **Dining:** 2 restaurants. **Activities:** rental boats, rental canoes, marina, fishing, hiking trails. **Fee:** guides & boat tours of island, kayaks. **Guest Services:** coin laundry.

JACKSON pop. 36,316

BAYMONT INN-JACKSON
Phone: (517)789-6000

Hotel
$71-$180

Address: 2035 Holiday Inn Dr 49202 **Location:** I-94, exit 138 (US 127), just nw. **Facility:** Smoke free premises. 67 units, some kitchens. 2 stories (no elevator), interior corridors. **Guest Services:** valet laundry, wireless Internet.

COMFORT INN & SUITES
Phone: 517/768-0088

Hotel
Rates not provided

Address: 2435 Shirley Dr 49202 **Location:** I-94, exit 138 (US 127), just n. **Facility:** Smoke free premises. 70 units. 3 stories, interior corridors. *Some:* safes (fee). *Some:* high-speed Internet. **Pool(s):** heated indoor. **Activities:** whirlpool, exercise room. **Guest Services:** valet and coin laundry, wireless Internet.

COUNTRY INN & SUITES BY CARLSON
Phone: (517)788-6400

Hotel
$119-$159

Address: 3506 O'Neill Dr 49202 **Location:** I-94, exit 137 (Airport Rd), just s. **Facility:** Smoke free premises. 78 units. 3 stories, interior corridors. **Amenities:** high-speed Internet. **Pool(s):** heated indoor. **Activities:** whirlpool, exercise room. **Guest Services:** valet and coin laundry, wireless Internet. *(see ad p. 6)*

FAIRFIELD INN BY MARRIOTT
Phone: (517)784-7877

Hotel
$122-$155

Address: 2395 Shirley Dr 49202 **Location:** I-94, exit 138 (US 127), just n to Springport Rd, then just e. **Facility:** Smoke free premises. 57 units. 3 stories, interior corridors. **Terms:** cancellation fee imposed. **Pool(s):** heated indoor. **Activities:** whirlpool. **Guest Services:** valet laundry, wireless Internet.

AAA Benefit:
Members save a minimum 5% off the best available rate.

HAMPTON INN BY HILTON
Phone: (517)789-5151

Hotel
$109-$159

Address: 2225 Shirley Dr 49202 **Location:** I-94, exit 138 (US 127), just n to Springport Rd, then just e. **Facility:** Smoke free premises. 63 units. 3 stories, interior corridors. **Terms:** 1-7 night minimum stay, cancellation fee imposed. **Pool(s):** heated indoor. **Activities:** whirlpool, exercise room. **Guest Services:** valet and coin laundry, wireless Internet.

AAA Benefit:
Members save up to 10% everyday!

--- **WHERE TO DINE** ---

BELLA NOTTE RISTORANTE
Phone: 517/782-5727

Italian
$8-$32

The soft glow of carriage lights illuminates hand-painted murals and creates a romantic courtyard setting in which guests dine on varied Italian-American dishes. Sautéed Michigan whitefish with pistachio risotto and fettuccine Alfredo grace a menu that also lists pizza and panini. **Bar:** full bar. **Hours:** 11 am-10 pm, Fri & Sat-11 pm. Closed major holidays; also Sun. **Address:** 137 W Michigan Ave 49201 **Location:** Downtown. **Parking:** on-site and street.

DARYL'S DOWNTOWN
Phone: 517/782-1895

American
$9-$28

The large open space of this downtown storefront restaurant is warmed with the use of hardwood floors, soft wood accents, Tiffany lamps and a large fish tank near the kitchen. A good-size menu of favorites from steak to seafood is well prepared and creatively presented. **Bar:** full bar. **Reservations:** suggested. **Hours:** 11 am-10 pm, Thurs-Sat to midnight. Closed major holidays; also Sun. **Address:** 151 W Michigan Ave 49201 **Location:** Downtown. **Parking:** on-site and street.

FINLEY'S AMERICAN GRILL
Phone: 517/787-7440

American
$8-$21

Residing near Westwood Mall, this restaurant offers a wide variety of predictable menu items including chargrilled steak, baby back ribs and seafood combinations. **Bar:** full bar. **Hours:** 11 am-10 pm, Fri & Sat-11 pm; to 7 pm 12/24. Closed: 11/24, 12/25. **Address:** 1602 W Michigan Ave 49201 **Location:** On I-94 business route; corner of Michigan Ave and Brown St.

JONESVILLE pop. 2,337

--- **WHERE TO DINE** ---

ROSALIE'S ROADHOUSE
Phone: 517/849-2120

American
$8-$15

In a converted house, this casual dining spot exudes country charm. Locals gather for wholesome meals of homemade soup, salad, steak, fajitas, burgers, lasagna and specialty pizzas, submarine sandwiches, wraps and panini large enough to share. The breads and pizza dough are made fresh daily. **Bar:** full bar. **Hours:** 11 am-9 pm, Fri & Sat-10 pm. Closed major holidays; also Sun. **Address:** 417 W Chicago St 49250 **Location:** On US 12; center.

KALAMAZOO pop. 77,145

BAYMONT INN & SUITES
Phone: (269)372-7999

Hotel
$58-$170

Address: 2203 S 11th St 49009 **Location:** US 131, exit 36B (Stadium Dr), just w. **Facility:** Smoke free premises. 87 units. 4 stories, interior corridors. **Terms:** cancellation fee imposed. **Guest Services:** valet and coin laundry, wireless Internet.

BEST WESTERN HOSPITALITY INN

Phone: (269)381-1900

Hotel
$80-$130

Address: 3640 E Cork 49001 **Location:** I-94, exit 80 (Sprinkle Rd), just nw. **Facility:** Smoke free premises. 124 units. 3 stories, interior corridors. **Amenities:** video games (fee). **Pool(s):** heated indoor. **Activities:** sauna, whirlpool, exercise room. **Guest Services:** valet and coin laundry, wireless Internet. **Free Special Amenities:** full breakfast and high-speed Internet.

/ SOME UNITS FEE FEE FEE

AAA Benefit:
Members save up to 20%, plus 10% bonus points with free rewards program.

BEST WESTERN PLUS KALAMAZOO SUITES

Phone: (269)350-5522

Hotel
$89-$190

Address: 2575 S 11th St 49009 **Location:** US 131, exit 36B (Stadium Dr), just w. **Facility:** Smoke free premises. 64 units, some efficiencies. 4 stories, interior corridors. **Terms:** cancellation fee imposed. **Amenities:** high-speed Internet. **Pool(s):** heated indoor. **Activities:** whirlpool, exercise room. **Guest Services:** valet and coin laundry, wireless Internet. **Free Special Amenities:** expanded continental breakfast and high-speed Internet.

CALL
/ SOME UNITS FEE

AAA Benefit:
Members save up to 20%, plus 10% bonus points with free rewards program.

CANDLEWOOD SUITES

Phone: (269)270-3203

Extended Stay
Contemporary Hotel
$109-$139

Address: 3443 Retail Place Dr 49048 **Location:** I-94, exit 80 (Sprinkle Rd), just s. **Facility:** Smoke free premises. 95 efficiencies. 4 stories, interior corridors. **Amenities:** high-speed Internet. **Activities:** exercise room, gazebo, barbecue grills. **Guest Services:** complimentary and valet laundry, wireless Internet.
CALL

/ SOME UNITS FEE

CLARION HOTEL

Phone: (269)385-3922

Hotel
$110-$160

Address: 3600 E Cork St 49001 **Location:** I-94, exit 80 (Sprinkle Rd), just n, then just w. **Facility:** Smoke free premises. 149 units. 6 stories, interior corridors. **Terms:** cancellation fee imposed. **Activities:** exercise room. *Fee:* game room. **Guest Services:** valet laundry, wireless Internet.
/ SOME UNITS

COMFORT INN DOWNTOWN KALAMAZOO

Phone: (269)384-2800

Hotel
$120-$150

Address: 739 W Michigan Ave 49007 **Location:** Jct Michkal Ave; downtown. **Facility:** Smoke free premises. 60 units. 3 stories, interior corridors. **Parking:** no self-parking. **Amenities:** high-speed Internet. **Activities:** exercise room. **Guest Services:** valet and coin laundry, wireless Internet.
CALL

FAIRFIELD INN BY MARRIOTT

Hotel
$94-$120

Phone: (269)344-8300

Address: 3800 E Cork St 49001 **Location:** I-94, exit 80 (Sprinkle Rd), just nw. **Facility:** Smoke free premises. 117 units. 3 stories, interior/exterior corridors. **Terms:** cancellation fee imposed. **Amenities:** video games (fee). **Pool(s):** heated outdoor. **Activities:** exercise room. **Guest Services:** valet laundry, wireless Internet.

FAIRFIELD INN-WEST

Hotel
$90-$115

Phone: (269)353-6400

Address: 6420 Cracker Barrel Dr 49009 **Location:** I-94, exit 72 (9th St), just s. **Facility:** Smoke free premises. 62 units. 3 stories, interior corridors. **Terms:** cancellation fee imposed. **Pool(s):** heated indoor. **Guest Services:** valet laundry, wireless Internet.

HALL HOUSE BED & BREAKFAST

Historic Bed & Breakfast
$110-$210

Phone: 269/343-2500

Address: 106 Thompson St 49006 **Location:** US 131, exit 38A, 2.9 mi e on W Main St. **Facility:** Set on a wooded hillside near downtown, this 1923 Georgian Revival inn offers themed rooms. Smoke free premises. 5 units. 3 stories (no elevator), interior corridors. **Terms:** check-in 4:30 pm, age restrictions may apply, 14 day cancellation notice-fee imposed. **Guest Services:** wireless Internet.

HAMPTON INN & SUITES

Hotel
$99-$169

Phone: (269)372-1010

Address: 5059 S 9th St 49009 **Location:** I-94, exit 72 (9th St), 0.5 mi n. **Facility:** Smoke free premises. 78 units. 3 stories, interior corridors. **Terms:** 1-7 night minimum stay, cancellation fee imposed. **Amenities:** video games (fee). **Pool(s):** heated indoor. **Activities:** whirlpool, exercise room. **Guest Services:** valet and coin laundry, wireless Internet.

HAMPTON INN BY HILTON

Hotel
$89-$125

Phone: (269)344-7774

Address: 1550 E Kilgore Rd 49001 **Location:** I-94, exit 78 (Portage Rd), just n, then just w. **Facility:** Smoke free premises. 64 units. 3 stories, interior corridors. **Terms:** 1-7 night minimum stay, cancellation fee imposed. **Pool(s):** heated indoor. **Activities:** whirlpool. **Guest Services:** valet laundry, wireless Internet.

HENDERSON CASTLE BED & BREAKFAST, MEETINGS AND BANQUETS

Historic Bed & Breakfast
$150-$300

Phone: (269)344-1827

Address: 100 Monroe St 49006 **Location:** US 131, exit 38A, 2.9 mi e. **Facility:** The 1895 castle is perched on a hilltop near downtown. With fiber-optic lights in some rooms, the property is recommended for blind guests. Smoke free premises. 6 units, some cottages. 3 stories (no elevator), interior corridors. **Terms:** office hours 9 am-5 pm, check-in 4 pm, 15 day cancellation notice-fee imposed. **Activities:** sauna, whirlpool, steamroom, rooftop hot tub, board games. *Fee:* massage. **Guest Services:** wireless Internet.

HOLIDAY INN EXPRESS

Hotel
$109-$119

Phone: (269)373-0770

Address: 3630 E Cork St 49001 **Location:** I-94, exit 80 (Sprinkle Rd), just n, then just w. **Facility:** Smoke free premises. 64 units. 3 stories, interior corridors. **Amenities:** high-speed Internet. **Pool(s):** heated indoor. **Activities:** exercise room. **Guest Services:** valet laundry, wireless Internet.

HOLIDAY INN-WEST

Hotel
$129-$134

Phone: (269)375-6000

Address: 2747 S 11th St 49009 **Location:** US 131, exit 36B (Stadium Dr), just w. **Facility:** Smoke free premises. 182 units. 4 stories, interior corridors. **Terms:** check-in 4 pm. **Amenities:** video games (fee). **Pool(s):** heated indoor. **Activities:** whirlpool, exercise room. *Fee:* game room. **Guest Services:** valet and coin laundry, area transportation-train station, wireless Internet. *(see ad p. 344)*

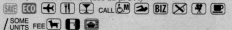

FREE local telephone calls and newspaper

QUALITY INN

Hotel
$70-$150

Phone: (269)381-7000

Address: 3820 Sprinkle Rd 49001 **Location:** I-94, exit 80 (Sprinkle Rd), 0.3 mi s. **Facility:** Smoke free premises. 52 units. 3 stories, interior corridors. **Pool(s):** heated indoor. **Activities:** limited exercise equipment. **Guest Services:** valet laundry, wireless Internet. **Free Special Amenities: expanded continental breakfast and high-speed Internet.**

[SAVE] [icons] / SOME UNITS FEE [icons]

RADISSON PLAZA HOTEL & SUITES

Hotel
Rates not provided

Phone: 269/343-3333

Address: 100 W Michigan Ave 49007 **Location:** Jct Michigan Ave and Rose St; downtown. Located in a historic area. **Facility:** This fashionable hotel with luxury accommodations is in town and within walking distance of the shops of the Kalamazoo Mall. Smoke free premises. 341 units, some efficiencies. 9 stories, interior corridors. **Parking:** on-site (fee) and valet. **Terms:** check-in 4 pm. **Amenities:** high-speed Internet. *Some:* safes. **Dining:** Webster's Prime, Zazios, see separate listings, entertainment. **Pool(s):** heated indoor. **Activities:** saunas, whirlpool, spa. **Guest Services:** valet laundry, wireless Internet. *(see ad p. 345)*

[SAVE] [ECO] [icons] / SOME UNITS [icons]

FREE local telephone calls and high-speed Internet

RED ROOF INN-WEST #7025

Hotel
$50-$110 4/1-11/1
$50-$100 11/2-4/30

Phone: (269)375-7400

Address: 5425 W Michigan Ave 49009 **Location:** US 131, exit 36B (Stadium Dr), just nw. **Facility:** Smoke free premises. 108 units. 2 stories (no elevator), exterior corridors. **Amenities:** safes (fee). **Guest Services:** wireless Internet. **Free Special Amenities: local telephone calls.**

[SAVE] CALL [icons] / SOME UNITS [icons]

RESIDENCE INN BY MARRIOTT

Extended Stay Hotel
$125-$160

Phone: (269)349-0855

Address: 1500 E Kilgore Rd 49001 **Location:** I-94, exit 78 (Portage Rd), just n, then just w. **Facility:** Smoke free premises. 83 kitchen units. 2 stories (no elevator), interior corridors. **Terms:** check-in 4 pm, cancellation fee imposed. **Amenities:** high-speed Internet. **Pool(s):** heated outdoor. **Activities:** whirlpool, exercise room, sports court. **Guest Services:** valet and coin laundry, wireless Internet.

AAA Benefit:
Members save a minimum 5% off the best available rate.

[ECO] [icons] CALL [icons] / SOME UNITS FEE [icons]

STAYBRIDGE SUITES-KALAMAZOO

Extended Stay Hotel
$99-$199

Phone: (269)372-8000

Address: 2001 Seneca Ln 49008 **Location:** US 131, exit 36A (Stadium Dr), 0.3 mi e. Adjacent to West Towne Mall. **Facility:** Smoke free premises. 95 efficiencies, some two bedrooms. 3 stories, interior corridors. **Amenities:** high-speed Internet. **Pool(s):** heated indoor. **Activities:** whirlpool, barbecue grills, patio, exercise room. **Guest Services:** valet and coin laundry, wireless Internet. [icons] CALL [icons] / SOME UNITS FEE [icons]

▼ See AAA listing p. 343 ▼

▼ See AAA listing p. 344 ▼

STUART AVENUE INN BED AND BREAKFAST
Phone: 269/342-0230

Historic Bed
& Breakfast
$109-$189

Address: 229 Stuart Ave 49007 **Location:** US 131, exit 38A, 3 mi e on W Main St. Located in a historic district. **Facility:** Elegantly restored, the Victorian house with its award-winning gardens is decorated with hand-painted wallpapers, Belgian lace curtains and many period antiques. Smoke free premises. 7 units. 3 stories (no elevator), interior corridors. **Terms:** 30 day cancellation notice-fee imposed. **Guest Services:** wireless Internet.

TOWNEPLACE SUITES BY MARRIOTT KALAMAZOO
Phone: (269)353-1500

Extended Stay
Hotel
$114-$139

Address: 5683 S 9th St 49009 **Location:** I-94, exit 72 (9th St), just s. **Facility:** Smoke free premises. 80 efficiencies. 3 stories, interior corridors. **Terms:** cancellation fee imposed. **Amenities:** high-speed Internet. **Pool(s):** heated indoor. **Activities:** gas barbecue grill, patio, exercise room. **Guest Services:** valet and coin laundry, wireless Internet.

> **AAA Benefit:**
> Members save a minimum 5% off the best available rate.

--- **WHERE TO DINE** ---

ASIAGO'S BAKERY & DELI
Phone: 269/544-7230

Deli
$6-$13

Specializing in deli-style sandwiches, wraps, soups and salads, this small, upbeat eatery also offers diners a selection of pizzas, calzones and pastas. Locals frequent this place for eat-in, take-out or delivery meals. **Hours:** 7 am-9 pm, Sun 11 am-7 pm. Closed major holidays. **Address:** 6997 W Q Ave 49009 **Location:** I-94, exit 72 (9th St), 1.2 mi sw to 8th St, then 3 mi s.

BENNUCCI'S CHICAGO OVEN & GRILL
Phone: 269/385-2222

American
$7-$23

Specializing in Chicago-style deep-dish pizza, this casual eatery also prepares hand-cut prime rib, steaks, chicken and pasta. The intimate dining room, with its relaxed Italian villa theme, features a brick fireplace and salad bar. **Bar:** full bar. **Hours:** 11 am-10 pm, Fri & Sat-11 pm, Sun 4 pm-10 pm. Closed major holidays. **Address:** 3717 E Cork St 49001 **Location:** I-94, exit 80 (Sprinkle Rd), just n.

BRAVO RESTAURANT & CAFE
Phone: 269/344-7700

American
$10-$34

This delightful Italian/American eatery makes good use of its wood-burning ovens in preparing cuisine that is at once delightful, well-prepared and delicious. The atmosphere is casually chic and blends restrained traditional touches and attentive service in an entirely non-smoking environment. **Bar:** full bar. **Reservations:** suggested. **Hours:** 11:30 am-10 pm, Fri-11 pm, Sat 5 pm-11 pm, Sun 10:30 am-2 & 4-9 pm. Closed major holidays. **Address:** 5402 Portage Rd 49002 **Location:** I-94, exit 78 (Portage Rd), just s.

COSMO'S CUCINA
Phone: 269/344-5666

American
$13-$22

Above a pub, the comfortable, second-floor dining room offers a large patio and a creative menu that features such diverse items as lamb tenderloin, fresh fish specials and penne with meatballs. **Bar:** full bar. **Hours:** 5 pm-10 pm, Sat also 8:30 am-2 pm, Sun 8:30 am-2 pm. Closed major holidays; also Mon. **Address:** 804 W Vine St 49007 **Location:** On S Westnedge Ave, just w; center. **Parking:** street only.

EPIC BISTRO & BIN 359
Phone: 269/342-1300

American
$14-$27

The stylish and contemporary restaurant is popular with theatergoers. With a menu that changes seasonally, the kitchen uses regional ingredients and global influences to create dramatic items such as braised lamb shank, cornmeal-dusted rainbow trout and grilled ancho chile barbecue pork rib-eye. **Bar:** full bar. **Hours:** 5 pm-10 pm, Fri & Sat-11 pm, Sun-9 pm. Closed major holidays. **Address:** 359 S Kalamazoo Mall, Suite 103 49007 **Location:** Downtown; in Epic Center. **Parking:** on-site (fee) and street.

FOOD DANCE RESTAURANT AND MARKET
Phone: 269/382-1888

American
$8-$28

The restaurant is known as something of a "food haven"—from the herb garden at the entry to the 10-foot-tall asparagus painted as a mural inside. Besides the eclectic interior, diners enjoy interesting grilled and cold sandwich combinations such as white cheddar and tomatoes or smoked ham with horseradish and red onion. Dinner selections include pasta dishes, entree salads or fresh fish, such as grilled sesame-ginger salmon. **Bar:** full bar. **Hours:** 7 am-10 pm, Fri & Sat-11 pm, Sun 8 am-3 pm. Closed major holidays. **Address:** 401 E Michigan Ave 49007 **Location:** Jct Pitcher St; downtown.

THE GREAT LAKES SHIPPING COMPANY
Phone: 269/375-3650

American
$8-$33

Serving a variety of fresh fish, slow-roasted prime rib, choice aged steaks, and creatively prepared chicken and pasta, this nautically themed restaurant has something to suit everyone's taste. The large salad bar offers many fresh items. **Bar:** full bar. **Hours:** 5 pm-10 pm, Fri & Sat-11 pm. Closed: major holidays, 12/24. **Address:** 4525 W KL Ave 49006 **Location:** US 131, exit 36A, just e on Stadium Dr, 0.3 mi n on Drake Ave, then just e.

GREAT WALL OF CHINA
Phone: 269/343-9888

Chinese
$4-$11

The stand-alone restaurant has two dining sections with booth and table seating. On the menu is a fine selection of reasonably priced entrees and combination plates, which are served in generous portions. **Bar:** full bar. **Hours:** 11 am-10 pm, Fri-11 pm, Sat noon-11 pm, Sun noon-10 pm. Closed: 12/25. **Address:** 3025 S Westnedge Ave 49008 **Location:** At Fairfax Ave.

LONDON GRILL-SINGAPORE
Phone: 269/381-9212

Provincial British
$6-$20

The weekend Celtic music in this bistro makes for happy times, but the pleasingly presented dishes featuring curries and fresh seafood delights any day of the week. **Bar:** full bar. **Hours:** 11 am-2 & 5-10 pm, Fri & Sat 4 pm-11 pm, Sun 5 pm-9 pm. Closed major holidays. **Address:** 214 E Michigan Ave 49007 **Location:** Just e of Westnedge Ave; downtown. **Parking:** street only.

OAKWOOD BISTRO
Phone: 269/344-5400

American
$7-$20

Hidden in a strip mall, the restaurant is one of the better-kept secrets of the local dining scene. Informed diners flock to the comfortably laid-back dining room to enjoy the eclectic menu and extensive selection of wines and martinis. While the menu changes seasonally, fresh seafood is a highlight among traditional France- and Asia-inspired dishes. **Bar:** full bar. **Hours:** 11 am-10 pm; Sunday brunch 8:30 am-2 pm. Closed major holidays. **Address:** 3003 Oakland Dr 49006 **Location:** Just n of jct Whites Rd; in shopping plaza.

OLDE PENINSULA BREW PUB & RESTAURANT
Phone: 269/343-2739

American
$8-$18

Pub foods, fresh seafood, great pasta and more than two dozen beers are served in one of the city's oldest buildings. **Bar:** full bar. **Hours:** 11 am-11 pm, Wed & Thurs-midnight, Fri & Sat-1 am, Sun noon-11 pm. Closed major holidays. **Address:** 200 E Michigan Ave 49007 **Location:** Just e of Westnedge Ave; downtown. **Parking:** street only.

RYKSE'S RESTAURANT & BAKERY
Phone: 269/372-3838

American
$6-$12

This family style restaurant offers homemade soup, a variety of vegetarian dishes, "crunchy" baked chicken and they all can be topped off with a selection from the many fresh-baked goods, including giant cinnamon rolls. **Hours:** 6:30 am-8 pm, Mon-3 pm. Closed major holidays; also Sun. **Address:** 5924 Stadium Dr 49009 **Location:** US 131, exit 36B (Stadium Dr), 0.5 mi w.

THE UNION
Phone: 269/384-6756

American
$6-$22

Specializing in grilled and roasted meats, the menu also features locally caught fish and freshly picked produce. It's a great place to hobnob before or after the game. **Bar:** full bar. **Hours:** 11 am-11 pm, Fri-midnight, Sat noon-midnight. Closed major holidays; also Sun. **Address:** 125 S Kalamazoo Mall 49007 **Location:** Jct E Michigan Ave; downtown. **Parking:** street only. CALL ⊜M

WEBSTER'S PRIME
Phone: 269/343-4444

American
$21-$55

The open display kitchen with its embossed copper front and Old World ambience set the stage for a classic steakhouse experience. White tablecloths, monogrammed china, and subdued lighting combine to create a sophisticated dining environment. The menu focuses on prime steaks and chops with vegetables and toppings offered a la carte. A number of pasta and seafood selections also are offered. Noteworthy is the three-course prix fixe that can be paired with a choice of wine or beer. **Bar:** full bar. **Reservations:** suggested. **Hours:** 5 pm-10 pm, Fri & Sat-11 pm. Closed: 1/1; also Sun. **Address:** 100 W Michigan Ave 49007 **Location:** Jct Michigan Ave and Rose St; downtown; in Radisson Plaza Hotel & Suites. **Parking:** on-site and valet. CALL ⊜M

ZAZIOS
Phone: 269/384-2650

Italian
$9-$35

The knowledgeable staff provides friendly service in a lively setting characterized by vibrant decor. Entrees range from custom pizza and pasta dishes to well-prepared seafood and steak preparations. Excellent selections reside in the on-site wine cellar. **Bar:** full bar. **Reservations:** suggested. **Hours:** 11 am-4 & 5-10 pm, Fri & Sat-11 pm. Closed: 11/24; also Sun. **Address:** 100 W Michigan Ave 49007 **Location:** Jct Michigan Ave and Rose St; downtown; in Radisson Plaza Hotel & Suites. **Parking:** on-site and valet. CALL ⊜M

KALKASKA pop. 2,226

ALL SEASONS RESORT
Phone: 231/258-0000

Hotel
Rates not provided

Address: 760 S Cedar St 49646 **Location:** On US 131 and SR 72, 0.8 mi e. **Facility:** Smoke free premises. 61 units. 2 stories (no elevator), interior corridors. **Parking:** winter plug-ins. **Pool(s):** heated indoor. **Activities:** whirlpool, snowmobiling, exercise room. *Fee:* game room. **Guest Services:** wireless Internet.

KENTWOOD pop. 45,255   (See map and index starting on p. 324)

COMFORT INN
Phone: (616)957-2080   **45**

Hotel
$67-$126

Address: 4155 28th St SE 49512 **Location:** I-96, exit 43A, 1.5 mi w on SR 11. **Facility:** Smoke free premises. 106 units. 3 stories, interior corridors. **Activities:** exercise room. **Guest Services:** coin laundry, wireless Internet.

COURTYARD BY MARRIOTT GRAND RAPIDS AIRPORT
Phone: (616)954-0500   **44**

Hotel
$135-$173

Address: 4741 28th St SE 49512 **Location:** I-96, exit 43A, 0.8 mi w on SR 11. **Facility:** Smoke free premises. 84 units. 3 stories, interior corridors. **Terms:** cancellation fee imposed. **Pool(s):** heated indoor. **Activities:** whirlpool, exercise room. **Guest Services:** valet and coin laundry, wireless Internet.

AAA Benefit:
Members save a minimum 5% off the best available rate.

EXTENDED STAYAMERICA GRAND RAPIDS-KENTWOOD
Phone: (616)977-6750   **49**

Extended Stay Hotel
$43-$70

Address: 3747 29th St SE 49512 **Location:** I-96, exit 43A, 2 mi w on SR 11, then just s. **Facility:** Smoke free premises. 104 kitchen units. 3 stories, interior corridors. **Terms:** office hours 7 am-11 pm, cancellation fee imposed. **Guest Services:** coin laundry, wireless Internet.

(See map and index starting on p. 324)

THE GATEHOUSE SUITES

Phone: 616/957-8111 **46**

Extended Stay Hotel
Rates not provided

Address: 2701 E Beltline Ave 49546 **Location:** Jct SR 11 and E Beltline Ave (SR 37). **Facility:** Smoke free premises. 96 kitchen units. 2 stories (no elevator), exterior corridors. **Pool(s):** heated outdoor. **Activities:** whirlpool, exercise room, sports court, basketball, volleyball. **Guest Services:** valet and coin laundry, wireless Internet.

HILTON GRAND RAPIDS AIRPORT

Phone: (616)957-0100 **43**

Hotel
S88-S166

Address: 4747 28th St SE 49512 **Location:** I-96, exit 43A, 0.5 mi w on SR 11. **Facility:** Smoke free premises. 226 units. 4 stories, interior corridors. **Terms:** 1-7 night minimum stay, cancellation fee imposed. **Amenities:** video games (fee). **Dining:** Spinnaker, see separate listing. **Pool(s):** heated indoor. **Activities:** sauna, whirlpool, exercise room. **Guest Services:** valet laundry, area transportation-within 2 mi, wireless Internet.

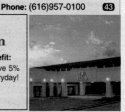

Hilton

AAA Benefit:
Members save 5% or more everyday!

FREE high-speed Internet and airport transportation

HOLIDAY INN GRAND RAPIDS AIRPORT

Phone: (616)285-7600 **51**

Hotel
$79-$169

Address: 3063 Lake Eastbrook Blvd SE 49512 **Location:** I-96, exit 43A, 2 mi w on SR 11, then just s. **Facility:** Smoke free premises. 148 units. 3 stories, interior corridors. **Parking:** winter plug-ins. **Amenities:** video games (fee), high-speed Internet. **Pool(s):** heated indoor. **Activities:** whirlpool, exercise room. **Guest Services:** valet and coin laundry, area transportation-within 2 mi, wireless Internet.

RAMADA PLAZA HOTEL

Phone: (616)949-9222 **47**

Hotel
$64-$144

Address: 3333 28th St SE 49512 **Location:** Jct SR 11 and E Beltline Ave (SR 37). Located at Woodland Shopping Mall. **Facility:** Smoke free premises. 181 units. 5 stories, interior corridors. **Terms:** check-in 4 pm, cancellation fee imposed. **Amenities:** Fee: video games, safes. **Pool(s):** heated indoor. **Activities:** whirlpool, waterslide, exercise room. Fee: game room. **Guest Services:** valet and coin laundry, area transportation-within 2 mi, wireless Internet. **Free Special Amenities: high-speed Internet and airport transportation.**

SLEEP INN

Phone: (616)975-9000 **48**

Hotel
$56-$63

Address: 4284 29th St 49512 **Location:** I-96, exit 43A, 1 mi w on SR 11, then just s on Acquest Ave. **Facility:** Smoke free premises. 78 units. 3 stories, interior corridors. **Pool(s):** heated indoor. **Activities:** whirlpool, exercise room. Fee: game room. **Guest Services:** valet and coin laundry, wireless Internet.

STAYBRIDGE SUITES

Phone: (616)464-3200 **50**

Extended Stay Hotel
$119-$149

Address: 3000 Lake Eastbrook Blvd SE 49512 **Location:** I-96, exit 43A, 2 mi w on SR 11, then just s. **Facility:** Smoke free premises. 94 efficiencies, some two bedrooms. 3 stories, interior corridors. **Amenities:** high-speed Internet, safes. **Pool(s):** heated outdoor. **Activities:** whirlpool, exercise room. **Guest Services:** complimentary and valet laundry, area transportation-within 3 mi, wireless Internet.

———— WHERE TO DINE ————

SEOUL GARDEN

Phone: 616/956-1522 **24**

Asian
$6-$18

The contemporary restaurant serves a wide selection of sushi and Asian cuisine, including tempting dishes such as chicken and vegetable tempura, and shrimp teriyaki served with miso soup, salad and rice. **Bar:** full bar. **Hours:** 11 am-10 pm, Fri & Sat-11 pm. Closed: 11/24, 12/25; also Sun. **Address:** 3321 28th St SE 49546 **Location:** Just w of jct SR 11 and E Beltline (SR 37); at Woodland Mall.

SPINNAKER

Phone: 616/957-0100 **23**

American
$8-$40

The dining room offers a wide selection of specialties such as teriyaki roasted halibut, chicken Mediterranean, cowboy steak and herb-crusted pork tenderloin. It's a place that's popular with the locals for its award-winning Sunday brunch. **Bar:** full bar. **Hours:** 6:30 am-10 pm, Sat from 7 am, Sun 7 am-2 pm. **Address:** 4747 28th St SE 49512 **Location:** I-96, exit 43A, 0.5 mi w on SR 11; in Hilton Grand Rapids Airport.

YEN CHING

Phone: 616/940-4111

Chinese
$6-$28

Mandarin and Szechuan dishes are served in a casual atmosphere. **Bar:** full bar. **Hours:** 10:30 am-9:30 pm, Fri & Sat-10:30 pm, Sun noon-9 pm. Closed: 7/4, 12/25. **Address:** 4605 28th St SE 49508 **Location:** On SR 11; in Roaring '20s Mall.

LAKE ORION —See Detroit p. 281.

LANSING pop. 119,128—See also East Lansing p. 314

COUNTRY INN & SUITES BY CARLSON
Phone: (517)827-7000

Hotel
$94-$174

Address: 6511 Centurion Dr 48917 **Location:** I-496, exit 1 (Creyts Rd), just n. **Facility:** Smoke free premises. 87 units, some two bedrooms. 3 stories, interior corridors. **Terms:** cancellation fee imposed. **Amenities:** high-speed Internet. **Pool(s):** heated indoor. **Activities:** whirlpool, exercise room. **Guest Services:** valet and coin laundry, wireless Internet. **Free Special Amenities:** expanded continental breakfast and high-speed Internet. *(see ad p. 6)*

COURTYARD BY MARRIOTT
Phone: (517)482-0500

Hotel
$125-$160

Address: 2710 Lake Lansing Rd 48912 **Location:** US 127, exit Lake Lansing Rd, just w. **Facility:** Smoke free premises. 129 units. 2 stories (no elevator), interior corridors. **Terms:** cancellation fee imposed. **Amenities:** video games (fee), high-speed Internet. **Pool(s):** heated indoor. **Activities:** whirlpool, exercise room. **Guest Services:** valet and coin laundry, wireless Internet.

AAA Benefit:
Members save a minimum 5% off the best available rate.

FREE full breakfast and high-speed Internet

FAIRFIELD INN BY MARRIOTT-WEST
Phone: (517)886-1066

Hotel
$81-$104

Address: 810 Delta Commerce Dr 48917 **Location:** I-96, exit 93B (SR 43/Saginaw Hwy), 0.4 mi e; behind Bennigans. **Facility:** Smoke free premises. 64 units. 3 stories, interior corridors. **Terms:** cancellation fee imposed. **Pool(s):** heated indoor. **Activities:** whirlpool. **Guest Services:** valet laundry, wireless Internet.

AAA Benefit:
Members save a minimum 5% off the best available rate.

HAMPTON INN OF LANSING
Phone: (517)627-8381

Hotel
$89-$116

Address: 525 N Canal Rd 48917 **Location:** I-96, exit 93B (SR 43/Saginaw Hwy), just e. **Facility:** Smoke free premises. 105 units. 3 stories, interior corridors. **Terms:** 1-7 night minimum stay, cancellation fee imposed. **Amenities:** high-speed Internet. **Pool(s):** heated indoor. **Activities:** whirlpool, exercise room. **Guest Services:** valet and coin laundry, wireless Internet.

AAA Benefit:
Members save up to 10% everyday!

FREE expanded continental breakfast and high-speed Internet

LEXINGTON LANSING HOTEL
Phone: (517)323-7100

Hotel
$150-$300

Address: 925 S Creyts Rd 48917 **Location:** I-496, exit 1 (Creyts Rd), just n. Located in an office park. **Facility:** Smoke free premises. 212 units. 5 stories, interior corridors. **Terms:** cancellation fee imposed. **Amenities:** video games (fee), high-speed Internet. **Dining:** Christie's Bistro, see separate listing. **Pool(s):** heated indoor. **Activities:** whirlpool, kid's activity area, exercise room, sports court. **Guest Services:** valet laundry, area transportation-within 10 mi, wireless Internet. **Free Special Amenities:** high-speed Internet and airport transportation.

MOTEL 6 LANSING WEST #1089
Phone: (517)321-1444

Motel
$45-$55

Address: 7326 W Saginaw Hwy 48917 **Location:** I-96, exit 93B (SR 43/Saginaw Hwy), just e. Located in a quiet area. **Facility:** Smoke free premises. 104 units. 1 story, exterior corridors. **Pool(s):** outdoor. **Guest Services:** coin laundry, wireless Internet.

QUALITY INN UNIVERSITY PLACE

Hotel
$89-$149

Address: 3121 E Grand River Ave 48912 **Location:** On I-96 business route and SR 43, just e of US 127. **Facility:** Smoke free premises. 105 units. 2 stories (no elevator), interior corridors. **Terms:** check-in 4 pm, cancellation fee imposed. **Amenities:** safes (fee). **Pool(s):** heated indoor. **Activities:** whirlpool, domed recreation center, exercise room. *Fee:* game room. **Guest Services:** valet and coin laundry, area transportation-within 7 mi, wireless Internet. *(see ad below)*

Phone: (517)351-1440

FREE full breakfast and high-speed Internet

▼ *See AAA listing p. 404* ▼

QUALITY SUITES HOTEL

Hotel
$79-$99

Phone: (517)886-0600

Address: 901 Delta Commerce Dr 48917 **Location:** I-96, exit 93B (SR 43/Saginaw Hwy), 0.3 mi e to Bennigan's, then just n. **Facility:** Smoke free premises. 117 units. 4 stories, interior corridors. **Activities:** sauna, whirlpool, exercise room. **Guest Services:** valet laundry, area transportation-within 5 mi, wireless Internet. **Free Special Amenities: expanded continental breakfast and manager's reception.**

RADISSON HOTEL LANSING

[fyi]
Hotel
$179-$289

Phone: (517)482-0188

Under major renovation, scheduled to be completed August 2011. **Last rated:** ♥♥♥ **Address:** 111 N Grand Ave 48933 **Location:** Corner of Michigan and Grand aves; downtown. **Facility:** Smoke free premises. 256 units. 11 stories, interior corridors. **Parking:** valet and street only. **Terms:** check-in 4 pm. **Amenities:** video games (fee). *Some:* safes. **Dining:** Capitol City Grille, see separate listing. **Pool(s):** heated indoor. **Activities:** sauna, whirlpool, exercise room. **Guest Services:** valet and coin laundry, wireless Internet.

RED ROOF INN-WEST #7020

Hotel
$47-$68

Phone: (517)321-7246

Address: 7412 W Saginaw Hwy 48917 **Location:** I-96, exit 93B (SR 43/Saginaw Hwy), just e. Located in a commercial area. **Facility:** Smoke free premises. 81 units. 2 stories (no elevator), exterior corridors. **Amenities:** *Fee:* video games, safes. **Guest Services:** wireless Internet. **Free Special Amenities: local telephone calls.**

RESIDENCE INN BY MARRIOTT WEST

Extended Stay
Hotel
$110-$120

Phone: (517)886-5030

Address: 922 Delta Commerce Dr 48917 **Location:** I-96, exit 93B (SR 43/Saginaw Hwy), 0.4 mi e; behind Bennigan's. **Facility:** Smoke free premises. 78 units, some two bedrooms, efficiencies and kitchens. 3 stories, interior corridors. **Terms:** cancellation fee imposed. **Pool(s):** heated indoor. **Activities:** whirlpool, exercise room, sports court. **Guest Services:** valet and coin laundry, wireless Internet.

AAA Benefit:
Members save a minimum 5% off the best available rate.

SPRINGHILL SUITES BY MARRIOTT LANSING

Hotel
$98-$125

Phone: (517)627-0002

Address: 111 S Marketplace Blvd 48917 **Location:** I-96, exit 93A (SR 43/Saginaw Hwy), just w, then 0.5 mi s. **Facility:** Smoke free premises. 104 units. 3 stories, interior corridors. **Terms:** cancellation fee imposed. **Amenities:** high-speed Internet. **Pool(s):** heated indoor. **Activities:** whirlpool, exercise room. **Guest Services:** valet and coin laundry, wireless Internet.

AAA Benefit:
Members save a minimum 5% off the best available rate.

—— WHERE TO DINE ——

BENSON'S VINAIGRETTES

American
$8-$14

Phone: 517/703-9616

This cozy, family-run restaurant serves fresh, wholesome selections at reasonable prices. Selections range from freshly prepared soups and sandwiches to rotating preparations of comfort foods such as mac and cheese, roasted chicken and pork tenderloin. Desserts are prepared fresh in house. **Hours:** 11 am-8 pm, Fri & Sat-9 pm. Closed major holidays; also Sun. **Address:** 940 Elmwood St 48917 **Location:** I-96/69, exit SR 43 (W Saginaw Hwy), 1.5 mi e; adjacent to Lansing Mall.

CAPITOL CITY GRILLE

American
$10-$22

Phone: 517/482-0188

The sleek and upscale restaurant is a popular gathering spot for local government officials and visitors. The extensive a la carte menu of contemporary American cuisine includes selections ranging from hamburgers to prime steaks. Breakfast and lunch buffets are well-priced choices for diners looking for a few different options. **Bar:** full bar. **Hours:** 6:30 am-10 pm. **Address:** 111 N Grand Ave 48933 **Location:** Corner of Michigan and Grand aves; downtown; in Radisson Hotel Lansing. **Parking:** valet and street only.

CHRISTIE'S BISTRO

American
$8-$35

Phone: 517/323-4190

Tucked away off the floor of the hotel lobby, the bistro evokes a European alleyway restaurant with its sky mural on the ceiling, chunks of exposed brick on the walls and framed, shuttered mirrors adding to the decor. The menu provides standards ranging from soups and sandwiches to steaks, chicken, fish and pasta dishes. **Bar:** full bar. **Hours:** 6:30 am-midnight, Sat & Sun from 7 am. **Address:** 925 S Creyts Rd 48917 **Location:** I-496, exit 1 (Creyts Rd), just n; in Lexington Lansing Hotel.

THE CLADDAGH IRISH PUB

Irish
$8-$18

Phone: 517/484-2523

Nooks and crannies dotted throughout lend to the Irish pub's character. A large selection of imported beers complements typical pub food, including fish and chips, shepherd's pie, Celtic corned beef and cabbage, beef and Guinness stew, bangers and mash, and an array of sandwiches and burgers. **Bar:** full bar. **Hours:** 11 am-11 pm, Fri & Sat-midnight, Sun-9 pm. Closed: 12/25. **Address:** 2900 Towne Center Blvd 48912 **Location:** Jct US 127 and Lake Lansing Rd, just w; in west end of Eastwood Towne Center.

CLARA'S RESTAURANT

American
$8-$18

Phone: 517/372-7120

Built in 1905, this fun family restaurant, once a railroad station, has a long menu with something to please everyone. The chicken Hawaiian is delicious. **Bar:** full bar. **Hours:** 11 am-10 pm, Fri & Sat-11 pm, Sun 10 am-10 pm. Closed major holidays. **Address:** 637 E Michigan Ave 48912 **Location:** Downtown; just e of Capitol Building Complex.

FINLEY'S AMERICAN GRILL

Phone: 517/323-4309

American
$6-$15

Everyone is welcome at this casual family restaurant. Baby-back ribs and such succulent steak as top sirloin and New York strip are popular specialties on a menu that centers on good basic fare. The uniformed staff provides friendly, prompt service. **Bar:** full bar. **Hours:** 11 am-10 pm, Fri & Sat-11 pm, Sun-9 pm. Closed: 11/24, 12/25. **Address:** 5615 W Saginaw Hwy 48917 **Location:** I-96, exit 93B (SR 43/Saginaw Hwy), 2 mi e.

MITCHELL'S FISH MARKET

Phone: 517/482-3474

Seafood
$17-$30

A variety of fresh, never-frozen fish is flown in daily, and market availability determines the daily specials. Diners may order fish grilled, broiled, blackened or steamed in the Shanghai style with ginger, spinach and sticky rice. Among other choices are steak, pasta and chicken selections. **Bar:** full bar. **Reservations:** suggested. **Hours:** 11:30 am-10 pm, Fri & Sat-11 pm, Sun-9 pm. **Address:** 2975 Preyde Blvd 48912 **Location:** US 127, exit Lake Lansing Rd, just w; in Eastwood Towne Center. CALL &M

P.F. CHANG'S CHINA BISTRO

Phone: 517/267-3833

Chinese
$10-$21

Trendy, upscale decor provides a pleasant backdrop for New Age Chinese dining. Appetizers, soups and salads are a meal by themselves. Vegetarian plates and sides, noodles, meins, chicken and meat dishes are created from exotic, fresh ingredients. **Bar:** full bar. **Hours:** 11 am-11 pm, Fri & Sat-midnight. Closed: 11/24, 12/25. **Address:** 2425 Lake Lansing Rd 48912 **Location:** US 127, exit Lake Lansing Rd, just w; in Eastwood Towne Center. CALL &M

LAPEER pop. 9,072

BEST WESTERN LAPEER INN

Phone: (810)667-9444

Hotel
$89-$109

Address: 770 West St 48446 **Location:** I-69, exit 155 (SR 24), 2 mi n. **Facility:** Smoke free premises. 89 units. 2 stories (no elevator), interior corridors. **Amenities:** *Some:* high-speed Internet, safes. **Pool(s):** heated indoor. **Activities:** whirlpool, indoor recreation center, exercise room. *Fee:* game room. **Guest Services:** valet and coin laundry, wireless Internet. **Free Special Amenities: continental breakfast and use of on-premises laundry facilities.**

AAA Benefit:
Members save up to 20%, plus 10% bonus points with free rewards program.

 /SOME UNITS

THE LAPEER HOTEL

Phone: (810)245-7700

Hotel
$95-$135

Address: 927 Demille Rd 48446 **Location:** I-69, exit 155 (SR 24), 1.2 mi n, then just e. **Facility:** Smoke free premises. 72 units. 3 stories, interior corridors. **Terms:** cancellation fee imposed. **Pool(s):** heated indoor. **Activities:** whirlpool, exercise room. **Guest Services:** valet and coin laundry, wireless Internet. CALL &M /SOME UNITS FEE

——— WHERE TO DINE ———

E.G. NICK'S

Phone: 810/664-6200

American
$8-$20

Located in a bustling retail area near the interstate, this casual restaurant offers a menu of old favorites and innovative dishes including planked whitefish and their house specialty of basted ribs. **Bar:** full bar. **Hours:** 11 am-10 pm, Fri & Sat-11 pm, Sun noon-9 pm. Closed: 11/24, 12/25. **Address:** 825 S Main St 48446 **Location:** 0.5 mi s on SR 24 and 21. CALL &M

LELAND pop. 2,033

——— WHERE TO DINE ———

THE COVE

Phone: 231/256-9834

American
$9-$24

Window tables and patio seating afford great views of Lake Michigan and the Manitou Islands. Seafood chowder and varied preparations of whitefish, such as macadamia nut whitefish, garlic Parmesan whitefish and campfire whitefish, are menu specialties. **Bar:** full bar. **Reservations:** suggested, in season. **Hours:** Open 5/15-10/31; 11 am-9 pm, Fri & Sat-10 pm; hours may vary. **Address:** 111 River St 49654 **Location:** Just w of Main St. **Parking:** street only.

LEXINGTON pop. 1,104

INN THE GARDEN BED & BREAKFAST

Phone: 810/359-8966

Historic Bed
& Breakfast
$90-$140

Address: 7156 Huron Ave 48450 **Location:** Center of town. **Facility:** Spacious grounds and a small greenhouse provide fresh herbs and produce for the breakfasts at this attractive Victorian-style house. Smoke free premises. 4 units, some two bedrooms. 3 stories (no elevator), interior corridors. **Terms:** check-in 4 pm, 2 night minimum stay - seasonal and/or weekends, 7 day cancellation notice. **Guest Services:** wireless Internet.

LINCOLN PARK —See Detroit p. 282.

LINWOOD

—— WHERE TO DINE ——

LINWOOD CORNERS RESTAURANT

Phone: 989/697-5141

American
$4-$12

Home-style comfort foods, such as roast turkey, pork chops, steak and good-old apple pie, make up the bulk of this casual restaurant's family-oriented menu. **Hours:** 5 am-8 pm. Closed: 12/25; also for dinner 12/24. **Address:** 44 N Huron Ave 48634 **Location:** I-75, exit 173, 2.3 mi e on Linwood Rd, then 0.3 mi n on SR 13.

LIVONIA —See Detroit p. 282.

LUDINGTON pop. 8,357

BEST WESTERN SPLASH PARK INN

Phone: (231)843-2140

Hotel
$75-$180

Address: 5005 W US 10 49431 **Location:** US 31, exit 170B, 1 mi w. **Facility:** Smoke free premises. 87 units, some two bedrooms and kitchens. 2-3 stories (no elevator), interior corridors. **Parking:** winter plug-ins. **Amenities:** *Some:* video games, high-speed Internet. **Pool(s):** heated indoor. **Activities:** sauna, whirlpool, waterslide, picnic area, playground, exercise room, horseshoes, shuffleboard. *Fee:* game room. **Guest Services:** coin laundry, wireless Internet. **Free Special Amenities:** expanded continental breakfast and high-speed Internet.

AAA Benefit:
Members save up to 20%, plus 10% bonus points with free rewards program.

CARTIER MANSION BED & BREAKFAST AND CONFERENCE CENTER

Phone: (231)843-0101

Historic Bed
& Breakfast
$99-$225

Address: 409 E Ludington Ave 49431 **Location:** US 31, exit 170B, 2.8 mi w on US 10. **Facility:** This stately B&B features antiques, original chandeliers and parquet floors. A library houses nearly 1,000 volumes to entertain guests. Smoke free premises. 5 units. 3 stories (no elevator), interior corridors. **Terms:** office hours 8 am-9 pm, check-in 4 pm, 2 night minimum stay - seasonal and/or weekends, 7 day cancellation notice. **Guest Services:** wireless Internet. **Free Special Amenities: full breakfast and high-speed Internet.**

HOLIDAY INN EXPRESS

Phone: (231)845-7004

Hotel
$89-$249

Address: 5323 W US 10 49431 **Location:** US 31, exit 170B, 1.3 mi w. **Facility:** Smoke free premises. 102 units, some two bedrooms and kitchens. 2-3 stories, interior corridors. **Terms:** check-in 4 pm, 2 night minimum stay - seasonal and/or weekends, cancellation fee imposed. **Amenities:** safes. *Some:* video games (fee), high-speed Internet. **Pool(s):** heated indoor. **Activities:** sauna, whirlpool, barbecue grill, playground, exercise room, horseshoes, shuffleboard. *Fee:* game room. **Guest Services:** valet and coin laundry, wireless Internet.

THE LAMPLIGHTER BED & BREAKFAST

Phone: 231/843-9792

Bed & Breakfast
$100-$170

Address: 602 E Ludington Ave 49431 **Location:** US 31, exit 170B, 2.8 mi w on US 10. **Facility:** This restored turn-of-the-20th-century Victorian home has European-style elegance. Multi-course breakfasts are served on antique china and crystal. Smoke free premises. 5 units. 2 stories (no elevator), interior corridors. **Terms:** office hours 8 am-9 pm, check-in 4 pm, 2 night minimum stay - seasonal and/or weekends, age restrictions may apply, 7 day cancellation notice-fee imposed. **Guest Services:** wireless Internet. **Free Special Amenities: full breakfast and high-speed Internet.**

VIKING ARMS INN

Phone: 231/843-3441

Motel
$60-$160 4/1-9/4
$55-$85 9/5-4/30

Address: 930 E Ludington Ave 49431 **Location:** US 31, 2.2 mi w on US 10. Opposite Memorial Medical Center. **Facility:** Smoke free premises. 45 units. 1 story, interior/exterior corridors. **Terms:** age restrictions may apply, cancellation fee imposed. **Pool(s):** heated outdoor. **Activities:** whirlpool. **Guest Services:** wireless Internet. **Free Special Amenities: continental breakfast and high-speed Internet.**

—— WHERE TO DINE ——

P. M. STEAMERS

Phone: 231/843-9555

Seafood
$10-$30

Across from the city marina, the casual waterfront restaurant is a comfortable place for family dining. The menu includes a good selection of steaks, seafood, pizza and burgers—as well as mouthwatering desserts. Sunday brunch is popular during summer. **Bar:** full bar. **Reservations:** suggested. **Hours:** 5 pm-9 pm, Sat from 4 pm; hours may vary. Closed: 11/24, 12/25. **Address:** 502 W Loomis St 49431 **Location:** Corner of Loomis and Lewis sts; center.

SCOTTY'S

Phone: 231/843-4033

American
$5-$25

Popular dishes include the roast prime rib of beef - the specialty of the house along with several seafood dishes such as their "renowned" lake perch or the seafood kabob. Booths available for more intimate dining. **Bar:** full bar. **Reservations:** suggested. **Hours:** 11:30 am-2 & 5-9 pm, Fri & Sat-10 pm; to 10 pm, Sun 9 am-1 pm 6/1-9/30. Closed major holidays. **Address:** 5910 E Ludington Ave 49431 **Location:** 1.8 mi w of jct US 10 and 31.

MACKINAC ISLAND pop. 523 (See map and index starting on p. 360)

GRAND HOTEL

▽▽▽ ▽▽▽ ▽▽▽
Classic Historic
Resort Hotel
$498-S728

Address: Mackinac Island 49757 **Location:** On Mackinac Island. **Facility:** This historic 1887 hotel sits on beautifully landscaped grounds overlooking the Straits of Mackinac. A strict dress policy goes into effect at 6 pm. Designated smoking area. 385 units, some two bedrooms and cottages. 6 stories, interior corridors. **Parking:** no self-parking. **Terms:** open 5/4-10/28, check-in 4 pm, 10 day cancellation notice-fee imposed. **Amenities:** safes, honor bars. **Dining:** 3 restaurants, entertainment. **Pool(s):** heated outdoor. **Activities:** sauna, whirlpools, 4 tennis courts, recreation programs in season, bocci, croquet, exercise trail, rental bicycles, hiking trails, jogging, exercise room, horseshoes, volleyball. *Fee:* golf-18 holes, horseback riding, massage, game room. **Guest Services:** valet laundry, wireless Internet, beauty salon. *(see ad below)*

Phone: (906)847-3331 **39**

[SAVE] [ECO] [icons] CALL [icons] [BIZ] [icons]
/SOME UNITS

FREE full breakfast and high-speed Internet

▼ See AAA listing above ▼

Create complete trip routings and custom place maps with the TripTik® Travel Planner on AAA.com or CAA.ca

(See map and index starting on p. 360)

HARBOUR VIEW INN

Historic Hotel
S89-S299

Phone: (906)847-0101   **37**

Address: 6860 Main St 49757 **Location:** 4 blks e. **Facility:** The manor was built in 1820 as a home for the granddaughter of a chief of the Ottawa Indian Nation. Many rooms offer harbor or garden views. Smoke free premises. 84 units. 4 stories, interior corridors. **Parking:** no self-parking. **Terms:** open 5/6-10/22, 2 night minimum stay - weekends, 10 day cancellation notice-fee imposed. **Guest Services:** wireless Internet.
(see ad below)

FREE continental breakfast and local telephone calls

THE INN ON MACKINAC

Bed & Breakfast
$79-$289

Phone: (906)847-3360   **36**

Address: 6896 Main St 49757 **Location:** 3 blks e. **Facility:** Smoke free premises. 44 units. 5 stories, interior corridors. **Parking:** no self-parking. **Terms:** open 5/6-10/8, 2-3 night minimum stay - seasonal and/or weekends, 14 day cancellation notice-fee imposed. **Activities:** whirlpool. **Guest Services:** wireless Internet.

▼ *See AAA listing above* ▼

Harbour View Inn

MACKINAC ISLAND

Overlooking

Mackinac Island's

Historic Harbor

83 Uniquely Decorated

Guest Rooms & Suites

Complimentary Deluxe

Continental Breakfast

♥♥ *Membership Discounts on Select Dates*

Box 1207 · Mackinac Island · Michigan · 49757
www.harbourviewinn.com

906-847-0101

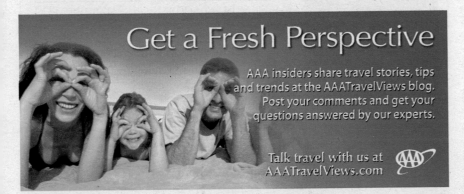

(See map and index starting on p. 360)

ISLAND HOUSE HOTEL

◆◆◆
Historic
Hotel
S99-S375

Address: 6966 Main St 49757 **Location:** 3 blks e. **Facility:** Accommodations vary in this renovated 1852 historic hotel. Smoke free premises. 96 units, some two bedrooms. 4 stories, interior corridors. **Parking:** no self-parking. **Terms:** open 5/3-10/24, check-in 4 pm, 2 night minimum stay - weekends, 3 day cancellation notice-fee imposed. **Amenities:** *Some:* safes. **Dining:** 2 restaurants. **Pool(s):** heated indoor. **Activities:** sauna, whirlpool, rental bicycles. **Guest Services:** wireless Internet. *(see ad below)*

Phone: 906/847-3347   38

[SAVE] [¶] [Y] [🏊] [BIZ] [✕] [👤] / SOME UNITS [📶] [▣] [☕]

▼ See AAA listing above ▼

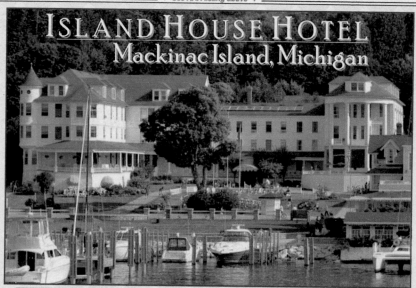

HISTORIC HOTELS
of AMERICA
NATIONAL TRUST FOR HISTORIC PRESERVATION®

Discover the Charm
of a Mackinac Island stay...

MACKINAC ISLAND'S OLDEST HOTEL, ESTABLISHED 1852

Air Conditioning • Indoor Heated Pool
Two Restaurants On-Site • Private Baths
96 Guest Rooms • Packages Available
Part of Mackinac
Island State Park

RESERVATIONS
(800) 626-6304
theislandhouse.com

(See map and index starting on p. 360)

LAKE VIEW HOTEL AND CONFERENCE CENTER

Phone: (906)847-3384   **41**

Historic
Hotel
$104-$435

Address: 7542 Main St 49757 **Location:** Center. Opposite Star Line Ferry Dock. **Facility:** The restored 1858 hotel offers a variety of units, attractive public areas and an enclosed courtyard with pool and spa. Close to shops and dining. Smoke free premises. 85 units. 4 stories, interior corridors. **Parking:** no self-parking. **Terms:** open 5/6-10/23, 3 day cancellation notice-fee imposed. **Pool(s):** heated indoor. **Activities:** sauna, whirlpool. **Guest Services:** wireless Internet. *(see ad below)*

SAVE ▯▯ ▯ CALL ▯ ▯ ▯ ▯ / SOME UNITS ▯

(See map and index starting on p. 360)

MURRAY HOTEL

Classic Hotel

$79-$305

Phone: (906)847-3360 **40**

Address: 7260 Main St 49757 **Location:** Center. Opposite Arnold Ferry Dock. **Facility:** Guest rooms at this quaintly decorated 1882 hotel in a lively area vary in size and comfort. A fudge shop and deli are in the lobby. Smoke free premises. 69 units. 4 stories, interior corridors. **Parking:** no self-parking. **Terms:** open 5/6-10/9, 2-3 night minimum stay - seasonal and/or weekends, 14 day cancellation notice-fee imposed. **Activities:** whirlpool. **Guest Services:** wireless Internet.

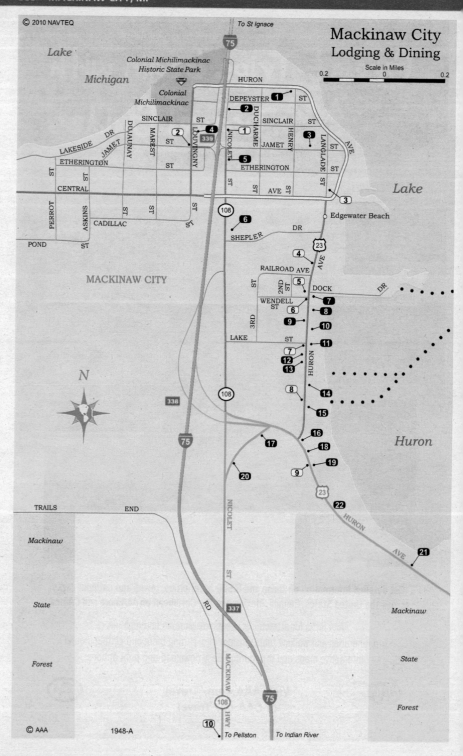

© 2010 NAVTEQ

Mackinaw City
Lodging & Dining

Scale in Miles
0.2   0   0.2

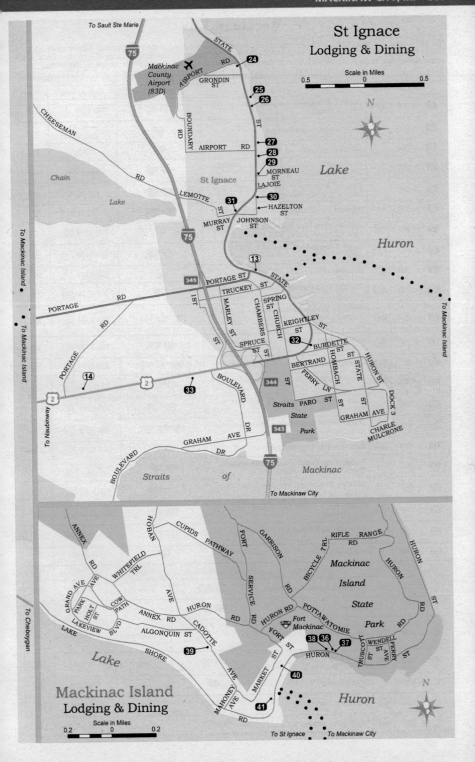

St Ignace
Lodging & Dining

Mackinac Island
Lodging & Dining

Mackinaw City

This index helps you "spot" where approved lodgings and restaurants are located on the corresponding detailed maps. Lodging daily rate range is for comparison only and show the property's high season. Restaurant rate range is a combination of lunch and/or dinner. Turn to the listing page for more detailed rate information and consult display ads for special promotions.

MACKINAW CITY

Map Page	OA	Lodgings	Diamond Rated	High Season	Page
❶ / p. 360	AAA	Super 8 Bridgeview - see ad starting on p. 378, on insert	◈◈	$39-$198 SAVE	388
❷ / p. 360		Econo Lodge at the Bridge	◈	Rates not provided	383
❸ / p. 360		Lamplighter Motel	◈	$32-$97	387
❹ / p. 360		Holiday Inn Express at the Bridge - see ad p. 385, inside back cover	◈◈	$49-$159	385
❺ / p. 360		Days Inn & Suites "Bridgeview Lodge" - see ad p. 377, inside back cover	◈◈	$57-$270	377
❻ / p. 360		Baymont Inn & Suites-Mackinaw City	◈◈	$89-$220	372
❼ / p. 360	AAA	Best Western Plus Dockside Waterfront Inn - see ad starting on p. 364, on insert	◈◈◈	$38-$298 SAVE	372
❽ / p. 360	AAA	Super 8-Beachfront - see ad p. 386, on insert	◈◈	$39-$199 SAVE	387
❾ / p. 360	AAA	Rainbow Motel	◈	$32-$164 SAVE	387
❿ / p. 360	AAA	Comfort Inn Lakeside - see ad p. 375, on insert	◈◈	$38-$198 SAVE	374
⓫ / p. 360	AAA	Hamilton Inn Select-Beachfront - see ad starting on p. 366, inside front cover, on insert	◈◈◈	$38-$288 SAVE	384
⓬ / p. 360	AAA	Econo Lodge Bayview - see ad on insert, p. 380	◈◈	$39-$199 SAVE	383
⓭ / p. 360	AAA	Comfort Suites - see ad p. 369, on insert	◈◈◈	$39-$299 SAVE	374
⓮ / p. 360	AAA	Ramada Waterfront - see ad p. 382, on insert	◈◈	$39-$199 SAVE	387
⓯ / p. 360	AAA	Days Inn Lakeview - see ad on insert, p. 376	◈◈	$38-$198 SAVE	377
⓰ / p. 360	AAA	Clarion Hotel Beachfront - see ad starting on p. 370, on insert	◈◈◈	$39-$278 SAVE	374
⓱ / p. 360	AAA	Best Western Thunderbird Inn	◈◈	$49-$200 SAVE	372
㉒ / p. 360	AAA	Bridge Vista Beach Hotel & Convention Center - see ad on insert, p. 373	◈◈	Rates not provided SAVE	372
⓲ / p. 360	AAA	Fairview Beachfront Inn - see ad on insert, p. 368	◈◈	$38-$198 SAVE	383
⓳ / p. 360	AAA	Quality Inn & Suites Beachfront - see ad p. 381, on insert	◈◈	$38-$198 SAVE	387
⓴ / p. 360	AAA	Americas Best Value Inn Mackinaw City	◈◈	$49-$209 SAVE	372
㉑ / p. 360		The Beach House	◈	$49-$197	372

Map Page	OA	Restaurants	Diamond Rated	Cuisine	Meal Range	Page
① / p. 360	AAA	Chippewa Room at Audie's	◈◈	American	$14-$24	388
② / p. 360		Darrow's Family Restaurant	◈◈	American	$6-$12	389
③ / p. 360	AAA	Dixie's Saloon & O'Reilly's Irish Pub - see ad on insert, p. 383	◈◈	American	$8-$28	389
④ / p. 360	AAA	Nonna Lisa's Italian Ristorante - see ad on insert	◈◈	Italian	$10-$28	389
⑤ / p. 360		Anna's Country Buffet	◈	American	$7-$16	388
⑥ / p. 360	AAA	Admiral's Table	◈◈	American	$7-$25	388
⑦ / p. 360	AAA	Lighthouse Restaurant	◈◈	American	$10-$32	389

Map Page	OA	Restaurants (cont'd)	Diamond Rated	Cuisine	Meal Range	Page
8 / p. 360	AAA	**Embers of Mackinaw City**	◇◇	American	$6-$16	389
9 / p. 360	AAA	**Blue Water Grill & Bar**	◇◇	American	$8-$28	388
10 / p. 360	AAA	**Neath the Birches**	◇◇	American	$12-$36	389

ST. IGNACE

Map Page	OA	Lodgings	Diamond Rated	High Season	Page
24 / p. 360		Carol's Tradewinds Motel	◇	Rates not provided	418
25 / p. 360		Kewadin Casino Lakefront Inn	◇◇	$59-$109	418
26 / p. 360	AAA	**Days Inn Lakefront & Suites**	◇◇◇	$81-$189 SAVE	418
27 / p. 360	AAA	**Quality Inn Lakefront - see ad p. 420**	◇◇	$48-$174 SAVE	420
28 / p. 360		Holiday Inn Express Lakefront	◇◇	$79-$249	418
29 / p. 360		Comfort Inn	◇◇	Rates not provided	418
30 / p. 360	AAA	**Best Western Plus Harbour Pointe Lakefront - see ad p. 417**	◇◇◇	$79-$220 SAVE	417
31 / p. 360	AAA	**Budget Host Inn & Suites - see ad p. 419**	◇◇	$66-$152 SAVE	418
32 / p. 360	AAA	**Aurora Borealis Motor Inn - see ad p. 416**	◇	$49-$99 SAVE	416
33 / p. 360		Super 8 of St. Ignace	◇◇	$58-$148	420

Map Page	OA	Restaurants	Diamond Rated	Cuisine	Meal Range	Page
13 / p. 360	AAA	**The Galley Restaurant & Bar**	◇◇	American	$6-$25	420
14 / p. 360		Timmy Lee's Pub	◇◇	American	$7-$16	421

MACKINAC ISLAND

Map Page	OA	Lodgings	Diamond Rated	High Season	Page
36 / p. 360		The Inn on Mackinac	◇◇	$79-$289	355
37 / p. 360	AAA	**Harbour View Inn - see ad p. 355**	◇◇	$89-$299 SAVE	355
38 / p. 360	AAA	**Island House Hotel - see ad p. 356**	◇◇	$99-$375 SAVE	356
39 / p. 360	AAA	**Grand Hotel - see ad p. 354**	◇◇◇◇	$498-$728 SAVE	354
40 / p. 360		Murray Hotel	◇	$79-$305	358
41 / p. 360	AAA	**Lake View Hotel and Conference Center - see ad p. 357**	◇◇	$104-$435 SAVE	357

▼ *See AAA listing p. 384* ▼

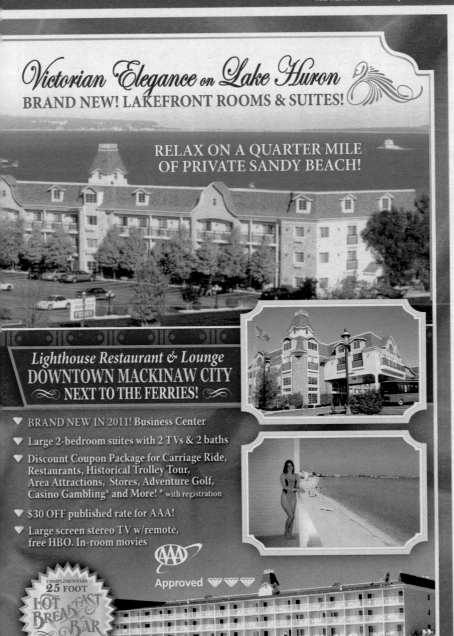

▼ See AAA listing p. 383 ▼

▼ See AAA listing p. 374 ▼

▼ See AAA listing p. 374 ▼

MACKINAW CITY pop. 859 (See map and index starting on p. 360)

AMERICAS BEST VALUE INN MACKINAW CITY

Motel
$49-$209

Phone: (231)436-5544 **20**

Address: 112 Old US 31 49701 **Location:** I-75, exit 337 northbound, 0.5 mi n; exit 338 southbound, 0.5 mi s. **Facility:** Smoke free premises. 73 units. 2 stories (no elevator), exterior corridors. **Terms:** open 5/1-10/25, check-in 4 pm, cancellation fee imposed. **Pool(s):** heated indoor. **Activities:** whirlpool. **Guest Services:** coin laundry, wireless Internet. **Free Special Amenities: expanded continental breakfast and high-speed Internet.**

BAYMONT INN & SUITES-MACKINAW CITY

Hotel
$89-$220

Phone: (231)436-7737 **6**

Address: 109 S Nicolet St 49701 **Location:** I-75, exit 338 southbound, just n. Located at entrance to Mackinaw Crossings. **Facility:** Smoke free premises. 77 units. 3 stories, interior corridors. **Terms:** open 5/1-10/24. **Pool(s):** heated indoor. **Activities:** whirlpool, exercise room. **Guest Services:** coin laundry, wireless Internet.

THE BEACH HOUSE

Cottage
$49-$197

Phone: 231/436-5353 **21**

Address: 11490 W US 23 49701 **Location:** 1.3 mi s. Located on Lake Huron. **Facility:** Smoke free premises. 28 units, some cottages. 1 story, exterior corridors. **Terms:** open 5/15-9/24, 14 day cancellation notice-fee imposed. **Pool(s):** heated indoor. **Activities:** whirlpool, limited beach access, basketball, horseshoes, volleyball. **Guest Services:** wireless Internet.

BEST WESTERN PLUS DOCKSIDE WATERFRONT INN

Motel
$38-$298

Phone: (231)436-5001 **7**

Address: 505 S Huron Ave 49701 **Location:** I-75, exit 337 northbound, 0.5 mi n to US 23, 0.3 mi e, then just n; exit 338 southbound, 0.8 mi se on US 23, then just n. Located on Lake Huron. **Facility:** Smoke free premises. 112 units, some two bedrooms. 4 stories, exterior corridors. **Terms:** 3 day cancellation notice-fee imposed. **Amenities:** Some: video games (fee). **Pool(s):** heated indoor. **Activities:** whirlpool, limited beach access, rental paddleboats, sun deck, exercise room. Fee: game room. **Guest Services:** coin laundry, area transportation-within 1 mi, wireless Internet.

(see ad starting on p. 364 & on insert)

AAA Benefit: Members save up to 20%, plus 10% bonus points with free rewards program.

FREE full breakfast and high-speed Internet

BEST WESTERN THUNDERBIRD INN

Motel
$49-$200

Phone: (231)436-5433 **17**

Address: 146 Old US 31 49701 **Location:** I-75, exit 337 northbound, just ne; exit 338 southbound, 0.7 mi se. **Facility:** Smoke free premises. 48 units. 2 stories (no elevator), exterior corridors. **Terms:** open 5/1-10/1, check-in 4 pm, cancellation fee imposed. **Amenities:** Some: high-speed Internet. **Pool(s):** heated indoor. **Activities:** whirlpool, playground. **Guest Services:** coin laundry, wireless Internet. **Free Special Amenities: expanded continental breakfast and high-speed Internet.**

AAA Benefit: Members save up to 20%, plus 10% bonus points with free rewards program.

BRIDGE VISTA BEACH HOTEL & CONVENTION CENTER

Hotel
Rates not provided

Phone: 231/436-9812 **22**

Address: 1027 S Huron St 49701 **Location:** I-75, exit 337 northbound, 0.5 mi n to US 23, then 0.3 mi e; exit 338 southbound, 0.8 mi se on US 23. **Facility:** Smoke free premises. 101 units, some two bedrooms. 3 stories, interior corridors. **Amenities:** safes (fee). Some: video games (fee). **Pool(s):** 2 heated indoor. **Activities:** whirlpool, waterslide, lifeguard on duty, limited beach access, indoor water park, lazy river, exercise room. Fee: game room. **Guest Services:** coin laundry, area transportation-within 1 mi, wireless Internet.

(see ad on insert & p. 373)

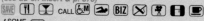

FREE full breakfast and high-speed Internet

▼ See AAA listing p. 372 ▼

(See map and index starting on p. 360)

CLARION HOTEL BEACHFRONT

Phone: (231)436-5539

Hotel
$39-$278

Address: 905 S Huron Ave 49701 **Location:** I-75, exit 337 northbound, 0.5 mi n to US 23, then 0.3 mi e; exit 338 southbound, 0.8 mi se on US 23. Located on Lake Huron. **Facility:** Smoke free premises. 115 units, some two bedrooms. 3-4 stories, exterior corridors. **Terms:** cancellation fee imposed. **Amenities:** *Some:* video games (fee). **Pool(s):** heated indoor. **Activities:** whirlpool, limited beach access, sun deck, playground, exercise room. **Guest Services:** coin laundry, area transportation-within 1 mi, wireless Internet.
(see ad starting on p. 370 & on insert)

FREE full breakfast and high-speed Internet

COMFORT INN LAKESIDE

Phone: (231)436-5057

Motel
$38-$198

Address: 611 S Huron Ave 49701 **Location:** I-75, exit 337 northbound, 0.5 mi n to US 23, 0.3 mi e, then just n; exit 338 southbound, 0.8 mi se on US 23, then just n. Located on Lake Huron. **Facility:** Smoke free premises. 60 units. 3 stories, exterior corridors. **Terms:** 3 day cancellation notice. **Amenities:** *Some:* video games (fee). **Pool(s):** heated indoor. **Activities:** whirlpool, limited beach access, exercise room. **Guest Services:** area transportation-within 1 mi, wireless Internet. *(see ad p. 375 & on insert)*

FREE full breakfast and high-speed Internet

COMFORT SUITES

Phone: (231)436-5929

Hotel
$39-$299

Address: 720 S Huron Ave 49701 **Location:** I-75, exit 337 northbound, 0.5 mi n to US 23, just e to Huron Ave, then just n; exit 338 southbound, 0.8 mi se on US 23, then just n. Opposite ferry boat docks. **Facility:** Smoke free premises. 50 units, some two bedrooms. 4 stories, interior/exterior corridors. **Terms:** check-in 4 pm, 3 day cancellation notice-fee imposed. **Amenities:** *Some:* video games (fee). **Pool(s):** heated indoor. **Activities:** sauna, whirlpool, waterslide, beach access, exercise room. **Fee:** game room. **Guest Services:** coin laundry, area transportation-within 1 mi, wireless Internet.
(see ad p. 369 & on insert)

FREE full breakfast and high-speed Internet

▼ See AAA listing p. 374 ▼

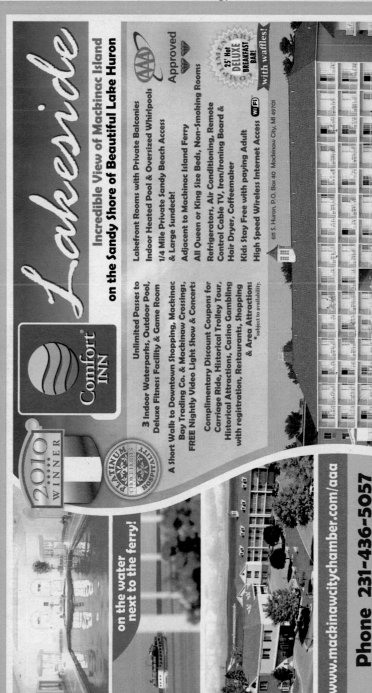

▼ See AAA listing p. 375 ▼

Overlooking Lake Huron & Mackinac Island!

— FREE —
25 foot Hot Breakfast Bar

Discount Savings Coupons for
Carriage Ride, Historical Trolley Tour,
Historical Attractions, Restaurants,
Shopping & Area Attractions

RIGHT NEXT
TO THE FERRY!

AAA
Approved

$30 OFF 2011 Published Rate for AAA Members!

Days Inn.
LAKEVIEW
825 South Huron Mackinaw City, MI 49701

- **Unlimited Passes to 3 Indoor Waterparks, Fitness Facility, Game Room, Heated Outdoor Pool, Indoor Whirlpool Spa & Private Sandy Beach!**
- **Close to Downtown Shopping, Mackinac Bay Trading Co. & Mackinaw Crossings, FREE Nightly Video Light Show, Concerts & Theater**
- **Lakefront Rooms with Private Balconies**
- **Indoor Heated Pool & Whirlpools**
- **Adjacent to Mackinac Island Ferry**
- **Refrigerators, Air Conditioning, Remote Control Cable TV, Iron/Ironing Boards, Hair Dryers & Coffeemaker**
- **Kids Stay Free with paying Adult**
- **High Speed Wireless Internet Access WiFi**

www.mackinawcitychamber.com/aaa

RESERVATIONS **231-436-5557**
TOLL-FREE **1-800-436-8807**

(See map and index starting on p. 360)

DAYS INN & SUITES "BRIDGEVIEW LODGE" Phone: (231)436-8961 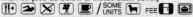 **5**

Motel
$57-$270

Address: 206 N Nicolet St 49701 **Location:** I-75, exit 339; at bridge. **Facility:** Smoke free premises. 59 units. 3 stories, interior/exterior corridors. **Terms:** open 4/30-10/31, check-in 4 pm. **Pool(s):** heated indoor. **Activities:** whirlpool, sun deck. **Guest Services:** wireless Internet. *(see ad below & inside back cover)*

DAYS INN LAKEVIEW Phone: (231)436-5557 **15**

Motel
$38-$198

Address: 825 S Huron Ave 49701 **Location:** I-75, exit 337 northbound, 0.5 mi n to US 23, then 0.3 mi e; exit 338 southbound, 0.8 mi se on US 23. Located next to ferry boat docks. **Facility:** Smoke free premises. 84 units. 2 stories (no elevator), exterior corridors. **Terms:** 3 day cancellation notice-fee imposed. **Amenities:** *Some:* video games (fee). **Pool(s):** heated indoor. **Activities:** whirlpool, beach access, putting green, playground. **Guest Services:** coin laundry, area transportation-within 1 mi, wireless Internet. *(see ad on insert & p. 376)*

FREE full breakfast and high-speed Internet

▼ See AAA listing p. 388 ▼

▼ See AAA listing p. 379 ▼

▼ See AAA listing p. 387 ▼

▼ See AAA listing p. 387 ▼

(See map and index starting on p. 360)

ECONO LODGE AT THE BRIDGE

Phone: 231/436-5026

Motel
Rates not provided

Address: 412 N Nicolet St 49701 **Location:** I-75, exit 339. **Facility:** Smoke free premises. 32 units. 1-2 stories (no elevator), exterior corridors. **Guest Services:** wireless Internet.

ECONO LODGE BAYVIEW

Phone: (231)436-5777 12

Motel
$39-$199

Address: 712 S Huron Ave 49701 **Location:** I-75, exit 337 northbound, 0.5 mi n to US 23, 0.3 mi e, then just n; exit 338 southbound, 0.8 mi se on US 23, then just n. Opposite ferry boat docks. **Facility:** Smoke free premises. 71 units, some cabins. 1-2 stories (no elevator), exterior corridors. **Terms:** 3 day cancellation notice-fee imposed. **Amenities:** *Some:* video games (fee). **Pool(s):** heated outdoor. **Activities:** whirlpool, beach access, water park privileges, playground, exercise room. **Guest Services:** coin laundry, area transportation-within 1 mi, wireless Internet. *(see ad on insert & p. 380)*

FREE full breakfast and high-speed Internet

FAIRVIEW BEACHFRONT INN

Phone: (231)436-8831 18

Motel
$38-$198

Address: 907 S Huron St 49701 **Location:** 0.8 mi se on US 23. Located on Lake Huron. **Facility:** Smoke free premises. 60 units, some two bedrooms. 2-3 stories (no elevator), exterior corridors. **Terms:** 3 day cancellation notice-fee imposed. **Amenities:** *Some:* video games (fee). **Pool(s):** heated indoor. **Activities:** whirlpools, beach access, indoor water park. **Guest Services:** area transportation-within 1 mi, wireless Internet. *(see ad on insert & p. 368)*

FREE full breakfast and high-speed Internet

▼ See AAA listing p. 389 ▼

(See map and index starting on p. 360)

HAMILTON INN SELECT-BEACHFRONT

Hotel
$36-$288

Address: 701 S Huron Ave 49701 **Location:** I-75, exit 337 northbound, 0.5 mi n to US 23, 0.3 mi e, then just n; exit 338 southbound, 0.8 mi se on US 23, then just n. Located on Lake Huron. **Facility:** Smoke free premises. 132 units, some two bedrooms. 4 stories, interior corridors. **Parking:** winter plug-ins. **Terms:** 3 day cancellation notice-fee imposed. **Amenities:** *Some:* video games (fee). **Pool(s):** heated indoor. **Activities:** whirlpool, limited beach access, rental paddleboats, snowmobiling, exercise room. **Guest Services:** coin laundry, area transportation-within 1 mi, wireless Internet, tanning facilities. *(see ad starting on p. 366, inside front cover & on insert)*

Phone: (231)436-5005 ⑪

FREE full breakfast and high-speed Internet

(See map and index starting on p. 360)

HOLIDAY INN EXPRESS AT THE BRIDGE

Hotel
$49-$159

Address: 364 Louvigny 49701 **Location:** I-75, exit 339. **Facility:** Smoke free premises. 102 units, some two bedrooms. 4 stories, interior corridors. **Terms:** check-in 4 pm. **Pool(s):** heated indoor. **Activities:** sauna, whirlpool, snowmobiling, sun deck, exercise room. **Guest Services:** coin laundry, wireless Internet.
(see ad below & inside back cover)

Phone: (231)436-7100 **4**

▼ *See AAA listing above* ▼

▼ See AAA listing p. 387 ▼

(See map and index starting on p. 360)

LAMPLIGHTER MOTEL
Phase: 231/436-5350 **3**

Motel
$32-$97

Address: 303 Jamet St 49701 **Location:** I-75, exit 339, just n of town. Located in a quiet area. **Facility:** Smoke free premises. 11 units, some two bedrooms and efficiencies. 1 story, exterior corridors. **Terms:** open 5/1-11/1. **Guest Services:** wireless Internet. ⊗ 💻 / SOME UNITS ⊟ ▣

QUALITY INN & SUITES BEACHFRONT
Phone: (231)436-5051 **19**

Motel
$38-$198

Address: 917 S Huron Ave 49701 **Location:** 1 mi se on US 23. Located on Lake Huron. **Facility:** Smoke free premises. 74 units, some two bedrooms. 1-4 stories, exterior corridors. **Terms:** check-in 4 pm, 3 day cancellation notice-fee imposed. **Amenities:** *Some:* video games (fee). **Pool(s):** heated indoor. **Activities:** sauna, whirlpool, limited beach access. **Guest Services:** area transportation-within 1 mi, wireless Internet. *(see ad p. 381 & on insert)*

FREE full breakfast and high-speed Internet

RAINBOW MOTEL
Phone: 231/436-5518 **9**

Motel
$32-$164

Address: 602 S Huron Ave 49701 **Location:** I-75, exit 337 northbound, 0.5 mi n to US 23, 0.3 mi e, then just n; exit 338 southbound, 0.8 mi se on US 23, then just n. **Facility:** Smoke free premises. 29 units. 1 story, exterior corridors. **Terms:** open 5/12-10/17, 3 day cancellation notice. **Pool(s):** heated indoor. **Activities:** whirlpools, putting green, playground, limited exercise equipment, basketball. **Guest Services:** wireless Internet. **Free Special Amenities: local telephone calls and high-speed Internet.**

RAMADA WATERFRONT
Phone: (231)436-5055 **14**

Hotel
$39-$199

Address: 723 S Huron Ave 49701 **Location:** I-75, exit 337 northbound, 0.5 mi n to US 23, just e to Huron Ave, then just n; exit 338 southbound, 0.8 mi se on US 23, then just n. Located on Lake Huron. **Facility:** Smoke free premises. 42 units, some two bedrooms. 3 stories, interior corridors. **Terms:** 3 day cancellation notice-fee imposed. **Amenities:** *Some:* video games (fee). **Pool(s):** heated indoor. **Activities:** whirlpools, limited beach access, exercise room. **Guest Services:** coin laundry, area transportation-within 1 mi, wireless Internet. *(see ad p. 382 & on insert)*

FREE full breakfast and high-speed Internet

SUPER 8-BEACHFRONT
Phone: (231)436-7111 **8**

Motel
$39-$199

Address: 519 S Huron Ave 49701 **Location:** I-75, exit 337 northbound, 0.5 mi n to US 23, 0.3 mi e, then just n; exit 338 southbound, 0.8 mi se on US 23, then just n. Located on Lake Huron. **Facility:** Smoke free premises. 59 units. 2 stories (no elevator), exterior corridors. **Terms:** 3 day cancellation notice-fee imposed. **Amenities:** *Some:* video games (fee). **Pool(s):** heated indoor. **Activities:** sauna, whirlpool, limited beach access. **Guest Services:** area transportation-within 1 mi, wireless Internet. *(see ad p. 386 & on insert)*

FREE full breakfast and high-speed Internet

(See map and index starting on p. 360)

SUPER 8 BRIDGEVIEW

Hotel
$39-$198

Phone: (231)436-5252 **①**

Address: 601 N Huron Ave 49701 **Location:** I-75, exit 339 northbound, just n, then just e. Opposite Straits of Mackinac. **Facility:** Smoke free premises. 65 units. 2-3 stories, interior/exterior corridors. **Terms:** 3 day cancellation notice-fee imposed. **Amenities:** *Some:* video games (fee). **Pool(s):** heated indoor. **Activities:** sauna, whirlpool, beach access, limited exercise equipment. *Fee:* game room. **Guest Services:** coin laundry, area transportation-within 1 mi, wireless Internet. *(see ad starting on p. 378 & on insert)*

SAVE 🍴 🏊 ✕ 🐾 🛢 ☕ / SOME UNITS FEE 🐕 📺

FREE full breakfast and high-speed Internet

—— WHERE TO DINE ——

ADMIRAL'S TABLE

American
$7-$25

Phone: 231/436-5687 **⑥**

Visit the warm, inviting restaurant for such favorites as prime rib and Great Lakes whitefish. Servers in sport tops, shorts and sneakers pass through the restaurant, which is appointed in a nautical theme. The seasonal breakfast buffet is especially popular. **Bar:** full bar. **Hours:** Open 5/3-10/20; 7 am-9 pm; to 10 pm 7/1-9/5. **Address:** 502 S Huron Ave 49701 **Location:** Center; opposite ferry boat docks.

ANNA'S COUNTRY BUFFET

American
$7-$16

Phone: 231/436-5195 **⑤**

Although the buffet is popular at breakfast, lunch and dinner, diners still may order from a menu of traditional favorites. The laid-back dining room is near the water and the ferries to Mackinac Island. The service here is friendly. **Bar:** full bar. **Hours:** Open 5/1-10/31; 8 am-9 pm; hours may vary. **Address:** 416 S Huron Ave 49701 **Location:** Just se; opposite ferry boat docks.

BLUE WATER GRILL & BAR

American
$8-$28

Phone: 231/436-7818 **⑨**

Located just south of town, this casual restaurant offers a good selection of seafood, steaks and finger foods. During the summer, seating is nice on the breezy patio. **Bar:** full bar. **Hours:** Open 5/10-10/20; 4 pm-10 pm; hours may vary. **Address:** 918 S Huron Ave 49701 **Location:** Just s on US 23.

CHIPPEWA ROOM AT AUDIE'S

American
$14-$24

Menu on AAA.com

Phone: 231/436-5744 **①**

American Indian artwork and knickknacks enhance the dining room, where guests can enjoy the leisurely atmosphere. Six tasty preparations of whitefish stand out on the varied menu. The dessert array includes many tempting choices. This place offers a good choice for casual family dining. **Bar:** full bar. **Reservations:** suggested. **Hours:** 5 pm-10 pm; seasonal hours vary. **Closed:** 11/24, 12/25. **Address:** 314 Nicolet St 49701 **Location:** I-75, exit 339; at bridge.

(See map and index starting on p. 360)

DARROW'S FAMILY RESTAURANT
Phone: 231/436-5514   2

American
$6-$12

Old-fashioned, home-style cooking includes such specialties as fresh whitefish, hamburgers and pie. **Hours:** Open 4/29-10/25; 7:30 am-8 pm, Fri & Sat-9 pm. **Address:** 1106 Louvigny St 49701 **Location:** I-75, exit 339, just w.

DIXIE'S SALOON & O'REILLY'S IRISH PUB
Phone: 231/436-5449   3

American
$8-$28

The impressive two-story restaurant—with its massive wood beams, attractive wood decor and warm atmosphere—welcomes all. Booths along the windows on the lower and upper levels provide a view of the water and ferry docks. Choice cuts of steak stand out amid a selection of American dishes and snacks. **Bar:** full bar. **Hours:** 11 am-10 pm; hours may vary. Closed: 11/24, 12/25. **Address:** 401 E Central St 49701 **Location:** Corner of Central St and Huron Ave; center. **Parking:** street only. *(see ad on insert & p. 383)*

EMBERS OF MACKINAW CITY   *Menu on AAA.com*
Phone: 231/436-5773   8

American
$6-$16

The restaurant's specialty is its smorgasbord, a tempting array of such selections as roast beef, broasted chicken, Cajun whitefish, crab legs and shrimp stir-fry. A daily breakfast buffet also is available. Service is prompt and pleasant. **Bar:** full bar. **Hours:** Open 4/1-10/31; 8 am-9 pm; hours may vary. **Address:** 810 S Huron Ave 49701 **Location:** 0.5 mi s on US 23.

LIGHTHOUSE RESTAURANT
Phone: 231/436-5191   7

American
$10-$32

Tender prime rib, whitefish and all-you-can-eat crab legs are favorite selections at this comfortable restaurant, a hot spot with the tourist crowd. The dining room features a copper-top bar, wall-mounted brass lamps and lighthouse-motif candles. **Bar:** full bar. **Hours:** Open 4/1-11/15; 5 pm-9 pm; seasonal hours vary. **Address:** 618 S Huron Ave 49701 **Location:** I-75, exit 337 northbound, 0.5 mi n to US 23, 0.8 mi e, then just n; exit 338 southbound, 0.8 mi se on US 23, then just n. CALL

NEATH THE BIRCHES
Phone: 231/436-5401   10

American
$12-$36

In a natural wooded setting, the restaurant has been serving the area for more than 35 years. Slow-roasted prime rib, which includes homemade bread and a salad bar visit, is a succulent choice. Service is warm and friendly. **Bar:** full bar. **Hours:** Open 5/1-10/22; 4 pm-9 pm, Fri & Sat-10 pm; hours may vary. **Address:** 14277 N Mackinaw Hwy 49701 **Location:** I-75, exit 337 northbound; exit 338 southbound, 1 mi s of blinker on Old US 31 (SR 108).

NONNA LISA'S ITALIAN RISTORANTE
Phone: 231/436-7901   4

Italian
$10-$28

The popular dining room is filled with unique wood furnishings. Families enjoy the waterfalls and wildlife scene while waiting for their wood-fired pizza, pasta or steaks. **Bar:** full bar. **Hours:** Open 4/1-11/30; 11 am-11 pm; hours may vary. **Address:** 312 S Huron Ave 49701 **Location:** Just s; at Mackinaw Bay Trading Company. *(see ad on insert)*

MACOMB —See Detroit p. 284.

MADISON HEIGHTS —See Detroit p. 284.

MANISTEE pop. 6,586

DAYS INN
Phone: (231)723-8385

Hotel
$71-$140

Address: 1462 Manistee Hwy 49660 **Location:** 1.3 mi s on US 31. **Facility:** Smoke free premises. 93 units. 2 stories (no elevator), interior corridors. **Parking:** winter plug-ins. **Terms:** check-in 4 pm. **Pool(s):** heated indoor. **Activities:** whirlpool. **Guest Services:** coin laundry, wireless Internet. **Free Special Amenities:** expanded continental breakfast and high-speed Internet.

LITTLE RIVER CASINO RESORT
Phone: 231/723-1535

Hotel
Rates not provided

Address: 2700 Orchard Hwy 49660 **Location:** Jct US 31 and SR 22. **Facility:** Located in a rural area, this casino is popular with the locals and the folks who drive here from downstate. 292 units, some two bedrooms. 2-4 stories, interior corridors. **Parking:** on-site and valet, winter plug-ins. **Terms:** check-in 4 pm. **Amenities:** safes. *Some:* honor bars. **Dining:** Willows, see separate listing. **Pool(s):** heated indoor. **Activities:** sauna, whirlpool, snowmobiling, playground, exercise room. **Fee:** massage. **Guest Services:** wireless Internet.

—— WHERE TO DINE ——

BOATHOUSE GRILL
Phone: 231/723-2300

American
$7-$19

Overlooking the scenic Manistee River, this restaurant is open, light and airy, with lots of windows. Menu favorites include New York strip steak, Great Lakes perch, pan-fried walleye and a black bean sandwich. **Bar:** full bar. **Hours:** 11 am-9 pm, Sun 10 am-2 pm. Closed: 12/25 & Easter. **Address:** 440 W River St 49660 **Location:** 0.5 mi w of jct US 31. **Parking:** street only.

RICO'S ROADHOUSE
Phone: 231/723-3721

American
$7-$22

This friendly place offers a variety of dishes that include the traditional prime rib, steaks and seafood as well as a few international dishes. **Bar:** full bar. **Hours:** 11 am-9 pm, Fri & Sat-10 pm; hours may vary. Closed: 12/25 & Easter. **Address:** 900 Caberfae Hwy 49660 **Location:** Jct US 31, 1.4 mi e on SR 55.

WILLOWS

Phone: 231/723-1535

American
$10-$30

Away from the noise of the casino, the casual restaurant employs friendly staff members and lines up a good selection of dishes on the buffet line. **Bar:** full bar. **Hours:** 8 am-11 pm. **Address:** 2700 Orchard Way 49660 **Location:** Jct US 31 and SR 22; in Little River Casino Resort. **Parking:** on-site and valet.

MANISTIQUE pop. 3,583

BUDGET HOST INN

Phone: (906)341-2552

Motel
$65-$95 4/1-9/30
$55-$70 10/1-4/30

Address: 6031 W US Hwy 2 49854-9108 **Location:** On US 2, 3.5 mi e. **Facility:** 26 units. 1 story, exterior corridors. **Parking:** winter plug-ins. **Terms:** cancellation fee imposed. **Pool(s):** heated outdoor. **Activities:** snowmobiling, playground. **Guest Services:** wireless Internet.

COMFORT INN

Phone: (906)341-6981

Hotel
$80-$160 4/1-10/9
$80-$109 10/10-4/30

Address: 617 E Lakeshore Dr 49854 **Location:** 0.5 mi e on US 2. Opposite Lake Michigan. **Facility:** Smoke free premises. 57 units. 2 stories (no elevator), interior corridors. **Amenities:** safes (fee). **Activities:** whirlpool, exercise room. **Guest Services:** coin laundry, wireless Internet.

ECONO LODGE LAKESHORE

Phone: (906)341-6014

Motel
$59-$119

Address: 1101 E Lakeshore Dr 49854 **Location:** 1.5 mi e on US 2. Opposite Lake Michigan. **Facility:** Smoke free premises. 32 units. 1 story, interior/exterior corridors. **Parking:** winter plug-ins. **Activities:** whirlpool, exercise room. **Guest Services:** wireless Internet.

PENINSULA POINTE HOTEL

Phone: (906)341-3777

Hotel
$76-$119

Address: 955 E Lakeshore Dr 49854 **Location:** 1.4 mi e on US 2. Opposite Lake Michigan. **Facility:** Smoke free premises. 54 units. 2 stories (no elevator), interior corridors. **Amenities:** safes (fee). **Guest Services:** coin laundry, wireless Internet.

MARENISCO

ROOT CELLAR RESORT

Phone: 906/842-3535

Motel
$44-$249 12/1-4/30
$25-$129 4/1-11/30

Address: N11071 E Shore Rd 49947 **Location:** 4 mi n on SR 64 from jct US 2, 9.5 mi ne on E Shore Rd. **Facility:** Designated smoking area. 17 units, some two bedrooms and cabins. 2 stories (no elevator), exterior corridors. **Parking:** winter plug-ins. **Terms:** 2 night minimum stay - seasonal and/or weekends, cancellation fee imposed. **Activities:** rental boats, boat dock, fishing, snowmobiling, playground, horseshoes, volleyball. **Guest Services:** wireless Internet.

MARINE CITY pop. 4,652

THE HEATHER HOUSE

Phone: 810/765-3175

Historic Bed
& Breakfast
$135-$195

Address: 409 N Main St 48039 **Location:** I-94, exit 248 (Marine City Hwy), 14 mi e on SR 29. **Facility:** Overlooking the St. Clair River, this Queen Anne-style house features two turrets and a wraparound porch that affords a great view of passing boats. Smoke free premises. 5 units. 3 stories (no elevator), interior corridors. **Terms:** 7 day cancellation notice-fee imposed.

—— **WHERE TO DINE** ——

RIVIERA RESTAURANT

Phone: 810/765-9030

American
$6-$15

Views of the ferry dock and St. Clair River contribute to the nautical theme in the diner-style restaurant. The menu offers lake perch and cod, as well as soups, sandwiches, burgers and pasta. Homemade pies are a treat. **Bar:** full bar. **Hours:** 7 am-9 pm, Fri & Sat-10 pm. Closed: 11/24, 12/25. **Address:** 475 S Water St 48039 **Location:** I-94, exit 248 (Marine City Hwy), 14.5 mi e on SR 29.

MARQUETTE pop. 19,661

BIRCHMONT MOTEL

Phone: (906)228-7538

Motel
$56-$76 6/21-10/23
$46-$66 4/27-6/20

Address: 2090 US 41 S 49855 **Location:** On US 41, 1.8 mi n of jct SR 28; 4.3 mi s of downtown. Opposite Lake Superior. **Facility:** Smoke free premises. 29 units, some two bedrooms and efficiencies. 2 stories (no elevator), exterior corridors. **Terms:** open 4/27-10/23, office hours 7:30 am-11 pm. **Pool(s):** heated outdoor. **Guest Services:** wireless Internet. **Free Special Amenities:** continental breakfast and high-speed Internet.

BUDGET HOST-BRENTWOOD MOTOR INN

Phone: 906/228-7494

Motel
$64-$70 4/1-11/15
$53-$62 11/16-4/30

Address: 2603 US 41 W 49855 **Location:** On US 41 and SR 28, 2.8 mi w. **Facility:** Smoke free premises. 41 units. 2 stories (no elevator), exterior corridors. **Parking:** winter plug-ins. **Guest Services:** wireless Internet. **Free Special Amenities:** continental breakfast and high-speed Internet.

CEDAR MOTOR INN

Motel
$49-$96

Phone: (906)228-2280

Address: 2523 US Hwy 41 W 49855 **Location:** On US 41 and SR 28, 2.8 mi w. **Facility:** Smoke free premises. 44 units. 2 stories (no elevator), interior/exterior corridors. **Terms:** 3 day cancellation notice. **Pool(s):** heated indoor. **Activities:** sauna, whirlpool, sun deck. **Guest Services:** wireless Internet. **Free Special Amenities: continental breakfast and high-speed Internet.**

COMFORT SUITES

Hotel
$109-$149

Phone: (906)228-0028

Address: 2463 US 41 W 49855 **Location:** On US 41 and SR 28, 2.5 mi w. **Facility:** Smoke free premises. 83 units. 3 stories, interior corridors. **Parking:** winter plug-ins. **Amenities:** safes (fee). **Pool(s):** heated indoor. **Activities:** sauna, whirlpool, ski wax room, bike storage, exercise room. **Guest Services:** valet and coin laundry, wireless Internet.

COUNTRY INN & SUITES BY CARLSON

Hotel
$104-$160

Phone: (906)225-1300

Address: 2472 US 41 W 49855 **Location:** On US 41 and SR 28, 2.8 mi w. **Facility:** Smoke free premises. 84 units. 3 stories, interior corridors. **Parking:** winter plug-ins. **Amenities:** high-speed Internet. **Pool(s):** heated indoor. **Activities:** whirlpool, exercise room. **Guest Services:** valet and coin laundry, wireless Internet. *(see ad p. 6)*

DAYS INN

Hotel
$71-$91

Phone: (906)225-1393

Address: 2403 US 41 W 49855 **Location:** On US 41 and SR 28, 2.3 mi w. **Facility:** Smoke free premises. 65 units. 3 stories, interior corridors. **Parking:** winter plug-ins. **Terms:** 3 day cancellation notice. **Amenities:** safes (fee). **Pool(s):** heated indoor. **Activities:** sauna, whirlpools, ski wax room, playground. **Guest Services:** valet laundry, wireless Internet.

HOLIDAY INN

Hotel
$114-$159

Phone: (906)225-1351

Address: 1951 US 41 W 49855 **Location:** On US 41 and SR 28, 1.8 mi w. **Facility:** Smoke free premises. 191 units. 5 stories, interior corridors. **Pool(s):** heated indoor. **Activities:** sauna, whirlpool, exercise room. **Guest Services:** valet and coin laundry, wireless Internet.

LANDMARK INN

(note: Landmark Inn diamond rating)

Classic
Hotel
$134-$409

Phone: (906)228-2580

Address: 230 N Front St 49855 **Location:** Jct Ridge St; downtown. **Facility:** The renovated 1930s European-style hotel features a luxurious grand lobby and guest rooms with elegant bedding and comfortable seating. Smoke free premises. 63 units, some two bedrooms. 6 stories, interior corridors. **Terms:** cancellation fee imposed. **Amenities:** high-speed Internet. **Activities:** exercise room. **Guest Services:** valet laundry, area transportation-within 10 mi, wireless Internet. **Free Special Amenities: high-speed Internet and local transportation.**

RAMADA MARQUETTE

Hotel
$85-$125

Phone: (906)228-6000

Address: 412 W Washington St 49855 **Location:** 0.5 mi w on US 42 business route. **Facility:** Smoke free premises. 112 units. 2-7 stories, interior corridors. **Terms:** cancellation fee imposed. **Pool(s):** heated indoor. **Activities:** sauna, whirlpool, exercise room. *Fee:* game room. **Guest Services:** wireless Internet.

SUPER 8

Hotel
$58-$81

Phone: (906)228-8100

Address: 1275 US 41 W 49855 **Location:** On US 41 and SR 28, 1 mi w. **Facility:** Smoke free premises. 80 units. 2 stories (no elevator), interior corridors. **Parking:** winter plug-ins. **Terms:** cancellation fee imposed. **Pool(s):** heated indoor. **Activities:** sauna, whirlpool. **Guest Services:** coin laundry, wireless Internet.

———— **WHERE TO DINE** ————

GREAT HUNAN

Chinese
$5-$14

Phone: 906/226-8649

Seafood is what it's all about at this restaurant. Menu favorites include the seafood combination, which blends crab, fresh fish and vegetables in a tasty sauce. Otherwise, you can't go wrong with the excellent selection and great value of traditional choices. Service is friendly and attentive. **Hours:** 11:30 am-9 pm, Fri & Sat-10 pm, Sun noon-8:30 pm. Closed: 11/24. **Address:** 2680 US 41 W 49855 **Location:** On US 41 and SR 28, 2.8 mi w.

THE VIERLING RESTAURANT & MARQUETTE HARBOR BREWERY

American
$5-$21

Phone: 906/228-3533

An antique bar, stained-glass windows and varied memorabilia decorate the casual 1883 saloon, which is restored to an Old World elegance. A good selection of microbrewed beers complements such dishes as Lake Superior whitefish, ribs and steak. **Bar:** full bar. **Hours:** 11 am-10 pm. Closed major holidays; also Sun. **Address:** 119 S Front St 49855 **Location:** Corner of Front and Main sts. **Parking:** street only. **Historic**

MARSHALL pop. 7,459

ARBOR INN OF HISTORIC MARSHALL

Motel
$45-$69

Phone: 269/781-7772

Address: 15435 W Michigan Ave 49068 **Location:** I-69, exit 36 (Michigan Ave), just w. Located in semi-rural area by small lake. **Facility:** Smoke free premises. 48 units, some kitchens. 1 story, exterior corridors. **Parking:** winter plug-ins. **Pool(s):** outdoor. **Guest Services:** wireless Internet.

FREE continental breakfast and local telephone calls

COMFORT INN

Hotel
$80-$200

Phone: (269)789-7890

Address: 204 Winston Dr 49068 **Location:** I-69, exit 36 (Michigan Ave), just se. **Facility:** Smoke free premises. 60 units. 2 stories (no elevator), interior corridors. **Amenities:** safes (fee). **Pool(s):** heated indoor. **Activities:** sauna, whirlpool, limited exercise equipment. **Guest Services:** valet laundry, wireless Internet.

HAMPTON INN-MARSHALL

Hotel
Rates not provided

Phone: 269/789-0131

Address: 325 Sam Hill Dr 49068 **Location:** I-94, exit 110 (SR 227), just s. Located in a commercial area. **Facility:** Smoke free premises. 73 units. 3 stories, interior corridors. **Terms:** check-in 4 pm. **Amenities:** high-speed Internet. *Some:* video games. **Pool(s):** heated indoor. **Activities:** exercise room. **Guest Services:** valet and coin laundry, wireless Internet.

HOLIDAY INN EXPRESS-MARSHALL

Hotel
Rates not provided

Phone: 269/789-9301

Address: 329 Sam Hill Dr 49068 **Location:** I-94, exit 110 (SR 227), just s. Located in a commercial area. **Facility:** Smoke free premises. 66 units. 3 stories, interior corridors. **Terms:** check-in 4 pm. **Amenities:** high-speed Internet. **Pool(s):** heated indoor. **Activities:** exercise room. **Guest Services:** valet laundry, wireless Internet.

ROSE HILL INN B & B

Historic Bed
& Breakfast
$109-$250

Phone: (269)789-1992

Address: 1110 Verona Rd 49068 **Location:** Fountain Circle, just n to Mansion St, then 0.7 mi w; downtown. **Facility:** An elegant 1860 Italianate-style mansion with a large front porch, the B&B is set on three acres of groomed grounds which include a tennis court. Smoke free premises. 6 units. 2 stories, interior corridors. **Terms:** age restrictions may apply, 7 day cancellation notice-fee imposed. **Pool(s):** heated outdoor. **Activities:** tennis court, billiards. **Guest Services:** wireless Internet.

------ **WHERE TO DINE** ------

PASTRAMI JOE'S DELI & TAKE-OUT MARKET

Deli
$5-$16

Phone: 269/781-8800

Just a few steps away from the downtown shops, the eatery's small front patio is a popular spot both to enjoy some of the freshly made sandwiches and to people-watch. **Hours:** 11 am-7 pm, Sat-3 pm. Closed major holidays; also Sun. **Address:** 105 N Jefferson St 49068 **Location:** Downtown. **Parking:** on-site and street.

SCHULER'S RESTAURANT & PUB   *Menu on AAA.com*

American
$11-$33

Phone: 269/781-0600

A visit to historic Marshall should include this popular, almost 100-year-old landmark. Along with top-notch service from a friendly waitstaff, patrons enjoy fresh baked bread and carefully prepared specialties that include prime rib, London broil and whitefish, served in generous portions. The menu is adjusted summer and winter to offer varied and new entrees. In-house prepared desserts will tempt even the most strong-willed of dieters. **Bar:** full bar. **Reservations:** suggested. **Hours:** 11 am-9 pm, Fri & Sat-10 pm. Closed: 12/25. **Address:** 115 S Eagle St 49068 **Location:** Just e of US 27 and Fountain Circle; 1 mi s of I-94. **Classic Historic** CALL ☾Ⓜ

MARYSVILLE pop. 9,684

SUPER 8 MOTEL PORT HURON/MARYSVILLE

Hotel
$57-$167

Phone: (810)364-7500

Address: 1484 Gratiot Blvd 48040 **Location:** I-94, exit 266 (Gratiot Blvd), 1 mi e, then 0.3 mi s of Port Huron on I-94 business loop. Located in a secluded area. **Facility:** Smoke free premises. 70 units, some two bedrooms. 2 stories, interior/exterior corridors. **Pool(s):** heated indoor. **Activities:** whirlpool, exercise room. *Fee:* game room. **Guest Services:** coin laundry, wireless Internet.

------ **WHERE TO DINE** ------

JUNCTION BUOY ON THE RIVER

American
$8-$21

Phone: 810/364-5730

On the St. Clair River, the relaxed restaurant has a nautical theme and boasts a beautiful view across the shores to Canada. The restaurant can be reached by both car and boat. On the menu are fresh fish, steaks, burgers, sandwiches and pasta dishes, as well as homemade soups and salads. The outdoor patio opens seasonally. **Bar:** full bar. **Hours:** 11 am-10 pm, Fri & Sat-11 pm, Sun noon-9 pm. Closed: 11/24, 12/25. **Address:** 1415 River Rd 48040 **Location:** I-94, exit 266, 2.5 mi e on Gratiot Blvd, 0.6 mi s on Busha Hwy, then 0.6 mi e.

MEARS

DUNES WATERFRONT RESORT

Hotel
Rates not provided

Phone: 231/873-5500

Address: 1180 N Shore Dr 49436 **Location:** US 31, exit 149, 7 mi w to Silver Lake, follow signs. Located on Silver Lake. **Facility:** Smoke free premises. 72 units. 4 stories, interior corridors. **Terms:** open 4/3-10/10. **Pool(s):** heated indoor. **Activities:** whirlpool, beach access, boat dock. *Fee:* game room. **Guest Services:** coin laundry, wireless Internet.

SIERRA SANDS FAMILY LODGE

Motel
$59-$160

Phone: 231/873-1008

Address: 7990 W Hazel Rd 49436 **Location:** US 31, exit Hart/Mears, 6 mi w to Silver Lake, follow signs. **Facility:** Smoke free premises. 41 units, some two bedrooms and kitchens. 2 stories (no elevator), exterior corridors. **Terms:** open 4/1-10/31, office hours 6 am-11 pm, 2 night minimum stay - seasonal and/or weekends, 7 day cancellation notice-fee imposed. **Pool(s):** heated outdoor. **Activities:** whirlpool, picnic area with grills, playground. **Guest Services:** wireless Internet.

MENOMINEE pop. 9,131

AMERICINN OF MENOMINEE

Hotel
$84-$139

Phone: (906)863-8699

Address: 2330 10th St 49858 **Location:** 0.8 mi n on US 41. Located on shores of Green Bay. **Facility:** Smoke free premises. 62 units. 2 stories (no elevator), interior corridors. **Terms:** cancellation fee imposed. **Pool(s):** heated indoor. **Activities:** whirlpool, boat ramp, playground. **Guest Services:** coin laundry, wireless Internet.

ECONO LODGE ON THE BAY

Hotel
$60-$140

Phone: (906)863-4431

Address: 2516 10th St 49858 **Location:** 1 mi n on US 41. Located on shores of Green Bay. **Facility:** Smoke free premises. 49 units, some efficiencies. 2 stories (no elevator), interior corridors. **Parking:** winter plug-ins. **Activities:** sauna, exercise room. **Guest Services:** wireless Internet, tanning facilities.

—— WHERE TO DINE ——

BERGS' LANDING

American
$12-$30

Phone: 906/863-8034

Jack Daniels New York strip stands out on a menu of traditionally prepared steak and seafood choices. The nautically appointed dining room overlooks Green Bay. The atmosphere is lively and upbeat, as is the staff, which provides efficient service. **Bar:** full bar. **Hours:** 5 pm-9 pm, Fri & Sat-10 pm, Sun-8 pm; hours may vary. Closed major holidays. **Address:** 450 1st St 49858 **Location:** US 41, 0.6 mi e on 10th Ave to 1st St, then 0.3 mi s along the lakefront; in historic district.

SCHLOEGEL'S BAY VIEW

American
S6-$12

Phone: 906/863-7888

Guests can enjoy panoramic views of Green Bay from the quiet dining room, attractively decorated with local art. The menu lists a wide selection of family-style foods. Homemade pies and fresh bread and "pasties" make mouths water. Service is friendly. **Hours:** 6:30 am-8:30 pm; hours may vary. Closed: 11/24, 12/25. **Address:** 2720 10th St 49858 **Location:** 1 mi n on US 41. CALL &M

MIDLAND pop. 41,685

BEST WESTERN VALLEY PLAZA RESORT

Hotel
$90-$130

Phone: (989)496-2700

Address: 5221 Bay City Rd 48642 **Location:** US 10, exit Midland/Bay City Rd. **Facility:** Smoke free premises. 162 units. 2 stories, interior corridors. **Terms:** check-in 4 pm, cancellation fee imposed. **Amenities:** safes (fee). *Some:* high-speed Internet. **Dining:** 2 restaurants. **Pool(s):** heated indoor. **Activities:** sauna, whirlpool, putting green, ice skating, exercise room, basketball, horseshoes, volleyball. *Fee:* bowling lanes, movie theater, game room. **Guest Services:** valet laundry, wireless Internet. **Free Special Amenities: expanded continental breakfast and high-speed Internet.**

AAA Benefit:
Members save up to 20%, plus 10% bonus points with free rewards program.

FAIRVIEW INN & SUITES

Hotel
$89-$125

Phone: (989)631-0070

Address: 2200 W Wackerly St 48640 **Location:** Jct US 10 and Eastman Rd. **Facility:** Smoke free premises. 90 units. 2 stories, interior corridors. **Parking:** winter plug-ins. **Pool(s):** heated indoor. **Activities:** whirlpool, exercise room. **Guest Services:** coin laundry, wireless Internet.

HAMPTON INN

Hotel
Rates not provided

Phone: 989/837-4000

Address: 6701 Eastman Ave 48642 **Location:** US 10, exit Eastman Rd, just n. Opposite Midland Mall. **Facility:** Smoke free premises. 87 units. 3 stories, interior corridors. **Terms:** check-in 4 pm. **Pool(s):** heated indoor. **Activities:** whirlpool, exercise room. **Guest Services:** valet and coin laundry, wireless Internet.

AAA Benefit:
Members save up to 10% everyday!

THE H HOTEL

Hotel
$104-$164

Phone: (989)839-0500

Address: 111 W Main St 48640 **Location:** Corner of Main and Ashman sts; downtown. **Facility:** Smoke free premises. 103 units. 6 stories, interior corridors. **Terms:** cancellation fee imposed. **Pool(s):** heated indoor. **Activities:** whirlpool, jogging, exercise room. *Fee:* bicycles. **Guest Services:** valet laundry, wireless Internet.

MIDLAND RESORT & CONFERENCE CENTER

Hotel
$62-$82

Phone: (989)631-4220

Address: 1500 W Wackerly St 48640 **Location:** Jct US 10 and Eastman Rd. **Facility:** Smoke free premises. 211 units. 2 stories (no elevator), interior/exterior corridors. **Parking:** winter plug-ins. **Terms:** check-in 4 pm, cancellation fee imposed. **Amenities:** video games. *Some:* high-speed Internet. **Pool(s):** heated indoor. **Activities:** sauna, whirlpool, indoor recreation area, basketball, volleyball. *Fee:* racquetball court, game room. **Guest Services:** valet and coin laundry, wireless Internet.

PLAZA SUITES HOTEL

Hotel
$90-$200

Phone: (989)496-2700

Address: 5221 Bay City Rd 48642 **Location:** US 10, exit Midland/Bay City Rd. **Facility:** Smoke free premises. 74 units. 2 stories (no elevator), interior corridors. **Terms:** check-in 4 pm. **Amenities:** safes (fee). *Some:* high-speed Internet. **Activities:** *Fee:* bowling lanes, movie theater. **Guest Services:** valet laundry, wireless Internet.

SLEEP INN OF MIDLAND

Hotel
$76-$90

Phone: (989)837-1010

Address: 2100 W Wackerly St 48640 **Location:** Jct US 10 and Eastman Rd. **Facility:** Smoke free premises. 77 units. 3 stories, interior corridors. **Pool(s):** heated indoor. **Activities:** sauna, exercise room. **Guest Services:** coin laundry, wireless Internet.

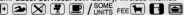

SPRINGHILL SUITES MIDLAND

Phone: (989)837-2700

Contemporary Hotel
$121-$154

Address: 800 Joe Mann Blvd 48642 **Location:** US 10, exit Eastman Ave, 1 mi e. **Facility:** Smoke free premises. 96 units. 3 stories, interior corridors. **Parking:** winter plug-ins. **Terms:** cancellation fee imposed. **Amenities:** high-speed Internet. **Pool(s):** heated indoor. **Activities:** whirlpool, exercise room. **Guest Services:** complimentary and valet laundry, area transportation-Corporate Centers for Dow Corning & Dow Chemical, wireless Internet.

> **AAA Benefit:**
> Members save a minimum 5% off the best available rate.

——— WHERE TO DINE ———

CHINA PALACE

Phone: 989/832-3177

Chinese
$6-$19

In business since the mid-1980s, the restaurant has several dining areas, all of which are decorated in an Oriental motif. Mongolian beef is among the delicious dishes of Mandarin, Szechuan, Hunan and Shanghai cuisine. The atmosphere is family-friendly. **Bar:** full bar. **Hours:** 11 am-9:15 pm, Fri-10:15 pm, Sat noon-10:15 pm, Sun noon-8:15 pm; hours may vary. Closed major holidays. **Address:** 1908 S Saginaw Rd 48640 **Location:** Just n of US 10 business route.

ENTRE AMIGOS

Phone: 989/832-6348

Mexican
$5-$16

As the name implies, the popular restaurant is a place for friends, who often gather here for traditional Mexican dishes. **Bar:** full bar. **Hours:** 11 am-10 pm, Fri & Sat-11 pm. Closed: 11/24, 12/25. **Address:** 2600 N Saginaw Rd, Suite A 48640 **Location:** Jct US 10 and Eastman Rd, 1 mi s, 0.5 mi w.

GENJI JAPANESE STEAKHOUSE

Phone: 989/495-6000

Japanese
$10-$35

The popular restaurant offers a sushi bar and several dining areas with knife-wielding chefs preparing traditional Japanese dishes that may include chicken, seafood or steak. **Bar:** full bar. **Hours:** 11 am-2 & 4:30-9:30 pm, Sat 3:30 pm-10:30 pm, Sun noon-2 & 3:30-9 pm. Closed: 11/24, 12/25. **Address:** 2929 S Saginaw St 48640 **Location:** Just s of US 10 business route.

MILAN pop. 4,775

SLEEP INN & SUITES

Phone: (734)439-1400

Hotel
$60-$150

Address: 1230 Dexter St 48160 **Location:** US 23, exit 27 (Carpenter Rd), just w. **Facility:** Smoke free premises. 64 units. 3 stories, interior corridors. **Terms:** cancellation fee imposed. **Amenities:** safes. **Pool(s):** heated indoor. **Activities:** exercise room. **Guest Services:** coin laundry, wireless Internet.

MILFORD —See Detroit p. 286.

MIO pop. 2,016

HINCHMAN ACRES RESORT

Phone: (989)826-3267

Cottage
$70-$150

Address: 702 N Morenci St 48647 **Location:** 0.5 mi n on SR 33 and 72. Located on the Au Sable River. **Facility:** Smoke free premises. 11 cottages. 1 story, exterior corridors. **Terms:** open 4/1-11/30, 2-7 night minimum stay - seasonal and/or weekends, 30 day cancellation notice-fee imposed. **Activities:** limited beach access, rental canoes, fishing, rental tubes & rafts, indoor recreation area, ORV access trail, hiking trails, playground, basketball, horseshoes, shuffleboard, volleyball. *Fee:* game room. **Guest Services:** coin laundry, wireless Internet.

MIO MOTEL

Phone: 989/826-3248

Motel
Rates not provided

Address: 415 N Morenci St 48647 **Location:** Just n on SR 33 and 72. **Facility:** Smoke free premises. 24 units. 2 stories (no elevator), exterior corridors. **Parking:** winter plug-ins.

MONROE pop. 22,076

HAMPTON INN

Phone: 734/289-5700

Hotel
Rates not provided

Address: 1565 N Dixie Hwy 48162 **Location:** I-75, exit 15 (SR 50), just e. **Facility:** Smoke free premises. 74 units. 3 stories, interior corridors. **Amenities:** video games (fee), high-speed Internet. **Pool(s):** heated indoor. **Activities:** exercise room. **Guest Services:** valet and coin laundry, wireless Internet.

> **AAA Benefit:**
> Members save up to 10% everyday!

QUALITY INN & SUITES

Phone: (734)242-6000

Hotel
$79-$150

Address: 1225 N Dixie Hwy 48162 **Location:** I-75, exit 15 (SR 50), just w. **Facility:** Smoke free premises. 161 units, some two bedrooms and efficiencies. 4 stories, interior corridors. **Pool(s):** heated indoor. **Activities:** whirlpool, exercise room. *Fee:* game room. **Guest Services:** valet and coin laundry, wireless Internet.

—— WHERE TO DINE ——

BOLLES HARBOR CAFE

◆◆◆ ◆◆◆

American
$5-$20

Phone: 734/457-2233

Family-owned and operated, the cozy, nautically themed shanty restaurant seems perfectly suited in the midst of a busy marina. Breakfasts feature Dutch baby apple pancakes and cinnamon-raisin French toast, while lunches and dinners center on sandwiches, burgers and homemade daily specials. **Hours:** 6 am-9 pm, Sun-2 pm. Closed major holidays; also Mon. **Address:** 13986 Laplaisance Rd 48161 **Location:** I-75, exit 11 (Laplaisance Rd), 1 mi e.

DOLCE VITA ITALIAN GRILLE

◆◆◆ ◆◆◆

Italian
$6-$22

Phone: 734/241-6100

Two large, silver figurines greet diners just inside the casually sophisticated dining room. Focusing on a mix of Northern and Southern Italian specialties, the menu lists such meat, fresh seafood and pasta preparations as lamb chops a la menta, salmon bella vista and ravioli bolognese. **Bar:** full bar. **Hours:** 11 am-10 pm, Fri & Sat-11 pm, Sun noon-9 pm. Closed: 12/25. **Address:** 391 N Telegraph Rd 48162 **Location:** Just s of jct US 24 (Telegraph Rd) and Stewart Rd; in Foodtown Plaza. CALL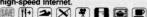

JOE'S FRENCH-ITALIAN INN

◆◆◆ ◆◆◆

Italian
$6-$23

Phone: 734/289-2800

Stained glass and an attractive mural carry out an Italian theme in this quiet, casual restaurant. A menu of French and Italian specialties includes preparations of seafood, prime rib and veal in addition to a lengthy selection of pasta dishes. **Bar:** full bar. **Reservations:** suggested. **Hours:** 11 am-9:30 pm, Fri-10 pm, Sat 4 pm-10 pm, Sun 4 pm-9:30 pm. Closed major holidays. **Address:** 2896 N Dixie Hwy 48162 **Location:** I-75, exit 15 (SR 50), 2 mi e.

MUGSY'S GRILLE & BAR

◆◆◆ ◆◆◆

American
$7-$18

Phone: 734/242-2330

The comfortable sports bar-type restaurant serves pizzas, hamburgers and fish specials. Homemade desserts end the meal on a high note. **Bar:** full bar. **Hours:** 11 am-11 pm, Sun 8 am-9 pm. Closed major holidays. **Address:** 15425 S Dixie Hwy 48161 **Location:** I-75, exit 11 (Laplaisance Rd), 1 mi nw, 0.8 mi w on Dunbar Rd, then just n on Monroe St. CALL

MOUNT CLEMENS —See Detroit p. 286.

MOUNT PLEASANT pop. 25,946

BAYMONT INN-MOUNT PLEASANT

◆◆◆ ◆◆◆

Hotel
$62-$179

Phone: (989)775-5555

Address: 5858 E Pickard St 48858 **Location:** Jct US 127 and SR 20 E, just e. **Facility:** Smoke free premises. 102 units. 3 stories, interior corridors. **Parking:** winter plug-ins. **Pool(s):** heated indoor. **Activities:** whirlpool. **Guest Services:** coin laundry, wireless Internet.

BEST WESTERN INN

◆◆◆ ◆◆◆

Hotel
$59-$179

Phone: (989)772-1101

Address: 5770 E Pickard St 48858 **Location:** Jct US 127 and SR 20 E, just e. **Facility:** Smoke free premises. 51 units. 1 story, interior corridors. **Parking:** winter plug-ins. **Pool(s):** heated indoor. **Activities:** sauna, whirlpool. **Guest Services:** wireless Internet. **Free Special Amenities: expanded continental breakfast and high-speed Internet.**

Best Western

AAA Benefit:
Members save up to 20%, plus 10% bonus points with free rewards program.

COMFORT INN & SUITES HOTEL AND CONFERENCE CENTER

◆◆◆

Hotel
Rates not provided

Phone: 989/772-4000

Address: 2424 S Mission St 48858 **Location:** 2 mi s on US 127 business route. **Facility:** Smoke free premises. 138 units. 2 stories (no elevator), interior corridors. **Parking:** winter plug-ins. **Terms:** check-in 4 pm. **Pool(s):** heated indoor. **Activities:** exercise room. **Fee:** game room. **Guest Services:** valet and coin laundry, wireless Internet.

FAIRFIELD INN & SUITES

◆◆◆

Hotel
$103-$131

Phone: (989)775-5000

Address: 2525 S University Park Dr 48858 **Location:** 2 mi s on US 127 business route. **Facility:** Smoke free premises. 74 units. 3 stories, interior corridors. **Terms:** cancellation fee imposed. **Pool(s):** heated indoor. **Activities:** whirlpool, hiking trails, exercise room. **Guest Services:** valet and coin laundry, wireless Internet.

AAA Benefit:
Members save a minimum 5% off the best available rate.

GREEN SUITES

◆◆◆ ◆◆◆

Motel
Rates not provided

Phone: 989/772-1703

Address: 1900 Summerton Rd 48858 **Location:** Jct US 127 and SR 20, just e on SR 20, then just n. **Facility:** Smoke free premises. 42 units, some kitchens. 2 stories (no elevator), exterior corridors. *Bath:* shower only. **Terms:** check-in 4 pm. **Guest Services:** wireless Internet.

HAMPTON INN

Hotel
Rates not provided

Phone: 989/772-5500

Address: 5205 E Pickard Rd 48858 **Location:** Jct US 127 and SR 20, just w on SR 20. **Facility:** Smoke free premises. 89 units. 3 stories, interior corridors. **Parking:** winter plug-ins. **Terms:** check-in 4 pm. **Amenities:** video games (fee). **Pool(s):** heated indoor. **Activities:** whirlpool, exercise room. **Guest Services:** valet and coin laundry, wireless Internet.

MT. PLEASANT INN & SUITES

Hotel
$59-$126

Phone: (989)772-7777

Address: 5500 E Pickard Rd 48858 **Location:** Jct US 127 and SR 20. **Facility:** Smoke free premises. 82 units. 3 stories, interior corridors. **Guest Services:** wireless Internet.

SOARING EAGLE CASINO & RESORT

Resort
Hotel
Rates not provided

Phone: 989/775-7777

Address: 6800 Soaring Eagle Blvd 48858 **Location:** Jct US 127 and SR 20, 1.5 mi e on SR 20, just s on Leaton Rd. **Facility:** Native American artwork adorns the resort, which offers casual and fine dining, recreational facilities, a casino and luxurious guest rooms. Smoke free premises. 516 units. 7 stories, interior corridors. **Parking:** on-site and valet. **Terms:** check-in 4 pm. **Amenities:** safes. **Dining:** 3 restaurants, also, Siniikaung Steak & Chop House, The Water Lily, see separate listings, entertainment. **Pool(s):** heated indoor. **Activities:** whirlpools, steamrooms, exercise room, spa. **Guest Services:** valet laundry, area transportation, wireless Internet, tanning facilities.

(see ad p. 397 & p. 96)

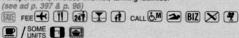

FREE newspaper and high-speed Internet

SUPER 8

Hotel
$63-$148

Phone: (989)773-8888

Address: 2323 S Mission St 48858 **Location:** 1.8 mi s on US 127 business route. **Facility:** Smoke free premises. 140 units. 3 stories, interior corridors. **Parking:** winter plug-ins. **Amenities:** video games (fee). **Guest Services:** coin laundry, wireless Internet.

── WHERE TO DINE ──

THE GRAND TRAVERSE PIE COMPANY

Breads/Pastries
$4-$7

Phone: 989/779-2743

The aromas of freshly baked fruit pies, spinach quiche and made-to-order sandwiches stimulate the appetites of those who enter the cute cafe's large, open bakery. The bakery also offers complimentary Wi-Fi. **Hours:** 8 am-9 pm, Sun 10 am-7 pm. Closed major holidays. **Address:** 1218 S Mission St 48858 **Location:** Between Bellows and Preston sts.

THE ITALIAN OVEN

Italian
$8-$17

Phone: 989/773-6836

The casual dining atmosphere of this restaurant provides a great spot for friends and family to gather for a hearty meal. The reasonably-priced menu features pizzas, baked pastas, juicy steaks, eggplant or chicken parmigiana, fish, and the signature "stromboli" calzones. Crayons at the tables allow guests to exercise their artistic talents on butcher paper tablecloths while awaiting the arrival of steaming entrees from the wood-fired oven. **Bar:** full bar. **Hours:** 11 am-10 pm, Fri & Sat-11 pm. Closed: 11/24, 12/25 & Easter. **Address:** 2336 S Mission St 48858 **Location:** 1.8 mi s on US 127 business route.

LA SEÑORITA

Mexican
$5-$12

Phone: 989/772-1331

With its inviting Mexican décor, this is a fun restaurant for casual or family dining. The menu features mesquite-grilled entrees and sizzling fajitas. **Bar:** full bar. **Hours:** 11 am-10 pm, Fri & Sat-11 pm; to midnight, Sun noon-10 pm 5/29-9/4. Closed: 11/24, 12/24, 12/25 & Easter. **Address:** 1516 S Mission St 48858 **Location:** 2.8 mi s on US 127 business route.

MOUNTAINTOWN STATION

American
$9-$30

Phone: 989/775-2337

Formerly the busy Mount Pleasant Railroad Depot and telegraph office, the station building was redesigned in 1995 to house a bustling microbrewery, restaurant and wine shop. The informal dining room is often packed with guests enjoying one of the house specialties, which include ribs, steaks and prime rib, or one of the many other menu options ranging from burgers and pasta to seafood, pork chops and chicken. Varied handcrafted beers are brewed on site. **Bar:** full bar. **Hours:** 4 pm-10 pm, Fri & Sat from 11:30 am, Sun 11:30 am-9 pm. Closed major holidays. **Address:** 506 W Broadway 48858 **Location:** Just w of jct Main St; downtown.

PIXIE

American
$3-$7

Phone: 989/772-7494

A Mount Pleasant tradition, the retro 1950s diner serves a full complement of hamburgers and hot dogs, as well as a variety of shakes. Diners are invited to earn a place on the walls of fame by eating so many hot dogs or hamburgers within a set time period; it's not an easy feat. **Hours:** 10 am-11 pm, Fri & Sat-midnight, Sun 11 am-11 pm. Closed major holidays. **Address:** 302 N Mission St 48858 **Location:** Just s of jct W Pickard St.

SINIIKAUNG STEAK & CHOP HOUSE

Phone: 989/775-5106

Steak
$8-$40

Located just off the casino floor, the quiet atmosphere provides a nice respite from the noisy gaming area. While the lunch menu offers a variety of reasonably priced offerings including entree salads, burgers and sandwiches, brick oven pizzas and steaks, dinner selections are on the more expensive side but feature larger portions of various cuts of beef, as well as a few chicken and fish options. **Bar:** full bar. **Hours:** 11:30 am-11 pm. **Address:** 6800 Soaring Eagle Dr 48858 **Location:** Jct US 127 and SR 20, 1.5 mi e on SR 20, just s on Leaton Rd; in Soaring Eagle Casino & Resort. **Parking:** on-site and valet. CALL 🛗M

THE WATER LILY

Phone: 989/775-7777

American
$8-$38

For a special occasion or night to remember, visit this casual, yet upscale, spot. Choose from a wide variety of dishes—from American to seafood to wild game. Representative of the excellent fare is the Western elk tenderloin with red onion marmalade, savory plum cornbread stuffing and lingonberry cognac glace. Wine recommendations are well-paired with each dish. **Bar:** full bar. **Reservations:** suggested. **Hours:** 7 am-noon & 5-11 pm; Sunday brunch 10:30 am-2 pm. **Address:** 6800 Soaring Eagle Dr 48858 **Location:** US 127, 1.5 mi e on SR 20, just s on Leaton Rd; in Soaring Eagle Casino & Resort. CALL 🛗M

MUNISING pop. 2,539

ALGER FALLS MOTEL

Phone: 906/387-3536

Motel
$45-$175

Address: E9427 E Hwy M-28 49862 **Location:** 2 mi e on SR 28 and 94. **Facility:** Smoke free premises. 17 units, some cottages. 1 story, exterior corridors. **Parking:** winter plug-ins. **Terms:** 2 night minimum stay - seasonal. **Activities:** heated garage for snowmobiles. *Fee:* game room. **Guest Services:** coin laundry, wireless Internet. **Free Special Amenities:** local telephone calls and high-speed Internet. SAVE ⊠ 🛏 🖨 / SOME UNITS FEE 🐾

AMERICINN LODGE & SUITES OF MUNISING

Phone: (906)387-2000

Hotel
$90-$170 9/8-4/30
$70-$170 4/1-9/7

Address: E9926 E Hwy M-28 49854 **Location:** On SR 28, 2.7 mi e. Located in a quiet area just outside of town. **Facility:** Smoke free premises. 62 units. 3 stories, interior corridors. **Terms:** cancellation fee imposed. **Amenities:** high-speed Internet. **Pool(s):** heated indoor. **Activities:** sauna, whirlpool, waterslide. **Guest Services:** coin laundry, wireless Internet. CALL 🛗M 🏊 ⊠ 🖥 / SOME UNITS FEE 🐾 🛏 🖨

SUNSET MOTEL ON THE BAY

Phone: (906)387-4574

Motel
$60-$105

Address: 1315 Bay St 49862 **Location:** 1 mi e on E Munising Ave (CR H58). Located on Munising Bay. **Facility:** 19 units, some two bedrooms, efficiencies and houses. 1-2 stories (no elevator), exterior corridors. **Terms:** office hours 8 am-11 pm. **Activities:** beach access, boat dock, fishing, kayak rentals, grills and picnic tables, playground. **Guest Services:** wireless Internet. **Free Special Amenities:** preferred room (subject to availability with advance reservations) and high-speed Internet. SAVE ⊠ 🛏 🖨 🖥 / SOME UNITS FEE 🐾

SUPER 8-MUNISING

Phone: 906/387-2466

Hotel
Rates not provided

Address: E9681 E Hwy M-28 49862 **Location:** On SR 28, 2.5 mi e. **Facility:** Smoke free premises. 43 units. 2 stories (no elevator), interior corridors. **Parking:** winter plug-ins. **Activities:** sauna, whirlpool, limited exercise equipment. **Guest Services:** coin laundry, wireless Internet. ⊠ 🐾 🛏 / SOME UNITS 🖥

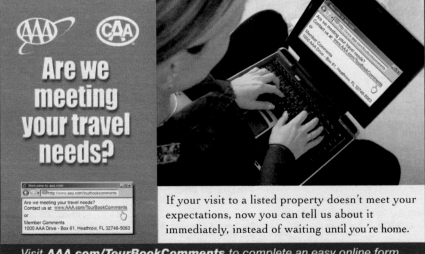

TERRACE MOTEL

Motel
$40-$68

Phone: 906/387-2735

Address: 420 Prospect St 49862 **Location:** 0.5 mi e, just off SR 28. Located in a quiet residential area. **Facility:** Smoke free premises. 18 units, some two bedrooms. 1 story, exterior corridors. **Terms:** office hours 8 am-10 pm, cancellation fee imposed. **Activities:** sauna, heated garage for snowmobiles, billiards, playground, basketball. **Guest Services:** wireless Internet. **Free Special Amenities: high-speed Internet.**

------ WHERE TO DINE ------

DOGPATCH

American
$5-$15

Phone: 906/387-9948

Established in 1966, the restaurant is a great place to take children for a casual meal. The menu lists country-style breakfasts, a great selection of sandwiches and charbroiled steaks. The popular seafood buffet with all the fixings is served every night. **Bar:** full bar. **Hours:** 7 am-10 pm; hours may vary. Closed: 11/24, 12/25. **Address:** 325 E Superior St 49862 **Location:** Just off SR 28; center.

SYDNEY'S RESTAURANT

American
$7-$24

Phone: 906/387-3748

The casual restaurant features a unique Australian theme with kangaroos and koala bears on display and a menu that presents prime steaks, chops and an abundance of seafood. The service is efficient and laid-back. **Bar:** full bar. **Hours:** 6 am-9 pm. Closed major holidays. **Address:** 400 Cedar St M-28 49862 **Location:** On SR 28, just ne of jct CR H58.

MUSKEGON pop. 40,105

COMFORT INN

Hotel
$85-$160

Phone: (231)739-9092

Address: 1675 E Sherman Blvd 49444 **Location:** Jct US 31 and CR B72, exit Sherman Blvd. Located next to a shopping mall. **Facility:** Smoke free premises. 117 units, some efficiencies. 2 stories (no elevator), interior corridors. **Terms:** cancellation fee imposed. **Amenities:** safes (fee). **Pool(s):** outdoor, heated indoor. **Activities:** whirlpool, exercise room. *Fee:* game room. **Guest Services:** coin laundry, wireless Internet.

HOLIDAY INN-MUSKEGON HARBOR

Hotel
$129-$209 6/1-4/30
$79-$199 4/1-5/31

Phone: (231)722-0100

Address: 939 3rd St 49440 **Location:** Center. **Facility:** Smoke free premises. 201 units. 8 stories, interior corridors. **Terms:** check-in 4 pm. **Amenities:** video games (fee). **Pool(s):** heated indoor. **Activities:** whirlpool, steamroom, exercise room. **Guest Services:** valet laundry, wireless Internet.

NAUBINWAY

------ WHERE TO DINE ------

ANCHOR IN NAUBINWAY

Deli
$4-$8

Phone: 906/477-1120

This log-framed deli has a sitting area with a fireplace and large-screen TV. Guests can relax and enjoy a specialty drink, sandwich, smoothie or dessert. **Hours:** 8 am-9 pm, Fri & Sat-10 pm; hours may vary. Closed: 11/24, 12/25. **Address:** W11623 US 2 49762

NEWBERRY pop. 2,686

COMFORT INN TAHQUAMENON FALLS

Hotel
Rates not provided

Phone: 906/293-3218

Address: 13954 Hwy M-28 49868 **Location:** Jct SR 28 and 123. **Facility:** Smoke free premises. 54 units. 2 stories (no elevator), interior corridors. **Activities:** sauna, whirlpool, snowmobiling, limited exercise equipment. *Fee:* game room. **Guest Services:** coin laundry, wireless Internet.

------ WHERE TO DINE ------

TIMBER CHARLIE'S FOOD, SPIRITS & GIFTS

American
$5-$25

Phone: 906/293-3363

Baby back ribs, Italian and Mexican fare and a tempting variety of sizzling steaks make up the restaurant's varied menu. Knotty pine walls and wildlife art contribute to the rustic atmosphere. Tourists and locals alike frequent the casual eatery. **Bar:** full bar. **Hours:** 7 am-9 pm, Sat & Sun-10 pm; hours may vary. Closed: 11/24, 12/25; also for dinner 12/24. **Address:** 110 Newberry Ave 49868 **Location:** On SR 123, north side of town. **Parking:** street only.

NEW BUFFALO pop. 2,200

FAIRFIELD INN & SUITES

Hotel
$80-$100

Phone: (269)586-2222

Address: 11400 Holiday Dr 49117 **Location:** I-94, exit 1 (La Porte Rd). **Facility:** Smoke free premises. 105 units. 4 stories, interior corridors. **Terms:** cancellation fee imposed. **Amenities:** high-speed Internet. **Pool(s):** heated indoor/outdoor. **Activities:** whirlpool, exercise room. **Guest Services:** coin laundry, wireless Internet. *(see ad below)*

AAA Benefit:
Members save a minimum 5% off the best available rate.

HARBOR COUNTRY HOTEL

Hotel
Rates not provided

Phone: 269/469-4193

Address: 18800 La Porte Rd 49117 **Location:** I-94, exit 1 (La Porte Rd), just w. **Facility:** Smoke free premises. 69 units. 3 stories, interior corridors. **Amenities:** *Some:* high-speed Internet. **Pool(s):** heated indoor. **Activities:** whirlpool, limited exercise equipment. **Guest Services:** coin laundry, wireless Internet.

THE HARBOR GRAND

Hotel
$129-$389

Phone: (269)469-7700

Address: 111 Oselka Dr 49117 **Location:** I-94, exit 1 (La Porte Rd), 2 mi w. Overlooking marina. **Facility:** Smoke free premises. 54 units. 4 stories, interior corridors. **Terms:** check-in 4 pm, 2 night minimum stay - weekends, cancellation fee imposed. **Amenities:** *Some:* high-speed Internet. **Pool(s):** heated indoor. **Activities:** whirlpool, bicycles, exercise room. **Fee:** massage. **Guest Services:** wireless Internet.

▼ See AAA listing above ▼

Complete Vacation Planning

AAA.com/Travel and **CAA.ca/Travel** – everything you need to plan and book your vacations, backed by the travel experts at local AAA/CAA offices.

HOLIDAY INN EXPRESS HOTEL & SUITES Phone: (269)469-1400

Hotel
$79-$299

Address: 11500 Holiday Dr 49117 **Location:** I-94, exit 1 (La Porte Rd), just w. **Facility:** Smoke free premises. 80 units. 3 stories, interior corridors. **Parking:** winter plug-ins. **Terms:** check-in 4 pm, 3 day cancellation notice-fee imposed. **Amenities:** *Some:* high-speed Internet. **Pool(s):** heated indoor. **Activities:** whirlpool, exercise room. *Fee:* game room. **Guest Services:** coin laundry, wireless Internet. CALL / SOME UNITS FEE

―――― WHERE TO DINE ――――

REDAMAK'S *Menu on AAA.com* Phone: 269/469-4522

American
$5-$10

A local institution, this casual and informal restaurant is known for its freshly prepared hamburgers, which are cut and ground on the premises. **Bar:** full bar. **Hours:** Open 4/1-10/23 & 3/1-4/30; noon-10:30 pm. Closed: Easter. **Address:** 616 E Buffalo St 49117 **Location:** I-94, exit 1 (La Porte Rd), 1 mi w, then 0.4 mi n.

RETRO CAFE' *Menu on AAA.com* Phone: 269/469-1800

American
$6-$14

The charming, country-style restaurant combines the coziness of a limited number of tables and the bright, cheerful feel of an interior complete with a wall of sepia-tone family pictures. Inventive creations make a strong showing on the breakfast and lunch menu. **Hours:** Open 4/1-2/1 & 3/15-4/30; 8:30 am-3 pm. Closed: 11/24, 12/25; also Tues. **Address:** 801 W Buffalo St 49117 **Location:** I-94, exit 1 (La Porte Rd), 1 mi w, then 0.5 mi s on SR 12. CALL

THE STRAY DOG BAR & GRILL Phone: 269/469-2727

American
$10-$18

Within walking distance of the beach, the popular hangout features a brick fireplace and pictures of all types of dogs on its walls. In the summer, guests wait at the bar for the prized patio seats. The standard bar menu lists hamburgers, sandwiches, pizza and a few daily specials. **Bar:** full bar. **Hours:** noon-11 pm. Closed major holidays. **Address:** 245 N Whittaker St 49117 **Location:** I-94, exit 1 (La Porte Rd), 2 mi w; overlooking marina. **Parking:** on-site and street.

NILES pop. 12,204

HOLIDAY INN EXPRESS Phone: (269)684-3900

Hotel
$99-$119 4/1-11/30
$89-$109 12/1-4/30

Address: 1265 S 11th St (M-51) 49120 **Location:** I-80/90, exit 77, n on SR 933 (which becomes SR 51), then 3.5 mi n. **Facility:** Smoke free premises. 51 units, some efficiencies. 3 stories, interior corridors. **Parking:** winter plug-ins. **Amenities:** high-speed Internet. **Pool(s):** heated indoor. **Activities:** exercise room. **Guest Services:** wireless Internet. **Free Special Amenities:** expanded continental breakfast and high-speed Internet.

NORTHVILLE —See Detroit p. 286.

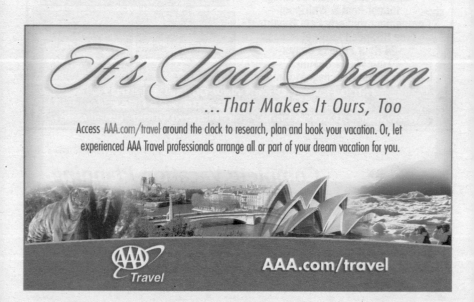

NORTON SHORES pop. 22,527

BAYMONT INN

Hotel
$63-$142

Phone: 231/798-0220

Address: 4677 Harvey Rd 49441 **Location:** US 31, exit Sternberg Rd, just e to Harvey Rd, then 1 mi n. **Facility:** Smoke free premises. 60 units. 2 stories (no elevator), interior corridors. **Terms:** 2 night minimum stay - seasonal and/or weekends, cancellation fee imposed. **Amenities:** safes (fee). **Pool(s):** heated indoor. **Activities:** sauna, whirlpool, exercise room. **Guest Services:** valet and coin laundry, wireless Internet.

FAIRFIELD INN & SUITES BY MARRIOTT

Hotel
$99-$149

Phone: (231)799-0100

Address: 1520 Mt Garfield Rd 49444 **Location:** US 31, exit Sternberg Rd, just e to Harvey Rd, then 0.5 mi s. **Facility:** Smoke free premises. 83 units. 3 stories, interior corridors. **Parking:** winter plug-ins. **Terms:** cancellation fee imposed. **Amenities:** high-speed Internet. **Pool(s):** heated indoor. **Activities:** whirlpool, exercise room. **Guest Services:** valet and coin laundry, wireless Internet.

> **AAA Benefit:**
> Members save a minimum 5% off the best available rate.

HAMPTON INN OF MUSKEGON

Hotel
$99-$199

Phone: (231)799-8333

Address: 1401 E Ellis Rd 49441 **Location:** Just se of jct I-96 and US 31; I-96, exit 1A westbound, follow signs to race track; US 31, exit Sternberg Rd, just e to Harvey Rd, 0.4 mi n, then just w. **Facility:** Smoke free premises. 81 units. 4 stories, interior corridors. **Terms:** 1-7 night minimum stay, cancellation fee imposed. **Pool(s):** heated indoor. **Activities:** whirlpool, exercise room. **Guest Services:** valet laundry, wireless Internet.

> **AAA Benefit:**
> Members save up to 10% everyday!

—— WHERE TO DINE ——

EGG ROLL HOUSE

Chinese
$6-$10

Phone: 231/798-9888

At The Points.Shopping Center, the Chinese restaurant is popular for its Mandarin cuisine. **Hours:** 11 am-9:30 pm, Sun 11:30 am-8 pm. Closed: 1/1, 11/24, 12/24, 12/25. **Address:** 1084 E Sternberg Rd 49441 **Location:** US 31, exit Sternberg Rd, just w.

HOUSE OF CHAN AND JOE'S STEAK HOUSE
Chinese
$8-$30

Phone: 231/733-9624

On the Chinese restaurant's menu are Cantonese dishes, combination plates and some American food. **Bar:** full bar. **Hours:** 11 am-9:30 pm, Fri-10:30 pm, Sat 4 pm-10:30 pm, Sun 11 am-8:30 pm. Closed: 12/25; also Mon. **Address:** 375 Gin Chan Ave 49444 **Location:** Just s of US 31 business route.

TONY'S BISTRO
Continental
$7-$22

Phone: 231/739-7196

The modern family-owned bistro has been operating in the area since 1969. On the menu is a good selection of steak, ribs, chops and seafood, including popular choices of stone-fired oven pizza and Athenian Greek salads. **Bar:** full bar. **Reservations:** suggested, weekends. **Hours:** 11 am-10 pm, Fri & Sat-11 pm, Sun 4 pm-10 pm; hours may vary. Closed major holidays. **Address:** 212 Seminole Rd 49444 **Location:** Jct US 31 business route; 2.8 mi w of US 31.

NORWAY

AMERICINN LODGE & SUITES OF NORWAY

Hotel
$83-$88 6/1-4/30
$81-$86 4/1-5/31

Phone: (906)563-7500

Address: 6002 W US Hwy 2 49870 **Location:** 0.7 mi w. **Facility:** Smoke free premises. 45 units. 2 stories (no elevator), interior corridors. **Pool(s):** heated indoor. **Activities:** sauna, whirlpool, snowmobiling. **Guest Services:** coin laundry, wireless Internet.

NOVI —See Detroit p. 287.

OKEMOS

COMFORT INN-E. LANSING/OKEMOS
Hotel
$79-$189

Phone: (517)347-6690

Address: 2187 University Park Dr 48864 **Location:** I-96, exit 110 (Okemos Rd), just n, then just e. Located in University Commerce Park. **Facility:** Smoke free premises. 90 units. 2 stories (no elevator), interior corridors. **Amenities:** high-speed Internet. **Guest Services:** valet laundry, wireless Internet.

FAIRFIELD INN BY MARRIOTT

Hotel
$89-$114

Address: 2335 Woodlake Dr 48864 **Location:** I-96, exit 110 (Okemos Rd), just n, then just w. Located in an office park. **Facility:** Smoke free premises. 78 units. 2 stories (no elevator), interior corridors. **Terms:** cancellation fee imposed. **Amenities:** *Some:* high-speed Internet. **Pool(s):** heated indoor. **Activities:** whirlpool, exercise room. **Guest Services:** valet laundry, wireless Internet.

HAMPTON INN & SUITES

Phone: 517/349-6100

Hotel
Rates not provided

Address: 2200 Hampton Pl 48864 **Location:** I-96, exit 110 (Okemos Rd), just n. **Facility:** Smoke free premises. 100 units. 3 stories, interior corridors. **Terms:** check-in 4 pm. **Pool(s):** heated indoor. **Activities:** whirlpool, exercise room. **Guest Services:** valet and coin laundry, wireless Internet.

HOLIDAY INN EXPRESS & SUITES

Phone: (517)349-8700

Hotel
$98-$104

Address: 2209 University Park Dr 48864 **Location:** I-96, exit 110 (Okemos Rd), just n, then just e. Located in University Commerce Park. **Facility:** Smoke free premises. 160 units. 2 stories (no elevator), interior corridors. **Terms:** check-in 4 pm, cancellation fee imposed. **Amenities:** high-speed Internet, safes (fee). **Pool(s):** heated indoor. **Activities:** sauna, whirlpool, exercise room. **Guest Services:** valet and coin laundry, area transportation-within 5 mi, wireless Internet.

STAYBRIDGE SUITES - LANSING/OKEMOS

Phone: (517)347-3044

Extended Stay Hotel
$89-$199

Address: 3553 Meridian Crossing Dr 48864 **Location:** I-96, exit 110 (Okemos Rd), just n. **Facility:** Smoke free premises. 95 efficiencies, some two bedrooms. 3 stories, interior corridors. **Amenities:** high-speed Internet. **Pool(s):** heated indoor. **Activities:** whirlpool, gas barbecue grills, theater room, exercise room. **Guest Services:** valet and coin laundry, wireless Internet.
(see ad p. 350)

—— WHERE TO DINE ——

BUDDIES PUB & GRILL

Phone: 517/347-0443

American
$7-$15

A local fixture for more than 15 years, the extensive menu of this restaurant covers the full gamut of pub and comfort foods, everything from burgers to deep-dish pizza, pastas, chicken dinners and pot roast. Not surprisingly, a giant plate of gooey nachos, large enough to feed three, is one of the most popular menu items. Locals sometimes pop in to see if chicken pot pie is on the day's menu. The chef doesn't make the chicken pot pie often, but when he does the locals flock in! **Bar:** full bar. **Hours:** 11 am-1 am, Sun 9 am-midnight. Closed major holidays. **Address:** 1937 W Grand River Ave 48864 **Location:** Jct Okemos Rd, 1 mi e.

DUSTY'S CELLAR

Phone: 517/349-5150

American
$8-$25

Trellised grapevines on the ceiling and a large vineyard mural frame this small, intimate dining room, which is entered through a wine store. An extensive selection of wines complements dishes that employ tropical flavors from areas as far-flung as Hawaii, Florida and the Caribbean. Among menu accents are New Zealand lamb chops, diver scallops and Lake Superior whitefish. **Bar:** full bar. **Hours:** 11 am-10 pm, Fri & Sat-11 pm, Sun 11 am-3 & 4-9 pm. Closed major holidays. **Address:** 1839 Grand River Ave 48864 **Location:** Jct Okemos Rd, 1 mi e.

GILBERT & BLAKE'S STEAK AND SEAFOOD GRILLE

Phone: 517/349-1300

American
$8-$36

The trendy, upscale dining room offers a sophisticated yet casual ambience in which to enjoy one of many prime steak or fresh fish selections. Seafood is flown in daily, but for those not in the mood for seafood, the menu also features a variety of pastas and chicken dishes, as well as a children's menu. Once a month the restaurant offers a reservations-only wine tasting dinner where a selection of wines from a particular vineyard is paired with pre-set menu selections. **Bar:** full bar. **Hours:** 11 am-10 pm, Fri & Sat-11 pm, Sun noon-9 pm. Closed major holidays. **Address:** 3554 Okemos Rd 48864 **Location:** I-96, exit 110 (Okemos Rd), just n.

THE GRAND TRAVERSE PIE COMPANY

Phone: 517/381-7437

Deli
$5-$8

A large, open, working bakery greets guests as they enter into this cute little cafe. The aromas of freshly baked fruit pies, spinach quiche and made-to-order sandwiches will certainly stimulate the appetite. **Hours:** 6:30 am-8:30 pm, Sat 8 am-5:30 pm, Sun 10 am-3 pm. Closed major holidays. **Address:** 3536 Meridian Crossing Dr 48864 **Location:** I-96, exit 110 (Okemos Rd), just n, then just w; in Meridian Crossing Development.

MARU SUSHI & GRILL

Phone: 517/349-7500

Japanese
$5-$26

The small, ultra-trendy restaurant offers a creative, fun ambience for diners. Favorite sushi standbys such as dynamite rolls and California rolls are served, as well as a nice selection of sashimi. There's a lengthy list of signature rolls and also fish-free veggie rolls. For those who don't care for sushi in any form, the restaurant serves steak, chicken and shrimp hibachi grills served with rice and vegetables. **Bar:** full bar. **Hours:** 11:30 am-2:30 & 4:30-9:30 pm, Sun 4 pm-9 pm. **Address:** 5100 Marsh Rd 48864 **Location:** Jct Grand River Ave, just n.

STILLWATER GRILL

American
$8-$25

Phone: 517/349-1500

The huge restaurant became popular almost immediately, which translates to a short wait for seating, even on weeknights. Intimate booths, hand-painted murals and copper accents give the room a stylish air, and the open kitchen prepares a menu that focuses on both steaks and several nightly fresh fish or pasta specials. **Bar:** full bar. **Reservations:** suggested. **Hours:** 11 am-10 pm, Sat from 3 pm, Sun 3 pm-9 pm. Closed: 7/4, 11/24, 12/25. **Address:** 3544 Meridian Crossing Dr 48864 **Location:** I-96, exit 110 (Okemos Rd), just n.

ONEKAMA pop. 647

ALPINE MOTOR LODGE-BUDGET HOST

Motel
$59-$95 4/1-8/31
$59-$85 9/1-4/30

Phone: (231)889-4281

Address: 8127 US 31 49675 **Location:** Jct 8 Mile Rd. **Facility:** Smoke free premises. 25 units. 1 story, exterior corridors. **Terms:** office hours 8 am-11 pm, 2 night minimum stay - seasonal and/or weekends. **Pool(s):** heated outdoor. **Activities:** miniature golf, picnic area with grills, playground, horseshoes. **Guest Services:** wireless Internet.

ONSTED pop. 813

—— **WHERE TO DINE** ——

RANDY'S ROADHOUSE BBQ

Barbecue
$9-$20

Phone: 517/467-2190

This restaurant's turn-of-the-20th-century décor includes leaded-glass chandeliers, antique furnishings and Tiffany-style lamps. The extensive menu focuses on barbecue items, with smoked ribs as a house specialty. Family platters offer good value for groups of four to six people as they include ribs, chicken and fixings like coleslaw, a choice of side vegetables and bread. **Bar:** full bar. **Hours:** Open 4/7-12/20; 4 pm-9 pm, Sat noon-10 pm, Sun noon-8 pm. Closed: 12/24, 12/25; also Mon & Tues. **Address:** 7305 US 12 49265 **Location:** 0.3 mi e.

ONTONAGON pop. 1,769

PETERSON'S COTTAGES

Cottage
$85-$275

Phone: 906/884-4230

Address: 22608 Lakeshore Rd 49953 **Location:** 1.5 mi sw on SR 64. Located on shores of Lake Superior. **Facility:** Designated smoking area. 16 units, some houses and cottages. 1 story, exterior corridors. **Parking:** winter plug-ins. **Terms:** office hours 8 am-10 pm, check-in 4 pm, 30 day cancellation notice-fee imposed. **Activities:** beach access, canoeing, paddleboats, cross country skiing, snowmobiling, bicycles, playground, horseshoes, volleyball. *Fee:* kayaks, snowshoes, pavilion. **Guest Services:** coin laundry, wireless Internet.

OSCODA pop. 992

AMERICINN LODGE & SUITES OF OSCODA

Hotel
$79-$219

Phone: (989)739-1986

Address: 720 E Harbor St 48750 **Location:** Just w of US 23; at Smith and 2nd sts. Located on the Au Sable River. **Facility:** Smoke free premises. 47 units. 2 stories (no elevator), interior corridors. **Amenities:** high-speed Internet. **Pool(s):** heated indoor. **Activities:** sauna, whirlpool, boat dock, fishing. **Guest Services:** coin laundry, wireless Internet. **Free Special Amenities: expanded continental breakfast and high-speed Internet.**

—— **WHERE TO DINE** ——

TAIT'S BILL OF FARE

American
$5-$25

Phone: 989/739-1518

Next to the movie theater, the downtown restaurant presents a menu of well-prepared traditional dishes. **Bar:** full bar. **Hours:** 11:30 am-3:30 & 4:30-9:30 pm; hours may vary. Closed major holidays; also Sun 9/6-6/15. **Address:** 111 E Dwight Ave 48750 **Location:** Just e of US 23; downtown.

WILTSE'S BREW PUB & FAMILY RESTAURANT

American
$6-$24

Phone: 989/739-2231

Craft-brewed ale and lager are brewed on the premises. A good selection of main dishes, from specialties like Paul Bunyan's mess burger served with everything but the kitchen sink to sirloin tips, have been popular dishes here for more than 18 years. **Bar:** full bar. **Hours:** 7 am-9 pm, Fri & Sat-10 pm; to 10 pm, Fri & Sat-11 pm 5/30-9/6. Closed: 11/24, 12/25. **Address:** 5606 N F41 48750 **Location:** On CR F41, 1 mi nw of US 23.

OWOSSO pop. 15,713

—— **WHERE TO DINE** ——

EDDIE O'FLYNN'S

American
$6-$15

Phone: 989/723-6741

Antique furnishings and knickknacks, including plenty of 1950s memorabilia, adorn the dining room. The expansive menu lists ribs, steak, fish, burgers, salad, stir-fry and pitas, plus a variety of tempting desserts. Breakfast on the weekend is a delicious treat. **Bar:** full bar. **Hours:** 11 am-10 pm, Fri-11 pm, Sat 4 pm-11 pm, Sun noon-4 pm. Closed major holidays; also Sun 5/30-9/6. **Address:** 2280 W SR 21 48867 **Location:** On SR 21, 1.8 mi w.

PARADISE pop. 4,191

BEST WESTERN LAKEFRONT INN & SUITES

Hotel
$118-$165

Phone: (906)492-3770

Address: 8112 N SR 123 49768 **Location:** On SR 123, just s. Located on shores of Whitefish Bay. **Facility:** Smoke free premises. 41 units. 3 stories, interior corridors. **Parking:** winter plug-ins. **Terms:** cancellation fee imposed. **Amenities:** *Some:* high-speed Internet. **Pool(s):** heated indoor. **Activities:** sauna, whirlpool, limited beach access, snowmobiling. **Guest Services:** coin laundry, wireless Internet. **Free Special Amenities:** expanded continental breakfast and high-speed Internet.

AAA Benefit:
Members save up to 20%, plus 10% bonus points with free rewards program.

PARADISE INN

Hotel
$39-$109

Phone: 906/492-3940

Address: 8359 N Whitefish Point Rd (Hwy M-123) 49768 **Location:** On SR 123; center. **Facility:** Smoke free premises. 36 units. 2 stories (no elevator), interior corridors. **Parking:** winter plug-ins. **Terms:** cancellation fee imposed. **Activities:** snowmobiling. **Guest Services:** coin laundry, wireless Internet. **Free Special Amenities:** continental breakfast and high-speed Internet.

PAW PAW pop. 3,363

COMFORT INN & SUITES

Hotel
$65-$139

Phone: (269)655-0303

Address: 153 Ampey Rd 49079 **Location:** I-94, exit 60 (SR 40), just nw. **Facility:** 65 units, some kitchens. 2 stories, interior corridors. **Pool(s):** heated indoor. **Activities:** sun deck, exercise room. **Guest Services:** valet and coin laundry, wireless Internet.

------ WHERE TO DINE ------

LA CANTINA RISTORANTE ITALIANO

Italian
$12-$24

Phone: 269/657-7033

Raffini-wrapped Chianti bottles adorn the entryway to this comfortable restaurant, which boasts large picture windows overlooking a serene brook. The menu features a wide range of traditional Italian dishes. **Bar:** full bar. **Reservations:** suggested. **Hours:** 5 pm-10 pm, Sun-8 pm. Closed major holidays; also Mon. **Address:** 139 W Michigan Ave 49079 **Location:** Downtown. **Parking:** on-site and street.

PELLSTON pop. 600

------ WHERE TO DINE ------

DAM SITE INN

American
$16-$39

Phone: 231/539-8851

Family-style preparations of chicken, steak and seafood are what the casual restaurant is all about. In business since 1953, the establishment offers views of the dam from many dining room windows. Service is friendly and efficient. **Bar:** full bar. **Hours:** Open 4/19-10/31; 5 pm-9 pm, Sun 3 pm-8 pm. Closed: Mon except 7/1-8/31. **Address:** US 31 49769 **Location:** On US 31, 1.5 mi s of town; near dam on Maple River.

PENTWATER pop. 958

COMFORT INN & SUITES

Hotel
Rates not provided

Phone: 231/869-8000

Address: 7576 S Pere Marquette Hwy 49449 **Location:** US 31, exit 158, 0.3 mi w. **Facility:** Smoke free premises. 56 units. 2 stories, interior corridors. **Parking:** winter plug-ins. **Pool(s):** heated indoor. **Activities:** whirlpool, exercise room. **Guest Services:** coin laundry, wireless Internet.

------ WHERE TO DINE ------

THE BROWN BEAR

American
$4-$12

Phone: 231/869-5444

This restaurant offers huge hamburgers, fried chicken and a variety of submarine sandwiches. **Bar:** full bar. **Hours:** 11 am-11 pm, Sun from noon. Closed: major holidays, 12/24. **Address:** 278 S Hancock St 49449 **Location:** Between 2nd and 3rd sts. **Parking:** street only.

PETOSKEY pop. 6,080

BEST WESTERN INN OF PETOSKEY

Motel

$49-$159

Address: 1300 Spring St 49770 **Location:** 1.3 mi s on US 131. **Facility:** Smoke free premises. 81 units, some two bedrooms. 2 stories (no elevator), interior/exterior corridors. **Pool(s):** heated indoor. **Activities:** sauna, whirlpool, exercise room. *Fee:* game room. **Guest Services:** wireless Internet. **Free Special Amenities: expanded continental breakfast and high-speed Internet.**

 / SOME UNITS

Phone: (231)347-3925

AAA Benefit:
Members save up to 20%, plus 10% bonus points with free rewards program.

DAYS INN PETOSKEY

Motel

$53-$116

Address: 1420 Spring St 49770 **Location:** 1.3 mi s on US 131. **Facility:** Smoke free premises. 134 units. 2 stories (no elevator), exterior corridors. **Amenities:** safes. **Activities:** limited exercise equipment. **Guest Services:** coin laundry, wireless Internet. *(see ad below)*

 / SOME UNITS FEE

Phone: (231)348-3900

FREE expanded continental breakfast and high-speed Internet

HAMPTON INN & SUITES

Hotel

$99-$219 4/1-9/5
$99-$189 9/6-4/30

Address: 920 Spring St 49770 **Location:** 1.2 mi s on US 131. **Facility:** Smoke free premises. 77 units. 4 stories, interior corridors. **Terms:** 1-7 night minimum stay, cancellation fee imposed. **Amenities:** video games (fee). **Pool(s):** heated indoor. **Activities:** whirlpool, exercise room. **Guest Services:** valet and coin laundry, wireless Internet.

/ SOME UNITS FEE   FEE

Phone: (231)348-9555

AAA Benefit:
Members save up to 10% everyday!

HOLIDAY INN EXPRESS HOTEL & SUITES

Hotel

$79-$299

Address: 1751 US 131 S 49770 **Location:** I-75, exit 282, w on SR 32 to US 131 N. **Facility:** Smoke free premises. 82 units, some two bedrooms, efficiencies and kitchens. 5 stories, interior corridors. **Terms:** check-in 4 pm, 2 night minimum stay - seasonal and/or weekends. **Amenities:** *Some:* high-speed Internet. **Pool(s):** heated indoor. **Activities:** sauna, whirlpool, sun deck, exercise room. **Guest Services:** valet and coin laundry, area transportation-within 5 mi, wireless Internet. *(see ad inside back cover & below)*

Phone: (231)487-0991

▼ *See AAA listing above* ▼

ExpressPetoskey.com

Holiday Inn **Express** & Suites

"VALLEY VIEW"

- 82 Luxurious Guest Rooms & Suites
- Two Club Level Suite Floors w/ 2 Room & 2 Bath Suites Featuring Deluxe Presidential Suites & 2000 sq.ft. Penthouse Suite w/ Full Kitchens, Private Balcony & Fireplaces
- Free Express Start Hot Breakfast Bar
- Hi-Speed Wireless Internet • 2 Elevators
- Private Balconies overlooking Little Traverse Bay and Bear River Valley • 24 Hour Casino Shuttle
- Meeting, Conference & Hospitality Room
- Golf, Skiing, Casino & Dining Packages
- Interior Corridor • Business Center
- Fitness Facility • Group Friendly
- Complimentary Limousine Shuttle to Casino, Dining & Shopping

Toll Free: **888-497-0105** • **231-487-0991**
Reservations Call Toll Free: **1-800-HOLIDAY** (800-465-4329)
1751 US 131 South, Petoskey, MI 49770

ODAWA HOTEL

Phone: 231/347-6041

Hotel
$69-$159

Address: 1444 US 131 S 49770 **Location:** 1.5 mi s. **Facility:** 137 units. 5 stories, interior corridors. **Parking:** winter plug-ins. **Terms:** check-in 4 pm, 3 day cancellation notice-fee imposed. **Pool(s):** heated indoor. **Activities:** whirlpool. **Guest Services:** valet and coin laundry, wireless Internet. **Free Special Amenities: expanded continental breakfast and high-speed Internet.**

── WHERE TO DINE ──

CITY PARK GRILL

Phone: 231/347-0101

American
$6-$26

Ernest Hemingway is reputed to have spent a fair amount of time at the massive 100-year-old mirrored cherry bar that dominates this casual restaurant. Honey-grilled pork chops marinated in jalapeños, soy sauce and Dijon mustard lead a Continental menu that offers a wide range of choices. **Bar:** full bar. **Hours:** 11:30 am-9 pm, Fri & Sat-10 pm. Closed: 11/24, 12/24, 12/25. **Address:** 432 E Lake St 49770 **Location:** Center. **Parking:** street only.

JULIENNE TOMATOES

Phone: 231/439-9250

Deli
$7-$9

Don't be surprised to find this popular spot packed with locals over the lunch hour who know that house rules state the largest tables in the tiny dining room are communal. The sofas facing a small TV are also a top spot to sip a coffee or enjoy one of the many specialty sandwiches prepared fresh to order. The menu also offers a variety of soups made from scratch, fresh salads and a rotating selection of decadent dessert options. Breakfast is served daily from 8 to 11 am. **Hours:** 8 am-4 pm. Closed major holidays; also Sun. **Address:** 421 Howard St 49770 **Location:** Downtown. **Parking:** street only.

SIDE DOOR SALOON

Phone: 231/347-9291

American
$8-$15

Tucked away from the hustle and bustle of the downtown tourist district, this is a favorite spot among locals and visitors in the know. The warm and cozy saloon offers a menu packed with pub favorites ranging from nachos and quesadillas to wraps, steaks and fresh fish. Locals swear that the burgers are the best in northern Michigan and the whitefish tostadas are definitely worth a try. **Bar:** full bar. **Hours:** 11 am-10 pm. Closed major holidays; also Sun. **Address:** 1200 N US 31 49770 **Location:** Just w of jct SR 119.

VILLA RISTORANTE ITALIANO

Phone: 231/347-1440

Italian
$23-$33

Gnocchi and shrimp with gorgonzola represent traditional preparations of Italian cuisine at this restaurant. The homemade Italian ice cream is hard to top as a meal finisher. **Bar:** full bar. **Reservations:** suggested, in season. **Hours:** 5 pm-10 pm; hours may vary. Closed major holidays; also Sun. **Address:** 887 Spring St 49770 **Location:** US 131, just s of jct US 31.

PLAINWELL pop. 3,933

COMFORT INN

Hotel
Rates not provided

Phone: 269/685-9891

Address: 622 Allegan St 49080 **Location:** US 131, exit 49A, just e. **Facility:** Smoke free premises. 63 units. 2 stories (no elevator), interior corridors. **Pool(s):** heated indoor. **Activities:** whirlpool, exercise room. **Guest Services:** wireless Internet.

SAVE ▮+ ➔ BIZ ✕ ▯ ▦ / SOME UNITS FEE ▭ ▯ ▦

—— WHERE TO DINE ——

LONDON GRILL-BOMBAY

Provincial British
$7-$20

Phone: 269/685-1877

The quintessential British pub, this small, lively space is adorned with British and Colonial Indian memorabilia. A small menu reflects a mix of both British pub favorites and Indian curries. **Bar:** full bar. **Hours:** 11 am-10 pm, Fri & Sat-11 pm, Sun & Mon-9 pm. Closed major holidays. **Address:** 200 E Bridge St 49080 **Location:** US 131, exit 49A, 2 mi e; center. **Parking:** street only. CALL ⑤M

PLYMOUTH —See Detroit p. 290.

PONTIAC —See Detroit p. 291.

PORTAGE pop. 44,897

—— WHERE TO DINE ——

THE CRAFTSMAN CHOP COMPANY

American
$8-$20

Phone: 269/327-2000

The family-friendly spot offers a comfortable dining atmosphere. Guests will find reasonable prices on a menu with good variety. Steaks, seafood and pasta dishes are highlights, and sandwiches include a Kobe beef burger or grilled chicken with pineapple sandwich. Kids will enjoy selections from the enticing children's menu. **Bar:** full bar. **Reservations:** suggested. **Hours:** 11:30 am-9 pm, Fri & Sat-10 pm. Closed major holidays. **Address:** 6905 Sears Dr 49024 **Location:** I-94, exit 76A (Westnedge Ave S), 1.4 mi s, then just w on Romence; behind Sears in Crossroads Mall. CALL ⑤M

FIELDSTONE GRILL

American
$7-$24

Phone: 269/321-8480

Using a wood-burning grill, stone pizza oven and rotisserie, the kitchen staff prepares Pacific seafood dishes, including seared sea scallops and wood-grilled Atlantic salmon. Diners also savor appetizer pizzas, fresh pasta dishes and wood-grilled steaks in the northwoods lodge-like setting, which incorporates floor-to-ceiling windows and a fieldstone fireplace. **Bar:** full bar. **Hours:** 11 am-10 pm, Sun 10 am-2 & 4-9 pm; hours may vary. Closed major holidays. **Address:** 3970 W Center Ave 49024 **Location:** US 131, exit Center Ave, 0.5 mi e; in Woodbridge Shopping Village. CALL ⑤M

PORT AUSTIN pop. 737

LAKE STREET MANOR BED & BREAKFAST

Historic Bed
& Breakfast
$60-$90

Phone: 989/738-7720

Address: 8569 Lake St 48467 **Location:** Just s on SR 53 (Van Dyke Rd); downtown. **Facility:** Near Saginaw Bay, this late-1800s Victorian summer home offers a fenced garden. Smoke free premises. 5 units. 2 stories (no elevator), interior/exterior corridors. **Bath:** some shared. **Terms:** open 4/1-1/15, 2 night minimum stay - seasonal and/or weekends, 3 day cancellation notice-fee imposed. **Activities:** whirlpool, barbecue grills, bicycles. ✕ ⓩ

LAKE VISTA MOTEL & COTTAGES RESORT

Motel
$78-$239

Phone: 989/738-8612

Address: 168 W Spring St 48467 **Location:** SR 25 (Spring St), 0.5 mi w. **Facility:** Designated smoking area. 23 units, some two bedrooms and kitchens. 1-2 stories (no elevator), exterior corridors. **Terms:** open 4/10-11/15, 2 night minimum stay - seasonal and/or weekends, 14 day cancellation notice-fee imposed. **Amenities:** Some: high-speed Internet. **Pool(s):** heated outdoor. **Activities:** fishing, barbecue grills, gazebos, horseshoes. Fee: miniature golf. **Guest Services:** coin laundry, wireless Internet. SAVE ➔ ✕ ⓩ ▯ ▦ / SOME UNITS ▯

—— WHERE TO DINE ——

THE BANK 1884

American
$6-$23

Phone: 989/738-5353

In an 1884 bank, the dining room displays historical touches from the 19th and early 20th centuries. The menu features something for every palate, including mouthwatering steaks and fresh seafood, as well as pasta, burgers and tableside-prepared salads. Fresh fish, such as perch, is a standout at this spot, which is just two blocks from the local wharf. **Bar:** full bar. **Reservations:** suggested. **Hours:** Open 5/1-11/1; 11 am-9 pm. Closed major holidays. **Address:** 8646 Lake St 48467 **Location:** Just s of jct SR 53 (Van Dyke Rd) and 25 (Spring St); downtown. **Parking:** street only.

BREAKERS ON THE BAY LAKEFRONT RESTAURANT

American
$18-$33

Phone: 989/738-5101

On the shores of Lake Huron, the dining room features a wall of windows to enhance the spectacular views, and when the weather's good, outside seats further make the most of them. The menu focuses on traditional dishes, including steak and seafood offerings such as local lake perch, Alaskan salmon, beef tenderloin and prime rib. Other options include pork loin chops, stuffed chicken, rack of lamb or the simple sirloin burger. Specialty tropical cocktails are among beverage options. **Bar:** full bar. **Reservations:** suggested. **Hours:** 5 pm-9 pm. Closed: Tues; Mon & Wed in winter. **Address:** 1404 Post Austin 48467 **Location:** 4 mi w on SR 25 (Spring St).

THE FARM RESTAURANT

Regional American
$10-$24

Phone: 989/874-5700

Located 2 miles from Port Austin, this converted farmhouse uses locally grown ingredients to create innovative dishes. **Bar:** full bar. **Hours:** Open 5/15-9/30; 5 pm-10 pm, Sun 4 pm-9 pm. Closed: Mon. **Address:** 699 Port Crescent Rd 48467 **Location:** 1.5 mi w of jct SR 53 (Van Dyke Rd) and Port Crescent Rd.

THE STOCK POT

American
$5-$8

Phone: 989/738-7111

Friendly and unpretentious staff members readily serve up homemade comfort foods, ranging from breakfast selections, sandwiches and to-die-for burgers to the varied soups that give this place its name. For dessert, it's hard to top fresh pies baked on site. **Hours:** 6 am-7 pm; to 2 pm off season. Closed major holidays. **Address:** 8714 Lake St 48467 **Location:** Just s on SR 53 (Van Dyke Rd); downtown. **Parking:** street only.

PORT HURON pop. 32,338

BAYMONT INN & SUITES

Hotel
$62-$107

Phone: (810)364-8000

Address: 1611 Range Rd 48074 **Location:** I-94, exit 269 (Range Rd), just w. Opposite an outlet mall. **Facility:** Smoke free premises. 60 units. 2 stories (no elevator), interior corridors. **Amenities:** safes (fee). **Pool(s):** heated indoor. **Activities:** whirlpool, exercise room. **Guest Services:** coin laundry, wireless Internet. **Free Special Amenities: expanded continental breakfast and high-speed Internet.**

BEST WESTERN HOSPITALITY INN

Hotel
$60-$120

Phone: (810)987-1600

Address: 2282 Water St 48060 **Location:** I-94, exit 274 (Water St), just n. Located in a quiet area. **Facility:** Smoke free premises. 63 units. 3 stories, interior corridors. **Pool(s):** heated indoor. **Activities:** exercise room. **Guest Services:** valet and coin laundry, wireless Internet. **Free Special Amenities: full breakfast and high-speed Internet.**

AAA Benefit:
Members save up to 20%, plus 10% bonus points with free rewards program.

COMFORT INN

Hotel
$80-$160

Phone: (810)982-5500

Address: 1700 Yeager St 48060 **Location:** I-94, exit 274 (Water St), just s, then just w. Located in a quiet area. **Facility:** Smoke free premises. 80 units. 2 stories (no elevator), interior corridors. **Terms:** check-in 4 pm. **Amenities:** safes (fee). **Pool(s):** heated indoor. **Activities:** whirlpool, exercise room. **Guest Services:** valet and coin laundry, wireless Internet.

FAIRFIELD INN BY MARRIOTT

Hotel
$79-$94

Phone: (810)982-8500

Address: 1635 Yeager St 48060 **Location:** I-94, exit 274 (Water St), just s, then just w. Located in a quiet area. **Facility:** Smoke free premises. 62 units. 3 stories, interior corridors. **Terms:** cancellation fee imposed. **Amenities:** high-speed Internet. **Pool(s):** heated indoor. **Activities:** whirlpool, patio, exercise room. **Guest Services:** valet and coin laundry, wireless Internet.

AAA Benefit:
Members save a minimum 5% off the best available rate.

HAMPTON INN

Hotel
Rates not provided

Phone: 810/966-9000

Address: 1655 Yeager St 48060 **Location:** I-94, exit 274 (Water St), just s, then just w. Located in a quiet area. **Facility:** 70 units. 3 stories, interior corridors. **Amenities:** video games (fee). **Some:** high-speed Internet. **Pool(s):** heated indoor. **Activities:** whirlpool, exercise room. **Guest Services:** valet and coin laundry, wireless Internet.

AAA Benefit:
Members save up to 10% everyday!

QUALITY INN & SUITES

Hotel
Rates not provided

Phone: 810/987-5999

Address: 1720 Hancock St 48060 **Location:** Business Loop I-69 and 94 E, then e. Located beside Blue Water Bridge. **Facility:** Designated smoking area. 96 units. 4 stories, interior corridors. **Amenities:** Some: video games. **Pool(s):** heated indoor. **Activities:** whirlpool, indoor playland, exercise room. **Fee:** game room. **Guest Services:** valet and coin laundry, wireless Internet.

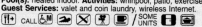

——— WHERE TO DINE ———

BISTRO 1882

American
$7-$30

Phone: 810/966-6900

Tucked away almost under the Blue Water Bridge, this small and intimate dining room offers a modest but creative menu in a classy dining room warmed with exposed brick walls and upscale lighting. **Bar:** full bar. **Reservations:** suggested. **Hours:** 11 am-9 pm, Sun from 10 am. Closed: 12/25. **Address:** 2333 Gratiot Ave 48060 **Location:** I-94, exit SR 25 (downtown), 0.6 mi s on Hancock, then just w.

DAYBREAK CAFE

Comfort Food
$6-$12

Phone: 810/966-5000

The focus is on homestyle foods at reasonable prices at this family-run diner. The menu concentrates on breakfast foods, burgers and sandwiches and even offers a number of healthful options for calorie counters. **Hours:** 6 am-9 pm, Sun-4 pm. Closed major holidays. **Address:** 3910 24th Ave 48060 **Location:** Jct Kraft Rd.

POWER'S DINER

American
$5-$15

Phone: 810/985-5130

Reminiscent of a 1950s diner, the small restaurant has black-and-white tile floors, sparkly red booths and the music of the Big Bopper and Elvis pouring from loudspeakers. Patrons find this a fun place to grab a hamburger, French fries and milk shake. **Hours:** 7 am-8 pm, Thurs-9 pm, Fri & Sat-11 pm. Closed major holidays. **Address:** 1209 Military St 48060 **Location:** Just s of Swing Bridge; downtown.

QUAY STREET BREWING COMPANY   *Menu on AAA.com*

American
$6-$15

Phone: 810/982-4100

Situated on the riverfront, this microbrewery not only offers a variety of hand-crafted brews but also features selections from other Michigan microbreweries. As well as offering traditional bar foods, the menu features a few surprises, such as a house version of Louisiana's famous muffuletta and grilled lamb burgers. **Bar:** full bar. **Hours:** 11:30 am-9 pm, Fri & Sat-10 pm, Sun noon-8 pm. Closed major holidays. **Address:** 330 Quay St 48060 **Location:** Adjacent to drawbridge; downtown. **Parking:** street only. CALL ⬥M

TOM MANIS RESTAURANT

American
$5-$15

Phone: 810/982-9021

A local favorite, the menu at the popular diner spans a wide range of comfort foods, including eggs, omelets, pancakes, chicken, steaks, ribs, burgers and Coneys. **Hours:** 6 am-8 pm, Sat from 8 am, Sun 8 am-3 pm. Closed major holidays. **Address:** 1232 10th St 48060 **Location:** I-94, exit 274 (Water St), 1.2 mi e, then 0.6 mi s.

PORTLAND pop. 3,798

BEST WESTERN AMERICAN HERITAGE INN

Hotel
$70-$150

Phone: (517)647-2200

Address: 1681 Grand River Ave 48875 **Location:** I-96, exit 77, just n. **Facility:** Smoke free premises. 48 units. 2 stories (no elevator), interior corridors. **Amenities:** *Some:* high-speed Internet. **Pool(s):** heated indoor. **Activities:** whirlpool. *Fee:* game room. **Guest Services:** coin laundry, wireless Internet. **Free Special Amenities: continental breakfast and high-speed Internet.**

SAVE CALL ⬥M 🛎 ✕ 🎥 🖥 / SOME UNITS FEE 🐾 🛗 🧳

AAA Benefit:
Members save up to 20%, plus 10% bonus points with free rewards program.

PORT SANILAC pop. 658

THE RAYMOND HOUSE AND INN

Historic Bed & Breakfast
$85-$95 4/1-10/31
$75-$85 11/1-4/30

Phone: 810/622-8800

Address: 111 S Ridge St 48469 **Location:** On SR 25; just s of downtown. **Facility:** This elegant house in a sleepy harbor village, is walking distance from the Lake Huron waterfront and the Port Sanilac Lighthouse. Smoke free premises. 7 units. 3 stories (no elevator), interior corridors. *Bath:* some shared. **Guest Services:** wireless Internet. 🍴➜ ✕

ROCHESTER —See Detroit p. 292.

ROCHESTER HILLS —See Detroit p. 293.

ROGERS CITY pop. 3,322

—— **WHERE TO DINE** ——

WATERS EDGE

American
$9-$40

Phone: 989/734-4747

The restaurant delivers such well-prepared food as whitefish, prime rib, chicken and pasta. The nautically themed dining room, affords views of Lake Huron. For dessert, try the Kentucky Derby pie. **Bar:** full bar. **Reservations:** suggested. **Hours:** Open 5/1-9/11; 4 pm-9 pm. Closed: 1/1, 12/25; also Sun-Tues. **Address:** 530 W Third St 49779 **Location:** 1 mi nw on US 23 business route.

ROMULUS —See Detroit p. 293.

ROSEVILLE —See Detroit p. 296.

ROYAL OAK —See Detroit p. 296.

SAGINAW pop. 61,799

AMERICAS BEST VALUE INN SAGINAW

Hotel
Rates not provided

Phone: 989/755-0461

Address: 1408 S Outer Dr 48601 **Location:** I-75, exit 149B (SR 46), just w. **Facility:** Smoke free premises. 158 units. 4 stories, interior corridors. **Amenities:** video games. *Some:* high-speed Internet. **Pool(s):** heated indoor. **Activities:** sauna, whirlpool, racquetball court, exercise room. *Fee:* game room. **Guest Services:** coin laundry, wireless Internet.

🍽 🛎 ✕ 🎥 🖥 / SOME UNITS FEE 🐾 🛗

COMFORT SUITES BY CHOICE HOTELS

Hotel
$81-$125

Phone: (989)797-8000

Address: 5180 Fashion Square Blvd 48603 **Location:** I-675, exit 6, 0.6 mi w on Tittabawassee Rd. **Facility:** Smoke free premises. 66 units. 3 stories, interior corridors. **Pool(s):** heated indoor. **Activities:** whirlpool. **Guest Services:** valet laundry, wireless Internet.

FAIRFIELD INN BY MARRIOTT

Hotel
$81-$104

Phone: (989)797-6100

Address: 5200 Fashion Square Blvd 48603 **Location:** I-675, exit 6, 0.5 mi w on Tittabawassee Rd. **Facility:** Smoke free premises. 76 units. 3 stories, interior corridors. **Parking:** winter plug-ins. **Terms:** cancellation fee imposed. **Pool(s):** heated indoor. **Activities:** whirlpool. **Guest Services:** valet laundry, wireless Internet.

AAA Benefit:
Members save a minimum 5% off the best available rate.

FOUR POINTS BY SHERATON SAGINAW

Hotel
Rates not provided

Phone: 989/790-5050

Address: 4960 Towne Centre Rd 48604 **Location:** I-675, exit 6, just w on Tittabawassee Rd. **Facility:** Smoke free premises. 142 units. 6 stories, interior corridors. **Pool(s):** heated indoor/outdoor. **Activities:** sauna, whirlpool, exercise room. **Guest Services:** valet and coin laundry, wireless Internet. **Free Special Amenities:** expanded continental breakfast and high-speed Internet.

FOUR POINTS
BY SHERATON

AAA Benefit:
Members get up to 15% off, plus Starwood Preferred Guest® bonuses.

INN AT SAGINAW CARDINAL SQUARE

Hotel
Rates not provided

Phone: 989/792-7666

Address: 2222 Tittabawassee Rd 48604 **Location:** Jct I-675. **Facility:** Smoke free premises. 120 units. 2 stories (no elevator), interior corridors. **Parking:** winter plug-ins. **Pool(s):** heated outdoor. **Activities:** exercise room. **Guest Services:** valet laundry, wireless Internet.

MONTAGUE INN

Country Inn
$85-$195

Phone: 989/752-3939

Address: 1581 S Washington Ave 48601 **Location:** 1.5 mi s on SR 13. Located on the shores of Lake Linton. **Facility:** This restored Georgian mansion, with pewabic-tiled walls and showers, is set on manicured grounds overlooking Lake Linton and Ojibway Island. Smoke free premises. 17 units. 2-3 stories, interior corridors. **Terms:** 7 day cancellation notice-fee imposed. **Guest Services:** wireless Internet.

RAMADA INN & SUITES

Hotel
$71-$134

Phone: (989)793-7900

Address: 3325 Davenport Ave 48602 **Location:** I-675, exit 3, 2 mi w on SR 58. **Facility:** Smoke free premises. 95 units. 2 stories, interior corridors. **Terms:** cancellation fee imposed. **Amenities:** high-speed Internet. **Activities:** exercise room. **Guest Services:** area transportation-within 3 mi, wireless Internet.

RESIDENCE INN BY MARRIOTT

Extended Stay
Hotel
$149-$159

Phone: (989)799-9000

Address: 5230 Fashion Square Blvd 48604 **Location:** I-675, exit 6, 0.8 mi w, then just n. **Facility:** Smoke free premises. 68 units. 3 stories, interior corridors. **Terms:** cancellation fee imposed. **Amenities:** high-speed Internet. **Pool(s):** heated indoor. **Activities:** whirlpool, pool table, exercise room, sports court. **Guest Services:** valet and coin laundry, wireless Internet.

AAA Benefit:
Members save a minimum 5% off the best available rate.

SPRINGHILL SUITES BY MARRIOTT

Hotel
$129-$139

Phone: (989)792-2800

Address: 5270 Fashion Square Blvd 48604 **Location:** I-675, exit 6, 0.8 mi w, then just n. **Facility:** Smoke free premises. 79 units. 3 stories, interior corridors. **Terms:** cancellation fee imposed. **Amenities:** high-speed Internet. **Pool(s):** heated indoor. **Activities:** whirlpool, exercise room. **Guest Services:** valet and coin laundry, wireless Internet.

── WHERE TO DINE ──

FORBIDDEN CITY RESTAURANT *Menu on AAA.com*

Chinese
$5-$22

Phone: 989/799-9340

A local fixture since 1973, this comfortable restaurant is decorated with red tablecloths, wood accents and Oriental artwork. The focus is on Mandarin-style food, such as almond chicken and Mongolian beef. Try the crab cheese appetizers or the vegetable bean curd soup. Service is professional and friendly. **Bar:** full bar. **Reservations:** suggested, weekends. **Hours:** 11 am-9:30 pm, Fri & Sat-10 pm, Sun noon-9 pm. Closed major holidays; also for lunch 9/4 & for dinner 12/24. **Address:** 4024 Bay Rd 48603 **Location:** SR 58, 2 mi n on SR 84; in Town Campus Mall.

GENJI JAPANESE STEAKHOUSE

Japanese
$10-$35

Phone: 989/497-9900

This popular restaurant offers a sushi bar and several dining areas with knife-wielding chefs preparing traditional Japanese dishes that may include chicken, seafood and steak. **Bar:** full bar. **Hours:** 11 am-2 & 4:30-10 pm, Sat 3:30 pm-10:30 pm, Sun noon-9 pm. Closed: 11/24, 12/25. **Address:** 3870 Bay Rd 48603 **Location:** On SR 84, 1.8 mi n of SR 58.

HELLO SUSHI

Japanese
$6-$23

Phone: 989/790-0022

This is the place to go for sushi in Saginaw, and it's conveniently close to several shopping centers. **Bar:** beer & wine. **Hours:** 11 am-9:30 pm, Fri & Sat-10 pm. Closed major holidays; also Sun. **Address:** 2575 Tittabawassee Rd 48604 **Location:** I-675, exit 6, 0.5 mi w.

HUNAN RESTAURANT

Chinese
$5-$18

Phone: 989/792-0303

Hunan, Szechuan and Mandarin dishes, such as beef with broccoli and sweet and sour pork, are served in plentiful portions. The quiet dining rooms are decorated with classy, Oriental appointments. Servers are friendly and adept at follow-up. **Bar:** full bar. **Hours:** 11:15 am-9:30 pm, Fri & Sat-10 pm, Sun noon-9 pm. Closed major holidays. **Address:** 3109 Bay Plaza 48604 **Location:** SR 58, 2.5 mi n on SR 84; opposite Fashion Square Mall.

KABOB AND CURRY HOUSE

Indian
$8-$16

Phone: 989/497-4400

As the name implies, this restaurant offers a selection of traditional Indian dishes from vegetarian delights to non-vegetarian dinners such as boti kebab: tender pieces of lamb marinated in yogurt, ginger, garlic and spices and cooked in the charbroiler. **Bar:** beer & wine. **Hours:** 5 pm-9 pm; hours may vary. Closed major holidays; also Sun & Mon. **Address:** 4070 Bay Rd 48603 **Location:** SR 84, 2 mi n of SR 58.

LOS CUATRO AMIGOS

Mexican
$4-$16

Phone: 989/799-1700

As the name implies, the popular restaurant is a place for friends, who can choose from all of the traditional Mexican dishes. **Bar:** full bar. **Hours:** 11 am-10 pm, Fri & Sat-10:30 pm. Closed: 11/24, 12/25. **Address:** 4570 Bay Rd 48603 **Location:** SR 58, 2.5 mi n on SR 84; at Fashion Square Mall.

SULLIVAN'S

American
$5-$15

Phone: 989/799-1940

Serving the area since 1946, the restaurant delivers home-cooked daily specials, as well as such dishes as seafood, Swiss steak and chicken. Soups and sandwiches are favorite lighter fare. Wood and brass accents lend to the contemporary feel. **Bar:** full bar. **Hours:** 7 am-9 pm; hours may vary. Closed: 11/24, 12/25. **Address:** 5235 Gratiot Rd 48603 **Location:** 5 mi w on SR 46.

TONY'S

American
$4-$12

Phone: 989/249-8669

The restaurant is well known in the area for its steak sandwiches and WOP salad, as well as huge portions for breakfast, lunch and dinner. Save room for one of the tempting desserts. **Hours:** 7 am-9:30 pm, Fri & Sat-10:30 pm, Sun 8 am-8 pm. Closed major holidays. **Address:** 4880 Fashion Square Blvd 48603 **Location:** I-675, exit 6, 0.7 mi w on Tittabawassee Rd, then just s.

ST. CLAIR pop. 5,802

—— WHERE TO DINE ——

RIVER CRAB

Seafood
$6-$36

Phone: 810/329-2261

Overlooking the St. Clair River, the restaurant is warm and romantic—a perfect spot for couples. The menu lists a lengthy selection of daily fish specials, such as salmon in a flavorful mustard sauce. **Bar:** full bar. **Reservations:** suggested. **Hours:** 11:30 am-9:30 pm, Fri & Sat-10 pm, Sun 10 am-2 & 3-9 pm; Sunday brunch. Closed: 12/25. **Address:** 1337 N River Rd 48079 **Location:** Adjacent to River Crab Blue Water Inn. **Parking:** on-site and valet.

ST. IGNACE pop. 2,678 (See map and index starting on p. 360)

AURORA BOREALIS MOTOR INN

Motel
$49-$99

Phone: 906/643-7488 [32]

Address: 635 W US 2 49781 **Location:** 1 mi e of bridge tollgate on I-75 business route and US 2. **Facility:** Smoke free premises. 56 units. 2 stories (no elevator), exterior corridors. **Terms:** open 4/1-11/15, check-in 3:30 pm. **Guest Services:** wireless Internet. *(see ad below)*

FREE early check-in/late check-out and high-speed Internet

Read, Share, Ask, Plan. Join the travel
conversation at AAATravelViews.com.

(See map and index starting on p. 360)

(See map and index starting on p. 360)

BUDGET HOST INN & SUITES

Hotel
$66-$152

Phone: (906)643-9666 **31**

Address: 700 N State St 49781 **Location:** 1.8 mi n of bridge tollgate on I-75 business route. **Facility:** Smoke free premises. 58 units, some two bedrooms. 2 stories, interior/exterior corridors. **Parking:** winter plug-ins. **Terms:** cancellation fee imposed. **Pool(s):** heated indoor. **Activities:** whirlpool, snowmobiling, playground. *Fee:* game room. **Guest Services:** coin laundry, wireless Internet. *(see ad p. 419)*

FREE full breakfast and high-speed Internet

CAROL'S TRADEWINDS MOTEL

Motel
Rates not provided

Phone: 906/643-9388 **24**

Address: 1190 N State St 49781 **Location:** 3 mi n of bridge tollgate on I-75 business route. Opposite Lake Huron. **Facility:** Smoke free premises. 25 units. 1 story, exterior corridors. *Bath:* shower only. **Terms:** open 4/15-10/20. **Guest Services:** wireless Internet.

COMFORT INN

Hotel
Rates not provided

Phone: 906/643-7733 **29**

Address: 927 N State St 49781 **Location:** 2 mi n of bridge tollgate on I-75 business route. Located on Lake Huron. **Facility:** Smoke free premises. 100 units. 4 stories, interior corridors. **Terms:** open 5/16-10/24. **Pool(s):** heated indoor. **Activities:** whirlpool, playground. **Guest Services:** wireless Internet.

DAYS INN LAKEFRONT & SUITES

Hotel
$81-$189

Phone: (906)643-8008 **26**

Address: 1067 N State St 49781 **Location:** 2.8 mi n of bridge tollgate on I-75 business route. Located on Lake Huron. **Facility:** Smoke free premises. 105 units. 2-3 stories, interior corridors. **Pool(s):** heated indoor. **Activities:** sauna, whirlpools, exercise room, volleyball. *Fee:* game room. **Guest Services:** coin laundry, wireless Internet.

FREE expanded continental breakfast and high-speed Internet

HOLIDAY INN EXPRESS LAKEFRONT

Hotel
$79-$249

Phone: (906)643-0200 **28**

Address: 965 N State St 49781 **Location:** 2.3 mi n of bridge tollgate on I-75 business route. **Facility:** Smoke free premises. 85 units. 4 stories, interior corridors. **Pool(s):** heated indoor. **Activities:** whirlpool, exercise room. **Guest Services:** coin laundry, wireless Internet.

KEWADIN CASINO LAKEFRONT INN

Motel
$59-$109

Phone: (906)643-8411 **25**

Address: 1131 N State St 49781 **Location:** 3 mi n of bridge tollgate on I-75 business route. Located on Lake Huron. **Facility:** 71 units. 2 stories (no elevator), interior/exterior corridors. **Terms:** open 5/1-10/31. **Pool(s):** heated indoor. **Activities:** whirlpool, snowmobiling, indoor recreation area, playground. **Guest Services:** wireless Internet.

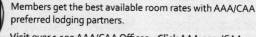

(See map and index starting on p. 360)

KEWADIN SHORES CASINO & HOTEL   Phone: 906/643-7071

Hotel
Rates not provided

Address: 3015 Mackinac Tr 49781 **Location:** I-75, exit 348, just e to CR H63 (Mackinac Tr), then 2.6 mi n. Located on Lake Huron. **Facility:** On the shores of Lake Huron, this modern, small-scale hotel features some rooms with a view of the lake. 81 units. 3 stories, interior corridors. **Parking:** winter plug-ins. **Terms:** check-in 4 pm. **Pool(s):** heated indoor. **Activities:** whirlpool, beach access, snowmobiling, exercise room. *Fee:* game room. **Guest Services:** wireless Internet.

▼ See AAA listing p. 418 ▼

(See map and index starting on p. 360)

QUALITY INN LAKEFRONT

Motel
$48-$174

Phone: (906)643-7581 ㉗

Address: 1021 N State St 49781 **Location:** 2.3 mi n of bridge tollgate on I-75 business route. Located on Lake Huron. **Facility:** Smoke free premises. 66 units. 3 stories, exterior corridors. **Terms:** open 4/15-10/31, 3 day cancellation notice-fee imposed. **Pool(s):** heated indoor. **Activities:** whirlpool, sun deck. **Guest Services:** wireless Internet.

(see ad below) [SAVE] 🅃📶 🏊 ❎ 🔋 💻

FREE expanded continental breakfast and local telephone calls

SUPER 8 OF ST. IGNACE

Hotel
$58-$148

Phone: (906)643-7616 ㉝

Address: 923 W US 2 49781 **Location:** I-75, exit 344B, 0.5 mi w. **Facility:** Smoke free premises. 61 units. 3 stories, interior corridors. **Pool(s):** heated indoor. **Activities:** whirlpool, snowmobiling. **Guest Services:** coin laundry, wireless Internet. 🅃📶 🏊 ❎ 📷 💻 / SOME UNITS 🔋

──────── **WHERE TO DINE** ────────

THE GALLEY RESTAURANT & BAR   *Menu on AAA.com*

American
$6-$25

Phone: 906/643-7960 ⑬

On the shores of Lake Huron, the restaurant features photographs of freighters, lighthouses and ships as well as wildlife prints of ducks and loons. Great Lakes whitefish, trout and juicy roast prime rib are well-prepared and flavorful. **Bar:** full bar. **Hours:** Open 5/1-10/23; 7 am-10 pm; hours may vary. **Address:** 241 N State St 49781 **Location:** Center.

Are we meeting your travel needs?

If your visit to an establishment listed in a AAA TourBook or CampBook guide doesn't meet your expectations, tell us about it.

Complete an easy online form at **AAA.com/TourBookComments**.

(See map and index starting on p. 360)

TIMMY LEE'S PUB

Phone: 906/643-8344 (14)

American
$7-$16

One of the few local spots open year round, the decor is simple and the six flat-screen TVs are always tuned to sports. The menu offers a variety of comforting options ranging from burgers and sandwiches to locally caught whitefish and hand-tossed pizzas. **Bar:** full bar. **Hours:** 11 am-2:30 am, Sun from noon. **Address:** W 748 US 2 49781 **Location:** On US 2, 2 mi w.

ST. JOSEPH pop. 8,789

THE BOULEVARD INN & BISTRO

Phone: 269/983-6600

Hotel
Rates not provided

Address: 521 Lake Blvd 49085 **Location:** I-94, exit 23, 5 mi n on Red Arrow Hwy, just w on Broad St, then just s; downtown. **Facility:** Smoke free premises. 82 units, some two bedrooms. 7 stories, interior corridors. **Terms:** check-in 4 pm. **Amenities:** high-speed Internet, safes (fee). **Dining:** Bistro On The Boulevard, see separate listing. **Activities:** exercise room. **Guest Services:** valet laundry, wireless Internet.

HOLIDAY INN EXPRESS HOTEL & SUITES

Phone: (269)982-0004

Hotel
$109-$199 5/2-4/30
$109-$129 4/1-5/1

Address: 3019 Lake Shore Dr 49085 **Location:** I-94, exit 23, 3.5 mi n. **Facility:** Smoke free premises. 82 units. 3 stories, interior corridors. **Terms:** cancellation fee imposed. **Amenities:** high-speed Internet. *Some:* video games. **Pool(s):** heated indoor. **Activities:** whirlpool, exercise room. **Guest Services:** valet and coin laundry, wireless Internet.

SILVER BEACH HOTEL

Phone: 269/983-7341

Hotel
Rates not provided

Address: 100 Main St 49085 **Location:** I-94, exit 27 eastbound, 5 mi nw to Main St; exit 33 westbound, 4.8 mi w on Business Rt I-94, then nw to Main St. **Facility:** Smoke free premises. 160 units. 7 stories, interior corridors. **Amenities:** safes (fee). **Pool(s):** heated indoor. **Activities:** sauna, whirlpool, children's play area, exercise room. *Fee:* game room. **Guest Services:** valet and coin laundry, wireless Internet.

— WHERE TO DINE —

BISTRO ON THE BOULEVARD

Phone: 269/983-3882

American
$9-$28

This bistro presents a seasonally changing menu of Mediterranean dishes, such as shrimp pastis and steak frites, that incorporate local and international ingredients. The patio, which faces the water, is a popular seating spot. **Bar:** full bar. **Hours:** 6:30-10 am, 11:30-1:30 & 5:30-10 pm; seasonal hours may vary. Closed: 1/1, 12/25. **Address:** 521 Lake Blvd 49085 **Location:** I-94, exit 23, 5 mi n on Red Arrow Hwy, just w on Broad St, then just s; downtown; in The Boulevard Inn & Bistro.

CAFFE TOSI

Phone: 269/983-3354

Deli
$5-$12

This cozy, coffee shop-inspired deli showcases most of its menu items under a large glass counter. The menu focuses on fresh soups and salads, and a wide variety of Italian sandwich options all are prepared on breads baked daily at a neighboring bakery. A variety of freshly prepared dessert items also are available. **Bar:** beer & wine. **Hours:** 7 am-8 pm, Sat from 8 am, Sun 8 am-4 pm. Closed major holidays. **Address:** 516 Pleasant St 49085 **Location:** Between State St and Lake Blvd; downtown. **Parking:** street only.

CHAN'S GARDEN RESTAURANT

Phone: 269/983-2609

Chinese
$6-$10

Serving the area since 1970, the casual, unpretentious restaurant serves varied entrees, including combination plates, to patrons seated in its booths. **Bar:** beer & wine. **Hours:** 11 am-9 pm, Fri-9:30 pm, Sat noon-9:30 pm, Sun 11:30 am-9 pm. Closed: 11/24, 12/25 & Easter. **Address:** 310 State St 49085 **Location:** Center. **Parking:** street only.

CLEMENTINE'S

Phone: 269/983-0990

American
$7-$20

This is an informal family restaurant located next to the marina and a short walk from downtown. The menu features a lot of salads and lighter entrees with the house specialty being a hot apple dumpling dessert. **Bar:** full bar. **Hours:** 11 am-10 pm, Fri & Sat-11 pm, Sun noon-10 pm. Closed major holidays. **Address:** 1235 Broad St 49085 **Location:** I-94, exit 27 (SR 63), 2.6 mi n to Napier Ave, 0.3 mi e to Langley Ave, then 1 mi n.

PUMP HOUSE GRILLE

Phone: 269/983-0001

American
$7-$24

In the downtown area, the relaxed but upscale bistro is known for its signature item: deep-fried dill pickles. Many selections, including baby back ribs and slow-cooked prime rib, are prepared in the on-site smoker. **Bar:** full bar. **Hours:** 11 am-10 pm, Fri & Sat-11 pm. Closed major holidays. **Address:** 214 State St 49085 **Location:** Downtown. **Parking:** on-site and street.

SCHU'S GRILL & BAR

Phone: 269/983-7248

American
$8-$26

Rustic appointments give the casual dining room the ambience of a warm, inviting lodge. Traditional comfort foods, ranging from burgers and steaks to pasta and overstuffed sandwiches, please all members of the family. The local crowd flocks to this place. **Bar:** full bar. **Hours:** 11 am-10 pm, Fri & Sat-11 pm, Sun noon-10 pm; hours may vary. Closed: 12/25. **Address:** 505 Pleasant St 49085 **Location:** Jct Lake Blvd; downtown. **Parking:** on-site and street.

ST. LOUIS pop. 4,494

—— WHERE TO DINE ——

FRANCESCO'S BISTRO

Italian
$6-$24

Phone: 989/681-2213

This restaurant offers a good selection of Italian and American dishes, pizzas and finger foods. Couples and families can relax in the inviting dining room, attended by friendly, prompt servers. **Bar:** full bar. **Hours:** 11 am-8:30 pm, Sun-3 pm; hours may vary. Closed major holidays. **Address:** 1875 W Monroe Rd 48880 **Location:** On SR 46, 1 mi e of US 127.

SANDUSKY pop. 2,745

DEMOTT'S WEST PARK INN

Hotel
Rates not provided

Phone: 810/648-4300

Address: 440 W Sanilac Rd 48471 **Location:** On SR 46; center. **Facility:** Smoke free premises. 29 units. 1-2 stories (no elevator), interior/exterior corridors. **Parking:** winter plug-ins. **Guest Services:** valet laundry, wireless Internet.

SAUGATUCK pop. 1,065—See also Douglas p. 313

BEST WESTERN PLAZA HOTEL OF SAUGATUCK

Hotel
$89-$239

Phone: (269)857-7178

Address: 3457 Blue Star Hwy 49453 **Location:** I-196, exit 41, 1.3 mi sw on CR A2. **Facility:** Smoke free premises. 52 units. 2 stories (no elevator), interior corridors. **Terms:** 2 night minimum stay - seasonal, cancellation fee imposed. **Amenities:** *Some:* high-speed Internet. **Pool(s):** heated indoor. **Activities:** whirlpool, exercise room. **Guest Services:** coin laundry, wireless Internet. **Free Special Amenities: continental breakfast and high-speed Internet.**

AAA Benefit:
Members save up to 20%, plus 10% bonus points with free rewards program.

SAUGATUCK'S VICTORIAN INN

Bed & Breakfast
$110-$225

Phone: 269/857-3325

Address: 447 Butler St 49453 **Location:** Downtown. **Facility:** Built in 1905 as the residence of the Koenig Hardware store owners, the inn includes an art gallery on the premises. Smoke free premises. 7 units. 2 stories (no elevator), interior corridors. **Terms:** 2 night minimum stay - seasonal and/or weekends, 7 day cancellation notice-fee imposed. **Guest Services:** wireless Internet. **Free Special Amenities: full breakfast and high-speed Internet.**

—— WHERE TO DINE ——

PUMPERNICKEL'S EATERY

American
$6-$9

Phone: 269/857-1196

This informal eatery serves breakfast, a number of items from the grill, and sandwiches served on thick-sliced bread, flour tortillas or plain bagels. The famous cinnamon rolls should not be missed. **Bar:** full bar. **Hours:** 8 am-4 pm; seasonal hours may vary. **Address:** 202 Butler St 49453 **Location:** Downtown. **Parking:** street only.

SAULT STE. MARIE pop. 16,542

BEST WESTERN SAULT STE. MARIE

Hotel
$70-$94

Phone: (906)632-2170

Address: 4335 I-75 Business Loop 49783 **Location:** I-75, exit 392, 0.3 mi ne. **Facility:** Smoke free premises. 53 units. 2 stories, interior corridors. **Pool(s):** heated indoor. **Activities:** sauna, snowmobiling, exercise room. *Fee:* game room. **Guest Services:** coin laundry, wireless Internet. **Free Special Amenities: expanded continental breakfast and early check-in/late check-out.**

AAA Benefit:
Members save up to 20%, plus 10% bonus points with free rewards program.

BUDGET HOST CRESTVIEW INN

Motel
$59-$99

Phone: (906)635-5213

Address: 1200 Ashmun St 49783 **Location:** I-75, exit 392, 2.8 mi ne on I-75 business loop. **Facility:** Smoke free premises. 43 units. 1 story, exterior corridors. **Parking:** winter plug-ins. **Guest Services:** wireless Internet. **Free Special Amenities: continental breakfast and high-speed Internet.**

DAYS INN

Hotel
$56-$90

Phone: (906)635-5200

Address: 3651 I-75 Business Spur 49783 **Location:** I-75, exit 392, 0.8 mi ne on I-75 business loop. **Facility:** Smoke free premises. 84 units. 2 stories, interior corridors. **Terms:** cancellation fee imposed. **Amenities:** safes (fee). *Some:* high-speed Internet. **Pool(s):** heated indoor. **Activities:** whirlpool, snowmobiling, limited exercise equipment. **Guest Services:** valet and coin laundry, wireless Internet. **Free Special Amenities: expanded continental breakfast and high-speed Internet.**

KEWADIN CASINO HOTEL & CONVENTION CENTER

Hotel
Rates not provided

Phone: 906/632-0530

Address: 2186 Shunk Rd 49783 **Location:** I-75, exit 392, 2 mi ne on I-75 business loop, 1.5 mi e on Marquette Ave, then just s. **Facility:** American Indian artwork adorns this casino hotel which has over 200,000 square feet for the casino and entertainment specials. 319 units. 2-6 stories, interior corridors. **Amenities:** Some: high-speed Internet. **Pool(s):** heated indoor. **Activities:** sauna, whirlpool, steamrooms, snowmobiling, exercise room. Fee: game room. **Guest Services:** valet laundry, wireless Internet.

PARK INN

Hotel
Rates not provided

Phone: 906/632-6000

Address: 3525 I-75 Business Spur 49783 **Location:** I-75, exit 392, 0.7 mi ne. **Facility:** Smoke free premises. 59 units, some efficiencies. 3 stories, interior corridors. **Parking:** winter plug-ins. **Amenities:** Some: high-speed Internet. **Pool(s):** heated indoor. **Activities:** sauna, whirlpool, snowmobiling, limited exercise equipment. **Guest Services:** coin laundry, wireless Internet.

SUPER 8

Hotel
$53-$72

Phone: 906/632-8882

Address: 3826 I-75 Business Loop 49783 **Location:** I-75, exit 392, 0.5 mi ne. **Facility:** Smoke free premises. 57 units. 2 stories (no elevator), interior corridors. **Activities:** snowmobiling. **Guest Services:** coin laundry, wireless Internet.

WHERE TO DINE

THE ANTLER'S

American
$7-$20

Phone: 906/632-3571

More than 200 mounted animals and a bell-and-whistle sound display lend to the casual ambience of the large, noisy restaurant. A tasty homemade barbecue sauce wakes up the flavor in slow-cooked baby back ribs. Service is friendly and efficient. **Bar:** full bar. **Hours:** 11 am-10 pm; hours may vary. **Closed:** 11/24, 12/24, 12/25 & Easter. **Address:** 804 E Portage Ave 49783 **Location:** 0.5 mi e.

CUP OF THE DAY

Deli
$4-$8

Phone: 906/635-7272

As you might guess from the name, the restaurant specializes in coffee drinks. The menu centers on lighter fare—salad, sandwiches and delicious dessert. A wide variety of juice is available at the raw juice bar. **Hours:** 7 am-8 pm. **Closed:** 1/1, 11/24, 12/25. **Address:** 406 Ashmun St 49783 **Location:** Center. **Parking:** street only.

FRANK'S PLACE

American
$4-$14

Phone: 906/632-7487

This well-established family restaurant is close to the locks, and serves breakfast all day as well as a number of items on the menu from meatball soup, to sandwiches, to traditional dinners. **Hours:** 6 am-8 pm, Thurs-Sat to 9 pm; hours may vary. Closed: 12/25. **Address:** 123 W Portage Ave 49783 **Location:** Just w of I-75 business loop; downtown. **Parking:** street only.

FREIGHTERS

American
$7-$38

Phone: 906/632-4211

Overlooking the Soo Locks and a little park below, the intimate restaurant is a comfortable spot for casual upscale dining. The daily specials are always a treat. **Bar:** full bar. **Hours:** 7 am-10 pm; hours may vary. **Address:** 240 W Portage Ave 49783 **Location:** Just w of I-75 business loop; downtown; in Ramada Plaza Hotel Ojibway.

GREAT WALL

Chinese
$7-$14

Phone: 906/635-1188

This restaurant features a popular buffet, which has a great selection of Hunan, Szechuan and Cantonese favorites. **Bar:** beer & wine. **Hours:** 11 am-9:30 pm, Fri & Sat-10:30 pm, Sun 11:30 am-9:30 pm; hours vary off season. Closed: 11/24, 12/25. **Address:** 3440 I-75 Business Spur 49783 **Location:** I-75, exit 392, 0.9 mi ne on I-75 business spur.

STUDEBAKERS

American
$8-$23

Phone: 906/632-4262

An interesting collection of old Studebaker pictures—as well as parts and other period collectibles—decorates the restaurant, which is likely to stir feelings of nostalgia. The specialty is whitefish, which is served pan-fried, broiled or deep-fried. **Bar:** full bar. **Hours:** 7 am-9 pm, Fri & Sat-10 pm; to 10 pm 6/1-10/15. Closed: 11/24, 12/25. **Address:** 3583 I-75 Business Spur 49783 **Location:** I-75, exit 392, 0.8 mi ne.

SAWYER

SUPER 8

Hotel
$58-$104

Phone: (269)426-8300

Address: 12850 Super Dr 49125 **Location:** I-94, exit 12 (Sawyer Rd), just e. **Facility:** Smoke free premises. 61 units. 3 stories, interior corridors. **Pool(s):** heated indoor. **Guest Services:** coin laundry, wireless Internet. **Free Special Amenities: expanded continental breakfast and high-speed Internet.**

SILVER CITY

MOUNTAIN VIEW LODGES

Cottage
$165-$265

Phone: 906/885-5256

Address: 34042 M-107 49953 **Location:** Jct SR 64, 0.8 mi w. Located on shores of Lake Superior. **Facility:** 11 cottages. 1 story, exterior corridors. **Terms:** office hours 9 am-8 pm, check-in 4 pm, 30 day cancellation notice-fee imposed. **Activities:** limited beach access, snowmobiling. **Guest Services:** wireless Internet.

SOUTHFIELD —See Detroit p. 298.

SOUTHGATE —See Detroit p. 302.

SOUTH HAVEN pop. 5,021

CARRIAGE HOUSE AT THE HARBOR BED & BREAKFAST

Bed & Breakfast
$125-$275

Phone: 269/639-2161

Address: 118 Woodman Ave 49090 **Location:** I-196, exit 20, 0.9 mi w, just n on Broadway, across the bridge, 0.3 mi w on Dyckman, then just s on North Shore Dr. Located in a residential area. **Facility:** Just a block from Lake Michigan, this B&B is decorated with antiques and offers rooms with gas fireplaces or views of the harbor. Smoke free premises. 12 units, some kitchens. 3 stories (no elevator), interior corridors. **Terms:** 2 night minimum stay - weekends, age restrictions may apply, 15 day cancellation notice-fee imposed. **Activities:** Fee: massage. **Guest Services:** wireless Internet.

COMFORT SUITES

Hotel
$79-$209

Phone: (269)639-2014

Address: 1755 Phoenix St 49090 **Location:** I-196, exit 20, 0.5 mi e. **Facility:** Smoke free premises. 61 units. 3 stories, interior corridors. **Amenities:** high-speed Internet, safes. **Pool(s):** heated indoor. **Activities:** limited exercise equipment. **Guest Services:** coin laundry, wireless Internet. **Free Special Amenities: continental breakfast and high-speed Internet.**

HAMPTON INN SOUTH HAVEN

Hotel
$79-$199

Phone: (269)639-8550

Address: 04299 Cecilia Dr 49090 **Location:** I-196, exit 20, just e. **Facility:** Smoke free premises. 62 units. 3 stories, interior corridors. **Terms:** check-in 4 pm, 1-7 night minimum stay, cancellation fee imposed. **Amenities:** video games (fee). **Pool(s):** heated indoor. **Activities:** whirlpool, exercise room. **Guest Services:** valet and coin laundry, wireless Internet. **Free Special Amenities: expanded continental breakfast and high-speed Internet.**

INN AT THE PARK BED & BREAKFAST

Bed & Breakfast
$125-$275

Phone: 269/639-1776

Address: 233 Dyckman Ave 49090 **Location:** I-196, exit 20, 0.9 mi w, just n on Broadway, then just w; across the bridge. **Facility:** Stained glass and sun-filled common areas add to the appeal of this Victorian-style B&B. Rooms have fireplaces and some have flat-screen TVs. Smoke free premises. 9 units. 2 stories (no elevator), interior corridors. **Terms:** office hours 8 am-8 pm, 2 night minimum stay - weekends, age restrictions may apply, 10 day cancellation notice-fee imposed. **Activities:** *Fee:* massage. **Guest Services:** wireless Internet.

SAND CASTLE INN

Bed & Breakfast
$135-$295 4/1-10/31
$135-$185 11/1-4/30

Phone: 269/639-1110

Address: 203 Dyckman Ave 49090 **Location:** I-196, exit 20, 0.9 mi w, just n on Broadway, then just w; across the bridge. **Facility:** The inn offers a retreat-like ambiance and is within walking distance of the river, the lake and downtown. All guest rooms have exterior patios. Smoke free premises. 10 units. 3 stories (no elevator), interior/exterior corridors. *Bath:* shower only. **Terms:** 2-3 night minimum stay - seasonal and/or weekends, age restrictions may apply, 10 day cancellation notice-fee imposed. **Pool(s):** heated outdoor. **Guest Services:** wireless Internet.

THE VICTORIA RESORT B&B

Bed & Breakfast
$95-$215

Phone: 269/637-6414

Address: 241 Oak St 49090 **Location:** I-196, exit 20, 0.9 mi w, just n on Broadway to Dyckman Ave, just w to Park Ave, 0.4 mi n, then just e. **Facility:** This property offers varied rooms and cottages on shady grounds. Smoke free premises. 14 units, some cottages. 2 stories (no elevator), interior corridors. **Terms:** office hours 9 am-8 pm, 2 night minimum stay - seasonal and/or weekends, age restrictions may apply, 7 day cancellation notice-fee imposed. **Pool(s):** outdoor. **Activities:** tennis court, bicycles, basketball, shuffleboard. **Guest Services:** wireless Internet.

—— **WHERE TO DINE** ——

CAPTAIN NEMOS

American
$5-$9

Phone: 269/637-5372

The casual diner is known for its vast selection of ice cream and soda treats, which make a fitting ending to any of a number of comfort foods, including burgers, sandwiches and fish and chips. The staff is friendly. **Hours:** 5:30 am-10 pm; Fri & Sat-11 pm; hours may vary. Closed major holidays. **Address:** 407 Phoenix St 49090 **Location:** I-196, exit 20, 1.2 mi w. **Parking:** street only.

CLEMENTINE'S
American
$7-$20

Phone: 269/637-4755

This is a relaxed, family restaurant located right downtown. The menu offers many salad and lighter entrees with the house specialty being a hot apple dumpling dessert. **Bar:** full bar. **Hours:** 11 am-10 pm, Fri & Sat-11 pm, Sun noon-10 pm. Closed major holidays. **Address:** 500 Phoenix St 49090 **Location:** I-196, exit 20, 1.1 mi w; downtown. **Parking:** street only. CALL

HAWKSHEAD
American
$8-$39

Phone: 269/639-2146

Located in a converted Tudor house, this relaxing space with large, floor-to-ceiling windows allows a good view of the golf course and landscaped gardens. A creative touch is evident on the continental menu that not only offers steaks and duck but also such seafood as shrimp and locally caught whitefish. **Bar:** full bar. **Reservations:** suggested. **Hours:** 11 am-9 pm; hours may vary. Closed: 1/1, 11/24, 12/25; also Sun-Tues 11/1-3/31. **Address:** 523 Hawks Nest Dr 49090 **Location:** I-196, exit 22 (N Shore Dr), just e, 2.5 mi n on 71st St/103rd Ave, then 0.4 mi e.

THE IDLER RIVERBOAT
American
$7-$23

Phone: 269/637-8435

Located in Old Harbor, the floating riverboat restaurant has many windows that look out on the natural settings. An open-air lounge is on the top deck. The menu focuses on tempting appetizers and a range of pub food such as burgers, fish and chips and sandwiches. Many guests take advantage of the large drink menu and enjoy a cocktail while taking in the harbor view. **Bar:** full bar. **Reservations:** suggested, weekends. **Hours:** Open 5/15-9/11; 11 am-11 pm, Fri & Sat-midnight, Sun-9 pm. **Address:** 515 Williams St, #10 49090 **Location:** I-196, exit 20, 1 mi w, then just n on Center St; in Old Harbor Village. **Parking:** street only.

PHOENIX STREET CAFE
American
$7-$20

Phone: 269/637-3600

Posters of bygone days, mostly from the Chicago World's Fair and the railroads and trains of the 1930s, adorn the walls of this cheerful downtown restaurant. Breakfast is served in addition to house-made soups and sandwiches and dinner entrées such as meatloaf, chicken Parmesan and stuffed walleye. **Bar:** full bar. **Hours:** 7 am-3 & 5-9 pm, Sun & Mon-3 pm. Closed: 11/24, 12/25 & Easter. **Address:** 523 Phoenix St 49090 **Location:** I-196, exit 20, 1 mi w; downtown. **Parking:** on-site and street.

THIRSTY PERCH WATERING HOLE & GRILLE
American
$7-$19

Phone: 269/639-8000

As the name suggests, the popular and spacious sports bar offers plenty of local and imported beers to wash down fresh seafood, steaks and pub snacks. **Bar:** full bar. **Hours:** 11:30 am-10 pm, Fri & Sat-11 pm. Closed: 12/25. **Address:** 272 Broadway 49090 **Location:** I-196, exit 20, 1 mi w to Broadway. **Parking:** on-site and street.

SPRING LAKE pop. 2,514

GRAND HAVEN WATERFRONT HOLIDAY INN

Hotel
$109-$199 4/1-9/4
$109-$140 9/5-4/30

Phone: (616)846-1000

Address: 940 W Savidge St 49456 **Location:** On SR 104, just e of US 31. Located on the river. **Facility:** Smoke free premises. 123 units. 4 stories, interior corridors. **Terms:** check-in 4 pm, cancellation fee imposed. **Pool(s):** heated indoor. **Activities:** whirlpool, exercise room. *Fee:* charter fishing. **Guest Services:** valet and coin laundry, wireless Internet.

SPRUCE

—— WHERE TO DINE ——

ROSA'S LOOKOUT INN   Phone: 989/471-2118

Italian
$13-$34

Established in 1934, the award-wining Italian steakhouse serves specialties such as chargrilled prime rib, walleye platter and stuffed pork filet with champagne-wine sauce. **Bar:** full bar. **Hours:** 4 pm-9 pm, Fri & Sat-10 pm; hours may vary. Closed major holidays. **Address:** 6808 US 23 S 48762 **Location:** 1.1 mi n of CR F41.

STERLING pop. 533

—— WHERE TO DINE ——

IVA'S CHICKEN DINNERS   Phone: 989/654-3552

American
$8-$18

Family-owned since 1938, the restaurant-in a late-19th-century house-features family- and plate-style chicken, steak, chops and seafood. Pictures around the inviting dining room are of a religious nature. Servers are friendly and efficient. **Bar:** full bar. **Hours:** 11:30 am-8 pm; hours may vary. Closed: 1/1, 12/25; also Tues 11/16-1/14 & Mon-Wed 1/15-5/15. **Address:** 201 Chestnut St 48659 **Location:** I-75, exit 195, 1.8 mi e on Sterling Rd/State St, then 0.3 mi s on Saginaw St, follow signs.

STERLING HEIGHTS —See Detroit p. 302.

STEVENSVILLE pop. 1,191

CANDLEWOOD SUITES   Phone: (269)428-4400

Extended Stay Hotel
$139-$179 5/18-4/30
$79-$109 4/1-5/17

Address: 2567 W Marquette Woods Rd 49127 **Location:** I-94, exit 23 (Red Arrow Hwy), just w. **Facility:** Smoke free premises. 51 efficiencies. 3 stories, interior corridors. **Terms:** cancellation fee imposed. **Amenities:** high-speed Internet. **Activities:** whirlpool, outdoor patio grill area, exercise room. **Guest Services:** complimentary and valet laundry, area transportation (fee), wireless Internet.

COMFORT SUITES   Phone: (269)428-4888

Hotel
$90-$200

Address: 2633 W Marquette Woods Rd 49127 **Location:** I-94, exit 23 (Red Arrow Hwy), just w. **Facility:** Smoke free premises. 65 units, some two bedrooms. 3 stories, interior corridors. **Amenities:** high-speed Internet. **Pool(s):** heated indoor. **Activities:** sauna, whirlpool, exercise room. **Guest Services:** valet and coin laundry, wireless Internet.

HAMPTON INN OF ST. JOSEPH I-94   Phone: (269)429-2700

Hotel
$98-$161

Address: 5050 Red Arrow Hwy 49127 **Location:** I-94, exit 23 (Red Arrow Hwy), just se. **Facility:** Smoke free premises. 75 units. 3 stories, interior corridors. **Terms:** 1-7 night minimum stay, cancellation fee imposed. **Amenities:** video games (fee). **Pool(s):** heated indoor. **Guest Services:** valet laundry, wireless Internet.

> **AAA Benefit:**
> Members save up to 10% everyday!

—— WHERE TO DINE ——

BIT OF SWISS PASTRY SHOPPE   Phone: 269/429-1661

Breads/Pastries
$3-$6

Mouthwatering pastries await in the tiny storefront attached to the bakery known among locals as "Michiana's best-kept secret." This award-winning bakery has been creating sugary masterpieces for more than 40 years, and many are produced for local shops and restaurants. Guests peruse the glass cases to select from treats such as chocolate mousse, Napoleans, buttercream tortes, German chocolate and Bavarian cakes, carrot cake, cheesecakes, fruit tarts, tiramisu, creme brulee and artisan breads. **Hours:** 8 am-6 pm. Closed major holidays; also Sun & Mon. **Address:** 4333 Ridge Rd 49127 **Location:** I-94, exit 23 (Red Arrow Hwy), 1 mi n, then 1 mi w on Glenlord Rd; behind Tosi's Restaurant.

GRANDE MERE INN

WWWWW
American
$15-$40

Phone: 269/429-3591

The popular restaurant is a local favorite for fresh seafood specialties, including blue gill and lake perch, as well as succulent ribs. Pretty views of the countryside and outside flower garden add to the experience. An attentive staff is watchful, even when the place is packed. Desserts don't disappoint. **Bar:** full bar. **Reservations:** suggested. **Hours:** 4:30 pm-close. Closed: 1/1, 12/25; also Sun & Mon. **Address:** 5800 Red Arrow Hwy 49127 **Location:** I-94, exit 23 (Red Arrow Hwy), 1.5 mi s.

STURGIS pop. 11,285

HAMPTON INN

WWWW
Hotel
$85-$129

Phone: (269)651-4210

Address: 71451 S Centerville Rd (SR 66) 49091 **Location:** I-80/90, exit 121 (SR 66), 0.4 mi n. **Facility:** Smoke free premises. 59 units. 3 stories, interior corridors. **Terms:** 1-7 night minimum stay, cancellation fee imposed. **Amenities:** video games (fee). **Pool(s):** heated indoor. **Activities:** whirlpool, exercise room. **Guest Services:** wireless Internet.

| AAA Benefit: |
| Members save up to 10% everyday! |

SUTTONS BAY pop. 589

RED LION MOTOR LODGE

WWW
Motel
$95-$195 4/1-10/27
$59-$95 10/28-4/30

Phone: 231/271-6694

Address: 4290 S West Bay Shore Rd 49682 **Location:** 5 mi s on SR 22. Opposite the bay on main highway. **Facility:** Smoke free premises. 19 units, some two bedrooms, efficiencies and cottages. 1 story, exterior corridors. **Parking:** winter plug-ins. ⊠ ✆ / SOME UNITS FEE 🐾 🛏 🖼 🖥

──── WHERE TO DINE ────

BOONE'S PRIME TIME PUB

WWW
American
$7-$24

Phone: 231/271-6688

The restaurant serves great steaks, seafood, and burgers in a cozy tavern atmosphere. **Bar:** full bar. **Hours:** 11 am-10 pm, Sun from noon; hours may vary. Closed: 11/24, 12/25 & Easter. **Address:** 102 N St Joseph Ave 49682 **Location:** On SR 22; center. **Parking:** street only.

TAWAS CITY pop. 2,005

BAY INN TAWAS

WWW
Hotel
$63-$135

Phone: (989)362-0088

Address: 1020 W Lake St 48763 **Location:** 1.5 mi s on US 23. **Facility:** Smoke free premises. 42 units. 2 stories (no elevator), interior corridors. **Terms:** check-in 4 pm, 3 day cancellation notice. **Pool(s):** heated indoor. **Activities:** whirlpool, playground. **Fee:** game room. **Guest Services:** coin laundry, wireless Internet. **Free Special Amenities: expanded continental breakfast and high-speed Internet.** SAVE ⊠ 🗡 🛏 🖼 🖥 / SOME UNITS FEE 🐾

──── WHERE TO DINE ────

CRYSTAL BAY

WWW
American
$5-$20

Phone: 989/362-3887

Located opposite Tawas Bay, the popular restaurant offers a variety of salads, sandwiches, hot lunches and a full dinner menu. Guests would be well-advised to ask the owner/chef about the desserts, as each one is a work of art. **Bar:** full bar. **Hours:** 8 am-9 pm, Sun-2 pm. Closed: 7/4, 12/25. **Address:** 448 W Lake St 48763 **Location:** Just s on US 23.

TAYLOR —See Detroit p. 303.

TECUMSEH pop. 8,574

──── WHERE TO DINE ────

EVANS STREET STATION

WWW
American
$8-$34

Phone: 517/424-5555

Ansel Adams prints adorn the walls of this upscale, yet comfortable, family-owned restaurant. Global influences permeate the creative menu, which features a wide range of seafood, pasta and steaks. **Bar:** full bar. **Hours:** 11:30 am-9 pm, Fri & Sat-10 pm. Closed: 1/1, 12/25; also Sun & Mon. **Address:** 110 S Evans St 49286 **Location:** Just s of SR 50; 15 mi w of US 23, exit 17 (Dundee); downtown. CALL 🔗M 🔲

THOMPSONVILLE pop. 457

CRYSTAL MOUNTAIN RESORT & SPA

WWWW
Resort Hotel
$139-$259

Phone: (231)378-2000

Address: 12500 Crystal Mountain Dr 49683 **Location:** On SR 115, 2 mi w. **Facility:** This scenic year-round resort on Michigan's Lower Peninsula features golf as well as downhill and cross-country skiing. Smoke free premises. 263 units, some two bedrooms, three bedrooms, kitchens, houses, cottages and condominiums. 1-3 stories (no elevator), interior/exterior corridors. **Terms:** check-in 5 pm, 2-3 night minimum stay - seasonal, 14 day cancellation notice-fee imposed. **Dining:** 3 restaurants. **Pool(s):** 2 heated outdoor, heated indoor. **Activities:** whirlpools, outside water playground, climbing wall, cross country skiing, snowmobiling, ice skating, recreation programs, rental bicycles, hiking trails, exercise room, spa. **Fee:** golf-36 holes, golf equipment, golf instruction, practice center, family golf clinic & junior golf privileges, 2 tennis courts, downhill skiing, alpine slide. **Guest Services:** coin laundry, wireless Internet. **Free Special Amenities: local telephone calls and high-speed Internet.** SAVE ECO 🍴 🍷 🛗 🚲 ⊠ 🗡 🛏 🖼 🖥 / SOME UNITS FEE 🐾

THREE RIVERS pop. 7,328

HOLIDAY INN EXPRESS HOTEL & SUITES

Hotel
$81-$138

Phone: (269)278-7766

Address: 1207 W Broadway St 49093 **Location:** Jct US 131 and SR 60 (W Broadway St), 0.3 mi s on US 131. **Facility:** Smoke free premises. 56 units. 2 stories, interior corridors. **Amenities:** high-speed Internet. **Pool(s):** heated indoor. **Activities:** whirlpool, exercise room. **Guest Services:** valet and coin laundry, wireless Internet.

SUPER 8

Hotel
$62-$115

Phone: (269)279-8888

Address: 689 Super 8 Way 49093 **Location:** Jct US 131 and SR 60 (W Broadway St), 0.3 mi s on US 131. **Facility:** Smoke free premises. 56 units. 3 stories, interior corridors. **Pool(s):** heated indoor. **Activities:** picnic pavilion, exercise room. **Guest Services:** wireless Internet.

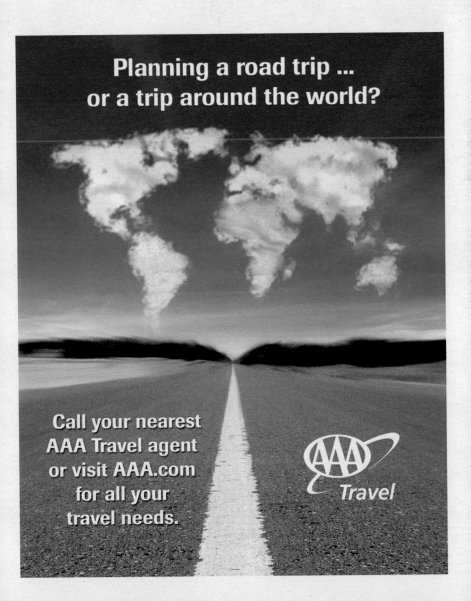

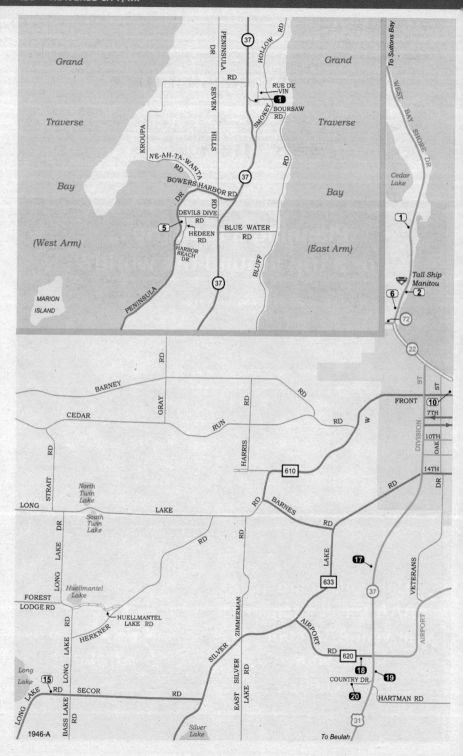

1946-A

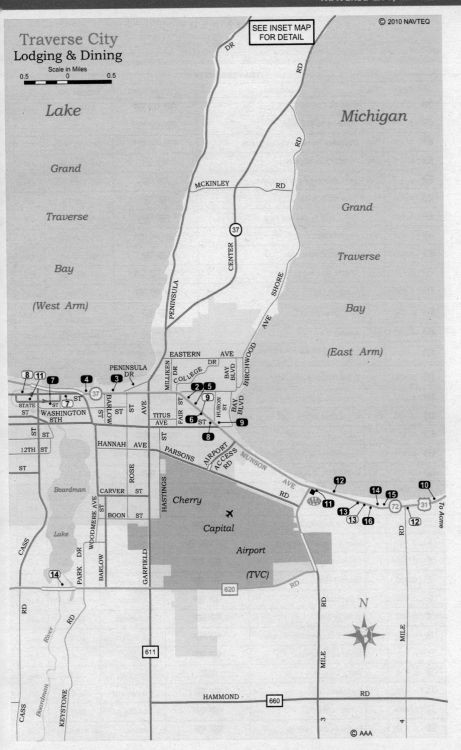

© 2010 NAVTEQ

Traverse City
Lodging & Dining

Scale in Miles

SEE INSET MAP
FOR DETAIL

Lake

Grand

Traverse

Bay

(West Arm)

Michigan

Grand

Traverse

Bay

(East Arm)

MCKINLEY   RD

37

PENINSULA

CENTER

SHORE   AVE

BIRCHWOOD   AVE

EASTERN   AVE

PENINSULA
DR

MILLIKEN
DR

COLLEGE
DR

BAY
BLVD

37

BARLOW   ST

AVE

TITUS
AVE

FAIR   ST

HURON   ST

BAY
BLVD

STATE
ST

WASHINGTON
8TH

7   ST

ST

ST

ST

6   ST

8

9

2 5

9

ST

HANNAH   AVE

12TH   ST

ST

PARSONS

HASTINGS

AIRPORT

ACCESS   RD

MUNSON   AVE

ROSE   ST

CARVER   ST

BOON   ST

WOODMERE AVE

ST

Boardman

Lake

Cherry

Capital

Airport

(TVC)

12

11

13

14

16

15

72

31

10

12

To Acme

CASS

PARK   DR

BARLOW

GARFIELD

620

River   RD

KEYSTONE

CASS

Boardman

611

HAMMOND   660   RD

MILE

MILE

3

4

N

© AAA

Traverse City

This index helps you "spot" where approved lodgings and restaurants are located on the corresponding detailed maps. Lodging daily rate range is for comparison only and show the property's high season. Restaurant rate range is a combination of lunch and/or dinner. Turn to the listing page for more detailed rate information and consult display ads for special promotions.

TRAVERSE CITY

Map Page	OA	Lodgings	Diamond Rated	High Season	Page
1 / p. 430		Chateau Chantal Bed & Breakfast	◈◈◈	$155-$560	434
2 / p. 430	AAA	**Cambria Suites Hotel**	◈◈◈	$119-$369 [SAVE]	434
3 / p. 430	AAA	**Bayshore Resort - see ad p. 434**	◈◈◈	$87-$260 [SAVE]	433
4 / p. 430	AAA	**Holiday Inn, West Bay**	◈◈	$79-$199 [SAVE]	437
5 / p. 430	AAA	**Best Western Four Seasons**	◈◈	$69-$259 [SAVE]	434
6 / p. 430		Days Inn & Suites	◈◈	$51-$153	435
7 / p. 430		Park Place Hotel - see ad p. 437	◈◈	$90-$290	437
8 / p. 430	AAA	**Comfort Inn**	◈◈◈	$79-$279 [SAVE]	435
9 / p. 430		Traverse Victorian Inn	◈◈	$110-$189	438
10 / p. 430	AAA	**Cherry Tree Inn & Suites**	◈◈◈	$64-$369 [SAVE]	435
11 / p. 430		Hampton Inn	◈◈◈	$89-$189	437
12 / p. 430		Park Shore Resort	◈◈	Rates not provided	437
13 / p. 430	AAA	**Quality Inn**	◈◈	$50-$200 [SAVE]	438
14 / p. 430		The Grand Beach Resort Hotel - see ad p. 438	◈◈◈	Rates not provided	436
15 / p. 430		Sugar Beach Resort Hotel - see ad p. 438	◈◈◈	Rates not provided	438
16 / p. 430		AmericInn of Traverse City	◈◈	$89-$199	433
17 / p. 430	AAA	**Great Wolf Lodge - see ad p. 112**	◈◈◈	$149-$279 [SAVE]	436
18 / p. 430		Courtyard by Marriott	◈◈◈	$99-$134	435
19 / p. 430		Baymont Inn & Suites-Traverse City	◈◈	$76-$144	433
20 / p. 430		Fairfield Inn & Suites by Marriott	◈◈	$79-$169	436

Map Page	OA	Restaurants	Diamond Rated	Cuisine	Meal Range	Page
① / p. 430		Tuscan Bistro	◈◈	Italian	$8-$20	441
② / p. 430		Apache Trout Grill	◈◈	American	$8-$27	438
⑤ / p. 430		Mission Table Restaurant	◈◈◈	American	$22-$36	440
⑥ / p. 430		Freshwater Lodge	◈◈	American	$7-$19	440
⑦ / p. 430		Bubba's Restaurant & Bar	◈◈	American	$5-$23	440
⑧ / p. 430		Poppycock's	◈◈	American	$9-$23	441
⑨ / p. 430		Cottage Cafe	◈◈	American	$7-$16	440
⑩ / p. 430		North Peak Brewing Company	◈◈	American	$6-$18	441
⑪ / p. 430		Mode's Bum Steer	◈◈	Steak	$6-$29	440
⑫ / p. 430		Don's Drive In	◈	American	$3-$9	440
⑬ / p. 430		Red Mesa Grill	◈◈	International	$6-$18	441
⑭ / p. 430		Panda North	◈◈	Asian	$6-$16	441
⑮ / p. 430		Boone's Long Lake Inn	◈◈	American	$14-$38	438

TRAVERSE CITY pop. 14,532   (See map and index starting on p. 430)

AMERICINN OF TRAVERSE CITY

Phone: (231)938-0288   🔢16

Hotel
$89-$199

Address: 1614 US 31 N 49686 **Location:** On US 31, 4.4 mi e. **Facility:** Smoke free premises. 47 units. 2 stories, interior corridors. **Terms:** 2 night minimum stay - seasonal and/or weekends. **Pool(s):** heated indoor. **Activities:** whirlpool. **Guest Services:** coin laundry, wireless Internet.

BAYMONT INN & SUITES-TRAVERSE CITY

Phone: (231)933-4454   🔢19

Hotel
$76-$144

Address: 2326 N US 31 S 49684 **Location:** 3.5 mi s on SR 37. **Facility:** Smoke free premises. 119 units. 3 stories, interior corridors. **Parking:** winter plug-ins. **Amenities:** video games (fee). **Pool(s):** heated indoor. **Activities:** whirlpool, exercise room. **Guest Services:** valet and coin laundry, wireless Internet.

BAYSHORE RESORT

Phone: (231)935-4400   🔢3

Hotel
$87-$260

Address: 833 E Front St 49686 **Location:** 0.8 mi e on US 31. Located on Grand Traverse Bay. **Facility:** Smoke free premises. 120 units. 4 stories, interior corridors. **Terms:** check-in 4 pm, 2 night minimum stay - seasonal and/or weekends, cancellation fee imposed. **Amenities:** high-speed Internet. **Pool(s):** heated indoor. **Activities:** whirlpool, beach access, rental boats, rental paddleboats, exercise room. **Fee:** jet boats, personal watercraft, game room. **Guest Services:** coin laundry, wireless Internet. (see ad p. 434)

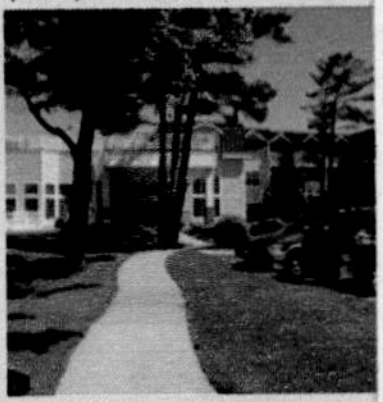

FREE expanded continental breakfast and high-speed Internet

▼ See AAA listing p. 210 ▼

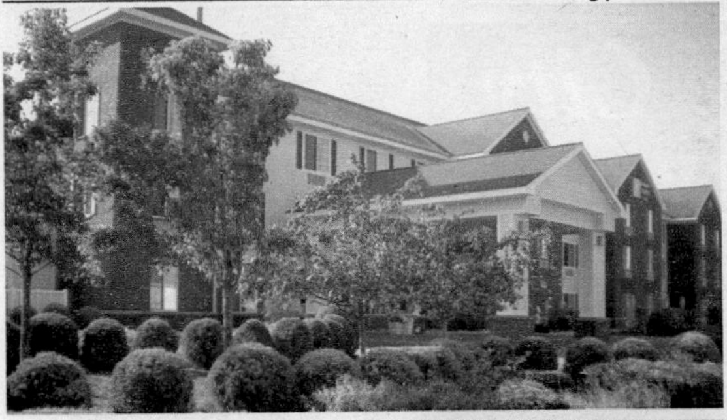

(See map and index starting on p. 430)

BEST WESTERN FOUR SEASONS

Hotel
$69-$259

Phone: (231)946-8424 **5**

Address: 305 Munson Ave 49686 **Location:** 2 mi e on US 31. **Facility:** Smoke free premises. 50 units, some efficiencies. 1-2 stories (no elevator), interior corridors. **Parking:** winter plug-ins. **Terms:** 2 night minimum stay - seasonal and/or weekends. **Amenities:** *Some:* high-speed Internet. **Pool(s):** heated indoor. **Activities:** whirlpool, movie nights. *Fee:* game room. **Guest Services:** area transportation-within 10 mi, wireless Internet. **Free Special Amenities: full breakfast and airport transportation.**

AAA Benefit:
Members save up to 20%, plus 10% bonus points with free rewards program.

CAMBRIA SUITES HOTEL

Hotel
$119-$369

Phone: (231)778-9000 **2**

Address: 255 Munson Ave 49686 **Location:** 1.8 mi e on US 31. **Facility:** Smoke free premises. 92 units. 3 stories, interior corridors. **Parking:** winter plug-ins. **Terms:** 2 night minimum stay - seasonal and/or weekends. **Amenities:** high-speed Internet. **Pool(s):** indoor. **Activities:** whirlpool, exercise room. **Guest Services:** valet and coin laundry, area transportation-within 10 mi, wireless Internet. **Free Special Amenities: high-speed Internet and airport transportation.**

CHATEAU CHANTAL BED & BREAKFAST

Bed & Breakfast
$155-$560

Phone: 231/223-4110 **1**

Address: 15900 Rue de Vin 49686 **Location:** 12 mi n on SR 37. **Facility:** Evening wine tastings are offered at this elegant property set on a high ridge with sweeping views of the vineyards and bay. Smoke free premises. 11 units, some two bedrooms and kitchens. 2-3 stories, interior corridors. **Terms:** office hours 8 am-7 pm, 2 night minimum stay - weekends, cancellation fee imposed. **Activities:** cross country skiing, exercise room. **Guest Services:** wireless Internet.

▼ See AAA listing p. 433 ▼

(See map and index starting on p. 430)

CHERRY TREE INN & SUITES

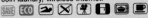

Hotel
$64-$369

Phone: (231)938-8888 🔟

Address: 2345 US 31 N 49686 **Location:** On US 31, 5.7 mi e. Located on Grand Traverse Bay. **Facility:** Smoke free premises. 76 units, some efficiencies and kitchens. 4-5 stories, interior corridors. **Terms:** 2 night minimum stay - seasonal and/or weekends, cancellation fee imposed. **Amenities:** safes. *Fee:* video games. **Pool(s):** heated indoor. **Activities:** whirlpool, limited beach access, putting green, library, playground, exercise room. *Fee:* personal watercraft, game room. **Guest Services:** coin laundry, wireless Internet.

FREE expanded continental breakfast and high-speed Internet

COMFORT INN

Hotel
$79-$279

Phone: (231)778-8000 8️⃣

Address: 460 Munson Ave (US 31) 49686 **Location:** 2.3 mi e on US 31. **Facility:** 62 units, some kitchens. 2 stories, interior corridors. **Terms:** 2 night minimum stay - seasonal and/or weekends. **Pool(s):** heated indoor. **Activities:** whirlpool, exercise room. *Fee:* game room. **Guest Services:** coin laundry, wireless Internet. **Free Special Amenities: full breakfast and airport transportation.**

COURTYARD BY MARRIOTT

Hotel
$99-$134

Phone: (231)929-1800 18️⃣

Address: 3615 S Airport Rd W 49684 **Location:** 3.2 mi s on US 31, just w. **Facility:** Smoke free premises. 83 units. 3 stories, interior corridors. **Terms:** cancellation fee imposed. **Amenities:** video games. **Pool(s):** heated indoor. **Activities:** whirlpool, exercise room. **Guest Services:** valet and coin laundry, wireless Internet.

AAA Benefit:
Members save a minimum 5% off the best available rate.

DAYS INN & SUITES

Hotel
$51-$153

Phone: (231)941-0208 6️⃣

Address: 420 Munson Ave 49686 **Location:** 2 mi e on US 31. **Facility:** Smoke free premises. 179 units. 2 stories, interior corridors. **Parking:** winter plug-ins. **Terms:** 2 night minimum stay - seasonal and/or weekends, cancellation fee imposed. **Amenities:** safes. **Dining:** Cottage Cafe, see separate listing. **Pool(s):** heated indoor. **Activities:** whirlpool, picnic area with grills, playground, exercise room. **Guest Services:** coin laundry, wireless Internet.

▼ See AAA listing p. 210 ▼

(See map and index starting on p. 430)

FAIRFIELD INN & SUITES BY MARRIOTT

Hotel
$79-$169

Address: 3701 N Country Dr 49684 **Location:** 3.6 mi s on SR 37. Located in a quiet area. **Facility:** Smoke free premises. 85 units. 3 stories, interior corridors. **Parking:** winter plug-ins. **Terms:** cancellation fee imposed. **Amenities:** high-speed Internet. **Pool(s):** heated indoor. **Activities:** whirlpool, exercise room. **Guest Services:** valet and coin laundry, wireless Internet.

Phone: (231)922-7900   [20]

THE GRAND BEACH RESORT HOTEL

Hotel
Rates not provided

Address: 1683 US 31 N 49686 **Location:** On US 31, 4.5 mi e. Located on Grand Traverse Bay. **Facility:** Smoke free premises. 105 units, some with kitchens. 3 stories, interior corridors. **Pool(s):** heated indoor. **Activities:** whirlpool, beach access, exercise room. **Fee:** paddleboats, jet boats, personal watercraft, game room. **Guest Services:** coin laundry, wireless Internet. *(see ad p. 438)*

Phone: 231/938-4455   [14]

GREAT WOLF LODGE

Hotel
$149-$279

Address: 3575 N US 31 S 49684 **Location:** 2.3 mi s on US 31 and SR 37. **Facility:** Smoke free premises. 280 units, some two bedrooms. 4 stories, interior corridors. **Terms:** check-in 4 pm, 3 day cancellation notice-fee imposed. **Amenities:** video games (fee). **Pool(s):** heated outdoor, 2 heated indoor. **Activities:** whirlpools, waterslide, indoor water park, recreation programs, exercise room, spa. **Fee:** game room. **Guest Services:** coin laundry, wireless Internet. *(see ad p. 112)*

Phone: (231)941-3600   [17]

(See map and index starting on p. 430)

HAMPTON INN

Hotel
$89-$189

Address: 1000 US 31 N 49686 **Location:** On US 31 and SR 72, 4.3 mi e. Opposite state park beach area. **Facility:** Smoke free premises. 124 units. 4 stories, interior corridors. **Terms:** check-in 4 pm, 1-7 night minimum stay, cancellation fee imposed. **Amenities:** video games (fee). **Pool(s):** heated indoor. **Activities:** whirlpool, exercise room. **Guest Services:** valet laundry, wireless Internet.

Phone: (231)946-8900 ⓫

HOLIDAY INN, WEST BAY

Hotel
$79-$199

Address: 615 E Front St 49686 **Location:** 0.5 mi e on US 31. Located along the bay. **Facility:** Smoke free premises. 179 units. 4 stories, interior corridors. **Terms:** check-in 4 pm. **Dining:** 2 restaurants. **Pool(s):** heated outdoor, heated indoor. **Activities:** sauna, whirlpool, beach access, rental boats, boat dock, exercise room. **Fee:** sailboats, personal watercrafts, game room. **Guest Services:** valet and coin laundry, wireless Internet.

Phone: (231)947-3700 ❹

PARK PLACE HOTEL

Hotel
$90-$290

Address: 300 E State St 49684 **Location:** Corner of E State and Park sts; downtown. **Facility:** Smoke free premises. 140 units. 4-10 stories, interior corridors. **Parking:** winter plug-ins. **Terms:** check-in 4 pm, 2 night minimum stay - seasonal and/or weekends, 3 day cancellation notice-fee imposed. **Amenities:** video games (fee), high-speed Internet. **Pool(s):** heated indoor. **Activities:** sauna, whirlpool, exercise room. **Guest Services:** valet laundry, wireless Internet. *(see ad below)*

Phone: (231)946-5000 ❼

PARK SHORE RESORT

Hotel
Rates not provided

Address: 1401 US 31 N 49686 **Location:** On US 31, 3.2 mi e. Located on Grand Traverse Bay. **Facility:** Smoke free premises. 80 units, some efficiencies. 4 stories, interior corridors. **Terms:** check-in 4 pm. **Amenities:** high-speed Internet, safes (fee). **Pool(s):** heated indoor. **Activities:** whirlpool, limited beach access, exercise room. **Fee:** paddleboats, sailboats, jet boats, personal watercraft, pontoons, parasailing, game room. **Guest Services:** valet and coin laundry, wireless Internet.

Phone: 231/947-3800 ⓬

▼ *See AAA listing above* ▼

(See map and index starting on p. 430)

QUALITY INN

Hotel
$50-$200

Address: 1492 US 31 N 49686 **Location:** On US 31, 3.3 mi e. **Facility:** Smoke free premises. 96 units. 2-3 stories, interior/exterior corridors. **Parking:** winter plug-ins. **Terms:** check-in 4 pm. **Amenities:** video games, safes (fee). **Pool(s):** heated indoor. **Activities:** whirlpool. **Guest Services:** wireless Internet. **Free Special Amenities: expanded continental breakfast and high-speed Internet.** **Phone:** (231)929-4423   **13**

 / SOME UNITS FEE

SUGAR BEACH RESORT HOTEL

Hotel
Rates not provided

Address: 1773 US 31 N 49686 **Location:** On US 31, 4.8 mi e. Located on Grand Traverse Bay. **Facility:** Smoke free premises. 106 units, some three bedrooms and kitchens. 3 stories, interior corridors. **Parking:** winter plug-ins. **Pool(s):** heated indoor. **Activities:** whirlpool, beach access, exercise room. **Fee:** paddleboats, boat dock, jet boats, personal watercraft, game room. **Guest Services:** coin laundry, wireless Internet. *(see ad below)* **Phone:** 231/938-0100   **15**

TRAVERSE VICTORIAN INN

Hotel
$110-$189 4/1-8/16
$69-$149 8/17-4/30

Address: 461 Munson Ave 49686 **Location:** 2.4 mi e on US 31. **Facility:** Smoke free premises. 67 units. 2 stories (no elevator), interior corridors. **Terms:** office hours 8 am-11 pm, 2 night minimum stay - weekends. **Pool(s):** heated indoor. **Activities:** whirlpool. **Guest Services:** wireless Internet. **Phone:** (231)947-5525   **9**

 / SOME UNITS FEE

─── **WHERE TO DINE** ───

APACHE TROUT GRILL

American
$8-$27

On the bay, the restaurant affords good views of the water from inside and on the seasonal patio. Specialties include seafood and steaks, as well as a number of mixed-grill items. **Bar:** full bar. **Hours:** 11 am-10 pm, Fri-11 pm, Sat noon-11 pm, Sun noon-9 pm. Closed: 1/1, 11/24, 12/25. **Address:** 13671 S West-Bay Shore Dr 49684 **Location:** 2 mi n on SR 22; jct SR 22 and 72.   **Phone:** 231/947-7079   **2**

BOONE'S LONG LAKE INN

American
$14-$38

Well worth any wait time, the 18-ounce New York strip steak is still the house favorite but don't miss out on trying one of the nightly specials or the fresh seafood. **Bar:** full bar. **Hours:** 4 pm-10 pm, Sat-11 pm, Sun noon-10 pm. Closed: 11/24, 12/25; also for dinner 12/24. **Address:** 7208 Secor Rd 49684 **Location:** 5.5 mi sw, 1.3 mi s on US 31, 4 mi sw on Silver Lake Rd, then 1.5 mi w.   **Phone:** 231/946-3991   **15**

Traveling is an adventure.

Keeping track of your money shouldn't be.

AAA Travel Money is the convenient and secure way to take your money with you wherever you roam. Explore your Travel Money options to select the best way for you to travel with your money on your next adventure.

 Visit your participating AAA office or visit online at AAA.com/travelmoney.

(See map and index starting on p. 430)

BUBBA'S RESTAURANT & BAR
Phone: 231/995-0570 (7)

American
$5-$23

Just about any night of the week, locals fill the seats at this popular, bustling hot spot. Known for its wide selection of juicy burgers, the menu also offers wraps and sandwiches, tacos and fajitas, plus steaks, chicken, and fish and chips. The grand traverse salad is loaded with local dried cherries and definitely worth a try, but those not partial to greens should lean toward the "Bubba salad"—featuring tortil'a chips, cheddar cheese and house-made salsa. **Bar:** full bar. **Hours:** 7 am-10 pm, Fri & Sat-midnight, Sun noon-9 pm, Mon 11 am-10 pm. Closed major holidays. **Address:** 428 E Front St 49686 **Location:** Between Boardman Ave and Wellington St; downtown. **Parking:** street only.

COTTAGE CAFE
Phone: 231/947-9261 (9)

American
$7-$16

The family-style restaurant delivers such familiar fare as pot pies, beef stew, shepherd's pie and local whitefish. Antiques, knicknacks and pictures decorate the dining room, which resembles a cozy cottage. Service is courteous and efficient. **Bar:** full bar. **Hours:** 7 am-10 pm. Closed: 12/25. **Address:** 420 Munson Ave 49684 **Location:** 2 mi e on US 31; in Days Inn & Suites.

DON'S DRIVE IN
Phone: 231/938-1860 (12)

American
$3-$9

This 1950s diner still has the great burgers and shakes being served in the atmosphere of that era. **Hours:** 10:30 am-10 pm; hours vary off season. Closed: 1/1, 11/24, 12/25. **Address:** 2030 US 31 N 49686 **Location:** On US 31, 4.8 mi e.

FRESHWATER LODGE
Phone: 231/932-4694 (6)

American
$7-$19

Opposite the bay, the restaurant nurtures a warm, up-north atmosphere, in part due to its high stone fireplaces and hunting and fishing memorabilia. Hand-cut lodge steak is marinated in a sweet and savory sauce then flame-broiled to the patron's liking. **Bar:** full bar. **Hours:** 11 am-11 pm, Fri & Sat-midnight, Sun 10 am-10 pm. Closed: 11/24, 12/25. **Address:** 13890 S West Bayshore Dr 49684 **Location:** On SR 22, just n of SR 72.

THE GRAND TRAVERSE PIE COMPANY
Phone: 231/922-7437

Deli
$6-$8

This flagship shop for the growing Midwest chain features a large open working bakery, which greets guests as they enter into this cute little cafe. The aromas of freshly baked fruit pies, spinach quiche and made-to-order sandwiches will certainly stimulate the appetite. **Hours:** 7 am-7 pm, Sat 8 am-6 pm, Sun 10 am-4 pm. Closed major holidays. **Address:** 525 W Front St 49684 **Location:** Just e of SR 37; downtown. CALL

MISSION TABLE RESTAURANT
Phone: 231/223-4222 (5)

American
$22-$36

Casually upscale dining is the mode in the restored home on West Bay. Representative of the distinctive cuisine are dishes such as filet mignon served with mashed Yukon gold potatoes and fresh seasonal vegetables using a cabernet franc reduction. The Jolly Pumpkin in back is also a delightful place to eat. **Bar:** full bar. **Reservations:** required. **Hours:** 5 pm-10 pm, Fri & Sat-11 pm; hours may vary. Closed: 11/24, 12/24, 12/25. **Address:** 13512 Peninsula Dr 49686 **Location:** 0.8 mi n on SR 37, 8.8 mi nw. **Historic**

MODE'S BUM STEER
Phone: 231/947-9832 (11)

Steak
$6-$29

This small, loud tavern is one of the best places in town for steaks and prime rib. Children under 8 are not allowed after 5 pm. **Bar:** full bar. **Hours:** 11 am-midnight, Fri & Sat-1 am. Closed: 12/25. **Address:** 125 E State St 49684 **Location:** Center.

(See map and index starting on p. 430)

NORTH PEAK BREWING COMPANY

American
$6-$18

Phone: 231/941-7325   ⑩

Located downtown, beers brewed on location, serving wood-fired pizza, snacks and steaks. **Bar:** full bar. **Hours:** 11 am-11 pm, Fri & Sat-midnight, Sun-10 pm; hours may vary. Closed: 11/24, 12/25. **Address:** 400 W Front St 49686 **Location:** Downtown.

PANDA NORTH

Asian
$6-$16

Phone: 231/929-9722   ⑭

On the river at Logans Landing, the restaurant prepares a tempting selection of Japanese, Chinese, Thai and Vietnamese dishes. **Reservations:** suggested, weekends. **Hours:** 11 am-9:30 pm, Fri & Sat-10:30 pm, Sun noon-9:30 pm. Closed: 11/24, 12/25. **Address:** 2038 S Airport Rd 49684 **Location:** 3.5 mi s on US 31 and SR 37, then 2 mi e.

POPPYCOCK'S

American
$9-$23

Phone: 231/941-7632   ⑧

Upbeat and eclectic, this popular local spot specializes in casual contemporary cuisine. On the menu are a variety of sandwiches and pastas, pork chops, fresh Lake Michigan whitefish, oven-roasted chicken, New York strip steak and even an extensive vegetarian menu. Patrons can choose from the long list of appetizers and small plates that are perfect for sharing. Tempting house-made desserts are on display in the pastry case. Live jazz is featured Friday and Saturday nights. **Bar:** full bar. **Hours:** 11 am-9 pm, Fri & Sat-11 pm. Closed major holidays. **Address:** 128 E Front St 49684 **Location:** Between Cass and Union sts; downtown. **Parking:** street only. CALL ⓛⓂ

RED MESA GRILL

International
$6-$18

Phone: 231/938-2773   ⑬

Diners soak up the popular restaurant's fun and jovial atmosphere as they nosh on such appetizers as Cuban black bean cakes. Main courses include specialties of jerk barbecue salmon, corn-roasted walleye and tempting Argentinean pork churrasco. **Bar:** full bar. **Hours:** 11 am-10 pm, Fri & Sat-11 pm. Closed: 11/24, 12/25. **Address:** 1544 US 31 N 49686 **Location:** 4.2 mi e.

TUSCAN BISTRO

Italian
$8-$20

Phone: 231/922-7795   ①

Opposite the West Grand Traverse Bay, this restaurant and lounge has a number of well-prepared Italian dishes. **Bar:** full bar. **Hours:** 11 am-10 pm, Sun-9 pm; hours may vary. Closed: 11/24, 12/25. **Address:** 12930 S West Bay Shore Dr 49684 **Location:** On SR 22, 1 mi n of SR 72. CALL ⓛⓂ

TRENTON — See Detroit p. 304.

TROY — See Detroit p. 304.

UNION PIER

SANDPIPER INN

Bed & Breakfast
$200-$295 4/1-10/31
$110-$195 11/1-4/30

Phone: 269/469-1146

Address: 16136 Lakeview Ave 49129 **Location:** I-94, exit 6 (Union Pier Rd), 2 mi w. **Facility:** Overlooking Lake Michigan, the "singing sands" of the beach are just down a flight of stairs from this stylish property. Smoke free premises. 9 units. 3 stories (no elevator), interior corridors. **Terms:** office hours 9 am-7 pm, check-in 4 pm, 2 night minimum stay - weekends, age restrictions may apply, 14 day cancellation notice-fee imposed. **Activities:** limited beach access, bicycles. **Guest Services:** wireless Internet. **Free Special Amenities:** full breakfast and high-speed Internet.

SAVE ⓘ⊕ ✕

—— WHERE TO DINE ——

FRANKIE'S PLACE

American
$11-$37

Phone: 269/469-9865

The cozy dining room, with its simple elegance and contemporary appeal, provides a romantic setting for a special occasion or fine night out. The menu offers creative preparations along the lines of filet mignon served on mushroom puff pastry, grilled lamb loin with tomato-olive relish, oven-roasted organic chicken, Parmesan-encrusted halibut and sautéed black cod. As a treat, house-spun cotton candy is served in flower pots at the end of the meal. **Bar:** full bar. **Reservations:** suggested. **Hours:** 5 pm-10 pm, Fri & Sat-11 pm. Closed major holidays; also Mon & Tues 5/26-9/1. **Address:** 16036 Red Arrow Hwy 49129 **Location:** I-94, exit 6 (Union Pier Rd), 1 mi w. ⬊

RED ARROW ROADHOUSE

American
$6-$20

Phone: 269/469-3939

From the outside, the eatery is the quintessential roadhouse of the '40s and '50s, while inside is a cozy, casual interior of knotty pine and mounted trophy heads. This spot is a popular draw for locals and want-to-be locals. The menu centers on creative interpretations of such classics as broasted chicken dinners, broiled Lake Superior whitefish, crispy Baja fish tacos and a variety of comfort foods. **Bar:** full bar. **Hours:** 5 pm-10 pm, Fri-11 pm, Sat noon-11 pm, Sun noon-10 pm; seasonal hours may vary. Closed major holidays. **Address:** 15710 Red Arrow Hwy 49129 **Location:** I-94, exit 6 (Union Pier Rd), 1 mi w, then 0.5 mi n. ⬊

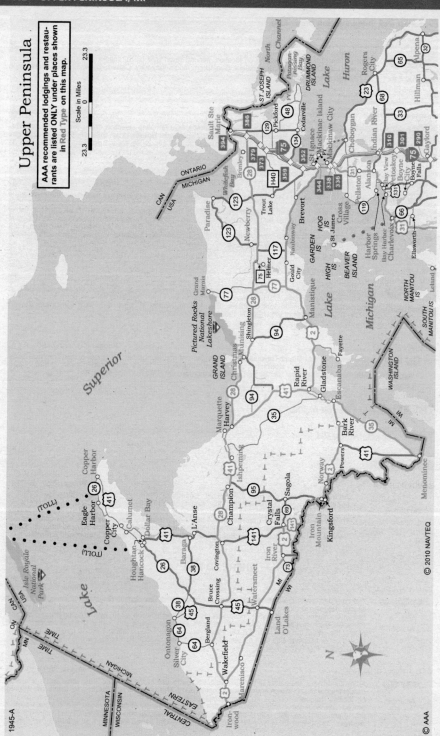

Upper Peninsula

AAA recommended lodgings and restaurants are listed ONLY under places shown in Red Type on this map.

Scale in Miles

23.3   0   23.3   23.3

1945-A

© AAA

© 2010 NAVTEQ

Upper Peninsula

UPPER PENINSULA

To help you more easily locate accommodations in the Upper Peninsula region of Michigan, please see the map on page. You can find accommodation listings under the alphabetical header for each city whose name appears on the map in red type.

UTICA —See Detroit p. 307.

WALKER pop. 21,842 (See map and index starting on p. 324)

BAYMONT INN & SUITES-GRAND RAPIDS NORTH

Phone: (616)735-9595 **14**

Hotel
$76-$134

Address: 2151 Holton Ct NW 49544 **Location:** I-96, exit 28 (Walker Ave), just s. **Facility:** Smoke free premises. 85 units. 4 stories, interior corridors. **Terms:** cancellation fee imposed. **Amenities:** video games (fee). **Pool(s):** heated indoor. **Activities:** whirlpool, exercise room. **Guest Services:** coin laundry, wireless Internet.

HAMPTON INN- GRAND RAPIDS NORTH

Phone: (616)647-1000 **13**

Hotel
$99-$124

Address: 500 Center Dr NW 49544 **Location:** I-96, exit 30, just n on Alpine Rd, then 0.3 mi e. Located behind a small mall. **Facility:** Smoke free premises. 84 units. 4 stories, interior corridors. **Parking:** winter plug-ins. **Terms:** 1-7 night minimum stay, cancellation fee imposed. **Amenities:** video games (fee). **Pool(s):** heated indoor. **Activities:** whirlpool, exercise room. **Guest Services:** valet laundry, wireless Internet.

> **AAA Benefit:**
> Members save up to 10% everyday!

HOLIDAY INN EXPRESS HOTEL & SUITES

Phone: (616)647-4100 **11**

Hotel
$89-$189

Address: 358 River Ridge Dr NW 49544 **Location:** I-96, exit 30, just n on Alpine Rd, then 0.3 mi e. Located behind a small mall. **Facility:** Smoke free premises. 94 units. 3 stories, interior corridors. **Amenities:** video games (fee), high-speed Internet. **Pool(s):** heated indoor. **Activities:** whirlpool, sun deck, exercise room. **Fee:** game room. **Guest Services:** valet and coin laundry, wireless Internet.

QUALITY INN GRAND RAPIDS NORTH

Phone: (616)791-8500 **15**

Hotel
$70-$84

Address: 2171 Holton Ct 49544 **Location:** I-96, exit 28 (Walker Ave), just s. **Facility:** Smoke free premises. 56 units. 2 stories (no elevator), interior corridors. **Pool(s):** heated indoor. **Activities:** whirlpool, limited exercise equipment. **Guest Services:** coin laundry, wireless Internet.

SPRINGHILL SUITES BY MARRIOTT

Phone: (616)785-1600 **12**

Hotel
$116-$148

Address: 450 Center Dr 49544 **Location:** I-96 and SR 37, exit Alpine Rd, just ne. Located behind a small mall. **Facility:** Smoke free premises. 76 units. 3 stories, interior corridors. **Parking:** winter plug-ins. **Terms:** cancellation fee imposed. **Amenities:** video games. **Pool(s):** heated indoor. **Activities:** whirlpool, exercise room. **Guest Services:** valet and coin laundry, wireless Internet.

> **AAA Benefit:**
> Members save a minimum 5% off the best available rate.

WARREN —See Detroit p. 308.

WATERFORD —See Detroit p. 311.

WATERSMEET

DANCING EAGLES RESORT LAC VIEUX DESERT CASINO

Phone: 906/358-4949

Hotel
$45-$90

Address: N5384 US Hwy 45 49969 **Location:** 1.8 mi n of US 2. **Facility:** Although the casino is in a rural area, it is recommended that you make reservations for a room ahead of time, as it's very popular with gamblers. Smoke free premises. 132 units. 2 stories, interior corridors. **Parking:** winter plug-ins. **Terms:** check-in 4 pm, cancellation fee imposed. **Pool(s):** heated indoor. **Activities:** sauna, whirlpool, snowmobiling, limited exercise equipment. **Fee:** golf-18 holes. **Guest Services:** coin laundry, wireless Internet.

WATERVLIET pop. 1,843

SURFARI JOE'S

Phone: (269)463-7946

Hotel
$129-$179 4/1-9/3
$99-$149 9/4-4/30

Address: 8258 Arnt Blvd 49098 **Location:** I-94, exit 41, just n. **Facility:** Smoke free premises. 96 units, some two bedrooms. 3 stories, interior corridors. **Pool(s):** heated indoor. **Activities:** exercise room. **Fee:** water park, game room. **Guest Services:** valet and coin laundry, wireless Internet.

WEST BLOOMFIELD —See Detroit p. 311.

WEST BRANCH pop. 1,926

—— WHERE TO DINE ——

THE WILLOW TREE RESTAURANT OF WEST BRANCH

American
$8-$42

Phone: 989/345-0660

This contemporary restaurant with three fireplaces and a cheery staff provides a warm atmosphere to enjoy dishes such as the all-natural Angus prime rib, fresh Lake Michigan perch and pasta. **Bar:** full bar. **Hours:** 11 am-9:30 pm, Fri & Sat-10 pm, Sun 10 am-9 pm. Closed: 12/25. **Address:** 633 Court St 48661 **Location:** I-75, exit 215, 1.6 mi e on SR 55, then 0.7 mi s on SR 30.

Discover The Jewel

WESTLAND —See Detroit p. 311.

WHITE CLOUD pop. 1,420

THE SHACK

Hotel
Rates not provided

Phone: 231-924-6683

Address: 2263 W 14th St 49349 **Location:** 0.5 mi s on SR 37, 5.5 mi w on 8th St and Post Rd. Located on Robinson Lake. **Facility:** Smoke free premises. 44 units, some two bedrooms. 1-2 stories (no elevator), interior/exterior corridors. **Activities:** paddleboats, fishing, cross country skiing, horseshoes, shuffleboard, volleyball. **Guest Services:** wireless Internet.

WHITEHALL pop. 2,884

COMFORT INN

Hotel
$72-$250

Phone: (231)893-4833

Address: 2822 N Durham Rd 49461 **Location:** US 31, exit 128, just e. **Facility:** Smoke free premises. 74 units, some two bedrooms. 3 stories, interior corridors. **Parking:** winter plug-ins. **Amenities:** safes (fee). *Some:* high-speed Internet. **Pool(s):** heated indoor. **Activities:** exercise room. *Fee:* game room. **Guest Services:** valet laundry, wireless Internet.

WHITMORE LAKE pop. 6,574

BEST WESTERN WHITMORE LAKE

Motel
$80-$130

Phone: (734)449-2058

Address: 9897 Main St 48189 **Location:** US 23, exit 53, just e. **Facility:** Smoke free premises. 61 units, some two bedrooms and kitchens. 2 stories (no elevator), exterior corridors. **Parking:** winter plug-ins. **Amenities:** safes. *Some:* high-speed Internet. **Pool(s):** heated indoor. **Activities:** sauna. **Guest Services:** coin laundry, wireless Internet. **Free Special Amenities:** expanded continental breakfast and high-speed Internet.

AAA Benefit:
Members save up to 20%, plus 10% bonus points with free rewards program.

WILLIAMSTON pop. 3,441

ACORN MOTEL

Motel
$66

Phone: (517)655-6793

Address: 2346 E Grand River Ave 48895 **Location:** I-96, exit 117 (Williamston), 1.5 mi n, then 0.7 mi e on SR 43. **Facility:** Smoke free premises. 8 units. 1 story, exterior corridors. **Parking:** winter plug-ins. **Terms:** office hours 8 am-10 pm, 3 day cancellation notice-fee imposed. **Guest Services:** wireless Internet.

—— WHERE TO DINE ——

CB'S BUCKET BAR AND GRILLE

American
$8-$23

Phone: 517/655-1000

The emphasis is on the food at this cozy yet casual restaurant on downtown's quaint main street. On the menu are varied steaks, fish selections and pasta dishes, as well as an extensive appetizer menu including crab cakes, spinach and artichoke dip, cheese bread and calamari fries and a rotating assortment of freshly prepared desserts. **Bar:** full bar. **Hours:** 11 am-11 pm; Sunday brunch 10 am-2 pm. Closed major holidays. **Address:** 132 Grand River Ave 48895 **Location:** I-96, exit 117 (Williamston), 1.5 mi n; downtown. **Parking:** street only.

RED CEDAR GRILL

American
$8-$25

Phone: 517/655-3766

An eclectic mixture of art and mirrors adorns the walls of this casual, open concept restaurant. A large and varied menu features a number of creatively prepared dishes and makes for interesting reading in its own right. **Bar:** full bar. **Hours:** 11 am-9 pm, Fri & Sat-11 pm, Sun noon-9 pm. Closed major holidays. **Address:** 150 E Grand River Ave 48895 **Location:** I-96, exit 117 (Williamston), 1.5 mi n; downtown.
CALL

WIXOM —See Detroit p. 311.

WOODHAVEN —See Detroit p. 312.

WYOMING pop. 69,368   (See map and index starting on p. 324)

HAMPTON INN GRAND RAPIDS SOUTH

Hotel
$99-$139

Address: 755 54th St SW 49509 **Location:** US 131, exit 78 (54th St). **Facility:** Smoke free premises. 138 units. 4 stories, interior corridors. **Terms:** check-in 4 pm, 1-7 night minimum stay, cancellation fee imposed. **Pool(s):** heated indoor. **Activities:** whirlpool, exercise room. *Fee:* game room. **Guest Services:** valet and coin laundry, wireless Internet.

Phone: (616)261-5500   **32**

> **AAA Benefit:**
> Members save up to 10% everyday!

HYATT PLACE GRAND RAPIDS - SOUTH

Hotel
$89-$179

Address: 2150 Metro Ln 49519 **Location:** SR 6, exit 5 (Byron Center Ave), just ne. Located in Metro Health Village. **Facility:** Smoke free premises. 113 units. 5 stories, interior corridors. **Terms:** cancellation fee imposed. **Amenities:** high-speed Internet. **Pool(s):** heated indoor. **Activities:** sun patio, exercise room. **Guest Services:** valet laundry, area transportation-within 5 mi, wireless Internet. **Free Special Amenities: continental breakfast and high-speed Internet.**

Phone: (616)724-1234   **33**

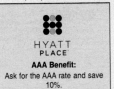

HYATT PLACE

> **AAA Benefit:**
> Ask for the AAA rate and save 10%.

SUPER 8

Hotel
$42-$53

Address: 727 44th St SW 49509 **Location:** US 131, exit 79. **Facility:** Smoke free premises. 62 units. 3 stories (no elevator), interior corridors. **Parking:** winter plug-ins. **Terms:** cancellation fee imposed. **Amenities:** safes (fee). **Guest Services:** wireless Internet.

Phone: (616)530-8588   **31**

TRAVELODGE

Hotel
$45-$67

Address: 65 28th St SW 49548 **Location:** On SR 11, 0.4 mi e of US 131. **Facility:** Smoke free premises. 54 units. 2 stories (no elevator), interior/exterior corridors. **Amenities:** safes (fee). **Pool(s):** heated indoor. **Activities:** exercise room. **Guest Services:** coin laundry, wireless Internet. **Free Special Amenities: expanded continental breakfast and high-speed Internet.**

Phone: (616)452-1461   **30**

—— WHERE TO DINE ——

ARNIE'S

American
$6-$15

Freshly baked artisan breads and Scandinavian danish complement the sandwiches, salads and soups, as well as other traditional dishes. **Hours:** 6:30 am-10 pm, Fri-10:30 pm, Sat 7 am-10:30 pm, Sun 8 am-3 pm. Closed: 11/24, 12/25. **Address:** 777 54th St 49509 **Location:** US 131, exit 78 (54th St), just w.

Phone: 616/532-5662   **20**

ORIENTAL FOREST

Chinese
$6-$12

Open seven days a week, the restaurant features an all-you-can-eat buffet with a variety of Chinese dishes. **Hours:** 11 am-10 pm; hours may vary. **Address:** 5316 Clyde Park SW 49509 **Location:** US 131, exit 78 (54th St), just w.

Phone: 616/538-9988   **19**

YPSILANTI pop. 22,362   (See map and index starting on p. 213)

ANN ARBOR MARRIOTT YPSILANTI AT EAGLE CREST

Resort Hotel
$159-$169

Address: 1275 S Huron St 48197 **Location:** I-94, exit 183 (Huron St), just se. **Facility:** The property, bordered by Ford Lake and a golf course, has a country-club setting. Smoke free premises. 235 units. 8 stories, interior corridors. **Parking:** winter plug-ins. **Terms:** cancellation fee imposed. **Amenities:** high-speed Internet. **Pool(s):** heated indoor. **Activities:** sauna, whirlpool, boat dock, tennis court, walking trail, exercise room. *Fee:* golf-18 holes, driving range. **Guest Services:** valet laundry, wireless Internet. **Free Special Amenities: early check-in/late check-out and high-speed Internet.**

Phone: (734)487-2000   **21**

Marriott.
HOTELS & RESORTS

> **AAA Benefit:**
> Members save 5% or more off best available rate.

PARISH HOUSE INN

Historic Bed & Breakfast
$99-$150

Address: 103 S Huron St 48197 **Location:** I-94, exit 183 (Huron St), 0.5 mi n; downtown. Located in historic district. **Facility:** This 1893 Queen Anne-style inn was formerly a parsonage. Smoke free premises. 8 units. 3 stories (no elevator), interior corridors. **Terms:** check-in 4 pm, 7 day cancellation notice. **Guest Services:** wireless Internet.

Phone: 734/480-4800   **20**

(See map and index starting on p. 213)

—— WHERE TO DINE ——

CAFE LUWAK

Deli
$4-$6

Phone: 734/482-8050   ㉙

The casual restaurant has warm hardwood floors and a hand-written chalkboard menu. Patrons find this a great stop for a light meal, such as a sandwich with in-house smoked turkey, a freshly made salad and a Stroh's ice cream cone. **Hours:** 8 am-9 pm, Thurs-Sat to 10 pm. Closed major holidays. **Address:** 42 E Cross St 48198 **Location:** In Depot Town. **Parking:** street only.

HAAB'S

American
$6-$27

Phone: 734/483-8200   ㉚

A local landmark since 1934, the longtime favorite is known for its rustic-looking dining room and traditional menu of delicious, well-prepared beef and seafood. Once a year, its prices reflect those of 1934. **Bar:** full bar. **Reservations:** suggested, weekends. **Hours:** 11 am-9 pm, Fri & Sat-10 pm. Closed: 12/25. **Address:** 18 W Michigan Ave 48197 **Location:** Downtown. **Parking:** street only.

PUB 13 RESTAURANT & DUELING PIANOS

American
$5-$20

Phone: 734/485-4120   ㉛

Two dueling pianos provide an entertaining—yet loud and boisterous—backdrop for a meal of standard American bar classics, including burgers, chicken and steak. Entertainment. **Bar:** full bar. **Hours:** 4 pm-midnight. Closed: 12/25. **Address:** 13 N Washington St 48197 **Location:** Between Michigan Ave and Pearl St; in historic district. **Parking:** street only.

Wisconsin

Pepin
© Walter Bibikow
Danita Delimont Stock
Photography

ABBOTSFORD pop. 1,956

RODEWAY INN

◆◆ ◆◆
Hotel
Rates not provided

Phone: 715/223-3337

Address: 300 E Elderberry Rd 54405 **Location:** SR 29, exit 132 (SR 13), just se. **Facility:** Smoke free premises. 60 units. 3 stories, interior corridors. **Parking:** winter plug-ins. **Pool(s):** heated indoor. **Activities:** whirlpool, snowmobile trails access, walking trail, exercise room. **Guest Services:** coin laundry, wireless Internet. 🛗 CALL 🛗M 🏊 ✕ 🎞 💻 / SOME UNITS FEE 🐕 🔋 🖥

——— WHERE TO DINE ———

BJ'S ABBY CAFÉ

◆◆ ◆◆
American
$5-$12

Phone: 715/223-3943

Simple, made-from-scratch entrees and homemade desserts are the draw at the popular diner. The country decor is representative of the surrounding farming community. **Hours:** 6 am-9 pm, Fri-10 pm. Closed: 12/25. **Address:** 206 E Spruce St 54405 **Location:** On Business Rt SR 29; downtown.

ALGOMA pop. 3,357

ALGOMA BEACH MOTEL

◆
Motel
$59-$199

Phone: (920)487-2828

Address: 1500 Lake St 54201 **Location:** Jct SR 54, 0.4 mi s on SR 42. Located on the shores of Lake Michigan. **Facility:** Smoke free premises. 29 units, some efficiencies. 1-2 stories (no elevator), interior/exterior corridors. **Terms:** office hours 8 am-8 pm, 2-3 night minimum stay - seasonal, 3 day cancellation notice. **Activities:** beachside picnic tables & grills. **Guest Services:** wireless Internet. **Free Special Amenities: continental breakfast and high-speed Internet.**
 SAVE CALL 🛗M ✕ 🎞 🔋 / SOME UNITS FEE 🐕 🍽

SCENIC SHORE INN

◆
Motel
$54-$71 4/1-9/6
$50-$64 9/7-4/30

Phone: 920/487-3214

Address: 2221 Lake St 54201 **Location:** Jct SR 54, 0.8 mi s on SR 42. Opposite Lake Michigan. **Facility:** Smoke free premises. 13 units. 2 stories (no elevator), exterior corridors. **Parking:** winter plug-ins. **Terms:** office hours 7:30 am-10 pm, 2 night minimum stay - seasonal and/or weekends, 3 day cancellation notice. **Amenities:** Some: high-speed Internet. **Activities:** picnic tables, grills. **Guest Services:** wireless Internet. ✕ 🎞 🔋 / SOME UNITS FEE 🐕

ANTIGO pop. 8,560

DAYS INN

◆◆ ◆◆
Hotel
$55-$91

Phone: (715)623-0506

Address: 525 Memory Ln 54409 **Location:** 0.4 mi n of jct SR 64 E and US 45, just w. **Facility:** Smoke free premises. 45 units. 2 stories, interior corridors. **Pool(s):** heated indoor. **Activities:** whirlpool. **Guest Services:** wireless Internet. 🛗 🏊 ✕ 🎞 💻 / SOME UNITS FEE 🐕 🔋 🖥

HOLIDAY INN EXPRESS & SUITES ANTIGO

◆◆ ◆◆◆
Hotel
$79-$99

Phone: (715)627-7500

Address: 2407 Neva Rd 54409 **Location:** Just n of jct SR 64 E and US 45, just e. **Facility:** Smoke free premises. 60 units. 3 stories, interior corridors. **Amenities:** high-speed Internet. Some: video games. **Pool(s):** heated indoor/outdoor. **Activities:** whirlpool, exercise room, game room. **Guest Services:** valet laundry, wireless Internet. 🛗 CALL 🛗M 🏊 ✕ 🎞 💻 / SOME UNITS FEE 🐕 🔋 🖥

SUPER 8-ANTIGO

◆◆ ◆◆
Hotel
$59-$103

Phone: (715)623-4188

Address: 535 Century Ave 54409 **Location:** On US 45 at SR 64 E. **Facility:** Smoke free premises. 52 units. 2 stories (no elevator), interior corridors. **Parking:** winter plug-ins. **Amenities:** safes (fee). **Pool(s):** heated indoor. **Activities:** sauna, whirlpool, adjacent snowmobile trail. **Guest Services:** wireless Internet. 🛗 CALL 🛗M 🏊 ♿ ✕ 🎞 🔋 💻 / SOME UNITS FEE 🐕 🖥

——— WHERE TO DINE ———

DIXIE LUNCH 5TH AVE

◆◆ ◆◆
American
$3-$14

Phone: 715/623-4634

Open since 1945, this family-owned eatery bakes fresh homemade pies every day and turns out one of the best cheeseburgers around. Breakfast is served all day. **Hours:** 5 am-10 pm, Fri-11 pm, Sun 6 am-2 pm. Closed: 12/25 & Easter. **Address:** 716 5th Ave 54409 **Location:** Jct SR 64 and 47, just e. CALL 🛗M

APPLETON pop. 70,087

BEST WESTERN FOX VALLEY INN

Hotel
$79-$200

Phone: (920)731-4141

Address: 3033 W College Ave 54914 **Location:** US 41, exit 137 (SR 125), 0.5 mi e. Located in a commercial area. **Facility:** Smoke free premises. 100 units. 2 stories (no elevator), interior corridors. **Parking:** winter plug-ins. **Amenities:** *Some:* high-speed Internet. **Pool(s):** heated indoor. **Activities:** whirlpool, domed recreation area, exercise room. **Guest Services:** valet and coin laundry, area transportation-within 5 mi, wireless Internet. **Free Special Amenities: continental breakfast and high-speed Internet.**

AAA Benefit:
Members save up to 20%, plus 10% bonus points with free rewards program.

CAMBRIA SUITES

Hotel
Rates not provided

Phone: 920/733-0101

Address: 3940 N Gateway Dr 54913 **Location:** US 41, exit 144 (Ballard Rd), just ne. **Facility:** Smoke free premises. 105 units. 4 stories, interior corridors. **Amenities:** high-speed Internet. **Pool(s):** heated indoor. **Activities:** whirlpool, exercise room. **Guest Services:** valet and coin laundry, wireless Internet.

CANDLEWOOD SUITES

Extended Stay
Hotel
$68-$179

Phone: (920)739-8000

Address: 4525 W College Ave 54914 **Location:** Just w of US 41. **Facility:** 82 units, some efficiencies and kitchens. 3 stories, interior corridors. **Parking:** winter plug-ins. **Terms:** office hours 7 am-11 pm, check-in 4 pm. **Amenities:** high-speed Internet. **Activities:** exercise room. **Guest Services:** complimentary laundry, wireless Internet.

COMFORT SUITES APPLETON AIRPORT

Hotel
$75-$175

Phone: (920)730-3800

Address: 3809 W Wisconsin Ave 54914 **Location:** US 41, exit 138 (Wisconsin Ave), just e. Located in a commercial area. **Facility:** Smoke free premises. 130 units, some kitchens. 2 stories (no elevator), interior corridors. **Parking:** winter plug-ins. **Amenities:** safes (fee). *Some:* high-speed Internet. **Pool(s):** heated indoor. **Activities:** sauna, whirlpool, exercise room. **Fee:** game room. **Guest Services:** valet and coin laundry, area transportation-within 5 mi, wireless Internet.

COPPERLEAF BOUTIQUE HOTEL & SPA

Phone: (920)749-0303

Boutique Contemporary Hotel
$109-$275

Address: 300 W College Ave 54911 **Location:** US 41, exit 137 (SR 125), 3 mi e of US 41; downtown. Located in a commercial area. **Facility:** This impressive hotel has an extensive spa, luxurious lobby and spacious guest rooms with elegant bedding and upholstered oversize seating. Smoke free premises. 73 units. 6 stories, interior corridors. **Parking:** on-site (fee). **Amenities:** high-speed Internet, safes (fee), honor bars. **Dining:** Black & Tan Grille, see separate listing. **Activities:** whirlpool, exercise room, spa. **Guest Services:** valet laundry, area transportation-within 5 mi, wireless Internet.

FREE full breakfast and high-speed Internet

COUNTRY INN & SUITES BY CARLSON

Phone: (920)830-3240

Hotel
$99-$140

Address: 355 Fox River Dr 54913 **Location:** US 41, exit 137 (SR 125), just nw. Located in a commercial area. **Facility:** Smoke free premises. 106 units. 3 stories, interior corridors. **Parking:** winter plug-ins. **Terms:** 3 day cancellation notice-fee imposed. **Amenities:** video games (fee). **Pool(s):** heated indoor. **Activities:** whirlpool, limited exercise equipment. *Fee:* game room. **Guest Services:** valet and coin laundry, area transportation-mall, wireless Internet. *(see ad p. 6)*

DAYS INN

Phone: (920)733-5551

Hotel
$44-$161

Address: 210 Westhill Blvd 54914 **Location:** US 41, exit 137 (SR 125), just e. Located in a commercial area. **Facility:** Smoke free premises. 102 units. 2 stories (no elevator), interior corridors. **Activities:** limited exercise equipment. **Guest Services:** coin laundry, wireless Internet.

EXTENDED STAYAMERICA-APPLETON-FOX CITIES

Phone: (920)830-9596

Extended Stay Hotel
$42-$70

Address: 4141 Boardwalk Ct 54915 **Location:** US 41, exit 137 (SR 125), just w on College Ave, then just s on Nicolet Rd. **Facility:** Smoke free premises. 107 efficiencies. 3 stories, interior corridors. **Parking:** winter plug-ins. **Terms:** office hours 7 am-11 pm, cancellation fee imposed. **Guest Services:** coin laundry, wireless Internet.

FAIRFIELD INN BY MARRIOTT

Phone: (920)954-0202

Hotel
$107-$137

Address: 132 N Mall Dr 54913 **Location:** US 41, exit 137 (SR 125), just nw. Located in a commercial area. **Facility:** Smoke free premises. 63 units. 3 stories, interior corridors. **Parking:** winter plug-ins. **Terms:** cancellation fee imposed. **Amenities:** *Some:* high-speed Internet. **Pool(s):** heated indoor. **Activities:** whirlpool. **Guest Services:** valet laundry, wireless Internet.

FRANKLIN STREET INN BED & BREAKFAST

Phone: 920/993-1711

Historic Bed & Breakfast
$99-$219

Address: 318 E Franklin St 54911 **Location:** US 41, exit 137 (College Ave), 3.5 mi e to Drew St, just s to E Franklin St, then just e. **Facility:** The 1897 Queen Anne Victorian home features an inviting wraparound porch, impressive period antique furniture and a wide variety of lovely artwork. Smoke free premises. 4 units. 3 stories (no elevator), interior corridors. **Terms:** check-in 4 pm, age restrictions may apply, 21 day cancellation notice-fee imposed. **Activities:** *Fee:* massage. **Guest Services:** wireless Internet.

GRANDSTAY HOTEL & SUITES

Phone: (920)993-1200

Hotel
$99-$198

Address: 300 Mall Dr 54913 **Location:** US 41, exit 137 (SR 125), just nw. **Facility:** Smoke free premises. 80 units. 3 stories, interior corridors. **Parking:** winter plug-ins. **Amenities:** video games (fee), high-speed Internet. **Pool(s):** heated indoor. **Activities:** whirlpool, exercise room. **Guest Services:** valet laundry, wireless Internet. **Free Special Amenities:** continental breakfast and high-speed Internet.

HAMPTON INN APPLETON

Phone: (920)954-9211

Hotel
$79-$249

Address: 350 Fox River Dr 54913 **Location:** US 41, exit 137 (SR 125), just nw. Located in a commercial area. **Facility:** Smoke free premises. 122 units. 4 stories, interior corridors. **Terms:** 1-7 night minimum stay, cancellation fee imposed. **Amenities:** video games (fee), high-speed Internet. **Pool(s):** heated indoor. **Activities:** whirlpool, sun deck, exercise room. **Guest Services:** valet laundry, area transportation-within 5 mi, wireless Internet.

HOLIDAY INN APPLETON

Phone: (920)735-9955

Hotel
$109-$279

Address: 150 Nicolet Rd 54914 **Location:** US 41, exit 137 (SR 125), just sw. **Facility:** Smoke free premises. 227 units. 2-8 stories, interior corridors. **Parking:** winter plug-ins. **Terms:** check-in 4 pm, cancellation fee imposed. **Pool(s):** heated indoor. **Activities:** whirlpool, exercise room. *Fee:* game room. **Guest Services:** valet and coin laundry, area transportation-mall, wireless Internet.

LA QUINTA INN & SUITES APPLETON COLLEGE AVENUE

Phone: (920)734-7777

Hotel
$69-$129

Address: 3730 W College Ave 54914 **Location:** US 41, exit 137 (SR 125), just e. Located in a commercial area. **Facility:** Smoke free premises. 98 units, some efficiencies. 2 stories, interior corridors. **Parking:** winter plug-ins. **Amenities:** video games (fee). **Pool(s):** heated indoor. **Activities:** sauna, whirlpool, indoor children's play area, mini arcade room, exercise room. **Guest Services:** valet and coin laundry, area transportation-mall, wireless Internet.

LA QUINTA INN APPLETON FOX RIVER MALL AREA

Phone: (920)734-6070

Motel
$49-$99

Address: 3920 W College Ave 54914 **Location:** US 41, exit 137 (SR 125), just e. Located in a commercial area. **Facility:** 83 units. 1-2 stories (no elevator), interior/exterior corridors. **Parking:** winter plug-ins. **Amenities:** video games (fee). *Some:* high-speed Internet. **Pool(s):** heated outdoor. **Guest Services:** valet and coin laundry, wireless Internet.

MICROTEL INN & SUITES

Phone: (920)997-3121

Hotel
$49-$144

Address: 321 Metro Dr 54913 **Location:** US 41, exit 137 (SR 125), just nw. Located in a commercial area. **Facility:** Smoke free premises. 79 units. 3 stories, interior corridors. **Parking:** winter plug-ins. **Activities:** whirlpool, limited exercise equipment. **Guest Services:** valet laundry, wireless Internet.

RADISSON PAPER VALLEY HOTEL

Phone: (920)733-8000

Hotel
$80-$450

Address: 333 W College Ave 54911 **Location:** US 41, exit 137 (SR 125), 3 mi e; downtown. **Facility:** Smoke free premises. 388 units. 7 stories, interior corridors. **Parking:** on-site (fee). **Terms:** cancellation fee imposed. **Amenities:** video games (fee). **Dining:** Vince Lombardi's Steakhouse, see separate listing. **Pool(s):** heated indoor. **Activities:** sauna, whirlpool, exercise room. *Fee:* game room. **Guest Services:** valet laundry, wireless Internet.

RESIDENCE INN BY MARRIOTT

Phone: 920/954-0570

Extended Stay Hotel
$150-$160

Address: 310 Metro Dr 54913 **Location:** US 41, exit 137 (SR 125), just nw on Mall Dr. Located in a commercial area. **Facility:** Smoke free premises. 66 units, some two bedrooms, efficiencies and kitchens. 3 stories, interior corridors. **Parking:** winter plug-ins. **Terms:** cancellation fee imposed. **Amenities:** high-speed Internet. **Pool(s):** heated indoor. **Activities:** whirlpool, sun deck, exercise room, sports court. **Guest Services:** valet and coin laundry, wireless Internet.

> **AAA Benefit:**
> Members save a minimum 5% off the best available rate.

SETTLE INN & SUITES APPLETON-FOX RIVER MALL AREA

Phone: (920)560-3000

Motel
$89-$229

Address: 1565 Federated Dr 54913 **Location:** US 41, exit 138. **Facility:** Smoke free premises. 81 units. 3 stories, interior corridors. **Parking:** winter plug-ins. **Amenities:** high-speed Internet. **Pool(s):** heated indoor. **Activities:** whirlpool, exercise room. **Guest Services:** valet and coin laundry, area transportation-within 5 mi, wireless Internet. **Free Special Amenities: expanded continental breakfast and high-speed Internet.**

── WHERE TO DINE ──

BEEFEATERS BRITISH GRILLE & ALE HOUSE

Phone: 920/730-8300

British
$9-$19

This modern English pub has polished cherry wood trim, stone accent walls and comfortable banquette seating. The menu lists a wide variety of traditional British favorites along with fine steaks, seafood and many sandwiches and appetizers. **Bar:** full bar. **Hours:** 11 am-10 pm, Fri & Sat-11 pm. **Address:** 2331 E Evergreen Dr 54913 **Location:** US 41, exit 144 to Ballard Rd, just ne.

BLACK & TAN GRILLE

Phone: 920/380-4745

American
$22-$40

Within walking distance of the performing arts center, this upscale restaurant features a contemporary menu and ambience. On the menu are Black Angus steaks, king salmon, yellowfin tuna, game and seafood dishes, as well as seasonal fresh vegetables. Guests can relax in the upscale lounge while waiting for a table. **Bar:** full bar. **Reservations:** suggested. **Hours:** 5 pm-9 pm, Sun-8 pm. Closed major holidays. **Address:** 300 W College Ave 54911 **Location:** US 41, exit 137 (SR 125), 3 mi e of US 41; downtown; in Copperleaf Boutique Hotel & Spa.

FRATELLOS WATERFRONT RESTAURANT

Phone: 920/991-0000

American
$8-$27

Gourmet pizza and Cap'n Crunch chicken are prepared in the wood-stone oven of the open display kitchen. Beers are created in the second-story brewery loft, and burgers, sandwiches and pasta complete the menu. Seating is available in the dining room or on the seasonal patio. **Bar:** full bar. **Hours:** 11 am-10 pm; seasonal hours may vary. Closed: 11/24, 12/25 & Easter. **Address:** 4301 W Wisconsin Ave 54915 **Location:** US 41, exit 138 (Wisconsin Ave), just sw; in Fox River Mall.

GEORGE'S STEAK HOUSE

Phone: 920/733-4939

Steak
$8-$30

A tradition since the 1940s, the relaxed, casual steakhouse appeals to families and business professionals. Representative of steak and seafood choices are prime rib au jus, flounder and the 24-ounce porterhouse. **Bar:** full bar. **Reservations:** suggested. **Hours:** 11 am-2 & 5-10 pm, Fri & Sat-10:30 pm. Closed: 1/1, 11/24, 12/25; also Sun. **Address:** 2208 S Memorial Dr 54911 **Location:** 1.4 mi s on SR 47 from jct SR 73.

GRAZIES ITALIAN GRILL

Phone: 920/996-9999

Italian
$8-$19

This restaurant has a neighborhood bar feel and offers wraps, wood-fired pizza and pasta made from scratch for dishes such as seafood pescatore with sautéed shrimp and scallops. Entertainment. **Hours:** 11 am-10 pm, Fri & Sat-11 pm. Closed: 11/24, 12/25 & Easter. **Address:** W6157 Lorna Ln 54915 **Location:** US 41, exit 145 (SR 441), 3.7 mi s to CR KK, then 0.6 mi e to Coop Rd. CALL

THE MACHINE SHED

Phone: 920/830-2326

American
$6-$20

Hearty portions of made-from-scratch farm-style cooking include specialties of pork and beef. The restaurant is dedicated to the American farmer and uses real dairy products and locally produced meats. Friendly servers don overalls. **Bar:** full bar. **Hours:** 6 am-9 pm, Fri & Sat-10 pm, Sun 7 am-9 pm. Closed: 1/1, 11/24, 12/25. **Address:** 220 N Fox River Dr 54913 **Location:** US 41, exit 137 (SR 125), just nw. CALL

NAKASHIMA OF JAPAN

Phone: 920/739-6057

Japanese
$7-$43

Highly skilled cooks offer quite a show while preparing meals at the table. Offerings include nigiri sushi and a variety of beef, chicken and fresh seafood dishes. This is the place to go for a great show and wonderful teppanyaki cooking. **Bar:** full bar. **Reservations:** suggested. **Hours:** 5 pm-10 pm, Sat 4 pm-9 pm. Closed major holidays. **Address:** 4100 W Pine St 54915 **Location:** I-41, exit 136/CR BB/Prospect Ave, 0.3 mi CR BB, then 0.5 mi n on S Van Dyke Rd. CALL

THE SEASONS   *Menu on AAA.com*

Phone: 920/993-9860

American
$12-$38

Fresh ingredients and attractive entree presentations make this American bistro popular with both business and leisure guests. Complemented by an extensive wine list, the menu, which changes seasonally, always features fresh fish. Delicious desserts are made in-house. Patio dining is offered in season, and smoking is permitted only in the lounge. **Bar:** full bar. **Reservations:** suggested. **Hours:** 11 am-10 pm, Sat from 4 pm. Closed major holidays; also Sun. **Address:** 213 S Nicolet Rd 54914 **Location:** US 41, exit 137 (SR 125), just sw; in Nicolet Square.

VICTORIA'S

Phone: 920/730-9595

Italian
$5-$28

Huge servings of fresh, flavorful food are the norm at the centrally located eatery. Among the numerous menu selections are Sicilian and Italian specialties, salads, seafood, made-to-order gourmet pizzas and create-your-own pasta dishes with a variety of sauces and meats. **Bar:** full bar. **Hours:** 11 am-9 pm. Closed: 11/24, 12/25 & Easter; also for dinner 12/24. **Address:** 503 W College Ave 54911 **Location:** Jct Walnut St, 2.7 mi e of US 41, exit 137 (SR 125); downtown. **Parking:** street only.

VINCE LOMBARDI'S STEAKHOUSE

Phone: 920/380-9390

Steak
$20-$62

This restaurant is a shrine to the former Green Bay Packers coach. The restaurant abounds with memorabilia of a personal nature and equipment and photographs depicting his many football exploits. The restaurant appeals to those hungry for some of the finest steak in this area and those looking for a glimpse into the life of the legend and the man. The atmosphere is decidedly upscale but with a casual ambience. **Bar:** full bar. **Reservations:** suggested. **Hours:** 4 pm-10 pm, Sun-9 pm. Closed: 1/1, 7/4, 12/24. **Address:** 333 W College Ave 54911 **Location:** US 41, exit 137 (SR 125), 3 mi e; downtown; in Radisson Paper Valley Hotel.

ARBOR VITAE

—— **WHERE TO DINE** ——

MARTY'S PLACE NORTH

Phone: 715/356-4335

American
$11-$37

A warm, "up-north" ambience pervades the cozy dining room, which features log walls, stone accents and wildlife prints. The restaurant is known locally for specialty dinners of stuffed orange roughy, veal Oscar, roast duck and Oriental steak. **Bar:** full bar. **Hours:** 4:30 pm-10 pm; hours may vary. Closed: 11/24, 12/24, 12/25; also week of Easter. **Address:** 2721 US 51 N 54568 **Location:** 5.8 mi n on US 51 from jct SR 47.

ARKDALE

NORTHERN BAY CONDOS & CASTLE COURSE

Phone: 608/339-2090

Condominium
$245-$475

Address: 1844 20th Ave 54613 **Location:** 2.9 mi w on SR 21, 3 mi s on CR Z, 0.9 mi w on Czech Ave, then 0.4 mi se. **Facility:** These spacious units are located on the golf course or along the lakefront. Smoke free premises. 109 units, some two bedrooms, three bedrooms, kitchens and houses. 3 stories, interior corridors. **Terms:** office hours 7 am-10 pm, check-in 4 pm, 2 night minimum stay - seasonal, cancellation fee imposed. **Amenities:** high-speed Internet. **Pool(s):** heated outdoor. **Activities:** whirlpool, beach access, fishing, 2 tennis courts, snowmobile trails, ATV trails, playground, volleyball. *Fee:* paddleboats, boat dock, pontoons, personal watercraft, golf-18 holes, bicycles, game room. **Guest Services:** complimentary laundry, wireless Internet.

ASHLAND pop. 8,620

AMERICINN OF ASHLAND
Phone: (715)682-9950

Hotel
$99-$199 4/1-10/23
$79-$169 10/24-4/30

Address: 3009 Lake Shore Dr E 54806 **Location:** On US 2, 2.1 mi e of jct SR 13 S. **Facility:** Smoke free premises. 94 units. 2 stories, interior corridors. **Parking:** winter plug-ins. **Amenities:** *Some:* high-speed Internet. **Pool(s):** heated indoor. **Activities:** sauna, whirlpool, waterslide, limited beach access, paddleboats, bicycles, exercise room, game room. **Guest Services:** coin laundry, wireless Internet. **Free Special Amenities: expanded continental breakfast and high-speed Internet.**

ASHLAND LAKE SUPERIOR LODGE
Phone: 715/682-5235

Hotel
$130-$150

Address: 30600 US Hwy 2 54806 **Location:** 2.5 mi w. **Facility:** Smoke free premises. 60 units. 2 stories (no elevator), interior/exterior corridors. **Parking:** winter plug-ins. **Terms:** 7 day cancellation notice. **Amenities:** high-speed Internet. **Pool(s):** heated indoor. **Activities:** whirlpool, exercise room. **Free Special Amenities: high-speed Internet.**

LAKE SUPERIOR LODGE
Phone: 715/682-5235

Hotel
$130-$150

Address: 30600 US Hwy 2 54806 **Location:** 2.5 mi w. **Facility:** Smoke free premises. 60 units. 2 stories (no elevator), interior/exterior corridors. **Parking:** winter plug-ins. **Terms:** 7 day cancellation notice. **Amenities:** high-speed Internet. **Pool(s):** heated indoor. **Activities:** whirlpool, exercise room.

SUPER 8
Phone: (715)682-9377

Hotel
$59-$126

Address: 1610 W Lake Shore Dr 54806 **Location:** On US 2 at 16th Ave. **Facility:** Smoke free premises. 70 units. 2 stories (no elevator), interior corridors. **Parking:** winter plug-ins. **Amenities:** high-speed Internet. **Pool(s):** heated indoor. **Activities:** whirlpool. **Guest Services:** coin laundry, wireless Internet.

—— WHERE TO DINE ——

THE BREAKWATER CAFE
Phone: 715/682-8388

American
$6-$15

The casual, family-friendly restaurant delivers an all-day menu of breakfast choices, plus sandwiches, soups, salads and burgers. The views of Lake Superior are beautiful. Delicious homemade baked goods include caramel rolls and doughnuts. **Hours:** 5 am-10 pm; to 9 pm in winter. Closed: 12/25. **Address:** 1808 Lake Shore Dr E 54806 **Location:** On US 2, 1.2 mi e of jct SR 13 S.

L.C. WILMARTH'S DEEP WATER GRILLE & SOUTH SHORE BREWERY
Phone: 715/682-4200

American
$8-$20

Just west of downtown, the upscale, nautical-themed restaurant harbors a notable brewpub on site. While traditional pub favorites can be found, the kitchen takes full advantage of the locally grown produce and freshly caught fish in its creative daily specials. **Bar:** full bar. **Reservations:** suggested. **Hours:** 11 am-10 pm. Closed major holidays. **Address:** 808 W Main St 54806 **Location:** Center.

PLATTER RESTAURANT
Phone: 715/682-2626

American
$9-$27

A charmingly restored turn-of-the-20th-century home welcomes diners. Country Victorian decor sets the stage. Regional cuisine shows interest both for a contemporary, unusual contrast of flavors and a respect for tradition. Squash bisque is drizzled with maple syrup, roasted duck is accompanied with perfumes of citrus and cranberries, and planked fish—a fish fillet backed on a maple board—echoes of Lake Superior old times and methods. **Bar:** full bar. **Reservations:** suggested. **Hours:** 4:30 pm-10 pm. Closed major holidays; also Sun & Mon in winter. **Address:** 315 Turner Rd 54806 **Location:** 2 mi w on US 2, follow signs for Prentice Park, then just s.

BAILEYS HARBOR —See Door County p. 463.

BALDWIN pop. 2,667

AMERICINN LODGE & SUITES OF BALDWIN
Phone: (715)684-5888

Hotel
$70-$185

Address: 500 Baldwin Plaza Dr 54002 **Location:** I-94, exit 19 (US 63), just ne. **Facility:** Smoke free premises. 65 units. 2 stories, interior corridors. **Parking:** winter plug-ins. **Pool(s):** heated indoor. **Activities:** whirlpool. **Guest Services:** coin laundry, wireless Internet.

SUPER 8
Phone: (715)684-2700

Hotel
$58-$71

Address: 2110 10th Ave 54002 **Location:** I-94, exit 19 (US 63), just se. **Facility:** Smoke free premises. 61 units. 2 stories, interior corridors. **Parking:** winter plug-ins. **Terms:** cancellation fee imposed. **Pool(s):** heated indoor. **Activities:** whirlpool. *Fee:* game room. **Guest Services:** coin laundry, wireless Internet.

BALSAM LAKE pop. 950

—— WHERE TO DINE ——

PARADISE LANDING RESTAURANT
Phone: 715/485-3210

American
$9-$32

Overlooking Balsam Lake, the restaurant has the look and feel of a lodge, with a large stone fireplace and antler chandelier. The menu focuses on regionally available fish, grilled rib-eye and homemade sauces. **Bar:** full bar. **Reservations:** suggested. **Hours:** Open 4/1-1/1; 11 am-9 pm, Fri & Sat-10 pm, Sun 9 am-8 pm; hours may vary. Closed: 1/1, 11/24, 12/24, 12/25; also Mon-Wed 9/4-5/27. **Address:** 264 CR I 54810 **Location:** 1 mi n.

BARABOO pop. 10,711

BEST WESTERN BARABOO INN

Hotel
$70-$135

Address: 725 W Pine St 53913 **Location:** On US 12, 0.3 mi n of SR 33. **Facility:** Smoke free premises. 82 units. 3 stories, interior corridors. **Terms:** 7 day cancellation notice. **Amenities:** *Some:* high-speed Internet. **Pool(s):** heated indoor. **Activities:** whirlpool, exercise room. **Guest Services:** coin laundry, wireless Internet. **Free Special Amenities: local telephone calls and newspaper.**

Phone: (608)356-1100

AAA Benefit:
Members save up to 20%, plus 10% bonus points with free rewards program.

CLARION HOTEL & CONVENTION CENTER

Hotel
$70-$155 7/2-4/30
$80-$92 4/1-7/1

Address: 626 W Pine St 53913 **Location:** On US 12, 0.3 mi n of SR 33. **Facility:** Smoke free premises. 84 units, some two bedrooms. 5 stories, interior corridors. **Terms:** check-in 4 pm, 3 day cancellation notice-fee imposed. **Pool(s):** heated indoor. **Activities:** sauna, whirlpool, exercise room. **Fee:** game room. **Guest Services:** coin laundry, wireless Internet.

Phone: (608)356-6422

PINEHAVEN BED & BREAKFAST

Bed & Breakfast
$99-$145

Address: E13083 Hwy 33 53913 **Location:** On SR 33, 4.8 mi e from jct US 12. Located in a quiet rural area. **Facility:** The outstanding feature of this B&B is its scenic location amid rolling hills, a farm pond and mature conifers; a gazebo offers panoramic views. Smoke free premises. 5 units, some two bedrooms and kitchens. 2 stories (no elevator), interior/exterior corridors. **Terms:** open 4/1-10/31, 2 night minimum stay - seasonal and/or weekends, age restrictions may apply, 7 day cancellation notice-fee imposed. **Activities:** boating, fishing, hiking trails. **Free Special Amenities: full breakfast and high-speed Internet.**

Phone: 608/356-3489

—— WHERE TO DINE ——

COPPER OAK STEAKHOUSE & LOUNGE

Steak
$15-$40

The Copper Oak Steak House is located in the Ho-Chunk Casino and Convention Center, just a couple of miles south of the Wisconsin Dells. It offers a fine-dining experience and specializes in steak, charbroiled over a combination of Wisconsin hickory and Texas mesquite, and lobster. Other menu offerings include escargot, Maryland crab cakes, lobster mashed potatoes, Northwoods breast of duckling, chicken, scallops, twice-baked potatoes and more. **Bar:** full bar. **Hours:** 5 pm-10 pm. **Address:** S 3214 US 12 53913 **Location:** I-90/94, exit 92 (US 12), 2.5 mi s; in Ho-Chunk Casino & Hotel.

Phone: 608/356-6210

LOG CABIN FAMILY RESTAURANT AND BAKERY

American
$5-$17

Made of log construction, this restaurant is popular with locals and visitors alike. The food tastes great, and many items are homemade. Breakfast is served all day. **Hours:** 6 am-10 pm. Closed: 11/24, 12/25 & Easter; also for dinner 12/24. **Address:** 1215 8th St 53913 **Location:** 2.5 mi e on SR 33 from jct US 12.

Phone: 608/356-8034

SUNRISE CLIFFS CAFE

American
$4-$13

The family-oriented cafe serves breakfast, lunch and dinner. **Hours:** 7 am-5 pm. **Address:** S 3214 US 12 53913 **Location:** I-90/94, exit 92 (US 12), 2.5 mi s; in Ho-Chunk Casino & Hotel.

Phone: 608/356-6210

BARRON pop. 3,284

BARRON MOTEL & RV CAMPGROUND

Motel
$63-$73

Address: 1521 E Division Ave 54812 **Location:** On US 8, 1 mi e of jct SR 25 N. **Facility:** Smoke free premises. 11 units. 1 story, exterior corridors. **Parking:** winter plug-ins.

Phone: 715/637-3154

BAYFIELD pop. 611

THE BAYFIELD INN

Hotel
Rates not provided

Address: 20 Rittenhouse Ave 54814 **Location:** Just s of SR 13. **Facility:** Smoke free premises. 21 units. 2 stories (no elevator), interior corridors. **Parking:** winter plug-ins. **Guest Services:** wireless Internet.

Phone: 715/779-3363

BAYFIELD ON THE LAKE

Condominium
$120-$325

Address: 10 S 1st St 54814 **Location:** Just s of SR 13. Located on lakefront. **Facility:** The property offers large accommodations, many with balconies or patios that showcase the view of the bay. Designated smoking area. 9 kitchen units, some two and three bedrooms. 3 stories (no elevator), interior corridors. **Parking:** winter plug-ins. **Terms:** check-in 4 pm, 2 night minimum stay - seasonal and/or weekends, 10 day cancellation notice-fee imposed. **Guest Services:** complimentary laundry.

Phone: 715/779-3621

COOPER HILL HOUSE

Phone: 715/779-5060

Historic Bed
& Breakfast
$99-$125 4/1-10/15
$99-$109 10/16-4/30

Address: 33 S 6th St 54814 **Location:** On SR 13: **Facility:** This quiet home has an old-fashioned charm; guest rooms are furnished with heirlooms and antiques. Smoke free premises. 4 units. 2 stories (no elevator), interior corridors. **Terms:** 2 night minimum stay - seasonal and/or weekends, age restrictions may apply, 7 day cancellation notice-fee imposed. **Guest Services:** wireless Internet.

OLD RITTENHOUSE INN

Phone: 715/779-5111

Historic
Country Inn
$130-$325

Address: 301 Rittenhouse Ave 54814 **Location:** Just w on SR 13. **Facility:** Two late-1800s Victorian mansions decorated with antiques make up this stately hillside inn; most rooms have fireplaces and some have bay views. Smoke free premises. 20 units. 3 stories (no elevator), interior corridors. **Parking:** winter plug-ins. **Terms:** check-in 3:30 pm, 10 day cancellation notice-fee imposed. **Dining:** restaurant, see separate listing. **Guest Services:** area transportation-marina, wireless Internet. / SOME UNITS

—— WHERE TO DINE ——

THE EGG TOSS BAKERY CAFE

Phone: 715/779-5181

American
$5-$10

Early-risers appreciate the compelling aroma of warm, freshly baked bread that comes from the small, colorful cafe. Fresh preserves and a few Mexican influences give comfort foods an international flair. **Hours:** 7 am-1 pm; seasonal hours vary. Closed: 12/25 & Easter. **Address:** 41 Manypenny Ave 54814 **Location:** Center. **Parking:** street only.

OLD RITTENHOUSE INN

Phone: 715/779-5111

Continental
$5-$50

In a restored 1890 mansion, this charming, Victorian-style restaurant offers incredible atmosphere for diners who seek romance and fine dining. The decor is classic and elegant yet not intimidating in the least. The wait staff is thoroughly knowledgeable about the constantly changing menu. The various courses of the prix fixe menu do not disappoint. Everything is fresh, well prepared and a joy to eat. **Bar:** full bar. **Reservations:** suggested. **Hours:** 7-10 am, 11-1:30 & 5-9 pm; seasonal hours may vary. Closed: 12/25. **Address:** 301 Rittenhouse Ave 54814 **Location:** Just w on SR 13; in Old Rittenhouse Inn. **Historic**

BEAVER DAM pop. 15,169

BEST WESTERN CAMPUS INN MOTOR LODGE

Phone: (920)887-7171

Hotel
$80-$120

Address: 815 Park Ave 53916 **Location:** US 151, exit 132 (SR 33), just w. **Facility:** Smoke free premises. 94 units. 2-4 stories, interior corridors. **Pool(s):** heated indoor. **Activities:** whirlpool, billiards, table tennis, exercise room. *Fee:* game room. **Guest Services:** valet and coin laundry, wireless Internet. **Free Special Amenities:** continental breakfast and high-speed Internet.

AAA Benefit:
Members save up to 20%, plus 10% bonus points with free rewards program.

SUPER 8

Phone: (920)887-8880

Hotel
$57-$81

Address: 711 Park Ave 53916 **Location:** US 151, exit 132 (SR 33), just w. **Facility:** Smoke free premises. 50 units. 3 stories (no elevator), interior corridors. **Parking:** winter plug-ins. **Guest Services:** coin laundry, wireless Internet. / SOME UNITS FEE

—— WHERE TO DINE ——

BENVENUTO'S ITALIAN GRILL

Phone: 920/887-7994

Italian
$6-$16

The casual eatery's menu comprises Italian and American fare, including gourmet calzones, pasta, ribs, wood-fired pizza, meatball sandwiches, steaks, mushroom and mozzarella burgers, walleyed pike and popcorn shrimp. **Bar:** full bar. **Hours:** 11 am-10 pm, Fri & Sat-11 pm. Closed: 11/24, 12/24, 12/25. **Address:** 831 Park Ave 53916 **Location:** US 151, exit 132 (SR 33), just sw.

DOS GRINGO'S MEXICAN RESTAURANT & CANTINA

Phone: 920/887-0800

Mexican
$8-$24

Since 1986, the restaurant has been serving daily prepared Mexican cuisine to people in Dodge County. Diners start with complimentary fresh chips and salsa, then move on to fajita wraps, quesadillas, burritos and the like. Mexican art and terra cotta-colored walls add up to south-of-the-border ambience. Patio seating is an option in nice weather. **Bar:** full bar. **Hours:** 11 am-10 pm, Fri & Sat-10:30 pm, Sun 11 am-9 pm. Closed major holidays. **Address:** 210 S Spring St 53916 **Location:** Downtown. **Parking:** street only.

WALKER'S FAMILY RESTAURANT

Phone: 920/885-9041

American
$4-$12

The family restaurant touts its baked chicken and Friday fish fry but also serves all-day breakfast items and home-cooked specials for lunch and dinner. This place also makes its own breads and pastries. **Hours:** 6 am-10 pm. Closed: 12/25. **Address:** 813 Park Ave 53916 **Location:** US 151, exit 132 (SR 33), just sw; adjacent to Best Western Campus Inn Motor Lodge.

BELMONT pop. 871

BAYMONT INN & SUITES

Hotel
$63-$117

Phone: (608)762-6900

Address: 103 W Moundview Ave 53510 **Location:** US 151, exit 26, just w. **Facility:** 50 units. 2 stories (no elevator), interior corridors. **Terms:** cancellation fee imposed. **Amenities:** safes (fee). **Pool(s):** heated indoor. **Activities:** whirlpool, limited exercise equipment. *Fee:* game room. **Guest Services:** wireless Internet.

BELOIT pop. 35,775

BELOIT INN

Hotel
$109-$219

Phone: (608)362-5500

Address: 500 Pleasant St 53511 **Location:** Downtown. **Facility:** Smoke free premises. 54 units, some efficiencies. 4 stories, interior corridors. **Terms:** cancellation fee imposed. **Amenities:** high-speed Internet. *Some:* honor bars. **Dining:** Cafe Belwah, see separate listing. **Activities:** exercise room. **Guest Services:** complimentary laundry, area transportation, wireless Internet. **Free Special Amenities: expanded continental breakfast and high-speed Internet.**

COMFORT INN OF BELOIT

Hotel
Rates not provided

Phone: 608/362-2666

Address: 2786 Milwaukee Rd 53511 **Location:** I-90, exit 185A, just w; at I-43 and SR 81. **Facility:** Smoke free premises. 54 units. 2 stories (no elevator), interior corridors. **Parking:** winter plug-ins. **Pool(s):** heated indoor. **Activities:** whirlpool, exercise room. **Guest Services:** coin laundry, wireless Internet. **Free Special Amenities: continental breakfast and high-speed Internet.**

ECONO LODGE

Hotel
Rates not provided

Phone: 608/365-8680

Address: 3002 Milwaukee Rd 53511 **Location:** I-90, exit 185A, just sw; at I-43 and SR 81. **Facility:** Smoke free premises. 62 units. 2 stories (no elevator), interior corridors. **Parking:** winter plug-ins. **Amenities:** safes (fee). **Guest Services:** coin laundry, wireless Internet. **Free Special Amenities: expanded continental breakfast and high-speed Internet.**

FAIRFIELD INN & SUITES

Hotel
$109-$119

Phone: (608)365-2200

Address: 2784 Milwaukee Rd 53511 **Location:** I-90, exit 185A, just sw; at I-43 and SR 81. Located in a commercial area. **Facility:** Smoke free premises. 94 units. 3 stories, interior corridors. **Parking:** winter plug-ins. **Terms:** cancellation fee imposed. **Pool(s):** heated indoor. **Activities:** whirlpool, exercise room. **Guest Services:** valet and coin laundry, wireless Internet.

AAA Benefit:
Members save a minimum 5% off the best available rate.

HOLIDAY INN EXPRESS

Hotel
$99-$150 4/1-10/13
$89-$119 10/14-4/30

Phone: (608)365-6000

Address: 2790 Milwaukee Rd 53511 **Location:** I-90, exit 185A, just sw; at I-43 and SR 81. **Facility:** Smoke free premises. 73 units. 2 stories, interior corridors. **Parking:** winter plug-ins. **Amenities:** *Some:* high-speed Internet. **Pool(s):** heated indoor. **Activities:** whirlpool, exercise room. **Guest Services:** valet and coin laundry, wireless Internet.

RODEWAY INN

Motel
$44-$85

Phone: (608)364-4000

Address: 2956 Milwaukee Rd 53511 **Location:** I-90, exit 185A, 0.3 mi w. **Facility:** Smoke free premises. 77 units. 1 story, interior/exterior corridors. **Parking:** winter plug-ins. **Guest Services:** coin laundry, wireless Internet. **Free Special Amenities: continental breakfast and high-speed Internet.**

—— WHERE TO DINE ——

BUTTERFLY CLUB FINE DINING

American
$12-$29

Phone: 608/362-8577

Established in 1924, this picturesque rural restaurant features seasonal deck dining. In addition to USDA prime Angus steak, poultry and seafood, diners can try the fish fry on Wednesday and Friday. Cinnamon rolls accompany all meals. **Bar:** full bar. **Reservations:** suggested. **Hours:** 5 pm-9:30 pm, Fri 4:30 pm-10 pm, Sat 5 pm-10 pm, Sun noon-8 pm. Closed: 1/1, 7/4, 12/24, 12/25; also Mon. **Address:** 5246 E CR X 53511 **Location:** I-90, exit 185B, 1.5 mi e on I-43, exit 2, then 0.5 mi e.

CAFE BELWAH

American
$6-$28

Phone: 608/363-1110

This restaurant features a lounge and offers good food in an upscale setting. Patio seats overlooking the Rock River. **Bar:** full bar. **Hours:** 6:30-10 am, 11-2 & 5-9 pm, Fri & Sat 6:30 am-10 & 5-10 pm; Sunday brunch 7 am-1 pm. Closed major holidays. **Address:** 500 Pleasant St 53511 **Location:** Downtown; in Beloit Inn.

DOMENICO'S PIZZA & RESTAURANT

Italian
$4-$19

Phone: 608/365-9489

The downtown Italian restaurant offers pizza, steaks, ribs, seafood and pasta selections. **Bar:** full bar. **Hours:** 11 am-11 pm, Fri-midnight, Sat noon-midnight, Sun noon-10:30 pm. Closed: 12/25. **Address:** 547 E Grand Ave 53511 **Location:** Downtown. **Parking:** street only.

BERLIN pop. 5,305

COUNTRYSIDE LODGE

Motel
$74-$125

Phone: (920)361-4411

Address: 227 Ripon Rd 54923 **Location:** On SR 49, at CR F. Located in a commercial area. **Facility:** Smoke free premises. 20 units. 2 stories (no elevator), interior corridors. **Parking:** winter plug-ins. **Terms:** office hours 7 am-11 pm, cancellation fee imposed. **Activities:** exercise room. **Guest Services:** valet laundry, wireless Internet. ⊠ 🖥 / SOME UNITS FEE 🐕 🛏 🖥

—— **WHERE TO DINE** ——

JEFF'S ON THE SQUARE

American
$8-$15

Phone: 920/361-4847

Broasted chicken and fish, seafood, steaks, ribs and pizza are some of the carefully prepared items that keep locals coming back. The rich cheesecake is made in house. The restaurant may be busy at peak times. **Bar:** full bar. **Hours:** 4 pm-10 pm, Fri from 11 am. Closed major holidays; also Mon. **Address:** 116 N Capron St 54923 **Location:** Center. **Parking:** street only.

BIRCHWOOD pop. 518

COBBLESTONE BED & BREAKFAST

Bed & Breakfast
$87-$135

Phone: (715)354-3494

Address: 319 S Main St 54817 **Location:** 0.8 mi e of jct SR 48 and Main St; center. **Facility:** Smoke free premises. 5 units, some two bedrooms. 2 stories (no elevator), interior corridors. **Parking:** on-site and street. **Terms:** 8 day cancellation notice-fee imposed. **Activities:** croquet, dart board, horseshoes. **Guest Services:** wireless Internet. 🍴 ⊠ / SOME UNITS ☎

BLACK RIVER FALLS pop. 3,618

BEST WESTERN-ARROWHEAD LODGE & SUITES

Hotel
$70-$100

Phone: (715)284-9471

Address: 600 Oasis Rd 54615 **Location:** I-94, exit 116 (SR 54), just ne. **Facility:** Smoke free premises. 141 units. 2-3 stories, interior corridors. **Parking:** winter plug-ins. **Amenities:** safes (fee). **Pool(s):** heated indoor. **Activities:** whirlpool, rental paddleboats, hiking trails, jogging, exercise room. **Guest Services:** coin laundry, wireless Internet. **Free Special Amenities:** expanded continental breakfast.

AAA Benefit:
Members save up to 20%, plus 10% bonus points with free rewards program.

SAVE 🍴 🍸 CALL 🚭 M 🏊 ⊠ 🎣 🛏 📺 🖥 / SOME UNITS FEE 🐕

COMFORT INN

Hotel
$94-$134

Phone: (715)284-0888

Address: W10170 Hwy 54 E 54615 **Location:** I-94, exit 116 (SR 54), just nw. **Facility:** Smoke free premises. 75 units. 2 stories, interior corridors. **Parking:** winter plug-ins. **Amenities:** high-speed Internet. **Pool(s):** heated indoor. **Activities:** whirlpool, waterslide, exercise room. **Guest Services:** coin laundry, wireless Internet. CALL 🚭 M 🏊 BIZ ⊠ 🎣 🖥 / SOME UNITS 🛏 🖥

DAYS INN

Hotel
$57-$123

Phone: (715)284-4333

Address: 919 Hwy 54 E 54615 **Location:** I-94, exit 116 (SR 54), just w. **Facility:** Smoke free premises. 84 units. 2 stories (no elevator), interior corridors. **Parking:** winter plug-ins. **Pool(s):** heated indoor. **Activities:** sauna, whirlpool. *Fee:* game room. **Guest Services:** coin laundry, wireless Internet. 🍴 CALL 🚭 M 🏊 FEE 🎣 ⊠ 🎣 🖥 / SOME UNITS FEE 🐕 🛏 🖥

BOSCOBEL pop. 3,047

THE RIVER INN AND BANQUET FACILITY

Hotel
$66-$140

Phone: 608/375-8000

Address: 1700 Elm St 53805 **Location:** Just s on US 61. **Facility:** Smoke free premises. 40 units. 2 stories (no elevator), interior corridors. **Parking:** winter plug-ins. **Terms:** cancellation fee imposed. **Pool(s):** heated indoor. **Activities:** sauna, whirlpool, limited exercise equipment. **Guest Services:** wireless Internet, tanning facilities. CALL 🚭 M 🏊 ⊠ 🎣 / SOME UNITS 🛏 🖥 🖥

BOULDER JUNCTION pop. 958

BOULDER JUNCTION MOTOR LODGE

Motel
$55-$105

Phone: 715/385-2825

Address: 10432 Main St 54512 **Location:** Just w on CR K. **Facility:** Smoke free premises. 20 units. 1 story, interior corridors. **Parking:** winter plug-ins. **Terms:** office hours 6:30 am-10 pm, 2 night minimum stay - seasonal and/or weekends, 3 day cancellation notice-fee imposed. **Activities:** whirlpool, fish cleaning facilities. **Guest Services:** wireless Internet. 🍴 ⊠ 🛏

—— **WHERE TO DINE** ——
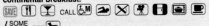

THE GUIDE'S INN
American
$15-$43

Phone: 715/385-2233

This restaurant offers Continental cuisine prepared by a chef certified by the American Culinary Association. Fresh ingredients, complimentary fresh French bread and appetizer tray, and a wide menu variety are hallmarks. **Bar:** full bar. **Hours:** 5 pm-9 pm; hours may vary. Closed: 12/24, 12/25 & Easter. **Address:** Hwy M 54512 **Location:** Just s on CR M and K.

BROOKFIELD —See Milwaukee p. 557.

BROWN DEER —See Milwaukee p. 560.

BURLINGTON pop. 9,936

AMERICINN LODGE & SUITES OF BURLINGTON

Phone: (262)534-2125

Hotel
$92-$112 4/1-8/31
$82-$102 9/1-4/30

Address: 2709 Browns Lake Dr 53105 **Location:** 3 mi n on SR 36 and 83, jct CR W. Located in a commercial area. **Facility:** Smoke free premises. 50 units, some two bedrooms and efficiencies. 2 stories (no elevator), interior corridors. **Terms:** 7 day cancellation notice. **Pool(s):** heated indoor. **Activities:** whirlpool. **Guest Services:** coin laundry, wireless Internet.

——— WHERE TO DINE ———

THE COTTONPICKER

Phone: 262/534-5151

American
$6-$42

Window tables in the country-themed dining room overlook a pretty courtyard landscape and soothing pond. The menu comprises well-prepared entrees such as prime rib, steak Oscar and roast duck. The sinful chocolate mocha cheesecake stands out among the tempting desserts. **Bar:** full bar. **Reservations:** suggested. **Hours:** 11:30 am-9:30 pm, Sun 10 am-2 & 2:30-9 pm. Closed: 11/24, 12/25; also for dinner 12/24. **Address:** 2600 S Browns Lake Dr 53105 **Location:** 3 mi n on SR 36 and 83, jct CR W.

CADOTT pop. 1,345

COUNTRYSIDE MOTEL

Phone: 715/289-4000

Motel
$60-$100

Address: 545 Lavorata Rd 54727 **Location:** SR 29, exit 91 (SR 27), just s. Located in a rural setting. **Facility:** Smoke free premises. 18 units. 1 story, interior corridors. **Parking:** winter plug-ins. **Terms:** office hours 8 am-10 pm. **Activities:** playground. **Guest Services:** wireless Internet.

CALEDONIA

——— WHERE TO DINE ———

SEBASTIANS

Phone: 262/681-5465

American
$18-$39

The family-owned-and-operated restaurant offers fine country dining in a casual atmosphere. Fresh fish, choice meats, distinctive sauces and homemade desserts are notable. Great care is given to the presentation of all courses. **Bar:** full bar. **Reservations:** suggested. **Hours:** 5 pm-9 pm, Fri & Sat-9:30 pm. Closed major holidays; also Sun. **Address:** 6025 Douglas Ave 53402 **Location:** On SR 32; jct 5 Mile Rd.

CAMERON pop. 1,546

BLACK BEAR MOTEL

Phone: (715)458-2111

Motel
$45-$60

Address: 201 S 1st St 54822 **Location:** On US 8 and CR SS. **Facility:** Smoke free premises. 20 units. 1 story, exterior corridors. **Parking:** winter plug-ins. **Terms:** cancellation fee imposed. **Guest Services:** wireless Internet.

CAMP DOUGLAS pop. 592

——— WHERE TO DINE ———

TARGET BLUFF GERMAN' HAUS

Phone: 608/427-6542

German
$6-$25

Unique hand-painted murals of castles and countryside adorn the walls of this Bavarian-themed restaurant. The menu consists of Old World German specialties as well as traditional American favorites. A few seafood dishes are also offered. **Bar:** full bar. **Hours:** 11 am-10 pm. Closed: 11/24, 12/25; also for dinner 12/24, Mon in winter. **Address:** 208 SR 12 & 16 54618 **Location:** I-90/94, exit 55, just s.

CEDARBURG —See Milwaukee p. 560.

CHILTON pop. 3,708

BEST WESTERN STANTON INN

Phone: (920)849-3600

Hotel
$75-$150

Address: 1101 E Chestnut St 53014 **Location:** Jct US 151 and SR 32/57. **Facility:** Smoke free premises. 48 units. 2 stories (no elevator), interior corridors. **Amenities:** high-speed Internet. **Pool(s):** heated indoor. **Activities:** whirlpool. *Fee:* game room. **Guest Services:** valet and coin laundry, wireless Internet. **Free Special Amenities:** continental breakfast and high-speed Internet.

AAA Benefit:
Members save up to 20%, plus 10% bonus points with free rewards program.

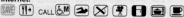

CHIPPEWA FALLS pop. 12,925

AMERICINN MOTEL & SUITES OF CHIPPEWA FALLS

Phone: (715)723-5711

Hotel
$85-$146

Address: 11 W South Ave 54729 **Location:** 2 mi s on SR 124, access via CR J. **Facility:** Smoke free premises. 61 units. 2 stories, interior corridors. **Parking:** winter plug-ins. **Terms:** cancellation fee imposed. **Pool(s):** heated indoor. **Activities:** whirlpool, waterslide. *Fee:* game room. **Guest Services:** valet laundry, wireless Internet.

COUNTRY INN & SUITES BY CARLSON

Phone: (715)720-1414

Hotel
$88-$129

Address: 1021 W Park Ave 54729 **Location:** Jct SR 124 and CR J. **Facility:** Smoke free premises. 62 units. 2 stories (no elevator), interior corridors. **Parking:** winter plug-ins. **Pool(s):** heated indoor. **Activities:** whirlpool. **Guest Services:** valet and coin laundry, wireless Internet. *(see ad p. 6)*

HOLIDAY INN EXPRESS HOTEL & SUITES

Phone: (715)723-4654

Hotel
$70-$149

Address: 12858 26th Ave 54729 **Location:** US 53, exit 94 (SR 124 N/CR 00), just e. **Facility:** Smoke free premises. 84 units. 3 stories, interior corridors. **Parking:** winter plug-ins. **Terms:** cancellation fee imposed. **Amenities:** high-speed Internet. **Pool(s):** heated indoor. **Activities:** whirlpool, exercise room. *Fee:* game room. **Guest Services:** valet and coin laundry, wireless Internet.

—— WHERE TO DINE ——

THE FILL INN STATION

Phone: 715/723-6551

American
$5-$18

This converted gas station features original brick pillars and a monkey wrench on the door. The menu consists of hand-made pizza, sandwiches and salad, prepared-to-order beef and buffalo burgers and a few Mexican dishes. **Bar:** full bar. **Hours:** 11 am-10 pm. Closed major holidays; also Sun. **Address:** 104 W Columbia St 54729 **Location:** Corner of Bay and Columbia sts; downtown.

CLINTONVILLE pop. 4,736

COBBLESTONE INN & SUITES

Phone: (715)823-2000

Hotel
$80-$110

Address: 175 Waupaca St 54929 **Location:** Jct US 45 and CR C. **Facility:** Smoke free premises. 30 units. 2 stories (no elevator), interior corridors. **Activities:** exercise room. **Guest Services:** coin laundry, wireless Internet.

COLUMBUS pop. 4,479

SUPER 8-COLUMBUS

Phone: (920)623-8800

Hotel
$61-$106

Address: 219 Industrial Dr 53925 **Location:** US 151, exit 118 (SR 16/60), just ne. **Facility:** Smoke free premises. 50 units. 3 stories, interior corridors. **Parking:** winter plug-ins. **Pool(s):** heated indoor. **Activities:** whirlpool, exercise room. **Guest Services:** coin laundry, wireless Internet.

—— WHERE TO DINE ——

CAPRI STEAK HOUSE

Phone: 920/623-4818

Steak
$6-$35

The downtown restaurant offers quality food in an old-fashioned supper club-type atmosphere. Daily specials as well as steaks and seafood are available. **Hours:** 11:30 am-1:30 & 5-9:30 pm, Fri & Sat-10 pm, Sun 4:30 pm-8:30 pm. Closed: 1/1, 11/24, 12/24, 12/25; also Mon. **Address:** 126 S Ludington 53925 **Location:** Downtown. **Parking:** street only.

CRANDON pop. 1,961

BEST WESTERN CRANDON INN & SUITES

Phone: (715)478-4000

Hotel
$90-$135

Address: 9075 E Pioneer St 54520 **Location:** 0.5 mi e on US 8 and SR 32. **Facility:** Smoke free premises. 46 units. 2 stories, interior corridors. **Parking:** winter plug-ins. **Amenities:** safes (fee). **Pool(s):** heated indoor. **Activities:** whirlpool, exercise room. **Guest Services:** coin laundry, wireless Internet. **Free Special Amenities: continental breakfast and early check-in/late check-out.**

AAA Benefit:
Members save up to 20%, plus 10% bonus points with free rewards program.

FOUR SEASONS MOTEL

Phone: 715/478-3377

Motel
$55-$80

Address: 304 W Glen St 54520 **Location:** 0.5 mi w on US 8. **Facility:** Smoke free premises. 20 units. 1 story, interior/exterior corridors. **Parking:** winter plug-ins. **Terms:** office hours 8 am-10 pm, cancellation fee imposed. **Guest Services:** wireless Internet.

CRITVITZ pop. 998

CRITVITZ LODGE

Hotel
$81-$90 4/1-10/31
$76-$85 11/1-4/30

Phone: 715/854-7014

Address: 215 Hall Ave 54114 **Location:** Just w of US 141. **Facility:** Smoke free premises. 20 units. 1 story, interior corridors. **Parking:** winter plug-ins. **Terms:** cancellation fee imposed. **Amenities:** high-speed Internet. **Activities:** exercise room. **Guest Services:** wireless Internet.

CUMBERLAND pop. 2,280

CUMBERLAND INN & SUITES

Hotel
$70-$130 4/1-9/30
$66-$120 10/1-4/30

Phone: (715)822-5655

Address: 1650 Elm St 54829 **Location:** 0.5 mi e on US 63. **Facility:** Smoke free premises. 41 units. 2 stories (no elevator), interior corridors. **Parking:** winter plug-ins. **Terms:** office hours 7 am-11 pm, 7 day cancellation notice-fee imposed. **Pool(s):** heated indoor. **Activities:** whirlpool. **Guest Services:** coin laundry, wireless Internet.

—— WHERE TO DINE ——

5 O'CLOCK CLUB

American
$14-$32

Phone: 715/822-2924

This restaurant offers a wide variety of flavorful foods in a rural and picturesque setting on a lakeshore. The dining room sports a fun nautical theme. Menu offerings range from fresh seafood and steak to pasta and Chinese fare. Homemade desserts are presented tableside on a tray. **Bar:** full bar. **Reservations:** suggested. **Hours:** 5 pm-9 pm. Closed major holidays; also Mon, Sun 9/5-5/29. **Address:** 2639 7th St 54829 **Location:** 3.5 mi n on US 63 from jct SR 48, then 0.4 mi e.

DARLINGTON pop. 2,418

SUPER 8 DARLINGTON

Hotel
$54-$86

Phone: (608)776-8830

Address: 201 Christensen Dr 53530 **Location:** On SR 81, just w of jct SR 23. **Facility:** Smoke free premises. 40 units. 2 stories (no elevator), interior corridors. **Pool(s):** heated indoor. **Activities:** whirlpool, exercise room. **Guest Services:** wireless Internet.

—— WHERE TO DINE ——

RIVERWOOD FAMILY RESTAURANT

American
$6-$13

Phone: 608/776-8910

The good family restaurant dishes up hearty portions. **Bar:** beer only. **Hours:** 6 am-9 pm, Fri & Sat-10 pm. Closed: 12/25. **Address:** 128 S Main St 53530 **Location:** Center.

DE FOREST pop. 7,368

COMFORT INN & SUITES

Hotel
$69-$129

Phone: (608)846-9100

Address: 5025 County Hwy V 53532 **Location:** I-90/94, exit 126 (CR V), just w. **Facility:** Smoke free premises. 79 units, some efficiencies. 3 stories, interior corridors. **Parking:** winter plug-ins. **Amenities:** high-speed Internet, safes (fee). **Pool(s):** heated indoor. **Activities:** whirlpool, exercise room. *Fee:* game room. **Guest Services:** valet and coin laundry, wireless Internet.

HOLIDAY INN EXPRESS

Hotel
$99-$109 4/1-11/1
$95-$105 11/2-4/30

Phone: (608)846-8686

Address: 7184 Morrisonville Rd 53532 **Location:** I-90/94, exit 126 (CR V), just e. **Facility:** Smoke free premises. 70 units. 3 stories, interior corridors. **Parking:** winter plug-ins. **Pool(s):** heated indoor. **Activities:** whirlpool, exercise room. **Guest Services:** valet and coin laundry, wireless Internet.

—— WHERE TO DINE ——

DE FOREST FAMILY RESTAURANT

American
$5-$14

Phone: 608/846-6910

The family-owned restaurant offers home cooking at a good value. Breakfast is served all day, and homemade bread and carry-out are available. **Hours:** 6 am-10 pm, Sun-9 pm. **Address:** 505 W North St 53532 **Location:** I-90/94, exit 126 (CR V), 1 mi e.

PINE CONE RESTAURANT

American
$6-$16

Phone: 608/249-8778

Easily accessed from the interstate, the restaurant is a favorite of truckers, who come in for large portions of home-style cooking. **Hours:** 24 hours. **Address:** 6162 US 51 53532 **Location:** I-94, exit 132, 0.6 mi n.

Travel Basics: Keep a AAA/CAA Atlas
in every vehicle in the household.

DELAFIELD —See Milwaukee p. 561.

DELAVAN pop. 7,956

COMFORT SUITES

Hotel
Rates not provided

Phone: 262/740-1000

Address: 313 Bauer Pkwy 53115 **Location:** I-43, exit 21 (SR 50), just w, just n, then just w. **Facility:** Smoke free premises. 80 units. 3 stories, interior corridors. **Parking:** winter plug-ins. **Amenities:** high-speed Internet, safes (fee). **Pool(s):** heated indoor. **Activities:** whirlpool, exercise room. *Fee:* game room. **Guest Services:** coin laundry, wireless Internet.

LAKE LAWN RESORT

Resort
Hotel
$79-$349

Phone: (262)728-7950

Address: 2400 E Geneva St 53115 **Location:** I-43, exit 21 (SR 50), 1 mi e. Located in a rural area. **Facility:** Water views enhance many guest rooms at this lakefront resort, which is set on sprawling, tree-covered grounds. Smoke free premises. 284 units, some efficiencies and houses. 2 stories, interior/exterior corridors. **Terms:** check-in 4 pm, 2-4 night minimum stay - seasonal and/or weekends, 3 day cancellation notice-fee imposed. **Amenities:** video games (fee). *Some:* high-speed Internet, safes, honor bars. **Pool(s):** heated outdoor, heated indoor. **Activities:** whirlpool, rental boats, rental paddleboats, fishing, lighted tennis court, ice skating, recreation programs, walking trail, aircraft runway, playground, exercise room, spa, basketball. *Fee:* sailboats, marina, cruise boat, kayaks, pontoons, golf-18 holes, miniature golf, driving range, cross country skiing, bicycles, game room. **Guest Services:** valet laundry, area transportation (fee)-within 20 mi, wireless Internet.

SKY LODGE INN & SUITES

Hotel
$59-$199

Phone: (262)728-9399

Address: 5560 SR 50 53115 **Location:** On SR 50, just se of jct CR F. **Facility:** Smoke free premises. 38 units. 2 stories (no elevator), interior corridors. **Parking:** winter plug-ins. **Pool(s):** heated indoor. **Activities:** whirlpool. *Fee:* game room. **Guest Services:** wireless Internet.

SUPER 8-DELAVAN

Hotel
$72-$126

Phone: (262)728-1700

Address: 518 Borg Rd 53115 **Location:** I-43, exit 21 (SR 50), just w. Located in a commercial area. **Facility:** Smoke free premises. 69 units. 2 stories (no elevator), interior corridors. **Parking:** winter plug-ins. **Amenities:** safes (fee). **Activities:** limited exercise equipment. **Guest Services:** coin laundry, wireless Internet.

——— WHERE TO DINE ———

MILLIE'S RESTAURANT & SHOPPING VILLAGE

American
$6-$18

Phone: 262/728-2434

On beautiful landscaped grounds with English gardens, the charming restaurant comprises five dining rooms decorated with antiques. The menu outlines Pennsylvania Dutch-style dinners, sandwiches and salads. Pancakes in various flavors are a hit among the all-day breakfast dishes. **Bar:** full bar. **Hours:** 8 am-4 pm. Closed: Tues-Fri 1/1-2/28 & Mon 9/2-6/30. **Address:** N 2484 CR O 53115 **Location:** 3.5 mi s on 2nd St (which becomes CR O); jct S Shore Dr.

DE PERE pop. 20,559

KRESS INN, AN ASCEND COLLECTION HOTEL

Hotel
$90-$110

Phone: (920)403-5100

Address: 300 Grant St 54115 **Location:** US 41, exit 163 (Main Ave), 1 mi e, then just s on 3rd St. Located on St. Norbert College campus. **Facility:** Smoke free premises. 46 units, some efficiencies. 3 stories, interior corridors. **Bath:** shower only. **Amenities:** high-speed Internet. **Activities:** limited exercise equipment. **Guest Services:** valet laundry, wireless Internet.

SLEEP INN & SUITES GREEN BAY/DE PERE

Hotel
$70-$150

Phone: (920)338-8800

Address: 1600 Lawrence Dr 54115 **Location:** US 41, exit 161. **Facility:** Smoke free premises. 76 units. 3 stories, interior corridors. **Terms:** cancellation fee imposed. **Amenities:** high-speed Internet, safes (fee). **Pool(s):** heated indoor. **Activities:** whirlpool, exercise room. **Guest Services:** valet and coin laundry, wireless Internet.

——— WHERE TO DINE ———

THE ABBEY BAR & GRILLE

American
$6-$12

Phone: 920/336-7242

More than 30 draft beers and a selection of wines pair with the tavern's burgers, classic sandwiches, salads, pizza and the pasta-vegetable skillet dish. **Bar:** full bar. **Hours:** 11 am-10 pm. Closed: 11/24, 12/25 & Easter. **Address:** 303 Reid St 54115 **Location:** Between 3rd and 4th sts; downtown.

A'S RESTAURANT & MUSIC CAFE

Phone: 920/336-2277

American
$6-$25

Ambience abounds at the welcoming spot, where musicians perform several times a week and the atmosphere evokes a French cafe. Sit down to a plate of flavor-rich Greek shrimp, rack of lamb, stuffed tenderloin or Mediterranean chicken. **Bar:** full bar. **Reservations:** suggested. **Hours:** 11 am-1:30 & 5-9:30 pm, Sat from 5 pm. Closed major holidays; also Sun & Mon. **Address:** 112 N Broadway 54115 **Location:** On east side of bridge; center.

BILOTTI'S PIZZA & ITALIAN GARDEN

Phone: 920/336-1811

Pizza
$8-$21

Named after the Bilotti family and in operation since 1956, the restaurant uses only the highest quality ingredients in the family's famous sauces and recipes. Owners take pride in their stature as the oldest Italian restaurant in Brown County. **Bar:** full bar. **Hours:** 11 am-12:30 am, Fri & Sat-1:30 am, Sun-11:30 pm. **Address:** 113 N Broadway 54115 **Location:** Just n on SR 57; downtown. **Parking:** street only.

CALIENTE-LA FIESTA MEXICANA

Phone: 920/336-8737

Mexican
$7-$12

In an older building, the corner restaurant has a cozy dining room with wood floors, a tin ceiling and booths along the window. Tempting Mexican dishes line the menu. **Bar:** full bar. **Hours:** 3 pm-11 pm; hours may vary. Closed: 11/24, 12/25. **Address:** 623 George St 54115 **Location:** Just e of bridge on CR G; downtown. **Parking:** street only.

LEGENDS BREWHOUSE & EATERY

Phone: 920/336-8036

American
$7-$16

The eatery's hand-crafted microbrews are perfect accompaniments to a good selection of comfort foods, burgers, sandwiches and salads. **Bar:** full bar. **Hours:** 11 am-10 pm, Fri & Sat-11 pm. Closed: 11/24, 12/25. **Address:** 875 Heritage Rd 54115 **Location:** From east side of bridge, 1.4 mi s on SR 57 and CR X; jct CR PP and X. CALL

UNION HOTEL

Phone: 920/336-6131

American
$8-$30

The setting is casually upscale in the restored hotel dining room. Among specials are pork hocks with bourbon gravy, stuffed Dover sole and traditional steaks. Guests can enjoy a drink in the old-style lounge while admiring the historical features of this unique hotel/restaurant. **Bar:** full bar. **Hours:** 11:30 am-1 & 5:30-9 pm, Sat from 5:15 pm, Sun 5 pm-8:30 pm; hours may vary. Closed major holidays. **Address:** 200 N Broadway 54115 **Location:** Just n on SR 57; downtown.

DODGEVILLE pop. 4,220

BEST WESTERN QUIET HOUSE & SUITES

Phone: (608)935-7739

Hotel
$70-$110

Address: 1130 N Johns St 53533 **Location:** On US 18, just e of jct SR 23. **Facility:** Smoke free premises. 39 units. 2 stories (no elevator), interior corridors. **Parking:** winter plug-ins. **Pool(s):** heated indoor/outdoor. **Activities:** whirlpool, exercise room. **Guest Services:** wireless Internet. **Free Special Amenities:** expanded continental breakfast and high-speed Internet. *(see ad p. 544)*

AAA Benefit:
Members save up to 20%, plus 10% bonus points with free rewards program.

PINE RIDGE MOTEL

Phone: 608/935-3386

Motel
$49-$85 4/1-10/31
$35-$49 11/1-4/30

Address: 405 CR YZ 53533 **Location:** 0.5 mi e of jct SR 23. Large vehicle parking on site. **Facility:** Smoke free premises. 22 units. 1 story, exterior corridors. **Parking:** winter plug-ins. **Terms:** 3 day cancellation notice-fee imposed. **Guest Services:** wireless Internet. **Free Special Amenities:** room upgrade (subject to availability with advance reservations) and high-speed Internet.

SUPER 8 OF DODGEVILLE

Phone: (608)935-3888

Hotel
$59-$79

Address: 1308 Johns St 53533 **Location:** Just n of US 18. **Facility:** Smoke free premises. 43 units. 2 stories (no elevator), interior corridors. **Parking:** winter plug-ins. **Terms:** 14 day cancellation notice. **Activities:** whirlpool, limited exercise equipment. **Guest Services:** coin laundry, wireless Internet.

FREE expanded continental breakfast and high-speed Internet

—— WHERE TO DINE ——

GOLDEN CROWN CHINESE RESTAURANT

Phone: 608/935-1717

Chinese
$6-$12

The chain restaurant offers good value and large portions; order to go or eat in. **Hours:** 11 am-9 pm, Fri & Sat-10 pm. Closed major holidays. **Address:** 1210 N Bequette St 53533 **Location:** On SR 23, just n of jct US 18.

Door County

BAILEYS HARBOR pop. 1,003

—— WHERE TO DINE ——

COYOTE ROADHOUSE

American
$7-$22

Phone: 920/839-9192

This popular tavern roadhouse welcomes families to visit for delicious steaks, ribs, fish and finger foods, which may be enjoyed inside with a drink or on the deck overlooking Kangaroo Lake. **Bar:** full bar. **Hours:** 11 am-10 pm; hours may vary. Closed: 11/24, 12/25. **Address:** 3026 County Rd "E" 54202 **Location:** 1.5 mi w of SR 57.

EGG HARBOR pop. 250

LANDMARK RESORT

Condominium
$84-$414

Phone: (920)868-3205

Address: 7643 Hillside Rd 54209 **Location:** 1 mi sw on CR G and Hillside Tr; 1 mi nw of SR 42 from jct Hillside Tr. Located on a bluff overlooking Green Bay. **Facility:** Smoke free premises. 294 kitchen units, some two and three bedrooms. 2-3 stories, interior corridors. **Terms:** check-in 4 pm, 3 day cancellation notice-fee imposed. **Pool(s):** 3 heated outdoor, heated indoor. **Activities:** whirlpools, steamrooms, 5 tennis courts (3 lighted), cross country skiing, snowmobiling, exercise room, basketball, horseshoes, shuffleboard, volleyball. **Fee:** game room. **Guest Services:** coin laundry, wireless Internet. *(see ad p. 464)*

FREE high-speed Internet and use of on-premises laundry facilities

LULL-ABI INN OF EGG HARBOR

Motel
$65-$199

Phone: (920)868-3135

Address: 7928 Egg Harbor Rd 54209 **Location:** On SR 42, just n. **Facility:** Smoke free premises. 24 units, some two bedrooms and kitchens. 2 stories (no elevator), exterior corridors. **Terms:** open 4/23-10/23, office hours 7:30 am-7:30 pm, 2 night minimum stay - weekends, 14 day cancellation notice. **Activities:** whirlpool. **Guest Services:** complimentary laundry, wireless Internet.

▼ See AAA listing p. 469 ▼

▼ See AAA listing p. 463 ▼

THE SHALLOWS

Resort Motel
$95-$425 6/24-11/1
$75-$360 4/29-6/23

Phone: (920)868-3458

Address: 7353 Horseshoe Bay Rd, Hwy G 54209 **Location:** On CR G, 2.5 mi s. Located on the shores of Green Bay. **Facility:** Views of the lake and exceptionally maintained rooms make guests want to stay and never leave. Some units have a fireplace. Smoke free premises. 34 units, some two bedrooms, efficiencies, houses and cottages. 1-2 stories (no elevator), exterior corridors. **Terms:** open 4/29-11/1, office hours 7 am-10 pm, 2-7 night minimum stay - seasonal and/or weekends, 30 day cancellation notice-fee imposed. **Amenities:** *Some:* high-speed Internet. **Pool(s):** heated outdoor. **Activities:** whirlpool, beach access, boating, canoeing, fishing, kayaks, tennis court, lakeside evening campfires, bicycles, playground, basketball. **Guest Services:** wireless Internet. *(see ad below)*

 / SOME UNITS FEE

FREE continental breakfast and high-speed Internet

—— **WHERE TO DINE** ——

TRIO RESTAURANT

Italian
$15-$25

Phone: 920/868-2090

The monthly changing menu samples a good variety of well-prepared French and Italian country "peasant" foods, all served in hearty portions. The atmosphere has the flavor and energy of an upbeat bistro. **Bar:** beer & wine. **Reservations:** suggested. **Hours:** Open 5/10-10/25; 5 pm-9 pm, Fri & Sat-9:30 pm. **Address:** 4655 CR E 54209 **Location:** On SR 42, jct CR E.

VILLAGE CAFE

American
$6-$10

Phone: 920/868-3342

Known for homemade delights, the restaurant specializes in lighter fare. Gourmet omelets and fresh fruit are popular selections from the breakfast menu. For lunch, diners favor specialty salads, burgers and sandwiches. **Bar:** beer & wine. **Hours:** 7 am-8 pm; hours may vary. **Address:** 7918 Egg Harbor Rd 54209 **Location:** On SR 42, just n of jct CR E.

▼ *See AAA listing above* ▼

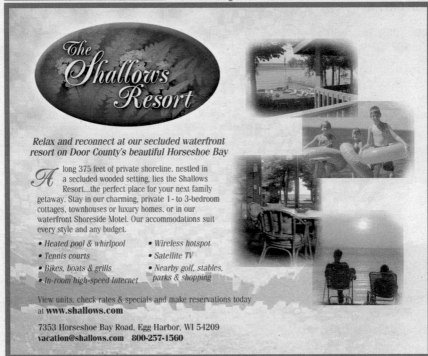

ELLISON BAY

―――― WHERE TO DINE ――――

MINK RIVER BASIN SUPPER CLUB   Phone: 920/854-2250

American
$15-$34

The menu samples a wide variety of home-style selections, ranging from fresh fish, pasta and duck to prime rib and baby back ribs. Premium wine created from Door County fruit include some non-alcoholic selections. The dessert bar is especially popular. **Bar:** full bar. **Hours:** 5 pm-8:30 pm, Sat & Sun-9:30 pm; hours vary in winter. Closed: 11/24, 12/25. **Address:** 12010 Hwy 42 54210 **Location:** On SR 42; center.

ROWLEYS BAY   Phone: 920/854-2385

American
$6-$17

Overlooking a picturesque lake, the country dining room is a quaint spot for home cooking and tempting bakery treats. Especially popular is the fish boil, offered on Saturday nights, as well as the breakfast, lunch and dinner smörgåsbords, available June through October. **Bar:** full bar. **Hours:** Open 5/15-10/15; 7:30 am-2 & 5-8 pm. **Address:** 1041 CR ZZ 54210 **Location:** 3.5 mi se on Mink River Rd; 6 mi ne of Sister Bay; in Wagon Trail Resort & Vacation Homes.

T. ASHWELL'S   Phone: 920/854-4306

American
$19-$49

Well-manicured grounds surround the contemporary high-end dining room and the screened-in dining patio. Traditional dishes prepared with a twist differ from what is common in the area. Fine steaks, lamb, pork tenderloin and seafood are often featured on the ever-changing seasonally directed menu. Fridays and Saturdays always feature something special. The wait staff is as polished and knowledgeable as it is friendly. **Bar:** full bar. **Reservations:** suggested. **Hours:** Open 5/16-2/28; 5:30 pm-9 pm; hours may vary. Closed: Tues. **Address:** 11976 Mink River Rd 54210 **Location:** Jct SR 42, just e.

EPHRAIM pop. 353

TROLLHAUGEN LODGE, B&B INN, MOTEL & LOG CABIN   Phone: 920/854-2713

Motel
$69-$169

Address: 10176 Hwy 42 54211 **Location:** 0.6 mi n of Village Hall. **Facility:** Smoke free premises. 14 units, some cabins. 1-2 stories (no elevator), interior/exterior corridors. *Bath:* shower only. **Terms:** open 5/1-10/31, office hours 7:30 am-8 pm, 2 night minimum stay - seasonal, cancellation fee imposed. **Activities:** whirlpool, hiking trails. **Guest Services:** wireless Internet. **Free Special Amenities: local telephone calls and high-speed Internet.**

FISH CREEK

HOMESTEAD SUITES   Phone: 920/868-3748

Hotel
$89-$229 4/1-10/27
$89-$169 10/28-4/30

Address: 4006 Main St 54212 **Location:** 0.3 mi n on SR 42. Located next to Peninsula State Park. **Facility:** Smoke free premises. 64 units, some condominiums. 2 stories (no elevator), interior/exterior corridors. **Terms:** office hours 7:30 am-10 pm, 2-3 night minimum stay - seasonal and/or weekends, 21 day cancellation notice-fee imposed. **Pool(s):** 2 heated outdoor, heated indoor. **Activities:** sauna, whirlpools, exercise room, game room. **Guest Services:** coin laundry, wireless Internet.

JULIE'S PARK CAFE & MOTEL   Phone: 920/868-2999

Motel
$49-$106

Address: 4020 Hwy 42 54212 **Location:** On SR 42, 0.3 mi n. Located at entrance to Peninsula State Park. **Facility:** Smoke free premises. 13 units, some two bedrooms. 1 story, exterior corridors. **Terms:** open 4/29-11/1, 2-3 night minimum stay - weekends, 10 day cancellation notice-fee imposed. **Guest Services:** wireless Internet.

SETTLEMENT COURTYARD INN & LAVENDER SPA   Phone: 920/868-3524

Hotel
$109-$399 4/1-12/31
$259-$299 1/1-4/30

Address: 9126 Hwy 42 54212 **Location:** On SR 42, 1 mi s. Located in a quiet residential area. **Facility:** Smoke free premises. 34 units, some two bedrooms, three bedrooms and houses. 2 stories (no elevator), interior corridors. **Parking:** winter plug-ins. **Terms:** 10 day cancellation notice-fee imposed. **Pool(s):** heated outdoor. **Activities:** hiking trails, horseshoes. *Fee:* massage. **Guest Services:** coin laundry, wireless Internet. **Free Special Amenities: local telephone calls and early check-in/late check-out.** *(see ad p. 467)*

THE WHITE GULL INN   Phone: (920)868-3517

Historic
Country Inn
$160-$295

Address: 4225 Main St 54212 **Location:** Just w of SR 42; center. **Facility:** The 1896 country inn has nicely-appointed guest rooms, most with a gas fireplace; phone ahead for seasonal closures. Smoke free premises. 17 units, some cottages. 1-2 stories (no elevator), interior/exterior corridors. **Terms:** office hours 7:30 am-9 pm, 2 night minimum stay - weekends, 14 day cancellation notice-fee imposed. **Dining:** restaurant, see separate listing. **Guest Services:** wireless Internet.

—— WHERE TO DINE ——

ENGLISH INN   Phone: 920/868-3076

American
$18-$35

Three attractive dining areas feature an English theme with lots of wood and beautiful stained glass. Whitefish, seafood casserole and prime rib stand out on the menu, which also lists dishes and salads for patrons with a lighter appetite. Entertainment. **Bar:** full bar. **Hours:** Open 5/3-10/31; 5 pm-9 pm; hours may vary. **Address:** 3713 Hwy 42 54212 **Location:** On SR 42, 2 mi n.

WHITE GULL INN   Phone: 920/868-3517

American
$8-$28

In an 1896 country inn appointed with period antiques, diners enjoy hearty breakfasts of cherry-stuffed French toast or traditional fish boils at dinner. Dishes such as crabmeat and wild rice salad are delicious and satisfying. Servers are pleasant. **Bar:** beer & wine. **Reservations:** suggested, for dinner. **Hours:** 7:30 am-2:30 & 5-8 pm; hours may vary. Closed: 11/24, 12/25. **Address:** 4225 Main St 54212 **Location:** Just w of SR 42; center; in The White Gull Inn. **Parking:** street only.

GILLS ROCK

HARBOR HOUSE INN   Phone: 920/854-5196

Bed & Breakfast
$129-$159

Address: 12666 SR 42 54210 **Location:** Center. Across from Weborg's Wharf. **Facility:** Smoke free premises. 12 units. 1-2 stories (no elevator), interior/exterior corridors. **Terms:** open 4/1-10/31, office hours 8 am-8 pm, 2 night minimum stay - seasonal and/or weekends, 14 day cancellation notice-fee imposed. **Activities:** sauna, whirlpool, grills, rental bicycles. **Guest Services:** wireless Internet.

MAPLE GROVE MOTEL   Phone: 920/854-2587

Motel
Rates not provided

Address: 809 SR 42 54210 **Location:** On SR 42, 0.3 mi e; 1.5 mi w of car ferry. Located in a rural area. **Facility:** Smoke free premises. 6 units, some two bedrooms. 1 story, exterior corridors. *Bath:* shower only. **Terms:** open 5/1-11/1, office hours 8 am-9 pm.

▼ See AAA listing p. 466 ▼

SISTER BAY pop. 886

COUNTRY HOUSE RESORT

Resort Motel
$72-$179

Phone: (920)854-4551

Address: 2468 Sunnyside Rd 54234 **Location:** Jct SR 42 and 57, 0.3 mi s on SR 42 to Highland Ave, just w. **Facility:** The motel features gorgeous gardens and landscaping with fountains and picnic tables on a tranquil wooded lot along the lake. Smoke free premises. 46 units. 2 stories (no elevator), exterior corridors. **Terms:** office hours 7 am-10:30 pm, 2-3 night minimum stay - seasonal and/or weekends, age restrictions may apply, 14 day cancellation notice-fee imposed. **Pool(s):** heated outdoor. **Activities:** whirlpool, boating, boat dock, fishing, bicycles, hiking trails, horseshoes, shuffleboard, volleyball. **Guest Services:** wireless Internet. *(see ad below)*

ECO SAVE 🏊 ✕ 📷 🖥 📺 / SOME UNITS FEE 🐕 📷

FREE continental breakfast and high-speed Internet

VOYAGER INN

Motel
$66-$99

Phone: 920/854-4242

Address: 10490 SR 57 54234 **Location:** Jct SR 42, 0.5 mi se. Located in a quiet area. **Facility:** Smoke free premises. 29 units. 2 stories (no elevator), interior/exterior corridors. **Terms:** open 5/6-10/30, office hours 8 am-10 pm, 14 day cancellation notice-fee imposed. **Pool(s):** heated outdoor. **Activities:** sauna, whirlpool, horseshoes. **Guest Services:** wireless Internet. 🏊 ✕ 🖥 📺

--- **WHERE TO DINE** ---

CARROLL HOUSE

Breakfast
$4-$7

Phone: 920/854-7997

The family restaurant is packed for breakfast. It's known for the ample portions it serves. **Hours:** Open 5/8-10/21; 7 am-2 pm; hours may vary. **Address:** 645 S Bayshore Dr 54234 **Location:** 0.4 mi s on SR 42.

SISTER BAY CAFE

Norwegian
$6-$21

Phone: 920/854-2429

The downtown restaurant delivers Norwegian specialties, such as lapskaus, meatballs and salmon. Entrees are attractively presented. The dining room is appointed with well-coordinated Scandinavian decor, including watercolors and flags. **Bar:** beer & wine. **Hours:** Open 4/1-10/31; 8 am-3 & 5-8:30 pm; hours may vary. **Address:** 611 N Bayshore Dr 54234 **Location:** On SR 42; downtown.

STURGEON BAY pop. 9,437

AMERICINN LODGE & SUITES OF STURGEON BAY   Phone: (920)743-5898

Hotel
$89-$179 4/1-10/31
$69-$139 11/1-4/30

Address: 622 S Ashland Ave 54235 **Location:** On SR 42/57, 0.5 mi s of jct CR C/S. **Facility:** Smoke free premises. 45 units. 2 stories, interior corridors. **Parking:** winter plug-ins. **Terms:** 2 night minimum stay - seasonal and/or weekends, cancellation fee imposed. **Pool(s):** heated indoor. **Activities:** sauna, whirlpool. **Guest Services:** coin laundry, wireless Internet.

 / SOME UNITS FEE

BEST WESTERN MARITIME INN   Phone: (920)743-7231

Hotel
$61-$121

Address: 1001 N 14th Ave 54235 **Location:** 1 mi n on Business Rt SR 42/57 at jct N 14th Ave. **Facility:** Smoke free premises. 90 units. 2 stories (no elevator), interior corridors. **Parking:** winter plug-ins. **Pool(s):** heated indoor. **Activities:** whirlpool. *Fee:* game room. **Guest Services:** valet laundry, wireless Internet. **Free Special Amenities: expanded continental breakfast and high-speed Internet.**

SAVE CALL / SOME UNITS FEE

AAA Benefit:
Members save up to 20%, plus 10% bonus points with free rewards program.

WHITE LACE INN   Phone: 920/743-1105

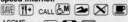
Bed & Breakfast
$70-$235

Address: 16 N 5th Ave 54235 **Location:** Between Michigan and Louisiana sts; downtown. **Facility:** Close to downtown, the Victorian-style inn has tastefully-decorated rooms situated in four historic homes; breakfast is served in the main house. Smoke free premises. 18 units. 2 stories (no elevator), interior corridors. **Terms:** office hours 7:30 am-10:30 pm, age restrictions may apply, 14 day cancellation notice-fee imposed. **Guest Services:** wireless Internet. *(see ad p. 463)*

SAVE / SOME UNITS

FREE full breakfast and high-speed Internet

———— WHERE TO DINE ————

THE NEIGHBORHOOD PUB & GRILL   Phone: 920/743-7018

American
$7-$23

The popular restaurant and pub features a wide variety of food options, including steaks, chops, pasta, pizza, grilled chicken, fish, sandwiches and salads. **Bar:** full bar. **Hours:** 11 am-10 pm, Fri & Sat-11 pm. Closed: 11/24, 12/25 & Easter. **Address:** 1407 Egg Harbor Rd 54235 **Location:** 1 mi n on Business Rt SR 42/57 at jct N 14th Ave.

The previous listings were for the Door County.
This page resumes the alphabetical listings of cities in Wisconsin.

DYCKESVILLE

———— WHERE TO DINE ————

SWEET SEASONS   Phone: 920/866-9691

American
$5-$18

The family restaurant offers home-style dishes, made-from-scratch bread and excellent thin-crust pizzas. Locals crowd this place for Sunday breakfast. **Bar:** beer & wine. **Hours:** 6 am-8 pm, Fri & Sat-9 pm. Closed: 11/24, 12/25 & Easter. **Address:** 6189 Tielens Rd 54217 **Location:** SR 57, exit CR DK/P (Dyckesville), 0.5 mi w.

EAGLE RIVER pop. 1,443

BEST WESTERN PLUS DERBY INN

Hotel
$81-$190

Address: 1800 Hwy 45 N 54521 **Location:** On US 45, 1 mi n. **Facility:** Smoke free premises. 47 units. 2 stories (no elevator), interior corridors. **Parking:** winter plug-ins. **Terms:** 2 night minimum stay - seasonal, 3 day cancellation notice. **Amenities:** high-speed Internet. **Pool(s):** heated indoor. **Activities:** sauna, whirlpool, snowmobiling. *Fee:* game room. **Guest Services:** coin laundry, wireless Internet.

Phone: (715)479-1600

AAA Benefit:
Members save up to 20%, plus 10% bonus points with free rewards program.

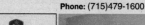

FREE expanded continental breakfast and high-speed Internet

CHANTICLEER INN

Resort
Hotel
$69-$175

Phone: 715/479-4486

Address: 1458 E Dollar Lake Rd 54521 **Location:** 2 mi e on SR 70, 0.5 mi n. Located on a chain of lakes. **Facility:** Condos, motel units and one- to three-bedroom villas are offered at this resort on a chain of lakes. Smoke free premises. 55 units, some two bedrooms, three bedrooms, efficiencies, kitchens and houses. 1-3 stories (no elevator), exterior corridors. **Parking:** winter plug-ins. **Terms:** office hours 8 am-9 pm, 2 night minimum stay - seasonal and/or weekends, cancellation fee imposed. **Activities:** beach access, rental boats, rental canoes, boat dock, fishing, tennis court, cross country skiing, snowmobiling, hiking trails, jogging, playground, basketball, volleyball. *Fee:* pontoon boat, kayaks, game room. **Guest Services:** coin laundry, wireless Internet. **Free Special Amenities: local telephone calls and high-speed Internet.**

DAYS INN

Hotel
$62-$131

Phone: (715)479-5151

Address: 844 Railroad St N 54521 **Location:** On US 45, 0.5 mi n. **Facility:** Smoke free premises. 93 units. 2 stories (no elevator), interior corridors. **Parking:** winter plug-ins. **Pool(s):** heated indoor. **Activities:** sauna, whirlpool, snowmobiling. *Fee:* game room. **Guest Services:** coin laundry, wireless Internet.

SUPER 8

Motel
$61-$122

Phone: (715)477-0888

Address: 200 W Pine St 54521 **Location:** On SR 70; center. **Facility:** Smoke free premises. 51 units. 2 stories, interior corridors. **Parking:** winter plug-ins. **Terms:** cancellation fee imposed. **Amenities:** safes (fee). **Pool(s):** heated indoor. **Activities:** sauna, whirlpool. *Fee:* game room. **Guest Services:** coin laundry, wireless Internet.

—— WHERE TO DINE ——

RIVERSTONE RESTAURANT & TAVERN

American
$10-$29

Phone: 715/479-8467

Delightful entrees, many prepared with local ingredients, delicious hearth breads and homemade desserts are good menu selections. Salads are prepared tableside by friendly staff. Wines are stored in a glass, climate-controlled wine room set off the dining area. **Bar:** full bar. **Hours:** 4:30 pm-10 pm, Sun 10 am-1 pm; hours may vary. **Address:** 219 N Railroad St 54521 **Location:** Just n on US 45; on side street.

EAST TROY pop. 3,564

COUNTRY INN & SUITES BY CARLSON

Hotel
$79-$229

Address: 2921 O'Leary Ln 53120 **Location:** I-43, exit 36, at jct SR 120. Located in a commercial residential area. **Facility:** Smoke free premises. 51 units. 2 stories (no elevator), interior corridors. **Parking:** winter plug-ins. **Terms:** cancellation fee imposed. **Pool(s):** heated indoor. **Activities:** whirlpool. **Guest Services:** valet and coin laundry, wireless Internet. *(see ad p. 6)*

Phone: (262)642-2100

—— WHERE TO DINE ——

ROMA'S RISTORANTE

Italian
$6-$30

Phone: 262/642-5353

Folks in the mood for a taste of Italian food can try fettuccine, manicotti, cannelloni, lasagna or pizza. Among other choices are veal, ribs, chicken and steak. **Bar:** full bar. **Hours:** 11 am-2 & 4-10 pm, Sat-11 pm. Closed: major holidays, 12/24; also Mon. **Address:** N8416 CR ES 53120 **Location:** I-43, exit 38, just w on CR 20, then just n.

EAU CLAIRE pop. 61,704

AMERICINN MOTEL & SUITES OF EAU CLAIRE
Phone: (715)874-4900

Hotel
$75-$175

Address: 6200 Texaco Dr 54703 **Location:** I-94, exit 59, jct US 12. **Facility:** Smoke free premises. 50 units. 2 stories, interior corridors. **Parking:** winter plug-ins. **Terms:** cancellation fee imposed. **Pool(s):** heated indoor. **Activities:** whirlpool, pool table. **Guest Services:** coin laundry, wireless Internet. **Free Special Amenities:** continental breakfast and high-speed Internet.

ANTLERS MOTEL
Phone: 715/834-5313

Motel
$56-$69

Address: 2245 S Hastings Way 54701 **Location:** Jct US 12 and Business US 53. **Facility:** Smoke free premises. 33 units. 1-2 stories (no elevator), exterior corridors. **Parking:** winter plug-ins. **Activities:** playground. **Guest Services:** wireless Internet. **Free Special Amenities:** continental breakfast and high-speed Internet.

BAYMONT INN & SUITES
Phone: (715)839-7100

Hotel
$75-$95

Address: 4075 Commonwealth Ave 54701 **Location:** I-94, exit 70, 0.8 mi n on US 53, just w on CR AA (Golf Rd), then just s. **Facility:** Smoke free premises. 87 units. 2 stories (no elevator), interior corridors. **Parking:** winter plug-ins. **Pool(s):** heated indoor. **Activities:** sauna. **Guest Services:** valet and coin laundry, wireless Internet.

BEST WESTERN PLUS TRAIL LODGE HOTEL & SUITES
Phone: (715)838-9989

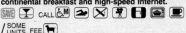
Hotel
$90-$150

Address: 3340 Mondovi Rd 54701 **Location:** I-94, exit 65, just n. **Facility:** Smoke free premises. 85 units. 3 stories, interior corridors. **Parking:** winter plug-ins. **Amenities:** *Some:* high-speed Internet. **Pool(s):** heated indoor. **Activities:** whirlpool, exercise room. *Fee:* game room. **Guest Services:** valet and coin laundry, wireless Internet. **Free Special Amenities:** expanded continental breakfast and high-speed Internet.

AAA Benefit:
Members save up to 20%, plus 10% bonus points with free rewards program.

COMFORT INN
Phone: (715)833-9798

Hotel
$59-$139

Address: 3117 Craig Rd 54701 **Location:** I-94, exit 65, 1.3 mi n on SR 37; just s of jct US 12. **Facility:** Smoke free premises. 56 units. 2 stories (no elevator), interior corridors. **Parking:** winter plug-ins. **Amenities:** high-speed Internet. **Pool(s):** heated indoor. **Activities:** whirlpool. **Guest Services:** wireless Internet.

COUNTRY INN & SUITES BY CARLSON
Phone: 715/832-7289

Hotel
Rates not provided

Address: 3614 Gateway Dr 54701 **Location:** I-94, exit 70, 0.8 mi n on US 53, then just ne on CR AA (Golf Rd). **Facility:** Smoke free premises. 58 units. 3 stories, interior corridors. **Parking:** winter plug-ins. **Amenities:** high-speed Internet. **Pool(s):** heated indoor. **Activities:** whirlpool. **Guest Services:** valet laundry, wireless Internet. *(see ad p. 6)*

DAYS INN
Phone: (715)834-3193

Hotel
$49-$80

Address: 2305 Craig Rd 54701 **Location:** I-94, exit 65, 1.3 mi n on SR 37; just w of jct US 12. **Facility:** Smoke free premises. 98 units, some kitchens. 2 stories (no elevator), interior corridors. **Parking:** winter plug-ins. **Activities:** limited exercise equipment. **Guest Services:** coin laundry, wireless Internet.

ECONO LODGE
Phone: (715)833-8818

Hotel
Rates not provided

Address: 4608 Royal Dr 54701 **Location:** I-94, exit 68, just n on SR 93, just w on Golf Rd, then just s. **Facility:** Smoke free premises. 36 units. 1 story, interior corridors. **Parking:** winter plug-ins. **Guest Services:** wireless Internet.

GRANDSTAY RESIDENTIAL SUITES
Phone: (715)834-1700

Extended Stay Hotel
$100-$169

Address: 5310 Prill Rd 54701 **Location:** I-94, exit 70, 0.8 mi n on US 53. **Facility:** Smoke free premises. 53 efficiencies, some two bedrooms. 3 stories, interior corridors. **Amenities:** high-speed Internet. **Pool(s):** heated indoor. **Activities:** whirlpool, putting green, barbecue grill, playground, exercise room, basketball. **Guest Services:** valet and coin laundry, wireless Internet. **Free Special Amenities:** continental breakfast and high-speed Internet.

HAMPTON INN
Phone: 715/833-0003

Hotel
Rates not provided

Address: 2622 Craig Rd 54701 **Location:** I-94, exit 65, 1.3 mi n on SR 37; just s of jct US 12. **Facility:** Smoke free premises. 105 units. 3 stories, interior corridors. **Amenities:** video games (fee). **Pool(s):** heated indoor. **Activities:** whirlpool, limited exercise equipment. **Guest Services:** valet laundry, wireless Internet. **Free Special Amenities:** expanded continental breakfast and high-speed Internet.

AAA Benefit:
Members save up to 10% everyday!

HOLIDAY INN CAMPUS AREA

Phone: (715)835-2211

Hotel
$70-$139

Address: 2703 Craig Rd 54701 **Location:** I-94, exit 65, 1.3 mi n on SR 37; just w of jct US 12. **Facility:** Smoke free premises. 137 units. 2 stories (no elevator), interior corridors. **Terms:** cancellation fee imposed. **Dining:** Green Mill Restaurant & Bar, see separate listing. **Pool(s):** heated indoor. **Activities:** whirlpool, exercise room. *Fee:* game room. **Guest Services:** valet and coin laundry, wireless Internet.

METROPOLIS RESORT

Phone: 715/852-6000

Boutique
Hotel
Rates not provided

Address: 5150 Fairview Dr 54701 **Location:** I-94, exit 68 (SR 93), just w. **Facility:** This family-oriented property features a waterpark. Smoke free premises. 106 units, some two bedrooms. 3 stories, interior corridors. **Amenities:** high-speed Internet, safes. **Activities:** whirlpool, waterslide, water park, exercise room. *Fee:* game room. **Guest Services:** valet laundry, wireless Internet. **Free Special Amenities: full breakfast and children's activities.**

OTTER CREEK INN

Phone: 715/832-2945

Bed & Breakfast
$110-$210

Address: 2536 Hillcrest Pkwy 54720 **Location:** US 53, exit US 12 E (Clairemont Ave), just e. **Facility:** On a hillside along Otter Creek, this English Tudor is decorated in a country-Victorian theme and features some rooms with a gas fireplace. Smoke free premises. 6 units. 3 stories (no elevator), interior corridors. *Bath:* shower only. **Terms:** check-in 4 pm, age restrictions may apply, 8 day cancellation notice. **Pool(s):** heated outdoor. **Guest Services:** wireless Internet.

THE PLAZA HOTEL & SUITES

Phone: (715)834-3181

Hotel
$79-$199

Address: 1202 W Clairemont Ave 54701 **Location:** I-94, exit 65, 1.3 mi n on SR 37; just w of jct US 12. **Facility:** Smoke free premises. 233 units. 2-4 stories, interior corridors. **Parking:** winter plug-ins. **Amenities:** *Some:* high-speed Internet. **Pool(s):** heated indoor. **Activities:** whirlpool, exercise room. *Fee:* game room. **Guest Services:** valet and coin laundry, wireless Internet.

RAMADA CONVENTION CENTER

Phone: (715)835-6121

Hotel
$62-$107

Address: 205 S Barstow St 54701 **Location:** Jct S Barstow and Gibson sts; downtown. **Facility:** Smoke free premises. 123 units. 8 stories, interior corridors. **Amenities:** safes (fee). **Pool(s):** heated indoor. **Activities:** exercise room. **Guest Services:** valet and coin laundry, area transportation, wireless Internet.

SLEEP INN & SUITES CONFERENCE CENTER

Phone: (715)874-2900

Hotel
$59-$117

Address: 5872 N 33rd Ave 54703 **Location:** SR 29, exit 69 (CR T), just sw. **Facility:** 72 units. 3 stories, interior corridors. **Parking:** winter plug-ins. **Terms:** cancellation fee imposed. **Amenities:** *Some:* high-speed Internet. **Pool(s):** heated indoor. **Activities:** whirlpool, exercise room. *Fee:* game room. **Guest Services:** coin laundry, wireless Internet.

—— **WHERE TO DINE** ——

FANNY HILL DINNER THEATRE

Phone: 715/836-8184

American
$19-$35

A quaint Victorian charm infuses the dining room, which is decorated with enchanting seasonal accents. Many windows afford panoramic river valley views. Grilled pork tenderloin stands out on a menu of creative entrees. **Bar:** full bar. **Reservations:** suggested. **Hours:** 5 pm-close, Sun 9:30 am-2 pm. Closed major holidays; also Mon-Wed. **Address:** 3919 Crescent Ave 54703 **Location:** I-94, exit 65, just n, 0.5 mi w on Short Rd, just s on Ferry St, then 1.5 mi w; in Fanny Hill.

FISCHERS' ON THE GREEN

Phone: 715/832-9711

American
$21-$44

The dining room affords a panoramic view of the golf course grounds, while the interior catches the eye with accents such as wood ceiling beams and dark wood crown molding. Served directly from a muffin tin, the popovers here are a must. Also offered are incredibly tender hand-cut dry-aged steaks, lamb chops and delectable seafood dishes, including the Alaskan king crab cake. **Bar:** full bar. **Reservations:** suggested. **Hours:** 5 pm-9 pm, Fri & Sat-10 pm. Closed major holidays; also Sun. **Address:** 2333 Hillcrest Pkwy 54720 **Location:** US 53, exit US 12 E (Clairemont Ave), 0.7 mi e; in Hillcrest Country Club.

GREEN MILL RESTAURANT & BAR

Phone: 715/839-8687

American
$8-$18

The eatery prepares top-notch pizzas; a good variety of appetizers, salads, sandwiches and pasta; and some steaks and seafood. Diablo wings are a great way to start the meal. **Bar:** full bar. **Hours:** 6 am-midnight. **Address:** 2703 Craig Rd 54701 **Location:** I-94, exit 65, 1.3 mi n on SR 37; just w of jct US 12; in Holiday Inn Campus Area.

MIKE'S SMOKEHOUSE

Phone: 715/834-8153

Barbecue
$5-$10

Locals consider the smokehouse one of the area's top barbecue joints. The plank-wood exterior makes this place resemble a roadside shack, but inside is a cozy and inviting setting. The house specialty is Texas-style barbecue, including hickory-smoked beef, ribs and chicken and fish cooked in a wood-burning oven. **Bar:** full bar. **Hours:** 11 am-9 pm, Fri & Sat-9:30 pm. Closed major holidays. **Address:** 2235 N Clairemont Ave 54703 **Location:** 1 mi n of jct US 12 and CR E. **Parking:** street only.

MILWAUKEE BURGER CO. GRILL & BAR

American
$7-$15

Phone: 715/834-6503

A visit to Wisconsin would be incomplete without a sampling of beer cheese soup and deep-fried cheese curds, both of which can be had here. Also on the menu are deep-fried pickles, hand-cut french fries with assorted seasonings, salads, sandwiches, chicken wings and burgers. Diners who can polish off the 3-pound Big Milwaukee burger in less than 30 minutes get a prize. Margaritas and beer are popular, and even classic milk shakes and malts come in "adulterated" versions. **Bar:** full bar. **Hours:** 11 am-10 pm, Sun-9 pm. Closed: 11/24, 12/25 & Easter. **Address:** 2620 E Clairemont Ave 54701 **Location:** Just w of US 53 and 12. CALL &M

MONA LISA'S RESTAURANT
Italian
$7-$24

Phone: 715/839-8969

In historic downtown, the trendy restaurant prepares creative and contemporary Italian cuisine, which contrasts with the decor: wood floors and lofty high ceilings from a century ago. Local markets and friends' gardens provide inspiration for the weekly menu. Fish, pasta and meat dishes are interpreted with flair. Guests can order from an extensive list of martinis or choose from among a good variety of wines by the glass. **Bar:** full bar. **Hours:** 4 pm-10 pm. Closed: 1/1, 11/24, 12/24, 12/25; also Sun & Mon. **Address:** 428 Water St 54703 **Location:** At 5th Ave; downtown. **Parking:** street only.

NORTHWOODS PUB & GRILL

American
$6-$23

Phone: 715/552-0510

Bustling with activity and the happy laughter of friends out for a good time, the local pub proudly features homemade beers and sodas. The thematic decor incorporates canoes, wood beams and artifacts reminiscent of Alaska. The menu suggests culinary explorations of elk, deer and buffalo steaks, while trout, walleye and salmon complete the Nordic feast. Well-known American fare is also featured. **Bar:** full bar. **Hours:** 7 am-10 pm, Fri & Sat-11 pm, Sun 8 am-8 pm. Closed: 11/24, 12/25. **Address:** 3560 Oakwood Mall Dr 54701 **Location:** I-94, exit 70, just nw; at end of Oakwood Mall.

RANDY'S FAMILY RESTAURANT
American
$6-$12

Phone: 715/839-8449

Family operated for more than 40 years, the nice, casual restaurant serves generous portions of tasty comfort foods, including an extensive selection of tempting fresh pies. Each meal, including the daily specials, is accompanied by a complimentary cup of warm, homemade vanilla pudding. Breakfast is served all day. **Hours:** 6 am-9 pm, Fri & Sat-10 pm. Closed major holidays; also Sun. **Address:** 1132 W MacArthur Ave 54701 **Location:** I-94, exit 65, 1.3 mi n on SR 37; just s of jct US 12. CALL &M

SWEETWATERS RESTAURANT & BAR

American
$8-$25

Phone: 715/834-5777

Preparations of seafood, steak and pasta are attractively presented. The casual setting offers seating conducive to small groups, families and couples, in addition to seasonal tables outdoors. **Bar:** full bar. **Reservations:** suggested. **Hours:** 11 am-9 pm, Fri-10 pm, Sat 4 pm-10 pm, Sun 4 pm-9 pm. Closed: 12/25. **Address:** 1104 W Clairemont Ave 54701 **Location:** Just w of jct US 12 and SR 37.

EDGERTON pop. 4,933

COMFORT INN

Hotel
$79-$129

Phone: (608)884-2118

Address: 11102 N Goede Rd 53534 **Location:** I-90, exit 163, just e. **Facility:** Smoke free premises. 50 units. 2 stories (no elevator), interior corridors. **Parking:** winter plug-ins. **Terms:** cancellation fee imposed. **Pool(s):** heated indoor. **Activities:** whirlpool. **Guest Services:** coin laundry, wireless Internet. CALL &M ⊠ ✕ ▣ ▤ / SOME UNITS FEE 🐾 ▤ ▣

EGG HARBOR —See Door County p. 463.

ELKHART LAKE pop. 1,021

THE OSTHOFF RESORT

Resort Condominium
$210-$720 4/1-9/30
$190-$530 10/1-4/30

Phone: (920)876-3366

Address: 101 Osthoff Ave 53020 **Location:** 0.5 mi w of SR 67 via CR A/J, 0.4 mi nw. Located in a rural area. **Facility:** All accommodations at this rural, family-oriented resort are contemporary in style and offer balconies and gas fireplaces; some have lake views. Smoke free premises. 241 units, some two bedrooms, three bedrooms and efficiencies. 4 stories, interior corridors. **Parking:** on-site and valet. **Terms:** check-in 4 pm, 2-4 night minimum stay - seasonal and/or weekends, cancellation fee imposed. **Amenities:** video games (fee), high-speed Internet. **Dining:** 2 restaurants, also, Lola's on the Lake, see separate listing. **Pool(s):** 2 heated outdoor, heated indoor. **Activities:** saunas, whirlpools, rental boats, rental canoes, rental paddleboats, fishing, tennis court, cross country skiing, ice skating, recreation programs, bocci, rental bicycles, hiking trails, jogging, exercise room, spa, basketball, volleyball. **Fee:** sailboats, waterskiing, game room. **Guest Services:** valet and coin laundry, area transportation-within village, wireless Internet. *(see ad p. 545)*

SAVE ECO FEE ✈ ⊤⊦ ▽ 🛌 ⊠ BIZ ✕ ▤ ▣ ▤ ▣

FREE newspaper and high-speed Internet

VICTORIAN VILLAGE RESORT

Phone: 920/876-3323

Resort
Hotel
Rates not provided

Address: 276 Victorian Village Dr 53020 **Location:** SR 23, exit 67, 0.6 mi w of SR 67 via CR A/J, then 0.4 mi nw. **Facility:** Amid extensively landscaped grounds on the banks of Elkhart Lake, the hotel offers a variety of guest rooms and condominium units. Smoke free premises. 65 units, some two bedrooms, three bedrooms, kitchens and houses. 2-4 stories, interior/exterior corridors. **Terms:** Office hours 6 am-midnight, check-in 4 pm. **Dining:** entertainment. **Pool(s):** heated outdoor, heated indoor. **Activities:** whirlpool, beach access, rental boats, rental canoes, rental paddleboats, boat dock, waterskiing, fishing, playground. **Guest Services:** valet laundry, wireless Internet.

---- WHERE TO DINE ----

LOLA'S ON THE LAKE

Phone: 920/876-5840

American
$11-$29

The gorgeous, sophisticated dining spot has lovely modern chandeliers, elegant floral arrangements, tabletops draped in crisp white linen and excellent lake views. The patio dining area is inviting in season. The menu features upscale haute cuisine with fine steaks, fish, lamb, bison, seafood, free-range chicken and Berkshire pork. The wait staff is polished and attentive. **Bar:** full bar. **Reservations:** suggested. **Hours:** 11 am-9 pm, Fri & Sat-10 pm, Sun 9 am-9 pm. **Address:** 101 Osthoff Ave 53020 **Location:** 0.5 mi w of SR 67 via CR A/J, 0.4 mi nw; in The Osthoff Resort.

ELKHORN pop. 7,305

AMERICINN LODGE & SUITES OF ELKHORN

Phone: (262)723-7799

Hotel
$92-$112 4/1-8/31
$82-$102 9/1-4/30

Address: 210 E Commerce Ct 53121 **Location:** I-43, exit 25, just s. Located in a commercial area. **Facility:** Smoke free premises. 57 units, some two bedrooms, efficiencies and kitchens. 2 stories, interior corridors. **Parking:** winter plug-ins. **Pool(s):** heated indoor. **Activities:** whirlpool, exercise room. **Guest Services:** coin laundry, wireless Internet.

HAMPTON INN ELKHORN

Phone: (262)743-2360

Hotel
$99-$149 4/1-9/30
$89-$129 10/1-4/30

Address: 40 W Hidden Trail Dr 53121 **Location:** Jct SR 67/12, just s. **Facility:** Smoke free premises. 64 units. 3 stories, interior corridors. **Terms:** 1-7 night minimum stay, cancellation fee imposed. **Amenities:** high-speed Internet. **Pool(s):** heated indoor. **Activities:** whirlpool, exercise room. **Guest Services:** valet laundry, wireless Internet.

> **AAA Benefit:**
> Members save up to 10% everyday!

ELLISON BAY —See Door County p. 466.

EPHRAIM —See Door County p. 466.

FIFIELD

---- WHERE TO DINE ----

NORTHWOODS SUPPER CLUB

Phone: 715-762-4447

American
$4-$20

Generous portions of traditional favorites, such as succulent prime rib, are what the family-oriented restaurant is all about. The Saturday prime rib buffet and Friday night fish fry are popular offerings, as are the wholesome and flavorful homemade soups. **Bar:** full bar. **Reservations:** suggested. **Hours:** 4:30 pm-9 pm; hours may vary off season. Closed: 12/24, 12/25; also Sun. **Address:** N14066 S Flambeau Ave 54524 **Location:** Jct SR 13 and 70.

FISH CREEK —See Door County p. 466.

FITCHBURG

CANDLEWOOD SUITES

Phone: (608)271-3400

Extended Stay
Hotel
$99-$129

Address: 5421 Caddis Bend 53711 **Location:** US 12/18, exit 260 (Fish Hatchery/CR D), 1.5 mi s. **Facility:** Smoke free premises. 79 kitchen units. 4 stories, interior corridors. **Terms:** cancellation fee imposed. **Amenities:** high-speed Internet. **Pool(s):** heated indoor. **Activities:** whirlpool. **Guest Services:** complimentary and valet laundry, wireless Internet.

QUALITY INN & SUITES

Phone: (608)274-7200

Hotel
$89-$149

Address: 2969 Cahill Main 53711 **Location:** US 12/18, exit 260 (Fish Hatchery/CR D), 1.5 mi s at CR PD (McKee Rd). **Facility:** Smoke free premises. 107 units. 4 stories, interior corridors. **Amenities:** high-speed Internet, safes (fee). **Dining:** Tuscany Mediterranean Grill, see separate listing. **Pool(s):** heated indoor. **Activities:** whirlpool, exercise room. **Fee:** game room. **Guest Services:** valet and coin laundry, area transportation-within 2 mi, wireless Internet.

—— WHERE TO DINE ——

BENVENUTO'S ITALIAN GRILL

Italian
$6-$20

Phone: 608/278-7800

The casual eatery's menu comprises Italian and American fare, including gourmet calzones, pasta, ribs, wood-fired pizza, meatball sandwiches, steaks, mushroom and mozzarella burgers, walleyed pike and popcorn shrimp. **Bar:** full bar. **Hours:** 11 am-10 pm. Closed: 11/24, 12/24, 12/25. **Address:** 2949 Triverton Pike Dr 53711 **Location:** Just w of jct CR D (Fish Hatchery Rd) and PD (McKee Rd).

PANCAKE CAFE

American
$7-$11

Phone: 608/204-7040

The newly built, upscale cafe prepares great breakfasts and sandwiches. High-quality ingredients include grade AA extra-large eggs, sausage prepared from a custom recipe, freshly-squeezed orange and grapefruit juices and Hawaiian Kona coffee. **Hours:** 7 am-2 pm, Fri & Sat-8 pm, Sun-3 pm. Closed: 11/24, 12/25. **Address:** 6220 Nesbitt Rd 53719 **Location:** US 12/14 (Beltline), exit 258 (Verona Rd), 1.8 mi s to CR PDW (McKee Rd), just w to Nesbitt Rd, then 0.5 mi s. CALL

TUSCANY MEDITERRANEAN GRILL

Italian
$6-$32

Phone: 608/270-1684

The sophisticated grill is one of the city's newest fine-dining establishments. Seafood, steak, pizza and regional cuisine make up the menu. **Bar:** full bar. **Hours:** 5 pm-10 pm. Closed major holidays. **Address:** 2969 Cahill Main 53711 **Location:** US 12/18, exit 260 (Fish Hatchery/CR D), 1.5 mi s at CR PD (McKee Rd); in Quality Inn & Suites. CALL

FOND DU LAC pop. 42,203

COMFORT INN FOND DU LAC

Hotel
$70-$210

Phone: (920)921-4000

Address: 77 Holiday Ln 54937 **Location:** US 41, exit 97 (Military Rd), just sw. Located in a commercial area. **Facility:** Smoke free premises. 78 units. 2 stories (no elevator), interior corridors. **Parking:** winter plug-ins. **Terms:** cancellation fee imposed. **Amenities:** safes (fee). **Pool(s):** heated indoor. **Activities:** whirlpool, exercise room. **Fee:** game room. **Guest Services:** valet and coin laundry, area transportation-within 10 mi, wireless Internet.

COUNTRY INN & SUITES BY CARLSON

Hotel
$99-$259

Phone: (920)924-8800

Address: 121 Merwin Way 54937 **Location:** US 41, exit 97 (Military Rd), just w to Rolling Meadows, then just n. Located in a commercial area. **Facility:** Smoke free premises. 65 units, some two bedrooms. 3 stories, interior corridors. **Parking:** winter plug-ins. **Amenities:** high-speed Internet. **Pool(s):** heated indoor. **Activities:** whirlpool, exercise room. **Guest Services:** valet and coin laundry, wireless Internet. *(see ad p. 6)* CALL

EXECUTIVE LODGE OF FOND DU LAC

Hotel
$49-$89

Phone: 920/923-2020

Address: 649 W Johnson St 54935 **Location:** US 41, exit 99 (Johnson St), 0.3 mi e on SR 23. Located in a commercial area. **Facility:** Smoke free premises. 48 units. 2 stories (no elevator), interior corridors. **Parking:** winter plug-ins (fee). **Pool(s):** heated indoor. **Activities:** whirlpool. **Guest Services:** valet laundry, wireless Internet.

HOLIDAY INN

Hotel
$119-$329 7/18-4/30
$119-$179 4/1-7/17

Phone: (920)923-1440

Address: 625 W Rolling Meadows Dr 54937 **Location:** US 41, exit 97 (Military Rd), just sw. Located in a commercial area. **Facility:** Smoke free premises. 139 units. 2 stories (no elevator), interior corridors. **Parking:** winter plug-ins. **Amenities:** Some: high-speed Internet. **Pool(s):** heated indoor. **Activities:** whirlpool, indoor recreational area, exercise room, shuffleboard. **Fee:** game room. **Guest Services:** valet and coin laundry, area transportation-within 10 mi, wireless Internet.

MICROTEL INN & SUITES

Hotel
$58-$114

Phone: (920)929-4000

Address: 920 S Military Rd 54935 **Location:** US 41, exit 97 (Military Rd). Located in a commercial area. **Facility:** Smoke free premises. 79 units. 3 stories, interior corridors. **Activities:** whirlpool, limited exercise equipment. **Guest Services:** valet laundry, wireless Internet.

RAMADA PLAZA HOTEL

Historic
Hotel
$69-$269

Phone: (920)923-3000

Address: 1 N Main St 54935 **Location:** Jct E Division St, 0.3 mi s of SR 23; downtown. Located in the business district. **Facility:** This renovated 1923 hotel has luxurious public spaces. Smoke free premises. 132 units. 8 stories, interior corridors. **Pool(s):** heated indoor. **Activities:** sauna, whirlpool, exercise room. **Guest Services:** valet laundry, wireless Internet.

SUPER 8-FOND DU LAC

Hotel
$45-$162

Phone: (920)922-1088

Address: 391 N Pioneer Rd 54935 **Location:** US 41, exit 99 (SR 23), just n on east frontage road (CR VV). Located in a commercial area. **Facility:** Smoke free premises. 45 units. 2 stories (no elevator), interior corridors. **Parking:** winter plug-ins. **Terms:** 3 day cancellation notice-fee imposed. **Amenities:** safes. **Guest Services:** coin laundry, wireless Internet.

—— **WHERE TO DINE** ——

COOL RIVER GRILLE   **Phone:** 920/922-4696

American
$6-$17

Diners can watch their favorite sport while dining on a sandwich and drink of choice at this sports bar and grill. **Bar:** full bar. **Hours:** 11 am-10 pm, Thurs-Sat to 11 pm. Closed major holidays. **Address:** 99 W Pioneer Rd 54935 **Location:** 1.1 mi e of jct US 151 and CR W (Pioneer Rd).

FRIAR TUCK'S   **Phone:** 920/921-4027

American
$6-$16

"Ye hearty" sandwiches are prepared on a choice of many fresh breads baked in house. Daily homemade soup is also popular. All appetizers are prepared in the deep "friar." Servers are dressed in brown monks' garb. **Bar:** full bar. **Hours:** 11 am-10 pm, Fri & Sat-11 pm. Closed major holidays; also for dinner 12/24. **Address:** 570 W Johnson St 54935-3132 **Location:** On SR 23, 1 mi e of jct US 41.

GINO'S ITALIAN   **Phone:** 920/906-9999

Italian
$6-$18

This popular restaurant features Chicago-style pizza as well as dishes such as fettuccine Alfredo, tortellini carbonara, chicken cacciatore and shrimp scampi, all served in a warm, cozy, relaxed environment. **Bar:** full bar. **Hours:** 11 am-10 pm. Closed major holidays; also for dinner 12/24. **Address:** 584 W Johnson St 54935-3132 **Location:** On SR 23, 1 mi e of jct US 41.

ROLLING MEADOWS FAMILY RESTAURANT   **Phone:** 920/922-9140

American
$7-$16

The menu covers a broad territory, with an extensive selection of sandwiches, salads and soups, all-day breakfast choices and steak, seafood and Italian entrees. Desserts are homemade. The Friday night fish fry and weekend prime rib specials are popular. **Bar:** full bar. **Hours:** 6 am-9 pm. Closed: 11/24. **Address:** 947 S Rolling Meadows Dr 54937 **Location:** Just nw of jct US 41 and 151.

SCHREINER'S RESTAURANT   **Phone:** 920/922-0590

American
$6-$18

This popular restaurant has been serving up homestyle meals of comfort food since 1938. The in-house bakery produces fresh desserts daily, and diners can get breakfast all day. Tours of the kitchen are available upon request. **Bar:** full bar. **Hours:** 6:30 am-8 pm. Closed: 11/24, 12/25 & Easter. **Address:** 168 N Pioneer Rd 54935 **Location:** Jct US 41 and SR 23.

FONTANA pop. 1,600

—— **WHERE TO DINE** ——

**GORDY'S BOAT HOUSE BAR & RESTAURANT &
COBALT LOUNGE**   **Phone:** 262/275-6800

American
$7-$22
CALL

Across the street from the marina, this nautical restaurant presents an extensive menu of excellent lunch and dinner fare. **Bar:** full bar. **Hours:** Open 4/2-10/31; 11 am-9 pm. **Address:** 336 Lake Ave 53125 **Location:** On west shore of Lake Geneva, 0.5 mi e of SR 67 (Valley View Dr). **Parking:** street only.

FORT ATKINSON pop. 11,621

HOLIDAY INN EXPRESS HOTEL & SUITES   **Phone:** (920)563-3600

Hotel
$104-$194

Address: 1680 Madison Ave 53538 **Location:** Jct SR 26 Bypass and US 12. **Facility:** Smoke free premises. 78 units. 3 stories, interior corridors. **Parking:** winter plug-ins. **Pool(s):** heated indoor. **Activities:** whirlpool, exercise room. *Fee:* game room. **Guest Services:** valet and coin laundry, wireless Internet. CALL

—— **WHERE TO DINE** ——

CHINA BUFFET   **Phone:** 920/563-6000

Chinese
$6-$14

The all-you-can-eat buffet offers a large selection of Chinese, Japanese and American items along with a salad bar and a dessert bar. Guests also can order directly from the menu. **Bar:** beer & wine. **Hours:** 10:30 am-10 pm, Fri & Sat-11 pm, Sun 11 am-10 pm. Closed major holidays. **Address:** 1525 Janesville Ave 53538 **Location:** 2 mi s on SR 26 business route. CALL

FORT ATKINSON FAMILY RESTAURANT   **Phone:** 920/563-6324

American
$6-$12

On the south side of town, the local favorite offers a good variety of American homestyle dishes at reasonable prices. **Hours:** 5 am-9 pm. Closed major holidays. **Address:** 1620 Janesville Ave 53538 **Location:** 2.5 mi s on SR 26 business route.

SALAMONE'S   **Phone:** 920/563-9213

Pizza
$6-$23

Delicious deep-dish and thin-crust pizzas are made from fresh ingredients at the family-owned restaurant. Some traditional dishes, including pasta and sausage with marinara sauce, are also listed on the dinner menu. Italian background music and beautiful murals add to the ambience. A brew pub is adjacent. **Bar:** full bar. **Hours:** 4 pm-10 pm, Fri & Sat-11 pm. Closed major holidays; also Tues. **Address:** 1245 Madison Ave 53538 **Location:** On US 12; just nw of downtown.

FOX POINT —See Milwaukee p. 561.

FRANKLIN —See Milwaukee p. 562.

FRIENDSHIP pop. 698

—— **WHERE TO DINE** ——

FAMILY AFFAIR RESTAURANT

Phone: 608/339-9747

American
$6-$17

Lake views from the dining room lend to a relaxed atmosphere. Locals favor this popular restaurant for a great breakfast menu and homemade soups. **Bar:** beer only. **Hours:** 7 am-8 pm, Fri & Sat-9 pm; to 7 pm, Fri & Sat-8 pm 12/1-4/30. Closed: 11/24, 12/25. **Address:** 208 N Main St 53934 **Location:** 0.5 mi n on SR 13. CALL &M 🔧

GENESEE DEPOT —See Milwaukee p. 562.

GERMANTOWN —See Milwaukee p. 562.

GILLS ROCK —See Door County p. 467.

GLENDALE —See Milwaukee p. 563.

GRAFTON —See Milwaukee p. 564.

GRANTSBURG pop. 1,369

WOOD RIVER MOTEL

Phone: 715/463-2541

Motel
$68-$125

Address: 703 W SR 70 54840 **Location:** 1 mi w on SR 70. **Facility:** Smoke free premises. 21 units. 2 stories (no elevator), exterior corridors. **Parking:** winter plug-ins. **Terms:** office hours 6:30 am-10 pm, 3 day cancellation notice-fee imposed. **Guest Services:** coin laundry, wireless Internet. **Free Special Amenities:** local telephone calls and high-speed Internet.

SAVE 📶 CALL &M ⊠ / SOME UNITS FEE 🛒 🔒 🖥

GREEN BAY pop. 102,313

✈ Airport Accommodations

OA	AUSTIN STRAUBEL INTERNATIONAL AIRPORT	Diamond Rated	High Season	Page
AAA	Airport Settle Inn, 1 mi e of airport	◆◆	$71-$189 SAVE	477
AAA	Airport Wingate by Wyndham, at entrance to airport	◆◆◆	$81-$170 SAVE	477
AAA	Extended Stay Airport, 1 mi e of airport	◆◆	$60-$75 SAVE	479
AAA	Radisson Hotel & Conference Center, across from airport	◆◆◆	$115-$199 SAVE	480

AIRPORT SETTLE INN

Phone: (920)499-1900

◆◆
Hotel
$71-$189

Address: 2620 S Packerland Dr 54313 **Location:** US 41, exit 165, 1 mi w on SR 172, then just s on CR EB. **Facility:** Smoke free premises. 115 units. 2 stories, interior corridors. **Parking:** winter plug-ins. **Terms:** cancellation fee imposed. **Pool(s):** heated indoor. **Activities:** whirlpool, exercise room. *Fee:* game room. **Guest Services:** valet laundry, area transportation-casino, wireless Internet.

SAVE ✈ 📶 🏊 BIZ ⊠ 🍴 / SOME UNITS 🔒 🖥

AIRPORT WINGATE BY WYNDHAM

Phone: (920)617-2000

◆◆◆
Hotel
$81-$170

Address: 2065 Airport Dr 54313 **Location:** US 41, exit 165, 2 mi w on SR 172. Opposite a casino. **Facility:** Smoke free premises. 80 units. 3 stories, interior corridors. **Amenities:** video games (fee), high-speed Internet, safes. **Activities:** whirlpool, exercise room. **Guest Services:** valet and coin laundry, wireless Internet. **Free Special Amenities: expanded continental breakfast and high-speed Internet.** SAVE ✈ 📶 BIZ ⊠ 🍴 🔒 🖥 💻

ALOFT GREEN BAY

Contemporary
Hotel
$89-$189

Phone: (920)884-0800

Address: 465 Pilgrim Way 54304 **Location:** US 41, exit 163B, just e. **Facility:** Smoke free premises. 105 units. 4 stories, interior corridors. *Bath:* shower only. **Terms:** cancellation fee imposed. **Amenities:** high-speed Internet, safes. **Pool(s):** heated indoor. **Activities:** whirlpool, billiards, outdoor courtyard, exercise room. **Guest Services:** valet and coin laundry, wireless Internet. **Free Special Amenities: high-speed Internet and airport transportation.**

AAA Benefit:
Enjoy the new twist, get up to 15% off Starwood Preferred Guest® bonuses.

AMERICINN LODGE & SUITES GREEN BAY EAST

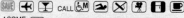
Hotel
Rates not provided

Phone: 920/964-0177

Address: 2628 Manitowoc Rd 54311 **Location:** I-43, exit 181, just w. **Facility:** Smoke free premises. 67 units. 3 stories, interior corridors. **Amenities:** high-speed Internet. **Pool(s):** heated indoor. **Activities:** sauna, whirlpool, waterslide, exercise room. **Guest Services:** coin laundry, wireless Internet.

AMERICINN LODGE & SUITES OF GREEN BAY WEST

Hotel
Rates not provided

Phone: 920/434-9790

Address: 2032 Velp Ave 54303 **Location:** US 41, exit 170, 0.3 mi w. **Facility:** Smoke free premises. 81 units. 3 stories, interior corridors. **Parking:** winter plug-ins. **Pool(s):** heated indoor. **Activities:** whirlpool, exercise room. **Guest Services:** coin laundry, wireless Internet.

THE ASTOR HOUSE

Historic Bed
& Breakfast
$99-$179

Phone: (920)432-3585

Address: 637 S Monroe Ave 54301 **Location:** On SR 57, just s of jct SR 54. **Facility:** This restored 1888 home, close to downtown and Lambeau Field, has modern amenities such as gas fireplaces and in-room whirlpools. Smoke free premises. 5 units. 3 stories (no elevator), interior corridors. **Terms:** check-in 4 pm, age restrictions may apply, 14 day cancellation notice-fee imposed. **Amenities:** *Some:* high-speed Internet. **Guest Services:** wireless Internet.

BAYMONT INN-GREEN BAY

Hotel
$53-$284

Phone: (920)494-7887

Address: 2840 S Oneida St 54304 **Location:** US 41, exit 164 (Oneida St), just e. **Facility:** Smoke free premises. 77 units. 2 stories (no elevator), interior corridors. **Parking:** winter plug-ins. **Terms:** cancellation fee imposed. **Amenities:** video games. **Guest Services:** wireless Internet.

BAY MOTEL

Motel
$49-$70

Phone: 920/494-3441

Address: 1301 S Military Ave 54304 **Location:** US 41, exit 167 (Lombardi Ave), 0.4 mi to Marlee, then 0.6 mi n. **Facility:** Smoke free premises. 53 units. 1 story, exterior corridors. **Parking:** winter plug-ins. **Dining:** Bay Family Restaurant, see separate listing. **Guest Services:** wireless Internet. **Free Special Amenities: newspaper and high-speed Internet.**

BEST WESTERN GREEN BAY INN

Hotel
$59-$399

Phone: (920)499-3161

Address: 780 Armed Forces Dr 54304 **Location:** US 41, exit 167 (Lombardi Ave), 1.4 mi e to Holmgren Way, then just s. **Facility:** Smoke free premises. 145 units. 2 stories (no elevator), interior corridors. **Amenities:** *Some:* high-speed Internet. **Pool(s):** heated indoor. **Activities:** sauna, whirlpool. *Fee:* game room. **Guest Services:** valet and coin laundry, wireless Internet. **Free Special Amenities: expanded continental breakfast and high-speed Internet.**

AAA Benefit:
Members save up to 20%, plus 10% bonus points with free rewards program.

CAMBRIA SUITES-LAMBEAU FIELD

Hotel
$99-$399

Phone: (920)569-8500

Address: 1011 Tony Canadeo Run 54304 **Location:** US 41, exit 167 (Lombardi Ave), 1.7 mi e, then just s. **Facility:** Smoke free premises. 127 units. 5 stories, interior corridors. **Terms:** cancellation fee imposed. **Amenities:** high-speed Internet. **Pool(s):** indoor/outdoor. **Activities:** whirlpool, exercise room. **Guest Services:** valet and coin laundry, wireless Internet.

CLARION HOTEL

Hotel
$89-$109 1/1-4/30
$79-$99 4/1-12/31

Phone: (920)437-5900

Address: 200 Main St 54301 **Location:** Jct Adams St; downtown. Opposite Washington Commons. **Facility:** Smoke free premises. 146 units. 7 stories, interior corridors. **Amenities:** video games. **Pool(s):** heated indoor. **Activities:** sauna, whirlpool, exercise room. **Guest Services:** complimentary and valet laundry, wireless Internet.

COMFORT INN BY CHOICE HOTELS

Hotel
$69-$159

Phone: (920)498-2060

Address: 2841 Ramada Way 54304 **Location:** US 41, exit 164 (Oneida St), just e to Ramada Way, then just n. **Facility:** Smoke free premises. 60 units. 2 stories (no elevator), interior corridors. **Parking:** winter plug-ins. **Amenities:** safes (fee). **Pool(s):** heated indoor. **Activities:** whirlpool. **Guest Services:** valet laundry, wireless Internet.

COMFORT SUITES

Phone: (920)499-7449

Hotel
$95-$300

Address: 1951 Bond St 54303 **Location:** US 41, exit 169 (SR 29/Shawano), just e, 0.5 mi n on Taylor St, then just w. **Facility:** Smoke free premises. 116 units. 2 stories, interior corridors. **Terms:** 3 day cancellation notice. **Amenities:** video games (fee), high-speed Internet, safes. **Pool(s):** heated outdoor, heated indoor. **Activities:** whirlpools, waterslide, indoor water park, exercise room. **Guest Services:** valet and coin laundry, wireless Internet. **Free Special Amenities: full breakfast and airport transportation.**

COUNTRY INN & SUITES BY CARLSON

Phone: (920)336-6600

Hotel
$99-$150

Address: 2945 Allied St 54304 **Location:** US 41, exit 164 (Oneida St), just nw. Located next to a bowling alley. **Facility:** Smoke free premises. 75 units. 2 stories, interior corridors. **Parking:** winter plug-ins. **Terms:** 3 day cancellation notice-fee imposed. **Pool(s):** heated indoor. **Activities:** whirlpool, sun deck, limited exercise equipment. *Fee:* game room. **Guest Services:** valet and coin laundry, wireless Internet. *(see ad p. 6)*

COUNTRY INN & SUITES BY CARLSON EAST

Phone: (920)288-0101

Hotel
$89-$259

Address: 850 Keplern Dr, Suite A 54311 **Location:** I-43, exit 183 (Mason St), just e. Located in an office park. **Facility:** Smoke free premises. 106 units. 3 stories, interior corridors. **Parking:** winter plug-ins. **Terms:** cancellation fee imposed. **Amenities:** high-speed Internet. **Pool(s):** heated indoor. **Activities:** whirlpool, sun deck, exercise room. *Fee:* game room. **Guest Services:** valet and coin laundry, wireless Internet. *(see ad p. 6)*

DAYS INN-LAMBEAU FIELD

Phone: (920)498-8088

Hotel
$54-$224

Address: 1978 Holmgren Way 54304 **Location:** US 41, exit 167 (Lombardi Ave), 1.4 mi e, then just s. **Facility:** 77 units. 2 stories (no elevator), interior corridors. **Parking:** winter plug-ins. **Amenities:** high-speed Internet. **Pool(s):** heated indoor. **Activities:** whirlpool, exercise room. **Guest Services:** coin laundry, wireless Internet.

ECONO LODGE INN & SUITES

Phone: 920/494-8790

Hotel
Rates not provided

Address: 2815 Ramada Way 54304 **Location:** US 41, exit 164 (Oneida St), just e to Ramada Way, then just n. **Facility:** Smoke free premises. 78 units. 2 stories (no elevator), interior corridors. **Parking:** winter plug-ins. **Pool(s):** heated indoor. **Activities:** whirlpool. *Fee:* game room. **Guest Services:** coin laundry, wireless Internet.

EXTENDED STAY AIRPORT

Phone: (920)499-3600

Hotel
$60-$75

Address: 1639 Commanche Ave 54313 **Location:** US 41, exit 165, 1 mi w on SR 172, then just s. **Facility:** Smoke free premises. 76 efficiencies. 2 stories, interior corridors. **Parking:** winter plug-ins. **Guest Services:** valet and coin laundry, area transportation-casino, wireless Internet. **Free Special Amenities: high-speed Internet and airport transportation.**

FAIRFIELD INN BY MARRIOTT

Phone: (920)497-1010

Hotel
$114-$119

Address: 2850 S Oneida St 54304 **Location:** US 41, exit 164 (Oneida St), just e. **Facility:** Smoke free premises. 62 units. 3 stories, interior corridors. **Terms:** cancellation fee imposed. **Pool(s):** heated indoor. **Activities:** whirlpool, exercise room. **Guest Services:** valet laundry, wireless Internet.

AAA Benefit:
Members save a minimum 5% off the best available rate.

HAMPTON INN GREEN BAY

Phone: (920)498-9200

Hotel
$89-$269

Address: 2840 Ramada Way 54304 **Location:** US 41, exit 164 (Oneida St), just e. **Facility:** Smoke free premises. 114 units. 4 stories, interior corridors. **Terms:** 1-7 night minimum stay, cancellation fee imposed. **Amenities:** video games (fee). **Pool(s):** heated indoor. **Activities:** whirlpool, exercise room. **Guest Services:** valet laundry, wireless Internet.

AAA Benefit:
Members save up to 10% everyday!

HILTON GARDEN INN

Phone: (920)405-0400

Hotel
$89-$107

Address: 1015 Lombardi Ave 54304 **Location:** US 41, exit 167 (Lombardi Ave), 1.6 mi e. **Facility:** Smoke free premises. 123 units. 5 stories, interior corridors. **Terms:** 1-7 night minimum stay, cancellation fee imposed. **Amenities:** high-speed Internet. **Pool(s):** heated indoor. **Activities:** whirlpool, exercise room. **Guest Services:** valet and coin laundry, wireless Internet.

AAA Benefit:
Members save 5% or more everyday!

HOLIDAY INN & SUITES - GREEN BAY STADIUM

Phone: (920)569-4248

Hotel
$99-$139

Address: 2785 Ramada Way 54304 **Location:** US 41, exit 164 (Oneida St), just e. **Facility:** Smoke free premises. 118 units. 4 stories, interior corridors. **Amenities:** high-speed Internet, safes. **Pool(s):** heated indoor. **Activities:** whirlpool, sun deck, exercise room. **Guest Services:** valet and coin laundry, area transportation-within 5 mi, wireless Internet.

HOTEL SIERRA GREEN BAY

Phone: (920)432-4555

Hotel
$79-$399

Address: 333 Main St 54301 **Location:** Between Adams and Madison sts; downtown. **Facility:** Smoke free premises. 241 units. 8 stories, interior corridors. **Amenities:** high-speed Internet. **Pool(s):** heated indoor. **Activities:** sauna, whirlpool, steamroom, exercise room. *Fee:* massage. **Guest Services:** valet and coin laundry, wireless Internet. **Free Special Amenities: full breakfast and high-speed Internet.** [SAVE] 🚫 🍴 🍽 CALL 🔐M 🏊 ✕ 🎬 🔌 📠 🖥

QUALITY INN & SUITES

Phone: (920)437-8771

Hotel
$59-$300

Address: 321 S Washington St 54301-4214 **Location:** On east side of Fox River, just s of Walnut St (SR 29); downtown. **Facility:** Smoke free premises. 100 units, some kitchens. 2 stories, interior corridors. **Parking:** winter plug-ins. **Amenities:** high-speed Internet, safes (fee). **Pool(s):** heated indoor. **Activities:** whirlpool, putting green, exercise room, game room. **Guest Services:** valet and coin laundry, wireless Internet. 🚫 🍴 🏊 ✕ 🎬 🔌 📠 🖥 🖥 / SOME UNITS 🐾

RADISSON HOTEL & CONFERENCE CENTER

Phone: (920)494-7300

Hotel
$115-$199

Address: 2040 Airport Dr 54313 **Location:** US 41, exit 165, 2 mi w on SR 172. Connected to a casino. **Facility:** Smoke free premises. 387 units. 3-6 stories, interior corridors. **Terms:** cancellation fee imposed. **Amenities:** video games (fee), high-speed Internet. **Dining:** 3 restaurants. **Pool(s):** heated indoor. **Activities:** sauna, whirlpool, exercise room. *Fee:* game room. **Guest Services:** valet laundry, area transportation-within 5 mi, wireless Internet. *(see ad below)*

[SAVE] 🚫 🍴 🍽 🏊 BIZ ✕ 🎬 🖥 / SOME UNITS FEE 📞 FEE 🖥

FREE local telephone calls and high-speed Internet

Create complete trip routings and custom place maps
with the TripTik® Travel Planner on AAA.com or CAA.ca

RAMADA PLAZA HOTEL & CONFERENCE CENTER

Hotel
S71-S215

Phone: (920)499-0631

Address: 2750 Ramada Way 54304 **Location:** US 41, exit 164 (Oneida St), just e. **Facility:** Smoke free premises. 145 units. 5 stories, interior corridors. **Terms:** check-in 4 pm, 2-3 night minimum stay - seasonal and/or weekends. **Amenities:** *Fee:* video games, safes. **Pool(s):** heated indoor. **Activities:** sauna, whirlpool, waterslide, indoor water park, exercise room, game room. **Guest Services:** valet laundry, area transportation-within 5 mi, wireless Internet. *(see ad below)*

FREE preferred room (subject to availability with advance reservations) and high-speed Internet

RESIDENCE INN BY MARRIOTT

Extended Stay
Hotel
$143-$183

Phone: (920)435-2222

Address: 335 W St. Joseph St 54301 **Location:** SR 172, exit Riverside Dr, 1.1 mi n on SR 57, then just e. **Facility:** Smoke free premises. 96 kitchen units, some two bedrooms. 2 stories (no elevator), exterior corridors. **Terms:** cancellation fee imposed. **Amenities:** high-speed Internet. **Pool(s):** heated outdoor. **Activities:** whirlpool, exercise room, sports court. **Guest Services:** valet and coin laundry, wireless Internet.

AAA Benefit:
Members save a minimum 5% off the best available rate.

SUBURBAN EXTENDED STAY HOTEL

Extended Stay
Hotel
$69-$199

Phone: (920)430-7040

Address: 1125 E Mason St 54301 **Location:** US 41, exit 168 (Mason St), 4 mi e. **Facility:** Smoke free premises. 86 efficiencies. 3 stories, interior corridors. **Terms:** check-in 4 pm. **Amenities:** high-speed Internet. **Activities:** exercise room. **Guest Services:** complimentary laundry, wireless Internet.

SUPER 8

Hotel
$44-$175

Phone: (920)494-2042

Address: 2868 S Oneida St 54304 **Location:** US 41, exit 164 (Oneida St), just e. **Facility:** Smoke free premises. 83 units. 2 stories (no elevator), interior corridors. **Parking:** winter plug-ins. **Amenities:** high-speed Internet. **Activities:** sauna, whirlpool. **Guest Services:** valet and coin laundry, wireless Internet.

SUPER 8 GREEN BAY I-43

Hotel
$44-$116

Phone: (920)406-8200

Address: 2911 Voyager Dr 54311 **Location:** I-43, exit 183 (Mason St), just e. Located in an office park. **Facility:** Smoke free premises. 60 units. 2 stories (no elevator), interior corridors. **Terms:** 30 day cancellation notice-fee imposed. **Amenities:** safes (fee). **Pool(s):** heated indoor. **Activities:** sauna, whirlpool, exercise room. **Guest Services:** valet laundry, wireless Internet.

▼ See AAA listing above ▼

TRAVELODGE GREEN BAY/LAMBEAU

Hotel
$53-$179

Phone: (920)499-3599

Address: 2870 Ramada Way 54304 **Location:** US 41, exit 164 (Oneida St), just e. **Facility:** Smoke free premises. 102 units. 2 stories (no elevator), interior corridors. **Activities:** exercise room. **Guest Services:** coin laundry, wireless Internet.

—— WHERE TO DINE ——

BAY FAMILY RESTAURANT

American
$6-$14

Phone: 920/494-3441

The casual restaurant is popular for its menu of reasonably priced food and friendly service. Breakfast is served all day, and the menu includes salads, deluxe burgers and sandwiches, as well as standard fare. **Bar:** full bar. **Hours:** 6 am-8 pm, Sun-3 pm. Closed: 11/24, 12/25; also for dinner 12/24 & 1/1. **Address:** 1301 S Military Ave 54304 **Location:** US 41, exit 167 (Lombardi Ave), 0.4 mi e to Marlee, then 0.6 mi n; in Bay Motel.

BRETT FAVRE'S STEAKHOUSE

American
$13-$26

Phone: 920/499-6874

You'll find this restaurant close to Lambeau Field, where many of the football pictures that decorate the walls were taken. Here they offer a selection of steaks, prime rib, seafood, pasta, poultry and a few Southern dishes. Fish fry on Friday nights. **Bar:** full bar. **Hours:** 4 pm-10 pm, Sat from 3 pm, Sun 3 pm-9 pm. Closed: 11/24, 12/25. **Address:** 1004 Brett Favre Pass 54304 **Location:** US 41, exit 167 (Lombardi Ave), 1.6 mi e; behind Hilton Garden Inn.

EVES SUPPER CLUB

American
$10-$40

Phone: 920/435-1571

Overlooking the Fox River, the casual restaurant affords great fourth-floor views. Steak and seafood specialties include tenderloin, rib-eye and walnut-crusted baked salmon. For dessert, try one of the cheesecakes. Service is friendly and efficient. **Bar:** full bar. **Hours:** 11 am-2 & 5-close, Sat from 5 pm. Closed major holidays; also Sun. **Address:** 2020 Riverside Dr 54301 **Location:** 1 mi n on SR 57 from jct SR 172.

GRAZIES PASTA COMPANY

Italian
$7-$17

Phone: 920/499-6365

This restaurant has a neighborhood bar and offers wraps, wood-fired pizza and pasta made from scratch for dishes such as seafood pescatore with sautéed shrimp and scallops. **Bar:** full bar. **Hours:** 11 am-10 pm, Fri & Sat-11 pm. Closed: 11/24, 12/25 & Easter. **Address:** 2851 S Oneida St 54304 **Location:** US 41, exit 164 (Oneida St), just e.

JULIE'S CAFE & CATERING

American
$4-$10

Phone: 920/494-4585

The casual restaurant overlooks a small lake with a water fountain. The dining room has high raftered ceilings and a country ambience. The universal menu features many sandwiches, wraps, pasta and primarily breakfast items. **Bar:** full bar. **Hours:** 5 am-9 pm. Closed: 11/24, 12/25. **Address:** 2130 Velp Ave 54303 **Location:** US 41, exit 170, 0.4 mi w.

KROLL'S WEST

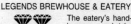

American
$4-$11

Phone: 920/497-1111

On the west side of the stadium, the restaurant has been serving its "Kroll's hamburgers" since 1931 and now also offers a good selection of traditional meals. **Bar:** full bar. **Hours:** 10:30 am-midnight, Fri & Sat-1 am. Closed major holidays. **Address:** 1990 S Ridge Rd 54304 **Location:** US 41, exit 167 (Lombardi Ave), 0.8 mi e, then just e.

LEGENDS BREWHOUSE & EATERY

American
$7-$16

Phone: 920/339-8970

The eatery's hand-crafted microbrews are perfect accompaniments to a good selection of comfort foods, burgers, sandwiches and salads. **Bar:** full bar. **Hours:** 11 am-10 pm, Fri & Sat-11 pm. Closed: 11/24, 12/25. **Address:** 940 Waube Ln 54304 **Location:** US 41, exit 164 (Oneida St), just w. CALL ⑤M

LEGENDS BREWHOUSE & EATERY

American
$7-$16

Phone: 920/662-1111

The eatery's hand-crafted microbrews are perfect accompaniments to a good selection of comfort foods, burgers, sandwiches and salads. **Bar:** full bar. **Hours:** 11 am-10 pm, Fri & Sat-11 pm. Closed: 11/24, 12/25. **Address:** 2840 Shawano Ave 54313 **Location:** US 41, exit 169 (Shawano Ave), 1.2 mi w on SR 29 and 32, then 0.5 mi n on CR J. CALL ⑤M

LORELIE

German
$5-$16

Phone: 920/432-5921

A limited selection of German dishes—plus well-seasoned steak—are listed on the family-operated restaurant's menu. The place is filled with locals, who enjoy catching up with their friends at other tables. The service is friendly and efficient. **Bar:** full bar. **Hours:** 11:30 am-1:30 & 5-9:30 pm, Sat from 5 pm. Closed major holidays; also Sun. **Address:** 1412 S Webster Ave 54301 **Location:** 1.8 mi n from jct SR 172.

LOS BANDITOS EAST

Mexican
$6-$18

Phone: 920/432-9462

The downtown restaurant is well known for its Mexican dishes and friendly service. **Bar:** full bar. **Hours:** 11 am-10 pm, Fri & Sat-11 pm, Sun 4 pm-10 pm. Closed major holidays. **Address:** 1258 Main St 54302 **Location:** 2.1 mi e of downtown on US 141/SR 29.

LOS BANDITOS WEST

Mexican
$6-$18

Phone: 920/494-4505

Just west of US 41, this eatery is well known for its Mexican dishes. **Bar:** full bar. **Hours:** 11:30 am-11:30 pm, Sun 4 pm-10 pm. Closed major holidays. **Address:** 2335 W Mason St 54303 **Location:** US 41, exit 168 (Mason St), just w.

MACKINAWS GRILL & SPIRITS

American
$7-$27

Phone: 920/406-8000

The rustic restaurant presents an extensive menu that lists a little something for everyone, or so it claims. Bands perform every Friday in the cabin bar. **Bar:** full bar. **Hours:** 11 am-10 pm, Sun from 9 am. Closed: 1/1, 11/24, 12/25. **Address:** 2925 Voyager Dr 54311 **Location:** I-43, exit 183 (Mason St).

MANDARIN GARDEN

Chinese
$6-$12

Phone: 920/499-4459

This well-established restaurant has been serving reasonably priced Chinese dishes for many years. **Bar:** full bar. **Hours:** 11 am-3 & 4:30-9:30 pm, Fri & Sat-10 pm, Sun 4:30 pm-9 pm. Closed: 12/25. **Address:** 2394 S Oneida St 54304 **Location:** US 41, exit 164 (Oneida St), 1.2 mi ne.

MARTY'S BOSTON CRAB

Seafood
$10-$45

Phone: 920/884-2722

Not far from Lambeau Field, this restaurant highlights everything to celebrate about fish. "Marty's Specialties" include salmon, mahi mahi, swordfish or Cajun-marinated catfish. For those who aren't so fish-friendly, the menu features some steaks and poultry items. **Bar:** full bar. **Hours:** 4 pm-10 pm. Closed: 11/24, 12/25. **Address:** 875 Lombardi Ave 54304 **Location:** US 41, exit 167 (Lombardi Ave), 2 mi e. CALL

PRIME QUARTER STEAKHOUSE

American
$12-$25

Phone: 920/498-8701

Grill your own USDA choice steak over a live hickory charcoal grill. All dinners include unlimited salad bar, baked potato, and Texas style toast. **Bar:** full bar. **Hours:** 5 pm-10 pm, Sat from 4 pm, Sun 4 pm-9 pm. Closed major holidays. **Address:** 2610 S Oneida St 54304 **Location:** US 41, exit 164 (Oneida St), 0.6 mi ne.

ROZZI'S ITALIAN DELI

Deli
$7-$9

Phone: 920/434-6717

This small, mom-and-pop Italian deli is located in a small shopping complex and offers freshly made sandwiches with meats from a wide selection. All the sandwiches are made with provolone cheese, tomatoes, onions, lettuce, mayonnaise and Italian dressing and include a small pasta side salad or fresh soup of the day. Guests can place orders to go or eat at one of the limited tables. **Hours:** 10:30 am-7:30 pm, Sat-4 pm, Sun-3 pm. Closed: 12/25 & Easter. **Address:** 2450 Velp Ave 54304 **Location:** US 41, exit 170, 1 mi w; in Glendale Crossing Shopping Center.

SAMMY'S PIZZA AND RESTAURANT

Italian
$7-$21

Phone: 920/499-6644

The family business has been serving pizzas in the area since 1958. The menu also lists a large selection of delicious-tasting dishes made from recipes created at home. **Bar:** full bar. **Hours:** 11 am-10:30 pm, Fri-12:30 am. Closed: 11/24, 12/25 & Easter. **Address:** 2161 S Oneida St 54304 **Location:** US 41, exit 164 (Oneida St), 1.9 mi ne.

TASTE OF INDIA
Indian
$8-$12

Phone: 920/338-9200

This casual restaurant prepares a broad choice of vegetarian and non-vegetarian dishes, many of which can be enjoyed from the lunch buffet. **Bar:** full bar. **Hours:** 11:30 am-3 & 5-10 pm; hours may vary. Closed: Mon. **Address:** 930 Waube Ln 54304 **Location:** US 41, exit 164 (Oneida St), just w.

TEN-0-ONE
American
$6-$21

Phone: 920/432-9787

It shouldn't be hard to find this corner restaurant, which is decorated with a bit of Green Bay nostalgia and serves a wide variety of menu offerings, from sandwiches, steaks and prime rib to fresh seafood, pasta and Mexican dishes. **Bar:** full bar. **Hours:** 11 am-10 pm, Fri-11 pm, Sun 4 pm-10 pm; hours may vary. Closed: 11/24, 12/25 & Easter. **Address:** 1001 Main St 54302 **Location:** Just e of downtown on US 141/SR 29.

TITLETOWN BREWING COMPANY
American
$8-$20

Phone: 920/437-2337

The microbrewery serves hand-crafted ales and root beer as well as delicious dishes and tempting specials. An 85-foot clock tower, hardwood floors and historical artwork decorate the restored 1899 train depot. **Bar:** full bar. **Hours:** 11 am-10 pm; hours may vary. Closed: 11/24, 12/25. **Address:** 200 Dousman St 54303 **Location:** On SR 29; west end of Fox River Bridge, just w of downtown.

THE WELLINGTON RESTAURANT

Phone: 920/499-2000

American
$18-$36

On the edge of town, the restaurant is known as a great place for steak. Also on the menu is a selection of fresh seafood, pork and poultry. The relaxing ambience is highlighted by an English motif, soft background music and large windows overlooking the lawn. **Bar:** full bar. **Reservations:** suggested. **Hours:** 5 pm-9 pm. Closed major holidays; also Sun. **Address:** 1060 Hansen Rd 54304 **Location:** US 41, exit 164 (Oneida St), 0.5 mi ne, then 0.5 mi w.

GREENFIELD —See Milwaukee p. 564.

GREEN LAKE pop. 1,100

BAY VIEW MOTEL & RESORT

Phone: 920/294-6504

Motel
$65-$245

Address: 439 Lake St 54941 **Location:** 0.3 mi se. **Facility:** Smoke free premises. 17 units, some efficiencies. 1 story, exterior corridors. **Parking:** winter plug-ins. **Terms:** office hours 8 am-10 pm, 2 night minimum stay - seasonal and/or weekends, 14 day cancellation notice-fee imposed. **Activities:** rental boats, boat dock, fishing. *Fee:* pontoon boats. **Guest Services:** wireless Internet.

HEIDEL HOUSE RESORT & SPA

Phone: (920)294-3344

Resort
Hotel
$99-$609

Address: 643 Illinois Ave 54941 **Location:** 1.4 mi s of jct SR 23/73 (S Futon St/CR D) and CR A, 0.7 mi e. Across from Tuscumbia Golf Course. **Facility:** The entire family will find plenty of activities at this four-season resort, situated on 20 acres of wooded lakefront land. Smoke free premises. 190 units. 2-4 stories, interior/exterior corridors. **Terms:** 2 night minimum stay - seasonal and/or weekends, 3 day cancellation notice. **Dining:** 3 restaurants. **Pool(s):** heated outdoor, heated indoor. **Activities:** sauna, whirlpools, limited beach access, rental boats, rental paddleboats, fishing, 2 tennis courts, exercise room, spa. *Fee:* boat tours, pontoons. **Guest Services:** valet and coin laundry, area transportation (fee)-within 10 mi, wireless Internet. *(see ad below)*

FREE preferred room (subject to availability with advance reservations) and high-speed Internet

LAKESIDE MOTEL

Phone: (920)294-3318

Motel
$70-$150

Address: 488 South St 54941 **Location:** Just w of downtown on Business Rt SR 23. **Facility:** Smoke free premises. 15 units. 1 story, interior/exterior corridors. **Parking:** winter plug-ins. **Terms:** open 5/1-10/30, cancellation fee imposed.

▼ *See AAA listing above* ▼

——— WHERE TO DINE ———

NORTON'S OF GREEN LAKE

American
$6-$32

Phone: 920/294-6577

Overlooking Green Lake, this eatery has a nautical theme. Evening fare features Canadian Walleye, salmon, assorted shellfish, chicken, chops, steak and pasta. Homemade soup and salad are included with many entrees. Lunch menu offers wide variety of finger foods, sandwiches and burgers. Patio seating for lunch. Boat docking available. **Bar:** full bar. **Hours:** 5 pm-close, Fri-Sun also 11:30 am-2:30 pm; seasonal hours may vary. Closed: 12/25; also for dinner 12/24, Mon & Tues. **Address:** 380 S Lawson Dr 54941 **Location:** 0.7 mi w on Business Rt SR 23. CALL 🅼

HARTFORD —See Milwaukee p. 564.

HAYWARD pop. 2,129

AMERICINN OF HAYWARD

Hotel
$85-$195

Phone: (715)634-2700

Address: 15601 US Hwy 63 54843 **Location:** Just n of jct SR 77. **Facility:** Smoke free premises. 42 units. 2 stories, interior corridors. **Parking:** winter plug-ins. **Pool(s):** heated indoor. **Activities:** sauna, whirlpool. **Fee:** pool table. **Guest Services:** wireless Internet.

COMFORT SUITES

Hotel
$99-$199

Phone: (715)634-0700

Address: 15586 CR B 54843 **Location:** 0.5 mi s of jct SR 27. **Facility:** Smoke free premises. 60 units. 2 stories, interior corridors. **Parking:** winter plug-ins. **Amenities:** high-speed Internet, safes (fee). **Pool(s):** heated indoor. **Activities:** sauna, whirlpool, rental paddleboats, boat dock, fishing, sun deck, cross country skiing, snowmobiling, barbecue grills, exercise room. **Fee:** game room. **Guest Services:** coin laundry, wireless Internet.

EDELWEISS MOTEL

Motel
$39-$105

Phone: 715/634-4679

Address: Hwy 27 S & Park Rd 54843 **Location:** On SR 27, 1.8 mi s of jct US 63. **Facility:** Smoke free premises. 8 units. 1 story, exterior corridors. **Parking:** winter plug-ins. **Guest Services:** valet laundry, wireless Internet.

THE FLAT CREEK INN & SUITES

Hotel
$87-$165 4/1-10/31
$77-$137 11/1-4/30

Phone: (715)634-4100

Address: 10290 Hwy 27 S 54843 **Location:** On SR 27 S, 0.7 mi s of jct US 63. **Facility:** Smoke free premises. 66 units. 2 stories, interior corridors. **Terms:** 2 night minimum stay - seasonal and/or weekends. **Pool(s):** heated indoor. **Activities:** whirlpool, access to snowmobile trails, snowmobile parking. **Fee:** game room. **Guest Services:** wireless Internet. **Free Special Amenities:** full breakfast and high-speed Internet.

GRAND PINES RESORT

Resort Cottage
$79-$465

Phone: 715/462-3564

Address: 9993 N Grand Pines Ln 54843 **Location:** 8.5 mi e on CR B. **Facility:** Handcrafted furniture completes the eclectic and North Woods-theme decor of these cabins and motel units. Smoke free premises. 32 units, some cottages. 1-2 stories (no elevator), exterior corridors. **Terms:** 2-7 night minimum stay - seasonal and/or weekends, 30 day cancellation notice-fee imposed. **Amenities:** Some: high-speed Internet. **Activities:** limited beach access, rental boats, fishing, pontoon, snowmobile trail, playground. **Fee:** game room.

ROSS' TEAL LAKE LODGE AND TEAL WING GOLF CLUB

Cabin
$170-$350

Phone: 715/462-3631

Address: 12425 N Ross Rd 54843 **Location:** On SR 77, 20 mi ne of jct US 63. Located in Chequamegon-Nicolet National Forest. **Facility:** This family-owned lakefront resort features a challenging golf course. Smoke free premises. 18 cabins. 1-2 stories, exterior corridors. **Parking:** winter plug-ins. **Terms:** 21 day cancellation notice-fee imposed. **Pool(s):** heated outdoor. **Activities:** sauna, rental boats, rental canoes, boat dock, fishing, driving range, cross country skiing, snowshoeing, bocci, croquet, bicycles, hiking trails, jogging, playground, horseshoes, shuffleboard, volleyball. **Fee:** fishing instruction & guide service, hydro bikes, pontoon boats, golf-18 holes, golf instruction, game room. **Guest Services:** coin laundry, wireless Internet.

SUPER 8

Hotel
$47-$133

Phone: (715)634-2646

Address: 10444 N SR 27 54843 **Location:** On SR 27, 0.3 mi s of jct US 63. **Facility:** Smoke free premises. 45 units. 1-2 stories (no elevator), interior/exterior corridors. **Parking:** winter plug-ins. **Pool(s):** heated indoor. **Activities:** whirlpool. **Guest Services:** wireless Internet.

——— WHERE TO DINE ———

CHIPPEWA INN

German
$14-$36

Phone: 715/462-3648

In a quiet, secluded location on the Chequamegon-Nicolet National Forest scenic drive, the restaurant delivers a mixture of American dishes—such as charbroiled Kansas City dry-aged steaks, chops, ribs and seafood—and German specialties of Wiener schnitzel, bratwurst, sauerbraten and potato pancakes. This place is known for its relish tray, which features assorted fresh vegetables, pickled vegetables, herring and cheese spread. **Bar:** full bar. **Reservations:** suggested. **Hours:** 5 pm-10 pm; seasonal hours vary. Closed: Tues. **Address:** 9702 N CR B 54843 **Location:** Jct CR A, 15 mi e. CALL 🅼

CLUB 77

American
$12-$30

Phone: 715/462-3712

Just outside of town, this well-known restaurant features excellent food served in a casual, unpretentious setting. Unlike most restaurants, this one provides diners a tray of crudités, a cheese fondue and diced bread for dipping. Locals and out-of-towners frequent this place for hearty meals. **Bar:** full bar. **Reservations:** suggested. **Hours:** Open 5/25-9/6; 5 pm-9 pm; hours may vary. **Address:** 12695 E State Hwy 77 54843 **Location:** On SR 77, 7 mi e. CALL ⓈM

COOPER'S FAMILY RESTAURANT

American
$5-$15

Phone: 715/634-8850

The popular eatery is known for its breakfasts, as well as its hearty portions and good value. **Hours:** 5:30 am-8 pm. Closed: 12/25. **Address:** 10604 Beal Ave 54843 **Location:** Jct SR 27 and Beal Ave. CALL ⓈM

THE NORSKE NOOK

Norwegian
$5-$13

Phone: 715/634-4928

This quaint, renowned restaurant serves homemade Norwegian dishes in addition to sandwiches and breakfast. The on-premises bakery produces fresh bread and an excellent selection of pies. Seasonally changing menus include lefse specialties. **Hours:** 5:30 am-8 pm, Sun from 7 am. Closed: 12/25 & Easter. **Address:** Hwy 27 S 54843 **Location:** 0.3 mi s of jct US 63. CALL ⓈM

OLD HAYWARD EATERY AND BREW PUB

American
$7-$23

Phone: 715/934-2337

Locally owned and operated, the restaurant entices guests with freshly brewed beer, Italian entrees, homemade soups, pizza from a wood-fired oven and nightly dinner specials such as the Friday night fish fry. Access to this place is convenient. **Bar:** full bar. **Hours:** 11 am-10 pm. Closed: 11/24, 12/25. **Address:** 15546 CR B 54843 **Location:** 1 mi e of jct US 63/SR 27.

HAZELHURST pop. 1,267

——— WHERE TO DINE ———

JACOBI'S OF HAZELHURST

Continental
$16-$31

Phone: 715/356-5591

This intimate restaurant is easily recognized by its pastel house-like exterior with beautiful seasonal flower landscaping. A complimentary appetizer is served. Soup, bread and dessert are all made in-house. Try the signature garlic-stuffed beef filet. **Bar:** full bar. **Hours:** 5 pm-9 pm, Sat-10 pm; hours may vary. Closed: Sun & Mon 10/15-5/1. **Address:** 9820 Cedar Falls Rd 54531 **Location:** 0.3 mi s on US 51, 0.3 mi w on Oneida St.

HILLSBORO pop. 1,302

HOTEL HILLSBORO

Hotel
$80-$125 4/1-11/30
$75-$110 12/1-4/30

Phone: 608/489-3000

Address: 1235 Water Ave (Hwy 33) 54634 **Location:** SR 33 and 80/82, just w. **Facility:** Smoke free premises. 44 units. 2 stories (no elevator), interior corridors. **Terms:** cancellation fee imposed. **Amenities:** high-speed Internet. **Pool(s):** heated indoor. **Activities:** whirlpool, patios, limited exercise equipment. **Guest Services:** coin laundry, wireless Internet. **Free Special Amenities: continental breakfast and high-speed Internet.**

SAVE ⒯⒧ ⓨ CALL ⓈM ⌖ ✕ ▦ ▢ / SOME UNITS FEE 🐾 ▯ ▭

HOWARDS GROVE pop. 2,792

——— WHERE TO DINE ———

LOG CABIN RESTAURANT

American
$4-$23

Phone: 920/565-2712

The third-generation-family-owned restaurant gets nods for its hearty portions and friendly service. An outdoor seating area opens seasonally. **Bar:** full bar. **Hours:** 11 am-8:30 pm. Closed major holidays. **Address:** 633 Madison Ave 53083 **Location:** Jct SR 32 and Madison Ave, just e. CALL ⓈM

HUBERTUS —See Milwaukee p. 564.

HUDSON pop. 8,775

BEST WESTERN PLUS HUDSON HOUSE INN

Hotel
$80-$100

Phone: (715)386-2394

Address: 1616 Crestview Dr 54016 **Location:** I-94, exit 2 (CR F), 0.7 mi w on south frontage road (Crestview Dr). **Facility:** Smoke free premises. 100 units. 1-2 stories, interior corridors. **Parking:** winter plug-ins. **Terms:** 3 day cancellation notice. **Amenities:** high-speed Internet. **Pool(s):** heated indoor. **Activities:** sauna, whirlpool, exercise room. **Guest Services:** wireless Internet, beauty salon. **Free Special Amenities: continental breakfast and high-speed Internet.**

SAVE ⒯⒧ ⓨ ⌖ ✕ ▦ ▢ / SOME UNITS ▯ ▭

AAA Benefit:
Members save up to 20%, plus 10% bonus points with free rewards program.

FAIRFIELD INN BY MARRIOTT

Hotel
$100-$110

Phone: (715)386-6688

Address: 2400 Center Dr 54016 **Location:** I-94, exit 2 (CR F), 0.3 mi s. **Facility:** Smoke free premises. 63 units. 3 stories, interior corridors. **Terms:** cancellation fee imposed. **Amenities:** *Some:* high-speed Internet. **Pool(s):** heated indoor. **Activities:** whirlpool. **Guest Services:** valet laundry, wireless Internet.

HOLIDAY INN EXPRESS

Hotel
Rates not provided

Phone: 715/386-6200

Address: 1200 Gateway Blvd 54016 **Location:** I-94, exit 2 (CR F), 0.3 mi s. **Facility:** Smoke free premises. 68 units. 3 stories, interior corridors. **Terms:** check-in 4 pm. **Pool(s):** heated indoor. **Activities:** whirlpool, exercise room. **Guest Services:** valet and coin laundry, wireless Internet.

QUALITY INN

Hotel
$65-$120

Phone: (715)386-6355

Address: 811 Dominion Dr 54016 **Location:** I-94, exit 2 (CR F), 1 mi w on south frontage road (Crestview Dr). **Facility:** Smoke free premises. 60 units, some efficiencies. 2 stories (no elevator), interior corridors. **Terms:** check-in 4 pm, cancellation fee imposed. **Pool(s):** heated indoor. **Activities:** whirlpool. **Guest Services:** coin laundry, wireless Internet.

SUPER 8 OF HUDSON

Hotel
$56-$144

Phone: (715)386-8800

Address: 808 Dominion Dr 54016 **Location:** I-94, exit 2 (CR F), 1 mi w on south frontage road (Crestview Dr). **Facility:** Smoke free premises. 53 units. 2 stories (no elevator), interior corridors. **Parking:** winter plug-ins. **Terms:** cancellation fee imposed. **Pool(s):** heated indoor. **Activities:** whirlpool. **Guest Services:** coin laundry, wireless Internet. **Free Special Amenities:** continental breakfast and high-speed Internet.

—— WHERE TO DINE ——

BARKER'S BAR & GRILL

American
$8-$24

Phone: 715/386-4123 30

The casual pub offers 16 beers on tap as well as a great selection of bottled beers to complement made-to-order sandwiches, burgers, salads and various chicken, pork and steak entrees. **Bar:** full bar. **Hours:** 11 am-11 pm. Closed: 11/24, 12/25. **Address:** 413 2nd St 54016 **Location:** Downtown. **Parking:** street only.

GREEN MILL RESTAURANT & BAR

American
$8-$19

Phone: 715/386-9900

The eatery prepares top-notch pizzas; a good variety of appetizers, salads, sandwiches and pasta; and some steaks and seafood. Diablo wings are a great way to start the meal. **Bar:** full bar. **Hours:** 11 am-10 pm. Closed: 12/25. **Address:** 2410 Gateway Ct 54016 **Location:** I-94, exit 2 (CR F), just s.

SAN PEDRO CAFE

Caribbean
$8-$24

Phone: 715/386-4003 29

Fresh, flavorful ingredients are staples at the trendy restaurant. Tropical salsa, Caribbean and jerk spices and a variety of peppers add zing to homemade recipes. Wood-fired pizzas and seafood preparations are popular. **Bar:** full bar. **Hours:** 11 am-10 pm, Fri-11 pm, Sat 8 am-11 pm, Sun 8 am-10 pm. Closed: 1/1, 11/24, 12/25. **Address:** 426 2nd St 54016 **Location:** Downtown. **Parking:** street only.

HURLEY pop. 1,818

DAYS INN OF HURLEY

Hotel
$77-$117

Phone: (715)561-3500

Address: 13355 N US Hwy 51 54534 **Location:** Jct US 2 and 51, 0.4 mi s on US 51. **Facility:** Smoke free premises. 70 units. 2 stories (no elevator), interior corridors. **Parking:** winter plug-ins. **Pool(s):** heated indoor. **Activities:** sauna, whirlpool, snowmobiling, ATV trails. **Fee:** game room. **Guest Services:** coin laundry, wireless Internet.

—— WHERE TO DINE ——

KIMBALL INN

American
$8-$15

Phone: 715/561-4095

The friendly owner is often found in the dining room discussing the food or what's happening in the area. The menu lists a good selection of classic dinners, as well as a number of Italian dishes. **Bar:** full bar. **Hours:** 4 pm-11 pm; hours may vary. Closed: 11/24, 12/25 & Easter; also Mon. **Address:** 6622 US 2 54534 **Location:** On US 2, 3.7 mi w.

—— *The following restaurant has not been evaluated by AAA but is listed for your information only.* ——

PETRUSHA'S

Phone: 715/561-9888

Not evaluated. Go south of town, and you'll find this well-established family restaurant. **Address:** Rt 1, US 51 54534 **Location:** On US 51, 0.9 mi s.

IRON RIDGE pop. 998

IRON RIDGE INN MOTEL

Hotel
$62-$98

Phone: 920/387-4090

Address: 129 S Main St 53035 **Location:** Jct SR 67, just e on CR S. **Facility:** Smoke free premises. 20 units, some kitchens. 2 stories (no elevator), interior corridors. **Parking:** winter plug-ins. **Terms:** office hours 7 am-10 pm, cancellation fee imposed. **Pool(s):** heated indoor. **Activities:** whirlpool, limited exercise equipment. *Fee:* game room. **Guest Services:** wireless Internet.

JACKSON —See Milwaukee p. 564.

JANESVILLE pop. 59,498

BEST WESTERN JANESVILLE

Hotel
$89-$149

Phone: (608)756-4511

Address: 3900 Milton Ave 53546 **Location:** I-90, exit 171A (SR 26), just e. **Facility:** Smoke free premises. 105 units. 2-3 stories, interior corridors. **Pool(s):** heated indoor. **Activities:** whirlpool, atrium recreation area, exercise room. *Fee:* game room. **Guest Services:** valet and coin laundry, wireless Internet. **Free Special Amenities:** room upgrade and preferred room (each subject to availability with advance reservations).

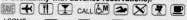

AAA Benefit:
Members save up to 20%, plus 10% bonus points with free rewards program.

ECONO LODGE - JANESVILLE

Hotel
Rates not provided

Phone: 608/754-0251

Address: 3520 Milton Ave 53545 **Location:** I-90/39, exit 171A, just sw via Frontage Rd. **Facility:** Smoke free premises. 57 units. 2 stories (no elevator), interior corridors. **Amenities:** safes (fee). **Guest Services:** coin laundry, wireless Internet.

HAMPTON INN-JANESVILLE

Hotel
$89-$109

Phone: (608)754-4900

AAA Benefit:
Members save up to 10% everyday!

Address: 2400 Fulton St 53546 **Location:** I-90, exit 171A (SR 26), just ne. **Facility:** Smoke free premises. 99 units. 3 stories, interior corridors. **Parking:** winter plug-ins. **Terms:** 1-7 night minimum stay, cancellation fee imposed. **Amenities:** *Some:* high-speed Internet. **Pool(s):** heated indoor. **Activities:** whirlpool. **Guest Services:** valet laundry, wireless Internet.

HOLIDAY INN EXPRESS & JANESVILLE CONFERENCE CENTER

Hotel
$109-$139

Phone: (608)756-3100

Address: 3100 Wellington Pl 53546 **Location:** I-90, exit 171C (US 14), just e. **Facility:** Smoke free premises. 142 units. 5 stories, interior corridors. **Pool(s):** heated indoor. **Activities:** whirlpool, exercise room. **Guest Services:** valet and coin laundry, area transportation-within 5 mi, wireless Internet.

—— WHERE TO DINE ——

HHFFRRRGGH INN RESTAURANT & BAR

American
$6-$20

Phone: 608/741-8833

The family-owned restaurant offers good old American homestyle cooking, such as meatloaf with mashed potatoes, all in large portions and at reasonable prices. **Bar:** full bar. **Hours:** 11 am-9 pm, Fri & Sat-10 pm. Closed major holidays. **Address:** 731 S Wuthering Hills 53545 **Location:** US 14, just w.

MILWAUKEE GRILL

American
$8-$26

Phone: 608/754-1919

A local favorite, the eatery offers a wide variety of beers as well as an extensive menu of American-style dishes including salads, sandwiches, burgers, fish, seafood, chicken, steaks and chops, all served in large portions. **Bar:** full bar. **Hours:** 11 am-10 pm, Fri & Sat-11 pm, Sun 7 am-10 pm. Closed major holidays. **Address:** 2601 Morse St 53545 **Location:** I-90, exit 171A (SR 26), just nw.

MO'S TAASBAG

American
$6-$16

Phone: 608/754-5667

The local sports bar offers "starting line ups" (appetizers), "super bowls" (soups), "Spring training" (light sandwiches) and burgers. **Bar:** full bar. **Hours:** 11 am-8 pm, Fri & Sat-9 pm. **Address:** 2339 Milton Ave 53545 **Location:** Just w of SR 26.

PEKING CHINESE RESTAURANT

Chinese
$6-$18

Phone: 608/752-9177

Ornate Oriental appointments, such as hanging lamps and sconces, decorate the cozy dining room. Northern Mandarin and Szechuan specialties, as well as chef specials of Szechuan squid and Peking duck, are served in large portions. The luncheon menu offers an exceptionally good value. Family dinners are available in the evening. **Bar:** full bar. **Hours:** 11 am-2:15 & 4-9 pm. Closed major holidays; also Sun. **Address:** 2632 Milton Ave 53545 **Location:** On SR 26, 0.4 mi s of jct US 14.

JEFFERSON pop. 7,338

RODEWAY INN

Motel
Rates not provided

Phone: 920/674-4404

Address: 1456 S Ryan Ave 53549 **Location:** On SR 26, 1.2 mi s of jct US 18. Located in a commercial area. **Facility:** Smoke free premises. 41 units. 2 stories (no elevator), interior corridors. **Parking:** winter plug-ins. **Terms:** office hours 6 am-11 pm. **Pool(s):** heated indoor. **Activities:** whirlpool. **Guest Services:** coin laundry, wireless Internet.

JOHNSON CREEK pop. 1,581

DAYS INN-JOHNSON CREEK
Hotel
$63-$108

Phone: (920)699-8000

Address: W4545 Linmar Ln 53038 **Location:** I-94, exit 267 (SR 26), just ne. **Facility:** Smoke free premises. 45 units. 2 stories (no elevator), interior corridors. **Parking:** winter plug-ins. **Pool(s):** heated indoor. **Activities:** whirlpool, exercise room. *Fee:* game room. **Guest Services:** coin laundry, wireless Internet.

——— WHERE TO DINE ———

FIESTA GARIBALDI MEXICAN RESTAURANT & BAR
Mexican
$6-$16

Phone: 920/699-8989

Music plays in the background of the Mexican-style cantina, where diners nosh on tacos, tostadas, burritos and traditional dinners. **Bar:** full bar. **Hours:** 11 am-10 pm, Fri & Sat-11 pm. Closed major holidays. **Address:** 310 Milwaukee St 53038 **Location:** I-94, exit 267 (SR 26), 0.9 mi s, then just w.

HI-WAY HARRY'S STEAKHOUSE

Steak
$9-$24

Phone: 920/699-4444

First-timers shouldn't let the name or location right off the interstate and across from Johnson Creek Outlet Center deceive them. This place provides romantic high booth areas, a bar, a soothing waterfall feature and a baby grand piano. Steak and seafood are the main fare. The patio opens in season. **Bar:** full bar. **Reservations:** suggested. **Hours:** 11 am-10 pm, Fri & Sat-11 pm, Sun 10:30 am-8 pm; Sunday brunch. Closed: 11/24, 12/25. **Address:** 710 Glover Ln 53038 **Location:** I-94, exit 267 (SR 26), just n.

KENOSHA pop. 90,352

BEST WESTERN EXECUTIVE INN
Hotel
$80-$300

Phone: (262)857-7699

Address: 7220 122nd Ave 53142 **Location:** I-94, exit 344 (SR 50), just nw. Located in a commercial area. **Facility:** Smoke free premises. 115 units. 4 stories, interior corridors. **Amenities:** *Some:* high-speed Internet. **Pool(s):** heated indoor. **Activities:** whirlpool, exercise room. *Fee:* game room. **Guest Services:** valet and coin laundry, wireless Internet. **Free Special Amenities:** full breakfast and high-speed Internet.

AAA Benefit:
Members save up to 20%, plus 10% bonus points with free rewards program.

BEST WESTERN HARBORSIDE INN & KENOSHA CONFERENCE CENTER
Hotel
$80-$150

Phone: (262)658-3281

Address: 5125 6th Ave 53140 **Location:** Just ne of jct SR 32 and 158; downtown. **Facility:** Smoke free premises. 111 units. 5 stories, interior corridors. **Amenities:** high-speed Internet. **Pool(s):** heated indoor. **Activities:** whirlpool. *Fee:* game room. **Guest Services:** valet and coin laundry, wireless Internet. **Free Special Amenities:** full breakfast and room upgrade (subject to availability with advance reservations).

AAA Benefit:
Members save up to 20%, plus 10% bonus points with free rewards program.

CANDLEWOOD SUITES
Extended Stay Hotel
$99-$119

Phone: (262)842-5000

Address: 10200 74th St 53142 **Location:** SR 50, exit 104th Ave, just n. **Facility:** Smoke free premises. 90 efficiencies. 3 stories, interior corridors. **Terms:** cancellation fee imposed. **Amenities:** high-speed Internet. **Activities:** picnic area with grills, exercise room. **Guest Services:** valet and coin laundry, wireless Internet. **Free Special Amenities:** newspaper and high-speed Internet.

COMFORT SUITES KENOSHA

Hotel
$72-$129

Phone: (262)857-3450

Address: 7206 122nd Ave 53142 **Location:** I-94, exit 344 (SR 50), just nw. Located in a commercial area. **Facility:** Smoke free premises. 72 units. 3 stories, interior corridors. **Pool(s):** heated indoor. **Activities:** whirlpool, limited exercise equipment. *Fee:* game room. **Guest Services:** valet and coin laundry, wireless Internet. **Free Special Amenities:** full breakfast and high-speed Internet.

COUNTRY INN & SUITES BY CARLSON

Hotel
$99-$140

Phone: (262)857-3680

Address: 7011 122nd Ave 53142 **Location:** I-94, exit 344 (SR 50), just nw. Located in a commercial area. **Facility:** Smoke free premises. 89 units. 3 stories, interior corridors. **Parking:** winter plug-ins. **Terms:** 3 day cancellation notice-fee imposed. **Pool(s):** heated indoor. **Activities:** whirlpool, exercise room. **Guest Services:** valet and coin laundry, wireless Internet. *(see ad p. 6)*

--------- **WHERE TO DINE** ---------

BOAT HOUSE PUB & EATERY

American
$6-$35

Phone: 262/654-9922

Appointed in a nautical theme, the restaurant affords great views of Lake Michigan, particularly from the seasonal outdoor seating. Although the menu focus is on seafood, other offerings include sandwiches, barbecue chicken and ribs, weekly specials and homemade soups such as fresh clam chowder. Courtesy customer docking is available. **Bar:** full bar. **Hours:** 11 am-close, Sun from 9 am. Closed: 12/25. **Address:** 4917 7th Ave 53140 **Location:** Just ne of jct SR 32 and 158; downtown.

MANGIA

Italian
$9-$30

Phone: 262/652-4285

Among outstanding offerings are fresh seafood, wonderful pasta and daily specials. Aromas of rosemary, garlic and a hint of smoke from the wood-burning oven waft through the air. Representative of delectable in-house desserts are tiramisu and crème brûlée. **Bar:** full bar. **Reservations:** suggested. **Hours:** 11:30 am-2 & 5-8:30 pm, Fri-10 pm, Sat 5 pm-10 pm, Sun 4 pm-9 pm. Closed major holidays; also Mon, Sun 1/1-3/31. **Address:** 5717 Sheridan Rd 53140 **Location:** On SR 32 N, 0.4 mi n of jct SR 50.

KEWAUNEE pop. 2,806

--------- **WHERE TO DINE** ---------

PORT O'CALL

American
$6-$22

Phone: 920/388-4883

Overlooking the harbor, the casual restaurant and lounge affords a good view of the activities on the water. **Bar:** full bar. **Hours:** 11 am-9 pm; hours may vary. Closed major holidays. **Address:** 310 Milwaukee St 54216 **Location:** On SR 42; center.

KIMBERLY pop. 6,146

HILTON GARDEN INN

Hotel
$96-$106

Phone: (920)730-1900

Address: 720 Eisenhower Dr 54136 **Location:** US 41, exit 145 (SR 441), 2.7 mi s to CR CE, then 0.4 mi e. **Facility:** 125 units. 5 stories, interior corridors. **Terms:** 1-7 night minimum stay, cancellation fee imposed. **Amenities:** high-speed Internet. **Pool(s):** heated indoor. **Activities:** whirlpool, sun deck, exercise room. **Guest Services:** valet and coin laundry, wireless Internet.

AAA Benefit:
Members save 5% or more everyday!

SUPER 8 - KIMBERLY

Hotel
$59-$116

Phone: (920)788-4400

Address: 761 Truman St 54136 **Location:** US 41, exit 145 (SR 441), 2.7 mi s to CR CE, then 0.4 mi e. **Facility:** Smoke free premises. 63 units. 2 stories (no elevator), interior corridors. **Amenities:** safes (fee). **Pool(s):** heated indoor. **Activities:** sauna, whirlpool, exercise room. **Guest Services:** valet laundry.

KOHLER pop. 1,926

THE AMERICAN CLUB

Classic Historic
Resort Hotel
$325-$1442 4/1-10/31
$205-$1133 11/1-4/30

Phone: (920)457-8000

Address: 419 Highland Dr 53044 **Location:** I-43, exit 126, 0.5 mi w on SR 23, then 1 mi s on CR Y and Highland Dr. Located in a residential area. **Facility:** Built in 1918 for workers of the Kohler Company, this grand resort offers extensive grounds and year-round recreational activities. Smoke free premises. 240 units. 3 stories, interior corridors. **Parking:** on-site and valet. **Terms:** check-in 4 pm, 7 day cancellation notice-fee imposed. **Amenities:** video games (fee), high-speed Internet, safes, honor bars. **Dining:** The Horse & Plow, The Immigrant Restaurant & Winery, The Wisconsin Room, see separate listings. **Pool(s):** 3 heated indoor. **Activities:** saunas, whirlpools, steamrooms, rental canoes, rental paddleboats, fishing, ice skating, tobogganing, recreation programs, rental bicycles, hiking trails, jogging, spa. *Fee:* charter fishing, golf-72 holes, 6 lighted indoor tennis courts, cross country skiing, dog sledding, carriage rides, trap shooting, bird hunting, history & Kohler factory tours, horseback riding. **Guest Services:** valet laundry, area transportation-within village, wireless Internet. *(see ad p. 543)*

FREE continental breakfast and newspaper

INN ON WOODLAKE

Hotel
Rates not provided

Phone: 920/452-7800

Address: 705 Woodlake Rd 53044 **Location:** I-43, exit 126, 0.5 mi w on SR 23, 0.5 mi s on CR Y and Highland Dr; in Woodlake Shopping Center. **Facility:** Smoke free premises. 121 units. 3 stories, interior corridors. **Terms:** check-in 4 pm. **Amenities:** high-speed Internet. **Activities:** putting green, hiking trails, jogging. *Fee:* fishing, privileges at The American Club. **Guest Services:** valet and coin laundry, area transportation-health club, village & whistling straits, wireless Internet. *(see ad p. 543)*

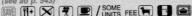

—— WHERE TO DINE ——

BLACKWOLF RUN

American
$8-$35

Phone: 920/457-4446

In the golf course clubhouse, the impressive Canadian log cabin structure overlooks the Sheboygan River and the course. The seasonally changing menu features hearty portions of foods from the heartland. Specialties include Angus beef, wild game, seafood and free-range chicken. **Bar:** full bar. **Reservations:** suggested. **Hours:** 6 am-10 pm; 11 am-3 & 6-10 pm 11/1-4/30. Closed: Sun & Mon 11/1-4/30. **Address:** 1111 W Riverside Dr 53044 **Location:** I-43, exit 126, 0.5 mi w on SR 23, then 1 mi s on CR Y and Highland Dr; in Blackwolf Run Golf Course Club House; at The American Club. CALL &M

CUCINA

Italian
$10-$40

Phone: 920/452-3888

Made-in-house pasta, veal, prime steaks, seafood and gourmet pizza are among the traditional dishes available at this elegant dining spot. Fresh ingredients, eye-catching dessert presentations and professional service complete the dining experience. The six grand white columns, domed ceiling and luxurious full-length draperies in the dining room set the stage for a fine-dining experience. Window tables and the seasonal terrace overlook Wood Lake. **Bar:** full bar. **Reservations:** suggested. **Hours:** 11 am-9 pm, Fri & Sat-10 pm; to 10 pm 5/1-10/1. Closed: 1/1, 11/24, 12/25. **Address:** 725 E Woodlake Rd 53044 **Location:** I-43, exit 126, 0.5 mi w on SR 23, then 0.5 mi s on CR Y and Highland Dr; in Woodlake Shopping Center. CALL &M

THE HORSE & PLOW

American
$8-$20

Phone: 920/457-8888

Comfortable booths, lovely glass and a caring staff make this a popular spot. The menu offers a wide variety of items such as Wisconsin three-cheese soup, Sheboygan sausage, quesadillas, wings, burgers, sandwiches and salads. A big-screen TV keeps sports fans up-to-date on the latest events. **Bar:** full bar. **Hours:** 11 am-10 pm. **Address:** 419 Highland Dr 53044 **Location:** I-43, exit 126, 0.5 mi w on SR 23, then 1 mi s on CR Y and Highland Dr; in The American Club. CALL &M

THE IMMIGRANT RESTAURANT & WINERY

Regional American
$30-$48

Phone: 920/457-8888

What once housed a bowling alley and laundry for immigrant workers now celebrates the heritage of people who helped grow Kohler Co. into a multinational corporation. The menu is contemporary, and adventurous offerings incorporate international influences. Service is formal and detailed while remaining refreshingly unpretentious. For a special treat, consider the seven-course degustation menu paired with specially selected wines. Semi-formal attire. **Bar:** full bar. **Reservations:** suggested. **Hours:** 6 pm-10 pm. Closed: Sun & Mon 11/1-4/30. **Address:** 419 Highland Dr 53044 **Location:** I-43, exit 126, 0.5 mi w on SR 23, then 1 mi s on CR Y and Highland Dr; in The American Club. **Parking:** on-site and valet. CALL &M

THE WISCONSIN ROOM

Regional American
$18-$40

Phone: 920/457-8888

The main dining room is luxurious and features a menu of Wisconsin and regional specialties incorporating products from the upper Midwest. The wine list is exclusively American. **Bar:** full bar. **Reservations:** suggested. **Hours:** 6:30 am-11 & 6-9 pm, Sat 6:30 am-11:30 & 6-10 pm, Sun 9 am-1 & 6-9 pm. **Address:** 419 Highland Dr 53044 **Location:** I-43, exit 126, 0.5 mi w on SR 23, then 1 mi s on CR Y and Highland Dr; in The American Club. **Parking:** on-site and valet.

LA CROSSE pop. 51,818

AMERICAS BEST VALUE INN

Hotel
$52-$110 4/1-10/31
$48-$84 11/1-4/30

Phone: (608)781-3070

Address: 2622 Rose St 54603 **Location:** I-90, exit 3, just s. **Facility:** Smoke free premises. 110 units. 2 stories (no elevator), interior corridors. **Parking:** winter plug-ins. **Terms:** cancellation fee imposed. **Activities:** exercise room. **Guest Services:** coin laundry, wireless Internet.

BEST WESTERN PLUS RIVERFRONT HOTEL

Hotel
$110-$150

Phone: (608)781-7000

Address: 1835 Rose St 54603 **Location:** I-90, exit 3, 1 mi s on US 53. **Facility:** Smoke free premises. 119 units. 2 stories (no elevator), interior corridors. **Parking:** winter plug-ins. **Amenities:** high-speed Internet. **Dining:** entertainment. **Pool(s):** heated indoor. **Activities:** whirlpool, boat dock, indoor domed water park, miniature golf, exercise room, volleyball. *Fee:* boat tours, game room. **Guest Services:** valet and coin laundry, area transportation-Amtrak station, wireless Internet. **Free Special Amenities:** early check-in/late check-out and high-speed Internet.

AAA Benefit:
Members save up to 20%, plus 10% bonus points with free rewards program.

BROOKSTONE INN

Hotel
$59-$140 11/1-4/30
$59-$110 4/1-10/31

Phone: (608)781-1400

Address: 1830 Rose St 54603 **Location:** I-90, exit 3, 1 mi s on US 53. **Facility:** Smoke free premises. 84 units. 3 stories, interior corridors. **Pool(s):** heated indoor. **Activities:** whirlpool. **Guest Services:** valet laundry, wireless Internet. *(see ad below)*

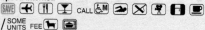

FREE expanded continental breakfast and high-speed Internet

CANDLEWOOD SUITES

Extended Stay Hotel
$89-$159

Phone: (608)785-1110

Address: 56 Copeland Ave 54603 **Location:** I-90, exit 3, 2 mi s on US 53. **Facility:** Smoke free premises. 92 kitchen units. 4 stories, interior corridors. **Terms:** cancellation fee imposed. **Amenities:** high-speed Internet. **Activities:** barbecue grill, exercise room. **Guest Services:** complimentary and valet laundry, wireless Internet. **Free Special Amenities:** local telephone calls and high-speed Internet.

▼ *See AAA listing above* ▼

Stay. Play. Dine. Save. Visit AAA.com/Travel
or CAA.ca/Travel for Information To Go!

COURTYARD BY MARRIOTT-DOWNTOWN MISSISSIPPI RIVERFRONT

Phone: (608)782-1000

Hotel
$129-$159

Address: 500 Front St 54601 **Location:** Just w of US 53; downtown. **Facility:** Smoke free premises. 78 units, some kitchens. 3 stories, interior corridors. **Terms:** cancellation fee imposed. **Amenities:** high-speed Internet. **Pool(s):** heated indoor. **Activities:** whirlpool, exercise room. **Guest Services:** valet and coin laundry, area transportation-Amtrak & bus station, wireless Internet.

> **AAA Benefit:**
> Members save a minimum 5% off the best available rate.

DAYS HOTEL & CONFERENCE CENTER

Phone: (608)783-1000

Hotel
$58-$116

Address: 101 Sky Harbour Dr 54603 **Location:** I-90, exit 2, just sw; on French Island. **Facility:** Smoke free premises. 146 units. 2 stories (no elevator), interior corridors. **Amenities:** high-speed Internet. **Pool(s):** heated indoor. **Activities:** whirlpool, limited exercise equipment. *Fee:* game room. **Guest Services:** valet laundry, wireless Internet.

ECONO LODGE

Phone: (608)781-0200

Hotel
$49-$99

Address: 1906 Rose St 54603 **Location:** I-90, exit 3, 0.9 mi s on US 53. **Facility:** Smoke free premises. 71 units. 2 stories (no elevator), interior corridors. **Terms:** cancellation fee imposed. **Activities:** whirlpool. **Guest Services:** coin laundry, wireless Internet. **Free Special Amenities: expanded continental breakfast and high-speed Internet.**

GRANDSTAY RESIDENTIAL SUITES HOTEL OF LA CROSSE

Phone: (608)796-1615

Extended Stay
Hotel
$89-$209

Address: 525 Front St N 54601 **Location:** I-90, exit 3; downtown. **Facility:** Smoke free premises. 55 kitchen units, some two bedrooms. 4 stories, interior corridors. **Terms:** 2 night minimum stay - seasonal and/or weekends, cancellation fee imposed. **Amenities:** high-speed Internet. **Pool(s):** heated indoor. **Activities:** whirlpool, exercise room, basketball. **Guest Services:** valet and coin laundry, wireless Internet. **Free Special Amenities: continental breakfast and high-speed Internet.**

HOLIDAY INN HOTEL & SUITES

Phone: (608)784-4444

Hotel
$70-$159

Address: 200 Pearl St 54601 **Location:** Downtown. **Facility:** Smoke free premises. 114 units. 5 stories, interior corridors. **Parking:** on-site (fee). **Terms:** check-in 4 pm. **Amenities:** *Some:* high-speed Internet. **Pool(s):** heated indoor. **Activities:** whirlpool, exercise room. **Guest Services:** valet and coin laundry, area transportation-Amtrak & bus station, wireless Internet.

HOWARD JOHNSON HOTEL LA CROSSE

Phone: (608)781-0400

Hotel
$53-$107

Address: 2150 Rose St 54603 **Location:** I-90, exit 3, 0.8 mi s on US 53. **Facility:** Smoke free premises. 99 units. 2 stories (no elevator), interior corridors. **Activities:** limited exercise equipment. **Guest Services:** coin laundry, wireless Internet.

RADISSON HOTEL LA CROSSE

Phone: (608)784-6680

Hotel
$129-$249

Address: 200 Harborview Plaza 54601 **Location:** Just w of US 53; downtown. **Facility:** Smoke free premises. 169 units. 8 stories, interior corridors. **Terms:** cancellation fee imposed. **Amenities:** *Some:* high-speed Internet, safes. **Dining:** Three Rivers Lodge, see separate listing. **Pool(s):** heated indoor. **Activities:** whirlpool, exercise room. **Guest Services:** valet laundry, area transportation-Amtrak & bus station, wireless Internet. **Free Special Amenities: newspaper and high-speed Internet.**

SETTLE INN

Phone: (608)781-5100

Hotel
$65-$120 4/1-10/31
$60-$120 11/1-4/30

Address: 2110 Rose St 54603 **Location:** I-90, exit 3, 0.9 mi s on US 53. **Facility:** Smoke free premises. 101 units. 2 stories (no elevator), interior corridors. **Amenities:** video games (fee). **Pool(s):** heated indoor. **Activities:** whirlpool, limited exercise equipment. **Guest Services:** valet laundry, wireless Internet.

——— **WHERE TO DINE** ———

BUZZARD BILLY'S RESTAURANT

Phone: 608/796-2277

Cajun
$6-$20

If you like a festive atmosphere and love authentic Cajun food, such as seafood gumbo, jambalaya, po'boy sandwiches and voodoo tuna, this is your stop. Starting off with gator fingers, seafood-stuffed mushrooms or even buzzard eggs are a great beginning. Rich and tasty soups as well as filling salads of various toppings are also on the menu. **Bar:** full bar. **Hours:** 11:30 am-10 pm, Fri-11 pm, Sat 11 am-11 pm, Sun 11 am-10 pm. Closed: major holidays, 12/24. **Address:** 222 Pearl St 54601 **Location:** Downtown. **Parking:** street only.

DIGGER'S STING RESTAURANT

Phone: 608/782-3796

American
$6-$36

The theme is of a NYC mobster-style restaurant with dark wood paneling and pictures of famous celebrities in black and white, as well as old-style jukebox. Known for its prime rib, it also feature tasty sirloin and filet mignon as well as smoky-flavored baby back ribs. Great seafood of scallops, shrimp and numerous fish offerings and tasty salads are also available. **Bar:** full bar. **Hours:** 11 am-10 pm, Mon-9 pm, Sat-10:30 pm. Closed major holidays; also Sun. **Address:** 122 N 3rd St 54601 **Location:** Downtown. **Parking:** street only.

EDWARDO'S PIZZA WAGON

Phone: 608/783-8282

American
$9-$20

Family owned and operated since 1955, the restaurant prepares pizzas in a wood-fired oven. Natural ingredients, custom dough and fresh vegetables make the pizza a standout. An extensive beer selection is offered. **Bar:** full bar. **Hours:** 4 pm-10:30 pm, Fri & Sat-10:45 pm, Sun-10 pm. Closed: 11/24, 12/25. **Address:** 1930 Rose St 54601 **Location:** I-90, exit 3, 0.5 mi s. CALL

HACKBERRY'S

Phone: 608/784-5798

American
$7-$22

Over a food co-op with which it partners, this restaurant uses the freshest seasonal fruits and vegetables. Clean, classic lines are part of the appeal of the decor. **Bar:** beer & wine. **Hours:** 11 am-9 pm, Sat & Sun from 9 am. Closed: 11/24, 12/24, 12/25. **Address:** 315 5th Ave S 54601 **Location:** Downtown. CALL

HUCK FINN'S ON THE WATER

Phone: 608/791-3595

American
$8-$29

A great place to enjoy a view of the shoreline through three glass walls, the restaurant offers a must-try artichoke dip as well as tasty chicken tortilla soup and a decadently fudgy yum-yum brownie cake. **Bar:** full bar. **Hours:** 11 am-9 pm; Sun 10 am-1:30 pm 10/1-4/30. Closed: 1/1, 11/24, 12/25; also Mon 10/1-4/30. **Address:** 127 Marina Dr 54601 **Location:** Downtown.

PICKERMAN'S SOUPS & SANDWICHES

Phone: 608/782-7087

American
$4-$8

Guests can get a quick bite to eat at the locally owned soup and sandwich restaurant in the heart of historic downtown. The signature bread is made from a secret family recipe, and oven-fresh cookies are baked on site. **Hours:** 10:30 am-7:30 pm. Closed major holidays; also Sun. **Address:** 327 Jay St 54601 **Location:** Corner of US 53 and Jay St, just n of jct US 53 and 14. **Parking:** street only.

PIGGY'S RESTAURANT

Phone: 608/784-4877

American
$9-$26

Hickory-smoked, American-cut pork chops, baby back ribs, prime steak and seafood are specialties at this restaurant with views of the Mississippi River. The comprehensive wine list is lengthier than the menu. The antique wood bar is a focal point of the dining room. **Bar:** full bar. **Reservations:** suggested. **Hours:** 11 am-2 & 5-9 pm, Fri & Sat-10 pm. Closed major holidays. **Address:** 501 Front St S 54601 **Location:** Just w of jct US 53 and King St.

THREE RIVERS LODGE

Phone: 608/793-5018

American
$5-$24

Just off the La Crosse River, the cozy, lodge-style restaurant affords beautiful views of the outdoor scenery. Among offerings at breakfast, lunch and dinner are modern Midwestern interpretations of wild rice soup, pan-fried walleyed pike and rotisserie chicken. Hearty plates redefine the local hot dish. **Bar:** full bar. **Hours:** 6:30 am-10 pm. **Address:** 200 Harborview Plaza 54601 **Location:** Just w of US 53; downtown; in Radisson Hotel La Crosse.

LADYSMITH pop. 3,932

AMERICINN LODGE & SUITES OF LADYSMITH

Phone: (715)532-7811

Hotel
$67-$135

Address: 700 W 9th St S 54848 **Location:** On SR 27, 0.5 mi s of US 8. **Facility:** Smoke free premises. 41 units. 2 stories (no elevator), interior corridors. **Parking:** winter plug-ins. **Terms:** 3 day cancellation notice. **Amenities:** high-speed Internet. **Pool(s):** heated indoor. **Activities:** sauna, whirlpool, limited exercise equipment. **Guest Services:** coin laundry, wireless Internet. CALL / SOME UNITS

AMERICINN MOTEL & SUITES OF LADYSMITH

Phone: 715/532-6650

Hotel
Rates not provided

Address: 800 W College Ave 54848 **Location:** On SR 27, 0.5 mi s of US 8. **Facility:** Smoke free premises. 38 units. 2 stories (no elevator), interior corridors. **Parking:** winter plug-ins. **Amenities:** high-speed Internet. **Pool(s):** heated indoor. **Activities:** sauna, whirlpool, pool table. **Guest Services:** coin laundry, wireless Internet. CALL / SOME UNITS FEE

—— **WHERE TO DINE** ——

LADYSMITH FAMILY RESTAURANT

Phone: 715/532-3755

American
$5-$13

In a small shopping mall, this eatery offers hearty servings of good, wholesome food. **Reservations:** suggested. **Hours:** 6 am-9 pm. Closed: 12/25. **Address:** 820 Miner Ave W 54848 **Location:** Jct SR 27 (W 9th St N) and 8, just s; in mini mall. CALL

LAKE GENEVA pop. 7,148

BELLA VISTA SUITES HOTEL

Phone: (262)248-2100

Hotel
$215-$305 4/1-12/31
$165-$215 1/1-4/30

Address: 335 Wrigley Dr 53147 **Location:** Just s of SR 50. Across from Lake Geneva. **Facility:** Smoke free premises. 39 units, some two bedrooms, efficiencies and kitchens. 4 stories, interior corridors. **Parking:** winter plug-ins. **Terms:** check-in 4 pm, 2 night minimum stay - seasonal and/or weekends, 3 day cancellation notice-fee imposed. **Pool(s):** heated indoor. **Activities:** whirlpool, exercise room, spa. **Fee:** boat dock. **Guest Services:** valet laundry, wireless Internet. **Free Special Amenities:** continental breakfast and high-speed Internet. SAVE CALL

BUDGET HOST DIPLOMAT MOTEL

Phone: (262)248-1809

Motel

$58-$106

Address: 1060 Wells St 53147 **Location:** 1 mi s of SR 50. Located in a commercial residential area. **Facility:** Smoke free premises. 23 units. 2 stories (no elevator), exterior corridors. **Parking:** winter plug-ins. **Terms:** office hours 7 am-11 pm, 7 day cancellation notice-fee imposed. **Pool(s):** heated outdoor. **Guest Services:** wireless Internet. **Free Special Amenities:** early check-in/late check-out and high-speed Internet.

COMFORT SUITES

Phone: 262/248-2300

Hotel

Rates not provided

Address: 300 E Main St 53147 **Location:** SR 50, 1 mi w of US 12. **Facility:** Smoke free premises. 80 units. 3 stories, interior corridors. **Amenities:** high-speed Internet, safes (fee). **Pool(s):** heated indoor. **Activities:** whirlpool, exercise room. *Fee:* game room. **Guest Services:** coin laundry, wireless Internet.

THE COVE OF LAKE GENEVA

Phone: (262)249-9460

Condominium

$149-$299 4/1-10/15

$99-$159 10/16-4/30

Address: 111 Center St 53147 **Location:** Just s of SR 50. Across from Lake Geneva. **Facility:** Gas fireplaces are featured in all of the property's accommodations. Smoke free premises. 210 units, some two bedrooms, efficiencies and kitchens. 4 stories, interior corridors. **Terms:** 2 night minimum stay - seasonal and/or weekends, 3 day cancellation notice-fee imposed. **Amenities:** high-speed Internet. **Dining:** Houlihan's, see separate listing. **Pool(s):** 2 heated outdoor, heated indoor. **Activities:** sauna, whirlpools, lighted tennis court, exercise room, basketball. *Fee:* massage, game room. **Guest Services:** coin laundry, wireless Internet.

GENERAL BOYD'S BED & BREAKFAST

Phone: 262/248-3543

Bed & Breakfast

$110-$160

Address: W2915 S Lake Shore Dr 53147 **Location:** Jct SR 50 and S Lake Shore Dr, 2.7 mi s of downtown. Located in a rural area. **Facility:** On 5 acres of landscaped grounds and gardens, this spacious 1843 Colonial Revival farmhouse is accented with a large collection of antiques. Smoke free premises. 4 units. 2 stories (no elevator), interior corridors. **Terms:** office hours 8 am-10 pm, 2 night minimum stay - seasonal and/or weekends, age restrictions may apply, 7 day cancellation notice-fee imposed. **Activities:** croquet, walking trail, horseshoes, barn for guest activities, basketball, horseshoes. **Guest Services:** wireless Internet.

GRAND GENEVA RESORT & SPA

Phone: (262)248-8811

Resort

Hotel

$129-$449

Address: 7036 Grand Geneva Way 53147 **Location:** On SR 50, just e of jct US 12. Located in a quiet area. **Facility:** This sprawling spa resort features Frank Lloyd Wright-inspired architecture and has multiple golf courses on its 1,300 acres of rolling countryside. Smoke free premises. 355 units. 3 stories, interior corridors. **Parking:** on-site and valet. **Terms:** check-in 4 pm, 2-3 night minimum stay - weekends, 3 day cancellation notice-fee imposed. **Amenities:** video games (fee). **Dining:** Geneva ChopHouse, Ristorante Brissago, see separate listings, entertainment. **Pool(s):** heated outdoor, 2 heated indoor. **Activities:** saunas, whirlpools, steamrooms, rental boats, access to nearby Moose Mountain indoor/outdoor water park, snowshoes, recreation programs, hiking trails, playground, spa, basketball, volleyball. *Fee:* golf-36 holes, 6 tennis courts (2 indoor, 6 lighted), downhill & cross country skiing, ice skating, 3845 ft lighted airport runway, rock climbing wall, bicycles, horseback riding. **Guest Services:** valet laundry, wireless Internet, beauty salon.

HARBOR SHORES ON LAKE GENEVA

Hotel
$87-$299

Phone: (262)248-9181

Address: 300 Wrigley Dr 53147 **Location:** Just s of SR 50. **Facility:** Smoke free premises. 108 units. 5 stories, interior corridors. **Terms:** check-in 4 pm, 3 day cancellation notice-fee imposed. **Amenities:** *Some:* high-speed Internet. **Pool(s):** heated outdoor, heated indoor. **Activities:** sauna, whirlpools, exercise room. **Guest Services:** valet laundry, wireless Internet.

FREE continental breakfast and high-speed Internet

TIMBER RIDGE LODGE & WATER PARK AT GRAND GENEVA

Hotel
$129-$425

Phone: (262)249-3400

Address: 7020 Grand Geneva Way 53147 **Location:** SR 50, just e of jct US 12. Located in a quiet area. **Facility:** Smoke free premises. 219 efficiencies, some two bedrooms. 3 stories, interior corridors. **Parking:** winter plug-ins. **Terms:** check-in 4 pm, 3 day cancellation notice-fee imposed. **Amenities:** high-speed Internet. **Pool(s):** heated outdoor, heated indoor. **Activities:** whirlpools, waterslide, 4 lighted tennis courts, children's activity center, horseback riding, playground, sports court, basketball, volleyball. *Fee:* golf-36 holes, downhill & cross country skiing, spa privileges, game room. **Guest Services:** coin laundry, wireless Internet.

——— WHERE TO DINE ———

GENEVA CHOPHOUSE

Steak
$18-$51

Phone: 262/248-8811

The restaurant features a polished and refined tiered dining room with rich dark-wood accents and superb views of a perfectly manicured golf course just outside. Adding to the energy of the room is the open display kitchen, where guests can watch the chefs busy at their craft. Fine steaks, chops and seafood are the primary draws, and they meet up with the sauces and toppings of the patron's choosing. Service is attentive, and the food is skillfully prepared. **Bar:** full bar. **Reservations:** suggested. **Hours:** 5:30 pm-10 pm; Sunday brunch 10 am-2 pm. **Closed:** Sat. **Address:** 7036 Grand Geneva Way 53147 **Location:** On SR 50, just e of jct US 12; in Grand Geneva Resort & Spa. **Parking:** on-site and valet.

GINO'S EAST OF CHICAGO

Pizza
$9-$19

Phone: 262/248-2525

The popular Chicago-style pizza restaurant furthers an ultra-casual ambience through its wood walls and floors and red-checkered tablecloths. On the menu are deep-dish and thin-crust pizzas, as well as many fine pasta dishes and sandwiches. **Bar:** full bar. **Hours:** 11 am-9 pm, Fri & Sat-10 pm. **Address:** 300 Wrigley Dr 53147 **Location:** Just s of SR 50; in Harbor Shores on Lake Geneva.

HOULIHAN'S

American
$8-$23

Phone: 262/248-7047

This busy eatery provides a comfortable atmosphere for gathering with friends or family. Menu favorites include the goat cheese bruschetta, stuffed chicken and the triple berry cobbler. **Bar:** full bar. **Hours:** 11 am-10 pm, Fri & Sat-11 pm. **Address:** 111 Center St 53147 **Location:** Just s of SR 50; in The Cove of Lake Geneva.

KIRSCH'S RESTAURANT

American
$22-$35

Phone: 262/245-5756

By the lake, this restaurant offers a variety of dishes made from USDA beef and local farm produce. Light summer breezes cool the patio, where guests can look out over the lake. **Bar:** full bar. **Reservations:** suggested. **Hours:** 5 pm-10 pm, Sun 11 am-9 pm. **Closed:** 1/1, 12/24. **Address:** W4190 West End Rd 53147 **Location:** SR 50 E, 0.4 mi on Red Chimney Rd.

POPEYE'S ON LAKE GENEVA

American
$8-$26

Phone: 262/248-4381

Offering casual dining with a spectacular view of Geneva Lake, the restaurant features a full menu including its famous broccoli-cheese soup and award-winning homemade apple pie, as well as flame-roasted chicken, pig and lamb on an outdoor barbecue pit during summer. **Bar:** full bar. **Hours:** 11 am-9:30 pm; 11:30 am-8:30 pm in winter. **Closed:** 11/24, 12/25. **Address:** 811 Wrigley Dr 53147 **Location:** Downtown. **Parking:** street only.

RISTORANTE BRISSAGO

Northern Italian
$16-$51

Phone: 262/248-8811

Careful attention is paid to the preparation of traditional pastas, wood-roasted pizza and veal dishes in this dining room overlooking the Wisconsin countryside. Service is professional and attentive. The imported Milano sorbets are wonderful. **Bar:** full bar. **Reservations:** suggested. **Hours:** 5:30 pm-10 pm, Sun also 10 am-2 pm. **Closed:** Mon. **Address:** 7036 Grand Geneva Way 53147 **Location:** On SR 50, just e of jct US 12; in Grand Geneva Resort & Spa. **Parking:** on-site and valet.

SCUTTLEBUTTS

American
$6-$21

Phone: 262/248-1111

The casual restaurant features a selection of flavorful gourmet burgers, sandwiches and salads, as well as a handful of Swedish specialties. Large windows in the dining room look out over Lake Geneva. Key lime pie and specialty ice cream desserts are wonderful. **Bar:** full bar. **Hours:** 6:30 am-9 pm, Fri & Sat-10 pm; hours may vary in winter. **Address:** 831 Wrigley Dr 53147 **Location:** Just s of SR 50; lakeside. **Parking:** street only.

LAKE MILLS pop. 4,843

AMERICAS BEST VALUE INN

Hotel
$60-$120

Phone: (920)648-3800

Address: W 7614 Oasis Ln 53551 **Location:** I-94, exit 259 (SR 89), just n. **Facility:** Smoke free premises. 43 units. 2 stories (no elevator), interior corridors. **Terms:** cancellation fee imposed. **Pool(s):** heated indoor. **Activities:** patio/picnic. **Guest Services:** valet laundry, wireless Internet.

--- **WHERE TO DINE** ---

PINE KNOLL RESTAURANT

American
$6-$37

Phone: 920/648-2303

Supper club fare revolves around such choices as breaded or broiled seafood, hand-cut steaks and succulent ribs. Patrons also can opt for lighter fare. Rolling farmland characterizes the rural setting. Dining room decor evokes Early American influences. Sunday brunch is popular. **Bar:** full bar. **Hours:** 5 pm-8:30 pm, Fri & Sat-9:30 pm, Sun 10:30 am-7:30 pm. Closed: 1/1, 12/24, 12/25; also Mon-Wed. **Address:** N7755 Hwy 89 53551 **Location:** I-94, exit 259 (SR 89), 3 mi n.

LANCASTER pop. 4,070

BEST WESTERN WELCOME INN

Hotel
$73-$78

Address: 420 W Maple St 53813 **Location:** Just w of downtown square. **Facility:** Smoke free premises. 22 units. 2 stories (no elevator), interior corridors. **Amenities:** *Some:* high-speed Internet. **Guest Services:** coin laundry, wireless Internet. **Free Special Amenities: expanded continental breakfast and high-speed Internet.** [SAVE]

Phone: (608)723-4162

LAND O'LAKES pop. 882

SUNRISE LODGE

Cottage
$85-$210

Address: 5894 W Shore Dr 54540 **Location:** 2 mi s on US 45, 2.8 mi e on CR E, then 1 mi n. Located on west shore of Lac Vieux Desert. **Facility:** Smoke free premises. 24 units, some houses and cottages. 1-2 stories (no elevator), exterior corridors. **Parking:** winter plug-ins. **Terms:** 21 day cancellation notice-fee imposed. **Activities:** rental boats, rental canoes, boat dock, fishing, miniature golf, tennis court, cross country skiing, snowmobiling, recreation programs in season, badminton, baseball, exercise trail, soccer, bicycles, playground, basketball, horseshoes, shuffleboard, volleyball, game room. *Fee:* pontoons. **Guest Services:** wireless Internet.

Phone: 715/547-3684

LITTLE CHUTE pop. 10,476

COUNTRY INN & SUITES BY CARLSON-APPELTON NORTH

Hotel
$125-$299 1/1-4/30
$115-$299 4/1-12/31

Address: 130 Patriot Dr 54140 **Location:** US 41, exit 146, just e on CR N. **Facility:** Smoke free premises. 66 units, some efficiencies. 3 stories, interior corridors. **Terms:** 3 day cancellation notice. **Amenities:** high-speed Internet. **Pool(s):** heated indoor. **Activities:** whirlpool, waterslide, indoor water park, exercise room. *Fee:* game room. **Guest Services:** valet and coin laundry, wireless Internet. *(see ad p. 6)*

Phone: (920)788-8080

LODI pop. 2,882

BEST WESTERN COUNTRYSIDE INN

Hotel
$70-$200

Address: W 9250 Prospect Dr 53555 **Location:** I-90/94, exit 119, just w. **Facility:** Smoke free premises. 53 units, some kitchens. 2 stories, interior corridors. **Parking:** winter plug-ins. **Amenities:** high-speed Internet. **Pool(s):** heated indoor. **Activities:** whirlpool, exercise room. *Fee:* game room. **Guest Services:** coin laundry, wireless Internet. **Free Special Amenities: continental breakfast and early check-in/late check-out.**

Phone: (608)592-1450

LODI VALLEY SUITES

Hotel
$70-$135

Address: 1440 N Hwy 113 53555 **Location:** 1.5 mi n of jct SR 60. **Facility:** Smoke free premises. 26 units. 2 stories (no elevator), interior corridors. **Parking:** winter plug-ins. **Terms:** 2-3 night minimum stay - weekends, 3 day cancellation notice. **Pool(s):** heated indoor. **Guest Services:** wireless Internet.

Phone: (608)592-7331

LOMIRA pop. 2,233

COUNTRY HEARTH INN & SUITES

Hotel
Rates not provided

Address: 645 East Ave 53048 **Location:** US 41, exit 85 (SR 67), just nw. **Facility:** Smoke free premises. 60 units. 2 stories (no elevator), interior corridors. **Amenities:** safes (fee). **Pool(s):** heated indoor. **Activities:** whirlpool, patio, exercise room. **Guest Services:** wireless Internet.

Phone: 920/269-7477

LUCK pop. 1,210

——— WHERE TO DINE ———

CAFE WREN

American
$5-$11

Light meals composed of fresh ingredients and complemented by a selection of organic coffee and tea make this eclectic small-town eatery a worthy find. **Bar:** beer & wine. **Hours:** 7 am-7 pm, Sat & Sun 8 am-5 pm. Closed: 11/24, 12/25 & Easter. **Address:** 2596 State Hwy 35 54853 **Location:** 0.5 mi n of jct SR 48.

Phone: 715/472-4700

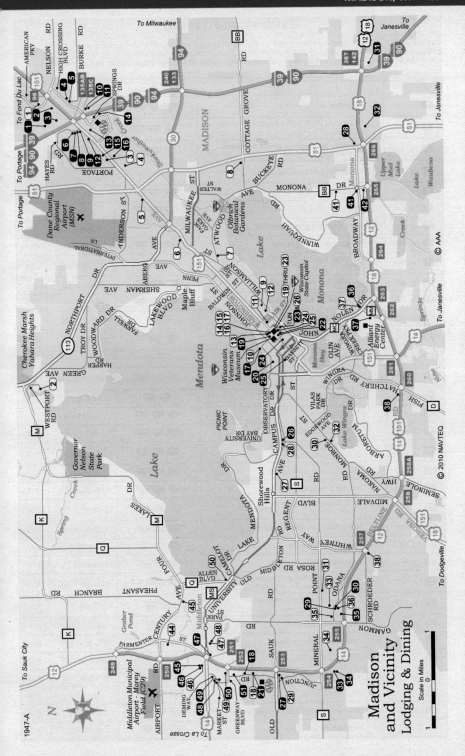

Madison
and Vicinity
Lodging & Dining

Scale in Miles

© 2010 NAVTEQ

© AAA

Madison and Vicinity

This index helps you "spot" where approved lodgings and restaurants are located on the corresponding detailed maps. Lodging daily rate range is for comparison only and show the property's high season. Restaurant rate range is a combination of lunch and/or dinner. Turn to the listing page for more detailed rate information and consult display ads for special promotions.

MADISON

Map Page	OA	Lodgings	Diamond Rated	High Season	Page
❶ / p. 499		Cambria Suites	▽▽▽	Rates not provided	507
❷ / p. 499		La Quinta Inn & Suites Madison American Center	▽▽▽	$69-$129	513
❸ / p. 499	AAA	**Holiday Inn Madison at The American Center** - see ad p. 512	▽▽▽	$139-$199 SAVE	512
❹ / p. 499	AAA	**GrandStay Residential Suites**	▽▽▽	Rates not provided SAVE	511
❺ / p. 499		Staybridge Suites	▽▽▽	$89-$199	515
❻ / p. 499		Hampton Inn-East	▽▽▽	$99-$209	511
❼ / p. 499	AAA	**Red Roof Inn-Madison #7052**	▽▽	$59-$94 SAVE	514
❽ / p. 499		Residence Inn by Marriott	▽▽▽	$126-$161	514
❾ / p. 499	AAA	**Comfort Inn & Suites - Airport** - see ad p. 508	▽▽	$69-$149 SAVE	508
❿ / p. 499		Fairfield Inn & Suites Madison East	▽▽▽	$125-$160	511
⓫ / p. 499		Courtyard by Marriott-Madison East	▽▽▽	$152-$194	509
⓬ / p. 499	AAA	**Econo Lodge of Madison** - see ad p. 510	▽▽	$55-$99 SAVE	511
⓭ / p. 499	AAA	**Best Western Plus East Towne Suites** - see ad p. 504	▽▽▽	$80-$210 SAVE	504
⓮ / p. 499	AAA	**Microtel Inn & Suites**	▽▽	$50-$67 SAVE	513
⓯ / p. 499	AAA	**Crowne Plaza Hotel Madison** - see ad p. 509	▽▽▽	$99-$209 SAVE	509
⓰ / p. 499		Baymont Inn & Suites	▽▽	$49-$121	504
⓱ / p. 499		The Edgewater	▽▽▽	$129-$419	511
⓲ / p. 499		Comfort Suites-Madison	▽▽▽	$79-$134	509
⓳ / p. 499		The Madison Concourse Hotel and Governor's Club - see ad p. 507	▽▽▽	$154-$284	513
⓴ / p. 499		The Dahlmann Campus Inn	▽▽▽	$140-$185	510
㉑ / p. 499		Holiday Inn Hotel & Suites	▽▽▽	$109-$229	512
㉒ / p. 499	AAA	**Best Western Plus Inn on the Park** - see ad p. 505	▽▽▽	$119-$259 SAVE	504
㉓ / p. 499	AAA	**Hilton Madison Monona Terrace**	▽▽▽	$139-$299 SAVE	512
㉔ / p. 499	AAA	**Hyatt Place Madison**	▽▽▽	$99-$299 SAVE	513
㉕ / p. 499	AAA	**Doubletree Hotel-Madison**	▽▽▽	$109-$349 SAVE	510
㉖ / p. 499	AAA	**Best Western Plus InnTowner & The Highland Club** - see ad p. 506, p. 155	▽▽▽	$119-$299 SAVE	505
㉗ / p. 499		Extended Stay Deluxe Madison West	▽▽	$56-$95	511
㉘ / p. 499	AAA	**Days Inn of Madison**	▽▽	$65-$116 SAVE	510
㉙ / p. 499	AAA	**AmericInn Madison West** - see ad p. 503	▽▽▽	$77-$120 SAVE	503
㉚ / p. 499	AAA	**Radisson Hotel Madison**	▽▽▽	$69-$199 SAVE	513
㉛ / p. 499	AAA	**Magnuson Grand Hotel Madison**	▽▽▽	$79-$199 SAVE	513
㉜ / p. 499		Sleep Inn & Suites	▽▽▽	$69-$139	514
㉝ / p. 499		Homewood Suites by Hilton Madison West	▽▽▽	$99-$209	513
㉞ / p. 499		Hampton Inn & Suites	▽▽▽	$99-$209	511

MADISON (cont'd)

Map Page	OA	Lodgings (cont'd)	Diamond Rated	High Season	Page
35 / p. 499	AAA	**Best Western West Towne Suites**	◆◆	$79-$179 SAVE	507
36 / p. 499	AAA	**Sheraton Madison Hotel**	◆◆◆	Rates not provided SAVE	514
37 / p. 499	AAA	**Clarion Suites Madison-Central**	◆◆◆	$80-$220 SAVE	507
38 / p. 499		Super 8-Madison	◆◆	$59-$99	515

Map Page	OA	Restaurants	Diamond Rated	Cuisine	Meal Range	Page
1 / p. 499		Erin's Snug Irish Pub	◆◆	Irish	$7-$20	516
2 / p. 499		The Mariner's Inn	◆◆	Steak	$14-$40	517
3 / p. 499	AAA	**Imperial Garden-East**	◆◆	Chinese	$7-$30	517
4 / p. 499		Laredo's	◆	Mexican	$6-$16	517
5 / p. 499		Prime Quarter Steak House	◆	Steak	$12-$27	518
6 / p. 499	AAA	**Ella's Kosher Style Deli & Ice Cream Parlor**	◆	Deli	$4-$12	516
7 / p. 499		Monty's Blue Plate Diner	◆◆	American	$5-$13	517
8 / p. 499		Dairyland Family Restaurant	◆◆	American	$7-$15	516
9 / p. 499		Eldorado Grill	◆◆	Southwestern	$8-$20	516
10 / p. 499		Admiralty Dining Room	◆◆◆	American	$9-$45	515
11 / p. 499		Bellini Italian Restaurant	◆◆	Italian	$12-$28	515
12 / p. 499		Bandung Restaurant	◆◆	Indonesian	$7-$17	515
13 / p. 499		The Blue Marlin	◆◆	Seafood	$9-$46	515
14 / p. 499		L'Etoile	◆◆◆	Regional American	$29-$42	517
15 / p. 499		The Old Fashioned Tavern & Restaurant	◆◆	American	$5-$29	518
16 / p. 499		Cafe Soleil	◆	Deli	$5-$10	515
17 / p. 499		Harvest	◆◆◆	American	$16-$28	517
18 / p. 499		George's Chop House	◆◆	American	$9-$30	516
19 / p. 499		The Casbah Restaurant & Lounge	◆◆	Mediterranean	$11-$21	516
20 / p. 499		Cafe Continental	◆◆	Italian	$9-$35	515
21 / p. 499		Tutto Pasta Cucina Italiana	◆◆	Italian	$7-$18	518
22 / p. 499		Marigold Kitchen	◆	American	$4-$11	517
23 / p. 499		Johnny Delmonico's	◆◆◆	Steak	$10-$47	517
24 / p. 499		Ocean Grill	◆◆◆	Seafood	$9-$30	518
25 / p. 499		The Tornado Club Steak House	◆◆◆	Steak	$14-$44	518
26 / p. 499	AAA	**Capitol Chophouse**	◆◆◆	Steak	$9-$45	516
27 / p. 499		Smoky's Club	◆◆	Steak	$10-$36	518
28 / p. 499		Lulu's	◆◆	Middle Eastern	$7-$24	517
29 / p. 499		Biaggi's Ristorante Italiano	◆◆◆	Italian	$8-$23	515
30 / p. 499		Pasqual's Salsaria & Southwestern Deli	◆	Southwestern	$6-$12	518
31 / p. 499		Otto's Restaurant & Bar	◆◆◆	Mediterranean	$15-$32	518
32 / p. 499		Bluephies	◆◆	American	$6-$15	515
33 / p. 499		Delaney's Charcoal Steaks	◆◆◆	Steak	$13-$45	516

Map Page	OA	Restaurants (cont'd)	Diamond Rated	Cuisine	Meal Range	Page
㉞ / p. 499		Pedro's Mexican Restaurante	▽▽	Mexican	$5-$17	518
㉟ / p. 499		Sa-Bai Thong	▽▽	Thai	$6-$17	518
㊱ / p. 499		China One West	▽	Chinese	$8-$11	516
㊲ / p. 499		Heartland Grill	▽▽	American	$8-$27	517
㊳ / p. 499		Copper Top Family Restaurant	▽	American	$5-$15	516

MONONA

Map Page	OA	Lodgings	Diamond Rated	High Season	Page
㊶ / p. 499		AmericInn of Madison South/Monona	▽▽	$99-$199	572
㊷ / p. 499		Country Inn & Suites By Carlson, Madison - see ad p. 6	▽▽▽	$99-$140	573

Map Page	OA	Restaurant	Diamond Rated	Cuisine	Meal Range	Page
㊶ / p. 499		Rossario's	▽▽	Italian	$7-$19	573

MIDDLETON

Map Page	OA	Lodgings	Diamond Rated	High Season	Page
㊺ / p. 499		Courtyard by Marriott Madison West/Middleton	▽▽▽	$134-$171	523
㊻ / p. 499	AAA	**Country Inn & Suites By Carlson, Madison West - see ad p. 508, p. 6**	▽▽▽	$114-$169 SAVE	523
㊼ / p. 499		Staybridge Suites by Holiday Inn	▽▽▽	$109-$149	524
㊽ / p. 499		Residence Inn by Marriott-Madison West/Middleton	▽▽▽	$152-$194	524
㊾ / p. 499		Hilton Garden Inn Madison West/Middleton	▽▽▽	$99-$209	524
㊿ / p. 499		Fairfield Inn & Suites by Marriott-Madison West	▽▽▽	$98-$125	524
51 / p. 499		Marriott Madison West	▽▽▽	$143-$183	524

Map Page	OA	Restaurants	Diamond Rated	Cuisine	Meal Range	Page
㊹ / p. 499		Fitzgerald's of Middleton	▽▽	American	$6-$35	524
㊺ / p. 499		Stamm House at Pheasant Branch	▽▽	American	$8-$26	525
㊻ / p. 499		P.F. Chang's China Bistro	▽▽▽	Chinese	$10-$23	525
㊼ / p. 499		Louisianne's Etc	▽▽▽	Cajun	$13-$36	525
㊽ / p. 499		Hubbard Avenue Diner	▽▽	American	$7-$12	524
㊾ / p. 499		Johnny's Italian Steakhouse	▽▽▽	Steak	$10-$30	525
㊿ / p. 499	AAA	**Imperial Garden Chinese Restaurant**	▽▽▽	Chinese	$5-$18	524

MADISON pop. 208,054   (See map and index starting on p. 499)

(See map and index starting on p. 499)

BAYMONT INN & SUITES

Hotel
$49-$121

Phone: (608)241-3861 **16**

Address: 4202 E Towne Blvd 53704 **Location:** I-90/94, exit 135A (US 151), 0.5 mi w. **Facility:** Smoke free premises. 92 units. 2 stories, interior corridors. **Activities:** exercise room. **Guest Services:** valet and coin laundry, wireless Internet.

BEST WESTERN PLUS EAST TOWNE SUITES

Hotel
$80-$210

Phone: (608)244-2020 **13**

Address: 4801 Annamark Dr 53704 **Location:** I-90/94, exit 135A (US 151) southbound; exit 135C (High Crossing Blvd) northbound, just sw on US 151. **Facility:** Smoke free premises. 122 units. 4 stories, interior corridors. **Parking:** winter plug-ins. **Amenities:** high-speed Internet. **Pool(s):** heated indoor. **Activities:** whirlpool, exercise room. **Guest Services:** valet laundry, wireless Internet. *(see ad below)*

AAA Benefit: Members save up to 20%, plus 10% bonus points with free rewards program.

FREE full breakfast and airport transportation

BEST WESTERN PLUS INN ON THE PARK

Hotel
$119-$259

Phone: (608)285-8000 **22**

Address: 22 S Carroll St 53703 **Location:** Downtown. Opposite the Wisconsin State Capitol. **Facility:** Smoke free premises. 215 units. 9 stories, interior corridors. **Parking:** valet only. **Terms:** cancellation fee imposed. **Amenities:** high-speed Internet. **Pool(s):** heated indoor. **Activities:** whirlpool, exercise room. **Guest Services:** valet laundry, area transportation-University of Wisconsin, wireless Internet. *(see ad p. 505)*

AAA Benefit: Members save up to 20%, plus 10% bonus points with free rewards program.

FREE newspaper and early check-in/late check-out

(See map and index starting on p. 499)

BEST WESTERN PLUS INNTOWNER & THE HIGHLAND CLUB

Hotel
$119-$299

Phone: (608)233-8778 26

Address: 2424 University Ave 53726 **Location:** 2.3 mi nw. **Facility:** Smoke free premises. 176 units. 4 stories, interior corridors. **Amenities:** *Some:* high-speed Internet. **Pool(s):** heated indoor. **Activities:** whirlpool, exercise room. **Guest Services:** valet laundry, area transportation-within 2 mi, wireless Internet. *(see ad p. 506 & p. 155)*

AAA Benefit:
Members save up to 20%, plus 10% bonus points with free rewards program.

FREE full breakfast and high-speed Internet

▼ See AAA listing p. 504 ▼

Madison's Only Capitol Square Hotel

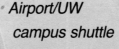

BEST WESTERN PLUS

Complimentary

- Airport/UW campus shuttle
- Valet parking
- Wireless & High-speed Internet
- Business center

Steps From

- Monona Terrace
- State Street
- Overture Center
- Kohl Center/UW Campus

800-279-8811
608-285-8000
reservations@innonthepark.net

22 S. Carroll St., Madison, WI 53703
www.innonthepark.net

(See map and index starting on p. 499)

BEST WESTERN WEST TOWNE SUITES

 Hotel
$79-$179

Phone: (608)833-4200 35

Address: 650 Grand Canyon Dr 53719 **Location:** US 12 and 14, exit 255 (Gammon Rd), just e on Odana Rd, then just sw. **Facility:** Smoke free premises. 101 units, some efficiencies. 2 stories (no elevator), interior corridors. **Parking:** winter plug-ins. **Activities:** exercise room. **Guest Services:** valet and coin laundry, wireless Internet.

AAA Benefit:
Members save up to 20%, plus 10% bonus points with free rewards program.

FREE full breakfast and high-speed Internet

CAMBRIA SUITES

Hotel
Rates not provided

Phone: 608/241-7070 1

Address: 5045 Eastpark Blvd 53718 **Location:** I-90/94, exit 135A (US 151), just w. **Facility:** Smoke free premises. 121 units. 6 stories, interior corridors. **Amenities:** high-speed Internet. **Pool(s):** heated indoor. **Activities:** whirlpool, exercise room. **Guest Services:** valet and coin laundry, area transportation-within 7 mi, wireless Internet.

CLARION SUITES MADISON-CENTRAL

Hotel
$80-$220

Phone: (608)284-1234 37

Address: 2110 Rimrock Rd 53713 **Location:** US 12 and 18, exit 262 (Rimrock Rd), just nw. Located next to Alliant Energy Center. **Facility:** Smoke free premises. 140 units, some efficiencies. 8 stories, interior corridors. **Terms:** cancellation fee imposed. **Amenities:** high-speed Internet. **Pool(s):** heated indoor. **Activities:** whirlpool, exercise room. **Guest Services:** valet and coin laundry, area transportation-downtown, wireless Internet. **Free Special Amenities:** full breakfast and high-speed Internet.

▼ See AAA listing p. 513 ▼

(See map and index starting on p. 499)

▼ *See AAA listing above* ▼

▼ *See AAA listing p. 523* ▼

(See map and index starting on p. 499)

COMFORT SUITES-MADISON

Hotel
$79-$134

Address: 1253 John Q Hammons Dr 53717 **Location:** US 12 and 14, exit 252 (Greenway Blvd), just sw. **Facility:** Smoke free premises. 95 units. 3 stories, interior corridors. **Parking:** winter plug-ins. **Amenities:** safes (fee). *Some:* high-speed Internet. **Pool(s):** heated indoor. **Activities:** whirlpool, exercise room. *Fee:* game room. **Guest Services:** valet and coin laundry, area transportation-within 5 mi, wireless Internet.

Phone: (608)836-3033 **18**

COURTYARD BY MARRIOTT-MADISON EAST

Hotel
$152-$194

Address: 2502 Crossroads Dr 53718 **Location:** I-90/94, exit 135C (High Crossing Blvd). **Facility:** Smoke free premises. 127 units. 4 stories, interior corridors. **Parking:** winter plug-ins. **Terms:** cancellation fee imposed. **Amenities:** video games (fee), high-speed Internet. **Pool(s):** heated indoor. **Activities:** whirlpool, exercise room. **Guest Services:** valet and coin laundry, wireless Internet.

Phone: (608)661-8100 **11**

> **AAA Benefit:**
> Members save a minimum 5% off the best available rate.

CROWNE PLAZA HOTEL MADISON

Hotel
$99-$209

Address: 4402 E Washington Ave 53704 **Location:** I-90/94, exit 135A (US 151), 0.4 mi w. **Facility:** Smoke free premises. 226 units. 6 stories, interior corridors. **Terms:** check-in 4 pm, cancellation fee imposed. **Amenities:** video games (fee). **Dining:** 2 restaurants. **Pool(s):** heated indoor. **Activities:** whirlpool, exercise room. *Fee:* game room. **Guest Services:** valet and coin laundry, area transportation-within 4 mi, wireless Internet. *(see ad below)*

Phone: (608)244-4703 **15**

FREE room upgrade (subject to availability with advance reservations) and high-speed Internet

---

▼ See AAA listing above ▼

(See map and index starting on p. 499)

THE DAHLMANN CAMPUS INN

Hotel
$140-$185

Phone: (608)257-4391   ㉒

Address: 601 Langdon St 53703 **Location:** Just e of jct Lake St; downtown, at University of Wisconsin-Madison campus. **Facility:** Smoke free premises. 74 units. 7 stories, interior corridors. **Terms:** cancellation fee imposed. **Amenities:** high-speed Internet. *Some:* safes. **Activities:** exercise room. **Guest Services:** valet laundry, wireless Internet.

DAYS INN OF MADISON

Hotel
$65-$116

Phone: (608)223-1800   ㉘

Address: 4402 E Broadway Service Rd 53716 **Location:** US 12 and 18, exit 266 (US 51), just ne. **Facility:** Smoke free premises. 65 units. 3 stories, interior corridors. **Pool(s):** heated indoor. **Activities:** whirlpool, exercise room. **Guest Services:** complimentary laundry, wireless Internet.

FREE expanded continental breakfast and high-speed Internet

DOUBLETREE HOTEL-MADISON

Hotel
$109-$349

Phone: (608)251-5511   ㉕

Address: 525 W Johnson St 53703 **Location:** 0.5 mi sw of Capitol Square. Adjacent to University of Wisconsin-Madison campus. **Facility:** Smoke free premises. 163 units. 7 stories, interior corridors. **Terms:** 1-7 night minimum stay, cancellation fee imposed. **Amenities:** video games (fee), safes. **Pool(s):** heated indoor. **Activities:** whirlpool, exercise room. **Guest Services:** valet laundry, area transportation-campus area, hospitals & Menona Terrace, wireless Internet. **Free Special Amenities:** high-speed Internet and local transportation.

DOUBLETREE
HOTELS·SUITES·RESORTS·CLUBS

AAA Benefit:
Members save 5% or more everyday!

▼ See AAA listing p. 511 ▼

(See map and index starting on p. 499)

ECONO LODGE OF MADISON

Hotel
$55-$99

Phone: (608)241-4171 **12**

Address: 4726 E Washington Ave 53704 **Location:** I-90/94, exit 135A (US 151), just w. **Facility:** Smoke free premises. 99 units. 2 stories (no elevator), interior corridors. **Parking:** winter plug-ins. **Amenities:** safes (fee). **Guest Services:** coin laundry, wireless Internet. *(see ad p. 510)*

FREE continental breakfast and high-speed Internet

THE EDGEWATER

Classic
Hotel
$129-$419

Phone: (608)256-9071 **17**

Address: 666 Wisconsin Ave 53703 **Location:** On Lake Mendota, 0.3 mi n of Capitol Square. **Facility:** In the Manson district, this classic hotel offers lakeshore views and the ability to walk by the lake. A conference center and restaurant are on site. Smoke free premises. 107 units. 5-8 stories, interior corridors. **Amenities:** high-speed Internet. **Dining:** Admiralty Dining Room, see separate listing. **Activities:** exercise room. *Fee:* massage. **Guest Services:** valet laundry, area transportation-within 3.5 mi, wireless Internet.

EXTENDED STAY DELUXE MADISON WEST

Extended Stay
Hotel
$56-$95

Phone: (608)833-2121 **27**

Address: 45 Junction Ct 53717 **Location:** SR 12, exit 253 (Old Sauk Rd), just w. **Facility:** Smoke free premises. 73 kitchen units. 3 stories, interior corridors. **Terms:** cancellation fee imposed. **Pool(s):** heated outdoor. **Activities:** exercise room. **Guest Services:** coin laundry, wireless Internet.

FAIRFIELD INN & SUITES MADISON EAST

Hotel
$125-$160

Phone: (608)661-2700 **10**

Address: 2702 Crossroads Dr 53718 **Location:** I-90/94, exit 135C (US 151/High Crossing Blvd). **Facility:** Smoke free premises. 130 units. 4 stories, interior corridors. **Terms:** cancellation fee imposed. **Amenities:** high-speed Internet. **Pool(s):** heated indoor. **Activities:** whirlpool, exercise room. **Guest Services:** valet and coin laundry, area transportation-within 5 mi, wireless Internet.

> **AAA Benefit:**
> Members save a minimum 5% off the best available rate.

GRANDSTAY RESIDENTIAL SUITES

Extended Stay
Hotel
Rates not provided

Phone: 608/241-2500 **4**

Address: 5317 High Crossing Blvd 53718 **Location:** I-90/94, exit 135C (US 151/High Crossing Blvd), 0.5 mi e. **Facility:** Smoke free premises. 53 efficiencies, some two bedrooms. 3 stories, interior corridors. **Amenities:** high-speed Internet. **Pool(s):** heated indoor. **Activities:** whirlpool, putting green, children's play area, patio with grill, exercise room, basketball. **Guest Services:** valet and coin laundry, wireless Internet. **Free Special Amenities: continental breakfast and high-speed Internet.**

HAMPTON INN & SUITES

Hotel
$99-$209

Phone: (608)271-0200 **34**

Address: 483 Commerce Dr 53719 **Location:** US 12, exit 261B, just n. **Facility:** Smoke free premises. 132 units. 5 stories, interior corridors. **Terms:** 1-7 night minimum stay, cancellation fee imposed. **Amenities:** high-speed Internet. **Pool(s):** heated indoor. **Activities:** whirlpool, waterslide, exercise room. **Guest Services:** valet and coin laundry, area transportation-within 5 mi, wireless Internet.

> **AAA Benefit:**
> Members save up to 10% everyday!

HAMPTON INN-EAST

Hotel
$99-$209

Phone: (608)244-9400 **6**

Address: 4820 Hayes Rd 53704 **Location:** I-90/94, exit 135A (US 151), just w to Hayes Rd, then just ne. **Facility:** Smoke free premises. 115 units. 4 stories, interior corridors. **Parking:** winter plug-ins. **Terms:** 1-7 night minimum stay, cancellation fee imposed. **Pool(s):** heated indoor. **Activities:** whirlpool, exercise room. **Guest Services:** valet laundry, wireless Internet.

> **AAA Benefit:**
> Members save up to 10% everyday!

Stay. Play. Dine. Save. Visit AAA.com/Travel or CAA.ca/Travel for Information To Go!

(See map and index starting on p. 499)

HILTON MADISON MONONA TERRACE

Hotel
$139-$299

Address: 9 E Wilson St 53703 **Location:** 2 blks e of Capitol Square; downtown. **Facility:** Smoke free premises. 240 units. 13 stories, interior corridors. **Parking:** valet only. **Terms:** 1-7 night minimum stay, cancellation fee imposed. **Amenities:** *Fee:* video games, high-speed Internet. **Dining:** Capitol Chophouse, see separate listing, entertainment. **Pool(s):** heated indoor. **Activities:** whirlpool, exercise room. **Guest Services:** valet laundry, area transportation-hospitals & attractions, wireless Internet.

Phone: (608)255-5100   **23**

AAA Benefit:
Members save 5% or more everyday!

HOLIDAY INN HOTEL & SUITES

Hotel
$109-$229

Address: 1109 Fourier Dr 53717 **Location:** US 12 and 14, exit 253 (Old Sauk Rd), just w, then 0.4 mi n on Excelsior Rd. **Facility:** Smoke free premises. 157 units. 4 stories, interior corridors. **Parking:** winter plug-ins. **Amenities:** high-speed Internet. *Fee:* game room. **Dining:** George's Chop House, see separate listing. **Pool(s):** heated indoor. **Activities:** whirlpool, waterslide, indoor water park, exercise room. *Fee:* game room. **Guest Services:** valet and coin laundry, area transportation-within 5 mi, wireless Internet.

Phone: (608)826-0500   **21**

HOLIDAY INN MADISON AT THE AMERICAN CENTER

Hotel
$139-$199

Address: 5109 W Terrace Dr 53718 **Location:** I-90/94 W, exit 135B, just w. **Facility:** Smoke free premises. 138 units. 5 stories, interior corridors. **Parking:** winter plug-ins. **Terms:** check-in 4 pm. **Amenities:** high-speed Internet, safes. **Pool(s):** heated indoor. **Activities:** whirlpool, exercise room. **Guest Services:** valet and coin laundry, area transportation-within 5 mi, wireless Internet. **Free Special Amenities:** high-speed Internet and local transportation. *(see ad below)*

Phone: (608)249-4220   **3**

▼ See AAA listing above ▼

STAY IMPRESSED.

Holiday Inn Madison at The American Center
5109 W Terrace Dr.
Madison, WI 53718
608-249-4220 · 1-800-Holiday
holidayinn.com

(See map and index starting on p. 499)

HOMEWOOD SUITES BY HILTON MADISON WEST

Extended Stay Hotel
$99-$209

Address: 479 Commerce Dr 53719 **Location:** US 12, exit 261B, just n. **Facility:** Smoke free premises. 122 efficiencies, some two bedrooms. 5 stories, interior corridors. **Terms:** 1-7 night minimum stay, cancellation fee imposed. **Amenities:** high-speed Internet. **Pool(s):** heated indoor. **Activities:** whirlpool, putting green, grills, gazebo, exercise room. **Guest Services:** valet and coin laundry, area transportation-within 5 mi, wireless Internet.

Phone: (608)271-0600 〔33〕

HYATT PLACE MADISON

Hotel
$99-$299

Address: 333 W Washington Ave 53703 **Location:** 2.5 blks sw of Capital Square; downtown. **Facility:** Smoke free premises. 151 units. 11 stories, interior corridors. **Terms:** cancellation fee imposed. **Amenities:** high-speed Internet. **Pool(s):** heated indoor/outdoor. **Activities:** exercise room. **Guest Services:** valet laundry, area transportation-within 2 mi, wireless Internet. **Free Special Amenities: continental breakfast and high-speed Internet.**

Phone: (608)257-2700 〔24〕

LA QUINTA INN & SUITES MADISON AMERICAN CENTER

Hotel
$69-$129

Address: 5217 E Terrace Dr 53718 **Location:** US 151, exit 98B (American Pkwy), just sw. **Facility:** Smoke free premises. 120 units, some efficiencies. 4 stories, interior corridors. **Amenities:** video games (fee). **Pool(s):** heated indoor. **Activities:** whirlpool, exercise room. **Guest Services:** valet and coin laundry, area transportation-within 5 mi, wireless Internet.

Phone: (608)245-0123 〔2〕

THE MADISON CONCOURSE HOTEL AND GOVERNOR'S CLUB

Hotel
$154-$284

Address: 1 W Dayton St 53703 **Location:** Just n of Capitol Square; downtown. **Facility:** Smoke free premises. 356 units. 13 stories, interior corridors. **Parking:** valet only. **Terms:** cancellation fee imposed. **Pool(s):** heated indoor. **Activities:** sauna, whirlpool, exercise room. **Fee:** massage, game room. **Guest Services:** valet laundry, area transportation-university vicinity & restaurants, wireless Internet. *(see ad p. 507)*

Phone: (608)257-6000 〔19〕

MAGNUSON GRAND HOTEL MADISON

Hotel
$79-$199

Address: 3510 Mill Pond Rd 53718 **Location:** I-90, exit 142B, just e on US 12 and 18, then w on south frontage road. **Facility:** Smoke free premises. 100 units. 4 stories, interior corridors. **Terms:** cancellation fee imposed. **Amenities:** high-speed Internet, safes (fee). **Pool(s):** heated indoor. **Activities:** whirlpool, exercise room. **Guest Services:** valet and coin laundry, area transportation-within 15 mi, wireless Internet.

Phone: (608)224-1500 〔31〕

FREE expanded continental breakfast and preferred room (subject to availability with advance reservations)

MICROTEL INN & SUITES

Hotel
$50-$67

Address: 2139 E Springs Dr 53704 **Location:** I-90/94, exit 135A (US 151), just s, then 0.5 mi e. **Facility:** Smoke free premises. 100 units. 3 stories, interior corridors. **Parking:** winter plug-ins. **Terms:** cancellation fee imposed. **Activities:** exercise room. **Guest Services:** wireless Internet. **Free Special Amenities: continental breakfast and high-speed Internet.**

Phone: (608)242-9000 〔14〕

RADISSON HOTEL MADISON

Hotel
$69-$199

Address: 517 Grand Canyon Rd 53719 **Location:** US 12 and 14, exit 255 (Gammon Rd), 0.5 mi e on Odana Rd. Located in a commercial area. **Facility:** Smoke free premises. 153 units. 2 stories, interior corridors. **Terms:** cancellation fee imposed. **Amenities:** high-speed Internet. **Some:** safes. **Pool(s):** heated indoor. **Activities:** whirlpool, exercise room. **Guest Services:** valet laundry, area transportation-within 3 mi, wireless Internet. **Free Special Amenities: full breakfast and high-speed Internet.**

Phone: (608)833-0100 〔30〕

(See map and index starting on p. 499)

RED ROOF INN-MADISON #7052　　　　　　　　　Phone: (608)241-1787

Motel
$59-$94 5/18-4/30
$55-$90 4/1-5/17

Address: 4830 Hayes Rd 53704 **Location:** I-90/94, exit 135A (US 151), just sw. **Facility:** Smoke free premises. 108 units. 2 stories (no elevator), exterior corridors. **Amenities:** safes (fee). **Guest Services:** wireless Internet.

RESIDENCE INN BY MARRIOTT　　　　　　　　　Phone: (608)244-5047 **8**

Extended Stay
Hotel
$126-$161

Address: 4862 Hayes Rd 53704 **Location:** I-90/94, exit 135A (US 151), just sw to Hayes Rd, then just ne. **Facility:** Smoke free premises. 66 units, some two bedrooms. 3 stories, interior corridors. **Terms:** cancellation fee imposed. **Pool(s):** heated indoor. **Activities:** whirlpool, exercise room, sports court. **Guest Services:** valet and coin laundry, wireless Internet.

SHERATON MADISON HOTEL　　　　　　　　　Phone: 608/251-2300 **36**

Hotel
Rates not provided

Address: 706 John Nolen Dr 53713 **Location:** US 12 and 18, exit 263 (John Nolen Dr), just n. **Facility:** Smoke free premises. 239 units. 8 stories, interior corridors. **Dining:** Heartland Grill, see separate listing. **Pool(s):** heated indoor. **Activities:** whirlpool, exercise room. **Guest Services:** valet laundry, area transportation-within 5 mi, wireless Internet. **Free Special Amenities:** early check-in/late check-out and local transportation.

SLEEP INN & SUITES　　　　　　　　　Phone: (608)221-8100 **32**

Hotel
$69-$139

Address: 4802 Tradewinds Pkwy 53718 **Location:** US 12/14/18/151, exit 266, 0.5 mi se, then 0.6 mi on Dutch Mill Rd. **Facility:** Smoke free premises. 89 units. 3 stories, interior corridors. **Pool(s):** heated indoor. **Activities:** whirlpool, exercise room. **Fee:** game room. **Guest Services:** valet and coin laundry, wireless Internet.

(See map and index starting on p. 499)

STAYBRIDGE SUITES

Extended Stay
Hotel
$89-$199

Phone: (608)241-2300 **5**

Address: 3301 City View Dr 53718 **Location:** I-90/94, exit 135C (US 151/High Crossing Blvd), just e. **Facility:** Smoke free premises. 90 efficiencies, some two bedrooms. 3 stories, interior corridors. **Terms:** 3 day cancellation notice. **Amenities:** high-speed Internet. **Pool(s):** heated indoor. **Activities:** whirlpool, patio with gas grill, library, exercise room. **Guest Services:** valet and coin laundry, wireless Internet.

SUPER 8-MADISON

Hotel
$59-$99

Phone: (608)258-8882 **38**

Address: 1602 W Beltline Hwy 53713 **Location:** US 12 and 18, exit 260B (CR D), just w on N Frontage Rd. **Facility:** Smoke free premises. 88 units. 3 stories, interior corridors. **Parking:** winter plug-ins. **Terms:** 2 night minimum stay - seasonal and/or weekends. **Pool(s):** heated indoor. **Activities:** whirlpool, limited exercise equipment. **Guest Services:** coin laundry, wireless Internet.

—— WHERE TO DINE ——

ADMIRALTY DINING ROOM

American
$9-$45

Phone: 608/661-6582 **10**

An elegant dining room, extensive wine list, good Continental cuisine and great views of Lake Mendota add up to a fine-dining event at this spot. **Bar:** full bar. **Hours:** 6:30-10 am, 11:30-2 & 5:30-9 pm, Sat 7:30 am-11 pm, Sun 7:30 am-10 & 11-2 pm. Closed major holidays. **Address:** 666 Wisconsin Ave 53703 **Location:** On Lake Mendota, 0.3 mi n of Capitol Square; in The Edgewater.

BANDUNG RESTAURANT

Indonesian
$7-$17

Phone: 608/255-6910 **12**

The exotic tastes and spices of various regions of Indonesia come out in the restaurant's well-seasoned dishes. Indonesian arts, crafts and batik decorate the dining area. **Bar:** beer & wine. **Hours:** 11 am-2 & 5-9 pm, Fri & Sat-10 pm, Sun 4 pm-8 pm. Closed major holidays. **Address:** 600 Williamson St 53703 **Location:** Just e of jct N Blair St; downtown.

BELLINI ITALIAN RESTAURANT

Italian
$12-$28

Phone: 608/250-0097 **11**

Creative Italian-American dishes are served in the beautifully restored landmark church, which features original stained-glass windows and woodwork. The menu includes mouthwatering pastas and pizzas, as well as the delicious dessert specialty: cheesecake wrap. **Bar:** full bar. **Reservations:** suggested. **Hours:** 4:30 pm-9 pm, Fri-10 pm, Sat 5 pm-10 pm. **Address:** 401 E Washington Ave 53703 **Location:** Just e of Capitol Square; downtown. **Parking:** street only.

BENVENUTO'S ITALIAN GRILL

Italian
$8-$19

Phone: 608/241-1144

The casual eatery's menu comprises Italian and American fare, including gourmet calzones, pasta, ribs, wood-fired pizza, meatball sandwiches, steaks, mushroom and mozzarella burgers, walleyed pike and popcorn shrimp. **Bar:** full bar. **Hours:** 11 am-10 pm. Closed: 11/24, 12/24, 12/25. **Address:** 1849 Northport Dr 53704 **Location:** 1 mi nw of jct SR 113 (Northport Dr/Penn Ave) and CR CV (Packers Ave).

BIAGGI'S RISTORANTE ITALIANO

Italian
$8-$23

Phone: 608/664-9288 **29**

Cool, upscale decor surrounds diners who savor freshly prepared creations. Delicious combinations of quality, unusual ingredients make for an adventurous dining experience. **Bar:** full bar. **Hours:** 11 am-9:30 pm, Fri & Sat-10:30 pm, Sun-9 pm. Closed: 11/24, 12/25. **Address:** 601 Junction Rd 53717 **Location:** US 12 and 14, exit 253 (Old Sauk Rd), just w; in Portofino Place Shopping area.

THE BLUE MARLIN

Seafood
$9-$46

Phone: 608/255-2255 **13**

Grilled seafood dishes center on fresh tuna, swordfish, salmon and live Maine lobster. **Bar:** full bar. **Reservations:** suggested. **Hours:** 5 pm-9 pm, Tues-Thurs to 10 pm, Fri 11 am-2:30 & 5-10 pm. Closed: 7/4. **Address:** 101 N Hamilton St 53703 **Location:** Just n of Capitol Square; downtown. **Parking:** street only.

BLUEPHIES

American
$6-$15

Phone: 608/231-3663 **32**

This modern restaurant's menu offers everything from Southwestern dishes to old-fashioned comfort food. Among the extensive dinner options are the meatloaf dinner, peppercorn-encrusted tuna dinner, sweet potato quesadilla and lots of vegetarian options. Brunch is served on Saturday and Sunday. **Bar:** full bar. **Reservations:** suggested. **Hours:** 11 am-9 pm, Fri-10 pm, Sat 8 am-10 pm, Sun 8 am-9 pm. Closed: 11/24, 12/24, 12/25. **Address:** 2701 Monroe St 53711 **Location:** US 12/14, exit 258 (Verona Rd), 2 mi nw; in Knickerbocker Place.

CAFE CONTINENTAL

Italian
$9-$35

Phone: 608/251-4880 **20**

A zinc bar is the centerpiece of the trendy Parisian-themed dining room, marked by hanging lamps, high ceilings and soft lighting. The menu centers on creatively prepared pasta, gourmet pizza and Continental cuisine. In-house desserts are rich. **Bar:** full bar. **Reservations:** suggested. **Hours:** 11 am-2 & 4-9 pm, Sat & Sun 9 am-3 pm. Closed: 11/24, 12/24, 12/25. **Address:** 108 King St 53703 **Location:** Just e of Capitol Square; downtown. **Parking:** street only.

CAFE SOLEIL

Deli
$5-$10

Phone: 608/251-0500 **16**

Across from the farmer's market, the casual soup-and-sandwich spot lavishes the same attention to fresh local and certified organic ingredients that has made the upstairs L'Etoile restaurant famous. **Hours:** 7:30 am-2:30 pm, Sat from 6:30 am. Closed major holidays; also Sun. **Address:** 25 N Pinckney St 53703 **Location:** On Capitol Square; downtown. **Parking:** street only.

(See map and index starting on p. 499)

CAPITOL CHOPHOUSE
Phone: 608/255-0165 ㉖

Steak
$9-$45

The clubby steakhouse has become known for its serious steaks, which are dry-aged for 28 days, and incredibly fresh seafood. **Bar:** full bar. **Reservations:** suggested. **Hours:** 11:30 am-2 & 5-10 pm, Sat from 5 pm. Closed: Sun. **Address:** 9 E Wilson St 53703 **Location:** 2 blks e of Capitol Square; downtown; in Hilton Madison Monona Terrace. CALL ♿Ⓜ

THE CASBAH RESTAURANT & LOUNGE
Phone: 608/255-2272 ⑲

Mediterranean
$11-$21

Right off the downtown square, the three-story restaurant and lounge serves Mediterranean food in either a casual environment or a space marked by eclectic King Tut-style decor. **Bar:** full bar. **Reservations:** suggested. **Hours:** 11 am-2 & 5-10 pm, Sun-9 pm. Closed major holidays. **Address:** 119 E Main St 53703 **Location:** Downtown. **Parking:** street only.

CHINA ONE WEST
Phone: 608/833-5288 ㊱

Chinese
$8-$11

Between two lodgings, this is a great place to experience a taste of Chinese cuisine. A multitude of delightful dishes is presented in a buffet format. **Bar:** beer only. **Hours:** 10:30 am-10 pm, Fri & Sat-11 pm. **Address:** 518 Grand Canyon Dr 53719 **Location:** US 12/14, exit 255 (Gammon Rd), just n, then 0.5 mi e on Odana Rd.

COPPER TOP FAMILY RESTAURANT
Phone: 608/271-4588 ㊳

American
$5-$15

Easily accessed from the Beltline, the family-owned restaurant specializes in breakfast. However, varied American, Mexican and Chinese dishes—from meatloaf to chicken stir-fry—also can be sampled in the diner-style setting. **Hours:** 6 am-9 pm, Sun-8 pm. **Address:** 5401 W Beltline Hwy 53711 **Location:** US 14, exit 257 (S Whitney Way), just sw.

DAIRYLAND FAMILY RESTAURANT
Phone: 608/222-9232 ⑧

American
$7-$15

The family-owned restaurant caters to locals with homestyle cooking, including homemade soups, steak, seafood, sandwiches and pasta dishes. **Hours:** 6 am-9 pm. Closed: 11/24, 12/24, 12/25. **Address:** 716 Cottage Grove Rd 53716 **Location:** Jct US 51 (Stoughton Rd) and Cottage Grove Rd.

DELANEY'S CHARCOAL STEAKS
Phone: 608/833-7337 ㉝

Steak
$13-$45

Established in 1973, the restaurant prepares prime rib, chicken, chops and select fresh seafood. However, top billing goes to the steaks, which are cut on the premises from USDA prime and choice aged Black Angus steer loins and served on a hot sizzler for that old-fashioned steakhouse feeling. **Bar:** full bar. **Hours:** 5 pm-9:30 pm, Fri & Sat-10 pm. Closed major holidays; also Sun. **Address:** 449 Grand Canyon Dr 53719 **Location:** US 12, exit 255 (Gammon Rd), just n, just e, then just n. CALL ♿Ⓜ

ELDORADO GRILL
Phone: 608/280-9378 ⑨

Southwestern
$8-$20

The old candy factory has been transformed into a warm and authentic Western atmosphere. The menu reflects an eclectic combination of Tex-Mex, Southwestern and Mexican cuisine with an upscale twist. Specialties include four-cheese chile relleno, beef tenderloin with chipotle blue butter, catfish Mariposa and the chocolate ancho pecan pie dessert. The bar features more than 60 types of tequila. **Bar:** full bar. **Reservations:** suggested. **Hours:** 5 pm-9 pm, Thurs also 11 am-2 pm, Fri & Sat 5 pm-10 pm, Sun 9 am-2 pm. Closed major holidays. **Address:** 744 Williamson St 53703 **Location:** Jct Winnebago St and E Washington Ave (US 151), 0.6 mi w.

ELLA'S KOSHER STYLE DELI & ICE CREAM PARLOR
Phone: 608/241-5291 ⑥

Deli
$4-$12

The extensive menu centers primarily on kosher sandwiches and salad. Antique and motorized toys, which decorate the charming restaurant, please adults and children alike. Noteworthy on the dessert menu is the delicious, old-fashioned frozen custard. **Bar:** beer & wine. **Hours:** 10 am-10 pm, Fri & Sat-11 pm; Fri & Sat-midnight 6/1-8/31. **Address:** 2902 E Washington Ave 53704 **Location:** I-90/94, exit 135A (US 151), 3 mi w.

ERIN'S SNUG IRISH PUB
Phone: 608/242-7616 ①

Irish
$7-$20

The fun experience begins from the moment guests notice the double-decker bus parked out front. Beautiful decor is found throughout, and Irish ballads play overhead. Open-mic nights and live entertainment are offered on weekends. The menu has something for everyone, from traditional Irish favorites such as bangers and mash or corned beef and cabbage to more American choices such as steaks or seafood. Also offered are a kids' menu and an extensive beer selection. **Entertainment. Bar:** full bar. **Hours:** 11 am-11 pm, Fri & Sat-2 am, Sun 9 am-10 pm. **Address:** 4601 American Pkwy 53718 **Location:** I-151, exit 98B, just nw. CALL ♿Ⓜ

GEORGE'S CHOP HOUSE
Phone: 608/826-0555 ⑱

American
$9-$30

This hybrid steakhouse exerts a subtle Tuscan influence in both its attractive decor and food. In addition to eight 21-day-aged steaks, this place serves such Italian favorites as calamari fritte, salmone alla griglia and lasagna Bolognese. **Bar:** full bar. **Hours:** 6:30 am-9:30 & 5-9 pm, Sat & Sun 7 am-11 am. Closed: 11/24, 12/25. **Address:** 1109 Fourier Dr 53717 **Location:** US 12 and 14, exit 253 (Old Sauk Rd), just w, then 0.4 mi n on Excelsior Rd; in Holiday Inn Hotel & Suites. CALL ♿Ⓜ

GRANITE CITY FOOD & BREWERY
Phone: 608/829-0700

American
$8-$25

The popular restaurant and brewery caters to travelers, business professionals, sports enthusiasts and children. The varying menu centers on American fare. Favorites include honey-rosemary filet mignon, barbecue ribs, a nice array of salads and classic sandwiches. Save room for one of the tasty, large-portioned desserts. Five to six beer varieties are brewed on the premises. **Bar:** full bar. **Hours:** 11 am-midnight, Fri-1 am, Sat 9 am-1 am, Sun 10 am-10 pm. **Address:** 72 West Towne Mall 53719 **Location:** US 12, exit 254; in West Towne Mall. CALL ♿Ⓜ

(See map and index starting on p. 499)

HARVEST | Phone: 608/255-6075 (17)

American
$16-$28

Affording a stunning view of the capitol building, the intimate French-American restaurant presents a weekly changing menu. Fresh, locally grown and certified organic produce comes from the weekend farmer's market across the street. **Bar:** full bar. **Reservations:** suggested. **Hours:** 5:30 pm-9 pm, Fri & Sat 5 pm-10 pm. Closed major holidays; also Sun. **Address:** 21 N Pinckney St 53703 **Location:** On Capitol Square; downtown. **Parking:** street only. CALL

HEARTLAND GRILL | Phone: 608/258-9505 (37)

American
$8-$27

Just off the Beltline, the Frank Lloyd Wright prairie-style setting encourages patrons to relax over preparations of stylish Midwestern cuisine. **Bar:** full bar. **Reservations:** suggested. **Hours:** 6:30 am-2 & 5-9 pm, Sat & Sun from 7 am. Closed: 11/24, 12/24, 12/25. **Address:** 706 John Nolen Dr 53713 **Location:** US 12 and 18, exit 263 (John Nolen Dr), just n; in Sheraton Madison Hotel. CALL

IMPERIAL GARDEN-EAST *Menu on AAA.com* | Phone: 608/249-0466 (3)

Chinese
$7-$30

Traditional specialties—such as cashew chicken, Mongolian beef and the happy family platter—are filling and flavorful. Also featured is a sushi bar. An attractive tiger carving is among beautiful Asian appointments in the moderately upscale dining room. Lighting is subtle. **Bar:** full bar. **Hours:** 11 am-2 & 4-9:30 pm, Fri-10:30 pm, Sat 11:30 am-10:30 pm, Sun 11:30 am-9 pm. Closed: 11/24, 12/24, 12/25; also for lunch 1/1 & 7/4. **Address:** 4214 E Washington Ave 53704 **Location:** I-90/94, exit 135A (US 151), 0.5 mi w. CALL

JOHNNY DELMONICO'S | Phone: 608/257-8325 (23)

Steak
$10-$47

Near the State Capitol, the stylish and trendy dining room specializes in premium aged steaks, fresh fish and other seafood. Menu options include oysters on the half shell, free-range chicken, French-style pork chops, roasted lamb shank and sirloin burgers. Seating is comfortable, and the service is refined. **Bar:** full bar. **Reservations:** suggested. **Hours:** 11 am-2 & 5-9 pm, Fri-10 pm, Sat 5 pm-10 pm. Closed: 11/24, 12/25. **Address:** 130 S Pinckney St 53703 **Location:** Corner of Doty St; downtown. CALL

LA BAMBA | Phone: 608/277-9522

Mexican
$5-$13

Flavorful food is prepared in front of patrons of the casual restaurant, which stays open for late-night eating. Portions are ample. **Hours:** 11 am-2 am, Fri & Sat-3 am. Closed: 11/24, 12/25. **Address:** 710 S Gammon Rd 53719-1302 **Location:** US 12, exit 255 (Gammon Rd), just s. CALL

LAREDO'S | Phone: 608/240-9701 (4)

Mexican
$6-$16

One of the city's past "Best of Madison" award-winners, the restaurant offers tasty Mexican food at a reasonable price. Included on the menu are casuelon (grilled rib-eye and chicken served with rice and beans) and steak ranchero (grilled T-bone steak with a choice of tomatillo or supreme sauce). Guests also can pick from numerous varieties of chimichangas, enchiladas, quesadillas, burritos, tacos and vegetarian dishes. **Bar:** full bar. **Hours:** 11 am-10 pm, Fri-10:30 pm, Sun noon-10 pm. Closed: 7/4, 11/24, 12/25. **Address:** 4001 Lien Rd 53704 **Location:** I-90/94, exit 135A (US 151), just w.

L'ETOILE | Phone: 608/251-0500 (14)

Regional American
$29-$42

This restaurant is known for using locally grown, fresh ingredients. The chef and proprietor takes pride in selecting Wisconsin grown vegetables, seasonings, dairy products and meats for the seasonally changing menu. Great attention is given to food presentation. There is a team approach to service. **Bar:** full bar. **Reservations:** suggested. **Hours:** 5:30 pm-close, Sat from 5 pm. Closed: Sun. **Address:** 1 S Pinckney St 53703 **Location:** On Capitol Square; downtown. **Parking:** street only.

LULU'S | Phone: 608/233-2172 (28)

Middle Eastern
$7-$24

The city's oldest Middle Eastern restaurant focuses on Arabic lamb, chicken and beef dishes; appetizers of hummus, tabbouleh and baba ghanoush; and daily specials such as couscous, kebabs, moussaka and spinach pie. Lending to the elegant decor are rugs on the walls, swags of material hanging from the ceiling, decorative jugs and Moroccan artwork. **Hours:** 11 am-2 & 4-9:30 pm, Fri & Sat 11 am-9:30 pm. Closed: Sun. **Address:** 2524 University Ave 53705 **Location:** Just w of jct Highland Ave; near University of Wisconsin-Madison.

MARIGOLD KITCHEN | Phone: 608/661-5559 (22)

American
$4-$11

Across from Capitol Square, the small storefront restaurant sees lines of in-the-know locals queue out the door and into the street on farmers market weekends. Dishes are made from certified organic and market-fresh seasonal ingredients. In addition to traditional fare, the menu lists some breakfast and lunch items that take unexpected twists, including duck confit hash and chile-poached eggs. **Bar:** full bar. **Hours:** 7 am-3 pm, Sat-2 pm, Sun 8 am-2 pm. Closed major holidays. **Address:** 118 S Pinckney St 53703 **Location:** Just s of the square; center.

THE MARINER'S INN | Phone: 608/246-3120 (2)

Steak
$14-$40

Located on the north shore of Lake Mendota, the restaurant offers a straight forward seafood menu along with a few beef selections. You can enjoy a view of a picturesque marina and the lake from most tables. **Bar:** full bar. **Hours:** 5 pm-9 pm, Fri & Sat 4:30 pm-10 pm, Sun 4:30 pm-9 pm. Closed: major holidays, 12/24; also Super Bowl Sun. **Address:** 5339 Lighthouse Bay Dr 53704 **Location:** 6 mi n on SR 113, just w on CR M, 0.3 mi se on Westport Rd, then just w. CALL

MONTY'S BLUE PLATE DINER | Phone: 608/244-8505 (7)

American
$5-$13

This popular neighborhood diner serves all-day breakfast items, burgers, homestyle entrees, pasta dishes, pastries, sandwiches, soups and many vegetarian options. On Fridays, guests can partake of the fish fry. **Hours:** 7 am-9 pm, Fri-10 pm, Sat 7:30 am-10 pm, Sun 7:30 am-9 pm. Closed: 11/24, 12/25. **Address:** 2089 Atwood Ave 53704 **Location:** 0.7 mi s of jct Winnebago St and E Washington Ave. **Parking:** street only.

(See map and index starting on p. 499)

OCEAN GRILL
Phone: 608/285-2582   24

Seafood
$9-$30

With its flying fish, high-definition aquarium, high-backed booths and view into the bustling, open-concept kitchen, the chic, urban restaurant nurtures an atmosphere of comfort and liveliness. The three-season patio affords views of the Capitol and Monona Terrace. Good wines, including many by-the-glass choices, pair with selections from the extensive seafood menu. **Bar:** full bar. **Hours:** 11 am-2 & 5-9 pm, Fri-10 pm, Sat 5 pm-10 pm. Closed major holidays; also Sun. **Address:** 117 Martin Luther King Jr Blvd 53703 **Location:** Downtown. **Parking:** street only.

THE OLD FASHIONED TAVERN & RESTAURANT
Phone: 608/310-4545 15

American
$5-$29

Beer, brats and cheese! Everything that makes Wisconsin great can be found here. In the case of the former, you'll find more than 150 flavors of Wisconsin brews. **Bar:** full bar. **Hours:** 11 am-midnight, Sun 9 am-10 pm, Mon & Tues 11 am-10:30 pm. Closed major holidays. **Address:** 23 N Pinckney St 53703 **Location:** On Capitol Square; downtown. **Parking:** street only. CALL ♿M

OTTO'S RESTAURANT & BAR
Phone: 608/274-4044 31

Mediterranean
$15-$32

Set in a beautifully restored 1870s stone farmhouse, this restaurant offers fine Mediterranean cuisine and certified Angus steaks. The upscale lounge, seasonal patio dining and live jazz are among the highlights of this restaurant, but the real stars are the beautifully adorned entrées, including grilled salmon in grape leaves, oven-roasted sea bass and grilled loin lamb chops. **Bar:** full bar. **Reservations:** suggested. **Hours:** 5 pm-9 pm, Sat-9:30 pm. Closed major holidays; also Sun, Mon & week of Thanksgiving. **Address:** 6405 Mineral Point Rd 53705 **Location:** US 12/14, exit 254 (Mineral Point Rd), 1 mi e.

PASQUAL'S SALSARIA & SOUTHWESTERN DELI
Phone: 608/238-4419 30

Southwestern
$6-$12

Guacamole and margaritas are standouts at the quick-service Southwestern-style eatery in the historic Dudgeon-Monroe neighborhood. Diners order from the board. **Bar:** beer & wine. **Hours:** 10 am-9 pm, Thurs & Fri-10 pm, Sat 8 am-10 pm, Sun 8 am-8 pm. Closed major holidays. **Address:** 2534 Monroe St 53711 **Location:** US 12/18, exit 258A (S Seminole Hwy), 0.6 mi n to Nakoma St, then 0.6 mi ne. **Parking:** on-site and street.

PEDRO'S MEXICAN RESTAURANTE
Phone: 608/833-9229 34

Mexican
$5-$17

Sizzling fajitas are a big hit at this restaurant which delivers favorites from burritos and tacos to enchiladas and nachos. Complimentary fresh chips and salsa accompany all meals. Stucco walls, tile flooring and colorful decorations add to the south-of-the-border atmosphere. **Bar:** full bar. **Hours:** 11 am-11 pm, Fri & Sat-midnight, Sun-10 pm. Closed: 11/24, 12/25; also for dinner 12/24. **Address:** 499 D'Onofrio Dr 53719 **Location:** US 12/14, exit 254 (Mineral Point Rd), just e, then just s. CALL ♿M

PRIME QUARTER STEAK HOUSE
Phone: 608/244-3520 5

Steak
$12-$27

Diners choose from a selection of fine USDA choice steak, tuna or salmon and then can enjoy a beverage and socialize as their grill their own steak over an open charcoal pit. All entrees are the same price and include all-you-can-eat baked potatoes, Texas toast and the salad bar. **Bar:** full bar. **Reservations:** suggested. **Hours:** 5 pm-10 pm, Sat from 4 pm, Sun 4 pm-9 pm. Closed major holidays. **Address:** 3520 E Washington Ave 53704 **Location:** On US 151, just w of jct US 51. CALL ♿M

QUIVEY'S GROVE STONE HOUSE, STABLE GRILL
Phone: 608/273-4900

American
$6-$27

The converted 1855 rural mansion and rustic stable are appointed with period furnishings. The menu includes dishes such as baked trout, roast duck, roast pork and the chicken-and-mushroom-filled popover. The 5-acre estate is in the historic district. **Bar:** full bar. **Hours:** 11 am-2:30 & 4:30-9 pm, Fri & Sat-10 pm. Closed: 5/30, 7/4, 9/5, 12/24; also Sun. **Address:** 6261 Nesbitt Rd 53719 **Location:** US 18/151, exit CR PD, just w, then 0.6 mi s. **Historic** CALL ♿M

SA-BAI THONG
Phone: 608/828-9565 35

Thai
$6-$17

The eatery is a hot destination for an adventure in tastes of the East. Delicious dishes, made from fresh ingredients and with homemade sauces, are created using old family recipes. **Bar:** full bar. **Reservations:** suggested. **Hours:** 11 am-2:30 & 4-9 pm, Fri-10 pm, Sat 11 am-10 pm, Sun 11 am-9 pm. Closed: 11/24, 12/25. **Address:** 6802 Odana Rd 53719 **Location:** US 12/14, exit 255 (Gammon Rd), 0.3 mi e.

SMOKY'S CLUB
Phone: 608/233-2120 27

Steak
$10-$36

The popular, established restaurant attracts much of its clientele from the university. Complimentary bread baskets and relishes on ice, along with homemade soups and succulent, sizzling steaks served with fries or hash browns, satisfy the heartiest appetites. Smoking is allowed only in the lounge. **Bar:** full bar. **Hours:** 5 pm-9 pm, Fri & Sat-10 pm. Closed major holidays; also Sun. **Address:** 3005 University Ave 53705 **Location:** 0.5 mi e of jct Midvale Blvd. CALL ♿M

THE TORNADO CLUB STEAK HOUSE
Phone: 608/256-3570 25

Steak
$14-$44

Enjoy the cozy atmosphere in this dark supper club-type restaurant known for their delicious, tender steaks and located right off Capitol Square. **Bar:** full bar. **Reservations:** suggested. **Hours:** 5 pm-10 pm. Closed: 11/24, 12/25. **Address:** 116 S Hamilton St 53703 **Location:** Just s of capitol; downtown. **Parking:** street only.

TUTTO PASTA CUCINA ITALIANA
Phone: 608/250-9000 21
Italian
$7-$18

The family-owned-and-operated restaurant mixes contemporary and traditional elements in its fresh preparations of pasta, pizza, poultry, seafood, lamb and veal, all made from authentic recipes. The indoor sidewalk cafe invites relaxed dining. **Bar:** full bar. **Hours:** 11 am-10 pm, Sun 3:30 pm-9 pm. Closed: 11/24, 12/25. **Address:** 107 King St 53703 **Location:** Downtown.

MANITOWISH WATERS pop. 646

—— WHERE TO DINE ——

BLUE BAYOU INN
Phone: 715/543-2537

Cajun
$15-$30

The lakefront restaurant delivers authentic Louisiana Cajun-Creole cuisine, with choices such as seafood gumbo, jambalaya and shrimp Creole with steamed rice and vegetables. A nice selection of beer and wine is available. **Bar:** full bar. **Reservations:** suggested. **Hours:** Open 5/24-10/31; 5 pm-10 pm. Closed major holidays; also Sun. **Address:** 288 US Hwy 51 54545 **Location:** At Spider Lake Bridge, 3 mi s of CR W.

MICHAEL'S PARLOR
Phone: 715/543-2550

American
$5-$12

Homemade baked goods, flavorful soup and hearty chili are tasty, basically prepared favorites at the quaint country cafe. Breakfast selections are served well into the afternoon. During the summer, the soda fountain brings in a good crowd. **Bar:** beer only. **Hours:** 6 am-4 pm; hours may vary. Closed: 11/24, 12/25. **Address:** 397 S US 51 54545 **Location:** On US 51, 5 mi s.

MANITOWOC pop. 34,053

AMERICINN LODGE & SUITES OF MANITOWOC
Phone: 920/684-3344

Hotel
Rates not provided

Address: 5020 Hecker Rd 54220 **Location:** I-43, exit 149, just sw. Located in a semi-commercial area. **Facility:** Smoke free premises. 64 units. 2 stories (no elevator), interior corridors. **Parking:** winter plug-ins. **Amenities:** high-speed Internet. **Pool(s):** heated indoor. **Activities:** whirlpool, snowmobiling, exercise room. **Guest Services:** coin laundry, wireless Internet.

BEST WESTERN LAKEFRONT HOTEL
Phone: (920)682-7000

Hotel
$69-$89

Address: 101 Maritime Dr 54220 **Location:** I-43, exit 152, 4.2 mi e on SR 42 N, then 1 mi s. Located on the water's edge. **Facility:** Smoke free premises. 109 units. 3 stories, interior corridors. **Terms:** check-in 4 pm. **Amenities:** high-speed Internet. **Pool(s):** heated indoor. **Activities:** sauna, whirlpool. **Guest Services:** valet laundry, area transportation-car ferry, wireless Internet. **Free Special Amenities:** local telephone calls and high-speed Internet.

AAA Benefit:
Members save up to 20%, plus 10% bonus points with free rewards program.

COMFORT INN BY CHOICE HOTELS
Phone: (920)683-0220

Hotel
$59-$114

Address: 2200 S 44th St 54220 **Location:** I-43, exit 149, just e. **Facility:** Smoke free premises. 47 units. 2 stories (no elevator), interior corridors. **Amenities:** safes (fee). **Activities:** exercise room. **Guest Services:** valet laundry, wireless Internet.

ECONO LODGE

Phone: 920/682-8271

Hotel
Rates not provided

Address: 908 Washington St 54220 **Location:** On US 151 business route; downtown. **Facility:** Smoke free premises. 53 units. 2 stories (no elevator), interior corridors. **Parking:** winter plug-ins. **Guest Services:** wireless Internet. **Free Special Amenities: continental breakfast and high-speed Internet.** [SAVE] 🍽 ⊠ 🎦 📷 🖥 🖨 / SOME UNITS FEE 🐕

HOLIDAY INN MANITOWOC

Phone: (920)682-6000

Hotel
$119-$159

Address: 4601 Calumet Ave 54220 **Location:** I-43, exit 149, just e. **Facility:** Smoke free premises. 204 units. 3 stories, interior corridors. **Amenities:** video games (fee). **Pool(s):** heated indoor. **Activities:** sauna, whirlpool, playground, exercise room. **Guest Services:** valet laundry, wireless Internet. 🏊 🍽 🍸 CALL 🅶M 🏊 ⊠ 🎦 🖥 / SOME UNITS FEE 🐕 🖨 🖼

——— **WHERE TO DINE** ———

FOUR SEASONS

Phone: 920/683-1444

American
$6-$15

The casual restaurant features an extensive menu of simple recipes and offers a coffee-shop ambience that is both comfortable for families and popular with the locals. Breakfast is served all day, and desserts and breads are made on the premises. **Bar:** full bar. **Hours:** 5:30 am-11 pm; hours may vary. **Address:** 3950 Calumet Ave 54220 **Location:** I-43, exit 149, 0.9 mi e.

LUIGI'S ITALIAN RESTAURANT

Phone: 920/684-4200

Italian
$7-$20

Diners who crave pizza need look no further. This restaurant's menu lists traditional, pan or Chicago-style stuffed pizzas. Also offered are hot and cold Italian sandwiches, pasta dinners and, of course, Italian dinners, which include salad and garlic bread with a choice of pasta or soup. **Bar:** full bar. **Hours:** 11 am-9:30 pm, Fri-Sun to 10 pm. Closed major holidays; also Mon. **Address:** 6124 Calumet Ave 54220 **Location:** I-43, exit 149, 1 mi w on US 151.

MARINETTE pop. 11,749

BEST WESTERN RIVERFRONT INN

Phone: (715)732-1000

Hotel
$80-$96

Address: 1821 Riverside Ave 54143 **Location:** Just w of US 41; downtown. Located close to the river. **Facility:** Smoke free premises. 120 units. 6 stories, interior corridors. **Amenities:** video games, high-speed Internet. **Pool(s):** heated indoor. **Activities:** whirlpool, limited exercise equipment. **Guest Services:** valet and coin laundry, wireless Internet. **Free Special Amenities: room upgrade (subject to availability with advance reservations) and high-speed Internet.**
[SAVE] 🍽 🍸 🏊 ⊠ 🎦 🖥 / SOME UNITS 🖨 🖼

AAA Benefit:
Members save up to 20%, plus 10% bonus points with free rewards program.

COMFORT INN OF MARINETTE

Phone: (715)732-2321

Hotel
$75-$130

Address: 2180 Roosevelt Rd 54143 **Location:** 2 mi s on US 41. **Facility:** Smoke free premises. 48 units. 2 stories (no elevator), interior corridors. **Parking:** winter plug-ins. **Amenities:** safes (fee). *Some:* high-speed Internet. **Activities:** exercise room. **Guest Services:** coin laundry, wireless Internet.
🍽 ⊠ 🎦 🖨 🖼 🖥

——— **WHERE TO DINE** ———

JOHN & SUE'S MEMORY LANE

Phone: 715/735-3348

American
$5-$14

Step back into the 1950s at this casual restaurant known for its home-style sandwiches and chargrilled burgers. Soup, chili, bread and old-fashioned dessert are made in-house. Breakfast is served all day. **Hours:** 6 am-8 pm; hours may vary. Closed: 12/25. **Address:** 1378 Main St 54143 **Location:** 0.5 mi s of US 41; downtown.

MARSHFIELD pop. 18,800

BAYMONT INN & SUITES-MARSHFIELD

Phone: (715)384-5240

Hotel
$76-$112

Address: 2107 N Central Ave 54449 **Location:** On SR 97; 1.6 mi n of SR 13. **Facility:** Smoke free premises. 60 units. 2 stories, interior corridors. **Amenities:** safes (fee). **Pool(s):** heated indoor. **Activities:** whirlpool, exercise room. **Guest Services:** valet laundry, wireless Internet.
🍽 CALL 🅶M 🏊 ⊠ 🎦 🖥 🖨 / SOME UNITS FEE 🐕

COMFORT INN

Phone: (715)387-8691

Hotel
$67-$110

Address: 114 E Upham St 54449 **Location:** On SR 97; 0.8 mi n of jct SR 13. Located in a commercial area. **Facility:** Smoke free premises. 46 units. 2 stories (no elevator), interior corridors. **Parking:** winter plug-ins. **Pool(s):** heated indoor. **Activities:** whirlpool. **Guest Services:** wireless Internet.
🍽 CALL 🅶M 🏊 ⊠ 🎦 🖥 / SOME UNITS FEE 🐕 🖨 🖼

HOLIDAY INN & CONFERENCE CENTER

Phone: (715)486-1500

Hotel
$104-$134

Address: 750 S Central Ave 54449 **Location:** Jct SR 13 and 97, 0.5 mi s on Business Rt 13. **Facility:** Smoke free premises. 91 units. 3 stories, interior corridors. **Amenities:** high-speed Internet, safes. **Pool(s):** heated indoor. **Activities:** whirlpool, waterslide, exercise room. *Fee:* game room. **Guest Services:** valet and coin laundry, area transportation-medical complex, wireless Internet.
🍽 🍸 CALL 🅶M 🏊 ⊠ 🎦 🖥 🖨 🖼

—— WHERE TO DINE ——

ROYAL TOKYO

Japanese
$11-$26

Phone: 715/486-8868

Skilled teppanyaki chefs put on quite a show as they prepare your food before your eyes on heated steel grills. Visitors tend to socialize at the large tables in this professionally restored train depot. Miso soup, a variety of sushi and entrees of beef, seafood and chicken highlight the menu. **Bar:** full bar. **Reservations:** required. **Hours:** 4:30 pm-9 pm. Closed major holidays; also Mon. **Address:** 112 E Veterans Pkwy 54449 **Location:** Just e of jct SR 97 and 13; downtown. CALL 🚹M

MAUSTON pop. 3,740

BEST WESTERN PARK OASIS INN

Hotel
$85-$150

Phone: (608)847-6255

Address: W5641 Hwy 82 E 53948 **Location:** I-90/94, exit 69, just se. **Facility:** Smoke free premises. 53 units, some kitchens. 3 stories, interior corridors. **Parking:** winter plug-ins. **Amenities:** safes (fee). *Some:* high-speed Internet. **Pool(s):** heated outdoor, heated indoor. **Activities:** sauna, whirlpool, horseshoes. *Fee:* game room. **Guest Services:** coin laundry, wireless Internet. **Free Special Amenities:** local telephone calls and high-speed Internet.

AAA Benefit:
Members save up to 20%, plus 10% bonus points with free rewards program.

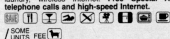
/ SOME UNITS FEE 🐾

COUNTRY INN & SUITES BY CARLSON

Hotel
$77-$150

Phone: 608/847-5959

Address: 1001 SR 82 53948 **Location:** I-90/94, exit 69, just ne. **Facility:** Smoke free premises. 61 units. 2 stories (no elevator), interior corridors. **Parking:** winter plug-ins. **Terms:** cancellation fee imposed. **Pool(s):** heated indoor. **Activities:** whirlpool. **Guest Services:** coin laundry, wireless Internet. *(see ad p. 6)*

 FEE / SOME UNITS FEE 🐾

SUPER 8

Motel
$74-$122

Phone: (608)847-2300

Address: 1001A Hwy 82 E 53948 **Location:** I-90/94, exit 69, just ne. **Facility:** Smoke free premises. 49 units. 2 stories (no elevator), interior corridors. **Parking:** winter plug-ins. **Pool(s):** heated indoor. **Activities:** whirlpool, picnic area with gas grill. **Guest Services:** coin laundry, wireless Internet.

/ SOME UNITS FEE 🐾

—— WHERE TO DINE ——

PARK OASIS RESTAURANT

American
$4-$16

Phone: 608/847-6543

Patrons frequent this place for hearty servings of home-cooked food. **Bar:** beer & wine. **Hours:** 6 am-10 pm. **Address:** W5641 Hwy 82 E 53948 **Location:** I-90/94, exit 69, just se.

MAYVILLE pop. 4,902

THE AUDUBON INN

Historic
Country Inn
$64-$129

Phone: (920)387-5858

Address: 45 N Main St 53050 **Location:** On SR 67; center. **Facility:** The 1896 Victorian inn features a turret and stained-glass windows; rooms sport Shaker-style decor, four-poster beds and a double whirlpool bath. Smoke free premises. 16 units. 3 stories, interior corridors. **Parking:** street only. **Terms:** office hours 10 am-5 pm, 7 day cancellation notice-fee imposed. **Dining:** The Beaumont Restaurant, see separate listing. **Guest Services:** wireless Internet.

CALL 🚹M FEE / SOME UNITS

THE MAYVILLE INN

Hotel
$64-$99

Phone: 920/387-1234

Address: 701 S Mountin Dr 53050 **Location:** 1.3 mi w on SR 28. Adjacent to a large park. **Facility:** Smoke free premises. 29 units. 2 stories, interior corridors. **Parking:** winter plug-ins. **Terms:** office hours 6 am-10 pm. **Guest Services:** valet laundry, wireless Internet.

CALL 🚹M FEE / SOME UNITS

—— WHERE TO DINE ——

THE BEAUMONT RESTAURANT

American
$10-$26

Phone: 920/387-5858

Diners browse a seasonally changing menu at this charming restaurant, which features beautiful stained-glass windows. Among menu options are the whiskey pork chop with grilled apples, citrus-glazed chicken, bacon carbonara, chicken pot pie, fine steaks and crab-stuffed chicken. **Bar:** full bar. **Hours:** 5 pm-9 pm, Sunday brunch 1st Sun of each month 10 am-2 pm. Closed: 12/25; also Sun & Mon. **Address:** 45 N Main St 53050 **Location:** On SR 67; center; in The Audubon Inn. **Parking:** street only. CALL 🚹M

MAZOMANIE pop. 1,485

—— WHERE TO DINE ——

THE OLD FEED MILL

American
$7-$24

Phone: 608/795-4909

Country cooking is dished up at a wonderfully restored 1857 flour feed mill furnished with antiques. Each day, the restaurant grinds its own flour for use in breads and pastries. Pot roast and pot pie are mouthwatering choices, as is scrumptious bread pudding from the dessert menu. **Bar:** full bar. **Hours:** 11 am-8 pm, Fri & Sat-9 pm, Sun 10 am-8 pm. Closed: 1/1, 12/25; also Mon 4/1-5/28 & 9/5-3/31, Tues & Wed 1/1-3/31. **Address:** 114 Cramer St 53560 **Location:** 0.3 mi n of US 14.

MEDFORD pop. 4,350

AMERICINN MOTEL OF MEDFORD

Hotel
$74-$89

Phone: (715)748-2330

Address: 435 S 8th St 54451 **Location:** On SR 13, 0.5 mi s of jct SR 64. **Facility:** Smoke free premises. 37 units. 2 stories (no elevator), interior corridors. **Parking:** winter plug-ins. **Terms:** cancellation fee imposed. **Pool(s):** heated indoor. **Activities:** sauna, whirlpool. **Guest Services:** wireless Internet.

WOODLANDS INN & SUITES

Motel
$70-$124

Phone: (715)748-3995

Address: 854 N 8th St 54451 **Location:** On SR 13, 0.6 mi n of jct SR 64. **Facility:** Smoke free premises. 27 units, some kitchens. 1 story, interior corridors. **Parking:** winter plug-ins. **Terms:** cancellation fee imposed. **Pool(s):** heated indoor. **Activities:** whirlpool. **Guest Services:** wireless Internet.

—— WHERE TO DINE ——

MEDFORD CAFE

American
$7-$10

Phone: 715/748-2233

This restaurant features homey, contemporary decor in a country and patriotic theme. The menu consists of a selection of traditional sandwiches and burgers, as well as a variety of country dinners. **Hours:** 6 am-9 pm. Closed: 11/24, 12/24, 12/25. **Address:** 403 S 8th St 54451 **Location:** On SR 13, 0.5 mi s of jct SR 64.

MENOMONIE pop. 14,937

COUNTRY INN & SUITES BY CARLSON

Hotel
$70-$120

Phone: (715)235-5664

Address: 320 Oak Ave 54751 **Location:** I-94, exit 41 (SR 25), just se. **Facility:** Smoke free premises. 68 units. 3 stories, interior corridors. **Parking:** winter plug-ins. **Terms:** cancellation fee imposed. **Amenities:** high-speed Internet. **Pool(s):** heated indoor. **Activities:** whirlpool, exercise room. **Guest Services:** valet and coin laundry, wireless Internet. *(see ad p. 6)*

MENOMONIE MOTEL 6 #4109

Hotel
$46-$69

Phone: (715)235-6901

Address: 2100 Stout St 54751 **Location:** I-94, exit 41 (SR 25), just se. **Facility:** 63 units. 3 stories, interior corridors. **Parking:** winter plug-ins. **Guest Services:** coin laundry, wireless Internet.

QUALITY INN & SUITES

Hotel
Rates not provided

Phone: 715/233-1500

Address: 1721 Plaza Dr NE 54751 **Location:** I-94, exit 45 (CR B), just sw. **Facility:** Smoke free premises. 61 units. 3 stories, interior corridors. **Amenities:** high-speed Internet, safes. **Pool(s):** heated indoor. **Activities:** whirlpool, limited exercise equipment. **Guest Services:** coin laundry, wireless Internet. **Free Special Amenities: expanded continental breakfast and high-speed Internet.**

SUPER 8-MENOMONIE

Hotel
$52-$58

Phone: (715)235-8889

Address: 1622 N Broadway 54751 **Location:** I-94, exit 41 (SR 25), just s. **Facility:** Smoke free premises. 80 units. 3 stories, interior corridors. **Parking:** winter plug-ins. **Amenities:** safes (fee). **Pool(s):** heated indoor. **Activities:** whirlpool. **Guest Services:** coin laundry, wireless Internet.

—— WHERE TO DINE ——

GREEN MILL RESTAURANT & BAR

American
$8-$18

Phone: 715/235-3000

The eatery prepares top-notch pizzas; a good variety of appetizers, salads, sandwiches and pasta; and some steaks and seafood. Diablo wings are a great way to start the meal. **Bar:** full bar. **Hours:** 11 am-10 pm. Closed: 12/25. **Address:** 1827 N Broadway 54751 **Location:** I-94, exit 41 (SR 25), just sw.

JAKE'S SUPPER CLUB

Steak
$9-$25

Phone: 715/235-2465

Five miles north of the city on beautiful Tainter Lake, this supper club offers a good selection of appetizers, salads, sandwiches, steaks and seafood along with its specialty prime rib. **Bar:** full bar. **Reservations:** suggested. **Hours:** 3:30 pm-10 pm, Sat from 11 am, Sun from 10 am. Closed: 12/25. **Address:** E 5690 CR D 54751 **Location:** 5 mi n to CR D, 0.5 mi e. **Parking:** street only.

MEQUON —See Milwaukee p. 565.

MERRILL pop. 10,146

AMERICINN LODGE & SUITES OF MERRILL
                Phone: (715)536-7979

Hotel
$89-$149

Address: 3300 E Main St 54452 **Location:** US 51, exit 208, 0.5 mi w on SR 64. **Facility:** Smoke free premises. 45 units. 2 stories (no elevator), interior corridors. **Parking:** winter plug-ins. **Terms:** cancellation fee imposed. **Amenities:** high-speed Internet, safes (fee). **Pool(s):** heated indoor. **Activities:** whirlpool. *Fee:* game room. **Guest Services:** coin laundry.

SUPER 8
                Phone: (715)536-6880

Hotel
$47-$108

Address: 3209 E Main St 54452 **Location:** US 51, exit 208, 0.5 mi w on SR 64. **Facility:** Smoke free premises. 57 units. 2 stories (no elevator), interior corridors. **Parking:** winter plug-ins. **Amenities:** *Some:* high-speed Internet. **Pool(s):** heated indoor. **Activities:** sauna, whirlpool. **Guest Services:** valet and coin laundry, wireless Internet.

MIDDLETON pop. 15,770   (See map and index starting on p. 499)

COUNTRY INN & SUITES BY CARLSON, MADISON WEST
      Phone: (608)831-6970 **46**

Hotel
$114-$169

Address: 2212 Deming Way 53562 **Location:** US 12/14, exit 251A, 0.3 mi w on University Ave, then just n. **Facility:** Smoke free premises. 84 units. 3 stories, interior corridors. **Parking:** winter plug-ins. **Terms:** cancellation fee imposed. **Amenities:** high-speed Internet. **Pool(s):** heated indoor. **Activities:** whirlpool, exercise room. **Guest Services:** valet and coin laundry, wireless Internet.
(see ad p. 508 & p. 6)

FREE newspaper and high-speed Internet

COURTYARD BY MARRIOTT MADISON WEST/MIDDLETON
      Phone: (608)203-0100 **45**

Hotel
$134-$171

Address: 2266 Deming Way 53562 **Location:** US 12/14, exit 252 (Greenway Blvd), just w. **Facility:** Smoke free premises. 136 units. 4 stories, interior corridors. **Terms:** cancellation fee imposed. **Amenities:** high-speed Internet. **Pool(s):** heated indoor. **Activities:** whirlpool, exercise room. *Fee:* massage. **Guest Services:** valet and coin laundry, wireless Internet.

AAA Benefit:
Members save 5% or more off best available rate.

(See map and index starting on p. 499)

FAIRFIELD INN & SUITES BY MARRIOTT-MADISON WEST

Hotel
$98-$125

Address: 8212 Greenway Blvd 53562 **Location:** US 12/14, exit 252 (Greenway Blvd), just w. **Facility:** Smoke free premises. 103 units. 3 stories, interior corridors. **Parking:** winter plug-ins. **Terms:** cancellation fee imposed. **Amenities:** video games (fee). **Pool(s):** heated indoor. **Activities:** whirlpool, exercise room. **Guest Services:** valet and coin laundry, wireless Internet.

Phone: (608)831-1400 〔50〕

AAA Benefit:
Members save a minimum 5% off the best available rate.

HILTON GARDEN INN MADISON WEST/MIDDLETON

Hotel
$99-$209

Address: 1801 Deming Way 53562 **Location:** US 12/14, exit 252 (Greenway Blvd), just w, then just n; in Greenway Station. **Facility:** Smoke free premises. 133 units. 4 stories, interior corridors. **Parking:** winter plug-ins. **Terms:** 1-7 night minimum stay, cancellation fee imposed. **Amenities:** video games (fee), high-speed Internet. **Pool(s):** heated indoor. **Activities:** whirlpool, exercise room. **Fee:** game room. **Guest Services:** valet and coin laundry, area transportation-within 5 mi, wireless Internet.

Phone: (608)831-2220 〔49〕

AAA Benefit:
Members save 5% or more everyday!

MARRIOTT MADISON WEST

Hotel
$143-$183

Address: 1313 John Q Hammons Dr 53562 **Location:** US 12/14, exit 252 (Greenway Blvd), just w. **Facility:** Smoke free premises. 292 units. 10 stories, interior corridors. **Terms:** check-in 4 pm, cancellation fee imposed. **Amenities:** high-speed Internet (fee). **Pool(s):** heated indoor. **Activities:** whirlpool, sun deck, exercise room. **Guest Services:** complimentary and valet laundry, area transportation-within 5 mi, wireless Internet.

Phone: (608)831-2000 〔51〕

AAA Benefit:
Members save 5% or more off best available rate.

RESIDENCE INN BY MARRIOTT-MADISON WEST/MIDDLETON

Extended Stay Hotel
$152-$194

Address: 8400 Market St 53562 **Location:** US 12/14, exit 252 (Greenway Blvd), just w, then just n; in Greenway Station. **Facility:** Smoke free premises. 122 units, some two bedrooms, efficiencies and kitchens. 4 stories, interior corridors. **Terms:** cancellation fee imposed. **Amenities:** high-speed Internet. **Pool(s):** heated indoor. **Activities:** whirlpool, grill area, exercise room, sports court. **Guest Services:** valet and coin laundry, area transportation-within 5 mi, wireless Internet.

Phone: (608)662-1100 〔48〕

AAA Benefit:
Members save a minimum 5% off the best available rate.

STAYBRIDGE SUITES BY HOLIDAY INN

Extended Stay Hotel
$109-$149

Address: 7790 Elmwood Ave 53562 **Location:** US 12/14, exit 251 (University Ave), just nw. **Facility:** Smoke free premises. 91 units, some two bedrooms and efficiencies. 3 stories, interior corridors. **Terms:** cancellation fee imposed. **Amenities:** high-speed Internet. **Pool(s):** heated indoor. **Activities:** whirlpool, sun deck, board games, barbecue grills, library, exercise room. **Guest Services:** valet and coin laundry, wireless Internet.

Phone: (608)664-5888 〔47〕

——— WHERE TO DINE ———

CHIN'S ASIA FRESH

Asian
$4-$8

Relax in the warm, yet airy inviting atmosphere while catching a quick meal in, or pick it your food to go. Every meal is quickly made to order in a wok. **Bar:** beer & wine. **Hours:** 11 am-9 pm, Sun-8 pm. Closed: 12/25 & Easter. **Address:** 8414 Old Sauk Rd 53562-4367 **Location:** US 12/14, exit 253 (Old Sauk Rd), just w.

Phone: 608/827-7721

FITZGERALD'S OF MIDDLETON

American
$6-$35

The classic Wisconsin supper club prepares great steaks and seafood. Locals flock here on Fridays for the fish fry. If these aren't good enough reasons to visit, diners can factor in friendly service and an inviting atmosphere. **Bar:** full bar. **Hours:** 11 am-2 & 5-9 pm, Fri 11 am-2 & 4:30-9:30 pm, Sat 5 pm-9:30 pm, Sun 10 am-2 & 4:30-8:30 pm; Sunday brunch. Closed: 1/1, 12/24, 12/25; also Mon. **Address:** 3112 Parmenter St 53562 **Location:** On US 12, just n of jct US 14.

Phone: 608/831-7107 〔44〕

HUBBARD AVENUE DINER

American
$7-$12

It's hard to go wrong with anything on a menu that lists choices ranging from burgers and sandwiches to classic meatloaf with mashed potatoes. Delicious, baked-from-scratch desserts beckon from the display case at the entry. The classic American diner features an award-winning 1940s design. **Bar:** beer & wine. **Hours:** 7 am-9 pm, Fri-10 pm, Sat 7:30 am-10 pm, Sun 7:30 am-9 pm. Closed: 11/24, 12/25. **Address:** 7445 Hubbard Ave 53562 **Location:** US 12/14, exit 251 (University Ave), just e to Aurora St, then just s.

Phone: 608/831-6800 〔48〕

IMPERIAL GARDEN CHINESE RESTAURANT *Menu on AAA.com*

Chinese
$5-$18

This restaurant has a large menu selection of traditional pork, beef, chicken, lamb, duck and seafood dishes. There are also some vegetarian entrees including rice and noodles. This restaurant is well-established and locally popular. **Bar:** full bar. **Hours:** 11 am-2 & 4-9:30 pm, Fri-10:30 pm, Sat 4 pm-10:30 pm, Sun 4 pm-9 pm. Closed: 7/4, 11/24, 12/25. **Address:** 2039 Allen Blvd 53562 **Location:** US 12/14, exit 251 (University Ave), 1.7 mi e.

Phone: 608/238-6445 〔50〕

(See map and index starting on p. 499)

JOHNNY'S ITALIAN STEAKHOUSE　　　　　　　Phone: 608/831-3705　

Steak
$10-$30

The music of Frank Sinatra, Dean Martin and Sammy Davis Jr. provide the background sound in this modern-day throwback to a classic steakhouse. The martini bar features wood-paneled walls and granite lounge tables, while the dining room sports oversize booths and velvet privacy curtains. The menu focuses on steaks ranging from classic preparations to the house Steak de Burgo or Drunken Steak, and also offers traditional Italian plates, including a variety of pastas, chicken and veal dishes. **Bar:** full bar. **Reservations:** suggested. **Hours:** 11 am-10 pm, Fri & Sat-11 pm, Sun-9 pm. Closed: 11/24, 12/25. **Address:** 8390 Market St 53562 **Location:** US 12/14, exit 252 (Greenway Blvd), just w, then just n; in Greenway Station. CALL 🅱Ⓜ

LOUISIANNE'S ETC　　　　　　　　　　　　Phone: 608/831-1929　47

Cajun
$13-$36

The piquant Creole flavors of New Orleans infuse colorfully presented dishes of seafood, beef and chicken. Original stone walls and soft lighting give the dining room an almost cavernous feel. The sounds of live jazz resonate off the walls. **Bar:** full bar. **Reservations:** suggested. **Hours:** 5 pm-close. Closed major holidays; also Sun. **Address:** 7464 Hubbard Ave 53562 **Location:** Southeast of jct US 12 and University Ave via Parmenter. **Parking:** street only.

P.F. CHANG'S CHINA BISTRO　　　　　　　　Phone: 608/831-2488　46

Chinese
$10-$23

Trendy, upscale decor provides a pleasant backdrop for New Age Chinese dining. Appetizers, soups and salads are a meal by themselves. Vegetarian plates and sides, noodles, meins, chicken and meat dishes are created from exotic, fresh ingredients. **Bar:** full bar. **Hours:** 11 am-10 pm, Fri & Sat-11 pm. Closed: 11/24, 12/25. **Address:** 2237 Deming Way 53562 **Location:** US 12/14, exit 252 (Greenway Blvd), just w. CALL 🅱Ⓜ

STAMM HOUSE AT PHEASANT BRANCH　　　　Phone: 608/831-5835　45

American
$8-$26

The restored 1847 stone tavern has housed everything from a post office to runaway slaves on the Underground Railroad. Today it is home to one of the area's best-loved restaurants. The most popular menu item is chicken and dumplings, served in a good-size helping. Entrees are served with a delicious side of green bean salad and fresh dinner rolls. **Bar:** full bar. **Hours:** 5 pm-10 pm; seasonal hours may vary. Closed major holidays; also Mon & Tues. **Address:** 6625 Century Ave 53562 **Location:** US 14, 1 mi e.

MILTON pop. 5,132

―――― **WHERE TO DINE** ――――

LIBERTY STATION　　　　　　　　　　　　Phone: 608/868-2873

American
$6-$17

The former train station depot has been converted to a restaurant and bar. The decor and signs still point to the building's origins; wait staff is dressed in engineer bib overalls, adding to the theme. **Bar:** full bar. **Hours:** 4:30 pm-9 pm, Fri & Sat 11 am-10 pm, Sun 11 am-7 pm. Closed: 11/24, 12/24, 12/25 & Easter; also Mon. **Address:** 231 Front St 53563 **Location:** I-90, exit 163 (SR 59), 2 mi e.

Destination Milwaukee
pop. 596,974

Polish Fest,
Milwaukee.
(See mention
page 176)

© Susan Ruggles / age fotostock

Milwaukee is naturally a great spot for water sports: Not only is the city right on Lake Michigan, it's also divided in half by the Milwaukee River.

Those who would rather stay dry can hit the malls, cheer on the area's sports teams and attend a performance at the opera or ballet.

Visit Milwaukee

Shopping at Mayfair, Wauwatosa.
(See mention page 176)

*P*laces included in this AAA Destination City:

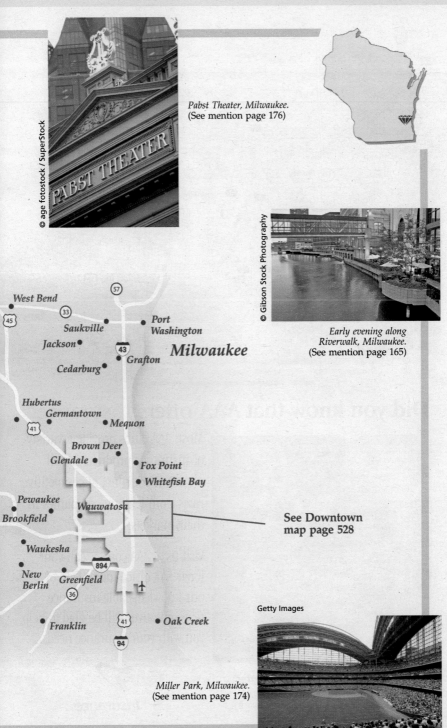

Pabst Theater, Milwaukee.
(See mention page 176)

© age fotostock / SuperStock

© Gibson Stock Photography

Early evening along
Riverwalk, Milwaukee.
(See mention page 165)

West Bend

57

33

45

Saukville

Jackson

Cedarburg

Port
Washington

43

Grafton

Milwaukee

Hubertus

Germantown

41

Mequon

Brown Deer

Glendale

Fox Point

Whitefish Bay

Pewaukee

Wauwatosa

Brookfield

Waukesha

894

New
Berlin   Greenfield

36

Franklin

41

Oak Creek

94

See Downtown
map page 528

Getty Images

Miller Park, Milwaukee.
(See mention page 174)

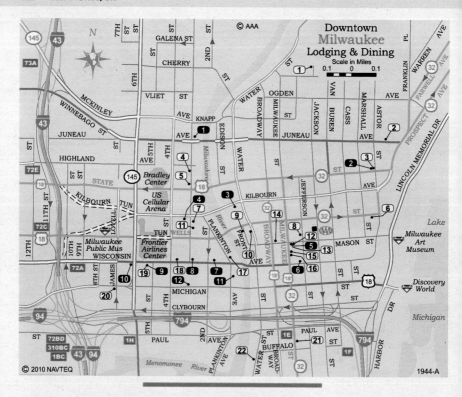

Did you know that AAA offers Insurance?

Insure With Someone You Trust®

Most[1] AAA clubs provide a variety of insurance products for all phases of your life, at competitive rates from leading companies in their markets.

Visit us at AAA.com or call your local AAA office today. One of our knowledgeable insurance representatives will be glad to help you with your insurance needs.

[1]Due to state regulations and local restrictions, insurance is not available through all AAA clubs.

Downtown Milwaukee

This index helps you "spot" where approved lodgings and restaurants are located on the corresponding detailed maps. Lodging daily rate range is for comparison only and show the property's high season. Restaurant rate range is a combination of lunch and/or dinner. Turn to the listing page for more detailed rate information and consult display ads for special promotions.

DOWNTOWN MILWAUKEE

Map Page	OA	Lodgings	Diamond Rated	High Season	Page
1 / p. 528	AAA	**Aloft Milwaukee Downtown** - see ad p. 535	▽▽▽	$89-$209 SAVE	535
2 / p. 528	AAA	**Comfort Inn & Suites Downtown Lakeshore**	▽▽	$100-$149 SAVE	535
3 / p. 528		InterContinental Milwaukee	▽▽▽	$119-$309	536
4 / p. 528	AAA	**Hyatt Regency Milwaukee**	▽▽▽	$89-$309 SAVE	536
5 / p. 528		Hotel Metro-Milwaukee	▽▽▽	$179-$359	536
6 / p. 528	AAA	**The Pfister Hotel** - see ad p. 539	▽▽▽▽	$139-$2000 SAVE	539
7 / p. 528	AAA	**Hampton Inn & Suites Milwaukee Downtown** - see ad p. 537	▽▽▽	$129-$189 SAVE	536
8 / p. 528	AAA	**Best Western Inn Towne Hotel**	▽▽	$79-$139 SAVE	535
9 / p. 528		Hilton Milwaukee City Center	▽▽▽	Rates not provided	536
10 / p. 528	AAA	**Doubletree Milwaukee City Center**	▽▽▽	$99-$209 SAVE	536
11 / p. 528		Residence Inn-Downtown Milwaukee	▽▽▽	$179-$209	539
12 / p. 528		Courtyard by Marriott Milwaukee Downtown	▽▽▽	$189-$229	536

Map Page	OA	Restaurants	Diamond Rated	Cuisine	Meal Range	Page
① / p. 528	AAA	**Sanford Restaurant**	▽▽▽▽	American	$31-$39	541
② / p. 528		Osteria del Mondo	▽▽▽	Italian	$15-$35	541
③ / p. 528		Aura	▽▽	International	$22-$50	539
④ / p. 528	AAA	**Mader's German Restaurant**	▽▽	German	$8-$33	540
⑤ / p. 528	AAA	**Old German Beer Hall**	▽	German	$1-$6	541
⑥ / p. 528		Bacchus	▽▽▽	American	$21-$45	539
⑦ / p. 528		Calderone Club	▽▽	Italian	$11-$36	540
⑧ / p. 528		Watts Tea Shop	▽▽	American	$7-$16	542
⑨ / p. 528		Safe House	▽▽	American	$8-$26	541
⑩ / p. 528		Sabor Brazilian Churrascaria	▽▽	Brazilian	$15-$49	541
⑪ / p. 528		The King & I Restaurant	▽▽	Thai	$7-$26	540
⑫ / p. 528		Mason Street Grill	▽▽▽	American	$9-$50	540
⑬ / p. 528		Metro Bar & Cafe	▽▽▽	American	$9-$42	540
⑭ / p. 528		Karl Ratzsch's Restaurant	▽▽▽	German	$7-$32	540
⑮ / p. 528		Carnevor	▽▽▽	Steak	$25-$75	540
⑯ / p. 528		Umami Moto	▽▽▽	Asian	$14-$45	542
⑰ / p. 528		Mo's: A Place for Steaks	▽▽▽	Steak	$17-$99	541
⑱ / p. 528		The Capital Grille	▽▽▽	American	$10-$40	540
⑲ / p. 528		Milwaukee Chop House	▽▽▽	American	$23-$48	541
⑳ / p. 528		Butch's Old Casino Steakhouse	▽▽	Steak	$23-$50	540
㉑ / p. 528		Coquette Cafe	▽▽	French	$8-$21	540
㉒ / p. 528		Milwaukee Ale House	▽▽	American	$7-$22	540

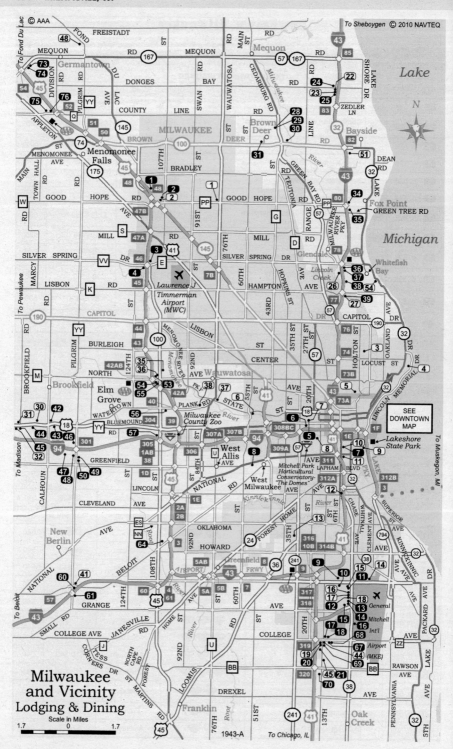

Milwaukee
and Vicinity
Lodging & Dining

Scale in Miles

1943-A

✈ Airport Accommodations

Map Page	OA	GENERAL MITCHELL INTERNATIONAL	Diamond Rated	High Season	Page
12 / p. 530	AAA	**Best Western Plus Milwaukee Airport Hotel & Conference Center, 0.6 mi w of terminal**	◆◆◆	$99-$139 [SAVE]	542
14 / p. 530	AAA	**Clarion Hotel Airport, 0.5 mi w of terminal**	◆◆◆	$109-$189 [SAVE]	546
17 / p. 530		Country Inn & Suites By Carlson, Milwaukee Airport, 2.3 mi s of terminal	◆◆◆	$99-$140	546
20 / p. 530		Crowne Plaza Milwaukee Airport Hotel, 2.9 mi sw of terminal	◆◆◆	$79-$149	547
18 / p. 530	AAA	**Hampton Inn-Milwaukee Airport, 2.7 mi s of terminal**	◆◆◆	$89-$149 [SAVE]	547
16 / p. 530	AAA	**Hilton Garden Inn Milwaukee Airport, 0.7 mi sw of terminal**	◆◆◆	$98-$170 [SAVE]	548
10 / p. 530	AAA	**Holiday Inn & Suites Milwaukee Airport, 1.3 mi w of terminal**	◆◆◆	$129-$179 [SAVE]	549
21 / p. 530		Holiday Inn Express & Suites Milwaukee Airport, 3 mi s of terminal	◆◆◆	$90-$139	550
15 / p. 530	AAA	**Hyatt Place Milwaukee Airport, 0.5 mi w of terminal**	◆◆◆	$99-$169 [SAVE]	550
13 / p. 530	AAA	**Super 8-Milwaukee Airport, 0.5 mi w of terminal**	◆◆	$58-$85 [SAVE]	551
11 / p. 530	AAA	**Wyndham Milwaukee Airport Hotel & Convention Center, 0.5 mi w of terminal**	◆◆◆	$84-$225 [SAVE]	551
69 / p. 530		Comfort Suites Milwaukee Airport, 2.9 mi s of terminal	◆◆◆	$79-$129	566
68 / p. 530		Days Inn Milwaukee Airport, 2.8 mi s of terminal	◆	$49-$74	566
67 / p. 530		MainStay Suites Oak Creek, 2.8 mi s of terminal	◆◆◆	$88-$210	566

Milwaukee and Vicinity

This index helps you "spot" where approved lodgings and restaurants are located on the corresponding detailed maps. Lodging daily rate range is for comparison only and show the property's high season. Restaurant rate range is a combination of lunch and/or dinner. Turn to the listing page for more detailed rate information and consult display ads for special promotions.

MILWAUKEE

Map Page	OA	Lodgings	Diamond Rated	High Season	Page
1 / p. 530	AAA	**Hilton Garden Inn Milwaukee Park Place**	◆◆◆	$79-$159 [SAVE]	548
2 / p. 530		Comfort Suites at Park Place	◆◆◆	$99-$219	546
3 / p. 530		Hampton Inn-Milwaukee NW	◆◆◆	$99-$119	548
4 / p. 530	AAA	**Hyatt Place Milwaukee-West**	◆◆◆	$99-$169 [SAVE]	550
5 / p. 530		Ambassador Hotel	◆◆◆	$119-$399	542
6 / p. 530		Ambassador Inn at Marquette	◆◆	$79-$259	542
7 / p. 530	AAA	**The Iron Horse Hotel - see ad p. 538**	◆◆◆	$149-$329 [SAVE]	551
8 / p. 530	AAA	**Best Western Woods View Inn - see ad p. 544**	◆◆	$64-$125 [SAVE]	542
9 / p. 530	AAA	**Sleep Inn & Suites**	◆◆◆	$80-$130 [SAVE]	551
10 / p. 530	AAA	**Holiday Inn & Suites Milwaukee Airport - see ad p. 549**	◆◆◆	$129-$179 [SAVE]	549
11 / p. 530	AAA	**Wyndham Milwaukee Airport Hotel & Convention Center - see ad p. 553**	◆◆◆	$84-$225 [SAVE]	551
12 / p. 530	AAA	**Best Western Plus Milwaukee Airport Hotel & Conference Center**	◆◆◆	$99-$139 [SAVE]	542
13 / p. 530	AAA	**Super 8-Milwaukee Airport**	◆◆	$58-$85 [SAVE]	551
14 / p. 530	AAA	**Clarion Hotel Airport - see ad p. 546**	◆◆◆	$109-$189 [SAVE]	546

MILWAUKEE (cont'd)

Map Page	OA	Lodgings (cont'd)	Diamond Rated	High Season	Page
15 / p. 530	AAA	**Hyatt Place Milwaukee Airport**	◆◆◆	$99-$169 SAVE	550
16 / p. 530	AAA	**Hilton Garden Inn Milwaukee Airport - see ad p. 548**	◆◆◆	$98-$170 SAVE	548
17 / p. 530		Country Inn & Suites By Carlson, Milwaukee Airport - see ad p. 6	◆◆◆	$99-$140	546
18 / p. 530	AAA	**Hampton Inn-Milwaukee Airport - see ad p. 547**	◆◆◆	$89-$149 SAVE	547
20 / p. 530		Crowne Plaza Milwaukee Airport Hotel	◆◆◆	$79-$149	547
21 / p. 530		Holiday Inn Express & Suites Milwaukee Airport	◆◆◆	$90-$139	550

Map Page	OA	Restaurants	Diamond Rated	Cuisine	Meal Range	Page
1 / p. 530		Yen Ching Restaurant	◆◆	Chinese	$5-$13	556
2 / p. 530		Branded Steer	◆◆	Steak	$5-$24	555
3 / p. 530		West Bank Cafe	◆◆	Vietnamese	$5-$17	556
4 / p. 530		Bartolotta's Lake Park Bistro	◆◆◆	French	$12-$49	555
5 / p. 530		Roots Restaurant & Cellar	◆◆	Regional American	$18-$36	556
6 / p. 530		Saz's State House	◆◆	American	$7-$27	556
7 / p. 530		Envoy	◆◆	American	$8-$25	555
8 / p. 530	AAA	**Dream Dance Steak**	◆◆◆◆	Regional American	$24-$46	555
9 / p. 530	AAA	**Rip Tide Seafood Bar & Grill**	◆◆	Seafood	$9-$38	556
10 / p. 530		Smyth	◆◆◆	Regional American	$8-$44	556
11 / p. 530		Botanas Mexican Cuisine	◆◆	Mexican	$6-$20	555
12 / p. 530		Old Town Serbian Gourmet Restaurant	◆◆	Eastern European	$6-$19	556
13 / p. 530		Omega Family Restaurant	◆◆	Greek	$6-$23	556
14 / p. 530		The Packing House	◆◆	Steak	$6-$37	556
15 / p. 530	AAA	**America's House of Steaks**	◆◆◆	American	$10-$30	555
16 / p. 530		Final Approach	◆◆	American	$5-$15	555
17 / p. 530		Jalapeno Loco	◆◆	Mexican	$6-$19	555
18 / p. 530	AAA	**Lake City Restaurant & Lounge**	◆◆	Steak	$8-$26	555
19 / p. 530		Houlihan's	◆◆◆	American	$9-$22	555

MEQUON

Map Page	OA	Lodgings	Diamond Rated	High Season	Page
24 / p. 530		The Chalet Motel of Mequon	◆◆	$59-$159	565
25 / p. 530	AAA	**Best Western Quiet House & Suites - see ad p. 544**	◆◆	$84-$239 SAVE	565

Map Page	OA	Restaurants	Diamond Rated	Cuisine	Meal Range	Page
22 / p. 530		Ferrante's Mequon	◆◆	Italian	$6-$18	565
23 / p. 530		Centennial Bar & Grille	◆◆	American	$7-$25	565

BROWN DEER

Map Page	OA	Lodgings	Diamond Rated	High Season	Page
28 / p. 530		Holiday Inn Express	◆◆◆	$104-$144	560
29 / p. 530		Candlewood Suites	◆◆◆	$95-$144	560
30 / p. 530	AAA	**Four Points by Sheraton Milwaukee North**	◆◆◆	$79-$259 SAVE	560

BROWN DEER (cont'd)

Map Page	OA	Lodgings (cont'd)	Diamond Rated	High Season	Page
31 / p. 530		Courtyard by Marriott Milwaukee North Brown Deer	◆◆◆	$139-$149	560

GLENDALE

Map Page	OA	Lodgings	Diamond Rated	High Season	Page
34 / p. 530		Residence Inn by Marriott Milwaukee/Glendale	◆◆◆	$129-$135	563
35 / p. 530		Radisson Hotel Milwaukee North Shore	◆◆◆	$89-$229	563
36 / p. 530		Baymont Inn & Suites Glendale/Milwaukee Northeast	◆◆	$49-$73	563
37 / p. 530		La Quinta Inn & Suites Milwaukee Bayshore Area	◆◆◆	$79-$159	563
38 / p. 530		La Quinta Inn Milwaukee Glendale Hampton Ave	◆◆	$52-$109	563
39 / p. 530	AAA	**Hilton Milwaukee River - see ad p. 549**	◆◆◆	$97-$197 [SAVE]	563

Map Page	OA	Restaurants	Diamond Rated	Cuisine	Meal Range	Page
26 / p. 530		The Bavarian Inn	◆◆	German	$6-$18	564
27 / p. 530		Anchorage Restaurant - see ad p. 549	◆◆◆	Seafood	$8-$24	563

BROOKFIELD

Map Page	OA	Lodgings	Diamond Rated	High Season	Page
42 / p. 530		TownePlace Suites by Marriott	◆◆	$149-$159	559
43 / p. 530		Courtyard by Marriott/Brookfield	◆◆◆	$149-$169	558
44 / p. 530	AAA	**Doubletree Hotel Milwaukee/Brookfield - see ad p. 558**	◆◆◆	$80-$199 [SAVE]	558
45 / p. 530		Homestead Studio Suites Hotel-Milwaukee/Brookfield	◆◆	$51-$85	558
46 / p. 530	AAA	**Sheraton Milwaukee Brookfield - see ad p. 552**	◆◆◆	$109-$269 [SAVE]	559
47 / p. 530	AAA	**Residence Inn by Marriott Milwaukee-Brookfield**	◆◆◆	$139-$209 [SAVE]	559
48 / p. 530	AAA	**Best Western Plus Midway Hotel & Suites-Brookfield**	◆◆◆	$99-$159 [SAVE]	557
49 / p. 530	AAA	**Brookfield Suites Hotel & Convention Center**	◆◆◆	$99-$395 [SAVE]	557
50 / p. 530	AAA	**Country Inn & Suites By Carlson, Milwaukee-West - see ad p. 557, p. 6**	◆◆◆	$99-$269 [SAVE]	557

Map Page	OA	Restaurants	Diamond Rated	Cuisine	Meal Range	Page
30 / p. 530		Taste of India	◆◆	Indian	$7-$17	560
31 / p. 530		Kopp's Frozen Custard	◆	American	$5-$10	559
32 / p. 530		Louise's	◆◆	Italian	$9-$23	560

WAUWATOSA

Map Page	OA	Lodgings	Diamond Rated	High Season	Page
53 / p. 530		Radisson Hotel Milwaukee West	◆◆◆	$109-$209	569
54 / p. 530		Extended StayAmerica-Milwaukee-Wauwatosa	◆◆	$51-$85	569
55 / p. 530		Holiday Inn Express Milwaukee West-Medical Center	◆◆	$109-$139	569
56 / p. 530		Crowne Plaza Milwaukee-Wauwatosa	◆◆◆	$99-$179	569
57 / p. 530		Super 8 of Milwaukee West	◆◆	$71-$80	569

Map Page	OA	Restaurants	Diamond Rated	Cuisine	Meal Range	Page
35 / p. 530		Maggiano's Little Italy	◆◆◆	Italian	$11-$38	570
36 / p. 530		RJ's Garden & Grille	◆◆	American	$9-$27	570

Map Page	OA	Restaurants (cont'd)	Diamond Rated	Cuisine	Meal Range	Page
37 / p. 530		Ristorante Bartolotta	◆◆◆	Northern Italian	$16-$37	570
38 / p. 530		Eddie Martini's	◆◆◆	Traditional American	$9-$39	569

NEW BERLIN

Map Page	OA	Lodgings	Diamond Rated	High Season	Page
60 / p. 530		Holiday Inn Express Hotel & Suites-New Berlin	◆◆◆	$99-$169	565
61 / p. 530		La Quinta Inn & Suites Milwaukee SW New Berlin	◆◆◆	$59-$139	565

Map Page	OA	Restaurant	Diamond Rated	Cuisine	Meal Range	Page
41 / p. 530		Mi Cocina Mexican Restaurant	◆◆	Mexican	$6-$15	566

GREENFIELD

Map Page	OA	Lodging	Diamond Rated	High Season	Page
64 / p. 530		Golden Key Motel	◆	$45-$85	564

OAK CREEK

Map Page	OA	Lodgings	Diamond Rated	High Season	Page
67 / p. 530		MainStay Suites Oak Creek	◆◆◆	$88-$210	566
68 / p. 530		Days Inn Milwaukee Airport	◆	$49-$74	566
69 / p. 530		Comfort Suites Milwaukee Airport	◆◆◆	$79-$129	566
70 / p. 530		La Quinta Inn Milwaukee Airport / Oak Creek	◆◆	$59-$105	566

Map Page	OA	Restaurants	Diamond Rated	Cuisine	Meal Range	Page
44 / p. 530		Branded Steer	◆◆	Steak	$5-$24	566
45 / p. 530		Nick's and Friends Family Restaurant	◆◆	American	$6-$13	566

GERMANTOWN

Map Page	OA	Lodgings	Diamond Rated	High Season	Page
73 / p. 530		Country Inn & Suites By Carlson - see ad p. 6	◆◆◆	$94-$129	562
74 / p. 530		AmericInn Lodge & Suites of Germantown	◆◆	$80-$100	562
75 / p. 530		Holiday Inn Express Milwaukee NW-Germantown	◆◆◆	$99-$149	562
76 / p. 530	AAA	**Super 8-Germantown/Milwaukee**	◆◆	$61-$70 SAVE	562

Map Page	OA	Restaurant	Diamond Rated	Cuisine	Meal Range	Page
48 / p. 530		Jerry's Old Town	◆◆	Barbecue	$18-$43	562

FOX POINT

Map Page	OA	Restaurant	Diamond Rated	Cuisine	Meal Range	Page
51 / p. 530		North Shore Bistro	◆◆◆	American	$11-$20	561

WHITEFISH BAY

Map Page	OA	Restaurant	Diamond Rated	Cuisine	Meal Range	Page
54 / p. 530		Jack Pandl's Whitefish Bay Inn	◆◆	American	$7-$29	571

DOWNTOWN MILWAUKEE (See map and index starting on p. 528)

ALOFT MILWAUKEE DOWNTOWN

Phone: (414)226-0122 **1**

Hotel
$89-$209

Address: 1230 N Old World Third St 53212 **Location:** I-43, exit 73A, just se. **Facility:** Smoke free premises. 160 units. 5 stories, interior corridors. *Bath:* shower only. **Parking:** valet only. **Terms:** cancellation fee imposed. **Amenities:** safes. **Pool(s):** heated indoor. **Activities:** exercise room. **Guest Services:** valet and coin laundry, wireless Internet. *(see ad below)*

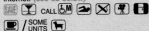

AAA Benefit: Enjoy the new twist, get up to 15% off Starwood Preferred Guest® bonuses.

FREE newspaper

BEST WESTERN INN TOWNE HOTEL

Phone: (414)224-8400 **8**

Hotel
$79-$139

Address: 710 N Old World 3rd St 53203 **Location:** Corner of Wisconsin Ave and N Old World 3rd St. Located in a commercial area. **Facility:** Smoke free premises. 103 units. 12 stories, interior corridors. **Parking:** no self-parking. **Terms:** 7 day cancellation notice-fee imposed. **Amenities:** *Some:* high-speed Internet. **Activities:** exercise room. **Guest Services:** valet laundry, wireless Internet. **Free Special Amenities: full breakfast and high-speed Internet.**

AAA Benefit: Members save up to 20%, plus 10% bonus points with free rewards program.

COMFORT INN & SUITES DOWNTOWN LAKESHORE

Phone: (414)276-8800 **2**

Hotel
$100-$149

Address: 916 E State St 53202 **Location:** Between Marshall and Astor sts. Located in a residential area. **Facility:** Smoke free premises. 159 units, some kitchens. 5 stories, interior corridors. **Parking:** on-site (fee). **Amenities:** video games (fee). **Dining:** Aura, see separate listing. **Activities:** exercise room. **Guest Services:** valet and coin laundry, area transportation-downtown, wireless Internet. **Free Special Amenities: expanded continental breakfast and high-speed Internet.**

(See map and index starting on p. 528)

COURTYARD BY MARRIOTT MILWAUKEE DOWNTOWN

Hotel
$189-$229

Address: 300 W Michigan St 53203 **Location:** I-794, exit 1A (Plankinton Ave), just n, then just w. **Facility:** Smoke free premises. 169 units. 6 stories, interior corridors. **Parking:** on-site (fee) and valet. **Terms:** cancellation fee imposed. **Amenities:** high-speed Internet. **Pool(s):** heated indoor. **Activities:** whirlpool, exercise room. **Guest Services:** valet and coin laundry, wireless Internet.

Phone: (414)291-4122 ⓬

AAA Benefit:
Members save a minimum 5% off the best available rate.

DOUBLETREE MILWAUKEE CITY CENTER

Hotel
$99-$209

Address: 611 W Wisconsin Ave 53203 **Location:** Corner of W Wisconsin Ave and 6th St. Located in a commercial area. **Facility:** Smoke free premises. 243 units. 10 stories, interior corridors. **Parking:** valet only. **Terms:** 1-7 night minimum stay, cancellation fee imposed. **Pool(s):** heated outdoor. **Activities:** exercise room. **Guest Services:** complimentary and valet laundry, wireless Internet. **Free Special Amenities:** newspaper and high-speed Internet.

Phone: (414)273-2950 ⓾

DOUBLETREE
HOTELS·SUITES·RESORTS·CLUBS

AAA Benefit:
Members save 5% or more everyday!

HAMPTON INN & SUITES MILWAUKEE DOWNTOWN

Hotel
$129-$189

Address: 176 W Wisconsin Ave 53203 **Location:** I-794, exit 1D (Plankinton Ave), 0.3 mi n, then just w. Located in a commercial area. **Facility:** Smoke free premises. 138 units. 10 stories, interior corridors. **Parking:** on-site (fee). **Terms:** 1-7 night minimum stay, cancellation fee imposed. **Amenities:** video games (fee). **Pool(s):** heated indoor. **Activities:** whirlpool, exercise room. **Fee:** game room. **Guest Services:** valet laundry, wireless Internet. *(see ad p. 537)*

Phone: (414)271-4656 ❼

AAA Benefit:
Members save up to 10% everyday!

FREE full breakfast and high-speed Internet

HILTON MILWAUKEE CITY CENTER

Hotel
Rates not provided

Address: 509 W Wisconsin Ave 53203 **Location:** Corner of W Wisconsin Ave and 5th St. **Facility:** Smoke free premises. 730 units. 24 stories, interior corridors. **Parking:** on-site (fee). **Terms:** check-in 4 pm. **Amenities:** video games (fee). *Some: Fee:* high-speed Internet. **Dining:** Milwaukee Chop House, see separate listing. **Activities:** whirlpool, indoor water park, exercise room. *Fee:* game room. **Guest Services:** valet laundry, wireless Internet.

Phone: 414/271-7250 ❾

AAA Benefit:
Members save 5% or more everyday!

HOTEL METRO-MILWAUKEE

Hotel
$179-$359

Address: 411 E Mason St 53202 **Location:** Corner of Mason and Milwaukee sts. Located in the theater/financial district. **Facility:** Smoke free premises. 63 units, some two bedrooms. 6 stories, interior corridors. **Parking:** valet only. **Terms:** cancellation fee imposed. **Amenities:** high-speed Internet, safes, honor bars. **Dining:** Metro Bar & Cafe, see separate listing. **Activities:** sauna, bicycles, exercise room, spa. **Guest Services:** valet laundry, wireless Internet.

Phone: (414)272-1937 ❺

HYATT REGENCY MILWAUKEE

Hotel
$89-$309

Address: 333 W Kilbourn Ave 53203 **Location:** At N 3rd St. Walkway to Midwest Express Center and Grand Ave Mall. **Facility:** Smoke free premises. 481 units. 18 stories, interior corridors. **Parking:** on-site (fee) and valet. **Terms:** cancellation fee imposed. **Amenities:** video games (fee), safes. **Activities:** exercise room. **Guest Services:** valet laundry, wireless Internet. **Free Special Amenities:** local telephone calls and newspaper.

Phone: (414)276-1234 ❹

HYATT
HOTELS & RESORTS ®

AAA Benefit:
Ask for the AAA rate and save 10%.

INTERCONTINENTAL MILWAUKEE

Hotel
$119-$309

Address: 139 E Kilbourn Ave 53202 **Location:** At Water St. **Facility:** Smoke free premises. 221 units. 10 stories, interior corridors. **Parking:** on-site (fee) and valet. **Terms:** cancellation fee imposed. **Amenities:** video games (fee), high-speed Internet, safes. *Some:* honor bars. **Activities:** saunas, steamrooms, sun deck. **Guest Services:** valet laundry, wireless Internet.

Phone: (414)276-8686 ❸

(See map and index starting on p. 528)

▼ See AAA listing p. 536 ▼

destination: unforgettable.

Ready to recharge? Let your friends at Hampton help connect you to a perfect getaway. We're delighted to offer special rates for AAA members.* • Complimentary On the House® hot breakfast • Indoor pool & whirlpool • 100% Smoke free • 100% Hampton satisfaction guarantee

Hampton Inn & Suites

we love having you here.*

free high-speed internet

free hot breakfast

show your card and save

Hampton Inn & Suites • 176 W Wisconsin Ave. Milwaukee, WI 53203

414-271-4656 • www.milwaukeedowntownsuites.hamptoninn.com

©2010 Hilton Worldwide. 10% discount off published rates. Subject to availability. Valid for stays Apr. 1, 2011 – Mar. 31, 2012. Discount exclude taxes, gratuities and incidental charges. Offer valid for AAA members only and is not transferable. AAA card required at check-in.

Sensible Spending:**SMART.**   Real Discounts:**INGENIOUS.**

Your AAA/CAA card can get you discounts on everything from clothing and jewelry to prescriptions and books.
Visit **AAA.com/discounts** and start saving today.

Show Your Card & Save®

(See map and index starting on p. 528)

(See map and index starting on p. 528)

THE PFISTER HOTEL

Classic Historic Hotel
$139-$2000

Phone: (414)273-8222   **6**

Address: 424 E Wisconsin Ave 53202 **Location:** Corner of E Wisconsin Ave and Jefferson St. **Facility:** Built in 1893 by Milwaukee industrialist Guido Pfister, this landmark hotel is now home to an impressive collection of Victorian art. Smoke free premises. 307 units, some two bedrooms. 8-23 stories, interior corridors. **Parking:** on-site (fee) and valet. **Terms:** cancellation fee imposed. **Amenities:** safes. *Fee:* video games, high-speed Internet. **Dining:** Mason Street Grill, see separate listing, entertainment. **Pool(s):** heated indoor. **Activities:** exercise room, spa. **Guest Services:** valet laundry, wireless Internet. Affiliated with A Preferred Hotel. *(see ad below)*

FREE newspaper

RESIDENCE INN-DOWNTOWN MILWAUKEE

Extended Stay Hotel
$179-$209

Phone: (414)224-7890   **11**

AAA Benefit:
Members save a minimum 5% off the best available rate.

Address: 648 N Plankinton Ave 53203 **Location:** I-794, exit 1D (Plankinton Ave), just n at Wisconsin Ave. Located on the Riverwalk. **Facility:** Smoke free premises. 131 units, some two bedrooms, efficiencies and kitchens. 8 stories, interior corridors. **Parking:** on-site (fee). **Terms:** cancellation fee imposed. **Amenities:** high-speed Internet. **Activities:** exercise room. **Guest Services:** valet and coin laundry, wireless Internet.

─── WHERE TO DINE ───

AURA

International
$22-$50

Phone: 414/272-1011   **3**

Patrons who enter the restaurant's visually stimulating atmosphere can experience a slice of L.A. in Milwaukee. The creative menu lists interesting dishes that draw their inspiration from various points around the globe. Servers are attentive and personable. **Bar:** full bar. **Reservations:** suggested. **Hours:** 5 pm-10 pm. Closed: Sun & Mon. **Address:** 1011 N Astor St 53202 **Location:** Between Marshall and Astor sts; in Comfort Inn & Suites Downtown Lakeshore. **Parking:** on-site and valet.

BACCHUS

American
$21-$45

Phone: 414/765-1166   **6**

Locally acclaimed as one of the city's most upscale eateries, the look of the dining room suggests that this is a place for power lunches and business meals, but also the spot to get together with family and friends. The menu boasts foie gras, caviar, Strauss lamb and Maine lobster. Not to be forgotten are the luscious desserts using Valrhona chocolate. **Bar:** full bar. **Reservations:** suggested. **Hours:** 5:30 pm-9 pm, Fri-10 pm, Sat 5 pm-10 pm. Closed major holidays; also Sun. **Address:** 925 E Wells St 53202 **Location:** Corner of E Wells St and N Prospect Ave. **Parking:** on-site (fee) and street.

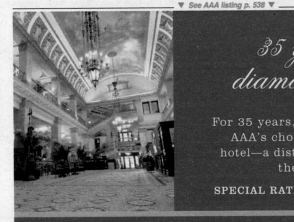

(See map and index starting on p. 528)

BUTCH'S OLD CASINO STEAKHOUSE
Phone: 414/271-8111 (20)

Steak
$23-$50

Convenient to many local hotels, this cozy, eclectically decorated dining room is shaped like a roulette wheel. A local favorite, the menu lists a variety of well-prepared steaks as well as daily seafood preparations. **Bar:** full bar. **Hours:** 5 pm-10 pm, Fri & Sat-11 pm. Closed major holidays; also Sun. **Address:** 555 N James Lovell St 53233 **Location:** Just n of W Clybourn St; across from Greyhound Bus Station. **Parking:** street only.

CALDERONE CLUB
Phone: 414/273-3236 (7)

Italian
$11-$36

A city staple for more than 30 years, this Italian bistro-style restaurant is a do not miss. Patrons sit down to hand-made pasta and pizza, in addition to steaks, seafood and daily specials. **Bar:** full bar. **Hours:** 11 am-10 pm, Fri-11 pm, Sat noon-midnight, Sun 4 pm-10 pm. Closed major holidays. **Address:** 842 N Old World 3rd St 53203 **Location:** At Kilbourn Ave. **Parking:** street only.

THE CAPITAL GRILLE
Phone: 414/223-0600 (18)

American
$10-$40

An English men's club comes to mind in the quiet, relaxed setting, enhanced by dark wood and rich upholstery. Perfectly prepared steaks, fresh seafood and lamb line the menu. **Bar:** full bar. **Reservations:** suggested. **Hours:** 11:30 am-3 & 5-10 pm, Fri-11 pm, Sat 5 pm-11 pm. Closed: 7/4, 11/24, 12/25; also Super Bowl Sun. **Address:** 310 W Wisconsin Ave 53203 **Location:** Corner of W Wisconsin Ave and Milwaukee St. **Parking:** valet only. CALL 🚹🅼

CARNEVOR
Phone: 414/223-2200 (15)

Steak
$25-$75

As the name might indicate, this is a meat-eater's mecca. The menu bursts with high-end steaks from wet-aged filet mignon and New York strip steak to dry-aged reserve cuts including bone-in rib-eye and imported Kobe beef filet mignon. Salmon, lobster, chicken and Alaskan king crab legs are also on the menu. The steaks are served with varied toppings or sauces. The energetic, low-lit dining room is designed as though guests are eating on the inside of a dinosaur. **Bar:** full bar. **Reservations:** suggested. **Hours:** 5 pm-10 pm, Thurs-Sat to 11 pm. Closed major holidays; also Sun. **Address:** 724 N Milwaukee St 53202 **Location:** Between E Wisconsin Ave and Mason St. **Parking:** valet and street only.

COQUETTE CAFE
Phone: 414/291-2655 (21)

French
$8-$21

In a historic building, the lively French-style cafe offers a menu of fine bistro cuisine. Among choices are mussels, cassoulet, pork chops, roast chicken and thin-crust French-style pizzas. **Bar:** full bar. **Reservations:** suggested. **Hours:** 11 am-10 pm, Fri-11 pm, Sat 5 pm-11 pm. Closed major holidays; also Sun. **Address:** 316 N Milwaukee St 53202 **Location:** Just s of St Paul St; center; in Historic Third Ward. **Parking:** on-site and street.

KARL RATZSCH'S RESTAURANT
Phone: 414/276-2720 (14)

German
$7-$32

Since 1904, the German-themed restaurant has offered a detailed and charming Old World atmosphere in which carefully prepared dishes are served by exceptionally professional, friendly servers. Beverage options include a good variety of wines and imported beers. **Bar:** full bar. **Reservations:** suggested. **Hours:** 4:30 pm-9 pm, Wed-Fri also 11:30 am-2 pm, Sat 11:30 am-2 & 4:30-10 pm. Closed major holidays; also Sun. **Address:** 320 E Mason St 53202 **Location:** Jct N Milwaukee St. **Parking:** valet and street only. **Historic** CALL 🚹🅼

THE KING & I RESTAURANT
Phone: 414/276-4181 (11)

Thai
$7-$26

Just steps away from most major downtown venues and hotels, the restaurant sports decor that may seem at odds with the image of a Thai restaurant. However, the well-prepared food is a local favorite for a reason. **Bar:** full bar. **Hours:** 11:30 am-11 pm, Sat from 5 pm, Sun 4 pm-9 pm. Closed major holidays. **Address:** 830 N Old World 3rd St 53203 **Location:** Jct E Wells St. **Parking:** street only.

MADER'S GERMAN RESTAURANT   *Menu on AAA.com*
Phone: 414/271-3377 (4)

German
$8-$33

This family-owned-and-operated restaurant has been a local favorite since 1902. All meals are prepared in the German tradition with a Continental flair. The German-style setting incorporates many medieval pieces of weaponry, steins, wood carvings and glassware. Beer lovers can choose from more than 200 imported and domestic beers to go with oxtail soup or sauerbraten. Alternately, the wine lists features more than 100 vintages. Homemade apple or cherry strudel is delicious. **Bar:** full bar. **Reservations:** suggested. **Hours:** 11:30 am-9 pm, Fri & Sat-10 pm, Sun 11 am-9 pm; Sunday brunch. Closed: 12/25. **Address:** 1041 N Old World 3rd St 53203 **Location:** Jct W State and N 3rd sts. **Parking:** on-site and valet. **Historic**

MASON STREET GRILL
Phone: 414/298-3131 (12)

American
$9-$50

New to the city, this restaurant is the place to go for wood-grilled steaks, homemade desserts and a warm atmosphere. Entertainment. **Bar:** full bar. **Reservations:** suggested. **Hours:** 11:30 am-2 & 5-10 pm, Sat from 5 pm, Sun 5 pm-9 pm. **Address:** 425 E Mason Ave 53202 **Location:** Corner of E Mason Ave and N Jefferson St; in The Pfister Hotel. **Parking:** valet only. CALL 🚹🅼

METRO BAR & CAFE
Phone: 414/225-3270 (13)

American
$9-$42

The stylish see-and-be-seen restaurant offers an ever-changing menu that features fresh, seasonal ingredients as well as serious steaks and seafood. **Bar:** full bar. **Hours:** 6 am-2 & 5-10 pm, Sat & Sun from 7 am. **Address:** 411 E Mason St 53202 **Location:** Corner of Mason and Milwaukee sts; in Hotel Metro-Milwaukee. **Parking:** valet and street only. CALL 🚹🅼

MILWAUKEE ALE HOUSE
Phone: 414/226-2337 (22)

American
$7-$22

Located in the Historic Third Ward of Milwaukee, this brick and timber warehouse overlooks the river with both inside and outside dining. Offering classic favorites and home brewed beers. **Bar:** full bar. **Hours:** 11 am-10 pm, Sun-9 pm. Closed major holidays. **Address:** 233 N Water St 53202 **Location:** Just n of jct Chicago St; in Historic Third Ward. **Parking:** street only. CALL 🚹🅼

(See map and index starting on p. 528)

MILWAUKEE CHOP HOUSE

Phone: 414/390-4562 ⑲

American
$23-$48

A contemporary flair punctuates the traditional steakhouse downtown. Tender steaks and fresh seafood merit praise. The old-time supper club interior features elegant gold-leaf chandeliers, mahogany trim and elegant tables draped with white cloths. **Bar:** full bar. **Reservations:** suggested. **Hours:** 5 pm-10 pm, Sun-9 pm. Closed major holidays; also Sun. **Address:** 633 N 5th St 53202 **Location:** Corner of W Wisconsin Ave and 5th St; in Hilton Milwaukee City Center. **Parking:** on-site (fee). CALL &M

MO'S: A PLACE FOR STEAKS

Phone: 414/272-0720 ⑰

Steak
$17-$99

As the name suggests, this quietly elegant yet comfortable restaurant is serious about its enormous steaks. Offering a butcher's selection of steaks, the restaurant also offers a wide variety of fresh and imported seafood. Desserts merit consideration. **Bar:** full bar. **Hours:** 5 pm-11 pm, Sat-midnight. Closed major holidays; also Sun. **Address:** 720 N Plankinton Ave 53203 **Location:** Jct E Wisconsin Ave. **Parking:** valet and street only. CALL &M

OLD GERMAN BEER HALL   *Menu on AAA.com*

Phone: 414/226-2728 ⑤

German
$1-$6

In the historic Third Ward, this place is fashioned after the beer halls in Munich and celebrates the German heritage of Milwaukee. Each of the beer steins lining the counters and shelves represents an active beer club member. Guests enjoy one-liter mugs of imported hofbrauhaus beer while partaking in fresh-baked pretzels and Usinger sausages like knackwurst, weisswurst, landjaeger and the ubiquitous bratwurst. For something different, try the smoked pork chop of curried bratwurst. **Bar:** full bar. **Hours:** 11 am-2 am. Closed: 12/25. **Address:** 1009 N Old World 3rd St 53203 **Location:** Jct W State St. **Parking:** street only.

OSTERIA DEL MONDO

Phone: 414/291-3770 ②

Italian
$15-$35

In the heart of Milwaukee, the osteria is an importation of Italy—its foods, its wine, its desserts and its ambience. Murals, sketches and paintings of the Sistine Chapel surround the intimate yet spacious setting. Diners can opt for any of three tasting menus or order a la carte. Food is impressively prepared with fresh ingredients and many made-in-house sauces. Excellent fish, veal, lamb, short ribs, pasta and steak options are often on the seasonally changing menu. **Bar:** full bar. **Reservations:** suggested. **Hours:** 5:30 pm-10 pm, Fri & Sat-11 pm. Closed: 11/24, 12/24, 12/25; also Sun. **Address:** 1028 E Juneau Ave 53202 **Location:** Jct N Waverly Pl; in Knickerbocker Hotel. **Parking:** valet and street only.

SABOR BRAZILIAN CHURRASCARIA

Phone: 414/431-3106 ⑩

Brazilian
$15-$49

Modeled after Brazilian gauchos and their legendary churrasco (barbecue), this place delights patrons with the robust flavors of slow-roasted meats served at the table upon request. Diners just turn over a card at the table and gauchos serve from one of 12 cuts of fire-roasted meats. The buffet lines up fresh salad offerings and roasted vegetables. **Bar:** full bar. **Reservations:** suggested. **Hours:** 11:30 am-1:30 & 5-9 pm, Fri-10 pm, Sat & Sun 5 pm-close. **Address:** 777 N Water St 53202 **Location:** Just n of McKinley. **Parking:** valet and street only. CALL &M

SAFE HOUSE

Phone: 414/271-2007 ⑨

American
$8-$26

A city landmark for 40 years, this establishment carries the spy theme throughout. This holds true for the menu, which lists spy burgers, the Egyptian spy palace and other fare designed for the ultimate in intrigue. **Bar:** full bar. **Reservations:** suggested. **Hours:** 11:30 am-2:30 & 5-9 pm, Fri & Sat-9:45 pm, Sun 4 pm-8 pm; Sun 11:30 am-9 pm 5/28-9/1. Closed major holidays. **Address:** 779 N Front St 53202 **Location:** Between Wells and Mason sts, just e of Water St. **Parking:** no self-parking.

SANFORD RESTAURANT

Phone: 414/276-9608 ①

American
$31-$39

In a small residential building, the cozy, intimate dining room is home to a wonderful adventure. The competent, smartly attired wait staff employs a seamless team approach to service, making guests feel special and at ease. The ever-changing menu offers three-, four-, five- and seven-course options. Cuisine is as varied as the market and often includes game dishes. Presentations are creative and eye-appealing, and everything is prepared to order. **Bar:** full bar. **Reservations:** suggested. **Hours:** 5:30 pm-9 pm, Fri-10 pm, Sat 5 pm-10 pm. Closed major holidays; also Sun. **Address:** 1547 N Jackson St 53202 **Location:** Southeast corner of N Jackson and Pleasant sts. **Parking:** valet and street only. CALL &M

(See map and index starting on p. 528)

UMAMI MOTO

Asian
$14-$45

Phone: 414/727-9333 16

This hip, high-energy dining hot spot is in an area filled with trendy restaurants and bars. This place has it going on in the kitchen with superb contemporary Asian cuisine that incorporates many fresh organic ingredients and high-end items such as Kobe beef, kung pao duck, sea bass, lobster, Japanese sunfish and black bass. The varied menu also presents a good number of sushi and sashimi items. The wait staff is as energetic as the music that plays in the background. **Bar:** full bar. **Reservations:** suggested, weekends. **Hours:** 5 pm-10 pm, Thurs-Sat to 11 pm, Sun 4 pm-9 pm. **Address:** 718 N Milwaukee St 53202 **Location:** Between E Wisconsin Ave and Mason St. **Parking:** valet only. CALL ⓂM

WATTS TEA SHOP

American
$7-$16

Phone: 414/291-5120 8

This family-owned-and-operated restaurant, a local favorite, was established in 1926 and is on the second floor of the George Watts & Son Inc. Building. It is known for its homemade bread, soup, salad, sandwiches and dessert. Afternoon tea is from 2:30 to 4 pm daily. **Reservations:** suggested. **Hours:** 9 am-4 pm. Closed major holidays; also Sun. **Address:** 761 N Jefferson St 53202 **Location:** Jct E Mason and N Jefferson sts. **Parking:** valet only. **Historic** CALL ⓂM

MILWAUKEE pop. 596,974 (See map and index starting on p. 530)

AMBASSADOR HOTEL

Hotel
$119-$399

Phone: (414)345-5000 5

Address: 2308 W Wisconsin Ave 53233 **Location:** I-94, exit 308 (US 41), just n to Wisconsin Ave (US 18) exit, then 1.5 mi e; jct N 24th St. **Facility:** Smoke free premises. 120 units. 8 stories, interior corridors. **Terms:** check-in 4 pm, cancellation fee imposed. **Amenities:** high-speed Internet, safes, honor bars. **Dining:** Envoy, see separate listing. **Activities:** exercise room. *Fee:* massage. **Guest Services:** valet and coin laundry, area transportation-downtown, wireless Internet.

📶 🍸 CALL ⓂM BIZ ✕ 🎦 💻 / SOME UNITS FEE 🐕

AMBASSADOR INN AT MARQUETTE

Hotel
$79-$259

Phone: (414)342-0000 6

Address: 2301 W Wisconsin Ave 53233 **Location:** I-94, exit 308 (US 41), just n to Wisconsin Ave (US 18) exit, then 1.5 mi e. **Facility:** Smoke free premises. 40 units, some kitchens. 3 stories, interior corridors. **Terms:** check-in 4 pm, cancellation fee imposed. **Amenities:** high-speed Internet, safes. **Activities:** exercise room. **Guest Services:** valet laundry, area transportation-downtown, wireless Internet.

📶 CALL ⓂM BIZ ✕ 🎦 🛗 🖥 💻

BEST WESTERN PLUS MILWAUKEE AIRPORT HOTEL & CONFERENCE CENTER

Hotel
$99-$139

Phone: (414)769-2100 12

Address: 5105 S Howell Ave 53207 **Location:** I-94, exit 318 (Airport), 1.1 mi e, then just n on Howell Ave (SR 38). **Facility:** Smoke free premises. 140 units. 2-3 stories, interior corridors. **Amenities:** safes (fee). *Some:* high-speed Internet. **Dining:** Lake City Restaurant & Lounge, see separate listing. **Pool(s):** heated indoor. **Activities:** whirlpool, exercise room. **Guest Services:** valet and coin laundry, wireless Internet. **Free Special Amenities:** full breakfast and room upgrade (subject to availability with advance reservations).

AAA Benefit:
Members save up to 20%, plus 10% bonus points with free rewards program.

SAVE ✈ 🍽 CALL ⓂM 🏊 BIZ ✕ 🎦 🛗 🖥 💻

BEST WESTERN WOODS VIEW INN

Hotel
$64-$125

Phone: (414)671-6400 8

Address: 5501 W National Ave 53214 **Location:** I-94, exit 308B, 0.5 mi s on Miller Pkwy, then 0.5 w on SR 59. Adjacent to Veterans Hospital. **Facility:** Smoke free premises. 61 units, some kitchens. 3 stories, interior corridors. **Amenities:** safes (fee). *Some:* high-speed Internet. **Pool(s):** heated indoor. **Activities:** whirlpool, sun deck, exercise room. **Guest Services:** valet laundry, wireless Internet. *(see ad p. 544)*

AAA Benefit:
Members save up to 20%, plus 10% bonus points with free rewards program.

SAVE 🍽 CALL ⓂM 🏊 ✕ 🎦 💻 / SOME UNITS 🛗 🖥

FREE continental breakfast and high-speed Internet

TourBook Comments

Are we meeting your travel needs?

If your visit to an establishment listed in a AAA TourBook or CampBook guide doesn't meet your expectations, tell us about it.

Complete an easy online form at **AAA.com/TourBookComments.**

▼ See AAA listing p. 542 ▼

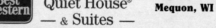

(See map and index starting on p. 530)

▼ See AAA listing p. 473 ▼

Comfortable.
Elegant.

Spacious accommodations, the perfect lakeshore location, Aspira Spa,
a cooking school, casual fine dining, and all the services and amenities you'd
expect of a AAA Four Diamond resort. Genuine, friendly staff and a host
of activities guaranteed to make you feel right at home.
The elegant and the comfortable meet at The Osthoff Resort.

THE
OSTHOFF
RESORT™
Your place on the lake.

ASPIRA
THE SPA

Elkhart Lake, WI • 800.876.3399 • www.osthoff.com

Complete Vacation Planning

AAA.com/Travel and **CAA.ca/Travel** – everything
you need to plan and book your vacations, backed
by the travel experts at local AAA/CAA offices.

(See map and index starting on p. 530)

CLARION HOTEL AIRPORT

Hotel
$109–$189

Phone: (414)481-2400   **14**

Address: 5311 S Howell Ave 53207 **Location:** I-94, exit 318 (Airport), 1.1 mi e on SR 38. Located in a commercial area. **Facility:** Smoke free premises. 180 units, some two bedrooms. 3 stories, interior corridors. **Pool(s):** heated indoor. **Guest Services:** valet and coin laundry, wireless Internet. *(see ad below)*

FREE continental breakfast and airport transportation

COMFORT SUITES AT PARK PLACE

Hotel
$99–$219

Phone: (414)979-0250   **2**

Address: 10831 W Park Pl 53224 **Location:** US 41/45, exit 47B (Good Hope Rd), just e. **Facility:** Smoke free premises. 120 units, some efficiencies. 4 stories, interior corridors. **Terms:** cancellation fee imposed. **Amenities:** safes. **Pool(s):** heated indoor. **Activities:** whirlpool, exercise room. **Fee:** game room. **Guest Services:** valet and coin laundry, wireless Internet.

COUNTRY INN & SUITES BY CARLSON, MILWAUKEE AIRPORT

Hotel
$99–$140

Phone: (414)762-6018   **17**

Address: 6200 S 13th St 53221 **Location:** I-94, exit 319, just e on College Ave (CR ZZ). **Facility:** Smoke free premises. 81 units. 3 stories, interior corridors. **Terms:** 3 day cancellation notice-fee imposed. **Pool(s):** heated indoor. **Activities:** whirlpool, exercise room. **Fee:** game room. **Guest Services:** valet and coin laundry, wireless Internet. *(see ad p. 6)*

▼ See AAA listing above ▼

(See map and index starting on p. 530)

CROWNE PLAZA MILWAUKEE AIRPORT HOTEL   Phone: (414)764-5300

Hotel
$79-$149

Address: 6401 S 13th St 53221 **Location:** I-94, exit 319, just se on College Ave. **Facility:** Smoke free premises. 193 units. 5 stories, interior corridors. **Amenities:** high-speed Internet. **Pool(s):** heated indoor. **Activities:** whirlpool, exercise room. **Guest Services:** valet laundry, wireless Internet.

HAMPTON INN-MILWAUKEE AIRPORT   Phone: (414)762-4240 **18**

Hotel
$89-$149

Address: 1200 W College Ave 53221 **Location:** I-94, exit 319, just e on College Ave (CR ZZ). Located in a commercial area. **Facility:** Smoke free premises. 104 units. 3 stories, interior corridors. **Terms:** 1-7 night minimum stay, cancellation fee imposed. **Amenities:** video games (fee). **Pool(s):** heated indoor. **Activities:** whirlpool, exercise room. **Guest Services:** valet and coin laundry, area transportation-within 2 mi, wireless Internet. *(see ad below)*

AAA Benefit:
Members save up to 10% everyday!

FREE expanded continental breakfast and airport transportation

AAA.com/Travel or CAA.ca/Travel ...
Destination Information and Ideas.

(See map and index starting on p. 530)

HAMPTON INN-MILWAUKEE NW

Hotel
$99-$119

Address: 5601 N Lovers Lane Rd 53225 **Location:** US 45, exit 46 (Silver Spring Dr), just ne. Located in a commercial area. **Facility:** Smoke free premises. 107 units. 4 stories, interior corridors. **Terms:** 1-7 night minimum stay, cancellation fee imposed. **Amenities:** video games (fee), high-speed Internet. **Pool(s):** heated indoor. **Activities:** whirlpool, exercise room. **Guest Services:** valet laundry, wireless Internet.

Phone: (414)466-8881   ③

HILTON GARDEN INN MILWAUKEE AIRPORT

Hotel
$98-$170

Address: 5890 S Howell Ave 53207 **Location:** I-94, exit 318 (Airport), 1.1 mi e to Howell Ave (SR 38), then 0.5 mi s. **Facility:** Smoke free premises. 143 units. 3 stories, interior corridors. **Terms:** 1-7 night minimum stay, cancellation fee imposed. **Amenities:** high-speed Internet. **Pool(s):** heated indoor. **Activities:** whirlpool, outdoor patio, exercise room. **Guest Services:** valet and coin laundry, wireless Internet. *(see ad below)*

Phone: (414)481-8280   ⑯

FREE high-speed Internet and airport transportation

HILTON GARDEN INN MILWAUKEE PARK PLACE

Hotel
$79-$159

Address: 11600 W Park Pl 53224 **Location:** US 45, exit 47B (Good Hope Rd), just ne. Adjacent to a business park. **Facility:** Smoke free premises. 184 units. 3 stories, interior corridors. **Terms:** 1-7 night minimum stay, cancellation fee imposed. **Amenities:** high-speed Internet. **Pool(s):** heated indoor. **Activities:** sauna, whirlpool, sun deck, exercise room. **Guest Services:** valet and coin laundry, area transportation-within 5 mi, wireless Internet. **Free Special Amenities:** newspaper and high-speed Internet.

Phone: (414)359-9823   ①

▼ See AAA listing above ▼

(See map and index starting on p. 530)

HOLIDAY INN & SUITES MILWAUKEE AIRPORT

Hotel
$129-$179 4/1-10/1
$109-$149 10/2-4/30

Phone: (414)482-4444   **10**

Address: 545 W Layton Ave 53207 **Location:** I-94, exit 317, 1.3 mi e. Located in a commercial/residential area. **Facility:** Smoke free premises. 130 units, some efficiencies and kitchens. 3 stories, interior corridors. **Amenities:** high-speed Internet. **Pool(s):** heated indoor. **Activities:** whirlpool, exercise room. *Fee:* game room. **Guest Services:** valet and coin laundry, area transportation-within 2 mi, wireless Internet. *(see ad below)*

[SAVE] ✈ 🍴 ☕ CALL &M 🛁 BIZ ✗ 🎥 🖥 📷 💻
/SOME UNITS FEE 🐾

FREE high-speed Internet and airport transportation

▼ See AAA listing p. 563 ▼

▼ See AAA listing above ▼

(See map and index starting on p. 530)

HOLIDAY INN EXPRESS & SUITES MILWAUKEE AIRPORT

Hotel
$90-$139

Phone: (414)563-4000 **21**

Address: 1400 W Zellman Ct 53221 **Location:** I-94, exit 319, 0.4 mi e on College Ave (CR ZZ) to S 13th St, then just s. **Facility:** Smoke free premises. 115 units. 3 stories, interior corridors. **Pool(s):** heated indoor. **Activities:** whirlpool, waterslide, exercise room. **Guest Services:** valet and coin laundry, wireless Internet.

 / SOME UNITS

HYATT PLACE MILWAUKEE AIRPORT

Hotel
$99-$169

Phone: (414)744-3600 **15**

Address: 200 W Grange Ave 53207 **Location:** I-94, exit 318 (Airport), 1.1 mi e, just n on Howell Ave (SR 38), then just w. Located in a commercial area. **Facility:** Smoke free premises. 99 units. 4 stories, interior corridors. **Terms:** cancellation fee imposed. **Amenities:** video games (fee), high-speed Internet. **Pool(s):** heated indoor. **Activities:** exercise room. **Guest Services:** valet and coin laundry, wireless Internet. **Free Special Amenities:** continental breakfast and high-speed Internet.

HYATT
PLACE

AAA Benefit:
Ask for the AAA rate and save 10%.

HYATT PLACE MILWAUKEE-WEST

Hotel
$99-$169

Phone: (414)462-3500 **4**

Address: 11777 W Silver Spring Dr 53225 **Location:** US 45, exit 46 (Silver Spring Dr), just w. Located in a commercial area. **Facility:** Smoke free premises. 121 units. 4 stories, interior corridors. **Terms:** cancellation fee imposed. **Amenities:** video games (fee), high-speed Internet. **Pool(s):** heated indoor. **Activities:** exercise room. **Guest Services:** valet and coin laundry, wireless Internet. **Free Special Amenities:** continental breakfast and high-speed Internet.

HYATT
PLACE

AAA Benefit:
Ask for the AAA rate and save 10%.

(See map and index starting on p. 530)

THE IRON HORSE HOTEL

Phone: (414)374-4766 ❼

Boutique Hotel
$149-$329

Address: 500 W Florida St 53204 **Location:** Jct 6th St. **Facility:** In a renovated 100-year-old factory designed to reflect industrial Milwaukee, the hotel mixes the old and the new in common areas and oversize rooms. Smoke free premises. 100 units. 6 stories, interior corridors. **Parking:** valet only. **Terms:** cancellation fee imposed. **Amenities:** video games (fee), high-speed Internet, safes, honor bars. **Dining:** Smyth, see separate listing. **Activities:** exercise room. *Fee:* massage. **Guest Services:** valet laundry, wireless Internet. *(see ad p. 538)*

FREE newspaper and high-speed Internet

SLEEP INN & SUITES

Phone: (414)831-2000 ❾

Hotel
$80-$130

Address: 4600 S 6th St 53221 **Location:** I-94/US 41, exit 317 (Layton Ave), 1.5 mi e. **Facility:** Smoke free premises. 82 units. 3 stories, interior corridors. **Amenities:** high-speed Internet. **Pool(s):** heated indoor. **Activities:** whirlpool, exercise room. **Guest Services:** coin laundry, wireless Internet. **Free Special Amenities: expanded continental breakfast and high-speed Internet.**

SUPER 8-MILWAUKEE AIRPORT

Phone: (414)481-8488 ❶❸

Hotel
$58-$85

Address: 5253 S Howell Ave 53207 **Location:** I-94, exit 318 (Airport), 1.1 mi e, then just n on SR 38 (Howell Ave). **Facility:** Smoke free premises. 116 units. 3 stories, interior corridors. **Amenities:** safes (fee). **Activities:** whirlpool. **Guest Services:** valet and coin laundry, wireless Internet. **Free Special Amenities: expanded continental breakfast and high-speed Internet.**

WYNDHAM MILWAUKEE AIRPORT HOTEL & CONVENTION CENTER

Phone: (414)481-8000 ❶❶

Hotel
$84-$225

Address: 4747 S Howell Ave 53207 **Location:** I-94, exit 318 (Airport), 1.1 mi e to Howell Ave (SR 38), then 0.7 mi n. Located in a commercial area. **Facility:** Smoke free premises. 508 units. 2-6 stories, interior corridors. **Terms:** cancellation fee imposed. **Amenities:** video games (fee). *Some:* high-speed Internet. **Dining:** America's House of Steaks, see separate listing. **Pool(s):** heated outdoor, heated indoor. **Activities:** exercise room. **Guest Services:** valet and coin laundry, wireless Internet. *(see ad p. 553)*

FREE high-speed Internet and airport transportation

(See map and index starting on p. 530)

▼ See AAA listing p. 559 ▼

(See map and index starting on p. 530)

▼ See AAA listing p. 551 ▼

Are we meeting your travel needs?

If your visit to an establishment listed in a AAA TourBook or CampBook guide doesn't meet your expectations, tell us about it.

Complete an easy online form at **AAA.com/TourBookComments**.

If you're texting
or talking on the phone
while you drive,
who's focusing on driving?

Stay Focused
Keep your mind on the road.

(See map and index starting on p. 530)

———— **WHERE TO DINE** ————

AMERICA'S HOUSE OF STEAKS
Phone: 414/615-8094 ⑮

American
$10-$30

This dressed-up supper club specializes in high-quality aged steak that is hand cut on the premises, as well as New Zealand rack of lamb, duck and rotisserie chicken. **Bar:** full bar. **Hours:** 5 pm-10 pm. Closed: Sun. **Address:** 4747 S Howell Ave 53207 **Location:** I-94, exit 318 (Airport), 1.1 mi e to Howell Ave (SR 38), then 0.7 mi n; in Wyndham Milwaukee Airport Hotel & Convention Center. CALL ⟨⟩M

BARTOLOTTA'S LAKE PARK BISTRO
Phone: 414/962-6300 ④

French
$12-$49

A fabulous view of Lake Michigan grabs patrons as they dine at this elegant restaurant. A striking exterior and stylishly decorated interior each lend to the bistro feel. Menu offerings capture the essence of French cooking with wonderful herbs and sauces. Specialties include grilled Atlantic salmon and filet medallions au poivre. The praline parfait reflects with a creative presentation and scrumptious flavor. **Bar:** full bar. **Reservations:** suggested. **Hours:** 11:30 am-2 & 5:30-9 pm, Fri-10 pm, Sat 5 pm-10 pm, Sun 10 am-2 & 5:30-8:30 pm; Sunday brunch. Closed major holidays. **Address:** 3133 E Newberry Blvd 53211 **Location:** I-43, exit 74 (Locust St), 2 mi e to Lake Dr, then just s; in Lake Park. CALL ⟨⟩M

BOTANAS MEXICAN CUISINE
Phone: 414/672-3755 ⑪

Mexican
$6-$20

This large, bustling and popular restaurant presents an extensive menu of traditional Mexican items from carne asada, burritos and quesadillas to enchiladas, tacos and ceviche. Also available are several fine seafood choices, including tilapia, red snapper and shrimp. Shortly after arriving to the table, guests are served freshly prepared chips and salsa. The wait staff is efficient. **Bar:** full bar. **Hours:** 11 am-10 pm. Closed major holidays. **Address:** 816 S 5th St 53204 **Location:** Between W National Ave and W Walker St. **Parking:** street only.

BRANDED STEER
Phone: 414/359-1349 ②

Steak
$5-$24

Western style punctuates the meal, atmosphere and decor at this place. Lasso steaks, pork or chicken from the wood-grill rotisserie share menu space with soups, sandwiches, salads and Black Angus beef burgers. **Bar:** full bar. **Hours:** 10:30 am-midnight, Sat & Sun from 8 am. **Address:** 10950 W Good Hope Rd 53224 **Location:** US 41/45, exit 47B (Good Hope Rd), then right. CALL ⟨⟩M

DREAM DANCE STEAK *Menu on AAA.com*
Phone: 414/847-7883 ⑧

Regional
American
$24-$46

This refined oasis inside the Potawatomi Bingo Casino has a seasonally changing menu that leans toward steak, but it's not the typical, clubby steakhouse. Offerings may include venison, kangaroo, Kobe beef, Walleye pike and shrimp. The Wisconsin influence can be seen in such items as a veal chop schnitzel, cheese curd fritters and local artisanal cheeses. The chef may cure game with root beer or create "Lobsterwurst." The wine list is tantalizing for its variety and reasonable prices. **Bar:** full bar. **Reservations:** suggested. **Hours:** 5 pm-9 pm, Fri & Sat-10 pm. Closed major holidays; also Sun & Mon. **Address:** 1721 W Canal St 53233 **Location:** In Potawatomi Bingo Casino. **Parking:** on-site and valet. CALL ⟨⟩M

ENVOY
Phone: 414/345-5015 ⑦

American
$8-$25

The small, yet elegant, art deco dining room boasts an intimate bistro appeal while offering a cosmopolitan experience. Seasonally changing preparations of multi-ethnic, nouveau American cuisine emphasize fresh regional ingredients, and diners are sure to delight in the imaginative offerings. Live jazz is played in the lounge on weekends. **Bar:** full bar. **Hours:** 6:30 am-10 pm. **Address:** 2308 W Wisconsin Ave 53233 **Location:** I-94, exit 308 (US 41), just n to Wisconsin Ave (US 18) exit, then 1.5 mi e; jct N 24th St; in Ambassador Hotel.

FINAL APPROACH
Phone: 414/744-7060 ⑯

American
$5-$15

Across Howell Avenue from General Mitchell International Airport, the small restaurant serves burgers and sandwiches in a homey atmosphere. **Bar:** full bar. **Hours:** 11 am-10 pm, Fri & Sat-11 pm. Closed major holidays. **Address:** 4959 S Howell Ave 53207 **Location:** I-94, exit 318 (Airport), 1.1 mi e to Howell Ave (SR 38), then 0.4 mi n.

HOULIHAN'S
Phone: 414/570-3003 ⑲

American
$9-$22

This busy eatery provides a comfortable atmosphere for gathering with friends or family. Menu favorites include the goat cheese bruschetta, stuffed chicken and the triple berry cobbler. **Bar:** full bar. **Hours:** 6 am-10 pm. **Address:** 6331 S 13th St 53221 **Location:** I-94, exit 319, just e on College Ave (CR ZZ); in Ramada Plaza Milwaukee Airport.

JALAPENO LOCO
Phone: 414/483-8300 ⑰

Mexican
$6-$19

There's no need to fly south, as a taste of Mexico is available right here. Chimichangas, burritos, fajitas, quesadillas, flautas and more are served in a warm and friendly atmosphere. **Bar:** full bar. **Hours:** 11 am-10 pm, Fri & Sat-11 pm. Closed major holidays. **Address:** 5067 S Howell Ave 53207 **Location:** Jct Layton Ave, 0.5 mi s.

LAKE CITY RESTAURANT & LOUNGE *Menu on AAA.com*
Phone: 414/831-3659 ⑱

Steak
$8-$26

The casual restaurant offers its signature home-smoked ribs and specialty cut steaks, in addition to pasta, sandwiches, salads and fish. **Bar:** full bar. **Hours:** 11 am-10 pm, Fri & Sat-11 pm. Closed major holidays. **Address:** 5105 S Howell Ave 53207 **Location:** I-94, exit 318 (Airport), 1.1 mi e, then just n on Howell Ave (SR 38); in Best Western Plus Milwaukee Airport Hotel & Conference Center. CALL ⟨⟩M

(See map and index starting on p. 530)

OLD TOWN SERBIAN GOURMET RESTAURANT
Phone: 414/672-0206

Eastern European
$6-$19

Flavorful foods and unusual recipes are the draw at the family-operated restaurant, a local fixture for more than 30 years. Old World decor and ethnic background music set the mood. Among selections of Serbian/European cuisine are preparations of chicken, beef, lamb, fish and veal. Locals favor such hearty, made-from-scratch entrees as moussaka, goulash and Burak beef. **Bar:** full bar. **Reservations:** suggested. **Hours:** 11:30 am-2:30 & 5-10 pm, Sat & Sun from 5 pm. Closed: Mon. **Address:** 522 W Lincoln Ave 53207 **Location:** I-94, exit 312B (W Lincoln Ave), just w. CALL 🅖🅜

OMEGA FAMILY RESTAURANT
Phone: 414/645-6595 ⑬

Greek
$6-$23

The lengthy menu dabbles in many varieties of food, ranging from barbecue and seafood dishes to traditional Italian and Greek cuisine. Breakfast items are served all day. Plates are piled high with tasty offerings. Baked goods are homemade. **Bar:** beer & wine. **Hours:** 24 hours. **Address:** 3473 S 27th St 53215 **Location:** I-894, exit 9 (SR 241), 0.9 mi n. CALL 🅖🅜

THE PACKING HOUSE
Phone: 414/483-5054 ⑭

Steak
$6-$37

Diners can choose from a variety of cuts and preparations, including garlic-stuffed filet, beef Wellington and filet Oscar. Seafood—such as Canadian walleye and king crab legs—also is offered. Rounding out the menu are a few vegetarian dishes, prime rib, chops, ribs and poultry. **Bar:** full bar. **Reservations:** suggested. **Hours:** 11 am-2 & 4-10 pm, Sat from 4 pm, Sun 10 am-1:30 & 4-9 pm. Closed: for dinner 12/24. **Address:** 900 E Layton Ave 53207 **Location:** 0.5 mi e of Howell Ave (SR 38). CALL 🅖🅜

RIP TIDE SEAFOOD BAR & GRILL   *Menu on AAA.com*
Phone: 414-271-8433 ⑨

Seafood
$9-$38

Patrons watch the boats come and go in the harbor from the relaxed dining room or inviting summer patio downtown. Among menu delights are a must—crab cakes—as well as scallops and Atlantic salmon. **Bar:** full bar. **Hours:** 11 am-10 pm, Fri & Sat-11 pm, Sun 10 am-9 pm; call ahead for hours in winter. Closed: 11/24, 12/25. **Address:** 649 E Erie St 53202 **Location:** Jct Milwaukee St, 0.5 mi se along the lake. **Parking:** street only. CALL 🅖🅜

ROOTS RESTAURANT & CELLAR
Phone: 414/374-8480 ⑤

Regional American
$18-$36

Perched on a bluff overlooking Commerce Street, this contemporary American restaurant highlights the finest in both Wisconsin and organic ingredients. One of the leading members of the farmer-chef owned restaurant movement, the chef owns a greenhouse and 9 acres of organic farmyard and produces many of his own ingredients. **Bar:** full bar. **Reservations:** suggested. **Hours:** 5 pm-9 pm, Fri-10 pm, Sun 10 am-2 & 5-9 pm. Closed major holidays. **Address:** 1818 N Hubbard St 53212 **Location:** I-43, exit North Ave, just e to Martin Luther King Dr, 0.5 mi s to W Vine St, then 0.4 mi e. **Parking:** street only. CALL 🅖🅜

SAZ'S STATE HOUSE
Phone: 414/453-2410 ⑥

American
$7-$27

The popular, bustling restaurant has been serving tasty food since 1976. Fall-off-the-bone pork and beef barbecue with Saz's own award-winning sauces is the big draw. The recipe for delicious cottage fries has been perfected over many years. **Reservations:** suggested. **Hours:** 11 am-9:30 pm, Fri & Sat-11 pm, Sun 10:30 am-9 pm. Closed: 1/1, 11/24, 12/24, 12/25. **Address:** 5539 W State St 53208 **Location:** Jct Hawley Rd overpass.

SMYTH
Phone: 414/831-4615 ⑩

Regional American
$8-$44

The restaurant's rustic dining room has 300-year-old pine columns, wood floors, light-colored brick walls and a Route 66 theme in the artwork. Midwestern cuisine emphasizes foods common in Wisconsin, including veal chops, prime steaks, venison, chicken, pork loin, Great Lakes bluegill fillets and Wisconsin cured meats and cheeses. The wait staff is polished and enthusiastic. **Bar:** full bar. **Reservations:** suggested. **Hours:** 11 am-10 pm, Sun 7 am-3 pm. **Address:** 500 W Florida 53204 **Location:** Jct 6th St; in The Iron Horse Hotel. **Parking:** valet only.

WEST BANK CAFE
Phone: 414/562-5555 ③

Vietnamese
$5-$17

In a residential neighborhood, the restaurant is simple and unpretentious. The menu is anything but ordinary, with thick curries that are slightly sweet and catfish cooked in a Vietnamese clay pot. Vegetarian and European entrees also are offered. **Bar:** full bar. **Hours:** 5:30 pm-9:30 pm. Closed major holidays. **Address:** 732 E Burleigh St 53212 **Location:** Jct N Fratney St.

YEN CHING RESTAURANT
Phone: 414/353-6677 ①

Chinese
$5-$13

Sweet and sour pork and almond chicken are among examples of Mandarin cuisine on the restaurant's extensive menu. The decor is Oriental, with carved, red-stained wood throughout. Servers exhibit strong knowledge of the menu and preparation style. **Bar:** full bar. **Hours:** 11:30 am-2 & 4:30-9:30 pm, Fri & Sat 4:30 pm-10 pm. Closed: 7/4, 11/24; also Sun. **Address:** 7630 W Good Hope Rd 53223 **Location:** Just w of SR 181 (76th St).

The Milwaukee Vicinity

BROOKFIELD pop. 38,649   (See map and index starting on p. 530)

BEST WESTERN PLUS MIDWAY HOTEL & SUITES-BROOKFIELD

Hotel
$99-$159

Phone: (262)786-9540   **48**

Address: 1005 S Moorland Rd 53005 **Location:** I-94, exit 301A (Moorland Rd), just s. Located in a commercial area. **Facility:** Smoke free premises. 124 units. 6 stories, interior corridors. **Parking:** winter plug-ins. **Amenities:** *Some:* high-speed Internet, honor bars. **Pool(s):** heated indoor. **Activities:** sauna, whirlpool, domed recreation area, exercise room. *Fee:* game room. **Guest Services:** valet and coin laundry, area transportation (fee)-within 10 mi, wireless Internet. **Free Special Amenities:** expanded continental breakfast and high-speed Internet.

BROOKFIELD SUITES HOTEL & CONVENTION CENTER

Hotel
$99-$395

Phone: (262)782-2900   **49**

Address: 1200 S Moorland Rd 53005 **Location:** I-94, exit 301A (Moorland Rd), just s. **Facility:** Smoke free premises. 203 units, some two bedrooms. 5 stories, interior corridors. **Terms:** check-in 4 pm. **Pool(s):** heated indoor. **Activities:** sauna, whirlpool, steamroom, exercise room. **Guest Services:** valet and coin laundry, wireless Internet. **Free Special Amenities:** full breakfast and high-speed Internet.

COUNTRY INN & SUITES BY CARLSON, MILWAUKEE-WEST

Hotel
$99-$269

Phone: (262)782-1400   **50**

Address: 1250 S Moorland Rd 53005 **Location:** I-94, exit 301A (Moorland Rd), just se. Located in a commercial area. **Facility:** Smoke free premises. 149 units. 3 stories, interior corridors. **Amenities:** video games (fee), high-speed Internet. **Dining:** 2 restaurants. **Pool(s):** heated indoor. **Activities:** whirlpool, exercise room. *Fee:* game room. **Guest Services:** valet and coin laundry, area transportation-local business park, wireless Internet. *(see ad below & p. 6)*

FREE early check-in/late check-out and room upgrade (subject to availability with advance reservations)

▼ *See AAA listing above* ▼

(See map and index starting on p. 530)

COURTYARD BY MARRIOTT/BROOKFIELD

Hotel
$149-$169

Address: 16865 W Bluemound Rd 53005 **Location:** I-94, exit 297 eastbound, 2.2 mi e on US 18; exit 301B westbound, 1.5 mi n on Moorland Rd, then 0.3 mi w on US 18. **Facility:** Smoke free premises. 148 units. 3 stories, interior corridors. **Terms:** cancellation fee imposed. **Amenities:** high-speed Internet. **Pool(s):** heated indoor. **Activities:** whirlpool, sun deck, exercise room. **Guest Services:** valet and coin laundry, wireless Internet.

Phone: (262)821-1800 **43**

DOUBLETREE HOTEL MILWAUKEE/BROOKFIELD

Hotel
$80-$199

Address: 18155 W Bluemound Rd 53045 **Location:** I-94, exit 297, 1.5 mi e on US 18. Located in a business park. **Facility:** Smoke free premises. 177 units. 3 stories, interior corridors. **Terms:** 1-7 night minimum stay, cancellation fee imposed. **Amenities:** high-speed Internet (fee). **Pool(s):** heated indoor. **Activities:** whirlpool, complete locker room facilities, exercise room. **Guest Services:** valet laundry, wireless Internet. *(see ad below)*

Phone: (262)792-1212 **44**

FREE newspaper and preferred room (subject to availability with advance reservations)

HAMPTON INN MILWAUKEE/BROOKFIELD

Hotel
$89-$189

Address: 575 N Barker Rd 53045 **Location:** I-94, exit 297, just e on US 18. Located in a commercial area. **Facility:** Smoke free premises. 119 units. 4 stories, interior corridors. **Terms:** 1-7 night minimum stay, cancellation fee imposed. **Amenities:** video games (fee). **Pool(s):** heated indoor. **Activities:** whirlpool, exercise room. **Guest Services:** valet laundry, wireless Internet.

Phone: (262)796-1500

HOMESTEAD STUDIO SUITES HOTEL-MILWAUKEE/BROOKFIELD

Extended Stay Hotel
$51-$85

Address: 325 N Brookfield Rd 53045 **Location:** I-94, exit 297, 1.1 mi e on US 18, then just e. Located in a quiet area. **Facility:** Smoke free premises. 137 efficiencies. 3 stories, interior corridors. **Terms:** office hours 6 am-10 pm, cancellation fee imposed. **Guest Services:** coin laundry, wireless Internet.

Phone: (262)782-9300 **45**

▼ See AAA listing above ▼

(See map and index starting on p. 530)

LA QUINTA INN MILWAUKEE WEST BROOKFIELD

Hotel
$59-$115

Phone: (262)782-9100

Address: 20391 W Bluemound Rd 53045 **Location:** I-94, exit 297, just e on US 18. **Facility:** Smoke free premises. 96 units. 3 stories, interior corridors. **Parking:** winter plug-ins. **Amenities:** video games (fee). **Activities:** exercise room. **Guest Services:** valet and coin laundry, wireless Internet.

QUALITY INN-MILWAUKEE/BROOKFIELD

Hotel
$69-$149

Phone: (262)785-0500

Address: 20150 W Bluemound Rd 53045 **Location:** I-94, exit 297, just e on US 18. **Facility:** Smoke free premises. 129 units. 3 stories, interior/exterior corridors. **Parking:** winter plug-ins. **Amenities:** safes (fee). **Pool(s):** heated outdoor. **Activities:** exercise room. **Guest Services:** valet and coin laundry, wireless Internet. **Free Special Amenities:** full breakfast and high-speed Internet.

RESIDENCE INN BY MARRIOTT MILWAUKEE-BROOKFIELD

Extended Stay Hotel
$139-$209

Phone: (262)782-5990   **47**

Address: 950 S Pinehurst Ct 53005 **Location:** I-94, exit 301A, just s. **Facility:** Smoke free premises. 104 units, some two bedrooms, efficiencies and kitchens. 2 stories (no elevator), exterior corridors. **Terms:** check-in 4 pm, cancellation fee imposed. **Amenities:** high-speed Internet. **Pool(s):** heated outdoor. **Activities:** whirlpool, exercise room, sports court. **Guest Services:** valet and coin laundry, area transportation-within 5 mi, wireless Internet. **Free Special Amenities:** full breakfast and manager's reception.

AAA Benefit:
Members save a minimum 5% off the best available rate.

SHERATON MILWAUKEE BROOKFIELD

Hotel
$109-$289

Phone: (262)786-1100   **46**

Address: 375 S Moorland Rd 53005 **Location:** I-94, exit 301B (Moorland Rd), just n. Located in a commercial area. **Facility:** Smoke free premises. 389 units. 6 stories, interior corridors. **Terms:** cancellation fee imposed. **Amenities:** high-speed Internet (fee). **Pool(s):** heated outdoor, heated indoor. **Activities:** whirlpool, exercise room. **Guest Services:** valet and coin laundry, wireless Internet. *(see ad p. 552)*

AAA Benefit:
Members get up to 15% off, plus Starwood Preferred Guest® bonuses.

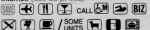

FREE full breakfast and newspaper

TOWNEPLACE SUITES BY MARRIOTT

Extended Stay Hotel
$149-$159

Phone: (262)784-8450   **42**

Address: 600 N Calhoun Rd 53005 **Location:** I-94, exit 297 eastbound, 2.1 mi e on US 18; exit 301B (Moorland Rd) westbound, 1.5 mi n, then 0.4 mi w on US 18. Located in a commercial area. **Facility:** Smoke free premises. 112 kitchen units, some two bedrooms. 2-3 stories, interior corridors. **Terms:** cancellation fee imposed. **Amenities:** high-speed Internet. **Pool(s):** heated outdoor. **Activities:** gas grill, exercise room. **Guest Services:** valet and coin laundry.

AAA Benefit:
Members save a minimum 5% off the best available rate.

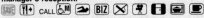

——— WHERE TO DINE ———

JAKE'S RESTAURANT

American
$19-$37

Phone: 262/781-7995

On a small hilltop in a rural area, the restaurant has been a local favorite since the 1970s. Although the exterior and interior design is rustic in appearance, tables are set in an intimate style and a large fireplace central to the dining room offers romantic charm. The menu is varied with poultry, steak, pork chops, prime rib and seafood choices, as well as a few seasonal selections. **Bar:** full bar. **Hours:** 5 pm-9 pm, Fri & Sat-9:30 pm; hours may vary. Closed: major holidays, 12/24; also Sun. **Address:** 21445 W Gumina Rd 53072 **Location:** Just n off SR 190, 1.7 mi e of jct SR 164.

KOPP'S FROZEN CUSTARD

American
$5-$10

Phone: 262/789-9490   **31**

Street sign postings tempt dessert lovers with the daily flavors complementing the standard chocolate and vanilla. Milwaukee draws raves for its frozen custard, and Kopp's is among the many outlets that offer this dairy treat. **Hours:** 10:30 am-10 pm, Fri & Sat-11 pm. Closed: 12/25. **Address:** 18880 W Bluemound Rd 53045 **Location:** I-94, exit 297, 1.1 mi e on US 18.

(See map and index starting on p. 530)

LOUISE'S

Phone: 262/784-4275　**32**

Italian
$9-$23

Easily recognizable by its gray exterior and set back from the main road, the contemporary dining room serves a mix of traditional Italian favorites prepared with subtle Californian influences. The open kitchen features a wood-burning oven that produces a wide range of hand-made pizzas. **Bar:** full bar. **Hours:** 11 am-11 pm, Fri & Sat-midnight. Closed major holidays. **Address:** 275 Regency Ct 53045 **Location:** I-94, exit 297, 0.5 mi e on US 18, at jct 190th St and Bluemound Rd. CALL 🛆M

PANO'S BAR & GRILL

Phone: 262/782-8670

American
$7-$21

The steakhouse and sports bar offers something for everyone, including chicken, pork chops, salad, shrimp, beef and kebabs. Enjoy the casual, relaxed atmosphere of the dining room or the more exciting vibe in the sports pub. **Bar:** full bar. **Hours:** 11 am-11 pm, Sun from 9 am. Closed: 1/1, 12/25. **Address:** 20290 W Bluemound Rd 53045 **Location:** I-94, exit 297, just e on US 18.

TASTE OF INDIA

Phone: 262/796-8200　**30**

Indian
$7-$17

This restaurant is located at the back of a small strip mall near the Wyndham Garden Hotel-Brookfield. It features a small buffet lunch and an expanded à la carte menu at dinner with a sampling of vegetarian, meat and seafood dishes. There is an excellent selection of Indian breads available as well. **Bar:** beer & wine. **Hours:** 11:30 am-3 & 5-10 pm, Fri & Sat-10:30 pm. **Address:** 17800 Bluemound Rd, Suite 7 53045 **Location:** I-94, exit 297, 1.6 mi e on US 18; in Brookmound Plaza.

YOKOSO JAPANESE RESTAURANT

Phone: 262/782-8880

Japanese
$8-$29

Patrons of the casual eatery can sample hirame ponzu, seaweed salad, happy avocado, gyoza, sashimi platter, king crab California roll, spider maki and more. **Hours:** 11 am-2 & 4:30-10 pm, Fri & Sat 4:30 pm-11 pm, Sun 4:30 pm-9 pm. Closed major holidays. **Address:** 20101 W Bluemound Rd 53045 **Location:** I-94, exit 297, just e on US 18; in Westown Shopping Center.

BROWN DEER pop. 12,170　(See map and index starting on p. 530)

CANDLEWOOD SUITES

Phone: (414)355-3939　**29**

Extended Stay
Hotel
$95-$144

Address: 4483 W Schroeder Dr 53223 **Location:** Just nw of SR 100 and 57. **Facility:** Smoke free premises. 75 efficiencies. 3 stories, interior corridors. **Terms:** cancellation fee imposed. **Amenities:** high-speed Internet. **Activities:** exercise room. **Guest Services:** complimentary and valet laundry, wireless Internet. CALL 🛆M 🗙 📷 🔲 🖼 💻 / SOME UNITS FEE 🐕

COURTYARD BY MARRIOTT MILWAUKEE NORTH BROWN DEER

Phone: (414)355-7500　**31**

Hotel
$139-$149

Address: 5200 W Brown Deer Rd 53223 **Location:** On SR 100, 0.7 mi w of jct SR 57. **Facility:** Smoke free premises. 122 units. 4 stories, interior corridors. **Terms:** cancellation fee imposed. **Amenities:** high-speed Internet. **Pool(s):** heated indoor. **Activities:** whirlpool, gazebo, exercise room. **Guest Services:** valet and coin laundry, wireless Internet.

AAA Benefit:
Members save a minimum 5% off the best available rate.

🍴 CALL 🛆M 🏊 🗙 📷 💻 / SOME UNITS 🔲 🖼

FOUR POINTS BY SHERATON MILWAUKEE NORTH

Phone: (414)355-8585　**30**

Hotel
$79-$259

Address: 8900 N Kildeer Ct 53209 **Location:** On SR 100, just e of jct SR 57. Located in a quiet area. **Facility:** Smoke free premises. 149 units. 6 stories, interior corridors. **Terms:** cancellation fee imposed. **Amenities:** high-speed Internet. **Pool(s):** heated outdoor, heated indoor. **Activities:** sauna, whirlpool, exercise room. **Guest Services:** valet laundry, area transportation-within 5 mi, wireless Internet.

FOUR POINTS
BY SHERATON
AAA Benefit:
Members get up to 15% off, plus Starwood Preferred Guest® bonuses.

SAVE ✈ 🍴 🍸 CALL 🛆M 🏊 BIZ 🗙 📷 💻 / SOME UNITS 🔲 🖼

HOLIDAY INN EXPRESS

Phone: (414)355-1300　**28**

Hotel
$104-$144

Address: 4443 W Schroeder Dr 53223 **Location:** Just nw of jct SR 100 and 57. **Facility:** Smoke free premises. 78 units. 3 stories, interior corridors. **Terms:** cancellation fee imposed. **Pool(s):** heated indoor. **Activities:** exercise room. **Guest Services:** valet laundry, wireless Internet. CALL 🛆M 🏊 BIZ 🗙 📷 💻 / SOME UNITS 🔲 🖼

CEDARBURG pop. 10,908

WASHINGTON HOUSE INN

Phone: (262)375-3550

Historic Bed
& Breakfast
$125-$315

Address: W62 N573 Washington Ave 53012 **Location:** Jct Colombia Rd; downtown. Located in a boutique shopping area. **Facility:** Furnished with period antiques, collectibles and reproductions, this inn offers some fireplace rooms and all with high-end beds. Smoke free premises. 34 units. 3 stories, interior corridors. **Activities:** sauna. *Fee:* massage. **Guest Services:** valet laundry, wireless Internet. CALL 🛆M FEE 🧖 🗙 📷 / SOME UNITS 🔲 💻

—— **WHERE TO DINE** ——

CREAM & CREPE CAFE

Phone: 262/377-0900

American
$5-$10

Soups, sandwiches, entrees and dessert crepes are served in a rustic old mill. **Hours:** 10 am-8 pm, Sun 11 am-5 pm, Mon 10 am-5 pm. Closed major holidays. **Address:** N70 W6340 Bridge Rd 53012 **Location:** Downtown; at Cedar Creek Settlement. **Parking:** on-site and street. **Historic**

DELAFIELD pop. 6,472

THE DELAFIELD HOTEL

Phone: (262)646-1600

Boutique
Hotel
$159-$498

Address: 415 Genesee St 53018 **Location:** I-94, exit 285, 0.4 mi n on CR C (Genesee St). **Facility:** The luxurious hotel occupies a quiet setting on the edge of town and features large guest rooms with elegant bedding, plush seating and lush baths. Smoke free premises. 38 units. 3 stories, interior corridors. **Parking:** on-site and valet. **Amenities:** high-speed Internet, safes, honor bars. **Guest Services:** valet laundry, wireless Internet. **Fee:** area transportation-within 10 mi. **Free Special Amenities: newspaper and high-speed Internet.**

HOLIDAY INN EXPRESS

Phone: (262)646-7077

Hotel
$109-$159 4/1-9/30
$99-$130 10/1-4/30

Address: 3030 Golf Rd 53018 **Location:** I-94, exit 287, just n, then just e. **Facility:** Smoke free premises. 84 units. 3 stories, interior corridors. **Parking:** winter plug-ins. **Pool(s):** heated indoor. **Activities:** whirlpool, exercise room. **Guest Services:** valet laundry, wireless Internet. **Free Special Amenities: full breakfast and high-speed Internet.**

LA QUINTA INN & SUITES MILWAUKEE DELAFIELD

Phone: (262)395-1162

Hotel
$59-$139

Address: 2801 Hillside Dr 53018 **Location:** I-94, exit 287, just s on SR 83, then just e. **Facility:** Smoke free premises. 96 units. 3 stories, interior corridors. **Parking:** winter plug-ins. **Amenities:** video games (fee). **Pool(s):** heated indoor. **Activities:** whirlpool, exercise room. **Guest Services:** valet and coin laundry, wireless Internet.

—— **WHERE TO DINE** ——

FISHBONE'S

Phone: 262/646-4696

Cajun
$13-$29

This is the place to be for ragin' Cajun in a great atmosphere of upbeat, bright colors and artwork. Menu options include tempting jambalaya, Cajun pasta dishes and desserts such as bourbon pecan pie. Diners may have to remind themselves they're along the banks of Lake Nagawicka in Wisconsin and not on Bourbon Street in Louisiana. **Bar:** full bar. **Reservations:** suggested, Fri & Sat. **Hours:** Open 4/1-9/30 & 2/2-4/30; 4 pm-11 pm, Fri & Sat-midnight, Sun-9 pm. Closed major holidays; also Mon. **Address:** 1704 Milwaukee St 53018 **Location:** I-94, exit 287, just n, then just w.

SAXE'S CASUAL FINE DINING

Phone: 262/968-4600

American
$7-$30

Baked ribs coated in barbecue sauce as well as fresh fish specials are among traditional American menu selections. Art deco lighting and attractive art decorate the Southwestern dining room. The menu of tempting desserts changes frequently. **Bar:** full bar. **Hours:** 11:30 am-10 pm, Sun 8 am-9 pm, Tues & Wed 3:30 pm-10 pm. Closed: 11/24, 12/25; also Mon. **Address:** W 325 S 1767 Mickle Rd 53018 **Location:** I-94, exit 287, 2.7 mi s on SR 83, then 0.4 mi w on US 18.

SEVEN SEAS ON NAGAWICKA LAKE

Phone: 262/367-3903

International
$21-$48

An extensive wine list complements creative preparations of seafood, beef and poultry, including choices such as roast goose with cherry compote or broiled Atlantic salmon with dill-hollandaise sauce. The lovely lakefront setting makes it easy to unwind. **Bar:** full bar. **Hours:** 4 pm-9 pm, Fri & Sat-10 pm, Sun 10:30 am-2 & 4-9 pm; Sunday brunch. Closed: 5/30, 9/5, 12/25; also Tues. **Address:** 1807 Nagawicka Rd 53029 **Location:** I-94, exit 287, 1.2 mi n on SR 83, then 0.7 mi w.

WATER STREET BREWERY LAKE COUNTRY

Phone: 262/646-7878

American
$8-$26

Served here are a variety of salads, sandwiches, pasta and some seafood and steak preparations, in addition to homemade pot pie and daily soup specials. Several beers, including seasonal specialties, are brewed on the premises. The dining room reflects a Western flair. **Bar:** full bar. **Hours:** 11 am-11 pm, Fri & Sat-midnight. Closed: 11/24, 12/25. **Address:** 3191 Golf Rd 53018 **Location:** I-94, exit 287, just nw.

FOX POINT pop. 7,012 (See map and index starting on p. 530)

—— **WHERE TO DINE** ——

NORTH SHORE BISTRO

Phone: 414/351-6100 ⑸

American
$11-$20

The new bistro offers diners a casual and airy setting as a backdrop for some innovative dishes. A great example is the shrimp and corn tamale crafted by chef Michael Wolf. Lined with warm wood and decorated with a changing collection of lively artwork, the bistro has become a reliable spot for fine casual dining on the North Shore. **Bar:** full bar. **Hours:** 11 am-10 pm, Fri & Sat-11 pm, Sun 4 pm-9 pm. Closed: 11/24, 12/25. **Address:** 8649 N Port Washington Rd 53217 **Location:** Jct I-43 and Brown Deer Rd; in River Point Village.

FRANKLIN pop. 29,494

STAYBRIDGE SUITES MILWAUKEE AIRPORT SOUTH   Phone: (414)761-3800

Extended Stay Hotel
$99-$159

Address: 9575 S 27th St 53132 **Location:** I-94, exit 322 (Ryan Rd), 0.6 mi w at jct 27th St. **Facility:** Smoke free premises. 118 efficiencies, some two bedrooms. 5 stories, interior corridors. **Terms:** cancellation fee imposed. **Amenities:** high-speed Internet. **Pool(s):** heated indoor. **Activities:** whirlpool, small movie theater, gazebo area with grills, exercise room. **Guest Services:** complimentary and valet laundry, wireless Internet.

GENESEE DEPOT

——— WHERE TO DINE ———

THE UNION HOUSE   Phone: 262/968-4281

American
$18-$37

In a quaint, historic inn, the restaurant presents a menu of fresh fish, poultry and creative preparations of wild game. Tempting desserts are prepared in house. The highly developed wine list is well rounded, and a large selection of single-malt scotches also is available. Service is friendly, professional and knowledgeable. **Bar:** full bar. **Reservations:** suggested. **Hours:** 4:30 pm-9 pm, Fri & Sat-10 pm. Closed major holidays; also Sun & Mon. **Address:** S42 W31320 Hwy 83 53127 **Location:** Downtown. **Historic**

GERMANTOWN pop. 13,700 (See map and index starting on p. 530)

AMERICINN LODGE & SUITES OF GERMANTOWN   Phone: (262)502-9750   [74]

Hotel
$80-$100

Address: W190 N10862 Commerce Cir 53022 **Location:** US 41 and 45, exit Lannon/Mequon rds, just e on SR 167 to Maple Rd. Located in a quiet area. **Facility:** Smoke free premises. 47 units. 2 stories, interior corridors. **Parking:** winter plug-ins. **Terms:** cancellation fee imposed. **Pool(s):** heated indoor. **Activities:** whirlpool. **Guest Services:** coin laundry, wireless Internet.

COUNTRY INN & SUITES BY CARLSON   Phone: (262)251-7700   [73]

Hotel
$94-$129

Address: W188 N11020 Maple Rd 53022 **Location:** US 41 and 45, exit Lannon/Mequon rds, just e on SR 167. Located in a commercial area. **Facility:** Smoke free premises. 62 units. 2 stories, interior corridors. **Parking:** winter plug-ins. **Amenities:** high-speed Internet. **Pool(s):** heated indoor. **Activities:** whirlpool, exercise room. **Guest Services:** valet and coin laundry, wireless Internet. *(see ad p. 6)*

HOLIDAY INN EXPRESS MILWAUKEE NW-GERMANTOWN   Phone: (262)255-1100   [75]

Hotel
$99-$149

Address: W177 N9675 Riversbend Ln 53022 **Location:** US 41 and 45, exit CR Q (County Line Rd), just w. Located in a commercial area. **Facility:** Smoke free premises. 74 units. 2 stories, interior corridors. **Amenities:** video games (fee). **Pool(s):** heated indoor. **Activities:** whirlpool, sun deck, limited exercise equipment. **Guest Services:** valet and coin laundry, wireless Internet.

SUPER 8-GERMANTOWN/MILWAUKEE   Phone: (262)255-0880   [76]

Hotel
$61-$70

Address: N96 W17490 County Line Rd 53022 **Location:** US 41 and 45, exit CR Q (County Line Rd), just w. Located in a commercial area. **Facility:** Smoke free premises. 98 units. 2 stories (no elevator), interior corridors. **Parking:** winter plug-ins. **Terms:** 2 night minimum stay - seasonal and/or weekends, cancellation fee imposed. **Pool(s):** heated indoor. **Activities:** whirlpool, sun deck. **Guest Services:** coin laundry, wireless Internet. **Free Special Amenities:** expanded continental breakfast and high-speed Internet.

——— WHERE TO DINE ———

JERRY'S OLD TOWN   Phone: 262/251-4455   [48]

Barbecue
$18-$43

Patrons go hog wild over the delicious homemade food and eclectic swine decor of the laid-back restaurant, which was founded in 1878. Servings of dishes such as tender barbecue ribs, corn-fed steer steak, blackened seafood and Cajun chicken satisfy all appetites. The huge "pig slop" ice cream dessert is worth a squeal of delight. **Bar:** full bar. **Reservations:** suggested. **Hours:** 4 pm-10 pm, Fri & Sat-10:30 pm, Sun-9 pm. Closed major holidays. **Address:** N 116 W 15841 Main St 53022 **Location:** 0.4 mi n on SR 145 from jct SR 167, just nw on Fond Du Lac Ave, then just w.

GLENDALE pop. 13,367   (See map and index starting on p. 530)

BAYMONT INN & SUITES GLENDALE/MILWAUKEE NORTHEAST   **Phone:** (414)961-7272

Hotel
$49-$73

Address: 5485 N Port Washington Rd 53217 **Location:** I-43, exit 78A (Silver Spring Dr), just se. Located in a commercial area. **Facility:** Smoke free premises. 122 units. 3 stories, interior corridors. **Parking:** winter plug-ins. **Activities:** exercise room. **Guest Services:** coin laundry, wireless Internet.

HILTON MILWAUKEE RIVER   **Phone:** (414)962-6040

Hotel
$97-$197

Address: 4700 N Port Washington Rd 53212 **Location:** I-43, exit 77A northbound, just e on Hampton Ave; exit 78A (Silver Springs Dr) southbound, just e, then just s. Located in a quiet area. **Facility:** Smoke free premises. 161 units. 5 stories, interior corridors. **Terms:** 1-7 night minimum stay, cancellation fee imposed. **Amenities:** video games (fee). **Dining:** Anchorage Restaurant, see separate listing. **Pool(s):** heated indoor. **Activities:** exercise room. **Guest Services:** valet laundry, wireless Internet. *(see ad p. 549)*

AAA Benefit:
Members save 5% or more everyday!

FREE continental breakfast and high-speed Internet

LA QUINTA INN & SUITES MILWAUKEE BAYSHORE AREA   **Phone:** (414)962-6767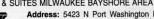

Hotel
$79-$159

Address: 5423 N Port Washington Rd 53217 **Location:** I-43, exit 78A (Silver Spring Dr), just se. Located in a commercial area. **Facility:** Smoke free premises. 109 units, some efficiencies. 4 stories, interior corridors. **Amenities:** video games (fee). **Pool(s):** heated indoor. **Activities:** whirlpool, exercise room. **Fee:** game room. **Guest Services:** valet and coin laundry, area transportation-within 5 mi, wireless Internet.

LA QUINTA INN MILWAUKEE GLENDALE HAMPTON AVE   **Phone:** (414)964-8484

Hotel
$52-$109

Address: 5110 N Port Washington Rd 53217 **Location:** I-43, exit 78A (Silver Spring Dr), 0.4 mi se. Located in a quiet area. **Facility:** Smoke free premises. 103 units, some efficiencies. 3 stories, interior corridors. **Parking:** winter plug-ins. **Amenities:** video games (fee). **Guest Services:** valet laundry, wireless Internet.

RADISSON HOTEL MILWAUKEE NORTH SHORE   **Phone:** (414)351-6960

Hotel
$89-$229

Address: 7065 N Port Washington Rd 53217 **Location:** I-43, exit 80 (Good Hope Rd), just e. **Facility:** Smoke free premises. 133 units. 3 stories, interior corridors. **Terms:** cancellation fee imposed. **Amenities:** high-speed Internet, safes. **Pool(s):** heated indoor. **Activities:** whirlpool, exercise room. **Fee:** game room. **Guest Services:** valet laundry, wireless Internet.

RESIDENCE INN BY MARRIOTT MILWAUKEE/GLENDALE   **Phone:** (414)352-0070

Extended Stay
Hotel
$129-$135

Address: 7275 N Port Washington Rd 53217 **Location:** I-43, exit 80 (Good Hope Rd), just e. Located in a residential/commercial area. **Facility:** Smoke free premises. 96 kitchen units. 2 stories (no elevator), exterior corridors. **Terms:** check-in 4 pm, cancellation fee imposed. **Pool(s):** heated outdoor. **Activities:** whirlpool, barbecue grill area, limited exercise equipment. **Guest Services:** valet and coin laundry, wireless Internet.

AAA Benefit:
Members save a minimum 5% off the best available rate.

——— WHERE TO DINE ———

ANCHORAGE RESTAURANT   **Phone:** 414/962-4710

Seafood
$8-$24

Great Lakes fresh fish and other seafood from the Gulf of Mexico and the Pacific and Atlantic oceans is offered along with traditional flavorful soups and sauces. Red snapper soup packs a punch. Tables overlook the Milwaukee River. **Bar:** full bar. **Reservations:** suggested. **Hours:** 6:30 am-2 & 4:30-10 pm, Sat from 7 am, Sun 7 am-1 & 4:30-9 pm. Closed: 11/24, 12/25. **Address:** 4700 N Port Washington Rd 53212 **Location:** I-43, exit 77A northbound, just e on Hampton Ave; exit 78A (Silver Springs Dr) southbound, just e, then just s; in Hilton Milwaukee River. *(see ad p. 549)*

(See map and index starting on p. 530)

THE BAVARIAN INN

German
$6-$18

Phone: 414/964-0300 26

Ethnic decor and a festive atmosphere add to the charm of the relaxed restaurant, a favorite for great German food. Menu choices include bratwurst, potato pancakes, pork chops, spaetzle and potato salad. The daily luncheon buffet and Sunday brunch are popular. Guests can enjoy the traditional Friday fish fry while soaking up live entertainment. **Bar:** full bar. **Hours:** 11:30 am-2 & 5-9 pm, Fri-9:30 pm, Sat 5 pm-9 pm, Sun 10:30 am-2 pm. Closed: 12/24, 12/25; also Mon. **Address:** 700 W Lexington Blvd 53217 **Location:** I-43, exit 78A (Silver Spring Dr), just s; 0.4 mi w of Port Washington Rd.

GRAFTON pop. 10,312

BAYMONT INN & SUITES MILWAUKEE-GRAFTON

Hotel
$61-$179

Phone: (262)387-1180

Address: 1415 Port Washington Rd 53024 **Location:** I-43, exit 92 (SR 60), just w, then just s. Located in a quiet area. **Facility:** Smoke free premises. 67 units. 4 stories, interior corridors. **Parking:** winter plug-ins. **Terms:** cancellation fee imposed. **Pool(s):** heated indoor. **Activities:** whirlpool, exercise room. **Guest Services:** coin laundry, wireless Internet.

HAMPTON INN & SUITES

Hotel
$99-$169

Phone: (262)474-1000

Address: 2633 Washington St 53024 **Location:** I-43, exit 92 (SR 60), just s. **Facility:** Smoke free premises. 83 units. 4 stories, interior corridors. **Terms:** 1-7 night minimum stay, cancellation fee imposed. **Amenities:** high-speed Internet. **Pool(s):** heated indoor. **Activities:** whirlpool, exercise room. **Guest Services:** valet and coin laundry, wireless Internet. **Free Special Amenities:** expanded continental breakfast and high-speed Internet.

Hampton

AAA Benefit:
Members save up to 10% everyday!

—— **WHERE TO DINE** ——

THE CHARCOAL GRILL AND ROTISSERIE

Barbecue
$7-$19

Phone: 262/375-1700

A casual, family-friendly atmosphere prevails at this welcoming spot for fun and great food. The menu lists barbecue ribs, grilled burgers and woodstone pizzas. **Bar:** full bar. **Hours:** 11 am-11 pm, Sun 9 am-9 pm. Closed: 11/24, 12/25. **Address:** 1200 N Port Washington Rd 53024 **Location:** I-43, exit 92 (SR 60), just w.

GREENFIELD pop. 35,476   (See map and index starting on p. 530)

GOLDEN KEY MOTEL

Motel
$45-$85

Phone: 414/543-5300 64

Address: 3600 S 108th St 53228 **Location:** I-894, exit 3, 0.5 mi w on Beloit Rd (CR T), then just n on SR 100. Located in a commercial area. **Facility:** Smoke free premises. 23 units. 2 stories (no elevator), interior/exterior corridors. **Terms:** cancellation fee imposed. **Amenities:** high-speed Internet. **Pool(s):** heated outdoor. **Guest Services:** wireless Internet.

HARTFORD pop. 10,905

AMERICINN OF HARTFORD

Hotel
Rates not provided

Phone: 262/673-2200

Address: 1527 E Sumner St 53027 **Location:** US 41, exit SR 60, 5 mi w. Located in a commercial area. **Facility:** Smoke free premises. 45 units. 2 stories (no elevator), interior corridors. **Parking:** winter plug-ins. **Pool(s):** heated indoor. **Activities:** whirlpool. **Guest Services:** coin laundry, wireless Internet.

HUBERTUS

—— **WHERE TO DINE** ——

THE NEW FOX & HOUNDS

American
$9-$32

Phone: 262/628-1111

Once a hunt club, the 1845 log cabin was converted to a restaurant in 1933. Stone fireplaces burn during the chilly winter months. **Bar:** full bar. **Reservations:** suggested. **Hours:** 4 pm-9 pm, Fri-10 pm, Sat 11 am-10 pm, Sun 10 am-9 pm. **Address:** 1298 Friess Lake Rd 53033 **Location:** 6 mi w on SR 167 of jct US 45, then 1 mi s at sign.

JACKSON pop. 4,938

COMFORT INN & SUITES OF JACKSON

Hotel
$69-$119

Phone: (262)677-1133

Address: W227 N 16890 Tillie Lake Ct 53037 **Location:** US 41, exit 64 (SR 60), 2.9 mi w at jct US 45. Located next to a business park. **Facility:** Smoke free premises. 54 units. 2 stories (no elevator), interior corridors. **Terms:** cancellation fee imposed. **Pool(s):** heated indoor. **Activities:** whirlpool, patio deck with grills. **Fee:** game room. **Guest Services:** valet and coin laundry, wireless Internet.

MEQUON pop. 21,823 (See map and index starting on p. 530)

BEST WESTERN QUIET HOUSE & SUITES
Phone: (262)241-3677

Hotel
$84-$239

Address: 10330 N Port Washington Rd 53092 **Location:** I-43, exit 85 (Mequon Rd), just w on SR 167, then 1 mi s. Located in a commercial area. **Facility:** Smoke free premises. 54 units. 2 stories (no elevator), interior corridors. **Terms:** cancellation fee imposed. **Amenities:** *Some:* high-speed Internet. **Pool(s):** heated indoor/outdoor. **Activities:** whirlpool, exercise room. **Guest Services:** valet laundry, wireless Internet. **Free Special Amenities: continental breakfast and airport transportation.**
(see ad p. 544)

THE CHALET MOTEL OF MEQUON
Phone: (262)241-4510 24

Motel
$59-$159

Address: 10401 N Port Washington Rd 53092 **Location:** I-43, exit 85 (Mequon Rd), just w on SR 167, then 1 mi s. Located in a commercial area. **Facility:** Smoke free premises. 53 units. 2 stories (no elevator), exterior corridors. **Terms:** 2-3 night minimum stay - seasonal and/or weekends, cancellation fee imposed. **Guest Services:** complimentary laundry, wireless Internet.

—— WHERE TO DINE ——

CENTENNIAL BAR & GRILLE
Phone: 262/241-4353 23

American
$7-$25

This restaurant prides itself on its food, and it shows. Flashes of creativity are evident in the extensive variety of sandwiches, homemade soups and entrees made with quality ingredients. A 100-year-old decorative wood bar is the centerpiece of the dining room, which has the atmosphere of a casual pub. **Bar:** full bar. **Hours:** 11:30 am-9 pm, Wed & Thurs-10 pm, Fri & Sat-10:30 pm, Sun 10 am-9 pm. Closed: Easter. **Address:** 10352 N Port Washington Rd 53092 **Location:** I-43, exit 85 (Mequon Rd), just w on SR 167, then 1 mi s.

FERRANTE'S MEQUON
Phone: (262)241-5420 22

Italian
$6-$18

Serving the city for 25 years, the casual, locally owned restaurant is a neighborhood tradition for pizza. Also on the menu are burgers, Friday fish fry, steaks, seafood and pasta dishes. **Bar:** full bar. **Hours:** 11:30 am-2 & 5-9:30 pm, Fri 4:30 pm-10:30 pm, Sat 4 pm-10:30 pm, Sun & Mon 4 pm-9 pm. Closed major holidays. **Address:** 10404 N Port Washington Rd 53092 **Location:** I-43, exit 83 (US 167), 1.4 mi n; corner of Donger Bay and Port Washington rds.

MUKWONAGO pop. 6,162

SLEEP INN
Phone: 262/363-9970

Hotel
Rates not provided

Address: 945 Greenwald Ct 53149 **Location:** I-43, exit 43, just nw. **Facility:** Smoke free premises. 61 units. 2 stories, interior corridors. **Parking:** winter plug-ins. **Amenities:** safes (fee). **Pool(s):** heated indoor. **Activities:** whirlpool. **Guest Services:** valet laundry, wireless Internet.

—— WHERE TO DINE ——

FORK IN THE ROAD
Phone: 262/363-7849

American
$8-$20

The casual and handsome downtown restaurant has wood floors, red columns and dark wood tables. Among the excellent variety of menu items are preparations of fish, steaks, chicken, pasta, salads, sandwiches and flatbreads, in addition to home-cooked macaroni and cheese or thick meatloaf stuffed with Wisconsin cheese and served with garlic mashed potatoes, red sauce and onion rings. The wait staff is friendly and efficient. **Bar:** full bar. **Hours:** 11:30 am-9:30 pm, Fri & Sat-10 pm. Closed: Sun. **Address:** 215 N Rochester St 53149 **Location:** I-43, exit 43, 1 mi n on SR 83.

NEW BERLIN pop. 38,220 (See map and index starting on p. 530)

HOLIDAY INN EXPRESS HOTEL & SUITES-NEW BERLIN
Phone: (262)787-0700 60

Hotel
$99-$169 4/1-8/31
$89-$159 9/1-4/30

Address: 15451 W Beloit Rd 53151 **Location:** I-43, exit 57 (Moorland Rd), just ne. Located in a commercial area. **Facility:** Smoke free premises. 101 units. 4 stories, interior corridors. **Terms:** cancellation fee imposed. **Amenities:** video games (fee). **Pool(s):** heated indoor. **Activities:** whirlpool, exercise room. **Guest Services:** valet and coin laundry, wireless Internet.

LA QUINTA INN & SUITES MILWAUKEE SW NEW BERLIN
Phone: (262)717-0900 61

Hotel
$59-$139

Address: 15300 W Rock Ridge Rd 53151 **Location:** I-43, exit 57 (Moorland Rd), just se. Located in a quiet area. **Facility:** Smoke free premises. 88 units. 4 stories, interior corridors. **Amenities:** video games (fee). **Pool(s):** heated indoor. **Activities:** whirlpool, exercise room. **Guest Services:** valet and coin laundry, wireless Internet.

(See map and index starting on p. 530)

—— WHERE TO DINE ——

THE CHARCOAL GRILL AND ROTISSERIE

Phone: 262/432-3000

American
$7-$20

Fine steaks, chops, chicken and pizza are featured at this casual dining spot. Entrees are attractively presented, and the dining room sports a northwoods theme. **Bar:** full bar. **Hours:** 11 am-10 pm, Sun 9 am-9 pm. Closed: 11/24, 12/25. **Address:** 15375 W Greenfield Ave 53151 **Location:** I-94, exit 301A, 0.5 mi s on Moorland Rd, then just e. CALL ⌖M

MI COCINA MEXICAN RESTAURANT

Phone: 262/780-9952   ㊶

Mexican
$6-$15

Mexican food is prepared with mild flavor, but those who like it spicy can take advantage of the hot sauce dish that's part of the serving. On the menu are chicken, steak, pork and seafood dishes, as well as fajitas, chimichangas, quesadillas and enchiladas. **Bar:** full bar. **Hours:** 11 am-10 pm, Fri & Sat-10:30 pm, Sun noon-9 pm. Closed major holidays. **Address:** 15366 W Beloit Rd 53151 **Location:** I-43, exit 57 (Moorland Rd), just ne.

OAK CREEK pop. 28,456   (See map and index starting on p. 530)

COMFORT SUITES MILWAUKEE AIRPORT

Phone: (414)570-1111   ㊳

Hotel
$79-$129

Address: 6362 S 13th St 53154 **Location:** I-94, exit 319 (College Ave), just e on CR 22, then just s. **Facility:** Smoke free premises. 138 units, some two bedrooms. 3 stories, interior corridors. **Amenities:** high-speed Internet, safes (fee). **Pool(s):** heated indoor. **Activities:** whirlpool, patio & sun deck, limited exercise equipment. **Fee:** game room. **Guest Services:** valet and coin laundry, area transportation-within 3 mi, wireless Internet.

ECO ⊁ ⫨ CALL ⌖M 🏊 ⊠ 🎥 🖥 📷 💻 / SOME UNITS FEE 🐾

DAYS INN MILWAUKEE AIRPORT

Phone: (414)764-1776   ㊲

Hotel
$49-$74

Address: 1201 W College Ave 53154 **Location:** I-94, exit 319 (College Ave), just e. **Facility:** Smoke free premises. 107 units. 2 stories (no elevator), interior corridors. **Activities:** limited exercise equipment. **Guest Services:** coin laundry, wireless Internet.

⊁ ⫨ CALL ⌖M ⊠ 🎥 💻 / SOME UNITS 🐾 FEE 🖥 FEE 📷

LA QUINTA INN MILWAUKEE AIRPORT / OAK CREEK

Phone: (414)762-2266   ㊱

Hotel
$59-$105

Address: 7141 S 13th St 53154 **Location:** I-94, exit 320 (Rawson Ave), just se. Located in a commercial area. **Facility:** Smoke free premises. 99 units. 3 stories, interior corridors. **Parking:** winter plug-ins. **Amenities:** video games (fee). **Activities:** exercise room. **Guest Services:** valet and coin laundry, wireless Internet. ⊁ ⫨ CALL ⌖M ⊠ 🎥 💻 / SOME UNITS 🐾 🖥 📷

MAINSTAY SUITES OAK CREEK

Phone: (414)571-8800   ㊷

Historic Resort
Hotel
$88-$210

Address: 1001 W College Ave 53154 **Location:** I-94, exit 319 (College Ave), just e. **Facility:** All guest rooms reflect high quality and have comfortable mattresses. Smoke free premises. 76 efficiencies, some two bedrooms. 3 stories, interior corridors. **Amenities:** high-speed Internet, safes (fee). **Activities:** patio with grill, exercise room. **Guest Services:** valet and coin laundry, wireless Internet.

⊁ ⫨ CALL ⌖M BIZ ⊠ 🎥 🖥 📷 💻 / SOME UNITS FEE 🐾

—— WHERE TO DINE ——

BRANDED STEER

Phone: 414/571-8672   ㊹

Steak
$5-$24

Lasso steaks, pork and chicken are cooked on a wood grill rotisserie at the Western-style restaurant. Also on the menu are soups, sandwiches, salads and Black Angus beef burgers. **Bar:** full bar. **Hours:** 11 am-midnight. Closed: 11/24, 12/25. **Address:** 1299 W College Ave 53154 **Location:** I-94, exit 319 (College Ave), just e. CALL ⌖M

NICK'S AND FRIENDS FAMILY RESTAURANT

Phone: 414/766-1100   ㊺

American
$6-$13

Owned by family and friends, this restaurant prepares good American home cooking that's priced to be a good value. This place opens for breakfast, lunch and dinner. **Bar:** full bar. **Hours:** 5 am-9 pm, Sun from 6 am. Closed: 12/24, 12/25. **Address:** 6874 S 13th St 53154 **Location:** On CR V; just n of jct CR BB.
CALL ⌖M

OCONOMOWOC pop. 12,382

HILTON GARDEN INN OCONOMOWOC

Phone: (262)200-2222

Hotel
$90-$200

Address: 1443 Pabst Farms Cir 53066 **Location:** I-94, exit 282 (SR 67), just e. **Facility:** Smoke free premises. 100 units. 3 stories, interior corridors. **Terms:** 1-7 night minimum stay, cancellation fee imposed. **Amenities:** high-speed Internet. **Pool(s):** heated indoor. **Activities:** whirlpool, sun deck, exercise room. **Guest Services:** valet and coin laundry, wireless Internet. **Free Special Amenities:** preferred room (subject to availability with advance reservations) and high-speed Internet.

SAVE 🍴 🍷 CALL ⌖M 🏊 BIZ ⊠ 🎥 🖥 📷 💻

OLYMPIA RESORT, SPA & CONFERENCE CENTER

Phone: (262)369-4999

Resort
Hotel
$99-$250

Address: 1350 Royale Mile Rd 53066 **Location:** I-94, exit 282 (SR 67), 1 mi n. **Facility:** Recreational activities are bountiful including a ski area with chair lifts, tennis courts, a golf course and a 17,000 square foot spa. Smoke free premises. 256 units. 4 stories, interior corridors. **Terms:** cancellation fee imposed. **Pool(s):** heated outdoor, heated indoor. **Activities:** saunas, whirlpools, steamrooms, indoor virtual golf simulator, horseback riding, playground, spa, shuffleboard, volleyball. *Fee:* game room. **Guest Services:** valet and coin laundry, wireless Internet, tanning facilities. *Fee:* area transportation-within 5 mi. **Free Special Amenities: local telephone calls and high-speed Internet.**

STAYBRIDGE SUITES MILWAUKEE WEST

Phone: (262)200-2900

Extended Stay
Hotel
$99-$139

Address: 1141 Blue Ribbon Dr 53066 **Location:** I-94, exit 282 (SR 67), just s. Located near a medical facility. **Facility:** Smoke free premises. 128 efficiencies, some two bedrooms. 3 stories, interior corridors. **Terms:** 3 day cancellation notice-fee imposed. **Amenities:** high-speed Internet. **Pool(s):** heated indoor. **Activities:** whirlpool, putting green, mini movie theater, patio with grill, exercise room. **Guest Services:** complimentary and valet laundry, area transportation-within 5 mi, wireless Internet. **Free Special Amenities: full breakfast and high-speed Internet.**

—— **WHERE TO DINE** ——

AROUND THE LAKES FAMILY RESTAURANT

Phone: 262/569-8965

American
$7-$22

Homemade food is prepared from fresh ingredients at this cheery restaurant. **Hours:** 5 am-10 pm. **Address:** 515 E Wisconsin Ave 53066 **Location:** Center.

SPINNAKER'S RESTAURANT & BAR

Phone: 262/567-9691

American
$7-$33

In a lovely setting overlooking downtown's Lac La Belle, the popular restaurant serves seafood, pasta, prime rib, steaks, sandwiches and salads. The dining room presents a well-coordinated nautical theme. In the summer, patrons can dine on the screened outdoor porch, while during winter, seats near the stone fireplace are cozy. **Bar:** full bar. **Hours:** 11 am-2 & 4-9 pm, Fri & Sat-9:30 pm, Sun 4 pm-8 pm; hours may vary in winter. Closed major holidays. **Address:** 128 W Wisconsin Ave 53066 **Location:** On SR 16; center.

OKAUCHEE

—— **WHERE TO DINE** ——

GOLDEN MAST INN

Phone: 262/567-7047

German
$14-$39

From their entrance into a grand Bavarian-style restaurant with high ceilings and liberal use of wood, rock and glass to their last bite of apple strudel, diners are treated to a decidedly German experience. Although the menu lists seafood and steak, the key elements are dumpling soups, Wiener schnitzel, beef rouladen and sauerbraten. A menu of casual fare is presented on the patio. Views of Okauchee Lake from the dining room are delightful. **Bar:** full bar. **Hours:** 5 pm-9 pm, Fri & Sat-10 pm, Sun 11 am-8 pm; Sunday brunch. Closed: Mon. **Address:** W349 N5293 Lacy's Ln 53069 **Location:** SR 16, exit 178 (Sawyer), 1 mi n, follow signs.

PEWAUKEE pop. 11,783

COMFORT SUITES

Phone: (262)506-2000

Hotel
$90-$160

Address: N14 W 24121 Tower Pl 53072 **Location:** I-94, exit 294 (SR 164 N), just nw. **Facility:** Smoke free premises. 94 units, some efficiencies. 3 stories, interior corridors. **Parking:** winter plug-ins. **Terms:** check-in 4 pm. **Amenities:** video games (fee). **Pool(s):** heated indoor. **Activities:** whirlpool, exercise room. **Guest Services:** valet and coin laundry, wireless Internet.

RADISSON HOTEL PEWAUKEE

Phone: (262)506-6300

Hotel
$129-$179

Address: N14 W 24140 Tower Pl 53072 **Location:** I-94, exit 294 (CR J), just nw. **Facility:** Smoke free premises. 118 units, some two bedrooms and kitchens. 3 stories, interior corridors. **Terms:** cancellation fee imposed. **Amenities:** high-speed Internet. *Some:* safes. **Dining:** Thunder Bay Grille, see separate listing. **Pool(s):** heated indoor. **Activities:** whirlpool, exercise room. **Guest Services:** valet laundry, wireless Internet.

—— **WHERE TO DINE** ——

BUBBA'S FROZEN CUSTARD

Phone: 262/695-8189

American
$2-$7

Hungry folks can get a quick bite to eat at the locally-owned hamburger place. Specialty sundaes feature many ice cream flavors, including pecan toffee crunch, mud pie, chocolate turtle and Heath bar. **Hours:** 11 am-9:30 pm, Fri & Sat-10 pm. Closed major holidays. **Address:** 1276 Capitol Dr 53072 **Location:** I-94, exit 294 (CR J), 2.6 mi n, then 0.4 mi w of jct SR 74/190E and CR J.

THE MACHINE SHED

Phone: 262/523-1322

American
$7-$24

Antiques and farm implements decorate the decidedly rustic dining room. Tried-and-true comfort foods—such as pot roast, ham and roast pork—please every member of the family. The Friday night fish fry draws a hungry crowd. Servers in overalls are friendly and prompt. **Bar:** full bar. **Hours:** 6 am-10 pm, Sun 7 am-9 pm. Closed: 1/1, 11/24, 12/24, 12/25. **Address:** N14 W24145 Tower Pl 53072 **Location:** I-94, exit 294 (SR 164 N), just nw.

THUNDER BAY GRILLE

American
$7-$22

Phone: 262/523-4244

Wooden chairs, antlers on the walls and canoes in the rafters contribute to the folksy northwoods atmosphere at this casual restaurant. The large variety of foods includes homemade soup, a variety of tapas, hand-cut steaks, fresh fish, pasta, slow-roasted prime rib and hardwood-smoked ribs. Outdoor courtyard dining is offered in season, and a plush lounge seating area features fully upholstered white high-back chairs. **Bar:** full bar. **Hours:** 11 am-10 pm, Fri & Sat-11 pm, Sun 10 am-9 pm. Closed: 1/1, 11/24, 12/24, 12/25. **Address:** N14 W 24130 Tower Pl 53072 **Location:** I-94, exit 294 (SR 164 N), just nw; in Radisson Hotel Pewaukee. CALL M

PORT WASHINGTON pop. 10,467

COUNTRY INN & SUITES BY CARLSON

Hotel
$84-$129 10/1-4/30
$79-$129 4/1-9/30

Phone: (262)284-2100

Address: 350 E Seven Hills Rd 53074 **Location:** I-43, exit 100, just w. **Facility:** Smoke free premises. 85 units. 3 stories, interior corridors. **Pool(s):** heated indoor. **Activities:** whirlpool, exercise room. *Fee:* game room. **Guest Services:** coin laundry, wireless Internet. *(see ad p. 6)*

HOLIDAY INN HARBORVIEW

Hotel
$89-$229 4/1-10/29
$89-$189 10/30-4/30

Phone: (262)284-9461

Address: 135 E Grand Ave 53074 **Location:** On SR 33; waterfront of Lake Michigan; downtown. Located between shops and harbor. **Facility:** Smoke free premises. 96 units. 5 stories, interior corridors. **Parking:** winter plug-ins. **Pool(s):** heated indoor. **Activities:** sauna, whirlpool, fishing, exercise room. *Fee:* game room. **Guest Services:** valet and coin laundry, wireless Internet. **Free Special Amenities: preferred room (subject to availability with advance reservations) and high-speed Internet.**

─── WHERE TO DINE ───

BEANIES MEXICAN RESTAURANT

American
$7-$15

Phone: 262/284-7200

Just off the waterfront, the tiny restaurant hits the spot for those seeking tasty food at a reasonable price. In addition to Mexican favorites, subs and burgers make up the menu. Complimentary chips and salsa accompany every meal. **Bar:** full bar. **Hours:** 11 am-9 pm, Fri & Sat-10 pm. Closed: 11/24, 12/25 & Easter. **Address:** 102 E Grand Ave 53074 **Location:** On SR 32; downtown.

TELLO'S GRILLE & CAFE

Mexican
$2-$15

Phone: 262/268-1133

In a historic hotel building, the restaurant offers not only great Mexican dishes but also Greek and American fare. Locals often congregate at this popular spot. **Bar:** full bar. **Hours:** 8 am-10 pm. Closed: 1/1, 12/25. **Address:** 200 W Grand Ave 53074 **Location:** Center. CALL M

SAUKVILLE pop. 4,068

SUPER 8- SAUKVILLE

Hotel
$59-$95

Phone: (262)284-9399

Address: 180 Foster Rd 53080 **Location:** I-43, exit 96, just s. **Facility:** Smoke free premises. 70 units. 2 stories (no elevator), interior corridors. **Parking:** winter plug-ins. **Activities:** sauna, whirlpool, limited exercise equipment. **Guest Services:** wireless Internet.

WAUKESHA pop. 64,825

BEST WESTERN WAUKESHA GRAND

Hotel
$75-$160

Phone: (262)524-9300

Address: 2840 N Grandview Blvd 53072 **Location:** I-94, exit 293, just s on CR T. **Facility:** Smoke free premises. 92 units. 3 stories, interior corridors. **Terms:** cancellation fee imposed. **Pool(s):** heated indoor. **Activities:** whirlpool, exercise room. **Guest Services:** coin laundry, wireless Internet. **Free Special Amenities: expanded continental breakfast and high-speed Internet.**

EXTENDED STAYAMERICA-MILWAUKEE-WAUKESHA

Extended Stay Hotel
$47-$80

Phone: (262)798-0217

Address: 2520 Plaza Ct 53186 **Location:** I-94, exit 297, just e on SR 18, then just s. **Facility:** Smoke free premises. 122 efficiencies. 3 stories, interior corridors. **Parking:** winter plug-ins. **Terms:** cancellation fee imposed. **Guest Services:** coin laundry, wireless Internet.

MARRIOTT MILWAUKEE WEST

Hotel
$175-$185

Phone: (262)574-0888

Address: W231 N1600 Corporate Ct 53186 **Location:** I-94, exit 295 (CR F), just n. **Facility:** Smoke free premises. 281 units. 6 stories, interior corridors. **Terms:** check-in 4 pm, cancellation fee imposed. **Amenities:** high-speed Internet (fee). **Pool(s):** heated indoor. **Activities:** whirlpool, exercise room. **Guest Services:** valet and coin laundry, wireless Internet.

AAA Benefit:
Members save 5% or more off best available rate.

SUPER 8 - WAUKESHA

Hotel
$53-$68

Phone: (262)786-6015

Address: 2510 Plaza Ct 53186 **Location:** I-94, exit 297, just n w on CR JJ (Bluemound Rd). **Facility:** Smoke free premises. 96 units, some efficiencies. 3 stories (no elevator), interior corridors. **Amenities:** safes (fee). **Guest Services:** coin laundry, wireless Internet.

------ **WHERE TO DINE** ------

GYROS CORNER WEST

Greek
$5-$12

Phone: 262/544-0211

Families come here for gyros, chicken and pork shish kebabs, an extensive choice of American dishes and all-day breakfast items. **Hours:** 5 am-9 pm, Sat-10 pm. Closed major holidays. **Address:** 1538 E Moreland Blvd 53186 **Location:** 1 mi e of jct US 18 and SR 164.

WEISSGERBER'S GASTHAUS RESTAURANT

German
$9-$28

Phone: 262/544-4460

Everything from the Old World decor to the servers in ethnic period uniforms to the authentic cuisine lend to a Bavarian experience here. The menu features a special Bavarian bean soup, sausage lovers' selections and a few American favorites. The tortes and pies are made in house. **Bar:** full bar. **Reservations:** suggested. **Hours:** 11:30 am-2 & 5-9 pm, Fri & Sat 4:30 pm-10 pm. Closed: 5/30, 7/4, 9/5; also Sun. **Address:** 2720 N Grandview Blvd 53188 **Location:** I-94, exit 293, just s on CR T.

WAUWATOSA pop. 47,271 (See map and index starting on p. 530)

CROWNE PLAZA MILWAUKEE-WAUWATOSA

Hotel
$99-$179

Phone: (414)475-9500   **56**

Address: 10499 Innovation Dr 53226 **Location:** US 45, exit Watertown Plank Rd, just n. **Facility:** Smoke free premises. 198 units. 8 stories, interior corridors. **Parking:** no self-parking, winter plug-ins. **Amenities:** high-speed Internet. **Pool(s):** heated indoor. **Activities:** whirlpool, walking path, exercise room. **Guest Services:** valet laundry, area transportation-within 5 mi, wireless Internet.

EXTENDED STAYAMERICA-MILWAUKEE-WAUWATOSA

Extended Stay
Hotel
$51-$85

Phone: (414)443-1909   **54**

Address: 11121 W North Ave 53226 **Location:** US 45, exit 42A, just n. **Facility:** Smoke free premises. 122 efficiencies. 3 stories, interior corridors. **Terms:** office hours 7 am-11 pm, cancellation fee imposed. **Guest Services:** coin laundry, wireless Internet.

HOLIDAY INN EXPRESS MILWAUKEE WEST-MEDICAL CENTER

Hotel
$109-$139

Phone: (414)778-0333   **55**

Address: 11111 W North Ave 53226 **Location:** US 45, exit 42A, just n on SR 100, then just w. Located in a commercial area. **Facility:** Smoke free premises. 121 units. 3 stories, interior corridors. **Amenities:** video games (fee). **Activities:** exercise room. *Fee:* game room. **Guest Services:** valet laundry, area transportation-within 5 mi, wireless Internet.

RADISSON HOTEL MILWAUKEE WEST

Hotel
$109-$209

Phone: (414)257-3400   **53**

Address: 2303 N Mayfair Rd 53226 **Location:** US 45, exit 42A, just n on SR 100 at North Ave. Across from shopping center. **Facility:** Smoke free premises. 151 units. 8 stories, interior corridors. **Terms:** cancellation fee imposed. **Amenities:** video games (fee), high-speed Internet. **Dining:** RJ's Garden & Grille, see separate listing. **Pool(s):** heated indoor. **Activities:** sauna, exercise room. **Guest Services:** valet laundry, wireless Internet.

SUPER 8 OF MILWAUKEE WEST

Hotel
$71-$80

Phone: (414)257-0140   **57**

Address: 115 N Mayfair Rd 53226 **Location:** I-94, exit 304B, just n on SR 100. **Facility:** 120 units. 2 stories (no elevator), interior corridors. **Activities:** limited exercise equipment. **Guest Services:** coin laundry, wireless Internet.

------ **WHERE TO DINE** ------

EDDIE MARTINI'S

Traditional
American
$9-$39

Phone: 414/771-6680   **38**

The casually elegant 1940s-style supper club is locally known for excellent food and professional service. Steak, chops and seafood are prepared with high-quality ingredients. Signature items include the ocean martini appetizer and bread pudding dessert. **Bar:** full bar. **Reservations:** suggested. **Hours:** 11:30 am-2 & 5-10 pm, Fri-11 pm, Sat 5 pm-11 pm, Sun 5 pm-9 pm. Closed major holidays. **Address:** 8612 W Watertown Plank Rd 53226 **Location:** US 45, exit 40, 0.7 mi e.

(See map and index starting on p. 530)

MAGGIANO'S LITTLE ITALY

Phone: 414/978-1000 (35)

Italian
$11-$38

Diners savor scrumptious, traditional favorites served in a bustling atmosphere reminiscent of Little Italy. The dining area projects an early-20th-century feel; loud conversations bouncing off high ceilings evoke a sense of the Roaring '20s. **Bar:** full bar. **Reservations:** suggested. **Hours:** 11:15 am-10 pm, Fri & Sat-11 pm, Sun noon-9 pm. Closed: 12/25. **Address:** 2500 N Mayfair Rd 53226 **Location:** SR 100, exit 42A (W North Ave), just e, then just n; in Mayfair Mall. CALL &M

RISTORANTE BARTOLOTTA

Phone: 414/771-7910 (37)

Northern Italian
$16-$37

The bustling trattoria captures the essence of rustic, peasant-style cooking. Roasted chicken and veal are cooked in a large, wood-burning oven. Duck, lamb and fresh seafood are included in other creative offerings, as well as varied pasta dishes. Service is upscale and attentive. The strictly Italian wine list remains true to its roots. In season, a few outdoor tables are available. **Bar:** full bar. **Reservations:** suggested. **Hours:** 5:30 pm-9 pm, Fri-10 pm, Sat 5 pm-10 pm, Sun 5 pm-8 pm. Closed major holidays. **Address:** 7616 W State St 53213 **Location:** Just w of jct Wauwatosa Ave; downtown. **Parking:** street only. CALL &M

RJ'S GARDEN & GRILLE

Phone: 414/257-3400 (36)

American
$9-$27

Convenient to the Mayfair Shopping Mall, the contemporary hotel restaurant has an art deco motif. The menu offers salads, sandwiches and a variety of fresh catches prepared to order. The patio is open seasonally. **Bar:** full bar. **Reservations:** suggested. **Hours:** 6:30 am-10 pm. Closed: 1/1, 12/25. **Address:** 2303 N Mayfair Rd 53226 **Location:** US 45, exit 42A, just n on SR 100 at North Ave; in Radisson Hotel Milwaukee West. CALL &M

WEST BEND pop. 28,152

COUNTRY INN & SUITES BY CARLSON

Phone: (262)334-9400

Hotel
$89-$199

Address: 2000 Gateway Ct 53095 **Location:** US 45, exit 68 (Paradise Dr), just se. Located in a commercial area. **Facility:** Smoke free premises. 58 units. 3 stories, interior corridors. **Parking:** winter plug-ins. **Terms:** cancellation fee imposed. **Amenities:** high-speed Internet. **Pool(s):** heated indoor. **Activities:** whirlpool. **Guest Services:** valet laundry, wireless Internet. *(see ad p. 6)*

HAMPTON INN & SUITES

Phone: (262)438-1500

Hotel
$99-$129

Address: 1975 S 18th Ave 53095 **Location:** US 45 S, exit 68 (Paradise Dr). **Facility:** Smoke free premises. 83 units. 4 stories, interior corridors. **Terms:** 1-7 night minimum stay, cancellation fee imposed. **Amenities:** high-speed Internet. **Pool(s):** heated indoor. **Activities:** whirlpool, exercise room. **Guest Services:** valet and coin laundry, wireless Internet. **Free Special Amenities:** newspaper and high-speed Internet.

AAA Benefit:
Members save up to 10% everyday!

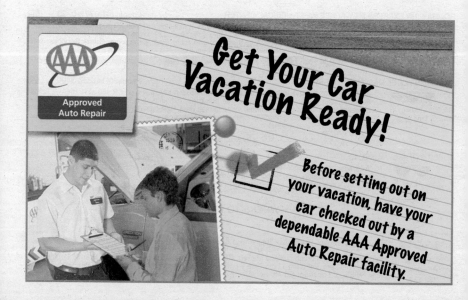

——— WHERE TO DINE ———

JUMBO'S FROZEN CUSTARD

American
$3-$6

Phone: 262/334-5400

Frozen custard and jumbo burgers are specialties at the pleasant quick-serve eatery. **Hours:** 10:30 am-10 pm, Fri & Sat-10:30 pm. Closed: 11/24, 12/25. **Address:** 1014 S Main St 53095 **Location:** US 45, exit 68 (Paradise Dr), 0.4 mi e, then 0.6 mi s.

OMICRON FAMILY RESTAURANT

American
$5-$14

Phone: 262/335-0777

Reasonably priced selections of primarily comfort foods mingle with an array of all-day breakfast items and some Greek fare on the diverse menu. The atmosphere is family-friendly and unpretentious. Several beers and wines are listed. **Bar:** beer & wine. **Hours:** 6 am-10 pm, Fri & Sat-11 pm. Closed: 12/24, 12/25. **Address:** 1505 S Main St 53095 **Location:** US 45, exit 68 (Paradise Dr), 0.4 mi e, then 0.3 mi n.

WHITEFISH BAY pop. 14,163 (See map and index starting on p. 530)

——— WHERE TO DINE ———

JACK PANDL'S WHITEFISH BAY INN

American
$7-$29

Phone: 414/964-3800 (54)

This designated county landmark has been operated by the same family since 1915. Fresh deboned whitefish is the house specialty, but the German pancakes are also notable. **Bar:** full bar. **Reservations:** suggested. **Hours:** 11:30 am-10 pm, Fri & Sat-10:30 pm, Sun 10 am-9 pm. Closed major holidays. **Address:** 1319 E Henry Clay St 53217 **Location:** On SR 32; 0.6 mi s of jct Silver Spring Dr.

Miller Brewery Tour and Visitor Center / © Scott White / Photolibrary

This ends listings for the Milwaukee Vicinity.
The following page resumes the alphabetical listings of cities in Wisconsin.

MINERAL POINT pop. 2,617

QUALITY INN

Hotel
$68-$90

Phone: (608)987-4747

Address: 1345 Business Park Rd 53565 **Location:** On US 151; 0.6 mi n of jct SR 23 and 39. **Facility:** Smoke free premises. 50 units. 2 stories (no elevator), interior corridors. **Parking:** winter plug-ins. **Amenities:** safes. **Pool(s):** heated indoor. **Activities:** whirlpool. **Guest Services:** coin laundry, wireless Internet. [icons] CALL [icons] / SOME UNITS FEE [icons]

------ **WHERE TO DINE** ------

BREWERY CREEK

American
$8-$18

Phone: 608/987-3298

With its walls of limestone, original oak ceiling joints and pine plank flooring, the quaint establishment exudes English charm. In fact, many furnishings were imported from England pubs. The menu combines staple pub items, such as burgers, with pastas, steaks and daily chef's specials. Patrons can sip a tasty microbrew or a homemade root beer. **Bar:** beer & wine. **Hours:** 11:30 am-8 pm, Fri & Sat-8:30 pm, Sun-3 pm. Closed: Mon; Sun-Wed 11/1-5/31. **Address:** 23 Commerce St 53565 **Location:** Downtown. **Parking:** street only.

MINOCQUA pop. 4,859

AMERICINN OF MINOCQUA

Hotel
$64-$159

Phone: (715)356-3730

Address: 700 Hwy 51 54548 **Location:** On US 51; downtown. Across from Torpy Park. **Facility:** Smoke free premises. 82 units. 2 stories (no elevator), interior corridors. **Parking:** winter plug-ins. **Amenities:** high-speed Internet. **Pool(s):** heated indoor. **Activities:** sauna, whirlpool, limited exercise equipment. **Guest Services:** coin laundry, wireless Internet.

[icons] CALL [icons] / SOME UNITS FEE [icons]

BEST WESTERN PLUS CONCORD INN

Hotel
$80-$183

Phone: (715)356-1800

Address: 320 Front St 54548 **Location:** On US 51; downtown. Across from Torpy Park. **Facility:** Smoke free premises. 52 units. 3 stories, interior corridors. **Parking:** winter plug-ins. **Amenities:** *Some:* high-speed Internet. **Pool(s):** heated indoor. **Activities:** whirlpool. *Fee:* game room. **Guest Services:** wireless Internet. **Free Special Amenities: expanded continental breakfast and high-speed Internet.**

[icons] CALL [icons] / SOME UNITS FEE [icons]

AAA Benefit:
Members save up to 20%, plus 10% bonus points with free rewards program.

COMFORT INN-MINOCQUA

Hotel
$59-$130

Phone: (715)358-2588

Address: 8729 Hwy 51 N 54548 **Location:** On US 51 at SR 70 W. **Facility:** Smoke free premises. 51 units. 2 stories (no elevator), interior corridors. **Parking:** winter plug-ins. **Amenities:** safes (fee). **Pool(s):** heated indoor. **Activities:** whirlpool, board games. **Guest Services:** wireless Internet.

[icons] / SOME UNITS FEE [icons]

THE WATERS OF MINOCQUA

Hotel
$69-$406

Phone: (715)358-4000

Address: 8116 Hwy 51 S 54548 **Location:** On US 51, 1 mi s. **Facility:** Smoke free premises. 106 units. 3 stories, interior corridors. **Parking:** winter plug-ins. **Terms:** 5 day cancellation notice-fee imposed. **Amenities:** high-speed Internet. **Dining:** 2 restaurants. **Pool(s):** heated indoor, heated indoor/outdoor. **Activities:** whirlpool, water park, cross country skiing, snowmobiling, exercise room. *Fee:* game room. **Guest Services:** coin laundry, wireless Internet. **Free Special Amenities: expanded continental breakfast and children's activities.**

[icons] CALL [icons] / SOME UNITS FEE [icons]

------ **WHERE TO DINE** ------

MAMA'S SUPPER CLUB

Italian
$9-$32

Phone: 715/356-5070

Overlooking a small lake, the dining room is charming and casual. The menu centers on traditional Italian preparations, such as Sicilian veal and a wide variety of pasta. Also on the menu are some American dishes, including a succulent tenderloin steak. **Bar:** full bar. **Hours:** 5 pm-10 pm. Closed: major holidays, 12/24. **Address:** 10486 Hwy 70 54548 **Location:** 3 mi w of town.

NORWOOD PINES SUPPER CLUB

American
$12-$28

Phone: 715/356-3666

This restaurant offers an authentic northwoods supper club experience complete with a traditional menu, friendly service and warm decor. Supper clubs are a tradition in rural Wisconsin. The scent of pine trees fill the entry. **Bar:** full bar. **Hours:** 5 pm-10 pm. Closed: 11/24, 12/25; also Sun. **Address:** 10171 Hwy 70 W 54548 **Location:** On SR 70, 2 mi w of jct US 51.

MONONA pop. 8,018 (See map and index starting on p. 499)

AMERICINN OF MADISON SOUTH/MONONA

Hotel
$99-$199

Phone: (608)222-8601 [41]

Address: 101 W Broadway 53716-3901 **Location:** US 12/18, exit 265 (Monona Dr), just nw. **Facility:** Smoke free premises. 61 units. 3 stories, interior corridors. **Parking:** winter plug-ins. **Amenities:** high-speed Internet. **Pool(s):** heated indoor. **Activities:** sauna, whirlpool, game room. **Guest Services:** coin laundry, wireless Internet.

[icons] CALL [icons] / SOME UNITS FEE [icons]

(See map and index starting on p. 499)

COUNTRY INN & SUITES BY CARLSON, MADISON

Phone: (608)221-0055 ⓐ42

Hotel
$99-$140

Address: 400 River Pl 53716 **Location:** US 12/18, exit 265 (Monona Dr), just nw. **Facility:** Smoke free premises. 87 units. 3 stories, interior corridors. **Terms:** cancellation fee imposed. **Pool(s):** heated indoor. **Activities:** whirlpool, exercise room. *Fee:* game room. **Guest Services:** valet and coin laundry, wireless Internet. *(see ad p. 6)*

 CALL ⬛ 🏊 ❌ 📷 🗄 🖥 🖵 / SOME UNITS FEE 🐾

------ WHERE TO DINE ------

ROSSARIO'S

Phone: 608/221-3940 ⓐ41

Italian
$7-$19

Locally owned and operated for the past 30 years, the popular restaurant focuses on homemade Italian specialties, steak, grilled trout, prime rib and the Friday fish fry. **Bar:** full bar. **Hours:** 11 am-2 & 5-9 pm, Sat 4:30 pm-9 pm, Sun 4 pm-8 pm. Closed major holidays; also Mon & Tues. **Address:** 6001 Monona Dr 53716 **Location:** US 12/18, exit 265 (Monona Dr), 0.6 mi n.

MONROE pop. 10,843

AMERICINN LODGE & SUITES OF MONROE

Phone: (608)328-3444

Hotel
$90-$140

Address: 424 4th Ave 53566 **Location:** On SR 69 S, 0.4 mi s of jct SR 81/11. **Facility:** 54 units. 2 stories (no elevator), interior corridors. **Parking:** winter plug-ins. **Terms:** cancellation fee imposed. **Pool(s):** heated indoor. **Activities:** whirlpool, billiards. **Guest Services:** coin laundry, wireless Internet. ECO CALL ⬛ 🏊 ❌ 📷 🗄 🖥 🖵

GASTHAUS MOTEL

Phone: (608)328-8395

Motel
$59-$99 4/1-10/31
$59-$79 11/1-4/30

Address: 685 30th St 53566 **Location:** 1.5 mi s on SR 69. **Facility:** Smoke free premises. 24 units, some kitchens. 1 story, exterior corridors. **Parking:** winter plug-ins. **Guest Services:** wireless Internet. **Free Special Amenities:** early check-in/late check-out and high-speed Internet.

SAVE CALL ⬛ ❌ 🖵 / SOME UNITS FEE 🐾 🗄

SUPER 8 OF MONROE

Phone: (608)325-1500

Hotel
$63-$135

Address: 500 6th St 53566 **Location:** On SR 69 S, 0.5 mi s of jct SR 81/11. **Facility:** Smoke free premises. 54 units. 2 stories (no elevator), interior corridors. **Parking:** winter plug-ins. **Amenities:** high-speed Internet. **Pool(s):** heated indoor. **Activities:** whirlpool, limited exercise equipment. **Guest Services:** wireless Internet.

ECO 🏊 BIZ ❌ 📷 🗄 🖥 🖵 / SOME UNITS FEE 🐾

------ WHERE TO DINE ------

BAUMGARTNER'S CHEESE STORE & TAVERN

Phone: 608/325-6157

Deli
$4-$12

A retail cheese outlet adjoins this tavern, where guests enjoy locally brewed beers, Wisconsin cheeses and assorted soups, sandwiches and sausages. The locals like their Limburger cheese with mustard and onion on rye bread with a cup of hearty chili. In business since 1931, this place claims to be the state's oldest cheese store. **Bar:** full bar. **Hours:** 8 am-11 pm. **Address:** 1023 16th Ave 53566 **Location:** Downtown. **Parking:** street only. **Historic**

SWISS ALPS RESTAURANT

Phone: 608/325-5900

Swiss
$7-$20

The family restaurant with a Swiss theme offers large portions of menu items such as Wiener schnitzel, chicken cordon bleu and Swiss Alps kalberwurst, as well as sandwich specialties such as bratwurst and hoagies. **Hours:** 6 am-9 pm. **Address:** 804 4th Ave W 53566 **Location:** SR 11, just s.

WORLD BUFFET

Phone: 608/329-5959

Chinese
$6-$15

A rarity in these parts, this Chinese restaurant serves ample portions of quick-serve food, offers a dine-in buffet and allows for take-out service. **Hours:** 11 am-10 pm, Fri & Sat-10:30 pm, Sun-9:30 pm. **Address:** 145 7 1/2 St 53566 **Location:** SR 69, 1 mi w. CALL ⬛

MONTELLO pop. 1,397

------ WHERE TO DINE ------

TIMBERS SUPPER CLUB

Phone: 920/293-4589

American
$12-$26

Prime rib and barbecue ribs are served daily in the popular, family-owned and operated restaurant. The modest dining room is in a tree grove in the beautiful Wisconsin countryside. Daily specials, homemade soups, broiled or fried seafood, some pork and poultry entrees and lighter selections complete the menu. **Bar:** full bar. **Hours:** 5 pm-close. Closed: 11/24, 12/24, 12/25; also Tues & Wed. **Address:** N 7085 SR 22 54960 **Location:** On SR 22, 8 mi n; between Wautoma and Montello; 2.7 mi n of jct CR J.

MUKWONAGO —See Milwaukee p. 565.

NEENAH pop. 24,507

BEST WESTERN PLUS BRIDGEWOOD RESORT HOTEL

Hotel
$139

Address: 1000 Cameron Way 54956 **Location:** US 41, exit 131 (US 10), just e to Green Bay Rd, then 0.8 mi s. **Facility:** Smoke free premises. 95 units, some two bedrooms. 3 stories, interior corridors. **Amenities:** high-speed Internet, safes (fee). **Pool(s):** heated indoor. **Activities:** whirlpools, mini water slide, cross country skiing, hiking trails, jogging, exercise room. *Fee:* golf-9 holes. **Guest Services:** valet and coin laundry, wireless Internet.

Phone: (920)720-8000

AAA Benefit:
Members save up to 20%, plus 10% bonus points with free rewards program.

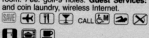

FREE full breakfast and high-speed Internet

DAYS INN OF FOX CITIES

Motel
$46-$212

Phone: (920)720-9020

Address: 495 S Green Bay Rd 54956 **Location:** US 41, exit 131 (Winneconne Ave), just e, then just n. Located in a commercial area. **Facility:** Smoke free premises. 51 units. 2 stories, interior corridors. **Parking:** winter plug-ins. **Terms:** cancellation fee imposed. **Pool(s):** heated indoor. **Activities:** whirlpool. **Guest Services:** coin laundry, wireless Internet.

HOLIDAY INN NEENAH RIVERWALK

Hotel
$75-$149

Phone: (920)725-8441

Address: 123 E Wisconsin Ave 54956 **Location:** US 41, exit 132 (Main St), 2 mi e; downtown. Located in a commercial area. **Facility:** Smoke free premises. 107 units. 7 stories, interior corridors. **Pool(s):** heated indoor. **Activities:** whirlpool, exercise room. *Fee:* game room. **Guest Services:** valet and coin laundry, wireless Internet.

NEILLSVILLE pop. 2,731

SUPER 8-NEILLSVILLE

Hotel
$59-$81

Phone: (715)743-8080

Address: 1000 E Division St 54456 **Location:** US 10, jct Boon and Division St. **Facility:** Smoke free premises. 39 units. 2 stories (no elevator), interior corridors. **Parking:** winter plug-ins. **Amenities:** high-speed Internet. **Pool(s):** heated indoor. **Activities:** whirlpool. **Guest Services:** wireless Internet.

NEW BERLIN —See Milwaukee p. 565.

NEW GLARUS pop. 2,111

CHALET LANDHAUS INN

Hotel
$85-$225

Phone: 608/527-5234

Address: 801 Hwy 69 53574 **Location:** On SR 69. **Facility:** Smoke free premises. 67 units. 3-4 stories, interior corridors. **Parking:** winter plug-ins. **Pool(s):** heated indoor. **Activities:** sauna, whirlpool, steamroom, exercise room. **Guest Services:** coin laundry, wireless Internet. **Free Special Amenities:** expanded continental breakfast and high-speed Internet.

SWISS AIRE MOTEL

Hotel
$59-$99

Phone: 608/527-2138

Address: 1200 Hwy 69 53574 **Location:** Just s of jct SR 39/69. **Facility:** Smoke free premises. 26 units. 1 story, interior/exterior corridors. **Activities:** picnic area. **Guest Services:** wireless Internet. **Free Special Amenities:** local telephone calls and high-speed Internet.

NEW LISBON pop. 1,436

TRAVELERS INN OF NEW LISBON

Hotel
$58-$159

Phone: (608)562-5141

Address: 1700 E Bridge St 53950 **Location:** I-90/94, exit 61 (SR 80), just ne. **Facility:** Smoke free premises. 61 units. 3 stories, interior corridors. **Amenities:** safes. **Pool(s):** heated indoor. **Activities:** whirlpool. **Guest Services:** wireless Internet.

NEW LONDON pop. 7,085

AMERICINN LODGE & SUITES OF NEW LONDON
Phone: (920)982-5700

Hotel
$79-$189 4/1-11/30
$59-$159 12/1-4/30

Address: 1404 N Shawano St 54961 **Location:** US 45, exit US 54, just n. Located in a commercial area. **Facility:** Smoke free premises. 49 units, some kitchens. 2 stories, interior corridors. **Parking:** winter plug-ins. **Terms:** cancellation fee imposed. **Amenities:** high-speed Internet. **Pool(s):** heated indoor. **Activities:** whirlpool, limited exercise equipment. **Guest Services:** coin laundry, wireless Internet.

------ WHERE TO DINE ------

HALF NELSON'S
Phone: 920/982-1600

American
$4-$23

The dining room is filled with sports photographs and memorabilia. On the menu is a selection of pasta, ribs, steak and Mexican dishes, as well as perch and walleye for those who enjoy fish. Booth and table seating are available. **Bar:** full bar. **Hours:** 11 am-9 pm, Fri & Sat-10 pm. Closed: 11/24, 12/25 & Easter. **Address:** 1601 N Shawano St 54961 **Location:** US 45, exit US 54, just n.

NEW RICHMOND pop. 6,310

AMERICINN MOTEL & SUITES OF NEW RICHMOND
Phone: (715)246-3993

Hotel
$69-$95

Address: 1020 S Knowles Ave 54017 **Location:** Just s on SR 65. **Facility:** Smoke free premises. 45 units. 2 stories (no elevator), interior corridors. **Parking:** winter plug-ins. **Terms:** cancellation fee imposed. **Pool(s):** heated indoor. **Activities:** sauna, whirlpool. **Guest Services:** coin laundry, wireless Internet.

OAK CREEK —See Milwaukee p. 566.

OCONOMOWOC —See Milwaukee p. 566.

OKAUCHEE —See Milwaukee p. 567.

ONALASKA pop. 14,839

BAYMONT INN & SUITES LACROSSE-ONALASKA
Phone: (608)783-7191

Hotel
$80-$179

Address: 3300 Kinney Coulee Rd N 54650 **Location:** I-90, exit 5, just ne. **Facility:** Smoke free premises. 67 units. 3 stories, interior corridors. **Parking:** winter plug-ins. **Pool(s):** heated indoor. **Activities:** whirlpool, exercise room. **Guest Services:** valet and coin laundry, wireless Internet.

COMFORT INN BY CHOICE HOTELS
Phone: (608)781-7500

Hotel
$60-$200

Address: 1223 Crossing Meadows Dr 54650 **Location:** I-90, exit 4, just e on SR 157, then w on CR SS. **Facility:** Smoke free premises. 69 units. 2 stories (no elevator), interior corridors. **Parking:** winter plug-ins. **Pool(s):** heated indoor. **Activities:** whirlpool. **Guest Services:** wireless Internet.

HAMPTON INN OF ONALASKA
Phone: (608)779-5000

Hotel
$89-$159

Address: 308 Hampton Ct 54650 **Location:** I-90, exit 5, 0.4 mi e on SR 16, just w on CR OS, then just s on Market Dr. **Facility:** Smoke free premises. 107 units. 3 stories, interior corridors. **Parking:** winter plug-ins. **Terms:** 1-7 night minimum stay, cancellation fee imposed. **Amenities:** video games (fee). **Pool(s):** heated indoor. **Activities:** whirlpool, exercise room. **Guest Services:** valet and coin laundry, wireless Internet.

> **AAA Benefit:**
> Members save up to 10% everyday!

HOLIDAY INN EXPRESS
Phone: (608)783-6555

Hotel
$109-$159

Address: 9409 Hwy 16 54650 **Location:** I-90, exit 5, 1 mi e. **Facility:** Smoke free premises. 75 units. 3 stories, interior corridors. **Parking:** winter plug-ins. **Pool(s):** heated indoor. **Activities:** whirlpool, exercise room. **Guest Services:** valet and coin laundry, wireless Internet.

MICROTEL INN
Phone: (608)783-0833

Hotel
$49-$113

Address: 3240 N Kinney Coulee Rd 54650 **Location:** I-90, exit 5, just ne. **Facility:** Smoke free premises. 63 units. 3 stories, interior corridors. **Parking:** winter plug-ins. **Terms:** cancellation fee imposed. **Guest Services:** valet and coin laundry, wireless Internet.

STONEY CREEK INN

Hotel
Rates not provided

Phone: 608/781-3060

Address: 3060 S Kinney Coulee Rd 54650 **Location:** I-90, exit 5, just se. **Facility:** Smoke free premises. 157 units. 4 stories, interior corridors. **Parking:** winter plug-ins. **Amenities:** high-speed Internet. **Pool(s):** heated indoor/outdoor. **Activities:** sauna, whirlpool, theater, exercise room. *Fee:* game room. **Guest Services:** valet and coin laundry, area transportation-Amtrak & bus station, wireless Internet.

—— WHERE TO DINE ——

CIATTI'S ITALIAN RESTAURANT

Italian
$7-$20

Phone: 608/781-8686

Both authentic and more innovative Italian dishes are served in an upscale setting. Also offered are grilled steaks, seafood and wines from an extensive list. **Bar:** full bar. **Hours:** 11 am-10 pm, Sun-9 pm. Closed: 1/1, 12/25. **Address:** 9348 US Hwy 16 54650 **Location:** I-90, exit 5, 1 mi w; in Valley Plaza Shopping Center.

MANNY'S MEXICAN COCINA

Mexican
$8-$20

Phone: 608/781-5601

The large metal sailfish statue on the grounds indicates that seafood is king at this distinctive Mexican restaurant. Manny and his team emphasize the use of freshly-made sauces and fish that is flown in daily. Seafood nachos share space with white sea bass with a citrus-based sauce that is light on calories but heavy on taste. The term "a la cocina fresca" means "made from in the kitchen," and patrons notice that difference after the first bite. **Bar:** full bar. **Hours:** 11 am-9:30 pm, Fri & Sat-10:30 pm. Closed: 11/24, 12/25. **Address:** 301 Hampton Ct 54650 **Location:** I-90, exit 5, 0.4 mi e on SR 16, just w on CR 0S, then just s.

SEVEN BRIDGES RESTAURANT

American
$8-$24

Phone: 608/783-6103

This restaurant offers nice views of the Black River and Lake Onalaska, especially at sunset. The walls are adorned with wildlife prints, and pictures of the local history. **Bar:** full bar. **Hours:** 5 pm-9 pm, Fri & Sat-10 pm. Closed: 11/24, 12/25. **Address:** 910 2nd Ave N 54650 **Location:** I-90, exit 3, 2 mi n on SR 35.

TRADITIONS RESTAURANT　*Menu on AAA.com*

American
$25-$30

Phone: 608/783-0200

In historic downtown, the upscale, fine-dining restaurant is in a restored bank and lets patrons dine in the vault for a more intimate experience. The palate-tempting, monthly changing menu reflects the tastes of the season. **Bar:** beer & wine. **Reservations:** suggested. **Hours:** 5:30 pm-10 pm. Closed major holidays; also Sun & Mon. **Address:** 201 Main St 54650 **Location:** I-90, exit 3, 1 mi n on SR 35.

OREGON pop. 7,514

—— WHERE TO DINE ——

THE DEBROUX

American
$6-$17

Phone: 608/835-3435

The dining room reflects on its historic past with stamped-tin ceilings and hardwood maple floors. The family-oriented menu includes many house specials such as charbroiled steaks and seafood. Among the many desserts are freshly baked pie and old-fashioned soda fountain creations. **Hours:** 6 am-8 pm, Fri & Sat-8:30 pm, Sun 7 am-7:30 pm. Closed: 11/24, 12/24, 12/25. **Address:** 101 S Main St 53575 **Location:** Center. **Parking:** street only.

MARIA'S PIZZA & RESTAURANT

Italian
$7-$18

Phone: 608/835-5455

The cozy restaurant offers a classic Italian menu including Sicilian dishes. Homemade lasagna, spaghetti, and a large selection of pizza are favorites. **Hours:** 4 pm-midnight, Fri & Sat-1 am, Sun-10 pm. Closed major holidays; also Mon. **Address:** 134 Main St 53575 **Location:** Center. **Parking:** street only.

OSCEOLA pop. 2,421

RIVER VALLEY INN & SUITES

Hotel
$75-$135

Phone: 715/294-4060

Address: 1030 Cascade St 54020 **Location:** Just n on SR 35. **Facility:** Smoke free premises. 31 units. 2 stories (no elevator), interior corridors. **Parking:** winter plug-ins. **Terms:** cancellation fee imposed. **Pool(s):** heated indoor. **Activities:** whirlpool, board games. **Guest Services:** coin laundry, wireless Internet. **Free Special Amenities:** continental breakfast and high-speed Internet.

OSHKOSH pop. 62,916

COMFORT SUITES

Hotel
$70-$170

Phone: (920)230-7378

Address: 400 S Koeller St 54902 **Location:** US 41, exit 117 (9th Ave), just e. **Facility:** Smoke free premises. 80 units. 4 stories, interior corridors. **Pool(s):** heated indoor. **Activities:** whirlpool, exercise room. *Fee:* game room. **Guest Services:** valet and coin laundry, wireless Internet.

FAIRFIELD INN BY MARRIOTT

Phone: (920)233-8504

Hotel
$80-$95

Address: 1800 S Koeller St 54902 **Location:** US 41, exit 117 (9th Ave), 0.8 mi s on east frontage road. Located in a commercial area. **Facility:** Smoke free premises. 57 units. 3 stories, interior corridors. **Parking:** winter plug-ins. **Terms:** cancellation fee imposed. **Pool(s):** heated indoor. **Activities:** whirlpool. **Guest Services:** valet laundry, wireless Internet.

> **AAA Benefit:**
> Members save a minimum 5% off the best available rate.

HAWTHORN INN & SUITES

Phone: (920)303-1133

Hotel
$109-$449

Address: 3105 S Washburn St 54904 **Location:** US 41, exit 116 (SR 44), just w, then just s. **Facility:** Smoke free premises. 77 units, some efficiencies. 3 stories, interior corridors. **Parking:** winter plug-ins. **Terms:** cancellation fee imposed. **Pool(s):** heated indoor. **Activities:** whirlpool, waterslide, patio deck with grills, exercise room. **Guest Services:** valet and coin laundry, wireless Internet.

HILTON GARDEN INN OSHKOSH

Phone: (920)966-1300

Hotel
$89-$125

Address: 1355 W 20th Ave 54902 **Location:** US 41, exit 116 (SR 44), 0.5 mi e. Located next to the airport. **Facility:** Smoke free premises. 126 units. 3 stories, interior corridors. **Parking:** winter plug-ins. **Terms:** 1-7 night minimum stay, cancellation fee imposed. **Amenities:** high-speed Internet. **Pool(s):** heated indoor. **Activities:** whirlpool, exercise room. **Guest Services:** valet and coin laundry, area transportation-within 10 mi, wireless Internet.

> **AAA Benefit:**
> Members save 5% or more everyday!

HOLIDAY INN EXPRESS HOTEL & SUITES

Phone: (920)303-1300

Hotel
$104-$189

Address: 2251 Westowne Ave 54904 **Location:** US 41, exit 119, 0.4 mi w of jct SR 21. Located in a commercial area. **Facility:** Smoke free premises. 69 units, some two bedrooms. 3 stories, interior corridors. **Parking:** winter plug-ins. **Terms:** cancellation fee imposed. **Pool(s):** heated indoor. **Activities:** whirlpool, exercise room. **Guest Services:** valet and coin laundry, wireless Internet.

LA QUINTA INN OSHKOSH

Phone: (920)233-4190

Hotel
$49-$102

Address: 1950 Omro Rd 54902 **Location:** US 41, exit 119, jct SR 21. Located in a commercial area. **Facility:** Smoke free premises. 97 units. 2 stories (no elevator), interior corridors. **Parking:** winter plug-ins. **Amenities:** video games (fee). *Some:* high-speed Internet. **Guest Services:** valet laundry, wireless Internet.

--- **WHERE TO DINE** ---

FRATELLO'S RESTAURANT & FOX RIVER BREWING COMPANY

Phone: 920/232-2337

American
$7-$26

Nine microbrews are crafted on the premises of this restaurant on the Fox River. Seasonal boat docking and patio dining are available. Menu selections include gourmet pizza, pasta, burgers and a few steak and seafood entrees. **Bar:** full bar. **Hours:** 11 am-10 pm, Fri & Sat-11 pm. Closed: 12/25. **Address:** 1501 Arboretum Dr 54901 **Location:** US 41, exit 119, 1 mi e on SR 21.

FRIAR TUCK'S

Phone: 920/231-9555

American
$6-$12

"Ye hearty" sandwiches are prepared on a choice of many fresh breads baked in house. Daily homemade soup is also popular. All appetizers are prepared in the deep "friar." Servers are dressed in brown monks' garb. **Bar:** full bar. **Hours:** 11 am-10 pm, Fri & Sat-11 pm. Closed major holidays. **Address:** 1651 W South Park Ave 54903 **Location:** US 41, exit 116 (SR 44), 0.4 mi e.

LARA'S TORTILLA FLATS

Phone: 920/233-4440

Northern Mexican
$7-$16

Delicious food is made from scratch with fresh ingredients and served with complimentary chips and a choice of salsa. Notable are the daily specials and traditional desserts, such as cookies and caramel, cinnamon chips and ice cream flower. The service staff is attentive. **Bar:** full bar. **Hours:** 11 am-9 pm, Thurs-Sat to 10 pm. Closed major holidays; also Sun. **Address:** 715 N Main St 54901 **Location:** Center.

MR. CINDER'S

Phone: 920/426-2288

American
$5-$16

The restaurant is locally known for its great chargrilled sandwiches, casual atmosphere and good American-style food. **Bar:** full bar. **Hours:** 11 am-10 pm, Sun-9 pm. Closed major holidays. **Address:** 2010 W 9th Ave 54904 **Location:** Jct US 41.

THE ROXY SUPPER CLUB

Phone: 920/231-1980

American
$6-$27

The downtown supper club-themed restaurant offers great all-American down-home cooking in large portions. **Bar:** full bar. **Hours:** 11 am-10 pm, Fri & Sat-11 pm, Sun 8 am-10 pm. **Address:** 571 N Main St 54901 **Location:** Center. **Parking:** on-site and street.

OSSEO pop. 1,669

—— WHERE TO DINE ——

NORSKE NOOK RESTAURANT & BAKERY
Phone: 715/597-3069

Norwegian
$5-$13

This quaint, renowned restaurant serves homemade Norwegian dishes in addition to sandwiches and breakfast. The on-premise bakery produces fresh bread and an excellent selection of pies. Menus change seasonally and includes lefse specialties. **Hours:** 5:30 am-8 pm, Sun from 8 am. Closed: 11/24, 12/25 & Easter. **Address:** 13804 W 7th St 54758 **Location:** I-94, exit 88 (US 10), 0.8 mi w. **Parking:** street only.
CALL 👤M

PEMBINE

THE FOUR SEASONS RESORT ON MISCAUNO ISLAND
Phone: (715)324-5244

Resort
Hotel
$89-$219

Address: N16800 Shoreline Dr 54156 **Location:** From US 141, 8.5 mi e on CR Z, follow signs. **Facility:** Over the years, this 100-year-old hotel has undergone many changes. It offers modern facilities and rooms. Designated smoking area. 57 units, some two bedrooms and efficiencies. 3 stories, interior corridors. **Parking:** winter plug-ins. **Terms:** 3 day cancellation notice. **Amenities:** safes. *Some:* video games (fee). **Dining:** 2 restaurants. **Pool(s):** heated indoor. **Activities:** sauna, whirlpool, rental boats, rental canoes, boat dock, fishing, sun deck, golf-9 holes, 2 lighted tennis courts, cross country skiing, rental bicycles, hiking trails, jogging, exercise room, basketball, horseshoes, volleyball. *Fee:* charter fishing, pontoon boat, massage, game room. **Guest Services:** coin laundry, wireless Internet, tanning facilities. **Free Special Amenities: expanded continental breakfast and high-speed Internet.**

SAVE 🍴 🍸 🏋 🏊 BIZ ✕ 🔌 📠 💻

PEPIN pop. 878

GREAT RIVER AMISH INN
Phone: 715/442-5400

Motel
$65-$75

Address: 311 3rd St 54759 **Location:** On SR 35; center. **Facility:** Smoke free premises. 7 units. 1 story, exterior corridors. **Parking:** winter plug-ins. **Guest Services:** wireless Internet.
🍴 ✕ 🔌 📠 💻

—— WHERE TO DINE ——

HARBOR VIEW CAFE
Phone: 715/442-3893

American
$10-$33

The ambience of this restaurant is highlighted by the historic feel and location on the Mississippi River. A chalkboard that changes twice a day presents creative cuisine made with fresh ingredients. Fresh halibut is noteworthy, and other highlights include Norwegian meatballs, beef tenderloin, saffron-braised chicken and freshly made desserts. **Bar:** full bar. **Hours:** Open 4/1-11/25 & 3/15-4/30; 11 am-2:30 & 5-8 pm, Thurs-Sat to 9 pm, Sun noon-7:30 pm; seasonal hours vary. Closed: Easter; also Tues & Wed. **Address:** 100 1st St 54759 **Location:** Just w of SR 35 on Lake Pepin; center. **Parking:** street only.

PEWAUKEE —See Milwaukee p. 567.

PLATTEVILLE pop. 9,989

COUNTRY INN & SUITES BY CARLSON
Phone: (608)348-7373

Hotel
$81-$118

Address: 630 S Water St 53818 **Location:** Jct US 151 and SR 80/81. **Facility:** Smoke free premises. 49 units. 2 stories (no elevator), interior corridors. **Terms:** cancellation fee imposed. **Pool(s):** heated indoor. **Activities:** whirlpool. **Guest Services:** coin laundry, wireless Internet. *(see ad p. 6)*
🍴 CALL 👤M 🏊 ♿ ✕ 🎦 💻 / SOME UNITS 🔌

MOUND VIEW INN
Phone: 608/348-9518

Hotel
$65-$150

Address: 1755 E Business Hwy 151 53818 **Location:** On US 151, exit 21, just w. **Facility:** Smoke free premises. 32 units. 2 stories, interior corridors. **Parking:** winter plug-ins. **Terms:** 3 day cancellation notice. **Activities:** whirlpool, limited exercise equipment. *Fee:* miniature golf. **Guest Services:** wireless Internet. 🍴 ✕ 🎦 🔌 📠 / SOME UNITS FEE 🐾

SUPER 8
Phone: (608)348-8800

Hotel
$55-$82

Address: 100 Hwy 80/81 S 53818 **Location:** Jct US 151 and SR 80. **Facility:** Smoke free premises. 72 units. 2 stories, interior corridors. **Parking:** winter plug-ins. **Activities:** whirlpool, steamroom, gazebo, access to walking & bike trail. **Guest Services:** coin laundry, wireless Internet. **Free Special Amenities: expanded continental breakfast and high-speed Internet.**
SAVE 🍴 CALL 👤M ♿ ✕ 🎦 💻 / SOME UNITS FEE 🐾 🔌 📠

—— WHERE TO DINE ——

ARTHUR HOUSE
Phone: 608/348-7899

American
$8-$20

The family-owned restaurant features nightly specials and a children's menu. Prime rib, roast duckling, pond-raised catfish and roast pork loin are among menu options. Nationally known comedy acts provide weekend entertainment. **Bar:** full bar. **Reservations:** suggested. **Hours:** 11 am-2 & 5-9 pm, Fri & Sat-10 pm, Sun 10 am-2 pm. Closed: 12/24, 12/25; also Mon & Tues. **Address:** 9315 Hwy 80 N 53818 **Location:** N on SR 80 to Arthur; on left side of SR 80.

PLEASANT PRAIRIE pop. 16,136

HOLIDAY INN EXPRESS HOTEL & SUITES
Phone: (262)942-6000

◆◆◆ ▼▼▼
Hotel
$89-$189

Address: 7887 94th Ave 53158 **Location:** I-94, exit 344 (SR 50), 1.5 mi e, then 0.3 mi s. **Facility:** Smoke free premises. 81 units, some efficiencies. 3 stories, interior corridors. **Parking:** winter plug-ins. **Amenities:** *Some:* high-speed Internet. **Pool(s):** heated indoor. **Activities:** whirlpool, exercise room. **Guest Services:** valet and coin laundry, wireless Internet.

LA QUINTA INN PLEASANT PRAIRIE KENOSHA
Phone: (262)857-7911

▼▼▼
Hotel
$55-$125

Address: 7540 118th Ave 53158 **Location:** I-94, exit 344 (SR 50), just e. Located in a quiet area. **Facility:** Smoke free premises. 91 units. 2 stories (no elevator), interior corridors. **Parking:** winter plug-ins. **Amenities:** video games (fee). *Some:* high-speed Internet. **Guest Services:** valet laundry, wireless Internet.

RADISSON HOTEL & CONFERENCE CENTER KENOSHA
Phone: (262)857-3377

◆◆◆ ▼▼▼
Hotel
$99-$199

Address: 11800 108th St 53158 **Location:** I-94, exit 347 (SR 165), just s on east frontage road. Located in a quiet area. **Facility:** Smoke free premises. 120 units. 6 stories, interior corridors. **Amenities:** video games (fee); high-speed Internet. *Some:* safes. **Pool(s):** heated indoor. **Activities:** whirlpool, picnic area, exercise room. **Guest Services:** valet and coin laundry, area transportation-within 5 mi, wireless Internet.

PLOVER pop. 10,520

AMERICINN OF PLOVER
Phone: (715)342-1244

◆◆
Hotel
$74-$109 7/1-4/30
$69-$109 4/1-6/30

Address: 1501 American Dr 54467 **Location:** I-39, exit 153 (CR B), just nw. **Facility:** Smoke free premises. 64 units. 2 stories (no elevator), interior corridors. **Parking:** winter plug-ins. **Pool(s):** heated indoor. **Activities:** sauna, whirlpool, exercise room. **Guest Services:** wireless Internet. **Free Special Amenities:** expanded continental breakfast and high-speed Internet.

COMFORT INN
Phone: (715)342-0400

▼▼▼
Hotel
$69-$99

Address: 1560 American Dr 54467 **Location:** I-39, exit 153 (CR B), just w. **Facility:** Smoke free premises. 68 units. 3 stories, interior corridors. **Amenities:** high-speed Internet. **Pool(s):** heated indoor. **Activities:** whirlpool, exercise room. **Guest Services:** valet and coin laundry, wireless Internet.

HAMPTON INN
Phone: (715)295-9900

▼▼▼
Hotel
$89-$119

Address: 3090 Village Park Dr 54467 **Location:** I-39, exit 153 (CR B), just sw. **Facility:** Smoke free premises. 64 units. 3 stories, interior corridors. **Terms:** 1-7 night minimum stay, cancellation fee imposed. **Amenities:** high-speed Internet. **Pool(s):** heated indoor. **Activities:** whirlpool, exercise room. **Guest Services:** valet laundry, wireless Internet.

> **AAA Benefit:**
> Members save up to 10% everyday!

—— WHERE TO DINE ——

THE CHARCOAL GRILL AND ROTISSERIE
Phone: 715/295-0100

◆◆ ▼▼
Barbecue
$7-$20

The grill is located in the shopping mall area. **Bar:** full bar. **Hours:** 11 am-10 pm, Sun from 9 am. Closed: 11/24, 12/25. **Address:** 190 Crossroads Dr 54467 **Location:** I-39, exit 156, just e.

HUDSON'S GRILL
Phone: 715/343-2890

▼▼
American
$6-$20

Memorabilia from the 1950s and '60s creates the atmosphere here. The menu lists a good variety of sandwiches, burgers and some entrees, such as baked spaghetti and chicken linguine. **Bar:** full bar. **Hours:** 11 am-10 pm, Fri & Sat-11 pm. Closed: 11/24, 12/25. **Address:** 1250 Commerce Pl 54467 **Location:** I-39, exit 156, just e.

SKY CLUB
Phone: 715/341-4000

◆◆◆ ▼▼
American
$14-$21

This well-established restaurant has been an area fixture since 1961. The restaurant is known for home-style cooking, and guests do not leave hungry! An extensive salad bar is set up at all times. Bread, soup, salad dressings and cheesecakes are made in-house. USDA Choice steaks are served sizzling, and there is a good selection of fresh seafood. **Bar:** full bar. **Reservations:** suggested. **Hours:** 5 pm-9 pm, Fri 4 pm-10 pm, Sat 5 pm-10 pm, Sun 10 am-9 pm. Closed: 12/24; also Mon. **Address:** 2200 Post Rd 54467 **Location:** US 51 business route, 0.7 mi n of jct SR 54.

SPRINGVILLE WHARF
Phone: 715/544-0336

▼▼▼
American
$6-$22

Patrons enjoy ample portions of home-cooking, like the chicken breast with broccoli sandwich, in a relaxed Northwoods atmosphere. **Bar:** full bar. **Hours:** 11 am-9 pm, Fri & Sat-10 pm. Closed: 1/1, 11/24, 12/25. **Address:** 1800 Post Rd 54467 **Location:** Jct SR 51, 1.2 mi n on SR 51 business route/Plover Rd.

PLYMOUTH pop. 7,781

AMERICINN MOTEL OF PLYMOUTH

Hotel
$99-$259

Phone: (920)892-2669

Address: 1708 Eastern Ave 53073 **Location:** On Business Rt SR 23, 1 mi w of jct SR 57. **Facility:** Smoke free premises. 38 units. 2 stories (no elevator), interior corridors. **Parking:** winter plug-ins. **Terms:** 2 night minimum stay - seasonal and/or weekends. **Pool(s):** heated indoor. **Activities:** sauna, whirlpool. **Guest Services:** valet laundry, wireless Internet.

BAYMONT INN & SUITES

Hotel
$89-$293

Phone: (920)893-6781

Address: 678 Walton Dr 53073 **Location:** On SR 57, just sw of jct SR 23 and 57. **Facility:** Smoke free premises. 61 units. 3 stories, interior corridors. **Parking:** winter plug-ins. **Terms:** 3 day cancellation notice-fee imposed. **Amenities:** high-speed Internet. **Pool(s):** heated indoor. **Activities:** whirlpool, exercise room. **Guest Services:** valet and coin laundry, wireless Internet.

------ **WHERE TO DINE** ------

52 STAFFORD ST

Irish
$7-$28

Phone: 920/893-0552

In a bed and breakfast in the heart of Wisconsin's famous Kettle Moraine area, the restaurant presents a menu of dishes prepared with an Irish flair. Freshwater fish, steaks and chops share menu space with several unusual dishes. **Bar:** full bar. **Hours:** 5 pm-9 pm, Fri & Sat-9:30 pm, Sun-8:30 pm. Closed major holidays. **Address:** 52 Stafford St 53073 **Location:** Center.

EXCHANGE BANK COFFEE HOUSE

American
$4-$8

Phone: 920/893-2326

In a historic bank, the restaurant features the personal service and friendly smiles that make the simple fare and great coffees even more enjoyable. **Hours:** 6 am-5:30 pm, Fri-8 pm, Sat-3 pm, Sun-1:30 pm. Closed major holidays. **Address:** 301 E Mill St 53073 **Location:** Center. **Parking:** street only.

PORTAGE pop. 9,728

BEST WESTERN RESORT & CONFERENCE CENTER

Hotel
$69-$156

Phone: (608)742-2200

Address: 2701 S CR CX 53901 **Location:** I-39, exit 92, just s, then 0.5 mi w. **Facility:** Smoke free premises. 99 units. 5 stories, interior corridors. **Amenities:** *Some:* high-speed Internet. **Pool(s):** heated indoor. **Activities:** sauna, whirlpool, exercise room. *Fee:* game room. **Guest Services:** coin laundry, wireless Internet. *(see ad p. 611)*

FREE continental breakfast and high-speed Internet

COMFORT SUITES

Hotel
$74-$189

Phone: (608)745-4717

Address: N5780 Kinney Rd 53901 **Location:** I-90/94, exit 108A (SR 78). **Facility:** Smoke free premises. 83 units. 3 stories, interior corridors. **Parking:** winter plug-ins. **Pool(s):** heated indoor. **Activities:** whirlpools, limited exercise equipment. *Fee:* game room. **Guest Services:** coin laundry, wireless Internet. **Free Special Amenities:** expanded continental breakfast and high-speed Internet.

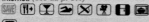

SUPER 8-PORTAGE

Hotel
$53-$58

Phone: (608)742-8330

Address: 3000 New Pinery Rd 53901 **Location:** I-39, exit 92, just s. **Facility:** Smoke free premises. 61 units. 2 stories (no elevator), interior corridors. **Parking:** winter plug-ins. **Amenities:** safes (fee). **Activities:** board games. **Guest Services:** coin laundry, wireless Internet.

── WHERE TO DINE ──

HITCHING POST

American
$6-$20

Phone: 608/742-8208

Known for homemade soups and generous portions, the local favorite has the look of a Western saloon and eatery. Steak, lobster, ribs are just some of the offerings. **Bar:** full bar. **Hours:** 11 am-9:30 pm, Fri & Sat-10 pm. Closed: 7/4, 11/24, 12/25; also Sun. **Address:** 2503 W Wisconsin St 53901 **Location:** I-39, exit 89, just n, then just w. CALL [M]

PORT WASHINGTON —See Milwaukee p. 568.

PRAIRIE DU CHIEN pop. 6,018

AMERICINN LODGE & SUITES OF PRAIRIE DU CHIEN

Hotel
$90-$140

Phone: (608)326-7878

Address: 130 S Main St 53821 **Location:** On US 18 W; east end of Mississippi River Bridge. **Facility:** Smoke free premises. 44 units. 2 stories (no elevator), interior corridors. **Amenities:** *Some:* high-speed Internet. **Pool(s):** heated indoor. **Activities:** whirlpool, limited exercise equipment. **Guest Services:** coin laundry, wireless Internet. [icons] CALL [M] [icons]

BEST WESTERN BLUFFVIEW INN & SUITES

Hotel
$80-$120

Phone: (608)326-4777

Address: 37268 US Hwy 18 S 53821 **Location:** On US 18, 1.9 mi e of jct SR 27 N. **Facility:** Smoke free premises. 42 units. 2 stories (no elevator), interior/exterior corridors. **Parking:** winter plug-ins. **Amenities:** *Some:* high-speed Internet. **Pool(s):** heated indoor. **Activities:** whirlpool, exercise room. **Guest Services:** wireless Internet.

[SAVE] [icons] CALL [M] [icons] / SOME UNITS FEE [icon]

AAA Benefit:
Members save up to 20%, plus 10% bonus points with free rewards program.

FREE full breakfast and high-speed Internet

COUNTRY INN & SUITES BY CARLSON

Hotel
$80-$149

Phone: (608)326-5700

Address: 1801 Cabela's Ln 53821 **Location:** On SR 35, 2 mi n of jct US 18/SR 35 S and 27 N. **Facility:** Smoke free premises. 64 units. 3 stories, interior corridors. **Parking:** winter plug-ins. **Amenities:** *Some:* video games. **Pool(s):** heated indoor. **Activities:** whirlpool, waterslide, indoor water park, exercise room. *Fee:* game room. **Guest Services:** coin laundry, wireless Internet. **Free Special Amenities: expanded continental breakfast and high-speed Internet.** *(see ad p. 6)*

[SAVE] [icons] CALL [M] [icons] / SOME UNITS FEE [icons]

DELTA MOTEL

Motel
Rates not provided

Phone: 608/326-4951

Address: 1733 S Marquette Rd 53821 **Location:** On US 18, 1.6 mi se of jct SR 27 N. **Facility:** Smoke free premises. 16 units. 1 story, exterior corridors. **Parking:** winter plug-ins. **Activities:** picnic area. **Guest Services:** area transportation-Riverboat Casino. [icons] / SOME UNITS [icon]

MICROTEL INN & SUITES

Hotel
$55-$129

Phone: (608)326-8476

Address: 1833 S Marquette Rd 53821 **Location:** On US 18, 1.6 mi se of jct SR 27 N. **Facility:** Smoke free premises. 59 units. 3 stories, interior corridors. **Amenities:** high-speed Internet. **Pool(s):** heated indoor/outdoor. **Activities:** whirlpool. **Guest Services:** coin laundry, wireless Internet. **Free Special Amenities: continental breakfast and high-speed Internet.**

[SAVE] [icons] CALL [M] [icons] / SOME UNITS [icons]

SUPER 8-PRAIRIE DU CHIEN

Hotel
$54-$90

Phone: 608/326-8777

Address: 1930 S Marquette Rd 53821 **Location:** On US 18, 1.9 mi e of jct SR 27 N. **Facility:** Smoke free premises. 30 units. 2 stories (no elevator), interior/exterior corridors. **Parking:** winter plug-ins. **Guest Services:** wireless Internet.

[icons] CALL [M] [icons] / SOME UNITS FEE [icon]

WINDSOR PLACE INN

Hotel
Rates not provided

Phone: 608/326-7799

Address: 1936 S Marquette Rd 53821 **Location:** On US 18, 1.9 mi e of jct SR 27 N. **Facility:** Smoke free premises. 35 units. 2 stories (no elevator), interior corridors. **Parking:** winter plug-ins. **Amenities:** high-speed Internet. **Pool(s):** heated indoor. **Activities:** whirlpool. **Guest Services:** wireless Internet. [icons]

—— **WHERE TO DINE** ——

EDDIE'S IRISH PUB

American
$4-$12

Phone: 608/326-6625

Beautiful decor in the style of an Irish pub enhances the setting, where diners sit down to a large selection of both domestic and foreign beers with tasty sandwiches. Classic hamburgers, Reuben's, various wraps and, of course, fish and chips are just a few of the selections available. **Bar:** full bar. **Hours:** 11 am-10 pm, Thurs-Sat to 11 pm. Closed: 12/24, 12/25. **Address:** 800 S Marquette Rd 53821 **Location:** On US 18, 8 mi e at jct SR 27 N. CALL &M

FORT MULLIGAN'S GRILL PUB

American
$6-$23

Phone: 608/326-0639

Homemade appetizers, sandwiches, salads, pasta, steaks, seafood and fajitas are served at the downtown eatery. **Bar:** full bar. **Hours:** 11 am-9:30 pm, Fri & Sat-10 pm, Sun-8 pm, Mon-8:30 pm. Closed: 11/24, 12/24, 12/25 & Easter. **Address:** 214 W Blackhawk Ave 53821 **Location:** Just n of US 18 W; downtown.

HUCKLEBERRY'S RESTAURANT

American
$6-$16

Phone: 608/326-5488

Recommended by locals, the mom-and-pop restaurant is a great place to get good, filling food. **Bar:** full bar. **Hours:** 6 am-9 pm, Fri & Sat-10 pm, Sun-8 pm; Fri & Sat-11 pm 6/1-10/31. Closed: 11/24, 12/25; also for dinner 1/1. **Address:** 1916 S Marquette Rd 53821 **Location:** On US 18, 1.9 mi e of jct SR 27 N. CALL &M

JEFFER'S BLACK ANGUS

Steak
$11-$32

Phone: 608/326-2222

An Old World supper club atmosphere prevails in the restaurant, which presents an extensive menu. Offerings include appetizers of shrimp cocktail and calamari, filet mignon and porterhouse steaks cooked on an open grill, fried chicken, baby back ribs, chicken Alfredo, frog legs, shrimp scampi, king crab legs, salmon and surf and turf. **Bar:** full bar. **Hours:** 4:30 pm-9 pm, Fri & Sat-10 pm. Closed: 11/24, 12/24, 12/25. **Address:** 37640 US 18 53821 **Location:** On US 18, 2 mi s of jct SR 27/35. CALL &M

PRAIRIE DU SAC pop. 3,231

—— **WHERE TO DINE** ——

BLUE SPOON CAFE

American
$7-$17

Phone: 608/643-0837

The cozy cafe is adorned with granite tables, wood floors and lots of country charm. Guests can enjoy wonderful homemade soups and delicious sandwiches made from carved-to-order delicatessen meats and freshly baked breads. For a sweet treat, indulge in smooth, freshly churned custard or homemade cheesecake. Seasonal dining on the patio lends to panoramic views overlooking the Wisconsin River. **Bar:** beer & wine. **Hours:** 6 am-8 pm, Fri & Sat-9 pm, Sun 8 am-3 pm. Closed: 1/1, 11/24, 12/25. **Address:** 550 Water St 53578 **Location:** Downtown. **Parking:** on-site and street. CALL &M

RACINE pop. 81,855

COMFORT INN RACINE

Hotel
$69-$150

Phone: (262)886-6055

Address: 1154 Prairie Dr 53406 **Location:** I-94, exit 333, 4.3 mi e on SR 20. Located in a commercial area. **Facility:** Smoke free premises. 80 units. 2 stories (no elevator), interior corridors. **Parking:** winter plug-ins. **Amenities:** safes (fee). **Activities:** whirlpool, limited exercise equipment. **Guest Services:** valet and coin laundry, wireless Internet.

 CALL &M ✕ ✈ ▤ ▥ ▭ / SOME UNITS FEE 🐾

FAIRFIELD INN BY MARRIOTT

Hotel
$81-$104

Phone: (262)886-5000

Address: 6421 Washington Ave 53406 **Location:** I-94, exit 333, 4.9 mi e on SR 20. Located in a commercial area. **Facility:** Smoke free premises. 63 units. 3 stories, interior corridors. **Parking:** winter plug-ins. **Terms:** cancellation fee imposed. **Pool(s):** heated indoor. **Activities:** whirlpool. **Guest Services:** valet laundry, wireless Internet.

AAA Benefit:
Members save a minimum 5% off the best available rate.

▤ CALL &M ➤ ♿ ✕ ✈ ▭ / SOME UNITS ▥ ▭

RACINE MARRIOTT HOTEL

Hotel
$159-$164

Phone: (262)886-6100

Address: 7111 Washington Ave 53406 **Location:** I-94, exit 333, 4 mi e on SR 20. Located in a commercial area. **Facility:** Smoke free premises. 222 units. 5 stories, interior corridors. **Terms:** cancellation fee imposed. **Amenities:** high-speed Internet (fee). **Pool(s):** heated indoor. **Activities:** whirlpool, exercise room. **Guest Services:** valet laundry, wireless Internet.

AAA Benefit:
Members save 5% or more off best available rate.

 FEE 🏊 ▤ ▾ CALL &M ➤ BIZ ✕ ✈ ▭ / SOME UNITS FEE 🐾 FEE ▥ FEE ▭

RADISSON HOTEL RACINE HARBOURWALK

Phone: (262)632-7777

Hotel
$119-$209 4/1-8/31
$99-$199 9/1-4/30

Address: 223 Gaslight Cir 53403 **Location:** Just e of Lake Ave; center. Located on harborside. **Facility:** Smoke free premises. 121 units, some efficiencies and kitchens. 3 stories, interior corridors. **Parking:** on-site (fee). **Terms:** 2 night minimum stay - seasonal and/or weekends, cancellation fee imposed. **Amenities:** video games (fee), high-speed Internet. **Pool(s):** heated indoor. **Activities:** whirlpool, exercise room. **Guest Services:** valet and coin laundry, wireless Internet.

FREE high-speed Internet and airport transportation

SUPER 8-RACINE

Phone: (262)884-0486

Hotel
$49-$90

Address: 1150 Oakes Rd 53406 **Location:** I-94, exit 333, 4 mi e on SR 20. Located in a commercial area. **Facility:** Smoke free premises. 60 units. 3 stories, interior corridors. **Parking:** winter plug-ins. **Guest Services:** coin laundry, wireless Internet. **Free Special Amenities: continental breakfast and local telephone calls.**

------- **WHERE TO DINE** -------

CHARCOAL GRILL & ROTISSERIE

Phone: 262/884-9400

American
$8-$20

The Western and sports-themed dining spot serves good pizzas, burgers, ribs, pasta and rotisserie chicken. The daily buffet features a different pasta along with a variety of pizzas and a fine salad bar. **Bar:** full bar. **Hours:** 11 am-10 pm, Fri & Sat-11 pm. Closed major holidays. **Address:** 8300 Washington Ave 53406 **Location:** I-94, exit 333, 3.6 mi e on SR 20.

CHARTROOM CHARLIES

Phone: 262/632-9901

Seafood
$5-$15

Boaters can tether their watercraft at the Chartroom dock and wander up for a casual meal in a seaside atmosphere. This place is on the banks of the Root River at Racine's harbor. **Bar:** full bar. **Hours:** 11 am-9 pm, Fri-11 pm, Sat-10 pm. Closed major holidays; also Mon. **Address:** 209 Dodge St 53402 **Location:** Just n of jct SR 32 and 38.

CORNER HOUSE

Phone: 262/637-1295

American
$10-$31

Specializing in succulent prime rib servings from petite to large, the restaurant has been owned and operated by the same family since 1945. The Friday night fish fry is popular. Most meals are geared toward hearty appetites, but an extensive lighter fare menu is also available. A complete list of foreign and domestic wines is offered. **Bar:** full bar. **Reservations:** suggested, weekends. **Hours:** 5 pm-9:30 pm, Fri & Sat-10:30 pm, Sun 4 pm-9 pm. Closed: 7/4, 12/24; also Super Bowl Sun. **Address:** 1521 Washington Ave 53403 **Location:** On SR 20, 0.3 mi w of jct SR 32.

DINO'S

Phone: 262/634-1993

Italian
$8-$24

In a residential area, this restaurant has been in the same family for 54 years. Large portions of homemade Italian pasta are well worth stopping in for. **Bar:** full bar. **Hours:** 4 pm-9 pm, Fri & Sat-10 pm. Closed: 7/4, 11/24, 12/24 & Easter. **Address:** 1816 16th St 53403 **Location:** SR 32, 0.4 mi w on 16th St; in residential area.

INFUSINO'S RESTAURANT

Phone: 262/633-3173

Italian
$8-$21

In business and serving the community for more than 35 years, this local favorite offers homemade pasta and pastries at a great value. **Bar:** full bar. **Reservations:** suggested. **Hours:** 11 am-11 pm, Fri & Sat-1 am. Closed major holidays. **Address:** 3225 Rapids Dr 53404 **Location:** Just se of jct SR 38 and CR MM.

JOSE'S BLUE SOMBRERO

Phone: 262/886-5600

Mexican
$7-$17

The restaurant and cantina considers itself a non-traditional Mexican restaurant. Besides the standard Mexican fare, the menu lists Buffalo wings dipped in spicy salsa, potato skins, shrimp fajitas, fish tacos and salmon with chipotle sauce. **Bar:** full bar. **Hours:** 11 am-10 pm, Fri & Sat-11 pm. Closed: 11/24, 12/25; also Sun. **Address:** 6430 Washington Ave 53406-3920 **Location:** I-94, exit 333, 5.3 mi e.

SALUTE AUTHENTIC ITALIAN RESTAURANT

Phone: 262/633-9117

Italian
$7-$19

A casual family atmosphere prevails at this place, where the menu lists an excellent selection of pasta, chicken, veal, steak and seafood dishes, in addition to pizza. **Bar:** full bar. **Reservations:** suggested. **Hours:** 11:30 am-2 & 4:30-9 pm, Fri-10 pm, Sat 4:30 pm-10 pm. Closed major holidays; also Sun. **Address:** 314 Main St 53403 **Location:** Just s of jct SR 32 and 38; downtown. **Parking:** street only.

THE SUMMIT

Phone: 262/886-9866

American
$8-$28

The casual restaurant is a local favorite for traditionally prepared seafood, pasta, steak, chicken and veal. Daily specials and homemade desserts don't disappoint. Friday nights usher in the all-you-can-eat fish fry. **Bar:** full bar. **Reservations:** suggested. **Hours:** 11:30 am-2 & 5-9 pm, Fri 11:30 am-2 & 4:30-10 pm, Sat 5 pm-10 pm, Sun 10 am-1:30 & 4-8 pm. Closed: 7/4. **Address:** 6825 Washington Ave 53406 **Location:** I-94, exit 333, 4.4 mi e on SR 20.

REEDSBURG pop. 7,827

QUALITY INN

Hotel
Rates not provided

Phone: 608/524-8535

Address: 2115 E Main St 53959 **Location:** 1.5 mi e on SR 23 and 33. **Facility:** Smoke free premises. 50 units, some three bedrooms and kitchens. 2 stories (no elevator), interior corridors. **Parking:** winter plug-ins. **Amenities:** *Some:* high-speed Internet. **Pool(s):** heated indoor. **Activities:** whirlpool. **Guest Services:** wireless Internet. ⊞ 🏊 ✕ 📷 🛗 📠 💻 /SOME UNITS FEE 🐾

SUPER 8-REEDSBURG

Hotel
$45-$108

Phone: (608)524-2888

Address: 1470 E Main St 53959 **Location:** 0.8 mi e on SR 23 and 33. **Facility:** Smoke free premises. 49 units. 3 stories (no elevator), interior corridors. **Parking:** winter plug-ins. **Terms:** cancellation fee imposed. **Pool(s):** heated indoor. **Activities:** whirlpool. **Guest Services:** wireless Internet. *Fee:* tanning facilities. ⊞ 🏊 ✕ 📷 🛗 📠 ☕

—— WHERE TO DINE ——

DONNIE'S RESTAURANT LLC

American
$6-$22

Phone: 608/524-8664

Each of the renovated Victorian home's small dining rooms has a distinct personality, and Green Bay Packer history finds its way into the mix on some walls. Patrons savor homemade soups and daily specials, such as liver and onions, prime rib and great all-you-can-eat fish on Fridays. **Bar:** full bar. **Reservations:** suggested. **Hours:** 6 am-9 pm, Fri & Sat-10 pm, Sun-8:30 pm. Closed: 12/25. **Address:** 1020 E Main St 53959 **Location:** 0.5 mi e on SR 23 and 33. CALL 🔊

RHINELANDER pop. 7,735

AMERICAS BEST VALUE INN

Motel
$61-$110

Phone: (715)369-5880

Address: 667 W Kemp St 54501 **Location:** On Business Rt US 8, just e of jct SR 47. **Facility:** Smoke free premises. 42 units. 2 stories, interior corridors. **Parking:** winter plug-ins. **Amenities:** high-speed Internet. **Guest Services:** wireless Internet. ⊞ CALL 🔊 👥 ✕ 📷 💻 /SOME UNITS FEE 🐾 🛗 📠

AMERICINN LODGE & SUITES OF RHINELANDER

Hotel
$74-$165

Phone: (715)369-9600

Address: 648 W Kemp St 54501 **Location:** On Business Rt US 8, 0.3 mi e of jct SR 47. **Facility:** Smoke free premises. 51 units. 2 stories, interior corridors. **Parking:** winter plug-ins. **Pool(s):** heated indoor. **Activities:** sauna, whirlpool, putting green, snowmobiling. **Guest Services:** coin laundry, wireless Internet. 🚹 ⊞ 🏊 ✕ 💻 /SOME UNITS 🛗 📠

BEST WESTERN CLARIDGE MOTOR INN

Hotel
$89-$130

Phone: (715)362-7100

Address: 70 N Stevens St 54501 **Location:** Between Davenport and Rives sts; downtown. **Facility:** Smoke free premises. 80 units, some kitchens. 2-4 stories, interior corridors. **Parking:** winter plug-ins. **Amenities:** *Some:* high-speed Internet. **Pool(s):** heated indoor. **Activities:** whirlpool, pool table, indoor recreational area, exercise room. *Fee:* game room. **Guest Services:** valet and coin laundry, wireless Internet. **Free Special Amenities:** high-speed Internet and airport transportation. 🆂 🚹 ⊞ 🍽 🍸 CALL 🔊 🏊 ✕ 💻 /SOME UNITS FEE 🐾 📠

AAA Benefit:
Members save up to 20%, plus 10% bonus points with free rewards program.

COMFORT INN

Motel
$89-$169

Phone: (715)369-1100

Address: 1490 Lincoln St 54501 **Location:** On Business Rt US 8, 2.6 mi e of jct SR 47. **Facility:** Smoke free premises. 51 units. 2 stories (no elevator), interior corridors. **Parking:** winter plug-ins. **Terms:** cancellation fee imposed. **Amenities:** high-speed Internet. **Pool(s):** heated indoor. **Activities:** sauna, whirlpool. **Guest Services:** wireless Internet. CALL 🔊 🏊 👥 ✕ 📷 💻 /SOME UNITS FEE 🐾 🛗 📠

QUALITY INN

Hotel
Rates not provided

Phone: 715/369-3600

Address: 668 W Kemp St 54501 **Location:** On Business Rt US 8, just e of jct SR 47. **Facility:** Smoke free premises. 100 units. 2 stories (no elevator), interior corridors. **Parking:** winter plug-ins. **Amenities:** high-speed Internet. **Pool(s):** heated indoor. **Activities:** sauna, whirlpool, exercise room. *Fee:* game room. **Guest Services:** valet and coin laundry, wireless Internet. 🚹 ⊞ CALL 🔊 🏊 ✕ 📷 💻 /SOME UNITS FEE 🐾 🛗 📠

—— WHERE TO DINE ——

AL-GEN DINNER CLUB

Steak
$12-$25

Phone: 715/362-2230

Constructed in 1932 using straightened hayrack wires, this log restaurant has a warm interior highlighted with rock fireplaces and wildlife prints. Barbecue ribs and walleye fillets are popular. **Bar:** full bar. **Reservations:** suggested, Sat. **Hours:** 5 pm-10 pm; hours may vary. Closed: 12/24, 12/25; also Mon. **Address:** 3428 Faust Lake Rd 54501 **Location:** 2.4 mi e on Business Rt US 8, just n.

THE RHINELANDER CAFE & PUB
Phone: 715/362-2918

American
$5–$39

Situated downtown and very popular with the locals, you can expect friendly service and a warm atmosphere. **Bar:** full bar. **Reservations:** suggested. **Hours:** 7 am-10 pm; hours may vary. Closed: 11/24, 12/25; also for dinner 12/24. **Address:** 33 N Brown 54501 **Location:** Between Davenport and Rives sts; downtown.

WOLFF'S LOG CABIN
Phone: 715/362-2686

American
$6–$16

A wide selection of reasonably priced items makes up the menu at the modern restaurant. **Bar:** full bar. **Hours:** 6:30 am-9:30 pm. Closed: 11/24, 12/25. **Address:** 721 W Kemp St 54501 **Location:** On Business Rt US 8, just e of jct SR 47.

RICE LAKE pop. 8,320

AMERICINN MOTEL & SUITES OF RICE LAKE
Phone: 715/234-9060

Hotel
Rates not provided

Address: 2906 Pioneer Ave S 54868 **Location:** US 53, exit 140 (CR O), 0.7 mi e. **Facility:** Smoke free premises. 43 units. 2 stories (no elevator), interior corridors. **Parking:** winter plug-ins. **Pool(s):** heated indoor. **Activities:** whirlpool. **Fee:** game room. **Guest Services:** valet and coin laundry, wireless Internet.

BEST WESTERN INN
Phone: (715)234-7017

Hotel
$77–$85

Address: 2835 S Main St 54868 **Location:** US 53, exit 140 (CR O), 1 mi e. **Facility:** Smoke free premises. 63 units. 2 stories (no elevator), interior corridors. **Parking:** winter plug-ins. **Amenities:** high-speed Internet. **Pool(s):** heated indoor. **Activities:** sauna, whirlpool, exercise room. **Guest Services:** valet laundry, wireless Internet. **Free Special Amenities:** expanded continental breakfast and high-speed Internet.

AAA Benefit:
Members save up to 20%, plus 10% bonus points with free rewards program.

MICROTEL INN & SUITES
Phone: (715)736-2010

Hotel
$62–$80

Address: 2771 Decker Dr 54868 **Location:** US 53, exit 140 (CR O), just ne. **Facility:** Smoke free premises. 56 units. 3 stories, interior corridors. **Parking:** winter plug-ins. **Activities:** limited exercise equipment. **Guest Services:** wireless Internet.

WHERE TO DINE

ADVENTURES A SPORTING CAFE' & PUB
Phone: 715/434-4040

American
$6–$22

Serving fresh fish, hand-cut steaks and homemade soups in a Northwoods setting, the sports bar restaurant offers an inviting, warm atmosphere with its roaring fireplace and lodge-style decor. This one shouldn't be missed. **Bar:** full bar. **Hours:** 11 am-10:30 pm, Fri-11 pm, Sun 10 am-9 pm. Closed: 11/24, 12/25. **Address:** 2901 College Dr 54868 **Location:** US 53, exit 140 (CR O), 0.5 mi e.

LEHMAN'S SUPPER CLUB
Phone: 715/234-2428

American
$4–$41

On the southeast side of town, this restaurant has been in the same family since 1934 and offers such specialties as aged steak, several types of fish, ribs, chicken and pasta dishes. Dinner entrees include a relish dish, soup and salad. Desserts are available. **Bar:** full bar. **Reservations:** suggested. **Hours:** 11 am-9:30 pm, Fri & Sat-10 pm, Sun-9 pm. Closed: 1/1, 11/24, 12/24, 12/25; also Mon. **Address:** 2911 S Main St 54868 **Location:** SR 53, exit 140 (CR O).

NORSKE NOOK RESTAURANT & BAKERY
Phone: 715/234-1733

Norwegian
$6–$12

Norwegian specialties, sandwiches, breakfast dishes and freshly baked breads and pies are the attraction at the relaxed restaurant. **Hours:** 6 am-8 pm, Sun from 8 am; seasonal hours may vary. Closed: 11/24, 12/25 & Easter. **Address:** 2900 Pioneer Ave 54868 **Location:** US 53, exit 140 (CR O), 0.7 mi e.

RICHLAND CENTER pop. 5,114

THE CENTER LODGE
Phone: 608/647-8988

Hotel
$70–$90

Address: 100 Foundry Dr 53581 **Location:** 0.9 mi e on US 14. **Facility:** Smoke free premises. 45 units. 2 stories (no elevator), interior corridors. **Parking:** winter plug-ins. **Terms:** 10 day cancellation notice. **Pool(s):** heated indoor. **Activities:** whirlpool, exercise room. **Guest Services:** wireless Internet.

RAMADA INN
Phone: (608)647-8869

Hotel
$68–$109

Address: 1450 Veterans Dr 53581 **Location:** 0.5 mi e on US 14. **Facility:** Smoke free premises. 43 units. 2 stories, interior corridors. **Parking:** winter plug-ins. **Amenities:** Some: safes. **Pool(s):** heated indoor. **Activities:** whirlpool, exercise room. **Guest Services:** coin laundry, wireless Internet.

—— **WHERE TO DINE** ——

CAFE FIESTA FE

Tex-Mex
$6-$16

Phone: 608/647-4732

In a renovated downtown building, this surprising find is worth the stop. The friendly staff and Mexican motif complement the authentic Mexican dishes, many of which incorporate in-house-made sauces. Mexican wedding cake is worth a second taste. **Bar:** beer & wine. **Hours:** 11 am-9 pm, Mon-7 pm. Closed major holidays; also Sun. **Address:** 130 S Main St 53581 **Location:** 0.5 mi w of jct US 14/SR 80 (Main St).

RIPON pop. 6,828

AMERICINN LODGE & SUITES OF RIPON

Hotel
$69-$199

Phone: (920)748-7578

Address: 1219 W Fond du Lac St 54971 **Location:** 1.8 mi w on SR 23. **Facility:** Smoke free premises. 42 units. 2 stories (no elevator), interior corridors. **Parking:** winter plug-ins. **Terms:** cancellation fee imposed. **Amenities:** *Some:* high-speed Internet. **Pool(s):** heated indoor. **Activities:** sauna, whirlpool. *Fee:* game room. **Guest Services:** wireless Internet.

COMFORT SUITES AT ROYAL RIDGES

Hotel
$90-$259

Phone: (920)748-5500

Address: 2 Westgate Dr 54971 **Location:** 2 mi w on SR 23. **Facility:** Smoke free premises. 72 units. 3 stories, interior corridors. **Parking:** winter plug-ins. **Amenities:** safes (fee). **Pool(s):** heated indoor. **Activities:** whirlpool, limited exercise equipment. *Fee:* game room. **Guest Services:** coin laundry, wireless Internet.

RIPON WELCOME INN & SUITES

Hotel
Rates not provided

Phone: 920/748-2821

Address: 240 E Fond du Lac St 54971 **Location:** Jct SR 23 and 49. Located in a commercial residential area. **Facility:** Smoke free premises. 38 units. 2 stories (no elevator), interior corridors. **Parking:** winter plug-ins. **Terms:** office hours 6 am-11 pm. **Activities:** limited exercise equipment. **Guest Services:** valet laundry, wireless Internet.

RIVER FALLS pop. 12,560

CROSSINGS BY GRANDSTAY INN & SUITES

Hotel
$69-$140

Phone: (715)425-9500

Address: 1525 Commerce Ct 54022 **Location:** Just n of jct SR 65 and 35. **Facility:** Smoke free premises. 46 units. 2 stories, interior corridors. **Terms:** cancellation fee imposed. **Pool(s):** heated indoor. **Activities:** whirlpool. *Fee:* game room. **Guest Services:** coin laundry, wireless Internet. **Free Special Amenities:** continental breakfast and high-speed Internet.

RIVERVIEW HOTEL & SUITES

Hotel
$90-$160

Phone: (715)425-1045

Address: 100 Spring St 54022 **Location:** Downtown. **Facility:** Smoke free premises. 86 units. 3 stories, interior corridors. **Pool(s):** heated indoor. **Activities:** whirlpool, exercise room. **Guest Services:** coin laundry, wireless Internet.

ROME pop. 1,700

SHERMALOT MOTEL

Motel
$79-$125

Phone: 715/325-2626

Address: 1148 W Queens Way 54457 **Location:** 1.5 mi s on SR 13. **Facility:** Smoke free premises. 23 units. 2 stories (no elevator), exterior corridors. **Terms:** open 4/1-12/1, 3 day cancellation notice. **Activities:** boat ramp, fishing. *Fee:* pool & tennis privileges. **Guest Services:** wireless Internet.

ROTHSCHILD pop. 4,970

CANDLEWOOD SUITES - WAUSAU

Extended Stay
Hotel
$79-$149

Phone: (715)355-8900

Address: 803 Industrial Park Dr 54474 **Location:** I-39, exit 185 (Business Rt US 51), just se. **Facility:** Smoke free premises. 83 efficiencies. 3 stories, interior corridors. **Parking:** winter plug-ins. **Amenities:** high-speed Internet. **Activities:** snowmobiling, exercise room. **Guest Services:** complimentary laundry, wireless Internet.

COMFORT INN

Hotel
$63-$100

Phone: (715)355-4449

Address: 1510 County Hwy XX 54474 **Location:** I-39, exit 185 (Business Rt US 51), just se. Located in a commercial area. **Facility:** Smoke free premises. 60 units. 2 stories (no elevator), interior corridors. **Parking:** winter plug-ins. **Pool(s):** heated indoor. **Activities:** whirlpool. **Guest Services:** valet and coin laundry, wireless Internet.

GRAND LODGE BY STONEY CREEK

Phone: (715)241-6300

Hotel
$99-$349

Address: 805 Creske Ave 54474 **Location:** I-39, exit 185 (Business Rt US 51), just se. Located in a commercial area. **Facility:** Smoke free premises. 139 units, some two bedrooms and kitchens. 3 stories, interior corridors. **Terms:** 2 night minimum stay - seasonal and/or weekends, cancellation fee imposed. **Activities:** water park, exercise room. *Fee:* game room. **Guest Services:** valet and coin laundry, wireless Internet.

HOLIDAY INN HOTEL & SUITES

Phone: (715)355-1111

Hotel
$94-$159

Address: 1000 Imperial Ave 54474 **Location:** I-39, exit 185 (Business Rt US 51), just se. Located in a commercial area. **Facility:** 148 units. 4 stories, interior corridors. **Parking:** winter plug-ins. **Amenities:** *Some:* high-speed Internet. **Dining:** Green Mill Restaurant & Bar, see separate listing. **Pool(s):** heated indoor. **Activities:** whirlpool, exercise room. *Fee:* game room. **Guest Services:** valet and coin laundry, wireless Internet.

MOTEL 6 ROTHSCHILD

Phone: 715/355-3030

Hotel
Rates not provided

Address: 904 Industrial Park Ave 54474 **Location:** I-39, exit 185 (Business Rt US 51), just se. Located in a commercial area. **Facility:** 39 units. 2 stories (no elevator), interior corridors. **Parking:** winter plug-ins. **Pool(s):** heated indoor. **Activities:** whirlpool. **Guest Services:** wireless Internet.

STONEY CREEK INN

Phone: (715)355-6858

Hotel
$79-$180

Address: 1100 Imperial Ave 54474 **Location:** I-39, exit 185 (Business Rt US 51), just e. Located in a commercial area. **Facility:** Smoke free premises. 107 units. 3 stories, interior corridors. **Parking:** winter plug-ins. **Terms:** cancellation fee imposed. **Amenities:** high-speed Internet. **Pool(s):** heated indoor. **Activities:** sauna, whirlpool, snowmobiling, exercise room. *Fee:* game room. **Guest Services:** valet and coin laundry, wireless Internet.

------ **WHERE TO DINE** ------

GREEN MILL RESTAURANT & BAR

Phone: 715/355-9200

American
$8-$16

The eatery prepares top-notch pizzas; a good variety of appetizers, salads, sandwiches and pasta; and some steaks and seafood. Diablo wings are a great way to start the meal. **Bar:** full bar. **Hours:** 6:30 am-10 pm, Fri & Sat-11 pm. Closed: 7/4, 12/25. **Address:** 1000 Imperial Ave 54474 **Location:** I-39, exit 185 (Business Rt US 51), just se; in Holiday Inn Hotel & Suites.

ST. CROIX FALLS pop. 2,033

HOLIDAY INN EXPRESS HOTEL & SUITES

Phone: (715)483-5775

Hotel
$110-$135

Address: 2190 E US Hwy 8 54024 **Location:** On US 8, 1.3 mi e of jct SR 35 S. **Facility:** Smoke free premises. 80 units. 4 stories, interior corridors. **Parking:** winter plug-ins. **Terms:** cancellation fee imposed. **Amenities:** high-speed Internet. **Pool(s):** heated indoor. **Activities:** whirlpool, exercise room. *Fee:* game room. **Guest Services:** valet laundry, wireless Internet.

ST. GERMAIN pop. 1,932

------ **WHERE TO DINE** ------

GOLDEN PINES

Phone: 715/479-7178

American
$9-$35

In a massive log building with open beams, this charming restaurant is warm and inviting. The menu, with most dishes freshly prepared, include prime rib, roast duck, Wiener schnitzel, chops and seafood. Dessert selections include varieties of pies. **Bar:** full bar. **Reservations:** suggested. **Hours:** 4 pm-10 pm; hours may vary. Closed: 11/24, 12/25; also Sun 3/15-4/15. **Address:** 8000 Hwy 70 E 54558 **Location:** On SR 70, 1 mi e.

SAUK CITY pop. 3,109

CEDARBERRY INN

Phone: (608)643-6625

Hotel
$88-$157

Address: 855 Phillips Blvd 53583 **Location:** On US 12, 0.5 mi w. **Facility:** Smoke free premises. 44 units. 2 stories, interior corridors. **Parking:** winter plug-ins. **Pool(s):** heated indoor. **Activities:** sauna, whirlpool. *Fee:* game room. **Guest Services:** coin laundry, wireless Internet.

------ **WHERE TO DINE** ------

GREEN ACRES

Phone: 608/643-2305

American
$10-$35

This is the place to be for great certified Angus steaks and a popular Friday fish fry. The wine list features varieties from the local Wollersheim Winery. **Bar:** full bar. **Hours:** 4 pm-9 pm, Fri & Sat-10 pm. Closed: 11/24, 12/24, 12/25 & Easter. **Address:** 7437 Hwy 78 53583 **Location:** Jct US 12 and SR 78.

LEYSTRA'S VENTURE RESTAURANT

Phone: 608/643-2004

American
$6-$14

The building was built in 1900 as a wagon shop, became a milk plant in the 1940s, later became an ice cream and cheese shop and finally was remodeled into a restaurant in the 1970s. The locally owned and operated restaurant offers family-style menus, daily specials, sandwiches, salads and freshly baked pastries, as well as all-day breakfast items. **Reservations:** suggested. **Hours:** 6 am-8 pm, Fri-9 pm. Closed: 11/24, 12/25 & Easter. **Address:** 200 Phillips Blvd 53583 **Location:** Jct John Adams St and US 12; downtown.

SAUKVILLE —See Milwaukee p. 568.

SCHOFIELD pop. 2,117

COUNTRY INN & SUITES BY CARLSON, WAUSAU

Phone: (715)359-1881

Hotel
$78-$111

Address: 1520 Metro Dr 54476 **Location:** On Business Rt US 51, 1 mi n of jct SR 29. Located in a commercial area. **Facility:** Smoke free premises. 50 units, some two bedrooms and kitchens. 2 stories, interior corridors. **Parking:** winter plug-ins. **Terms:** cancellation fee imposed. **Pool(s):** heated indoor. **Activities:** whirlpool, limited exercise equipment. **Guest Services:** valet and coin laundry, wireless Internet. *(see ad p. 6)*

—— WHERE TO DINE ——

LOG CABIN RESTAURANT

Phone: 715/359-3669

American
$6-$17

A beautiful log cabin exterior and interior, right down to the stuffed animals on the high ceilings, marks this restaurant, where the motto is "real home-cooked foods without shortcuts." Breakfast is served anytime. **Bar:** beer & wine. **Hours:** 24 hours, Sun-9 pm, Mon 6 am-9 pm. **Address:** 1522 Metro Dr 54476 **Location:** 1.3 mi ne of jct Business Rt US 51 and SR 29.

SHAWANO pop. 8,298

COMFORT INN & SUITES

Phone: (715)524-9090

Hotel
$80-$190

Address: W7393 River Bend Rd 54166 **Location:** SR 29, exit 225, just n on SR 22. **Facility:** Smoke free premises. 65 units. 3 stories, interior corridors. **Amenities:** high-speed Internet, safes (fee). **Pool(s):** heated indoor. **Activities:** whirlpool, exercise room. **Guest Services:** valet and coin laundry, wireless Internet.

SUPER 8-SHAWANO

Phone: (715)526-6688

Motel
$49-$72

Address: 211 Waukechon St 54166 **Location:** 1.2 mi e on SR 29 business route; SR 29, exit 227, 1.8 mi n, then 1.1 mi w. **Facility:** 55 units. 2 stories (no elevator), interior corridors. **Parking:** winter plug-ins. **Amenities:** safes (fee). **Guest Services:** coin laundry, wireless Internet.

—— WHERE TO DINE ——

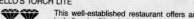

ANELLO'S TORCH LITE

Phone: 715/526-5680

American
$9-$25

This well-established restaurant offers an extensive menu selection of both American and Italian dishes, including traditional steak, chicken, seafood and barbecue ribs, as well as house specialties of delicious lasagna, manicotti and beef-roll sausage. **Bar:** full bar. **Hours:** 4 pm-10 pm; hours may vary. Closed: 11/24, 12/24. **Address:** 1276 E Green Bay St 54166 **Location:** 1.8 mi e on SR 29 business route.

SHEBOYGAN pop. 50,792

AMERICINN MOTEL & SUITES OF SHEBOYGAN

Phone: 920/208-8130

Hotel
Rates not provided

Address: 3664 S Taylor Dr 53081 **Location:** I-43, exit 123, just e. Located in a commercial area. **Facility:** Smoke free premises. 60 units. 3 stories, interior corridors. **Parking:** winter plug-ins. **Pool(s):** heated indoor. **Activities:** whirlpool. **Guest Services:** valet and coin laundry, wireless Internet.

BLUE HARBOR RESORT AND CONFERENCE CENTER

Phone: (920)452-2900

Hotel
$109-$449

Address: 725 Blue Harbor Dr 53081 **Location:** I-43, exit SR 23 E. **Facility:** Smoke free premises. 246 units, some houses. 1-4 stories, interior/exterior corridors. **Terms:** check-in 4 pm, 3 day cancellation notice-fee imposed. **Amenities:** video games (fee), high-speed Internet, safes. **Dining:** 4 restaurants. **Pool(s):** heated outdoor, heated indoor. **Activities:** whirlpool, waterslide, lifeguard on duty, water park, recreation programs, jogging, exercise room, spa. *Fee:* kayaks, shoreline cruises, game room. **Guest Services:** valet and coin laundry, area transportation (fee)-within 5 mi & water taxi, wireless Internet. *(see ad p. 193)*

COMFORT INN BY CHOICE HOTELS-SHEBOYGAN

Phone: (920)457-7724

Hotel
$89-$150

Address: 4332 N 40th St 53083 **Location:** I-43, exit 128, 0.3 mi e on Business Rt SR 42. Located in a commercial area. **Facility:** Smoke free premises. 59 units. 2 stories (no elevator), interior corridors. **Parking:** winter plug-ins. **Terms:** cancellation fee imposed. **Amenities:** safes (fee). **Pool(s):** heated indoor. **Activities:** whirlpool. **Guest Services:** valet laundry, wireless Internet.

GRANDSTAY RESIDENTIAL SUITES HOTEL

Phone: (920)208-8000

Extended Stay Hotel
$90-$170

Address: 708 Niagara Ave 53081 **Location:** Downtown. **Facility:** Smoke free premises. 71 efficiencies, some two bedrooms. 4 stories, interior corridors. **Terms:** cancellation fee imposed. **Amenities:** high-speed Internet. **Pool(s):** heated indoor. **Activities:** whirlpool, exercise room, basketball. **Guest Services:** valet and coin laundry, wireless Internet. **Free Special Amenities:** continental breakfast and high-speed Internet.

HARBOR WINDS HOTEL

Phone: 920-452-9000

Hotel
Rates not provided

Address: 905 S 8th St 53081 **Location:** Jct Riverfront Dr; s of downtown; on riverfront boardwalk. **Facility:** Smoke free premises. 28 units. 2 stories (no elevator), interior corridors. **Guest Services:** valet laundry, wireless Internet.

HOLIDAY INN EXPRESS SHEBOYGAN

Phone: (920)451-8700

Hotel
$129-$169

Address: 3823 Germaine Ave 53081 **Location:** I-43, exit 123, just se. **Facility:** Smoke free premises. 99 units. 3 stories, interior corridors. **Parking:** winter plug-ins. **Amenities:** high-speed Internet. **Pool(s):** heated indoor. **Activities:** exercise room. **Guest Services:** valet laundry, wireless Internet.

LA QUINTA INN SHEBOYGAN

Phone: (920)457-2321

Hotel
$59-$129

Address: 2932 Kohler Memorial Dr 53081 **Location:** I-43, exit 126, 1 mi e on SR 23. Located in a commercial area. **Facility:** Smoke free premises. 96 units, some kitchens. 2 stories (no elevator), interior corridors. **Parking:** winter plug-ins. **Amenities:** video games (fee). **Guest Services:** valet laundry, wireless Internet.

——— WHERE TO DINE ———

CITY STREETS-RIVERSIDE

Phone: 920/457-9050

American
$7-$40

Within walking distance of Lake Michigan and lake shore specialty shops, the restaurant is popular for its fresh seafood. The area's nautical theme is maintained in the dining room decor. Good choices include locally caught broiled whitefish and salmon. Steaks, grilled pork loin and other American dishes are also offered. **Bar:** full bar. **Hours:** 11 am-2 & 5-9 pm, Fri-10 pm, Sat 5 pm-10 pm. Closed: Sun. **Address:** 712 Riverfront Dr 53081 **Location:** E of 8th St on Virginia; in Riverfront District.

THE MUCKY DUCK SHANTY

Phone: 920/457-5577

American
$5-$17

On the docks overlooking the harbor, the eatery resembles a fishing shack from the outside, with its nautical theme and outside seating. Varied pasta dishes complement a menu that overwhelming focuses on seafood. **Bar:** full bar. **Hours:** 11 am-9 pm, Sun-8 pm. Closed: 11/24, 12/25 & Easter; also Super Bowl Sun. **Address:** 701 Riverfront Dr 53081 **Location:** E of 8th St; in Riverfront District.

RUPP'S LODGE DOWNTOWN

Phone: 920/459-8155

American
$6-$45

The family-owned restaurant delivers basic American fare—steaks, sandwiches and specials—with some selections of fresh local fish. The large salad bar is included with meals. Tables are nicely spaced throughout the supper club-style dining room. **Bar:** full bar. **Reservations:** suggested. **Hours:** 11 am-2 & 4-9 pm, Fri-10 pm, Sat 4 pm-10 pm, Sun 4 pm-9 pm. Closed major holidays. **Address:** 925 N 8th St 53081 **Location:** Downtown. **Parking:** street only.

TRATTORIA STEFANO

Phone: 920/452-8455

Italian
$12-$29

The informal and lively restaurant, with simple wood tables and a trendy decor, complements its fine Italian dishes with good selection of Italian wines. **Bar:** full bar. **Reservations:** suggested. **Hours:** 5 pm-9 pm, Fri & Sat-10 pm. Closed major holidays; also Sun. **Address:** 522 S 8th St 53081 **Location:** Downtown.

WHISTLING STRAITS

Phone: 920/565-6080

American
$9-$43

Whistling Straits Golf Resort opened in 1998 and offers two courses of dynamic contrast, one called Windswept and the other called Tranquil. The restaurant has a serene atmosphere and features American cuisine with a British Isles flair. **Bar:** full bar. **Reservations:** suggested. **Hours:** Open 4/1-12/31; 6 am-10 pm. Closed: 12/25. **Address:** N8501 County Rd LS 53083 **Location:** I-43, exit 128 (SR 42), just e to 40th St (Dairyland Rd), 4 mi n to CR FF, then 1 mi e.

SHEBOYGAN FALLS pop. 6,772

DAYS INN & SUITES

Hotel
$45-$225

Phone: (920)467-4314

Address: 600 Hwy 32 N 53085 **Location:** SR 23, exit 32 (Sheboygan Falls/Howards Grove), just w. **Facility:** Smoke free premises. 43 units. 2 stories (no elevator), interior corridors. **Amenities:** Some: high-speed Internet. **Pool(s):** heated indoor. **Activities:** sauna, whirlpool, limited exercise equipment. **Guest Services:** valet laundry, wireless Internet. **Free Special Amenities: expanded continental breakfast and high-speed Internet.**

THE ROCHESTER INN, A HISTORIC HOTEL

Historic Bed & Breakfast
$99-$169

Phone: 920/467-3123

Address: 504 Water St 53085 **Location:** Just e of downtown via CR PP. **Facility:** This 1848 Greek Revival B&B features two-level suites, four-poster beds, wet bars and large, jetted tubs. Smoke free premises. 6 units. 3 stories (no elevator), interior corridors. **Terms:** office hours 7 am-7 pm, 2 night minimum stay - seasonal and/or weekends, age restrictions may apply, 14 day cancellation notice-fee imposed. **Guest Services:** wireless Internet.

SHELL LAKE pop. 1,309

AMERICA'S BEST INN & SUITES

Hotel
$89-$189 6/2-4/30
$69-$155 4/1-6/1

Phone: (715)468-4494

Address: 315 Hwy 63 S 54871 **Location:** On SR 63, just s. **Facility:** Smoke free premises. 41 units. 2 stories (no elevator), interior corridors. **Parking:** winter plug-ins. **Terms:** cancellation fee imposed. **Amenities:** high-speed Internet. **Pool(s):** heated indoor. **Activities:** sauna, whirlpool, waterslide. **Guest Services:** coin laundry.

SIREN pop. 988

BEST WESTERN NORTHWOODS LODGE

Hotel
$69-$129

Phone: (715)349-7800

Address: 23986 SR 35 S 54872 **Location:** On SR 35 at SR 70 W and CR B E. **Facility:** Smoke free premises. 40 units. 2 stories, interior corridors. **Parking:** winter plug-ins. **Amenities:** high-speed Internet. **Pool(s):** heated indoor. **Activities:** sauna, whirlpool, board games. **Guest Services:** coin laundry, wireless Internet. **Free Special Amenities: continental breakfast and high-speed Internet.**

AAA Benefit:
Members save up to 20%, plus 10% bonus points with free rewards program.

THE LODGE AT CROOKED LAKE

Hotel
$89-$265

Phone: (715)349-2500

Address: 24271 SR 35 N 54872 **Location:** On SR 35, 0.5 mi n of jct SR 70. **Facility:** Smoke free premises. 60 units. 2 stories, interior corridors. **Parking:** winter plug-ins. **Terms:** 2 night minimum stay - seasonal and/or weekends. **Amenities:** high-speed Internet. **Pool(s):** heated indoor. **Activities:** sauna, whirlpool, fishing, cross country skiing, snowmobiling, bicycles, hiking trails, exercise room. **Fee:** miniature golf. **Guest Services:** valet laundry, wireless Internet. **Free Special Amenities: expanded continental breakfast and high-speed Internet.**

PINE WOOD MOTEL

Motel
$35-$65

Phone: 715/349-5225

Address: 23862 Hwy 35 S 54872 **Location:** On SR 35, 0.3 mi s of jct SR 70 W and CR B E. **Facility:** Smoke free premises. 14 units. 1 story, exterior corridors. **Parking:** winter plug-ins. **Terms:** cancellation fee imposed.

—— WHERE TO DINE ——

ADVENTURES RESTAURANT & PUB

American
$7-$18

Phone: 715/349-8500

It seems only right that diners can enjoy eating in a northwoods-themed restaurant up in the northwoods. Offering an extensive menu of pub favorites, the menu also features burgers, steaks and locally caught walleye. **Bar:** full bar. **Hours:** 11 am-10 pm, Fri & Sat-11 pm; seasonal hours may vary. Closed major holidays. **Address:** 7710 Park Rd W 54872 **Location:** On SR 35, 0.5 mi n of jct SR 70; beside The Lodge at Crooked Lake. CALL

SISTER BAY — See Door County p. 468.

SPARTA pop. 8,648

BEST WESTERN PLUS SPARTA TRAIL LODGE

Hotel
S89-$129

Address: 4445 Theatre Rd 54656 **Location:** I-90, exit 28 (SR 16), just w. **Facility:** Smoke free premises. 80 units. 3 stories, interior corridors. **Parking:** winter plug-ins. **Amenities:** high-speed Internet, safes. **Pool(s):** heated indoor. **Activities:** sauna, whirlpool, waterslide, exercise room. *Fee:* game room. **Guest Services:** coin laundry, wireless Internet. **Free Special Amenities: expanded continental breakfast and high-speed Internet.**

Phone: (608)269-2664

AAA Benefit:
Members save up to 20%, plus 10% bonus points with free rewards program.

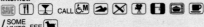
/ SOME UNITS FEE

COUNTRY INN & SUITES BY CARLSON

Hotel
$87-$148

Address: 737 Avon Rd 54656 **Location:** I-90, exit 25 (SR 27), just n. **Facility:** Smoke free premises. 61 units. 2 stories (no elevator), interior corridors. **Parking:** winter plug-ins. **Pool(s):** heated indoor. **Activities:** whirlpool. **Guest Services:** coin laundry, wireless Internet. *(see ad p. 6)*

Phone: (608)269-3110

 / SOME UNITS FEE

SUPER 8 SPARTA

Hotel
$71-$113

Address: 716 Avon Rd 54656 **Location:** I-90, exit 25 (SR 27), just n. **Facility:** Smoke free premises. 49 units. 2 stories (no elevator), interior corridors. **Parking:** winter plug-ins. **Amenities:** safes (fee). **Pool(s):** heated indoor. **Activities:** whirlpool, picnic facilities. **Guest Services:** coin laundry, wireless Internet.

Phone: (608)269-8489

/ SOME UNITS FEE

SPOONER pop. 2,653

BEST WESTERN AMERICAN HERITAGE INN

Hotel
Rates not provided

Address: 101 W Maple St 54801 **Location:** On SR 70, just e of US 63, 1 mi w of US 53. **Facility:** Smoke free premises. 45 units, some kitchens. 2 stories (no elevator), interior corridors. **Amenities:** high-speed Internet. **Pool(s):** heated indoor. **Activities:** sauna, whirlpool, snowmobiling, ATV trail, bicycle trails. *Fee:* game room. **Guest Services:** wireless Internet. **Free Special Amenities: expanded continental breakfast and high-speed Internet.**

Phone: 715/635-9770

AAA Benefit:
Members save up to 20%, plus 10% bonus points with free rewards program.

/ SOME UNITS FEE

COUNTRY HOUSE MOTEL & RV PARK

Motel
Rates not provided

Address: 717 S River St 54801 **Location:** On US 63, 0.5 mi s of jct SR 70. **Facility:** Smoke free premises. 23 units. 1-2 stories (no elevator), interior/exterior corridors. **Parking:** winter plug-ins (fee). **Amenities:** *Some:* high-speed Internet. **Pool(s):** heated indoor. **Activities:** whirlpool. *Fee:* video games. **Guest Services:** wireless Internet. **Free Special Amenities: local telephone calls and high-speed Internet.**

Phone: 715/635-8721

/ SOME UNITS FEE

INN TOWN MOTEL

Motel
$40-$70

Address: 801 River St 54801 **Location:** 0.8 mi n of jct US 63 and SR 70. **Facility:** Smoke free premises. 20 units. 1 story, exterior corridors. **Parking:** winter plug-ins. **Terms:** office hours 7 am-10 pm, 3 day cancellation notice-fee imposed. **Guest Services:** coin laundry, wireless Internet.

Phone: 715/635-3529

/ SOME UNITS FEE

—— **WHERE TO DINE** ——

FOXXY'S BAR AND GRILLE

American
$8-$33

A short drive from hotels, the popular, sometimes boisterous, restaurant is well known for its extensive menu. **Bar:** full bar. **Hours:** 4 pm-9 pm, Mon-8 pm. Closed: 7/4, 11/24, 12/25; also Sun. **Address:** N5295 Rocky Ridge Rd 54801 **Location:** Jct River and Elm sts, 1 mi w on Elm St.

Phone: 715/635-2399

SPRING GREEN pop. 1,444

HILL STREET BED & BREAKFAST

Bed & Breakfast
$85-$115

Address: 353 W Hill St 53588 **Location:** Just nw of downtown. **Facility:** Smoke free premises. 7 units. 2 stories (no elevator), interior corridors. *Bath:* some shared. **Terms:** check-in 4 pm, 2 night minimum stay - seasonal and/or weekends, age restrictions may apply, 7 day cancellation notice-fee imposed. **Guest Services:** wireless Internet.

Phone: 608/588-7751

THE HOUSE ON THE ROCK RESORT

Resort
Hotel
$125-$205

Phone: 608/588-7000

Address: 400 Springs Dr 53588 **Location:** 2.5 mi s on SR 23, 0.8 mi e on CR C. **Facility:** All units at this picturesque resort near the Wisconsin River have views of a golf course and surrounding wooded hills. Smoke free premises. 80 units. 4 stories, interior corridors. **Terms:** cancellation fee imposed. **Pool(s):** heated outdoor, 2 heated indoor. **Activities:** saunas, whirlpools, steamrooms, 2 lighted tennis courts, racquetball court, mountain biking, hiking trails, jogging, exercise room, spa, volleyball. *Fee:* golf-27 holes. **Guest Services:** wireless Internet.

ROUND BARN LODGE

Hotel
Rates not provided

Phone: 608/588-2568

Address: E 4830 Hwy 14 & 60 53588 **Location:** On US 14; just w of jct SR 23 N. **Facility:** Smoke free premises. 43 units, some two bedrooms. 1-2 stories (no elevator), interior/exterior corridors. **Parking:** winter plug-ins. **Pool(s):** heated indoor. **Activities:** whirlpool, exercise room. *Fee:* game room. **Guest Services:** wireless Internet.

SPRING VALLEY INN

Hotel
$85-$145

Phone: 608/588-7828

Address: 6279 CR C 53588 **Location:** On US 14 at CR C, 3 mi e. **Facility:** Smoke free premises. 35 units. 1 story, interior corridors. **Terms:** open 5/15-10/31. **Pool(s):** heated indoor. **Activities:** sauna, whirlpool, steamroom, water aerobics, sun deck, cross country skiing, snowmobiling, outdoor patio, hiking trails, exercise room. *Fee:* massage, game room. **Guest Services:** wireless Internet. **Free Special Amenities: full breakfast and high-speed Internet.**

THE USONIAN INN LLC

Motel
$69-$130 4/1-10/31
$59-$79 11/1-4/30

Phone: 608/588-2323

Address: E 5116 US Hwy 14 53588 **Location:** On US 14 at SR 23 S. **Facility:** Smoke free premises. 11 units. 1 story, exterior corridors. *Bath:* shower only. **Terms:** office hours 7:30 am-10 pm, 2 night minimum stay - seasonal and/or weekends, cancellation fee imposed. **Guest Services:** wireless Internet. **Free Special Amenities: local telephone calls and high-speed Internet.**

—— WHERE TO DINE ——

ARTHUR'S

Steak
$9-$32

Phone: 608/588-2521

Open only for dinner, this supper club is known for its steak and seafood specialties. Full dinners include the fresh salad bar with Wisconsin's finest aged cheddar. **Bar:** full bar. **Hours:** 5 pm-9 pm, Fri & Sat-9:30 pm, Sun 8 am-1 & 4:30-9 pm. **Address:** E4885 Hwy 23 & 14 53588 **Location:** Just w of jct US 14 and SR 23.

THE SHED

American
$4-$18

Phone: 608/588-9049

The small downtown restaurant and bar serves hearty helpings of filling food. It's known for its Friday night fish fry. **Bar:** full bar. **Hours:** 10:30 am-9 pm. Closed: 11/24 & Easter. **Address:** 123 N Lexington St 53588 **Location:** Center. **Parking:** street only.

SPRING GREEN GENERAL STORE

American
$5-$9

Phone: 608/588-7070

The trendy cafe prepares weekend breakfasts and an extensive selection of vegetarian offerings from scratch. **Bar:** beer & wine. **Hours:** 9 am-6 pm, Sat from 8 am, Sun 8 am-4 pm. Closed major holidays. **Address:** 137 S Albany St 53588 **Location:** Just w of SR 23. **Parking:** street only.

STANLEY pop. 1,898

AMERICA'S BEST INN STANLEY

Hotel
$54-$91

Phone: (715)644-3332

Address: 555 S Broadway 54768 **Location:** SR 29, exit 101 (CR H), just n. **Facility:** 36 units. 2 stories, interior corridors. **Parking:** winter plug-ins. **Terms:** cancellation fee imposed. **Activities:** whirlpool. **Guest Services:** wireless Internet.

STEVENS POINT pop. 24,551

A VICTORIAN SWAN ON WATER BED & BREAKFAST

Bed & Breakfast
$80-$150

Phone: 715-345-0595

Address: 1716 Water St 54481 **Location:** US 10, 0.7 mi w of jct US 51 business route, then 0.4 mi s. Located in a residential area. **Facility:** Smoke free premises. 4 units. 2 stories (no elevator), interior corridors. **Terms:** office hours 8 am-10 pm, age restrictions may apply, 14 day cancellation notice-fee imposed. **Guest Services:** wireless Internet.

COUNTRY INN & SUITES BY CARLSON

Hotel
$81-$144

Phone: (715)345-7000

Address: 301 Division St N 54481 **Location:** I-39, exit 161 (US 51 business route), 0.6 mi s. Located in a commercial area. **Facility:** Smoke free premises. 72 units. 3 stories, interior corridors. **Parking:** winter plug-ins. **Pool(s):** heated indoor. **Activities:** whirlpool, exercise room. **Guest Services:** coin laundry, wireless Internet. *(see ad p. 6)*

FAIRFIELD INN BY MARRIOTT

Hotel
$90-$95

Phone: (715)342-9300

Address: 5317 Hwy 10 E 54481 **Location:** I-39, exit 158A (US 10), just se. Located in a commercial area. **Facility:** Smoke free premises. 62 units. 3 stories, interior corridors. **Parking:** winter plug-ins. **Terms:** cancellation fee imposed. **Pool(s):** heated indoor. **Activities:** whirlpool, limited exercise equipment. **Guest Services:** valet laundry, wireless Internet.

> **AAA Benefit:**
> Members save a minimum 5% off the best available rate.

HOLIDAY INN EXPRESS

Hotel
$79-$139

Phone: (715)344-0000

Address: 1100 Amber Ave 54481 **Location:** I-39, exit 158 (US 10), 1 mi, then just n. **Facility:** Smoke free premises. 66 units. 3 stories, interior corridors. **Terms:** cancellation fee imposed. **Pool(s):** heated indoor. **Activities:** whirlpool, exercise room. **Guest Services:** valet and coin laundry, area transportation-within 5 mi, wireless Internet.

HOLIDAY INN HOTEL AND CONVENTION CENTER

Hotel
$89-$149

Phone: (715)344-0200

Address: 1001 Amber Ave 54481 **Location:** I-39, exit 158 (US 10), 1 mi e on US 10, then just n. **Facility:** Smoke free premises. 149 units, some two bedrooms. 3 stories, interior corridors. **Parking:** winter plug-ins. **Amenities:** high-speed Internet, safes. *Some:* video games. **Dining:** Rudy's Redeye Grill, see separate listing. **Pool(s):** heated indoor. **Activities:** whirlpool, waterslide, exercise room. *Fee:* game room. **Guest Services:** valet and coin laundry, area transportation-in town, wireless Internet.

LA QUINTA INN & SUITES STEVENS POINT

Hotel
$59-$119

Phone: (715)344-1900

Address: 4917 Main St 54481 **Location:** I-39, exit 158B (US 10), just sw. Located in a commercial area. **Facility:** Smoke free premises. 73 units. 3 stories, interior corridors. **Parking:** winter plug-ins. **Amenities:** video games (fee). **Pool(s):** heated indoor. **Activities:** whirlpool, exercise room. **Guest Services:** coin laundry, wireless Internet.

STAY INN & SUITES

Hotel
Rates not provided

Phone: 715/341-9090

Address: 159 Division St N 54481 **Location:** I-39, exit 161 (US 51 business route), 0.6 mi s. **Facility:** Smoke free premises. 86 units, some efficiencies. 2 stories (no elevator), interior corridors. **Activities:** exercise room. **Guest Services:** coin laundry, wireless Internet.

SUPER 8

Hotel
Rates not provided

Phone: 715/341-8888

Address: 247 N Division St 54481 **Location:** I-39, exit 161 (US 51 business route), 0.6 mi s. **Facility:** Smoke free premises. 56 units. 3 stories (no elevator), interior corridors. **Parking:** winter plug-ins. **Amenities:** safes (fee). **Guest Services:** coin laundry, wireless Internet.

—— **WHERE TO DINE** ——

@1800

American
$19-$37

Phone: 715/346-1800

The dining room has large windows that overlook a "northwoods" backyard with a wildlife feeding station. The chef makes use of organic and local ingredients, and is happy to accommodate dietary requests. The menu changes seasonally, and the entrees are nicely presented. Scrumptious desserts are prepared in-house. Lunch is served in the more casual Pagliace Taverna from 11 am Mon-Fri. **Bar:** full bar. **Reservations:** suggested. **Hours:** 11 am-2 & 5-9 pm, Sat from 5 pm. Closed major holidays; also Sun. **Address:** 1800 N Point Dr 54481 **Location:** I-39, exit 161 (US 51 business route), just sw; in Sentry Headquarters.

GRAZIES ITALIAN GRILL

Italian
$8-$17

Phone: 715-345-7808

This restaurant has a neighborhood bar and offers wraps, wood-fired pizza and pasta made from scratch for dishes such as seafood pescatore with sautéed shrimp and scallops. **Bar:** full bar. **Reservations:** suggested. **Hours:** 11 am-10 pm. Closed: 11/24, 12/25 & Easter. **Address:** 5327 Hwy 10 E 54481 **Location:** I-39, exit 158 (US 10), at US 51.

RUDY'S REDEYE GRILL

American
$7-$23

Phone: 715-344-9808

Offering breakfast, lunch and dinner, the menu boasts a wide variety of choices from a light lunch menu with homemade soups to more heartier dinner offerings of steak and fish dishes. No meal would be complete without the delicious carrot cake. **Bar:** full bar. **Reservations:** suggested. **Hours:** 6:30 am-10 pm. Closed: 12/25. **Address:** 1001 Amber Ave 54481 **Location:** I-39, exit 158 (US 10), 1 mi e, then just n; in Holiday Inn Hotel and Convention Center.

STOUGHTON pop. 12,354

COMFORT QUALITY HOTEL OF STOUGHTON

Hotel
$85-$180

Phone: 608-877-9000

Address: 660 Nygaard St 53589 **Location:** On US 51 business route, 0.7 mi nw of jct SR 138 S. Truck parking on premises. **Facility:** 50 units. 2 stories (no elevator), interior corridors. **Parking:** winter plug-ins. **Terms:** cancellation fee imposed. **Pool(s):** heated indoor. **Activities:** whirlpool, limited exercise equipment. **Guest Services:** valet and coin laundry, wireless Internet.

STURGEON BAY —See Door County p. 469.

STURTEVANT pop. 5,287

DAYS INN RACINE/STURTEVANT

Hotel
$50-$113

Phone: (262)884-6840

Address: 13340 Hospitality Ct 53177 **Location:** I-94, exit 333 (SR 20), just se. Located in a commercial area. **Facility:** Smoke free premises. 47 units. 2 stories (no elevator), interior corridors. **Parking:** winter plug-ins. **Pool(s):** heated indoor. **Activities:** exercise room. **Guest Services:** coin laundry, wireless Internet. **Free Special Amenities: continental breakfast and high-speed Internet.**

HOLIDAY INN EXPRESS-RACINE

Hotel
$119-$149 4/1-9/15
$99-$119 9/16-4/30

Phone: (262)884-0200

Address: 13339 Hospitality Ct 53177 **Location:** I-94, exit 333 (SR 20), just se. Located in a commercial area. **Facility:** Smoke free premises. 107 units. 3 stories, interior corridors. **Terms:** 3 day cancellation notice. **Pool(s):** heated indoor. **Activities:** whirlpool, exercise room. **Guest Services:** coin laundry, wireless Internet.

------ **WHERE TO DINE** ------

APPLE HOLLER

American
$5-$25

Phone: 262/886-8500

A popular tourist stop with orchards, hayrides, dinner theater and pig roasts, the restaurant prepares fare such as apple butter-smoked barbecue ribs; freshly grilled brats, hamburgers and hot dogs; carved beef; chicken; and sandwiches. Down-to-earth desserts include apple pie and gourmet chocolate chip cookies. **Bar:** full bar. **Hours:** 7 am-7:30 pm, Fri & Sat-8:30 pm; to 8 pm 1/1-2/28. Closed: 12/24, 12/25. **Address:** 5006 S Sylvania Ave 53177 **Location:** I-94, exit 335 (SR 11), just w, then 1 mi s.

SUN PRAIRIE pop. 20,369

QUALITY INN & SUITES-SUN PRAIRIE

Hotel
$69-$179

Phone: (608)834-9889

Address: 105 Business Park Dr 53590 **Location:** US 151, exit 103 (CR N), just n. **Facility:** Smoke free premises. 62 units. 2 stories (no elevator), interior corridors. **Parking:** winter plug-ins. **Terms:** cancellation fee imposed. **Amenities:** high-speed Internet, safes (fee). **Pool(s):** heated indoor. **Activities:** whirlpool, exercise room. **Guest Services:** valet and coin laundry, wireless Internet. **Free Special Amenities: expanded continental breakfast and high-speed Internet.**

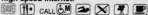

SUPERIOR pop. 27,368

BARKERS ISLAND INN

Hotel
$89-$189

Phone: (715)392-7152

Address: 300 Marina Dr 54880 **Location:** Just ne of US 2/53; on Barkers Island. Adjacent to the marina. **Facility:** Designated smoking area. 112 units. 2 stories, interior corridors. **Dining:** Captain Barkers, see separate listing. **Pool(s):** heated indoor. **Activities:** sauna, whirlpool. **Fee:** game room. **Guest Services:** coin laundry, wireless Internet. **Free Special Amenities: full breakfast and newspaper.**

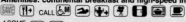

BEST WESTERN BAY WALK INN

Hotel
$60-$170

Phone: (715)392-7600

Address: 1405 Susquehanna Ave 54880 **Location:** Just e of US 2 on Belknap St. **Facility:** 50 units. 2 stories, interior corridors. **Parking:** winter plug-ins. **Amenities:** *Some:* high-speed Internet. **Pool(s):** heated indoor. **Activities:** sauna, whirlpool. **Guest Services:** coin laundry, wireless Internet. **Free Special Amenities: continental breakfast and high-speed Internet.**

AAA Benefit:
Members save up to 20%, plus 10% bonus points with free rewards program.

BEST WESTERN BRIDGEVIEW MOTOR INN

Hotel
$60-$189

Phone: (715)392-8174

Address: 415 Hammond Ave 54880 **Location:** 0.8 mi n at south end of Blatnik Bridge. **Facility:** Smoke free premises. 96 units. 2 stories, interior corridors. **Parking:** winter plug-ins. **Pool(s):** heated indoor. **Activities:** whirlpool, exercise room. **Fee:** game room. **Guest Services:** coin laundry, wireless Internet. **Free Special Amenities: expanded continental breakfast and high-speed Internet.**

AAA Benefit:
Members save up to 20%, plus 10% bonus points with free rewards program.

HOLIDAY INN EXPRESS

Hotel
$144-$154 6/2-4/30
$109-$119 4/1-6/1

Phone: (715)392-3444

Address: 303 2nd Ave E 54880 **Location:** Just n of jct US 2/53. **Facility:** 84 units. 3 stories, interior corridors. **Parking:** winter plug-ins. **Terms:** cancellation fee imposed. **Amenities:** high-speed Internet. **Pool(s):** heated indoor. **Activities:** whirlpool, exercise room. **Guest Services:** valet and coin laundry, wireless Internet.

SUPER 8 OF SUPERIOR

Hotel
$59-$117

Phone: (715)398-7686

Address: 4901 E 2nd St 54880 **Location:** 6 mi se on US 2/53. **Facility:** Smoke free premises. 40 units. 2 stories (no elevator), interior corridors. **Parking:** winter plug-ins. **Guest Services:** wireless Internet. 🛗 CALL ♿Ⓜ ✕ 📺 💻 / SOME UNITS 🛡 🖥

—— WHERE TO DINE ——

CAPTAIN BARKERS

American
$4-$23

Phone: 715/392-7152 ⑪

Diners can look out on the bay while enjoying a hearty breakfast, light lunch or steak and seafood for dinner. This eatery has a number of menu options. **Bar:** full bar. **Reservations:** suggested, weekends. **Hours:** 6:30 am-9 pm, Fri & Sat-10 pm; to 8 pm, Fri & Sat-9 pm in winter. **Address:** 300 Marina Dr 54880 **Location:** Just ne of US 2/53; on Barkers Island; in Barkers Island Inn. CALL ♿Ⓜ

GRIZZLY'S GRILL & SALOON

American
$8-$29

Phone: 715/392-5210

Patrons enjoy a casual dining experience in a rustic setting. The menu lists selections of barbecue ribs, USDA Choice steaks, pasta dishes and some healthy choices, as well as even a few Tex-Mex offerings. **Bar:** full bar. **Hours:** 11 am-midnight. Closed major holidays. **Address:** 3405 Tower Ave 54880 **Location:** 1.2 mi s on SR 35 from jct US 2.

THE HAMMOND STEAKHOUSE

Steak
$8-$30

Phone: 715/392-3269 ⑩

The popular steakhouse offers excellent value with its large portions. **Bar:** full bar. **Hours:** 5 pm-9 pm, Fri & Sat-10 pm. Closed: Tues. **Address:** 1402 N 5th St 54880 **Location:** 0.8 mi n; at south end of Blatnik Bridge.

THE SHACK SMOKEHOUSE & GRILLE

American
$7-$31

Phone: 715/392-9836 ⑫

Steak, seafood, chicken, prime rib and the house specialty smokehouse barbecue ribs—in addition to lunch choices of lighter fare—make up a diverse menu at the established restaurant. Service is friendly and unpretentious, and portion sizes are ample. **Bar:** full bar. **Hours:** 11 am-9 pm, Fri & Sat-10 pm, Sun-8 pm. Closed: 12/25; also for dinner 12/24. **Address:** 3301 Belknap St 54880 **Location:** 1.5 mi w. CALL ♿Ⓜ

THORP pop. 1,536

AMERICINN LODGE & SUITES OF THORP

Hotel
Rates not provided

Phone: 715/669-5959

Address: 203 1/2 W Hill St 54771 **Location:** US 29, exit 108 (SR 73), just nw. **Facility:** 42 units. 2 stories (no elevator), interior corridors. **Pool(s):** heated indoor. **Activities:** whirlpool, limited exercise equipment. **Fee:** game room. **Guest Services:** coin laundry, wireless Internet.
🛗 CALL ♿Ⓜ 🏊 📺 🛡 🖥 💻 / SOME UNITS FEE 🐾 ✕ 🖥

THREE LAKES

NORTHERNAIRE RESORT & SPA

Hotel
$99-$375 4/1-10/31
$79-$375 11/1-4/30

Phone: 715/546-2700

Address: 6990 Bengs Rd 54562 **Location:** 3.5 mi se on SR 32. Located on Shores of Deer Lake. **Facility:** Smoke free premises. 55 units, some two bedrooms and kitchens. 3 stories, interior corridors. **Parking:** winter plug-ins. **Terms:** 2-5 night minimum stay - seasonal and/or weekends, 3 day cancellation notice-fee imposed. **Pool(s):** heated indoor. **Activities:** whirlpools, boat dock, snowmobiling, hiking trails, exercise room, spa. **Fee:** game room. **Guest Services:** wireless Internet.
SAVE CALL ♿Ⓜ 🏊 ✕ 📺 🛡 🖥 💻

TOMAH pop. 8,419

AMERICINN LODGE & SUITES OF TOMAH

Hotel
$79-$159

Phone: (608)372-4100

Address: 750 Vandervort St 54660 **Location:** I-94, exit 143 (SR 21), just e. **Facility:** Smoke free premises. 45 units. 2 stories (no elevator), interior corridors. **Parking:** winter plug-ins. **Amenities:** Some: high-speed Internet. **Pool(s):** heated indoor. **Activities:** sauna, whirlpool. **Guest Services:** valet and coin laundry, wireless Internet.
🛗 CALL ♿Ⓜ 🏊 ✕ 📺 🛡 🖥 💻 / SOME UNITS FEE 🐾

COMFORT INN BY CHOICE HOTELS

Hotel
$74-$134

Phone: (608)372-6600

Address: 305 Wittig Rd 54660 **Location:** I-94, exit 143 (SR 21), just w. **Facility:** Smoke free premises. 52 units. 2 stories (no elevator), interior corridors. **Parking:** winter plug-ins. **Pool(s):** heated indoor. **Activities:** whirlpool. **Guest Services:** wireless Internet.
🛗 🏊 ✕ 📺 🛡 🖥 💻 / SOME UNITS FEE 🐾

CRANBERRY COUNTRY LODGE & CONVENTION CENTER

Phone: 608/374-2801

Hotel
$70-$145

Address: 319 Wittig Rd 54660 **Location:** I-94, exit 143 (SR 21), just w. **Facility:** Smoke free premises. 93 units. 3 stories, interior corridors. **Parking:** winter plug-ins. **Amenities:** high-speed Internet. **Pool(s):** 2 heated indoor. **Activities:** whirlpool, waterslide, water park, exercise room. *Fee:* game room. **Guest Services:** coin laundry, wireless Internet.

ECONO LODGE

Phone: (608)372-9100

Hotel
$57-$73

Address: 2005 N Superior Ave 54660 **Location:** I-94, exit 143 (SR 21), just w. **Facility:** Smoke free premises. 77 units. 2 stories (no elevator), interior/exterior corridors. **Parking:** winter plug-ins. **Terms:** cancellation fee imposed. **Pool(s):** heated indoor. **Activities:** whirlpool. **Guest Services:** coin laundry, wireless Internet.

HOLIDAY INN

Phone: (608)372-3211

Hotel
$110-$135 6/2-4/30
$85-$100 4/1-6/1

Address: 1017 E McCoy Blvd 54660 **Location:** I-94, exit 143 (SR 21), just e. **Facility:** Smoke free premises. 100 units. 2 stories (no elevator), interior corridors. **Pool(s):** heated indoor. **Activities:** sauna, whirlpool, catch and release fishing, 3-hole golf course, walking trail, exercise room, horseshoes, volleyball. *Fee:* game room. **Guest Services:** valet and coin laundry, wireless Internet.

LARK INN

Phone: (608)372-5981

Motel
$66-$128 4/1-10/31
$62-$102 11/1-4/30

Address: 229 N Superior Ave 54660 **Location:** I-94, exit 143 (SR 21), 1.5 mi s on US 12; I-90, exit 41, 2 mi n on US 12. **Facility:** Smoke free premises. 33 units, some two bedrooms and kitchens. 2 stories, interior/exterior corridors. **Parking:** winter plug-ins. **Activities:** gazebo. **Guest Services:** coin laundry, wireless Internet. *(see ad below)*

FREE expanded continental breakfast and high-speed Internet

SUPER 8-TOMAH

Hotel
$59-$139

Phone: (608)372-3901

Address: 1008 E McCoy Blvd 54660 **Location:** I-94, exit 143 (SR 21), just e. **Facility:** Smoke free premises. 65 units. 2 stories (no elevator), interior corridors. **Parking:** winter plug-ins. **Amenities:** safes (fee). **Guest Services:** coin laundry, wireless Internet.

 / SOME UNITS FEE

—— WHERE TO DINE ——

BURNSTAD'S EUROPEAN CAFE

American
$4-$25

Phone: 608/372-5355

This casual restaurant is adjacent to a quaint gift shop. The menu lists steak, seafood, pork and chicken dishes such as New York strip steak, cranberry pecan chicken and pork moutarde. Also available are some Italian entrees and items for guests with lighter appetites. Desserts are made from scratch in house. **Bar:** full bar. **Hours:** 9 am-9 pm, Sun-8 pm; to 8 pm, Fri & Sat-9 pm 9/1-5/31. Closed: 1/1, 11/24, 12/25; also for dinner 12/24. **Address:** 701 E Clifton St 54660 **Location:** I-90, exit 43 (SR 21), 1 mi n on US 12 and 16; in Burnstad's European Village.

MR. ED'S TEE PEE

American
$5-$21

Phone: 608/372-0888

Known for soups and prime rib, the local favorite presents a menu of varied seafood and pasta preparations. **Bar:** full bar. **Hours:** 10:30 am-10 pm. Closed: 1/1, 12/24, 12/25. **Address:** 812 Superior Ave 54660 **Location:** I-90, exit 43 (SR 21), 1.6 mi w on SR 12 (Superior Ave).

TOMAHAWK pop. 3,770

BEST WESTERN LAKE AIRE MOTEL

Motel
$75-$170

Phone: (715)453-5189

Address: N 11925 CR L 54487 **Location:** US 51, exit 234, 2.6 mi w to CR L, then 0.5 mi n. Located on Lake Nokomis. **Facility:** Smoke free premises. 25 units, some efficiencies and cottages. 2 stories (no elevator), exterior corridors. **Parking:** winter plug-ins. **Terms:** office hours 6:30 am-11:30 pm, 2-3 night minimum stay - seasonal and/or weekends. **Amenities:** Some: high-speed Internet. **Activities:** limited beach access, boat dock, fishing, sun deck, beach, snowmobiling, grills, horseshoes, volleyball. **Guest Services:** wireless Internet. **Free Special Amenities: continental breakfast and high-speed Internet.**

AAA Benefit:
Members save up to 20%, plus 10% bonus points with free rewards program.

RODEWAY INN & SUITES

Hotel
$70-$120

Phone: (715)453-8900

Address: 1738 E Comfort Dr 54487 **Location:** US 51, exit 229, just nw. **Facility:** Smoke free premises. 46 units. 3 stories, interior corridors. **Parking:** winter plug-ins. **Amenities:** high-speed Internet, safes (fee). **Pool(s):** heated indoor. **Activities:** whirlpool, limited exercise equipment. *Fee:* game room. **Guest Services:** coin laundry, wireless Internet.

CALL / SOME UNITS FEE

SUPER 8-TOMAHAWK

Hotel
$63-$86

Phone: (715)453-5210

Address: 108 W Mohawk Dr 54487 **Location:** US 51, exit 231, 1.4 mi w, then 0.6 mi s. **Facility:** Smoke free premises. 56 units, some two bedrooms. 3 stories, interior corridors. **Parking:** winter plug-ins. **Terms:** cancellation fee imposed. **Pool(s):** heated indoor. **Activities:** sauna, whirlpool, adjacent snowmobile trail. *Fee:* game room. **Guest Services:** coin laundry, wireless Internet.

 CALL / SOME UNITS FEE

—— WHERE TO DINE ——

TOMAHAWK FAMILY RESTAURANT

American
$6-$14

Phone: 715/453-4504

Best for breakfast and lunch, the popular restaurant puts forth a large menu of reasonably priced American, Mexican and Italian dishes, which are served in hearty portions. **Hours:** 6 am-10 pm. Closed: 1/1, 12/25. **Address:** 1020 N 4th St 54487 **Location:** On US 51 business route, 0.5 mi n of downtown. CALL

TWO RIVERS pop. 12,639

LIGHTHOUSE INN ON LAKE MICHIGAN

Hotel
$94-$156 4/1-10/31
$84-$145 11/1-4/30

Phone: (920)793-4524

Address: 1515 Memorial Dr 54241 **Location:** 0.3 mi s on SR 42. Located on the shore of Lake Michigan. **Facility:** Smoke free premises. 67 units. 2 stories (no elevator), interior corridors. **Pool(s):** heated indoor. **Activities:** whirlpool, fishing, fish freezer, rental bicycles, exercise room. **Guest Services:** valet and coin laundry, wireless Internet. **Free Special Amenities: local telephone calls and high-speed Internet.**

 / SOME UNITS

RED FOREST BED & BREAKFAST

Bed & Breakfast
$125-$130

Phone: (920)793-1794

Address: 1421 25th St 54241 **Location:** Just n of SR 42 on Washington St. **Facility:** The 1907 distinctive shingle-style home is highlighted with stained glass windows and sits in a quiet residential area. Smoke free premises. 4 units. 2 stories (no elevator), interior corridors. **Terms:** office hours 8 am-9 pm, age restrictions may apply, 7 day cancellation notice. **Guest Services:** wireless Internet.

VERONA pop. 7,052

HOLIDAY INN EXPRESS HOTEL & SUITES MADISON-VERONA

Hotel
$139-$209

Phone: (608)497-4500

Address: 515 W Verona Ave 53593 **Location:** On US 51 business route, exit 81, 1.8 mi w. **Facility:** Smoke free premises. 109 units. 3 stories, interior corridors. **Amenities:** high-speed Internet. **Pool(s):** heated indoor. **Activities:** whirlpool, exercise room. **Guest Services:** valet and coin laundry, area transportation-within 5 mi, wireless Internet.

SUPER 8-VERONA

Hotel
$54-$107

Phone: (608)848-7829

Address: 131 Horizon Dr 53593 **Location:** US 18 and 151, exit 94 southbound; exit 89 northbound, just n. **Facility:** Smoke free premises. 43 units. 2 stories, interior corridors. **Parking:** winter plug-ins. **Amenities:** high-speed Internet. **Pool(s):** heated indoor. **Activities:** whirlpool, exercise room. **Guest Services:** valet laundry, wireless Internet.

------- WHERE TO DINE -------

THE DRAFT HOUSE

American
$10-$16

Phone: 608/848-3158

Sports fans and families gather in this eatery, where they can watch their favorite team on any of many large TVs while noshing on a burger or sandwich. **Hours:** 11 am-10 pm. **Address:** 1010 Enterprise Dr 53593 **Location:** Jct CR M and Cross Country Rd, just e.

VIROQUA pop. 4,335

HICKORY HILL MOTEL

Motel
$64-$75 4/1-12/1
$54-$65 12/2-4/30

Phone: 608/637-3104

Address: US 14 S 3955 54665 **Location:** On US 14 and SR 27 and 82, 1.8 mi se. Located in a rural area. **Facility:** Smoke free premises. 25 units, some efficiencies. 1 story, exterior corridors. **Parking:** winter plug-ins. **Terms:** cancellation fee imposed. **Pool(s):** heated outdoor. **Activities:** picnic area. **Guest Services:** wireless Internet.

VERNON INN & SUITES

Hotel
$65-$175

Phone: 608/637-3100

Address: 1325 N Main St 54665 **Location:** On US 14 and SR 16 and 27, 1 mi n of center. **Facility:** Smoke free premises. 50 units, some two bedrooms. 2 stories (no elevator), interior corridors. **Parking:** winter plug-ins. **Terms:** check-in 4 pm. **Pool(s):** heated indoor. **Activities:** whirlpool. **Guest Services:** coin laundry, wireless Internet.

WASHBURN pop. 2,280

------- WHERE TO DINE -------

STEAK PIT INC

Steak
$7-$29

Phone: 715/373-5492

Beside Lake Superior, this older-style steakhouse affords views of the marina. Friendly, unpretentious servers bring out well-prepared meat and freshwater fish dishes. **Bar:** full bar. **Reservations:** suggested. **Hours:** 5 pm-close, Sun from 4 pm. **Closed:** 11/24, 12/25. **Address:** 125 Harborview Dr 54891 **Location:** Just e of SR 13.

WATERFORD pop. 4,048

BAYMONT INN & SUITES-WATERFORD

Hotel
$76-$188

Phone: (262)534-4100

Address: 750 Fox Ln 53185 **Location:** On SR 36, 1 mi s of jct SR 164. Located next to a residential area. **Facility:** Smoke free premises. 54 units. 3 stories, interior corridors. **Terms:** cancellation fee imposed. **Amenities:** video games (fee). **Pool(s):** heated indoor. **Activities:** whirlpool, sun deck, exercise room. **Guest Services:** valet and coin laundry, wireless Internet.

WATERTOWN pop. 21,598

HOLIDAY INN EXPRESS

Hotel
$104-$114 4/1-10/13
$99-$104 10/14-4/30

Phone: (920)262-1910

Address: 101 Aviation Way 53094 **Location:** On SR 26, 1.5 mi s of jct SR 19. **Facility:** Smoke free premises. 79 units. 2 stories, interior corridors. **Parking:** winter plug-ins. **Pool(s):** heated indoor. **Activities:** sauna, whirlpool, exercise room. **Guest Services:** valet and coin laundry, wireless Internet.

SUPER 8

Hotel
$64-$85

Phone: (920)261-1188

Address: 1730 S Church St 53094 **Location:** On SR 26, 1.5 mi s of jct SR 19. **Facility:** Smoke free premises. 45 units. 2 stories (no elevator), interior corridors. **Parking:** winter plug-ins. **Terms:** cancellation fee imposed. **Amenities:** Some: high-speed Internet. **Pool(s):** heated indoor. **Activities:** whirlpool, limited exercise equipment. **Fee:** game room. **Guest Services:** coin laundry, wireless Internet.

—— WHERE TO DINE ——

CHINA BUFFET

Chinese
$6-$14

Phone: 920/261-0737

The all-you-can-eat buffet offers a very large selection of Chinese, Japanese and American items along with a salad bar and a dessert bar, or order directly from the menu. **Bar:** beer & wine. **Hours:** 10:30 am-10 pm, Fri & Sat-11 pm, Sun 11 am-10 pm. Closed major holidays. **Address:** 1632 S Church St 53094 **Location:** On SR 26 of jct SR 19. CALL

ROSE GARDEN FAMILY RESTAURANT

American
$5-$14

Phone: 920/261-0006

The family restaurant opens early to serve breakfast and stays open with offerings of pizza and American favorites. **Hours:** 7 am-9 pm, Fri & Sat 24 hours, Sun 6 am-9 pm. Closed: 11/24, 12/24, 12/25. **Address:** 500 Bernard St 53094 **Location:** 0.6 mi s of jct SR 19 and 26.

STEAKFIRE GRILLE & BAR

Steak
$6-$20

Phone: 920/262-2222

This restaurant allows patrons to grill their own steaks or seafood, in addition to signature platters and steak sandwiches. The busy highway location makes for easy access. A fish fry is featured on Fridays. **Bar:** full bar. **Hours:** 11 am-10 pm. Closed: 12/25. **Address:** 1726 S Church St 53094 **Location:** On SR 26, 1.5 mi s of jct SR 19.

UPPER KRUST PIES & MORE

American
$6-$10

Phone: 920/206-9202

This popular restaurant has charming decor. Homemade pies are the big draw, but patrons shouldn't overlook the scrumptious soups, salads, pot pie, quiche and sandwiches, which are made daily from fresh ingredients. **Hours:** 7 am-8 pm, Sun 9 am-1:30 pm. Closed major holidays. **Address:** 1300 Memorial Dr 53098 **Location:** Jct SR 16/Frontage Rd and Memorial Dr, follow signs to hospital.

WAUKESHA —See Milwaukee p. 568.

WAUNAKEE pop. 8,995

—— WHERE TO DINE ——

CHINA WOK

Chinese
$8-$14

Phone: 608/849-9638

Lunch and dinner buffets line up selections of Cantonese, Szechuan and Hunan food. Guests can dine in or order their meals for carry-out. **Hours:** 11 am-10 pm. Closed: 7/4, 11/24, 12/25. **Address:** 204 S Century St, A-6 53597 **Location:** Jct SR 19 and 113, just s. CALL

REX'S INNKEEPER

American
$5-$23

Phone: 608/849-5011

Locally owned and operated, the restaurant offers a huge selection of your favorite home-style dishes. Located only seven miles from Madison, the eatery's delicious steaks, prime rib, seafood and Friday night fish fry are worth the drive. **Bar:** full bar. **Hours:** 11 am-2 & 4:30-9 pm, Fri-10 pm, Sat 4:30 pm-10 pm, Sun 4 pm-9 pm. Closed: major holidays, 12/24. **Address:** 301 N Century Ave 53597 **Location:** On SR 113. CALL

SPRING GARDEN RESTAURANT

American
$5-$13

Phone: 608/850-3732

Daily specials complement the breakfast dishes and American classics at the mom-and-pop restaurant. **Hours:** 6 am-9 pm, Sun-8 pm. Closed major holidays. **Address:** 225E S Century Ave 53597 **Location:** Just s of jct SR 19/113/CR Q. CALL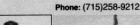

WAUPACA pop. 5,676

BEST WESTERN PLUS GRAND SEASONS HOTEL

Hotel
$80-$150

Phone: (715)258-9212

Address: 110 Grand Seasons Dr 54981 **Location:** Jct US 10 and SR 54 W. Located in a commercial area. **Facility:** Smoke free premises. 90 units. 3 stories, interior corridors. **Parking:** winter plug-ins. **Amenities:** safes (fee). Some: high-speed Internet. **Pool(s):** heated indoor. **Activities:** sauna, whirlpool, waterslide. Fee: game room. **Guest Services:** valet and coin laundry, wireless Internet.

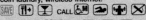

AAA Benefit:
Members save up to 20%, plus 10% bonus points with free rewards program.

FREE expanded continental breakfast and high-speed Internet

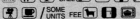

COMFORT SUITES AT FOXFIRE

Phone: 715/942-0500

Hotel
Rates not provided

Address: 199 Foxfire Dr 54981 **Location:** Jct US 10 and SR 54 W, 0.7 mi sw. **Facility:** Smoke free premises. 70 units. 3 stories, interior corridors. **Parking:** winter plug-ins. **Amenities:** high-speed Internet, safes (fee). *Some:* video games (fee). **Pool(s):** heated indoor. **Activities:** whirlpool, exercise room. *Fee:* game room. **Guest Services:** coin laundry, wireless Internet.

———— **WHERE TO DINE** ————

"CLEAR WATER HARBOR" WATERFRONT RESTAURANT & BAR

Phone: 715/258-9912

American
$5-$12

Patrons of this casual spot can sit indoors, where a picture window affords views out over the lakes, or on the deck, where they can bask in the summer sun. Specialties include the 'shroom burger, grilled fish, grilled chicken sandwiches, fresh crisp salads, homemade soups and desserts. The Friday fish fry is a local favorite. **Bar:** full bar. **Hours:** Open 4/21-9/25; 10 am-midnight. **Address:** N2757 Hwy QQ 54981 **Location:** 2 mi sw of jct US 10/SR 49/54 and CR QQ; on Taylor Lake.

WAUPUN pop. 10,718

INN TOWN MOTEL

Phone: 920/324-4211

Motel
Rates not provided

Address: 27 S State St 53963 **Location:** US 151, exit 146 (SR 49), 1 mi w on Main St, then just s. Located in a residential area. **Facility:** Smoke free premises. 16 units, some kitchens. 1 story, exterior corridors. **Parking:** winter plug-ins. **Terms:** office hours 8 am-11 pm. **Guest Services:** wireless Internet.

———— **WHERE TO DINE** ————

HELEN'S KITCHEN

Phone: 920/324-3441

American
$4-$10

A local favorite, this mom-and-pop operation serves fabulous breakfasts at a very good price. This place also satisfies with friendly, down-home hospitality. **Hours:** 5:45 am-8 pm, Fri-9 pm. Closed major holidays; also Sun. **Address:** 1116 W Main St 53963 **Location:** US 151, exit 146 (SR 49), 1.8 mi w.

WAUSAU pop. 38,426

BEST WESTERN MIDWAY HOTEL

Phone: (715)842-1616

Hotel
$70

Address: 2901 Hummingbird Rd 54401 **Location:** I-39, exit 190 (CR NN), just sw. **Facility:** Smoke free premises. 97 units. 2 stories (no elevator), interior corridors. **Parking:** winter plug-ins. **Amenities:** *Some:* high-speed Internet. **Pool(s):** heated indoor. **Activities:** whirlpool, domed recreation center, exercise room. *Fee:* game room. **Guest Services:** valet and coin laundry, area transportation-within 10 mi, wireless Internet. **Free Special Amenities:** expanded continental breakfast and airport transportation.

AAA Benefit:
Members save up to 20%, plus 10% bonus points with free rewards program.

COURTYARD BY MARRIOTT

Phone: (715)849-2124

Hotel
$112-$143

Address: 1000 S 22nd Ave 54401 **Location:** I-39, exit 191 (Sherman St), just se. Located in a quiet area. **Facility:** Smoke free premises. 84 units. 3 stories, interior corridors. **Parking:** winter plug-ins. **Terms:** cancellation fee imposed. **Amenities:** video games (fee), high-speed Internet. **Pool(s):** heated indoor. **Activities:** whirlpool, exercise room. **Guest Services:** valet and coin laundry, wireless Internet.

AAA Benefit:
Members save a minimum 5% off the best available rate.

DAYS INN

Phone: (715)842-0641

Motel
$49-$85

Address: 116 S 17th Ave 54401 **Location:** I-39, exit 192, just ne. Located in a commercial area. **Facility:** Smoke free premises. 120 units, some efficiencies. 2 stories (no elevator), interior corridors. **Parking:** winter plug-ins. **Activities:** limited exercise equipment. **Guest Services:** valet and coin laundry, wireless Internet.

DAYS INN & SUITES WAUSAU

Phone: (715)355-5501

Hotel
$53-$71

Address: 4700 Rib Mountain Dr 54401 **Location:** I-39, exit 188, just ne. Located in a commercial area. **Facility:** Smoke free premises. 50 units. 2 stories (no elevator), interior corridors. **Parking:** winter plug-ins. **Terms:** cancellation fee imposed. **Amenities:** safes (fee). **Pool(s):** heated indoor. **Activities:** whirlpool. **Guest Services:** coin laundry, wireless Internet. **Free Special Amenities:** expanded continental breakfast and high-speed Internet.

HAMPTON INN

Hotel
$89-$129

Phone: (715)848-9700

Address: 615 S 24th Ave 54401 **Location:** I-39, exit 191 (Sherman St), just ne. Located in a commercial area. **Facility:** 88 units. 3 stories, interior corridors. **Parking:** winter plug-ins. **Terms:** 1-7 night minimum stay, cancellation fee imposed. **Amenities:** video games (fee). **Pool(s):** heated indoor. **Activities:** whirlpool, exercise room. **Guest Services:** valet and coin laundry, wireless Internet. **Free Special Amenities:** expanded continental breakfast and high-speed Internet.

AAA Benefit:
Members save up to 10% everyday!

HOWARD JOHNSON INN & CONFERENCE CENTER

Hotel
$62-$80

Phone: (715)842-0711

Address: 2101 N Mountain Rd 54401 **Location:** I-39, exit 190 (CR NN), just se. **Facility:** Smoke free premises. 120 units. 2 stories (no elevator), interior corridors. **Parking:** winter plug-ins. **Amenities:** safes (fee). **Pool(s):** heated indoor. **Activities:** whirlpool, putting green, exercise room. *Fee:* game room. **Guest Services:** valet laundry, wireless Internet.

JEFFERSON STREET INN

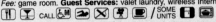

Hotel
$109-$325

Phone: (715)845-6500

Address: 201 Jefferson St 54403 **Location:** Just w of jct 2nd St; center. **Facility:** Smoke free premises. 100 units, some kitchens. 5 stories, interior corridors. **Parking:** on-site (fee). **Terms:** cancellation fee imposed. **Amenities:** video games (fee), high-speed Internet, honor bars. **Pool(s):** heated indoor. **Activities:** sauna, whirlpool, exercise room. *Fee:* massage. **Guest Services:** area transportation, wireless Internet.

FREE expanded continental breakfast and high-speed Internet

LA QUINTA INN WAUSAU

Hotel
$49-$109

Phone: (715)842-0421

Address: 1910 Stewart Ave 54401 **Location:** I-39, exit 192, just se. Located in a commercial area. **Facility:** Smoke free premises. 93 units. 2 stories (no elevator), interior corridors. **Parking:** winter plug-ins. **Amenities:** video games (fee). *Some:* high-speed Internet. **Pool(s):** heated indoor. **Activities:** whirlpool. **Guest Services:** valet laundry, wireless Internet.

RIB MOUNTAIN INN

Hotel
$69-$499

Phone: (715)848-2802

Address: 2900 Rib Mountain Way 54401 **Location:** I-39, exit 190 (CR NN), 1.2 mi w on N Mountain Rd (CR NN), then just s. Located in a residential area, adjacent to golf course & recreational area. **Facility:** 24 units, some two bedrooms, three bedrooms and kitchens. 2-3 stories, interior/exterior corridors. **Parking:** winter plug-ins. **Terms:** office hours 6 am-10 pm, 2-3 night minimum stay - seasonal and/or weekends, 3 day cancellation notice. **Activities:** sauna, whirlpool, cross country skiing, snowmobiling, snowshoeing, barbecue grills, bicycles, hiking trails. *Fee:* golf privileges, downhill skiing. **Guest Services:** complimentary laundry, wireless Internet.

ROSENBERRY INN

Historic Bed
& Breakfast
$90-$150

Phone: 715/842-5733

Address: 511 Franklin St 54403 **Location:** Between 5th and 6th sts; center. Located in a residential area. **Facility:** This B&B consists of two historic homes located across the street from one another. Smoke free premises. 8 units. 2 stories (no elevator), interior/exterior corridors. **Terms:** office hours 9 am-10 pm, 10 day cancellation notice-fee imposed. **Guest Services:** wireless Internet.

STEWART INN BED AND BREAKFAST

Historic Bed
& Breakfast
$150-$215

Phone: 715/849-5858

Address: 521 Grant St 54403 **Location:** Between 5th and 6th sts; center. Located in a residential area. **Facility:** The 100-year-old Arts and Crafts masterpiece by architect George W. Maher features period appointments, updated rooms and baths with steam showers. Smoke free premises. 5 units. 2 stories (no elevator), interior corridors. **Terms:** age restrictions may apply, 30 day cancellation notice-fee imposed. **Guest Services:** wireless Internet.

SUPER 8 WAUSAU

Hotel
$49-$72

Phone: (715)848-2888

Address: 2006 Stewart Ave W 54401 **Location:** I-39, exit 192, just se. Located in a commercial area. **Facility:** Smoke free premises. 84 units. 2 stories (no elevator), interior corridors. **Parking:** winter plug-ins. **Terms:** cancellation fee imposed. **Pool(s):** heated indoor. **Activities:** whirlpool, exercise room. **Guest Services:** valet and coin laundry, wireless Internet. **Free Special Amenities:** expanded continental breakfast and high-speed Internet.

—— **WHERE TO DINE** ——

2510 RESTAURANT

American
$5-$20

Phone: 715/845-2510

This well-established restaurant is locally popular. The menu is vast and varied, and a deli and bakery are attached. While reservations are not accepted, call-ahead seating is available. **Bar:** full bar. **Hours:** 7 am-10 pm, Sun-9 pm. Closed: 11/24, 12/25. **Address:** 2510 Stewart Ave 54401 **Location:** I-39, exit 192, 0.3 mi w on SR 52. **Parking:** on-site (fee).

ANNIE'S AMERICAN CAFE

American
$6-$15

Phone: 715/842-0846

Serving good, wholesome meals and homemade soups and desserts, the restaurant features a hearty breakfast and lunch buffet in addition to their regular menu offerings. **Hours:** 6 am-11 pm. Closed: 11/24, 12/25. **Address:** 305 S 18th Ave 54401 **Location:** I-39, exit 192, just ne.

CARMELO'S

Italian
$10-$29

Phone: 715/845-5570

Convenient to a ski area and golf course, the lively restaurant offers food that is homemade and tasty. Servers are friendly and reliable. **Bar:** full bar. **Hours:** 5 pm-close. Closed major holidays. **Address:** 3607 N Mountain Rd 54401 **Location:** I-39, exit 190 (CR NN), 0.9 mi w. CALL 👓M

EMMA KRUMBEE'S

American
$6-$12

Phone: 715/843-7171

The coffee shop-style restaurant prepares homemade baked goods using 29 varieties of apples. Counter, table or booth seating available. Menu is family favorites. **Hours:** 6 am-8 pm. Closed major holidays. **Address:** 2101 N Mountain Rd 54401 **Location:** I-39, exit 190 (CR NN), just se. CALL 👓M

HUDSON'S CLASSIC GRILL

American
$7-$15

Phone: 715/849-8586

Memorabilia from the '50s and '60s creates the atmosphere here. The menu lists a good variety of sandwiches and burgers, with some entrees such as baked spaghetti and chicken linguine. **Bar:** full bar. **Hours:** 11 am-10 pm, Fri & Sat-11 pm. Closed: 11/24, 12/25. **Address:** 2200 Stewart Ave 54402 **Location:** I-39, exit 192, just e. CALL 👓M

MICHAEL'S

American
$10-$30

Phone: 715/842-9856

Fresh seafood, veal specialties and gourmet pizza highlight the menu, which is bolstered by the popular Friday night fish fry. The chef gladly accommodates special requests. Desserts are presented tableside on a tray. **Bar:** full bar. **Hours:** 5 pm-10 pm. Closed major holidays; also Sun. **Address:** 2901 Rib Mountain Dr 54401 **Location:** I-39, exit 190 (CR NN), 0.5 mi se.

MINO'S CUCINA ITALIANA

Italian
$14-$34

Phone: 715/675-5939

Patrons can choose from classic dishes or the chef's creations. Seafood, pasta and pizza are popular. The tiramisu, which is made in house, is delicious. **Bar:** full bar. **Hours:** 5 pm-10 pm. Closed major holidays; also Sun. **Address:** 900 Golf Club Rd 54403 **Location:** On CR W, 1.3 mi n of jct SR 52 E; on east side of Wisconsin River. CALL 👓M

WAUTOMA pop. 1,998

AMERICINN LODGE & SUITES OF WAUTOMA

Hotel
$78-$169

Phone: (920)787-5050

Address: W7696 SR 21/73 54982 **Location:** On SR 21 and 73, 1.2 mi e. **Facility:** Smoke free premises. 49 units, some efficiencies. 2 stories (no elevator), interior corridors. **Parking:** winter plug-ins. **Terms:** cancellation fee imposed. **Amenities:** safes (fee). *Some:* high-speed Internet. **Pool(s):** heated indoor. **Activities:** whirlpool, picnic area. **Guest Services:** coin laundry, wireless Internet, tanning facilities.

🍴 CALL 👓M 🛄 FEE 🏊 ✕ 🖥 🖨 🖵 / SOME UNITS FEE 🐾

SUPER 8-WAUTOMA

Hotel
$54-$91

Phone: (920)787-4811

Address: W7607 SR 21/73 54982 **Location:** On SR 21 and 73, 1.5 mi e. **Facility:** Smoke free premises. 50 units. 2 stories (no elevator), interior corridors. **Parking:** winter plug-ins. **Pool(s):** heated indoor. **Activities:** sauna, whirlpool. **Guest Services:** coin laundry, wireless Internet.

🍴 CALL 👓M 🛄 ✕ 🎦 🖵 / SOME UNITS FEE 🐾 🖥 🖨

—— WHERE TO DINE ——

CHRISTIANOS PIZZA & REAL ITALIAN PASTA

Italian
$6-$17

Phone: 920/787-7262

A renovated office building houses this Italian restaurant. At 4 am, the owner comes in to bake all the breads for the day. Standouts here include the homemade sauces that accompany many dishes and pizzas and calzones baked in the brick oven. **Hours:** 11 am-10 pm, Fri & Sat-midnight. Closed: 12/24, 12/25; also Sun. **Address:** 200 W Main St 54982 **Location:** Just n of center; on Main St (SR 21). CALL ⟨&⟩M

WAUWATOSA —See Milwaukee p. 569.

WEST BEND —See Milwaukee p. 570.

WESTBY pop. 2,045

—— WHERE TO DINE ——

OLD TOWNE INN

American
$12-$38

Phone: 608/634-3991

This contemporary country restaurant lures patrons for a casual, quiet meal. Steak and seafood make up the bulk of a menu of tried-and-true favorites. On Tuesdays, diners can try Mexican fare, while succulent prime rib is the special on Wednesdays and weekends. **Bar:** full bar. **Reservations:** suggested. **Hours:** 5 pm-9 pm, Fri & Sat-10 pm. Closed: major holidays, 12/24; also Mon. **Address:** 100 E Old Town Rd 54667 **Location:** 0.5 mi s on US 14.

WESTFIELD pop. 1,217

WESTFIELD PIONEER MOTOR INN

Hotel
$75-$105 5/1-4/30
$65-$96 4/1-4/30

Phone: 608/296-2135

Address: 242 N Pioneer Rd 53964 **Location:** I-39, exit 113 (CR J and E), just nw. Located in a commercial area. **Facility:** Smoke free premises. 29 units. 2 stories (no elevator), interior corridors. **Parking:** winter plug-ins. **Terms:** cancellation fee imposed. **Guest Services:** wireless Internet.

WESTON pop. 12,079

FAIRFIELD INN & SUITES BY MARRIOTT

Hotel
$89-$114

Phone: (715)241-8400

Address: 7100 Stone Ridge Dr 54476 **Location:** SR 29, exit 173, just n. **Facility:** Smoke free premises. 87 units. 3 stories, interior corridors. **Terms:** cancellation fee imposed. **Amenities:** high-speed Internet. **Pool(s):** heated indoor. **Activities:** whirlpool, exercise room. **Guest Services:** valet and coin laundry, wireless Internet.

> **AAA Benefit:**
> Members save a minimum 5% off the best available rate.

WEST SALEM pop. 4,540

AMERICINN MOTEL & SUITES OF WEST SALEM

Hotel
$83-$153

Phone: (608)786-3340

Address: 125 Buol Rd 54669 **Location:** I-90, exit 12, just sw on CR C. **Facility:** Smoke free premises. 50 units. 2 stories (no elevator), interior corridors. **Parking:** winter plug-ins. **Pool(s):** heated indoor. **Activities:** sauna, whirlpool. Fee: game room. **Guest Services:** valet and coin laundry, wireless Internet.

WHITEFISH BAY —See Milwaukee p. 571.

WHITEWATER pop. 13,437

BAYMONT INN & SUITES
Hotel
$62-$116

Phone: (262)472-9400

Address: 1355 W Main St 53190 **Location:** On US 12 business route, 0.5 mi w of jct SR 59 W. **Facility:** Smoke free premises. 60 units. 2 stories (no elevator), interior corridors. **Parking:** winter plug-ins. **Terms:** cancellation fee imposed. **Amenities:** safes (fee). **Pool(s):** heated indoor. **Activities:** whirlpool, sun deck, exercise room. **Guest Services:** valet and coin laundry, wireless Internet. **Free Special Amenities:** expanded continental breakfast and high-speed Internet.

—— WHERE TO DINE ——

RANDY'S RESTAURANT & FUN HUNTERS BREWERY

American
$7-$34

Phone: 262/473-8000

Visitors can watch the brewing operation from the bar area of this laid-back restaurant. On the varied menu are entrees such as barbecue baby back ribs, steaks, seafood, chicken, pasta, sandwiches, burgers and salads. Tasty beverages include microbrewed beers and homemade root beer and cream soda. Historic area photographs adorn the walls. **Bar:** full bar. **Hours:** 11 am-9 pm, Fri & Sat-10:30 pm, Sun 10:30 am-9 pm. Closed: 1/1, 11/24, 12/25. **Address:** 841 E Milwaukee St 53190 **Location:** On US 12 business route; east end of town. CALL ⟨&⟩M

WILD ROSE pop. 765

—— WHERE TO DINE ——

PIONEER PUB

American
$4-$15

Phone: 920/622-4550

This looks much like a log cabin on the lake and actually sits on the shores of Wild Rose Mill Pond. The laid-back setting includes a tiered deck overlooking the water for those days when the weather is nice. Half-pound Angus burgers, charbroiled steaks, pizza and the Friday fish fry (a Wisconsin tradition) are specialties here. The menu also offers appetizers such as deep-fried cheese curds and breaded mushrooms, soups, salads, sandwiches, chicken, barbecue ribs, tuna and walleye dinners. **Bar:** full bar. **Hours:** 11 am-11 pm; seasonal hours may vary. **Address:** 480 Main St (Hwy 22) 54984 **Location:** Main St (SR 22); center. **Parking:** on-site and street. CALL 🏃M

WINDSOR pop. 2,533

DAYS INN

Hotel
$56-$126

Phone: (608)846-7473

Address: 6311 Rostad Cir 53598 **Location:** I-90/94, exit 131 (SR 19). **Facility:** Smoke free premises. 54 units. 3 stories, interior corridors. **Parking:** winter plug-ins. **Terms:** cancellation fee imposed. **Pool(s):** heated indoor. **Activities:** sauna, whirlpool, limited exercise equipment. **Guest Services:** coin laundry, wireless Internet. 🅗 CALL 🏃M 🔁 ✕ 🐾 🎦 📷 💬 / SOME UNITS FEE 🐕

—— WHERE TO DINE ——

THE RODESIDE GRILL

American
$6-$20

Phone: 608/846-1874

The log cabin restaurant and bar offers good food, spirits and a nice fireplace by which to get warm. It's just off the interstate for easy access. **Bar:** full bar. **Hours:** 11 am-9 pm, Fri & Sat-10 pm. Closed: 11/24, 12/24, 12/25. **Address:** 6317 Rostad Cir 53598 **Location:** I-90/94, exit 131 (SR 19), just e on SR 19. CALL 🏃M

Wisconsin Dells
Lodging & Dining

Scale in Miles
0.6   0   0.6

To Mauston
Rocky Arbor State Park

To Wisconsin Rapids

SEE INSET MAP FOR DETAIL

© 2010 NAVTEQ

BROADWAY ST

DELLS DAM

Mirror Lake

State Park

To Baraboo © AAA

To Madison

To Portage

Downtown
Wisconsin
Dells

Wisconsin River

Dells Boat Tours

BROADWAY

DELLS DAM

WISCONSIN AVE

MICHIGAN AVE

WASHINGTON AVE

1660-A

Wisconsin Dells

This index helps you "spot" where approved lodgings and restaurants are located on the corresponding detailed maps. Lodging daily rate range is for comparison only and show the property's high season. Restaurant rate range is a combination of lunch and/or dinner. Turn to the listing page for more detailed rate information and consult display ads for special promotions.

WISCONSIN DELLS

Map Page	OA	Lodgings	Diamond Rated	High Season	Page
1 / p. 605		Bridge View Motel	◆	$69-$189	610
2 / p. 605	AAA	**Indian Trail Motel**	◆	$39-$149 SAVE	613
3 / p. 605	AAA	**The Gables Motel**	◆	$39-$99 SAVE	611
4 / p. 605	AAA	**Black Hawk Motel**	◆	$40-$255 SAVE	609
5 / p. 605		Super 8-Wisconsin Dells	◆◆	$43-$103	614
6 / p. 605		Comfort Inn	◆◆	Rates not provided	611
7 / p. 605	AAA	**Best Western Ambassador Inn & Suites**	◆◆	$60-$219 SAVE	609
8 / p. 605	AAA	**AmericInn Lodge & Suites of Wisconsin Dells - see ad p. 610**	◆◆◆	$90-$180 SAVE	609
9 / p. 605		Atlantis Waterpark Hotel	◆◆	$59-$229	609
10 / p. 605		Raintree Resort	◆◆	$129-$499	614
11 / p. 605		Luna Inn & Suites	◆◆	$49-$169	613
12 / p. 605	AAA	**Caribbean Club Resort**	◆◆	$115-$415 SAVE	610
13 / p. 605		Hilton Garden Inn Wisconsin Dells	◆◆◆	$140-$210	613
14 / p. 605		American World Hotel-A Mt. Olympus Hotel and RV Resort	◆◆	Rates not provided	608
15 / p. 605		Holiday Inn Express - see ad p. 608	◆◆◆	$79-$179	613
16 / p. 605	AAA	**Ramada Wisconsin Dells**	◆◆◆	$68-$158 SAVE	614
17 / p. 605		Wintergreen Resort & Conference Center	◆◆◆	$75-$189	614
18 / p. 605	AAA	**Great Wolf Lodge - see ad p. 201**	◆◆◆	Rates not provided SAVE	613

Map Page	OA	Restaurants	Diamond Rated	Cuisine	Meal Range	Page
1 / p. 605		River Walk Pub	◆	American	$5-$15	616
2 / p. 605		Pedro's Mexican Restaurante	◆◆	Mexican	$7-$22	616
3 / p. 605		High Rock Cafe	◆◆	American	$6-$22	615
4 / p. 605		Monk's Bar and Grill	◆	American	$5-$12	615
5 / p. 605		Grandma Honey's Family Restaurant	◆	American	$5-$7	615
6 / p. 605		Mexicali Rose	◆◆	Mexican	$10-$19	615
7 / p. 605	AAA	**Paul Bunyan's "Northwoods Cook Shanty"**	◆	American	$8-$15	615
8 / p. 605		Ginza of Tokyo Japanese Steakhouse and Sushi Bar	◆◆◆	Japanese	$15-$38	614
9 / p. 605		Marley's	◆◆	Caribbean	$7-$21	615
10 / p. 605		Pizza Pub	◆◆	American	$8-$25	616
11 / p. 605		Wally's House of Embers	◆◆◆	American	$14-$35	616
12 / p. 605		The Del-Bar	◆◆◆	American	$17-$39	614
13 / p. 605		Mary's Place	◆	American	$5-$10	615
14 / p. 605		Brat House Grill	◆	Deli	$4-$9	614
15 / p. 605		Moosejaw Pizza & Dells Brewing Co	◆◆	American	$6-$30	615

Map Page	OA	Restaurants (cont'd)	Diamond Rated	Cuisine	Meal Range	Page
⑯ / p. 605	AAA	**Field's at the Wilderness**	◆◆◆	Steak	$20-$45	614
⑰ / p. 605		Howie's Restaurant	◆	Breads/Pastries	$4-$12	615
⑱ / p. 605		Sarento's	◆◆◆	Italian	$13-$36	616
⑲ / p. 605		R Place Italian Restaurant	◆◆	Italian	$11-$32	616
⑳ / p. 605		The Cheese Factory Restaurant	◆◆	Vegetarian	$5-$18	614
㉑ / p. 605		Monk's Bar & Grill at the Wilderness	◆◆	American	$7-$20	615
㉒ / p. 605		Buffalo Phil's Grille	◆◆	American	$12-$25	614
㉓ / p. 605		Kahunaville	◆◆	American	$8-$24	615

WISCONSIN DELLS pop. 2,418   (See map and index starting on p. 605)

AMERICAN WORLD HOTEL-A MT. OLYMPUS HOTEL AND RV RESORT   Phone: 608/253-4451   **14**

Hotel
Rates not provided

Address: 400 CR A & Hwy 12 53965 **Location:** I-90/94, exit 87 (SR 23), jct US 12 and CR A. **Facility:** Smoke free premises. 71 units. 3 stories, interior corridors. **Parking:** winter plug-ins. **Pool(s):** heated outdoor, 2 heated indoor. **Activities:** saunas, whirlpools, lighted tennis court, picnic pavilion, playground, sports court, basketball, volleyball. **Fee:** waterslide, game room. **Guest Services:** coin laundry, wireless Internet.

AMERICAS BEST VALUE DAY'S END MOTEL   Phone: (608)254-8171

Motel
$41-$152 4/1-9/4
$34-$118 9/5-4/30

Address: N 604 Hwy 12-16 53965 **Location:** I-90/94, exit 85 (US 12), 0.8 mi nw. **Facility:** Smoke free premises. 28 units. 1 story, exterior corridors. **Parking:** winter plug-ins. **Terms:** 3 day cancellation notice-fee imposed. **Pool(s):** heated outdoor. **Activities:** waterslide, miniature golf, picnic area with grills, playground. **Guest Services:** wireless Internet. *(see ad p. 609)*

FREE local telephone calls and high-speed Internet

▼ See AAA listing p. 613 ▼

Stay. Play. Dine. Save. Visit AAA.com/Travel
or CAA.ca/Travel for Information To Go!

(See map and index starting on p. 605)

AMERICINN LODGE & SUITES OF WISCONSIN DELLS
Phone: (608)254-1700

Hotel
$90-$180 4/1-9/1
$70-$130 9/2-4/30

Address: 550 State Hwy 13 53965 **Location:** I-90/94, exit 87 (SR 13), just e. **Facility:** Smoke free premises. 78 units. 3 stories, interior corridors. **Parking:** winter plug-ins. **Terms:** 3 day cancellation notice-fee imposed. **Amenities:** high-speed Internet, safes (fee). **Pool(s):** heated indoor. **Activities:** sauna, whirlpool, limited exercise equipment. **Guest Services:** coin laundry, wireless Internet. *(see ad p. 610)*

FREE expanded continental breakfast and high-speed Internet

ATLANTIS WATERPARK HOTEL
Phone: (608)253-6606 **9**

Hotel
$59-$229

Address: 1570 Wisconsin Dells Pkwy 53965 **Location:** I-90/94, exit 87 (SR 13), 1 mi e, then 1 mi n on US 12. **Facility:** Smoke free premises. 96 units, some two bedrooms. 4 stories, interior corridors. **Terms:** 2 night minimum stay - seasonal and/or weekends, 3 day cancellation notice-fee imposed. **Amenities:** *Some:* high-speed Internet. **Pool(s):** 3 heated outdoor, 3 heated indoor. **Activities:** sauna, waterslide. *Fee:* game room. **Guest Services:** coin laundry, wireless Internet.

BEST WESTERN AMBASSADOR INN & SUITES
Phone: (608)254-4477 **7**

Hotel
$60-$219

Address: 610 Frontage Rd S 53965 **Location:** I-90/94, exit 87 (SR 13), just e. **Facility:** Smoke free premises. 181 units, some two bedrooms and kitchens. 2-3 stories, interior corridors. **Parking:** winter plug-ins. **Terms:** check-in 4 pm, 3 day cancellation notice-fee imposed. **Pool(s):** heated outdoor, heated indoor. **Activities:** sauna, whirlpools, playground. *Fee:* game room. **Guest Services:** wireless Internet. **Free Special Amenities:** early check-in/late check-out and high-speed Internet.

AAA Benefit:
Members save up to 20%, plus 10% bonus points with free rewards program.

BLACK HAWK MOTEL
Phone: 608/254-7770 **4**

Motel
$40-$255 5/21-10/23
$36-$165 4/15-5/20

Address: 720 Race St 53965 **Location:** I-90/94, exit 87 (SR 13), 2 mi e on SR 13, 16 and 23. **Facility:** Smoke free premises. 75 units, some two bedrooms, kitchens and houses. 1-2 stories (no elevator), exterior corridors. **Terms:** open 4/15-10/23, 3 day cancellation notice-fee imposed. **Pool(s):** heated outdoor, heated indoor. **Activities:** saunas, whirlpools, waterslide, playground. *Fee:* game room. **Guest Services:** coin laundry, area transportation-train depot, wireless Internet. **Free Special Amenities:** early check-in/late check-out and high-speed Internet.

▼ See AAA listing p. 608 ▼

(See map and index starting on p. 605)

BRIDGE VIEW MOTEL

Motel
$69-$189

Phone: 608/254-6114 **❶**

Address: 1020 River Rd 53965 **Location:** Just n of SR 13; center. **Facility:** Smoke free premises. 17 units, some efficiencies. 2 stories (no elevator), exterior corridors. **Terms:** open 5/1-10/31, 3 day cancellation notice-fee imposed. **Pool(s):** heated outdoor. **Activities:** waterslide, playground.

CARIBBEAN CLUB RESORT

Vacation Rental
Condominium
$115-$415

Phone: (608)254-4777 **⓬**

Address: 1093 Canyon Rd 53965 **Location:** I-90/94, exit 92 (SR 12), 0.7 mi w on SR 12 to Canyon Rd, then 1.2 mi. **Facility:** Located in a quiet area overlooking a lake, the resort offers units with full kitchens and spacious living spaces; each room includes a whirlpool. Smoke free premises. 47 kitchen units, some two and three bedrooms. 2 stories (no elevator), interior corridors. **Terms:** office hours 9 am-10 pm, 2 night minimum stay - seasonal and/or weekends, 7 day cancellation notice-fee imposed. **Pool(s):** heated outdoor, heated indoor. **Activities:** sauna, whirlpool, limited beach access, canoeing, boat dock, pedal boats. **Guest Services:** complimentary laundry, wireless Internet. **Free Special Amenities: room upgrade (subject to availability with advance reservations) and high-speed Internet.**

▼ See AAA listing p. 609 ▼

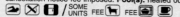

(See map and index starting on p. 605)

CHRISTMAS MOUNTAIN VILLAGE
Phone: (608)253-1000

Vacation Rental House
$129-$526 9/4-4/30
$129-$382 4/1-9/3

Location: I-90/94, exit 87 (SR 13), 0.4 mi ne to CR H, 4 mi sw, then just s. **Facility:** Individual homes and condos provide a restful place to build vacation memories; near a golf course, several campgrounds and a downhill ski area. 350 houses. 2 stories (no elevator), exterior corridors. **Terms:** check-in 4 pm, 2 night minimum stay - seasonal and/or weekends, 3 day cancellation notice-fee imposed. **Activities:** sauna, whirlpools, waterslide, paddleboats, kayaks, miniature golf, tennis court, downhill skiing, tobogganing, recreation programs in season, hiking trails, playground, exercise room, basketball, horseshoes, shuffleboard, volleyball, game room. Fee: golf-27 holes. **Guest Services:** coin laundry, wireless Internet.

CHULA VISTA RESORT
Phone: (608)254-8366

Resort Hotel
$139-$649

Address: 2501 N River Rd 53965 **Location:** From Wisconsin River Bridge, 3 mi n. **Facility:** On the Upper Dells of the Wisconsin River, this resort is popular with families due to the many recreational activities available. Smoke free premises. 620 units, some two bedrooms, three bedrooms, efficiencies and kitchens. 2-7 stories, interior/exterior corridors. **Terms:** check-in 4 pm, 2 night minimum stay - seasonal and/or weekends, 3 day cancellation notice-fee imposed. **Amenities:** Some: video games (fee). **Dining:** 4 restaurants. **Pool(s):** 4 heated outdoor, 2 heated indoor. **Activities:** whirlpools, waterslide, indoor & outdoor water park, recreation programs, playground, exercise room, spa. Fee: golf-18 holes, miniature golf, game room. **Guest Services:** coin laundry, area transportation-bus & train station, wireless Internet. (see ad p. 612)

FREE newspaper and high-speed Internet

COMFORT INN
Phone: 608/253-3711

Hotel
Rates not provided

Address: 703 N Frontage Rd 53965 **Location:** I-90/94, exit 87 (SR 13), just e. **Facility:** Smoke free premises. 75 units. 3 stories, interior corridors. **Parking:** winter plug-ins. **Terms:** check-in 4 pm. **Pool(s):** heated indoor. **Activities:** whirlpool, sun deck. **Guest Services:** wireless Internet.

THE GABLES MOTEL
Phone: 608/253-3831 [3]

Motel
$39-$99

Address: 822 Oak St 53965 **Location:** Just n of Broadway, US 16, SR 13 and 23; downtown. **Facility:** Smoke free premises. 30 units. 2 stories (no elevator), exterior corridors. **Parking:** winter plug-ins. **Terms:** 3 day cancellation notice. **Pool(s):** heated outdoor. **Guest Services:** wireless Internet. **Free Special Amenities:** local telephone calls and high-speed Internet.

▼ See AAA listing p. 580 ▼

▼ See AAA listing p. 611 ▼

(See map and index starting on p. 605)

GREAT WOLF LODGE

Hotel
Rates not provided

Phone: 608/253-2222　**18**

Address: 1400 Great Wolf Dr 53965 **Location:** I-90/94, exit 92 (US 12). **Facility:** Smoke free premises. 436 units, some two bedrooms, three bedrooms and kitchens. 3-4 stories, interior corridors. **Terms:** check-in 4 pm. **Amenities:** video games (fee). *Some:* safes. **Dining:** 3 restaurants. **Pool(s):** heated outdoor, heated indoor. **Activities:** whirlpools, waterslide, indoor/outdoor water park facilities with lazy river, exercise room, spa. *Fee:* game room. **Guest Services:** coin laundry, wireless Internet. *(see ad p. 201)*

HILTON GARDEN INN WISCONSIN DELLS

Hotel
$140-$210

Phone: (608)253-1100　**13**

AAA Benefit:
Members save 5% or more everyday!

Address: 101 E Hiawatha Dr 53965 **Location:** I-90/94, exit 92 (US 12), 1.7 mi n, then 0.6 mi e. **Facility:** Smoke free premises. 128 units. 4 stories, interior corridors. **Terms:** 1-7 night minimum stay, cancellation fee imposed. **Amenities:** video games (fee), high-speed Internet. **Pool(s):** heated indoor. **Activities:** whirlpools, exercise room. *Fee:* game room. **Guest Services:** coin laundry, wireless Internet.

HOLIDAY INN EXPRESS

Hotel
$79-$179

Phone: (608)253-3000　**15**

Address: 1033 Wisconsin Dells Pkwy S 53913 **Location:** I-90/94, exit 92 (US 12), 0.3 mi n. **Facility:** Smoke free premises. 113 units. 3 stories, interior corridors. **Terms:** check-in 4 pm. **Pool(s):** heated outdoor, heated indoor. **Activities:** whirlpool, waterslide, exercise room. *Fee:* game room. **Guest Services:** coin laundry, wireless Internet. **(see ad p. 608)**

INDIAN TRAIL MOTEL

Motel
$39-$149 5/1-9/5
$39-$119 9/6-10/16

Phone: (608)253-2641　**2**

Address: 1013 Broadway 53965 **Location:** I-90/94, exit 87 (SR 13), 2 mi e on SR 13, 16 and 23. **Facility:** Smoke free premises. 46 units, some houses. 1 story, exterior corridors. **Terms:** open 5/1-10/16, 2 night minimum stay - seasonal and/or weekends, 3 day cancellation notice-fee imposed. **Amenities:** *Some:* high-speed Internet. **Pool(s):** heated outdoor, heated indoor. **Activities:** sauna, whirlpool, playground. *Fee:* game room. **Guest Services:** coin laundry, wireless Internet. **Free Special Amenities:** early check-in/late check-out and high-speed Internet.

   / SOME UNITS

LUNA INN & SUITES

Motel
$49-$169

Phone: 608/253-2661　**11**

Address: 1111 Wisconsin Dells Pkwy 53965 **Location:** I-90/94, exit 92 (US 12), 2.8 mi n. **Facility:** Smoke free premises. 72 units. 2 stories (no elevator), interior/exterior corridors. **Terms:** open 5/1-10/30, 2 night minimum stay - seasonal and/or weekends, 3 day cancellation notice-fee imposed. **Pool(s):** heated outdoor, heated indoor. **Activities:** whirlpool, waterslide, playground. *Fee:* game room. **Guest Services:** coin laundry.

(See map and index starting on p. 605)

RAINTREE RESORT

◈◈◈
Hotel
$129-$499 4/1-8/31
$79-$299 9/1-4/30

Phone: (608)254-8700 ⑩

Address: 1435 Wisconsin Dells Pkwy 53965 **Location:** I-90/94, exit 89 (SR 23), 0.5 mi e, then 1.5 mi n on US 12. **Facility:** Smoke free premises. 158 units. 3-4 stories, interior corridors. **Terms:** 7 day cancellation notice-fee imposed. **Pool(s):** heated indoor, heated indoor/outdoor. **Activities:** whirlpools, waterslide, small indoor/outdoor water park with multiple children activity areas, exercise room. *Fee:* game room. **Guest Services:** coin laundry, wireless Internet.

🍽 🍸 CALL 🚭M 🏊 ✕ 🛗 🖥 💻

RAMADA WISCONSIN DELLS

◈◈◈
Hotel
$68-$158

Phone: (608)254-2218 ⑯

Address: 1073 Wisconsin Dells Pkwy S 53965 **Location:** I-90/94, exit 92 (US 12), 0.3 mi n. **Facility:** Smoke free premises. 71 units. 2 stories, interior corridors. **Parking:** winter plug-ins. **Terms:** check-in 4 pm, 2 night minimum stay - seasonal and/or weekends, cancellation fee imposed. **Pool(s):** heated indoor. **Activities:** sauna, whirlpool, exercise room. **Guest Services:** coin laundry, wireless Internet. **Free Special Amenities: expanded continental breakfast and high-speed Internet.** SAVE 🍽 CALL 🚭M 🏊 BIZ ✕ 🧖 🛗 🖥 💻

SUPER 8-WISCONSIN DELLS

◈◈◈
Hotel
$43-$103

Phone: (608)254-6464 ❺

Address: 800 CR H 53965 **Location:** I-90/94, exit 87 (SR 13), just e. **Facility:** Smoke free premises. 124 units. 3 stories, interior corridors. **Parking:** winter plug-ins. **Pool(s):** heated indoor. **Activities:** sauna, whirlpool. **Guest Services:** coin laundry, wireless Internet.

🍽 🏊 ✕ 🧖 💻 / SOME UNITS FEE 🐾 🛗 🖥

WINTERGREEN RESORT & CONFERENCE CENTER

◈◈◈
Hotel
$75-$189

Phone: 608-254-2285 ⑰

Address: 60 Gasser Rd 53965 **Location:** I-90/94, exit 92 (US 12), just n. Located next to a casino. **Facility:** Smoke free premises. 111 units, some three bedrooms. 3 stories, interior corridors. **Parking:** winter plug-ins. **Terms:** check-in 4 pm, 2 night minimum stay - seasonal and/or weekends, 3 day cancellation notice-fee imposed. **Pool(s):** heated outdoor, heated indoor. **Activities:** whirlpools, waterslide, mini water park, waterfalls, playground, exercise room. **Guest Services:** coin laundry, wireless Internet. 🍽 🍸 🏊 ✕ 🛗 🖥 💻

--------- **WHERE TO DINE** ---------

BRAT HOUSE GRILL

◈
Deli
$4-$9

Phone: 608/254-8505 ⑭

In an old church building, the full-service Internet cafe has 20 workstations and T1 connections for network gaming or online access. Diners can enjoy a sandwich and gourmet coffee while they browse. **Bar:** beer & wine. **Hours:** 11 am-11 pm. Closed: 12/25. **Address:** 49 Wisconsin Dells Pkwy S 53965 **Location:** I-90/94, exit 92 (US 12), 2 mi w.

BUFFALO PHIL'S GRILLE

◈◈
American
$12-$25

Phone: 608/254-7300 ㉒

With a lodge-style atmosphere, which is accented by a stone fireplace, this a great place to enjoy a bowl of chicken tortilla soup or a rack of barbecue ribs. There is plenty here to excite both the eyes and the palate. **Bar:** full bar. **Hours:** 11 am-10 pm, Fri & Sat-10:30 pm; to 11 pm in summer. **Address:** 150 Gasser Rd 53965 **Location:** I-90/94, exit 92 (US 12), just n.

THE CHEESE FACTORY RESTAURANT

◈◈
Vegetarian
$5-$18

Phone: 608/253-6065 ⑳

Fresh, flavorful ingredients, unusual international recipes and pleasant service are staples at the restored cheese factory. An authentic soda fountain, jukebox and waiters in bow ties add to the nostalgic mood. Homemade desserts are wonderful. **Hours:** 11 am-9 pm, Sun from 9 am; seasonal hours may vary. Closed: 12/25 & Easter; also Mon-Wed. **Address:** 521 Wisconsin Dells Pkwy S 53965 **Location:** I-90/94, exit 92 (US 12), 1.3 mi n. CALL 🚭M

THE DEL-BAR

◈◈◈
American
$17-$39

Phone: 608/253-1861 ⑫

Owned and operated by same family since 1943. Excellent aged steak and fresh seafood. Also featuring Wisconsin duck. Terrace dining in season. Warm atmosphere with soft lighting and soothing player piano background music. **Bar:** full bar. **Reservations:** suggested. **Hours:** 4:30 pm-9 pm, Fri & Sat-9:30 pm. Closed: 11/24, 12/24, 12/25. **Address:** 800 Wisconsin Dells Pkwy 53940 **Location:** I-90/94, exit 92 (US 12), 2.5 mi n on US 12 and SR 23. CALL 🚭M

FIELD'S AT THE WILDERNESS

◈◈◈◈
Steak
$20-$45

Phone: 608/253-1400 ⑯

Inspired by the architecture of Frank Lloyd Wright, the demurely elegant restaurant features a number of stone hearth fireplaces, waterfalls and an exhibition kitchen. The a la carte menu lists contemporary yet creative preparations of steak, chops and fresh seafood, as well as pizzas cooked in a wood-burning oven. **Bar:** full bar. **Reservations:** suggested. **Hours:** 4:30 pm-10 pm. Closed: 12/24, 12/25. **Address:** 511 E Adams St 53965 **Location:** I-90/94, exit 92 (US 12), 0.7 mi n. CALL 🚭M

GINZA OF TOKYO JAPANESE STEAKHOUSE AND SUSHI BAR

◈◈◈
Japanese
$15-$38

Phone: 608/254-8883 ⑧

The fun yet elegant restaurant is a sushi lover's delight. Guests have a choice of three seating areas: the sushi bar, communal hibachi tables and private tables where food is ordered a la carte. At the sushi bar, experts guide the uninitiated through menu options while chefs skillfully slice sashimi and hand-rolled sushi. At the more playful hibachi tables, guests sit back for the show as their own personal chef joins the table. During the busy season, it's a good idea to make reservations. **Bar:** full bar. **Hours:** 4:30 pm-9:30 pm, Fri 5 pm-10 pm, Sat 4 pm-10 pm, Sun 4:30 pm-9:30 pm; 4 pm-midnight in season. Closed: 12/25. **Address:** 1481 Wisconsin Dells Pkwy 53940 **Location:** I-90/94, exit 89 (SR 23), 0.5 mi e, then 1.5 mi n on US 12. CALL 🚭M

(See map and index starting on p. 605)

GRANDMA HONEY'S FAMILY RESTAURANT
Phone: 608/254-2444 ⑤

American
$5-$7

In an off-the-beaten-path house, the no-frills mom-and-pop restaurant is a favorite of locals for good food at a good value. **Hours:** 7 am-2 pm. Closed: 1/1, 12/25; also Thurs in winter. **Address:** 855 CR H 53965 **Location:** I-90/94, exit 87, 0.3 mi e (SR 13), then 0.3 mi nw. CALL ♿M

HIGH ROCK CAFE
Phone: 608/254-5677 ③

American
$6-$22

Above a retail store, the small, relaxed dining room offers guests a quiet view of the otherwise hectic downtown drag. The menu focuses on modern variations of traditional chicken, fish and steaks. **Bar:** beer & wine. **Hours:** 11 am-10 pm. Closed: 1/1, 11/24, 12/25. **Address:** 232 Broadway 53965 **Location:** Downtown. **Parking:** street only.

HOWIE'S RESTAURANT
Phone: 608/254-2076 ⑰

Breads/Pastries
$4-$12

Open for breakfast only, the eatery has been in business since 1958 offering quick-serve breakfasts with a few choices of lunch items such as burgers and sandwiches. **Hours:** Open 4/1-11/30 & 2/1-4/30; 7 am-noon; to 2 pm in summer. Closed major holidays. **Address:** 230 W Monroe Ave 53965 **Location:** I-90/94, exit 89 (SR 23 N), 0.5 mi e. CALL ♿M

KAHUNAVILLE
Phone: 608/254-5466 ㉓

American
$8-$24

Designed to resemble a tropical island paradise, the expansive dining area, with its fun-filled atmosphere, combines big-screen TVs, juggling bartenders and a children's play area. The menu lines up selections ranging from island-inspired pub classics to children's favorites. Oversize dessert portions are perfect for sharing. **Bar:** full bar. **Hours:** 4 pm-10 pm. **Address:** 1305 Kalahari Dr 53965 **Location:** I-90/94, exit 92 (US 12), just w; in Kalahari Resort. CALL ♿M

MARLEY'S
Phone: 608/254-1800 ⑨

Caribbean
$7-$21

This colorful, lively place is not just a restaurant; it is also an experience. Jamaican food, mostly seafood and fruity adult beverages, make up the menu. Little ones can check out the children's menu. **Bar:** full bar. **Hours:** 11 am-9 pm; to 10 pm in summer. Closed: 11/24, 12/25. **Address:** 1470 Wisconsin Dells Pkwy 53965 **Location:** 1.4 mi s of jct US 16, SR 13 and 23.

MARY'S PLACE
Phone: 608/393-8688 ⑬

American
$5-$10

From the whimsical cartoon-like hot dog that forms the signage outside to the arcade games inside to the train whistle the staff blows when guests' meals are ready, aspects of this eatery add up to a family-friendly experience. Quick, inexpensive meals along the lines of half-pound footlong hot dogs, hamburgers, Italian sandwiches, deep-fried white cheese curds and hot fudge sundaes can be ordered for dining in or taking out. **Hours:** 11 am-8 pm. Closed: 11/24, 12/25; also Mon & Tues off season. **Address:** 133 Wisconsin Dells Pkwy S 53965 **Location:** I-90/94, exit 92, 2 mi w on US 12.

MEXICALI ROSE
Phone: 608/254-6036 ⑥

Mexican
$10-$19

Next to the docks by the dam separating the Upper from Lower Dells on the Wisconsin River, this Mexican restaurant is a favorite among locals and tourists alike for its value-priced meals and festive atmosphere. Colorful murals adorning the walls, paper roses and colored lights strung from the ceiling, and piñata-themed sculptures all bring a sense of fiesta to the setting, in which many tables are positioned along large windows overlooking the river. The seasonal terrace also offers seating. **Bar:** full bar. **Hours:** 4:30 pm-10 pm; from 11 am in season. Closed: 11/24, 12/25. **Address:** 195 State Hwy 13 53967 **Location:** I-90/94, exit 87 (SR 13), 1.6 mi n. CALL ♿M

MONK'S BAR AND GRILL
Phone: 608/254-2955 ④

American
$5-$12

The smell of frying burgers wafts out onto the street from this tiny pub, and the burgers are among the best in the Dells. Made from a secret family recipe, the burgers are best with fried onions and melted cheese but taste heavenly no matter how they're prepared. The smoky pub filled with sports memorabilia offers limited seating. The houses specialty drink is the purple monkey, a sweet and icy treat. **Bar:** full bar. **Hours:** 11 am-midnight; seasonal hours vary. Closed: 11/24, 12/25. **Address:** 220 Broadway 53965 **Location:** Downtown. **Parking:** street only.

MONK'S BAR & GRILL AT THE WILDERNESS
Phone: 608/254-6665 ㉑

American
$7-$20

This newer downtown sports bar offers traditional grill fare with a unique twist. Must-tries are the signature chili and Monk's fabulous burgers, made daily with their own special blend of Angus beef. **Bar:** full bar. **Hours:** 11 am-10 pm, Fri & Sat-midnight. Closed: 12/24. **Address:** 45 Hillman Rd 53965 **Location:** I-90/94, exit 92 (US 12), 1 mi n. CALL ♿M

MOOSEJAW PIZZA & DELLS BREWING CO
Phone: 608/254-1122 ⑮

American
$6-$30

With pool tables and video games, the northwoods-lodge-inspired family restaurant can keep kids, and kids at heart, busy. The menu lists traditional pub favorites, such as pizza and hot dogs, as well as New York strip steaks and elk burgers. A brewpub is on site. **Bar:** full bar. **Hours:** 11 am-10:30 pm, Fri & Sat-11 pm. **Address:** 110 Wisconsin Dells Pkwy S 53965 **Location:** I-90/94, exit 92 (US 12), 1 mi n. CALL ♿M

PAUL BUNYAN'S "NORTHWOODS COOK SHANTY"
Menu on AAA.com   Phone: 608/254-8717 ⑦

American
$8-$15

In a main dining room that resembles a frontier log cabin with plastic gingham tablecloths and wood beams across the ceiling, guests enjoy meals of homemade barbecue, fried chicken and heartier all-you-can-eat fare, in addition to wonderful breakfasts. **Hours:** Open 4/1-10/28 & 3/23-4/30; 7 am-8 pm, Fri & Sat-9 pm. Closed: 3 days midweek in early spring & late fall. **Address:** 411 Hwy 13 53965 **Location:** I-90/94, exit 87 (SR 13), just e; look for large sign Paul Bunyan's Northwoods Restaurant. CALL ♿M

(See map and index starting on p. 605)

PEDRO'S MEXICAN RESTAURANTE

Mexican
$7-$22

Phone: 608-253-7233 ②

Sizzling fajitas are a big hit at this restaurant, which delivers favorites from burritos and tacos to enchiladas and nachos. Complimentary fresh chips and salsa accompany all meals. Stucco walls, tile flooring and colorful decorations add to the south-of-the-border atmosphere. **Bar:** full bar. **Hours:** 11 am-9:30 pm, Fri & Sat-10:30 pm; to 11 pm 5/29-9/4. Closed: 11/24, 12/24, 12/25. **Address:** 951 Stand Rock Rd 53965 **Location:** Just w of downtown on US 16, SR 13 and 23. CALL

PIZZA PUB

American
$8-$25

Phone: 608/254-7877 ⑩

With its large seating capacity, 50-item soup and salad bar, and menu of pasta, burgers and sandwiches, the family-oriented restaurant is a great spot to unwind. Also on the list of favorites are the specialty pizzas, which come in thin, pan or hand-tossed crust; the hand-tossed Big Kahuna pizza feeds six to eight people. Guests can hang out in the arcade area and lounge while waiting for their generous portion of reasonably priced food. Desserts make mouths water. Take-out service is an option. **Bar:** full bar. **Hours:** 11 am-10 pm. Closed: 11/24, 12/25. **Address:** 1455 Wisconsin Dells Pkwy 53965 **Location:** I-90/94, exit 87 (SR 13), 1 mi e, then 1 mi n on US 12. CALL

RIVER WALK PUB

American
$5-$15

Phone: 608/254-8215 ①

The restaurant/pub overlooking the Wisconsin River offers a quick bite to eat, including burgers, sandwiches and soups. This is also a great place to just relax and enjoy a beverage. **Hours:** 7 am-11 pm. Closed major holidays. **Address:** 911 River Rd 53965 **Location:** Just n of Broadway, US 16, SR 13 and 23; downtown.
CALL

R PLACE ITALIAN RESTAURANT

Italian
$11-$32

Phone: 608/253-9240 ⑲

The cozy Italian restaurant draws plenty of recommendations from locals for its large selection of tasty pasta dishes. **Bar:** full bar. **Hours:** 4 pm-9:30 pm, Fri & Sat-10 pm. Closed major holidays. **Address:** 444 Wisconsin Dells Pkwy S 53965 **Location:** I-90/94, exit 92 (US 12), 1.5 mi n.

SARENTO'S

Italian
$13-$36

Phone: 608/253-3300 ⑱

Chefs prepare Italian specialties, including delicious pasta, veal, chicken, seafood, steak, pizza, soups, salads and homemade desserts. The setting welcomes families. **Bar:** full bar. **Hours:** 4:30 pm-9 pm, Fri & Sat-9:30 pm. Closed: 11/24, 12/24, 12/25. **Address:** 441 Wisconsin Dells Pkwy S 53965 **Location:** I-90/94, exit 92 (US 12), 1.3 mi n, then 1.5 mi se. CALL

WALLY'S HOUSE OF EMBERS

American
$14-$35

Phone: 608/253-6411 ⑪

Casual dining in family owned restaurant since 1959. Famous for hickory smoked barbecue ribs. Also featuring Austrian veal and fresh fish. Private dining rooms are available in addition to seasonal outdoor patio dining. **Bar:** full bar. **Hours:** 4:30 pm-10 pm, Fri-Sun to 10:30 pm. Closed: 11/24, 12/24, 12/25. **Address:** 935 Wisconsin Dells Pkwy 53940 **Location:** I-90/94, exit 192 (US 12), 2.5 mi n. CALL

WISCONSIN RAPIDS pop. 18,435

AMERICAS BEST VALUE INN

Hotel
$50-$80

Phone: (715)423-8080

Address: 3410 8th St S 54494 **Location:** 1.9 mi s on SR 13 of jct SR 54 W. Located in a commercial area. **Facility:** Smoke free premises. 48 units. 2 stories (no elevator), interior corridors. **Parking:** winter plug-ins. **Amenities:** safes (fee). **Guest Services:** coin laundry, wireless Internet. **Free Special Amenities:** continental breakfast and high-speed Internet.

AMERICINN LODGE & SUITES OF WISCONSIN RAPIDS

Hotel
$89-$199

Phone: (715)424-3444

Address: 3010 8th St S 54494 **Location:** 1.4 mi s on SR 13. Located in a commercial area. **Facility:** Smoke free premises. 65 units. 2 stories (no elevator), interior corridors. **Parking:** winter plug-ins. **Pool(s):** heated indoor. **Activities:** whirlpool. **Fee:** game room. **Guest Services:** valet and coin laundry, wireless Internet.

HOTEL MEAD

Hotel
$89-$250

Phone: (715)423-1500

Address: 451 E Grand Ave 54494 **Location:** Just e of downtown. Located in a residential area. **Facility:** Smoke free premises. 157 units. 5 stories, interior corridors. **Terms:** check-in 4 pm, cancellation fee imposed. **Amenities:** high-speed Internet. **Dining:** Café Mulino, The Grand Avenue Grill, see separate listings. **Pool(s):** heated indoor. **Activities:** sauna, whirlpool, exercise room. **Fee:** game room. **Guest Services:** valet laundry, wireless Internet. **Free Special Amenities:** newspaper and high-speed Internet.

QUALITY INN

Hotel
$80-$110

Phone: (715)423-5506

Address: 3120 8th St S 54494 **Location:** 1.5 mi s on SR 13. Located in a commercial area. **Facility:** Smoke free premises. 36 units. 2 stories (no elevator), interior corridors. **Parking:** winter plug-ins. **Pool(s):** heated indoor. **Activities:** whirlpool. **Guest Services:** valet laundry, wireless Internet.

SLEEP INN & SUITES

Hotel
$85-$105

Phone: (715)424-6800

Address: 4221 8th St S 54494 **Location:** 1.3 mi s on SR 13 from jct SR 54. **Facility:** Smoke free premises. 57 units. 2 stories (no elevator), interior corridors. **Pool(s):** heated indoor. **Activities:** whirlpool. **Guest Services:** valet and coin laundry, wireless Internet.

—— WHERE TO DINE ——

CAFÉ MULINO

Italian
$6-$24

Phone: 715-422-7000

The lively, trattoria-style restaurant delivers regional specialties and traditional Italian cuisine, including pizza cooked in a wood-burning oven. Generous portions are an excellent value. The friendly, casual atmosphere is welcoming to families. **Bar:** full bar. **Reservations:** suggested. **Hours:** 11:30 am-2 & 4:30-9 pm, Sun 4 pm. **Address:** 451 E Grand Ave 54494 **Location:** Just e of downtown; in Hotel Mead.

FOUR STAR FAMILY RESTAURANT

American
$8-$17

Phone: 715/424-4554

The popular restaurant's menu selections are vast and varied, ranging from burgers, sandwiches and pitas to salads, pasta and Mexican specialties. All-day breakfast selections include crepes, waffles, omelets and Swedish pancakes. **Bar:** wine only. **Hours:** 5 am-10 pm. **Address:** 2911 8th St 54494 **Location:** 1.5 mi s on SR 13.

THE GRAND AVENUE GRILL

American
$7-$25

Phone: 715/422-7000

This traditional grill room offers time-tested favorites in a warm, relaxing atmosphere. Choice steak and seafood highlight the menu, which also lists roast duck, smoked pork chop and Wisconsin venison stew. The chef prepares several new specials weekly. Made-in-house desserts are presented tableside on a tray. Service is attentive and capable. Soft lighting, background music and tables draped in white cloth lend to a comfortable dining experience. **Bar:** full bar. **Hours:** 6:30-11 am, 11:30-1:30 & 5-9 pm, Fri & Sat-10 pm, Sun 6:30 am-2 pm. Closed: 12/25; also Mon & Tues. **Address:** 451 E Grand Ave 54494 **Location:** Just e of downtown; in Hotel Mead.

HONG KONG BUFFET

Asian
$8-$14

Phone: 715/424-5858

This large buffet lines up low-cholesterol choices, in addition to dishes prepared without monosodium glutamate. The well-rounded menu comprises shrimp, beef, chicken and mussel dishes, in addition to tasty fried calamari. **Bar:** beer only. **Hours:** 11 am-10 pm. Closed: 11/24. **Address:** 4531 8th St S, Suite 106 54494 **Location:** 3.4 mi n on SR 13 from jct SR 73.

WITTENBERG pop. 1,177

BEST WESTERN WITTENBERG INN

Hotel
$79

Phone: (715)253-3755

Address: W17267 Red Oak Ln 54499 **Location:** US 29, exit 198, just se. **Facility:** Smoke free premises. 63 units. 3 stories, interior corridors. **Parking:** winter plug-ins. **Terms:** cancellation fee imposed. **Amenities:** safes (fee). **Pool(s):** heated indoor. **Activities:** whirlpool, exercise room. *Fee:* game room. **Guest Services:** coin laundry, wireless Internet. **Free Special Amenities: expanded continental breakfast and high-speed Internet.**

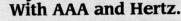

WOODRUFF pop. 1,982

—— WHERE TO DINE ——

PLANTATION SUPPER CLUB   *Menu on AAA.com*

American
$14-$27

Phone: 715-356-9000

First constructed in 1938 and operated by its current owners since 1970, this traditional northern Wisconsin supper club is well established. Friendly, attentive servers deliver homemade onion rings and giant lobster tail, both popular choices, as is the Friday night fish fry. Smoking is permitted in the lounge. **Bar:** full bar. **Hours:** 5 pm-9 pm; hours may vary. Closed: Mon. **Address:** 11084 Hwy 70 E 54568 **Location:** 1.5 mi n on US 51.

Offices

Cities with main offices are listed in **BOLD TYPE** and toll-free member service numbers in *ITALIC TYPE*.
All are closed Saturdays, Sundays and holidays unless otherwise indicated.
The addresses, phone numbers and hours for any AAA/CAA office are subject to change.
The type of service provided is designated below the name of the city where the office is located:

✛ Auto travel services, including books and maps, and on-demand TripTik ® routings.
● Auto travel services, including selected books and maps, and on-demand TripTik ® routings.
▪ Books/maps only, no marked maps or on-demand TripTik ® routings.
▲ Travel Agency Services, cruise, tour, air, car and rail reservations; domestic and international hotel reservations; passport photo services; international and domestic travel guides and maps; travel money products; and International Driving Permits. In addition, assistance with travel related insurance products including trip cancellation, travel accident, lost luggage, trip delay and assistance products.
○ Insurance services provided.
✖ Car Care Plus Facility provides car care services.

AAA NATIONAL OFFICE: 1000 AAA DRIVE, HEATHROW, FLORIDA 32746-5063, (407) 444-7000

MICHIGAN

ADRIAN—AAA MICHIGAN, 1325 N MAIN ST STE G, 49221. WEEKDAYS (M-F) 8:30-5:30. (517) 265-3400. ○

ALLEN PARK—AAA MICHIGAN, 18614 ECORSE RD, 48101. WEEKDAYS (M-F) 8:30-5:30. (313) 382-0522. ○

ALLEN PARK—AAA MICHIGAN, 3177 FAIRLANE DR, 48101. WEEKDAYS (M-F) 8:30-6:00. (313) 386-7000, *(800) 222-8852.* ✛▲○

ALMA—AAA MICHIGAN, 7336 ALGER RD, 48801. WEEKDAYS (M-F) 8:30-5:30. (989) 463-6200, *(800) 348-3439.* ○

ALPENA—AAA MICHIGAN, 2539 US 23 S, 49707. WEEKDAYS (M-F) 8:30-6:00. (989) 354-2151, *(800) 322-3014.* ✛▲○

ANN ARBOR—AAA MICHIGAN, 2650 CARPENTER RD, 48108. WEEKDAYS (M-F) 8:30-6:00. (734) 973-2800, *(800) 833-4613.* ✛▲○

ANN ARBOR—AAA MICHIGAN, 1750 PLYMOUTH RD, 48105. WEEKDAYS (M-F) 8:30-5:30. (734) 662-9350. ○

ANN ARBOR—AAA MICHIGAN, 1200 S MAIN ST, 48104. WEEKDAYS (M-F) 8:30-6:00. (734) 747-7000, *(877) 447-5490.* ✛▲○

BAD AXE—AAA MICHIGAN, 970 N VAN DYKE STE D, 48413. WEEKDAYS (M-F) 8:30-5:30. (989) 269-9989, *(866) 716-8885.* ○

BATTLE CREEK—AAA MICHIGAN, 5700 BECKLEY RD STE E20A, 49015. WEEKDAYS (M-F) 8:30-6:00. (269) 962-2500, *(800) 435-0320.* ✛▲○

BAY CITY—AAA MICHIGAN, 1111 S EUCLID AVE, 48706. WEEKDAYS (M-F) 8:30-6:00. (989) 686-2940, *(800) 322-4517.* ✛▲○

BIRMINGHAM—AAA MICHIGAN, 36801 N WOODWARD AVE, 48009. WEEKDAYS (M-F) 8:30-5:30. (248) 642-4477. ○

BIRMINGHAM—AAA MICHIGAN, 34802 WOODWARD AVE, 48009. WEEKDAYS (M-F) 8:30-6:00. (248) 433-8200. ✛▲○

BRIGHTON—AAA MICHIGAN, 8350 W GRAND RIVER AVE, 48116. WEEKDAYS (M-F) 8:30-6:00. (810) 229-7100. ✛▲○

BROWNSTOWN TOWNSHIP—AAA MICHIGAN, 19366 ALLEN RD STE D, 48183. WEEKDAYS (M-F) 8:30-5:30. (734) 479-1850, *(800) 217-2936.* ○

BURTON—AAA MICHIGAN, 2368 S CENTER RD, 48519. WEEKDAYS (M-F) 8:30-5:30. (810) 715-0745, *(800) 535-3441.* ○

CADILLAC—AAA MICHIGAN, 103 E PINE ST, 49601. WEEKDAYS (M-F) 8:30-5:30. (231) 775-7400. ○

CANTON—AAA MICHIGAN, 2017 N CANTON CENTER RD, 48187. WEEKDAYS (M-F) 8:30-6:00. (734) 844-0146, *(800) 844-0424.* ✛▲○

CANTON—AAA MICHIGAN, 41804 FORD RD, 48187. WEEKDAYS (M-F) 8:30-5:30. (734) 981-5100, *(800) 222-6424.* ○

CARO—AAA MICHIGAN, 810 S STATE ST STE B, 48723. WEEKDAYS (M-F) 8:30-5:30. (989) 673-1488, *(866) 890-1409.* ○

CHARLEVOIX—AAA MICHIGAN, 1002 BRIDGE ST, 49720. WEEKDAYS (M-F) 8:30-5:30. (231) 547-0111. ○

CHEBOYGAN—AAA MICHIGAN, 111 N MAIN ST, 49721. WEEKDAYS (M-F) 8:30-5:30. (231) 627-4088. ○

CHESTERFIELD—AAA MICHIGAN, 46484 GRATIOT AVE, 48051. WEEKDAYS (M-F) 8:30-5:30. (586) 598-9600. ○

CLARKSTON—AAA MICHIGAN, 6300 SASHABAW RD STE B, 48346. WEEKDAYS (M-F) 8:30-5:30. (248) 625-6920, *(800) 424-2967.* ○

CLARKSTON—AAA MICHIGAN, 6751 DIXIE HWY STE 103, 48346. WEEKDAYS (M-F) 8:30-5:30. (248) 620-9120. ○

CLARKSTON—AAA MICHIGAN, 6751 DIXIE HWY STE 112, 48346. WEEKDAYS (M-F) 8:30-5:30. (248) 625-4486. ○

CLINTON TOWNSHIP—AAA MICHIGAN, 37450 GARFIELD RD ST 400, 48036. WEEKDAYS (M-F) 8:30-5:30. (586) 228-1800. ○

COLDWATER—AAA MICHIGAN, 722 E CHICAGO RD, 49036. WEEKDAYS (M-F) 8:30-5:30. (517) 278-4544, *(800) 692-4544.* ○

COMMERCE TOWNSHIP—AAA MICHIGAN, 3050 UNION LAKE RD # 5A, 48382. WEEKDAYS (M-F) 8:30-5:30. (248) 366-2372, *(800) 470-1627.* ○

DEARBORN—AAA MICHIGAN, 21917 GARRISON ST, 48124. WEEKDAYS (M-F) 8:30-5:30. (313) 563-7390. ○

DEARBORN—AAA MICHIGAN, 25001 MICHIGAN AVE #1, 48124. WEEKDAYS (M-F) 8:30-5:30. (313) 563-4300. ○

DEARBORN HEIGHTS—AAA MICHIGAN, 23506 FORD RD, 48127. WEEKDAYS (M-F) 8:30-5:30. (313) 278-0840, *(800) 395-4140.* ○

DETROIT—AAA MICHIGAN, 719 GRISWOLD AVE STE 170, 48226. WEEKDAYS (M-F) 8:30-6:00. (313) 237-5500, *(800) 934-8209.* ✛▲○

DETROIT—AAA MICHIGAN, 7910 W OUTER DR, 48235. WEEKDAYS (M-F) 8:30-6:00. (313) 255-9310, *(800) 222-4416.* ✛▲○

DETROIT—AAA MICHIGAN, 13318 E JEFFERSON AVE, 48215. WEEKDAYS (M-F) 8:30-6:00. (313) 417-2393, *(800) 851-9694.* ✛▲○

DEXTER—AAA MICHIGAN, 7444 DEXTER-ANN ARBOR STK, 48130. WEEKDAYS (M-F) 8:30-5:30. (734) 426-3516, *(800) 690-1245.* ○

EAST LANSING—AAA MICHIGAN, 2843 E GRAND RIVER AV 150, 48823. WEEKDAYS (M-F) 8:30-5:30. (517) 333-7200, *(866) 581-2271.* ○

EAST LANSING—AAA MICHIGAN, 2200 COOLIDGE RD STE 12, 48823. WEEKDAYS (M-F) 8:30-5:30. (517) 332-6037, *(800) 263-0386.* ○

FARMINGTON HILLS—AAA MICHIGAN, 30038 ORCHARD LAKE RD, 48334. WEEKDAYS (M-F) 8:30-5:30. (248) 851-0400. ○

FARMINGTON HILLS—AAA MICHIGAN, 38751 W 12 MILE RD, 48331. WEEKDAYS (M-F) 8:30-6:00. (248) 553-3700, *(800) 224-1178.* ✛▲○

FARMINGTON HILLS—AAA MICHIGAN, 33120 W 12 MILE RD, 48334. WEEKDAYS (M-F) 8:30-5:30. (248) 489-1170. ○

FARMINGTON HILLS—AAA MICHIGAN, 28731 GRAND RIVER AVE, 48336. WEEKDAYS (M-F) 8:30-5:30. (248) 471-2345, *(800) 804-4545.* ○

FENTON—AAA MICHIGAN, 1219 N LEROY ST, 48430. WEEKDAYS (M-F) 8:30-5:30. (810) 714-5300, *(866) 222-5531.* ✪

FLINT—AAA MICHIGAN, 5009 W BRISTOL RD, 48507. WEEKDAYS (M-F) 8:30-6:00. (810) 230-8890, *(800) 552-5970.* ✚▲✪

FLINT—AAA MICHIGAN, 1388 W BRISTOL RD, 48507. WEEKDAYS (M-F) 8:30-5:30. (810) 232-0200, *(888) 430-4055.* ✪

GAYLORD—AAA MICHIGAN, 710 EDELWEISS VILLAGE PKY, 49735. WEEKDAYS (M-F) 8:30-5:30. (989) 732-9196, *(888) 732-9196.* ✪

GRAND RAPIDS—AAA MICHIGAN, 890 3 MILE RD NW STE 3, 49544. WEEKDAYS (M-F) 8:30-5:30. (616) 784-0053. ✪

GRAND RAPIDS—AAA MICHIGAN, 4650 PLAINFIELD NE, 49525. WEEKDAYS (M-F) 8:30-6:00. (616) 364-6111, *(800) 442-8304.* ✚▲✪

GRAYLING—AAA MICHIGAN, 2384 S I-75 BUS LOOP #A, 49738. WEEKDAYS (M-F) 8:30-5:30. (989) 348-2089, *(800) 905-4241.* ✪

GREENVILLE—AAA MICHIGAN, 210 S LAFAYETTE ST, 48838. WEEKDAYS (M-F) 8:30-5:30. (616) 754-5627. ✪

GROSSE POINTE—AAA MICHIGAN, 17640 MACK AVE, 48230. WEEKDAYS (M-F) 8:30-5:30. (313) 881-8900. ✪

GROSSE POINTE WOODS—AAA MICHIGAN, 19299 MACK AVE, 48236. WEEKDAYS (M-F) 8:30-6:00. (313) 343-6000, *(800) 293-7169.* ✚▲✪

HILLSDALE—AAA MICHIGAN, 69 E ST JOE ST, 49242. WEEKDAYS (M-F) 8:30-5:30. (517) 439-1408. ✪

HOLLAND—AAA MICHIGAN, 587 E 8TH ST, 49423. WEEKDAYS (M-F) 8:30-5:30. (616) 392-5171, *(888) 544-9204.* ✪

HOUGHTON—AAA MICHIGAN, 1107 RIDGE RD, 49931. WEEKDAYS (M-F) 8:30-5:30. (906) 483-3850, *(800) 819-0036.* ✪

HOWELL—AAA MICHIGAN, 843 E GRAND RIVER AVE, 48843. WEEKDAYS (M-F) 8:30-5:30. (517) 545-3932, *(800) 545-1740.* ✪

HOWELL—AAA MICHIGAN, 10051 E HIGHLAND RD #17, 48843. WEEKDAYS (M-F) 8:30-5:30. (810) 632-9949. ✪

JACKSON—AAA MICHIGAN, 1000 N WISNER STE 1, 49202. WEEKDAYS (M-F) 8:30-6:00. (517) 787-7300, *(800) 842-8999.* ✚▲✪

KALAMAZOO—AAA MICHIGAN, 3321 STADIUM DR STE B, 49008. WEEKDAYS (M-F) 8:30-5:30. (269) 375-3678. ✪

KALAMAZOO—AAA MICHIGAN, 2015 W CROSSTOWN PKWY, 49008. WEEKDAYS (M-F) 8:30-6:00. (269) 381-7100, *(800) 851-9662.* ✚▲✪

KENTWOOD—AAA MICHIGAN, 2560 E PARIS AVE SE, 49546. WEEKDAYS (M-F) 8:30-6:00. (616) 957-4455, *(800) 222-3103.* ✚▲✪

LAKE ORION—AAA MICHIGAN, 690 S LAPEER RD, 48362. WEEKDAYS (M-F) 8:30-5:30. (248) 693-3990, *(888) 909-9319.* ✪

LANSING—AAA MICHIGAN, 6242 W SAGINAW HWY, 48917. WEEKDAYS (M-F) 8:30-5:30. (517) 321-7434. ✪

LANSING—AAA MICHIGAN, 3415 EAST SAGINAW STE G, 48912. WEEKDAYS (M-F) 8:30-6:00. (517) 487-6171, *(800) 222-9905.* ✚▲✪

LAPEER—AAA MICHIGAN, 3056 DAVISON RD STE 5, 48446. WEEKDAYS (M-F) 8:30-5:30. (810) 667-3881. ✪

LATHRUP VILLAGE—AAA MICHIGAN, 28630 SOUTHFIELD RD # 134, 48076. WEEKDAYS (M-F) 8:30-5:30. (248) 569-7070. ✪

LIVONIA—AAA MICHIGAN, 19233 NEWBURGH, 48152. WEEKDAYS (M-F) 8:30-5:30. (734) 956-1060. ✪

LIVONIA—AAA MICHIGAN, 18499 FARMINGTON RD, 48152. WEEKDAYS (M-F) 8:30-5:30. (248) 474-0766, *(800) 424-6099.* ✪

LIVONIA—AAA MICHIGAN, 37383 SIX MILE RD, 48152. WEEKDAYS (M-F) 8:30-6:00. (734) 462-7000, *(800) 851-9691.* ✚▲✪

MACOMB TOWNSHIP—AAA MICHIGAN, 21851 HALL RD, 48044. WEEKDAYS (M-F) 8:30-6:00. (586) 469-4050, *(800) 551-4311.* ✚▲✪

MADISON HEIGHTS—AAA MICHIGAN, 160 W 13 MILE RD, 48071. WEEKDAYS (M-F) 8:30-5:30. (248) 585-6265. ✪

MARQUETTE—AAA MICHIGAN, 3020 US 41 W STE 12 & 13, 49855. WEEKDAYS (M-F) 8:30-6:00. (906) 225-6750, *(800) 526-4241.* ✚▲✪

MARYSVILLE—AAA MICHIGAN, 302 HURON BLVD, 48040. WEEKDAYS (M-F) 8:30-5:30. (810) 364-5667. ✪

MIDLAND—AAA MICHIGAN, 2800 RODD ST, 48640. WEEKDAYS (M-F) 8:30-5:30. (989) 835-3441, *(866) 681-1140.* ✪

MIDLAND—AAA MICHIGAN, 1900 S SAGINAW RD, 48640. WEEKDAYS (M-F) 8:30-6:00. (989) 832-6500, *(800) 322-4271.* ✚▲✪

MILFORD—AAA MICHIGAN, 512 HIGHLAND AVE, 48381. WEEKDAYS (M-F) 8:30-5:30. (248) 685-7000, *(800) 685-7228.* ✪

MONROE—AAA MICHIGAN, 7495 N TELEGRAPH RD, 48162. WEEKDAYS (M-F) 8:30-5:30. (734) 586-5555. ✪

MONROE—AAA MICHIGAN, 305 S TELEGRAPH RD, 48161. WEEKDAYS (M-F) 8:30-5:30. (734) 243-3030, *(800) 222-4421.* ✪

MT CLEMENS—AAA MICHIGAN, 205 S MAIN ST, 48043. WEEKDAYS (M-F) 8:30-5:30. (586) 465-1240. ✪

MT PLEASANT—AAA MICHIGAN, 913 E PICKARD STE L, 48858. WEEKDAYS (M-F) 8:30-5:30. (989) 772-6001, *(800) 888-8850.* ✪

MUSKEGON—AAA MICHIGAN, 5890 HARVEY ST STE B, 49444. WEEKDAYS (M-F) 8:30-5:30. (231) 739-9363, *(800) 851-9689.* ✪

NEW BALTIMORE—AAA MICHIGAN, 31631 23 MILE RD, 48047. WEEKDAYS (M-F) 8:30-5:30. (586) 598-1100, *(800) 459-3076.* ✪

NILES—AAA MICHIGAN, 815 E MAIN ST STE A, 49120. WEEKDAYS (M-F) 8:30-5:30. (269) 683-3500, *(800) 521-1428.* ✪

NORTHVILLE—AAA MICHIGAN, 42973 7 MILE RD, 48167. WEEKDAYS (M-F) 8:30-5:30. (248) 349-2110, *(800) 852-7629.* ✪

NOVI—AAA MICHIGAN, 47972 GRAND RIVER AVE, 48374. WEEKDAYS (M-F) 8:30-5:30. (248) 347-6969. ✪

ORION—AAA MICHIGAN, 3009 BALDWIN RD STE B, 48359. WEEKDAYS (M-F) 8:30-5:30. (248) 393-7702, *(866) 853-6600.* ✪

PETOSKEY—AAA MICHIGAN, 1321 SPRING ST, 49770. WEEKDAYS (M-F) 8:30-5:30. (231) 347-8284, *(800) 294-6503.* ✪

PLYMOUTH—AAA MICHIGAN, 1472 SHELDON RD, 48170. WEEKDAYS (M-F) 8:30-5:30. (734) 451-4501, *(800) 664-4158.* ✪

PORT HURON—AAA MICHIGAN, 933 LAPEER, 48060. WEEKDAYS (M-F) 8:30-6:00. (810) 987-4800, *(800) 462-9968.* ✚▲✪

PORTAGE—AAA MICHIGAN, 1209 E MILHAM STE B, 49002. WEEKDAYS (M-F) 8:30-5:30. (269) 344-3000. ✪

REDFORD—AAA MICHIGAN, 14807 TELEGRAPH RD, 48239. WEEKDAYS (M-F) 8:30-5:30. (313) 543-2255, *(800) 396-8143.* ✪

RICHMOND—AAA MICHIGAN, 66898 GRATIOT AVE, 48062. WEEKDAYS (M-F) 8:30-5:30. (586) 430-9971, *(800) 551-7398.* ✪

ROCHESTER HILLS—AAA MICHIGAN, 2490 WALTON BLVD STE 204, 48309. WEEKDAYS (M-F) 8:30-5:30. (248) 656-9616. ✪

ROCHESTER HILLS—AAA MICHIGAN, 200 DIVERSION ST STE 190, 48307. WEEKDAYS (M-F) 8:30-5:30. (248) 656-0900. ✪

ROCHESTER HILLS—AAA MICHIGAN, 901 E AUBURN RD, 48307. WEEKDAYS (M-F) 8:30-5:30. (248) 853-7005. ✪

SAGINAW—AAA MICHIGAN, 3785 BAY RD, 48603. WEEKDAYS (M-F) 8:30-6:00. (989) 790-3240, *(800) 322-1120.* ✚▲✪

SAGINAW—AAA MICHIGAN, 255 N CENTER RD STE 2, 48603. WEEKDAYS (M-F) 8:30-5:30. (989) 790-9308, *(888) 778-9950.* ✪

SALINE—AAA MICHIGAN, 1351 E MICHIGAN AVE, 48176. WEEKDAYS (M-F) 8:30-5:30. (734) 944-4851, *(800) 211-3011.* ✪

SHELBY TOWNSHIP—AAA MICHIGAN, 13464 22 MILE RD, 48315. WEEKDAYS (M-F) 8:30-5:30. (586) 254-5250. ✪

SHELBY TOWNSHIP—AAA MICHIGAN, 45700 MOUND RD, 48317. WEEKDAYS (M-F) 8:30-6:00. (586) 739-1400, *(800) 851-9690.* ✚▲✪

SHELBY TOWNSHIP—AAA MICHIGAN, 46520 VAN DYKE AVE, 48317. WEEKDAYS (M-F) 8:30-5:30. (586) 254-5630. ✪

SOUTH LYON—AAA MICHIGAN, 582 N LAFAYETTE ST, 48178. WEEKDAYS (M-F) 8:30-5:30. (248) 437-1729, *(800) 783-1729.* ✪

SOUTHGATE—AAA MICHIGAN, 14130 PENNSYLVANIA RD, 48195. WEEKDAYS (M-F) 8:30-5:30. (734) 283-9780. ✪

SOUTHGATE—AAA MICHIGAN, 15150 FORT ST, 48195. WEEKDAYS (M-F) 8:30-6:00. (734) 284-0800, *(800) 222-6612.* ✚ ▲ ✪

ST. CLAIR SHORES—AAA MICHIGAN, 31364 HARPER, 48082. WEEKDAYS (M-F) 8:30-5:30. (586) 296-6602. ✪

ST. JOSEPH—AAA MICHIGAN, 2090 NILES RD STE 200, 49085. WEEKDAYS (M-F) 8:30-5:30. (269) 982-0033, *(800) 800-1897.* ✪

STERLING HEIGHTS—AAA MICHIGAN, 3927 17 MILE RD, 48310. WEEKDAYS (M-F) 8:30-5:30. (586) 977-3333. ✪

STERLING HEIGHTS—AAA MICHIGAN, 38121 UTICA RD, 48312. WEEKDAYS (M-F) 8:30-5:30. (586) 978-9300. ✪

STERLING HEIGHTS—AAA MICHIGAN, 42934 SCHOENHERR RD, 48313. WEEKDAYS (M-F) 8:30-5:30. (586) 566-0200. ✪

TRAVERSE CITY—AAA MICHIGAN, 940 N US 31 N, 49686. WEEKDAYS (M-F) 8:30-6:00. (231) 947-8045, *(800) 442-1742.* ✚ ▲ ✪

TRENTON—AAA MICHIGAN, 3520 WEST RD, 48183. WEEKDAYS (M-F) 8:30-5:30. (734) 692-0880. ✪

TROY—AAA MICHIGAN, 125 E MAPLE RD, 48083. WEEKDAYS (M-F) 8:30-5:30. (248) 524-1660. ✪

TROY—AAA MICHIGAN, 25 E LONG LAKE RD, 48085. WEEKDAYS (M-F) 8:30-6:00. (248) 879-2030, *(877) 349-1514.* ✚ ▲ ✪

WARREN—AAA MICHIGAN, 29311 MOUND RD, 48092. WEEKDAYS (M-F) 8:30-6:00. (586) 754-2200, *(800) 843-6513.* ✚ ▲ ✪

WASHINGTON—AAA MICHIGAN, 64297 VAN DYKE RD, 48095. WEEKDAYS (M-F) 8:30-5:30. (586) 752-2710. ✪

WEST BRANCH—AAA MICHIGAN, 2204 S M 76 STE D, 48661. WEEKDAYS (M-F) 8:30-5:30. (989) 343-0534, *(866) 366-9876.* ✪

WESTLAND—AAA MICHIGAN, 8047 N WAYNE RD, 48185. WEEKDAYS (M-F) 8:30-5:30. (734) 525-5260. ✪

WHITE LAKE TWP—AAA MICHIGAN, 330 TOWN CENTER BLVD D101, 48386. WEEKDAYS (M-F) 8:30-6:00. (248) 618-3440, *(800) 222-2661.* ✚ ▲ ✪

WYOMING—AAA MICHIGAN, 1945 28TH ST SW, 49509. WEEKDAYS (M-F) 8:30-5:30. (616) 538-4431, *(800) 466-0237.* ✪

WISCONSIN

APPLETON—AAA WISCONSIN, 160 S MCCARTHY RD, 54914. WEEKDAYS (M-F) 8:30-5:30 (ADDITIONAL HOURS BY APPOINTMENT). (920) 738-4200, *(800) 236-1115.* ✚ ▲ ✪

BROOKFIELD—AAA WISCONSIN, 12635 W NORTH AVE, 53005. WEEKDAYS (M-F) 8:30-5:30 (ADDITIONAL HOURS BY APPOINTMENT). (262) 796-8960, *(800) 236-8863.* ✚ ▲ ✪

EAU CLAIRE—AAA WISCONSIN, 3430 OAKWOOD HILLS PKWY, 54701. WEEKDAYS (M-F) 8:30-5:30 (ADDITIONAL HOURS BY APPOINTMENT). (715) 836-8640, *(800) 236-0018.* ✚ ▲ ✪

FOND DU LAC—AAA WISCONSIN, 504A N ROLLING MEADOWS DR, 54937. WEEKDAYS (M-F) 8:30-5:30 (ADDITIONAL HOURS BY APPOINTMENT). (920) 923-4805, *(866) 823-7660.* ✚ ✪

GLENDALE—AAA WISCONSIN, 202 W SILVER SPRING DR, 53217. WEEKDAYS (M-F) 8:30-5:30 (ADDITIONAL HOURS BY APPOINTMENT). (414) 963-3060, *(800) 236-3061.* ✚ ▲ ✪

GRAFTON—AAA WISCONSIN, 1040 N PORT WASHINGTON RD, 53024. WEEKDAYS (M-F) 8:30-5:30 (ADDITIONAL HOURS BY APPOINTMENT). (262) 204-1000, *(866) 550-2046.* ✚ ▲ ✪

GREEN BAY—AAA WISCONSIN, 2285 S ONEIDA STE #1, 54304. WEEKDAYS (M-F) 8:30-5:30 (ADDITIONAL HOURS BY APPOINTMENT). (920) 498-6120, *(800) 236-7860.* ✚ ▲ ✪

JANESVILLE—AAA WISCONSIN, 2900 DEERFIELD DR STE 9C, 53546. WEEKDAYS (M-F) 8:30-5:30 (ADDITIONAL HOURS BY APPOINTMENT). (608) 755-3960, *(800) 608-0613.* ✚ ▲ ✪

KENOSHA—AAA WISCONSIN, 10320 75TH ST STE D, 53142. WEEKDAYS (M-F) 8:30-5:30 (ADDITIONAL HOURS BY APPOINTMENT). (262) 697-7280, *(866) 500-4904.* ✚ ▲ ✪

MADISON—AAA WISCONSIN, 2358 E SPRINGS DR STE 100, 53704. WEEKDAYS (M-F) 8:30-5:30 (ADDITIONAL HOURS BY APPOINTMENT). (608) 242-6000, *(866) 823-7662.* ✚ ▲ ✪

MADISON—AAA WISCONSIN, 8401 EXCELSIOR DR, 53717. WEEKDAYS (M-F) 8:30-6:00 (ADDITIONAL HOURS BY APPOINTMENT). (608) 836-6555, *(800) 236-5558.* ✚ ▲ ✪

MENOMONEE FALLS—AAA WISCONSIN, W176 N9348 RIVERCREST DR, 53051. WEEKDAYS (M-F) 8:30-5:30 (ADDITIONAL HOURS BY APPOINTMENT). (262) 257-7555, *(866) 812-4368.* ✚ ▲ ✪

MILWAUKEE—AAA WISCONSIN, 775 N JACKSON, 53202. WEEKDAYS (M-F) 8:30-5:30 (ADDITIONAL HOURS BY APPOINTMENT). (414) 224-8430, *(800) 434-8901.* ✚ ▲ ✪

MILWAUKEE—AAA WISCONSIN, 4433 S 27TH ST, 53221. WEEKDAYS (M-F) 8:30-6:00 (ADDITIONAL HOURS BY APPOINTMENT). (414) 423-2180, *(800) 236-8229.* ✚ ▲ ✪

ONALASKA—AAA WISCONSIN, 1125 MAIN ST STE 100, 54650. WEEKDAYS (M-F) 8:30-5:30 (ADDITIONAL HOURS BY APPOINTMENT). (608) 783-7412, *(800) 236-5999.* ✚ ▲ ✪

OSHKOSH—AAA WISCONSIN, 1496 W SOUTH PARK AVE, 54902. WEEKDAYS (M-F) 8:30-5:30 (ADDITIONAL HOURS BY APPOINTMENT). (920) 232-6150, *(866) 823-7665.* ✚ ▲ ✪

RACINE—AAA WISCONSIN, 5630 WASHINGTON AVE #7, 53406. WEEKDAYS (M-F) 8:30-5:30 (ADDITIONAL HOURS BY APPOINTMENT). (262) 636-8720, *(800) 254-4245.* ✚ ▲ ✪

SHEBOYGAN—AAA WISCONSIN, 3104 S BUSINESS DR, 53081. WEEKDAYS (M-F) 8:30-5:30 (ADDITIONAL HOURS BY APPOINTMENT). (920) 208-8900, *(866) 823-7664.* ✚ ▲ ✪

WAUKESHA—AAA WISCONSIN, 21505 E MORELAND BLVD 100, 53186. WEEKDAYS (M-F) 8:30-5:30 (ADDITIONAL HOURS BY APPOINTMENT). (262) 317-1250, *(800) 548-1077.* ✚ ▲ ✪

WAUSAU—AAA WISCONSIN, 4724 RIB MOUNTAIN DR, 54401. WEEKDAYS (M-F) 8:30-5:30 (ADDITIONAL HOURS BY APPOINTMENT). (715) 241-7222, *(866) 812-4370.* ✚ ▲ ✪

MICHIGAN-WISCONSIN
DRIVING DISTANCES

100 MILES IN US/KILOMETERS IN CANADA
2:00 AVERAGE TIME (EXCLUDING STOPS)

3677-J

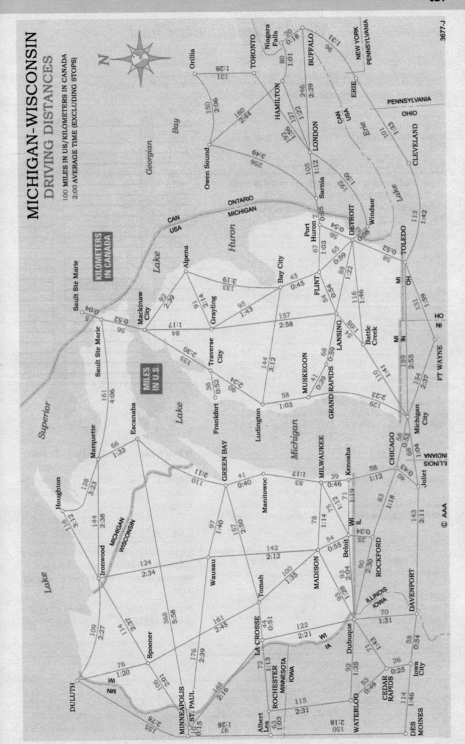

KILOMETERS IN CANADA

MILES IN U.S.

© AAA

Metric Equivalents Chart

TEMPERATURE

To convert Fahrenheit to Celsius, subtract 32 from the Fahrenheit temperature, multiply by 5 and divide by 9. To convert Celsius to Fahrenheit, multiply by 9, divide by 5 and add 32.

ACRES

1 acre = 0.4 hectare (ha)   1 hectare = 2.47 acres

MILES AND KILOMETRES

Note: A kilometre is approximately 5/8 or 0.6 of a mile. To convert kilometres to miles multiply by 0.6.

Miles/Kilometres		Kilometres/Miles	
15	24.1	30	18.6
20	32.2	35	21.7
25	40.2	40	24.8
30	48.3	45	27.9
35	56.3	50	31.0
40	64.4	55	34.1
45	72.4	60	37.2
50	80.5	65	40.3
55	88.5	70	43.4
60	96.6	75	46.6
65	104.6	80	49.7
70	112.7	85	52.8
75	120.7	90	55.9
80	128.7	95	59.0
85	136.8	100	62.1
90	144.8	105	65.2
95	152.9	110	68.3
100	160.9	115	71.4

Celsius ° / Fahrenheit °

Celsius		Fahrenheit
100	BOILING	212
37		100
35		95
32		90
29		85
27		80
24		75
21		70
18		65
16		60
13		55
10		50
7		45
4		40
2		35
0	FREEZING	32
-4		25
-7		20
-9		15
-12		10
-15		5
-18		0
-21		-5
-24		-10
-27		-15

LINEAR MEASURE

Customary	Metric
1 inch = 2.54 centimetres	1 centimetre = 0.4 inches
1 foot = 30 centimetres	1 metre = 3.3 feet
1 yard = 0.91 metres	1 metre = 1.09 yards
1 mile = 1.6 kilometres	1 kilometre = .62 miles

LIQUID MEASURE

Customary	Metric
1 fluid ounce = 30 millilitres	1 millilitre = .03 fluid ounces
1 cup = .24 litres	1 litre = 2.1 pints
1 pint = .47 litres	1 litre = 1.06 quarts
1 quart = .95 litres	1 litre = .26 gallons
1 gallon = 3.8 litres	

WEIGHT

If You Know:	Multiply By:	To Find:
Ounces	28	Grams
Pounds	0.45	Kilograms
Grams	0.035	Ounces
Kilograms	2.2	Pounds

PRESSURE

Air pressure in automobile tires is expressed in kilopascals. Multiply pound-force per square inch (psi) by 6.89 to find kilopascals (kPa).

24 psi = 165 kPa   28 psi = 193 kPa
26 psi = 179 kPa   30 psi = 207 kPa

GALLON AND LITRES

Gallons/Litres				Litres/Gallons			
5	19.0	12	45.6	10	2.6	40	10.4
6	22.8	14	53.2	15	3.9	50	13.0
7	26.6	16	60.8	20	5.2	60	15.6
8	30.4	18	68.4	25	6.5	70	18.2
9	34.2	20	76.0	30	7.8	80	20.8
10	38.0	25	95.0	35	9.1	90	23.4

Border Information

U.S. – Canada Border Information

For United States Residents Traveling to Canada

Border crossing requirements: Travelers are required to present proper travel documents for travel to Canada and to return to the United States.

Air travel: U.S. passport is required for travel by air to Canada and to the U.S.

Land or sea travel: Proof of citizenship and proof of identity is required for travel to Canada by land or sea. U.S. citizens returning to the U.S. from Canada by land or sea are required to present proper travel documents according to the Western Hemisphere Travel Initiative. Approved documents include a passport or passport card, Enhanced Driver's License, or NEXUS trusted traveler program card. Please refer to the U.S. Department of State's website travel.state.gov for the most current information on these requirements. Canada citizens should refer to the Canada Border Services Agency website cbsa-asfc.gc.ca.

U.S. resident aliens: Alien Registration Receipt Card (Green Card) in addition to passport from country of citizenship.

Minors: All children must have their own travel documents. In lieu of a U.S. passport or passport card, U.S. children under 16 traveling to and from Canada by land or sea may also present an original or copy of his or her birth certificate, a consular Report of Birth Abroad, or a Naturalization Certificate.

Single parents, grandparents or guardians traveling with a minor must show documentation of legal custody and provide proof of citizenship for each child (the minor's passport or a parent's passport that includes the child).

When a child is traveling with only 1 parent, that parent should have a notarized letter of consent from the other parent or legal custody documents.

When a child is traveling alone or with an individual other than a parent, the minor should have a notarized letter of consent with phone number(s) from both parents or a custody document.

Legal Issues: Persons with felony convictions, driving while intoxicated records or other offenses may be denied admittance into Canada. Contact the Canadian embassy or nearest consulate before travel.

Firearms: Canada has strict laws regarding the importing, exporting, possession, use, storage, display and transportation of firearms. These are federal laws that apply across the country.

Classes of Firearms:
- Non-restricted (most ordinary rifles and shotguns)
- Restricted (mainly handguns)
- Prohibited (full automatics, converted automatics, handguns with a barrel length of 105 m ($\approx$ 4 inches) or less, and .25 or .32 caliber handguns, among others)

Certain handguns used in International Shooting Union sporting competition are classified as restricted even though they meet the prohibited handgun definition.

Yes: To bring a non-restricted or restricted firearm into Canada you must:
- Be 18 years of age or older
- Declare firearm(s) at first point of entry
- Get an Authorization to Transport (ATT) from a provincial or territorial Chief Firearms Officer before arriving at point of entry (Note: ATT not issued for hunting or self-protection purposes);call 800-731-4000 for more information.

No: You may not bring into Canada a prohibited firearm or replica firearm, except replicas of firearms classified as antiques (a replica that looks exactly, or almost exactly, like a firearm but is not a firearm; it cannot discharge projectiles or discharges only harmless projectiles).

The Canada Border Services Agency is responsible for all customs procedures.

Yes:
- You may import non-restricted firearms for legitimate purposes: sporting or hunting; use in competitions; transit movement; or personal protection against wildlife in remote areas (customs officer must agree that circumstances warrant firearm possession)
- Register weapons with U.S. Customs before departure
- Upon return you must show proof that you had the weapon before departure
- Under certain circumstances individuals and businesses may import firearms

No: Non-residents may not import prohibited items.

Fees (in Canadian funds):

- Non-Resident Firearm Declaration – $25 covers all firearms listed on declaration
- Possession and acquisition license – $60 for non-restricted firearms; valid for 5 years
- Temporary Firearms Borrowing License (for non-residents) – $30; may renew once in a 12-month period at no extra cost; (800-731-4000)
- Imported firearm registration fee – No fee to register or transfer a firearm

Prohibited: Any large capacity cartridge magazine (limited to 5 rounds for semiautomatic rifles or shotguns, 10 rounds for handguns), any device designed to stop the sound of a firearm, any knife with a blade opened by spring pressure (e.g., switchblade), martial arts weapons (e.g., shuriken (shooting stars), nunchaku sticks), mace, blowguns, hand-held compact crossbows and any other weapons declared prohibited by regulation.

Yes: Hunters may bring in, duty-free, 200 rounds of ammunition; competition participants 1,500 rounds. Must show valid license or declaration to purchase ammunition. If planning to hunt in multiple provinces or territories, you must obtain a hunting license from each one.

No: Firearms forbidden in many of Canada's national and provincial parks, game reserves and adjacent areas.

Parks and Hunting Regulation Information:
Newfoundland and Labrador 800-563-6353 or 709-729-2830; Prince Edward Island 888-734-7529 or 902-629-2400; Nova Scotia 800-565-0000 ext 998 or 902-425-5781; New Brunswick 800-561-0123 or 506-789-4982; Quebec 800-363-7777 or 514-873-2015; Ontario 800-668-2746 or 416-314-0944; Manitoba 800-665-0040 or 204-945-3777; Saskatchewan 877-237-2273 or 306-787-2300; Alberta 800-661-8888 or 780-427-4321; British Columbia 800-663-6000 or 250-387-1642; Northwest Territories (Western NWT) 800-661-0788 or 867-873-4059; Nunavut (Eastern NWT) 800-491-7910; Yukon 867-667-5340.

Note: Provinces and territories also have their own laws regulating the transportation of firearms through their areas, usually in connection with their hunting regulations. For further information on the entry of firearms, applying for a license or to obtain authorization to transport a firearm, contact: Canadian Firearms Centre at 800-731-4000.

Personal Baggage:

- Admissible into Canada on a temporary basis without payment of duty and taxes
- Customs may require a refundable security deposit at time of entry
- Deposits not normally required for health- or pleasure-related visits as long as all items are exported at trip's end

Personal baggage that may be taken into Canada on a duty- and tax-free basis includes clothing and personal items, sporting goods, automobiles, vessels, aircraft, snowmobiles, cameras, personal computers, food products and other items appropriate for the purpose and duration of the visit.

Tobacco products – Those meeting age requirements (18 years in Alberta, Manitoba, Northwest Territories, Nunavut, Saskatchewan, Quebec and Yukon; 19 years in other provinces) may bring in 50 cigars, 200 cigarettes, 200 grams of tobacco and 200 tobacco sticks.

Alcohol – Those meeting age requirements (18 years in Alberta, Manitoba and Quebec; 19 years in other provinces and territories) may bring in limited alcoholic beverages: 40 ounces (1.14 L) of liquor, 1.6 quarts (1.5 L) of wine or 9 quarts (8.5 L) of beer or ale (equivalent to 24 12-ounce bottles or cans).

- Amounts exceeding the allowable quantities noted above are subject to federal duty and taxes, and provincial/territorial liquor fees
- Pay provincial fees at customs at the time of entry in all provinces and the Yukon
- Illegal to bring more than the allowable alcohol quantity into the Northwest Territories or Nunavut

Articles purchased at Canadian duty-free shops are subject to U.S. Customs exemptions and restrictions; those purchased at U.S. duty-free shops before entering Canada are subject to duty if brought back into the United States.

Prescription Drugs: Persons requiring medication while visiting Canada are permitted to bring it for their own use. Clearly identify and carry in original packaging with a label listing the drug and its intended use. Have a copy of the prescription and prescribing doctor's phone number.

Gifts: Items not exceeding $60 (CAN) in value,

excluding tobacco, alcoholic beverages and advertising matter, taken into or mailed to Canada are allowed free entry. Gifts valued at more than $60 are subject to regular duty and taxes on the excess amount.

Pets and Plants: You must have a certificate for a dog or cat age 3 months and older. It must clearly describe the animal, declare that the animal is currently vaccinated against rabies and have a licensed veterinarian signature.

- Collar tags are not sufficient proof of immunization
- Be sure the vaccination does not expire while traveling in Canada
- The certificate is also required to bring the animal back into the United States

Exempt From These Rules: Assist dogs; healthy puppies and kittens under 3 months old with a health certificate, signed by a licensed veterinarian, indicating that the animal is too young to vaccinate.

Plants or plant material must be declared. For information, contact: Canadian Food Inspection Agency (CFIA), 1400 Merivale Road, Ottawa, ON K1A 0Y9; 613-225-2342.

Radio Communication Equipment
- Cell phone, PCS phone, citizens band (CB) or Family Radio Service radio allowed without prior registration
- Use of aircraft, marine or amateur radio allowed without prior authorization
- All other types of radio transmitting stations allowed with authorization letter from Industry Canada's Radio - communication and Broadcasting Regulatory Branch

Special Permits: A CITIES (Convention on International Trade in Endangered Species) permit is required for any endangered species brought into Canada, including those kept as pets, and for any items made from them (e.g., coats, handbags, shoes). For information contact: Environment Canada, Canadian Wildlife Service at 819-997-1840.

An Export Permit may be required to take out of Canada objects more than 50 years old (e.g., fossils, archaeological artifacts, fine and decorative art, technological objects or books and archival material). Contact: Movable Cultural Property Program of

Canadian Heritage, 15 Eddy St., 3rd Floor, Gatineau, Quebec, Canada K1A 0M5; 819-997-0055.

An Import Permit may be required for the importation of clothing, textiles, steel and certain agricultural products in excess of minimum quantities. For information contact: Department of Foreign Affairs and Int'l Trade, Export and Import Controls Bureau, Tower C, 4th Floor, LB Pearson Bldg, 125 Sussex Dr., Ottawa, ON K1A 0G2.

Vehicles
- Vehicles entering Canada for touring, including trailers not exceeding 8 feet 6 inches (2.6 m) in width are generally subject to quick and routine entry procedures.
- To leave or store a car, trailer or other goods in Canada while you leave the country you must pay import duty and taxes or present a valid permit. Canadian Customs officials. issue permits at point of entry
- You may not store a vacation trailer in Canada during the off-season.
- Vehicle registration cards required for Canadian travel.
- If driving a car other than your own, you must have written permission from the owner to use it.
- If driving a rented car, you must possess a copy of the contract.
- A valid U.S. driver's license is valid in Canada for time period specified by the individual provinces and territories.
- In all Canadian provinces and territories except Alberta, British Columbia and Saskatchewan, it is illegal to use radar detectors, even if unplugged.
- Seat belts required for the driver and all passengers throughout Canada.

Headlights: Driving with daytime running lights is required for all car models after 1990.
- In Alberta, British Columbia, New Brunswick, and Prince Edward Island, lights must be turned on when light conditions restrict visibility to 500 feet (150 m).
- In Manitoba, lights must be turned on when light conditions restrict visibility to 200 feet (60 m).
- In Yukon, Nova Scotia, Northwest Territories and

Nunavut, headlights must remain on at all times.

- Elsewhere in Canada, driving with headlights on during all hours of the day is advised.

FINANCIAL RESPONSIBILITY LAWS IN CANADA

When an accident involves death, injury or property damage, Canadian provinces and territories require evidence of financial responsibility. You may be asked to show this evidence at any time.

U.S. motorists should check with their own U.S. insurance companies as to whether they are required to obtain and carry a yellow Non-Resident Inter-Province Motor Vehicle Liability Insurance Card (accepted as evidence of financial responsibility throughout Canada). Those not carrying proper proof may be subject to a substantial fine in some jurisdictions in Canada. If renting a vehicle, check with the rental car company.

The minimum liability insurance requirement is $200,000 (Canadian dollars) in all provinces and territories except Quebec, which requires $50,000. Should the courts' judgments exceed these figures, motorists held accountable are responsible for paying the full amount.

If traveling in Quebec, discuss your collision, disability and bodily injury coverages with your insurance agent. Since Quebec's minimum requirement does not include bodily injury, coverage of $200,000 or more is recommended. Consider additional coverage (i.e., trip accident policy).

For United States Residents Returning to the United States

U.S. citizens returning to the U.S. from Canada by air must have a passport. Those returning by land or sea are required to present proper travel documents according to the Western Hemisphere Travel Initiative.

Everyone who seeks entry into the United States – whether foreign visitors, U.S. citizens, or U.S. lawful permanent residents – must be inspected at the point of entry. Random searches may be conducted by U.S. Customs and Border Protection agents.

U.S. Exemptions for a Stay in Canada No Less Than 48 Hours

- You may bring back tax- and duty-free articles not exceeding $800 in retail value
- Any amount over the $800 exemption is subject to duty

- The exemption is allowed once every 30 days
- A family (related persons living in the same household) may combine its exemptions, even if articles claimed by one member exceed that individual's $800 amount.
- Exemptions based on fair retail value (keep receipts of all purchases as proof of fair retail value)
- Exemptions apply to articles acquired only for personal or household use or as gifts, but not intended for sale
- The exemption may include 100 cigars, 200 cigarettes and 1 liter of liquor per person over age 21 (customs enforces state liquor laws)
- All articles claimed under this exemption must accompany you on your return

U.S. Exemptions for a Stay in Canada Less Than 48 Hours

- You may bring back tax- and duty-free articles not exceeding $200 in retail value
- The exemption may include no more than 50 cigarettes, 10 cigars, 5 fluid ounces (150 milliliters) of alcoholic beverage or 150 milliliters of perfume containing alcohol
- A family may not combine purchases
- If purchases exceed the $200 exemption, you lose the exemption and all purchases become subject to duty
- All goods must be declared
- All articles claimed under this exemption must accompany you on your return

Gifts

- Gifts up to $100 fair retail value may be sent to friends or relatives in the United States provided no recipient receives more than 1 gift per day (need not be included in the $800 exemption)
- Gifts containing tobacco products, alcoholic beverages or perfume containing alcohol valued at more than $5 retail are excluded from this provision
- Write on outside of package the contents, retail value and "Unsolicited Gift"

Prohibited: Articles considered detrimental to the general welfare of the United States are prohibited entry: narcotics and dangerous drugs, drug paraphernalia, obscene articles and publications, seditious or treasonable matter, lottery tickets, hazardous items (fireworks, dangerous toys, toxic or poisonous substances) and switchblade knives. Any goods originating in embargoed countries, including the following: Western Balkans, Burma, Cote d'Ivoire, Cuba, Democratic Republic of Congo, Iran, Iraq, Liberia, Sierra Leone, Sudan, Syria and Zimbabwe. Please note embargoes are not limited to these countries.
Restricted items include automobiles, biological materials (disease organisms and vectors for

research), ceramic tableware, cultural treasures, firearms and ammunition, articles bearing marks or names copying or simulating trademarked articles or trade names (watches, cameras, perfumes), pirated copies of copyrighted articles (books, CDs, DVDs, audio- and video-tapes, computer programs), agricultural goods (plants and animal products) and pets, wildlife and fish.

You may bring into or take out of the United States an unlimited amount of money, however, if you transport more than $10,000 you must file a FinCen 105 with U.S. Customs. Failure to comply can result in civil, criminal and/or forfeiture penalties. Monies include currency, traveler's checks, U.S. or foreign coins in circulation, money orders and negotiable instruments or investment securities in bearer form. For a currency reporting flier contact: U.S. Customs, P.O. Box 7407, Washington, D.C. 20044.

While some agricultural products of Canadian origin (fruits, some plants with phyto-sanitary certificates, meats, etc.) may be brought into the United States, many are restricted to prevent the introduction of plant and animal pests and diseases. All must be declared at the U.S. border. Visit the Animal and Plant Health Inspection Service at www.aphis.usda.gov or U.S. Customs at www.cbp.gov/xp/cgov/travel/vacation/kbyg/ for more information.

For Canada Residents Traveling to the United States

Canadian citizens entering the U.S. by air are required to present a passport. Canadian citizens entering the U.S. by land or sea are required to present proper travel documents according to the Western Hemisphere Travel Initiative. Approved documents include a passport or passport card, Enhanced Driver's License, or NEXUS trusted traveler program card. Please refer to the U.S. Department of State's website travel.state.gov or the Canada Border Services Agency website cbsa-asfc.gc.ca for the most current information on these requirements.

If traveling to the United States with a child, carry documentation proving your custodial rights. A person under age 18 traveling to the United States alone or with only 1 parent or another adult, must have certified documentation proving that the trip is permitted by both parents.

United States Customs permits Canadian residents to bring, free of duty, for personal use and not intended for sale: clothing, personal items and equipment appropriate to the trip, including 200 cigarettes, 50 cigars or 2 kilograms of tobacco, or proportionate amounts of each, and 1 liter of alcoholic beverage.

Visitors in the United States for at least 72 hours who have not claimed this exemption in the preceding 6 months may bring gifts totaling $100 (US) retail value. Perfume containing alcohol and valued at more than $5 retail, tobacco products and alcoholic beverages are excluded from the gift provision.

Use of cell phones and General Radio Service Station (CB) is unrestricted.

For Canada Residents Returning to Canada

The Canada Border Services Agency allows Canadian residents to bring, free of duty and taxes, goods valued up to $400 (CAN) any number of times a year, provided the visit to the United States is 48 hours or more and all goods accompany the purchaser (written declaration may be required).

You may claim a $50 (CAN) exemption on goods, excluding alcoholic beverages and tobacco products, if returning after an absence of 24 hours or more and are not using any other exemption. If bringing back more than $50 worth of goods, the regular duty and tax rate is levied on the entire value. This exemption may apply any number of times in a year. No tobacco or alcohol may be carried if returning after an absence of less than 48 hours.

If returning after 7 days or more in the United States (not counting departure day from Canada) you may claim up to a $750 (CAN) exemption on goods. Goods, other than alcohol and tobacco products, need not accompany you (written declaration may be required).

Permitted within the $400 and $750 exemptions: up to 50 cigars, 200 cigarettes, 200 tobacco sticks and 200 grams (6.4 oz) of tobacco, and up to 1.14 liters (40 oz) of liquor or 1.5 liters (1.6 qts) of wine or 8.5 liters (9 qts) of beer or ale (or its equivalent of 24 12-ounce bottles or cans). You must meet the minimum age requirement of the province or territory entered to claim alcohol or tobacco products.

Special Tariff: When exceeding the $400 or $750 exemption, a special rate of 7 percent combined duty and taxes is levied on the next $300 value in goods (except tobacco and alcohol) exceeding the maximum exemptible amounts, provided goods are of U.S. origin. Regular duties apply on any additional amount. A 13 percent Harmonized Sales

Tax (HST), which combines a 5 percent Goods and Services Tax (GST) and 8 percent provincial component, is charged on most goods and services supplied in Nova Scotia, New Brunswick and Newfoundland and Labrador. For information contact the Canada Border Services Agency before departing Canada. All extra goods must accompany you.

All exemptions are individual and may not be combined with those of other people. You may be asked to verify the length of your visit. Dated receipts normally constitute proof. Gifts (excluding alcoholic beverages, tobacco products and advertising matter) up to $60 (CAN) retail may be sent from abroad free of duty or taxes. For gifts valued at more than $60 (CAN), duty and taxes apply to amount exceeding $60. Gifts sent from abroad do not count against personal exemptions; gifts brought back must be included in exemptions.

While AAA makes every effort to provide accurate and complete information, AAA makes no warranty, express or implied, and assumes no legal liability or responsibility for the accuracy or completeness of any information contained herein.

NATIONAL PARKS ENTRANCE FEES

At Canada's national parks, the basic per person or per family entry fee gives visitors access to the park, scenic outlooks, picnic areas and a variety of facilities. Additional fees are charged for visitors who choose to use other recreational services such as campgrounds, special interpretation programs and golf courses.

To receive a free Parks Canada vacation planner, phone (888) 773-8888. Detailed information about the services, benefits, entry fees and discounts at all national parks and historic sites is available by calling the following numbers:

(800) 748-7275 for Alberta;

(902) 426-3436 for Atlantic provinces (Newfoundland and Labrador, New Brunswick, Nova Scotia and Prince Edward Island);

(604) 513-4777 for British Columbia;

(888) 748-2928 for Manitoba;

(800) 748-7275 for Saskatchewan;

(800) 463-6769 for Québec;

(800) 661-0486 for Yukon.

Points of Interest Index

Index Legend

EVENTS-HOLIDAY

EVENTS-MUSIC

EVENTS-PAGEANTS, PARADES, DAYS

EVENTS-SHOWS

EVENTS-SPORTS

EXHIBITS & COLLECTIONS-GENERAL

EXHIBITS & COLLECTIONS-ANIMALS & BIRDS

EXHIBITS & COLLECTIONS-ART

EXHIBITS & COLLECTIONS-AVIATION

EXHIBITS & COLLECTIONS-CIVIL WAR

EXHIBITS & COLLECTIONS-DOLLS & TOYS

EXHIBITS & COLLECTIONS-HISTORICAL

EXHIBITS & COLLECTIONS-INDIAN

EXHIBITS & COLLECTIONS-MUSIC

EXHIBITS & COLLECTIONS-RELIGIOUS ITEMS

HISTORIC DOCUMENTS, MANUSCRIPTS & RARE BOOKS

HISTORIC SITES

MUSIC HALLS & OPERA HOUSES

NATURAL BRIDGES

NATURAL PHENOMENA

NATURE CENTERS

PARKS, NATIONAL

PERFORMING ARTS ORGANIZATIONS

RECREATION-WINTER ACTIVITIES

RELIGIOUS COLONIES

RESTORED VILLAGES & SETTLEMENTS

SHIPS & BOATS

SHOPS, FIRMS & STORES

⟦SAVE⟧ *Attraction Admission Discount Index*

Enjoy total reward flexibility

WORLDPOINTS® REWARDS

The AAA Credit Card With WorldPoints® Rewards

- Travel, cash, and merchandise rewards
- Low Introductory APR† offer

Call 866-665-3581 or visit AAA.com/CreditCard

Bed & Breakfast Lodgings Index

Some bed and breakfasts listed below might have historical significance.
Those properties are also referenced in the Historical index.

Country Inns Index

Some of the following country inns can also be considered as bed-and-breakfast operations.

Historical Lodgings & Restaurants Index

Some of the following historical lodgings can also be considered as bed-and-breakfast operations.

Historical Lodgings & Restaurants (cont'd)

Resorts Index

Many establishments are located in resort areas; however, the following
places have extensive on-premises recreational facilities:

Comprehensive City Index

Here is an alphabetical list of all cities appearing in this TourBook® guide. Cities are presented by state/province. Page numbers under the POI column indicate where points of interest text begins. Page numbers under the L&R column indicate where lodging and restaurant listings begin.

Comprehensive City Index (cont'd)

Comprehensive City Index (cont'd)

Comprehensive City Index (cont'd)

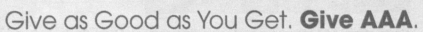

What do these items have in common? AAA members spend less.

Hertz offers AAA members exclusive discounts and benefits including:

- $6.99 daily fee for Hertz NeverLost® GPS rental
- 50% off SIRIUS XM Radio® rental
- Additional authorized driver at no charge*

- Free use of a child seat
- Special Internet pricing
- Member Satisfaction Guarantee
- 10% Off Fuel Purchase Option
- 10% Off U.S. prepaid rates

Show Your Card & Save®

SHOW YOUR AAA CARD AND SAVE

THE ONLY CAR RENTAL COMPANY ENDORSED BY AAA

hertz.com

FOR YOUR INFORMATION: Advance reservations are required. Discounts and benefits are valid at participating locations in the U.S., Canada and Puerto Rico. One child seat at no additional charge. Hertz NeverLost and SIRIUS XM Radio subject to availability. SIRIUS not available in Alaska, Hawaii or Puerto Rico. Discounts valued in local currency upon redemption and exclude applicable taxes and surcharges. Your valid AAA membership card or Hertz/AAA discount card must be presented at time of pickup. SIRIUS is a registered trademark of SIRIUS XM Radio, Inc.

*No charge for an additional authorized driver who is a AAA member, holds a major credit card in their name and meets standard rental qualifications.

® Reg. U.S. Pat. Off. © 2010 Hertz System, Inc.

| Visit | Over 1,100 AAA Offices | Click | AAA.com/Hertz | Call | 800-654-3080 |